Second Edition

Atlas of HUMAN POISONING and ENVENOMING

Second Edition

Atlas of HUMAN POISONING and ENVENOMING

James H. Diaz
LSUHSC
School of Public Health
New Orleans, Louisiana, USA

CRC Press
Taylor & Francis Group
Boca Raton London New York

CRC Press is an imprint of the
Taylor & Francis Group, an **informa** business

CRC Press
Taylor & Francis Group
6000 Broken Sound Parkway NW, Suite 300
Boca Raton, FL 33487-2742

Printed on acid-free paper
Version Date: 20140903

International Standard Book Number-13: 978-1-4665-0540-7 (Hardback)

Library of Congress Cataloging-in-Publication Data

Diaz, James H., author.
[Color atlas of human poisoning and envenoming]
Atlas of human poisoning and envenoming / James H. Diaz. -- Second edition.
p. ; cm.
Preceded by Color atlas of human poisoning and envenoming / by James Diaz. 1st ed. 2006.
Includes bibliographical references and index.
ISBN 978-1-4665-0540-7 (hardcover : alk. paper)
I. Title.
[DNLM: 1. Poisoning--Atlases. 2. Toxicology--Atlases. 3. Antidotes--Atlases. 4. Poisons--Atlases. 5. Toxins, Biological--Atlases. 6. Venoms--Atlases. QV 17]

RA1211
615.9--dc23 2014034121

Visit the Taylor & Francis Web site at
http://www.taylorandfrancis.com

and the CRC Press Web site at
http://www.crcpress.com

Contents

Preface ... ix

Acknowledgments ... xi

Author ... xiii

SECTION I General Medical Toxicology

Chapter 1 The Pharmacology of Human Poisoning and Envenoming ... 3

Chapter 2 General Poisoning Management ... 21

Chapter 3 Diagnostic Work-Up of the Poisoned Patient ... 37

Chapter 4 Poison Antidotes ... 53

Chapter 5 Toxicity of Antiseptics and Drug Additives ... 81

Chapter 6 Poisonings with Over-the-Counter and Opioid Analgesics ... 89

Chapter 7 Household Product Poisonings ... 105

Chapter 8 Drug and Illicit Substance Abuse ... 167

Chapter 9 Anticonvulsants and Sedative-Hypnotics ... 207

Chapter 10 Reproductive and Perinatal Toxicology and Teratogenesis 217

Chapter 11 Hypoglycemic and Other Endocrine Agent Toxicity 233

Chapter 12 Cardiovascular Drug Toxicity 241

Chapter 13 Antibiotic Toxicity 257

Chapter 14 Anticancer Drug Toxicity 269

Chapter 15 Environmental and Occupational Nephrotoxicology 281

Chapter 16 Neurotoxicology 309

SECTION II Environmental Toxicology

Chapter 17 Food Poisoning 359

Chapter 18 Seafood Poisoning 379

Chapter 19 Mushroom Poisonings 395

Chapter 20 Herbal Poisonings. 413

Chapter 21 Common Poisonous Household and Garden Plants 443

Chapter 22 Bites and Stings: Terrestrial Envenomings. 477

Chapter 23 Common Arthropod Vectors of Infectious Diseases 525

Chapter 24 Tick Paralysis 557

Chapter 25 Bites and Stings: Marine Envenomings 569

Chapter 26 Voodoo, Hoodoo, and Cajun Traditions and Poisonings 583

SECTION III Industrial and Occupational Toxicology

Chapter 27 Volatile Organic Chemicals 613

Chapter 28 Petrochemical Toxicity 629

Chapter 29 Industrial Gas Exposures and Occupational Lung Diseases 645

Chapter 30 Metal and Metalloid Poisonings 673

Chapter 31 Pesticide Poisonings: Insecticides, Rodenticides, and Herbicides 707

Chapter 32 Radiation Toxicology 727

Chapter 33 Chemical, Biological, and Radiological Weapons and Warfare 747

Chapter 34 Workplace Substance Abuse Monitoring 769

Chapter 35 Miscellaneous Toxicants 813

SECTION IV Epidemiology and Statistics for Toxicology

Chapter 36 Epidemiology and Statistics for Toxicology 843

Index 855

Preface

Since the first edition of this atlas was published in 2006, there have been many changes in the manner in which clinicians are examined for clinical competencies during their residencies, certified in their primary and secondary fields after completing training, and periodically recertified in all areas of their expertise. Some significant changes include annual computer-based examinations with passing scores required for residents to progress to advanced levels; computer-based national board certification examinations administered near the end of residency training and later after fellowships or periods of active practice; and computer-based national recertification examinations every 10 years. Today, most provider organizations, hospital staffs, and health insurance companies require proof of recertification by examination for their medical providers to maintain hospital practice privileges and to qualify for reimbursements of services.

All these required examinations share similarly structured test questions that are now redesigned to assess clinical acumen and judgment rather than rote recall. Frequently, the test questions will begin with an image of a patient, a radiograph or electrocardiogram, a lesion or wound, or a venomous animal or plant. Following a short vignette of the clinical encounter, typically a mini-history and physical examination, the examinee will face a series of multiple-choice questions based on the image and its vignette. Since the images are rarely analyzed or interpreted, examinees must quickly identify the images and any potential adverse outcomes and proceed to answer a series of questions that follow. Initial mistakes in analyzing and interpreting images and any associations with their accompanying vignettes will result in not one, but several, incorrect answers, in a required test–subject category.

The second edition of the *Atlas of Human Poisoning and Envenoming* will continue to serve as a visual and written reminder of the ubiquitous sources of toxins and toxoids in the environment and the outcomes of accidental and intentional toxic exposures in humans. The atlas has been redesigned as a ready resource with bulleted text, tables, and figure legends that resemble the vignettes that accompany national examination images to better prepare practitioners from several fields for image-intense, computer-based examinations in their respective fields. The atlas will be a useful study guide for emergency physicians, emergency medical service first responders, poison control center professionals, military physicians, family practitioners, physician assistants, preventive medicine and veterinary medicine practitioners, public health officers, occupational medicine specialists, pediatricians, and health science and medical students preparing for a professional lifetime of image-intense national examinations.

Several new chapters have been added to the second edition, including chapters on the prescription and illicit drug abuse epidemics, environmental and occupational nephrotoxicology and neurotoxicology, tick paralysis, and petrochemical toxicants. The atlas will conclude chapters on biological, chemical, and radiological warfare agents; workplace substance abuse screening and monitoring; and epidemiological design and statistical analysis of toxicological investigations.

Acknowledgments

The author acknowledges the encouragement and continuing support of the medical editors in Boca Raton, Florida, at CRC Press, LLC, and the Taylor & Francis Group, LLC, particularly Barbara Norwitz, senior editor, and Jill Jurgensen, senior project coordinator. The author also acknowledges the support and new image contributions provided by David K. Lirette, MS, MT-ASCP, PhD, assistant professor of public health in the Environmental and Occupational Health Sciences Program of the Louisiana State University School of Public Health in New Orleans, Louisiana. A medical technologist, analytical chemist, and forensic toxicologist by profession, Dr. Lirette is also a self-taught naturalist and an expert nature photographer as his images of venomous animals and poisonous plants attest (Figures A.1 and A. 2).

FIGURE A.1 A juvenile water moccasin, *Agkistrodon piscivorus*, or cottonmouth, has coloration similar to its relative, the copperhead, *Agkistrodon contortrix*, and is often mistaken for a nonpoisonous water snake until its coloration darkens to a more solid brown to black. Note the triangular-shaped head and thick midsection. (Courtesy of David K. Lirette, PhD, School of Public Health, Louisiana State University Health Sciences Center, New Orleans, Louisiana.)

FIGURE A.2 A golden paper wasp, *Polistes* species, perched on a leaf. Paper wasps build honey-combed "paper" nests under eaves, feed on nectar and small insects including caterpillars, and are considered as beneficial pollinators and biological pest controllers by gardeners. Although not as aggressive as honeybees and yellow jackets, paper wasps can sting repeatedly and cause anaphylactic shock–like reactions in susceptible human victims. (Courtesy of David K. Lirette, PhD, School of Public Health, Louisiana State University Health Sciences Center, New Orleans, Louisiana.)

Author

A native of New Orleans, Dr. James H. Diaz earned several degrees from Tulane University, including bachelor of science, doctor of medicine, master of health administration, diploma in tropical medicine, master of public health and tropical medicine, and doctor of public health. Dr. Diaz is board certified in anesthesiology, critical care medicine, pain management, general preventive medicine and public health, occupational/environmental medicine, and medical toxicology. Dr. Diaz served as a written and oral board examiner for the American Board of Anesthesiology from 1986 to 1996 and currently serves on the core examination committee of the American Board of Preventive Medicine. Dr. Diaz has published more than 200 original articles and chapters in scientific journals and textbooks as the first author. Dr. Diaz has published one scientific book on perinatal anesthesiology and critical care medicine, and another book on human toxicology, now in its second edition. Dr. Diaz authors the section on ectoparasite-borne infectious diseases in the current edition of *Mandell's Principles and Practice of Infectious Diseases*. Dr. Diaz currently serves as the professor of public health and preventive medicine in the School of Public Health, and professor of anesthesiology in the School of Medicine, at the Louisiana State University Health Sciences Center in New Orleans (LSUHSC). Dr. Diaz also serves as the program director of environmental and occupational health sciences at LSUHSC. Dr. Diaz's current academic and clinical research interests include (1) occupational and environmental toxicology; (2) environmental and tropical infectious diseases and injuries in international travelers; (3) emerging environmentally associated diseases and poisonings, particularly food-, water-, and vector-borne infectious diseases and poisonings; and (4) the impact of climate change on natural disasters and their public health outcomes.

In 2001, Dr. Diaz was elected to a lifetime membership in Delta Omega, the national public health honor society. In 2009, Dr. Diaz accepted the Allen A. Copping Award for excellence in teaching from LSUHSC. In 2009, Dr. Diaz was appointed to a 2-year advisory committee position on the Transportation Research Board of the National Academy in Washington, DC, to study risk factors in the transmission of infectious diseases aboard aircraft and on the impact of international air travel on the dissemination of arthropod-borne infectious diseases. In 2010, Dr. Diaz was awarded a U.S. Centers for Disease Control and Prevention Principal Investigator subcontract to study the health effects of biological and chemical exposures in children living in Federal Emergency Management Agency (FEMA) trailers in the Gulf States for prolonged periods following hurricanes Katrina and Rita. In 2011, Dr. Diaz was elected to the Hall of Fame of the New Orleans Anesthesia Society for his services to the specialty and to the society as its past president.

Section I

General Medical Toxicology

Chapter 1

The Pharmacology of Human Poisoning and Envenoming

Definitions 4
Absorption 4
Distribution 8
Metabolism 10
Liver Zones 11
Liver Zones: CYP 450 11
Excretion 14
First- vs. Zero-Order Kinetics 14
Poison Pharmacology 18

Definitions

- **Xenobiotics:** Foreign, natural, or man-made (synthetic) chemicals, including, drugs, pesticides, environmental, and industrial agents.
- **Pharmacokinetics:** The application of mathematical models to describe and predict the behavior of drugs during their absorption, distribution, metabolism, and elimination or excretion.
- **Pharmacodynamics:** The relationships of drug concentrations to their observed clinical effects.
- **Toxicokinetics:** The application of mathematical models to describe and predict the behavior of xenobiotics in toxic or excessive doses (overdoses—ODs) during their absorption, distribution, metabolism, and excretion.
- **Toxicodynamics:** The relationships of toxic concentrations of xenobiotics to their observed clinical effects.

Absorption

Routes of Absorption

Enteral Administration

- **Oral:** Variable absorption, yet most commonly used route; subjects all xenobiotics to *first-pass hepatic metabolism*; oral doses diluted by foods; intestinal absorption delayed by enteric coatings, drug concretions or bezoars, anticholinergics, H_2-blockers, sedatives, drug-induced pylorospasm.
- **Sublingual:** Xenobiotics enter systemic circulation without first pass avoiding gastric delays and inactivation. Ex: NTG.
- **Rectal:** Also avoids gastric delays and inactivation; useful during nausea and vomiting; provides shortcut to central circulation and *reduces first pass by 50%.*

Parenteral Administration

- **Intravascular:** Intravenous route most commonly used; avoids both GI tract and first-pass hepatic metabolism; useful for drugs poorly absorbed by or unstable in GI tract. Ex: Insulin, lidocaine.
- **Intramuscular and subcutaneous:** Good for slow, sustained delivery of depot preparations of drugs. Ex: Antibiotics.
- **Intrathecal and intraventricular:** Used primarily for cancer drugs, local anesthetics and antibiotics. Caution: use only sterile, preservative-free (polyethylene glycol, methyl paraben) meds to avoid *chemical arachnoiditis.*

Delayed GI Absorption

- **Delayed gastric emptying:** Often results from fatty meals, anticholinergics, antiserotoninergics (ondansetron), tricyclic antidepressants, barbiturates, ethanol, glutethimide, methaqualone, and opioids.

- **Drug coatings, bezoars, concretions:** Will all require initial disintegration prior to absorption. Ex: Enteric-coated tablets and long-acting preparations (ASA, theophylline, CCBs), *meprobamate* (Soma® [carisoprodal] concretions), foods (persimmons = phytobezoars).
- **Gastric outlet pylorospasm:** Most frequently caused by common gastric irritants. Ex: *Iron, salicylates.*

Routes vs. Rates of Absorption

Routes of Absorption

- **Enteral:** Oral, rectal.
- **Parenteral:** Intradermal, subcutaneous, intravascular (intravenous, intra-arterial), intramuscular.
- **Cutaneous:** Topical and transdermal.
- **Miscellaneous:** Inhalation, sublingual, transmucosal, intranasal, intrathecal, intraventricular.

Rates of Absorption

- **Fastest to slowest:** Intravascular ≥ inhalation > sublingual > intranasal > intramuscular > rectal > oral > subcutaneous > transmucosal > topical > transdermal.
- **Rate of absorption:** Predicts the onset of xenobiotics action.
- **Extent of absorption:** Predicts the bioavailability of the xenobiotic or the extent of its pharmacologic effect. Ex: digoxin has 75% bioavailability (Figures 1.1a and 1.1b).

Rates vs. Bioavailabilities (See Figure 1.1)

Decreasing Rate × Constant Bioavailability Blood concentrations of three poisons when bioavailability is constant and rate of absorption is decreasing over time.

Constant Rate × Decreasing Bioavailability Blood concentrations of three poisons when rate of absorption is constant and bioavailability is decreasing over time.

Physical Factors

- **Molecular weight (MW):** Low MW promotes rapid absorption by passive diffusion.
- **Blood flow:** ↑ blood flow favors ↑ absorption. Ex: Intestinal > gastric absorption.
- **Surface area:** ↑ surface area favors ↑ absorption. Ex: Intestinal > gastric absorption.
- **Contact time:** Absorption is inversely proportional to GI transit time. Ex: Cathartics speed transit time and limit absorption. Chelators enhance the bioavailability of safer, bound toxins, but have no impact on transit time or absorption, unless combined with cathartics. Ex: Deferoxamine and Fe, penicillamine and Cu, succimer and Pb, Prussian blue, and Tl.

Solubility, Polarity, pH

- **Water solubility:** Water-soluble (hydrophilic) xenobiotics cannot cross lipoprotein membranes and must filter through aqueous channels.

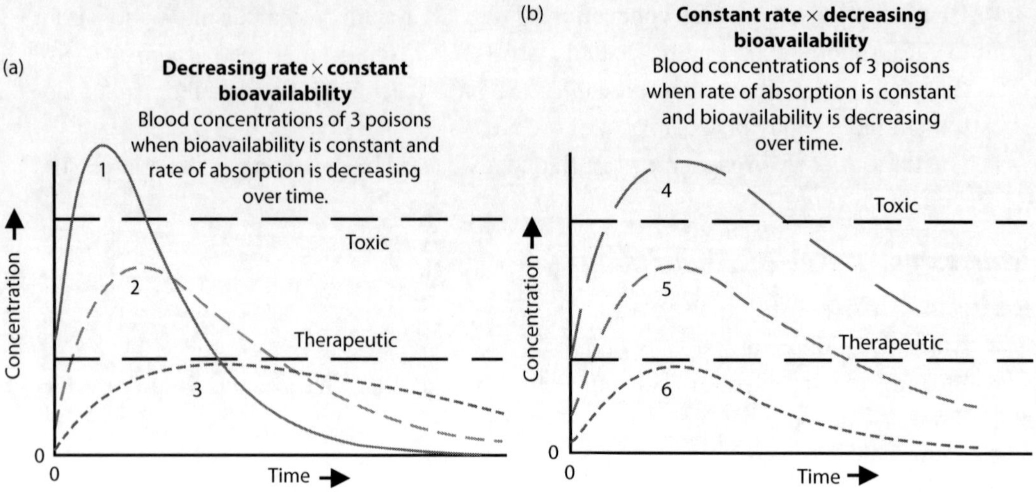

FIGURE 1.1 (a) The blood concentrations of three poisons when bioavailability is constant and rate of absorption is decreasing over time. (b) Constant rate × decreasing bioavailability. The blood concentrations of three poisons when rate of absorption is constant and bioavailability is decreasing over time.

- **Lipid solubility:** Lipid-soluble (lipophilic) xenobiotics readily cross lipoprotein membranes for ↑ absorption and often enter enterohepatic cycles that ↓ renal elimination. Ex: Opioids-fentanyls.
- **Polarity:** Lack of polarity or charge favors enhanced absorption by diffusion.
- **pH:** Acidic drugs (ASA) demonstrate ↑ absorption in the acidic stomach; basic drugs in the alkaline intestine (jejunum > ileum).

Toxin Transport Mechanisms 1

Passive Diffusion

- **Concentration gradient:** The gradient between high-to-low concentrations that provides the driving force for passive diffusion.
- **Saturation potential:** None; passive diffusion is not susceptible to saturation kinetics.
- **Energy source:** Concentration gradients alone.
- **Fick's Law of Diffusion:** Governs the rate of passive diffusion

$$dQ/dT = \mathrm{DAK}(C_1 - C_2)/h,$$

where:

D = Diffusion constant

A = Surface area of membrane

$C_1 - C_2$ = Difference in poison concentrations on either side of the membrane
h = Thickness of the membrane

Active Transport (See Figure 1.2)

- **Carrier protein:** Required for active transport against concentration gradients. Ex: H^+–Na–K ATPase gastric proton pump.
- **Saturation potential:** High; protein carriers are often saturated in overdoses, allowing drugs or toxins to accumulate in the central circulatory compartment.
- **Energy source:** Energy is always provided by the hydrolysis of ATP. Active transport is a highly energy-dependent process.

Toxin Transport Mechanisms 2 (See Figure 1.2)

Passive Diffusion

- **Favors:** Nonpolar, unionized weak acids and bases

Active Transport

- **Favors:** Specific xenobiotics

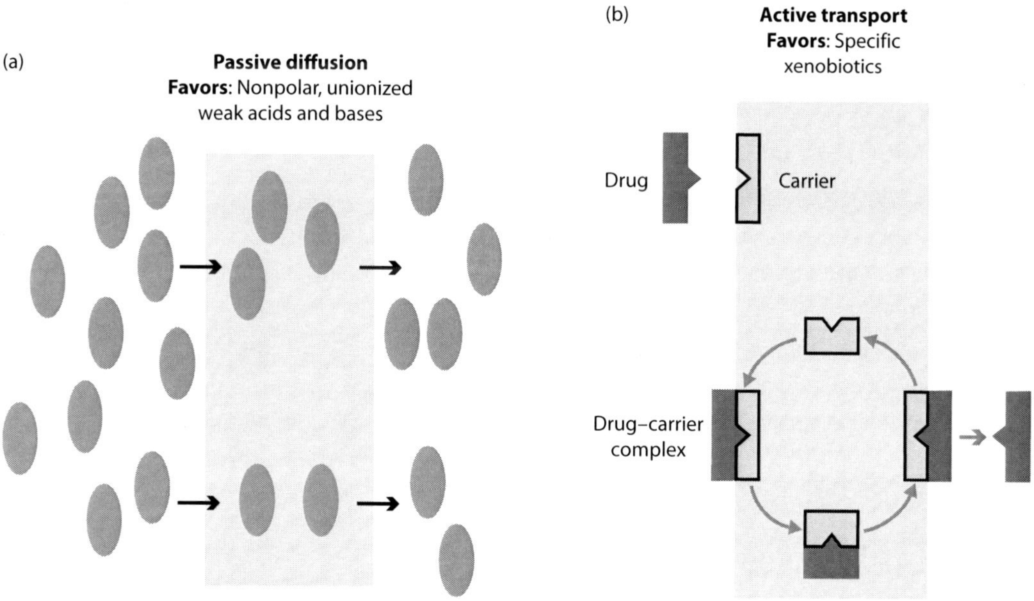

FIGURE 1.2 (a) Passive diffusion favors nonpolar, unionized weak acids and bases. (b) Active transport favors specific xenobiotics.

Distribution

Bound vs. Unbound Drugs

Bound Drugs

Specialized proteins bind xenobiotics in plasma-making toxins unavailable for distribution.

- **Albumin:** Binds *acidic ("A") drugs* with ↓ V_d = aspirin, phenoxyacetic acid herbicides, anticonvulsants, chlorpropamide, warfarin.
- **α-1-Acid glycoprotein:** Binds *basic ("B") drugs* with ↓ V_d = β-blockers, amide local anesthetics, tricyclic antidepressants (TCAs).
- **Specialized carrier proteins**: Exist in blood transferrin (Fe); in the kidney metallothionein (Cd, Pb, Hg); and in the retina melanin (chloroquine, quinine, chlorpromazine [CPZ]).

Unbound Drugs

Only unbound drugs freely distribute through membranes to tissues.

- **Bioavailability:** Applies to unbound drugs only.
- **Saturation kinetics:** Toxic overdoses often saturate protein binders and carriers (albumin, transferrin) making large concentrations of unbound drugs available for tissue distribution and organ toxicity. Ex: ASA-CNS toxicity; Fe-hepatotoxicity and cardiotoxicity.
- **Lab serum concentrations:** Of limited value because labs measure both bound and unbound drugs to determine total serum values that closely approximate plasma concentrations. Only unbound plasma concentrations are actively bioavailable.

Physiochemical Determinants

1. **Blood flow:** Determined by the cardiac output and accounts for initial distribution of xenobiotics and preferentially perfuses brain, liver, kidneys > muscle > fat > skin > bone.
2. **Drug structure:** *Uncharged, hydrophobic, and lipophilic* drugs readily cross lipoprotein membranes.
3. **Protein binding:** Plasma and specialized carrier proteins sequester xenobiotics in the central plasma compartment and often become saturated, resulting in ↑ plasma concentrations of unbound toxins. Ex: Acetaminophen (APAP) and glutathione.
4. **Physiologic barriers:** Protect downstream target organs from xenobiotic distribution and toxicity. Ex: Blood–brain barrier, placental barrier, blood–testis barrier.

Volume of Distribution (V_d)

Definitions and Relationships

- V_d is the theoretical volume of body water into which a drug distributes.
- V_d determines how much of a drug remains inside or outside of the central (plasma) compartment sampled by serum concentrations.

- V_d drugs with V_ds < 1 L/kg remain within the plasma compartment available for removal by hemodialysis (HD). Ex: ASA $V_d = 0.2$, ethylene glycol (antifreeze) = 0.6.
- V_d drugs with V_ds > 1 L/kg distribute from plasma to tissues and are unavailable for removal by HD. Ex: Digoxin $V_d = 5$, TCAs $V_d = 10–15$.

Determinants of the V_d

- Drug dose administered.
- Drug bioavailability (%).
- Peak plasma concentration.
- Formula: V_d = dose in mg/kg × bioavailability (%)/plasma concentration. Alternatively, plasma concentration = dose in mg/kg/V_d × weight in kg.

Classical Compartment Models

One-Compartment Model

- **Definition:** Xenobiotics rapidly enter the central compartment for rapid distribution to tissues; plasma concentrations mirror tissue concentrations (first-order kinetics).

Two-Compartment Model

- **Definition:** Most xenobiotics do not instantaneously equilibrate with tissues, but are initially distributed to highly perfused central tissues, and subsequently distributed to less perfused peripheral tissues. Ex: Digoxin, barbiturates, lidocaine (Figures 1.3a and 1.3b).

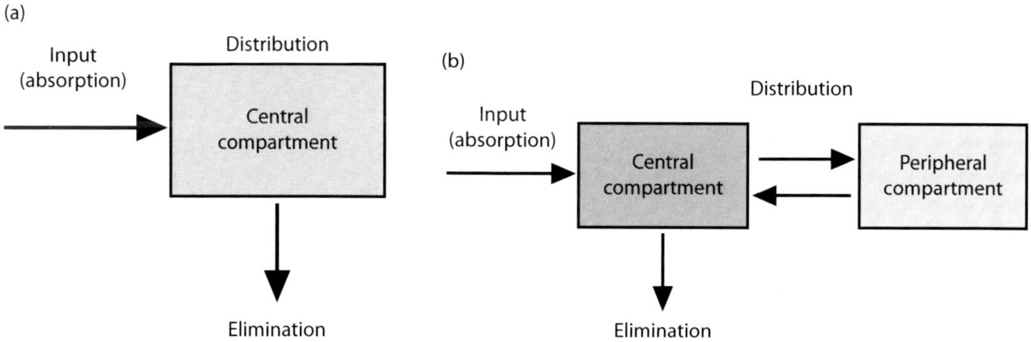

FIGURE 1.3 (a) One-compartment distribution model. Some xenobiotics rapidly enter the central circulatory compartment for rapid distribution to tissues; plasma concentrations mirror tissue concentrations. (b) Two-compartment distribution model. Most xenobiotics do not instantaneously equilibrate with tissues, but are initially distributed to highly perfused organs, and subsequently distributed to less perfused peripheral tissues. Ex: barbiturates, digoxin, lidocaine.

Metabolism

Metabolic Reactions

Phase I Hepatic Reactions (rxns)

- **Mechanisms:** Preparative or nonsynthetic rxns that often precede phase II rxns and either introduce hydrophilic polar groups to (by oxidation > reduction and hydrolysis) or expose polar groups (by dealkylation) on xenobiotics to ↓ their water solubility in preparation for further hepatic metabolism (by phase II) or renal elimination.
- **Enzymes:** All phase I enzymes are members of the hepatic microsomal (endoplasmic reticulum fraction) mixed function oxidase enzyme system (Cytochrome [CY] P 450).

Phase II Hepatic Reactions (rxns)

- **Mechanisms:** Synthetic reactions that often replace or follow, but rarely precede, phase I rxns, designed to conjugate polar groups, reduce electric charges, and assure complete water solubility for the ultimate renal elimination of xenobiotics. Conjugation occurs with glucuronide > sulfate, acetate, methyl groups, or amino acids (glycine > taurine and glutamic acid). Ex: Toluene-benzyl alcohol-*glycine* + *benzoic acid*-hippuric acid.
- **Enzymes:** Phase II hepatic enzymes may belong to either the microsomal (CYP450) or cytosolic fraction.

Common CYP450 Enzymes

Common CYP450 Hepatic Enzymes

- CYP1A1
- CYP1A2
- CYP2A6
- CYP2D6
- CYP2E1
- CYP3A4

Representative Enzyme Substrates

- PAHs
- Caffeine, theophylline
- Nicotine
- Debrisoquine
- APAP and *NAPQI*, ethanol
- Some APAP, many antiarrhythmics, oral contraceptive pills (OCPs), warfarin, HMGCoAs

Liver Zones

Drug–Drug Interactions

- **Hepatic enzyme inducers:** ↑ Substrate drug metabolism and ↓ therapeutic drug efficacy.
- **Anticonvulsants:** *Barbiturates*, carbamazepine, phenytoin, primidone.
- **Sedatives:** *Ethanol*, glutethimide.
- **Antibiotics:** *Rifampin* (↓ efficacy of oral contraceptive pills [OCPs]).
- **Miscellaneous:** Omeprazole, polycyclic aromatic hydrocarbons (PAHs), St. John's wort (can ↓ efficacy of SSRIs and has been associated with suicides in depressed patients on SSRIs).
- **Hepatic enzyme inhibitors:** ↓ Substrate drug metabolism, usually ↑ toxicity of drug, but ↓ toxicity of metabolites. Ex: *Cimetidine* for mushroom poisoning.
- **Antifungals:** All *azoles*.
- **Antibiotics:** All *macrolides*, many *quinolones*, chloramphenicol, primaquine, trimethoprim-sulfamethox*azole*, ciprofloxacin.
- **Antiretrovirals:** Ritonavir, indinivir.
- **Antiarrhythmics:** Amiodarone, β-blockers, quinidine, verapamil.
- **H_2-blockers and proton-pump inhibitors:** Cimetidine, ranitidine, omeprazole.
- Most antipsychotics and TCAs.
- **Miscellaneous:** allopurinol, OCPs, grapefruit juice.

Liver Zones: CYP 450

Pharmacogenetics

Genetic Polymorphisms

- **Definition:** Inherited (autosomal recessive, often X-linked), inter-individual differences in the structure and function of specific hepatic microsomal or cytosolic enzymes that alter either phase I or phase II hepatic metabolic reactions to promote or, more rarely, to reduce the toxicity of xenobiotics, usually therapeutically administered drugs. Ex: INH acetylators.

Common Genetic Polymorphisms

- **Fast vs. slow INH acetylators:** 95% of Asians and African/African American Blacks are fast (rapid) acetylators of INH at ↓ risk of INH neurotoxicity. 50% of Americans and >70% of Scandinavians are slow acetylators at ↑ risk of INH neurotoxicity.
- **Pseudocholinesterase deficiency:** 2% of Americans and most Inuits cannot metabolize ester local anesthetics (including cocaine) and succinylcholine with ↑ risks of toxicity: Cocaine-induced MI and CVA. Succinylcholine-prolonged paralysis.
- **G-6-PD (glucose-6-phosphate dehydrogenase) deficiency:** Common in Europeans and all dark-skinned races (provides malaria protection) and renders RBC's incapable

of responding to oxidative structural stresses imposed by oxidant drugs (chlorates, nitrites, sulfa), resulting in methemoglobinemia and hemolysis, often refractory to methylene blue.

Pharmaceutical Excipients

What Are Excipients?

- **Definition:** Excipients are the chemical ingredients other than active drug that are included in pharmaceutical preparations for a variety of reasons.
- **Uses:** Binders, coatings, colors, diluents, disintegrators, flavors, preservatives, sweeteners, solvents.

Commonly Used Excipients

- **Colors:** Dyes can cause allergic reactions. Ex: FD&C Reds 40 and 19, carnine, quinolone yellow.
- **Flavors:** Licorice (glycyrrhizic acid) inhibits cortisol metabolism causing hypertension (↑ BP) and hypokalemia (↓ K).
- **Sweeteners:** Aspartame is contraindicated in phenylketonurics.
- **Preservatives:** Benzyl alcohol in IV flush solutions and multi-dose vials can cause metabolic acidosis and shock in premies—*"Gasping Baby" Syndrome.*
- **Solvents:** Polyethylene glycol in IV drugs irritates veins and has caused metabolic acidosis, CV collapse, and acute renal failure after IV pushes or topical antimicrobial creams for extensive burns.

The Therapeutic Index (See Figure 1.4)

What Is the Therapeutic Index (TI)?

- **Definition:** The TI is the ratio of the dose of a drug that causes toxicity to the dose that produces the desired and intended effect. The TI can only be determined by administering increasing drug doses to volunteers and observing for toxic responses.

How Is Drug Safety Assessed? (By Large vs. Small TIs)

- **Large TI = a large therapeutic window:** Large doses of the drug are relatively safe to administer, unless drug allergy exists. Close patient monitoring is unnecessary due to the drug's safety profile. Ex: Penicillin, OCPs.
- **Small TI = a small therapeutic window:** Drug toxicity is possible even at low drug doses. Drug serum concentrations and early toxic effects must be closely monitored. Ex: Warfarin-INR, digoxin-dig levels, serum K, lithium-Li, and Na levels.

Large (Safe) vs. Small (Unsafe) TIs (See Figure 1.4)

- Large TI (penicillin)
- Small TI (lithium, warfarin)

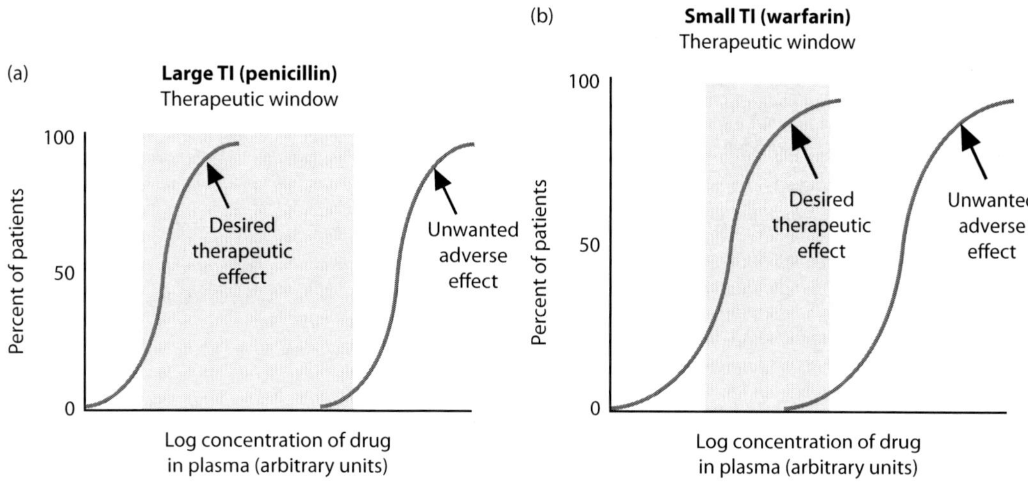

FIGURE 1.4 (a) Large therapeutic index. A large therapeutic index reflects a large therapeutic window in which large doses of a drug are relatively safe to administer, unless drug allergy exists. Ex: penicillin. (b) Small therapeutic index. A small therapeutic index reflects a small therapeutic window in which drug toxicity is possible even at low doses. Ex: digoxin, warfarin.

Dose–Response Relationships

Receptor Theory

- **Definition:** Many xenobiotics bind to specific protein receptors by ionic forces > hydrophobic or hydrophilic forces > weak Van der Waals forces to create a stable drug–receptor complex; the key to opening receptor-locked lipoprotein membrane barriers and entering organ and tissue compartments.

Receptor States

- **Agonist:** Xenobiotic that activates protein receptor and open barriers to tissues.
- **Partial agonist:** Xenobiotic that only partially activates protein receptor.
- **Antagonist:** Xenobiotic that totally prevents the binding of an agonist to its specific protein receptor.
- **Partial antagonist:** Xenobiotic that partially prevents the binding of an agonist to its specific protein receptor.
- **Competitive antagonist:** Xenobiotic that competes with the agonist for its receptor.
- **Noncompetitive antagonist:** Xenobiotic that interferes with agonist binding.

Efficacy vs. Potency (ED_{50})

How Effective Is the Drug?

- **Definition:** *Efficacy* is a measure of the maximal effective response produced by a drug. Efficacy depends on the number of drug–receptor complexes formed and the efficiency with which the activated complex produces a cellular response.

How Potent Is the Drug?

- **Definition:** *Potency* is a measure of how much of a drug is required to elicit a given response.

1. Potency is expressed as the *effective dose 50* [ED_{50}] or the dose of a drug that elicits 50% of the maximal response.
2. The lower the dose required for a given response, the more potent the drug.
3. Potent drugs have steep dose–response curves (plasma concentration vs. time) demonstrating that small ↑ in drug doses will elicit large changes in response. Ex: Digoxin, lithium, warfarin (Figures 1.4a and 1.4b).

Excretion

Drug Elimination Kinetics 1

First-Order Kinetics

The rate of a drug's elimination is directly proportional to its plasma concentration; the higher the concentration, the more rapid the drug elimination. Drug decay curve is curvilinear. Ex: 90% of all drugs.

Zero-Order Kinetics

The rate of a drug's elimination is independent of its concentration because (1) the drug's hepatic metabolizing enzyme system quickly becomes saturated to capacity, and (2) a constant, predictable amount of drug is eliminated per unit of time. Drug decay curve is linear. Ex: Ethanol.

First- vs. Zero-Order Kinetics

Drug Elimination Kinetics 1

See Figure 1.5.

Drug Elimination Kinetics 2

See Figure 1.6.

Combined Elimination Kinetics

- **Definition:** The rate of a drug's elimination is initially first order, and then switches to zero order when the drug's hepatic metabolizing enzyme system becomes saturated to capacity. Combined elimination kinetics is also known as *Michaelis–Menten* kinetics. Drug decay curve is initially curvilinear and then becomes more linear.

Plasma Clearance

Plasma Clearance

- **Definition:** Clearance (Cl) is measured as the volume of plasma cleared of a xenobiotic per unit of time.

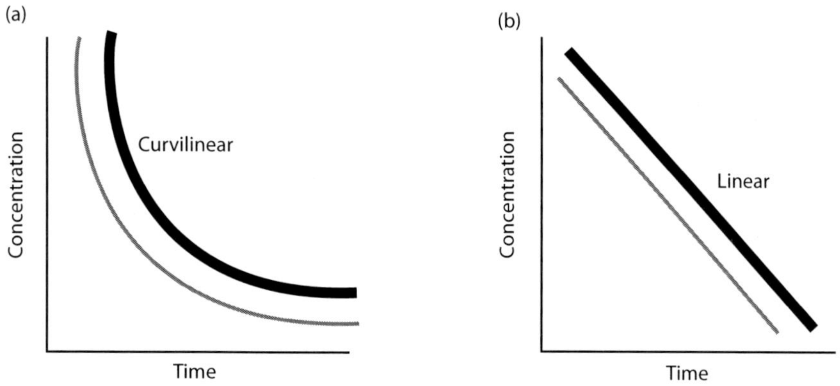

FIGURE 1.5 (a) First-order kinetics. The rate of a drug's elimination is directly proportional to its plasma concentration. Thus, the higher the drug concentration, the more rapid is the drug's elimination. Ex: most drugs. (b) Zero-order kinetics. The rate of the drug's elimination is independent of its concentration, and a constant amount of drug is eliminated per unit time. Ex: ethanol.

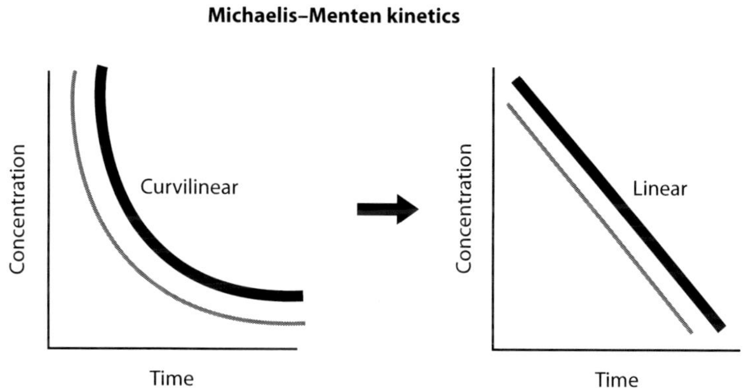

FIGURE 1.6 Michaelis–Menten kinetics. The rate of a drug's elimination is initially by first-order kinetics, and then switches to zero-order kinetics when the drug's hepatic metabolizing enzyme system becomes saturated to capacity.

Cl = *rate of elimination*/plasma concentration × time
= rate of elimination × V_d
= IV dose administered/area under $C \times t$

Renal Elimination

1. **Glomerular filtration (GF):** Dependent on cardiac output and renal perfusion, and independent of a drug's pH or lipid solubility; measured as the GF rate (GFR), normally 20% of renal plasma flow (600 mL/min) or *125 mL/min.*

2. **Proximal tubular secretion:** Drugs that are not eliminated in the glomerular filtrate may be removed by active transport using specific carrier proteins within the proximal tubules. Ex: Cadmium + metallothionein.
3. **Distal tubular reabsorption:** As high concentrations of uncharged, water-soluble (hydrophilic) phase I drug metabolites reach the distal convoluted tubules (DCTs), concentration gradients are created between the DCTs and the central circulatory compartment, allowing drug metabolites to be reabsorbed into plasma. Conversely, phase II hepatically metabolized drugs remain highly ionized, become trapped in the urine, and are unable to back diffuse into the central circulation. Ex: Alkalinization of the urine with sodium bicarbonate and forced diuresis with IV fluids will ion-trap acidic ASA and phenoxyacetic acid herbicide metabolites in the urine and augment GFR for enhanced elimination of toxic metabolites.

Enhanced Elimination

Corporeal Enhanced Elimination

- **Alkaline diuresis:** Traps weak acids and their metabolites (barbiturates, phenoxyacetic acid herbicides, salicylates—ASA) in the DCTs and enhances their renal excretion.
- **Gut dialysis:** Multiple doses of oral activated charcoal (AC) used to reverse diffusion gradients to back diffuse xenobiotics with low V_d s (<1 L/kg) from the plasma compartment back into the gut for fecal excretion. Ex: Multiple doses of AC for theophylline poisoning.

Extracorporeal Enhanced Elimination

- **Hemodialysis:** Most effective.
- **Hemoperfusion:** Only effective for drugs that are highly absorbed to AC. Ex: Theophylline.
- **Hemofiltration:** Effective for the slow and prolonged removal of high molecular weight (4500–40,000 Da) compounds, not amenable to hemodialysis (<500 Da).
- **Peritoneal dialysis:** Ineffective for the enhanced elimination of xenobiotics and not recommended.

Corporeal Enhanced Elimination

Multiple-Dose Activated Charcoal (AC)

Extracorporeal Enhanced Elimination

Indications for Enhanced Elimination

- Poisoned patients not responding to supportive care.
- Poisoned patients with impaired hepatic or renal elimination systems.
- Severely poisoned patients with ↑ drug concentrations associated with ↑ morbidity and mortality. Ex: Ethylene glycol, lithium.

- Poisoned patients at ↑ risks due to advanced age, pregnancy, or concurrent diseases.
- Poisoned patients with coexisting and nonresponsive volume or electrolyte disturbances. Ex: Fluid overload, acidosis, hyperkalemia.

Drug Factors Favoring the Use of Enhanced Elimination

- Low $V_d < 1$ L/kg
- Low molecular weight < 500 Da
- Water-soluble compounds
- Nonprotein-bound compounds
- Low endogenous renal clearance
- One-compartment model kinetics

Enhanced Elimination Techniques

- **Hemodialysis (HD):** Success requires that the toxin be of low MW and low V_d, water soluble, and not protein bound. Complications include bleeding, thrombosed access sites, and the elimination of therapeutic drugs, antidotes (folic acid), and water-soluble vitamins (vit K). Ex: Bromides, ethanol, *methanol*, *ethylene glycol*, chloral hydrate, *lithium*, *ASA*.
- **Hemoperfusion (HP):** Success requires that the toxin be highly adsorbed by AC. Preferred for poisoning with *theophylline* and *anticonvulsants* (carbamazepine, phenobarbital, and phenytoin).
- **Hemofiltration (HF):** Not as effective as HD or HP, but can be continued for days with fewer complications. Advantages include the ability to eliminate *high MW (4500–40,000 Da) and protein-bound toxins*. Preferred for toxins slowly eliminated from tissue binding sites, for example, aminoglycosides, lithium, and procainamide (Figures 1.5a, 1.5b, 1.6, and 1.7).

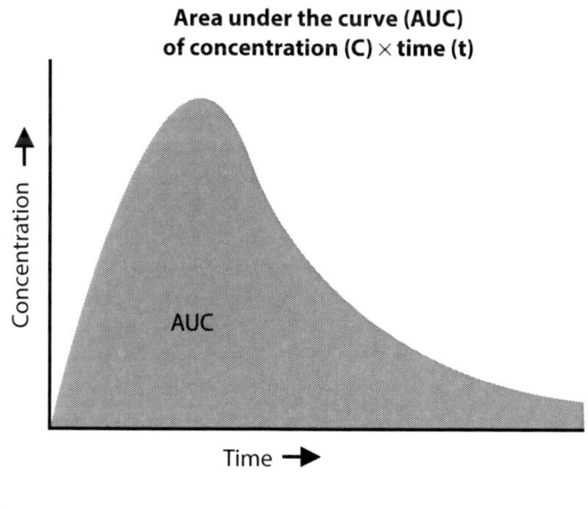

FIGURE 1.7 Plasma clearance. Plasma clearance is reflected by the area under the curve of a drug's plasma concentration over time, or clearance = the rate of elimination/plasma concentration × time.

Poison Pharmacology

Poisoning in Children 1

Epidemiology

- *67%* of all annual poisoning occur in children ≤19 years old.
- *Ingestion* is the route of exposure in *76%* of pediatric cases.
- *Children* <*5* years old have the highest CFRs and the highest rate of poisoning visits to Emergency Departments (EDs).

Ingested Agents

- *Cosmetics and personal care products* are the most commonly ingested nontoxic agents.
- *Medications* = 52% of ingestions.
- *Nonmedications* = 48% of ingestions.
- *Most lethal agents* = Cocaine, anticonvulsants, antidepressants (TCAs), iron > cleanings products, hydrocarbons.

Poisoning in Children 2

Most Commonly Ingested Agents

- Cosmetics/personal care
- Cleaning products
- Analgesics
- Plants
- Cough and cold preps
- Foreign bodies
- Topical agents
- Pesticides
- Vitamins

Hydrocarbons

Home Management

- **Ipecac:** Use only at home, only if directed by PCC, and within 1 h of ingestion. Avoid use with coma, convulsions, corrosives, coagulopathies, hydrocarbons, and in children <6 year old.
- **Position:** Left lateral decubitus, Trendelenburg.

Poisoning in Children 3

ED Management

- **Gastric lavage:** Only with airway protection and with life-threatening overdoses (TCAs) within 1 h of ingestion.

- Activated charcoal (AC): Administer 1 g/kg within the first hour of ingestion. Ineffective for alcohols and contraindicated for acids/alkalis/corrosives (caustics), hydrocarbons, metals (except thallium), and minerals (also metals).

PICU Management

- **Multi-dose-activated charcoal (MDAC):** Consider for life-threatening ingestions with drugs with high V_d's that are adsorbed to AC (HD unavailable) = carbamazepine, phenobarbital, theophylline.
- **Cathartics:** Only indicated with MDAC with *Mg citrate* preferred over > sorbitol. Consider *WBI* for slow-release drugs, iron, and lithium.

Poisoning in the Elderly

Behavioral and Physical Considerations

- **↓ muscle mass and ↑ fat:** Promotes ↑ V_d of lipophilic toxins. Ex: Benzodiazepines.
- **↑ total body water:** Promotes ↑ V_d of water-soluble toxins.

Compliance Problems

- **Age-related CNS problems:** Confusion, disorientation, depression, dementia
- **Dosing problems:** Multiple medications, drug tolerance

Pharmacokinetic Considerations

- **Absorption:** ↓ gastric acid secretion and ↓ gut motility
- **Distribution:** ↓ albumin binding and ↑ α-acid glycoprotein binding, ↓ gut and hepatic perfusion
- **Metabolism:** ↓ phase I hepatic metabolism; phase II hepatic metabolism remains unchanged
- **Excretion:** ↓ RPF = ↓ GFR = ↓ excretion by filtration

Chapter 2

General Poisoning Management

Preventing Absorption 22
Enhancing Elimination. 29
Physical Assessment 31
Pharmacokinetics. 33
Nontoxic Exposures. 35

Preventing Absorption

- Gastric emptying: Indications vs. contraindications
- Emesis vs. lavage?
- Activated charcoal
- Cathartics
- Whole bowel irrigation
- Alternative methods of GI emptying

Gastric Emptying?

Indications for Gastric Emptying 1

- **High-risk, potentially lethal ingestions:** Aspirin (ASA), calcium channel blockers (CCBs), chloroquine, colchicine, cyanide, TCAs, verapamil
- Recent ingestions, <1–2 h
- **Consequential toxicity:** Seizures, hypotension, arrhythmias
- **Ineffective or nonexistent antidotes:** CCBs, Fe, colchicine, paraquat, selenious acid
- **Enteric-coated or sustained-release tabs:** ASA, theophylline, verapamil
- **Agents that reduce GI motility:** Anticholinergics, opioids, sedative-hypnotics

Indications for Gastric Emptying 2

- **Agents that cause pylorospasm and gastric outlet obstruction:** ASA, meprobamate, iron
- **Agents that form concretions or masses:** ASA, enteric-coated and sustained release tabs, iron, meprobamate, phenobarbital

Contraindications to Gastric Emptying

- Caustic acid–alkali ingestions
- Hydrocarbon ingestions
- Sharp and pointed material ingestions
- Drug packet ingestions
- Bleeding diathesis, coagulopathies
- Esophageal varices and Mallory–Weiss tears
- Significant vomiting
- Nontoxic ingestions (Table 2.1)

Ipecac Emesis 1

Indications

- Witnessed ingestions
- Home use only
- Ingestions of objects too large for lavage tubes
- Ingestions by infants >6 months and small children (Figure 2.1)

Table 2.1 Nontoxic Home Products 1

Personal-Use Items	Art Supplies	Toys
Bath products, deodorants	Charcoal, chalk, clay, crayon	Bath toys
Shampoos, lotions	Latex paints	Caps
Cosmetics	Pens, pencils	Etch-a-Sketch®
Colognes	Glues	Play-Doh®
Hairsprays	Pastes	Toy cosmetics
Toothpastes	Watercolors	Teething rings

Contraindications

- Potential for compromised AW protective reflexes
- Imminent seizure or coma: INH, camphor
- Imminent deterioration: TCAs, propoxyphene, propranolol
- Caustic acid–alkali ingestions
- Hydrocarbon ingestions
- Sharp material ingestions
- Increased risks of bleeding
- Significant vomiting
- Nontoxic ingestions

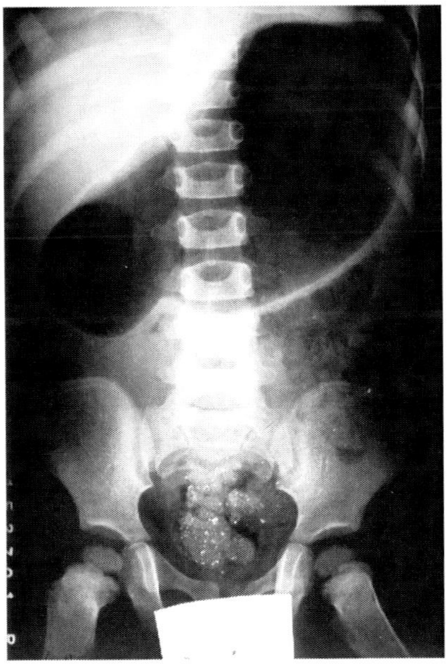

FIGURE 2.1 Nondissolving radiopacities in the gastrointestinal tract. Abdominal radiograph of a 3-year-old boy with a history of ingesting leaded paint chips peeling off doors and windows. Note radiopaque leaded paint chips in colon and rectum. (Courtesy of Carlos R. Gimenez, MD, Professor of Radiology, LSU School of Medicine, New Orleans, LA.)

Ipecac Emesis 2

Dose

- **Adults and children >5 years old:** 30 mL (2 tbsp), may repeat 1 time
- **Children 1–5 year old:** 15 mL (1 tbsp)
- **Infants 6–12 months old:** 10 mL (2 tsp)

Complications

- Intractable vomiting (rare), delayed emesis while unconscious
- Mallory–Weiss tears
- Pneumomediastinum
- Aspiration pneumonitis
- Delayed activated charcoal administration
- Electrolyte abnormalities
- Substance abuse = bulimia (Princess Diana, Karen Carpenter)

Emesis vs. Lavage?

- Orogastric lavage is preferable to ipecac-induced emesis in most of the hospital cases.
- Lavage has replaced emesis in all cases involving ingestions of toxic substances well adsorbed to activated charcoal.
- Reserve ipecac-induced emesis for witnessed ingestions at home, unless ipecac is contraindicated or activated charcoal administration is anticipated shortly.

Orogastric Lavage 1

Indications

- High-risk ingestions when a drug or toxin is still accessible in the stomach
- Ingestions that delay gastric emptying, cause gastric outlet obstruction, or form gastric concretions
- Ingestions of enteric-coated or sustained-release preparations

Contraindications

- Caustic acid or alkali ingestions
- Sharp material ingestions
- Drug packet ingestions
- Bleeding diathesis or increased risks of GI hemorrhage
- Prior significant emesis
- Nontoxic ingestions

Orogastric Lavage 2

Procedure

- Adults: 36–40 Fr orogastric tube (OG)
- Children: 22–28 Fr OG

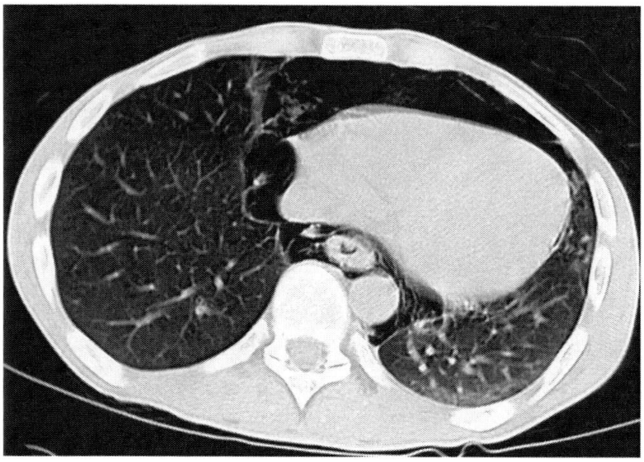

FIGURE 2.2 Orogastric tube-induced gastric perforation with pneumomediastinum. Computerized axial tomogram (CT) of the chest that demonstrates a huge pneumomediastinum surrounding the distal esophagus, heart, and descending thoracic aorta following the insertion of an orogastric tube for gastric lavage and activated charcoal (AC) administration. (Courtesy of Carlos R. Gimenez, MD, Professor of Radiology, LSU School of Medicine, New Orleans, LA.)

- ETT if AW compromised
- Left lateral decubitus
- Confirm OG place by x-ray
- Lavage in aliquots: Adults 250 mL and children 10 mL/kg of NS until clear, max 1 L for children
- Instill AC via OG tube (Figure 2.2)

Complications

- Inadvertent tracheal intubation or airway trauma
- Esophageal/gastric perforation with pneumomediastinum, mediastinitis, or hemorrhage
- Emesis
- Aspiration pneumonitis

Lavage-induced gastric perforation: *Pneumoperitoneum and pneumomediastinum* General Poison Mx

Activated Charcoal 1

Indications

- Activated charcoal (AC): Any substance known to bind to AC, especially highly toxic substances

- Multi-dose activated charcoal (MDAC): All drugs and toxins known to bind with small volumes of distribution (<1 L/kg), low renal clearance, little protein binding, and enterohepatic recirculation of toxic metabolites
- Drugs that reduce GI motility, form gastric concretions, and enteric-coated or sustained-release preparations

Contraindications

- Patients at risk for aspiration with unprotected AWs
- Caustic acid and alkali ingestions
- Ileus or small bowel obstruction
- Most hydrocarbon (need endoscopy) and heavy metal (or mineral) ingestions
- Most large volume (dose usually in g/kg) ingestions: Fe, Li, ethanol
- Single substance ingestions of iron, lithium, ethanol

Oral alkali (ammonia) burns: *AC contraindicated*

Activated Charcoal 2

Dose/Procedure

- Initial: *1 g/kg* for both adults and children, add sorbitol
- MDAC: *0.5–1.0 g/kg* q 1–4 h, no additional cathartics
- Consider NG and antiemetic to control vomiting
- Allow AC to leave the stomach before emptying

Complications

- Aspiration
- Emesis
- Obscuring GI mucosa limiting endoscopy to evaluate caustic burns
- Constipation
- Small bowel obstruction

Multiple-Dose AC

Cathartics 1

Indications

- Drugs or toxins that remain in the GI tract and may continue to be adsorbed to or desorbed from AC
- Combine only with the initial dose of AC or initial MDAC and do not repeat

Contraindications

- Abdominal trauma
- Intestinal ileus or small bowel obstruction
- Preexisting diarrhea

- Hypovolemia and dehydration
- Renal failure (Mg citrate and Mg sulfate)
- Routine use in children
- Prior cathartic dose(s)
- Hereditary fructose intolerance (sorbitol)

Cathartics 2

Dose

- **Sorbitol 70% is preferred:** For adults *1 g/kg* and for children 0.5 g/kg is administered.
- **10% Mg citrate:** A dose of *4 mL/kg* is administered for children and a max of 300 mL for adults is given.
- **Mg sulfate:** For adults *1 g/kg* and for children 0.5 g/kg is administered.

Complications

- Excessive diarrhea
- Emesis
- Electrolyte abnormalities
- Hypermagnesemia (Mg citrate and sulfate)
- Hypokalemia
- Hyponatremia
- Volume depletion and dehydration
- Hypernatremic dehydration (sorbitol)

Whole Bowel Irrigation 1

Indications

- **Sustained-release drugs:** Theophylline, CCBs, verapamil
- **Enteric-coated drugs:** Aspirin
- **Drugs or toxins not adsorbed by AC:** Iron, heavy metals, lithium
- **Slowly dissolving, solid substances:** Iron tablets, leaded paint chips, bezoars, and concretions
- **Crack vials:** Body stuffers, cocaine (Figure 2.3)
- **Drug packets:** Body packers, cocaine, and heroin

Contraindications

- Paralytic ileus or small bowel obstruction
- Abdominal trauma
- Rapidly absorbed drugs and toxins: Alcohols
- All liquid ingestions
- Hydrocarbon ingestions
- Caustic acid and alkali ingestions
- Parenterally administered drugs

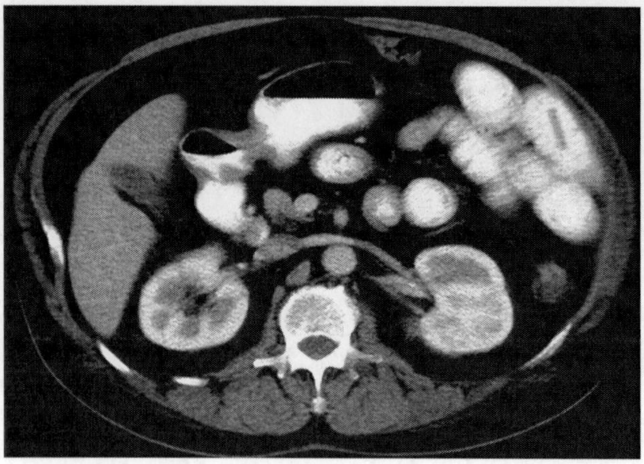

FIGURE 2.3 Body stuffer: Heroin. Axial abdominal oral and intravenous contrast-enhanced computerized tomogram (CT) at the level of the renal veins that demonstrated a rectangular container of heroin in a jejunal loop. (Courtesy of Carlos R. Gimenez, MD, Professor of Radiology, LSU School of Medicine, New Orleans, LA.)

Whole Bowel Irrigation 2

Dose

- **Adults:** 2 L/h
- **Children:** 0.5 L/h

Complications

- Vomiting, especially with rapid administration
- Bloating
- Decreased efficiency of activated charcoal
- Rectal itching from diarrhea

Alternative GI Emptying

Other Binding Agents

- **Cholestyramine and colestipol:** Methotrexate and organochlorine pesticides-lindane (Kwell®) and chlordecone (Kepone®)
- **Sodium polystyrene sulfonate (Kayexalate®):** Lithium and potassium
- **Ferric ferrocyanide (Prussian blue):** Thallium and cesium
- **Fuller's earth (DE):** Paraquat and diquat (Figure 2.4)

Surgical Emptying

- Rupture of cocaine drug packets
- Mechanical bowel obstruction by cocaine drug packets
- **Bezoars:** Aspirin, bromide, meprobamate

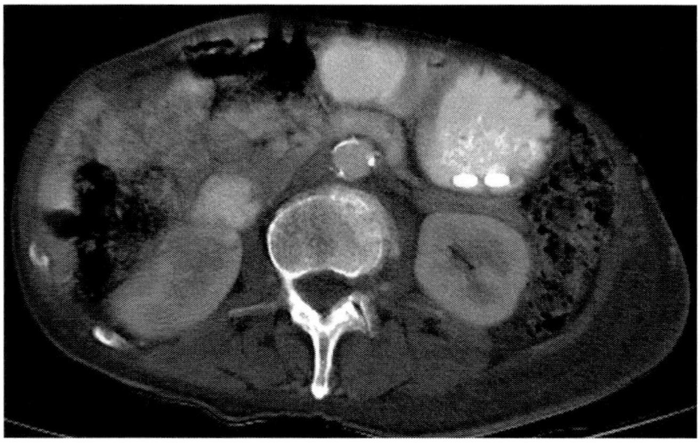

FIGURE 2.4 Slowly dissolving substances: Enteric-coated phenothiazine tablets in stomach. Axial oral and contrast-enhanced computerized tomogram (CT) at the stomach level that demonstrates two slowly dissolving radiopaque substances (enteric-coated phenothiazine tablets). (Courtesy of Carlos R. Gimenez, MD, Professor of Radiology, LSU School of Medicine, New Orleans, LA.)

Enhancing Elimination

Methods

- Manipulation of urine pH
- Forced diuresis
- Peritoneal dialysis
- Hemodialysis
- Charcoal hemoperfusion
- Continuous hemofiltration
- Plasmapheresis and exchange transfusion

Indications

- **Small volume of distribution:** Poison remains in the blood compartment and not distributed to tissues
- **Low endogenous renal clearance rate:** Alcohols, beta-blockers, lithium, phenytoin, paraquat, salicylates, theophylline
- Poisons that are not lipid soluble or highly protein bound

Urinary Alkalinization

- **Mech:** To trap weak acids in alkalinized tubular fluid to prevent tubular absorption and promote urinary excretion.

- **Indic:** Salicylates, phenobarbital, chlorpropamide, formic acid (methanol), chlorphenoxyacetic acid herbicides, methotrexate, myoglobinuria from rhabdomyolysis.
- **Comp:** Volume overload, metabolic alkalosis. Urine acidification not recommended.

Forced Diuresis

- **Mech:** To produce diuresis by volume expansion with Na-containing solutions, NS or LR. Often combined with diuretics.
- **Indic:** Not recommended except to protect the kidneys from myoglobinuria in extensive rhabdomyolysis.
- **Exception**: *Forced Cl diuresis with NaCl + mannitol* for *platinoid (cisplatin)* OD.
- **Comp:** Volume overload and electrolyte disturbances.

Peritoneal Dialysis

- **Mech:** To enhance the elimination of water-soluble, low MW, poorly protein-bound substances with low volumes of distribution
- **Indic:** Too slow to be useful and not recommended

Hemodialysis

- **Mech:** To enhance the elimination of *water-soluble, very low MW (<500 Da), non-protein-bound* compounds with a *low volume of distribution (<1 L/kg)* and *low endogenous renal clearance (<4 mL/kg/min)*
- **Indic:** Bromide, lithium, salicylates, all alcohols = ethylene glycol, methanol, isopropanol and chloral hydrate, and its 1° HC metabolite, trichloroethanol
- **Comp:** Bleeding, access comp, air embolism, nosocomial infection

Charcoal Hemoperfusion

- **Mech:** To enhance the elimination of compounds adsorbed by AC in an extracorporeal fashion; can be used in series with HD.
- **Indic:** Anticonvulsants: Carbamazepine, phenobarbital, and phenytoin; *theophylline; thallium (Exception: Only heavy metal adsorbed to AC).* In series *HP-HD:* Carbamazepine, theophylline, procainamide, thallium.
- **Comp:** Same as dialysis + charcoal embolization, leukopenia, thrombocytopenia, and hypocalcemia.

Continuous Hemofiltration

- **Mech:** To enhance the elimination of very high MW (10,000–40,000 Da) compounds by using the patient's arterial pressure (CAVH) or a blood pump (CVVH) to continuously perfuse a large pore size dialysis membrane
- **Indic:** To clear very large molecules, such as methotrexate, heparin, protamine, insulin, myoglobin, and antibiotics, especially vancomycin
- **Comp:** Same as HD 2° anticoagulation; removes therapeutic drugs = antibiotics

Plasmapheresis

- **Mech:** To enhance elimination of large MW compounds (>15,000 Da) that are not dialyzable and have limited endogenous metabolism. FFP and albumin are used to replace removed plasma.
- **Indic:** To remove protein-bound molecules, such as Ag/Ab complexes, as in serum sickness, multiple sclerosis, immune complex nephritis.
- **Comp:** Transfusion-related anaphylaxis or allergic manifestations.

Exchange Transfusion

- **Mech:** Same as plasmapheresis, but the replacement of removed blood is with WB or PRBCs
- **Indic:** Usually reserved for neonates
- **Comp:** All transfusion-related

Physical Assessment

- 1° survey and treatment: OD + ↓ mental status
- 2° survey and treatment
- Alcohol and drug combined OD
- Pregnant patient OD
- Caustic cutaneous and ocular injuries

Primary Survey and Tx

Primary Survey

- Clear the airway
- Assess and protect the C-spine
- Intubate comatose patients for ventilation, lavage, and AC
- Order ABGs and COHb
- ECG and temp monitoring
- Start IV, fluid load—NS or LR; draw CBC, glucose, electrolytes, liver function tests (LFTs), BUN, creatinine, tox screen
- Manage 3 seizure (sz) types: (1) *BZ responsive*-EtOH withdrawal; (2) *special antidote* required—*pyridoxine + INH, Gyromitra*; (3) motor ceases, EEG sz persists—CO

Primary Treatment = Coma Cocktail

- **Dextrose:** *0.5–1.0 g/kg* $D_{50}W$ ($D_{10}W$ for children) to manage or exclude hypoglycemia
- **Thiamine:** *100 mg* IV to manage or prevent alcoholic Wernicke–Korsakoff syndrome (unnecessary in children)
- **Naloxone:** *2 mg* IV for both children and adults
- **Oxygen** at high flow rates, 8–10 L/min

Secondary Survey and Tx

Secondary Survey

- Exclude heart murmurs = subacute bacterial endocarditis (SBE), intravenous drug users (IVDUs)
- Exclude brady and tachydysrhythmias = dig, ß-blockers, CCBs, tricyclic antidepressants (TCAs)
- Exclude silent abdomen = anticholinergics, opioids
- Examine extremities for needle tracks and evidence of heavy metal poisoning (Mees' lines, arsenical keratoses)

Secondary Treatment

- **Gastric emptying:** No emesis, lavage + initial AC with cathartic
- Consider enhanced elimination beginning with MDAC, no further cathartics
- Consider other modalities of enhanced elimination

General Poison Mx

Mees' lines: *Chronic arsenic and thallium poisoning*

Hyperkeratoses: *Chronic arsenic poisoning*

The Unknown Overdose

Contraindicated Treatments

- No analeptics
- No flumazenil
- No forced diuresis
- No urinary acidification
- No IA or IC antiarrhythmics
- No long-acting opioid antagonists (only naloxone)
- Choose appropriate vasopressor support 2° myocardial sensitization

Alcohol + Drug OD

- Give coma cocktail.
- Monitor CVP/PAP prior to fluid and inotropic treatment (tx).
- Suspect concomitant trauma or complications. Head CT?
- Secure ICU bed.
- Alcohol breath does not indicate intoxication, suspect combined etiologies. Sole EtOH ODs will awaken in 3–4 h.

Unusual Exposures

OD in Pregnancy

- Manage hypotension aggressively
- Maintain left lateral decubitus position
- Anticipate respiratory acidosis

- Avoid all unusual antidotes, except naloxone
- Maintain high index of suspicion for CO poisoning; measure COHb by co-oximetry; *HBO for COHb ≥ 15%*

Cutaneous and Ocular Exposures

- **Skin:** (1) PPE for EMS-OP and sodium azide poisoning of EMS; (2) remove and bag all clothing; (3) bathe patient (pt) with soap and water × 2; (4) never try to neutralize acid or base burns; (5) do not apply cream or grease → prolong contact and ↑ absorption and burn injury
- **Eye:** (1) topical anesthetic and lid retractor; (2) *1–2 L BSS* > NS > LR > H_2O irrigation; (3) pH strip to fornix → maintain pH 6.5–7.6

Diagnostic Odors of Xenobiotics

- **Bitter almond**—cyanide
- **Carrots**—water hemlock (cicutoxin)
- **Eggs, rotten**—H_2S, CS_2, mercaptans, disulfiram, *N*-acetylcysteine (NAC)
- **Fish**—zinc phosphide, aluminum phosphide
- **Garlic**—arsenic, DMSO, phosphorous, selenium, thallium
- **Hay**—phosgene
- **Mothballs**—camphor, naphthalene, *p*-dichlorobenzene
- **Pear**—paraldehyde
- **Shoe polish**—nitrobenzene
- **Tobacco**—nicotine
- **Rope, burnt**—marijuana, opium
- **Vinyl**—ethylchlorvynol (Placidyl®-*Jelly Bellies*)
- **Vinegar**—acetic acid
- **Violets**—terpenes, turpentine
- **Wintergreen**—methyl salicylate

Pharmacokinetics

- Drug compartment models
- Drug elimination patterns

Compartment Models 1

- **One Compartment:** Simple instantaneous equilibration model in which drug enters the central circulatory compartment and is rapidly distributed to tissues, with plasma concentrations determining proportional changes in tissue concentrations. Ex: Ethanol.
- **Two Compartment:** Most common model in which drug instantaneously distributes to two compartments, the more highly perfused central compartment and its viscera (brain, lungs, liver, kidneys) and the less perfused tissue compartments (muscle, fat, skin, bone). Ex: Barbiturates, volatile anesthetics.

Compartment Models 2

- **Three to Five Compartment:** Most complex model in which drug or toxin (especially heavy metals) distribute first to a central circulatory compartment, then to a highly perfused visceral compartment, and finally to the least perfused third compartment (bone, teeth, nails, hair). The soft tissue and bone compartments (cortical and trabecular) are often subdivided into labile and stable equilibrating subcompartments in a five-compartment model. Ex: Lead, cadmium.

Lead Three Compartment

- Lead distributes in a three-compartment model (Figure 2.5).

Lead Five Compartment

- Lead distributes in a five-compartment model (Figure 2.6).

Elimination Kinetics

- **First-order:** *Constant percentage or proportion* of drug eliminated per unit time. Plot of concentration vs. time is *curvilinear.* Log concentration plot—linear. Ex: Most drugs.
- **Zero-order:** *Constant fixed amount* of drug eliminated per unit time. Plot of concentration vs. time is *linear.* Log plot—curvilinear. Ex: Alcohol.

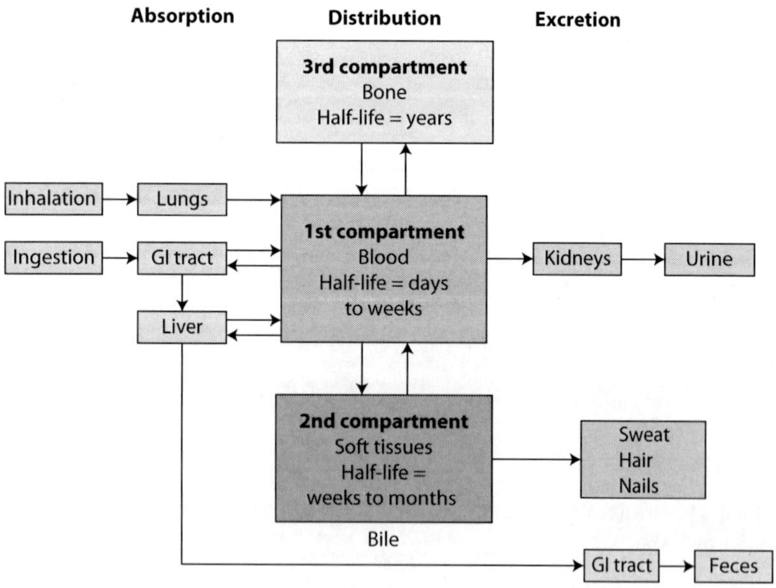

FIGURE 2.5 Ingested lead distributes in a three-compartment model. Ingested lead is distributed in a three-compartment model in which the heavy metal is initially distributed to a central circulatory compartment; then to a highly perfused visceral organ compartment; and finally to the least perfused third compartment composed of bone, teeth, nails, and hair.

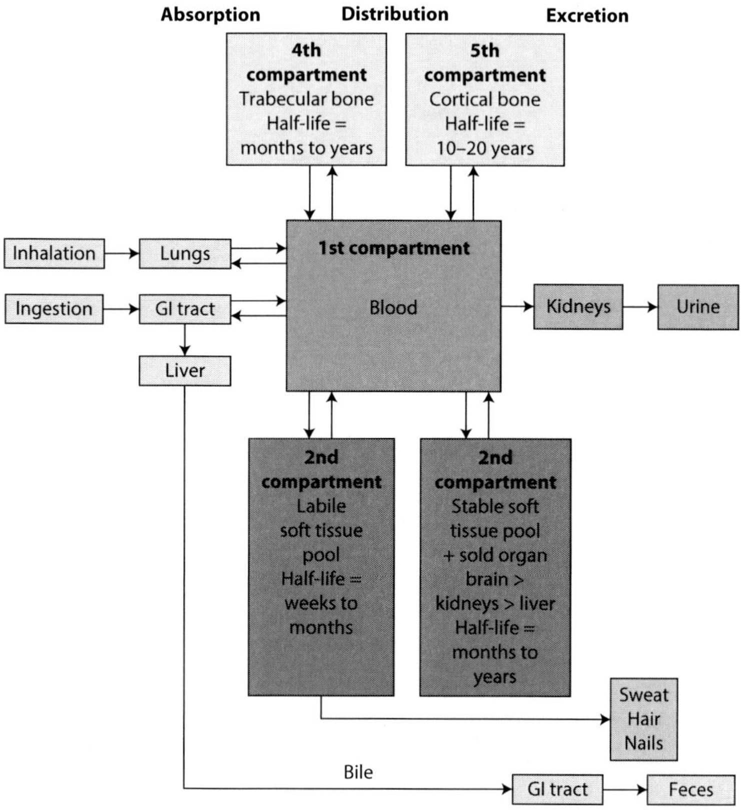

FIGURE 2.6 Ingested lead distributes in a five-compartment model. Ingested lead is distributed in a five-compartment model in which the heavy metal is initially distributed to a central circulatory compartment; then to a highly perfused visceral organ compartment; and finally to the least perfused third compartment composed of bone and soft tissues, subdivided into labile and stable subcompartments.

- **Michaelis–Menten:** Drug elimination pattern *changes* from first-order to zero-order as drug concentration increases, reflecting *saturation*. Both plots of concentration vs. time are *curvilinear.*

Nontoxic Exposures

- Epidemiology of nontoxic exposures
- Categorizing exposures as nontoxic
- Common nontoxic household exposures

Epid: Nontoxic Exposures

- More than 40% of poison exposures reported to Poison Control Centers are nontoxic exposures.

- Nontoxic exposures fall into two categories: (1) exposures to products unlikely to cause toxicity at any dose; and (2) exposures to products that are potential toxins, but at doses that are nontoxic, for example, acetaminophen ingestions <150 mcg/kg.

Categorizing Nontoxic Exp

- The product must be absolutely identified.
- There is only a single product exposure.
- The exposure must be unintentional.
- *Consumer Product Safety Commission (CPSC) warnings must not appear on labels: Caution, Warning, Danger!*
- A reliable approximation of the amount (dose/kg) of exposure must be made.
- The route of exposure must be assured by history.
- The exposed patient is symptom-free.
- Follow-up consultation must be available (Table 2.2).

Table 2.2 Nontoxic Home Products 2

Medications	Cleansers	Miscellaneous
Antacids, antibiotics	Fabric softeners	Matches, candles
Oral contraceptives, steroids	Bleach, 2–5%	Newspaper
Calamine lotion	Detergents	Grease, motor oils
Mineral oil	Most soaps	Incense, putty
Zinc and zirconium oxide	Dishwasher liquids	Spackle, silica gels

Chapter 3

Diagnostic Work-Up of the Poisoned Patient

Lab Assessment 38
Testing Methods 1 38
Testing Methods 2 38
Blood/Serum Levels. 39
Routine Serum Tox 39
Radiographic Assessment 40
Visualizing Toxins 40
Toxic Skeletal Changes 40
Chest X-Rays: Lungs 41
Chest X-Rays: Pleura, Mediastinum, Heart, and Great Vessels. 44
Abdominal X-Rays 45
Head CT. 46
Electrocardiogram (ECG) Assessment 47
ECG: Lytes and Temp 47
ECG: Dig and TCAs 49
ECG: Tachyarrhythmias. 50
ECG: Bradyarrhythmias. 52
ECG: Ischemia and Ectopy 52

Lab Assessment

Three Types of Lab Tests

- **Monitoring:** Requires precision. Ex: Gentamicin levels.
- **Screening:** Requires sensitivity. Ex: Employee drug tests.
- **Diagnostic:** Requires specificity. Ex: Drug toxicology screen.

Testing Methods (Sensitivity and Specificity + to +++)

- Chemical spot tests (+)
- Spectrophotometric assays (+)
- Immunoassays (++)
- Thin-layer chromatography (++)
- High-performance liquid chromatography (++)
- Gas chromatography (++)
- GC + mass spectrometry (+++)

Testing Methods 1

Chemical Spot Tests

- **Mechanism:** Identifies the chemical reactivity between a drug and its specific reagent
- **Indication:** Quick detection of single substances
- **Example:** + urine ferric chloride test for aspirin (also + for phenothiazines)

Spectrophotometric Tests

- **Mech:** Converts target drugs into identifiable ultraviolet (UV) light-absorbing compounds
- **Indic:** Co-oximetry (CO, COHb, CN) and colorimetry
- **Ex:** Replaced by immunoassays

Testing Methods 2

Immunoassays

- **Mech:** Wide applications; use drug-specific antibodies to identify toxic antigens, cross-reacting group antigens often yield false positives on screening immunoassays (ephedrine and methamphetamine)
- **Indic:** Employee drug testing; affords rapid turn around

Chromatographic Assays

- **Thin Layer Chromatography (TLC):** Drugs are spotted and coated onto plates, then coated with silica gels.
- **High Pressure Liquid Chromatography (HPLC):** Drugs are separated as liquids under ↑ pressures within tightly packed columns.

- **Gas Chromatography (GC):** Drugs are extracted as gases at specific temperatures, then detected.
- **Gas Chromatography/Mass Spectrometry (GC/MS):** Most sensitive/most specific; effluent gases from GC are extracted, then ionized, and detected by MS. Ex: opioid and amphetamine confirmation tests.

Blood/Serum Levels

Order for Diagnosis (OD)

- Acetaminophen *(>150 mcg/mL)*
- Carbon monoxide *(>15%)*
- Ethanol *(>0.08–0.10%)*
- Ethylene glycol *(>25 mg/dL)*
- Iron *(>500 mcg/dL)*
- Methanol *(>25 mg/dL)*
- MetHb *(>20–30%)*
- Salicylate *(>60 mg/dL)*
- Theophylline *(>90–100 mcg/mL)*

Order for Treatment

- Therapeutic monitoring for all diagnostics, except ethanol
- *Digoxin (>4 ng/mL)*
- Heavy metals: arsenic, lead, mercury
- *Lithium (>4 mEq/L)*
- Organophosphates (AchE)
- Phenobarbital *(>100 mcg/mL)*
- General Poison Mx

Routine Serum Tox

Toxins Detected

- Alcohols and analgesics
- Antihistamines
- Antidepressants
- Amphetamines
- Barbiturates and sedatives
- Benzodiazepines
- Cardiovascular drugs
- Opioids and neuroleptics
- **Misc:** Theophylline, caffeine, nicotine, sulfonylureas, strychnine

Toxins Not Detected

- **Too polar:** Antibiotics, diuretics, INH, lithium, metals
- **Too nonpolar:** Digoxin, steroids
- **Too volatile:** Anesthetics, volatile HCs
- **Too nonvolatile:** Plant alkaloids
- **Concentrations too low:** Very potent drugs taken in small doses—fentanyl, sufentanil, colchicine, and LSD
- **Toxic anions:** Bromide, cyanide, fluoride, and nitrites
- All **new** drugs

Radiographic Assessment

- Visualizing the toxin: Unknown vs. known toxins
- Toxin-induced skeletal changes
- Chest x-ray findings in poisonings
- Abdominal x-ray findings in poisonings
- Brain CT findings in poisonings

Visualizing Toxins

Unknown Toxin

- Radiopacity = ↑ physical density + ↑ atomic number
- Radiopaque meds contain constituents of *atomic no. >15*: Most heavy metals, barium, bismuth, calcium, *chlorine*, iron, lead, potassium
- *CCHIPES* = Anticipate radiopacity with: *C*hlorine and *c*hloral hydrate, *C*Cl_4, *h*eavy metals (As, Cd, Cr, Fe, Hg, Pb, Th, Tl), *i*ron, *p*henothiazines, *s*ustained-release and *E*CTs, *C*l-*s*olvents

Known Toxin

- **Iron:** Ferrous gluconate/sulfate
- **Heavy metals:** As, Cd, Cr, Fe, Hg, Pb, Tl
- **Toxins in packets and containers:** Packers and stuffers
- **Mothballs:** Paradi*chloro*benzene (densely radiopaque) > naphthalene > camphor (radiolucent)
- **Halogenated hydrocarbons:** ↑ *chlorine* groups—CCl_4, chloral hydrate, chloroform

Toxic Skeletal Changes

Increased Bone Density

- **Transverse metaphyseal bands:** Lead (arsenic) lines

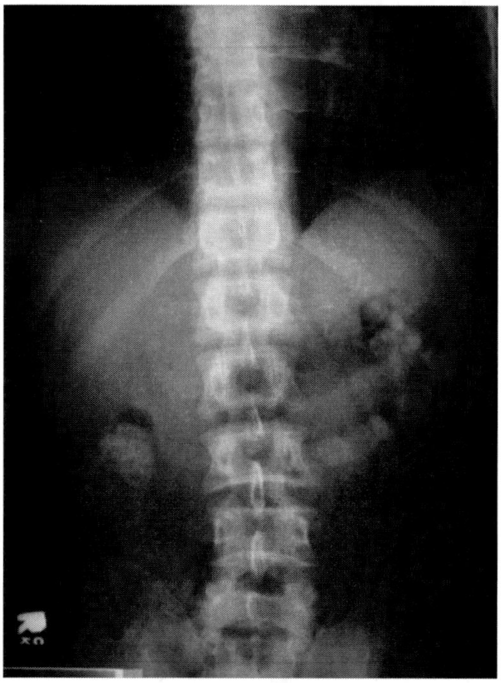

FIGURE 3.1 Bismuth subsalicylate (Pepto-Bismal®) abuse. Abdominal radiograph that demonstrates ascending right colon and transverse colon radiopaque substances in a patient with chronic bismuth subsalicylate abuse. (Courtesy of Carlos R. Gimenez, MD, Professor of Radiology, LSU School of Medicine, New Orleans, LA.)

- **Fluorosis (children and adults):** Otosclerosis, osteophytosis, ligament and tendon calcifications
- **Pediatric hypervitaminosis A:** Subperiosteal new bone and cortical hyperostosis
- **Pediatric hypervitaminosis D:** Generalized otosclerosis (Figure 3.1)

Decreased Bone Density

- **Corticosteroids:** Diffuse osteoporosis + focal osteonecrosis (AVN)
- **Adult hypervitaminosis D:** Diffuse osteoporosis, nephrocalcinosis
- **Focal, lytic osteomyelitis:** IVDUs-septic emboli in the sternum and sternoclavicular joints
- **Distal acro-osteolysis:** Vinyl chloride monomer (Figure 3.2)

Chest X-Rays: Lungs

Airspace Filling

- **Diffuse filling:** ARDS-noncardiogenic pulmonary edema = ASA, opioids, cocaine

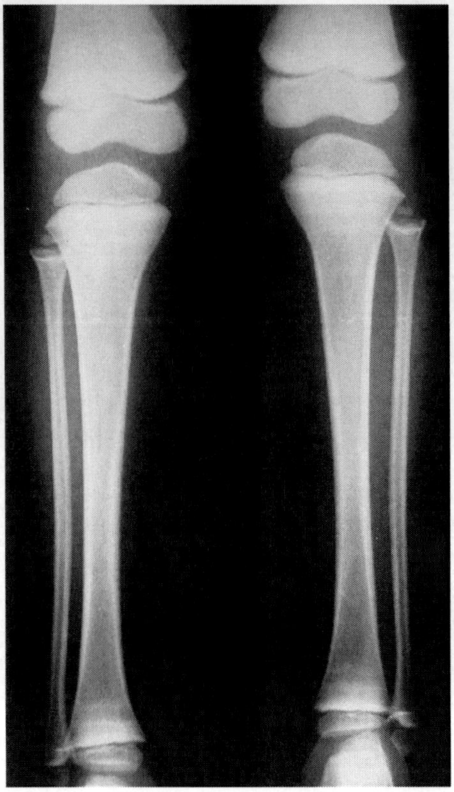

FIGURE 3.2 Metaphyseal "lead lines." Frontal long bone radiograph of the legs of a 3.5-year-old girl with a chronic history of ingesting lead paint chips. Note the thickened, transverse, radiodense metaphyseal "lead (or arsenic) lines" and the widening of the metaphyses. (Courtesy of Carlos R. Gimenez, MD, Professor of Radiology, LSU School of Medicine, New Orleans, LA.)

- **Diffuse:** Cardiogenic pulmonary edema: alcoholic and cobalt cardiomyopathy, cocaine cardiomyopathy
- **Diffuse:** Cholinergic bronchorrhea = OPs, carbamates, inhalants, low water solubility gases (NO_2, phosgene)
- **Focal filling:** Aspiration, especially HCs (Figures 3.3 and 3.4)

Interstitial Patterns

- **Reticulonodular:** Hypersensitivity pneumonitis (sulfa drugs—nitrofurantoin) and allergic alveolitis (farmer's lung, etc.)
- **Interstitial fibrosis:** Cytotoxic chemotherapeutics (busulfan, bleomycin, methotrexate, cyclophosphamide)
- **Phospholipidosis:** Amiodarone, injected particles—talcosis
- **Pneumoconioses:** Asbestos, beryllium, coal, silica

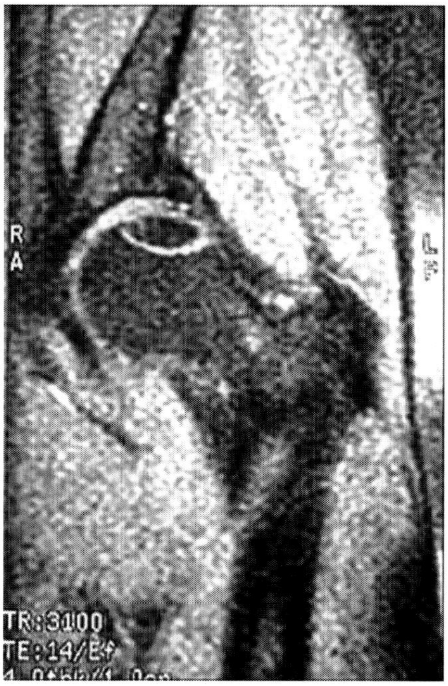

FIGURE 3.3 Steroid-induced osteonecrosis. Coronal magnetic resonance (MRI) of the left hip in a patient on chronic corticosteroid therapy that demonstrates the characteristic "double line" sign of steroid-induced osteonecrosis with inner and outer hyperintense rim lines. (Courtesy of Carlos R. Gimenez, MD, Professor of Radiology, LSU School of Medicine, New Orleans, LA.)

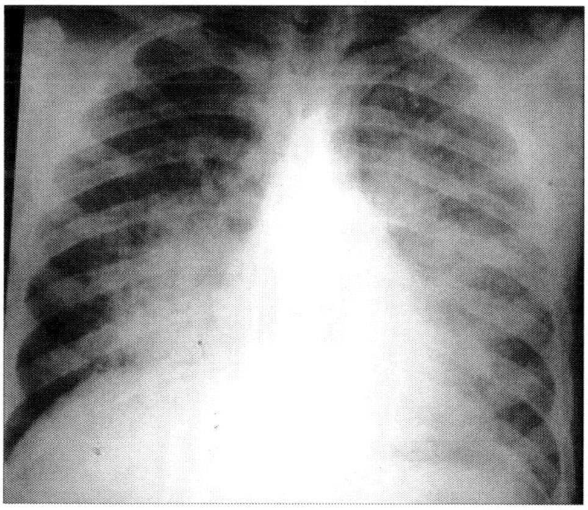

FIGURE 3.4 Noncardiogenic pulmonary edema: Heroin overdose. Frontal chest radiograph that demonstrates normal size and configuration of the cardiomediastinal silhouette with diffuse bilateral noncardiogenic pulmonary edema following heroin overdose. (Courtesy of Carlos R. Gimenez, MD, Professor of Radiology, LSU School of Medicine, New Orleans, LA.)

Chest X-Rays: Pleura, Mediastinum, Heart, and Great Vessels (Figures 3.5 and 3.6)

- **Pleural effusions:** Drug-induced lupus syndromes = hydralazine and procainamide; isoniazid, methyldopa, chlorpropamide; anthrax

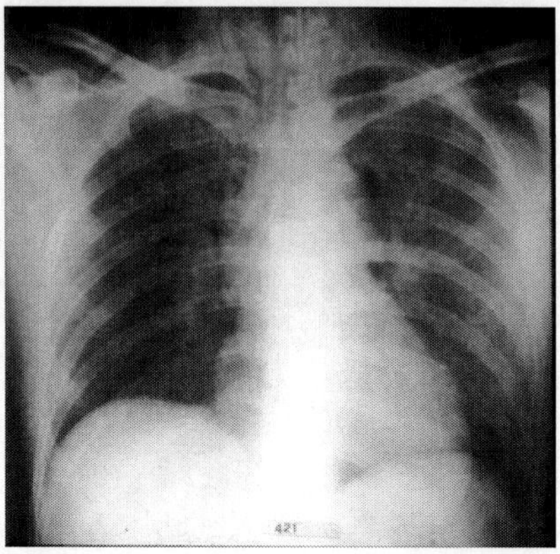

FIGURE 3.5 Pneumomediastinum: crack-cocaine inhalation. Frontal chest radiograph that demonstrates abnormal scattered radiolucencies in the mediastinum and the base of the neck consistent with pneumomediastinum and cervical subcutaneous emphysema following crack-cocaine inhalation. (Courtesy of Carlos R. Gimenez, MD, Professor of Radiology, LSU School of Medicine, New Orleans, LA.)

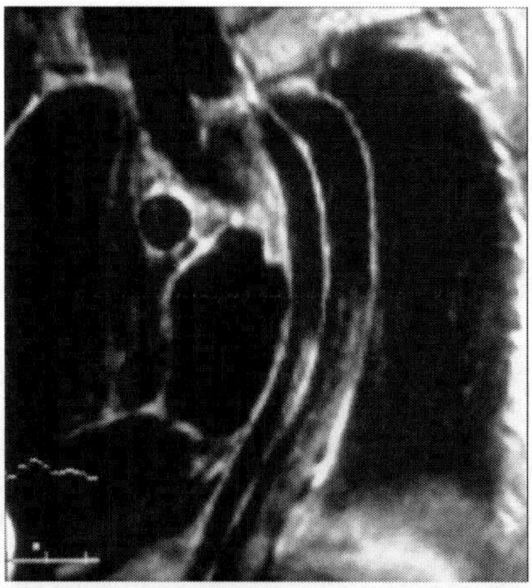

FIGURE 3.6 Cocaine-induced acute aortic dissection. Sagittal, oblique, T-1-weighted magnetic resonance image (MRI) of the chest demonstrating an intimal flap that divides the lumen of the descending aorta into a false lumen and a true lumen with blood flow, consistent with acute thoracic aortic dissection Type B in an intravenous crack-cocaine abuser. (Courtesy of Carlos R. Gimenez, MD, Professor of Radiology, LSU School of Medicine, New Orleans, LA.)

- **Pneumomediastinum:** Caustic-induced esophageal perforation, ipecac or alcohol-induced Mallory–Weiss syndrome
- **Pleural plaques:** Asbestosis
- **Hilar lymphadenopathy:** Phenytoin; anthrax, tularemia
- **Cardiomegaly:** Alcoholic and cobalt cardiomyopathy, cardiotoxic chemotherapeutics = adriamycin
- **Aortic dissection:** Cocaine, ergots

Abdominal X-Rays (Figures 3.7 through 3.9)

- **Pneumoperitoneum:** 2° GI perforation = caustics (acids, alkalis, iron), cocaine, ipecac, lavage tube

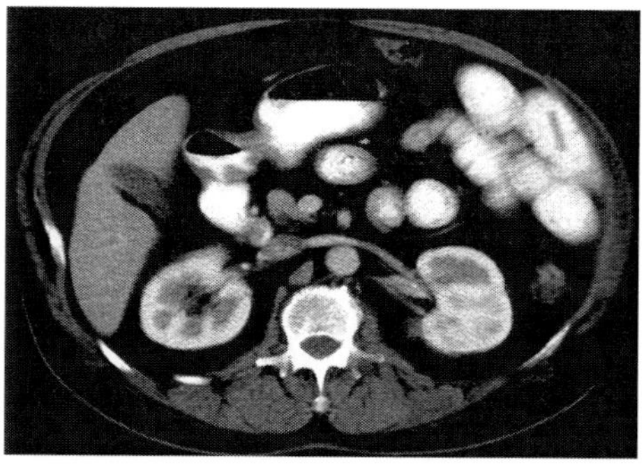

FIGURE 3.7 Body stuffer: heroin. Axial abdominal oral and intravenous contrast-enhanced computerized tomogram (CT) at the level of the renal veins that demonstrated a rectangular container of heroin in a jejunal loop. (Courtesy of Carlos R. Gimenez, MD, Professor of Radiology, LSU School of Medicine, New Orleans, LA.)

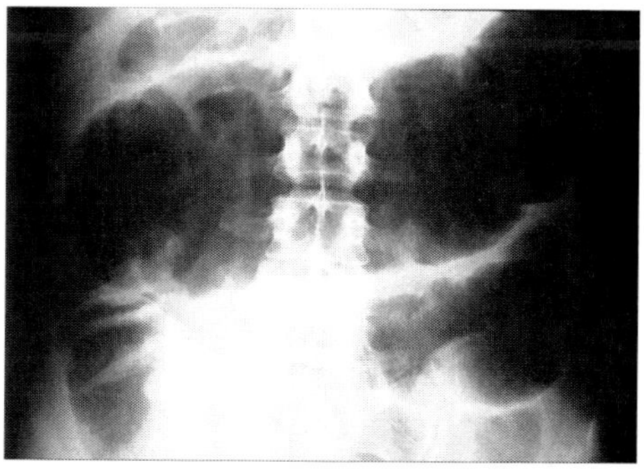

FIGURE 3.8 Opioid bowel: colonic ileus in a methadone abuser. Abdominal radiograph (KUB) that demonstrates air distension of the small bowel and transverse colon consistent with chronic constipation and colonic ileus in a methadone abuser. (Courtesy of Carlos R. Gimenez, MD, Professor of Radiology, LSU School of Medicine, New Orleans, LA.)

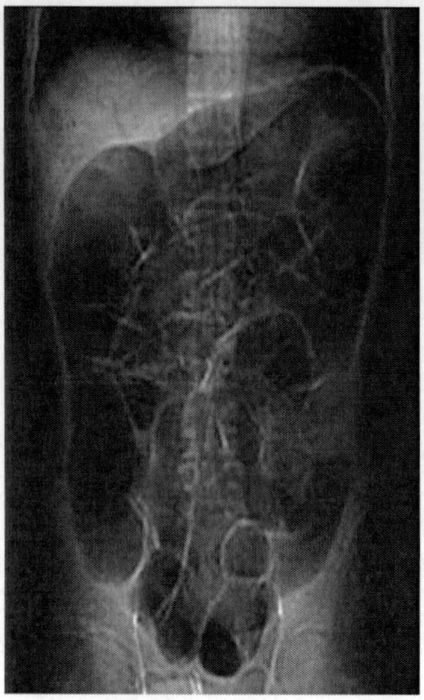

FIGURE 3.9 Cocaine-induced intestinal ischemia. Abdominal radiograph (KUB) demonstrating gas in the main portal vein and its intrahepatic primary and secondary branches with diffuse dilation and pneumotosis intestinalis of the small bowel and colon in a chronic cocaine abuser with acute mesenteric ischemia and multiple small bowel infarctions. Chronic ergot alkaloid ingestion may also be associated with acute mesenteric ischemia and small bowel infarction. (Courtesy of Carlos R. Gimenez, MD, Professor of Radiology, LSU School of Medicine, New Orleans, LA.)

- **Mechanical obstruction:** 2° gastric outlet bezoars, or SBO = enteric-coated tabs, concretions, body packers
- **Ileus:** 2° decreased GI motility = anticholinergics, TCAs, opioids, ischemic (cocaine, OCPs), ↓ K and ↓ Mg
- **Intramural gas:** 2° intestinal vasospasm, thrombosis, infarction = cocaine, ergots, OCPs
- **Radiodense FBs** = Barium, bismuth subsalicylate, bromide, calcium carbonate, clay (pica), iron, and other heavy metals, especially lead-paint chips

Head CT

- **Intracranial hemorrhage:** 2° intraparenchymal CVA and SAH = amphetamines, cocaine, ephedrine and pseudoephedrine, *phenylpropanolamine*, phencyclidine (PCP); or subdural = head trauma (alcohol, sedative-hypnotics, seizures)
- **Lucencies:** 2° basal ganglia necrosis = CO, CN, CS_2 H_2S, Mn, methanol; vasospasm = cocaine, ergots; septic emboli = IVDUs
- **Atrophy:** Cerebral and cerebellar = alcohol and toluene
- **Calcifications:** Basal ganglia = CO and Pb (Figure 3.10)

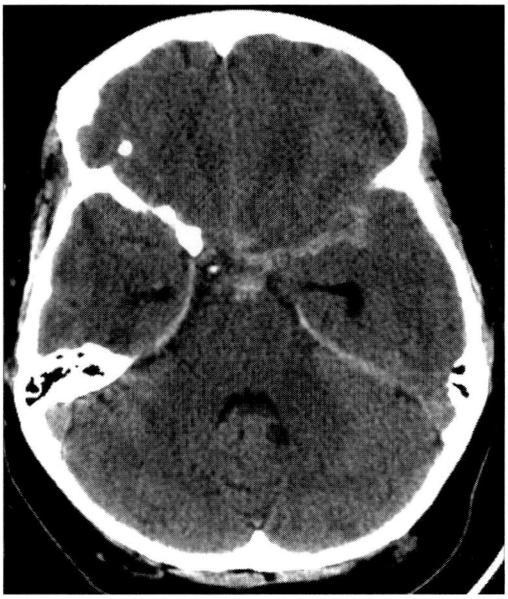

FIGURE 3.10 Subarachnoid hemorrhage: intravenous cocaine abuse. Cranial computerized axial tomogram (CT) at the level of the pons that demonstrates acute blood hyperdensities in the suprachiasmatic cistern extending into the left Sylvian fissure, consistent with acute subarachnoid hemorrhage following intravenous cocaine overdose. (Courtesy of Carlos R. Gimenez, MD, Professor of radiology, LSU School of Medicine, New Orleans, LA.)

Electrocardiogram (ECG) Assessment

- Electrolyte and temperature-induced arrhythmias
- Digoxin and TCA-induced arrhythmias
- Tachyarrhythmias
- Prolonged QT syndromes, ventricular tachycardia and torsades de pointes
- Bradyarrhythmias

ECG: Lytes and Temp

Electrolyte Disturbances

ECG: K Effects
Hyperkalemia: *No P, wide QRS, tall peak T*
Hypokalemia: *Shorter-inverted T, U wave*

- **Hyperkalemia:** Tall tented T waves and progressive widening of the QRS (Figure 3.11a)
- **Hypokalemia:** Progressive decrease in T wave amplitude with U waves, and eventual fusion of T and U waves (Figure 3.11b)

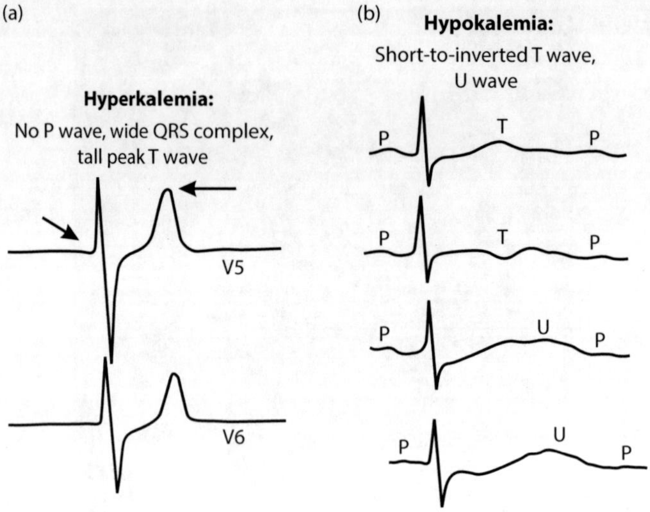

FIGURE 3.11 (a) Electrocardiographic evidence of hyperkalemia. Electrocardiogram (ECG) Lead II tracing in a patient with hyperkalemia that demonstrates no P wave, wide QRS complex, and a tall peaked T wave. (b) Electrocardiographic evidence of hypokalemia. Electrocardiogram (ECG) Lead II tracing in a patient with hypokalemia that demonstrates short-to-inverted T- and U waves.

ECG: Ca Effects

Hypercalcemia: *Short QT*
Hypocalcemia: *Prolonged QT*

- **Hypercalcemia:** Short QT and ST segments = antacids, vitamins A and D, HCTZ (Figure 3.12a)
- **Hypocalcemia:** Prolonged QT and ST segments = fluoride, hydrofluoric acid, SMFA rat poison, calcitonin, ethylene glycol, phosphates (Figure 3.12b)

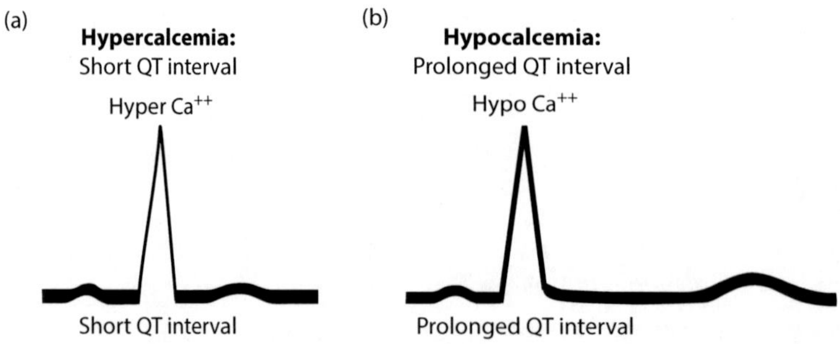

FIGURE 3.12 (a) Electrocardiographic evidence of hypercalcemia. Electrocardiogram (ECG) Lead II tracing in a patient with hypercalcemia that demonstrates a short QT interval. (b) Electrocardiographic evidence of hypocalcemia. Electrocardiogram (ECG) Lead II tracing in a patient with hypocalcemia that demonstrates a prolonged QT interval.

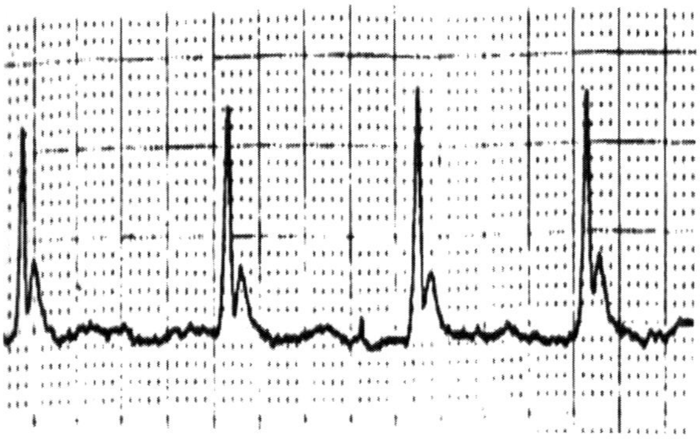

FIGURE 3.13 Electrocardiographic evidence of hypothermia (rectal temperature 24 degrees Centigrade). Note the characteristic J wave of Osborne embedded in the terminal phase of the QRS complex.

Hypothermia

- Progressive conduction block
- Progressive sinus bradycardia
- Prolonged PR and QT intervals
- Progressive widening of QRS 2° the *J-wave of Osborn*, located in the terminal phase of the QRS (Figure 3.13)

ECG: Dig and TCAs

Digoxin Effects

- Initial ectopic rhythms and PVCs (10–15%)
- Progressive bradycardia
- Increased PR interval to AV blocks
- Extrasystoles leading to tachyarrhythmias from delayed after-repolarizations (Figure 3.14a and b)
- Pathognomonic bidirectional VT

ECG: TCA Effects 1
TCA OD: *Prominent S wave in I and aVL, R wave in aVR*

ECG: TCA Effects 2
TCA OD: *S in I and aVL, R in aVR*

TCA Effects

- Sinus tachycardia
- Prolonged PR, QRS, QT intervals
- Prominent S in I and aVL, R in aVR

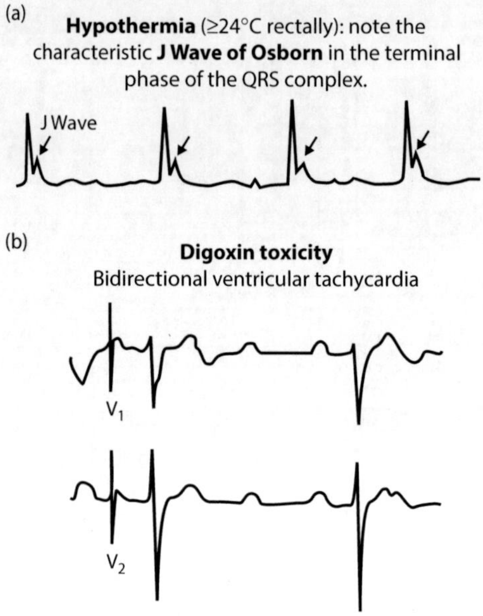

FIGURE 3.14 (a) Electrocardiographic evidence of digoxin toxicity. Electrocardiogram (ECG) Lead II tracing in a patient with digoxin toxicity that demonstrates (a) atrial tachycardia and atrioventricular conduction block and (b) bi-directional ventricular tachycardia, pathognomonic of digoxin toxicity.

- TCA OD: *Wide QRS complexes, respond to* $NaHCO_3$ (Figure 3.15)
- AV and bundle branch blocks
- All supraventricular and ventricular arrhythmias, including torsades de pointes
- Asystole

ECG: Tachyarrhythmias

- **Anticholinergics and antihistamines:** Block fast inward sodium channels (phase 0), like LAs
- **Adrenergic agonists:** ↑ cyclic AMP = all $ß_2$-agonists

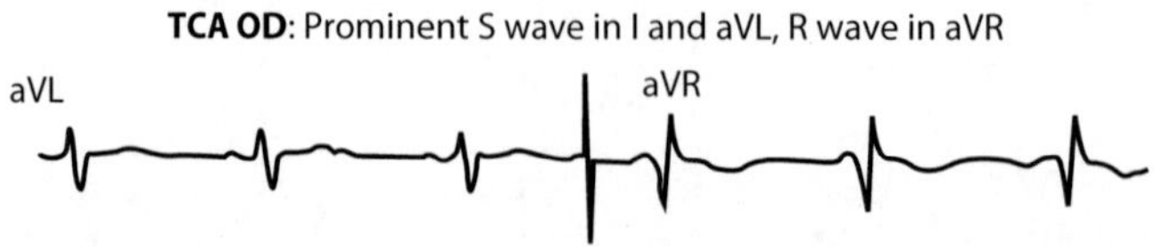

FIGURE 3.15 Electrocardiographic evidence of tricyclic antidepressant overdose. Electrocardiogram (ECG) tracing in a patient with a history of suicide attempt by tricyclic antidepressant overdose that demonstrates widened QRS complexes indicative of cardiac sodium channel blockade that should correct with intravenous sodium bicarbonate administration.

- **Phosphodiesterase inhibitors:** Also ↑ cyclic AMP = methylxanthines (theophylline, caffeine, theobromine) and amrinone; cause SVT, Afib/AF, SV/V tachyarrhythmias
- **Diet pills:** Amphetamine and serotonin effects + pulmonary HTN = phentermine, fenfluramine
- **Botanicals:** Sympathomimetics = khat, betel nut, ginseng (Ginseng abuse ayndrome [*GAS*]: ↑ HR, ↑ BP, insomnia, AM diarrhea)
- **Thyroid hormone:** Sinus tachycardia
- **Metals:** As = arsenic trioxide chemotherapy for leukemia: ↑ QT and torsades; Li = mimics ↓ K

ECG: Tachyarrhythmias

Ginseng (Panax spp.): HR abnormalities

Monkshood (Aconitum spp.): vagomimetic bradycardia, alternating ventricular-ventricular fibrillation in overdose

ECG: Tachycardias

Theophylline OD: Supraventricular tach

Astemizole/terfenadine: Torsades de pointes

ECG: Prolonged QT and VT

Prolonged QT and torsades de pointes

Milieu: ↓ K, ↓ Mg, ↓ Ca, bradycardia, ischemia, hypoxia

Toxins: Nonsedating antihistamines = astemizole and terfenadine, pentamidine, erythromycin, arsenic trioxide

Ventricular Tachycardia

- **Chloral hydrate** and all halogenated HCs that sensitize myocardium to catechols → VT (Figure 3.16)
- **Propoxyphene:** Norpropoxyphene, junctional tach, widening QRS → VT
- **Phenothiazines:** Quinidine—LA effects = ↑ QT and QRS → VT
- **Chloroquine:** Also has quinidine—LA effects → VT
- **Amantadine:** Blocks dopamine reuptake, ↑ QT → VT
- **Botanicals:** Na channel openers = aconitine—monkshood, azaleas/rhododendrons—grayanotoxins

ECG: Quinidine Effects

Quinidine OD: Notched P, long QT, inverted T

ECG: Bradycardias

Hypothermia: *J wave of Osborn*

CCB (verapamil) OD: *Sinus brady: 38 bpm*

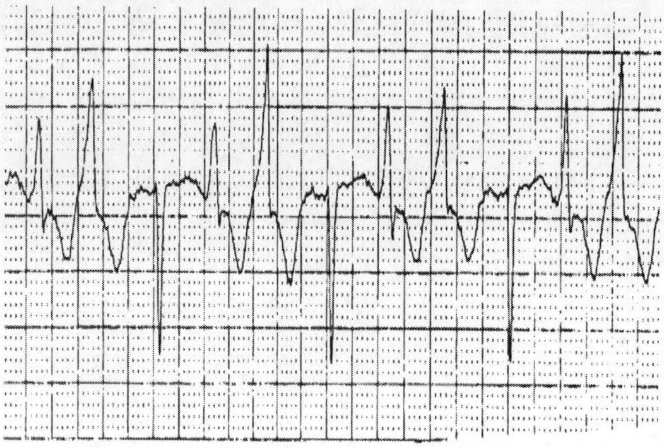

FIGURE 3.16 Electrocardiographic evidence of chloral hydrate toxicity. Electrocardiogram (ECG) tracing in a patient sedated with oral chloral hydrate for a magnetic resonance imaging procedure that demonstrates the ventricular ectopic or premature beats (premature ventricular contractions) characteristic of chlorinated hydrocarbon toxicity from chloral hydrate or halogenated hydrocarbon anesthetics (halothane and others) with myocardial sensitization to endogenous catecholamines.

ECG: Bradyarrhythmias

- **Class I Na channel blockers:** Type IA or quinidine–LA effects
- **Class II Beta-blockers:** Progressive bradycardia, AV blocks, complete heart block
- **Class IV Calcium channel blockers:** Decreased inotropy and AV conduction, smooth muscle vasodilation, progressive AV blocks
- **Ischemia:** ST and T changes, Q injury waves, vasospasm, hypoxia, MI = cocaine and ergot alkaloids
- Digitalis-associated bradyarrhythmias

ECG: Ischemia and Ectopy

Cocaine ischemia: *Precordial ST elevation*
Chloral hydrate OD: *Ventricular ectopy*

Chapter 4

Poison Antidotes

Toxidromes. 54
GI Decontaminants 56
Metal Chelators 59
Antivenoms and Antitoxins 62
Specific Antagonists. 67
Vitamins 70
Specific Antidotes 72
Nonspecific Antidotes 75

Outline

- Toxidromes and antidotes
- Gastrointestinal decontaminants
- Metal chelators
- Antivenoms and antitoxins
- Vitamins and antioxidants
- Specific antagonists
- Specific antidotes
- Nonspecific antidotes
- Poison antidotes

Toxidromes

1. **Parasympathetic Toxidromes:** Anticholinergic and cholinergic
2. **Sympathetic Toxidromes:** Sympathomimetic and hypermetabolic
3. **CNS Toxidromes:** Benzodiazepine and extrapyramidal
4. **Opioid Toxidromes:** Opioid and withdrawal

Parasympathetic

Anticholinergic Toxidrome

- **Features:** *"Blind as a bat, hot as Hades, red as a beet, dry as a bone, mad as a hatter"*= fever, tachycardia, dilated pupils, cycloplegia, dry flushed skin, exocrine gland hyposecretion, thirst, ↓ bowel sounds, urinary retention, delirium
- **Causes:** Belladonna alkaloids, antihistamines, TCAs, antipsychotics, anti-Parkinson drugs, Jimson weed (*Datura stramonium),* henbane, mandrake
- **Antidote:** Physostigmine

Cholinergic Toxidrome

- **Features:** Salivation, Lacrimation, Urination, Defecation, Emesis, or *SLUDE* = Muscarinic + miosis, bronchorrhea and bronchospasm = (*DUMBBELS*), ↓ HR. Nicotinic: weakness, fasciculations, paralysis, sweating. CNS: agitation/confusion, seizures, coma
- **Causes:** OPs, carbamates, "stigmines" and oximes; pilocarpine eye drops, nerve gases, echothiophate gtts = AchE inhibitors; *Clitocybe/Inocybe* (glutamic acid, ibotenic acid → muscimol) muscarinic mushrooms
- **Antidote:** Atropine +/– pralidoxime

Herbal Poisonings

CNS Tox: Belladonnas

- Mydriasis: Anticholinergic toxidrome (Figure 4.1)
- Miosis: Cholinergic and opioid toxidromes (Figure 4.2)

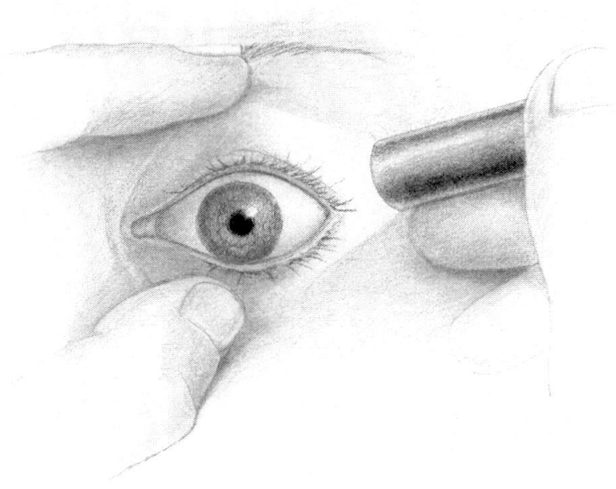

FIGURE 4.1 Mydriasis, left eye. Pupillary dilation or mydriasis characteristic of an anticholinergic toxidrome.

- Cholinergic toxidrome
- Clitocybe mushrooms
- Inocybe mushrooms

Tox: Sympathetic

Sympathomimetic Toxidrome

- **Features:** *"Fight or flight,"* hypertension, tachycardia, sweating, fever, excitation-psychomotor agitation, tremor, seizures, dilated pupils

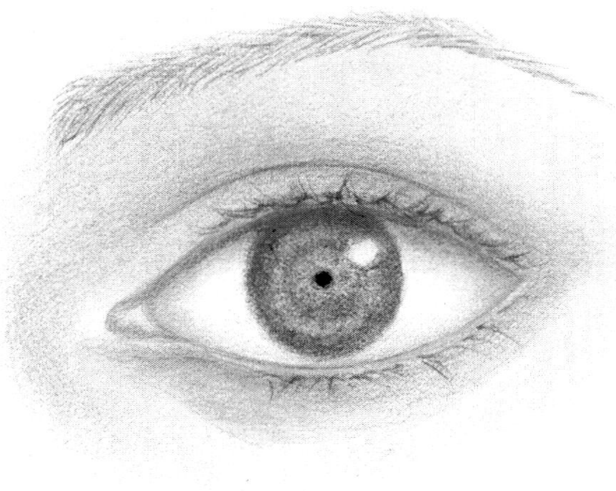

FIGURE 4.2 Miosis, left eye. Pupillary constriction or miosis characteristic of cholinergic and opioid toxidromes.

- **Causes:** Amphetamines/diet drugs, cocaine, theophylline, caffeine, methylphenidate; over-the-counter (OTC) cold medications, especially phenylpropanolamine (PPA), ephedrine, and pseudoephedrine
- **Antidote:** Beta-blockers

Hypermetabolic Toxidrome

- **Features:** *"Uncoupling of oxidative phosphorylation"* with high fever, tachycardia, hyperpnea, tachypnea, restlessness, convulsions, combined metabolic acidosis and respiratory alkalosis
- **Causes:** Salicylates (*ASA*), chlorphenoxy*acetic acid* herbicides (2,4-D and 3,4,5-T), dinitrophenol, phenol, triethyl tin, SMFA, and bromethalin
- **Antidote:** Lavage and activated charcoal, supportive

Toxidromes: CNS

Benzodiazepine Toxidrome

- **Features:** *"Coma with stable vital signs,"* mild sedation-to-complete unresponsiveness, amnesia, respiratory depression, loss of airway protective reflexes, mild hypotension
- **Causes:** Benzodiazepines, GHB
- **Antidote:** Flumazenil > physostigmine

Extrapyramidal Toxidrome

- **Features:** *"Drug-induced Parkinsonism,"* tremor, rigidity, opisthotonus, torticollis, dysphonia, oculogyric crisis = tardive dyskinesias
- **Causes:** Phenothiazines, butyrophenones (haloperidol, droperidol), metoclopramide, clomipramine
- **Antidote:** Diphenhydramine

Tox: Opioid

Opioid Toxidrome

- **Features:** Pinpoint pupils, somnolence, CNS depression, respiratory depression, bradycardia, hypotension, hypothermia, decreased GI motility, constipation
- **Causes:** All opioids, natural and synthetic, including propoxyphene, tramadol, codeine. Exception: α-2-agonists = clonidine and the imidazolines, oxymetazoline, and tetrahydrolozine
- **Antidote:** Naloxone

Withdrawal Toxidrome

- **Features:** Yawning, sneezing, runny nose, lacrimation, piloerection aka "goose bumps," abdominal cramps, diarrhea, restlessness, hallucinations, tachycardia, and hypertension

- **Causes:** Opioid, alcohol, barbiturate, benzodiazepine cessation withdrawal
- **Antidote:** "Cold turkey," agonists as substitutes (Ex: methadone, clonidine), antagonists for maintenance (naltrexone)
- Drug withdrawal syndromes

GI Decontaminants

- Activated charcoal
- Cathartics
- Diluents and neutralizers
- Syrup of ipecac
- Whole-bowel irrigation (WBI)
- Poison Antidotes

Decon: Activated Charcoal

Properties

- **Chem:** Pyrolyzed carbonaceous materials steamed and then CO_2-activated to create pores and ↑ adsorptive surface area
- **Mech:** Adsorption by H_2 ion bonding and van der Waals forces of agents that are nonionized, undissociated, not protein-bound, poorly-to-slowly absorbed, distributed (anticholinergics ↓ GI motility), and excreted
- **Contra indications:** Coma, seizures, vomiting, ileus, SBO, simultaneous PEG; alcohols, HCs, metals (except thallium), caustics, lithium

Applications

- **Use:** Most organic and inorganic materials, ASA, acetaminophen, anticonvulsants-barbiturates, phenytoin, glutethamide, theophylline, TCAs, pesticides
- **Dose:** Early (within 1–4 h) administration of a flavored 8:1 water slurry, 10:1 AC:drug, 1 g/kg bw. MDAC: 0.5 mg/kg
- **Side Effects (SE):** Vomiting, aspiration, diarrhea → constipation → SBO; AC is usually combined with a cathartic, particularly 70% sorbitol > Mg citrate, 4 mL/kg

Decontamination or Decon: Multiple-Dose AC

Properties

- **Chem:** Provides constant intestinal clearance by maintaining a *continuous diffusion gradient* between blood and gut (known as "gut dialysis")
- **Mech:** GI tract dialysis, especially for large ingestions, enteric or slow/sustained release-drug ingestions; to halt enterohepatic circulation of poisons
- **Contra:** Same as AC—coma, seizures, vomiting, ileus, SBO, simultaneous WBI; all alcohols, HCs, metals, caustics, lithium

Applications

- **Uses:** Digoxin, phenobarbital, carbamazepine, phenylbutazone, dapsone, methotrexate, naldolol, theophylline, ASA, TCAs, cyclosporine, propoxyphene
- **Dose:** 0.5 g/kg q 2–6 h, starting within 1 h of ingestion
- **SE:** Same as AC—vomiting, aspiration, diarrhea → constipation → Small Bowel Obstruction (SBO), add a cathartic only to first dose of AC, usually sorbitol 1 g/kg

Decon: Cathartics

Properties

- **Chem:** Saline and glucose-based cathartics composed of nonabsorbable cations (Mg, Na) that establish an osmotic gradient to draw water into gut.
- **Mech:** Mg citrate and sorbitol = osmotics.
- **Contra:** A dynamic ileus–SBO, abdominal trauma, diarrhea, renal failure (Mg citrate and sulfate), *congenital fructose intolerance* (sorbitol), more than initial dose of MDAC. All oil-based cathartics are hydrocarbons (HCs) (mineral oil), ↑ aspiration risk, and ↑ lipid-soluble *HC* and mothball absorption (camphor, paradichlorobenzene, naphthalene).

Applications

- **Use:** To reduce constipation with possible SBO from AC, to speed delivery of AC to SI, and to speed fecal elimination of poorly absorbed or sustained-release toxins
- **Dose:** Sorbitol 0.5–1.0 g/kg; Mg citrate 4 mL/kg; Mg sulfate 1 g/kg
- **SE:** N, V, D, abdominal cramping, dehydration-hypovolemia, ↓ Na, ↓ K, hyponatremic–hypokalemic metabolic alkalosis, ↑ Mg and renal failure (2° Mg citrate and sulfate), *unique hypernatremic dehydration (2° sorbitol)*

Diluents > Neutralizers

Properties of Diluents

- **Chem:** Water or milk to dilute ingested alkalis or weak acids
- **Mech:** Reduce caustic contact time with GI mucosa, modify and reduce the heat dissipated by the initial hydration and subsequent neutralization of the caustic at tissue (mucosal) expense
- **Contra:** All noncaustics and strong acids (HCl—careful removal via NG). Neutralization of caustics is not recommended, except for *nebulized $NaHCO_3$ for chlorine and chloramine gas inhalation*

Applications of Diluents

- **Use:** Dilution of alkalis and weak acids, for example, milk for ingested F or HF acid (calcium gluconate preferred), milk/ice cream as demulcents for calcium oxalate-containing plant ingestions
- **Dose:** Water or milk, 250 mL po, or 15 mL/kg bw

- **SE:** Could increase heat production by water or *HCl contact (zinc phosphide)*-↑ hydration and neutralization reactions; acute gastric distension with potential for vomiting and aspiration of caustics

Decon: Ipecac

Properties

- **Chem:** A *Cephaelis* spp. plant extract containing two powerful emetic plant alkaloids: *cephaline > emetine*
- **Mech:** (1) Local activation of peripheral sensory receptors in the first part of the duodenum; (2) central stimulation of the chemoreceptor trigger zone (CTZ)
- **Contra:** All HC and caustic ingestions, altered mental status, poor airway protective reflexes (↑ aspiration or seizure risks); bleeding diathesis; sharp object and battery ingestions

Applications

- **Use:** Best for *at-home* use immediately after (<30 min) ingestions without additional oral fluids.
- **Dose:** 1 tsp (10 mL) for infants 6–12 months, 15 mL (1 tbsp) for children, 30 mL (2 tbsp) for adults, may repeat once in 30 min.
- **SE:** Time delay to AC administration or specific antidote therapy in the ED, vagal bradycardia, prolonged vomiting → Mallory–Weiss esophageal tears, rarely cerebrovascular accident (CVA) or stroke in adults. Could be replaced by home AC slurries.

Decon: WBI

Whole Bowel Irrigation

- **Chem:** A nonabsorbable mixture of a *high MW polyethylene glycol (PEG)* solution and an electrolyte lavage solution (ELS)
- **Mech:** To flush out the entire GI tract without causing fluid and electrolyte shifts to reduce the mucosal contact time available for poison absorption
- **Contra:** Any preexisting GI pathology—ileus, SBO, GI perforation

Applications

- **Use:** *All sustained-release drug ingestions* (theophylline, CCBs—verapamil, fenfluramine); all poisons unabsorbed by AC (*iron*, lead, zinc, *lithium*); and for opioid body packers
- **Dose:** 0.5 L/h for children, 2 L/h for adults po or NG for 4–6 h
- **SE:** Gastric distension and vomiting (add an antiemetic), anal itching

Metal Chelators

- **Calcium disodium edetate ($CaNa_2EDTA$):** Lead
- **Deferoxamine:** Iron and aluminum

- **Dimercaprol (British Anti-Lewisite, BAL):** Pb, As, Hg
- **Succimer (dimethylsuccinic acid, DMSA):** Lead
- **D-Penicillamine:** Cu
- **Diethylene triamine penta-acetic acid (DTPA):** Chelates radioactive americium, curium, and plutonium
- **Prussian blue (ferric ferrocyanide):** Chelates radioactive cesium and thallium
- **Gallic acid:** Uranium
- **Disodium edetate (Na_2EDTA):** Pb
- **Deferoxamine:** Fe, Al
- **Dimercaprol (British Anti-Lewisite, BAL):** Pb, As, Hg
- **Succimer (dimethylsuccinic acid, DMSA):** Pb
- **D-Penicillamine:** Cu
- **Diethylene triamine pentaacetic acid (DTPA):** Chelates radioactive americium, curium, and plutonium
- **Prussian blue (ferric ferrocyanide):** Chelates radioactive cesium and thallium

Chelators: EDTA

Properties

- **Chem:** Water-soluble, calcium-containing ring-structured acid
- **Mech:** *Exchanges its ring-bound Ca for a heavy metal*, usually Pb, to form a stable, nonionized, water-soluble chelate that can be renally excreted
- **Contra:** Dehydration, renal dysfunction, CAD chelation, cadmium chelation, *sole therapy (without BAL initially) in Pb encephalopathy*—give BAL first, then EDTA 4 h later to ↓ brain Pb delivery by EDTA

Applications

- **Use:** To chelate Pb in lead poisoning; in conjunction with BAL initially to rapidly chelate Pb in Pb encephalopathy
- **Dose:** Intramuscularly (IM) in procaine or intravenously (IV) (preferred) diluted in NS over 8–24 h
- **SE:** Chelation and subsequent depletion of all essential metals ("*minerals*") (Cu, Co, Fe, Mn, Zn); elevated LFTs; calcinosis at injection sites; thrombophlebitis; nephrotoxicity 2° Pb release in kidneys during excretion

Chelators: Deferoxamine

Properties

- **Chem:** A water-soluble, specific iron chelator created by removing ferric iron (Fe^{3+}) from ferrioximine.
- **Mech:** Chelates extra free Fe and Fe in transit between transferrin and ferritin; but *will not chelate Fe complexed to Hb, ferritin, or hemosiderin*. Also *chelates aluminum* best.
- **Contra:** None.

Applications

- **Use:** To chelate Fe in Fe overdoses, massive transfusions, hemosiderosis, and thalassemia. To chelate aluminum in CRF.
- **Dose:** 1 g IM, then 0.5 g q 4–12 h; IV preferred = *15 mg/kg/min slowly.*
- **SE:** ↓ BP; *pulmonary toxicity* (ARDS); *oculotoxicity* (↓ vision, ↓ color vision, night blindness); and *ototoxicity* (deafness). Acts as *siderophage* for some bacteria that cannot absorb Fe- *Yersinia* and *Vibrio-* ↑ *V. vulnificus* sepsis risk. *Rose (vin rosé)-orange colored urine.*

Chelators: BAL

Properties

- **Chem:** Nonspecific metal chelator formulated in peanut oil and developed during World War II as an antidote for both Lewisite (arsine gas) and mustard vesicant gases.
- **Mech:** A sulfur-donating chelator that forms stable bonds with *soft metals*—especially *As* and *Hg*. Can also bind borderline soft metals, particularly *Pb*.
- **Contra:** Peanut allergy, liver dysfunction, G-6-PD deficiency 2° hemolysis, organic or methyl Hg poisoning.

Applications

- **Use:** To chelate As, elemental and inorganic Hg; to treat arsenical dermatitis; to use in conjunction with EDTA as initial chelation in Pb encephalopathy.
- **Dose:** Deep IM 2.5 mg/kg q 4–6 h × 4 doses; topical qsad.
- **SE:** Local injection site pain, peanut anaphylaxis, fever, ↑ BP and HR, N, V, HA. Can also chelate essential metals (especially Cu and Zn) and will chelate Fe during concomitant Fe therapy.
- Arsenical keratoses.

Chelators: Succimer

Properties

- **Chem:** DMSA, a more water-soluble *analog of BAL* that is less toxic and more specific for Pb, a borderline soft metal, than BAL.
- **Mech:** Same as BAL, but less toxic, *effective orally, will not chelate essential metals* (Cu, Co, Fe, Mn, Zn), and can be used with concomitant Fe therapy. Unlike BAL, succimer does not cause hemolysis in G-6-PD deficiency.
- **Contra:** None.

Applications

- **Use:** Primarily lead poisoning (BPb > 45 mcg/dL), unapproved for organic and inorganic Hg poisoning and As poisoning
- **Dose:** 30 mg/kg/day po × 5 day
- **SE:** Transient ↑ AST and multiple abdominal complaints—crampy abdominal pain, flatus, and diarrhea
- Pb chelation

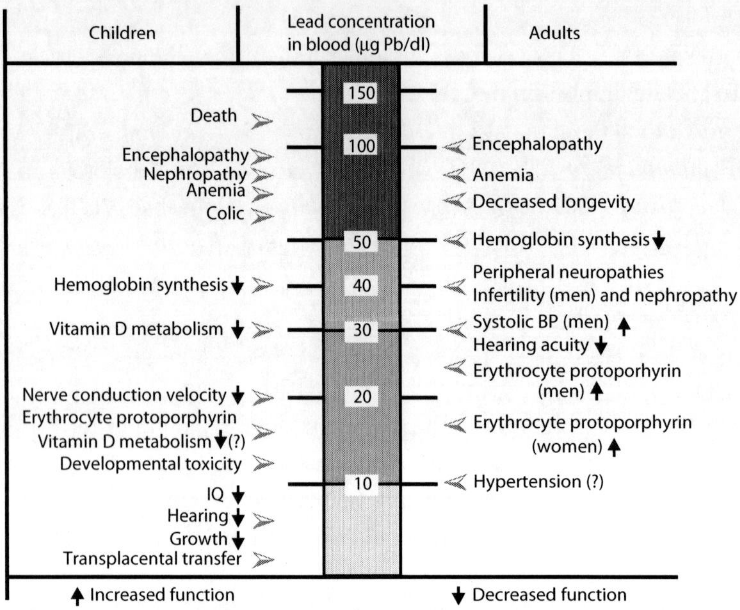

FIGURE 4.3 Clinical findings and blood lead levels. A correlation of the clinical findings and rising blood lead levels in children and adults. (From U.S. Government Document, Agency for Toxic Substances and Disease Registry.)

Chelators: Penicillamine

Properties

- **Chem:** A highly toxic, penicillin-derived, nonspecific metal chelator (Cu > As, Hg, Pb) that is orally titrated over weeks
- **Mech:** Same as succimer, but less effective and ↑ SEs; *works best for Cu*
- **Contra:** Penicillin allergy, preexisting skin diseases, or renal dysfunction

Applications

- **Uses:** Cu chelation in Wilson's disease (hepatolenticular degeneration)
- **Dose:** 10 mg/kg/day po ↑ 10 mg/kg/week to 30 mg/kg/day × 10 weeks
- **SE:** Severe N&V, pcn anaphylaxis, leukopenia, thrombocytopenia, eosinophilia, aplastic anemia, myopathy, *dermatitis-Stevens–Johnson syndrome*, nephrotic syndrome (Figure 4.3)

Antivenoms and Antitoxins

- **Reptile antivenoms:** Crotalid and Elapid antivenoms
- **Insect antivenoms:** *Centruroides* and *Latrodectus* antivenoms
- Botulinum antitoxin
- Digoxin-specific antibody fragments (Fab, DigiBind®)
- Crotalids

- Eastern diamondback
- Mojave rattlesnake

Crotalid Antivenom

Properties

- **Chem:** A polyvalent pit viper IgG antivenom prepared in horses hyperimmunized to venoms of the U.S. eastern and western diamondback rattlesnakes (*Crotalus* spp.) and the tropical fer-de-lance (*Bothrops* spp.).
- **Mech:** Direct Ag/Ab antagonism.
- **Contra:** Horse serum allergy, prior antivenom allergy, relative contraindication =+ skin test. Recently replaced by less antigenic ovine polyvalent Crotalid Fab (CroFab®), with Fabs from *eastern* and *western diamondbacks*, *Mojave*, and *water mocassin.*

Applications

- **Use:** Most rattlesnake envenomations, all *Mojave rattlesnake* bites (delayed neurotoxicity), 12% of copperhead and water moccasin (*Agkistrodon* spp.) envenomations.
- **Dose:** At least 5 vials diluted 1:10 in NS IV.
- **SE:** Hypersensitivity reactions (20–40%) = urticaria, anaphylactoid rxn, anaphylaxis. Serum sickness common (50+%) = rash, pruritus, urticaria, migratory arthralgias, lymphadenopathy, rarely immune-complex glomerulonephritis.

Elapids

Eastern coral snake
Western (TX) coral snake

- Corals
- Southern U.S. states
- Red, yellow/rarely white, and black bands
- "Red on yellow, kill a fellow; red on black, friend of Jack." Only works in North America (NA); not with albinos-cross breeds
- *Proterolgyphous*—small fixed fangs
- <1% of U.S. bites
- Second most potent venom in NA
- **Venom:** Neurotoxic
- **Distribution:** Florida, Louisiana, Alabama, Arizona, Texas = Western and Eastern Coral Snakes. Southeastern FL has highest distribution
- Venoms and toxins
- **Elapids:** "Red-on-yellow"
- Venoms and toxins
- **Elapids:** Coral snakes
- **Name:** Eastern coral snake
- **Latin:** *Micrurus fulvius fulvius*

- **Venom:** Neurotoxin
- **Diagnosis (Dx):** Shy, docile, nocturnal, bites-chews when disturbed, few local sx, 12–24 h later—paresis, paresthesias, fasciculations, dysarthria, dysphagia, ptosis, stridor, diplopia, resp. arrest
- **Antidote:** Equine bivalent (eastern + Texas)—5–10
- **Tx:** Mechanical ventilation in 15%

Micrurus fulvius fulvius

"Red on yellow, kill a fellow, red on black, venom lack."

- Sonoran coral snake (Micuroides euryxanthus)
- Arizona, Mexico, Central America, South America
- **Venom:** Less potent delayed neurotoxin
- **Dx:** Less severe neurotoxicity
- **Antivenom:** Not available in the United States but available in Mexico and Costa Rica; *only bivalent elapid antivenom—United States*
- **Tx:** Consider importing antivenom; supportive, observe for apnea and respiratory dysfunction for 24 h

Elapid Antivenom

Properties

- **Chem:** A polyvalent elapid IgG antivenom prepared in horses hyperimmunized to venoms of U.S. eastern and western (Texas) coral snakes only, but *not to the much less venomous Sonoran (Arizona/Mexico) coral snake*
- **Mech:** Direct Ag/Ab antagonism
- **Contra:** Horse serum allergy, prior antivenom reaction

Applications

- **Use:** All proven eastern and western coral snake bites, not Sonoran coral snakebites
- **Dose:** 3–5 vials, up to 10 vials
- **SE:** Since less antivenom is used for small coral snake envenomations, there are fewer hypersensitivity rxns; nevertheless, serum sickness remains a high possibility
- **Coral snake bites:** Florida, 2004–2009

Presenting Manifestations	
$N = 234$:	
Fang marks	85%
Local edema	40%
Paresthesia	35%

Nausea	30%
Vomiting	25%
Euphoria	15%
Vertigo and/or Tinnitus	15%
Diplopia	10%
Dyspnea	10%
Diaphoresis	10%
Muscle pain	10%
Fasciculations	5%
Confusion	5%

- **Management:** Antivenom
- **Manufacturer:** Wyeth, equine, bivalent, since 1967
- **Dose:** 3–5 vials; repeat × 1
- **Administer:** Prior to sx onset; will not reverse presenting signs or sx
- **Adverse effects (AEs):** Urticaria 35%, serum sickness 10%
- **Problem:** Wyeth stopped production in 2005; all vials now expired
- **Availability:** Coralmyn®, equine, polyvalent-Mexico; Suero Autiofidico Anti-coral®, equine, monovalent-Costa Rica
- **Recent coral snake bite case:** Florida, 2009
- **Source:** JN Bernstein, MD, FACEP, director Miami-Dade County, FL, PCC
- **Bite:** Intoxicated 39-year-old female picks up small brightly colored snake on picnic and is bitten on the right hand
- **1st hour:** Presents to local ED, + fang marks; observed for 3 hours and discharged as intoxicated
- **6th hour:** Returns to the same ED-c/o widespread allodynia, tinnitus, metallic taste; discharged as intoxicated
- **16 hours post-bite:** Drives to a distant ED with PCC c/o unbearable tinnitus, allodynia. PE: opisthotonic posture, no gag, dysarthric
- **Management (Mx):** Trachea intubated, mechanical ventilation × 5 weeks
- **Outcomes:** DC'ed 6 weeks, left foot drop 5th–7th weeks; neurologically intact by week 8
- **Moral:** Antivenom for all documented cases; even if expired or imported
- **Exotic snakebites:** United States vs. World
- Incidence of attack
- 7000–8000 reptile bites per year in the United States
- Rattlers majority
- 10–15% are dry bites
- 300,000–400,000 venomous snake bites per year internationally

- Mortality
    - Fewer than 12 deaths/year in the United States
    - 30,000–110,000 deaths/year worldwide
    - Up to 5× that amount face permanent morbidity
    - U.S. mortality rate
    - With antivenom treatment—0.28%
    - Without antivenom treatment—2.6%
    - Data derived from estimates
    - Worldwide: 5.4 million bites w/2.5 million envenomations and 125,000 deaths

Centruroides Antivenom

Properties

- **Chem:** Fab antivenom produced in horses, very expensive
- **Mech:** Direct Ag/Ab antagonism
- **Contra:** Most adults, reserve for severe envenomations in children

Applications

- **Use:** Severe (grade III–IV) U.S. scorpion envenomations in children <age 6
- **Dose:** 1–2 vials over 30 min each
- **SE:** Serum sickness less likely
- *Centruroides sculpturatus*

Latrodectus Antivenom

Properties

- **Chem:** *Latrodectus mactans*—specific IgG prepared in horses
- **Mech:** Direct Ag/Ab antagonism
- **Contra:** Prior allergy

Applications

- **Use:** Bites of *L. mactans, L. hesperus, L. bishopi,* and *L. geometricus* that are associated with severe abdominal pain, myospasm, respiratory insufficiency, and not responsive to intensive therapy
- **Dose:** 1 vial in 50 mL NS
- **SE:** Severe bronchospasm (↑ CFR), serum sickness in >85% of recipients

Botulinum Antitoxin

Properties

- **Chem:** Equine IgG antitoxins = trivalent (toxin types A, B, and E) and heptavalent (A, B, C, D, E, F, G)—*only for BW victims.*
- **Mech:** Direct Ag/Ab antagonism.
- **Contra:** None, botulism is fatal. Cannot be used to treat infant botulism.

Applications

- **Use:** Foodborne botulism before all toxin is bound and fixed to NMJ receptors. Infant botulism is managed supportively only with botulinum hyperimmune globulin (BIG).
- **Dose:** 1 or more vials diluted 1:10 IV q 2–4 h.
- **SE:** Hypersensitivity rxns and anaphylaxis common.

Digoxin-Specific Fab

Properties

- **Chem:** Purified Fb fragments of intact IgG anti-digoxin Abs. *No Fc fragments*, which do not bind Ag and ↑ *hypersensitivity* reaction potential.
- **Mech:** Direct Ag/Ab antagonism of intravascular free digoxin with enough cross-reactivity to also bind digitoxin and the natural cardiac glycosides from garden plants (oleander) and amphibians (toad bufodienolides).
- **Contra:** Hypercalcemia, concomitant Ca administration as in CCB overdose.

Applications

- **Use:** Dig toxicity = worsening AV block, VT, VF, rising K > 5 mEq/L; natural glycoside poisonings from plants such as foxglove, oleander, red squill; animals-toad bufodienolides
- **Dose:** Empiric 10–20 vials → 38 mg Fab per vial will bind 0.5 mg of digoxin
- **SE:** Acute hypokalemia, worsening of CHF, rash, potential for hypersensitivity and serum sickness

Digoxin-Specific Fab: Calculations

- Each vial of Dig Fab contains 38 mg of purified Fabs which will bind 0.5 mg of digoxin
- Digoxin has a bioavailability of 80%
- Digoxin dose known = digoxin dose ingested in mg × 0.8/0.5 mg = # vials of Dig Fab rounded up
- Digoxin level known = digoxin level in ng/mL × wt in kg/100 = # vials of Dig Fab rounded up
- Always round up the number of vials of Dig Fab to administer IV

Indications: DigiBind

- Natural cardiac glycosides—Foxglove digitalis
- Natural cardiac glycosides—Toad budodienolides
- Natural cardiac glycosides—Nerium oleander
- Natural cardiac glycosides—Thevetia peruviana

Specific Antagonists

- Calcium-CCB, K, and Mg antagonist
- Flumazenil-benzodiazepine antagonist

- Opioid antagonists
- Physostigmine-anticholinesterase (AchE) antagonist
- Protamine-heparin antagonist

CCB Antag: Calcium

Properties

- **Chem:** Ionized cation essential in all muscle and nerve functions, especially for excitation–contraction coupling in heart and peripheral circulation
- **Mech:** Direct antagonist to the cardiac effects of CCBs, K, and Mg and to the neurologic effects of Mg; *restores Ca in ethylene glycol* and *hydrofluoric acid (HF) poisoning*; complexes with F to limit HF burns
- **Contra:** Digitalis toxicity

Applications

- **Use:** CCB overdose, ↑ K, ↑ Mg, ethylene glycol poisoning, HF burns. Questionable use in β-blocker OD and to relieve myospasms after black widow spider bites.
- **Dose:** 1 g $CaCl_2$ = 3 g calcium gluconate.
- **SE:** ↑ Ca = N, V, constipation, hypertension, worsening digitalis toxicity, injection site tissue irritation.

Benzodiazepine (BZ) Antagonism: Flumazenil

Properties

- **Chem:** A competitive benzodiazepine (BZ) antagonist with little agonist effect
- **Mech:** Occupies the BZ receptor with high affinity and without causing functional change and displaces the BZ agonist
- **Contra:** In coma cocktails, BZ addiction, seizure disorders; can provoke seizures or arrhythmias in ODs with TCAs, carbamazepine, theophylline, chloroquine, chlorinated HCs, and chloral hydrate

Applications

- **Use:** To reverse pure BZ overdose or therapeutic BZ use for "conscious sedation"
- **Dose:** 1–3 mg IV slowly titrated 0.1 mg/min
- **SE:** *Seizure* and *arrhythmia induction* in those predisposed with preexisting seizure disorders, or in ODs with convulsants, theophylline, chlorinated hydrocarbons; resedation; rebound BZ respiratory depression

Opioid Antagonists

Properties

- **Chem:** Pure competitive opioid antagonists = naloxone, naltrexone, and nalmefene

- **Mech:** Competitive antagonists most potent at the *mu receptor*, subserving analgesia, respiratory and CNS depression
- **Contra:** Long-acting naltrexone should not be administered to the potentially opioid-dependent without an initial short-acting naloxone opioid withdrawal test

Applications

- **Use:** Naloxone to reverse mu receptor effects; questionable use in septic shock; Naltrexone > nalmefene for opioid and alcohol addiction
- **Dose:** 0.4 mg naloxone IV titrated to effect in 0.1 mg increments; long-acting naltrexone 50 mg po qd
- **SE:** Withdrawal in the opioid dependent, opioid resedation; rarely noncardiogenic pulmonary edema, HTN, and dysrhythmias

AchE Antag: Physostigmine

Properties

- **Chem:** An oxime carbamate (insecticide) reversible anticholinesterase
- **Mech:** Antagonizes AchE at both PNS and CNS sites reversing anticholinergic effects at central > muscarinic > nicotinic receptor sites by increasing Ach concentrations
- **Contra:** TCA OD, AV block bronchospastic disease, PVD, GI, or bladder outlet obstruction

Applications

- **Use:** Peripheral muscarinic (dry mucosa and skin, fever, flushing, mydriasis, tachycardia, urinary retention = *"red as a beet, dry as a bone, hot as Hades"*) and central (agitation, delirium, hallucinations, seizures = *"mad as a hatter"*) anticholinergic toxidrome; more effective reversal of CNS effects
- **Dose:** 1–2 mg IV slowly
- **SE:** Bradycardia, hypersalivation, bronchospasm; rapid administration = N, V, HA, and diaphoresis = cholinergic toxidrome = SLUDE

Heparin Antag: Protamine

Properties

- **Chem:** An electropositively charged protein derivative of salmon sperm
- **Mech:** Complexes with the electronegatively charged heparin with a greater affinity for heparin than for antithrombin-III, and *dissociates the heparin-AT-III complex* in favor of the protamine–heparin complex
- **Contra:** Prior protamine or fish (salmon) allergy, vasectomy, NPH and PZI insulin, sole administration without heparin

Applications

- **Use:** To reverse heparin activity, usually after cardiopulmonary bypass or PTCA

- **Dose:** 1–1.5 times the heparin dose (*1 mg of protamine will reverse 100 units of heparin*) based on an activated clotting time (ACT) normal of 150 sec
- **SE:** Hypotension 2° vasodilation, anaphylaxis, bleeding from platelet aggregation and quantitative thrombocytopenia

Vitamins

- Folic and folinic acids
- Hydroxocobalamin (cyanocobalamin-vitamin B_{12} precursor)
- Vitamin K (specifically vitamin K_1)
- Pyridoxine (vitamin B_6)
- Thiamine (vitamin B_1)
- Niacin (nicotinic acid) and niacinamide (nicotinamide)
- Toxic alcohols
- Methanol metabolism

Folic and Folinic acids

Properties

- **Chem:** An essential water-soluble vitamin, whose active form, folinic acid, is required for DNA (purine and thymidine) synthesis.
- **Mech:** Folic acid ↑ formic acid metabolism and ↓ formate levels in *methanol* and *formaldehyde* poisoning; dihydrofolate reductase (DHFR) converts folic acid into its active form, folinic acid. Ca chemotherapeutic *methotrexate* (MTX) *inhibits DHFR* and blocks folic acid → active folinic acid.
- **Contra:** Use only folinic acid for MTX OD.

Applications

- **Use:** Folic and folinic (leucovorin) acids can be used to ↓ formate levels in methanol (and formaldehyde) poisoning and ↓ risks of *oculotoxicity*; folinic acid, not folic acid, is the specific antidote for MTX OD.
- **Dose:** FA-70 mg, 1–2 mg/kg q 6 h; leucovorin-2x MTX dose in mg ASAP + q 6 h × 3d.
- **SE:** None; folic acid is useless for MTX (a DHFR inhibitor) OD; must use folinic acid, the activated form of folic acid.

Hydroxocobalamin

Properties

- **Chem:** A cobalt-containing active vitamin B_{12} (cyanocobalamin) precursor
- **Mech:** Displaces cyanide from cytochrome oxidase to form cyanocobalamin which is an essential vitamin that is either excreted in the urine unchanged and/or detoxified by the hepatic *thiosulfate-rhodanase-thiocyanate pathway*, especially during CN poisoning
- **Contra:** None

Applications

- **Use:** May administer along with thiosulfate for cyanide poisoning or individually
- **Dose:** 4 g IV, repeat × 1, max 8 g, coadminister 8 g sodium thiosulfate
- **SE:** Skin reddening, skin allergy

Vitamin K

Properties

- **Chem:** The *k*oagulation factor, an essential fat-soluble vitamin, which exists as two types: (1) the plant vitamin K_1s = phylloquinone > phytonadione (K_1); and (2) the bacterial vitamin K_2 = menaquinone (K_2), synthesized by GI bacteria, except in newborns without an established intestinal flora
- **Mech:** Activate clotting factors *II, VII, IX, X,* and *proteins S and C*
- **Contra:** Allergy to colloidal formulation

Applications

- **Use:** Warfarin (coumadin)-induced vitamin K_1 deficiency and bleeding, newborn vitamin K_2 deficiency, malabsorption syndromes, superwarfarin rodenticide poisonings
- **Dose:** 25–50 mg IV or sq, 50–100 mg po tid × 1–2 days
- **SE:** Anaphylactoid rxn from rapid IV administration, hematoma from IM admin, potentiates warfarin-induced skin necrosis in protein C/S deficiencies
- Vitamin K has to be activated first
- Warfarin blocks vitamin K activation
- Vitamin K activates II, VII, IX, X

Vitamins: Pyridoxine (B_6)

Properties

- **Chem:** The stable precursor to active vitamin B_6, a cofactor in the metabolism of neuro-transmitters, *GABA and 5-HT.*
- **Mech:** *Isoniazid* (INH) and *monomethylhydrazine* (MMH) poisoning-anticonvulsant effects mediated by enhanced GABA activity. *EG poisoning*—redirects the metabolism of EG away from the production of its toxic metabolite, oxalic acid.
- **Contra:** None; relative contra-preexisting peripheral neuropathy.

Applications

- **Use:** (1) INH OD and MMH poisoning (MMH = gyromitrin from *Gyromitra esculenta* mushrooms, MMH rocket fuel), (2) ethylene glycol poisoning
- **Dose:** INH-mg/mg to max 5 g; MMH-25 mg/kg, max 70 mg/kg; EG-100 mg/day to max 5 g
- **SE:** Acute neurotoxicity = ataxia, incoordination, seizures, ↑ CFR; chronic = *delayed sensory peripheral neuropathy-axonopathy*, potentially permanent

Vitamins: Thiamine (B_1)

Properties

- **Chem:** Water-soluble essential B vitamin that maintains the glycolytic pathway, produces ATP for cellular energy, and ensures nerve conduction
- **Mech:** Catalyzes pyruvate → acetyl CoA, links glycolysis to Kreb's cycle, promotes ATP generation
- **Contra:** None

Applications

- **Use:** (1) alcoholics and ethanol ODs, (2) coma cocktail for all altered mental status cases to prevent *wet beriberi* (high output CHF) and *dry beriberi* (Wernicke's encephalopathy + Korsakoff's psychosis, ↑ CFR), (3) coadminister with hypertonic dextrose, (4) *EG poisoning* to promote as a cofactor a less toxic metabolic pathway
- **Dose:** 100 mg IV or IM qd
- **SE:** Few; deficiency = wet (CHF) and dry (psychosis) beriberi
- Ethylene glycol metabolism

Vitamins: Niacin (B_3)

Properties

- **Chem:** Water-soluble, B-complex vitamin and essential precursor for NAD (and NADP) metabolism that also binds lipoproteins
- **Mech:** Protects hepatic pentose phosphate pathway; provides precursors to *pancreatic B-islet cells* for NAD (and NADP) production
- **Contra:** Preexisting allergy, ASA sensitivity, skin disorders

Applications

- **Use:** (1) Niacin in massive doses (10–100 × RDA) to ↓ TG and cholesterol levels; (2) niacinamide (nicotinamide) as a specific AD for *Vacor* (PNU) rodenticide poisoning to prevent toxic acute diabetes mellitus (IDDM)
- **Dose:** Niacinamide (nicotinamide)—500 mg IV stat, then 200 mg IV q 4 × 48 h
- **SE:** Potentially severe PG-mediated vasodilation, *flushing*, HA, N, V, D, niacin hepatitis

Specific Antidotes

- Ethanol
- Fomepizole (4-methylpyrazole)
- NAC
- Pralidoxime (2-PAM)
- Miscellaneous specific antidotes
  - **Hydroxocobalamin**
  - **Fomepizole (4-methylpyrazole)**

- **NAC**
- **Pralidoxime (2-PAM)**

Ethanol

Properties

- **Chem:** Acts as the highest affinity substrate for the hepatic enzyme *alcohol dehydrogenase* (ADH), which also metabolizes *EG to oxalic acid, methanol to formic acid, isopropanol to acetone*, with highly toxic metabolites
- **Mech:** Competitive antagonism of ADH to inhibit toxic alcohol metabolism
- **Contra:** None

Applications

- **Use:** To arrest the further metabolism of EG and methanol to their toxic metabolites
- **Dose:** IV (10%) or po (20–30%), load 0.8 g/kg IV or 8 mL/kg po over 20–60 min, to maintain a serum level of 100–150 mg/dL
- **SE:** IV—venous irritation and phlebitis, CNS depression, diuresis → dehydration → hyponatremia, hyperglycemia initially → hypoglycemia subsequently
- Poison antidotes

Fomepizole (4-MP)

Properties

- **Chem:** *A specific inhibitor of alcohol dehydrogenase* (ADH) that acts synergistically with ethanol in EG and methanol poisoning to occupy ADH
- **Mech:** 4-MP blocks ADH by complexation
- **Contra:** None

Applications

- **Use:** Alternative to or in combination with ethanol for ethylene glycol and methanol ingestions; and potentially for severe ethanol-disulfiram rxns
- **Dose:** IV load with 15 mg/kg, then 15 mg/kg q 12 h
- **SE:** N, HA, dizziness, rash, eosinophilia, ↑ LFTs
- Fomepizole for ethylene glycol and methanol

NAC

Properties

- **Chem:** A thiol (HS)-containing antioxidant and amino acid (cysteine) precursor deacetylated *in vivo* to cysteine that is required for glutathione synthesis
- **Mech:** Replenishes hepatic glutathione (an antioxidant-free O^- radical scavenger) in acetaminophen OD and limits the alternate path for P450 metabolism of acetaminophen to the toxic metabolite, NAPQI
- **Contra:** Do not coadminister with AC (20% adsorbed), separate administrations by 1–2 h

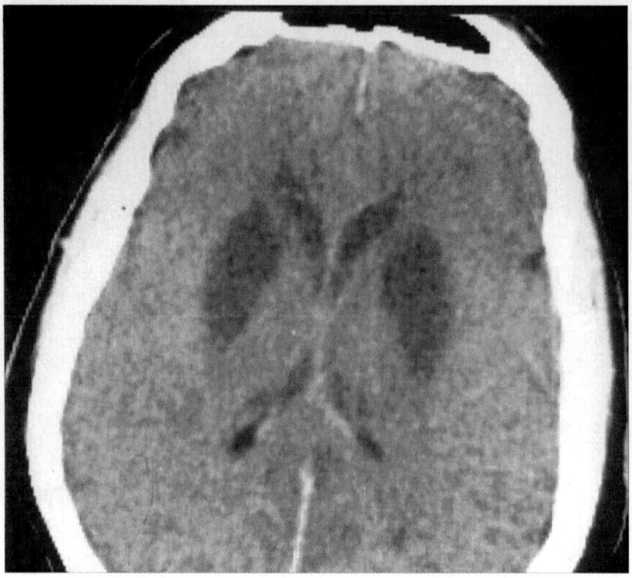

FIGURE 4.4 Cerebral effects of carbon monoxide poisoning. Cranial computerized axial tomogram (CT) at the level of the basal ganglia in a patient with atypical Parkinson's disease who suffered carbon monoxide poisoning in a house fire that demonstrates bilateral hypodensities in the basal ganglia. (Courtesy of Carlos R. Gimenez, MD, professor of radiology, LSU School of Medicine, New Orleans, LA.)

Applications

- **Use:** (1) All acetaminophen ODs, especially in patients with preexisting glutathione depletion (alcoholics-malnourished, HIV-AIDS, P450 inducing drugs); (2) free radical scavenging in poisonings with carbon tetrachloride, chloroform, dichloropropane, cyclophosphamide, pulegone-pennyroyal oil
- **Dose:** *"Rule of 7s"* = 140 (2 × 70) mg/kg po within 8 h, then 70 mg/kg q 4 h × 3 d for 17 doses in 72 h
- **SE:** Po-anticipate vomiting (co-admin antiemetic), IV (not approved)-coagulopathy, anaphylaxis (Figure 4.4)

Pralidoxime (2-PAM)

Properties

- **Chem:** An oxime carbamate and nonspecific cholinesterase (both acetyl and pseudo) reactivator
- **Mech:** Greater AchE reactivation at central and nicotinic (NMJ) over muscarinic sites, coadminister with atropine for better antimuscarinic coverage
- **Contra:** Sole use without atropine, relative contra-carbamate insecticide poisoning

Table 4.1 Miscellaneous Specific Antidotes

Drugs or Toxins	Specific Antidotes
Cesium	Prussian blue—potassium ferricyanoferrate (chelator)
Colchicine	Colchicine Fabs
Hydrofluoric acid	Calcium gluconate
Paraquat	Fuller's earth (binder)
Potassium	Sodium polystyrene sulfonate (binder)
Lindane	Cholestyramine (binder)
Lithium	Sodium polystyrene sulfonate (binder)
Methotrexate	Folinic acid (leucovorin)
Nickel	Dithiocarb (diethyldithiocarbamate)
Platinum	Dithiocarb (diethyldithiocarbamate)
Thallium	Prussian blue (chelator)
Uranium	Gallic acid
Warfarin	Vitamin K

Applications

- **Use:** Organophosphate pesticide and OP nerve gas poisoning, AchE will spontaneously reactivate in carbamate poisoning
- **Dose:** Admin 1–2 g diluted over 30 min within 24–48 h, repeat q 12 × 48 h
- **SE:** Rare-dizziness, blurred vision, and elevated DBP with rapid IV admin
- Misc. Specific antidotes (Table 4.1)
- Amiloride for Li-induced nephrogenic DI

Diabetes insipidus (DI): Central DI is due to ↓ ADH secretion by the posterior pituitary, but *nephrogenic DI*, a common AE of *lithium therapy*, is due to insensitivity of the kidney to ADH and is characterized by the production of large amounts of dilute urine. Tx: desmopressin, *amiloride*—a K-sparing diuretic (like triamterene) not associated with ↓K like thiazides that *blocks Li entry into renal epithelial Na channels.*

Nonspecific Antidotes

- Dextrose
- Glucagon
- Methylene blue, Cyanide Kit®, Cyanokit®
- Sodium bicarbonate
- Hyperbaric oxygen (HBO)
- Intravenous fat emulsion

Dextrose

Properties

- **Chem:** Precursor of glucose, the primary energy source for the brain
- **Mech:** Energy substrate
- **Contra:** Relative contraindications = cerebral ischemia, preemies at risk for intracranial hemorrhage, cardiac insufficiency—CHF

Applications

- **Use:** Empiric administration to all patients with coma or altered mental status
- **Dose:** $D_{50}W$, 0.5–1.0 g/kg bolus IV
- **SE:** Phlebitis at IV injection sites; seizures and intracranial hematoma in preemies; potential osmotic fluid overload in cardiac insufficiency

Glucagon

Properties

- **Chem:** Hormone secreted by pancreatic *alpha cells* in response to hypoglycemia
- **Mech:** Mobilizes glucose fuel stores; suppresses insulin release; provides *direct inotropic and chronotropic cardiac stimulation like β-agonists but outside the β receptor*; relaxes SM in lower esophageal sphincter, GI tract and biliary tree—all actions mediated via ↑ *cAMP*
- **Contra:** Insulin and oral hypoglycemic-induced hypoglycemia; not to be used in lieu of $D_{50}W$ in the initial therapy of comatose patients

Applications

- **Use:** To reverse overdoses of *β-blockers and calcium channel blockers*; to promote GI elimination of *ingested button batteries*
- **Dose:** Initial bolus, 50 mcg/kg IV
- **Side effects (SE):** Not arrhythmogenic, dose-dependent N&V, hyperglycemia, hypokalemia, allergic reactions from beef or pork glucagon preparations

Methylene Blue

Properties

- **Chem:** A *blue dye* initially used as a urinary antiseptic and weak antimalarial agent that is both a *Hb oxidizer* (high doses) and *reducer* (therapeutic low doses)
- **Mechanism:** Paradoxically both oxidizes oxyHb to metHb at high doses and reduces metHb back to oxyHb at low doses (therapeutic use) via the NADPH-metHb reductase pathway (with normal G-6-PD)
- **Contraindications:** Absolute (not variant) G-6-PD deficiency-no NADPH; ineffective for reducing H_2S-metHb in H_2S poisoning

Applications

- **Use:** To reverse metHb production by aniline dyes, sulfonamides, sulfones, nitrates and nitrites, phenols, $KMnO_4$; to reduce cyanmetHb in CN poisoning treated with nitrites
- **Dose:** 1–2 mg/kg IV over 5 m
- **SE:** metHb at high doses > 5 mg/kg and in G-6-PD deficiency, *blue skin*-mucosa-urine-vomit, ECG changes

Acquired Methemoglobinemia

Medications

- **Nitrites and nitrates:** Amyl and sodium nitrite, NTG, Nitroprusside, silver nitrate
- **Local anesthetics:** Prilocaine, lidocaine, benzocaine
- **Antibiotics:** Antimalarials (chloroquine, primaquine), dapsone, sulfonamides
- **Misc:** Pyridium, phenacetin, large doses (>5 mg/kg) of methylene blue

Toxic Chemical Exposures

- **Nitrites and nitrates:** Butyl and isobutyl nitrite, foods with nitrite or nitrate preservatives (processed meats), phenols-nitrophenol and phenacetin, silver nitrate, TNT, well-water nitrates (infants), nitrogen oxide gases (NO)
- Aniline dyes
- **Mothballs:** Naphthalene only
- **Misc:** Potassium permanganate

Cyanide Kits

Properties

- **Chem:** Cyanide antidote kits composed of (1) amyl nitrite pearls, (2) 3% IV sodium nitrite, and (3) 25% IV sodium thiosulfate
- **Mech:** Induce methemoglobinemia with (1) and (2) to bind CN and form cyan-metHb, unable to further poison cytochrome oxidase; to provide additional substrate with (3) in the presence of rhodanase and CN to form less toxic *thiocyanate for renal excretion*
- **Contra:** None

Applications

- **Use:** Complete kit-CN poisoning; IV sodium nitrite alone—hydrogen sulfide poisoning; thiosulfate alone—sodium nitroprusside concomitantly or SCN overdose with CN poisoning
- **Dose:** (1) Amyl nitrite—for inhalation only; (2) sodium nitrite—10 mL of the 3% solution IV diluted in 100 mL; (3) sodium thiosulfate-50 mL of the 25% solution IV vs. hydroxocobalamin (Cyanokit)
- **SE:** Methemoglobinemia—consider methylene blue, 1 mg/kg IV

Cyanide Kit

Properties

- **Chem:** A cobalt-containing active vitamin B_{12} (cyanocobalamin) precursor
- **Mech:** Displaces cyanide from cytochrome oxidase to form cyanocobalamin which is an essential vitamin that is either excreted in the urine unchanged and/or detoxified by the hepatic *thiosulfate-rhodanase-thiocyanate pathway*, especially during CN poisoning
- **Contra:** None

Applications

- **Use:** May administer along with thiosulfate for cyanide poisoning or individually
- **Dose:** 4 g IV, repeat × 1, max 8 g, coadminister 8 g sodium thiosulfate
- **SE:** Skin reddening, skin allergy

Sodium Bicarbonate 1

Properties

- **Chem:** Nonspecific antidote
- **Contra:** Pulmonary edema, CHF, renal failure, preemies at risk of intracranial hemorrhage

Applications

- **Dose:** 1–2 mEq/kg IV bolus
- **SE:** Metabolic alkalosis, ↑ HCO_3, ↑ Na, fluid overload, ↓ K, ↓ Ca
- Sodium bicarbonate 2 (Table 4.2)

Hyperbaric Oxygen

Properties

- **Chem:** HBO is the inhalation of oxygen at pressures > 1 atm
- **Mech:** (1) Elevates hydrostatic pressure and ↓ gas volume (air embolism, "bends"); (2) hastens dissociation of CO and H_2S from Hb; (3) hastens dissociation of CO from cytochrome oxidase; (4) inhibits leukocyte sequestration in brain and ↓ reperfusion injury
- **Contra:** Absolute-*tension pneumothorax, bleomycin* therapy; relative-sinus congestion, otosclerosis

Applications

- **Use:** Air embolism (H_2O_2), decompression sickness (N), CO poisoning, CO + CN poisoning, methylene chloride poisoning (hepatically biotransformed to CO), H_2S poisoning, CCL_4 hepatotoxicity (by inhibiting the hepatic microsomal oxidase system that produces toxic metabolites)
- **Dose:** NA, depth and length of "dive"
- **SE:** Otic barotrauma, especially ruptured TM, claustrophobia, sinus pain, filled tooth pain

Table 4.2 Mechanisms and Antidote Uses: Sodium Bicarbonate

Mechanisms	Antidote Uses
Overrides cardiac Na channel block by alkalinizing blood	TCAs, cocaine, all quinidine-like antiarrhythmics that block Na channels and increase QRS complex duration
Ionizes weak acids, trapping them in blood before receptor activation	Phenobarbital, ASA, formate
Ionizes weak acids, trapping them in urine and increasing tubular excretion	Phenobarbital, ASA, chlorpropamide, and chlorphenoxyacetic acid pesticides (2,4-D; 2, 4, 5-T)
Buffers metabolic acidosis	Ethylene glycol, methanol
Increases solubility of insoluble drugs methotrexate (MTX)	Methotrexate
Forced alkaline diuresis prevents myoglogin dissociation and reduces risks of acute tubular necrosis (ATN) from rhabdomyolysis	Rhabdomyolysis
Neutralizes inhaled acid gases, especially chlorine and chloramine gas	Chlorine and chloramine gas inhalation-nebulized $NaHCO_3$

HBO: CO Poisoning

Head CT of a patient with permanent mental status changes (and later Parkinsonism) following CO poisoning. Note characteristic *symmetrical lucencies of the globus pallidus bilaterally.* Neurotoxicity could have been prevented by early HBO.

Intravenous Fat Emulsion

- **Definition:** Intravenous fat emulsion (IFE) is an oily white mixture of triglycerides, egg whites, soybean oil, and glycerol used for parenteral nutrition and to deliver insoluble drugs (propofol) that is now indicated as a rescue antidote for local anesthetic (bupivacaine) toxicity and possible as an effective antidote for overdoses of B-blockers, CCBs, TCAs, and organophosphate pesticides.

Purported Mechanisms of Action (MoAs)

- To create a fat-soluble sink in the plasma compartment for lipid-soluble poisons to dissolve in
- To supply FFAs to mitochondria via carnitine translocase to produce ATP and augment cardiac energy
- To ↑ intracellular Ca in cardiac myocytes

Dose: Bolus *2 mL/kg or 100 mL 20% IFE*, then infuse another 2–4 mL/kg to 200 mL

Chapter 5

Toxicity of Antiseptics and Drug Additives

Outline . . . 82
Additives Tox . . . 82
Propylene Glycol . . . 82
Polyethylene Glycol . . . 83
Diethylene Glycol . . . 83
Benzyl Alcohol . . . 84
Bromines/Bromides . . . 84
Chlorobutanol . . . 84
Thimerosal . . . 85
Benzalkonium Chloride . . . 85
Phenol . . . 86
The Parabens . . . 86
Pharm Additive Tragedies . . . 86

Outline

- Definitions: Additives = Excipients
- Glycols: Propylene, polyethylene, and diethylene glycols
- Benzyl alcohol
- Bromines/bromides/bromates/boron
- Chlorobutanol
- Thimerosal
- Benzalkonium chloride
- Phenol
- Parabens: Methylparaben, propylparaben
- Additive tragedies: E-Ferol, Eosinophilia-Myalgia Syn

Additives Tox

Additives = Excipients

What Are Drug Excipients?

- **Definition:** Drug excipients are chemical ingredients other than the active drug that are included in pharmaceutical drug preparations for a variety of reasons.
- **Uses:** Binders, coatings, colors, diluents, disintegrators, flavors, nutrients, preservatives, sweeteners, and solvents.

Commonly Used Drug Excipients

- **Colors:** Dyes can cause allergic reactions. Ex: *yellow dye # 5 (tartrazine). FD&C Reds* 40 and 19, carnine, and quinolone yellow.
- **Flavors:** Licorice (*glycyrrhizic acid*) inhibits cortisol metabolism causing ↑ BP and ↓ K.
- **Sweeteners:** *Aspartame* is contraindicated in *phenylketonurics.*
- **Preservatives:** *Benzyl alcohol* in intravenous flush solutions and multidose vials can cause metabolic acidosis 2° ↑ benzoic acid and shock in preemie = *"Gasping Baby" syndrome.*
- **Solvents:** Polyethylene glycol in intravenous drugs irritates veins and can cause CV collapse on rapid IV push. Ex: diazepam, phenytoin.

Propylene Glycol

Pharmacokinetics and Uses

- **Pharmacology (Pharm):** Clear, odorless, viscous, volatile alcohol, sweet to taste, and rapidly absorbed; low Vd, metabolized by *alcohol dehydrogenase* (ADH) to *lactic and pyruvic acids.*
- **Uses:** Food and drug preservative, especially parenteral drugs (BZs, antidysrhythmics).

Toxicities

- *CV > Met > CNS > dermal*
  - **Cardiovascular (CV):** Vagomimetic and directly cardiotoxic on *rapid IV infusion*; ↓ HR and ↓ BP, apnea, wide QRS, ↓ T to inverted T, and ↑ ST
  - **Metabolic (Met):** Serum hyperosmolarity, *metabolic (lactic) acidosis* (after topical *silver sulfadiazine* in burns)
  - **CNS:** Intoxication → CNS depression, then excitation and seizures
  - **Dermatological (Derm):** Thrombophlebitis

Polyethylene Glycol

Pharmacokinetics and Uses

- **Pharm:** A family of high-molecular-weight alcohols also oxidized by *ADH* to acid metabolites; *high MWs limit GI absorption and are relatively insoluble = whole-bowel irrigation (WBI) solutions of PEG*
- **Uses:** Bowel preps and WBI solutions (GoLytely®) to cleanse gut, which are the common cosmetic and ointment additives

Toxicities

- **Renal > Met**; relatively nontoxic
  - **Renal:** Potential ATN in massive OD
  - **Metabolic:** High MW = serum hyperosmolarity, and production of lactic and pyruvic acids = *high-anion gap (and osmolal gap) metabolic acidosis*, as with propylene glycol

Diethylene Glycol

Pharmacokinetics and Uses

- **Pharm:** An industrial alcohol solvent and *antifreeze agent* with a low affinity for ADH with negligible metabolism
- **Uses:** Industrial solvent, illicitly substituted for propylene glycol as a solvent to *solubilize APAP* (Tylenol®) manufactured in developing countries (Haiti, etc.) = *Haitian diethylene glycol (DEG)-contaminated Tylenol* tragedy, 100s of deaths in children > women

Toxicities

- *Initial GI and renal > hepatic.*
  - **GI:** Initial N and V with severe abdominal cramps and pain.
  - **Renal:** Initial polyuria followed within 24 h by oliguria, then anuria and *ARF*. No oxaluria, crystaluria. High CFRs.
  - **Hepatic:** *Hepatoxicity* = hepatomegaly and jaundice.
- **Tx:** Supportive only with *hemodialysis* (HD); *ethanol and 4-MP ineffective* as antidotes.

Benzyl Alcohol

Pharmacokinetics and Uses

- **Pharm:** Colorless aromatic alcohol and metabolite of toluene hepatically oxidized rapidly to *benzoic acid*, then conjugated with glycine to form *hippuric acid*, and excreted in urine—except in preemies who *cannot glycine conjugate benzoic acid 2° hepatic immaturity*
- **Uses:** Common bacteriostatic additive in parenteral meds and IV flush solutions (gasping-baby syndrome in preemies)

Toxicities

- *CNS—Central > peripheral*
- **Gasping-baby syndrome:** ↑ Benzoic acid levels → *metabolic acidosis*, hypotonia, gasping respirations, seizures, ↓ HR, and ↓ BP → CV collapse; high CFRs
- **Demyelinization:** Transient MS-like paraplegia in LEs following intrathecal and epidural administration of LAs and other drugs (MTX) containing benzyl alcohol

Bromines/Bromides

- **Uses:** Emulsifiers and flavor carriers for soft drinks (colas, *Ruby Red Squirt*) and drugs (ipratropium bromide [Atrovent®], dextromethorphan bromide [Robitussin®], and pancuronium bromide [Pavulon®]); pesticides (methyl bromide); and permanent hair wave solutions

Toxicities

- *Dermal > CNS > GI*
  - **Dermal:** Bromoderma
  - **CNS:** Somnolence, sedation
  - **GI:** Nausea, vomiting, and diarrhea
  - **Antidote:** None
- **Tx:** Withdrawal; colchicine to ↓ pmn chemotaxis 2° microtubular arrest

Chlorobutanol

Pharmacokinetics and Uses

- **Pharm:** An antibacterial–antifungal–preservative *halogenated hydrocarbon* chemically similar to *trichloroethanol*, the active metabolite of *chloral hydrate* ("*Mickey Finn*")
- **Uses:** Antimicrobial preservative in cosmetics and drugs, especially injectables, otic, and ophthalmic topicals

Toxicities

- *CNS > CV > ocular*
  - **CNS:** *Sedative-hypnotic* effects, somnolence, inebriation–intoxication such as ethanol, then slurred speech, dysarthria, and seizures
  - **CV:** Halogenated hydrocarbon that *sensitizes the myocardium* → PVCs → Vtach-Vfib
  - **Ocular:** Cytotoxic to corneal epithelium, but less damaging than benzalkonium chloride

Thimerosal

Pharmacokinetics and Uses

- **Pharm:** An *organic mercury* compound, formerly contained in *Merthiolate® or Mercurochrome®*, old over-the-counter (OTC) topical antiseptics, contains 49% organic Hg by weight
- **Uses:** Contact lens disinfectant; vaccines, antivenin, and topical ointment *preservative*

Toxicities

- *Initial GI and CNS > renal*
  - **GI:** Initial severe vomiting → *hemorrhagic gastroenteritis.*
  - **CNS:** Altered mental status ("*Mad as a Hatter*"), fever, slurred speech, ataxia, and later autonomic and ascending sensorimotor peripheral polyneuropathies. No link to autism or developmental delay.

Benzalkonium Chloride

Pharmacokinetics and Uses

- **Pharm:** A quartenary ammonium cationic surfactant (similar to surfactants in glyphosphate–herbicides) with immediate antimicrobial activity and delayed cytotoxic activity.
- **Uses:** The most widely used *contact lens disinfectant* and opthalmic preservative 2° immediate onset and long duration of action and tissue penetration. In most ophthalmic preparations.

Toxicities

- *Ocular > ENT mucosal*
  - **Ocular:** Progressive *cytolytic degeneration of corneal epithelium* with eye pain and photophobia, chronic keratitis, especially in those predisposed by dry eyes (keratoconjunctivitis sicca), and ↑ prolonged contact lens use
  - **ENT:** Decreased viscosity of the normal protective mucus blanket

Phenol

Pharmacokinetics and Uses

- **Hx:** Sir Joseph Lister, 1827–1912, carbolic acid was the original surgical antiseptic solution.
- **Pharm:** Formerly *carbolic acid*, an oral antiseptic (Chloraseptic®) and *chemical peeling* agent; rapidly absorbed. Total dose should be < 50 mg/10 h.
- **Uses:** Preservative/diluent in injectable and oral meds, chemical peels, injectable neurolytic for cancer pain, and *diluent for lyophilized glucagon* powder.

Toxicities

- *CNS > CV: Vacuolar encephalopathy in preemies* 2° *hexachlorophene* (trichlorinated bisphenol) in *PhisoHex®* baths
    - **CNS:** Drowsiness, respiratory depression, and peripheral nerve dissolution (painful peripheral nerve regeneration possible, avoid use as a neurolytic for nonmalignant disease)
    - **CV:** Dysrhythmias, especially PVCs

The Parabens

Pharmacokinetics and Uses

- **Pharmacology:** The parahydroxybenzoic acids, both methylparaben and propylparaben, are often used in synergistic combination as antimicrobials and preservatives.
- **Uses:** The second most common preservatives in *cosmetics*, next to water.

Toxicities

- *Allergy > Repro > hepatic*
    - **Allergy:** High incidence of *allergic reactions* to food, drugs, and cosmetics containing > 0.1% (1 mg/mL) parabens
    - **Hepatic:** Displaces bilirubin from albumin- binding sites in newborns → kernicterus
    - **Repro:** Significant spermicidal activity → used in vaginal contraceptive creams

Pharm Additive Tragedies

- Haitian diethylene glycol (DEG)-contaminated acetaminophen (DEG-contaminated over-the-counter analgesics, cough syrups, and other elixirs continue to cause mass poisonings throughout the developing world)
- Polysorbate 80-contaminated E-ferol vitamin E supplement for preemies
- Contaminated L-tryptophan PMS and sleep aid = eosinophilia–myalgia syndrome

- Gasping-baby syndrome and benzyl alcohol
- Vacuolar encephalopathy and pHisoHex

The E-Ferol Tragedy

- **Pharm:** A vitamin E prep combined with *polysorbate emulsifiers* to prevent O_2 toxicity in preemies, similar to the multivitamin polysorbate 80-containing drops and injectable preps (*Poly-Vi-Sol®*, *Tri-Vi-Sol®*). E-ferol, and polysorbate-80 were recalled in the 1980s.
- **Syndrome:** Vasculopathic—hepatotoxicity = hepatomegaly—*intralobular cholestasis*, ascites, ARF, and ↓ *platelets* in preemies; *38 deaths.*

Eosinophilia–Myalgia Syndrome

- **Pharm:** Bacterially contaminated L-tryptophan amino acid supplement for insomnia, pre-menstrual syndrome (PMS), and anxiety. Recalled (U.S.) in 1989.
- **Syndrome:** Unexplained peripheral *eosinophilia* with severe *myalgias, mouth ulcers, arthralgias,* rashes, peripheral edema, cough, dyspnea, and ↑ LFTS. Findings closely resembled toxic rapeseed oil-poisoning cases in Spain, felt secondary to aniline contamination. Thousands of cases worldwide, mostly in women; *36 deaths.*
- Gasping babies and Benzyl alcohol
  - **Pharm:** Colorless aromatic alcohol and metabolite of toluene hepatically oxidized rapidly to *benzoic acid*, then conjugated with glycine to form *hippuric acid*, and excreted in urine—except in preemies who *cannot glycine conjugate benzoic acid* 2° *hepatic immaturity.*
  - **Gasping-baby syndrome:** ↑ Benzoic acid levels → *metabolic acidosis*, hypotonia, gasping respirations, seizures, ↓ HR, and ↓ BP → CV collapse; high case fatality rates (CFRs).
- pHisoHex: Hexachlorophene and vacuolar encephalopathy.

Toxicity

- **CNS:** Vacuolar encephalopathy in preemies 2° hexachlorophene (trichlorinated bisphenol) in PhisoHex® baths.

Chapter 6

Poisonings with Over-the-Counter and Opioid Analgesics

Outline 90
Acetaminophen (*N*-acetyl-para-aminiphenol) (APAP) vs. ASA 90
NSAID Outline 94
Opioids: Outline. 97

Outline

1. Acetaminophen (*N*-acetyl-para-aminophenol, APAP)
2. Aspirin (ASA)
3. Nonsteroidal anti-inflammatory drugs (NSAIDs)
4. Opioids (natural opium poppy derivatives and synthetics)

Acetaminopen (*N*-acetyl-para-aminiphenol) (APAP) vs. ASA

1. Epidemiology
2. Toxicology
3. Clinical manifestations
4. Acute vs. chronic poisoning
5. Diagnosis
6. Treatment

Epidemiology

APAP

1. >100,000 analgesic overdoses (ODs)/year, >200 deaths, *46% due to APAP.*
2. APAP OD hospitalizations > all other OD hospitalizations.
3. APAP has replaced ASA as the analgesic–antipyretic of choice, especially for children 2° safety profile, NAC antidote, ASA toxicity, and potential to precipitate Reye's Syn.
4. **APAP toxicity risk factors:** ↓ hepatic glutathione stores in chronic alcoholics and malnourished; P450 induction 2° isoniazid (INH) and anticonvulsants.

ASA

1. ASA = 26% analgesic deaths.
2. ASA + viral illness = Reye's (N, V, ↓ glucose, ↑ LFTs → hepatic encephalopathy).
3. OTC drugs contain APAP or ASA → toxicology screens should include both analgesics.
4. Pepto-Bismal® (bismuth subsalicylate)—8.7 mg ASA/mL.
5. ↑ ASA in ointments, liniments, keratolytics (Compound W®), and vaporizer oils = *methyl salicylate* (*oil of wintergreen*) = *1400 mg/mL* = >5 g/tsp = lethal in children!

Toxicology

APAP

1. *90%* of APAP is hepatically metabolized to harmless *glucuronide* (60%) and sulfate (30%) metabolites excreted in the urine.
2. *5–15%* of APAP is oxidized by the cytochrome P450 MFOs to potentially hepatotoxic *N-acetyl-p-benzoquinoneimine* (NAPQI).
3. NAPQI is normally immediately detoxified by hepatic glutathione conjugation to non-toxic metabolites.

ASA

1. ASA is rapidly absorbed in the stomach > SI, unless absorption is delayed by *pylorospasm*, hypomotility, gastric outlet obstruction, or *bezoar-concretion* formation.
2. ASA (1) centrally stimulates the brainstem respiratory center causing hyperventilation and respiratory alkalosis; (2) blocks the Krebs cycle uncoupling oxidative phosphorylation and ↓ ATP production; (3) promotes anaerobic metabolism with ketosis, lactic acidosis, and hypoglycemia.

APAP OD

1. In OD, ↑ NAPQI production outstrips hepatic ability to detoxify by glutathione conjugation. NAPQI covalently binds to and arylates hepatocytes causing massive *centrilobular hepatic necrosis*, reversible by NAC, a glutathione precursor and substitute. NAPQI causes proximal renal tubular necrosis and ARF in 25% of ODs.
2. **Therapeutic level:** 10–30 mcg/mL; *4 h-NAC action level >150 mcg/mL*; significant serum toxicity level >250 mcg/mL.

ASA OD

1. Adult ODs present with mixed respiratory and metabolic acidosis; children present only with metabolic acidosis (>40 mg/dL).
2. **Unique toxic effects include:** (1) Reye's syndrome; (2) noncardiogenic pulmonary edema 2° hypoxia and pulmonary vasodilation and HTN; (3) hypoprothrombinemia and platelet dysfunction; (4) GI = N, V, ↓ GI motility, hemorrhagic gastritis; (5) rhabdomyolysis 2° ↑ heat production; and (6) tinnitus preceding deafness (>20–45 mg/dL).

Clinical Manifestations

Acute APAP Poisoning

- **Phase 1 (0.5–24 h):** Asymptomatic or *nonspecific sx*, anorexia, malaise, N, V, pallor, diaphoresis
- **Phase 2 (24–72 h):** *Asymptomatic* onset of *hepatic injury*, *RUQ pain*, ↑ AST, then ↑ PT and RFTs
- **Phase 3 (72–96 h):** Hepatic necrosis, coagulopathy, *jaundice*, encephalopathy, coma, all LFTs ↑, renal failure (25%); ARDS, ATN, and pancreatitis possible
- **Phase 4 (4 days–2 weeks):** Recovery, complete hepatic *regeneration* in survivors

Acute ASA Poisoning

- **Early acute:** N, V, fever, diaphoresis, tinnitus, tachypnea
- **Late acute:** (1) CNS = tinnitus, then deafness, vertigo, ↑ fever, hyperventilation, agitation hyperactivity, delirium, hallucinations, coma; (2) acid–base = *respiratory alkalosis and met acidosis*; (3) GI distress; (4) coagulopathy; (5) metabolic = hypoglycemia, ketonemia, ketonuria, lactic acidemia; (5) pulmonary = tachypnea, hyperpnea, *noncardiogenic pulmonary edema* (NCPE) (Figure 6.1)

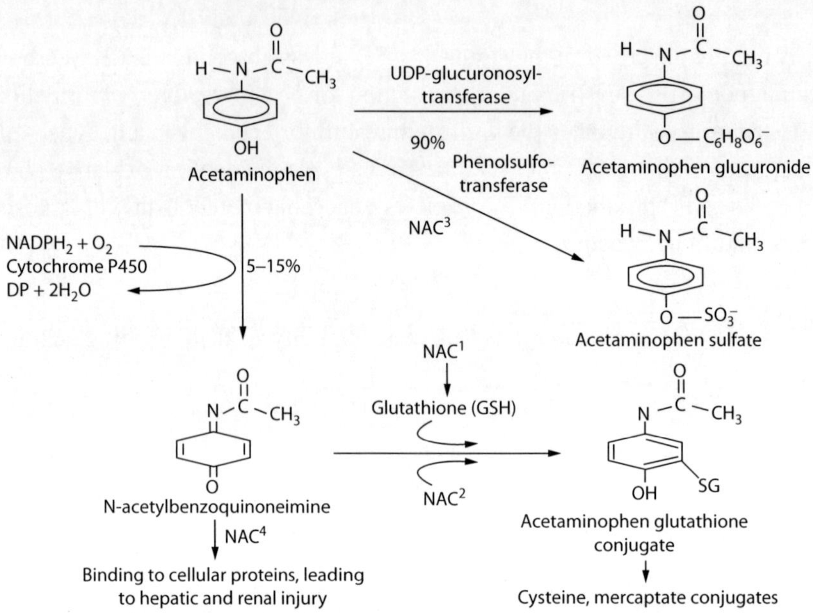

FIGURE 6.1 Acetaminophen (*N*-acetyl-para-aminophenol-APAP). Biotransformation pathways of toxicity. The biotransformation pathways and mechanisms of toxicity of acetaminophen or *n*-acetyl-para-aminophenol (APAP).

Chronic APAP Poisoning

- **Chronic:** Since APAP is a phenacetin metabolite, renal papillary necrosis and nephrotic syndrome are possible = *chronic analgesic nephropathy.*

Chronic ASA Poisoning

- **Chronic:** (1) Mainly a CNS constellation of *tinnitus*, *deafness*, dyspnea, hyperventilation, tachycardia, hyperthermia, CNS hyperactivity, agitation, confusion, slurred speech, hallucinations, seizures, coma; (2) chronic GI distress; (3) NCPE possible.

Diagnosis

APAP

1. OD >7.5 g in adults and >150 mg/kg in children.
2. **Identify sx and signs of hepatic injury:** [APAP] *4 h after OD* (<1 h useless, 2–4 h OK); AST if [APAP] above lower nomogram line or RUQ pain; if *AST is 1000* ± IU/L, check PT, BUN, and creatinine.
3. **High risk if:** [APAP] above lower line; [APAP] >10 mcg/mL and OD time unknown-order AST; nomogram crossing present-repeat AST in 4 h, r/o extend release-APAP.

ASA

1. **Obtain serum ASA:** Therapeutic 15–30 mg/dL, toxic >30–40, *action level 100 mg/dL*

Table 6.1 Acute vs. Chronic ASA Poisoning

Acute	Chronic
Age: Young	*Age:* Old
Etiology: Overdose	*Etiology:* Iatrogenic
Dx: Classic	*Dx:* Unrecognized
Assoc diseases: None	*Assoc diseases:* Chronic pain
Suicidal ideation: Yes	*Suicidal ideation:* No
Clinical: Rapid progression to >30 mg/dL	*Clinical:* CNS abnormalities, bleeding tendency, noncardiogenic pulmonary edema possible
Mortality: Rare	*Mortality:* 25%
Serum levels: High	*Serum levels:* Intermediate

2. **Confirm ASA by bedside $FeCl_3$ test:** Few drops (gtts) + 1 mL urine → *purple* + (also + for acetoacetic acid, diflunisalone, sulfasalizine, phenothiazines, phenylpyruvic acid, and phenylbutazone)
3. Pathognomonic respiratory alkalosis + metabolic acidosis (sole in children)
4. Confirm + urine ketones 2° anaerobic FA metabolism (Table 6.1 and Figure 6.2)

Treatment

APAP

1. Gastric emptying rarely indicated 2° rapid absorption
2. AC if OD <4 h, *separate AC* and *NAC by 1–2 h* to prevent adsorption of NAC (20%)
3. **NAC:** Supplies glutathione to detoxify NAPQI, effective up to 8 h post OD, can even *reverse NAPQI binding to hepatocytes*
4. **NAC dosing:** *Rule of 7s*—po load 140 mg/kg, maintain 70 mg/kg q 4 h × 17 doses × 72 h

ASA

1. Orogastric lavage + AC
2. Replace fluid, K, Na losses 2° hypermetabolism; monitor CVP or PAP (NCPE risk)
3. *Forced alkaline diuresis- alkalinize blood* and *urine*, IV $NaHCO_3$ (*not acetazolamide* = metabolic acidosis) for [ASA] >35 mg/dL, 1–2 mEq/kg bolus + infuse 3 amps/L at 2×EFR
4. Maintain arterial pH 7.45–7.50 and urine pH 7.5–8.0
5. Support ventilation to maintain respiratory alkalosis; high risk = respiratory acidosis + met acidosis

NAC

Complications

- **PO:** Nausea and vomiting common, add an antiemetic; diarrhea
- **IV:** Anaphylactoid reactions and anaphylaxis possible, not FDA approved in the United States

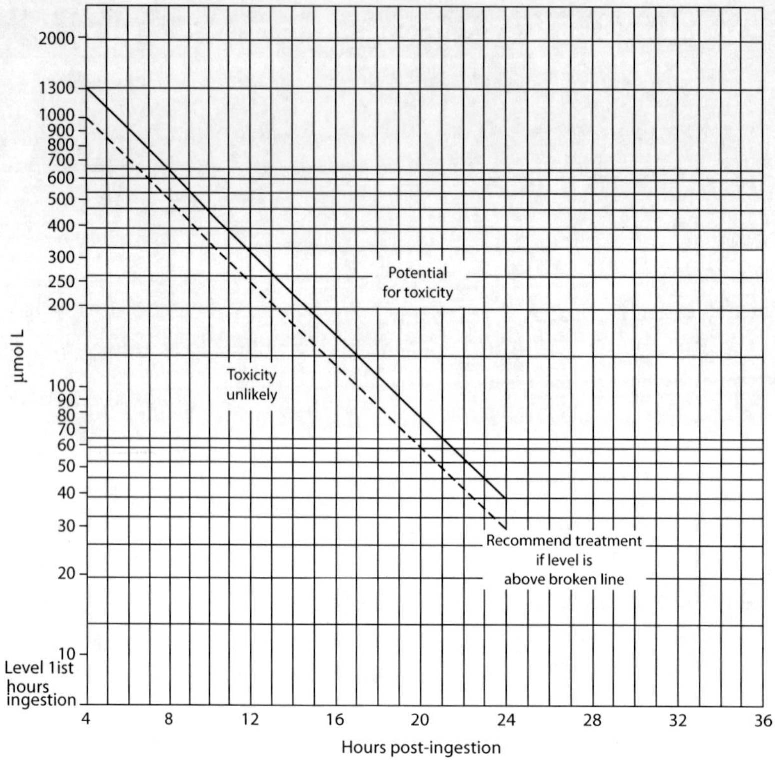

FIGURE 6.2 The acetaminophen (APAP) toxicity nomogram. The acetaminophen toxicity nomogram as determined by amount ingested and time needed for detoxification by non-toxic biotransformation routes. See text for instructions on how to interpret the nomogram.

Indications for IV NAC

1. Fulminant hepatic necrosis and liver failure
2. Persistently elevated [APAP] > 8 h post OD
3. APAP ODs during pregnancy

NSAID Outline

1. Epidemiology of NSAID OD
2. Classification of NSAIDs
3. Mechanism of NSAID toxicity
4. Diagnosis and general management of NSAID poisoning
5. Specific NSAID toxicities

Epidemiology

1. NSAIDs are now the most commonly prescribed medications with >73M Rx's/year costing $2.2B/year.

2. NSAID ODs cause more morbidity than mortality; CFRs are 6–7× higher for APAP and ASA ODs than NSAID ODs.
3. **Lethal ODs:** ASA > APAP > NSAIDs. **CFRs over 10 years:** ASA—0.38%; APAP—0.12%; NSAIDs—0.03%.
4. NSAIDs cause 25% of all reported adverse drug reactions, most commonly GI side effects.
5. Acute renal failure associated with NSAID use accounts for about *15% of drug-induced renal failure*, mostly in the elderly.

NSAID Classification

1. **Pyrazolones:** Phenylbutazone only (aplastic anemia)
2. **Fenamates:** The anthranilic acids, meclo*fenam*ate and me*fenam*ic acid (*epileptogenic*)
3. *A*cetic *a*cids; diclofen*ac*, etodol*ac*, indometh*ac*in, ketorol*ac*, nabumetone, sulind*ac*, tolmetin (*hepatotoxic*, *dermatotoxic*)
4. **Propionic acids:** Ibu*pro*fen, flurbi*pro*fen, keto*pro*fen, na*pro*xin (*nephrotoxic*, *hepatotoxic*, *ototoxic*)
5. **Oxicams:** Pir*oxicam* only (Feldene®)

NSAID: Tox Mechanisms

1. Most are nonspecific *COX-1* and *COX-2 inhibitors* that block the synthesis of PGs, which cause inflammation, fever, and pain.
2. Also block synthesis of the *gastric cytoprotective PGs, PGE_2*, and *PGI_2*, which maintain upper GI mucosal barrier → gastric and duodenal ulcers → 3% risk of hemorrhage or GI perforation.
3. Also block synthesis of *prostacyclines and thromboxanes* necessary for normal clotting mechanisms. NSAIDs increase bleeding risks by causing platelet dysfunction.
4. NSAIDs are mildly hepatotoxic and cause transient elevations in hepatic transaminases in 25% of patients. *Exception: Diclofenac* (Voltaren®) can cause massive *hepatocellular necrosis.*
5. NSAIDs are more nephrotoxic than hepatotoxic and can cause chronic renal failure, or *analgesic nephropathy*, by *blocking PG support of renal perfusion* and *GFR* with interstitial nephritis, nephrotic syndrome, and papillary necrosis in heavy NSAID abusers, especially the elderly (Figure 6.3).

Diagnosis and Management of NSAID Poisoning

Diagnosis

- **Acute OD:** *CNS depression*, respiratory depression, hypotension, hypothermia, GI distress, GI bleeding, ↑ *LFTs*, acute renal failure, rarely hallucinations and seizures
- **Chronic OD**: CRF in the elderly and alcoholics; *bleeding* and cognitive dysfunction and *dementia* in the elderly
- **Constellation of SEs:** GI, renal, hypersensitivity reactions (Stevens–Johnson syn), pulmonary, CNS, hematologic, drug–drug interactions

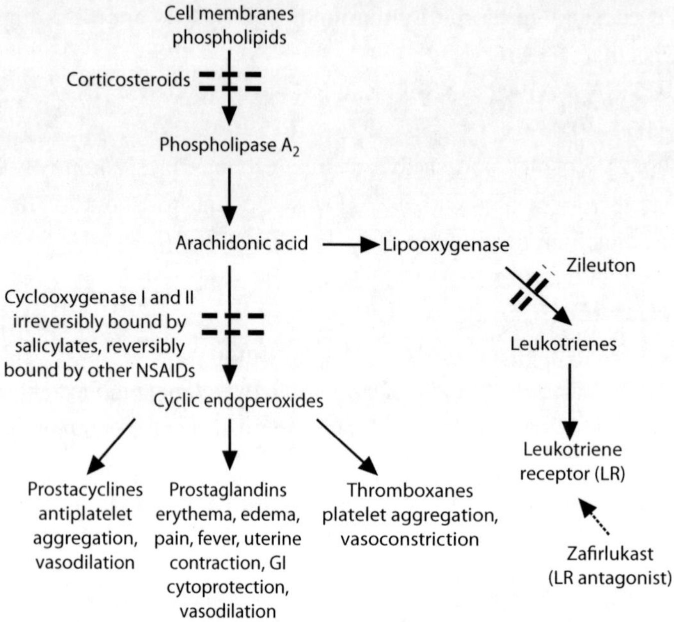

FIGURE 6.3 The mechanisms of toxicity of nonsteroidal anti-inflammatory drugs (NSAIDs). Comparative toxic biotransformation pathways of common over-the-counter nonsteroidal anti-inflammatory drugs (NSAIDs).

Management

1. Immediate orogastric lavage + AC, consider MDAC, support.
2. Add *misoprostel*, a PGE_2 analog, for GI mucosal cytoprotection in chronic NSAID users.
3. Switch to specific COX-2 inhibitors (**SEs:** Thrombogenic and become nonspecific in OD).
4. Hemodialysis is useless because of high protein binding of NSAIDs.
5. **Assess for systemic damage:** GI, hematologic, hepatic, renal.

Specific NSAID Adverse Effects

Significant Hematologic SEs

1. **↑ bleeding time from ↓ platelet aggregation:** All NSAIDs
2. **Agranulocytosis:** *Phenylbutazone*, naproxen
3. **Aplastic anemia:** Indomethacin, *phenylbutazone*, etodolac
4. **Hemolytic anemia:** Mefenamic acid (also epileptogenic)
5. **Neutropenia:** Indomethacin
6. **Thrombocytopenia:** Indomethacin, *ibuprofen*, naproxen

Drug–Drug Interactions

1. **All anticoagulants** and **ASA:** ↑ GI bleeding
2. **Antihypertensives:** Reduced efficacy

3. **Sulfonylureas:** Greater hypoglycemic effects
4. **Lithium:** ↑ toxicity
5. **Digoxin:** ↑ toxicity
6. **Aminoglycosides:** ↑ toxicity

Specific NSAID Toxicities

1. **Phenylbutazone:** Most toxic NSAID, seizures, coma, hemodynamic instability, NCPE, ARF, *agranulocytosis, aplastic anemia.* **Tx:** Immediate OG lavage + AC, MDAC, HD useless.
2. **Fenamates (anthranilic acids):** N, V, D (15%); muscle twitching and *seizures.* **Tx:** AW and seizure management (benzodiazepines [BZs]), lavage + AC, MDAC.
3. **Acetic acids:** N, abdominal cramps, drowsiness, HA, seizures; diclofen*ac* = *hepatocellular necrosis.* **Tx:** Lavage + AC.
4. **Propionic acids:** GI upset, seizures, apnea, coma, ARF, hepatotoxicity, *thrombocytopenia.* **Tx:** Lavage + AC.
5. **Oxicams:** Dizziness, blurred vision, coma. **Tx:** Lavage + AC.

Opioids: Outline

1. Opioid receptors, endogenous ligands, opioid agonists and antagonists
2. Opioid toxidrome and differential diagnosis
3. Clinical effects of opioids
4. Special consideration opioids
5. Management of opioid overdose (Table 6.2)

Opioids: Agonists/Antagonists

1. **Partial agonist:** Buprenorphine
2. **Agonists:** Codeine, dextromethorphan, diphenoxylate, fentanyl, heroin, hydrocodone, hydromorphone, loperamide, meperidine, methadone, morphine, oxycodone, paregoric-tincture of opium, propoxyphene, tramadol

Table 6.2 Opioids: Receptors

Opioid Receptor	Endo Ligand	Clinical Effects
Mu	Endorphins Naloxone-rev	Central analgesia, euphoria, respiratory depression, miosis, depend, pruritus, CV ↓
Kappa	Dynorphins Naloxone-rev	Spinal analgesia, dysphoria, psychomimesis
Delta	Enkephelins Naloxone-rev	Spinal analgesia, dopamine release modulation
Sigma	Not a receptor, not naloxone-reversible	Psychomimesis, seizures (pentazocine)

3. **Antagonists:** Nalmefene, naloxone, naltrexone
4. **Agonist–antagonists:** Butorphanol, nalbuphine, pentazocine

The Opioid Toxidrome

Opioid Toxidrome

1. Central CNS and respiratory depression
2. Miosis
3. *GI hypomotility* and *constipation*, GI sphincter spasm, ↑ hepatic intrabiliary pressures
4. ↓ *HR*, not true bradycardia
5. *Mild hypotension* from *histamine*-mediated pulmonary and peripheral vasodilation

Differential Diagnosis 3

1. All agonist opioids
2. All *alpha*$_2$ agonists = *clonidine* (central only) and *imidazolines* (central and peripheral agonists, used as mucosal decongestants)
3. **Benzodiazepines:** Sedation and *normal VS*
4. **PCP:** *Despite the miosis*, *nystagmus* is pathognomonic
5. **Phenothiazines:** Severe ↓ BP, dysrhythmias-*IA* effect (Figures 6.4 through 6.6)

Clinical Effects of Opioids

1. **Respiratory depression:** ↓ central ventilatory response to both hypoxia and hypercarbia, correlates better with ↓ TV > ↓ RR.
2. **Noncardiogenic pulmonary edema:** 2° (1) attempted inspiration against a closed glottis, or (2) naloxone-induced massive sympathetic discharge.
3. **CV effects:** Venous and arteriolar vasodilation, mild hypotension and decreased HR 2° histamine release.
4. *N.B. Propoxyphene* induces wide-complex dysrhythmias in a *quinidine-like (IA) effect*, responsive to $NaHCO_3$.

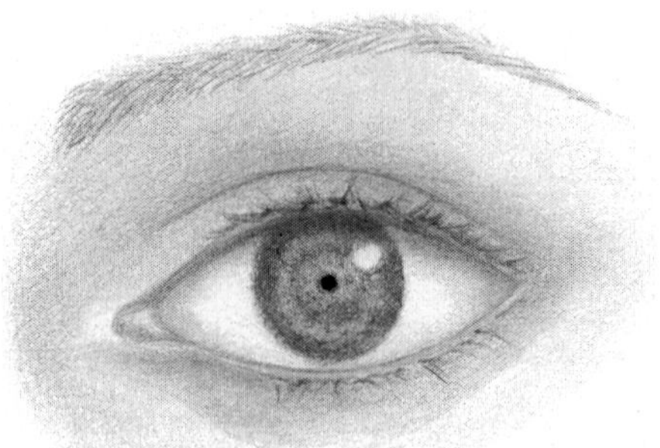

FIGURE 6.4 Opioid toxidrome. Miosis, left eye. Pupillary constriction or miosis characteristic of an opioid toxidrome.

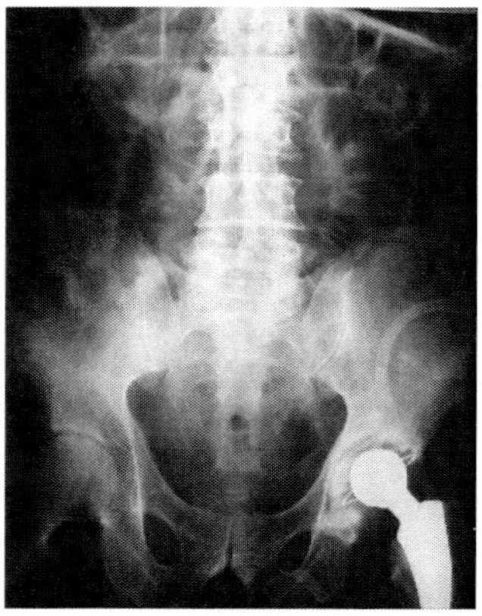

FIGURE 6.5 Opioid ileus. Heroin addict. Frontal abdominal radiograph (KUB) of a heroin addict consistent with adynamic bowel or opioid ileus that demonstrates diffuse bowel gas distension of the small bowel, ascending colon, and transverse colon. (Courtesy of Carlos R. Gimenez, MD, professor of radiology, LSU School of Medicine, New Orleans, LA.)

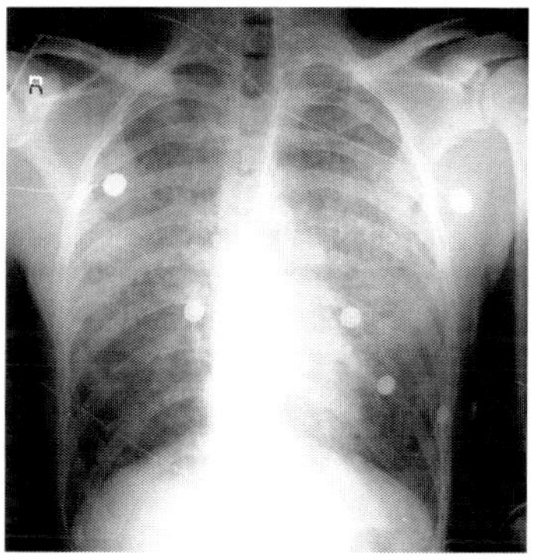

FIGURE 6.6 Noncardiogenic pulmonary edema. Aspirin overdose. Frontal chest radiograph of a patient following a suicide attempt by aspirin overdose that demonstrates noncardiogenic pulmonary edema characterized by normal size and configuration of the cardiomediastinal silhouette and diffuse bilateral pulmonary edema. (Courtesy of Carlos R. Gimenez, MD, professor of radiology, LSU School of Medicine, New Orleans, LA.)

5. **Miosis:** Inconsistent; meperidine and propoxyphene = normal pupils; but pentazocine (Talwin®), σ and κ agonists → dilated pupils.
6. **CNS:** OD commonly causes *seizures* 2° to hypoxia; seizures pathognomonic with *meperidine* and *propoxyphene* ODs; seizures occur at therapeutic doses of *tramadol* (Ultram®).
7. **Muscular rigidity:** Acute muscular rigidity with restricted ventilation with rapid IV *fentanyl.*
8. **N and V:** Apomorphine was a classic emetic, a dopamine agonist within the medullary CTZ.

Special Consideration Opioids

1. Agonists/antagonists and long-acting opioids (methadone, LAAM)
2. Meperidine and propoxyphene (*epileptogenic*)
3. Diphenoxylate and loperamide (*antidiarrheals*)
4. MPTP (Parkinsonism) and pentazocine (*psychomimetics*)
5. Tramadol and dextromethorphan (↑ serotonin = *serotonin syndrome*)
6. Clonidine and imidazolines (*central alpha2 agonists*)
7. Heroin body packers and narcotic adulterants (quinine strychnine, talc, and *China white* fentanyls)

Special Opioids

Agonists/Antagonists

- **Mech:** Synthetic drugs that are agonist at one opioid receptor, either mu or kappa, and antagonist at another, usually mu; may precipitate acute withdrawal in the opioid dependent.
- **Ex:** Butorphanol (Stadol®), nalbuphine (Nubain®), pentazocine (Talwin®, kappa agonist, and mu antagonist).

Long-Acting Opioids

- **Mech:** Synthetic agonists with long durations of action >24 h, provide long-term analgesia for cancer patients, maintenance for addicts, and support during withdrawal; OD problematic due to short naloxone reversal time (1 h), with resedation and resp depress.
- **Ex:** Methadone and MS-Contin® (24 h), levo-alpha-acetyl methadol (LAAM) T1/2 = 3 days.

Meperidine (Demerol®)

1. *Normeperidine metabolite* is neurotoxic → causing tremors, myoclonus, and *seizures*, especially in renal insufficiency.
2. Causes ↑ presynaptic *serotonin release* → can precipitate the *serotonin syndrome* (*hyperthermia, muscle rigidity*, and *CNS depression*), especially when combined with MAOIs or SSRIs. Tx for serotonin syndrome = cooling, benzodiazepines, nondepolarizing muscle relaxants.

Propoxyphene (Darvon®)

1. Both the parent drug and its *norpropoxyphene metabolite* have quinidine-like (Class IA) effects and cause ↑ *QRS widening* and dysrhythmias that are responsive to Na bicarbonate.
2. OD may produce acute *neurotoxicity* with *seizures* responsive to benzodiazepines more so than barbiturates.
3. Often formulated with *APAP*, suspect co-toxicities in OD, and monitor serum [APAP].

Antidiarrheals

Diphenoxylate (Lomotil®)

1. *Insoluble meperidine analog* that delays gastric emptying, coats gut, relaxes and immobilizes GI tract; used as an antidiarrheal.
2. *Formulated with atropine* for its antimuscarinic and antispasmodic effects; OD may manifest both anticholinergic and opioid toxidromes.
3. *Long T1/2* due to #1 and #2 dictates admission for lavage, AC, and naloxone infusion.

Loperamide (Immodium®)

1. *An OTC insoluble meperidine analog*, like diphenoxylate, that also immobilizes GI tract; also used as an antidiarrheal
2. *Safer than diphenoxylate because loperamide does not contain atropine* or delay gastric emptying, does not have a prolonged T1/2, and is not associated with prolonged retention of pills in the stomach

Methyl-Phenyl-Tetrahydropyridine (MPTP)

1. A meperidine analog and a neurotoxic by-product of the failed illicit laboratory synthesis of *meperidine.*
2. Intravenous drug users (IVDUs) become *"frozen addicts"* and develop classical *Parkinsonism* from selective destruction of dopamine-secreting substantia nigra cells; *resistant to l-dopa tx.*
3. MPTP is now used to induce *experimental Parkinsonism* in laboratory animals.

Pentazocine (Talwin®)

1. A synthetic agonist/antagonist that is an *agonist* at the *kappa* and *sigma* receptors (causing dysphoria and psychomimesis), but an *antagonist* at the *mu* receptor (thus producing little respiratory depression)
2. Formerly mixed with the blue antihistamine, *tripelennamine* = "*T's* for Talwin and *Blues for tripelennamine*"; but now mixed with *methylphenidate* (Ritalin®) for recreational abuse at all-night *Rave parties*

Tramadol (Ultram®)

1. A novel synthetic opioid that is a combined *mu opioid agonist* and a *serotonin/NE reuptake inhibitor*; only partially antagonized by naloxone.
2. Can cause *seizures* in therapeutic doses and characteristically in ODs. Seizures respond to benzodiazepine suppression, but may be precipitated by naloxone.
3. Can precipitate *serotonin syndrome*, like *SSRIs*, by *blocking serotinin reuptake*, especially in patients on MAOIs.

Dextromethorphan (Robitussin®)

1. An OTC synthetic opioid agonist with no analgesic activity that is for cough suppression, like codeine.

2. In OD, causes miosis, CNS depression; and *choreoathetosis* and *dystonia* 2° ↑ *serotonin release.* Also acts as a sigma agonist and can cause a PCP-like psychosis.
3. Formulated as a *hydrobromide salt* → *bromism*, CNS depression, ataxia, confusion, coma.
4. Can also precipitate *serotonin syndrome*, like *meperidine*, by ↑ presynaptic release of serotonin.

Clonidine (Catapress®)

1. *Centrally acting* $alpha_2$ *agonist* that produces an opioid toxidrome (lethargy, miosis, bradycardia, and respiratory depression) indistinguishable from mu agonists due to agonist activity overlap at the mu receptor
2. CNS and respiratory depression reversed by *naloxone* → admit for naloxone infusion 2° resedation
3. Used as a sympathetic blocker for HTN and RSD, and to provide sympatholysis during opioid withdrawal

Imidazolines (Afrin®, etc.)

1. *Combined central* and *peripheral* $alpha_2$ *agonists* used as nasal and conjunctival decongestants (oxymetazoline, tetrahydrozoline, xylometazoline) that produce an opioid toxidrome (bradycardia, hypotension, CNS, and respiratory depression) indistinguishable from mu agonists due to agonist activity overlap at the mu receptor
2. Partially naloxone-reversible, but prolonged duration of action (4–8 h) causes resedation

Heroin Body Packers (See Figures 6.7 through 6.9)

1. "Mules" who ingest large numbers of neatly and multiply wrapped packages of heroin (or cocaine) for smuggling, home catharsis, and later street distribution.
2. Abdominal x-rays confirm status and direct WBI with PEG in asymptomatic patients.
3. Symptomatic heroin packers can be managed medically with AC, naloxone infusion, and WBI. (*Symptomatic cocaine packers need surgery 2° GI ischemic necrosis* and ↑ *CFRs.*)

Narcotic Adulterants

1. **Quinine:** Disguises bitter taste of heroin → dysrhythmias, headache, vertigo, *tinnitus*, blurred vision, temporary–permanent *blindness.*
2. **Scopolamine:** CNS and peripheral anticholinergic toxidrome.
3. **Fentanyl analogs:** *China white* = fentanyl (100× MS), sufentanil (10× fent or 1000× MS), and methyl-fentanyl (6000× MS); superpotent fentanyl-adulterated heroin → respiratory arrest, coma and death. **Tx:** CPR, naloxone.
4. **Misc. adulterants:** Amphetamines, cocaine, lead-thallium, quinine, barium carbonate, talc, *strychnine.*

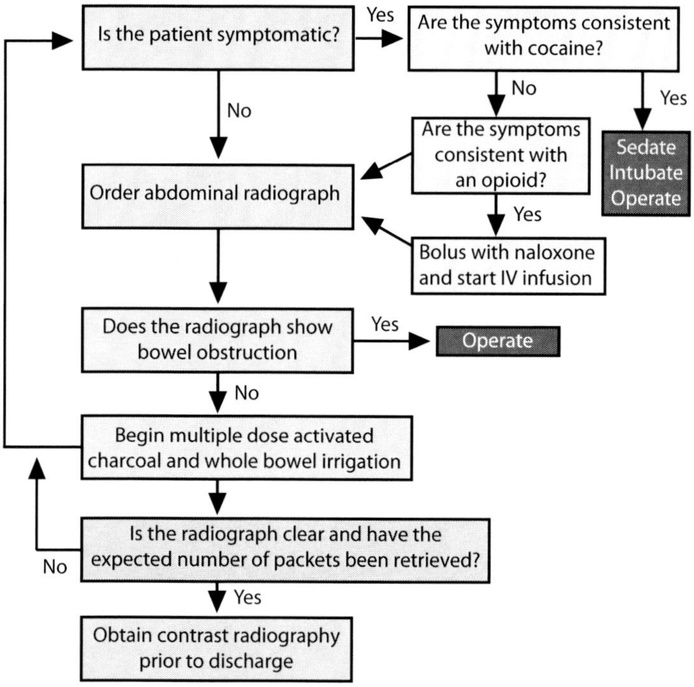

FIGURE 6.7 Management. Cocaine vs. heroin body packers. A flow chart outlining the clinical practice management strategies for body packers of cocaine or heroin.

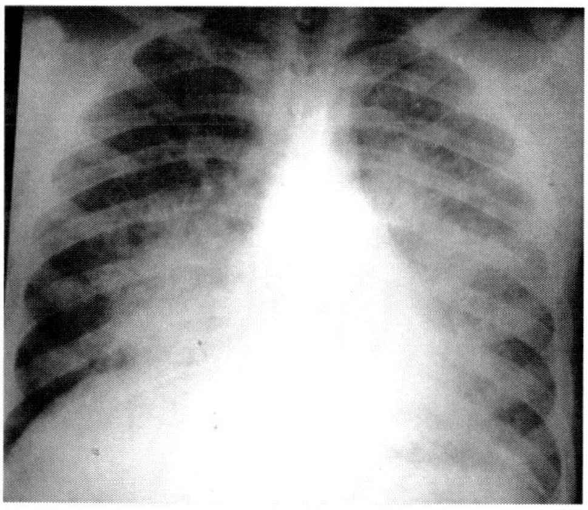

FIGURE 6.8 Noncardiogenic pulmonary edema. Heroin overdose. Frontal chest radiograph that demonstrates normal size and configuration of the cardiomediastinal silhouette with diffuse bilateral noncardiogenic pulmonary edema following heroin overdose. (Courtesy of Carlos R. Gimenez, MD, professor of radiology, LSU School of Medicine, New Orleans, LA.)

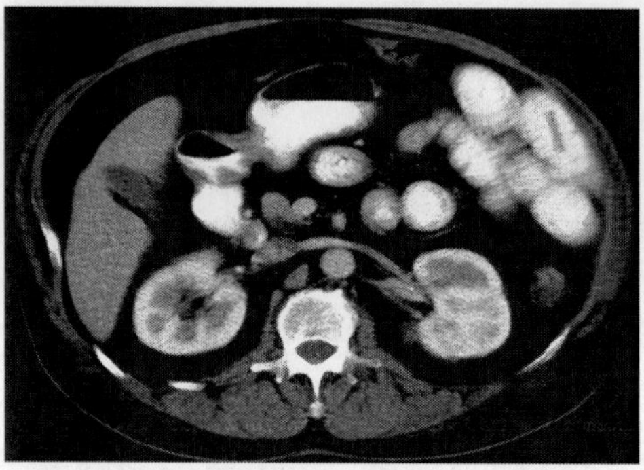

FIGURE 6.9 Body stuffer. Heroin. Axial abdominal oral and intravenous contrast-enhanced computerized tomogram (CT) at the level of the renal veins that demonstrated a rectangular container of heroin in a jejunal loop. (Courtesy of Carlos R. Gimenez, MD, professor of radiology, LSU School of Medicine, New Orleans, LA.)

Management of an Opioid Overdose

Acute OD Management

1. Low initial IV naloxone boluses (0.1–0.4 mg), rather than a single, large therapeutic bolus (2 mg) to avoid precipitating acute withdrawal in addicts or causing noncardiogenic pulmonary edema
2. Aim is to reverse respiratory depression and restore RR > 8
3. Intubate and ventilate if respiratory depression persists, administer 10 mg naloxone IV–no infusion, just prolonged mechanical ventilation

Naloxone Infusion

1. If diagnostic naloxone bolus is successful, *administer 2/3 of the initial dose IV per hour.*
2. If withdrawal develops, stop the infusion to let symptoms abate and restart at 1/2 rate.
3. If respiratory depression recurs during infusion, readminister 1/2 the initial bolus, and increase infusion rate by 1/2.

Chapter 7

Household Product Poisonings

Outline 106
Cleansers and Caustics. 106
Food Additives 115
Household Products 116
Hydrocarbons/Solvent/Fuels 119
Alcohols and Glycols. 122
Aliphatic Hydrocarbon. 127
Miscellaneous Toxicants 156

Outline

- Cleansers and caustics
- Miscellaneous household products
- Veterinary products
- Hydrocarbons
- Solvents
- Miscellaneous toxicants

Cleansers and Caustics

Acids (See Table 7.1)

1. **Bioavailability:** Acid exposures desiccate epithelial cells. An acid is a proton donator. Accidental ingestion, inhalation, and dermal contact are all ways of exposure (Tables 7.1 through 7.6 and Figures 7.1 through 7.4).
2. **Usages:**
   a. Acetic acid can be found in permanent wave neutralizers, and in a photographic stop bath.
   b. Boric acid can be found in roach powders, water softeners, and germicides.
   c. Formic acid, and formaldehyde can be found in deodorizing tablets, plastic menders, fumigants, and embalming agents.
   d. Hydrochloric acid can be found in metal and toilet bowl cleaners.
   e. Sulfuric acid can be found in automobile batteries and drain cleaners.
3. **Administration:** For primary use in a variety of cleansers. The product is not designed for ingestion or inhalation.
4. **Toxicity:** Exposure to acids can create complications including airway compromise, hemodynamic instability, vascular erosion, septic shock, perforation of the gastrointestinal (GI) tract, and infections from bacteria. Following acid ingestion, gastric and esophageal mucosa are equally affected.

Table 7.1 Sources and Uses of Acids

Acid Source	Acid Uses
Boric acid	Roach tablets
Formaldehyde metabolite (formic acid)	Tissue fixative, pesticide/fungicide effects in foam insulation
Hydrochloric (muriatic) acid	Toilet, brick, and tile cleaners
Hydrofluoric acid	Antirust products
Oxalic acid	Bleaches and whiteners
Selenious acid	Gun bluing agents
Sulfuric acid	Automotive batteries

5. **Upon overdose:** Irrigation with water or saline washes, surgical removal of burned skin, endoscopy, and bronchoscopy are used to determine the severity of the exposure. GI decontamination with activated charcoal with the addition of cathartic sorbitol if copious vomiting has not already occurred. If sorbitol is given separately, it should be diluted with an equal volume of water before administration. People with porphyria should avoid direct sunlight that exacerbated the dermal injury by porphyrins.

Alkali (See Table 7.2)

1. **Bioavailability:** Alkaline xenobiotics enter tissue surfaces and produce liquefaction necrosis. This process causes protein dissolution, collagen destruction, cell death, transmural thrombosis, cell membrane emulsification, and fat saponification.
2. **Usages:**
   a. Ammonia can be found in toilet bowl cleaners, hair dyes and tints, jewelry cleaners, floor strippers, glass cleaners, and wax removers.
   b. Benzalkonium chloride can be found in detergents.
   c. Sodium hydroxide (detergents, paint removers, drain cleaners and openers, and oven cleaners).
   d. Sodium borates, carbonates, phosphates, and silicates can be found in detergents, electric dishwasher preparations, and water softeners.
3. **Administration:** For primary use in a variety of cleansers. The product is not designed for ingestion or inhalation.
4. **Contraindication:** High exposure to alkalis can cause adverse reactions that include metallic alkalosis and edema. When they exceed the capacity of the kidneys to excrete this excess alkali, many health effects surface.
5. **Toxicity:** Exposure of alkalis to the eye can lead to perforation. Exposure to the esophagus demonstrates that erythema and edema of the mucosa occur followed by an inflammatory reaction into the submucosa and muscular layers. Caustic burns and strictures occur when ingested and airway compromise may also occur. Headache, nausea, and irritability may occur as well. Ammonia has good warning properties due to its odor and immediate symptoms of the mucous membrane, eye, and throat irritation. Lower airway involvement resulting in bronchospasm, pulmonary edema, and residual reactive airways disease have all been described following massive exposures, especially those who are entrapped in enclosed spaces.
6. **Upon overdose:** Management of esophageal strictures includes early endoscopic dilation. Exposure that results from splash injuries is treated with immediate irrigation for a minimum of 15 min with 0.9% sodium chloride, lactated Ringer solution, or tap water. Treatment is supportive with humidified oxygen and bronchodilators. Concentrated ammonia, such as 8.4% ammonia hydroxide, is extremely hazardous to the eyes. Therefore, following ocular irrigation in symptomatic patients, evaluation for the presence of corneal burns should be considered, and a careful ophthalmologic examination and consultation is warranted.

Table 7.2 Sources and Uses of Alkalis

Alkali Sources	Alkali Uses
Ammonium hydroxide (ammonia)	Glass, oven, and other hard surface cleaners (Windex®)
Potassium permanganate	Antiseptics, mouthwashes
Sodium hydroxide	Detergents
Sodium borates, carbonates, phosphates, and silicates	Detergents, dishwasher/scouring powders, water softeners
Sodium hypochlorite (Clorox®)	Bleaches, whiteners, tile surface cleansers, and disinfectants

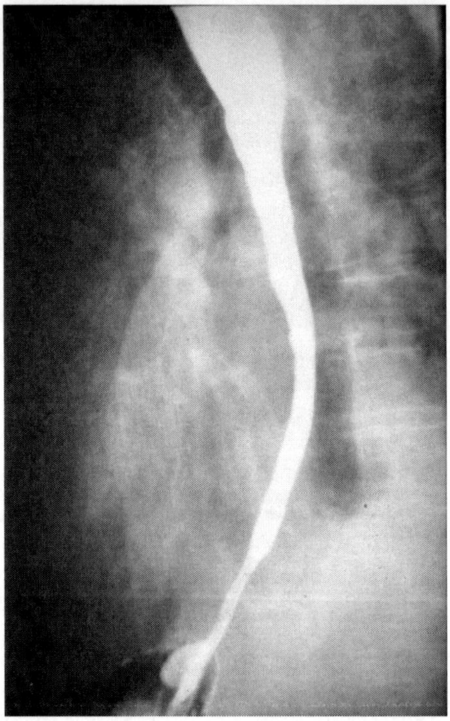

FIGURE 7.1 Esophageal stenosis following lye ingestion. Frontal esophagogram of an adolescent 8 months following intentional lye ingestion in a suicide attempt that demonstrates a gradual funnel-like tapering of the distal esophagus and concentric esophageal stenosis. (Courtesy of Carlos R. Gimenez, M, Professor of Radiology, LSU School of Medicine, New Orleans, LA. With permission.)

Bleach

1. **Bioavailability:** Bleach is used for disinfecting surfaces, cleaning clothing, as well as treating drinking water. However, it must be diluted to be used safely. Granular and industrial bleach, such as that used for bleaching or cleaning swimming pools, contains much higher concentrations of caustic agents and are more dangerous.

2. **Usages:** Bleach can be found in household-cleaning chemicals, tooth-bleaching products, hair-bleaching products, and used for treating drinking water.
3. **Administration:** Usually applied directly to the surface for cleaning effects. For primary use in a variety of cleansers. The product is not designed for ingestion or inhalation.
4. **Contraindication:** Do not use bleach when there are any open cuts and abrasions. In regard to hair bleaching, do not come in contact with bleach when the hair is coated with a metallic substance, such as hair-restoration products. Bleach is a contraindication if your teeth were treated with formaldehyde or if you have amalgam fillings.
5. **Toxicity:** It irritates the mucous membranes of the nose, mouth, and throat. It will cause nausea, vomiting, and diarrhea if ingested. If these symptoms are left untreated, they can lead to dehydration.
6. **Upon overdose:** Treatment includes removing the irritant, cleaning the skin, and treating any symptoms.

Detergents and Soaps

1. **Bioavailability:** Household detergents, such as laundry powders and dishwasher detergents, contain silicates, carbonates, and phosphates, and have the potential to induce caustic burns and strictures even when ingested unintentionally. Cationic detergents include quinolinium compounds, pyridinium compounds, and quaternary ammonium salts. These are frequently found in products for industrial use, as well as household fabric softeners.
2. **Usages:** Used to clean inanimate objects.
3. **Administration:** For primary use in a variety of cleansers. The product is not designed for ingestion or inhalation.
4. **Contraindication:** None.
5. **Toxicity:** A concentration >7.5% can cause severe burns. Esophageal burns, secondary to both alkali and acid exposures, are classified based on endoscopic visualization that employs a grading system similar to that used with burns of the skin. Grade I burns are generally described as hyperemia or edema of the mucosa without evidence of ulcer formation. Grade II burns include submucosal lesions, ulcerations, and exudates. Grade II lesions can be further divided into grade IIa, noncircumferential lesions, and grade IIb, near-circumferential injuries. Grade III burns are defined as deep ulcers and necrosis into the periesophageal tissues. Severe change in the acid level of blood (pH balance) leads to damage in all the body organs—loss of vision, severe pain in the throat, and severe pain or burning in the nose, eyes, ears, lips, or tongue.
6. **Upon overdose:** Follow through skin decontamination with soap and water, GI decontamination with activated charcoal with the addition of cathartic sorbitol if copious vomiting has not already occurred. If sorbitol is given separately, it should be diluted with an equal volume of water before administration. People with porphyria should avoid direct sunlight which exacerbates the dermal injury by porphyrins. Seek medical attention. The hospital will treat you with a breathing tube, bronchoscopy (camera

down the throat to see burns in the airways and lungs), endoscopy (camera down the throat to see burns in the esophagus and the stomach), fluids by IV, medicines to treat pain, oxygen, surgical removal of burned skin (skin debridement), and irrigation every few hours for several days.

Disinfectants and Topical Anti-Infectives (See Tables 7.3–7.5)

1. **Bioavailability:** Disinfectants are chemical agents used on inanimate objects to kill and inhibit microorganisms.
2. **Usages:**
   a. Formaldehydes are used as disinfectants and fumigants. Health-care workers are the most familiar with the use of formaldehyde for tissue fixtures and as an embalming agent.
   b. Phenols are known as carbolic acid and are one of the oldest antiseptic agents. It is used as a disinfectant, chemical intermediary, and nail cauterizer.
   c. Quaternary ammonium compounds are surface-active agents that are used as disinfectants, detergents, and sanitizers.
3. **Administration:** For primary use in a variety of cleansers. The product is not designed for ingestion or inhalation.
4. **Contraindication:** The most rapid systemic manifestation of formaldehyde poisoning is metabolic acidosis, resulting from both tissue injury and the conversion of formaldehyde into formic acid.
5. **Toxicity:**
   a. Formaldehyde exposure can lead to epigastric tenderness, hematemesis, cyanosis, hypotension, and tachypnea. Hypotension may be profound with decreased myocardial contractility, as well as hypovolemic shock, contributing to the cardiovascular instability. Early endoscopic findings include ulceration, necrosis, perforation, and hemorrhage of the stomach, with infrequent esophageal involvement. Headache, nausea, skin rash, sore throat, nasal congestion, and eye irritation are associated with the use of these polymers.
   b. Phenol exposure can cause systemic symptoms in the GI tract. Manifestations of systemic toxicity include CNS and cardiac symptoms. Local toxicity to the GI tract from the ingestion of phenol may result in nausea, painful oral lesions, vomiting, bloody diarrhea, dark urine, and severe abdominal pain. Phenol precipitates tissue protein and causes respirator alkalosis followed by metabolic acidosis; some phenols cause methemoglobinemia. Local gangrene occurs after prolonged contact with the tissue. Phenol is readily absorbed from the GI tract, causing diffuse capillary damage. Pentachlorophenol that has been used in terminal rinsing of diapers, has caused infant fatalities.
   c. Quaternary ammonium compounds are less toxic than phenol or formaldehyde. Most of the infrequent complications that are described result from ingestions of

Table 7.3 Household Antimicrobials

Antiseptics	Disinfectants	Sterilants
Antimicrobials applied to humans. Example: Alcohols, iodophors, chlorhexidine Alcohols Iodines Chlorines Oxidants Hydrogen peroxide (H_2O_2) Potassium permanganate ($KMnO_4$) Benzalkonium chloride	Antimicrobials applied only to inanimate objects Example: Bleach, formaldehyde, phenols Chlorine bleaches Phenols Boric acid Formaldehyde	Antimicrobials applied to inanimate objects to kill all microorganisms, including spores Example: Ethylene oxide, glutaraldehyde Ethylene oxide Gluaraldehyde

Table 7.4 Antiseptics: Iodines

Iodine (I)	Iodophor	Iodide
Elemental I Free I 2% Tincture of iodine Most toxic form of iodine, rarely used today	I + high-molecular-weight nontoxic iodine carrier (e.g., I + povidone = Betadine®) Relatively safe, mostly skin irritants, commonly used for surgical procedures	Reduced I–, multiple uses: 1. SSKI for hyperthyroidism 2. NaI added to table salt 3. X-ray contrast agents Least toxic forms of iodine

Table 7.5 Mothballs

Camphor	Naphthalene	*Para*-Dichlorobenzene
High toxicity	Moderate toxicity	Low toxicity
Not radiopaque	Faintly radiopaque	Densely radiopaque
Wet and oily	White and dry	White and oily
Float in tap and saltwater	Sink in tap, float in saltwater	Sink in both tap and saltwater
Treatment: Sedation, AC, nonoil cathartic = increased absorption	Treatment: AC, nonoil cathartic, methemoglobinemia possible, may require methylene blue therapy	Treatment: Not indicated, the safest mothball, most commonly used mothball today in the United States
Acute toxicity: CNS > GI; excitement, tremor, restlessness, seizures, apnea, coma, camphor-smelling breath, initial nausea, vomiting, cramps	Acute toxicity: Hematologic > GI > CNS; #1 hemolysis, methemoglobinemia possible, hemolysis in G-6-P deficiency, cyanosis, anemia, fever, nausea, vomiting, diarrhea, cramps	Acute toxicity: GI > hematologic; mucosal irritant, rarely causes hemolysis and jaundice
Chronic: Mimics Reye's syndrome–hepatic encephalopathy	Chronic: Aplastic anemia, jaundice, hepatic necrosis	Chronic: Rarely causes hepatic necrosis

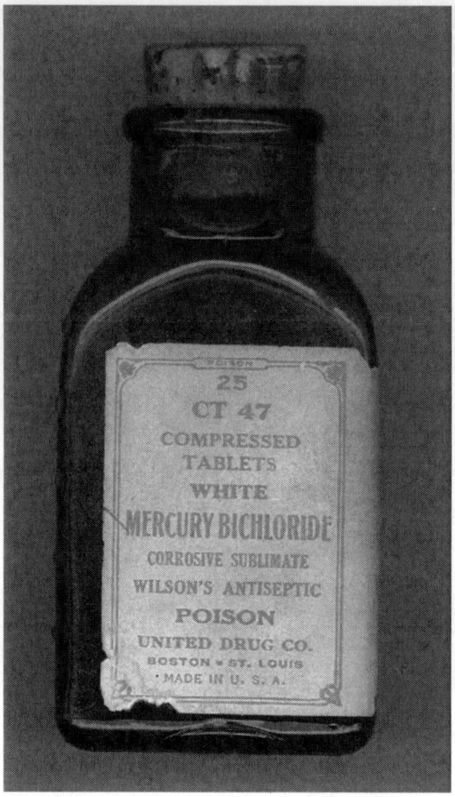

FIGURE 7.2 Over-the-counter mercury bichloride tablets, c. 1890s. Highly caustic, inorganic mercury compounds were commonly sold worldwide as over-the-counter topical antiseptics (mercuric chloride or mercuric bichloride) and infant teething powders (calomel) well into the twentieth century. Accidental ingestions may result in severe oropharyngeal and esophageal burns, hemorrhagic gastroenteritis, hypovolemic shock, acute tubular necrosis, and esophageal stenosis in survivors. (From the antique pharmaceutical collection of James H. Diaz, MD, DrPH.)

benzalkonium chloride. Complications of these ingestions include burns to the mouth and esophagus, CNS depression, elevated liver enzyme concentrations, metabolic acidosis, and hypotension.

d. **Upon overdose:** Immediate treatment of formaldehyde includes dilution with water. In phenol, isopropanol could also be considered as another treatment for dermal decontamination. Endoscopic evaluation, as needed to determine the extent of GI injury, and good supportive care are also recommended. Quaternary ammonium compounds are less toxic than formaldehyde and phenol, but emergency department evaluation should be considered for all patients who ingest more than a taste of a dilute (<1%) solution.

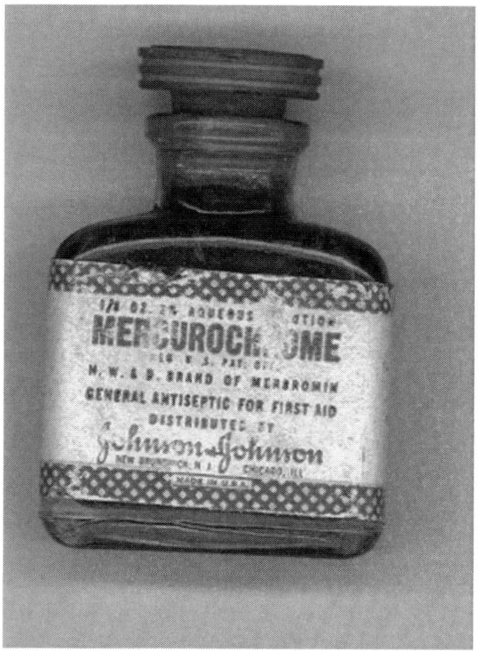

FIGURE 7.3 Mercurochrome (merbromin) antiseptic, official Boy Scout first aid kit, 1950s. The organic mercury compounds, mercurochrome (merbromin) and thimerosol (merthiolate), were also commonly sold over-the-counter worldwide as topical antiseptics well into the twentieth century. Thimerosol is still added to vaccines and pooled hyperimmune plasma immunoglobulins and antivenoms as a bacteriostatic and fungicidal preservative. Repeated topical applications or accidental ingestions of the organic mercurials may result in mercuric neurotoxicity with slurred speech, tremor, and chorea. (From the antique pharmaceutical collection of James H. Diaz, MD, DrPH.)

Swimming Pool Products

1. **Bioavailability:** The most common method of sanitizing swimming pool water is through the use of the chemical chlorine. Chlorine is dissolved into your swimming pool water and combines with bacteria and other organics in the water on a molecular level to kill these harmful contaminants. Once chlorine "combines" with the bacteria and organics in the swimming pool water, the chlorine becomes inactive and no longer works to sanitize your pool. The combined chlorine and organic contaminants are burned off by a weekly "shock treatment" and removed from the water by the pool-filter system. Another chemical commonly used to sanitize a swimming pool is called bromine. The chemical bromine is very similar to pool chlorine in the way that bromine kills bacteria and harmful contaminants, but the two pool chemicals react in different ways. Bromine is most commonly used to sanitize spas/hot tubs because it is more stable than chlorine in the warmer spa water temperatures, and because of the

lack of chemical odor in the water. The chemical bromine is preferred by many pool and spa owners because it causes less irritation of the skin and eyes. Since bromine is so stable, it can be harder to wash the chemical smell from your skin after bathing in a pool or spa that uses bromine. Bromine is available in tablet form and can be added to pool water using a chemical feeder to dissolve the tablets.

2. **Usages:** Chlorine and bromide are used to sanitize pools. The difference between chlorine and bromine is that once chlorine combines with bacteria or harmful organics to kill them, most of the chlorine is used up and will no longer work to sanitize your swimming pool. This "combined chlorine" will be burned off by the next shock treatment and removed from the pool water by the filter. When bromine combines with bacteria in pool water, the bromine is still active but combined with the bacteria and organic matter to neutralize these harmful contaminants.
3. **Administration:** For primary use in a variety of cleansers. The product is not designed for ingestion or inhalation.
4. **Contraindication:** None.
5. **Toxicity:** Function is progressively impaired by a poorly understood mechanism, with resulting inappropriateness of behavior, headache, apathy, irritability, confusion, muscle weakness, anorexia, weight loss, thickened speech, psychotic behavior, tremulousness, ataxia, and eventually coma. Delusions and hallucinations can occur. Bromide can lead to hypertension, increased intracranial pressure, and papilledema. Chronic use of bromides can also lead to dermatologic changes, with the hallmark characteristic of a facial acneiform rash. Toxicity with bromides during pregnancy may lead to accumulation of bromide in the fetus. A spurious laboratory result of hyperchloremia with decreased anion gap may result from bromide's interference with the chloride assay on older analyzers. So, an isolated elevated serum chloride concentration with neurologic symptoms should raise suspicion of possible bromide poisoning. Early inflammatory injury results from the formation of hydrochloric and hypochlorous acids and oxidants upon contact with moist membranes. Immediate ocular and upper airway irritation along with nausea and vomiting are common following mild exposures. More significant exposure results in coughing, hoarseness, and pulmonary edema, usually within 6 h, with some exposures leading to acute respiratory distress syndrome.
6. **Upon overdose:** Care is primarily supportive, with the use of humidified oxygen and bronchodilators as needed. Prophylactic antibiotics are not recommended. The role of inhaled steroids and nebulized sodium bicarbonate as a neutralizing therapy is controversial and is not recommended. Chlorine may cause dermal injury at high concentration, and skin decontamination may be required. Follow through skin decontamination with soap and water, GI decontamination with activated charcoal and the addition of cathartic sorbitol if copious vomiting has not already occurred. If sorbitol is given separately, it should be diluted with an equal volume of water before administration. People with porphyria should avoid direct sunlight which exacerbates the dermal injury by porphyrins.

Food Additives

Monosodium Glutamate

1. **Bioavailability:** Glutamate is an excitatory neurotransmitter that can stimulate the CNS neurons through activation of glutamate receptors, and may be the explanation for some of the neurologic symptoms described with ingestion.
2. **Usages:** MSG can be used to enhance the taste of certain dishes. It is usually used with meat, poultry, fish, sauces, soups, and vegetables. Alone and in excess, MSG does not have a pleasant taste. Because of its interaction with sodium chloride, MSG has been used to reduce salt intake.
3. **Administration:** Added to food that is administered orally.
4. **Contraindication:** MSG seems to have a connection to vitamin B12. Asthmatics seem to have allergic reactions to MSG.
5. **Toxicity:** Exposure can lead to a burning sensation of the upper torso, facial pressure, headache, flushing, chest pain, nausea and vomiting, and, infrequently, life-threatening bronchospasm and angioedema. MSG causes shudder attacks or a seizure-like syndrome in young children.
6. **Upon overdose:** Symptoms of a serious adverse reaction to MSG—chest pain, heart palpitations, throat swelling, and shortness of breath—require emergency medical attention.

Sulfites

1. **Bioavailability:** There are six sulfating agents that the Food and Drug Administration (FDA) allows manufacturers to add to food.
   a. Sodium sulfite
   b. Sodium bisulfite
   c. Sodium metabisulfite
   d. Sulfur dioxide
   e. Potassium bisulfite
   f. Potassium metabisulfite
2. **Usages:** Sulfites are food additives that are antioxidants used to preserve food. It keeps food from turning brown and preserves certain nutrients.
3. **Administration:** Added to food that is administered orally.
4. **Contraindication:** Exposure seems to negatively affect asthmatics.
5. **Toxicity:** Exposure seems to negatively affect asthmatics.
6. **Upon overdose:** The adverse reaction results from the body's inability to metabolize or deal with the sulfite. The amount of the substance required to trigger the onset of symptoms and the nature and severity of symptoms may vary among those with sulfite allergies. Treat specific symptoms. Follow through skin decontamination with soap and water, GI decontamination with activated charcoal with the addition of cathartic sorbitol if copious vomiting has not already occurred. If sorbitol is given

separately, it should be diluted with an equal volume of water before administration. People with porphyria should avoid direct sunlight that exacerbated the dermal injury by porphyrins.

Household Products

Aquarium Products

1. **Bioavailability:** There are a variety of products used to promote healthy living and growth among your personal aquatic life. Owing to the fact that toxic ingredients in the product could lead to the death of the aquatic life, many products are not considered toxic. However, all items have a toxicity level and at some point can cause negative health effects.
2. **Usages:** Common aquarium-cleaning products contain the following compounds:
   a. Sodium hydroxide
   b. Tartaric acid
   c. Formaldehyde
3. **Administration:** Aquarium products are to be applied to the surface as a cleaning agent. Ingestion and inhalation of fumes are not advised.
4. **Contraindication:** If there are any known allergies to the ingredients in the specific product at hand, do not expose yourself to it.
5. **Toxicity:** Most aquarium products have been classified as not being "harmful by ingestion." This is because of the lack of corroborating animal or human evidence. The material may be still damaging to the health of the individual, following ingestion, especially where preexisting organ (liver, kidney) damage is evident. These definitions of harmful or toxic substances are generally based on doses producing mortality (death) rather than those producing morbidity (disease, ill health). GI tract discomfort may produce nausea and vomiting. Although the chemicals are not thought to be an irritant, direct contact with the eye may produce transient discomfort characterized by tearing or conjunctival redness (as with windburn). The material is not thought to produce adverse health effects or skin irritation following contact. Good hygiene practice requires that exposure must be kept to a minimum and that suitable gloves must be used in an occupational setting. Long-term exposure to the product is not thought to produce chronic effects that are adverse to the health.
6. **Upon overdose:** Follow through skin decontamination with soap and water, GI decontamination with activated charcoal with the addition of cathartic sorbitol if copious vomiting has not already occurred. If sorbitol is given separately, it should be diluted with an equal volume of water before administration. People with porphyria should avoid direct sunlight which exacerbates the dermal injury by porphyrins.

Art Products

1. **Bioavailability:** Art and craft supplies that contain toxic substances, including potential human carcinogens, pose a significant danger to the health and safety of schoolchildren.
2. **Usages:** Asbestos, heavy metals, organic solvents, and other toxic ingredients found in some art and craft materials present risks to the health and safety of individuals using them.
3. **Administration:** Art products contain a wide range of items used to create a piece from the artist's imagination. All substances are not to be ingested or inhaled. Body art is considered as a form of art and therefore, some products are made to apply dermally for expression purposes.
4. **Contraindication:** Exposure to hazardous substances in art supplies occurs by three routes: inhalation, ingestion, and skin contact. Dusts, powders, vapors, gases, and aerosols may be readily inhaled and, therefore, they present a health hazard. Direct damage to the lungs may result from silica or asbestos present in dry earth clays. Organ damage may occur following inhalation of solvent vapors and subsequent absorption into the bloodstream. Ingestion of hazardous substances can occur by eating and drinking food that has been contaminated or more directly through oral contact with hands or tools used in art projects. This route of exposure is an important concern since children tend to experiment and put things in their mouths. Finally, skin contact with hazardous materials may result in local or internal effects. Caustic substances or solvents may cause local skin damage. Certain solvents can also pass through the skin into the bloodstream, resulting in damage to other organs.
5. **Toxicity:** Exposure to toxic materials may result in either acute or chronic illness. An acute illness may result from a relatively large exposure over a short period of time. An example would be the intoxication-like symptoms following deliberate or inadvertent ingestion of toxic solvents. A chronic illness may result from a relatively small exposure over a long period of time as, for example, degeneration of the nervous system from exposure to lead-containing products. While the symptoms of an acute illness are immediately apparent, this is not necessarily the case for a chronic illness. Chronic illness may arise at a later time due to the concentration of substances in the body (e.g., asbestos or lead), accumulated damage to the body, or the sensitization to a substance after repeated exposure.
6. **Upon overdose:** Follow through skin decontamination with soap and water, GI decontamination with activated charcoal with the addition of cathartic sorbitol if copious vomiting has not already occurred. If sorbitol is given separately, it should be diluted with an equal volume of water before administration. People with porphyria should avoid direct sunlight which exacerbates the dermal injury by porphyrins.

Batteries

1. **Bioavailability:** Most of button battery ingestions occur in children <5 years old.
2. **Usages:** Batteries are used to convert stored chemical energy into electrical energy.

3. **Administration:** Batteries come in a variety of sizes and are usually inserted into the object in which it needs energy to function.
4. **Contraindication:** N/a.
5. **Toxicity:** Batteries lodged in the esophagus may be asymptomatic initially or may present with pain, drooling, dysphagia, poor intake, cough, vomiting, or fever. Mechanisms of injury associated with button battery ingestion include electrical-current-induced soft-tissue injury and liquefaction necrosis, resulting from alkali exposure due to battery leakage or the *de novo* synthesis of the alkali at the surface of the battery.
6. **Upon overdose:** Plain radiographs should be obtained to locate the battery within the GI tract. Button batteries can be distinguished from coins on plain x-ray by demonstration of a double contour. Button batteries that are lodged in the esophagus can lead to potentially fatal complications and require immediate removal in consultation with a gastroenterologist or surgeon. Batteries that have passed into the stomach are likely to traverse the GI tract without complication.

Cosmetics, Dental Products, Hair Products, and Personal Hygiene Products

1. **Bioavailability:** Parabens, or parahydroxybenzoic acids, are a group of compounds widely employed as preservatives in cosmetics, food, and pharmaceuticals because of their bacteriostatic, fungistatic, and antioxidant properties. A survey conducted by the FDA identified the parabens as the second most common ingredients in cosmetic formulations, with water being the most common. Parabens are often used in combination, because the presence of two or more parabens is synergistic.
2. **Usages:** The following are ingredients found in various personal hygiene products:
   a. Diethanolamine can be found as a wetting/foaming agent in shampoos and lotions.
   b. Propylene glycol can be found in a variety of hair-care products and deodorants.
   c. Sodium lauryl sulfate is a common degreaser found in shower gels, soaps, shampoo, and toothpaste.

   The following are found in almost all personal hygiene products:
   d. Parabens are compounds that act as preservatives in cosmetics, food, and pharmaceuticals.
   e. Phthalates can be found in baby powder, shampoo, nail polishes, deodorants, perfumes, and lotions.
   f. Polyethylene glycol is used in a number of toothpastes as a dispersant; it binds water and helps keep xanthan gum uniformly distributed throughout the toothpaste. It is also under investigation for use in body armor and tattoos to monitor diabetes.
3. **Administration:** Personal hygiene products are usually applied dermally. Dental products are administered in the mouth but are typically not supposed to be ingested.

4. **Contraindication:** People with allergies to any of these chemical or known bowel obstructions usually have issues when applying these chemicals for use.
5. **Toxicity:**
   a. Diethanolamine was found to induce body and organ weight changes, clinical and histopathological changes, indicative of mild blood, liver, kidney, and testicular systemic toxicity.
   b. Extremely hazardous in case of skin contact (irritant), eye contact, ingestion, and inhalation. Skin inflammation is characterized by itching, scaling, reddening, or blistering.
   c. A preliminary study suggested that sodium lauryl sulfate in toothpaste caused the recurrence of aphthous ulcers, commonly referred to in some countries as canker sores or white sores. It has been shown to irritate the skin of the face with prolonged and constant exposure (more than an hour) in young adults. Sodium lauryl sulfate may worsen skin problems in individuals with chronic skin hypersensitivity, with some people being affected more than others. In animal studies, SDS appears to cause skin and eye irritation. Sodium lauryl sulfate temporarily diminishes the perception of sweetness, an effect commonly observed after recent use of toothpaste containing this ingredient.
   d. Parabens have the potential to cause breast cancer, uterine cancer, and most recently, skin cancer. Most recently, parabens have been reported to potentiate oxidative stress, nitric oxide production, and lipid peroxidation following ultraviolet (UV) light exposure in cultured-skin keratinocytes. This is of particular concern since parabens are commonly used as preservatives in skin-care products.
   e. Polyethylene glycol can cause diarrhea, hives, gas cramping, bloating, and nausea if ingested.
   f. Phthalates are known as endocrine disrupters.
6. **Upon overdose:** Seek medical attention immediately. Eye contact: Check for and remove any contact lenses. Immediately flush eyes with running water for at least 15 min, keeping the eyelids open. Skin contact: Wash immediately with plenty of water. Inhalation: Rest in a ventilated area. Ingestion: Do not induce vomiting. Examine the lips and mouth to ascertain whether the tissues are damaged, a possible indication that the toxic material was ingested. Some symptoms of polyethylene glycol overdose include diarrhea, thirst, confusion, and seizure.

Hydrocarbons/Solvent/Fuels

Aldehydes

Formaldehyde

1. **Chemistry:** A colorless gas with a pungent, irritating odor even at very low concentrations (below 1 ppm); vapors are flammable and explosive, and are commonly used and stored in solution = formalin (30–50% formaldehyde and up to 15% methanol stabilizer).

2. **Sources:**
    a. Primary sources
        i. **Breathing contaminated air:** Industry, wood products, automobile exhaust, cigarette smoke, paints and varnishes, carpets, and permanent press fabrics. Rural <suburban; indoor> outdoor
        ii. **Workplace:** Primarily formaldehyde-based resins industry; other professions: dentists, doctors, embalmers, nurses, pathologists, teachers, and students who handle preserved specimens in laboratories, veterinarians, and workers in the clothing industry or in furniture factories
    b. Secondary sources
        i. **Water:** Occasionally detected in rain and fog water
        ii. **Food:** Low levels naturally occur in a variety of foods, such as fruits, from use as a fumigant, fertilizer, or preservative
3. **Uses:**
    a. Manufacture of plastics, resins, and urea—formaldehyde foam insulation
    b. **Agricultural industry:** Fumigant, preventative for mildew in wheat and rot in oats, a germicide and fungicide for plants, an insecticide, and used in the manufacture of slow-release fertilizers
    c. Formaldehyde or formaldehyde-containing resins used in the manufacture of chelating agents, a wide variety of organic products, glass mirrors, explosives, artificial silk, and dyes
    d. Has been used as a disinfectant, germicide, and in embalming fluid
    e. Has also been used in the sugar, rubber, food, petroleum, pharmaceutical, and textile industries
    f. **Widely used consumer products:** Antiseptics and cleaning agents, carpets and permanent press fabrics, cigarettes, cosmetics, fertilizers, insulation for electrical uses (wiring and appliances), manufactured wood products (furniture, plywood, and particleboard), medicines and vitamins, paints and varnishes, and preserved foods
4. **Pharmacokinetics:** Readily absorbed from the respiratory and GI tracts, but poorly absorbed following dermal application. Quickly metabolizes to formate by the enzyme formaldehyde dehydrogenase; this appears to take place at the initial site of contact. Neither formaldehyde nor formate is stored to any significant extent in any tissue of the body; very little if any intact formaldehyde can be found in the blood. Formate is excreted in the urine (primarily as formic acid), incorporated into other cellular molecules, or oxidized to carbon dioxide and exhaled.
5. **Toxicity:** The exact mechanism by which formaldehyde exerts its irritant, corrosive, and cytotoxic effects is not known, but it is known that it can interact with molecules on cell membranes and in body tissues and fluids (proteins and DNA) and disrupt cellular functions. High concentrations cause precipitation of proteins, which results in cell death.

a. Irritates eye, skin, and respiratory tract; inhalation of vapors can produce narrowing of the bronchi and an accumulation of fluid in the lungs.
b. Children may be more susceptible than adults to the respiratory effects of formaldehyde.
c. **Formaldehyde solution (formalin):** Causes corrosive injury to the GI tract, especially the pharynx, epiglottis, esophagus, and stomach.
d. Ingestion of as little as 30 mL (1 ounce) of a solution containing 37% formaldehyde has been reported to cause death in an adult.
e. Systemic effects are primarily due to its metabolic conversion into formate and may include metabolic acidosis, circulatory shock, respiratory insufficiency, and acute renal failure.
f. Potent sensitizer and a probable human carcinogen.

6. **Treatment:**
   a. There is no antidote.
   b. Treatment consists of supportive measures including decontamination (flushing of skin and eyes with water), administration of supplemental oxygen, intravenous (IV) sodium bicarbonate and/or isotonic fluid, and hemodialysis.
   c. **Ingestion of formalin:** Emesis should not be induced. Victims who are conscious and able to swallow should be given 4–8 ounces of water or milk. Gastric lavage with a small-bore nasogastric (NG) tube should be considered if it can be performed within 1 h after ingestion. The effectiveness of activated charcoal administration is unknown, but it is suggested following lavage (administer activated charcoal at 1 g/kg, usual adult dose 60–90 g, and child dose 25–50 g).

Acroelin

1. **Chemistry:** Colorless or yellow liquid with a pungent, suffocating odor; highly flammable and burns to produce toxic gases (peroxides and oxides of carbon). It is volatile, producing toxic concentrations at room temperature; the odor may not provide adequate warning of hazardous concentrations; dissolves in water very easily; and quickly changes to a vapor when heated.
2. **Sources and uses:** Small amounts can be formed and can enter the air when trees, tobacco, other plants, gasoline, and oil are burned; used as a pesticide to control algae, weeds, bacteria, and mollusks. It is also used to make other chemicals.
3. **Pharmacokinetics:** No information on absorption, metabolism, and excretion in humans; in animals, 80%–90% is absorbed through inhalation and metabolized to thiol ethers; 30% is exhaled as CO_2 and 50%–60% is excreted via the urine.
4. **Toxicity:** Respiratory > CNS > cardiovascular > GI > dermal > ocular.
   a. **Respiratory:** Irritation of the respiratory tract increases airway resistance and tidal volume, decreases respiratory frequency, pulmonary edema, and death. Inhalation may also cause an asthmatic reaction in sensitized individuals.

b. **CNS and cardiovascular:** CNS depression, hypertension, and tachycardia.
c. **GI:** Burns of the lips, mouth, throat, esophagus, and stomach, nausea, vomiting, and diarrhea.
d. **Dermal:** Irritates the skin irritant, skin burns, erythema, and edema; children are more vulnerable to toxicants affecting the skin, because of their relatively larger surface area: body weight ratio.
e. **Ocular:** Eye irritation and damage to the cornea.

5. **Treatment:** No antidote.
   a. **Inhalation:** Supplemental oxygen by mask to patients who have respiratory symptoms; treat bronchospasm with an aerosolized bronchodilator such as albuterol. May cause hypertension and tachycardia, in which case, the use of bronchodilators that are known cardiac-sensitizing agents may pose enhanced risk; administer corticosteroids if persistent wheezing or hypersensitivity pneumonitis.
   b. **Skin/eye:** Flush the exposed skin and hair with copious amounts of water. Wash with soap and rinse thoroughly with water. Flush the exposed or irritated eyes with tepid water for 15 min.
   c. **Ingestion:** Do not induce emesis; slurry of activated charcoal at a dose of 1 g/kg (infant, child, and adult dose if the person is alert); 4–8 ounces of milk or water (not to exceed 15 mL/kg in a child if alert). Gastric lavage with a small NG tube if (1) a large dose has been ingested; (2) condition is evaluated within 30 min; (3) has oral lesions or persistent esophageal discomfort; and (4) the lavage can be administered within 1 h of ingestion; care must be taken when placing the gastric tube because blind gastric-tube placement may further injure the chemically damaged esophagus or stomach.

Alcohols and Glycols (See Table 7.6 and Figures 7.4 and 7.5)

Diethylene Glycol

1. **Pharmacokinetics:** An industrial alcohol solvent and antifreeze agent with a low affinity for ADH with negligible metabolism
2. **Uses:** Industrial solvent, illicitly substituted for propylene glycol to solubilize APAP (Tylenol) manufactured in developing countries
3. **Toxicities:** Initial GI and renal > hepatic:
   a. **GI:** Initial nausea and vomiting with severe abdominal cramps and pain
   b. **Renal:** Initial polyuria followed within 24 h by oliguria, then anuria, and acute renal failure
   c. **Hepatic:** Hepatotoxicity, hepatomegaly, and jaundice
   d. Epidemic poisoning in children manifested by liver failure, respiratory failure, neurotoxicity including seizures, optic neuritis, and paresthesias

4. **Treatment:** Supportive only with hemodialysis; ethanol and 4-methylpyrazole (4-MP) are ineffective as antidotes

Ethylene Glycol

1. **Chemistry:** EG is a synthetic liquid that absorbs water; is odorless, but has a sweet taste. It is a toxic alcohol similar to methanol in toxicity and lethality, with a characteristic delayed onset of toxicity.
2. **Uses:** Antifreeze (95%) and deicing solutions, refrigerating fluids, fire extinguishers, solar energy fluids, hydraulic brake fluids, and inks used in stamp pads, ballpoint pens, and print shops.
3. **Pharmacokinetics:** Rapidly absorbed orally, peaks within 1–4 h; rapidly metabolized by ADH to glycoaldehyde and by the glycoaldehyde dehydrogenase to its toxic metabolites, glycolic, glyoxalic, and oxalic acid. Pyridoxine and thiamine can serve as cofactors to promote nontoxic alternative routes of metabolism.
4. **Toxicity:** (1) CNS > (2) metabolic > (3) renal.
   a. **Initial GI toxicity:** Nausea and vomiting.
   b. **Toxic phases 1–3:**
      i. **Phase 1—CNS:** Ataxia, nauseas, vomiting, intoxication, inebriation, nystagmus, and progression to lethargy and coma within 4–8 h.
      ii. **Phase 2—Cardiovascular and metabolic:** Profound anion gap metabolic acidosis progressing to hypertension, tachycardia, tachypnea, and cardiovascular collapse.
      iii. **Phase 3—Renal:** Urinary excretion of toxic metabolites, especially oxalate, which combines with calcium to form oxalate crystals (calcium oxalate and hippuric acid); with calcium oxalate crystalluria causing nephrolithiasis, proteinuria, and hematuria, and progresses to acute tubular necrosis.
5. **Diagnosis:** Calcium oxalate crystalluria, urine fluorescein staining under UV Wood's lamp lighting, and serum EG levels by gas chromatography.
6. **Overdose management:**
   a. Initial management of activated charcoal is ineffective due to rapid absorption and delayed symptom onset of 4–8 h; ipecac contraindicated due to existing vomiting; sodium bicarbonate to correct acidosis and increase excretion of weak acids.
   b. **Antidote:** Ethanol (and/or 4-MP, and ADH inhibitor) as a preferred ADH substrate, 0.8 g/kg IV or 8 mL/kg orally, to maintain serum ethanol level of 100–150 mg/dL (EG:EtOH ratio = 1:4).
   c. **Enhanced elimination:** (1) Urinary alkalinization to promote urinary excretion of weak acid metabolites; (2) thiamin (100 mg IV) and pyridoxine (50 mg IV) every 6 h, to promote alternative nontoxic routes of metabolism; and (3) hemodialysis for EG levels > 25 mg/dL.
   d. **Correct hypocalcemia:** Treat hypocalcemia from massive calcium loss in a calcium oxalate crystalluria.

7. **EG ingestion:** Urinary calcium oxalate crystals (EG ingestion requires ethanol and 5,4-MP [fomipazole]) therapy, often with hemodialysis for serum EG levels > 25 mg/dL to prevent tubular necrosis.

Glycol Ethers

1. **Chemistry:** Most of them are clear, colorless liquids. Some have mild, pleasant odors or no smell at all; others (mainly the acetates) have strong odors. Some evaporate quickly and can easily reach hazardous levels in the air; others evaporate very slowly and are therefore less hazardous by inhalation. Structurally, the glycol ethers are categorized as EG ether or monopropylenes, dipropylene, or tripropylene glycol ethers.
2. **Uses:** Industrial solvents; may be used alone, or as an ingredient in products such as coatings (paints, varnishes, dyes, stains, inks, and semiconductor chip coatings), cleaners (for degreasing, dry cleaning, film cleaning, and circuit board manufacture), jet fuel deicing additives, brake fluids, and perfumes and cosmetics.
3. **Pharmacokinetics:** Absorbed by all routes, with low acute oral toxicity; some glycol ethers have high percutaneous absorption and it appears that absorption is enhanced in the presence of water. Eliminated primarily through the metabolisms of ADH and aldehyde dehydrogenase (ALDH).
4. **Toxicity:** Resembles toxic alcohol poisoning; CNS depression > high anion gap acidosis; toxicity is associated with its oxidation to the corresponding aldehyde and alkoxyacetic acid by cytosolic ADH and ALDH.
   a. **Acute:** Low exposure; inebriation, conjunctivitis, upper respiratory tract irritation, headache, nausea, and temporary corneal clouding. High doses; narcosis, pulmonary edema, and severe liver and kidney damage.
   b. **Chronic:** Fatigue, lethargy, nausea, anorexia, tremor, and anemia. Animal studies have reported anemia, reduced body weight gain, and irritation of the eyes and nose from inhalation exposure.
5. **Treatment:** Decontamination: Removal from sources of exposure; dispose off clothes and shoes; wash exposed skin thoroughly; and irrigate eyes until burning sensation

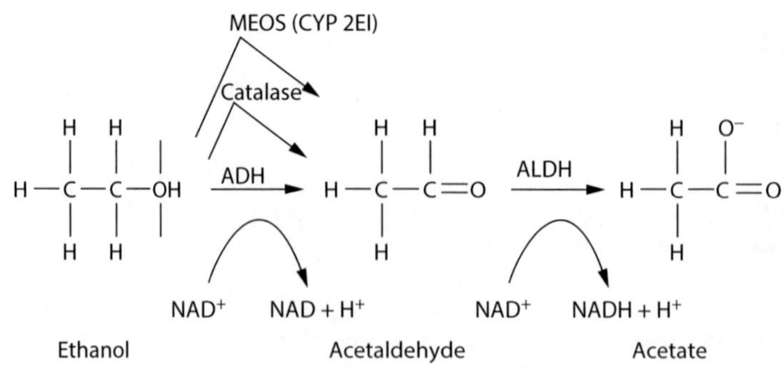

FIGURE 7.4 EG metabolism. The hepatic biotransformation reactions, which are responsible for the metabolism of EG, a common component of antifreeze.

ceases; Supportive measures: Assessment and stabilization of breathing and circulation; administration of oxygen if needed. Emesis should not be induced for risk of chemical pneumonitis; possible gastric lavage.

Isopropanol

1. **Chemistry:** 70% isopropyl alcohol or rubbing alcohol; clear, colorless, and volatile liquid with an acetone smell. Exception: It is the only alcoholic absorbed by activated charcoal.
2. **Uses:** Used in toiletries, disinfectants, window cleaners, and solvents.
3. **Pharmacokinetics:** Rapid all-route absorption, especially dermal and inhalation; low volume of distribution = 0.6 L/kg; and 50% is rapidly metabolized by ADH to acetone, the remaining 50% is metabolized and excreted by the kidneys > exhalation via lungs.
4. **Toxicity:** CNS > GI > pulmonary > metabolic:
   a. **CNS:** Three times more CNS depression than EtOH, lethargy, weakness, headache, ataxia, dysarthria, apnea, respiratory depression, and hypotension
      i. **Pulmonary and GI:** Acetone breath, hemorrhagic, gastritis, and hemorrhagic tracheobronchitis
      ii. **Metabolic:** Exception: Only toxic alcohol not causing metabolic acidosis or hypoglycemia; euglycemia is maintained, ketonemia, and ketonuria occur from acetone poisoning
      iii. **Diagnosing overdose:** Determine serum acetone levels; anticipate falsely elevated creatinine; arterial blood gases: pH will be normal and no metabolic acidosis; anticipate ketonemia and ketonuria from acetone metabolite; and breath acetone odor
5. **Management of overdose:**
   a. Immediate skin decontamination.
   b. Orogastric lavage and then AC. Exception: Only toxic alcohol to be well absorbed by activated charcoal.
   c. **Enhanced elimination:** Hemodialysis is very effective in a serious overdose, especially in children. Ethanol is not indicated because there is no need to block isopropanol's metabolism to acetone, which is relatively nontoxic and exhaled by the lungs and excreted in the urine.

Methanol

1. **Chemistry:** Methyl alcohol or wood alcohol: colorless liquid, completely miscible with water and organic solvents, and is very hygroscopic
2. **Uses:** Windshield-washing fluid, deicing solutions; carburetor cleaners, model airplane glues, canned heat (Sterno®), fuels, and paint removers/thinners
3. **Pharmacokinetics:** Rapid—all-route absorption, peaks 1/2–1 h; 85% is rapidly metabolized by hepatic ADH to form formaldehyde and formic acid metabolites that are responsible for retinal toxicity

Table 7.6 Pathophysiology and Management of Toxic Alcohol Poisonings

Alcohol	Uses	Toxic Dose	Action Level	Metabolism	Manifestations	Manegement
Isopropanol (rubbing alcohol)	Rubbing alcohol, nail polish remover	2–4 mL/kg	NA	Metabolized by ADH to acetone—exhale or urine secreted	Ketosis without acidosis, inebriation, ataxia, dysarthria, confusion, stupor, coma, acetone breath, hemorrhagic gastritis	Supportive, no ethanol
EG (antifreeze)	Antifreeze, coolants, brake fluids	1–1.5 mL/kg	>20–20 mg/dL	Metabolized by ADH to glycolic and oxalic acids. Oxalate combines with calcium to cause calcium oxalate crystalluria	Increased anion and decreased osmolal gaps, hypocalcemia with and increased QT and tetany; CNS (1–12 h): ataxia, nystagmus seizures, nausea–vomiting; cardiovascular/metabolic (12–27 h): hypertension, tachycardia, increased QT, tachypnea, cardiovascular collapse Renal (24–72 h/cardiovascular) tenderness, oliguria, urine fluorescein, acute renal failures	Alkalininze urine, thiamine, and pyriodoxine, to promote nontoxic metabolism, ethanol IV or 4-methylpyrazole, orally, hemodialysis
Methanol (wood alcohol)	Windshield washer, radiator fluid, Sterno fuel	<1 mL/kg	>50 mg/dL	Metabolized by ADH to formaldehyde and formic acid	Increased anion and osmolal gaps, intoxication. Nausea—vomiting, hemorrhagic gastritis, photophobia, blurred—reduced vision, "snowfield" blindness, retinal edema, hyperemic optic disks	Alkalinize urine, folic acid, to promote nontoxic metabolism, ethanol IV, hemodialysis

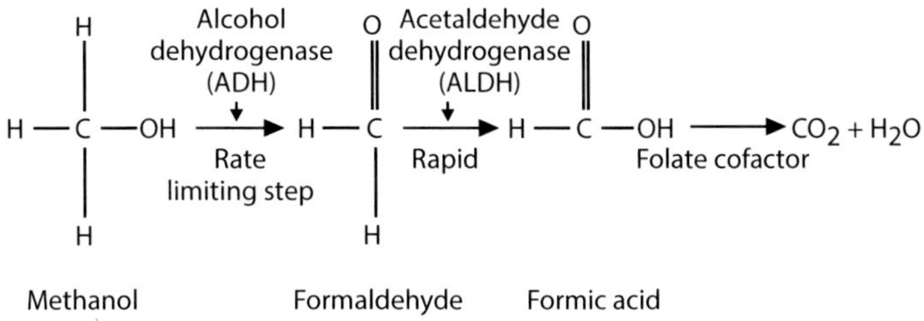

FIGURE 7.5 Methanol metabolism. The hepatic biotransformation reactions, which are responsible for the metabolism of methanol or wood alcohol.

4. **Toxicity:** Initial GI > eyes/CNS > metabolic:
   a. **Initial GI toxicity:** Nausea, vomiting, and cramping
   b. **Eye:** Dimmed and blurred vision, scotomata, dilated and sluggishly reactive pupils, hyperemic optic disk, retinal edema, and blindness
   c. **CNS:** Inebriation, headache, vertigo, meningismus, cerebral edema, seizure, and coma
   d. **Metabolic:** 24-h delayed onset and high anion gap metabolic acidosis, followed by oculotoxicity
5. **Overdose diagnosis:** Lactic acidosis, unique eye findings, and increased serum methanol levels by gas chromatography
6. **Overdose management:**
   a. **Initial management:** Activated charcoal ineffective due to rapid absorption and delayed symptom onset; ipecac contraindicated due to vomiting; and $NaCOH_3$ to correct acidosis
   b. **Antidotes:** Ethanol (and/or fomipazole [4-MP]) as a preferred ADH substrate; 0.8 g/kg IV or 8 mL/kg orally, to maintain serum EtOH level that is 100–150 mg/dL (MeOH:EtOH = 1:4)
   c. **Enhanced elimination:** (1) Urinary alkalization to promote renal excretion of undissociated formic acid; (2) folic acid, 150 mf IV every 4 h, to serve as a cofactor promoting the metabolism of formic acid to $CO_2 + H_2O$; and (3) hemodialysis for methanol levels > 25 mg/dL

Aliphatic Hydrocarbon

Hexane (n-Hexane)

1. **Chemistry:** Colorless liquid with a slightly disagreeable odor; highly flammable, and its vapors can be explosive.
2. **Sources and uses:** Made from crude oil; used in laboratories; used to extract vegetable oils from crops such as soybeans; cleaning agents in the printing, textile, furniture, and shoe-making industries; and glues used in the roofing and shoe and leather industries; gasoline, quick-drying glues are used in various hobbies, and rubber cement.

3. **Pharmacokinetics:** Absorbed by all routes, primarily by inhalation; absorption depends on the length and concentration of exposure; once absorbed, it is distributed to all the organs; body fat is metabolized in the liver by CYP; primary metabolites 2-hexanol, 2,5-hexanedione, and γ-valeroacetone; are mostly excreted via the urine within a day or two; and 10–20% is exhaled.
4. **Toxicity:** Is due to metabolites, primarily 2,5-hexanedione; causes peripheral neuropathy; for example, shoe workers in Japan and Italy in the 1960s and 1970s; symptoms reported were numbness of the feet and hands, followed by muscle weakness in the feet and lower legs; and paralysis of the arms and legs also developed.
5. **Diagnosis:** Urine analysis for levels of 2,5-hexanedione; must be done within 2–3 days after suspected exposure.
6. **Treatment:** Remove from the sources of exposures.
7. **Inhalation:** Removal from sources of exposure; assessment and stabilization of breathing and circulation; and administration of oxygen.
8. **Ingestion:** Emesis should not be induced for risk of chemical pneumonitis; gastric lavage maybe necessary.
9. **Skin/eyes:** Dispose of clothes and shoes; wash exposed skin thoroughly; and irrigate eyes until burning sensation ceases.

Mixtures (Gasoline and Kerosene)

Gasoline

1. **Chemistry:** Colorless, pale brown, or pink liquid, and is very flammable with a distinct odor; odor provides adequate warning of hazardous concentrations; vapors are heavier than air and may collect in low-lying areas; manufactured mixture that does not naturally exist in the environment; and contains more than 150 chemicals, including small amounts of benzene, toluene, automotive gasoline, and sometimes lead.
2. **Sources/uses:** Produced by the distillation, cracking, and reforming of crude oil; various additives influence the use and physical properties of the mixture; its primary use is as a fuel for reciprocating, spark ignition, and internal combustion engines in automobiles, trucks, and light aircraft.
3. **Pharmacokinetics:** Readily absorbed by the lungs, less readily absorbed by the GI tract, and poorly absorbed by intact skin. Skin burns may result from prolonged contact with gasoline. No data on absorption rate or metabolism; rate of absorption and excretion may vary due to various compounds found in gasoline.
4. **Toxicity:** CNS > cardiovascular > renal > GI > dermal/ocular:
   a. **CNS:** CNS excitation followed by CNS depression; confusion, giddiness, nausea, headache, blurred vision, dizziness, weakness, reactive airway dysfunction syndrome (RADS); massive exposures, rapid CNS depression, respiratory depression, seizures, loss of consciousness, coma, and death.

b. **Respiratory:** Irritation of the respiratory tract; pulmonary congestion, edema, acute exudative tracheobronchitis, and intrapulmonary hemorrhage; pulmonary aspiration of ingested gasoline may cause pneumonitis.
c. **Cardiovascular:** Gasoline vapors sensitize the myocardium to circulating epinephrine that may cause potentially fatal ventricular fibrillation.
d. **Renal:** Inhalation of massive amounts of gasoline may result in fatty degeneration of the proximal convoluted tubules, glomeruli, and renal failure; ingestion can cause oliguria, tubular necrosis, interstitial edema, and hematuria, reduced creatinine clearance and elevated serum creatinine, elevated urinary protein, glucose, and hemoglobin, and elevated BUN.
e. **GI:** Esophagitis, gastritis, degeneration of the epithelium, and mucositis of the oral cavity.
f. **Dermal:** Vapors can cause inflammation of the skin; prolonged contact with liquid gasoline causes significant irritation (e.g., irritant contacts dermatitis), degreasing, and burns; and redness and blisters.
g. **Ocular:** Irritation, burning pain, and transient corneal injury; chronic exposure can cause damage to the cornea, retina, and ciliary body.
h. **Carcinogenicity:** Classified group 2B, possibly carcinogenic to humans; classification is based on inadequate evidence of carcinogenicity in humans and limited evidence for carcinogenicity in experimental animals.
i. **Chronic excessive exposure:** Intentional gasoline abuse (sniffing) can cause irritability, tremor, nausea, insomnia, loss of memory, drowsiness, mental dullness, confusion, seizures, muscle spasms, altered vision, hallucinations, impaired gait, inflammation of the optic nerve, dizziness, and involuntary eye movement; and can cause kidney disease (i.e., renal tubular dysfunction); nerve disorders, causing motor weakness and muscular degeneration, can also occur in gasoline abusers. Abuse of leaded gasoline has been reported to cause brain disease (e.g., lead encephalopathy) (lead is no longer added to gasoline in the United States).

5. **Overdose diagnosis:** Lead blood and urine levels for leaded gasoline; increased thioether in urine, limited because it is not specific to gasoline exposure; and biomarkers of components such as benzene.
6. **Overdose treatment:** No antidote for gasoline poisoning; the treatment consists of the support of cardiovascular and respiratory functions.
   a. **Skin:** Flush exposed skin and hair with plain water for 2 min and then wash with soap.
   b. **Eyes:** Irrigate exposed or irritated eyes with plain water or saline for 15 min.
   c. **Ingestion:** Emesis should not be induced; gastric lavage and activated charcoal should not be used. Catharsis with magnesium or sodium sulfate is acceptable. If spontaneous vomiting occurs, it is important to watch for signs of pulmonary aspiration.

Fuel Oils/Kerosene

Fuel Oils				
Fuel oil no. 1 (the most widely used fuel oil)	Fuel oil no. 1-D	Fuel oil no. 2	Fuel oil no. 2-D	Fuel oil no. 4
Kerosene	Diesel fuel	Home-heating oil	Diesel fuel oil no. 2	Diesel fuel oil no. 4
Straight-run kerosene	Diesel fuel oil no. 1	Gas oil	Diesel fuel no. 2	Heavy residual fuel oil
Kerosene		No. 2 burner oil	Diesel oil no. 2	Marine diesel fuel
Range oil			No. 2 diesel	Residual fuel oil no. 4
Deobase (deodorized kerosene)				
Coal oil				
JP-5 (jet fuel)				

1. **Chemistry:** Fuel oils are a variety of yellowish-to-light-brown liquid mixtures that come from crude petroleum; composed of aliphatic (open-chain and cyclic compounds) and aromatic petroleum hydrocarbons composed of benzene and compounds similar to benzene; may contain small amounts of nitrogen, sulfur, and other elements such as additives; and differ from one another by their hydrocarbon compositions, boiling-point ranges, chemical additives, and uses. Common fuel oils: kerosene, diesel fuel, jet fuel, range oil, and home-heating oil.
2. **Sources and uses:** Produced by different petroleum-refining processes, depending on their intended uses; used as fuel for engines, lamps, heaters, furnaces, and stoves, or as solvents.
3. **Pharmacokinetics:** All routes of absorption; no relevant information is available on absorption metabolism or excretion of fuel oils. Kerosene has been found in small amounts in the brain, lung, liver, spleen, and kidney of exposed animals.
4. **Toxicity:** Respiratory > CNS > GI > cardiovascular > renal > dermal:
   a. **Initial after ingestion:** Vomiting, diarrhea, swelling of the stomach, stomach cramps, coughing, drowsiness, restlessness, irritability, and unconsciousness.
   b. **Reparatory:** Coughing, pneumonia, painful breathing, gagging, and choking leading to aspiration with bronchospasm; tachypnea; hypoxia; emphysema; and pneumonitis.
   c. **CNS:** Headache, light headedness, anorexia, poor coordination, and difficulty in concentrating; more severe: seizures, coma, and may even cause death (lipoid pneumonia).
   d. **GI:** Nausea, vomiting, hematemesis, and GI mucosal ulceration.

e. **Cardiovascular/renal:** Hypertension, tachycardia, cardiac arrhythmia, and renal failure.
f. **Dermal:** Itchy skin, red, and sore; blisters may occur and the skin may peel.

5. **Diagnosis:** No medical test; may use laboratory analysis for components such as benzene, toluene, and fuel oils; however, concentrations of these compounds in distilled fuels are so low that if they were detected in your blood, it might not indicate specific or exclusive exposure to fuel oils.
6. **Treatment:** Careful GI decontamination; no emesis or activated charcoal; and possible gastric lavage with small NG for large volumes.

Aromatic Hydrocarbons

Benzene

1. **Chemistry:** Made from petroleum; colorless liquid with sweet odor; highly flammable; evaporates quickly in air; heavier than air and dissolves slightly in water; formed from both natural processes and human activity.
2. **Uses and sources:** Used in industries that make rubber, lubricants, dyes, detergents, drugs, and pesticides; used in other chemicals such as styrene, cyclohexane; natural sources such as volcanoes and forest fires; and is a major component of crude oil, gasoline, and cigarette smoke.
3. **Pharmacokinetics:** Rapidly and extensively absorbed by inhalation and ingestion; absorption through the skin is rapid but not extensive, as most of it evaporates quickly and is distributed throughout the body; 50% of inhaled benzene is absorbed after a 4-h exposure to approximately 50 ppm benzene in air; an *in vivo* study on human volunteers indicated that approximately 0.05% of a benzene dose applied to the skin was absorbed; oral absorption has not been studied in the human body; and primarily concentrates in the liver, bone marrow, tissues with high perfusion rate (kidney), and tissues with high lipid content (brain). Primarily metabolized in the liver to phenol and other metabolites (e.g., hydroquinone, catechol, 1,2,4-trihydroxybenzene, and *S*-phenyl mercapturic acid), most of which are excreted via the urine and a smaller amount is excreted via the feces. Some of the liver metabolites travel to the bone marrow where they are further metabolized. Unmetabolized benzene is excreted via the lungs.
4. **Toxicity:** CNS > hematological/carcinogen > respiratory > cardiovascular > GI > dermal > ocular:
   a. **CNS:** Headache, light headedness, dizziness, nausea, impaired gait and blurred vision, tremors, respiratory depression and confusion, loss of consciousness, coma, and death.
   b. **Hematological:** Thrombocytopenia, aplastic anemia, pancytopenia, and acute myelogenous leukemia.
   c. **Respiratory and cardiovascular:** Respiratory tract irritation, fluid in the lungs, and respiratory arrest. Pulmonary aspiration of toxic vomitus may cause hemorrhagic inflammation of the lungs. Arrhythmias such as ventricular fibrillation.

d. **GI:** Nausea, vomiting, diarrhea, and death.
e. **Dermal:** Skin irritation, erythema, a burning sensation, and in more severe cases, edema and even blistering. Children are more vulnerable than adults to toxicants absorbed through the skin because of their surface area (body:weight ratio).
f. **Ocular:** Eye irritation and visual blurring, burning pain, and sloughing of the eye surface.

5. **Overdose diagnosis:**
   a. **Lab evaluation:** Complete blood count with differential, hematocrit, hemoglobin, erythrocyte count, erythrocyte indices (e.g., MCV, MCH, and MCHC), and platelet count. Plasma folate and vitamin B12 levels may be used to rule out megaloblastic anemia if the MCV is elevated. These laboratory tests will detect hematologic abnormalities that have been associated with relatively high levels of exposure to benzene.
   b. **Direct biological indicators:**
      i. **Phenol in the breath or blood:** Can be useful in certain occupation settings; testing must be conducted right after suspected exposure; and not an accurate measurement due to benzenes short biological half-life. Blood and breath are generally not clinically useful in any occupational settings.
      ii. **Urinary phenol concentrations:** Exposure to concentrations above 10 ppm, at low-level exposure, urinary phenol levels are unreliable.
      iii. **Other benzene metabolites:** *t,t*-muconic acid, and *S*-phenyl mercapturic acid. Analysis of urinary muconic acid appears to be a better indicator than phenol for chronic, low-level benzene exposure.
6. **Overdose management:**
   a. No antidote.
   b. **Inhalation:** Immediate removal from sources; administration of oxygen; monitoring and treatment of cardiopulmonary status.
   c. **Ingestion:** Emesis should not be induced; slurry of activated charcoal if the victim is alert and is able to swallow (at 1 mg/kg, usual adult dose 60–90 g, child dose 25–50 g). Gastric lavage.
   d. If the patient exhibits seizures, administer a benzodiazepine; diazepam (adult: 5–10 mg IV, repeat every 10–15 min as needed; child: 0.2–0.5 mg/kg IV, repeat every 5 min as needed); or lorazepam (adult: 4–8 mg IV; child: 0.05–0.1 mg/kg IV). Phenobarbital and/or phenytoin or fosphenytoin if seizures are uncontrollable or recur after diazepam 30 mg (adults) or 10 mg (children >5 years).
   e. **Skin/eyes:** Dispose of clothes and shoes; wash exposed skin thoroughly; irrigate eyes for 3–5 min or until burning sensation ceases.

Polycyclic Aromatic Hydrocarbons

1. **Chemistry:** A class of organic compounds produced by incomplete combustion or high-pressure processes; often consist of three or more fused benzene rings containing

only carbon and hydrogen; are solids with low volatility at room temperature; relatively insoluble in water; and most of them can be photooxidized and degraded to simpler substances. Some PAHs are manufactured; these pure PAHs usually exist as colorless, white, or pale yellow-green solids.

2. **Sources and uses:** A group of over 100 different chemicals formed during the incomplete burning of coal, oil and gas, garbage, or other organic substances such as tobacco or charbroiled meat; usually found as a mixture containing two or more of these compounds, such as soot. Manufactured PAHs are found in coal tar, crude oil, creosote, and roofing tar, but a few are used in medicines or to make dyes, plastics, and pesticides.
3. **Pharmacokinetics:** Absorbed by all routes; the percentage of absorption varies by structure and chemical properties; once absorbed, they enter the lymph, circulate in the blood, and are primarily metabolized in the liver and kidney; also metabolizes in the adrenal glands, testes, thyroid, lungs, skin, sebaceous glands, and small intestines; and initially transformed into epoxides, which are converted into dihydrodiol derivatives and phenols. Glucuronide and sulfate conjugates of these metabolites are excreted in the bile and urine. Glutathione conjugates are further metabolized to mercapturic acids in the kidney and are excreted in the urine; hydroxylated metabolites are excreted in human urine both as free hydroxylated metabolites and as hydroxylated metabolites conjugated to glucuronic acid and sulfate.
4. **Toxicity:** Formation of reactive metabolites and the biologically effective dose are key to PAH toxicity.
   Carcinogen > reparatory > GI > renal > dermal
   a. **Carcinogenicity:** Some parent PAHs are weak carcinogens that require metabolism to become more potent carcinogens. Diol epoxides—intermediate metabolites—are mutagenic and affect normal cell replication when they react with DNA to form adducts; well established in laboratory animals; associated with increased incidences of lung, skin, and bladder cancers with occupational exposure.
   b. **Respiratory:** Chronic bronchitis, chronic cough irritation, and bronchogenic cancer.
   c. **GI:** Excessive PAH intake in blackened and barbecued meats and fish associated with increased incidence of colon cancer.
   d. **Dermal:** Dermatitis, cutaneous photosensitization, and pilosebaceous reactions.
5. **Diagnosis:** Exposure history: Occupational history; occupation of the spouse and other household members; use of medications, including coal tar-containing dermatologic preparations; diet, especially charbroiled meats, alcohol consumption; smoking habits; and hobbies and recreational activities.
6. **Physical examination:** Review of all systems, with the knowledge that cancer is the most significant endpoint of chronic PAH toxicity; inspection of buccal mucosa and oropharynx may demonstrate leukoplakia or non-healing ulcerations that should be

biopsied to rule out oropharyngeal carcinomas. Arterial blood gases, a chest radiograph, and other monitoring might be indicated.

7. **Direct biological measures:** Blood and tissue measure of the parent PHA; not clinically useful because of limited knowledge of the significance of background levels in humans.
8. **Indirect biological measures:** Tests for PHA metabolites in tissues, blood, and urine; pyrene and its urinary metabolite, 1-hydroxypyrene are commonly used. Note: Although these tests can show that you have been exposed to PAHs, these tests cannot be used to predict whether any health effects will occur or to determine the extent or source of your exposure to the PAHs. It is not known how effective or informative the tests are after exposure is discontinued.
9. **Treatment:**
   a. **Inhalation:** Supportive measures: Periodic pulmonary function tests and chest x-ray.
   b. **Skin/eyes:** Decontamination: Remove contaminated clothing as soon as possible; wash the affected area thoroughly with soap and water; irrigate eyes; and a complete eye examination.

Toluene

1. **Chemistry:** Clear colorless liquid with a sweet, pungent, benzene-like odor that provides an adequate warning of hazardous concentrations; volatile, readily producing flammable and toxic concentrations at room temperature; vapor is heavier than air; and may accumulate in low-lying areas.
2. **Uses and sources:** Occurs naturally in crude oil and in the toluene tree; also produced in the process of making gasoline and other fuels from crude oil and making coke from coal; used in making paints, paint thinners, fingernail polish, lacquers, adhesives, and rubber; and in some printing and leather-tanning processes.
3. **Pharmacokinetics:** Absorbed by all routes, with inhalation being the primary route; peaks within 15–30 min after inhalation; rate of oral absorption is slower; and levels peak 1–2 h after ingestion. Percutaneous absorption is slow through intact skin and rarely produces toxicity; distributed to highly perfused and fatty tissues (brain, liver, and kidney), and primarily accumulates in adipose and other tissues with high fat content; 80% is oxidized in the liver to benzoic acid, which is then conjugated with glycine to form hippuric acid or with glucuronic acid to form benzoyl glucuronate; a small amount undergoes aromatic ring oxidation to form *ortho*- and *para*-cresols; most of it is excreted via the urine within 12 h after exposure; a small amount (up to 20%) is eliminated as free toluene in expired air; and <2% of the total toluene metabolites is excreted in the bile.
4. **Toxicity:** CNS > respiratory > renal > hematopoietic > metabolic:
   a. **CNS:** Headache, light headedness, dizziness, confusion, nausea, impaired judgment, impaired gait, and blurred vision; loss of consciousness, peripheral neuropathy, neuropsychiatric, and neurobehavioral disorders, coma, and death.

b. **Respiratory:** Tract irritant, bronchospasm, chemical pneumonitis, respiratory depression, and death. Can lead to RADS, a chemically or irritant-induced type of asthma.
c. **Cardiovascular and hepatic:** Ventricle arrhythmia; liver damage has been reported in solvent abusers.
d. **Metabolic and renal:** Anion gap metabolic, hypokalemia, hypocalcemia, proteinuria, hematuria, distal renal acidosis, and pyuria. **GI:** Irritates the stomach, causing nausea, vomiting, and diarrhea.
e. **Skin/eyes:** Irritation, burning pain, blistering, blepharospasm, conjunctivitis, and keratinitis.

5. **Overdose diagnosis:**
   a. **Laboratory evaluation:** Baseline studies should include the following: electrolytes with blood urea nitrogen and creatinine; complete blood count and smear; electrocardiogram (ECG) with rhythm monitoring; liver enzymes; urinalysis; creatine kinase; neuropsychologic assessment; and chest radiograph, if symptomatic. Baseline tests should be repeated in 3–6 months to detect delayed hepatic or renal abnormalities or both. A neuropsychological follow-up evaluation should also be carried out at this time. Patients with substantial chronic exposures should have annual reassessments.
   b. **Direct biological indicators:** Biologic samples for analysis must be obtained soon after exposure. A venous blood sample taken within 1 day after exposure can be used to confirm toluene exposure (normal for unexposed populations are 0.1 milligrams/deciliter [mg/dL]); however, the toluene level obtained will not correlate well to the degree of exposure or to symptoms. Analysis of exhaled air for toluene is only experimental.
   c. **Indirect biological indicators:** Hippuric acid urine concentration; Caution: Also produced from metabolism of other chemicals, including common food additives and is present in urine of the unexposed person. Hippuric acid levels of >2.5 grams per gram (g/g) creatinine suggest toluene exposure.
6. **Overdose management:**
   a. No antidote exists for toluene toxicity; treatment for toluene overdose consists of supportive care.
   b. **Inhalation:** Immediate removal from sources, support of cardiopulmonary function, and prevention of further absorption; may require low-flow oxygen (~40%) and hydration; severe cases might require assisted ventilation.
   c. **Ingestion:** Induction of emesis is contraindicated because of the risk of CNS depression and subsequent pulmonary aspiration from vomiting. Standard regimes for administering a cathartic and activated charcoal should be followed; if a large amount is ingested (>5 milliliters [mL] or >1 teaspoon) and is examined within 30 min of ingestion, the benefits of gastric lavage should be weighed against the risk of pulmonary aspiration. Ingestion of a small amount (<5 mL or <1 teaspoon)

can be treated by administering activated charcoal orally without emptying the gut. Activated charcoal should be used cautiously because it may be able to cause vomiting.

i. Metabolic acidosis is usually accompanied by severe hypokalemia; therefore, administration of bicarbonate should be avoided because bicarbonate can worsen hypokalemia by causing intracellular shifting of potassium.
ii. Hypocalcemia can occur after electrolyte replenishment; it should be corrected with IV calcium. Use appropriate supportive treatment to correct acute renal failure if it occurs.

d. **Skin/eyes:** Decontaminate or safely dispose off contaminated shoes and clothes; exposed skin should be washed thoroughly with soap and water; and eyes should be irrigated for at least 15 min.

Veterinary Products

1. Use of veterinary products
    a. Veterinary drugs, including antibiotics, antiparasitic medications, and vaccines, play an important role in the control and prevention of disease in all livestock.
    b. However, there is risk when working with animals and animal medicines.
    c. The U.S. Department of Agriculture (USDA), FDA, and the Environmental Protection Agency (EPA) have strict rules regulating the prescription, distribution, and use of animal medications and chemicals.
    d. Regulations on how a drug is stored, administered, and disposed of, ensure product safety to the producer, animal, consumer, and environment.
2. Drugs used for suicide
    a. Antibiotics
        i. Tilmicosin
            A. **Drug description:**
                I. Semisynthetic, bacteriostatic, macrolide antibiotic
                II. Calcium channel blocker
            B. **Usages include:**
                I. Suicide attempts
                II. Approved for treating specific infectious diseases (e.g., pneumonia) caused by *Pasturella* and *Actinobacillus* species in cattle and sheep
            C. **Administration:**
                I. Concentrated injectable drug at a dose of 300 mg/mL in a solvent of 25% propylene glycol
                II. Subcutaneous routes, but can be fatal to cattle and sheep if injected intravenously
            D. **Toxicity:**
                I. Doses in excess of 5 mL result in fatalities

II. Chest pain, shortness of breath, pulmonary edema, ECG abnormalities, myocardial depression, respiratory distress requiring intubation, negative inotropic effects, hypotension, and tachycardia progressing to dysrhythmias

III. Additional clinical signs and symptoms can include headache, nausea, dizziness, tachycardia, chest pain, anxiety, and severe pain at the injection site

E. **Upon overdose:**

I. No specific antidote for tilmicosin toxicity

II. Cardiovascular system is the target of toxicity and should be closely monitored

III. Supportive care with calcium chloride or possibly calcium gluconate infusions

IV. Negative inotropic effects of tilmicosin may be managed with IV dobutamine or dopamine

V. Hypotension should be managed with isotonic fluids

VI. β-Adrenergic antagonists, such as propranolol, should be avoided, as they exacerbated the negative inotropy of tilmicosin in dogs

VII. Routine use of epinephrine or norepinephrine is also discouraged due to worsened outcomes in animal studies

b. Euthanasia drugs

i. Vetanarcol

A. **Drug description:**

I. Available in a 100 mL bottle with each milliliter containing 162 mg of pentobarbital sodium salt, 20 mg of benzyl alcohol as a preservative, and 500 mg of propylene glycol as a vehicle

B. **Usages include:**

I. Suicide attempts

II. Narcosis

III. Euthanasia

IV. Tranquilizer

V. Anesthetic

C. **Administration:**

I. IV or intraperitoneal administration

II. 0.5–1.0 mL/kg injections

D. **Toxicity:**

I. Rapid CNS depression and cardiovascular collapse

II. Shallow breathing

III. Incoordination

IV. Difficulty in thinking

V. Slowed heart rate
VI. Coma
VII. Death
E. **Upon overdose:**
I. There is no direct antidote
II. Respiration must be maintained by artificial means until the drugs are removed from the body
III. Symptomatic and supportive care
ii. T-61
A. **Drug description:**
I. A mixture of three compounds containing embutramide, a general anesthetic, mebenzonium, a muscle relaxant, and tetracaine, a local anesthetic
B. **Usages include:**
I. Suicide attempts
II. Narcosis
III. Euthanasia
C. **Administration:**
I. IV injection
II. Oral ingestion
D. **Toxicity:**
I. Drowsiness, disorientation, muscle hypertonia, and upper limb myoclonus
II. Encephalopathy, jaundice, and a severe coagulopathy
E. **Upon overdose:**
I. High-dose (1.2 g/day) IV-reduced glutathione should be administered
II. Maintenance therapy to treat hepatic damage
3. Drugs used for substance abuse
a. Ketamine
i. **Drug description:**
A. Dissociative general anesthetic
B. *N*-methyl-D-aspartate receptor antagonist
C. White powder with a characteristic odor and is soluble in water and alcohol
ii. **Usages include:**
A. General anesthetic
B. Approved for use in cats and for restraint in subhuman primates
C. Treat certain types of neurological-mediated pain
D. Pre-euthanasia agent
E. Recreational purposes
iii. **Administration:**
A. IM 5–10 mg/kg

B. Intravascular (IV) 1–5 mg/kg
C. Snorted
D. Applied on smokeable materials
E. Consumed in drinks

iv. **Toxicity:**
A. Tachycardia, palpitations, nystagmus, slurred speech, increased intracranial and intraocular pressure, dizziness, anxiety, confusion, vivid dreams, agitation, and delirium
B. Nosebleeds can result from snorting the drug
C. Bronchodilatation, increased salivary secretions, and problems of verbalizing have also been reported
D. Additional pharmacological effects are hypertension, agitation, paranoid psychoses, hyperthermia, and seizures

e. **Upon overdose:**
A. Supportive care that includes cardiac, respiratory, vital sign, and neurologic status monitoring, and high-flow oxygen as needed
B. Potential pharmacological interventions are IV benzodiazepines such as midazolam, diazepam, or lorazepam for seizures, anxiety, and delirium
C. Dystonic reactions have been reported from ketamine and can be managed through the use of diphenhydramine

b. Carfentanil

i. **Drug description:**
A. Mu-opioid agonist
B. Highly water-soluble, clear liquid with no distinguishable odor
C. The medication is a schedule-II, ultrapotent narcotic with a clinical potency 10,000 times that of morphine and 100 times that of fentanyl

ii. **Usages include:**
A. Rapid immobilization and chemical capture of wildlife such as large hoof stock and exotic animals
B. Used by veterinarians in zoological parks and wildlife management environments to safely immobilize animals for examination, assessment, and procedures
C. Recreational purposes

iii. **Administration:**
A. Compounded dosage form in a concentration of 3 mg/mL, in 10-mL vials
B. Intramuscularly via darting
C. Absorption through mucous membranes (eyes, nose, and mouth)
D. Direct absorption through broken skin

iv. **Toxicity:**
A. Lethal human dose of carfentanil is unknown
B. Signs and symptoms of exposure are consistent with opioid toxicity

C. Pinpoint pupils
D. Respiratory depression
E. Depressed mental status
F. Other signs and symptoms include dizziness, lethargy, sedation, nausea, vomiting, shallow or absent breathing, cold clammy skin, weak pulse, loss of consciousness, and cardiovascular collapse secondary to hypoxia and death

v. **Upon overdose:**
A. Ideally, the veterinarian has established protocols whereby the antagonist agent is readily available when carfentanil is used.
B. Naloxone is the opioid antagonist used for the reversal of carfentanil and is the preferred treatment in human health-care settings.
C. Veterinary practitioners exposed in the field may self-administer the veterinary-labeled naltrexone 50 mg/mL concentration that is made via the same compounding pharmacy source.
D. The recommended dose for animal reversal is a ratio of 100 mg of naltrexone for every 1 mg of carfentanil delivered.
E. Basic supportive measures are necessary in the field immediately after exposure:
I. Topical or mucous membrane exposure to carfentanil should be flushed immediately with copious amounts of cool or room-temperature water.
II. An exposed patient will need the reversal agent within 60 s.
III. For full parenteral exposure via needle stick or dart in humans, administer 10 mg naloxone, if available, intravenously.
IV. If a vein cannot be accessed, administer the reversal intramuscularly every 3–5 min until CNS depression is antagonized.

c. Clenbuterol

i. **Drug description:**
A. Long-acting, β-2 adrenergic agonist
B. Known on the street as "Clen"

ii. **Usages include:**
A. Approved for use in horses as a bronchodilator in the management of chronic obstructive pulmonary disease
B. Bodybuilders ingest this drug for its repartitioning and anabolic effects.
I. Abused by bodybuilders due to its ability to increase the rate of muscle protein deposition, resulting in enlargement of muscle fibers and the promotion of lipolysis
C. Others ingest it for its reported weight-loss effects

iii. **Administration:**
A. Available as an oral syrup (72.5 mg/mL)

B. Clenbuterol-tainted cocaine
C. Clenbuterol-tainted heroin

iv. **Toxicity:**
A. Dose-dependent β-agonist adverse effects include headache, dizziness, vertigo, nervousness, palpitations, nausea, muscle tremors, chest pain, and tachycardia.
B. Hypotension, severe chest pain, and tachydysrhythmias including supraventricular tachycardia and atrial fibrillation, pulmonary edema, hyperglycemia, and myocardial ischemia are also reported.

v. **Upon overdose:**
A. There is no known antidote to clenbuterol.
B. Treatment with activated charcoal can be considered if the patient presents within 1–2 h of ingestion.
C. Basic supportive measurers such as IV fluid replacement and airway support should be utilized.
D. The administration of a short-acting, parenteral β-antagonist agent such as esmolol is an option, assuming the patient has no clinical contraindications.
E. For suspected cases of clenbuterol contaminated with cocaine, β-agonists are not recommended due to the potential for unopposed α-receptor stimulation.

d. Testosterone and estradiol

i. **Drug description:**
A. FDA-approved, over-the-counter implants.
B. The drugs are included on the Drug Enforcement Administration's exempt anabolic steroid list.
C. The implants also come in a form containing an antibiotic, tylosin, to prevent implant site infection and abscesses.

ii. **Usages include:**
A. Increase the rate of weight gain and improve feed efficiency in steers.
B. Increased the rate of weight gain in heifers fed in confinement for slaughter.
C. The ingredients contribute to more marbling in edible muscle tissues, which can result in more valuable cuts of beef, contributing to the overall palatability.
D. Performance-enhancing purposes.

iii. **Administration:**
A. Subcutaneous
B. 25 mg of testosterone and 2.5 mg estradiol benzoate

iv. **Toxicity:**
A. The adverse effects are seen over extended periods of use.
B. The vascular and cardiac abnormalities that present with the abuse of anabolic steroids are of a serious nature and include myocardial infarction, cerebrovascular accident, hypertension, and edema.

C. Subjective adverse effects include steroid-induced acne, sexual dysfunction, mood alterations, gynecomastia, insomnia, local site reactions, loss of hair, and testicular atrophy.
D. Serious adverse effects include possible hepatotoxicity and sudden death due to abuse of anabolic steroids.

v. **Upon overdose:**
A. Treatment is supportive and removal of the abusive agent(s).
B. There is no antidote for testosterone toxicity.

4. Drugs used as human therapeutics
a. Dimethyl sulfoxide (DMSO)

i. **Drug description:**
A. Dimethyl sulfoxide
B. Able to carry some drugs rapidly through the skin

ii. **Usages include:**
A. Approved uses only in horses and dogs
B. Liniment for horses
C. Treatment of increased intracranial pressure and/or cerebral edema in horses
D. Topical analgesia
E. Paint remover
F. Antifreeze

iii. **Administration:**
A. Topical
B. Intravenously

iv. **Toxicity:**
A. Neurotoxicity could be detected at doses as low as 0.3 mL/kg
B. High concentrations of DMSO (70–90%) results in immediate burning and stinging
C. Nausea and headaches
D. Garlic breath
E. Eye irritation
F. Hemolysis

v. **Upon overdose:**
A. Maintenance therapy for hepatic damage
B. Wash affected area thoroughly

b. Ivermectin

i. **Drug description:**
A. Class of medications called anthelmintics
B. 22,23-Dihydro derivative of avermectin B1, a macrocyclic lactone, produced by an actinomycete, *Streptomyces avermitilis*

ii. **Usages include:**
A. Antiparasitic

B. Used to treat strongyloidiasis (threadworm; infection with a type of roundworm that enters the body through the skin, moves through the airways, and lives in the intestines)
C. Also used to control onchocerciasis (river blindness; infection with a type of roundworm that may cause rash, bumps under the skin, and vision problems including vision loss or blindness)
D. Sometimes used to treat certain other roundworm infections, head or pubic lice infestation, and scabies

iii. **Administration:**
A. Oral ingestion

iv. **Toxicity:**
A. Rash, hives, seizure, headache, tingling of hands or feet, weakness, loss of coordination, stomach pain, nausea, vomiting, diarrhea, dizziness, swelling of the face, arms, hands, feet, ankles, or lower legs

v. **Upon overdose:**
A. Induction of emesis and/or gastric lavage as soon as possible
B. Followed by administration of purgatives and other routine overdose measures
C. Supportive care
D. Parenteral fluids and electrolytes, respiratory support, and presser agents if clinically significant hypotension is present

5. Human drugs used as animal therapeutics
   a. TCAs
      i. Amitriptyline
         A. **Drug description:**
            I. Elavil
            II. Tryptizol
            III. Laroxyl
            IV. One of the largest families of psychotropic drugs
            V. Blocks the reuptake of norepinephrine and serotonin at the neuronal membrane
         B. **Usages include:**
            I. Antidepressants
            II. Chronic pain
         C. **Administration:**
            I. Oral ingestion
            II. Subcutaneous injection
         D. **Toxicity:** Lethargy and ataxia can quickly progress to tachycardia, vomiting, mydriasis, vasodilation, hypotension, cardiac arrhythmias, vocalizing, dyspnea, pulmonary edema, seizures, coma, and death.

E. **Upon overdose:**
   I. The oral lethal dose for many TCAs is 15 mg/kg.
   II. Clinical signs of TCA overdose can appear as early as 30 min after ingestion, and death can occur within 1 or 2 h if a patient is not treated.
   III. Induced emesis.
   IV. Repeated doses of activated charcoal with a cathartic.
   V. Avoid magnesium salts as cathartics because of the decreased peristalsis caused by TCAs, which can result in increased magnesium absorption.
   VI. Sodium bicarbonate (2–3 mEq/kg slowly intravenously) is recommended if a patient is acidotic or hypotensive or if arrhythmias are present, because maintaining alkalosis ($pH > 7.5$) in experimentally dosed dogs prevented death.
   VII. Do not administer sodium bicarbonate therapy if you cannot monitor blood gases, because metabolic acidosis can be a serious complication.

b. Selective Serotonin Re-uptake Inhibitors (SSRIs) (antidepressants)
   i. Fluoxetine
      A. **Drug description:**
         I. Prozac
         II. Fontex
         III. Seronil
         IV. Antipsychotic drug
      B. **Usages include:**
         I. Treat canine sadness, separation anxiety and other behavioral problems
         II. Used to treat symptoms of psychiatric disorders such as schizophrenia and bipolar disorder
      C. **Administration:**
         I. Oral ingestion
      D. **Toxicity:**
         I. The minimum lethal dose of fluoxetine in dogs is greater than 100 mg/kg
         II. Lethargy, vomiting, and disorientation
         III. Unresponsiveness, coma, uncontrollable shaking
      E. **Upon overdose:**
         I. Safer in overdose when compared with traditional antidepressants such as the tricyclic antidepressants
         II. Regurgitation with hydrogen peroxide
         III. Activated charcoal every 6 h with a cathartic
         IV. Symptomatic and supportive care
         V. ECG monitoring is usually indicated to detect any cardiac abnormalities

Household Products

1. Aquarium products
   a. Trichlorfon
      i. **Drug description:**
         A. Dimethyl(2,2,2,trichloro-1-hydroxyethyl) phosphonate
         B. An organophosphate compound
         C. A pale clear, white or yellow crystalline powder
      ii. **Usages include:**
         A. Used as an insecticide
            I. Particularly used against *Diptera*
            II. Control of internal and external parasites
            III. Anthelmintic in the treatment of schistosomiasis
            IV. Treatment of *Hydra*, *Lernia* (anchor worms), parasitic copepods, monodigenetic and digenetic flukes, fish lice (*Argulus*), leeches
            V. Removal of snails
      iii. **Administration:**
         A. Dust
         B. Granular
         C. Emulsifiable concentrate
         D. Soluble powder
         E. Injectable solution
         F. Tablets
         G. Fly bait
      iv. **Toxicity:**
         A. Poisonings have occurred after oral, dermal, and inhalation exposure to trichlorfon.
         B. Indirect inhibitor of AChE.
         C. Sweating, visual disturbances, vomiting, diarrhea, chest and abdominal distress, pulmonary edema, respiratory depression, and muscle weakness and twitching.
      v. **Upon overdose:**
         A. If ingested, empty stomach and intestines by intubation, aspiration, and lavage, using activated charcoal slurry.
         B. Administer charcoal and cathartic. *Do not* induce vomiting.
         C. Insure a clear airway, by aspiration if necessary. Administer oxygen if needed.
         D. As an antidote, administer IV atropine (0.4–2 mg every 10–15 min), until atropinization is achieved.
         E. Severe poisoning may also require IV pralidoxime (1–2 g). This treatment may need to be repeated over several days.

F. Monitor patient for at least 72 h; symptoms may recur for as long as 5–14 days.

b. Copper sulfate

i. **Drug description:**

A. Copper is one of 26 essential trace elements occurring naturally in plant and animal tissue.

B. A strong irritant.

ii. **Usages include:** For treatment of freshwater and marine ichthyophthriasis or ich (*Cryptocaryon*), *Oodinium*, external parasites, fungus, and even algae (especially in ponds).

iii. **Administration:**

A. Soluble copper salts

B. Medicated wonder shells

C. Sequestered copper sulfate

iv. **Toxicity:**

A. Usual routes by which humans receive toxic exposure to copper sulfate are through skin or eye contact, as well as by inhalation of powders and dusts.

B. The lowest dose of copper sulfate that has been toxic when ingested by humans is 11 mg/kg.

C. Metallic taste in the mouth, burning pain in the chest and abdomen, intense nausea, vomiting, diarrhea, headache, sweating, shock, discontinued urination leading to yellowing of the skin.

D. Injury to the brain, liver, kidneys, and stomach and intestinal linings may also occur in copper sulfate poisoning.

v. **Upon overdose:**

A. There have been reports of human suicide resulting from the ingestion of gram quantities of this material.

B. Do *not* induce vomiting.

C. Give plenty of water to drink.

D. Start an early treatment of chelating agents.

I. Dimercaprol-2,3-dimercaptopropane-1-sulfonate (DMPS)

II. Penicillamine

III. Edetate calcium disodium

2. Art products

a. Paints

i. Methyl alcohol

A. **Drug description:**

I. A primary alcohol with the chemical formula CH_3OH.

II. It is colorless, volatile, flammable, and readily miscible in water.

III. It also has a light odor that is distinctly different from that of ethanol.

B. **Usages include:**

I. Paint thinner and strippers
II. Automotive windshield washer solvent
III. Gas line antifreeze
IV. Copy machine fluid
V. Fuel for small stoves
VI. Industrial solvent

C. **Administration:**
I. Oral ingestion
II. Topical

D. **Toxicity:**
I. Poisoning occurs over a number of hours.
II. While methanol itself is only mildly intoxicating, it is converted to highly toxic metabolites.
III. Responsible for acidosis, blindness, and potentially death.
IV. Patients usually describe blurred or misty vision, double vision, or changes in color perception.
V. There may be constricted visual field and, occasionally, total loss of vision.
VI. Characteristic visual dysfunctions include pupillary dilation and loss of pupillary reflex.
VII. Further signs and symptoms may be shallow respiration, cyanosis, tachypnea, coma, seizures, electrolyte disturbances, and various hemodynamic changes, including profound hypotension and cardiac arrest.
VIII. There may be mild to profound loss of memory, confusion, and agitation, which may progress to stupor and coma as the severity of the acidosis increases.
IX. The lethal dose of pure methanol is estimates to be 1–2 mL/kg; however, permanent blindness and death have been reported with as little as 0.1 mL/kg (6–10 mL in adults).

E. **Upon overdose:**
I. The three primary goals of therapy include treatment of
   Metabolic acidosis
   Inhibition of the methanol metabolism
   Enhanced elimination of the unmetabolized compound and existing toxic metabolites
II. Gastric decontamination is unlikely to be beneficial because methanol is rapidly and completely absorbed from the gut.
III. Ipecac-induced emesis is contraindicated due to the risk of rapid loss of consciousness.
IV. It is doubtful that activated charcoal has the ability to absorb significant amounts of methanol; however, it may be useful if a coingestant is suspected.

V. Sodium bicarbonate should be administered to correct serum pH.
VI. Fluid and electrolyte replacement, airway management, and the treatment of serious cardiovascular and neurological signs, such as hypotension and seizures, should also be a primary concern.
VII. The elimination of methanol may be enhanced by administering folic acid.

ii. Lead
A. **Drug description:**
I. Lead is a metal that occurs naturally in the Earth's crust, but human activity—mining, burning fossil fuels, and manufacturing—has caused it to become more widespread.
II. The use of lead-based paints for homes, children's toys, and household furniture has been banned in the United States since 1978.
But lead-based paint is still on walls and woodwork in many older homes and apartments.
B. **Usages include:**
I. Lead-based paint
II. Gasoline
III. Batteries
IV. Pipes
V. Pottery
VI. Roofing materials
VII. Some cosmetics
C. **Administration:**
I. Oral ingestion
II. Inhalation
III. Topical
D. **Toxicity:**
I. High blood pressure
II. Declines in mental functioning
III. Pain, numbness, or tingling of the extremities
IV. Muscular weakness
V. Memory loss
VI. Mood disorders
VII. Reduced sperm count, abnormal sperm
VIII. Miscarriage or premature birth in pregnant women
E. **Upon overdose:**
I. The first step in treating all degrees of lead poisoning is to remove the source of the contamination.
II. Chelation therapy.
III. EDTA therapy.

Doctors treat lead levels greater than 45 mcg/dL of blood with a chemical called ethylenediaminetetraacetic acid (EDTA).

b. Clay
  i. Cadmium
    A. **Drug description:**
      I. The form of cadmium that is of most interest for health effects from inhalation exposure is cadmium oxide because that is the main form of airborne cadmium.
    B. **Usages include:**
      I. Product found in clay
      II. Industrial workplaces
      III. Batteries
    C. **Administration:**
      I. Inhalation
      II. Oral ingestion
    D. **Toxicity:**
      I. Coughing and irritation of the throat and mucosa
      II. Severe dyspnea and wheezing
      III. Chest pain and precordial constriction
      IV. Weakness and malaise
      V. Anorexia, nausea, diarrhea, nocturia, abdominal pain, hemoptysis, and prostration
      VI. Severe pulmonary edema
      VII. Chemical pneumonitis
      VIII. Death
      IX. Increased concentrations of urinary beta-2 microglobulin
    E. **Upon overdose:**
      I. There is no effective treatment for cadmium toxicity.
      II. Vitamin D may be given for weak bones.
      III. Symptomatic and supportive care.
  ii. Silica dust
    A. **Drug description:**
      I. The material used for making pottery contains varying proportions of ball clay, china clay, and felspar, with 35% of finely ground quartz or "flint."
      II. Dust arising from such a mixture will originate silicosis after years of exposure.
    B. **Usages include:**
      I. Pottery
      II. Industrial workplaces
      III. Construction zones

C. **Administration:**
   I. Inhalation
   II. Oral ingestion
d. **Toxicity:**
   I. Impairment of lung function resulting from fibrosis of the lungs
   II. Development of tuberculosis
   III. Chronic cough
   IV. Fever
   V. Weight loss
E. **Upon overdose:**
   I. There is no specific treatment for silicosis
   II. Removing the source of silica exposure is important to prevent the disease from getting worse
   III. Supportive treatment includes cough medicine, bronchodilators, and oxygen if needed
   IV. Antibiotics prescribed for respiratory infections as needed

3. Batteries
   a. Manganese dioxide
      i. **Drug description:**
         A. Black to brown, solid, odorless material
      ii. **Usages include:**
         A. Dry-cell batteries
         B. Pigment
         C. Precursor to other manganese compounds
      iii. **Administration:**
         A. Oral ingestion
         B. Inhalation
         C. Topical
         D. Eye contact
      iv. **Toxicity:**
         A. Inhalation manganese dioxide fume can cause "fume metal fever."
            I. A flu-like illness characterized by chills, fever, aching muscles, dryness in the mouth and throat, headache.
         B. Chronic exposure to manganese dioxide can lead to manganese poisoning, called maganism.
            I. It primarily involves the CNS.
            II. Early symptoms include languor, sleepiness, poor appetite, and weakness in the legs.
         C. Later effects may include a stolid mask-like appearance of the face, muscle cramps, twitching and tremors, changes in mood and personality,

emotional disturbances such as uncontrollable laughter and a spastic gait with a tendency to fall while walking.

D. Later symptoms are identical to Parkinson's disease.

v. **Upon overdose:**

A. Treatment with levodopa has limited benefits in improvement of clinical symptoms.

B. In severe cases of Mn poisoning, EDTA chelation therapy has been recommended in order to reduce the body burden of Mn and to alleviate the symptoms.

4. Cosmetics

a. Petroleum-based products

i. **Drug description:** Petroleum products are highly complex chemical mixtures consisting predominantly of hydrocarbons.

ii. **Usages include:**

A. Petrolatum

B. Petroleum jelly

C. Mineral oil

D. Paraffin

E. Paraffin oil

F. Paraffin wax

G. Make-up

iii. **Administration:**

A. Oral ingestion

B. Inhalation

C. Topical

D. Eye contact

iv. **Toxicity:**

A. Petroleum hydrocarbon toxicity may involve the respiratory, GI, or integumentary systems or the CNS.

B. Pneumonia due to aspiration of hydrocarbons into the lungs is usually the most serious consequence of ingestion of these materials.

C. Development of sequelae such as aspiration pneumonia and CNS depression.

v. **Upon overdose:**

A. Management in most cases is symptomatic.

B. Supportive care.

C. Removal of source of petroleum.

5. Dental products

a. Zinc

i. **Drug description:**

A. Excess zinc has been found in products such as Fixodent and Poli-Grip denture creams. Zinc concentrations ranging from about 17,000 to 34,000 mug/g were identified.

ii. **Usages include:**

A. Denture cream
B. Dry-cell batteries
C. Food products
D. Dietary supplements
E. Cold medicines

iii. **Administration:** Oral ingestion

iv. **Toxicity:**

A. Nausea, vomiting, loss of appetite, abdominal cramps, diarrhea, and headaches.
B. Intakes of 150–450 mg of zinc per day have been associated with chronic effects such as low copper status, altered iron function, reduced immune function, and reduced levels of high-density lipoproteins.
C. Severe nerve damage and neurological disease, "human swayback disease."
D. Hypocupremia.

v. **Upon overdose:**

A. Remove source of zinc.
B. Increase copper intake to decrease absorption on zinc.
C. Symptomatic and supportive treatment.

f. Fluoride

i. **Drug description:** Fluoride has been described as an essential element needed for normal development and growth of animals and extremely useful for human beings.

ii. **Usages include:**

A. Toothpaste
B. Drinking water
C. Mouthwash

iii. **Administration:**

A. Oral ingestion
B. Inhalation

iv. **Toxicity:**

A. The amount of fluoride considered lethal when taken orally is 35–70 mg F per kg body weight. This is equivalent to 5–10 g sodium fluoride for a 70-kg adult and 1–2 g sodium fluoride for a 15-kg child.
B. Symptoms of acute toxicity occur rapidly: diffuse abdominal pain, diarrhea, vomiting, excess salivation, and thirst.
C. Excessive fluoride, more than 8 ppm in drinking water daily for many years, can lead to skeletal fluorosis.

I. Owing to chronic toxicity, bone density slowly increases; the joints stiffen and become painful.

II. The clinical signs of these stages are chronic joint pain, dose-related calcification of ligaments, osteosclerosis, possible osteoporosis of long bones, and in severe cases, muscle wasting and neurological defects.

v. **Upon overdose:**

A. Rapid measures to reduce fluoride absorption should be started by inducing vomiting and administrating large volume of calcium as in limewater or milk.

B. Because alkaline urine prevents fluoride reabsorption, it is suggested that expeditious manipulation of urinary pH by diuresis with an alkalinizing agent might favorably affect the clinical outcome in such cases.

6. Hair products

a. Lye relaxers

i. **Drug description:** Contains 2.5–3% concentrations of sodium hydroxide or potassium hydroxide

ii. **Usages include:**

A. Hair relaxers

B. Red Devil® Lye

C. Drano® drain opener

D. Easy Off® oven cleaner

E. Liquid Plumber® drain opener

iii. **Administration:**

A. Inhalation

B. Oral ingestion

C. Topical skin contact

D. Eye contact

iv. **Toxicity:**

A. Irritation and burning of the skin, eyes, nose, windpipe, and lungs.

B. One-time, high-level inhalation of sodium hydroxide may lead to swelling of the larynx and irreversible obstructive lung disease.

C. Early symptoms of ingestion include abdominal pain and vomiting.

D. Perforation of the GI tract and shock are also possible, and may not become apparent until several hours after ingestion.

E. Chronic effects resulting from long-term exposure to low concentrations of airborne sodium hydroxide include nose and throat irritation, chest pains, shortness of breath, and ulceration of the nasal passages.

F. Chronic skin exposure may cause dermatitis.

v. **Upon overdose:**

A. Rapid decontamination is critical.

I. Remove contaminated clothing and shoes. Immediately wash skin with plenty of water for at least 15 min

B. Do not induce vomiting.

I. Give 4–8 ounces of water or milk.

II. Do not administer activated charcoal or attempt to neutralize stomach contents.

b. Sodium lauryl sulfate (SLS)

i. **Drug description:**

A. Classified as an emulsifying, wetting, and/or solubilizing agent

B. A mixture of sodium alkyl sulfates, primarily sodium lauryl sulfate containing not more than a total of 8% of sodium sulfate and sodium chloride

ii. **Usages include:**

A. Cosmetics as an anionic surfactant with detergent, wetting, foaming, and emulsifying properties

B. Hair shampoos

C. Bubble baths

D. Hair dyes

E. Skin cleansing products

F. Skin moisturizers

iii. **Administration:**

A. Topical

B. Oral ingestion

C. Inhalation

iv. **Toxicity:**

A. Skin irritation

B. Mouth ulcers

C. Irritation of the gastrointestinal tract

v. **Upon overdose:**

A. In case of contact, immediately flush eye/skin with plenty of water.

B. Cover the irritated skin with an emollient.

C. Wash with a disinfectant soap and cover the contaminated skin with an antibacterial cream.

D. Do *not* induce vomiting unless directed to do so by medical personnel.

7. Personal hygiene products

a. Aluminum

i. **Drug description:** Aluminum is the most abundant metal in the Earth's crust, and is present in the environment combined with other elements.

ii. **Usages include:**

A. Deodorant

B. Nail polish

C. Mascara

iii. **Administration:**
   A. Oral ingestion
   B. Topical
   C. Inhalation
   D. Eye irritant
iv. **Toxicity:**
   A. Muscle weakness
   B. Bone pain
   C. Fractures that do not heal, especially in ribs and pelvis
   D. Altered mental status
   E. Premature osteoporosis
   F. Anemia
   G. Impaired iron absorption
   H. Impaired immunity
   I. Seizures
   J. Dementia/Alzheimer's disease
   K. Delayed growth in children
   L. **Spinal deformities:** scoliosis or kyphosis
v. **Upon overdose:**
   A. Deferoxamine mesylate
      i. Given to help eliminate aluminum from your body
   B. Removal of aluminum
   C. Symptomatic and supportive care

b. Fragrance
i. **Drug description:**
   A. Usually listed as "fragrance" (in the United States), or "parfum" (EU)
   B. Commonly used in cosmetic ingredients and personal care products, fragrance may contain up to 4000 separate ingredients, although typically most products use an average of 50–100 fragrance ingredients
   C. These ingredients have no restrictions and are not required to be listed separately
ii. **Usages include:**
   A. Perfumes
   B. Shampoos
   C. Face wash
   D. Make-up
   E. Moisturizer
   F. Dryer sheets
   G. Detergents
iii. **Administration:**
   A. Oral ingestion

B. Topical
C. Inhalation
D. Eye contact

iv. **Toxicity:**
A. Sensory irritation
B. Pulmonary irritation
C. Decreases in expiratory airflow velocity
D. Alterations of the functional observational battery indicative of neurotoxicity
E. Contact dermatitis

v. **Upon overdose:**
A. Removal of fragrance product
B. Symptomatic and supportive treatment

Miscellaneous Toxicants

Acrolein

Characteristics: Colorless or yellow liquid with a disagreeable odor.

Usage: An intermediate in the synthesis of polyester resin, polyurethane, propylene glycol, acrylic acid, acrylonitrile, and glycerol; a widely used biocide (algaecide, molluskicide, and herbicide).

Toxicity: Causes severe irritation to any exposed membrane. Severe exposure can cause pulmonary edema. Noncarcinogenic. Additional symptoms include fluid in lungs, coughing, difficulty breathing, skin redness, increased blood pressure, tearing eyes, rapid heart rate, and rapid breathing.

Bioavailability: Maybe found in soil, water, or air. Breaks down rapidly in the air by reacting with other chemicals and sunlight. Evaporates rapidly from soil and water. Found in tobacco smoke, automobile exhaust, and overheated cooking oil. Absorption from inhalation, ingestion, or dermal contact.

Diagnosis: Urine testing.

Treatment: No antidote. Treatment consists of respiratory and cardiovascular support, and flushing of exposed skin with water.

Acrylamides

Characteristics: A white, odorless crystalline water-soluble solid. Decomposes to form ammonia and carbon monoxide, carbon dioxide, and oxides of nitrogen.

Usage: Synthesis of polyacrylamides, which are used as thickeners. Used in wastewater treatment, gel electrophoresis, papermaking, ore processing, and fabrics. Also found in starchy foods, dried and pickled foods, coffee, and cigarettes.

Toxicity: Causes irritation to exposed mucous membranes, and neurotoxicity. Symptoms include sweating, urinary incontinence, speech disorders, myalgia, nausea, numbness, paresthesia, and weakening of the legs and hands. Carcinogenic and mutagenic characteristics.

Bioavailability: Absorption through skin, inhalation, eye contact, and ingestion.

Diagnosis: Based on a history of ingestion, air and water sampling, and assessment of symptoms.

Treatment: Removal of exposure source. No specific therapy exists.

Acrylates

Characteristics: A salt or ester of acrylic acid. Also known as propenoates. Colorless liquids.

Usage: Synthesis of plastics, resins, and acrylic acids, used in adhesives and coatings. Found in latex applications, polishes, leather finishes, paper coatings, and emulsion polymers. A marine phytoplankton's natural poisonous defense mechanism against protozoa.

Toxicity: Irritation to any exposed membrane. Symptoms include lung damage, coughing, wheezing, laryngitis, shortness of breath, headaches, nausea, vomiting, laryngospasms, fluid in lungs, mouth pain, abdominal pain, diarrhea, skin rash, and throat swelling.

Bioavailability: Absorption through skin, inhalation, eye contact, and ingestion.

Diagnosis: Based on history of dermal contact and inhalation.

Treatment: Decontamination and supportive measures. Gastric lavage or activated charcoal.

Amines

Characteristics: Broad group of organic compounds. Derived from ammonia. Separated into two classes (aliphatic amines and aromatic amines).

Usage: Used in dyes, drugs (neurotransmitters), and gas treatment/refinery.

Toxicity: Increased/abnormal central and peripheral nervous system activity (increased neurotransmitter release), causing tachycardia and dysrhythmias (coronary vasospasms and hypertension). Other general effects are weight loss, hyperactivity, confusion, agitation, anorexia, diaphoresis, and mydriasis, pulmonary edema, nausea, vomiting, hypertension, and euphoria.

Bioavailability: Absorption from ingestion or inhalation.

Diagnosis: Drug screening, glucose and electrolyte testing, urinalysis, CT scans, echocardiographs, and chest radiographs.

Treatment: Sedation, and gastric lavage or activated charcoal.

Aniline Compounds

Characteristics: Colorless, oily, pungent liquid. Mixes readily with most organic solvents.

Usage: Used in the manufacture of dyes, plastics, rubber, pharmaceuticals, urethane foams, herbicides/fungicides, photographic chemicals, and explosives.

Toxicity: Damages hemoglobin. Causes dizziness, headaches, irregular heartbeat, convulsions, and comas. Also lung, skin, and eye irritation.

Bioavailability: Inhalation, ingestion, and dermal absorption. Readily breaks down and does not bioaccumulate.

Diagnosis: Urinalysis. Methemoglobin measurement to determine severity of damage.

Treatment: Decontamination and cardiopulmonary support. Gastric lavage or activated charcoal.

Azides

Characteristics: Explosive chemicals. Exist in inorganic and organic form. Some are colorless, odorless, in solid, or in solution. High risk of explosion when shaken or heated. Some forms are toxic when mixed with water.

Usage: Production of pharmaceuticals (antivirals), freeze-drying equipment, airbags, nematocides/herbicides, and used as sample preservatives in labs.

Toxicity: Mutagenic/carcinogenic. strong methemoglobinemia effects, lowered blood pressure, bronchitis, headache, weakness, and irritation of the eyes, nose, throat, and lungs.

Bioavailability: Strong dermal and inhalation absorption.

Diagnosis: Based on history of exposure (dermal, inhalation, or ingestion) and assessment of symptoms.

Treatment: Decontamination (depends on types of azides) and supportive measures. Gastric lavage or activated charcoal.

Bromide Compounds

Characteristics: Reddish-brown volatile liquid. Highly corrosive and toxic.

Usage: Fire retardants, gasoline additives, some vegetable oils, drilling fluids, refrigerants, dyes, and pesticides. Potassium bromide and sodium bromide used as anticonvulsants and sedatives.

Toxicity: Target cochlear hairs and renal tubules. Severe GI irritant, bromism, bromoderma.

Bioavailability: Inhalation from industrial uses, ingestion, or dermal absorption.

Diagnosis: Based on history of exposure and assessment of symptoms.

Treatment: Usually with gastric lavage or activated charcoal.

Butadienes

Characteristics: Colorless, flammable hydrocarbons.

Usage: Production of synthetic rubber from petroleum, and nylon. Also found in automobile exhaust, plastics, cigarettes, and acrylics.

Toxicity: Irritation of eyes, nose, throat, and lungs. Blurred vision, fatigue, vertigo, and headaches. Carcinogenic. Elevated risk of heart disease.

Bioavailability: Dermal and inhalation absorption most common.

Diagnosis: Pulmonary function tests of nervous system depression.

Treatment: Removal of exposed sources and supportive measures.

Carbon Disulfide

Characteristics: Colorless volatile, highly flammable liquid with an ether-like odor.

Usage: A building block in organic chemistry, and an industrial and chemical solvent. Also released by volcanic eruptions and marshes. Used in the production of rayon, cellophane, carbon tetrachloride, rubber chemicals, and pesticides.

Toxicity: Highly toxic to the CNS. Chest pains, nausea, vomiting, dizziness, fatigue, headaches, mood changes, lethargy, blurred vision, delirium, convulsions, depression, stupor, restlessness, and unconsciousness. Additionally, chronic exposure associated with effects on skin, eyes, and reproductive system. Increased risk of Parkinsonism and lymphatic leukemia.

Bioavailability: Absorbed from inhalation, due to its volatility.

Diagnosis: Blood, urine, and breath testing.

Treatment: No known antidote. Removal of exposed sources and cardiovascular/respiratory support.

Chlorates

Characteristics: Powerful oxidizers. When mixed with combustible material, will readily deflagrate (burn at very low levels).

Usage: Pyrotechnics, antiseptics, matches, and herbicides.

Toxicity: GI irritation and methemoglobinemia.

Bioavailability: Absorbed from ingestion mainly.

Diagnosis: History of exposure and assessment of symptoms.

Treatment: Gastric lavage, activated charcoal, hemodialysis, peritoneal dialysis, or exchange transfusions.

Diamantes

Characteristics: Colorless or yellowish liquids with ammonia-like odor. Consists of many different types of amines (ethylene diamante, methylene diamine, phenylenediamine). Some are flammable and corrosive.

Usage: Color photography development, fuel additives, fungicides, adhesives, curing agents, lubricants, pharmaceuticals, and cattle feed additives.

Toxicity: Irritation to skin, respiratory system, liver, and kidneys. Symptoms, depending on type of diamine, include erythema, increased blood urea, tachycardia, hemolysis, increased blood potassium, decrease red blood cells, abdominal cramps, diarrhea, increased body temperature, coughing, blackish vomiting, headaches, chills, and muscle pain. Some forms are known to causing methemoglobinemia. Long-term exposure causes rhinitis, congestion, coughing, wheezing, dyspnea, and asthma.

Bioavailability: Absorption from inhalation and ingestion.

Diagnosis: Chest x-rays, eosinophil counts, and assessment of symptoms.

Treatment: Removal of exposure source and vital supportive measures.

Dibromochloropropane

Characteristics: Colorless liquid when pure. Dark brown color when mixed for commercial-grade liquids.

Usage: Pesticides.

Toxicity: Possibly carcinogenic. Acute toxicity in the CNS and causes pulmonary congestion. Irritation of the eyes and skin. Also causes GI distress and pulmonary edema when ingested. Long-term exposure causes reproductive and developmental problems, such as azoospermia and oligospermia.

Bioavailability: Inhalation, ingestion, and dermal absorption.

Diagnosis: Measured in breath and blood samples, biopsy, sperm counts, and blood-hormone levels.

Treatment: Flushing of skin, use of activated charcoal, oxygen, and respiratory supportive measures.

Dimethylacetamide

Characteristics: Colorless, water miscible, with a high boiling point.

Usage: A solvent for organic chemistry. Pharmaceuticals and plasticizers.

Toxicity: Irritation of the respiratory tract, GI tracts, eyes, and skin. Causes kidney damage, abdominal spasms, vomiting, sweating, weakness, headaches, depression, lethargy, disorientation, visual and auditory hallucinations, delusion, and emotional detachment.

Bioavailability: Inhalation, ingestion, and dermal absorption.

Diagnosis: History of exposure and assessment of symptoms.

Treatment: Removal of exposure, flushing with water, and respiratory supportive measures.

Dimethylformamide

Characteristics: Colorless, odorless liquid, which is miscible with water and most organic liquids. Degraded DMF often has a fishy smell, due to impurities. Has a low evaporation rate. Penetrates most plastics, and makes them swell.

Usage: Used as a solvent for chemical reactions, and in the production of acrylic fibers and plastics. Also used in pharmaceuticals, pesticides, adhesives, synthetic leathers, fibers, films, and surface coatings.

Toxicity: Possible carcinogenicity; possibly causes birth defects. Irritation of the respiratory tract, skin, and eyes, flushing of the face and increased blood pressure. Long-term exposure causes damage to digestive and hepatic system.

Bioavailability: Inhalation, ingestion, and dermal absorption. Not readily disposed of in the body.

Diagnosis: History of exposure and assessment of symptoms.

Treatment: Removal of exposure source, and supportive measures for respiratory and cardiovascular system, and liver function.

Dinitrobenzene

Characteristics: Extremely toxic crystalline solid. Explosive under high heat.

Usage: Used in explosives, such as ammunitions.

Toxicity: Causes methemoglobinemia, headaches, dizziness, and nausea. Extremely toxic, potentially fatal. Other symptoms include visual disturbance, central scotomas, bad taste/burning in mouth, dry throat, yellowing of hair, eyes, and skin, anemia, and liver damage.

Bioavailability: Inhalation, ingestion, or dermal absorption.

Diagnosis: Liver and blood tests.

Treatment: Removal of exposure source, induce vomiting immediately, and give an activated charcoal solution.

Dinitrotoluene

Characteristics: A pale yellow crystalline solid. A precursor to trinitrotoluene (TNT), used in the polymer industry.

Usage: Production of flexible polyurethane foams, deterrent coatings, and propellants.

Toxicity: Metallic taste in mouth, muscular weakness, headaches, appetite loss, giddiness, dizziness, nausea, insomnia, and tingling in extremities. Also causes pallor, cyanosis, anemia, and increased risk of heart disease, reproductive, and developmental defects. Carcinogenic.

Bioavailability: Primarily absorbed from inhalation or dermal exposure.

Diagnosis: Blood and urine analysis.

Treatment: Hemodialysis, diuresis, hyperbaric oxygen, methylene blue, or hemoperfusion.

Epichlorohydrin

Characteristics: Colorless, volatile, flammable liquid with a garlic-like odor. Insoluble in water, but miscible in most organic solvents. Hydrolyzes in water to form a carcinogen.

Usage: Production of glycerol, plastics, epoxy glues, and resins.

Toxicity: Irritation of the eyes, respiratory tract, and skin. Can cause nausea, vomiting, coughing, labored breathing, and pulmonary edema. Lethal at higher doses. Carcinogenic, especially in lungs.

Bioavailability: Inhalation, eye contact, and dermal absorption are the main routes.

Diagnosis: Chest x-ray, FEV tests, liver function test, and urinalysis.

Treatment: Removal of exposure source, oxygen administration, pulmonary resuscitation, and flushing with water.

Ethylene Dibromide

Characteristics: Colorless liquid with a sweet odor. Extremely toxic.

Usage: An additive to leaded gasoline, and a pesticide.

Toxicity: Irritation of the nose and throat, coughing, chest pain, dyspnea, bronchitis, pneumonitis, pulmonary edema, hemorrhage, and hydrocarbon pneumonitis. Additionally, airway dysfunction syndrome (RADS), mild depression, drowsiness, ocular conjunctivitis, severe liver damage, renal lesions, abdominal pain, nausea, vomiting, and diarrhea from ingestion and inhalation.

Bioavailability: Mainly from inhalation and ingestion.

Diagnosis: Serum bromide level testing, blood cell counts, glucose/electrolyte levels, liver function and renal function test, chest radiography, and arterial blood gas readings.

Treatment: Oxygen, bronchodilator, and epinephrine for inhalation treatment. Avoid induced vomiting, and use activated charcoal for ingestion treatment.

Ethylenediamine

Characteristics: Colorless liquid with an ammonia-like odor. Strongly basic.

Usage: Used in chemical synthesis as a building block, corrosion inhibitor in paints and coolants, animal feeds, color photography development, adhesives, fabric softeners, and curing agents for epoxies and dyes.

Toxicity: Irritation of exposed membranes.

Bioavailability: Absorption from inhalation and ingestion, but mainly dermal application

Diagnosis: Urinalysis. Only a small portion is excreted renally.

Treatment: Gastric lavage or activated charcoal.

Fluoride Compounds

Characteristics: Naturally occurring yellow-green gas with a sharp odor. Examples include hydrofluoric acid, sodium fluoride, calcium fluoride, and uranium hexafluoride. Extremely toxic in high amounts.

Usage: Used in dentistry, glass etching, propellants, and prescription drugs.

Toxicity: GI tract irritation. Yellowing of teeth, white spots, pitting, and tooth and bone damage at high amounts. Used to treat dental cavities and osteoporosis in low amounts.

Bioavailability: Absorption from ingestion. Readily absorbed in the small intestines.

Diagnosis: Urinalysis and bone marrow samples.

Treatment: Consumption of milk, calcium carbonate, or milk of magnesia.

Hexachloro-1,3-Butadiene

Characteristics: Colorless liquid with a turpentine-like odor.

Usage: Manufacture of rubber compounds, lubricants, fluid for gyroscopes, heat transfer liquids, and hydraulic fluids.

Toxicity: No studies on human toxicity. Toxic to kidneys and respiratory systems of animals. Carcinogenic to animals.

Bioavailability: Mainly absorbed by ingestion.

Diagnosis: Urinalysis or fat breakdown levels.

Treatment: Removal of exposure source.

Isocyanates

Characteristics: Very toxic carcinogens. Examples include toluene diisocyanate and methyl isocyanate.

Usage: Manufacture of polyols for polyurethane production.

Toxicity: Irritation of the respiratory tract, lungs, eyes and skin, asphyxiation, chest tightness, sputum production, inflammation of the bronchi, malaise, and shortness of breath; burning of lips, mouth, throat, esophagus, and stomach. Additionally, causes RADS, lightheadedness, headache, insomnia, impaired gait, loss of consciousness, and coma. Carcinogenic.

Bioavailability: Inhalation, ingestion, and dermal absorption.

Diagnosis: Chest x-ray and symptom assessment.

Treatment: Bronchodilators, and respiratory and cardiovascular support. Avoid emesis, and use activated charcoal.

Maleic Anhydride

Characteristics: Colorless or white solid with an acrid odor.

Usage: Formation of unsaturated polyester resins for boats and automobiles, buildings, piping, and electrical equipment, production of pesticides, and an oil additive to prolong engine oil life.

Toxicity: Conjunctivitis, photophobia, double vision; eye, nasal, and upper respiratory tract irritation; bronchial asthma, and dermatitis.

Bioavailability: Inhalation and dermal absorption are main routes.

Diagnosis: Radioallergosorbent and neurotoxicity tests.

Treatment: Decontamination, removal of exposure source, and supportive measures.

Mercaptans

Characteristics: Sulfur-containing compounds. Released from decaying organic matter.

Usage: Used in detecting natural gas leaks, pharmaceuticals, pesticides, plastics, and livestock feed. Found naturally in garlic and onions, gas oil fields, and skunk spray.

Toxicity: Depress CNS and respiratory paralysis. Additionally, hemolytic anemia, methemoglobinemia, internal bleeding, coma, myoclonic tremors, and emboli in pulmonary arteries.

Bioavailability: Inhalation, ingestion, and dermal absorption.

Diagnosis: Blood pressure testing, glucose and electrolyte levels, pulse oximetry, and chest radiography.

Treatment: Decontamination with water, removal of exposure source, transfusion, bronchodilators, diazepam, epinephrine, ventilation and oxygenation, and antibiotics to prevent respiratory infection.

Nitriles

Characteristics: Colorless or pale blue solids or liquids. A class of organic compounds, including amyl nitrile, nitric oxide, and alkyl nitrile.

Usage: Used in aphrodisiacs.

Toxicity: Headache, nausea, syncope, methemoglobinemia, hemolytic anemia, and Popper dermatitis. Nitric oxide is a vasodilator, but causes methemoglobin production at low levels.

Bioavailability: Inhalation, ingestion, and dermal absorption.

Diagnosis: History of exposure and assessment of symptoms.

Treatment: Cyanide antidote kits.

Phosphorus/Phosphides

Characteristics: Generally white, yellow, black, red, or colorless powders that are highly flammable. Toxicity and characteristics vary.

Usage: Used in fertilizers, fireworks, nerve agents, friction matches, explosives, pesticides, toothpaste, and detergents.

Toxicity: Damages hepatic system, chemical and thermal burns to exposed membranes, and damage to the cardiovascular system.

Bioavailability: Most common absorption is dermal, but can be ingested or inhaled.

Diagnosis: History of exposure and assessment of symptoms.

Treatment: Supportive measures for burns; gastric lavage or emesis, and then activated charcoal and sorbitol.

Phthalates

Characteristics: Esters of phthalic acid.

Usage: Primarily used as plasticizers in flexible polyvinyl chloride (PVC) production. Found in garden hoses, plastic bags, toys, medical tubing/bags, flooring, adhesives, cosmetics, soaps, raincoats, automotive plastics, solvents, fragrances, and deodorants.

Toxicity: Can cause mild GI discomfort, nausea, and vertigo. Additionally, acts as an endocrine disrupter, resulting in damage to the liver and testes, insulin resistance, obesity, and is potentially carcinogenic.

Bioavailability: Absorption from ingestion and dermal contact mainly.

Diagnosis: Urinalysis and blood tests.

Treatment: Dialysis and transfusions.

Polymers

Characteristics: A large class of natural and synthetic materials

Usage: Many different uses

Toxicity: Causes polymer fume fever—fever, chills, myalgias, coughing, and pneumonitis

Bioavailability: Absorption from ingestion or dermal contact, but mainly inhalation

Diagnosis: Assessment of symptoms

Treatment: Oxygen and supportive respiratory measures

Resins

Characteristics: Synthetic substances, similar to the resin hydrocarbons secreted by plants

Usage: Used herbal preparations, dental procedures, perfumes, varnishes, and adhesives

Toxicity: Extreme irritation of the GI, contact dermatitis, redness, swelling, burns, and itching

Bioavailability: Main absorbed dermally, but can be ingested or inhaled

Diagnosis: Patch test

Treatment: Supportive dermal measures

Styrene

Characteristics: Colorless volatile liquid that has a sweet odor.

Usage: Production of rubber, fiberglass, pipes, plastics, resins, insulation, containers, carpet backing, car parts, cigarette smoke, and a number of building materials.

Toxicity: Irritation of the eyes, respiratory tract, and GI tract. Long-term effects are headaches, fatigue, weakness, depression, and peripheral neuropathy.

Bioavailability: Inhalation, ingestion, and dermal absorption.

Diagnosis: Blood tests, urinalysis, and tissue biopsy.

Treatment: Avoid emesis. Flush with saline, gastric lavage, and activated charcoal.

Trimellitic Anhydride

Characteristics: White or colorless crystalline powder that is flammable and has a musty odor

Usage: Production of resins, polymers, adhesives, printing ink, dyes, and agricultural and pharmaceutical products

Toxicity: Irritation of exposed membranes, allergic reactions, coughing, rhinorrhea, dyspnea, malaise, chills, fever, muscle and joint aching, hypoxemia, anemia, and pulmonary disease—anemia

Bioavailability: Inhalation, ingestion, and dermal absorption

Diagnosis: Blood testing and assessment of symptoms

Treatment: Supportive measures

Triorthoscresyl Phosphate

Characteristics: Colorless or yellow, viscous liquid, that is insoluble in water.

Usage: A plasticizer in lacquers, varnishes, and PVC. Also a flame retardant in plastics and rubbers, gasoline additive, hydraulic fluid, and waterproofing.

Toxicity: Neurotoxic. GI disturbances, peripheral neuropathy, muscle cramps and weakness, paralysis, and wrist drop.

Bioavailability: Inhalation, ingestion, and dermal/ocular absorption.

Diagnosis: Electromyograms and nerve conduction velocity tests.

Treatment: Removal of exposure source and supportive measures. Avoid emesis, and conduct gastric lavage.

Xylidine

Characteristics: Yellow or brown flammable liquid. Weak amine-like odor.

Usage: Mainly used as a dye. Also in antioxidants, pharmaceuticals, organic chemicals, agrochemicals, and some rocket fuels.

Toxicity: Cyanosis, headaches, lethargy, fatigue, dyspnea, dysrhythmia, depression, seizures, and shock. Irritation of the eyes, skin, and respiratory tract. Long-term exposure can cause kidney and liver damage. Carcinogenic.

Bioavailability: Inhalation, ingestion, and dermal/ocular absorption.

Diagnosis: Hemoglobin and electrolyte levels, arterial blood gas, chest x-ray, and ECG.

Treatment: Avoid emesis. Use activated charcoal, oxygen, methylene blue, or exchange transfusion for extreme cases.

Chapter 8

Drug and Illicit Substance Abuse

Outline 168
Drug Abuse: Cocaine 168
Drug Abuse: Opioids Adulterants 181
Drug Abuse: Amphetamines 182
Drug Abuse—Hallucinogens: PCP 185
Drug Abuse: LSD and Other Hallucinogens 186
Drug Abuse: Plant Hallucinogens 188
Plant Hallucinogens: *Salvia divinorum* 189
Drug Abuse: Marijuana 190
Drug Abuse: Synthetic Cannabis 191
Drug Abuse: What Are "Bath Salts?" 191
Drug Abuse: "Date-Rape" Drugs 192
Prescription Drug (Rx) Abuse 193
Nonprescription (OTC) Drug Abuse 194
Volatile Substance Abuse 194
Drug Abuse: Anesthetic Drug Abuse 196
Inhalant Abuse: Nitrous Oxide 196
Anesthetic Drug Abuse: What Is Propofol? 197
Epilogue: Drug and Illicit Substance Abuse 200
References 205

Outline

- The National Institute of Drug Abuse (NIDA) "5": Federally mandatory drug screens in regulated industries (aviation, transportation, petrochemical, pipeline, mining, defense, health care)
  - *Cocaine and heroin* (opioids)—considered together as *formerly* the most commonly abused illicit drugs
  - Amphetamines
  - Phencyclidine (PCP)
  - Lysergic acid diethylamide (LSD)
  - Marijuana (THC)
  - The "date-rape" drugs
    - Gamma-hydroxybutyrate (GHB and GBL)
    - *Flunitrazepam*—Rohypnol, a benzodiazepine (BZ)
- New abused substances: "Bath salts," synthetic cannabis, prescription drugs (opioids), OTC drugs, anesthetics (propofol, ketamine, N_2O)
- Volatile organic compounds (VOCs) and other volatile gas abuse = sniffing → huffing → bagging

The NIDA 5: Street Names

- Cocaine (blow, bump, C, candy, coke, crack, flake, snow, toot)
- Amphetamines (crank, speed, ice, go)
- Phencyclidine (PCP, angel dust, hog, love boat, peace pill)
- Lysergic acid diethylamide (LSD, acid, blotter, cubes, yellow sunshine, blue heaven, purple haze)
- Marijuana (pot, weed, hemp, rope, grass, skunk, reefer, Mary Jane) and hashish (boom, hash, hemp, hemp oil)

Drug Abuse: Cocaine

Outline

- History and epidemiology of cocaine abuse
- Pharmacology and toxicology of cocaine abuse
- Cocaine abuse and its clinical manifestations
- General and specific treatment of cocaine intoxication

History and Epidemiology

History

- Cocaine is a natural plant alkaloid of the Central and South American cocoa plant.

- Peruvian Incas used cocaine-filled saliva as local anesthetics for ritual and war wound trephinations.
- Cocaine was an early ingredient of *Coca-Cola.*

Epidemiology

- Cocaine abuse is the most frequent drug-related cause of emergency department visits in the United States.
- Over 25 million Americans have tried cocaine at least once.
- Over 5 million Americans use cocaine one or more times a month.

Pharmacology and Toxicology

Pharmacology

- **Ester-type LA:** Rapid onset = inhalation: 1–3 min and peaks 20–30 min; IV: onset in seconds and peaks 3–5 min
- **Three routes of metabolism:** (#1) Hydrolysis by *plasma pseudocholinesterases* to *ecgonine methyl ester* (EME), major metabolite (50%); (#2) *nonenzymatic hydrolysis* to longest T1/2 metabolite, *benzoylecgonine* (40% drug screen marker); (#3) *hepatic N-demethylation* to *norcocaine* (10%)

Toxicology

- **Pseudocholinesterase deficiency:** 2% of Americans and most Inuits predisposes to ↑ toxicity 2° ineffective 1° metabolic pathway
- **LA effect** (IB)**:** 2° Na channel block centrally, peripherally, and in the myocardium
- **Vasoconstriction:** 2° Catecholamine RI → intense cerebral, coronary, and mesenteric vasoconstriction
- **Rostral-caudal CNS stimulation:** Euphoria, excitement, restlessness, tonic-clonic seizures 2° dopamine reuptake inhibition

Clinical Manifestations

Methods of Abuse

- **Snorting:** Nasally insufflated; "head shop" paraphernalia = spoons, dollar bills, and straws
- **Free-basing:** Home conversion of hydrochloride salt to pure cocaine base for inhalation or IV use by *flame processing* in volatile solvents—ether, benzene, alcohol (*Richard Pryor*)
- **Crack:** A highly purified and dry-processed smoke-able form of cocaine, available in small, inexpensive packages of "chips" or "rocks"
- **Hyperthermia:** 2° ↑ psychomotor *hyperactivity* and ↓ heat dissipation from vasoconstriction
- **CNS:** Mydriasis, seizures, ↑ CVAs = SAH, ICH, TIA

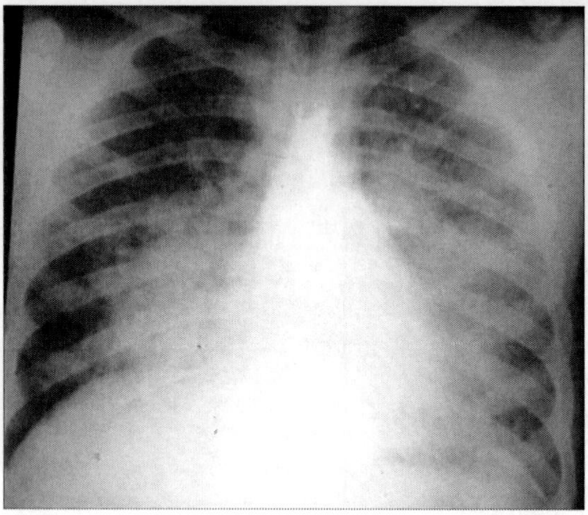

FIGURE 8.1 Noncardiogenic pulmonary edema: crack cocaine injection. Frontal chest radiograph that demonstrates normal size and configuration of the cardiomediastinal silhouette and bilateral diffuse pulmonary edema following the intravenous injection of crack cocaine. Noncardiogenic pulmonary edema may also follow opioid overdoses with the same radiographic patterns. (Courtesy of Carlos R. Gimenez, MD, Professor of Radiology, LSU School of Medicine, New Orleans, LA.)

- **Acute CV:** ↑ HR and BP, ↑ all tachyarrhythmias, angina, MI, vascular endothelial damage and platelet aggregation, SBE
- **Chronic CV:** CAD + LVH = dilated cardiomyopathy, PVD and acute aortic dissection
- **Pulmonary:** NCPE 2° PHTN; pneumomediastinum

Clinical Findings: CXR and ECG (See Figure 8.1)

Crack cocaine inhalation: *CXR noncardiogenic pulmonary edema*
Crack cocaine inhalation: *ECG myocardial injury, ST elevation, later Q-wave MI*

Clinical Findings: CT (See Figures 8.2 through 8.5)

Crack cocaine inhalation: *SAH 2° ruptured aneurysm*
Intravenous crack cocaine: *Septic cerebral emboli*

Clinical Findings: CXR

Crack cocaine inhalation: *Pneumomediastinum* (Figure 8.6)
Intravenous crack cocaine: *Dissecting thoracic aneurysms* (Figure 8.7)

- **Extensive Barotrauma:** Crack Cocaine Inhalation
- Subcutaneous emphysema in neck
- Pneumomediastinum
- Pneumopericardium
- Pneumothorax

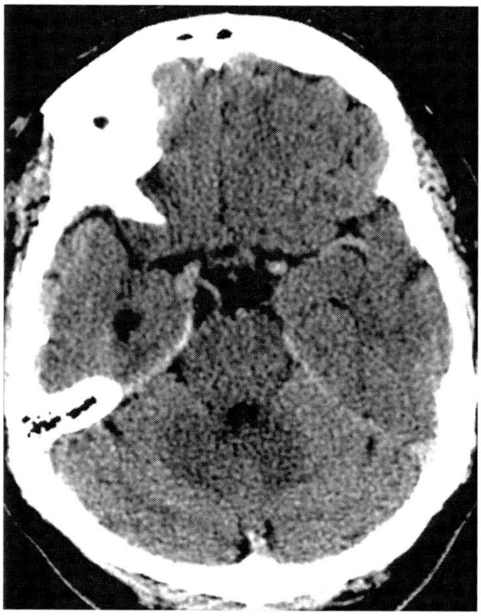

FIGURE 8.2 Intracranial aneurysm: crack cocaine inhalation. Cranial computerized axial tomogram (CT) at the level of the pons and the superior fourth ventricle in a crack cocaine abuser that demonstrates a right parasellar hyperdense rounded area consistent with a saccular aneurysm of the right posterior communicating artery. (Courtesy of Carlos R. Gimenez, MD, Professor of Radiology, LSU School of Medicine, New Orleans, LA.)

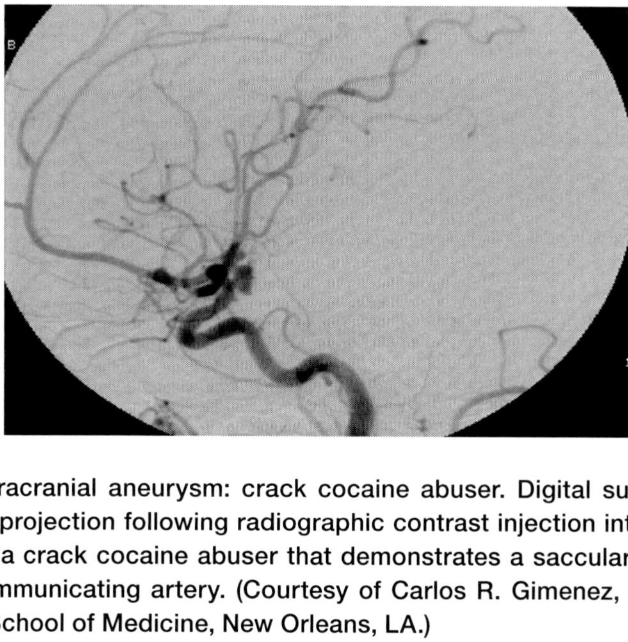

FIGURE 8.3 Intracranial aneurysm: crack cocaine abuser. Digital subtraction arteriogram in a lateral projection following radiographic contrast injection into the left internal carotid artery of a crack cocaine abuser that demonstrates a saccular aneurysm of the left posterior communicating artery. (Courtesy of Carlos R. Gimenez, MD, Professor of Radiology, LSU School of Medicine, New Orleans, LA.)

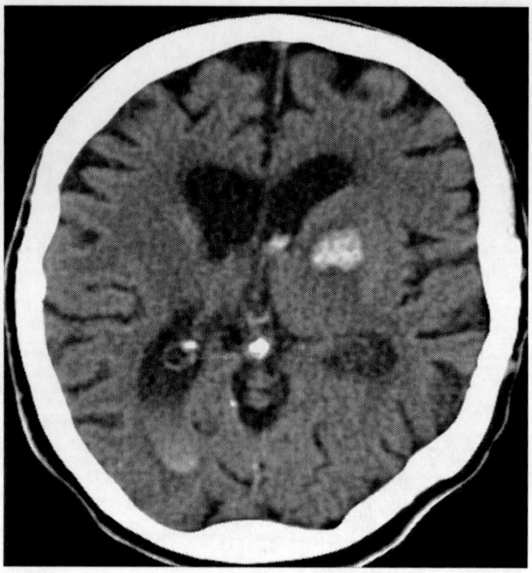

FIGURE 8.4 Intracranial and interventricular hemorrhage: crack cocaine inhalation. Noncontrast computerized axial tomogram (CT) of the brain at the level of the third ventricle in a crack cocaine abuser that demonstrates a hyperdense lesion in the left basal ganglia, asymmetry of the left frontal ventricular horn, and interventricular hemorrhage in the right ventricular horn consistent with hypertensive intracranial hemorrhage with disruption into the ventricular system. (Courtesy of Carlos R. Gimenez, MD, Professor of Radiology, LSU School of Medicine, New Orleans, LA.)

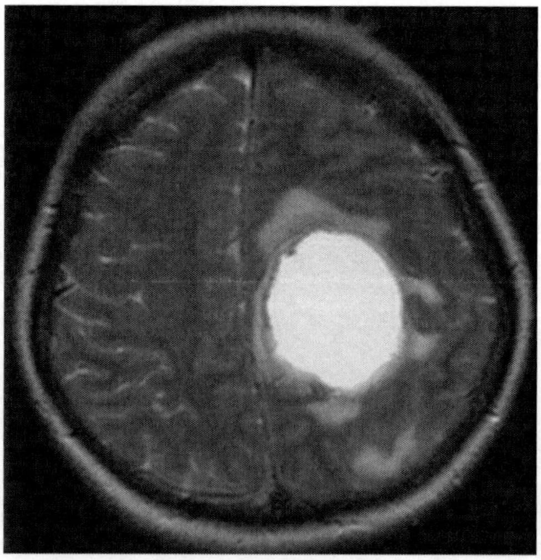

FIGURE 8.5 Septic cerebral emboli with brain abscess. Axial T1-weighted magnetic resonance image (MRI) of the brain at the level of the centrum semiovale that demonstrates a large cystic lesion with surrounding halos of vasogenic edema consistent with multiple septic emboli and resulting cerebral abscess in an intravenous crack cocaine abuser. (Courtesy of Carlos R. Gimenez, MD, Professor of Radiology, LSU School of Medicine, New Orleans, LA.)

(a)

(b)

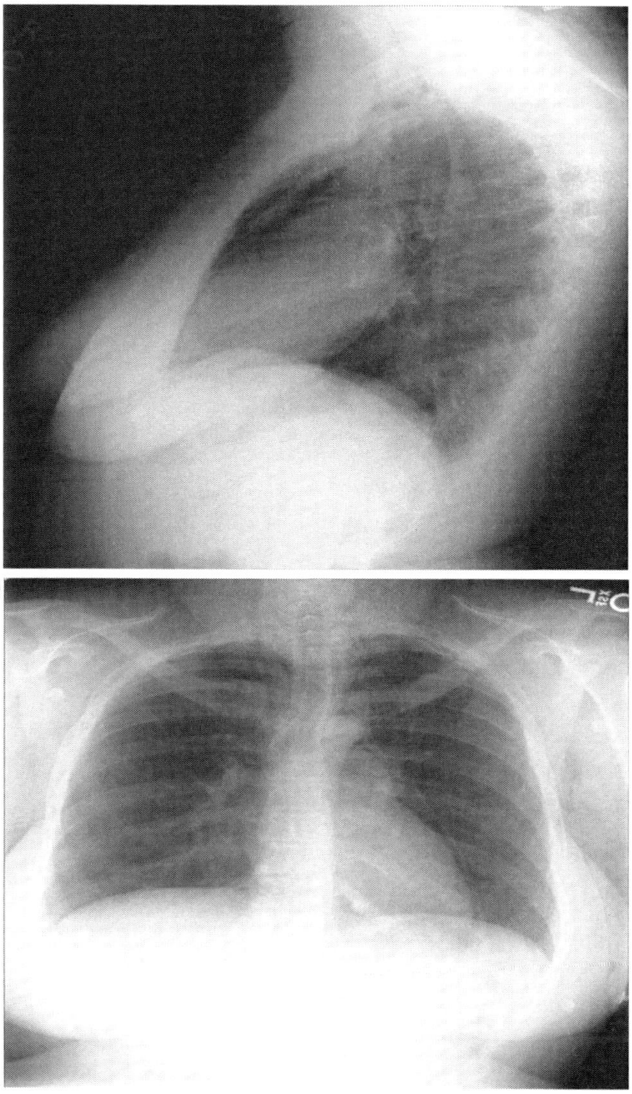

FIGURE 8.6 Pneumomediastinum following crack cocaine inhalation. Frontal (a) and lateral (b) chest radiographs that demonstrate radiolucencies throughout the left lung interstitium, mediastinum, and base of the neck consistent with pulmonary interstitial emphysema, pneumomediastinum, and subcutaneous soft tissue emphysema following crack cocaine inhalation. (Courtesy of Carlos R. Gimenez, MD, Professor of Radiology, LSU School of Medicine, New Orleans, LA.)

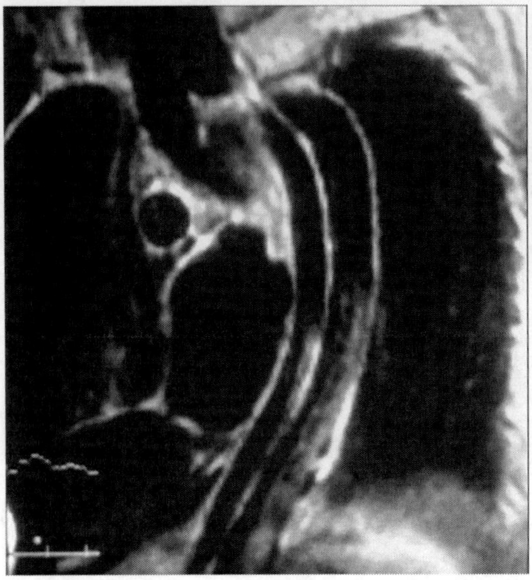

FIGURE 8.7 Dissecting thoracic aneurysm. Contrast-enhanced, T1-weighted, sagittal-oblique, computerized axial tomogram (CT) of the chest that demonstrates an intimal flap dividing the descending thoracic aorta into true and false lumens consistent with dissecting thoracic aneurysm Type B in an intravenous cocaine abuser. (Courtesy of Carlos R. Gimenez, MD, Professor of Radiology, LSU School of Medicine, New Orleans, LA.)

Clinical Manifestations (Continued)

- **Skeletal muscle:** Muscular hyperactivity and rigidity leading to muscle damage, $\uparrow$ CPK, *rhabdomyolysis*, myoglobinuria $\rightarrow$ ATN = ARF
- **GI vasoconstriction:** Mesenteric (gut) ischemia and mesenteric thrombosis $\rightarrow$ *bowel necrosis* (Figure 8.8)
- **Uteroplacental** and **fetal:** SAB, abruptio placenta, IUGR, microcephaly, and $\downarrow$ BW. *Cocaine OD: Fatal Mesenteric Thrombosis with Bowel Ischemia and Necrosis*

Cocaine-induced nasal and septal perforations after 5 years cocaine snorts: Tx = 0
Radial artery spasm after intra-arterial cocaine injection: Tx = amputation L thumb

Clinical Findings: CT

Abdominal CT: *Cocaine-induced intestinal ischemia*; bowel wall edema with *pneumatosis intestinalis* and air in mesenteric and portal veins

DDx and Labs

DDx of Sympathetic Toxidromes

- **Toxins:** Cocaine, PCP, amphetamines, MDMA, caffeine, hallucinogens, PPA, theophylline, ephedrine (ephedra—*ma huang*), pseudoephedrine, tyramine, MAOIs
- **Metabolic:** Thyrotoxicosis, pheochromocytoma, hypoglycemia

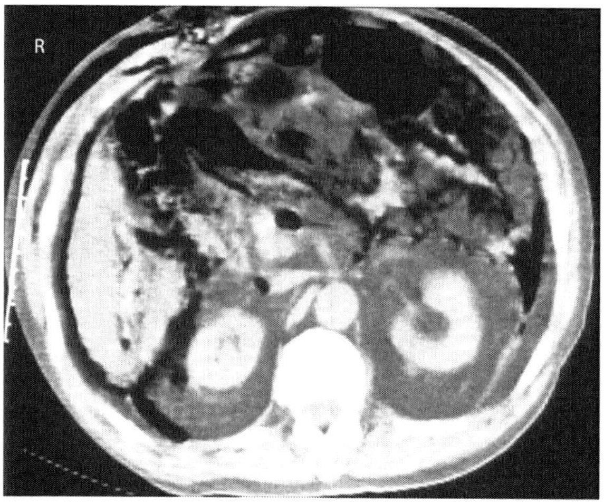

FIGURE 8.8 Fatal mesenteric infarction with small bowel perforation. Noncontrast, computerized axial tomogram (CT) of the abdomen at the level of the uncinate process of the pancreas that demonstrates bowel gas in the main portal vein and its intrahepatic branches, extraperitoneal emphysema in the properitoneal fat space and posterior pararenal space, pneumoperitoneum, and subcutaneous soft tissue emphysema following acute mesenteric infarction and subsequent small bowel perforation in an intravenous cocaine abuser. (Courtesy of Carlos R. Gimenez, MD, Professor of Radiology, LSU School of Medicine, New Orleans, LA.)

- **Withdrawal:** Ethanol, sedative-hypnotics
- **Neuropsychiatric:** Status epilepticus, mania, psychosis, schizophrenia

Diagnostic Tests

- **Labs:** Hyperglycemia, hypokalemia, ↑ CPK, and ↑ CPK-MB
- **ECG:** All tachydysrhythmias, ischemia, MI = Q + STE
- **Head CT:** All CVAs = SAH, ICH, IVH, ischemic cerebral infarcts, septic emboli
- **Abdominal x-rays:** Body packing mules vs. body stuffers; free air from perforated, necrotic bowel
- **MRI:** Dissecting aortic aneurysm, pneumatosis intestinalis, portal and mesenteric venous air emboli

General OD Mx

General Principles

- Assure AW and control motor hyperactivity and seizures with benzodiazepines and barbiturates.
- **Coma cocktail:** 1 g/kg $D_{50}W$ + 100 mg thiamine IV.
- **Externally cool:** Ice water baths.
- Avoid all neuroleptics and succinylcholine, which could exacerbate rhabdomyolysis.
- Treat SVTs with CCBs; treat QRS widening → $NaHCO_3$ and torsades de pointes → Mg.

Enhanced Elimination

- Initial AC + sorbitol, both at 1 g/kg, followed by MDAC for both body packers and body stuffers; monitor packers for packet rupture and need for surgical exploration.
- Consider WBI with PEG-ELS for hemodynamically stable packers and stuffers.
- Hydrate while monitoring CVP-PAP and *alkalinize urine with $NaHCO_3$ drip to protect kidneys from rhabdomyolysis*-induced myoglobinuria and ↑ risk of ATN.

Specific OD Mx

CV Toxicity

Hypertension (HTN): O_2, benzodiazepines for sedation, vasodilatation with *rapidly acting peripheral vasodilators*—phentolamine, NTG, and SCN

Pulmonary Edema: O_2, furosemide, MS, NTG

Angina: O_2, BZs, MS, ASA, NTG, CCBs (verapamil > diltiazem)

ST and **SVT:** O_2, BZs, CCBs, adenosine

VT and **VF:** O_2, BZs, $NaHCO_3$, cardioversion, defibrillation, consider lidocaine (avoid bretylium)

CNS Toxicity

- **Hyperthermia:** O_2, ice water baths, BZs (lorazepam > diazepam), vasodilators, non-depolarizing muscle relaxants
- **Agitation:** Sedation with BZs and barbiturates, if indicated
- **Rhabdomyolysis:** Hydrate while monitoring CVP-PAP, *alkalinize urine with $NaHCO_3$*, consider hemodialysis if ATN imminent

Mx: Body Packers vs. Stuffers

Body Packers

- Confirm by abdominal x-ray.
- Institute ECG monitoring.
- AC + cathartic, then MDAC to ↓ absorption and enhance elimination.
- WBI with PEG-ELS to ↓ GI mucosal contact time, speed transit, and ↑ elimination.
- Surgical removal for symptomatic patients with packet rupture.
- Follow-up imaging with abdominal x-rays; consider barium enema.

Body Stuffers

- Confirm by abdominal x-ray.
- Immediate orogastric lavage for recent ingestions.
- Institute ECG monitoring.
- AC + cathartic, MDAC to ↓ absorption and ↑ elimination.
- WBI with PEG-ELS to ↓ GI mucosal contact time, speed transit, and ↑ elimination.

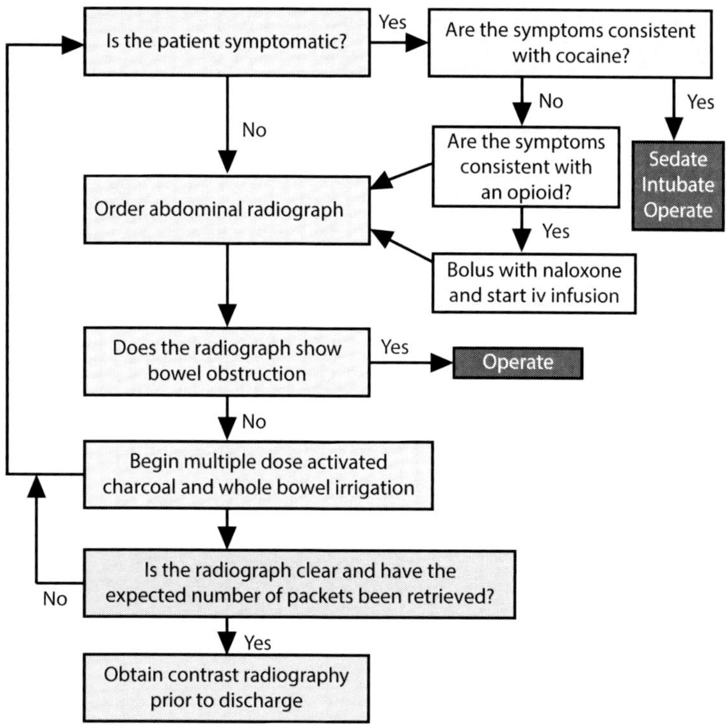

FIGURE 8.9 Management: cocaine vs. heroin body packers. A flowchart outlining the clinical practice management strategies for body packers of cocaine or heroin.

- Surgical removal for obstructed patients (ileocecal valve).
- Follow-up imaging with abdominal x-rays.

Heroin Body Packers (Figure 8.9)

- "Mules" who ingest large numbers of neatly and multiply wrapped packages of heroin (or cocaine) for smuggling, home catharsis, and later street distribution.
- Abdominal x-rays confirm status and direct WBI with PEG in asymptomatic patients.
- Symptomatic heroin packers can be managed medically with AC, naloxone infusion, and WBI. *(Symptomatic cocaine packers need surgery 2° GI ischemic necrosis and ↑ CFRs.)*

Opioids, Opioid Agonists, Antagonists, and Adulterants

- Agonists/antagonists and long-acting opioids (methadone, levo-alpha-acetyl-methadol [LAAM])
- Meperidine and propoxyphene (*epileptogenic*)
- Diphenoxylate and loperamide (*antidiarrheals*)
- MPTP-methyl-phenyl-tetra-hydropyridine (induces Parkinsonism) and pentazocine (*psychomimetics*)

- Tramadol and dextromethorphan (↑ serotonin = *serotonin syndrome*)
- Clonidine and imidazolines (*central alpha$_2$ agonists*)
- Heroin and narcotic adulterants (quinine strychnine, talc, *China white* fentanyls, etc.)

Special Opioids

Agonists/Antagonists

- **Mech:** Synthetic drugs that are agonist at one opioid receptor, either mu or kappa, and antagonist at another, usually mu; may precipitate acute withdrawal in the opioid-dependent.
- **Ex:** Butorphanol (Stadol®), nalbuphine (Nubain®), buprenorphine (Subutex®), pentazocine (Talwin®, kappa agonist and mu antagonist).

Long-Acting Opioids (Figure 8.10)

- **Mech:** Synthetic agonists with long durations of action of >24 h provide long-term analgesia for cancer patients, maintenance for addicts, and support during withdrawal; OD problematic due to short naloxone reversal time (1 h), with resedation and respiratory depression.
- **Ex:** Methadone and MS-Contin® (24 h), levo-alpha-acetyl methadol (LAAM) T1/2 = 3 days.

Meperidine (Demerol®)

- *Normeperidine metabolite* is neurotoxic → causing tremors, myoclonus, and *seizures*, especially in renal insufficiency.

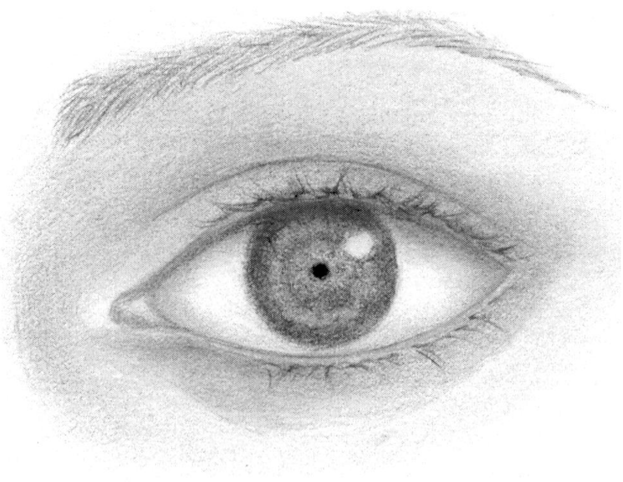

FIGURE 8.10 Miosis, right eye. Pupillary constriction or miosis is characteristic of an opioid toxidrome and overdoses with opioid receptor agonists.

- Causes ↑ presynaptic *serotonin release* → can precipitate the *serotonin syndrome* (*hyperthermia, muscle rigidity, and CNS depression*), especially when combined with MAOIs or SSRIs. Tx for serotonin syndrome = cooling, benzodiazepines, nondepolarizing muscle relaxants.

Propoxyphene (Darvon®)

- Both the parent drug and its *norpropoxyphene metabolite* have quinidine-like (Class IA) effects and cause ↑ *QRS widening* and dysrhythmias, which are responsive to Na bicarbonate.
- OD may produce acute *neurotoxicity* with *seizures* responsive to benzodiazepines more so than barbiturates.
- Often formulated with *APAP*, suspect cotoxicities in OD, and monitor serum [APAP].

Special Opioids: Antidiarrheals

Diphenoxylate (Lomotil®)

- **Insoluble meperidine analog** that delays gastric emptying, coats gut, relaxes, and immobilizes GI tract; used as an antidiarrheal.
- *Formulated with atropine* for its antimuscarinic and antispasmodic effects; OD may manifest both anticholinergic and opioid toxidromes.
- *Long T1/2* due to #1 and #2 dictates admission for lavage, AC, and naloxone infusion.

Loperamide (Immodium®)

- **An OTC insoluble meperidine analog**, like diphenoxylate, that also immobilizes GI tract; also used as an antidiarrheal.
- **Safer than diphenoxylate because loperamide** *does not contain atropine* or delay gastric emptying, does not have a prolonged T1/2, and is not associated with prolonged retention of pills in stomach.

Special Opioids: Miscellaneous

Methyl-Phenyl-Tetrahydropyridine (MPTP)

- A neurotoxic by-product of MPPP, a meperidine analog, manufactured during the failed illicit lab synthesis of *meperidine*.
- IVDUs become *frozen addicts* and develop classical *Parkinsonism* from selective destruction of dopamine-secreting substantia nigra cells; *resistant to L-dopa tx*.
- MPTP is now used to induce *experimental Parkinsonism* in laboratory animals.

Pentazocine (Talwin®)

- A synthetic agonist/antagonist that is *agonist* at the *kappa* and *sigma* receptors (causing dysphoria and psychomimesis), but *antagonist* at the *mu* receptor (thus producing little respiratory depression)

- Formerly mixed with the blue antihistamine, *tripelennamine* = "*T's for Talwin and Blues for tripelennamine*"; but now mixed with *methylphenidate* (Ritalin®) for recreational abuse at all-night *rave parties*

MPTP-Induced Parkinsonism

MPTP destroys CNS dopamine-secreting nigrostriatal cells.
MPTP-induced Parkinsonism is resistant to L-dopa.

Special Opioids: Opioid Agonists

Tramadol (Ultram®)

- A novel synthetic opioid that is a combined *mu opioid agonist* and a *serotonin/NE reuptake inhibitor*; only partially antagonized by naloxone. Replaced by tapentadol (Nucynta®).
- Can cause *seizures* in therapeutic doses and characteristically in ODs. Seizures respond to benzodiazepine suppression, but may be precipitated by naloxone.
- Can precipitate *serotonin syndrome*, like *SSRIs*, by *blocking serotonin reuptake*, especially in patients on MAOIs.

Dextromethorphan (Robitussin®)

- An OTC synthetic opioid agonist with no analgesic activity that is for cough suppression, like codeine.
- In OD, causes miosis, CNS depression, and *choreoathetosis* and *dystonia* 2° ↑ *serotonin release*. Also acts as a sigma agonist and can cause a PCP-like psychosis.
- Formulated as a *hydrobromide* salt → *bromism*, CNS depression, ataxia, confusion, coma.
- Can also precipitate *serotonin syndrome*, like *meperidine*, by ↑ presynaptic release of serotonin.

Special Opioids: Alpha Agonists

Clonidine (Catapress®)

1. *Centrally acting alpha$_2$ agonist* that produces an opioid toxidrome (lethargy, miosis, bradycardia and respiratory depression) indistinguishable from mu agonists due to agonist activity overlap at the mu receptor
2. CNS and respiratory depression reversed by *naloxone* → admit for naloxone infusion 2° resedation
3. Used as a sympathetic blocker for HTN and RSD, and to provide sympatholysis during opioid withdrawal

Imidazolines (Afrin®, etc.)

- *Combined central and peripheral alpha$_2$ agonists* used as nasal and conjunctival decongestants (oxymetazoline, tetrahydrozoline, xylometazoline) that produce an opioid toxidrome (bradycardia, hypotension, central CNS and respiratory depression) indistinguishable from mu agonists due to agonist activity overlap at the mu receptor

- Partially naloxone-reversible, but prolonged duration of action (4–8 h) causes resedation

Tx: Opioid OD

Acute OD Management

- Low initial IV naloxone boluses (0.1–0.4 mg), rather than a single, large therapeutic bolus (2 mg) to avoid precipitating acute withdrawal in addicts or causing noncardiogenic pulmonary edema.
- Aim is to reverse respiratory depression and restore RR > 8.
- Intubate and ventilate if respiratory depression persists, administer 10 mg naloxone IV—no infusion, just prolonged mechanical ventilation.

Naloxone Infusion

- If diagnostic naloxone bolus is successful, administer 2/3 of the initial dose IV per hour.
- If withdrawal develops, stop the infusion to let symptoms abate and restart at 1/2 rate.
- If respiratory depression recurs during infusion, readminister 1/2 the initial bolus, and increase infusion rate by 1/2.

Drug Abuse: Opioids Adulterants

Narcotic Adulterants

- **Quinine:** Disguises bitter taste of heroin → dysrhythmias, headache, vertigo, *tinnitus*, blurred vision, temporary–permanent *blindness*
- **Scopolamine:** CNS and peripheral anticholinergic toxidrome
- **Fentanyl analogs:** *China white* = fentanyl (100 × MS), sufentanil (10 × fent or 1000 × MS), and methyl-fentanyl (6000 × MS); superpotent fentanyl-adulterated heroin → respiratory arrest, coma and death
- Tx: CPR, naloxone
- **Miscellaneous adulterants:** Amphetamines, cocaine, quinine, lead–thallium, talc, *strychnine*, pesticides—barium carbonate, sodium monofluoroacetate

Adulteration of Commonly Abused Substances—Heroin: *Conclusions*

I. What are the most commonly used adulterants for heroin?
Whatever is at hand and is a white noncrystalline powder: Aspirin, APAP, boric acid roach pills, baby powder, vermiculite-diatomaceous earth (for swimming pool filters). Never salt or sugar crystals, used to adulterate cocaine.

II. What are the most commonly used criminal adulterants?
Whatever will be lethal and hard to find on tox screens post mortem: Strychnine, quinine, barium carbonate, sodium monofluoroacetate, thallium, arsenic.

Drug Abuse: Amphetamines

Outline

- Amphetamine pharmacology and abuse
- Prescription vs. designer vs. international amphetamines and their uses and abuses
- Acute vs. chronic amphetamine toxicity
- Management of amphetamine toxicity

Pharmacology and Abuse

Pharmacology

- **Mech:** (1) *Direct release of catecholamines*, particularly NE and dopa, from presynaptic terminals; (2) competitive *inhibition of catechol reuptake* at adrenergic terminals; (3) *5-HT release* at higher doses.
- **NE effects:** α and β-Adrenergic stimulation produce anorexia and alerting effects.
- **5-HT effects:** Altered perception and psychosis.
- **Met:** Lipid-soluble, high Vd, ↑ T1/2 and active metabolites, no COMT biodegradation.

Abuse

- **Prescription:** Used for ADHD, narcolepsy, and weight loss
- **Illicit:** Methamphetamine (ice, speed)—most common illicit drug produced by *clandestine drug labs*, 1° ingredient = *ephedrine*, adulterants = Pb and Hg
- **Designer:** MDMA (Ecstasy, claity, lover's speed, *Adam*) and MDEA (*Eve*)
- **International:** (1) *Khat*: active agent = *cathinone*, Arabia and East Africa (Somalia) = euphoria, alertness, anxiety, hyperactivity; (2) *ma huang*: Chinese *ephedrine* used as a bronchodilator for asthmatics and COPD

Rx vs. Designer

Prescription Amphetamines

- **ADHD and narcolepsy**: Amphetamine, dextroamphetamine, methamphetamine, methylphenidate (Ritalin® = most popular prescribed drug for preteens), pemoline
- **Weight reduction**: Amphetamine, methamphetamine, dexfenfluramine, phentermine, and fenfluramine (phen–fen: withdrawn by FDA)
- Pure methamphetamine = *ice* or *speed*

Designer Amphetamines

All are potent serotonin releasers; popular at all-night *rave parties*.

- Dimethoxyamphetamine: DOM or *STP*
- Methylene dioxyamphetamine: MDA, *love drug*
- Methylene dioxymethamphetamine: MDMA, *Ecstasy*, or *Adam*
- Methylene dioxyethamphetamine: MDEA, *Eve*

Acute vs. Chronic Toxicity

Acute Toxicity

- CNS > CV > Pulmonary
- **CNS:** *Mydriasis*, anorexia, euphoria, psychosis, *hyperthermia* → diaphoresis, HA, agitation—*hyperactivity* → tremor, seizures → muscle rigidity → *choreoathetosis* → *rhabdomyolysis* → *myoglobinuria* → *ATN-ARF*
- **CV:** Hypertension, tachycardia, tachydysrhythmias, vasospasm, angina, and MI
- **Pulm:** Tachypnea, pulmonary vasoconstriction and HTN

Chronic Toxicity

- **CV and pulmonary:** Catecholamine-induced dilated and valvular *cardiomyopathies*, mitral regurgitation (phen–fen), pulmonary hypertension (phen–fen), *necrotizing vasculitis* → ischemic colitis, permanent dopaminergic and serotonergic neurotransmitter depletion encephalopathy
  - *Phen–fen: 3D-echo—Valvular cardiomyopathy*
  - *Phen–fen: Color flow Doppler echo—Mitral regurgitation*
  - *Ruptured mitral valve—Diet therapy with phentermine–fenfluramine* (Figures 8.11 and 8.12)
- **Labs:** Hyperglycemia, leukocytosis, ↑ LFTs, ↑ CPK → *myoglobinuria*

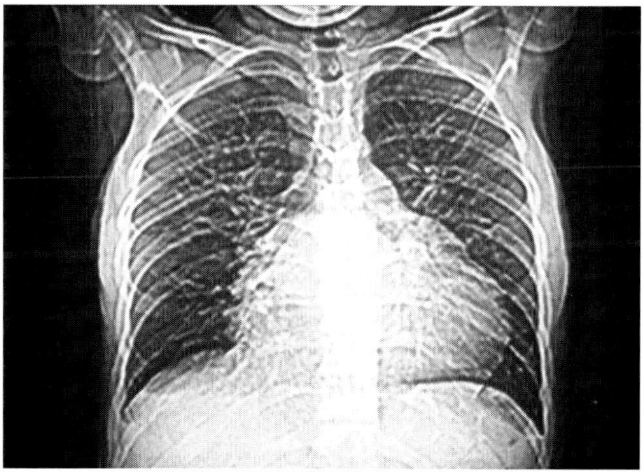

FIGURE 8.11 Phentermine–fenfluramine (amphetamine) cardiomyopathy. Digital subtraction frontal chest radiograph that demonstrates diffuse dilated cardiomegaly, predominantly of the left-sided cardiac chambers consistent with amphetamine-induced dilated cardiomyopathy in an obese patient taking an oral phentermine–fenfluramine combination for weight loss. (Courtesy of Carlos R. Gimenez, MD, Professor of Radiology, LSU School of Medicine, New Orleans, LA.)

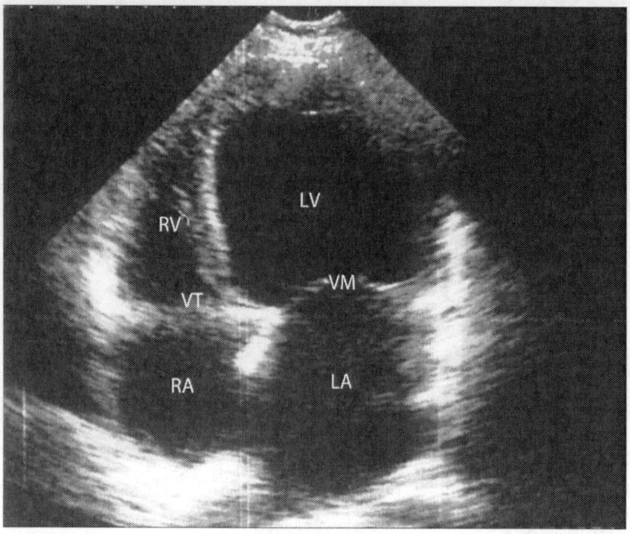

FIGURE 8.12 Phentermine–fenfluramine (amphetamine) cardiomyopathy with mitral valve prolapse. A cardiac ultrasound examination that demonstrates diffuse cardiomegaly predominantly of the left-sided cardiac chambers with mitral valve prolapse in an obese patient taking an oral phentermine–fenfluramine combination for weight loss. (Courtesy of Carlos R. Gimenez, MD, Professor of Radiology, LSU School of Medicine, New Orleans, LA.)

OD Management

General Management

- Restrain and sedate with BZs.
- Rapid external cooling with ice water baths.
- AC for recent oral ingestions.
- Administer coma cocktail, without naloxone: 1 g/kg $D_{50}W$ + thiamine 100 mg IV.
- *Avoid all neuroleptics* → ↑ temp, ↓ sz threshold, dystonia and choreoathetosis with neuroleptic malignant syndrome, may precipitate tachydysrhythmias.
- Monitor for rhabdomyolysis.

Specific Treatment

- **Agitation and restlessness:** BZs, IV diazepam
- **Seizures:** BZs > barbiturates
- **Hyperthermia:** Sedation + external cooling
- **Oral ingestions:** AC + sorbitol, both 1 g/kg
- **HTN:** Initially sedate with BZs, consider *peripheral vasodilators* for ease of titration—phentolamine, nitroglycerin, and sodium nitroprusside

Drug Abuse—Hallucinogens: PCP

Outline

- History and pharmacology of PCP
- Clinical and laboratory findings in PCP intoxication
- Management of PCP intoxication

Hx and Pharmacology

History of PCP

- Developed in the 1950s as a *dissociative anesthetic* for painful diagnostic procedures; ↑↑ postop psychomimesis.
- Some of the early congeners of PCP are still in use today as dissociative anesthetics, primarily *ketamine.*
- PCP was introduced to the San Francisco drug scene in the 1960s as the *PeaCePill.*

Pharmacology of PCP

- **Pharm:** Highly lipid-soluble weak base; 65% plasma protein bound; large Vd of 6.2 L/kg; hepatically metabolized to inactive metabolites; renal excretion
- **Mech:** *NMDA antagonists*, like *ketamine and dextromethorphan*, that inhibit the binding of glutamate to NMDA receptors centrally
- **Street use:** Sold as tabs, caps, or rock salt-like crystals and abused by smoking, insufflation, and ingestion

Clinical and Lab Findings

Clinical Manifestations

- **Ophthalmic:** *Exception*: *PCP is the only abused drug to cause miosis*—with blank stare, dysconjugate gaze, and *nystagmus—horizontal, vertical, and rotatory.*
- **CNS:** Disorientation, dysphoria, paranoia, dysarthria, jargonaphasia, auditory and visual *hallucinations*, agitation, hyperactivity, tremor, seizures, dystonia, torticollis, facial grimacing, opisthotonos, *rhabdomyolysis*, myoglobinuria, ATN, ARF.
- **Cardioresp:** HTN, sinus tachycardia, no cardioresp depression, tachypnea.

Lab Findings

- **WBC:** Leukocytosis
- **Lytes:** Hyperkalemia
- **Glucose:** Hypoglycemia
- **ABGs:** Metabolic acidosis
- **Enzymes:** Elevated muscle enzymes—LDH and CPK → myoglobinemia and myoglobinuria

- **Urine:** False-positive urine PCP tox screens from ketamine and dextromethorphan, other NMDA antagonists

Clinical Findings

PCP Miosis: Most CNS stimulants (amphetamines, cocaine, LSD) will cause mydriasis, with PCP being the only exception. PCP also characteristically causes nystagmus.

Management of PCP OD

General Management

- Restrain and sedate with BZs.
- Administer 100 mL $D_{50}W$ + 100 mg thiamine IV.
- Avoid syrup of ipecac (2° sz) and sedation with neuroleptics (↑ temp, ↓ sx threshold, ↑ dystonia).
- Orogastric lavage followed by AC, 1 g/kg + sorbitol, 1 g/kg.
- MDAC preferred over continuous NG suction.

Specific Treatment

- Monitor for elevated CPK and myoglobinuria, as rhabdomyolysis is associated with ↑ CFRs.
- If myoglobinuria occurs, protect kidneys with hydration, osmotic diuretics, and urinary alkalinization with $NaHCO_3$.

Drug Abuse: LSD and Other Hallucinogens

Outline

- Synthetic hallucinogens and their mechanisms of action
- Clinical presentation of LSD intoxication
- Management of LSD intoxication
- The plant hallucinogens: Lysergamides—morning glory, LSD-like; thujone—absinthe; myristicin—nutmeg; peyote—mescaline; wormwood—absinthe; belladonnas—nightshade, Jimson weed, angel's trumpet; diterpenoids—salvia

Hallucinogen Pharmacology

Common Hallucinogens

- **Lysergamides:** All natural and synthetic *ergot alkaloid* derivatives (*Claviceps purpurea*), such as LSD, and morning glory species (*Argyreia* and *Ipomoea*) and related Hawaiian baby woodrose seeds
- **Indolealkylamines:** Mushroom *psilocybin and psilocin*; *bufotenine* from *Bufo* spp. toads
- **Phenylethylamines:** *Mescaline* from peyote cactus, all *amphetamines* (especially the 5-HT releasers, MDMA and MDEA)
- **Cannabinols:** *Delta-9-THC* in marijuana and hashish

LSD Pharmacology

1. **Pharm:** Colorless, tasteless, and odorless powders that are rapidly absorbed mucosally; 80% protein bound; hepatically metabolized with no active metabolites and short durations of action, terminated by renal excretion.
2. **Mech:** All act as *serotonin releasers* and *agonists*, usually by promoting presynaptic serotonin release in the limbic system.

Clinical Manifestations

Acute Hallucinogen Toxicity

- **Initial autonomic effects:** Sympathomimetic with LSD, but GI (N and V) with peyote; then a constellation of *mydriasis*, dizziness, diaphoresis, piloerection, ataxia, tachypnea, HTN, and tachycardia
- **Later psychological effects:** Emotional lability = euphoria–dysphoria, *perceptual distortions*, visual (*psychedelic* colors) > auditory (sounds magnified) > tactile > olfactory *hallucinations*

Chronic Hallucinogen Toxicity

- Preexisting psychiatric illnesses predispose to chronic mental disturbances
- Extended psychoses possible: Schizophrenia
- Recurring panic reactions: mx by reassurance and support
- *Hallucinogen persisting perceptual disorder* (HPPD): aka *"purple haze"* = recurrence of flashbacks of earlier *bad trips*, triggered by exercise, stress, or illness

LSD Intoxication

General Management

- **"Coma cocktail" IV:** 100 mL $D_{50}W$ + 100 mg thiamine + 2 mg naloxone; secure AW
- **AC + sorbitol (1 g/kg):** For recent ingestions; ineffective once hallucinations begin
- **Acute panic reactions:** Quiet room—no stimuli, reassurance by nonjudgmental advocate
- **"Bad trip" dysphoria:** Sedation with BZs
- **Avoid excessive physical restraint:** 2° ↑ rhabdomyolysis risks with ↑ CFRs

Specific Treatment

- **HTN:** BZs initially, then vasodilators = phentolamine, nifedipine, SCN
- **Avoid all neuroleptics:** 2° α-Block-↓ BP, hyperthermia, and ↓ seizure threshold
- **Avoid β and mixed α- and β-blockers:** 2° Risks of unopposed α-adrenergic-mediated HTN
- **Hyperthermia:** Aggressive external cooling, IV hydration, BZs and MRs
- **Monitor for rhabdomyolysis:** ↑ CPK, myoglobinuria, protect renal function—diuresis + alkalinization

Drug Abuse: Plant Hallucinogens

- **Reps:** Morning glory ("LSD") and Hawaiian baby woodrose seeds, peyote cactus, nutmeg and mace (*Myristica fragrans*, resembles MDMA = *Ecstasy* toxicity)
- **Toxins:** *Lysergamide* (LSD-like), *mescaline*, and *myristicin* (MMDA)
- **Antidote:** None
- **Dx:** Initial N and V, diaphoresis, mental status changes, deep sleep (nutmeg), hallucinations
- **Tx:** GI decontamination, supportive

Neurotoxicity

Plant Hallucinogens

- *Morning glory* (Lysergamide)
- *Peyote cactus* (Mescaline)
- *Wormwood—absinthe* (Thujones)
- *Morning glory* (Lysergamide—LSD)

Hallucinogens

- *Hawaiian baby woodrose, Argyreia nervosa*: Like its relative morning glory's seeds, the seeds of the Hawaiian baby woodrose contain ergine, an *LSD-like compound* detected by mass spectrometry. Purchase 100 seeds for $10 online and use 10–12 per hallucinogenic trip.

Plant Hallucinogens: Morning Glory

Argyreia nervosa, Hawaiian baby woodrose: Seeds contain ergine, LSD derivative
Ipomoea purpurea, common morning glory: Seeds contain less LSD derivatives
Absinthe or wormwood (*Artemesia absinthium*)

- A ubiquitous herb that produces an oily terpene extract added to wines and liquors that contains *thujone*, a GABA and serotonin (5-HT) agonist that causes hallucinations. Example: Vincent van Gogh's right ear and his painting *Starry Night*.
- *Artemesia absinthium*: Note yellow blooms also contain thujone.

Nutmeg (*Myristica fragrans*)

- Indonesian and Caribbean tropical tree with fruit producing two spices from ground-up nut and *red* aril. Both contain *myristicin* and *elemicin*. *Myristicin*, a weak MAOI, is hepatically metabolized to amphetamine-like (MDMA) hallucinogens. Large doses must be consumed for psychoactive effects.
- *Nutmeg is the nut and mace is the red* covering or aril.

Belladonna Alkaloids: Atropa belladonna

Deadly nightshade (flowers)
Deadly nightshade (berries)

Belladonna Alkaloids

- **Reps:** Nightshade, jessamine, Jimson weed (thornapple), *Solandra* spp. (Angel's trumpet, common in NO)
- **Toxins:** *Atropine* = hyoscyamine, *scopolamine* = hyoscine
- **Antidote:** Physostigmine for CNS effects
- **Dx:** Atropine tox = F, dry mouth, tachycardia, ileus, urinary retention, hallucinations, seizures, "red as a beet, etc."
- **Tx:** GI decontamination
- *Datura stramonium* (Jimson weed—atropine antidote), *Brugmasia candida* (Angel's trumpet), *Solandra guttata* (Gold trumpet)

Neurotoxic Plant Poisonings

La Familia Belladonna

Datura stramonium	*Datura wrightii*	*Brugmasia candida*
Jimsonweed	Thorn apple	Angel's trumpet

Plant Hallucinogens: *Salvia divinorum*

- **Chem:** *Salvia divinorum*: diviner-seer's sage long used by Mazatec shamans of Oaxaca to induce visionary trances in spiritual ceremonies contains the diterpenoid, *salvinorum A*, unique *kappa opioid receptor agonist*
- **Epid (United States):** 2006: 1.8 M over age 12 had used
- **Methods:** Ingesting fresh leaves, extracts of dried leaves in seasonings, tinctures of leaves soaked in H_2O/EtOH

Salvia leaves and flowers (likes shade and rarely blooms)

- **Clin:** Spiritual and other visions, fluctuating mood–insight–connectedness–self-confidence–concentration–temperature sensations; lightheadedness, flying–floating; calmness– "afterglow."
- **Addiction potential:** Possible, low. Driving impaired.
- **Regulation:** Not scheduled, use is illegal in several states, including LA.
- **Availability:** Increasingly available on the Internet.

Salvia is sold locally in states where legal and on the Internet everywhere.

Plants—Nonamphetamine Appetite Suppressants

Hoodia gordonii: What Is *Hoodia*?

- **Def:** *Hoodia*, a cactus-like, spiny succulent native to Namib (SW Africa) and Kalahari Deserts (SE Africa) with tan, foul-smelling, bitter-tasting flowers, is used by indigenous bushmen for stamina/appetite suppression during droughts and treks. Unilever poised to market worldwide as appetite suppressant, but abandoned strategy (2008) 2° lack of evidence to support efficacy and safety.

- **Mechanism of action (MoA):** May be 2° steroid glycosides and bitter taste, which ↓ *cholecystokinin release*? *Available worldwide*: GNC and net.

Miscellaneous Serotonergic Hallucinogens

***Indolealkylamines**—Psilocybe mushrooms*

***Indolealkylamines**—Bufo alvarius—bufotenine*

Drug Abuse: Marijuana

Outline

- Epidemiology and pharmacology of marijuana usage
- Acute vs. chronic marijuana toxicity
- Diagnosis and management of marijuana toxicity

Epidemiology and Pharmacology

Epidemiology

- Marijuana is an oily, dried fibrous material obtained from the Indian hemp plant, *Cannabis sativa.*
- The most commonly used illegal substance in the United States.
- The most commonly abused substance in the world after nicotine, alcohol, and caffeine.
- Considered a *gateway drug* by DEA, NIDA, and SAMHSA.

Pharmacology

- *Δ-9-Tetrahydrocannibinol*: Psychoactive component.
- *Hashish* (smoked in pipes) and *hashish oil* (mixed with tobacco and smoked): *Cannabis* derivatives that contain higher concentrations of THC.
- THC is transported to the brain within 15 s of smoking to occupy specific *cannabinoid receptors* in the cerebral cortex.

Acute vs. Chronic Toxicity

Acute Marijuana Toxicity

- **Physiological effects:** Dose-related ↑ HR, BP stable, ↑ appetite, *conjunctival injection*, ↓ *intraocular pressure*, bronchodilation, weakness, muscle tremors, urinary retention, ↓ *testosterone levels.*
- **Psychological effects:** Dose-related, euphoria, relaxation, sensory alterations. Preexisting psychopathology may predispose to transient, acute psychotic reactions with paranoid delusions and hallucinations.

Chronic Marijuana Toxicity

- **Tolerance and dependence:** 2° repeated use
- **Withdrawal syndrome:** Irritability, restlessness, insomnia, and appetite loss
- **COPD and lung cancer:** Smoking induced
- **Congenital toxicity:** Neonatal and early childhood neurobehavioral and developmental disturbances
- **Male infertility:** ↓ testosterone levels, ↓ sperm count and motility, ↑ abnormal sperm morphology

Mx: Marijuana Intoxication

- **Motor vehicle and other transportation-related accidents:** Marijuana detected in 11–33% of cases (including mass transit and train accidents) and causes a prolonged (24 h) loss of judgment and motor skills needed for safe vehicular operation.
- **Acute psychotic reactions:** Sedation with BZs.
- **Pneumomediastinum:** Rare and 2° deep inhalation with alveolar overdistension rupture; supportive management with O_2.

Drug Abuse: Synthetic Cannabis

- Synthetic cannabis, best known in the United States as K2 or Spice, and sold in gas stations, head and smoke shops as herbal incense, is a combination of synthetic cannabinoids and herbs that when abused by smoking mimics the effects of THC and can cause chronic psychotic disorders in susceptible individuals with family histories of mental illness. Metabolites can be detected in urine, but not with NIDA 5 screens.
- **Street names:** K2, Spice, Spice Gold, Kronic (Australia).
- *K2 and Spice = synthetic cannabis.*

The Synthetic Cathinones

Natural Cathinone *(Khat)*

- *Synthetic cathinones'* parent compound, *cathinone* (*khat*), and its active metabolite (cathine), have been used as amphetamine-like euphoric stimulants and appetite suppressants for centuries, especially in the horn of Africa (Ethiopia and Somalia; *Blackhawk Down*) and in Yemen. In 2006, there were approximately 10 million chronic *khat* users worldwide. *Khat* users chew on the twigs or leaves of the *khat plant*, *Catha edulis.*
- *Khat* suppresses appetite during Ethiopian famine.
- *Khat* is now sold illegally throughout Europe.

Drug Abuse: What Are "Bath Salts?"

- Bath salts are synthetic cathinones, amphetamine-like powders, primarily methylenedioxypyrovalerone (MDPV) with 4× the potency of methylphenidate (Ritalin®,

Concerta®); sold in gas stations and convenience stores as "bath salts" for recreational abuse by ingestion, insufflation, rectal, and IV use. They cause a sympathetic toxidrome characterized by hallucinations and paranoia, often complicated by HTN and angina.

- **MoA:** Inhibits reuptake of dopamine and NE.
- **Street names:** Ivory Snow, Ivory Wave, Bolivian Bath, Bliss, Purple Wave, Super Coke, Peeve, Magic.

Drug Abuse: "Date-Rape" Drugs

- *Gamma-hydroxybutyrate* (GHB, gamma-hydroxybutyric acid) and its precursors or prodrugs: Gamma-butyrolactone (GBL) and 1, 4-butanediol (BD)
- Flunitrazepam (Rohypnol®)

"Date-Rape": GHB

Medical Toxicology

Toxicokinetics

- **Street names:** Liquid Ecstasy, Easy Lay.
- **GHB is an active GABA metabolite:** GHB is a naturally occurring CNS (brain) metabolite of GABA, the central inhibitory neurotransmitter.
- **Rapid oral absorption:** Peak onset in 15 min; duration 1.5–2 h.

Clinical Manifestations

- **CNS:** Initial relaxation, tranquility, *disinhibition*; followed rapidly by loss of consciousness, delirium, *amnesia*, rarely seizures
- **CP:** Bradycardia, mild hypotension, transient respiratory depression
- **GI:** Vomiting

"Date-Rape": GBL

Medical Toxicology

Toxicokinetics

- **Street names:** Liquid Ecstasy, Easy Lay, Russian Roulette, Ruffies.
- **GBL is a precursor drug or prodrug to GHB:** GBL is a sweet-smelling oily liquid, highly soluble in alcohol/water, used as stain/superglue remover, paint stripper. Highly lipophilic and rapidly converted to GHB by plasma lactonases causing intoxication at low doses and sedation and unconsciousness at higher doses. Potentiated by EtOH in potentially fatal combinations (Hester Stewart, medical student, died age 21, United Kingdom, 2009).
- **Rapid oral absorption:** Peak onset in 5–10 min; duration 1.5–2 h. Onset is more rapid than GHB. Easily available over the Internet.

GBL in liquid and powder forms for purchase on the Internet (seized by DEA).

"Date-Rape": GHB, GBL, BD

Use/Abuse and Mx

Methods of Use and Abuse

- **Licit use:** Narcolepsy, not FDA-approved in the United States
- **Ineffective use:** By *body builders* to promote rest, fasting, fat metabolism, muscle mass and ↑ growth hormone levels
- **Illicit use:** "Date-rape"

General Mx of OD

- **AW protection:** Monitor oxygenation and ventilation
- **Consider coma cocktail:** Flumazenil and naloxone ineffective
- **Atropine:** For bradycardia
- Consider *physostigmine* for reversal of CNS depression

"Date-Rape": Flunitrazepam

Toxicokinetics

- **Rohypnol®:** Foreign trade name, U.S. street drug
- **Short-acting benzodiazepine:** 7–10 times as potent as diazepam
- **Rapid oral absorption:** Peak onset in 15–20 min; duration 4–6 h

Clinical Manifestations and Mx

- Profound CNS depression with maintenance of stable vital signs; characteristic of BZs
- Anterograde *amnesia* common
- **General OD mx:** Supportive, protect AW, monitor oxygenation and ventilation
- **Antidote:** *Flumazenil*

Prescription Drug (Rx) Abuse

Prescription Rx Abuse—United States, 2012

- Rx drug abuse has exceeded illicit substance abuse.
- Commonly abused Rx's include opioid combinations (Vicodin®), methadone, BZs (Valium®, Xanax®), and Soma® (carisoprodol).
- Fatalities are ↑, especially from combinations of opioids + BZs + EtOH.
- Latest Rx's abused = dextromethorphan, propofol (Diprivan®), tramadol (Ultram®), buprenorphine (Suboxone®).

Miscellaneous prescription drug abuse (usually by athletes and sports figures):

- **Anabolic steroids:** Abused by weightlifters, baseball players, other athletes—aka *roids, juice, gym candy, pumpers.*
- **Beta-agonists:** All MDI beta-agonist bronchodilators have been abused to enhance performance by cyclists, runners—albuterol (Proventil®), and so on.

- **Erythropoietin:** Abused to increase oxygen-carrying capacity and stamina—Epogen®, *epo.*

Nonprescription (OTC) Drug Abuse

- **Pseudoephedrine:** All pseudoephedrine-containing drugs can be used to make illicit methamphetamines (MDMA and others) in small meth labs, including all decongestants and antihistamines + decongestants—Sudafed®, Claritin D®, Zyrtec D®, Allegra D®.
- **Dextromethorphan:** A codeine analog and cough suppressant dispensed as syrup, gel caps, tablets; Robitussin®, Delsym®.

OTC Drug Abuse: Dextromethorphan

- **DXM Chem:** Opioid analog, SSRI, NMDA antagonist such as PCP and ketamine, sigma agonist
- **Street names:** *Robo, robo-tripper, triple C* (Coricidin D®), *purple drank*
- **Methods:** Ingestion
- **Clin:** Dissociative—an "out of body experience," euphoria, vivid imagination, psychosis, hallucinations

Volatile Substance Abuse

Outline

VOCs commonly abused by adolescents (and celebrities)

Alkyl nitrites (poppers) #1

Aerosol propellants #2

- CFCs
- Nitrous oxide gas

Typewriter correction fluids/dry cleaning agents #3

- Trichloroethane
- Trichloroethylene
- Perchloroethylene

Butane lighter refills

- Propane gas canisters
- Gasoline

VOCs commonly abused in industries

Glues and paints: *Occupational #1*

- Benzene
- Toluene
- Naptha

- *n*-Hexane
- Xylene

Gasoline, kerosene
Liquid anesthetics (abused in health care industry)
- Ether, enflurane, desflurane, isoflurane

VOC Abuse: Methods

- **Techniques:** Sniffing → huffing → bagging
- **Agents:** Toluene (glues, paints) → fuels (butane, gasoline) → TCE and PCE (correction fluids—White Out®, Liquid Paper®) → dry cleaning fluids (acetone, CCl_4, TCE, PCE) → propellants (CFCs, nitrous oxide)
- **Acute tox:** *CNS* excitation, *euphoria*, hallucinations, ataxia, seizures, HA, respiratory depression > *CV* tachyarrhythmias → *"sudden sniffing death"* > *heme*—methemoglobinemia > *hepatotoxicity* (*CCL_4*) and *CO poisoning* (*methylene chloride*)
- **Chronic tox:** *"Glue-sniffers"* or toluene *encephalopathy*/chronic "painter's syndrome": Leukoencephalopathies characterized by memory and cognitive losses, dementia, insomnia, anxiety and depression, personality disorder, ataxia and chorea, peripheral neuropathy (*n*-hexane, MIBK)
- **Epidemiology:** 5–10% HS students; >60 deaths year/United States and much greater among street children in SE Asia and Africa; male:female = 5:1; butane lighter refills are the most commonly abused VOCs

VOC Abuse: Poppers

- **Chem:** Colorless liquids, vasodilating alkyl nitrites (amyl, butyl, isobutyl, and isopropyl) related to sildanafil (Viagra®). Available in drugs, air fresheners, video head–computer monitor cleaners.
- **Street names:** "Poppers" 2° popping sound on crushing ampoules of amyl nitrite (cyanide antidote); push, ram, rave, rush, snappers, liquid gold, locker room, and so on.
- **Regulation:** *None.*
- **Path:** Vasodilation, warmth, dizziness, acute sexual arousal. On OD and with chronic abuse may cause HA, ↓BP, arrhythmias, loss of consciousness, vision loss, retinal damage, blindness, methemoglobinemia, hemolysis, acute renal failure (G-6-PD), lipoid pneumonia on aspiration, angina–MI in older men with preexisting CAD.
- **Tx:** Restore BP immediately.
- **Antidote:** Methylene blue, works best for amyl.

Carcinogenic vs. Neurotoxic VOCs

Carcinogenic HCs

- Benzene—AML
- Vinyl chloride—hepatic angiosarcoma

- PAHs—colon cancer
- Formaldehyde—nasal and laryngeal cancers
- Chloroform and methylene chloride—liver cancers?
- CCl_4, TCE, perc—animal cancers only

CNS Leukoencephalopathies

- Toluene—paints and glues
- TCE—trigeminal neuralgia
- Glycol ethers and styrene

Peripheral Neuropathies

- *n*-Hexane—axonopathy
- Acrylamide and styrene
- Methyl-*n*-butyl ketone—axon (*MEK* and *MIBK nontoxic*)
- 2,5-*Hexanedione* (MBK and MNBK metabolite)
- CS_2 and ethylene oxide gas

Drug Abuse: Anesthetic Drug Abuse

Outline

- Nitrous oxide
- Ketamine (cat Valium, special K, vitamin K)
- Propofol (milk of amnesia)
- **Benzodiazepines:** Diazepam, midazolam, lorazepam
- **Opioids:** Morphine, meperidine, methadone, alfentanil, sufentanil, fentanyl
- **Opioid agonists:** Tramadol
- **Agonists/antagonists:** Buprenorphine

Inhalant Abuse: Nitrous Oxide

- **Use:** N_2O, a colorless, nonflammable, sweet-smelling greenhouse gas used as a dissociative anesthetic, propellant for spray cans and race cars, is abused for its euphoric effects.
- **Chem:** Oxidizes dietary B12 as cofactor for methionine (myelin) and THF (DNA) synthesis.
- **Path:** Toxic B12 deficiency, subacute combined degeneration of dorsal columns and LMNs (chronic myeloneuropathy), megaloblastic nonpernicious anemia.
- **Demi Moore:** *A nitrous oxide abuser.*
- **Street names:** Laughing/sweet gas, wank, whip-it, whippets, whip cream, cream, nossies.
- **High risk:** Medical personnel, adolescents, actors/actresses—celebrities (no drug screens, no needle marks, difficult to detect).

- **Clin:** Glove and stocking sensory loss, especially vibratory, but sparing most motor fx, pain and temperature sensation. Targets dorsal columns; ataxic, poor tandem gait.
- **Dx:** NCT, ↑↓ B12, ↑↑ MMA and homocysteine. *Tx*: B12 IM and po.
- *Demi Moore was hospitalized for* N_2O abuse, NYC, January 2012.

Anesthetic Drug Abuse: What Is Propofol?

Propofol is an alkylphenol derivative, 2,6-diisopropyl-phenol, marketed initially by AstraZeneca as Diprivan® (*Di*iso*pr*opyl *IV an*esthetic) and FDA-approved (1989) for use as a short-acting IV hypnotic-sedative for induction of GA, procedural sedation, and sedation for mechanical ventilation in an ICU.

Why Milk of Amnesia?

Propofol Chemistry

- Owing to its water insolubility, 1% propofol is formulated in a liquid emulsion of *10% soybean oil, 1.2% purified egg whites, 2.25% glycerol, with NaOH to alkalinize (causes ↑ pain on injection)* and 1 of the following preservatives: EDTA, benzyl alcohol,* or Na metabisulfite,† depending on the drug manufacturer.
- **The color is** glistening opaque white due to light scatter by oil droplets of soybean and egg phospholipids = "milk of amnesia."

Propofol: Propofol's Mechanism of Action—MoA?

Propofol's exact mechanisms of action are *unknown* but may include:

1. Direct activation of CNS $GABA_A$ receptors, ↓ channel closing time
2. Inhibition of NMDA receptors
3. Modulation of calcium influx through slow calcium-ion channels
4. CNS sodium channel blockade?

Like other sedative-hypnotics, propofol is a $GABA_A$ agonist. GABA inhibits CNS electrical transmission within the CNS.

Propofol Abuse

The recreational use and abuse of propofol has been increasing *among medical personnel* and *insomniacs* primarily for the following reasons:

- Propofol is *not scheduled as Class IV by the FDA* and is undetected by *urine tox screens.*

---

* "Gasping baby" syndrome in neonates.

† Allergic reactions to sulfites.

- Propofol *activates cannabinoid receptors* and causes euphoria highs, disinhibition, and hallucinations.
- Propofol induces *short* and *deep restful sleep* in night shift workers and insomniacs. Long-term use is *addictive.*
- *Four deaths* have now been reported from propofol self-administration.

The Michael Jackson (1958–2009) Case: Propofol Death

On June 25, 2009, Dr. Conrad Murray administered *25 mg* (2.5 mL) of propofol diluted in 1% lidocaine to Michael Jackson at his home, Neverland, in Beverly Hills, CA. In August 2009, the LA Coroner concluded that Michael Jackson died from *respiratory arrest from a mixture of propofol and two benzodiazepines*, (1) IV lorazepam on top of (2) po *diazepam* ingested earlier. On November 7, 2011, jurors found Dr. Conrad Murray guilty of involuntary manslaughter, and he was sentenced to 4 years in the LA County jail on November 29, 2011.

Propofol Infusion Syndrome

What Is the Propofol Infusion Syndrome (PRIS)?

Definition Propofol, a popular sedative-hypnotic, is commonly used for induction of general anesthesia and sedation in the intensive care unit (ICU). It is preferred over other agents for its rapid onset of action, rapid emergence from sedation, and reduced likelihood of nausea and vomiting. Despite these advantages, propofol may rarely cause a typically fatal condition known as propofol infusion syndrome, or PRIS [1–4]. The diagnosis of PRIS is usually by exclusion because patients often exhibit other potentially fatal comorbidities, including metabolic acidosis, acute renal failure, and rhabdomyolysis.

History The name “propofol infusion syndrome” was coined in 1998 when Bray summarized 13 more propofol-related deaths of children; all of whom exhibited a similar constellation of symptoms, including metabolic acidosis, lipemic serum, and refractory bradycardia progressing to asystole [2]. In 1996, Merinella was the first author to suggest that a propofol reaction should be included in the differential diagnosis of metabolic acidosis developing in adult patients during long-term sedation with propofol [3]. In 1998, the first case of PRIS in an adult was reported. In this case, nearly all of the earlier presenting signs of PRIS in pediatric patients were described, including hypoxia, metabolic acidosis, rhabdomyolysis, renal failure, and cardiac dysfunction [4].

Risk Factors Despite over 20 years of intensive research, the complete pathophysiological mechanisms responsible for PRIS have not been identified. Potential risk factors for PRIS include high-dose infusions of propofol for lengthy periods of time. These risk factors were first described in a series of five cases reported in 1992 in relatively healthy children with acute epiglottis or tracheobronchitis who died after being sedated with propofol in the ICU. In these cases, the pediatric patients developed metabolic acidosis, lipemic serum, and refractory bradycardia progressing to asystole [1].

Epidemiology The true incidence of PRIS is unknown. Roberts described 1017 critically ill patients receiving propofol infusions for longer than 24 h in 2009 and found the incidence of PRIS to be 1.1% [5]. Later, the Food and Drug Administration's MEDWATCH system analyzed 1139 suspected cases of PRIS and estimated an incidence of approximately 30% [6]. In addition to the confusion regarding the true incidence of PRIS, there remains no consensus on the management of PRIS other than early recognition and discontinuation of propofol.

Clinical Manifestations The clinical manifestations that have come to define PRIS include the development of metabolic acidosis, rhabdomyolysis (skeletal > cardiac); cardiac arrhythmias (including right bundle branch block, Brugada-like syndrome, atrial fibrillation, supraventricular tachycardia, ventricular tachycardia, ventricular fibrillation, and electromechanical dissociation); acute renal failure; lipemic serum; hepatomegaly; and fatal cardiac arrest [2]. It has been suggested that the onset of PRIS is related to the inhibition of intracellular energy production by mitochondria, possibly by the following two mechanisms: (1) inhibition of transportation of long-chain fatty acids into cells during the nutritionally deficient states of critical illnesses; and/or (2) inhibitory effects on the intracellular mitochondrial respiratory chain [7]. The metabolic derangements in PRIS appear to be triggered by (1) metabolic stress and high energy demand during critical illness in susceptible patients; (2) low carbohydrate supplies, especially in children; and (3) a high availability of fats, as in propofol's emulsion of soybean oil and egg whites [8,9]. However, anything that inhibits effective cellular aerobic respiration may result in lactic acidosis that, if left untreated, may result in rhabdomyolysis, hyperkalemia, and, ultimately, acute renal failure. Other risk factors for PRIS include respiratory infection, severe head injury, propofol sedation for more than 48 h at doses greater than 4 mg/kg/h, and increased catecholamine and glucocorticoid serum levels [8]. A meta-analysis by Fong et al. found that death from PRIS was more likely if a patient was younger than 18, received a vasopressor, or developed any of the following symptoms: cardiac arrhythmias, rhabdomyolysis, impairment in renal function, metabolic acidosis, or dyslipidemia [6].

Differential Diagnosis (See Table 8.1) Congenital cardiac conduction disorders, such as Brugada syndrome, an autosomal dominant disorder in right ventricular conduction, can result in sudden death. Genetic polymorphisms that affect lipid metabolism, such as medium-chain acyl-coenzyme A dehydrogenase deficiency may also be risk factors for PRIS and should be included in the differential diagnosis. Medications can also be a cause of laboratory derangements resembling PRIS. The medications that should be considered when ruling out PRIS either have the capability to cause muscle injury or have been shown to cause renal damage. Finally, miscellaneous conditions that need to be considered in the differential diagnosis of PRIS include the use of typical antipsychotics in bipolar patients and the presence of ongoing seizures in an epileptic patient, both of which can cause rhabdomyolysis.

Recommendations Today, a presumptive diagnosis of PRIS includes rhabdomyolysis, hyperkalemia, hyperlipidemia, and ARF in adults receiving high-dose propofol infusions

Table 8.1 A Differential Diagnosis of Propofol Infusion Syndrome (PRIS)

Congenital	Metabolic	Medications	Miscellaneous
Brugada syndrome	Hypoperfusion	HMG-CoA reductase inhibitors	Direct muscle injury
MCADD	Hypoxia	Corticosteroids	Hypoxia from traumatic lung Injury
Hereditary monogenic disorders	Sepsis	Renal toxic antibiotics	Seizures
	Diabetic ketoacidosis	ACE inhibitors/angiotensin receptor blockers	Immobilization
		Renal toxic chemotherapeutic	Myoclonus
		Agents	Neuroleptic malignant syndrome
		Cimetidine	Contrast-induced acute kidney injury
		Protease inhibitors	

MCADD: medium-chain acyl-coenzyme A dehydrogenase deficiency.

(>4 mg/kg/h) for prolonged (>48 h) periods. If possible, propofol should not be used as sedation for greater than 3 days. During propofol infusions, clinicians should monitor arterial blood gases, serum triglycerides, creatine kinase, all electrolytes (particularly potassium), serum lactate levels, and creatinine. The true incidence of PRIS remains unknown, and more objective criteria for its diagnosis need to be established. Future large prospective, randomized controlled trials comparing outcomes of several sedation protocols in ICU patients will be needed to determine the true incidence of PRIS, to identify genetically susceptible patients, and to develop clinical guidelines for propofol sedation without increasing risks of PRIS.

Epilogue: Drug and Illicit Substance Abuse

Prescription Drug Abuse Epidemic

Response Roles for Physicians

Today, several population health trends have developed, including a worldwide epidemic of prescription drug abuse and "drugged" driving. However, new research in prescription drug abuse has resulted in the identification of validated risk factors for substance abuse of all types, and a paradigm shift in the management and prevention of substance abuse.

Several significant changes have occurred in the selection of pharmaceutical substances to abuse and their regulation and criminalization in the United States and Europe over the past century. As trade expanded throughout the Pacific Rim nations after the Spanish–American War, Chinese and Filipino immigrants brought recreational opium use with them from Asia at a time when U.S. opiate abusers could easily and legally obtain opiates from their local physicians and pharmacists. Opiates were often prescribed for gastrointestinal and menstrual disorders, especially in women. In the late 1890s, some carbonated beverages even contained cocaine or lithium and were also prescribed for medical and mental disorders.

By the beginning of the twentieth century, the distribution of opium and cocaine, and later heroin, became linked to organized crime, and the Federal government responded by enacting a series of laws to control "illicit" drug distribution, beginning with the Harrison Narcotics Tax Act of 1914. Although Federal regulation of illegal drugs has continued over the years, the Controlled Substances Act of 1970 scheduled all prescribed medications by their abuse potentials. In 1914, one U.S. citizen in every 400 (0.25%) was addicted to a medication containing opium [10]. By 2008, however, over six million persons, or 2.5% of the U.S. population age 12 and older, reported past 30-day use of a prescribed psychotherapeutic drug for nonmedical purposes [11]. This is more than the total number of people in the United States today who abuse cocaine, heroin, amphetamines, benzodiazepines, and inhalants combined [11].

There is no denying the current epidemic of prescription drug abuse, drug-induced fatal overdoses, and "drugged" driving. Several factors have contributed to the development of this epidemic, including an increased recognition of pain as the "fifth vital sign"; a greater emphasis on treating pain, especially noncancer pain using opioids, as popularized by advocacy groups; and an overwhelming pharmaceutical industry response with new continuous-release and long-acting opioids. As a result, practitioners have dramatically increased their rates of opioid prescribing over the past two decades. From 1990 to 1996, prescriptions for four opioid analgesics increased significantly: morphine by 59%, fentanyl by 1168%, oxycodone by 23%, and hydromorphone by 19% [12]. From 1997 to 2001, prescriptions for three opioid analgesics confirmed further increasing use of morphine by 48.8%, fentanyl by 151.2%, and oxycodone by 347.9% [13]. Prescriptions for controlled substances increased faster and to a significantly greater extent than prescriptions for noncontrolled drugs [11]. From 1992 until 2002, the number of prescriptions for controlled drugs increased by 154.3% compared to an increase in prescriptions for noncontrolled drugs of only 56.6% at a time when the U.S. population only grew by only 13% [11]. As the number of prescriptions for controlled drugs grew, the number of people abusing controlled drugs for nonmedical reasons grew, especially among high-risk groups for substance abuse and drug overdose deaths.

Emergency department visits for prescription drug overdoses increased by over 100% from 627,291 visits in 2004 to 1,244,679 visits in 2009 (Figure 8.13) [14]. Prescription drug-induced overdose deaths also increased substantially over the same time periods [14]. In 2007, the U.S. Centers for Disease Control and Prevention (CDC) reported approximately 27,000 unintentional drug overdose deaths in the United States or 1 death every 19 min (Figure 8.14) [14]. Since 2003, more unintentional drug overdose deaths in the United States have involved opioid analgesics more than the number of annual deaths from cocaine and heroin overdoses combined (Figure 8.15) [14]. For every opioid overdose death, 9 persons are admitted for substance abuse treatment, 35 visit emergency departments, 161 admit to drug abuse or dependence, and 461 report nonmedical use of opioid analgesics [15]. Unintentional annual drug overdose deaths in the United States have now surpassed the annual number of automotive crash fatalities in 16 states; are more than double the annual number of murders in the United States

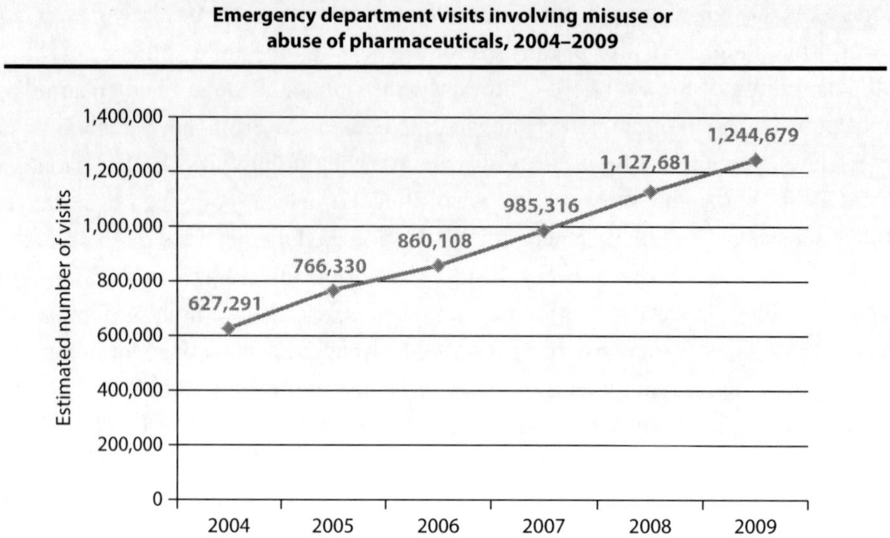

FIGURE 8.13 Increasing number of emergency department visits involving misuse or abuse of pharmaceuticals, 2004–2009. (Courtesy of the Substance Abuse and Mental Health Services Administration [SAMHSA], Drug Abuse Warning Network [DAWN], 2009.)

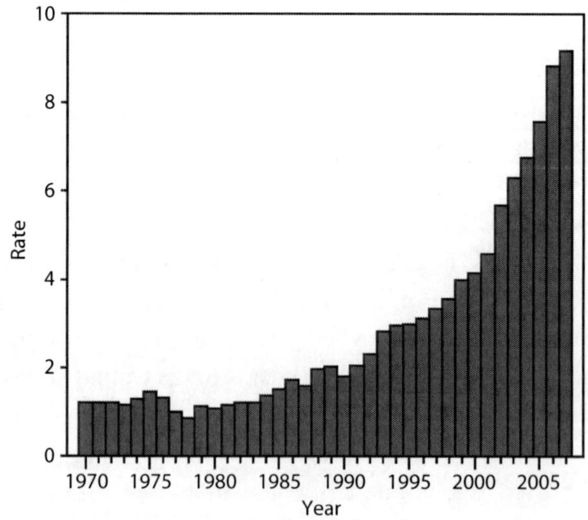

FIGURE 8.14 Increasing incidence rates for unintentional drug overdose deaths in the United States per 100,000 persons, 1970–2007. (Courtesy of the CDC.)

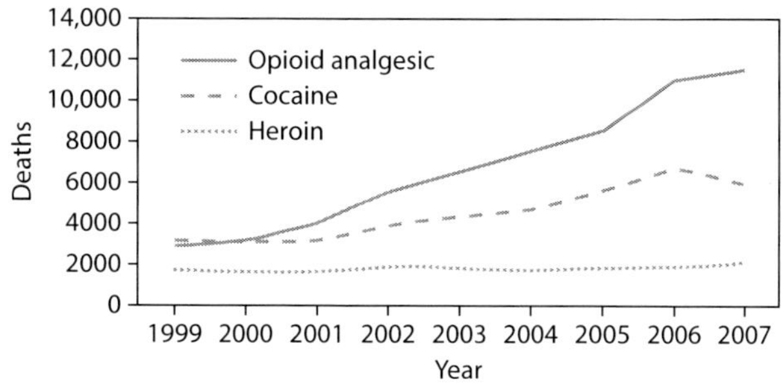

FIGURE 8.15 Increasing number of deaths per year from opioid analgesic overdoses compared to the deaths from overdoses of cocaine and heroin, United States, 1995–2007. (Courtesy of the CDC.)

(approximately 17,000/year); and are greater than the annual number of suicides (approximately 33,000/year) (Figure 8.16) [16]. The prescription opioid abuse epidemic has resulted in lives lost unnecessarily, families decimated, and spiraling direct annual health care costs, estimated at $72.5 billion in 2010 [17]. At the same time, the U.S. pharmaceutical industry has grossed billions of dollars annually in opioid sales.

In addition to drug overdose deaths, drivers are now operating vehicles while under the influence of controlled substances both when the medications are taken as properly prescribed and when the medications are taken for nonmedical and recreational reasons [11]. In 2009, Compton and Berning reported that 3.9% of weekend nighttime drivers were positive for

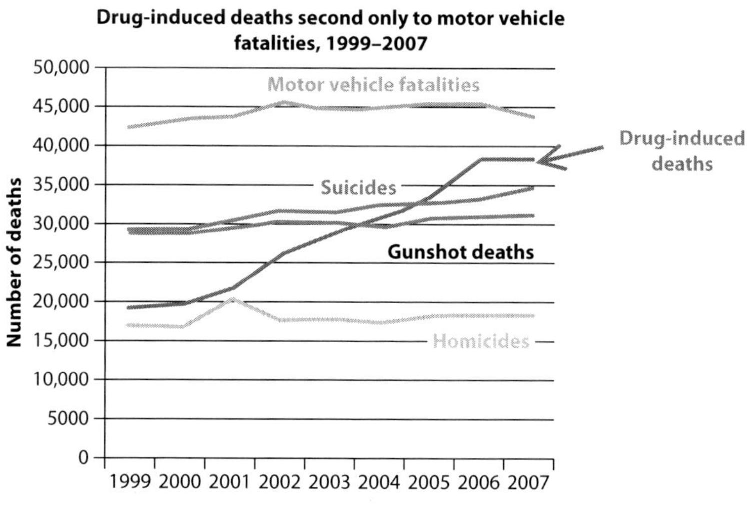

FIGURE 8.16 Drug-induced deaths per year compared to deaths from motor vehicle fatalities and other causes of death, United States, 1999–2010. (Courtesy of the CDC, National Center for Health Statistics [NCHS].)

controlled substances [18]. In a study of seriously injured motor vehicle crash victims admitted to the University of Maryland shock-trauma unit in 2004, Walsh and coauthors reported that 10.2% tested positive for opioids and 7.9% tested positive for anxiolytics, including benzodiazepines [19]. In a CDC study of motor vehicle crash fatalities in West Virginia in 2006, 7.9% of deceased drivers tested positive for opioids, and another 7.9% tested positive for anxiolytics, including benzodiazepines [11]. Not only are drugged drivers killing themselves in motor vehicle crashes, they are also injuring and killing their vehicular occupants and many other crash victims.

The most important high-risk groups for substance abuse include (1) non-Hispanic white males between the ages of 20–64 years often residing in poor or rural regions; (2) all young adults between the ages of 18–25, especially those reporting any lifetime use of controlled substances for nonmedical reasons; (3) persons who seek controlled substances from friends and relatives or visit emergency departments seeking opioid analgesics; (4) patients with chronic noncancer pain with manifestations of opioid dependence and tolerance; (5) medical personal with ease of access to opioid analgesics; and, even, (6) patients newly prescribed opioids after short-stay surgeries who exhibit a 44% increased risk of becoming long-term opioid users within 1 year [20,21].

In a recent retrospective cohort study of anesthesiology residents in training during the period 1975–2009 (N = 44,612 residents), Warner and coauthors reported that 384 (0.86%) had evidence of substance use disorder, primarily opioid abuse, with high relapse rates over 30 years (43%) and significant case fatality rates from drug overdoses (7.3%, n = 28) [20].

The nonmedical abuse of controlled substances is a common problem among high school and college students. In 2008, 4.7% of high school seniors used OxyContin®, 5.8% used Vicodin®, and 2.4% used Ritalin® nonmedically [22]. Among college students, the abuse of opioid analgesics and amphetamines used to treat attention deficit hyperactivity disorder (ADHD) is pervasive and intended to either improve academic performance with stimulants or enhance the intoxicating highs produced by other drugs, including alcohol. In a study of college undergraduates taking prescription medications, Garnier and coauthors reported that 61.7% diverted amphetamines to others, and 35.1% diverted opioid analgesics to others [23].

The high-risk groups for controlled substance abuse have now been identified and must be targeted for a combination of new interventions in order to curb the epidemic of substance abuse and overdose deaths. These interventions will include combinations of improved, guideline-directed prescribing practices by physicians, especially for chronic nonmalignant conditions, such as low back pain, now known to be unimproved by long-term opioids; prescription drug monitoring programs (PDMP) and enforcement regulations; drugged-driving regulations similar to alcohol-impaired driving laws; controlled substance medication disposal programs to prevent diversion; opioid overdose fatality reduction programs with broader distribution of naloxone for emergency administration, even by nonmedical personnel; and, most importantly, improved treatment programs with new tamper-proof and abuse-proof medications, especially agonist–antagonist combinations [24,25].

Historically, the management of opioid dependence has been with opioid substitution, initially with heroin for opium addiction and later with methadone for heroin addiction. Recently, there has been a major paradigm shift in the management and prevention of opioid abuse away from pure opioid agonist substitution. The newest medication treatment for opioid dependence is buprenorphine, a partial opioid agonist, which may be combined with naloxone in sublingual preparations to prevent abuse and diversion. Buprenorphine has several advantages over methadone for opioid substitution, including improved safety profiles; decreased risks of abuse and diversion, especially when combined with naloxone or implanted subdermally; and ease of administration in office-based practices rather than in licensed methadone clinics [24,25]. In a recent randomized, placebo-controlled trial over 6 months in 2007–2008, Ling and coinvestigators divided 163 adults between 18 and 65 years of age with confirmed opioid dependence into a study group of 108 subjects randomized to receive four buprenorphine implants (80 mg per implant) and a control group of 55 subjects randomized to receive four placebo implants. At 16 weeks, the study subjects receiving the buprenorphine implants reported significantly lower ratings of opioid cravings, significantly fewer opioid withdrawal symptoms, and were significantly less likely to use opioids as assessed by urine drug samples compared to control subjects with placebo implants [25].

In order to protect public health and to improve patient safety, new paradigms in managing and preventing substance abuse must be implemented now and will include educating the public and physicians about the misuse and abuse of controlled substances. Government will have to implement better state and Federal prescription drug monitoring programs; and health care providers will need to target high-risk groups for new interventional treatment strategies, such as intranasal naloxone rescue to prevent opioid overdose deaths, and buprenorphine–naloxone preparations and buprenorphine implants to replace traditional opioid substitution in methadone clinics. Clinicians must prepare now to respond to the substance abuse epidemic by reviewing the pharmacology of frequently abused illicit and prescribed drugs; by recommending multidisciplinary management strategies for substance abuse; and by adopting several of the new treatment modalities for substance abuse, including partial agonists, such as buprenorphine; antagonists, such as naloxone; and nonopioid substitutes, such as clonidine and gabapentin.

References

1. Parke TJ, Stevens JE, Rice ASC et al. Metabolic acidosis and fatal myocardial failure after propofol infusion in children: Five case reports. *BMJ.* 1992;305(6854):613–616.
2. Bray RJ. Propofol infusion syndrome in children. *Paediatr Anaesth.* 1998;8(6):491–499.
3. Marinella MA. Lactic acidosis associated with propofol. *Chest* 1996;109(1):292.
4. Hanna JP, Ramundo ML. Rhabdomyolysis and hypoxia associated with prolonged propofol infusion in children. *Neurology* 1998;50:301–303.
5. Roberts RJ, Barletta JF, Fong JJ, Schumaker G, Kuper PJ, Papadopoulos S, et al. Incidence of propofol-related infusion syndrome in critically ill adults: A prospective, multicenter study. *Crit Care.* 2009;13:R169.
6. Fong JJ, Sylvia L, Ruthazer R, Schumaker G, Kcomt M, Devlin JW. Predictors of mortality in patients with suspected propofol infusion syndrome. *Crit Care Med.* 2008;36(8):2281–2287.
7. Diedrich DA, Brown DR. PRIS in the ICU. *J Intens Care Med* 2011;26:59–72.
8. Motsch J, Roggenbach J. [Propofol infusion syndrome]. *Anaesthesist.* 2004;53:1009–22.
9. Otterspoor LC, Kalkman CJ, Cremer OL. Update on the propofol infusion syndrome in ICU management of patients with head injury. *Curr Opin Anaesthesiol* 2008;21:544–551.

10. Kandall SR. Women and addiction in the United States—1850–1920. In Wetherington CL and Roman AB, Eds. *Drug Addiction Research and the Health of Women* 1998, Rockville, MD, National Institute on Drug Abuse, pp. 33–52.
11. Dupont RL. Prescription drug abuse: An epidemic dilemma. *J Psychoactive Drugs* 2010;42:127–132.
12. Joranson DE, Ryan KM, Gilson AM, Dahl JL. Trends in medical use and abuse of opioid analgesics. *J Am Med Assoc* 2000;283:1710–1714.
13. Novak S, Nemeth WC, Lawson KA. Trends in medical use and abuse of sustained-release opioid analgesics: A revisit. *Pain Med* 2004;5:59–65.
14. CDC Grand Rounds: Prescription Drug Overdoses—A U.S. Epidemic. *Morb Mort Week Rep* 2012;61:10–13.
15. Noudreau D, Von Kroff M, Rutter CM et al. Trends in long-term opioid therapy for chronic non-cancer pain. *Pharmacoepidemiol Drug Safe* 2009;18:1166–1175.o. 5 in CDC Grand Rounds.
16. Heron M, Hoyert D, Murphy S, et al. Deaths: Final data for 2006. *National Vital Statis Rep* 2009;57:14.
17. CDC Vital Signs Issue: Prescription painkiller overdoses in the U.S.—November 2011. Available at http://www.cdc.gov/vitalsigns.
18. Compton R, Berning A. *Results of the 2007 National Roadside Survey of Alcohol and Drug Use by Drivers.* Traffic Safety Facts DOT HS 811 175. Washington, DC; National Highway and Traffic Safety Administration, National Center for Statistics and Analysis.
19. Walsh JM, Fiegel R, Cangianelli LA et al. Epidemiology of alcohol and other drug use among motor vehicle crash victims admitted to a Level-1 trauma center. *Traffic Inj Prev* 2004;5:254–260.
20. Warner DO, Berge K, Sun H et al. Substance use disorder among anesthesiology residents, 1975–2009. *J Am Med Assoc* 2013;310:2289–2296.
21. Alam A, Gomes T, Zheng H et al. Long-term analgesic use after low-risk surgery: A retrospective cohort study. *Arch Intern Med* 2012;172:425–430.
22. Johnston LD, O'Malley PM, Bachman JG, Schulenberg JE. *Monitoring the Future: National Results on Adolescent Drug Use, Overview of Key findings, 2008.* NIH Publication No. 09-7401, 2009. Bethesda, MD: National Institute on Drug Abuse.
23. Garnier LM, Arria AM, Caldeira KM et al. Sharing and selling of prescription medications in a college student sample. *J Clin Psychiatr* 2010;71:262–269.
24. Beletsky L, Rich JD, Walley AY. Prevention of fatal opioid overdose. *J Am Med Assoc* 2012;308: 1863–1864.
25. Ling W, Casadonte P, Bigelow G et al. Buprenorphine implants for treatment of opioid dependence: A randomized controlled trial. *J Am Med Assoc* 2010;304:1576–1583.

Chapter 9

Anticonvulsants and Sedative-Hypnotics

Sedative-Hypnotics 208
Marijuana 215

Sedative-Hypnotics (SHs)

Definitions

- **Anticonvulsants:** Drugs that can prevent or stop seizure activity, including sedative-hypnotics (e.g., barbiturates and benzodiazepines [BZs])
- **Sedatives:** Drugs that reduce activity, moderate excitement, and exert a calming effect
- **Hypnotics:** Drugs that produce drowsiness and facilitate sleep
- **Anxiolytics:** Sedative-hypnotics that also have antianxiety properties (e.g., BZs, zolpidem, and buspirone)

Classification

- **Barbiturates:** Ultra-short acting, short acting, intermediate acting, long acting
- **Nonbarbiturates:** BZs, alcohols, piperidinediones, paraldehyde, meprobamate, new anxiolytics—zolpidem, buspirone

Mechanism

- **Barbiturates and BZs:** Enhance inhibitory GABA-mediated chloride currents in CNS by binding at different receptor sites on the GABA receptor–Cl ionophore complex
- **Barbiturates and BZs:** Potentiate each other's sedative, hypnotic, and anticonvulsant effects
- BZs also exert muscle relaxant effects centrally and peripherally
- **Antidote for BZs:** Flumazanil, a pure BZ-receptor antagonist

Pharmacology

- SHs induce sleep by reducing time to sleep onset, reducing REM sleep, increasing stage 2 non-REM sleep. In overdose, SHs depress CNS to stage III anesthesia.
- Tolerance to sedation in 1 week.
- Barbiturates and BZs are rapidly absorbed in SI; as their lipid solubility increases, blood–brain barrier penetration increases, and CNS depression increases.
- Lipid-soluble barbiturates and BZs are highly protein bound, poorly filtered renally, and not dialyzable. BZs are hepatically biotransformed to active metabolites (oxazepam); barb met yields few active intermediates.

Diagnosis

Physical Findings

- **CNS:** Mydriasis, mild-mod ataxia, slurred speech, incoordination leads to increased CNS depression, stupor, coma; rarely euphoria-excitation (methaqualone), toxic psychosis (triazolam, flurazepam, glutethimide), and extrapyramidal effects (methaqualone).
- **Cardiovascular:** Myocardial depression due to hypotension and heart rate and smooth muscle vasodilation; rarely AT and SVT (alcohols, chloral hydrate, meprobamate).

- **Pulmonary:** Respiratory depression and arrest.
- **Metabolic:** Hypothermia (barbiturates, BZs, and bromides).

Lab and X-Ray Findings

- **Labs:** To rule out other causes of stupor and coma (especially metabolic and neurologic causes): Electrolytes, BUN, creatinine, glucose, serum alcohol and phenobarbital, LFTs, ABGs
- **Abdominal x-ray:** Gastric concretions with barbiturates and meprobamate
- **Endoscopy:** To break up and/or remove concretions

Pathognomonic Signs

- **Breath odor:** Chloral hydrate and paraldehyde = pear-like; ethchlorvynol (Placidyl®) = pungent plastic or vinyl smell
- **Skin:** (1) Barbiturate (6.0–6.5%) (and ethchlorvynol) blisters = bullous lesions on hands, buttocks, knees; (2) bromoderma = bromide acne = ulcerating acneiform eruption starts on face and spreads over body
- **Gastrointestinal:** Hemorrhagic gastritis unique to chloral hydrate overdose

Overdose Management

Basic Management

- **Airway protection:** Endotracheal tube (ETT) inserted for airway maintenance and aspiration protection
- **Orogastric lavage:** Reduced gastric motility and concretion potential
- **Initial AC (activated-charcoal) slurry:** 1 g/kg and cathartic
- **MDAC (multi-dose activated charcoal):** q 2–4 h, 0.5 g/kg, no additional cathartic, especially for phenobarbital, meprobamate, and glutethimide
- **WBI (whole-bowel irrigation)-polyethylene glycol/electrolyte solution (PEG/ELS):** For gastrointestinal concretions on x-ray (meprobamate) and overdoses with sustained-release SHs (diazepam and/or barbiturates)

Enhanced Elimination

- **Acid–base manipulation:** Urinary alkalinization only for phenobarbital (pKa = 7.21), $NaHCO_3$ 1–2 mEq/kg IV bolus, then 150 mEq/L D5W to keep arterial pH 7.45–7.50 and urine pH 7.5–8.0; replace K losses.
- **Hemoperfusion:** Preferred over HD for all SH overdoses, except bromides (HD only); due to low V_d, increased lipid solubility, increased water solubility, increased protein binding. HP very effective for phenobarbital and meprobamate.
- **Antidote:** Flumazenil for all BZs and zolpidem, can precipitate BZ-withdrawal reactions.

Bromates vs. Bromides

Bromates

- **Use:** Hair neutralizers and straighteners, bread preservatives.

- **Toxicity:** Like aminoglycosides, bromates target the hair cells of the cochlea and the renal tubules impairing their unique abilities to regulate electrochemical gradients. Bromate ototoxicity is permanent, but renal failure is reversible.
- **Treatment:** Lavage and AC.
- **Use:** Old nerve-headache tonics and sedatives (Bromo-Seltzer®); gas fumigant for soil, fruits, and vegetables; vehicle for some drugs (bromopheniramine and dextromethorphan).
- **Toxicity:** Severe gastrointestinal mucosal irritant, brown-stained tongue, progressive CNS depression = Bromism: headache, apathy, irritability leads to confusion, ataxia, tremor, dysarthria, psychosis leads to coma. Later Bromoderma = like ioderma with ulcerating facial acne; treatment = antibiotics and Retin-AR.
- **Treatment:** Lavage and AC, hemodialysis.
- **Note:** Bromoderma acne resembles ioderma acne, with weeping and ulcerating facial pustules and indicates long-term exposure to brominated or iodinated products.

Barbiturates

Barbiturate Classification

- Ultra-short acting (redistribution, then hepatic elimination): Methohexital, thiamylal, thiopental
- Short acting (hepatic > renal): Hexobarbital, pentobarbital, secobarbital
- Intermediate acting (hepatic > renal): Amobarbital, aprobarbital, butabarbital
- Long acting (mostly renal elimination): Barbital, phenobarbital, primidone

Barbiturate Pharmacology

Short and Intermediate Acting

- High pKa, very alkaline
- More lipid soluble
- More protein bound
- Rapid onset, short duration
- Almost completely metabolized hepatically
- Alkaline diuresis ineffective
- Enhanced elimination by hemoperfusion only

Long Acting

- Lower pKa, weak acids
- Less lipid soluble
- Less protein bound
- Slow onset, long duration
- Almost completely renally eliminated
- Enhanced elimination by multi-dose activated charcoal (MDAC), alkaline diuresis, and hemoperfusion > hemodialysis

Barbiturate Toxicity

- **CNS:** Slurred speech, ataxia, lethargy, confusion, headache progressing to anesthesia, coma, respiratory arrest, cerebral edema
- **Cardiovascular:** Direct myocardial depression, peripheral vasodilation, pulmonary edema, cardiac arrest
- **Dermal:** Barbiturate blisters = cutaneous bullae (6.5%)
- **Metabolic:** Hypothermia
- **Miscellaneous:** CYP-450 inducers, increase δ-ALA and contraindicated in porphyrias

Drug–Drug Interactions

- **Hepatic enzyme induction:** Increased metabolism of drugs
- **Synergistic CNS depression:** With other SHs and all CNS depressants (especially alcohol)
- **Increased production of δ-ALA:** Contraindicated in porphyrias
- **ASA and warfarin:** Displace barbiturates from their protein binding sites

Benzodiazepines (BZ)

BZ Classification

Short Acting (Half-Life <24 h)

- Alprazolam (Xanax®)
- Flurazepam (Dalmane®)
- Lorazepam (Ativan®)
- Midazolam (Versed®)
- Temazepam (Restoril®)
- Triazolam (Halcion®)
- Flunitrazepam (Rohypnol®, date-rape, not FDA approved)

Long Acting (Half-Life >24 h)

- Chlordiazepoxide (Librium®)
- Clonazepam (Klonopin®)—only BZ used as a chronic anticonvulsant
- Diazepam (Valium®)
- Oxazepam (Serax®)

BZ Toxicity

- **General:** Weakness, nausea, diarrhea, chest pain
- **CNS:** Headache, vertigo, blurred vision, obtundation, stupor, coma—all potentiated by coingestions, especially with alcohol
- **Cardiovascular:** VS well-maintained, not arrhythmogenic
- **Tolerance:** Occurs rapidly, within 1 week
- **Withdrawal:** Headache, tremor, weight loss, paresthesias, perceptual losses

Miscellaneous and Drug–Drug Interactions

- **Miscellaneous:** Triazolam (Halcion®) = toxic psychosis; flurazepam (DalmaneR) = nightmares and hallucinations
- **Synergistic CNS depression:** Potentiate the actions of all other CNS depressants
- **Cimetidine:** Inhibits hepatic microsomal enzymes and increased half-lives of all BZs, especially those with active metabolites (oxazepam)

"Date-Rape" Drugs

- Gamma-hydroxybutyrate (GHB, gammahydroxybutyric acid) and its precursors: gammabutyrolactone (GBL) and 1, 4-butanediol
- Flunitrazepam (Rohypnol®)
- **"Date-Rape":** GHB

Toxicology

Street names: Liquid Ecstasy, Easy Lay.

- **GABA metabolite:** A naturally occurring CNS (brain) metabolite of GABA, the inhibitory neurotransmitter
- **Rapid oral absorption:** Peak onset in 15 min; duration 1.5–2 h

Clinical Manifestations

- **CNS:** Initial relaxation, tranquility, disinhibition; followed rapidly by loss of consciousness, delirium, amnesia; rarely seizures
- **Cardiopulmonary:** Bradycardia, mild hypotension, transient respiratory depression
- **Gastrointestinal:** Vomiting

Use/Abuse and Management

Methods of Use and Abuse

- **Licit use:** Narcolepsy, not FDA approved in the United States
- **Ineffective use:** By body builders to promote rest, fasting, fat metabolism, muscle mass, and high growth hormone levels
- **Illicit use:** "Date-rape"

General Management of Overdose

- **Airway protection:** Monitor oxygenation and ventilation
- **Consider coma cocktail with thiamine and D50 W:** Flumazenil and naloxone ineffective
- **Atropine:** For bradycardia
- Consider physostigmine

Flunitrazepam

Toxicokinetics

- **Rohypnol®:** Foreign trade name, U.S. street drug

- **Short-acting benzodiazepine:** 7–10 times as potent as diazepam
- **Rapid oral absorption:** Peak onset in 15–20 min; duration 4–6 h

Clinical Manifestations and Management

- Profound CNS depression with maintenance of stable VS
- Anterograde amnesia common
- **General overdose management:** Supportive, protect airway, monitor oxygenation and ventilation
- **Antidote:** Flumazenil

Alcohols

Chloral Hydrate (Noctec®)

- **Pharmacology:** Severe gastrointestinal irritant, rapidly absorbed, first-pass active metabolite = trichloroethanol; "Mickey Finn" = chloral hydrate and ethanol.
- **CNS:** Mimics barbiturate overdose with stupor and coma; pathognomonic pear-like breath odor.
- **Gastrointestinal:** Nausea, vomiting, hemorrhagic gastritis with gastric and SI necrosis and gastrointestinal perforation; esophageal stricture.
- **Cardiovascular:** Myocardial sensitization leads to depression, ventricular arrhythmias = VT, VF, torsades. Treatment: β-blockers.
- **Miscellaneous:** Genotoxic, animal carcinogen.

Ethchlorvynol (Placidyl®)

- **Pharmacology:** Rapidly absorbed, 90% hepatically metabolized
- **CNS:** Central respiratory depression, stupor progressing to prolonged deep coma; pathognomonic plastic- or vinyl-smelling breath
- **Cardiovascular:** Myocardial depression = hypotension and bradycardia
- **Pulmonary:** Respiratory depression, pulmonary edema, especially after IV overdose
- **Dermal:** "Barbiturate blisters" on hands, knees, and buttocks
- **Treatment:** Hemoperfusion

Piperidinediones

Glutethimide (Doriden®)

- **Acute overdose:** Similar to barbiturate overdose, profound and prolonged coma like ethchlorvynol, sudden apnea, and seizures
- **Chronic overdose:** Toxic psychosis, ataxia, seizures, peripheral neuropathy
- **Miscellaneous:** Anticholinergic, thick bronchial secretions block major airways

Methyprylon (Noludar®)

- **Overdose:** Stupor, coma, hypotension, pulmonary edema, shock
- **Miscellaneous:** Cytochrome P-450 inducer, increases δ-ALA synthetase and contraindicated in porphyrias

Carbamates and Bromides

Meprobamate (Miltown®)

- **Overdose:** Can cause euphoria, seizures, coma, hypotension, respiratory depression, pulmonary edema, arrhythmias
- **Miscellaneous:** Forms large masses or bezoars of pills that can become concretions
- **Treatment:** Lavage and endoscopy to remove concretions, WBI with PEG-ELS if concretions detected in gastrointestinal tract on abdominal x-ray

Bromides

- **Overdose:** Old nerve tonics (Bromo-Seltzer) and nematocidal fumigants; very irritating to the gastrointestinal tract = increased vomiting; increased sedation leads to stupor and coma; bizarre neurological and psychological effects (bromism)
- **Bromism:** Bizarre behavior, delusions, hallucinations, headache, apathy, irritability, confusion, dysarthria, tremors, ataxia, anorexia-weight loss, bromoderma
- **Miscellaneous:** Spurious hyperchloridemia

Withdrawn Sedatives-Hypnotics

Methaqualone (Quaalude®)

- **Overdose:** CNS = euphoria (cause for abuse), fatigue, delirium, hypertonia, myoclonus, hyperreflexia, stupor-coma, respiratory arrest
- **Miscellaneous:** Withdrawal syndrome with agitation, delirium, seizures

Paraldehyde (Paral®)

- **Overdose:** An alcohol metabolite, overdose mimics ethanol intoxication, pear-smelling breath; formerly used to cover ethanol detoxification; causes a high anion gap metabolic acidosis
- Anion gap = $Na^+ - (Cl^- + HCO_3^-) = 12 \pm 4$ mEq/L = 8–16 mEq/L
- **MUDPPIILES:** Methanol, uremia, diabetic ketoacidosis, paraldehyde, phenformin, INH, iron, lactic acidosis, ethylene glycol, salicylates

New Anxiolytics

Buspirone (Buspar®)

- **Pharmacology:** Central serotonin and dopamine reuptake inhibitor
- **Overdose:** Gastrointestinal symptoms, drowsiness, dizziness, miosis, rarely dysphoria and extrapyramidal reactions, no cardiovascular and respiratory depressant effects

Zolpidem (Ambien®)

- **Pharmacology:** A non-BZ that has its own unique BZ receptor binding sites; unlike BZs, has little effect on the stages of sleep
- **Overdose:** Drowsiness, sensory distortion, psychotic reactions, rarely respiratory depression and coma; high CFR with co-ingestions (alcohol, SSRIs)
- **Antidote:** Flumazinil

Short-Term Anesthetics

Propofol (Diprivan®)

- **Pharmacology:** GABA enhancer
- **Overdose:** Transient apnea, dose-related respiratory depression and hypotension, not arrhythmogenic
- **Miscellaneous:** Lipemic serum due to high TGs; histamine and anaphylactoid reactions to soybean–egg emulsion formulation, rarely true anaphylaxis; supports bacterial overgrowth

Etomidate (Amidate®)

- **Pharmacology:** GABA enhancer
- **Overdose:** Same as propofol and involuntary muscle movements, rarely severe cardiovascular and respiratory depression
- **Miscellaneous:** Suppresses adrenal steroid hormone production—cortisol and aldosterone; no longer recommended for prolonged ICU sedation

Marijuana

Epidemiology

- Marijuana is an oily, dried fibrous material obtained from the Indian hemp plant, *Cannabis sativa.*
- The most commonly used illegal substance in the United States.
- The most commonly abused substance in the world after nicotine, alcohol, and caffeine.
- Considered a "gateway drug" by the DEA, NIDA, and the Substance Abuse and Mental Health Services Administration (SAMHSA).

Pharmacology

- Delta-9-THC is the psychoactive component.
- **Hashish (smoked in pipes) and hashish oil (mixed with tobacco and smoked):** All are Cannabis derivatives that contain higher concentrations of THC.
- THC is transported to the brain within 15 s of smoking to occupy specific cannabinoid receptors in the cerebral cortex.

Acute vs. Chronic Marijuana Toxicity

Acute Marijuana Toxicity

- **Physiological effects:** Dose-related tachycardia, blood pressure remains stable, increased appetite, dry (cotton) mouth, conjunctival injection, reduced intra-ocular pressure, bronchodilation, weakness, muscle tremors, urinary retention, low testosterone levels—impotence.

- **Psychological effects:** Dose-related euphoria, relaxation, sensory alterations. Preexisting psychopathology may predispose to transient, acute psychotic reactions with paranoid delusions and hallucinations.

Chronic Marijuana Toxicity

- **Tolerance and dependence:** Resulting from repeated use
- **Withdrawal syndrome:** Irritability, restlessness, insomnia, and appetite loss
- **COPD, oral and lung cancer:** Smoking induced
- **Congenital toxicity:** Neonatal and early childhood neurobehavioral and developmental disturbances
- **Male infertility:** The result of combinations of low testosterone levels, low sperm counts, reduced sperm motility, and greater abnormal sperm morphology

Management of Marijuana Intoxication

- **Motor vehicle and other transportation-related accidents:** Marijuana is detected in 11–33% of cases (including mass transit and train accidents) and associated with a prolonged (≥24 h) loss of judgment and motor skills needed for safe vehicular operation.
- **Acute psychotic reactions:** Sedation with BZs.
- **Pneumomediastinum:** Rare and the result of deep inhalation with alveolar overdistension and rupture; supportive management with O_2.

Chapter 10

Reproductive and Perinatal Toxicology and Teratogenesis

Outline 218
Epidemiology 218
Fertility, Potency, and Gestation 218
Pharmacokinetics of Pregnancy 221
Acute Poisoning in Pregnancy 223
Specific Poisonings in Pregnancy 224
Theophylline OD in Pregnancy 227
Substance Abuse in Pregnancy 229
Breastfeeding 231

Outline

1. Epidemiology of reproductive toxicology
2. Toxins affecting fertility, potency, and gestation
3. Pharmacokinetics of pregnancy and placental transfer
4. General management of acute poisonings in pregnancy
5. Specific management of acute poisonings in pregnancy
6. Neonatal pharmacokinetics and toxicokinetics
7. Substance abuse in pregnancy
8. Drugs and toxic exposures contraindicated during breastfeeding

Epidemiology

1. There are over *90,000 chemicals* used commercially in the United States, but *only 2200 (≤3%)* have been evaluated for mutagenic and teratogenic effects in animal models.
2. There are over *20 million women* of reproductive age in the U.S. workforce, but only 4–6% of birth defects are related to known drug or toxin exposures during pregnancy.
3. From *30–70%* of pregnant women use *3–10 different drugs during pregnancy*, especially vitamins, iron, analgesics, antipyretics, antimicrobials, antiemetics, theophylline, caffeine, ethanol, and nicotine.
4. From *15–25%* of pregnant women report licit drug use (ethanol > nicotine) or illicit drug use (marijuana > cocaine > heroin) or have positive urine drug screens during pregnancy.
5. Analgesics, vitamins, iron, antibiotics, theophylline, and psychotropic medications account for *50–79%* of reported toxic ingestions by pregnant women.

Fertility, Potency, and Gestation

1. Toxic male infertility and sexual dysfunction (See Tables 10.1 and 10.2)
2. Toxic female infertility and sexual dysfunction (See Tables 10.3 and 10.4)
3. Toxic aphrodisiacs and mechanisms of toxicity (See Table 10.5)
4. Toxic priapism and abortifacients

Toxic Priapism and Abortifacients

Priapism-Inducing Agents

1. **α-Blockers and vasodilators—mechanism:** *Erection = cholinergic stimulation* (↑ blood in) + α_2*-antagonism* (↓ blood out):
   Guanethidine (α_2-antagonism)
   Hydralazine (α_2-antagonism)

Labetalol (α_2-antagonism)
Phenothiazines (α_2-antagonism)
Prazosin (α_2-antagonism)
Trazadone (α_2-antagonism)
Yohimbine (α_2-antagonism)

Table 10.1 Male Infertility

Drugs or Toxins	Mechanisms of Infertility
Anabolic steroids	↓ *L*H (*L*eydig), ↓ sperm # and morph
Androgens	↓ Testosterone, ↓ sperm
Antineoplastics, radiation	Gonadal toxicity, ↓ sperm
Carbon disulfide	↓ LH, ↓ F*S*H (*S*ertoli), ↓ sperm
Cimetidine	↓ Sperm
Dibromochlorpropane	↓ Sperm
Epichlorohydrin	↓ Sperm
Ethanol	↓ *L*H (*L*eydig), ↓ sperm
Ethylene dibromide, glycol ethers	↓ Sperm
Lead	↓ Sperm
Opioids	↓ LH, ↓ testosterone, ↓ sperm
Sulfasalazine	↓ Sperm
Marijuana and tobacco	↓ Testosterone, ↓ sperm

Table 10.2 Male Sexual Dysfunction

Drugs or Toxins	Mechanisms of Dysfunction
Anabolic steroids	↓ Libido, impotence
Anticholinergics	Erectile failure
Antihypertensives (α_2-agonists)	Impotence, erectile failure (neurologic)
Antihypertensives (thiazides)	Erectile failure (vascular)
Cimetidine	↓ Libido, impotence
Dimethylaminoproprionitrile	Neurogenic bladder, erectile failure
Ethanol	Impotence, erectile failure
Lead	↓ Libido, erectile failure
Lithium	Erectile failure
MAOIs	↓ Libido, impotence
Opioids	↓ Libido
Phenothiazines	↓ Libido
TCAs	↓ Libido, impotence

Table 10.3 Female Infertility

Drugs or Toxins	Mechanisms of Infertility
Anabolic steroids	↓ LH and FSH
Antineoplastic agents, radiation	Gonadal toxicity
Carbon disulfide	↓ LH and FSH
Lead	↑ SABs and stillbirths
Oral contraceptives	Prolonged hypothalamic–pituitary axis shutdown
Thyroid	↓ Ovulation

Table 10.4 Female Sexual Dysfunction

Drugs or Toxins	Mechanisms of Dysfunction
Anabolic steroids	↓ libido
Cimetidine	↓ libido
Lithium	↓ libido
Opioids	↓ libido
Oral contraceptives	↓ libido
Phenothiazines	↓ libido
Tricyclic antidepressants	↓ libido
SSRIs	↓ libido

Table 10.5 Aphrodisiacs

Drugs or Toxins	Mechanisms of Toxicity
1. **Bufotoxins:** Bufodienolides; dried toad gland secretions contain cardioactive steroids = *love stone*, *rock hard*, Chan su	1. Cardiac glycoside (dig) toxicity; Tx = digoxin Fabs (DigiBind®)
2. **Cantharidin:** Crushed blister beetle = *Spanish fly*	2. Hemorrhagic blistering of mouth, GI and GU tracts; hemorrhagic bladder bullae; priapism; vaginal bleeding
3. **Lead additives:** For red color	3. Lead colic, anemia, basophilic stippling, infertility, impotency
4. **Nitrites:** Amyl (crushable-pop), butyl, isobutyl = "*poppers*"	4. HA, N, syncope, ↓ BP, reflex tachycardia, *methemoglobinemia*
5. **Yohimbine:** African *yohimbe* tree bark extract, an $\underline{\alpha}_2$-*antagonist* and *cholinergic agonist* = *yo-yo*	5. Unopposed α_1-mediated ↑ BP, ↑ HR, MI, mydriasis, diaphoresis, flushing; cholinergic-SLUDE and flushing; Tx: AC decon, then BZs

2. **Miscellaneous erection and priapism-inducing agents:**
   Androgens
   Anticoagulants
   Cantharidin (*Spanish fly*)

Abortifacients

1. **Quinine:** Oxytocic antimalarial
2. **Misoprostel:** Synthetic $PGE_{2\alpha}$ oxytocic used for therapeutic abortions (TAB)
3. **Mifepristone (RU-486):** "Morning-after" pill, an antiprogesterone that must be combined with PGE for TAB
4. **Pulegone (pennyroyal oil):** Hepatotoxicity 2° *glutathione depletion* (like APAP); **Tx:** NAC
5. **Black cohosh root:** Herbal preparation causing GI and GU mucosal toxicity (like cantharidin)

Pharmacokinetics of Pregnancy

Increase Free Drug Concentration

Factors ↑ Drug Absorption

1. ↓ gastric emptying
2. ↓ GI tract motility
3. ↑ GI content-mucosal contact time
4. ↑ skin and mucosal perfusion
5. ↑ RR and TV

Factors ↑ Drug Distribution

1. ↑ cardiac output
2. ↓ protein (albumin) binding
3. ↓ hepatic biotransformation
4. ↑ FFAs which release stored drugs and displace protein-bound drugs

Decrease Free Drug Concentration

Factors ↑ Drug Excretion

1. ↑ ECFV
2. ↑ RBF
3. ↑ GFR
4. ↑ Urine output

Placental Barrier Effects

1. Placental biotransformation
2. Placental ion trapping

Placental Transfer (See Table 10.6)

FDA Use-in-Pregnancy Ratings

A: Human RCTs show *no risk.*
Ex: Vitamins.

B: Animal studies show *no risk.*
Ex: APAP, penicillins, ampicillin.

C: Risk in humans *uncertain.*
Ex: Albuterol.

D: Evidence of risk in humans; use in pregnancy *not recommended unless benefits of the drug use outweigh its risks.*
Ex: Isoretinoin, tetracyclines.

X: Known *teratogens, use contraindicated in pregnancy.*
Ex: Iodine, quinine.

Mechanisms of Placental Transfer

1. **Factors ↑ Passive Diffusion:**
   a. ↓ MW
   b. ↑ Lipid solubility
   c. ↓ Ionization
   d. ↓ Protein binding
2. **Ion trapping of weak acid teratogens in the higher pH of fetal tissues in early gestation:** Isoretinoin (retinoic acid), phenytoin valproate (valproic acid), trimethadione, thalidomide, and warfarin

Table 10.6 D Drugs and X Teratogens

D = Contraindicated Drugs	Category X = Known Teratogens
Aminoglycosides: Deafness	*ACEIs:* Pulmonary hypoplasia
Anticonvulsants: Craniofacial defects (CFDs) and neural tube defects (NTDs)	*Carbamazepine:* CFDs and NTDs
Antineoplastics: Chromosomal damage and mutations	*Cocaine:* IUGR, vascular/limb ↓
Antithyroids, iodine: Neonatal cretinism and goiter	*Coumarin:* Fetal warfarin syn
NSAIDs: Premature PDA closure	*DES:* Vaginal adenosis and cancer
Progestogens and androgens: Female masculinization	*Ethanol (Toluene):* Fetal alcohol, CFDs
Sulfonamides: Neonatal jaundice and kernicterus	*Lithium:* Ebstein's anomaly
Sulfonylureas: Neonatal hypoglycemia	*Penicillamine:* Cutis laxa
	Misoprostel: Short limbs, Moebius syn
	Methotrexate: CFDs
	Methyl mercury: Minamata disease
	Phenytoin and retinoids: CFDs
	Tetracyclines: Teeth staining
	Thalidomide: Phocomelia
	Valproate: CFDs and NTDs

3. **Near-term maternal changes:** ↑ FFAs release maternal fat-stored drugs—BZs
4. **Near-term fetal changes:** ↑ *albumin* = ↑ fetal drug binding near term

Teratogenic Syndromes

Fetal Alcohol and Toluene Syndromes

Craniofacial defects:

- Hyperteleorism
- *Short philtrum*
- Flattened nasal bridge
- Low set ears

Microcephaly
Mental retardation
Limb defects possible

The VACTREL Association

See Figures 10.1 and 10.2.

Acute Poisoning in Pregnancy

Epidemiology

1. 2–12% of women who attempt suicide are pregnant.
2. 1–5% of pregnancy deaths are results of OD suicides.

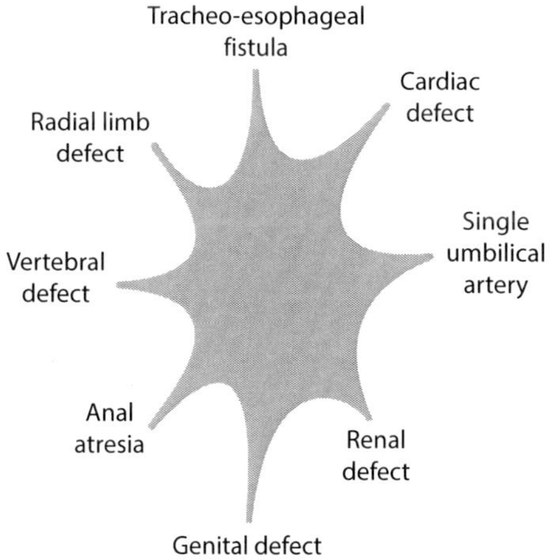

FIGURE 10.1 The VACTREL association 1. The VACTREL association is a constellation of birth defects that may occur in the rare pregnancies conceived during maternal birth control with oral contraceptive pills. The mnemonic VACTREL stands for vertebral anomalies (spina bifida), imperforate anus, congenital cardiac defects, tracheoesophageal fistula, and limb deformities (radial agenesis or dysplasia).

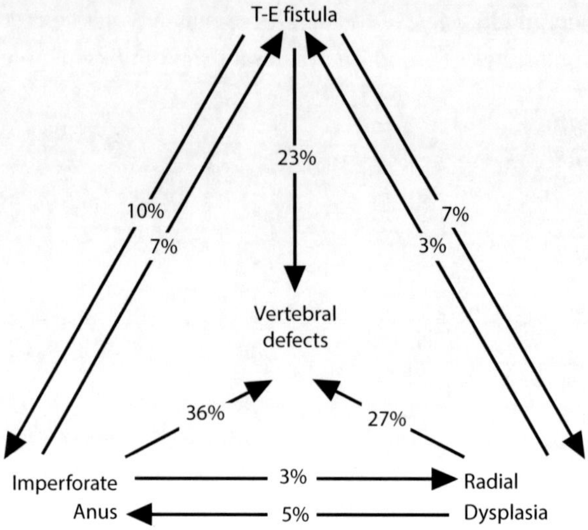

FIGURE 10.2 The VACTREL association 2. A diagram that indicated the ranges of joint association of congenital birth defects in the VACTREL association.

3. Analgesics, vitamins, iron, psychotropics, and theophylline account for 50–79% of drug ODs in pregnancy.
4. *Warning*: Chronic exposures to ethanol and most anticonvulsants will cause CFDs (carbamazepine, phenytoin, valproate) and/or NTDs (valproate).

General Management

1. Ipecac contraindicated 2° vomiting and ↑ preterm labor.
2. Coma cocktails should contain dextrose and naloxone.
3. AC is very useful 2° gastric axis shift and content stasis.
4. WBI with PEG-ELS is indicated for Fe OD; not AC adsorbed.
5. Most antidotes are FDA category C or better; only ethanol is category D.
6. Never withhold specific antidotes in pregnancy, especially NAC for APAP or HBO for CO.

Specific Poisonings in Pregnancy

1. Acetaminophen
2. Iron
3. Carbon monoxide
4. Theophylline

APAP ODs

APAP OD in Pregnancy

- **Epi:** The most commonly used and overdosed analgesic in pregnancy.

- **Mech:** Rapid glutathione depletion first in mother and then in fetus, with generation of hepatotoxic NAPQI metabolite**,** *mother > fetus.*
- **Mx:** NAC; *Warning*: Consider induction in late third trimester 2° ↑ CFRs; SAB and preterm labor often occur within weeks of *successful treatment with NAC.*

Fe ODs

Iron OD in Pregnancy

- **Epi:** Another common OD in pregnancy; maternal > fetal toxicity and fatality 2° placental barrier blocking large Fe transfers to fetus.
- **Mech:** Most Fe remains in the maternal circulation and can be chelated with *deferoxamine*, which is only minimally transferred across the placenta.
- **Mx:** Initial deferoxamine chelation; WBI for massive and slow-release Fe ODs as Fe is not adsorbed to AC.

Chelators: Deferoxamine

Properties

- **Chem:** A water-soluble, specific iron chelator created by removing ferric iron (Fe^{3+}) from ferrioximine
- **Mech:** Chelates extra free Fe and Fe in transit between transferrin and ferritin; but *will not chelate Fe complex to Hb, ferritin, or hemosiderin*
- **Contra:** None

Applications

- **Use:** To chelate Fe in Fe overdoses, massive transfusions, hemosiderosis, and thalassemia. To chelate aluminum in CRF.
- **Dose:** 1 g IM, then 0.5 g q 4–12 h; IV preferred = 15 mg/kg/min slowly.
- **SE:** ↓ BP; **pulmonary toxicity** (ARDS); *oculotoxicity* (↓ vision, ↓ color vision, night blindness); and *ototoxicity* (deafness). Acts as a *siderophage* for some bacteria that cannot absorb Fe—***Yersinia*** and ***Vibrio*** ↑ *V. vulnificus* sepsis risk. *Rose (vin rosé)-orange-colored urine.*

Pediatric Iron OD (See Table 10.7)

- **Epid:** 30% of pediatric ingestion deaths, 1999–2001
- **Fe content:** Ferrous gluconate 11–12%, ferrous sulfate 20%, ferrous fumarate 33%
- **Dose:** Toxic dose = *20–60 mg/kg*, fatal dose > 60 mg/kg; > 500 mcg/dL
- **MoA:** (1) *Caustic corrosion GI* mucosa, (2) severe *metabolic acidosis*, (3) *inhibition of oxidative phosphorylation*, (4) periportal *hepatic necrosis*, (5) GI *strictures in survivors*

Iron

- **Stages: I:** Bloody vomit and diarrhea within 6 h, **II:** Latency between 6 and 18 h, **III:** Acidosis and hypovolemic shock by 24 h, **IV:** Liver failure by day 2–3, **V:** GI strictures within weeks, repeated operations

Table 10.7 Pediatric Iron OD

Preps	Tab (mg)	% Fe	Mg Fe/tab
Ferrous gluconate	325	12%	40
Ferrous sulfate	325	20%	65
Ferrous fumarate	325	33%	107
Pedi multivitamin	NA	NA	10–18
Adult multivitamin	NA	NA	3–100
Prenatal multivitamin	NA	NA	10–100
Toxic dose	20–60 mg/kg ingested, >500 mcg/dL blood level		
Fatal dose	> 60 mg/kg ingested, >500 mcg/dL blood level		

- **Dx:** Radio-opaque pills in stomach (CHIPS), serum Fe > 500 mcg/dL, TIBC useless
- **Tx:** No ipecac or AC, IVFs, $NaHCO_3$, monitor LFTs, consider WBI, deferoxamine chelation = 100 mg chelates 8.5 mg Fe
- Deferoxamine chelation and urine color—useless, use serum Fe

Fe Chelating Agent

Deferoxamine*: *A specific chelator for iron only that is extracted from the bacterium ***Streptomyces pilosus***; *may be given IV* (*15 mg/kg/h*) > IM; *binds only free Fe and not Fe in transferrin or Hgb*; binds Fe on a molar basis 1-to-1, 100 mg binds 9 mg Fe; can acutely cause histamine-mediated vasodilation with ↓ BP, and *free radical-induced lung injury*; chronically associated with *hemosiderosis* and *Vibrio vulnificus and Yersinia enterocolitica* septicemia by serving as a siderophage for bacteria that cannot absorb iron.

CO Poisoning

Maternal CO Poisoning

- **Epi:** CO is the leading cause of all poison fatalities; fetal > maternal toxicity and fatality.
- **Mx:** Hyperbaric oxygen therapy.

Mechanisms

1. Fetus has 10–15% ↑ baseline COHb levels than mother.
2. In CO poisoning, fetus has 58% ↑ CO levels than mother.
3. Both maternal and fetal PO_2 ↓ by COHb, fetal (PO_2 = shift of O_2Hb dissociation curve ↓ tissue O_2).
4. Cellular hypoxia 2° inhibition mitochondrial cytochrome oxidase.

Neonatal toxicology

1. ↑ **Dermal absorption:** *Hexachlorophene (pHisoHex®)—vacuolar encephalopathy*, aniline dyes—*metHb*, I^- antiseptics—↓ thyroid.

2. ↑ **Protein binding:** Sulfonamides and ceftriaxone displace bilirubin from albumin = *kernicterus.*
3. ↓ **Hepatic P450 met:** ↑ concentration of phenytoin, phenobarb, theophylline; ↓ glucuronidation/glycine of *chloramphenicol = gray baby* and *benzyl alcohol = gasping baby.*
4. **General mx:** No ipecac and lavage 2° lyte and T losses; consider exchange trans > HD > HP for drug ODs.

Theophylline OD in Pregnancy

1. Theophylline pharmacology and toxicology
2. Initial and specific treatment of theophylline OD
3. Enhanced elimination techniques in theophylline OD

Theophylline OD

Pharmacology (See Table 10.8)

- **Serum levels:** Therapeutic levels 5–15 mcg/mL; *toxic ≥ 20 mcg/mL*; HP indicated > 90 mcg/mL anytime; and >40 with seizures, arrhythmias, refractory vomiting, or ↓ BP
- **Mech:** Antagonizes adenosine to ↓ histamine release and ↓ bronchospasm; inhibits cAMP- ↑ plasma catechols = SM relax, periph vasodilation, CV-CNS stimulation
- **Met:** Low Vd (0.5 L/kg); 50% protein-bound; 90% P450 biotransformed to inactive metabolites; 10% renal excretion

Toxicity

- **Forme fruste:** Severe N and V, tachyarrhythmias, seizures, ↓ BP, ↓ K, metabolic acidosis
- **CV:** Tachyarrhythmias 2° β_1 stimulation, ↓ BP 2° β_2 stimulation
- **GI:** Severe N and V, ↓ *K-hypokalemia*, hypovolemia

Table 10.8 Theophylline Metabolism

Increased Metabolism	Decreased Metabolism
Carbamazepine	Cimetidine
Phenobarbital	Quinolone antibiotics
Phenytoin	Macrolide antibiotics
Primidone	Mexilitene
Rifampin	Verapamil
Cigarette and marijuana—smoking	Reduced hepatic perfusion: Advancing age Intercurrent infections Congestive heart failure Hepatic failure

- **CNS:** Anxiety, tremor, agitation, hyperventilation, seizures–all 2° ↓ adenosine anticonvulsant activity
- **Metabolic:** ↓ K, ↓ Ca, ↓ PO_4, metabolic acidosis

Mx: Theophylline OD

Initial Assessment

1. ABCs and ECG monitor
2. **Labs:** Theophylline level, CBC, lytes, Ca, glucose, BUN, creatinine, coags
3. Avoid β-mimetics (↑ HR, ↓ BP)
4. Avoid ipecac and most antiemetics, especially phenothiazines (↑ arrhythmias)

GI Decontamination (See Figure 10.3 and Table 10.9)

1. **Gastric emptying:** No ipecac, granisetron > ondansetron (5-HT blockers) > metoclopramide for severe V; HP for refractory V.
2. **OG lavage:** Best to administer AC and sorbitol; limited by slow-release tabs, bezoars, and concretions.
3. **AC:** 1–2 g/kg, + sorbitol, 1 g/kg.
4. **MDAC:** 0.5 g/kg q 2 h, 0 cathartic.
5. **WBI:** For sustained-release preps.

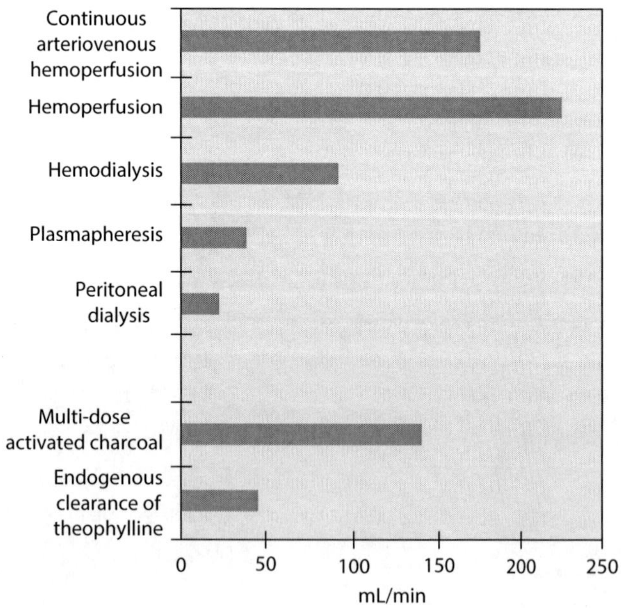

FIGURE 10.3 Theophylline overdose in pregnancy. Hemoperfusion offers the most rapid method for extracorporeal clearance of theophylline when ingested in toxic amounts during pregnancy.

Table 10.9 Theophylline Enhanced Elimination

Acute Charcoal Hemoperfusion	Chronic Theophylline Toxicity
1. Theophylline level >90 mcg/mL at any time	1. Risks with advancing age, intercurrent illnesses-infections, and reduced hepatic perfusion
2. Theophylline level >40 mcg/mL when combined with a. Seizures b. Hypotension, refractory to fluid loading c. Ventricular dysrhythmias d. Protracted vomiting, refractory to antiemetics	2. No role for either emesis or orogastric lavage, unless to instill AC via OG tube
	3. AC and MDAC for CV-stable patients
	4. Charcoal HP for unstable patients and for AC failures
	5. Monitor theophylline levels q 4–6 h until <20 mcg/kg

6. **Consider HP:** For levels > 40 mcg/mL complicated by sz, V, ↓ BP, ventricular arrhythmias; HP-HD for levels > 90 anytime.
7. **Antidotes:** Consider *adenosine and CCBs*. β-Blockers relatively contraindicated.

Specific Mx: Theophylline OD

CNS Toxicity

- **Agitation and restlessness, then seizures:** $D_{50}W$ + thiamine 100 mg for hypoglycemia; IV benzodiazepines > barbiturates
- **Refractory seizures:** Secure AW; BZs and barbs; consider MRs; control ventilation; avoid phenytoin
- **Status epilepticus:** Aggressive charcoal hemoperfusion to ↓ theophylline levels <40 mcg/mL

CV Toxicity

- **Hypotension:** Fluid load with NS or RL; as vasopressors, use pure α-agonists, norepinephrine or phenylephrine, titrated to effect; avoid mixed agonists with β_2-mediated vasodilation and ↓ BP.
- **Tachydysrhythmias:** Restore electrolyte balance, especially K and Ca; as antiarrhythmics, use *adenosine first and then CCBs* (verapamil > diltiazem) rather than β-blockers (*bronchospasm, ↓ BP possible*); consider lidocaine but it ↓ seizure threshold; charcoal HP for PVCs → VT.

Substance Abuse in Pregnancy

1. Alcohol and fetal alcohol syndrome (FAS)
2. Cocaine and fetal cocaine syndrome (FCS)
3. Opioids and neonatal withdrawal syndrome (NWS)

Alcohol and Cocaine Abuse

Alcohol Abuse and FAS

- **Epi:** 20% of pregnant women consume alcohol; 1–2% consume > 4 drinks/day; FAS => 2–3oz of ethanol/day (4–6 drinks/day) or with frequent binge drinking.
- **Mech of FAS:** *Craniofacial dysmorphogenesis* = early teratogenesis; MR and cortical defects occur late in gestation.
- **FAS:** IUGR, microcephaly, epicanthal folds, small palpebral fissures, cleft palate, *flat philtrum*—maxillary hypoplasia, micrognathia, MR.

Cocaine Abuse and FCS

- **Epi:** 1% of U.S. women use cocaine during pregnancy.
- **Mech of FCS:** Vasospastic and vascular disruptive effects on uteroplacental and fetal end circulations.
- **FCS:** IUGR, microcephaly, neurobehavioral abnormalities, vascular disruptive phenomena = *limb autoamputation* (Moebius syndrome), seizures, cerebral infarctions, visceral and GU defects.
- **OB complications:** Abruptio placenta, premature delivery.

Opioid Abuse and NWS

Opioid Abuse in Pregnancy

- **Epi:** 0.2% of pregnant women use heroin > methadone; 75,000 neonates/year are exposed to opioid abuse *in utero* and 60–90% manifest NWS.
- **Maternal comp:** Hepatitis, sepsis, septic emboli, SBE, STDs, AIDS.
- **OB comp:** SAB, premature delivery, stillbirth.
- **Neonatal comp:** SGA.
- **NWS:** Occurs within 24 h for heroin, but *delayed for days with methadone abuse*; increased incidence of SIDS × 1–2 year.

Neonatal Withdrawal Syndrome (See Table 10.10)

- **Mech:** Chronic opioid use ◊ tolerance, dependence, and ↑ # of CNS α_2-receptors

Table 10.10 Drug Withdrawal Syndromes

Adult Alcohol Withdrawal	Adult Opioid Withdrawal	Neonatal Opioid Withdrawal
Tremulousness	Anxiety	Tremulousness and hyperreflexia
Tachycardia	Tachycardia	Sinus rhythm
Tachypnea	Tachypnea	Tachypnea
Hypertension	Hypertension	Normotensive
Hyperthermia	Normothermia	Hypothermia
Diaphoresis	No diaphoresis	Diaphoresis
Altered level of consciousness (DTs)	Normal level of consciousness	Irritability and wakefulness

- **Def:** *WITHDRAWAL* = *w*akefulness, *i*rritability, *t*remulousness-↓ *t*emperature-*t*achypnea, *hyperactivity–h*yperreflexia, *d*iarrhea–*d*iaphoresis, *r*hinorrhea–*r*espiratory distress, *a*pnea–*a*utonomic dysfunction, *w*eight loss, *a*lkalosis (respiratory), and *l*acrimation
- **Tx:** Tincture of opium (*paregoric*) for withdrawal seizures

Breastfeeding

Toxicokinetics

1. Only *free drugs* are available for transfer from maternal plasma to breast milk.
2. **Membrane diffusion factors determine transfer:** Low MW, ↑ lipid solubility, ↓ ionization, and limited protein binding.
3. *Lipid solubility* = #1 determinant of milk transfer.
4. Large *MW* drugs, such as heparin and insulin, do not transfer.
5. Breast milk, with a *lower pH* = 7.0, will concentrate weak bases, like sulfacetamide.

Absolutely Contraindicated Drugs

1. **Bromocriptine:** ↓ lactation
2. **Antineoplastics and radiopharmaceuticals:** Carcinogenesis, myelosuppression, immunosuppression
3. **Ergotamines:** ↑ neonatal vomiting and seizures
4. Lithium
5. Metronidazole
6. Substances of abuse

Relatively Contraindicated Drugs

- Phenobarbital
- **Sulfonamides**: Kernicterus, hemolysis in G-6-PD-deficient neonates

Chapter 11

Hypoglycemic and Other Endocrine Agent Toxicity

Outline 234
Hypoglycemic Toxicity 234
Hepatotoxicity and Hypoglycemia 235
Hypoglycemic Manifestations 235
Endocrine: Thyroid-Active Agents 237
Endocrine: *Bone*-Active Agents 238
Hormones 238
Common Electrolyte Abnormalities Associated with Endocrinopathies and Drug Toxicities 239

Outline

- Definitions and epidemiology of hypoglycemia
- Etiologies of hypoglycemia
- Clinical manifestations of hypoglycemia
- Orally administered hypoglycemic agents
- Characteristics of routinely administered insulin preparations
- General and specific management of toxic hypoglycemia
- Surreptitious hypoglycemia
- Other endocrine agents

Hypoglycemic Toxicity

Definitions

- **Hypoglycemia:** Failure to maintain serum glucose > 60 mg/dL
- **Euglycemia:** Serum glucose level of 70–110 mg/dL
- **Therapeutic euglycemia maintenance:** 100–250 mg/dL

Epidemiology

- **Accidental insulin OD:** Most common cause of hypoglycemia 2° dose miscalculation and ↓ caloric intake or ↑ exercise level (Table 11.1)
- **Long-acting (LA) sulfonylureas:** Most common cause of noninsulin, drug-induced hypoglycemia, especially chlorpropamide and glyburide and glipizide
- **Market withdrawals:** (1) Biguanide, *phenformin*, withdrawn 1976, 2° *fatal lactic acidosis*; (2) *troglitazone* (Rezulin®), withdrawn 1990s, 2° *fatal hepatotoxicity*

Table 11.1 Insulin Pharmacokinetics

Classes of Insulin Preparations	Short (Rapid)-Acting	Intermediate-Acting	Long (Ultra)-Acting
Duration (h)	3–6	10–18	18–36
Examples of common insulin preparations	Regular insulin (Humulin®, Novolin®) Insulin aspart (Novolog®) Insulin lispro (Humalog®)	NPH insulin Lente insulin	PZI Ultralente insulin Insulin glargine (Lantus®)
Metabolism and excretion	Hepatic metabolism Renal excretion	Hepatic metabolism Renal excretion	Not metabolized Renal excretion only

Note: Common classes and examples of routinely administered insulin preparations that are often mixed on individual daily dosing schedules to permit the most precise therapeutic maintenance of euglycemia in type I (juvenile diabetes) and type II (adult-onset diabetes) insulin-dependent diabetics.

Etiologies of Hypoglycemia

- **Pathophysiological:** *Endocrinopathy* (Addison's disease, Sheehan syndrome); *neoplasms* (insulinomas, MEA I); *liver* disease (alcoholism, cirrhosis); *CRF* and hemodialysis; *miscellaneous* (AIDS, autoimmune diseases, pregnancy)
- **Drug-induced:** Oral hypoglycemic agents, parenteral insulin preparations
- **Food or drug potentiation of hypoglycemic agents:** Foods (unripe Jamaican ackee fruit—hypoglycin A [vomiting, hypoglycemia, CNS depression, seizures], ethanol); drugs (ACE inhibitors, β-*blockers*, *chloramphenicol*, disopyramide, MAOIs, *quinine–quinidine*, *salicylates*, sulfonamides)

Hepatotoxicity and Hypoglycemia

Ackee and Jamaican Vomiting Sickness

- **Rep:** Ackee tree
- **Toxins:** *Hypoglycin* A inhibits G-6-PD and causes *Jamaican vomiting sickness*
- **Antidote:** 50% dextrose
- **Dx:** Severe N and V, hypoglycemia-2° decreased gluconeogenesis, mental status Δs, hypothermia, metabolic acidosis, seizures, ↓ liver fx—centrilobular hepatic necrosis
- **Tx:** GI decontamination (lavage + AC)

Hypoglycemic Manifestations

Clinical Manifestations

2° Catecholamine Release

- **CV effects:** Arrhythmias (SVT, PVCs, at fib); HTN-HA; angina–ischemia, MI
- **Autonomic effects:** Anxiety, diaphoresis, dry mouth, pallor, piloerection
- **GI effects:** Hunger, nausea

2° Cerebral Glucose Depletion

- **Acute delirium:** Confusion, bizarre behavior, mania
- **Coma:** Posturing, CNS and respiratory depression, hypothermia, *preserved brainstem reflexes* (doll's eyes, oculocephalic, oculovestibular, and pupillary)
- **Focal neurologic deficits:** Mimics CVA, ataxia, weakness, hemiparesis, hemiplegia
- **Solitary or refractory seizures:** *No postictal periods*

Oral Hypoglycemics

- **Sulfonylureas:** Stimulate β-islet insulin release, first vs. second generation. *Meglitinides* have similar mechanisms of action (MoA).
- **Biguanides:** ↓ Hepatic production and ↓ peripheral utilization of glucose, *metformin* (Glucophage®); *phenformin* withdrawn 1976, 2° *fatal lactic acidosis* 2° inhibition gluconeogenesis.

- **Thiazolidinedione:** ↑ Insulin sensitivity peripherally, *troglitazone* (Rezulin®); withdrawn 2° *fatal hepatotoxicity.*
- **Small intestinal α-glucosidase inhibitors:** ↓ Intestinal absorption of glucose, do not cause hypoglycemia, often used with other hypoglycemics (sulfonylureas); *acarbose* (Precose®).
- **Other drugs causing hypoglycemia:** ACEIs, β-blockers, ASA—all salicylates, ethanol, hypoglycin A and valproic acid (↓ carnitine transport), islet poisons—Vacor (PNU—pyridylmethyl nitrophenyl urea rodenticide), alloxan, streptozocin.

Sulfonylureas

First generation—Few hypoglycemic events

- Acetohexamide (Dymelor®)
- Chlorpropamide (Diabenese®)
- Tolazamide (Tolinase®)
- Tolbutamide (Orinase®)

Second generation—All LA ↑ hypoglycemic events

- Glipizide (Glucotrol®)
- Glyburide (Diabeta®, Micronase®)

Sulfonylureas vs. Biguanides

Sulfonylureas

- **Mech:** Stimulate pancreatic beta cells to release preformed insulin
- **Type I IDDM:** Ineffective
- **Type II NIDDM:** Effective
- **Nondiabetics:** Can cause *severe hypoglycemia,* especially long-acting chlorpropamide and all second-generation sulfonylureas

Biguanides

- **Mech:** Do not stimulate insulin secretion, *inhibit hepatic gluconeogenesis* and promote tissue glucose uptake
- **Type I IDDM:** Ineffective
- **Type II NIDDM:** Effective
- **Nondiabetics:** Do not lower blood glucose

General and Specific OD Mx

Immediate General Mx

1. **Contraindicated treatments:** No ipecac 2° seizures, *no glucagon*

2. **Secure AW:** Left lateral decubitus
3. **Labs:** Glu, BUN-creatinine, lytes, Ca, Mg, CBC, ethanol level
4. **Coma cocktail:** $D_{50}W$, 1 g/kg, + thiamine, 100 mg
5. **Initial OG lavage:** Then AC + cathartic
6. **MDAC:** For long-acting (*chlorpropamide*) and enterohepatic-circulating (*glipizide*) agents
7. **Correct hypoglycemia = $D_{10}W$ maintenance:** Maintain relative euglycemia, 100–250 mg/dL

Specific Drug OD Mx

- **Urinary alkalinization:** Only for chlorpropamide, a *weak acid*; maintain urine pH 7.0–8.0.
- **Octreotide:** A semisynthetic long-acting *analog of somatostatin* with longer T1/2 that also *inhibits insulin secretion* in insulinomas, quinine–quinidine ODs, and sulfonylurea ODs (both classes stimulate insulin release).
- **Diazoxide (Hyperstat®):** Directly inhibits insulin secretion from insulinomas and sulfonylurea ODs; but *not recommended* because it is less effective than octreotide and will ↓ BP.

Surreptitious Hypoglycemia

Epidemiology

- **IDDM patients:** High-risk unintentional insulin ODs
- **Health care workers:** High-risk intentional insulin ODs; suicides, homicides, child abuse, and elder abuse (*Klaus von Bulow* case, Newport, RI)

Differential Lab Evaluation

- **Exogenous insulin-induced:** ↑ Insulin levels + ↑ insulin antibodies + ↓ *C-peptide levels.*
- **Sulfonylurea-induced:** ↑ Insulin levels + ↑ *C-peptide levels* + no insulin antibodies + urinary sulfonylurea metabolites present.
- C-peptide levels—*mirror endogenous and not exogenous insulin levels.* Only endogenous insulin and sulfonylureas, which stimulate endogenous insulin release can *increase C-peptide levels.*

Endocrine: Thyroid-Active Agents

Antithyroid Agents

- **β-Blockers:** ↓ Peripheral deiodination of less active T4 to more active *T3, which ↑↑ upregulates B receptors*
- **Propylthiouracil (PTU):** Inhibits thyroid synthesis of T3 and T4 and ↓ peripheral deiodination of T4 to T3
- **Methimazole:** Same as PTU, can cause agranulocytosis and cholestatic jaundice

Only two drugs can cause both hypothyroidism and hyperthyroidism:

- *Amiodarone*: Hypothyroidism in 25%
- *Lithium*: Hypothyroidism in 5–15%

Note: Only *T*4, levothyroxine (Synthroid®), is indicated for tx of hypothyroidism because it is more stable and induces less thyrotoxicity than T3.

Endocrine: *Bone*-Active Agents

Bone-Active Agents

- *Vitamin D*: ↑ Ca, "stones, bones, moans, groans"
- *Calcitonin*: ↓ Bone resorption
- *Bisphosphonates*: ↓ Bone resorption, esophagitis, jaw osteonecrosis

Hormones

Anabolic Steroids

- Testosterone and 12-α-alkylated androgens
- ↑LDL and ↓HDL =↑ CAD
- ↑ BPH and ↑ prostate cancer
- ↑ Testicular atrophy and ↑ infertility
- Mania and road rage
- Hepatotoxic cholestasis and ↑ liver cancer
- Peliosis hepatis

Anabolic Steroid Abuse and Peliosis Hepatis

- *Cycling*: Taking anabolic steroids (AS) for a period, stopping, and restarting
- *Stacking*: Using two or more AS simultaneously
- *Pyramiding*: Escalating the dose, frequency, and/or number of AS to a mid-cycle peak and then deescalating to zero
- *Peliosis hepatis*: Cystic blood-filled cavities scattered throughout liver associated with coagulopathy and liver rupture and failure

Estrogens

- Thromboembolism
- Breast and endometrial cancer
- Postmenopausal MI and CVA
- Hyperglycemia
- Hypertriglyceridemia

Common Electrolyte Abnormalities Associated with Endocrinopathies and Drug Toxicities

See Table 11.2.

Table 11.2 Electrolytes

	Sodium	Potassium	Calcium	Magnesium
↓	Lethargy, ↓ mental status, and ↑ seizures	Weakness, arreflexia, paralysis, flat T and U waves	Paresthesias, carpopedal spasms, tetany, seizures, long QT	Lethargy, weakness, reduced deep tendon reflexes (DTRs), tremor
	Polydipsia	Polyuria	Fluoride toxicity (fluorosis)	Beta-agonists
	Diuretics	Hyperventilation	Ethylene glycol (oxaluria)	Fluoride
	SIADH	Vomiting		Diuretics
	Lithium	Diarrhea		RTA
	Glycine irrigation (transurethral resection of the prostate or TURP)			
↑	Weakness, hypertension, tachycardia	Ascending paralysis, ↑ dig toxicity	N, V, ↓ mental status	Reduced DTRs, paralysis
	Dehydration	ADH antagonist diuretics	short QT interval	Antacid abuse
	Vomiting or emetics	Hypo-aldosteronism	Antacid and vitamin D abuse	$MgSO_4$ therapy tx
	Diarrhea or cathartics	Renal failure	Cholecalciferol rodenticide	
	Sorbitol (↑ Cl)			
	Excessive sweating: Organophosphate pesticide-induced Salivation, Lacrimation, Urination, Defecation, Emesis (SLUDE)			

Chapter 12

Cardiovascular Drug Toxicity

Cardiac Glycosides 242
β-Blockers 245
Calcium Channel Blockers 248
Classification of Antiarrhythmics 250
Miscellaneous Antihypertensives. 250
Drugs That Cause QT Prolongation and/or Torsades de Pointes. 254

Cardiac Glycosides

Etiology

- Digoxin is most often implicated.
- **Rarely implicated cardiac glycosides:** Digitoxin, ouabain, and lanatoside C (now used infrequently).
- **Plant glycoside ingestions:** Foxglove, oleander, lily-of-the-valley, and red squill.
- **Toad skin venom:** Presumed aphrodisiacs secreted by Bufo toads (family Bufonidae) that contain bufotoxins, especially from the bufadienolide class. The common U.S. species include Colorado River toad (*Bufo alvariusi*), cane toad (*Bufo marinus*), and the American toad.

Mechanisms

- Inhibition of the Na–K ATPase-dependent myocardial sarcolemmal pump
- Positive inotropic effect from elevated intracellular (cytosolic) Ca during systole
- **Direct and indirect vagomimetic effects = cause the most common side effects:** Nausea, vomiting, bradycardia, and heart block
- Peripheral vasodilation and reduced afterload

Plant Glycosides

- Foxglove (*Digitalis purpurea*)
- Oleander (*Nerium oleander*)

Natural Glycosides

- Lily-of-the-valley (*Convallaria majalis*)
- Cane toad (*Bufo marinus*)

Pharmacology

- **Slow absorption and onset:** IV 5–30 min; orally 1.5–6 h
- 25% protein binding
- **High volume of distribution (Vd):** 6–7 L/kg in adults, even greater in children
- **Half-life:** 1.6 days
- Limited hepatic metabolism and enterohepatic circulation
- 60–80% renal excretion
- **Narrow therapeutic index:** 0.5–2.0 ng/mL

Pathophysiology

- At toxic doses, digoxin suppresses the sinoatrial (SA) node, increasing atrial and ventricular automaticity causing extrasystoles and tachydysrhythmias: junctional tachycardia, atrial fibrillation, atrial flutter, and ventricular tachycardia (VT)—ventricular fibrillation (VF), pathognomonic bidirectional VT (torsades de pointes)

- Reduces conduction velocity in atria, ventricles, and atrioventricular (AV) node = increased PR interval, sinus bradycardia, SA and junctional blocks, and AV blocks
- **Noncardiac:** Anorexia, nausea, vomiting, cramps, confusion, hyperkalemia (blocks cytosolic K entry), and hypomagnesemia

Toxicity Effects: Adults vs. Children

Adults

- **Cardiac:** Sinus bradycardia, AV block, nonparoxysmal atrial tachycardia, premature ventricular contractions (PVCs), bigeminy, and bidirectional ventricular tachycardia (VT) (torsades de pointes), VF.
- **Noncardiac:** Anorexia, crampy abdominal pain, nausea (N) and vomiting (V), confusion, dizziness, fatigue, lethargy, and delirium. Unique visual disturbances: halos, yellow and green flashes and objects, and darkened and blurred vision.

Children

- **Cardiac:** Bradycardia, 1st–2nd degree AV Blocks, junctional rhythm, SA arrest, SA blocks, AV junctional tachycardia, and rarely VF
- **Noncardiac:** Lethargy and vomiting

Lab Diagnosis

Serum Digoxin Levels

- **Very narrow therapeutic index:** 0.5–2.0 ng/mL
- **Heightened toxicity caused by electrolyte changes and certain drugs:** Decreased levels of K–Mg–Ca, elevated Na, alkalosis, hypothyroidism, decreased level of O_2, catecholamines, CCBs, quinidine, amiodarone, diuretics (via hypokalemia), and enzyme inhibition by cimetidine
- Increased by digoxin-like immunoreactive substances (DLIS) and digoxin–Fabs

Endogenous Digoxin-Like Immunoreactive Substances Are Associated with

- Renal insufficiency
- Pregnancy
- Liver disease
- **Heart disease:** Congestive heart failure (CHF)
- **CNS insults:** Subarachnoid hemorrhage (SAH)
- **Endocrinopathies:** Insulin-dependent diabetes mellitus (IDDM) and acromegaly
- **Neonates:** Stress and elevated serum bilirubin levels
- **Adults:** Stress and drugs = spironolactone (via hyperkalemia)
- **Polyclonal digoxin radioimmunoassays (RIAs):** To clarify true increase [digoxin]

General Management

- Discontinue digoxin, gastrointestinal decontamination, especially with AC.
- Orogastric lavage preferred to emesis in a digoxin-toxic patient already vomiting.
- AC and sorbitol, then MDAC up to 1 g/kg every 2–4 h. Slow absorption and an enterohepatic circulation make digoxin very amenable to decontamination, with both AC and MDAC.
- **Steroid-binding resins:** Cholestyramine and colestipol bind digoxin and interrupt enterohepatic circulation along with MDAC.
- Hemoperfusion and hemodialysis ineffective due to high molecular weight and increased Vd.

Specific Management

- **Digoxin-specific antibody fragments—Fabs (DigiBind®):** Will decrease free digoxin, but elevate total serum digoxin levels; Fabs will also decrease levels of K and increase excretion of Fab-bound digoxin.
- **K > 5 mEq/L:** Fab > insulin and glucose > $NaHCO_3$ > sodium polystyrene sulfonate.
- **Supraventricular tachycardia (SVT):** Fab preferred over β-blockers.
- **AV block:** Fab preferred over pacemaker.
- **Ventricular tachycardia/ventricular fibrillation:** Cardioversion/defibrillation preferred over Fab, phenytoin, and lidocaine.
- **Contraindicated medications:** Isoproterenol and, especially, calcium, due to increased intracellular calcium stores.

Digoxin-Specific Fabs

Indications

- Rising K or K > 5 mEq/L at any time
- **Severe ventricular dysrhythmias:** VT, VF, and torsades de pointes
- Progressive bradydysrhythmias refractory to atropine
- Serum [dig] > 10–15 ng/mL anytime
- Ingestion of >4 mg of digoxin by a child, and >10 mg by an adult

Dose Calculations for Digoxin Fab Therapy

- Each vial of DigiBind® contains 38 mg of purified digoxin-specific Fabs that will bind exactly 0.5 mg of digoxin.
- Assume 80% bioavailability on absorption of ingested digoxin.
- **Example:** An adult who is 70 kg ingests # 50 tablets (0.25-mg tabs); 0.25 mg × 50 tablets ingested = 12.5 mg total digoxin ingested; 12.5 × 0.80 = 10 mg total digoxin absorbed; and 10/0.5 = 20 vials of DigiBind® are indicated.
- Give at least 5–20 vials of DigiBind® whenever treatment of digoxin toxicity is indicated.

β-Blockers (See Figure 12.1)

Overdose Epidemiology

- During 1989–1995, 5000 β-blocker overdoses were reported to the American Association of Poison Control Centers (AAPCCs), with 15 adult deaths and no pediatric deaths.
- Children <6 years old accounted for 1/3 of all exposures, but no deaths.
- Intentional β-blocker overdose occurred most commonly with propranolol, frequently prescribed to patients with suicidal ideations = anxious, nervous, hyperactive, stressed out, often with migraine headaches, and chronic pain syndromes or tremors.

β-Adrenergic Physiology

- Catecholamines (norepinephrine [NE], epinephrine) stimulate their β-adrenergic receptors that are coupled to G-proteins on myocardial, pulmonary, and vascular membrane surfaces.
- This stimulation increases intracellular cAMP, which in turn activates protein kinases, the ultimate end mediators of the cellular effects of β-receptor stimulation.
- **There are three (three) types of β-receptors:** β1, β2, and β3, with β1 subserving the cardiovascular effects of increasing cardiac contractility, intracardiac conduction velocity, cardiac automaticity, and renal renin secretion.
- Specific β1-receptor stimulation causes the cardiovascular effects of increased cardiac contractility, intracardiac conduction velocity, cardiac automaticity, and renal renin secretion.
- Specific β2-receptor stimulation causes peripheral arteriolar vasodilation, pulmonary bronchodilation, hepatic gluconeogenesis, and glycogenolysis, increased insulin secretion with hypoglycemia, and increased uptake by muscle resulting in serum hypokalemia.
- β3-receptor stimulation probably mediates thermogenesis and lipolysis.
- Even the most selective β-blockers will lose their selectivity in overdose.

Classification (Mean Half-Life = 5 h)

Nonselective β-Blockers (β1 and β2)

- Labetolol (also increased an α1-blocker)
- Nadolol (half-life = 10 h)
- Oxprenolol (exhibits intrinsic sympathetic activity [ISA])
- Pindolol (exhibits ISA)
- Propranolol (increased lipid solubility)
- Sotolol (increased half-life = 10 h)
- Timolol

β_1-Selective Blockers

- Acebutalol (ISA)
- Atenolol (increased H_2O solubility)
- Esmolol (very short acting)
- Metoprolol

Indications

- **Hypertension:** β1-selective > nonselectives, which also block bronchodilation and peripheral vasodilation and could exacerbate bronchospasm in obstructive pulmonary disease and lower-extremity claudication in peripheral vascular disease
- **Angina:** Reduces anginal attacks and decreases postmyocardial infarction mortality
- **Tachydysrhythmias:** Used in theophylline overdose, butadenosine is preferred over β-blockers
- **Tremor:** Propanolol over prescribed agitation, stage fright, and panic attacks ("shakes")
- Migraine headaches
- **Hyperthyroidism:** β-blockers moderate the sympathetic, hyperdynamic effects of thyroid storm

Side Effects

- **Bronchospasm:** Nonselectives prevent bronchodilation and promote bronchospasm in chronic obstructive pulmonary disease (COPD) patients.
- **High anaphylaxis risk:** Nonselectives block catechol's ability to reduce mast cell degranulation in patients with atopic allergies.
- **Hypoglycemia:** All β-blockers mask the sympathetic response to hypoglycemia and interfere with gluconeogenesis/glycogenolysis.
- **Withdrawal:** Rebound increased heart rate and elevated blood pressure on abrupt withdrawal can precipitate MI and CVA.

Toxicity

- **Asymptomatic:** 1/3 of all β-blocker overdoses
- **Mild toxicity:** Bradycardia, mild hypotension, and ECG—increased PR interval and widened QRS
- **Moderate toxicity:** Sinus arrest, AV block, severe hypotension, and hypoglycemia
- **Severe toxicity:** All of the above and cardiovascular collapse, delirium, coma, seizures (especially with propranolol overdose), respiratory depression, bronchospasm in COPD patients, and possibly, asthmatics

DDx: Drug-Induced Bradycardia

- **β-blockers:** Hypotension, depressed mental status, slightly elevated K, and ECG—prolonged PR interval and widened QRS

- **CCBs:** Hypotension, preserved mental status, and ECG—PR-prolonged interval and widened QRS complex
- **Digoxin:** Nausea and vomiting, hyperkalemia, hypertension, and mental status preserved; ECG—prolonged PR, ST changes, atrial, and then ventricular dysrhythmias
- **Na-channel blockers:** Seizures, hypotension, depressed mental status, and ECG—widened QRS complex
- **Cholinergics:** SLUDE, DUMBBELS, and ECG—sinus tachycardia or paradoxical bradycardia
- **α-Agonists: α1 = phenylpropanolamine (PPA):** Severe hypertension, intracranial hemorrhage (ICH), and sinus bradycardia; α2 = clonidine, imidazolines cause an opioid toxidrome, with pinpoint miosis and sinus bradycardia

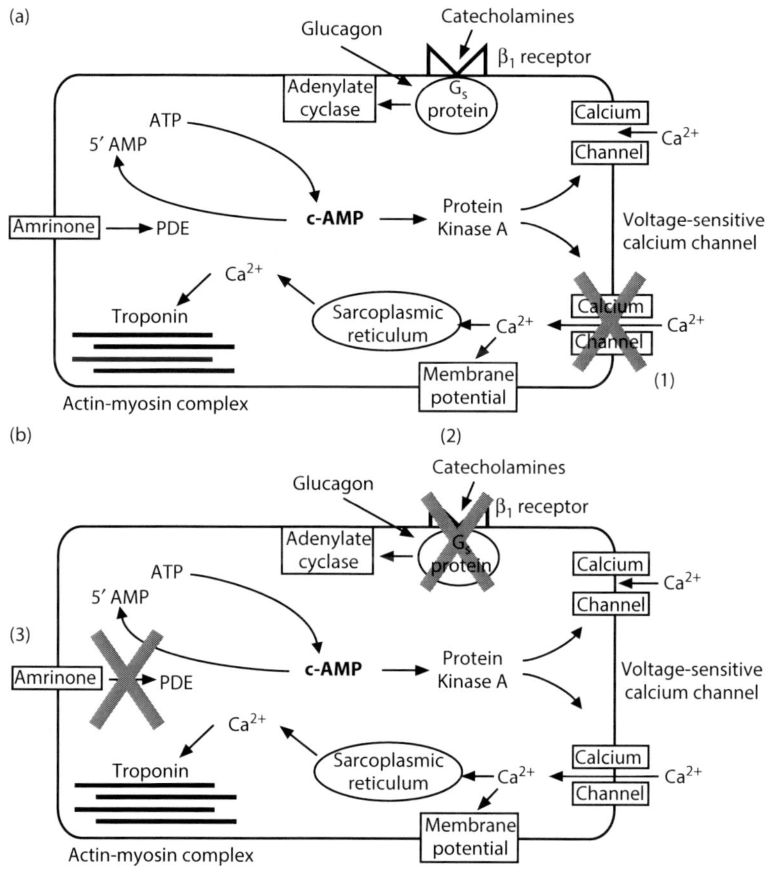

FIGURE 12.1 Cardiovascular adrenergic physiology and pharmacology. The cardiovascular molecular receptors and ionic channels and the mechanisms and (a) calcium channel blockers (CCBs): site of action (1); (b) β-receptor blockers (2) and phosphodiesterase inhibitors (3): sites of action.

General Overdose Management

- **Asymptomatic:** No ipecac, AC preferred over lavage with vagomimetic effects, and WBI for sustained-release preps
- **Mild toxicity:** All of the above and atropine for bradycardia and fluid bolus for hypotension
- **Moderate toxicity:** All of the above and glucagon (hormone secreted by pancreatic α-cells in response to decreased levels of glucose and elevated catechols); administer 2–5 mg bolus of glucagon IV push to bypass β-receptors and to increase intracellular cAMP; CaCl2 IV up to 1 g; and consider more atropine, up to 3 mg IV

Specific Management of Severe Toxicity

- General management and invasive monitoring.
- **Catecholamine infusion:** Dobutamine (β1) preferred over NE (α and β) and isoproterenol.
- Isoproterenol is the least-preferred catecholamine due to peripheral vasodilation with hypotension (from β2 stimulation).
- **Add a phosphodiesterase inhibitor:** Amrinone or milrinone to bypass β-receptors and increase intracellular cAMP restoring cardiac contractility.
- Consider IV insulin and glucose therapy.
- Consider ventricular pacing.
- Hemodialysis rarely indicated.

Calcium Channel Blockers (See Figure 12.1)

Epidemiology of CCB Overdose

- In 1995, there were more than 8300 CCB overdoses, >1000 caused moderate-to-major toxicity, with 69 deaths, mostly from sustained-release preparations.
- CCBs are No. 3 in prescribed drug overdoses, after No. 1 TCAs/SSRIs and No. 2 opioids.
- In 1989, verapamil, diltiazem, and nifedipine were among the top 20 prescribed drugs.

CCB Physiology

- Cardiac and smooth muscle cells (GI and vascular) require active influx of Ca through L-type, voltage-sensitive Ca channels for excitation–contraction coupling (ECC), and cardiac, vascular, and intestinal muscle conduction and contraction.
- Skeletal muscle depends on its own intracellular Ca stores for ECC and is unaffected by CCBs.
- Ca influx also modulates myocardial conduction by stimulating spontaneous depolarization (phase 4) in SA node and propagating conduction from the SA node and through the AV node.

CCB Pharmacology

- CCBs block L-type, slows Ca channels in cardiac and smooth muscle cells.
- CCBs limit Ca entry into cardiac and smooth muscle cells, reducing ECC and slowing intracardiac electrical conduction.
- Myocardial force of contraction and inotropy is decreased; conduction through the SA and AV nodes is reduced; and vascular smooth muscle relaxes, causing peripheral vasodilation and lowered blood pressure.
- CCBs are well absorbed orally, hepatically metabolized and highly protein bound, and have increased Vd (not dialyzable).

CCB Classification

- **Phenylalkylamines:** Exert the greatest effects on SA and AV normal conduction and cause profound negative inotropic effects in overdose:
  - Verapamil (Calan®)
- **Benzothiazepines:** Diltiazem (Cardizem®)
- **Dihydropyridines:** The largest, safest, and most frequently prescribed class of CCBs:
  - Nifedipine (Procardia®)
  - Nimodopine (Nimotop®)
  - Nicardipine (Cardene®)

CCB Indications

- Severe hypertension
- **Tachycardias:** Atrial fibrillation, atrial flutter, and reentrant SVT
- **High peripheral vascular resistance (PVR) with hypertension and/or vasospastic conditions:** Raynaud's phenomenon, Prinzmetal's angina, cardioesophageal spasm, vascular headaches, post-SAH, and cerebral vasospasm

Clinical Manifestations

Onset and Severity of Poisoning

- Toxicity presents within 2–3 h post ingestion with regular-release preparations.
- Toxicity may be delayed for 6 to 15 h with sustained-release preparations with half-lives >48 h.
- **Comorbidities:** CHF and advancing age magnify predisposition to and severity of toxicity from CCB overdoses.

Forme Fruste Clinical Presentation

- **Cardiovascular:** Myocardial depression with bradycardia and peripheral vasodilation = hypotension, decreased myocardial conduction = AV block may progress to complete heart block.

- **CNS:** Lightheadedness, dizziness, fatigue, lethargy, syncope, and rarely, coma. Severe CNS depression uncommon, as opposed to β-blocker toxicity with heart block and profound CNS depression.
- Reduced insulin release = hyperglycemia.
- **Pulmonary:** Noncardiogenic pulmonary edema (NCPE) from increased transcapillary hydrostatic pressure.

General Overdose Management

- **Gastrointestinal decontamination:** No ipecac due to rapid deterioration in the level of consciousness; immediate orogastric lavage within 1–2 h.
- **AC:** 1 g/kg and cathartic, then MDAC, 0.5 g/kg, especially for sustained-release preparations.
- **WBI:** WBI with PEG–ELS for sustained-release preparations, 1–2 L via NG and antiemetic.
- **Monitoring:** ECG, good IV access.

Specific Management

- **Atropine:** 0.5 mg IV every 2–3 min, to 3 mg.
- **10% $CaCl_2$:** 3 times more ionic calcium activity than calcium gluconate, dose = calcium chloride: 1 g IV (20 mg/kg); calcium gluconate: 3 g IV (60 mg/kg).
- **Vasopressor support:** Epinephrine > NE > phenylephrine > dopamine > dobutamine (β2) > isoproterenol (β2).
- **Glucagon:** Bypasses β-receptor to increase cAMP; administer 2–5 mg IV push over 1 min, infuse at 4 mg/h.
- **Phosphodiesterase inhibitor:** Amrinone > milrinone to bypass β-receptor and to increase intracellular cAMP.
- Intra-aortic balloon pump > cardiopulmonary bypass > extracorporeal membrane oxygenation% > pacemaker.
- Consider insulin and glucose therapy.

Classification of Antiarrhythmics

See Table 12.1.

Miscellaneous Antihypertensives

Sympatholytics

Classification

- **Central α2-agonists:** Clonidine (Catapress®), α-methyldopa (Aldomet® a prodrug that induces central α2-agonist activity), and imidazolines (eye/nose drops)
- **Ganglionic blockers:** Trimethaphan (Arfonad®)

Table 12.1 Vaughan–Williams Classifications of Antiarrhythmics

Class	Mechanisms	Toxicity	Examples
Class IA	Short-acting, open-state, Na channel block > K channel block	Widened QRS; prolonged QT, SA, and AV blocks; and torsades	Quindine Procainamide Disopyramide
Class IB	Increased effective refractory period; short-acting Na channel block	Biphasic CNS—cardiovascular toxicity—CNS > CV; little change in QRS and QT; sinus arrest; and AV block	Lidocaine Mexilitene Tocanide Phenytoin Propafenone
Class IC	Prolonged Na, K, and Ca channel blocks	Widened QRS, prolonged QT, SA, and AV blocks, and VT–VF	Ecainide Flecanide
Class II	β_1- and β_2-blockers, selective (β_1) and nonselective (β_1 and β_2)	Prolonged PR, widened QRS, bradycardia, AV block, bronchospasm, hyperglycemia, and hypotension	Esmolol (β_1) Labetolol (β_1, β_2) Propranolol (β_1, β_2)
Class III	K channel blockers, prolonged depolarization, and repolarization	Sinus bradycardia, profound negative inotropism, and severe hypotension	Amiodarone (hypothyroidism, pulmonary fibrosis, and corneal microdeposits) Bretylium (initial hypertension)
Class IV	L-type Ca channel blockers	Bradycardia and hypotension, AV blocks, lethargy and vertigo, little CNS depression	Verapamil Diltiazem Nifedipine
Unclassified: adenosine	Purine (adenosine) receptor agonist, very short half-life	Sinus arrest, asystole, bronchospasm, hypotension, methylxanthine-induced SVTs require larger doses due to adenosine receptor antagonism	Adenosine

- **Peripheral adrenergic blockers:** Guanethidine (Ismelin®), reserpine
- **Peripheral α1-blockers:** Prazosin (Minipress®)

Mechanisms, Indications, and Side Effects

- **Reduce central sympathetic outflow:** Indicated for hypertension, migraine, and opioid/EtOH withdrawal, as nasal decongestants; side effects include withdrawal, rebound hypertension, and α-methyldopa causes a Coomb and hemolytic anemia
- **Reduce postganglionic autonomic transmission:** Often used for deliberate hypotension to limit surgical blood loss
- **Reduce NE release from distal nerve terminals:** Initially used to treat hypertension, prior to newer antihypertensives
- Block postsynaptic α1-receptors in vascular smooth muscle

Toxicity

- **α2-Agonists:** Opioid toxidrome = miosis, bradycardia; hypotension and CNS depression may follow initial paradoxical hypertension, and hypothermia; CNS depression = lethargy, somnolence, and stupor
- **Ganglionic blockers:** Hypotension, constipation, and urinary retention
- **Peripheral blockers:** Hypotension, orthostasis, drowsiness, and diarrhea
- **Peripheral α1-blockers:** Hypotension, syncope, orthostasis, and CNS depression

Management

- No ipecac, AC, whole-bowel irrigation (WBI) for clonidine patch ingestions, naloxone drip, IV fluids, and sodium nitroprusside (SCN) for initial hypertension
- Crystalloid fluid boluses, direct-acting vasopressors—NE > phenylephrine
- Crystalloid fluid boluses and vasopressors (dopamine)

Diuretics

Classification

- **Thiazides:** HCTZ (Hydrodiuril®), chlorthalidone (Hygroton®)
- **Loop diuretics:** Furosemide (Lasix®), bumetanide (Bumex®), and ethacrynic acid (Edecrin®)
- **K-sparing diuretics:** Triamterene (Maxzide®), spironolactone (Aldactone®)

Mechanisms, Indications, and Side Effects

- **Limit Na and Cl reabsorption in distal convoluted tubule:** Indicated for hypertension, diuresis.
- **Limit K–Na–Mg reabsorption:** Indicated for digoxin toxicity.
- **Limit Na–K–Cl reabsorption in ascending loop:** Indicated for diuresis.
- **Limit Na and Cl reabsorption in distal convoluted tubule and collecting ducts, aldosterone antagonists:** Indicated for diuresis.
- **Side effects:** Hyperuricemia (gout), hyponatremia, hypokalemia, and ototoxicity; aldosterone antagonist may cause hyperkalemia and precipitate digitalis toxicity.

Toxicity

- **Hypovolemia:** From brisk diuresis.
- **Electrolyte disturbances:** Low serum Na, K, Cl, and Mg levels may be associated with altered mental status, muscle weakness, and digoxin toxicity.

Management

- Fluid replacement
- **Electrolyte replacement:** Restore normal Na, Cl, K, and Mg levels; consider sodium polystyrene sulfonate-binding agent for hyperkalemia from K-sparing diuretics; and monitor digoxin levels

Vasodilators

- **Direct smooth muscle vasodilators:**
  - Hydralazine (Apresoline®)
  - Minoxidil (Rogaine®)
  - Diazoxide (Hyperstat®)
  - SCN (Nipride®)

Mechanisms, Indications, and Side Effects

- **All:** Produce vascular smooth muscle relaxation with peripheral vasodilation and triggering of baroreceptor-mediated tachycardia; main uses—hypertension
- **Management of toxicity:** Fluids, α-pressors
- **Hydralazine:** Same indications, and lupus syndrome possible as a side effect, as with procaineamide
- **Minoxidil:** Same indications, and hair growth
- **Diazoxide:** Same, and immediate increase in glucose in the management of insulin and oral hypoglycemic overdoses
- **SCN:** Vasodilation via nitric oxide mechanism; cyanide (CN) toxicity possible
- (Lilly CN kit—sodium nitrite first, then sodium thiosulfate)

Angiotensin Blockers (See Figure 12.2)

Classification

- **Angiotensin-converting enzyme (ACE) inhibitors:** Captopril (Capoten®), enalapril (Vasotec®), lisinopril (Prinivil®), and quinapril (Accupril®)
- **Angiotensin II receptor blockers:** Losartan (Cozaar®), valsartan

Mechanisms, Indications, and Side Effects

- **ACE inhibitors:** Block the conversion of angiotensin I into II in lungs and vascular endothelium, reduced PVR, and lower blood pressure; indications—hypertension; side effects: reduced bradykinin breakdown in lungs, causing angioedema and cough
- **Management of toxicity:** Epinephrine, H1-blockers, and steroids
- **Angiotensin receptor blockers:** Decrease formation of angiotensin II at vascular receptor sites; indications—hypertension; side effects: few, bradykinin metabolism unaffected, no angioedema, and cough so common with ACE inhibitor therapy

Unclassified: Adenosine

- A naturally occurring nucleoside and G-protein with its own specific adenosine receptors; IV boluses of adenosine are indicated to rapidly terminate reentrant and theophylline-induced SVTs.
- **Mechanisms:** Provides an evanescent (10 s) calcium entry block and increases AV nodal refractory period; reduces action potentials and reduces automaticity.

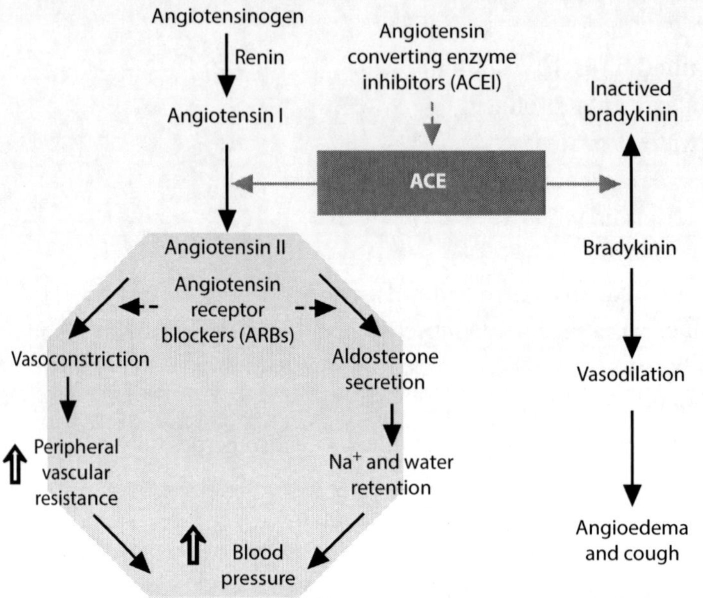

FIGURE 12.2 The renin–angiotensin–aldosterone (RAA) pathway and mechanisms of action. Flowchart demonstrating the RAA system and mechanisms of action and the sites of action of ACE inhibitors and angiotensin receptor blockers (ARBs).

- **Toxicities:** Transient asystole, atrial fibrillation, hypotension, and bronchospasm. All toxicities are potentiated by the antiplatelet agent, dipyridamole, an adenosine uptake inhibitor. Higher doses are required for methylxanthine overdoses due to adenosine receptor blockade.
- **Treatment of toxicity:** Supportive.

Class IA: Quinidine

- **Mechanism:** Na, K, and Ca channel blocker
- **Pharmacology:** An amide local anesthetic, with excellent mucosal absorption, d-isomer of quinine, the antimalarial from cinchona bark; rapidly absorbed orally; high Vd and protein binding
- **Toxicity:** Prolonged QT interval and widened QRS complex, VT, VF, torsades, hypotension, seizures, noncardiogenic pulmonary edema (NCPE), and cinchonism
- **Treatment:** Decontamination—no ipecac, orogastric lavage; IV fluids and vasoMech (a cardiac and peripheral Na channel blocker)

Drugs That Cause QT Prolongation and/or Torsades de Pointes

See Table 12.2.

Table 12.2 Drugs That Cause QT Prolongation and/or Torsades de Pointes

Definite TdP Risk	Associated with QT Prolongation and TdP but Unclear Risk
Antiarrhythmics (1, 7, 9.10,13–15, 65–75, 161, and 162)	
Quinindine Disopyramide Procainamide Amiodarone Ibutilide Sotalol Dofetilide Flecainide	Dronedarone Propafenone Mexiletine
Other Cardiac Drugs (5, 9, 76–78)	
Bepridil	Nicardipine Moexipril/HCTZ Ranolazine Isradipine
Antipsychotics (91–100,159)	
Haloperidol Thioridazine Chlorpromazine Mesoridazine Pimozide	Risperidone Paliperidone Iloperidone Clozapine Olanzapine Quetiapine Ziprasidone Aripiprazole Asenapine Sertinodole Sulpiride Amisulpride
Antidepressants (100–106)	
	Escitalopram Venlafaxine Maprotiline Citalopram Fluoxetine Paroxetine Sertraline Amitriptyline Nortriptyline Protriptyline Clomipramine Desipramine

Chapter 13

Antibiotic Toxicity

Outline 258
Penicillins (Pcns) 258
Cephalosporins. 258
Disulfiram Reactions 259
Mushroom Poisonings 259
Aminoglycosides 259
Aminoglycoside Ototoxicity 260
Chloramphenicol and Vancomycin 260
Quinolones and Macrolides 260
Sulfonamides and Tetracyclines. 261
Antifungals. 261
Antituberculous Agent Toxicity 262
TB and INH Epidemiology 262
INH Pharmacokinetics. 262
INH Mechanisms and Toxicity 263
INH Overdose (OD) Management. 264
Chronic INH Toxicity 265
Other Anti-TB Agents 265
Streptomycin 266
Antimalarial Toxicity 266
Other Antimalarials 268

Outline

- Antibiotic and antifungal agent toxicity
- Antituberculous agent toxicity
- Antimalarial agent toxicity
- Penicillins
- Cephalosporins
- Aminoglycosides
- Chloramphenicol
- Vancomycin
- Fluoroquinolones
- Macrolides
- Sulfonamides
- Tetracyclines
- Antifungals

Penicillins (Pcns)

Mechanism and Toxicity

- **Mech:** β-lactams that erode bacterial cell walls by inhibiting mucopeptide synthesis. Subgroup includes carbapenems (imipenem).
- **Tox:** GI (nausea [N], vomiting [V], diarrhea [D]) > allergy > CNS.
- **Allergy:** *5% manifest pcn sensitivities* = local pruritus, asthma; *1% develop anaphylaxis.* Tx: O_2, epi-NE, β_2-agonists, steroids, H_1 and H_2 blockers, theophylline, fluids. Consider glucagon for severe ↓ BP.
- **CNS:** Seizures 2° gamma-aminobutyric acid (GABA) inhibition by binding to the GABA picrotoxin receptor.
- **Tx:** BZs > barbs.

Unique Toxicities

- **Jarisch–Herxheimer Reaction:** Acute febrile response to Ag's from *lysed spirochetes* = myalgias, chills, fever, HA, rash
- **Hoigne Syndrome:** Local anesthetic toxicity rxn 2° *procaine* penicillin G = *seizures*, hallucinations, ↑ HR *and* BP
- **Hyperkalemia:** 2° K-pcn G administration in chronic renal failure (CRF) pts

Cephalosporins

Mechanism and Toxicity

- **Mech:** β-lactams like pcns that ↓ bacterial cell wall integrity
- **Tox:** Allergy > heme
- **Allergy:** 4% in general pop, but ↑ to *8% in those with a preexisting pcn allergy*

- **Heme:** Acute hemolysis
- **Acute OD:** Same as pcn, but not as life threatening
- **CNS:** Sz 2° GABA antagonism, like pcns *and* imipenem

Unique Cephalosporin Toxicities

- **n-Methylthiotetrazole (nMTT) side chain rxns:** *Disulfiram-like rxns* 2° inhibition aldehyde dehydrogenase = N, V, *and* flushing on ethanol (EtOH) consumption
- **nMTT-mediated hypoprothrombinemia:** 2° inhibition vit K epoxide reductase formation of active vitamin K
- **nMTT reps:** Cefazolin, cefotetan, cefamandole, moxalactam

Disulfiram Reactions

Antimicrobial-Induced Disulfiram Reactions

1. **Antibiotics:** nMTT-side chain cephalosporins, chloramphenicol, sulfonamides-nitrofurantoin
2. **Antifungals:** Metronidazole, griseofulvin
   - **Antivirals:** *Ritonavir.*
   - **Miscellaneous:** *Coprinus* spp. mushrooms; carbamates, oximes, diethyldithiocarbamate: All are related to disulfiram.

Mushroom Poisonings

Coprine Toxicity

- **Reps:** *Coprinus* spp.
- **Toxin:** Coprine metabolite = *l-aminocyclopropanol*, acetaldehyde dehydrogenase inhibitor, like disulfiram and diethyldithiocarbamate
- **Antidote:** None
- **Dx:** *Delayed* onset 0.5–2 h, *disulfiram-reaction* following ingestion of alcohol within 24–48 h with facial flushing, N and V, tachycardia, hypertension
- **Tx:** Supportive, IV fluids

Aminoglycosides

Mechanism and Toxicity

- **Mech:** Inhibit protein synthesis by blocking *30s RNA* ribosomal subunit
- **Reps:** Kanamycin, streptomycin, neomycin, gentamicin, tobramycin, amikacin
- **Tox:** Ototoxicity > renal > NMJ
- **Ototox:** 0.5–5%: (1) *cochlear dysfunction* = deafness; (2) *vestibular tox* = permanent tinnitus-vertigo from hair cell damage, same as bromates

Unique Aminoglycoside Toxicities

- Oto- and vestibular toxicity.

- **Nephrotoxicity:** ATN in the first week of tx.
- **Antidote:** *ticarcillin*-Na load protects the nephrotoxic effects *and* inactivates antimicrobial effects; removes 50% more drug than HD.
- **NM block:** 2° ↓ *presynaptic Ach release*, esp. in those on NMBs or with myasthenia gravis or botulism.

Aminoglycoside Ototoxicity

- Permanent (1) cochlear and (2) vestibular hair cell degeneration (G2)
  - Gentamicin
  - Tobramycin
- Cochlear toxicity alone
  - Amikacin
  - Kanamycin
  - Neomycin
- Permanent vestibular hair cell degeneration alone
  - **Streptomycin:** Anti-TB

Chloramphenicol and Vancomycin

Chloramphenicol

- **Mech:** Inhibits protein syn by blocking *50s* ribosomal subunit
- **Tox:** CV and *Gray baby* > heme
- **CV:** (1) Acute CV collapse in OD
- **Tx:** OG → AC, exchange trans in neonates (2) *Gray baby syn.*: ↓ BP, gray color, V, resp distress, hypoglycemia; 2° ↓ hepatic conjugation and ↓ renal ability to excrete free drug
- **Heme:** Dose-dependent BM suppression → aplastic anemia

Vancomycin

- **Mech:** ↓ glycopeptide polymerization → ↓ cell wall stability
- **Tox:** Derm/allergy > renal > heme
- **Derm:** 3.4% → *red man syn.*, a glycopeptide-induced anaphylactoid rxn with pruritus–urticaria–angioedema, ↓ BP, angina → CV collapse, seizures
- **Tx:** Slow IV adm, H_1-blockers
- **Renal:** Nephrotox 2° chronic use
- **Heme:** Rare neutropenia and ↓ plts

Quinolones and Macrolides

Fluoroquinolones

- **Reps:** Ciprofloxacin, oxfloxacin, norfloxacin, levofloxacin
- **Mech:** Inhibit DNA replication

- **Tox:** Soft tissue > CNS > renal
- **ST:** Target and damage developing *articular cartilage*, especially in *children and pregnancy*
- **CNS:** Rarely seizures 2° GABA inhibition, especially during concomitant theophylline tx
- **Renal:** Rarely renal failure

Macrolides

- **Reps:** Erythromycin estolate, erythromycin lactobionate, erythromycin stearate, clarithromycin, azithromycin.
- **Mech:** ↓ protein synthesis by inhibiting *50s* RNS ribosomal subunit.
- **Tox:** CV > drug–drug > hepatic toxicity > ototoxicity.
- **CV:** *Lactobionate* causes ↑ QT *and torsades* 2° K-channel block.
- **Drug–drug interactions:** Erythromycins *inhibit P450* = torsades when coadministered with *astemizole* or *terfenadine.*
- **Hepatotoxicity:** *Estolate* causes *cholestatic hepatitis* with chronic use.
- **Ototoxicity:** Reversible high-frequency hearing loss.
- **Cardiotoxicity: Erythromycin *lactobionate*:** Prolonged QT and torsades de pointes.

Sulfonamides and Tetracyclines

Sulfonamides

- **Mech:** Inhibit PABA metabolism required for folic acid synthesis
- **Tox:** GI (N *and* V) > dermal > heme > renal > metabolic
- **Derm:** Skin hypersensitivity
- **Heme:** BM suppression, especially with folic acid or B_{12} deficiency
- **Renal:** Nephrolithiasis
- **Metabolic:** Hypoglycemia
- **CRANK:** *c*rystalluria, *r*ash, *a*plastic *a*nemia, *n*, v, ↓ glu, *k*ernicterus

Tetracyclines

- **Reps:** Tetracycline, oxytetracycline, doxycycline, minocycline
- **Mech:** ↓ protein syn by binding to the *30s* RNA ribosomal subunit
- **Tox:** Dermal > bone > GI
- **Derm:** Sun-exposed skin develops hypersensitivity and *hyperpigmentation*
- **Bone:** *Discolors teeth* in children < 6–8-year-old and in fetuses > 12 weeks
- **GI:** N, V, epigastric pain

Antifungals

Amphotericin B

- **Mech:** Combines with ergosterol in the fungal cytoplasmic cell membrane, ↓ integrity, and ↑ porosity with leakage of cellular organelles

- **Tox:** Febrile syndrome > renal > heme
- **Febrile syndrome:** Fever (F), headache (HA), rigors, N, V, dyspnea, ↓ BP *and* HR, IV phlebitis *PreTx*: APAP, steroids, H_1-blockers
- **Renal:** *80% develop minor renal insufficiency*; later azotemia possible 2° renal tubular damage and renal artery vasoconstriction
- **Heme:** BM suppression = anemia, leukopenia, thrombocytopenia

Azoles

- **Mech:** Alter cell membranes to ↑ permeability
- **Triazoles:** Fluconazole, itraconazole
- **Imidazoles:** Miconazole, clotrimazole
- **Tox:** ↑ drug–drug interactions
- **Drug–drug:** Azoles inhibit CYP3A4, responsible for metabolizing many drugs: statins, H_1-blockers, steroids, BZs, CCBs

Antituberculous Agent Toxicity

- TB and INH toxicity and epidemiology
- INH pharmacology and toxicity
- Acute INH toxicity and management
- Chronic INH toxicity and management
- Other antituberculous agents and their toxicities and management

TB and INH Epidemiology

- TB is *epidemic* among *high-risk pops* of SE Asian immigrants, Native Americans, Inuits, alcoholics, prisoners, homeless, refugees, IVDUs, and HIV/AIDS.
- About *2 billion* people worldwide are infected with TB, with 10 million new cases/year, *and* 1 million deaths/year.
- Isonicotinyl hydrazide (INH) is among the most common causes of drug-induced *seizures* in the United States.
- 10–20% of patients taking INH will develop asymptomatic ↑ *ALT and AST* (2–3× nL); 10% of these will develop INH hepatitis (1% total) with a 10% CFR (0.1% total).
- INH toxicity risks: ↓ *acetylators (neuropathy)*, ↑ acetylators on rifampin (hepatotox), elderly, malnourished, alcoholics, liver dysfunction, INH + *rifampin* or *pyrazinamide* tx.

INH Pharmacokinetics

INH Pharmacology

- **Absorption:** Rapid po from GI tract, peak levels in 1–2 h
- **Very low Vd:** 0.6 L/kg

- **Low protein binding:** 10%
- **Mostly renally excreted:** 75–95%
- **Easily dialyzable:** 2° ↓ Vd, ↓ protein binding, and ↑ renal excretion

INH Metabolism (See Figure 13.1)

- **Hepatic metabolism:** Two pathways, (1) *acetylation* > (2) *dehydrazination*
- **Rapid acetylators:** An autosomal dominant trait present in 50% U.S. pop and 95% of Inuits, Chinese, Japanese, and Blacks—who have 30–50% less free INH than slow acetylators (most whites) with ↓ T1/2 vs. slow acetylators = ↑ INH toxicity risks only in slow acetylators also on rifampin (Figure 13.1)

INH Mechanisms and Toxicity

INH Mechanisms

Pyridoxine (or B_6 = cofactor for GABA synthesis) *antagonism* via three mech:

- **B_6 complex:** *Complexes directly with B_6* to form a large complex, not activated *and* excreted in urine.
- **INH hydrazones:** Dehydranization yields hydrazones that *inhibit pyridoxine phosphokinase*, the enzyme catalyzing activation of B_6 to an active form, pyridoxyl 5′-phosphate.
- **Inhibits pyridoxyl phosphate:** The active form of B_6 and final required cofactor for GABA synthesis = sz.

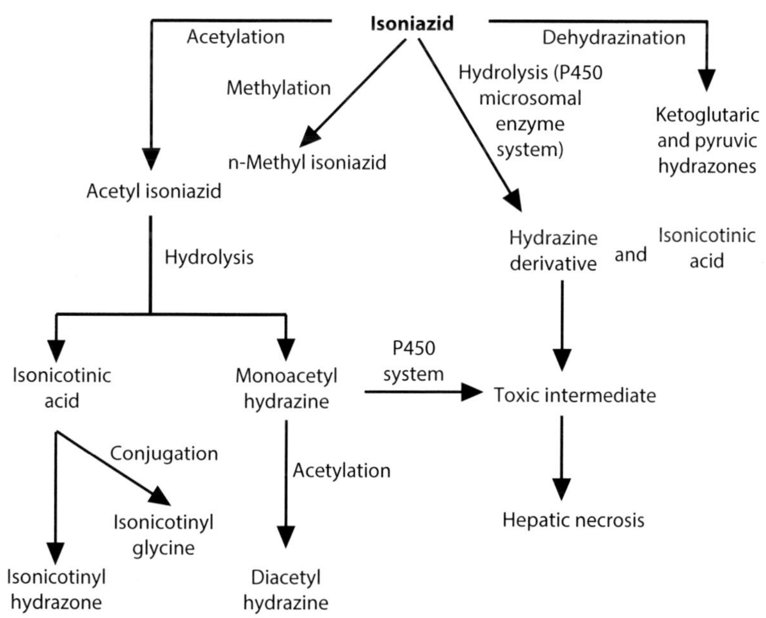

FIGURE 13.1 Isoniazid (INH) metabolism. The intrahepatic biotransformation pathways of isoniazid (INH) and the production of nontoxic and toxic intermediate metabolites.

INH Toxicity (See Figures 13.2 and 13.3)

- **Acute tox:** CNS > metabolic > GI
- *INH triad* = (1) refractory seizures, (2) metabolic acidosis, and (3) persistent coma
- **Initial GI:** N and V, then dizziness, hyperthermia, and ↓ BP
- **CNS:** Tonic–clonic sz, refractory status epilepticus (CFR 20%)
- **Met:** High anion gap metabolic acidosis mimicking diabetic ketoacidosis 2° sz and ↑ lactate
- **Toxic doses:** Seizures > 20 mg/kg; death > 50 mg/kg; LD_{50} > 80–150 mg/kg (Figures 13.2 and 13.3)

INH Overdose (OD) Management

General Mx of INH OD

- **No ipecac:** 2° ↑ seizures, AW loss, and aspiration risk
- **Secure AW:** Insert OG
- **Immediate OG lavage:** Then AC + cathartic
- **MDAC:** No cathartic
- **$NaHCO_3$:** Correct metabolic acidosis
- **Dialysis:** Reserve *HD and HP* for those with renal insufficiency

Specific Mx of INH OD

- **Pyridoxine (B_6):** For seizure control; use *1 g per g of INH* ingested or *70 mg/kg bolus*, to a max of 5 g
- **Repeat pyridoxine:** For refractory seizures and status epilepticus
- **Add diazepam:** *Diazepam and pyridoxine (B_6)* act together synergistically to enhance GABA's seizure-inhibition activity

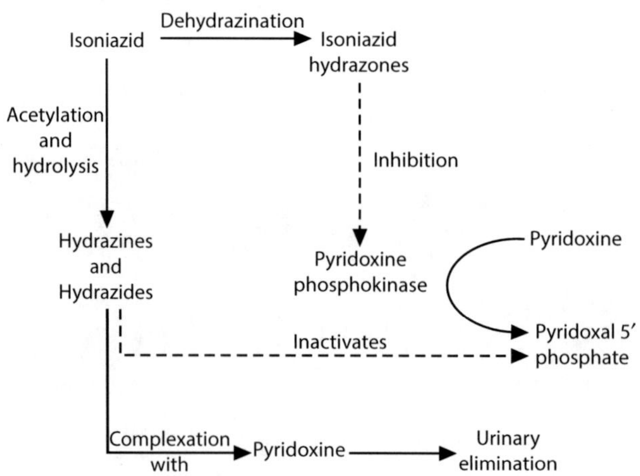

FIGURE 13.2 Isoniazid (INH) toxicity 1. The mechanisms and sites of action of isoniazid (INH)-mediated epileptogenic neurotoxicity.

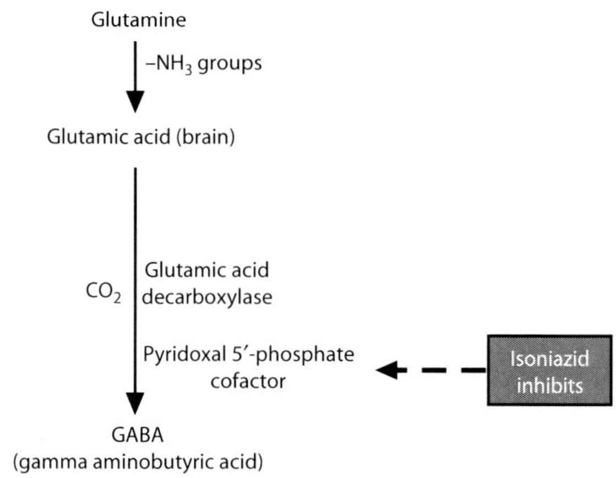

FIGURE 13.3 Isoniazid (INH) toxicity 2. Additional mechanisms and sites of action of isoniazid (INH)-mediated epileptogenic neurotoxicity.

Chronic INH Toxicity

Common SEs: #1 Hepatic

- **Adverse rxns:** *5.4%* will develop fever, rash, neuritis, or jaundice.
- **↑ LFTs:** *10%* develop asymptomatic ↑ *LFTs.*
- **INH hepatitis:** *1%* dev N, V, F, fatigue, RUQ pain 2° *hydrazine intermediates that covalently bind to hepatocytes → hepatic necrosis*, esp. in slow acetylators also taking rifampin (APAP mechanism).

Less Common SEs: #1 CNS

- **Optic neuritis:** Causes optic neuritis → optic atrophy.
- **Peripheral neuropathy:** 20% will develop a distal sensory *and* motor axonopathy.
- **Pellagra-like skin syndrome:** A triad of dermatitis, diarrhea, *and* dementia due to inability of *pyridoxyl 5′-phosphate to serve as a required cofactor in niacin synthesis* = niacin deficiency.

Other Anti-TB Agents

- Rifampin
- Ethambutol
- Pyrazinamide
- Streptomycin

Rifampin

- **Mech:** Antibiotic that inhibits DNA-dependent RNA polymerase
- **Pharm:** Well absorbed po, peaks 2–4 h, ↑ Vd 1.6 L/kg, 75% protein bound, enterohepatic circulation, 30% excreted, *potent P450 inducer*

- **Tox:** 6% GI (N, V) > dermal > hepatic
- **Derm:** *Red-orange staining* of skin, urine, tears, subcutaneous tissues with flushing, rash, pruritus
- **Hepatic:** 33% ↑ LFTs and 1% hepatitis with jaundice, esp. in slow rifampin inactivators, hx liver dis, INH co-tx
- **Tx:** OG, AC, MDAC, HD-HP ineffective

Ethambutol

- **Mech:** Antimetabolite that inhibits RNA synthesis
- **Pharm:** Well absorbed po, peaks 2–4 h, 20% metabolized, 50% excreted
- **Tox:** *Eye* > initial GI *and* CNS > metabolic
- **Ocular toxicity:** Optic neuritis, ↓ acuity, ↓ *red-green* color perception; all dose-related *and* reversible
- **GI, then CNS:** Initial N *and* crampy pain → confusion *and* hallucinations
- **Metabolic:** Inhibits renal uric acid excretion → acute gout

Pyrazinamide

- **Mech:** Bactericidal analog of nicotinic acid.
- **Pharm:** Well absorbed po, peaks in 2 h, partly metabolized, excreted by filtration.
- **Tox:** Hepatic > metabolic.
- **Hepatic:** 15% will develop acute hepatitis with CFR 2–3% 2° *acute hepatic necrosis.*
- **Met:** Inhibits renal uric acid excretion → acute gout.

Streptomycin

- **Mech:** *Aminoglycoside* that inhibits protein synthesis by binding to *30S* subunit of bacterial ribosomal RNA
- **Pharm:** IM only, peaks 1 h, 34% protein bound, T1/2 2–5 h, 89% excreted
- **Tox:** Ototox > NMJ block > heme > renal
- **Ototox:** Tinnitus, vertigo, dizziness, ataxia, *deafness*, congenital CN VIII damage
- **NM block:** ↓ *presynaptic Ach release*; reversed by Ca, not neostigmine
- **Heme:** Hemolytic anemia, IgG-mediated factor V inhibition → bleeding
- **Renal:** Aminoglycoside *nephrotoxicity*; no hepatotoxicity = exception

Antimalarial Toxicity

Outline: Antimalarials

- Current antimalarials
- Quinine and quinidine pharmacology and cinchonism
- General and specific management of quinine OD
- Toxicity and management of chloroquine OD
- Miscellaneous antimalarials and their toxicities

Current Antimalarials

- **Quinolines:** Quinine, quinidine, chloroquine, primaquine. Any combination of these with each other or with halofantrine increases the risk of torsades de pointes.
- **Dihydrofolate reductase inhibitors (FA inhibitors):** Proguanil, pyrimethamine, pyrimethamine + dapsone (Maloprim®), pyrimethamine + sulfadoxine (Fansidar®). All are folic acid inhibitors and can cause megaloblastic anemias.
- **Sulfonamides/sulfones:** Sulfonamides-sulfadoxine, dapsone. All can result in methemoglobinemia.
- **Antibiotics:** Tetracycline, doxycycline, azithromycin.
- **Miscellaneous:** Halofantrin, artemisinins. Artemisinins have short half-lives *and* must be combined with longer-acting antimalarials.

Quinine and Cinchonism

Pharm: Quinine and Quinidine

- **Source:** Quinine and quinidine, optical isomers, are extracts from the bark of the SA *Cinchona* tree
- ↑ **Absorption:** Rapid and complete po, peaks in 3 h
- ↑ **Protein binding:** 95%
- ↑ **Vd:** 1.8 L/kg
- ↑ **T1/2:** 6–8 h
- ↑ **Metabolism:** 80%
- ↓ **Renal excretion:** 20%

Cinchonism

- **Tox:** CNS > GI > derm > heme
- **CNS:** HA, dizzy-vertigo, confusion, syncope delirium, sz, coma
- **Eye:** *Mydriasis*, scotomata, diplopia, blurred vision, photophobia, visual field cuts, ↓ color vision
- **Ototox:** Tinnitus, deafness
- **CV:** IA = ↑ PR-QRS-QT; *torsades*, V tach, V fib, vasodilation → ↓ BP
- **GI/Endo:** ↑ N *and* V, ↑ insulin release-*hypoglycemia* (like *sulfonylureas*)
- **Derm:** Flushing, rash, angioedema
- **Heme:** Hemolysis in G-6-PD, ↓ plts
- **Misc:** *Oxytoxic*, premature labor

Quinine/Quinidine OD

General OD Management

- **No ipecac:** 2° emesis, seizures, aspiration
- **OG lavage:** Only for ingestions < 1 h

- **AC + cathartic:** 1 g/kg
- **MDAC:** 0.5 g/kg, no cathartic, q 2–4 h

Specific OD Management

- **Serum alkalinization:** To pH 7.45–7.50 for ↑ QRS and myocardial depression
- **Avoid IA and IC:** Antidysrhythmics → additive toxicities
- **Large Vd:** Renders HP and HD ineffective
- **Eye:** Monitor for retinal toxicity with baseline fundoscopy, visual fields, and color testing

Chloroquine Toxicity

CQ Pharm and Mechanisms

- **Epid:** Highest *CFR* of all antimalarials, narrow therapeutic index
- **Pharm:** Rapidly absorbed po, peaks 1–3 h, highly protein bound 70%, very long T1/2 40+ days, not dialyzable
- **Binds to tissues:** Liver, lungs, kidneys
- *Less ocular toxicity* than quinine/quinidine

CQ Toxicity and Mx

- **Tox:** CV and CNS > pulmonary > metabolic
- **CV:** Wide QRS, peripheral vasodilation, direct myocardial depression, severe ↓ BP → CV collapse
- **CNS:** CNS depression, HA, dizziness, seizures
- **Pulm:** Respiratory depression *and* sudden apnea possible
- **Met:** *Severe hypokalemia* → ↓ T wave, U waves, ↓ ST
- **Mx:** *Combined* epinephrine + *diazepam* = best antidote, mech?

Other Antimalarials

Mefloquine

- **Use:** CQ-resistant *P. falciparum*
- **Pharm:** Long T1/2 of 20 days
- **Tox:** CNS > CV > hepatic
- **CNS:** Hallucinations, nightmares, seizures, diffuse encephalopathy
- **CV:** ↓ BP, dysrhythmias

Primaquine

- **Use:** Relapsing malaria 2° *P. vivax* and *P. ovale*
- **Tox:** Less CNS toxicity than mefloquine
- **Methemoglobinemia:** Especially in G-6-PD deficients

Chapter 14

Anticancer Drug Toxicity

Chemotherapy Toxicity 270
Human Carcinogens 270
Classification 270
Epidemiology 275
Methotrexate: Outline 275
Anthracyclines/Antibiotics 279
Nitrogen Mustards 279
Platinoid Toxicity 280

Chemotherapy Toxicity

Outline

- Human carcinogenesis
- Classification of antineoplastic agents
- Epidemiology of chemotherapy toxicity
- Methotrexate toxicity and management
- Vincristine toxicity and management
- Anthracycline toxicity and management
- Nitrogen mustard toxicity and management
- Platinoid toxicity and management

Human Carcinogens (See Table 14.1)

- **Alkylating agents:** Cyclophosphamide, melphalan
- **Aromatics:** Aromatic amines, benzene, benzidene, and PAHs
- **Environmental toxins:** Aflatoxins, tobacco smoke, tars, soots, and hydrocarbon solvents—CCl_4
- **Hormones:** Estrogens (DES), anabolic steroids
- **Plastics:** Vinyl chloride monomer
- **Heavy metals:** Arsenic, cadmium, chromium, and nickel
- **Ionizing radiation:** Radon, x-rays
- **Nonionizing radiation:** *Ultraviolet* light
- **Miscellaneous drugs:** Chloramphenicol, phenytoin (Table 14.1)

Classification

- **Antimetabolites:** MTX—*DHFR and thymidine synthetase inhibitor* that prevents *activated, reduced folate* from serving as a cofactor for DNA and RNA synthesis. OD: mucositis, myelosuppression, and acute renal failure.
- **Antimitotics:** VCR and *vinblastine, vinca plant alkaloids* that *inhibit microtubular polymerization and arrest mitosis* at the metaphase, limiting cell movement and division. OD: seizures, encephalopathy, autonomic dysfunction, myelosuppression, and SIADH.
- **Antibiotics:** (1) The *anthracyclines* = *doxorubicin*, and so on; and (2) the *mycins* = adriamycin, *bleomycin, and* mitomycin. The anthracyclines are derived from the ***Streptomyces*** bacterium and release O^- *free radicals* (paraquat) causing severe cardiotoxicity, mucositis, and myelosuppression.
- **Alkylating agents:** (1) *Nitrogen mustards*, such as *cyclophosphamide,* causing *hemorrhagic cystitis* and myelosuppression; (2) heavy-metal *platinoids*, such as *cisplatin*, causing seizures, encephalopathy, retinal toxicity, ototoxicity, peripheral neuropathy, and nephrotoxicity (Table 14.2).

Table 14.1 Agents Associated with Human Carcinogenesis

Antineoplastic Drugs	
Agent	**Cancer Site**
Busulfan	Acute myeloid leukemia
Chlorambucil	Acute myeloid leukemia
Cyclophosphamide	Acute myeloid leukemia, bladder
Melphalan	Acute myeloid leukemia
Semustine (methyl CCNU)	Acute myeloid leukemia
Thiotepa	Leukemia
Treosulfan	Acute myeloid leukemia
MOPP-combined therapy	Acute myeloid leukemia
Etoposide in combo with cisplatin and bleomycin	Acute myeloid leukemia
Etoposide	
Chlomphazine	Bladder
Azathioprine	Non-Hodgkin lymphoma, skin
Cyclosporin	Non-Hodgkin lymphoma, skin, and multiple other sites
Methoxsalen + UV light	Skin
Plants with aristolochic acid	Renal pelvis, ureter
Aristolochic acid	
Analgesic mixtures containing phenacetin	
Phenacetin	Renal pelvis, ureter
Hormonal Treatments	
Agent	**Cancer Site**
Diethylstilbestrol	Breast (user) Vagina/cervix (*in utero* exp) Testicular (*in utero* exp)
Estrogen-only menopausal therapy	Endometrium, ovary
Combined estrogen–progestogen menopausal therapy	Endometrium (risk of diseases with number of days/months of progestrogen); breast
Combined estrogen–progestogen oral contraceptives	Breast, cervix, and liver (endometrium and ovary decreased)
Tamoxifen	Endometrium (breast decreased)
Personal Health	
Agent	**Tumor Sites**
Tobacco smoking	Oral cavity, oropharynx Nasopharynx, hypopharynx Esophagus (adenocarcinoma and squamous cell) Stomach, colorectum Liver, pancreas Nasal cavity and paranasal sinuses

(*continued*)

Table 14.1 (continued) Agents Associated with Human Carcinogenesis

Personal Health	
Agent	**Tumor Sites**
	Larynx, lung Uterine, cervix, and ovary (mucinous) Urinary bladder, kidney (body and pelvis) Ureter, bone marrow (myeloid leukemia)
Parenteral smoking (cancer in offspring)	Hepatoblastoma
Second-hand smoke	Lung
Smokeless tobacco	Oral cavity, esophagus, and pancreas
Betel quid with tobacco	Oral cavity, pharynx, and esophagus
Betel quid without tobacco	Oral cavity, esophagus
Alcohol consumption	Oral cavity, pharynx, larynx, esophagus, liver, colorectum, and female breast
Acetylaldehyde associated with alcohol consumption	Esophagus, head, and neck
Chinese-style salted fish	Nasopharynx
Indoor emissions from household combustion of coal	Lung
Chemicals	
Agent	**Tumor Sites**
Aromatic Amines	
4-Aminobiphenyl	Urinary bladder
Benzidine	Urinary bladder
Dyes metabolized to benzidine	
4,4′methylenebis(2-chloroaniline)	
2-Naphthylamine	Urinary bladder
Ortho-toluidine	Urinary bladder
Auramine production	Urinary bladder
Magenta production	Urinary bladder
PAH-Related Exposures	
Benzo(a)pyrene	
Soot (chimney sweeps)	Skin, lung
Coal gasification	Lung
Coal–tar distillation	Skin
Coke production	Lung
Coal–tar pitches (paving, roofing)	Lung
Aluminum production	Lung, urinary bladder
Other Chemicals	
Aflatoxins	Hepatocellular carcinoma

Table 14.1 (continued) Agents Associated with Human Carcinogenesis

Chemicals	
Agent	**Tumor Sites**
Benzene	Acute nonlymphocytic leukemia
Bis(chloromethyl)ether/chloromethylmethylether	Lung
1,3-Butadiene	Hematolymphatic organs
Dioxin (2,3,7,8 TCDD)	All cancers combined
2,3,7,8-Pentachlordibenzofuran	
3,3′,4,4′,5-Pentachlrobiphenyl (PCB-126)	
Ethylene oxide	Leukemia
Formaldehyde	Nasopharynx Leukemia (myeloid)
Sulfur mustard	Lung
Vinyl chloride	Hepatic angiosarcoma Hepatocellular carcinoma
Other Complex Exposures	
Iron and steel founding	Lung
Isopropyl alcohol manufacture using strong acids	Nasal cavity
Mineral oils	Skin
Occupational exposure as a painter	Lung, urinary bladder, and pleural mesothelioma
Rubber-manufacturing industry	Leukemia, lymphoma, urinary bladder, lung, and stomach
Shale oils	Skin
Strong inorganic acid mists	Larynx
Metals, Arsenic Dust, and Fibers	
Agent	**Tumor Sites**
Arsenic and inorganic arsenic compounds	Lung, skin, and urinary bladder
Beryllium and beryllium compounds	Lung
Cadmium and cadmium compounds	Lung
Chromium (VI) compounds	Lung
Nickel compounds	Lung, nasal cavity, and paranasal sinuses
Asbestos (chrysotile, crocidolite, amosite, tremolite, actinolite, and anthrophyllite)	Lung, mesothelioma, larynx, and ovary
Erionite	Mesothelioma
Silica dust, crystalline in the form of quartz or crystabalite	Lung
Leather dust	Nasal cavity and paranasal sinuses
Wood dust	Nasal cavity and paranasal sinuses, nasopharynx

(*continued*)

Table 14.1 (continued) Agents Associated with Human Carcinogenesis

Radiation	
Agent	**Tumor Sites**
Radon 222 and decay	Lung
Radium 224 and decay	Bone
Radium 226, radium 228, and decay	Bone, paranasal sinuses Mastoid process (only radium 226)
Thorium 232 and decay	Liver, extrahepatic biliary ducts Gall bladder Leukemia (excluding CLL)
Plutonium	Lung, liver, and bone
Phosphorus 32	Acute leukemia
Fission products, including strontium 90	Solid cancers, leukemia
Radioiodines, including iodine 131	Thyroid
Other	
X-radiation or γ- radiation	Salivary gland, esophagus Stomach, colon Lung, bone Skin (BCC) Female breast Urinary bladder Brain and CNS Leukemia (excluding CLL) Thyroid Kidney (atomic bomb survivors/medical pts) Multiple sites (*in utero* exp)
Solar radiation	Skin (BCC, SCC, and melanoma)
UV-emitting tanning devices	Skin (melanoma) Eye (melanoma, particularly choroid and ciliary body)
Biological Agents	
Agent	**Cancer Sites**
Epstein Barr virus	Nasopharyngeal carcinoma Burkitt's lymphoma
	Extranodal NK/T-cell lymphoma (nasal type) Hodgkin's lymphoma
Hepatitis B virus	Hepatocellular carcinoma
Hepatitis C virus	Hepatocellular carcinoma Non-Hodgkin's lymphoma
Kaposi's sarcoma herpes virus	Kaposi's sarcoma Primary effusion lymphoma

Table 14.1 (continued) Agents Associated with Human Carcinogenesis

Biological Agent	
Agent	**Cancer Sites**
HIV 1	Kaposi's sarcoma Non-Hodgkin's lymphoma Hodgkin's lymphoma Cancer of cervix, anus, and conjunctiva
HPV 16	Cervix, vagina, and vulva Penis, anus OP, tonsil, and oral cavity
Human T-cell lymphotrophic virus, type-1	Adult T-cell leukemia and lymphoma
Heliobacter pylori	Noncardiac gastric carcinoma Low-grade B-cell-associated lymphoid tissue (MALT) Gastric lymphoma
Clonorchis sinemsis	Cholangiosarcoma
Opsithochis viverrini	Cholangiosarcoma
Schistosoma haemetobium	Urinary bladder

Epidemiology

- Antineoplastic agents have a very *narrow therapeutic index; 90%* of ODs are unintentional; and *20%* result in moderate-to-severe toxicity.
- The antineoplastic agent OD has increased threefold over the past 10 years.
- *VCR* OD is the most frequently reported antineoplastic agent OD.
- *Anthracycline antibiotics* (doxorubicin) are the most toxic chemotherapeutics and can cause oxygen-free radical-induced cardiomyopathy with irreversible CHF and a high CFR of 48%.

Methotrexate: Outline

- MTX mechanisms, indications, and toxicities
- General and specific management of MTX OD
- General and specific management of intrathecal MTX OD

MTX: Mechanism and Toxicity

- **Mech:** Inhibits both *dihydrofolate reductase* and *thymidine (thymidylate) synthetase* making *reduced folate* unavailable for DNA and RNA synthesis (Figure 14.1).
- **Indic:** Lymphoma, lymphocytic leukemia, breast cancer, small cell carcinomas, trophoblastic disease, rheumatoid arthritis, psoriasis, and suppression of organ transplant rejection.

Table 14.2 Classification of AntiCancer Agents and Their Toxicities

Class	Agent	Toxicity	Overdose	Antidote
Alkylating agents	Mustards Chlorambucil Cyclophosphamide	Hemorrhagic cystitis, encephalopathy, and pulmonary fibrosis	Seizures, myocardial necrosis	Benzodiazepines
	Platinoids Cisplatin Carboplatin	Peripheral neuropathy, ototoxicity, retinal toxicity, distal tubular necrosis, acute renal failure, and myelosuppression	Seizures, encephalopathy, ototoxicity, and renal toxicity	DDTC (chelates platinum)
Antimetabolites	Methotrexate	Mucosities, acute renal failure, and elevated transaminases	Myelosuppression	Folinic acid (to block DHFR inhibition)
Antimitotics	Vinblastine VCR	Peripheral neuropathy, autonomic neuropathy	Seizures, encephalopathy, paralytic ileus, myelosuppression, and SIADH	Glutamic acid (to stabilize tubulin)
Antibiotics	Anthrcyclines Doxorubicin	Direct cardiotoxicity, congestive cardiomyopathy	Dysrhythmias, congestive heart failure	Digoxin
	Mycins Mithramycin	Pulmonary fibrosis	Respiratory failure	None, avoid high FO_2

Note: DHFR = dihydrofolate reductase; SIADH = syndrome of inappropriate secretion of antidiuretic hormone.

Toxicities

GI > renal > BM > CNS > pulmonary

- **GI:** N, V, **mucositis** = stomatitis, esophagitis, and diarrhea; hepatotoxicity = ↑ AST/ALT
- **Renal:** Oliguria and azotemia = acute renal failure
- **BM:** Pancytopenia
- **CNS:** Seizures, hemiparesis
- **Pulm:** Delayed (by 12–17 years) hypersensitivity pneumonitis (Figure 14.1)

General Management of MTX Overdose

- **Immediate gastric emptying:** Ipecac if witnessed ingestion
- **OG lavage:** Then AC, no cathartic
- **MDAC:** No cathartic
- **Cholestyramine:** Synergistic with MDAC in interrupting enterohepatic circulation

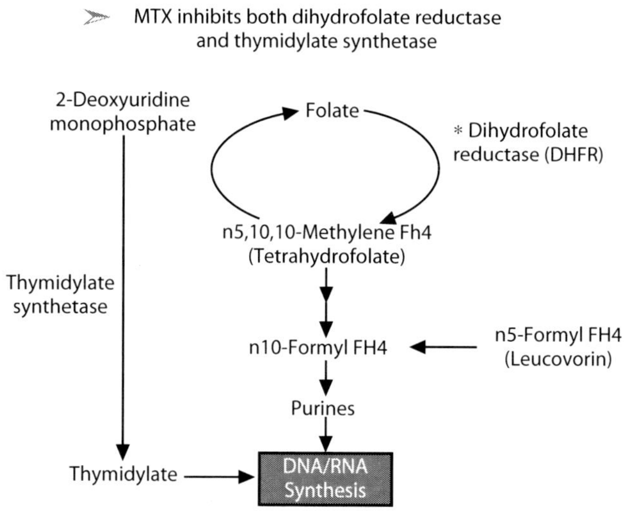

FIGURE 14.1 The mechanisms of action of MTX. The antineoplastic activities and sites of action of the commonly prescribed cancer chemotherapeutic agent, MTX.

- **Fluid loading:** For diuresis
- **Urinary alkalinization:** $NaHCO_3$; urine pH 7–8

Specific Mx MTX OD (See Figure 14.2)

- **Antidote:** *Leucovorin* (folinic acid)—restores reduced folate; monitor with ↓ MTX levels. *Folic acid ineffective*; not in active form.
- **Enhanced elimination: Hemoperfusion best:** HP > HP + HD > HD (removes both folic and folinic acids).
- **Granulocyte colony-stimulating factor (G-CSF):** For ↓ BM and pancytopenia.

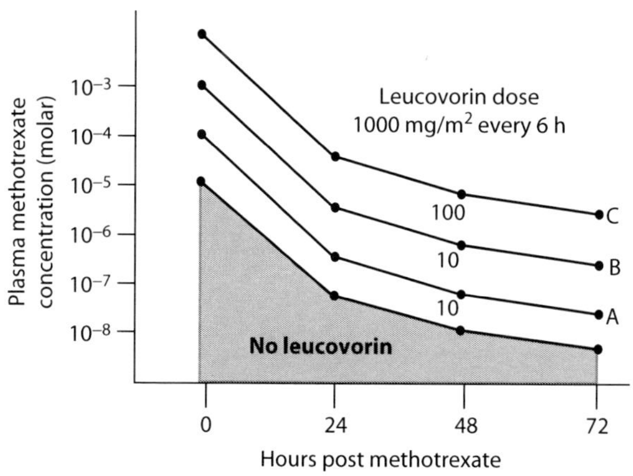

FIGURE 14.2 The management of MTX overdose with leucovorin. A clearance graph of the efficacy of leucovorin in the management of MTX overdose.

Intrathecal MTX OD

General Mx of IT MTX OD

- Upright, sitting posture
- **CSF drainage:** Same LP puncture site
- **CSF exchange:** 2–3 exchanges with equal parts (30 mL) of LR to CSF
- **CSF perfusion:** Ventriculostomy to LP irrigation with LR + 25 mL FFP per liter at 150 mL/h × 24 h

Specific Mx of IT MTX OD

- **High dose leucovorin rescue:** IV only; CNS toxic if given IT
- **Overhydration:** To promote renal excretion
- Urinary alkalinization
- **Dexamethasone IV:** To limit meningeal inflammation (Figure 14.2)

Vincristine: Outline

- VCR mechanisms, indications, and toxicities
- General and specific management of VCR OD
- Management of IT VCR OD and VCR extravasation

VCR: Mechanisms and Tox

Mechanisms and Indications

- **Mech:** VCR and VB are *periwinkle plant alkaloids* that, like *colchicine (crocus)* and *podophyllin (mayapple)*, bind to tubulin to prevent its polymerization into microtubules, arresting *mitosis* at the metaphase, and inhibiting cell movements and cell division.
- **Indic:** Leukemias, lymphomas, and solid tumors.

VCR Toxicities

- *CNS > BM > CV*
- **CNS:** Ascending periph neuropathy (axonopathy), seizures, encephalopathy, and autonomic dysfunction = paralytic ileus, atonic bladder; hypothalamic stimulation = fever and *SIADH*
- **BM:** Myelosuppression, VCR < VB
- **CV:** Necrotic MI 2° alkaloid-induced coronary vasospasm and platelet aggregation

General Mx of VCR OD

- **Oral OD:** Ipecac if witnessed, then OG lavage and AC
- **IV OD:** Most common, seizure mx with BZs > barbs, secure AW

Specific Mx of VCR OD

- **Antidote = glutamic acid:** May assist in the stabilization of tubulin promoting polymerization into microtubules and improving peripheral neuropathy

- **Leucovorin:** May limit neuropathy and myelosuppression by blocking VCR's inhibition of both DHFR and thymidylate synthetase

VCR IT OD and Extravasation

Mx: IT OD of VCR

- **High CFR:** 2° chemical arachnoiditis, ascending neuropathy, encephalopathy, and seizures
- **Posture:** Maintain upright for gravitational protection
- **CSF drainage:** Maintain LP site for drainage
- **CSF exchange:** 30 mL LR per 30 mL CSF × 3 exchanges
- **CSF perfusion:** LR + FFP 25 mL/L as for IT OD MTX

Mx: VCR Extravasation

- **Aspirate infusate:** From infiltrated IV site
- **Consider dilution:** Use NS
- **Hyaluronidase:** Id or subq to promote systemic absorption
- **Warm dry compresses:** To promote systemic absorption
- **Extremity elevation:** To limit further progression

Anthracyclines/Antibiotics

Anthracycline Toxicities

1. **Reps:** (1) Doxorubicin group and all *Streptomyces*-derived, cardiotoxic (↑ CHF) *free radical formers*; (2) mycins: adriamycin, bleomycin, and mitomycin
2. **Antidotes:** None
3. **Cardiotoxicity:** Monitor for 10% drop in EF
4. **Cardioprotectants:** Consider digoxin and verapamil to ↑ EF
5. **Myelosuppression:** Monitor CBC and platelets
6. **Enhanced elimination:** Only **HP**

Anthracycline Extravasation

1. DMSO as a *free radical scavenger*
2. Cold compresses
3. Extremity elevation

Nitrogen Mustards

Nitrogen Mustards: Tox and Mx

1. **Reps:** Cyclophosphamide, melphalan chlorambucil, and mechlorethamine
2. **Mech:** Form reactive intermediates that bind to nucleophilic moieties on DNA

3. **Tox:** Chlorambucil—seizures, CNS depression; cyclophosphamide—*hemorrhagic cystitis* in 10% and cardiotoxicity = arrhythmias and myocarditis
4. **Mx:** BZs for sz, AW, OG lavage, and AC

Mustard Extravasation

1. **Sodium thiosulfate:** Dilute solution id and subq to *inhibit tissue alkylation*
2. Cool compresses
3. Extremity elevation

Platinoid Toxicity

Platinoid Mechanism and Toxicity

- **Reps:** Platinum-containing cisplatin, carboplatin, and so on
- **Mech:** Form intra- and interstrand cross-links with DNA molecules when hydrolytically activated upon entering *low-chloride intracellular environments*
- **Tox:** CNS > renal > BM
- **CNS:** sz, encephalopathy, heavy-metal sensory periph neuropathy–axonopathy, retinal toxicity, ↓ color vision, and ototoxicity (high frequency)
- **Renal:** Dist tubular necrosis = ARF
- **BM:** Myelosuppression: ↓ RBCs and plts

Platinoid OD Mx

- **Renal protection:** By (1) *chloride diuresis*—0.9% NaCl + mannitol to maintain *high Cl diuresis* and ↑ Pt excretion; and (2) *nephroprotection* with two antidotes: *diethyldithiocarbamate* (DDTC) or its precursor *disulfiram* and *Na thiosulfate*, both of which chelate free Pt
- **Enhanced elimination:** Plasmapheresis only, especially for chelated Pt; HD ineffective

Chapter 15

Environmental and Occupational Nephrotoxicology

Pre-Test Questions . . . 282
Outline . . . 283
Nephrotoxicology: Epidemiology . . . 283
Nephrotoxicology: Pathophysiology . . . 283
Acute Renal Dysfunction . . . 284
Chronic Renal Dysfunction . . . 284
Indirect vs. Direct Causes of ARF . . . 285
Biomarkers of Renal Dysfunction . . . 285
Environmental Causes of ARF . . . 286
Environmental Causes of ARF from Pigment Nephropathies . . . 287
Environmental Causes of ARF from Pigment Nephropathies: Mushroom Poisonings . . . 287
Acute Anuric RF: *Amanita* Mushrooms . . . 287
Tricholoma magnivalere (Edible Matsutake or Pine Mushrooms) . . . 288
Orelline Nephrotoxicity . . . 288
Environmental Causes of ARF from Pigment Nephropathies: Plant Poisonings . . . 288
Environmental Causes of ARF from Pigment Nephropathies: Crustacean Palytoxin Poisoning . . . 291

Environmental Causes of ARF from Pigment Nephropathies: Snakebites . . 291
Environmental Causes of ARF from Pigment Nephropathies: Spider Bites 292
Environmental Causes of ARF from Pigment Nephropathies: Rodenticide Ingestions. 292
Phossy Jaw, Chronic Inorganic Phosphate Ingestion, and Bisphosphonate-Associated Mandibular Osteonecrosis 293
Occupational Causes of ARF: Heavy Metal-Induced Acute Tubulointerstitial Nephropathy 294
Cadmium 295
Lead Poisoning. 296
Mercury Poisoning. 297
ARF from Glomerular Nephropathies 298
Occupational Causes of ARF: Toxic Alcohols. 299
Ethylene Glycol Metabolism 300
Diethylene Glycol 301
Direct ARF: Acute Glomerular Nephropathy 301
Occupational Causes of ARF: Herbicides 302
Environmental Causes of ARF: Hymenoptera Stings 303
Environmental and Occupational Nephrotoxicology: CRF. 303
Nephrotoxic Plants Causing CRF 304
Chronic Renal Failure 2. 305
Environmental Nephrotoxicology: Parasitic Infections Schistosomiasis and Bladder Cancer 307
Conclusions 307
Post-Test Questions 307

Pre-Test Questions

1. The diagnosis of end-stage renal disease as being environmental or occupational exposure related in origin is rarely entertained because:
   a. Chronic renal disease causes most ESRD.
   b. Such causes have prolonged latencies.
   c. There is inadequate biomarker surveillance.
   d. All of the above.*
2. Heavy metal nephrotoxins target the:
   a. Glomerulus.
   b. Proximal convoluted tubule.*
   c. Distal convoluted tubule.
   d. Collecting duct.

* Correct.

Outline

Epidemiology
Pathophysiology
Acute vs. chronic renal dysfunction
Direct vs. indirect acute renal dysfunction
Sensitive vs. insensitive exposure biomarkers
Indirect acute renal dysfunction: physical stressors, pigment nephropathies
Acute tubulointerstitial nephropathy
Acute glomerular nephropathy
Chronic glomerular nephropathy
Misc. chronic nephropathies: vascular nephropathy, papillary necrosis, cystic disease, radiation nephritis
Environmental and occupational GU tract carcinogens
Lower GU tract disorders: urolithiasis, neurogenic bladder, bladder cancer, cystitis
Conclusions

Nephrotoxicology: Epidemiology

- Today, approximately *0.5 million persons are treated for ESRD* annually, and this group is *anticipated to increase* as the population ages.
- \$15–20 B is now spent annually on persons with ESRD.
- The diagnosis of ESRD as being *environmental or occupational* in origin is *rarely entertained*, as *chronic diseases cause most ESRD.*
- The true incidence of ESRD 2° to environmental and occupational exposures is unknown due to *prolonged subclinical latency periods* and *inadequate biomarker surveillance.*
- Environmental and occupational nephrotoxic exposures represent potentially *preventable* causes of ESRD.

Nephrotoxicology: Pathophysiology

(See Table 15.1)

- 20% of the cardiac output goes to the kidneys, *a fraction of which is filtered as the GFR* (125 mL/min = 180 L/day).
- 2/3 of the filtrate is reabsorbed in the *proximal tubule*, then concentrated and acidified distally.
- Environmental and occupational nephrotoxins are highly concentrated in the *proximal convoluted tubules.*
- Acute renal dysfunction from env/occ nephrotoxins often manifests as *acute tubular necrosis* (metals, mushrooms, organic solvents, pesticides).

Table 15.1 Major Environmental and Occupational Nephrotoxins Causing ARF and CRF

Acute Renal Failure			Chronic Renal Failure		
Pigment nephropathies (Indirect)	Acute Tubulo-interstitial Nephropathy (ATIN)	Acute Glomerulo-nephropathy (AGN)	Chronic Tubule-interstitial Nephropathy (CTIN)	Chronic Glomerulo-Nephropathy (CGN)	Vascular Nephropathy
Hemolysis: Arsine Anilines Nitrates nitrites Butoxy-ethanol Rhabdo-myolysis: Injuries Foods Bites Stings Pesticides	Pb Cd Hg	Silica HCs: VOCs Glycols: Ethylene glycol, diethylene glycol Petro-chemicals solvents Solvent inhalers Bypiridyl Pesticides	Cd (*itai-itai*) Pb Regional Balkan endemic nephropathy	Hg Nephrotic Syn AGBM+ Silica ANCA+ Org solvents AGBM+	Carbon disulfide CS_2

- Chronic renal dysfunction from env/occ nephrotoxins often manifests as *chronic tubulointerstitial nephritis* (Pb, Cd) or *chronic glomerulonephropathy* (Si, Br).

Acute Renal Dysfunction

Acute Renal Failure (ARF)

- **Predominant renal lesion:** *Acute tubular necrosis* = initial inflammatory tubular injury followed by necrosis sparing the glomerulus at 1st, but may later be associated with widespread necrosis.
- **Predominant location:** *Proximal tubule.*
- **Urine output:** Oliguria within hours to days to <500 mL/day.
- **Urinalysis:** Renal tubular cells, granular casts, little-to-no protein.
- **Labs:** ↑ BUN and creatinine, electrolyte abnormalities.
- **Px:** Recovery in 1–2 weeks, heralded by diuresis.

Chronic Renal Dysfunction

Chronic Renal Failure (CRF)

- **Predominant renal lesions:** Chronic tubulointerstitial nephritis or chronic, often membranous glomerulonephropathy.
- **Predominant locations:** Proximal tubule, interstitium, glomerulus.
- **UO:** Decreased to none.

- **U/A:** Tubulointerstitial nephritis = proteinuria (nephrotic syndrome-Hg), glycosuria, phosphaturia, calciuria <2 g/24 h, no cellular elements; glomerulonephropathy = ↑ RBC–WBC–epithelial cell casts.
- **Labs:** ↑ serum BUN, creatinine, potassium, ↓ calcium.
- **Px:** No recovery, renal replacement therapy required.

Indirect vs. Direct Causes of ARF

Indirect (Prerenal) Causes

1. *Systemic disorders*, physical stressors (heat stroke), circulatory depression (shock)
2. *Hemolysis–hemoglobinuria*-associated factors
3. *Rhabdomyolysis–myoglobinuria*-associated factors (may also be 2° physical stress = crush/electrical injuries, esp. in earthquakes; bites and stings)
4. *Methemoglobinuria*-secondary hemolysis-associated factors

Direct (Renal) Causes of ARF

Acute tubulointerstitial nephropathy:

1. Metals and elements
2. Metal chelation therapy
3. Nephrotoxic mushrooms

Acute glomerular nephropathy:

1. Metals
2. Solvents: organic, petrochemicals
3. Halogenated hydrocarbons
4. Glycols and derivatives (solvents and dispersants)
5. Pesticides

Biomarkers of Renal Dysfunction

(See Table 15.2)

Insensitive Tests for Env/Occ Nephrotoxicity

- Serum electrolytes
- Serum/urine osmolality, osmolar gap, anion gap
- Serum creatinine and BUN
- Urinalysis
- Urinary sediment
- GFR and creatinine clearance

Table 15.2 Most Sensitive Biomarkers of Renal Dysfunction

Glomerular Damage	Tubular Damage	Loop and Collecting Duct	Miscellaneous Biomarkers
High MW (>40,000 D) urinary plasma proteins: albumin, transferrin, IgG Glomerular components in serum or urine: fibronectin, laminin, sialic acids, anti-GBM ABs, prostanoids: TXB_2 and $PGF_1\alpha$	*Prox.: Low MW urine proteins:* ß-2-microglobulin (mg), α-1-mg, retinol binding protein *Enzymes: N*-acetylglucose-aminidase, total nonspecific AP, GGT, alanine aminopeptidase *Antigens:* Brush border (BB)-50 *Distal tubule:* *Kallikrein*	*Loop of Henle:* Tamm–Horsfall glycoprotein *Collecting tubule and interstitium:* *Prostanoids:* $PGF_2\alpha$ and PGE_2 *Renal biopsy* *Invasive and most sensitive and specific with immuno-fluorescent stains:*	*Pigments:* serum and urine free Hgb and Mgb. *Nonspecific proteins:* Glycoso-aminoglycans *Immune biomarkers:* Anti-GBM ABs ANA ANCA (Cytoplasmic > Perinuclear-ANCA) Anti-laminin ABs

More Sensitive Tests for Env/Occ Nephrotoxicity

- Glomerular level damage biomarkers
- Proximal tubular level damage biomarkers
- Distal tubular level biomarkers
- Loop of Henle damage biomarkers
- Immune and other nonspecific or site-unrelated biomarkers
- Renal biopsy

Environmental Causes of ARF

(See Table 15.3)

Table 15.3 Major Environmental and Occupational Causes of Acute Renal Dysfunction

Acute Renal Dysfunction		
Pigment (Indirect)	**ATIN**	**AGN**
Hemolysis: Arsine Anilines Nitros Butoxyethanol *Rhabdomyolysis:* Injuries Foods Bites Stings Pesticides	*Metals:* Pb Cd Hg	*Solvents and misc.:* Silica HCs: VOCs Glycols: EG, PG Petro solvents Solvent inhalers Bypiridyl Pesticides

Table 15.4 Environmental and Occupational Causes of ARF from Pigment Nephropathies

Hemoglobinuria	Myoglobinuria	Secondary Hemolysis
Arsine, stibene gas	*Poison plants/mushrooms:*	*Carboxy-hemoglobinemia*
Aniline dyes	Poison and water hemlocks,	Carbon monoxide
Benzene	hemp-nettle	*Methemoglobinemia*
Butoxyethanol (Corexit)	Crustacean palytoxin poisoning	*All aromatic–aliphatic nitro and*
Coal ars	*Bites and stings*:	*amine cmpds:*
Copper sulfate	Rattlesnake, Black Widow, Bee/wasp	Aniline dyes
Cresols	*Crush/electrical injuries*	Naphthalene
Ethylene glycol	*Gas:* Carbon monoxide	mothballs
Hydroquinone	*Inorganic metals*:	*Explosives*:
Isopropyl alcohol	Arsenic trioxide	Ethylene glycol dinitrate
Methyl chloride	Mercuric chloride	Trinitrophenol
Naphthalene	*Pesticides:*	(picric acid)
Phenol	Lindane, strychnine, zinc phosphide	*Herbicides*:
Sodium chlorate	*Glycols, alcohols*: EG,	Sodium chlorate dinitrophenol
Trimetallic anhydrides	Isopropyl, methanol	
Trinitrotoluene		

Environmental Causes of ARF from Pigment Nephropathies

(See Table 15.4)

Environmental Causes of ARF from Pigment Nephropathies: Mushroom Poisonings

Nephrotoxic Mushroom Poisonings Rhabdomyolysis: Tricholoma equestre

Rep: *Tricholoma equestre* (aka *T. flavovirens,* the "*edible*" yellow knight mushroom).

Epid: 1992–2001: 12 French patients experienced delayed rhabdomyolysis 24–72 h after ingesting cooked *T. equestre* mushrooms; 3 died.

Myotoxins: Unidentified, metabolites include triterpenoids, sterols, indoles, acetylenic compounds, and *yellow* pigment = 7,7′-bi-physicion.

Antidote: None.

Clin: N, V, fever, facial erythema, diaphoresis, weakness, leg myalgias, dark urine in 24–72 h.

Tx: Cooling blanket, IV fluid loading, mannitol-forced diuresis, continuous venomous hemofiltration, exchange tx, vasopressors.

Acute Anuric RF: *Amanita* Mushrooms

Nephrotoxic Amanita smithiana *(Often Confused with Matsutake Mushrooms)*

Tricholoma magnivalere (Edible Matsutake or Pine Mushrooms)

Mushroom Poisonings: Acute Anuric RF

Epid: Starting in the 1990s- ↑ reports acute anuric RF 1–6 days post ingestion *Amanita smithiana* (United States, Canada), *A. proxima* (France, Spain, Italy), *A. pseudoporphyria* (Japan) 2° confusion with edible *matsutake* mushrooms.

Toxin: Allenic norleucine (2-amino-4, 5-hexadienoic acid).

Antidote: None.

Dx: Severe N and V in 1–6 h, acute anuric RF-↑ BUN/Cr and AST/ALT in 1–6 days.

Tx: Hemodialysis × 1–4 weeks.

Orelline Nephrotoxicity

Reps: *Cortinarius* spp.

Toxins: *Orelline* and *orellanine*, both *nephrotoxic* bipyridyls, like paraquat and diquat

Antidote: None

Dx: Initial GI sx with HA and chills in 24–36 h, then delayed oliguric renal failure may develop days to weeks later

Tx: Hemoperfusion, hemodialysis, renal transplant

Environmental Causes of ARF from Pigment Nephropathies: Plant Poisonings

Water Hemlock Poisoning 1

Water Hemlock

Latin: *Cicuta maculata* L.

The *most poisonous plant in North America (NA)* containing the epileptogenic, *strychnine-like* neurotoxin, *cicutoxin*, in all parts, especially its *hollow tuberous roots*. Grows *worldwide* along the shores of freshwater and brackish rivers, streams, bayous, lagoons, lakes, bays, and *estuaries*.

Water Hemlock Poisoning 2

Water Hemlock: Cicutoxin

Hx: 1679 Wepfer-childhood poisonings (Ger.).; 1814 Stockbridge-3 cases, 2 deaths (United States); 1911 Egdahl reviewed 47 cases United Kingdom and United States, 21 deaths

Toxic parts: All, especially tuberous roots in spring; heat stable

Toxins: #1 Cicutoxin (diacetylene-diol); #2 cicutol (alcohol)

Epid: 1900–1975 83 U.S. cases, *CFR* 30%— most toxic U.S. plant—according to CDC and the AAPCC TESS

Water Hemlock Poisoning 3

Water Hemlock Poisoning

Toxicity: Water hemlock on ingestion or even *mucosal contact*[*] will induce initial cholinergic toxicity: Salivation, sweating, dizziness, diplopia, rigidity; then choreathetosis and seizures → *rhabdomyolysis, myoglobinuria*, ATN → ARF.

Antidote: None.

Tx: Supportive.

CFR: 30 + %.

Indirect Water Hemlock Poisoning: Haff Disease

Haff Disease

Def: A syndrome of afebrile muscle stiffness, rigidity, pain (myalgia); followed rapidly by rhabdomyolysis, myoglobinuria, potential ARF from ATN precipitated by the consumption of several spp. of cooked freshwater fish meat (often prepared as gefilte fish), and especially after eating fish liver and row

Treatment: Supportive

CFR: 1–10%

Haff Disease Synonyms

1. *Haff–Iuksovsk–Sartlansk disease*: Preferred Eastern European name for Haff disease
2. *Iuksovsk–Sartlansk disease*: Preferred name for Haff disease in Siberia
3. *Haff–Uchs disease*: Preferred name for Haff disease in Germany and former East Prussia, now Russia

Indirect Hemlock Poisoning: Food Vectors—Haff Disease

Ictiobus cyprinellus: Largemouth buffalo fish

Lota lota: European burbot

Indirect Water Hemlock Poisoning: DDx

Haff Disease = Indirect Water Hemlock

DDx: #1 statin (HMG-CoA reductase inhibitors)-induced rhabdomyolysis, ASA, codeine, amphetamine ODs, strychnine poisoning, crustacean/seafood/algal palytoxin poisoning. The exact etiology of Haff disease remains unknown but resembles similar toxidromes caused by cicutoxin following water hemlock ingestions and by palytoxin following contaminated seafood ingestions. All of these toxidromes are characterized by severe muscle pain and rhabdomyolysis.

Course: CPK ↑↑↑ >10,000, then ↓ over 3–5 days.

Outcomes: Lingering muscle stiffness, recovery unless ATN → ARF.

CFR: 1–10%.

---

[*] **Ped cases:** Lethal toy whistles made from hollow stems of water hemlock.

Cicuta maculata *L.: Water Hemlock*

History of Haff Disease 1

1924–1925: 1000+ cases reported, coastal *Konigsburg* (now Kalingrad, Russia) *Haff* (Old Ger., a "shallow lagoon"), East Prussia (Russia, since 1945), following consumption of cooked freshwater eel, pike, and, especially, burbot (*Lota lota*) and *burbot liver*

1928–1931: Sporadic cases along shores of Konigsberg Haff

1932–1933: 1000+ cases, 2nd Konigsberg Haff epidemic

1934: ? # cases reported, shores of Lake Onega, Russia

1942–1943: 12 cases (2 deaths), Lake Ymsen, near Mariestad, Sweden; following consumption of cooked eel, turbot, turbot liver

History of Haff Disease 2

1965: Leschchenko experimentally induced Haff disease in cats and mice by feeding them fresh carp from a contaminated lake in Russia.

1984: First three U.S. cases reported from Texas following the consumption of largemouth buffalo fish (*Ictiobus cyprinellus*).

1984–1985: 114 cases reported from Novosibirsk, Siberia following the consumption of freshwater "white fish."

1984–1986: Four cases reported from *California* following consumption of buffalo fish (primarily in Ukrainian immigrants preparing *gefilte* fish and others frying fish).

History of Haff Disease 3

1997: Six case cluster of Haff disease in the United States following consumption of largemouth buffalo fish harvested from *Mississippi-Missouri River Basin.*

2001: Eight cases of Haff disease reported from *South Central Louisiana* following consumption of freshly *boiled crayfish* sold by a common local vendor who also sold largemouth buffalo fish.

Food Tracebacks

U.S. Food Traceback Investigations: Both the CDC and FDA investigations of the buffalo fish-associated Haff disease cases implicated seafood vendors in LA and MO, who purchased freshwater seafood from commercial fishermen in the MS–MO River Basin. Tox screens by GC–MS detected no unknown toxins and excluded *organophosphates, arsenic, freshwater blue-green algal toxins*, especially *Microcystis aeruginosa* toxins (microcystin, nodularin), and *marine toxins* (ciguatoxin, saxitoxin). *Mouse bioassays* reproduced identical histopathology–rhabdomyolysis with renal tubular damage and necrosis.

Conclusion: Crayfish were slimed by toxic buffalo fish in the same bin. Boil crayfish before eating.

Environmental Causes of ARF from Pigment Nephropathies: Crustacean Palytoxin Poisoning

Agents and Toxins: Bioaccumulated *red algal gonyautoxins* and zoanthid coral palytoxin; endogenous tetrodotoxin.

LD_{50}: Gonyautoxins and tetrodotoxin (TTX)-9 mcg/kg; paly-0.15 mcg/kg.

Mech: Gony and TTX reversibly bind to outer pore of Na channels ↓ Na influx and depolarization; paly inhibits Na–K ATPase, Na and K can enter but not leave axon, Ca cannot enter, causing *hypocalcemic tetanic contractions.*

Vectors: Most Indo-Pacific xanthid crabs, terrestrial coconut crab, and Asian horseshoe crabs; herbivorous reef triggerfish and parrotfish (palytoxin).

Incubation: 10–15 min-3–4 h.

Sx: Palytoxin—initial N, V, D, facial-to-limb paresthesias; tonoclonic sz with rhabdomyolysis, myoglobinuria, ATN; CV collapse. Tetrodotoxin or TTX-resp paralysis.

Dx: Mouse bioassay, TLC, HPLC, ↑↑ serum CPK 2° *rhabdomyolysis.*

Tx: Protect AW; gastric emptying, OG lavage with $NaHCO_3$, then activated charcoal (AC), 1 g/kg; mechanical ventilation; consider multi-dose AC.

Prognosis (Px): CFR-TTX: 62%, CFR-palytoxin: >60%; most recover in ICU by 48 h–5 d.

Prev: Avoid unusual crab spp. and local crab "*miso*"—soups made from *tidal xanthid crabs*; always adhere to local seafood consumption advisories.

Environmental Causes of ARF from Pigment Nephropathies: Snakebites

Crotalids: Vipers/Rattlesnakes

Name: Timber (canebrake) rattler

Latin: *Crotalus horridus horridus*

Venom: "Mosaic of antigens"

Dx: Hemorrhagic bullae, tissue necrosis, ↑ edema, CV instability, coagulopathies = *thrombocytopenia + defibrinogenation** > *DIC*, ↑ fasciculations = *persistent muscular quivering (myokymia)* = hemolysis, rhabdomyolysis

Antidote: CroFab-mod envenom—5–10 vials, severe—10–40 vials

Tx: Immobilize limb, no ice, Ttox, antibiotics, pressors, blood prod-cryo, wound debride, rarely fasciotomy

* Recent death 53-year-old M FL.

Environmental Causes of ARF from Pigment Nephropathies: Spider Bites

Arachnids: Latrodectus 1

Name: Black widow

Latin: *Latrodectus mactans*

Venom: *Alpha-latrotoxin* causes Ach release and presynaptic stimulation of all muscarinic and nicotinic cholinergic receptors

Dx: *2 painful red spots*- in hrs—latrodectism = *facies latrodectismica*, N, V, salivation, urine retention, priapism, bronchorrhea, abdominal muscle cramps/rigidity, *rhabdomyolysis*, ↑ HR, and BP, restlessness, sz

Arachnids: Latrodectus 2

Name: Black widow, red hourglass spider

Latin: *Latrodectus mactans*

Antidote: *Latrodectus mactans* antivenom—a crude monovalent hyperimmune horse serum (IgG) antivenin

Tx: Ttox, cold packs, benzodiazepines for muscle relaxation >10% calcium gluconate for cramps does not work

Environmental Causes of ARF from Pigment Nephropathies: Rodenticide Ingestions

Rodenticides: High Toxicity

Strychnine

Phys: Bitter white powder, rodenticide and heroin adulterant

Source: *Strychnine tree*: *Strychnos nux-vomica* (Asia, Hawaii)

Mech: Blocks *glycine motor inhibition in spinal cord*

Onset: 10–20 min

Sx: *Sensorium remains intact* with twitching, hyperextension, *opisthotonos* → skeletal fxs, *trismus* → *risus sardonicus*, *rhabdomyolysis* → *ATN*

Anti: None

Tx: Immediate lavage + AC, BZs, barbs, muscle relaxants; support and quiet room to avoid triggering extensor spasms

Zinc Phosphide (Zn_3P_2)

Phys: Dark, gray powder, smells like rotten fish—attracts, rats, gophers, squirrels, domestic animals

Mech: Releases phosphine and zinc on contact with water and *gastric acid*

Onset: Within hours

Sx: Rotten fish breath, black vomit, rapid ↓ Ca, tetany 2° hypocalcemia, seizures, *rhabdomyolysis* → ATN, pulmonary edema 2° inhalation, CV collapse, ATN

Anti: None

Tx: Immediate dilution with water, milk, or $NaHCO_3$; then lavage-AC- cathartic; consider proton-pump inhibitor to ↓ gastric acid

Phosphorus: Red vs. Yellow?

Red Phosphorus

Use: Red "safety" matches; replaced yellow or white phosphorus on matches, 1940s.

Tox: Nonvolatile and *insoluble*; harmless when ingested.

Phossy jaw: Hyperphosphatemia and jaw osteonecrosis in German match factory workers exposed to white inorganic phosphorous, 1890s). Current "phossy jaw" exposures = bisphosphonates = jaw osteonecrosis in postmenopausal females taking bisphosphonates for osteoporosis prophylaxis.

Yellow (White) Phosphorus

Use: Rodenticides and incendiaries

Tox: Volatile and highly soluble

Skin: Burns; *"phossy jaw"= mandibular osteonecrosis*

GI: "Smoking" and luminescent vomitus and stools

CV: Direct myocardial depressant → ATN

Tx: Emesis → OG lavage with 0.1% $KMnO_4$ or 2% H_2O_2 to oxidize P to harmless PO_4s → then AC + sorbitol (not Mg or oil cathartics)

Phossy Jaw, Chronic Inorganic Phosphate Ingestion, and Bisphosphonate-Associated Mandibular Osteonecrosis

Chronic Inorganic Phosphorous Ingestions

2° workplace exposures (white phosphorous, OP pesticides) or drugs (bisphosphonates) may cause osteopenia/osteonecrosis.

Rodenticides: High Toxicity

Barium: Soluble vs. Insoluble?

Insoluble Barium

Rep: Barium sulfate

Use: Oral radiographic contrast agent: barium swallow, barium enema

Tox: *Insoluble* and harmless when ingested; radio-opaque contrast stays in GI tract

Tx: None indicated

Soluble Barium

Rep: Ba acetate, *carbonate*, chloride, hydroxide, nitrate, sulfide

Use: Rodenticides (*carbonate*)

Tox: Profound ↓↓ K 2° ↑ muscle membrane permeability, driving extracellular K into muscles

CP and renal: ↓ K = arrhythmias, CHF; *hypokalemic respiratory paralysis*; acute respiratory failure

Tx: OG lavage with *Na thiosulfate or* $MgSO_4$ → *soluble* $BaCO_3$ → harmless, *insoluble* $BaSO_4$

Occupational Causes of ARF: Heavy Metal-Induced Acute Tubulointerstitial Nephropathy

(See Tables 15.5 and 15.6)

Table 15.5 Major Environmental and Occupational Causes of ARF from Acute Tubulointerstitial Nephropathies

Metals, Elements, Chelators		Mushrooms
Metals	*Elements*	*Amanita smithiana*
Antimony	Bismuth	*Amanita proxima*
Arsenic	Lithium	*Amanita pseudoporphyria*
Cadmium	*Metal chelators*	*Cortinarius* spp.
Chromium	All deliver bound metals to PCTs:	*Pesticides*
Copper	EDTA (ethylene-diamine-tetraacetic acid)	White phosphorous
Iron	Penicillamine	Soluble *barium* solvents, depilatories, pesticides:
Lead		Ba arsenate, carbonate,
Mercury (esp. $HgCl_2$)		chloride, hydroxide, nitrate, and sulfide
Platinum		
Silver and gold		
Thallium		
Uranium (uranyl nitrate)		
Vanadium		

Table 15.6 Acute Renal Effects of Heavy Metal Exposures

Metal	ATN = PCT Necrosis	Fanconi Syndrome	CRF = CTIN or CRF	Nephrotic Syndrome
Cadmium	+	+	+	0
Copper	+	+	+	0
Gold	+	0	+	+
Mercury	+	0	+	+
Lead	+	+	+	0
Thallium	+	0	0	+

+: Typically present; 0: typically absent.

Cadmium

Uses and Exposures

Uses of Cadmium

Electroplating: Silverware.

Glazing: Pots, pans, most kitchen utensils.

Soldering: Internal copper conduit soldering in hot and cold vending machines. Warning: coffee and hot chocolate from hot beverage vending machines.

Batteries: Nickel–cadmium.

Paints and pigments

Film manufacture (replaced by digital technology).

Exposures to Cadmium

Vapor and fume inhalation: Occupational, especially cadmium arc welding

Ingestion: Cd-contaminated drinking water, acidic foods/liquids (fruit and vegetable juices), alcohols and wines contaminated by Cd leached from Cd-glazed containers and pitchers

Cadmium: Toxicology

Absorption/Distribution

- Inhalation > GI absorption
- Rapid transport to liver for binding with its specific metal transport protein, *metallothionein*
- Circulatory transport of *bound Cd to kidneys* for glomerular filtration and proximal tubular reabsorption
- Bound Cd concentrated in kidneys > bone > liver

Metabolism/Excretion

- Not biotransformed.
- As *hepatic* and *then renal metallothionein production is overwhelmed*, unbound Cd is distributed to *kidneys and bone*, where it establishes a reservoir pool (like lead in bone).
- Slow renal elimination with $T_{1/2}$ = 7–30 years.

Cadmium: Pathophysiology

- Once the stores of *metallothionein* binding protein are depleted and the *hepatorenal protein synthesizing capabilities are overwhelmed*, free toxic Cd is distributed to *kidneys > bone > liver.*
- Chronic Cd nephrotoxicity causes a *Fanconi's syndrome* of aminoaciduria, glucosuria, calciuria-hyperphosphaturia, metabolic acidosis (RTA) ↓ concentrating ability, and nephrolithiasis 2° ↑ excretion of Ca and P.
- Chronic urinary *calcium loss* results in *osteomalacia* with pathologic fractures ("*itai-itai*" or "ouch-ouch" disease).

- Chronic inhalation exposure causes emphysema that acutely mimics metal fume fever and later causes *pulmonary fibrosis.*
- Chronic Cd exposures cause ↑ *lung (and possibly prostate) cancers.*

Clinical Effects

Acute Toxicity

GI: N, V, D

Pulmonary: Acute chemical pneumonitis > mimics "metal fume fever" → pulmonary edema, ARDS, later pulmonary fibrosis

Renal: Proximal tubular dysfunction and proteinuria = *Fanconi's syndrome*

Chronic Toxicity

Pulm: Emphysema, pulmonary fibrosis, lung cancer

GU/renal: Reduced GFR, ↑ spilling of Ca and PO_4 in urine, CRF often associated with nephrolithiasis (Ca phosphate stones)

Bone: *Demineralization, osteomalacia*, pathologic fractures ("*itai-itai*" or "ouch-ouch" disease)

Diagnosis and Treatment

Diagnosis

- Urine > serum Cd
- **Serum Cd:** Unhelpful and not reflective of body burden as Cd is protein bound to its transporter protein metallothionein in kidneys > liver
- Urine metallothionein levels
- Increasing proteinuria and glucosuria reflecting early Fanconi's syndrome

Treatment

- Gastric evacuation and catharsis
- Pulmonary support
- Remove from exposure sources
- *Chelation is contraindicated as it will increase renal cadmium load* and further deplete metallothionein, *increasing nephrotoxicity*

Lead Poisoning

Pathophysiologic Effects

Primary Effects

1. Neurologic
2. Hematologic
3. *Renal*
4. Reproductive

Secondary Effects

5. Endocrine
6. Skeletal
7. Gastrointestinal
8. Cardiac

Lead Poisoning: Nephrotoxicity

Acute → Chronic Lead Nephropathy

- Adults > children
- Nuclear inclusions from lead–protein complexes in *proximal tubular cells* and their casts, *nephrotic syndrome common*
- **Fanconi syndrome:** Aminoaciduria, glycosuria, phosphaturia, fructosuria, citrauria, HCO_3 loss-renal tubular acidosis (RTA)
- CRF 2° tubular atrophy initially and later fibrosis
- Renovascular HTN 2° ↑ renin

"Saturnine" Gout

- **Saturn:** Roman god of agriculture and vineyards; red wines leach Pb out of lead, lead-glazed, and leaded glass decanters
- Adults—Common > children—Rare
- ↓ Renal uric acid excretion
- ↑ Serum uric acid
- **Gout:** Uric acid crystal deposition rare in joints (gouty arthropathy) and skin (tophi), no urolithiasis

Mercury Poisoning

Clinical Syndromes: Acute vs. Chronic Nephrotoxicity

- Acute inhalation of elemental Hg vapor
- *Acute ingestion of inorganic Hg salts*
- *Chronic elemental Hg poisoning*
- *Chronic inorganic Hg poisoning*
- Methyl (organic) Hg poisoning (Minamata disease)
- Chronic inorganic mercury ingestion in children = Mercurial acrodynia or *Pink* disease

Mercury: Pathophysiology

- Avid covalent binding to all sulfur-containing groups, especially the sulfhydryl groups, throughout the body.
- Widespread destruction of membranes and structural proteins (CNS) and disruption of enzyme and transport systems.

- *Elemental Hg* targets *lungs* (chemical pneumonitis, ARDS), *inorganic Hg* targets *GI* tract and *kidneys* (hemorrhagic gastroenteritis, ATN), *organic Hg* targets *CNS*, especially fetal CNS (Minamata disease).

Mercury: Acute Clinical Effects

Acute Elemental Inhalation

Pulmonary > GI > CNS

Pulm: Cough, chills, fever, dyspnea, *chemical pneumonitis*, pulmonary edema, ARDS, interstitial fibrosis

GI: Metallic taste, nausea, vomiting, diarrhea, dysphagia

CNS: Headaches, weakness, visual disturbances

Acute Inorganic Ingestion

GI > renal

GI: Metallic taste, oral pain and burning, nausea, vomiting, diarrhea, abdominal pain, *hemorrhagic gastroenteritis*, dehydration → orthostatic hypotension

Renal: *Proximal tubular necrosis* → ATN

Mercury: Chronic Clinical Effects

Elemental Mercury

Pulm > Renal > GI

Pulm: Pulmonary fibrosis, restrictive lung disease

Renal: *Fanconi's syndrome* = proteinuria → *nephrotic syndrome* 2° *autoimmune-glomerulonephritis (AGBM+)* →CRF

GI: Relatively nontoxic due to *negligible absorption* (e.g., after long-NG tube balloon rupture)

CNS: "Mad Hatter" syndrome post-inhalation exposures

Inorganic Mercury ("Mad Hatter" Syndrome)

CNS > Renal > GI

CNS: Intention tremor, ballismus, and *choreoathetosis* ("mad hatter" syndrome), *erethism* (anxiety, *easy blushing*, emotional lability, memory loss), *neurasthenia* (HA, depression, fatigue anorexia, weight loss)

GI: Metallic taste and a characteristic triad of (1) *gingivostomatitis*, (2) *loose teeth*, and (3) *salivary gland hyperplasia*

ARF from Glomerular Nephropathies

(See Tables 15.7, 15.8, and 15.9)

Table 15.7 Major Occupational Causes of ARF from Glomerular Nephropathies

Metals and Mixtures with Solvents	Halogenated Hydrocarbons (Solvents = Degreasers, Dry Cleaners)	Glycols and Derivatives (Solvents, Antifreeze)
Mercury *Silica* Silicon Organic solvent mixtures	CCl_4 and chloroform Dibromochloropropane Ethylene dibromide Ethylene dichloride Ethylene chlorohydrine Hexachlorobutadiene Methylene chloride Tetrachloroethane Trichloroethane Trichloroethylene Tetrachloroethylene Vinyllidine chloride	*Ethylene glycol* *Diethylene glycol* Propylene glycol (IV, otherwise insoluble) Dipropylene glycol Monoalkyl glycol ethers (cellusolves)
Petroleum distillates Diesel Gasoline *Pine distillate* Turpentine		*Non-halogenated HCs* Dioxane Phenol Toluene

Occupational Causes of ARF: Toxic Alcohols

Ethylene Glycol: Pharm and Tox

- **Chem:** A toxic alcohol similar to methanol in toxicity and lethality with a characteristic delayed onset of toxicity; used in antifreeze (95%), refrigerating fluids, fire extinguishers, solar energy fluids.
- **Pharm:** Rapidly absorbed po, peaks 1–4 h; rapidly metabolized by ADH to glycoaldehyde, then *glycolic, glyoxalic, and oxalic acids. Pyridoxine and thiamine* serve as cofactors to promote nontoxic alternative routes of metabolism.

Table 15.8 Additional Environmental and Occupational Exposure Causes of ARF from Acute Glomerular Nephropathies

Organic Solvent Mixtures		Pesticides
Abusive organic solvent inhalers: Baggers Huffers Sniffers	Pine distillate: *Turpentine* *Petroleum distillates*: Diesel oil Gasoline	Bipyridyls: *Diquat* Paraquat *Dinitrophenols Dinitro-o-cresols* *Pentachlorophenol* *Organic mercurials*
Acute Immune Complex Glomerulonephritis: *Bee and wasp stings* Trimetallic anhydides	*Acute toxic glomerulonephropathy* (anti-GBM AGN c/s lung disease, or Goodpasture's syndrome): Silica Mercury Mixtures of organic solvents	

Table 15.9 Hypersensitivity Reactions with Potential to Cause ARF

Type	Definitions	Mediators	Onset times	Examples
I	Immediate HS Anaphylaxis	IgE	Immediate to minutes	Bee stings Baker's asthma
II	Complement fixation	IgM > IgG, and C-immune complex nephritis	Hours	Transfusion reactions *Trimetallic anhydrides*
III	Antigen–antibody complex formation—deposition	IgM and IgG, potential renal deposition—acute tubulo-interstitial nephritis	12 h to 1–2 weeks	Bee/wasp stings Serum sickness hypersens. pneumonitis occ asthma
IV	Delayed HS-PPD+ cellular immunity	T-lymphocytes	24–72 h	*Beryllium* poison IV

- **Toxicity:** (1) CNS >(2) Metabolic >(3) Renal > initial GI N and V.
- **Toxic phases 1–3:** *Phase 1-CNS:* N, V, *intoxication*, inebriation, nystagmus, myoclonus, seizures, progressing to lethargy and coma in 4–8 h. *Phase 2-Metabolic:* profound *high anion gap metabolic acidosis* causing CV collapse. *Phase 3-Renal:* urinary excretion of toxic metabolites (calcium oxalate and hippuric acid); *calcium oxalate crystalluria* → nephrolithiasis → proteinuria and hematuria → ATN.

Ethylene Glycol Metabolism

Ethylene Glycol OD: Dx and Mx

Dx: Calcium oxalate *crystalluria*, urine *fluorescein* staining under ultraviolet Wood's lamp, serum EG levels by GC/MS

Urinalysis: *Ethylene Glycol Ingestion*: *Urinary calcium oxalate crystals* (ethylene glycol ingestion → management with intravenous *ethanol and /or fomepizole*

- **Initial mx:** AC ineffective 2° rapid absorption and delayed sx onset of 4–8 h; ipecac contraindicated 2° vomiting; $NaHCO_3$ to correct acidosis and ↑ excretion weak acids; antidotes = *ethanol*, an ADH competitor (and/or fomepizole, an ADH inhibitor, 15 mg/kg load, then 10–15 mg/kg until EG levels, 20 mg/dL*) as preferred ADH substrates, 0.8 g/kg IV or 8 mL/kg po, to maintain serum EtOH level of 100–150 mg/dL *(EG:EtOH ratio = 1:4)*
- **Enhanced elimination:** (1) Urinary alkalinization to promote urinary excretion of weak acid *metabolites*; (2) *thiamine*, 100 mg IV, and *pyridoxine*, 50 mg IV, q 6 h, to promote alternative nontoxic routes of metabolism; (3) *hemodialysis* for EG levels >25 *mg/dL* to prevent ATN

* *Fomepizole Rule of 15s.*

- **Correct hypocalcemia:** Treat hypocalcemia 2° massive calcium losses from calcium oxalate crystalluria

Diethylene Glycol

Pharmacokinetics and Uses

Pharm: An industrial alcohol solvent and anti-freeze agent with a pleasant sweet taste and with negligible metabolism.

Uses: Industrial solvent, illicitly substituted for propylene glycol as a solvent to solubilize APAP (Tylenol®), cough syrup, tooth powder, and other drugs manufactured in many developing countries. Continues to cause many deaths worldwide, mostly in children.

Toxicities

Initial GI and Renal > Hepatic.

GI: Initial N and V with severe abdominal cramps and pain.

Renal: Initial polyuria followed within 24 h by oliguria, then anuria and *ARF*. High CFRs.

Hepatic: *Hepatotoxicity* = hepatomegaly and jaundice.

Tx: Supportive only with *hemodialysis* (HD); *ethanol* and *4-MP ineffective* as antidotes.

Direct ARF: Acute Glomerular Nephropathy

Volatile Substance Abuse 1

Nephrotoxins Abused by Inhalation

VOCs commonly abused by adolescents
- Butane lighter refills #1
- Typewriter correction fluids #2
  - *Trichloroethane*
  - *Trichloroethylene*
  - *Perchloroethylene*
- Aerosol propellants #3
  - Nitrous oxide gas #1
  - CFCs
- Propane gas canisters

VOCs commonly abused by workers
- *Glues and paints:* occupational #1
  - *Benzene*
  - *Toluene*
  - *Naptha*
  - N-hexane
  - Xylene
- Gasoline, kerosene

Liquid anesthetics

Ether, *enflurane*, desflurane

Volatile Substance Abuse 2

- **Techniques:** Sniffing → huffing → bagging
- **Agents:** Toluene (glues, paints) → fuels (butane, gasoline) → TCE and PCE (typewriter correction fluids, Liquid Paper®) → dry cleaning fluids (acetone, CCl_4, TCE, PCE) → propellants (CFCs, nitrous oxide)
- **Acute tox:** *CNS*-excitation, euphoria, hallucinations, ataxia, seizures, HA, respiratory depression > *CV*-tachyarrhythmias → "*sudden sniffing death*" > *heme-methemoglobinemia* > *hepatotoxicity* (*CCl_4*) and *CO poisoning* (*methylene chloride*)
- **Chronic tox:** "*Glue-sniffers*" *or toluene encephalopathy/chronic* "*painter's syndrome*": leukoencephalopathies characterized by memory and cognitive losses, dementia, insomnia, anxiety and depression, personality disorder, ataxia and chorea, peripheral neuropathy (n-hexane, MIBK)
- **Epidemiology:** 5–10% HS students; >60 deaths year/United States and much greater among street children in SE Asia and Africa; male:female = 5:1; butane lighter refills are the most commonly abused VOCs

Occupational Causes of ARF: Herbicides

Bipyridyl Herbicides: Paraquat and Diquat 1

Paraquat phys: Water-soluble, *dark brown liquid, looks like coke*; rapid GI absorption, little skin and lung absorption; common suicide agent in India and SE Asia

Mech: Very corrosive to GI tract, superoxide radical damage to alveolar lining cells > kidneys; ↑↑ *pulmonary O_2 toxicity*

Onset: Immediate GI effects = N-V-D; subacute ATN in 1–5 days

Sx: GI ulceration → esophageal perforation → hemorrhagic pulmonary edema → "*diphtheritic membrane*" → late *pulmonary interstitial fibrosis* from O^- superoxide radical toxicity

Tx: No antidote; immediate adsorbent = AC > Fuller's earth > bentonite clay; no emesis and lavage 2° ↑ GI perforation risk; sorbitol cathartic; consider bilateral lung tx?; ↓↓ FIO_2

Diquat: Not taken up by alveolar lining cells, no oxygen toxicity, no residual interstitial fibrosis, little lung injury *only renal damage*

Bypyridyl Herbicides: Paraquat and Diquat 2

Paraquat

Renal toxicity: If the patient survives the acute cardiopulmonary effects (noncardiogenic pulmonary edema, then rapidly progressive fibrosis), proximal tubular dysfunction ensues within 2–6 days with glycosuria, amnioaciduria, and phosphaturia.

Tx: Early HP, HD, or both HP-HD. Peritoneal dialysis is ineffective.

Diquat and Morfamquat

Renal toxicity: Little to no pulmonary toxicity with both, but *pronounced proximal tubular dysfunction following diquat ingestions*. Morfamquat's renal toxicity is unknown—it is an animal nephrotoxin.

Tx: Same.

Environmental Causes of ARF: Hymenoptera Stings

Hymenoptera: Apids (Bees)

Names: Honeybee, bumble bee, carpenter bee

Latin: *Apis mellifera, Bombus* spp., *Xylocopa* spp.

Venom: Phospholipase A_2, hyaluronidase, *mellitin*, *apamin*, acid phosphatase, *allergen C, mast cell degranulating peptide**

Hymenoptera: Vespids (Wasps)

Name: Paper wasp, gold wasp, yellow jacket, white- (bald)-faced hornet

Latin: Vespids

Venom: *Kinins, antigen* 5, phospholipases, hyaluronidase, mast cell degranulating peptide

Dx: Same as Apids, consider desensitization

Tx: Scrape out stingers, prepare for anaphylaxis

Environmental and Occupational Nephrotoxicology: CRF

(See Tables 15.10, 15.11, and 15.12)

Table 15.10 Major Environmental and Occupational Exposure Causes of CRF

Chronic Renal Dysfunction		
CTIN: Metals	**CGN: Metals, Solvents, Autoimmune**	**Vascular Nephropathy: Only Carbon Disulfide**
Cd (*itai-itai*) Pb Region. environ. (Balkan endemic nephropathy = BEN)	Hg Nephro-tic syn, AGBM+ Silica ANCA+ Org solvents AGBM+	CS_2

* ↑ **Rxn risks:** Prior rxn, systemic mastocytosis, ↑ serum tryptase, *ACEI tx-↑ lung kinins.*

Table 15.11 Additional Environmental and Occupational Exposure Causes of CRF 1

Chronic Tubulointerstitial Nephropathy	Chronic Glomerulonephropathy	Vascular Nephropathy
Metals Cadmium Geranium Lead Mercury Uranium *Environmental:* *Balkan endemic nephropathy* *Herbal/analgesic nephropathy*	Metals Gold Mercury Elements Silica Bismuth tartrate *Organic solvents*	*Carbon disulfide* Nylon and Rayon manufacturing Synthetic silk and synthetic fabricmanufacturing

Table 15.12 Additional Environmental and Occupational Exposure Causes of CRF 2

Papillary Necrosis	Polycystic Disease	Radiation Nephritis
#1 = Excessive analgesic use: Phenacetin NSAIDs *Misc. chemicals:* Bromoethanamine Diphenylamine Diphenylmethyl alcohol Ethylenimine Methylaniline Phenylanthranilic acid PCBs and dioxins	*Experimental and teratogenic cystic agents:* Biphenyl Diphenylamine Diphenylthiazole *Miscellaneous:* Lithium Cisplatin	External therapeutic irradiation with cumulative doses > 2300 rads over 2–3 weeks may result in malignant hypertension, proteinuria, microhematuria, with degenerative changes of both tubular epithelial and glomerular endothelial cells.

Nephrotoxic Plants Causing CRF

Kidney stones, renal cancer: *Aristolochia* spp. (clematis vines), Balkan endemic nephropathy

Nephrogenic diabetes insipidus: Excessive excretion of dilute urine

Tx: DDAVP

Colchicum autumnale **(autumn crocus):** Colchicine, glory lily

Misc. drugs causing DI: # 1 = lithium, methoxyflurane, propoxyphene, demeclocycline, ifosfimide

SIADH: Reduced urine output, hypervolemia, dilutional hyponatremia

Tx: ↓ fluids, ↑ Na

Vinca alkaloids: Vinblastine, vincristine

Other chemotherapeutics: Cyclophosphamide, cisplatinum

Misc. drugs causing SIADH: # 1 = thiazides, chlorpropamide, TCAs, SSRIs, phenothiazines, valproic acid

CRF: Balkan Endemic Nephropathy

Balkan Endemic Nephropathy (BEN)

Dist: 1st desc. 1950s in Balkans among locals aged 50s–60s

Clin: Renal tubular acidosis, glycosuria, hyperuricosuria, hypouricemia, proteinuria <1 g/day

Path: Interstitial and peri-glomerular fibrosis, no inflammatory cell infiltrates, normal glomeruli; *transitional cell cancers develop in upper tracts in 30–40%*

Etiol: ?, Aristolochic acid-contaminated flour by seeds of *Aristolochia clematis*?

Tx: HD, screen for papillary transitional cell cancer

CRF: Chinese Herbal Nephropathy

Herbal (Chinese) Endemic Nephropathy (HEN)

Dist: 1st desc. 1991 in Belgium among women consuming Chinese herbal meds at a weight-loss clinic

Clin: Abnormalities of tubal function predominate as in BEN

Path: Interstitial and periglomerular fibrosis, no infiltrates, glomeruli normal, ↑ incidence transitional cell cancers

Etiol: *Aristolochia* spp. herbs containing aristolochic acid which can form DNA adducts in patients with HEN

Tx: HD, screen for transitional cell cancer in upper tracts

Chronic Renal Failure 2

Occupational Nephrotoxicology: Nonrenal Disorders—Berylliosis, Urolithiasis, and Bladder Disorders

(See Tables 15.13 and 15.14)

Berylliosis and Urolithiasis

Pathology: Be is a rare strategic metal that can induce an immunologic allergic response in sensitized patients to Be antigen causing a sarcoid (and TB)-like granulomatous lung disease characterized by the development of reactive granulomas (beryllium granulomas) with central multinucleated giant cells with Be deposits (Schaumann bodies), an inner surrounding cuff of lymphocytes, and outer rings of fibrous collagen. Similar lesions may also develop in the skin, lymph nodes, bronchi, and *kidneys.*

Renal: Urolithiasis occurs in 30% of cases 2° ↓ serum ca, ↑ urine Ca, ↑ serum uric acid.

Tx: Supportive.

Beryllium granuloma: Sarcoid-like granuloma with central giant cells and ringing cuffs of lymphocytes and collagen.

Table 15.13 Miscellaneous Environmental and Occupational Causes of Nonrenal Genitourinary Tract Abnormalities

Urolithiasis	Noncancerous Bladder Disorders	
Foodborne vs. environmental: ↑ *Worcestershire* sauce (unknown herbal lithogen-aristolochic acid?) *Metals*: *Cadmium, calcium* (calciuria) *Beryllium* (oxaluria) *Oxaluria:* *Antifreeze: ethylene glycol; vitamin C* *Melamine:* synthetic protein used in fertilizers and added to pet food and baby formula (China 04-07).	Neurogenic bladder: #1 = *dimethyl-aminoproprionitrile* (DMAPM)-poly-urethrane foam catalytic agent-sphincter denervation, *loss of detrusor tone, urinary retention* + distal peripheral neuropathy. #2 = *acrylamide*-grout-autonomic and peripheral neuropathy, neurogenic bladder.	Hemorrhagic cystitis: #1 = *turpentine* inhalation/ingestion, acrolein metabolite, accompanied by thrombocytopenia, urine smells like violets. *Pesticides* Toluidines Formamidines *Cancer chemotherapeutics* Cyclophosphamide Ifosfamide

Turpentine

Pine terpenes: Used in paints, varnishes, solvents, fragrances, wax-polishes, cleansers (PineSol®), topical meds (Vicks VapoRub®)

Pulm > renal > heme > CNS

Pulm: Aspiration pneumonitis

Renal: Pathognomonic *hemorrhagic cystitis* → ATN

Heme: Pathognomonic of turpentine = *TP thrombocytopenic purpura*

CNS: Excitation → depression

Tx: Same as for petroleum distillates

Test question: Urine smells like violets

Table 15.14 Environmental and Occupational Causes of Genitourinary Malignancies

Carcinogens	Kidney	Bladder	Prostate
Environmental	*Balkan endemic nephropathy 2° aristolochic acid* (transitional cell carcinomas) ? *Arsenic in drinking water*	*Arsenic in drinking water (major cause)* *Schistosoma haematobium* (Af.) Smoking (tar, *Cadmium*) TCE in drinking water	*Cadmium* in drinking water
Occupational	*Cadmium* welding (RR = 2.5–4.4)	*Arsenic* (major cause) Aniline dyes Aromatics, benzene Cd (paints, vending) Naphthylamine Nitrosamines (rubber)	*Cadmium* welding (RR = 1.7)

Environmental Nephrotoxicology: Parasitic Infections Schistosomiasis and Bladder Cancer

Urinary Tract Schistosomiasis: Causative Blood Fluke = Schistosoma haematobium

Transmission: Infective cercaria exit snail, penetrate, mature in bladder venous plexuses, adult female, lives in the bladder (Figure 15.1)

Diagnosis: By IVP, bladder ultrasound, and cystoscopic biopsy IVP

Findings: Malignant polyps, bladder filling defects

Histopathology: Squamous cell papillary bladder cancer; gravid female flukes and disintegrating eggs in biopsies

Conclusions

- Toxins are responsible for *over 1/3 (35%) of cases of ARF from ATN*, but chronic diseases remain responsible for significantly more cases of CRF than toxins.
- Always include a *detailed environmental* and *occupational exposure history* in the work-up of all patients with renal dysfunction.
- Arsenic, cadmium, and lead are commonly used in industrial processes and are ubiquitous *wastes in the soil* (paint chips, plywood) and *in drinking water* (*Note*: EPA just lowered the As MCL in drinking water 2° ↑ bladder cancer, especially in the South).
- Order *most sensitive biomarkers* if considering environmental/occupational nephrotoxicity.
- Purchase *organic herbs, mushrooms, fish, and fowl at groceries*, rather than foraging/hunting for them.

Post-Test Questions

1. Select the most sensitive biomarker of renal dysfunction.
   a. Serum perinuclear-ANCA (p-ANCA).
   b. Urine sediment.
   c. Serum BUN/creatinine.
   d. Urine ß-2-microglobulin.*
2. Select the best combination of renal protective measures in managing rhabdomyolysis following crush injuries.
   a. Early high-volume hydration with normal saline followed by bicarbonate correction of metabolic acidosis.*
   b. Late high-volume hydration with normal saline plus bicarbonate and mannitol.

* Correct

c. Early hydration with Ringer's lactate plus bicarbonate and mannitol.
d. Hydration with Ringer's lactate and bicarbonate only if urine pH < 6.5.

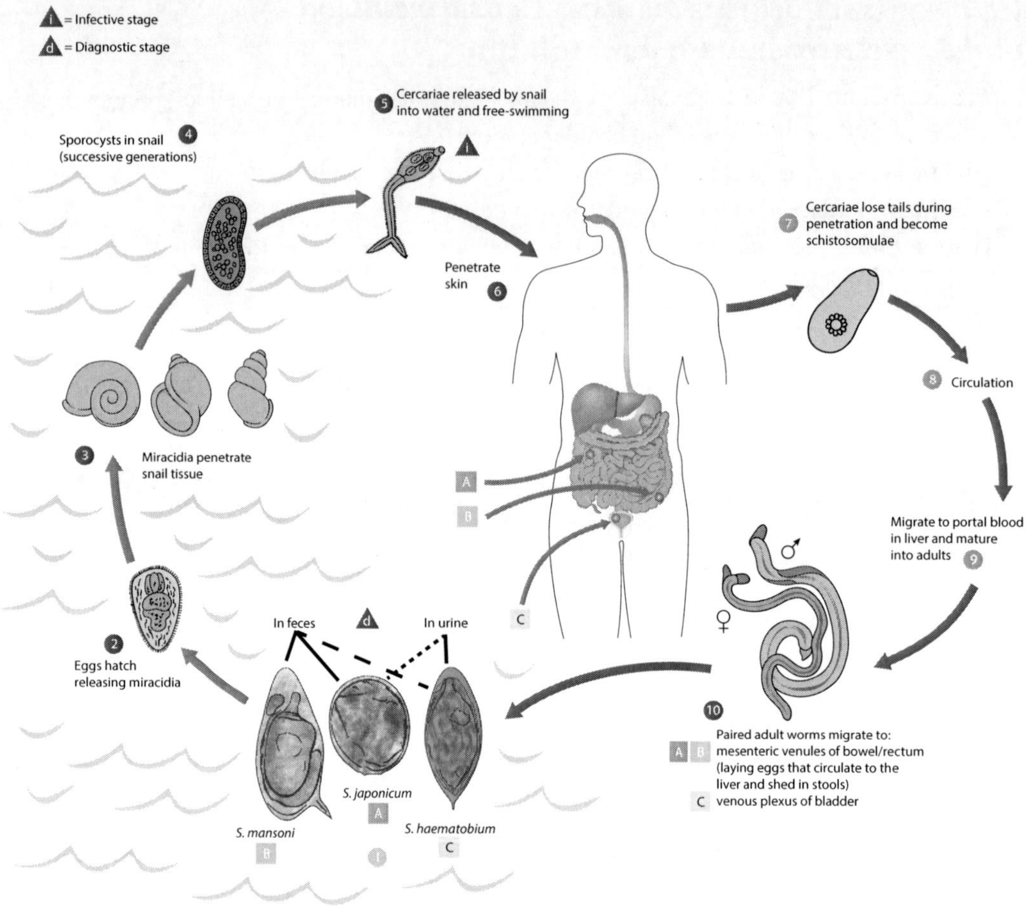

FIGURE 15.1 The comparative life cycles of the three parasitic blood flukes responsible for most cases of schistosomiasis worldwide. All schistosomes share freshwater snails as intermediate hosts that release penetrating infective stage cercariae into freshwater ecosystems. *Schistosoma haematobium* cercariae (C) preferentially migrate to the venous plexi of the bladder to mature into mating adults that release eggs in the urine. Chronic *S. haematobium* infections can cause bladder cancer diagnosed by filling defects on ultrasound and intravenous pyelogram (IVP) studies and gravid female flukes in bladder biopsy specimens. Treatment requires antiparasitic therapy and cystoscopic or open surgical resection of malignant lesions. (From The Public Health Image Library [PHIL] of the CDC. Available at http://www.dpd.cdc.gov/dpdx)

Chapter 16

Neurotoxicology

Outline .310
Objectives .311
Neuroanatomy .312
Pyramidal vs. Extrapyramidal? .313
Mechanisms of Neurotoxicity .313
Neuronopathy .314
Neurotoxic Opioids .314
Axonopathy .314
Transmission Neurotoxicity: "Transmissionopathy" .315
Toxic CNS Disorders .315
Neurodiagnostic Investigations 1 .315
Neurodiagnostic Investigations 2 .316
Occ NeuroTox .316
Toxic vs. Nontoxic Disorders? .317
Classical Neurologic Diagnoses .317
Neuropathology: GBS .318
DDx: 1° Organic vs. 2° Toxic? .318
DDx: Acute vs. Chronic Encephalopathy? .319
DDx: Extrapyramidal vs. Pyramidal? .319
DDx: Myeloneuropathy vs. Polyneuropathy? 320
Metals: Metals vs. "Minerals" 321
Metals: Carcinogenic vs. Neurotoxic 321

Arsenic 322
Lead 323
Lead Poisoning 324
Mercury 324
Mercury Poisoning 325
Thallium 326
Manganese 329
Minor Metal Poisoning 329
Neurotoxic Gases 331
Poison Gas 331
Cyanide 334
Hydrogen Sulfide 336
VOCs 338
Hydrocarbons 339
Toxic Alcohols 342
VOCs 345
Additives Tox 345
Pesticides 346
Outline 349
Neurotoxic Rodenticides 350
Low Tox Rodenticides 350
High Tox Rodenticides 352
Psychotropics 353
Insecticides 354
Herbicides 354
Conclusions 355

Outline

1. Neuroanatomy review
2. Neurodiagnostics review
3. General neurotoxicity syndromes
4. Differential diagnosis of neurotoxicity syndromes
   a. Congenital
   b. Acquired
      i. Occupational
      ii. Idiopathic
5. Specific neurotoxicity syndromes
   a. Metals
   b. Gases
   c. Hydrocarbons
      i. Solvents = VOCs

   d. Pesticides
      i. Insecticides
      ii. Rodenticides
      iii. Herbicides
6. Management
7. Hierarchy of prevention
8. Conclusions

Objectives

This session will focus on the identification of common workplace neurotoxins; their mechanisms of neurotoxicity; and the diagnosis, management, and prevention of acquired neurotoxic illnesses.

At the conclusion of this session, the student-learner should be able to

1. Describe common workplace neurotoxins and their mechanisms of neurotoxicity
2. Stratify the outcomes of neurotoxic disorders as upper motor neuron, autonomic, and lower motor neuron disorders
3. Describe the most common presentations of central, autonomic, and peripheral nervous system neurotoxic disorders
4. Discuss an evidence-based practice of determining the causality of and presenting a differential diagnosis of inherited, acquired, and idiopathic neurologic illnesses in workers
5. Demonstrate a systematic clinical approach to the diagnosis of suspected neurotoxic disorders, including recognizing pathognomonic features on the occupational history and physical examination and recommending appropriate investigations, consultations, and treatments

What Makes the Nervous System More Vulnerable to Injury?

1. High aerobic and glucose energy requirements:
   - Most sensitive organ system to loss of oxygen and glucose supply: basal ganglia > cortex > medulla ϖ spinal cord > peripheral nerves > autonomic nerves
2. Presence of long, complex cell structures:
   - Longest axons are most sensitive to damage

What Makes the Nervous System Less Vulnerable to Injury?

1. *Blood–brain barrier:*
   - Substances must pass through an endothelial cell "barrier"
   - Lipid-soluble substances penetrate the barrier more easily than water-soluble substances

- Barrier does not offer complete protection to spinal and autonomic ganglia, outside of CNS
- Not fully developed at birth

2. *Excess neuronal capacity:*
    - Symptoms delayed or worsen with age-related attrition
    - Injury manifests as latency or deterioration following cessation of exposure
    - Examples: MPTP and manganese-induced Parkinsonism, chronic glue-sniffer's and painter's encephalopathies
3. *Autoregulation of perfusion pressure:*
    - Cerebral perfusion pressure (CPP) = mean arterial pressure (MAP)–intracranial pressure (ICP).
    - Normal ICP = 10–12 mmHg.
    - MAP autoregulated 50–150.
    - Autoregulation mechanisms reset upward in all patients with essential hypertension, despite antihypertensive therapy. Thus, patients with head injuries need higher MAP to maintain CPP.

Neuroanatomy

Neuraxis

1. *CNS* = Brain and brainstem + spinal cord
2. *PNS* = Peripheral nerve + responding muscle
3. *ANS* = Sympathetic nervous system (NS) ("fight or flight" response) + Parasympathetic NS (Salivation, Lacrimation, Urination, Defecation, Emesis = "SLUDE" or Diarrhea, Urination, Miosis, Bronchorrhea, Bronchospasm, Emesis, Lacrimation, Salivation = "DUMBBELS")

Motor Neuron (Neurone)

1. *UMN* = Brain and brainstem + spinal cord to anterior horn motor cells, includes the CNs. Protected by blood–brain barrier (BBB).
2. *LMN* = Anterior horn to peripheral nerve + neuromuscular junction to muscle, includes the spinal dorsal root ganglia and the ANS ganglia. Not protected by BBB.

UMN Lesion

- Confined to pyramidal tracts
- Contralateral hemiparesis
- Muscles hypertonic
- No muscle atrophy
- Arms flexed, legs extended

- Hyperactive DTRs
- No fasciculations + pathological reflexes

LMN Lesion

- Confined to PNS
- Focal limited paresis
- Muscles flaccid
- Prominent muscle atrophy
- Flailing, unsure gait
- Hypoactive DTRs
- + Fasciculations; no pathological reflexes

Pyramidal vs. Extrapyramidal?

Pyramidal Tracts

- Temporoparietal motor cortex strips (*Homunculus*)
- Anterior pyramidal tracts
- Decussation of pyramids
- Lateral corticospinal tracts = relatively resistant to neurotoxins except lead and some VOCs
- Control proprioception, gait, and motor movement

Extrapyramidal Tracts

- Vestibular system
- Cerebellum
- Basal ganglia = caudate nucleus + globus pallidus + putamen + substantia nigra (SN) = most sensitive to inhaled neurotoxins
- Control resting tone, balance, positioning, and muscular coordination

Mechanisms of Neurotoxicity

Neurotoxic damage to

1. Cell body
   - Neuronopathy
2. Axon
   - Axonopathy
3. Myelin
   - Myelinopathy
4. Synapse or neuromuscular junction
   - "Transmissionopathy"

Neuronopathy

- Damage is irreversible
  - Examples:
    - Methyl mercury
    - MPTP = methyl-phenyl-tetrahydropyridine

Neurotoxic Opioids

Methyl-Phenyl-Tetrahydropyridine (MPTP)

1. A neurotoxic by-product of MPPP, a meperidine analog, manufactured during the failed illicit lab synthesis of *meperidine.*
2. IVDUs become *frozen addicts* and develop classical *Parkinsonism* from selective destruction of dopamine-secreting substantia nigra cells; *resistant to l-dopa tx, and resembles manganic Parkinsonism.*
3. MPTP is now used to induce *experimental Parkinsonism* in laboratory animals in order to test new anti-Parkinson drugs.

Axonopathy

- Damage is *reversible* in PNS; *irreversible* in CNS.
- All are sensorimotor neuropathies. Arsenic and thallium axonopathies are more sensory than motor.
- Autonomic dysfunction may be present.
- "Stocking and glove" distribution.

Examples: Axonopathy

- Carbon disulfide, nitrous oxide (mechanism = toxic B_{12} deficiency)
- *n*-Hexane:
  - Converted in body to toxic metabolite (*n*-hexanedione)
  - Potentiated by methyl *n*-butyl ketone (MNBK)
  - "Glue sniffer's" polyneuropathy ("polyaxonopathy")
  - Multiple foci of neurofilament damage
- Acrylamide monomer
- Arsenic (painful sensory peripheral axonopathy—glove and stocking)
- Thallium (painful sensory peripheral axonopathy)
- Trichloroethylene (TCE) → Remember TCE's unique toxicity = *degreaser's flush* (also caused by TE) and *trigeminal neuropathy*

Transmission Neurotoxicity: "Transmissionopathy"

Organophosphate Pesticides

1. Unopposed cholinergic activity ("transmissionopathy")
   - Acute, within hours of exposure
   - Causes "SLUDE" or "DUMBBELS"
2. Myopathy
   - Subacute, 1–4 days after exposure
   - Frequently involves respiratory muscles—hypoventilation
   - Recovery with supportive treatment

Toxic CNS Disorders

- Most common picture is a chronic encephalopathy—resembles alcoholic inebriation
- Compatible with mild diffuse CNS injury
- Acute inebriation, then chronic mood alterations, personality changes, asthenia, cognitive disturbances. Examples: painter's encephalopathy, glue-sniffer's encephalopathy, toluene encephalopathy
- Often misdiagnosed as alcoholism, Wernicke–Korsakoff psychosis, Alzheimer's
- Causes: Organometals (lead, manganese, mercury, tin), solvents (chlorinated hydrocarbons, mixtures, carbon disulfide, toluene), other VOCs (styrene)

Neurodiagnostic Investigations 1

Is Structural Integrity OK?

- Conventional x-rays
- Computed tomography (CT scans, ± contrast)
- Magnetic resonance imaging (MRI scans)
- Angiography
- Nerve and brain biopsy

Is Functional Integrity OK?

- Functional MRI
- Positron emission tomography (PET)
- Nerve conduction
- Electromyography
- Neuropsychological testing*
- CSF analysis: For protein, cells, immunoglobulins, microbes

* Most sensitive for early evidence of chronic encephalopathy.

Neurodiagnostic Investigations 2

Central Nervous System

- Imaging (CT, MRI, PET) studies usually normal unless very advanced disease.
- Other investigations (lumbar puncture, EEG) to rule out other causes, for example, postinfectious meningoencephalitis (West Nile, SLE, even influenza?) or GBS (*Campylobacter jejuni*).
- Most sensitive investigation is neuropsychological testing.
  - Testing is user-dependent.
  - Report should provide numerical scores on test.
- Include investigations for effects of exposure on other systems. (Ex: LFTs for VOC—solvents = CCL_4 and perchloroethylene).

"General" NeuroTox Syn: Outline

1. **Encephalopathy:** Mimics alcoholism, Wernicke–Korsakoff, dementia, Alzheimer's
2. **Parkinsonism:** Only difference between toxin-induced and acquired Parkinsonism is refractoriness to L-dopa therapy
3. **Upper motor neuron disease:** Resembles MS (UMN) and ALS (UMN + LMN)
4. **Lower motor neuron peripheral neuropathy:** Sensory and motor components often differ

Occ NeuroTox

"General" NeuroTox Syn

1. *Encephalopathy*—Irritability, headache, disorientation, inebriation, seizures, amnesia, psychosis, lethargy, somnolence, stupor, coma. Ex: Ethanol or isopropanol intoxication, glue-sniffer's encephalopathy, West Nile virus encephalopathy.
2. *Parkinsonism*—Pill-rolling and resting tremors, bradykinesia, masked facies, simian posture, cogwheel rigidity, shuffling-stiff gait, no arm swing. Ex: Ischemic; toxic (CO, Mn, MPTP); postinfectious; familial; and idiopathic Parkinson's disease (Michael J. Fox).
3. *Upper motor neuron disease*—Muscle weakness, spasticity, disuse atrophy, fasciculations, hyperreflexia, pathological reflexes (Babinski, rooting, etc.). May be painful. Ex: multiple sclerosis (MS), amyotropic lateral sclerosis (ALS).
4. *LMN peripheral neuropathy*—Painful paresthesias, allodynia, numbness, weakness, paralysis, areflexia, autonomic dysfunction (sweating, bladder and bowel dysfunction). Ex: Guillain–Barré syndrome (inflammatory demyelinating polyneuropathy), cauda equina syndrome (L3–S5 polyneuropathy), carpal tunnel syndrome (median neuropathy), acrylamide-induced axonopathy with neurogenic bladder.

Toxic vs. Nontoxic Disorders?

Primary (Classical) Neurologic Diseases

- Ischemic, drug/toxin-induced, postinfectious, and familial
- Parkinsonism = extrapyramidal
- Multiple sclerosis = UMN, acquired demyelinating
- Amyotrophic lateral sclerosis = U + LMN, hereditary demyelinating
- Guillain–Barré syndrome = postinfectious acquired
- Alzheimer's disease = UMN, inherited
- Wernicke–Korsakoff syndrome = UMN, acquired/inherited potential

Secondary (Acquired) Neurotoxic Syndromes

- Acute encephalopathy
- Chronic encephalopathy
- Parkinsonism
- Myeloneuropathy (UMN): Resembles MS
- Myeloneuropathy (UMN + LMN): Resembles ALS
- Polyneuropathy (LMN ± autonomic dysfunction)
- Diabetes, alcoholism, steroid, uremia-associated polyneuropathies (LMN)

Classical Neurologic Diagnoses

1. Parkinson's disease (*Parkinsonism*)
2. Multiple sclerosis (MS)
3. Amyotrophic lateral sclerosis (*ALS*)
4. Guillain–Barré syndrome (*GBS*)

Def: Parkinsonism

A syndrome of older adults (55+) caused by *dopamine neurotransmitter depletion* in the *substantia nigra* area of the *basal ganglia* and characterized by stiff, bradykinetic movements with tremors. Etiologies include (1) *ischemic* (cerebrovascular = >50%), (2) *postencephalitic or postinfectious (influenza, West Nile)*, (3) *drug*-induced, (4) *toxin*-nduced, (5) *familial* (1–10%), and (6) *idiopathic* Parkinsonism.

Def: Multiple Sclerosis

An autoimmune UMN disease of young adults (25–45 yo), especially females (3:1, female:male) caused by multiple demyelinated, *sclerotic plaques in the white matter* of the brain (*optic nerve, corpus callosum*) and spinal cord (*pyramidal tracts*) noted on CT and MRI and characterized by *exacerbations and remissions* of visual loss, gait disturbances, weakness, bladder and bowel dysfunction, incoordination, and behavioral changes. Exact initiating mechanisms of autoimmune activity are unknown and may include recurrent URIs in cold climates, with postinfectious circulating cytokines damaging myelin epitopes. Vitamin D deficiency may also play a role.

Neuropathology of MS

Myelin loss: *Periventricular white, sclerotic plaque PAS myelin stain, periventricular white matter (×15)*

Cytokine-mediated demyelination: *Immuno-stain, macrophages "eating" myelin sheaths*

Def: Amyotrophic Lateral Sclerosis

A progressive hereditary disease of older adults (55+) caused by *sclerotic destruction of anterior horn motor cells* (as in polio) and *lateral corticospinal* (pyramidal) tracts and characterized by weakness, atrophy, *fasciculations*, hyperreflexia, pathological reflexes, spasticity, and gait disturbances. Also known as *Lou Gehrig's disease*. ALS was the most common reason for patients to visit Dr. Kevorkian for assisted suicides. In addition to Lou Gehrig, actors Dudley Moore and David Niven died of ALS-like diseases.

Def: Guillain–Barré Syndrome

An acute *postviral or post-infection,** *demyelinating peripheral polyneuropathy* of young-middle-aged adults (25–55) characterized by distal paresthesias, then *weakness beginning in the legs and ascending to the thorax* with *transverse paraplegia* (permanent weakness in 65%) and *respiratory insufficiency* from hypoventilation. Also known as *ascending transverse myelitis and acute idiopathic inflammatory polyneuritis.*

Neuropathology: GBS

Diagnosis of GBS: Sural nerve bx: early GBS, DDx

1. Toxic acquired vs. 1° neurologic disorders
2. Acute vs. chronic encephalopathies
3. Parkinsonism (extrapyramidal) vs. upper motor neuron (pyramidal) disorders
4. Myeloneuropathy vs. polyneuropathy

DDx: 1° Organic vs. 2° Toxic?

Primary Neurologic

- Local and asymmetrical
- No temporal relationship to exposures

* Viral URI, influenza, HIV, CMV, EBV-infectious mononucleosis.

- No dose–response effect
- No "coasting" effect
- Progressive attrition
- Remissions only

Toxic (Secondary)

- Diffuse and symmetrical
- Temporal relationship to exposures
- Dose–response effect
- "Coasting" deterioration
- Age attrition
- Recovery is possible

DDx: Acute vs. Chronic Encephalopathy?

Acute Encephalopathy

- **Anat:** Diffuse cortical
- **Sx:** HA, disorientation, inebriation, seizures, lethargy, stupor, coma
- **Tox:** Alcohol, VOCs, anesthetics, glues, toluene, solvents, CO, CS_2, organochlorines

Chronic Encephalopathy

- Diffuse cortical
- Psychosis, aggression/depression, cognitive loss, dementia
- Chronic low-dose exposures to same toxins (*glue-sniffer's* encephalopathy), organophosphates

DDx: Extrapyramidal vs. Pyramidal?

Parkinsonism (Extrapyramidal)

- **Anat:** Basal ganglia
- **Sx:** Tremor, bradykinesia, cogwheel rigidity, shuffling gait
- **Tox:** CO, manganese, methanol

UMN Disorders (Pyramidal)

- Spinal cord and pyramidal tracts
- Muscle weakness, disuse atrophy, flailing gait
- Fasciculations
- Lead, organotin, manganese

DDx: Myeloneuropathy vs. Polyneuropathy?

Myeloneuropathy

- **Anat:** Cord and peripheral sensorimotor nerves
- **Sx:** Paresthesias, numbness, DTR +, path reflexes, "dying-back" or glove and stocking neuropathy = axonopathy
- **Tox:** N_2O abuse, hexacarbons, As, organophosphates
- **Acq:** B_{12} deficiency (subacute combined degeneration)

Polyneuropathy

- Peripheral sensorimotor and autonomic nerves
- Allodynia, neuropathic pain, weakness, reduced to absent deep tendon reflexes (DTRs), autonomic dysfunction (bladder and bowel)
- Acrylamide, *n*-hexane, PCBs, thallium, Pb, As, Hg

Specific Neurotoxic Syndromes

Heavy Metals

- Arsenic
- Lead
- Mercury
- Thallium
- Manganese
- Miscellaneous metals

Gases

- Carbon monoxide
- Hydrogen sulfide
- Carbon disulfide
- Ethylene oxide

Hydrocarbons

- Acrylamide
- Hexacarbons
- VOCs—solvents
- Trichloroethylene

Pesticides

- Organochlorines
- Organophosphates
- Rodenticides
- Herbicides

Metals: Metals vs. "Minerals"

Neurotoxic Heavy Metals

- Aluminum
- Arsenic
- Beryllium
- Cadmium
- Lead
- Mercury
- Thallium
- Thorium
- Uranium
- Vanadium

"Essential Minerals" Are Also Heavy Metals and Some Are Neurotoxic

- Boron
- Chromium
- Cobalt
- Copper
- Iron
- Manganese
- Molybdenum
- Nickel
- Vanadium
- Zinc

Metals: Carcinogenic vs. Neurotoxic

Carcinogenic Metals

- **Arsenic:** Bladder, liver, lung, skin
- **Cadmium:** Lung
- **Copper:** Vineyard sprayers' liver and lung cancers
- **Chromium:** Lung, nasal
- **Nickel:** Lung, nasal
- **Thorium:** Bile ducts, liver
- **Uranium:** Lung

Neurotoxic Metals

- **Aluminum:** Dementia
- **Arsenic:** Sensory axonopathy

- **Copper:** Lens degeneration
- **Lead:** Motor neuropathy
- **Manganese:** Parkinsonism
- **Mercury:** Erethism, peripheral neuropathy, Minamata disease
- **Selenium:** Anosomia
- **Thallium:** Sensory axonopathy
- **Tin:** Demyelinating encephalopathy/neuropathy

Arsenic

Toxicology

Absorption/Distribution

- Tasteless and odorless
- Well absorbed rapidly
- Pulmonary inhalation (arsine gas) > GI (inorganics) > dermal
- Systemic distribution, especially to liver and kidneys, but also to skin, hair, and nails
- Can remain as *radiopaque* metal sludge in SI → enterohepatic circulation

Metabolism/Excretion

- Rapid hepatic *methylation* to *methyl*arsinic acid (MAA) and di*methyl*arsinic acid (DMA)—methylation requires *glutathione*
- **Glutathione depletion**, common in alcoholics and malnourished, will ↓ methylation and ↑ toxicity
- Renal excretion (90%) > GI—fecal > dermal—hair and nails

Pathophysiology

1. Reduced glucose production from impaired gluconeogenesis from pyruvate
2. Reduced glucose uptake and utilization
3. Decreased production of high energy *ATP*
4. *Rapid glucose depletion* with severe *hypoglycemia*, especially in the CNS and PNS

Clinical Effects

Acute Toxicity

- **GI:** Initial sx = metallic taste, garlic breath, N, V, cramps, rice-water (cholera-like) diarrhea
- **CV:** Instability, orthostasis
- **CNS:** Encephalopathy, seizures, coma
- **Pulm:** ARDS and respiratory failure
- **Hepatorenal:** Rhabdomyolysis + acute hemolytic anemia → ATN, especially in glutathione-depleted (alcoholics)

Chronic Toxicity

- **PNS:** *Glove and stocking peripheral sensory neuropathy*, ↓ pain–touch–position–temp–vibration sensation, ↓ DTRs → *ascending flaccid paralysis*; partial sensorimotor recovery only, even after chelation
- **CNS:** Encephalopathy, CN palsies, dementia
- **Dermal:** Hyperpigmentation–hyperkeratosis → *skin cancer*, (squamous and basal cell ca, Bowen's disease), Mees' lines
- **Pulmonary:** *Lung cancer*

Dermal Effects

Arsenical hyperkeratoses
Arsenical epidermoid (squamous) cancer
Arsenical hyperkeratoses
Arsenical Bowen's disease
Arsenical Mees' lines (keratin destruction)
Diagnosis and Treatment

Diagnosis

- **Labs:** *Urine* spot As + 24-h urine As
- **R/O shellfish ingestion = organic As:** By liquid separation chromatography
- CBC, LFTs, RFTs, hair and nail As
- **X-rays:** Flat abdomen for *radiopaque sludge* in stomach and SI

Treatment

1. OG lavage if radiopaque sludge present, then whole bowel irrigation (WBI) with polyethylene glycol electrolyte (PEG) solution
2. Glucose and nutritional support
3. Monitor for respiratory failure using negative inspiratory forces (NIFs)
4. Chelation: *BAL* IM > succimer po > penicillamine po
5. Hemodialysis for ATN

Lead

- **Uses:** Batteries, alloys, ceramics, ammo, radiation shielding, former gas additive.
- **Routes:** Inhalation (adult), ingestion (child).
- **Syn:** Mostly motor polyneuropathy, less painful than arsenic and thallium sensory neuropathies. Adult: mimics ALS, frequently causes male infertility. Child: neuropsychiatric dysfunction, ADHD, IQ loss, behavioral problems.
- **Sx:** Wrist/foot drops, few sensory losses, lead colic (autonomic neuropathic constipation), infertility in males > females, chronic renal failure.

- **Tx:** Removal; EDTA IV, Succimer® po chelation.
- **Pv:** Workplace hygiene, abatement, blood Pb monitoring.

Lead Poisoning

Neurotoxicity

Central Nervous System (Targeted in Children)

- Inhibits Ach, dopa, NE, GABA, NMDA, glutamate trans, blocks vasc Ca channels and Na–K ATPase in mitochondria
- Targets cortex, cerebellum, and occipital lobes
- Acute encephalopathy- ↑ ICP, seizures and coma

Children: Hearing, cognition, IQ, developmental, motor and coordination disorders

Peripheral Nervous System (Targeted in Adults)

- Schwann cell necrosis and demyelination (adults)
- Reduced peripheral nerve conduction amplitude and velocity, UE > LE
- Motor > sensory peripheral neuropathy (Ddx: As and Tl)
- Wrist drop ("dangles") > foot drop

Mercury

Forms and Exposures

Elemental Hg	Inorganic Hg	Organic Hg
Ex: "Quicksilver"	Mercuric chloride	Methyl Hg
Dentists	Antiseptics	Seafood
Calibrated instruments (BP)	Disinfectants—taxidermy	Grain and seed fumigants
NG tubes	Batteries	Insecticides
Jewelers	Explosives	Fungicides
Electroplaters	Plastics (PVC)	Wood preservatives

Accidental Exposures

1. *Cantor tube, Hg-filled balloon used to decompress small bowel obstruction (SBO)*
2. *NG removed after balloon rupture-free elemental Hg*

Toxicology

Elemental Hg	**Inorganic Hg**	**Organic Hg**
Route: Inhalation	Ingestion (GI) > dermal (skin)	Predominantly GI
Distribution: CNS, kidney	CNS > Kidney > GI	CNS > fetus > kidney > liver
Excretion: Renal > GI	Renal > GI	Methyl: GI–fecal; aryl: renal

Pathophysiology

1. Avid covalent binding to all sulfur-containing groups, especially the *sulfhydryl groups*, throughout the body.
2. Widespread destruction of membranes and structural proteins (CNS) and disruption of enzyme and transport systems.
3. *Elemental Hg* targets *lungs* (chemical pneumonitis, ARDS), *inorganic Hg* targets *GI* tract and *kidneys* (hemorrhagic gastroenteritis, ATN), *organic Hg* targets *CNS*, especially fetal CNS (*Minamata disease*).

Mercury Poisoning

Clinical Syndromes

1. Acute inhalation of elemental Hg vapor
2. Acute ingestion of organic Hg salts
3. Chronic elemental Hg poisoning
4. Chronic inorganic Hg poisoning
5. Methyl (organic) Hg poisoning (Minamata disease)
6. Mercurial acrodynia

Acute Clinical Effects

Acute Elemental Inhalation

- Pulmonary > GI > CNS
- **Pulm:** Cough, chills, fever, dyspnea, *chemical pneumonitis*, pulmonary edema, ARDS, interstitial fibrosis
- **GI:** Metallic taste, nausea, vomiting, diarrhea, dysphagia
- **CNS:** Headaches, weakness, visual disturbances
- Acute inorganic ingestion
- GI > renal
- **GI:** Metallic taste, oral pain and burning, nausea, vomiting, diarrhea, abdominal pain, *hemorrhagic gastroenteritis*, dehydration → orthostatic hypotension
- **Renal:** *Proximal tubular necrosis* → ATN

Chronic Clinical Effects

Elemental Mercury

- Pulm > Renal > GI and CNS
- **Pulm:** Pulmonary fibrosis, restrictive lung disease
- **Renal:** *Fanconi's syndrome* = proteinuria → nephrotic syndrome 2° autoimmune glomerulonephritis, CRF
- **GI:** Relatively nontoxic due to *negligible absorption* (e.g., after long-NG tube balloon rupture)
- **CNS:** "Mad hatter" syndrome postinhalation

Inorganic Mercury ("Mad Hatter" Syndrome)

- CNS > Renal > GI
- **CNS:** Intention tremor, ballismus and *choreoathetosis* ("mad hatter" syndrome), *erethism* (anxiety, emotional lability, memory loss), *neurasthenia* (HA, depression, fatigue anorexia, weight loss)
- **GI:** Metallic taste and a characteristic triad of (1) *gingivostomatitis*, (2) *loose teeth*, and (3) *salivary gland hyperplasia*

Methyl Hg and Acrodynia

Methyl Hg Poisoning

- **Toxic form:** Inorganic Hg transformed by marine bacteria to organic methyl Hg—*bioconcentrated in the seafood chain*
- **Common name:** Minamata disease
- **Sx:** *Fetal neurotoxicity*, ↓ birth weight, MR—developmental delay, ataxia, seizures hypotonia—spasticity, deafness–blindness

Acrodynia (Pink Disease)

- **Toxic form:** Inorganic HgCl salts—*Calomel*, inorganic mercurial teething powder
- **Common name:** "Pink disease"
- **Sx:** *Pink papular rash* → hyperkeratoses on palms and soles → later *acral desquamation* → ulceration

Diagnosis and Management

Diagnosis	Emergency Mx	Specific Tx
Elemental: urine Hg > blood Hg	Elem: absor, decon, no vacuuming, haz mat 911-PPE	Inorganic: IM BAL + po succimer > penicillamine
Inorganic: urine Hg	Inorganic: EGD, WBI (PEG) for residual	Elemental: same as inorganic tx
Methyl Hg: blood Hg	Methyl Hg: NA	Methyl Hg: tx resist, succimer

Thallium

Properties and Uses

Properties

- Soft, pliable toxic metal
- Common component of granite and shale
- Behaves like $K^{\pm}$ ion in the body, interfering with nerve conduction, especially in the longest peripheral nerves → *painful, glove-and-stocking neuropathy*

Uses/Exposures

- Alloys and anticorrosives
- Optical lenses

- Coatings for lamp and lantern filaments (Coleman lanterns®)
- Jewelry
- Depilatories
- Rodenticide—outside the United States
- *Radioactive contrast agent*—thallium cardiac scan for EF ("dirty bomb")

Toxicology

Absorption/Distribution

- Rapidly absorbed by all routes
- Inhalation and ingestion > dermal
- Distributed rapidly throughout the body
- Partitions into a three-compartment model: First—blood, second—well-perfused organs, last—CNS, *no prolonged storage* in reservoirs, like Pb and Cd

Metabolism/Excretion

- Not metabolized
- *Does not persist in tissue storage sites*, like Pb and Cd in bone
- GI—fecal excretion (50 + %), unlike most other heavy metals > renal—urine excretion (25 + %) > sweat, hair, nails (<10%)

Pathophysiology

1. Thallium ions preferentially accumulate in all areas of *high K concentration*, particularly central and peripheral *nerves*, liver, and muscle, including cardiac muscle.
2. Thallium *replaces K* in all K-dependent enzyme systems.
3. Thallium *impairs nerve conduction and muscle membrane depolarization*: Sensory > motor, long nerves (LE) > short nerves (UE).
4. Thallium decreases mitotic activity (causing total alopecia) and combines with sulfhydryl groups, like arsenic, weakening keratin in nails → causing Mees' lines.
5. **Exception:** Unlike other heavy metal salts, thallium salts are substantially adsorbed to activated charcoal.

Clinical Effects

Immediate	**Intermediate**	**Late**	**Chronic**
3–4 h	Hours–days	2–4 weeks	Months
#1 = GI	#1 = PNS	#1 = Dermal	#1 = CNS
N, V, cramps, *constipation* (vagal neuropathy)	Painful ascend *peripheral neuropathy*, CN palsies	*Alopecia, Mees' lines*	Optic neuritis Ophthalmoplegia
Autonomic (X) neuropathy	Alopecia	Motor neuropathy	Memory and cognitive loss

Thallium: Dermal Effects

Thallium alopecia

Thallium—Mees' lines

Arsenic and Thallium—Mees' Lines

DDx: Alopecia and Mees' Lines

DDx of Total Toxic Alopecia

1. Thallium
2. Arsenic
3. Selenium
4. Colchicine
5. Vinca alkaloids, cancer chemotherapeutics
6. Boron

DDx of Mees' lines

1. Thallium
2. Arsenic
3. Mitotic inhibitors: Colchicine, dapsone
4. Antimetabolites: 5-FU

Diagnosis and Treatment

Diagnosis	Early Mx	Late Tx
24-h urine for atomic absorption spectroscopy	Lavage > emesis if no vomiting, WBI if x-ray +	MDAC + mannitol (osmotic cathartics only)
Urine > blood > hair and nails	Oral *Prussian blue* chelation	Prussian blue = K ferric ferrocyanide
Abdominal x-ray for radiopaque GI sludge-WBI-PEG if +	*MDAC* + cathartic, mannitol > sorbitol due to reduced GI motility	Prussian blue exchanges its K for *thallium* and *cesium* ions during chelation

Manganese

Exposures	Acute Toxicity	Chronic Tox	Treatment
Alloys welding solders	MnO_2-acute pneumonitis (manganic pn)	*Parkinsonism*—dopamine uniquely in globus pallidus and less so to absent in the substantia nigra	Early chelation only
Animal food additives	Conjunctivitis Dermatitis	Dystonia and intention tremor	$CaNa_2EDTA$
Fertilizers	GI caustic-mucosal and orogastric burns	Pulmonary fibrosis	L-dopa for Parkinson's disease

Manganese

- Controversial whether or not lower-level exposures cause more subtle neuropsychological changes including cognitive dysfunction
- Manganese-induced Parkinsonism
  - *Not* the same as other types of Parkinson's disease (postinfectious, familial, idiopathic, atherosclerotic), but resembles MPTP Parkinsonism

Mn-Induced Parkinsonism

- Clinically distinct from other forms of PD.
- Patients do not respond to dopamine replacement with L-dopa.
- Deteriorate even after removal from exposure.
- MRI normalizes by 6 months postexposure.
- Dopamine-labeled PET scan normal.
- Little role for whole-blood Mn measurement.

Heavy Metal Poisoning

- Racette et al. (2001) found significantly younger age at onset in Parkinson's disease patients who were welders compared to nonwelders (46 years vs. 63 years).
- No other clinical differences.
- Active area for litigation.

Minor Neurotoxicity

1. Copper
2. Selenium
3. Tin

Minor Metal Poisoning

Copper

Exposures	Acute Toxicity	Chronic Toxicity	Treatment
Alloys	GI: metallic taste, N, V, D, GI bleed, jaundice	Proximal tubular nephrotoxicity	Lavage
Electrical wiring		Wilson's disease (hepatolenticular degeneration)	Catharsis
			Chelation for Wilson's
Algicides Fungicides	*Metal fume fever*	↓ ceruloplasmin	Chelation—D-penicillamine only
	Hemolysis	*Lens—Blindness*	
		Cirrhosis	
Preservative Pigments	Irritant > allergic dermatitis	*Encephalopathy*	Liver transplant (Wilson's)

Selenium

Exposures	Acute Tox	Chronic Tox	Treatment
Gun bluing solvents	GI: garlic breath, N, V, watery D	GI distress, garlic breath, metal taste	Chelation contraindicated
			2° nephrotox
Alloys	Abdominal cramps	*Anosmia*, reactive AW	Activated charcoal
Antifungal shampoos (Selsun Blue®)	Dry hair, paresthesias	Antioxidant and anticancer effects? ↓ prostate ca	Add a cathartic

Selenium

Occupational Gustatory Toxicity: DDx of Garlic Breath

1. Garlic consumption
2. Selenium, selenious acid
3. Dimethyl sulfoxide (DMSO)
4. Phosphorus, zinc phosphide (rotten fish)
5. Arsenic
6. Tellurium
7. Thallium

Occupational Ototoxicity: DDx of Hearing Loss

Reversible Hearing Loss

Carbon monoxide

Irreversible Hearing Loss

- Bromates
- Heavy metals
  - Arsenic
  - Mercury
- Hydrocarbons
  - Styrene
  - Toluene
  - Xylene

Occupational Gustatory Toxicity: DDx of Olfactory Disturbances

Anosmia (Impairment or Complete Loss of Smell)

- Acrylic acid
- Cadmium
- Formaldehyde

- Hydrogen sulfide
- Selenium
- Sulfur dioxide
- Many VOCs

Cacosmia (Foul Smell) or Dysomia (Distorted Smell)

- DMSO
- Organochlorines
- Organophosphates
- Selenium

Tin

Exposures	Acute Tox	Chronic Tox	Treatment
Alloys—bronzes	Benign pneumoconiosis	*Peripheral demyelinating neuropathy*	Chelation with BAL
Solders		(organotins)	
Electroplating			
Cook utensils	Stannosis	*Encephalopathy*	#1 = *BAL*
Toothpastes	CXR +	*Cerebral edema*	BAL > DMSA
Algicides			
Fungicides			

Neurotoxic Gases

Outline

1. Carbon monoxide (CO)
2. Hydrogen cyanide (HCN)
3. Hydrogen sulfide (H_2S)
4. Carbon disulfide (CS_2): Supplied as a clear, colorless to faintly yellow liquid that volatilizes easily
5. Ethylene oxide (EtO)

Poison Gas

Basal Ganglia Toxins

- The basal ganglia toxins target specific nuclei in the basal ganglia (extrapyramidal control center) and can cause postexposure toxic Parkinsonism.
  1. Carbon monoxide
  2. Carbon disulfide

3. Hydrogen cyanide
4. Hydrogen sulfide
5. Manganese
6. Methanol
7. MPTP (methyl-phenyl-tetrahydropyridine)

Carbon Monoxide (CO)

1. Epidemiology
2. Pathophysiology
3. Clinical manifestations
4. Delayed effects
5. Diagnosis
6. Management

CO: Epidemiology

1. CO is the leading cause of poisoning morbidity and mortality in the United States, causing >5000 deaths/year.
2. 50 + % of the CO deaths/year are caused by auto exhausts; 500 CO deaths/year are caused by nonautos, such as stoves, fireplaces, gas heaters, generators, propane-powered indoor equipment (forklifts and Zamboni® ice resurfacers).
3. 3–24% of symptomatic patients with flu-like sx of HA, N, and dizziness, reporting to EDs/year have CO poisoning.
4. CO is the most common cause of fire deaths; smokers can have COHb levels of 6–10% increasing their susceptibility to CO poisoning.
5. 14–40% of discharged patients treated for CO poisoning will have delayed, permanent neurologic dysfunction, such as Parkinsonism.
6. Besides combustion of fossils fuels (oil, gas, coal, wood) and cigarette smoking, methylene chloride-containing paint strippers are the next highest contributors to human COHb levels. Methylene chloride is rapidly absorbed through the skin and lungs and later converted to CO by the liver over 12–24 h.

Carbon Monoxide

- **Use:** Fossil fuel combustion
- **Route:** Inhalation
- **Syn:** Acute encephalopathy → chronic *Parkinsonism*
- **Sx:** HA, dizziness, somnolence, stupor, coma, → *tremor, ataxia, bradykinesia, rigidity*
- **Tx:** Removal, 100%—hyperbaric O_2, L-dopa
- **Pv:** Engineering controls > PPE

CO: Clinical Manifestations

Severity =% COHb	Symptoms → Signs
Mild: 5–15%	Headache, nausea, dizziness → vomiting, no sequelae
Moderate: 15–25%	Obtundation, weakness, chest tightness, dyspnea → tachycardia, angina, tachypnea, ataxia, myonecrosis from disrupted myoglobin
Severe: >25%	Chest pain, palpitations, disorientation → PVCs, MI, ↓ BP, sz, coma, skin bullae, cherry-red skin color, CNS damage, death

CO: Pathophysiology

1. CO *binds to Hb* with an affinity 250 × greater than for O_2.
2. CO *shifts the oxyHb dissociation curve leftward*, decreasing oxygen unloading to tissues, causing tissue hypoxia and lactic acidosis.
3. CO also *binds to myoglobin*, impairing myocardial performance and causing *myonecrosis and myoglobinuria.*
4. CO can *displace NO from platelets*, causing peripheral vasodilation and hypotension.
5. CO interferes with cellular respiration by *binding to mitochondrial cytochrome oxidase (aa3)*, like CN, *uncoupling oxidative phosphorylation*, and contributing to tissue hypoxia and lactic acidosis.

CO: Delayed Effects

1. Patients rendered unconscious or >30 yo during CO exposure are more susceptible to delayed, often permanent, neurologic effects of CO poisoning.
2. Delayed neurologic effects = amnesia, agnosia, apraxia, dementia, incontinence, psychosis, chorea, cortical blindness, periph neuropathy, Parkinsonism.
3. Delayed neurologic sequelae can be predicted from acute changes on CT and MRI scans, especially *basal ganglia lesions* (globus pallidus) and ischemia of subcortical white matter.

Delayed CNS damage in CO poisoning: Bilateral lucent lesions of globus pallidus, secondary to ischemia–reperfusion injury

CO: Dx and Tx

Lab Diagnosis

- COHb level monitoring by *co-oximetry* only
- ABGs (normal PaO_2) and pulse oximetry (COHb) very unreliable
- ABGs to confirm lactic and metabolic acidosis
- Mildly elevated CPK 2° myonecrosis

Indications for Hyperbaric Oxygen (HBO)

Immediate HBO:

COHb > *25%*

COHb > 15% in pregnancy

Any local CNS findings: Syncope, seizures, coma, lateralizing neurologic signs

ECG: Myocardial ischemia, PVCs/any tachydysrhythmias

- *HBO after initial tx* (100% $O_2 \times$ 2–4 h): Persistent neurologic findings = HA, dizziness, confusion, and ataxia

Cyanide

1. Exposures and settings
2. Mechanisms of toxicity
3. Clinical manifestations
4. Diagnosis and management

CN: Exposures and Settings

CN Exposures

1. Suicides/homicides involving chemists and lab workers
2. Consumer product tampering
3. Residential fires involving fabrics and synthetics: Synthetic rubber, wool, silk, polyurethane, nitrocellulose
4. Ingestion of acetonitrile-based fake nail removers
5. Plants: (1) *Prunus* spp. pitted fruits = apricots, cherries, peaches, almonds; (2) *hydrangeas* → gut-transformed-*amygdalin* → HCN
6. Iatrogenic SCN infusions

Clinical Settings for CN Toxicity

1. Sudden collapse of an academic or industrial lab or chemical worker
2. Fire victims with coma and metabolic acidosis
3. Suicide or unexplained coma and acidosis
4. Ingestion of or access to artificial nail removers
5. Cancer pts on Laetrile® (amygdalin or CN-containing "anticancer" hoax) tx
6. ICU pts on prolonged SCN^- infusions

CN: Mechanisms

1. *Rapid absorption* via all routes with rapid membrane transit due to nonionization and low MW
2. Initial inhibition of cytochrome oxidase, shutting down electron transport chain, blocking aerobic ATP-energy production in mitochondria, causing cellular hypoxia

3. Stimulation of alternative *anaerobic routes of ATP-energy production* from pyruvate with lactate production, lactic and metabolic acidosis
4. Direct *CNS neurotoxicity* through lipid peroxidation and ischemia with greatest damage to the most O_2-sensitive areas of the brain in the basal ganglia

CN: Acute vs. Delayed Effects

Acute Manifestations

Unique: Bitter almond breath and body odor detectable by only 40% of the population

CNS: Predominant progressive sx of anxiety, agitation, confusion, lethargy, seizures, coma, central tachypnea → agonal bradypnea

CV: Initial ↓ HR and ↑ BP, then ↑ HR and ↓ BP, then myocardial failure

Skin: *Cherry-red skin color* → cyanosis

Delayed Manifestations

CNS neurotoxicity predominates: Confined to basal ganglia = globus pallidus, putamen, hippocampus (CT confirmation) → **Parkinsonism**, bradykinesia, dystonia, dysarthria, rigidity, L-dopa resistant.

Chronic low-level CN toxicity occurs in (1) *tobacco amblyopia* (male smokers with FHx), (2) *tropical (cassava root) ataxic neuropathy*, (3) *Leber's hereditary optic atrophy* (males, FHx).

Mechanism: *Low endogenous stores of detoxifying hydroxocobalamin* and *thiosulfate.*

CN: Management

Lab Diagnosis

- Assess for metabolic acidosis with ABGs, central venous gas, serum lactate, glucose, electrolytes, renal function tests—BUN, creatinine
- Request serum and gastric aspirate CN levels
- Obtain baseline ECG
- Monitor with co-oximetry for metHb and cyanmetHb after nitrites

Treatment

- **Decon:** Lavage + 1 g/kg AC, remove all contaminated clothes and wash skin.
- **Antidote:** Cyanide kit® = (1) *amyl nitrite* insufflation and/or (2) IV 3% *sodium nitrite*, 10 mL over 30 min, (3) IV 25% *sodium thiosulfate*, 50 mL.
- **Recently approved new tx:** The B_{12} precursor, *hydroxocobalamin*, used to displace CN from cytochrome oxidase to form cyanocobalamin (vitamin B_{12}) to be metabolized to nontoxic metabolites by the rhodanase–thiosulfate pathway. *Infuse 1 vial = 5 g over 15 min; may repeat × 1 for a max. dose == 10 g.*

Hydrogen Sulfide

1. H_2S exposures and settings for poisoning
2. Mechanisms of toxicity
3. Clinical manifestations
4. Management: diagnosis and treatment

H_2S: Sources and Mechanisms

H_2S Sources of Exposures

- **Natural gas:** Bacterial decomposition of proteins, including vegetation, human sewage, animal remains and wastes, decaying fish → marsh–swamp gas
- **Natural events:** Volcanoes, sulfur springs, natural gas fields, marine vent tube worms
- **Industrial:** Paper mills, oil/gas refineries, leather tanning and manufacture

H_2S Toxic Pathophysiology

1. *Rapid absorption* via lungs and easy membrane transit 2° high lipid solubility.
2. H_2S inhibits *cytochrome oxidase chain*, like CN, inhibiting oxidative phosphorylation and limiting ATP-energy production.
3. H_2S binds to endogenous metHb to form sulfmetHb with even greater affinity than it binds to mitochondrial cytochrome oxidase.
4. H_2S causes K-channel-mediated neuronal hyperpolarization and potentiates neuronal inhibition.

H_2S: Clinical Manifestations

Suspect H_2S Poisoning

- Anticipate a rapid "knock down" effect
- Rapid loss of consciousness
- *Blackening and/or darkening of pocket change and any jewelry items—watch, necklace, and so on*
- Breath and body odor *smell of rotten eggs*
- **Low odor threshold:** 0.02–0.13 ppm
- **Mucosal irritation:** 50–150 ppm
- **Rapid olfactory fatigue and paralysis:** 100–150 ppm
- **Knock down, death:** 1000 + *ppm*

Confirm Clinical Suspicions

- **HEENT:** Severe mucosal irritation and edema, *keratoconjunctivitis* → corneal epithelial ulcers ("*gas eye*"), rhinitis
- **CV:** Bradycardia, angina
- **Pulm:** Dyspnea, cyanosis, bronchitis, cough, hemoptysis, pulmonary edema
- **GI:** Nonspecific N&V

- **CNS:** HA, weakness, dysequilibrium, seizures, later memory loss and dementia in survivors, coma, *purple brain* at autopsy

H_2S: Management

Lab Diagnosis

- Assess for metabolic acidosis (ABGs) and elevated serum lactate levels
- Monitor metHb levels with co-oximetry
- *MRI*: To assess delayed and often permanent neuropsychiatric sequelae 2° subcortical white matter demyelination and globus pallidus degeneration

Treatment

- **Prehospital:** Evacuate with SCBA, provide high-flow oxygen, provide best AW, and support ventilation
- **Hospital:** Manage acidosis and provide inotropic support
- **Antidote:** (1) 3% *sodium nitrite*, 10 mL IV over 15 min, to induce *methHb → sulf-metHb*; (2) *HBO* if immediately available

Carbon Disulfide

- **Use:** Rayon and cellophane production, grain fumigant
- **Route:** Inhalation > dermal and ocular
- **Syn:** Acute encephalopathy, Parkinsonism-like manifestations—probably CO
- **Sx:** Acute dizziness, HA, delirium, seizures, ataxia, coma, arrhythmias. *Chronic-accelerated atherosclerosis* → CAD, psychosis, *polyneuropathy, optic nerve and retinal degeneration*, miscarriages, birth defects
- **Tx:** Removal, decontamination, oxygen
- **Pv:** Engineering controls > PPE

Ethylene Oxide

- **Chem:** Flammable, reactive gas; transported as volatile liquid
- **Uses:** Cleansers, degreasers, antifreeze, grain fumigant, medical sterilant
- **Syn:** Dermatitis, miscarriages, birth defects, peripheral neuropathy, leukemia
- **Sx:** Acute cough, bronchospasm, pneumonitis. Chronic neuropathy, mutagenesis, carcinogenesis
- **Tx:** Supportive
- **Pv:** Avoid exposures, ventilated gas sterilizers
- **DoT label:** EtO crosses your neighborhood daily

Common Ethylene Oxide Exposures

EtO Hospital Gas Autoclave

EtO degreasers

EtO dermatitis

VOCs

Outline: HCs and Alcohols

1. Halogenated hydrocarbons
   i. Petroleum distillates
   ii. Wood distillates
2. Toxic alcohols
   i. Ethanol
   ii. Isopropanol
   iii. Ethylene glycol
   iv. Methanol

HC Uses

- Adhesives and cements
- Fuels and propellants
- Paints and coatings
- Lacquers and varnishes
- Lubricants and oils
- Polishes and waxes
- Paint removers and strippers
- Paint thinners
- Solvents and degreasers
- Spot removers and dry cleaners
- Typewriter correction fluids (Liquid Paper®)

HC Classification

Mostly Petroleum Distillates

- Acetone and toluene
- Gasoline and benzene
- Butane and propane
- Carbon tetrachloride
- Methylene chloride (hepatically metabolized to CO)
- Trichloroethane
- Trichloroethylene
- Tetra(per)chloroethylene
- *n*-Hexane and *n*-heptane
- Methyl-isobutyl ketone
- Mineral spirits (Stoddard solvent)
- Styrene and xylene

Few Wood (Pine) Distillates

Pine oil
Turpentine

HC Epidemiology

- There are 60,000 HC exposures per year; 95% are unintentional; 60% involve children; 50% demonstrate minimal toxic effects; and 20% require treatment.
- There are 20 deaths per year from HC poisoning; 90% of these deaths occur in children under age 5; 30% of these deaths involve gasoline/motor oils; and 10% involve Freon® and propellants (usually in adolescent HC inhalation abusers).

HC Toxicology 1

1. **Pulmonary toxicity predominates:** Pulmonary (50%) > GI (5%) > *CNS (3%)* > CV > dermal > hematologic.
2. *Pulm toxicity* 2° aspiration → ↓surfactant → ARDS.
3. **HC pulmonary toxicity:** Determined by HC physical properties: ↓ *surface tension,* ↓ *viscosity,* ↑ *volatility.*
4. **Sx:** Gagging, coughing, choking → bronchospasm, rales, rhonchi, tachypnea, hypoxia → *hemorrhagic pulmonary edema*, methemoglobinemia (nitro-, nitrites, hydrazines), cyanosis → chronic URIs → bronchiectasis and pulmonary fibrosis.
5. **X-ray:** Pneumonitis, infiltrates, consolidating pneumonias, pleural effusions, barotrauma, upright gastric "*double-bubble*" sign = (1) air–HC + (2) HC–gastric fluid interfaces.

Hydrocarbons

Outline

1. Classification and uses of HCs
2. Epidemiology of HC poisoning
3. Toxicology of HC poisoning
4. Treatment of HC poisoning
5. Volatile HC substance abuse: "Sniffing" → "Huffing" → "Bagging"

HC Toxicology 2

1. **GI (5%):** Nausea, vomiting, hematemesis, GI mucosal ulcerations
2. **CNS (3%):** Seizures then coma 2° hypoxia and inhalation of volatile HC–"*anesthetics*" with progression from Stage II (excitement) to Stage IV anesthesia (coma)
3. **PNS:** Peripheral neuropathies
4. **CV:** *Myocardial sensitization* → dysrhythmias
5. **Dermal:** Defatting dry dermatitis, *oil boils, degreaser's flush* (especially trichloroethylene)
6. **Hematologic:** Methemoglobinemia, hemolysis, anemia, DIC

HC Treatment

1. **Careful GI decontamination:** No emesis! No activated charcoal! Possibly gastric lavage with small NG for large volumes, intentional ingestions, and highly toxic HCs: (*CHAMP*) = *C*amphor, *H*alogenated HCs, *A*romatic HCs, HCs associated with *M*etals, HCs associated with *P*esticides.
2. *No cathartics, especially no olive or mineral oil cathartics* (will increase absorption of lipophilic HCs), no prophylactic antibiotics or corticosteroids.
3. **Mechanical ventilation for ARDS:** Barotrauma risk = start with PEEP > HFJV > ECMO.
4. **CV:** Consider avoiding inotropic support during PEEP due to *myocardial sensitization* and arrhythmogenesis.

Volatile Substance Abuse

1. **Techniques:** Sniffing → huffing → bagging
2. **Agents:** Toluene (glues, paints) → fuels (butane, gasoline) → TCE and PCE (typewriter correction fluids, Liquid Paper®) → dry cleaning fluids (acetone, CCl_4, TCE, PCE)
3. **Acute tox:** *CNS*—excitation, *euphoria*, hallucinations, ataxia, seizures, HA, respiratory depression > *CV*—tachyarrhythmias → "*sudden sniffing death*" > *heme*-methemoglobinemia > *hepatotoxicity* (*CCL_4*) and *CO poisoning* (*methylene chloride*)
4. **Chronic tox:** *"Glue-sniffers" encephalopathy*/chronic "painter's syndrome": Leukoencephalopathies characterized by memory and cognitive losses, dementia, insomnia, anxiety and depression, personality disorder, ataxia and chorea, peripheral neuropathy (*n*-hexane, MIBK)

Carcinogenic vs. Neurotoxic

Carcinogenic HCs

1. Benzene—AML
2. Vinyl chloride—hepatic angiosarcoma
3. PAHs—colon cancer
4. Formaldehyde—nasal and laryngeal cancers
5. Chloroform and methylene chloride—liver cancers?
6. CCl_4, TCE, perc—animal cancers only

CNS Leukoencephalopathies

1. Toluene—paints and glues
2. TCE—degreaser's flush and trigeminal neuralgia (*tic doloreaux*)
3. Glycol ethers

Peripheral Neuropathies

1. *n*-Hexane—axonopathy
2. Methyl-*n*-butyl ketone—axonopathy (MEK and MIBK are nontoxic)

3. Acrylamide, styrene, xylene
4. 2,5-Hexanedione (*n*-hexane metabolite)
5. Carbon disulfide and ethylene oxide

TCE: Degreaser's Flush

Adult after ethanol ingestion = red, flushed face

Acrylamide

- **Use:** Grouting, tile-setting, water-proofing
- **Route:** Inhalation > skin absorption
- **Syn:** Myeloneuropathy— > polyneuropathy
- **Sx:** Weakness, numbness, paresthesias, ataxia, neurogenic bladder, hyperhidrosis
- **Tx:** Removal, supportive
- **Pv:** Engineering controls > PPE

Hexacarbons (n-hexane, MNBK)*

- **Use:** Solvents, adhesives, glues, molds, jet fuel
- **Route:** Inhalation ("glue sniffers" neuropathy)
- **Syn:** Demyelinating myeloneuropathy (mimics MS), progressing to chronic polyneuropathy
- **Sx:** Distal, symmetric paresthesia, numbness, anesthesia, weakness
- **Tx:** Removal, supportive
- **Pv:** Engineering controls > PPE

VOCs: Styrene versus Xylene

Styrene

- **Chem:** Synthesized from benzene
- **Uses:** Insulation, rubber, plastics, dental fillings, Styrofoam cups/plates, masonry paints
- **Route:** Inhalation > skin
- **Syn:** "Styrene sickness," dermatitis, peripheral neuropathy, irreversible ototoxicity
- **Sx**: SS = fatigue, HA, weakness, inebriation
- **Tx:** Supportive Pv: remove

Xylene

- **Chem:** Synthesized from benzene
- **Uses:** Paints, varnishes, thinners, degreasers, pesticides, aviation fuels
- **Route:** Inhalation > skin
- **Syn:** Peripheral neuropathy, dermatitis, irreversible ototoxicity

* Methyl-*n*-butyl-ketone (MNBK). *Note*: Unlike MNBK, methyl-ethyl-ketone and methyl-isobutyl ketone are nonneurotoxic and do not cause axonopathies.

- **Tx:** Supportive only
- **Pv:** Remove from the source of exposure

Wood Distillates

Pine Oil

- PineSol®
- Pine terpenes
- Pulm > CNS
- **Pulm:** Aspiration pneumonitis
- **CNS:** Excitation → depression
- **Tx:** Same as for the petroleum distillates

Turpentine

- Pine terpenes
- Pulm > renal > heme > CNS
- **Pulm:** Aspiration pneumonitis
- **Renal:** Pathognomonic *hemorrhagic cystitis* from acrolein metabolite → ATN
- **Heme:** Pathognomonic of *t*ur*p*entine = *TP thrombocytopenic purpura*
- **CNS:** Excitation → depression
- **Tx:** Same as for petroleum distillates

Toxic Alcohols

1. High anion gap vs. high osmol gap metabolic acidosis
2. Ethanol (ethyl alcohol, EtOH)
3. Isopropanol (isopropyl alcohol, rubbing alcohol)
4. Ethylene glycol (antifreeze)
5. Benzyl alcohol (antimicrobial preservative)
6. Methanol (methyl alcohol, wood alcohol)

Anion Gap Metabolic Acidosis

- **Def:** [Measured cations – measured anions] = $[Na^+] - [Cl^- + HCO_3^-]$ = 140 – [110 + 24] = 6
- **Normal range:** 3–11
- **High:** *MUDPPIILEESS* = *M*ethanol, *U*remia, *D*iabetic ketoacidosis, *P*araldehyde, *P*henformin, *I*NH, *I*ron, *L*actic acidosis, *E*thanol, *E*thylene glycol, *S*alicylates, and *S*olvents
- **Low:** *Bromides* (falsely elevated chloride levels)

Osmol Gap Metabolic Acidosis

- **Def:** [Measured osmolality – calculated osmolarity] = [mOsm/kg] – $[2Na^+ + Glu/18 + BUN/2.8]$
- **Normal range:** –14 to +10, nonspecific, wide range

- **High:** Ethanol, all toxic alcohols, lactic acidosis, renal failure, hyperlipidemias, hypertriglyceridemias, and hyperproteinemias (multiple myeloma)

Ethanol: Pharm and Tox

1. **Chem:** Colorless, odorless hydrocarbon; highly water-soluble and highly lipid-soluble; dependence and addiction possible
2. **Pharm:** Low MW, low *Vd = 0.6 L/kg*, rapidly diffusible; rapid gastric emptying and drinking without food increase absorption; hepatically oxidized by three pathways: #1 *ADH* (EtOH—(ADH) → Acetaldehyde—(Acet DH) → Acetyl CoA—(*thiamine cofactor*) → Kreb's TCA cycle → $CO_2 + H_2O$) > #2 *CYP450* (inducible metabolism) > #3 *hepatic peroxidase—catalase*
3. **Tox:** CNS > GI > metabolic
   CNS: Inebriation, disinhibition, incoordination, blurred vision, diplopia, confusion, CNS and respiratory depression
4. **GI:** Nausea, vomiting, cramping abdominal pain, gastric bleeding
5. **Met:** High-anion gap metabolic acidosis, hypoglycemia, hypokalemia, hypomagnesemia, hypophosphatemia, hyperamylasemia

Acute EtOH Intoxication

Blood Ethanol Levels% (mg/dL)	Clinical Manifestations
0.05% (50 mg/dL)	Disinhibition and incoordination
0.08% (80 mg/dL)a	↓ reaction time, auto driving impaired
0.20% (200 mg/dL)	N, V, confusion, staggering gait
0.30% (300 mg/dL)	Slurred speech, ↓ vision and ↓ sensation
0.40% (400 mg/dL)	↓ temp, ↓ glucose, amnesia, seizures
0.70% (700 mg/dL)	↓ DTRs, respiratory depression, loss of AW protective reflexes, aspiration pneumonia, coma, death

[a] Legally intoxicated in most states; otherwise 0.10% (100 mg/mL).

Ethanol OD: Dx and Mx

Diagnosis EtOH OD

1. **Blood ethanol levels:** Determine stage of intoxication
2. **Blood glucose:** R/o hypoglycemia
3. **CBC and lytes:** ↓ Na, ↓ K, ↓ Mg, ↓ Ca, ↓ P
4. **ABGs:** High-anion gap metabolic acidosis
5. **Serum amylase:** R/o pancreatitis
6. **Serum ammonia:** R/o hepatic encephalopathy 2° cirrhosis

Mx EtOH OD

1. Ipecac contraindicated
2. **OG lavage and AC:** Especially for coingestions

3. **Coma cocktail:** $D_{50}W$ 0.5–1.0 g/kg + *thiamine 100 mg IV*
4. Multivitamins and folate 1–5 mg IV
5. Slow rewarming
6. **Correct lytes:** ↓ K–Mg–P
7. **Enhanced elimination:** Hemodialysis very effective 2° ↓ MW and Vd, rarely indicated

Isopropanol: Pharm and Tox

1. **Chem:** 70% Isopropyl alcohol or rubbing alcohol; a clear, colorless volatile liquid with an acetone smell; used in toiletries, disinfectants, window cleaners, and solvents. *Exception*: *Adsorbed by AC*.
2. **Pharm:** Rapid all-route absorption, especially dermal and inhalation; low Vd = 0.6 L/kg; 80% rapidly *metabolized by ADH to acetone*, remaining 20% unmetabolized and excreted by kidneys > exhalation.
3. **Tox:** CNS > GI > Pulmonary > Metabolic.
4. **CNS:** 3× *more CNS depression than EtOH*, lethargy, weakness, HA, ataxia, apnea, respiratory depression, hypotension.
5. **Pulm and GI:** Acetone breath, hemorrhagic gastritis, and hemorrhagic tracheobronchitis.
6. **Metabolic:** *Exception*: only toxic alcohol *not causing metabolic acidosis or hypoglycemia*, euglycemia, ketonemia → ketonuria.

Isopropanol OD: Dx and Mx

Diagnosis

1. Determine serum acetone level.
2. Anticipate falsely elevated creatinine.
3. **ABGs:** pH will be normal, no acidosis.
4. **Glucose:** No hypoglycemia.
5. Anticipate **ketonemia** and **ketonuria** 2° acetone.
6. **Breath:** Acetone odor.

Management

1. Immediate skin decontamination
2. OG lavage, then AC: *Exception*: only toxic alcohol to be well adsorbed by AC
3. Enhanced elimination: *Hemodialysis* very effective in serious ODs, especially in children

Ethylene Glycol: Pharm and Tox

1. **Chem:** A toxic alcohol similar to methanol in toxicity and lethality with a characteristic delayed onset of toxicity; used in antifreeze (95%), refrigerating fluids, fire extinguishers, solar energy fluids.
2. **Pharm:** Rapidly absorbed po, peaks 1–4 h; rapidly metabolized by ADH to glycoaldehyde, then *glycolic, glyoxalic, and oxalic acids. Pyridoxine and thiamine* serve as cofactors to promote nontoxic alternative routes of metabolism.

3. **Toxicity:** (1) CNS > (2) Metabolic > (3) Renal > initial GI N and V.
4. **Toxic phases 1–3:** *Phase 1—CNS:* N, V, *intoxication*, inebriation, nystagmus, myoclonus, seizures, progressing to lethargy and coma in 4–8 h. *Phase 2—Metabolic:* Profound *high anion gap metabolic acidosis* causing CV collapse. *Phase 3—Renal:* Urinary excretion of toxic metabolites (calcium oxalate and hippuric acid); *calcium oxalate crystalluria* → nephrolithiasis → proteinuria and hematuria → ATN.

Ethylene Glycol OD: Dx and Mx

1. **Dx:** Calcium oxalate *crystalluria*, urine *fluorescein* staining under ultraviolet Wood's lamp, serum EG levels by gas chromatography
2. **Initial mx:** AC ineffective 2° rapid absorption and delayed sx onset of 4–8 h; ipecac contraindicated 2° vomiting; $NaHCO_3$ to correct acidosis and ↑ excretion weak acids; antidotes = *ethanol* (and/or 4-MP, 15 mg/kg load, then 15 mg/kg until EG levels, 20 mg/dL) as preferred ADH substrates, 0.8 g/kg IV or 8 mL/kg po, to maintain serum EtOH level of *100–150 mg/dL* (*EG:EtOH ratio = 1:4*)
3. **Enhanced elimination:** (1) Urinary *alkalinization* to promote urinary excretion of *weak acid metabolites*; (2) *thiamine*, 100 mg IV, and *pyridoxine*, 50 mg IV, q 6 h, to promote alternative nontoxic routes of metabolism; (3) *hemodialysis* for EG levels ≥ *25 mg/dL*
4. **Correct hypocalcemia:** Treat hypocalcemia 2° massive calcium losses from calcium oxalate crystalluria

VOCs

Ethylene Glycol Ingestion

Urinary calcium oxalate crystals (ethylene glycol ingestion → *ethanol and/or 4-MP* therapy indicated with *HD* for serum EG level > *25 mg/dL* to prevent ATN)

Additives Tox

Benzyl Alcohol

Pharmacokinetics and Uses

- **Pharm:** Colorless aromatic alcohol and metabolite of toluene hepatically oxidized rapidly to *benzoic acid*, then conjugated with glycine to form *hippuric acid*, excreted in urine—except in preemies who *cannot glycine conjugate benzoic acid 2° hepatic immaturity*
- **Uses:** Common bacteriostatic additive in parenteral meds and IV flush solutions (gasping baby syndrome in preemies)

Toxicities

- CNS—Central > Peripheral
- **Gasping baby syndrome:** ↑ benzoic acid levels → *metabolic acidosis*, hypotonia, gasping respirations, seizures, ↓ HR and ↓ BP → CV collapse; high CFRs

- **Demyelinization:** Transient MS-like paraplegia in LEs following intrathecal and epidural administration of LAs and other drugs (MTX) containing benzyl alcohol

Methanol: Pharm and Tox

1. **Chem:** Methyl alcohol or wood alcohol; used in windshield washing fluids, deicing solutions, carburetor cleaners, model airplane and canned heat (Sterno®) fuels, paint removers/thinners
2. **Pharm:** Rapid all-route absorption, peaks 1/2–1 h; 85% rapidly metabolized by hepatic ADH to *formaldehyde* and *formic acid* metabolites that are responsible for *retinal toxicity*
3. **Tox:** Eye/CNS > Metabolic > initial GI-N, V, and cramping
4. **Eye:** Dimmed and blurred vision, scotomata, dilated and sluggishly reactive pupils, *hyperemic optic disks*, retinal edema, blindness
5. **Metabolic:** *24 h delayed onset* of high anion gap metabolic acidosis, followed by oculotoxicity
6. **CNS:** Inebriation, HA, vertigo, meningismus, seizures, coma, later Parkinsonism

Methanol: Dx and Mx

1. **Dx:** Lactic acidosis, unique eye findings, increased serum levels by gas chromatography
2. **Initial mx:** AC ineffective 2° rapid absorption and delayed symptom onset; ipecac contraindicated 2° vomiting; *$NaHCO_3$* to correct acidosis; antidotes = *ethanol* (and/or 4-MP) as preferred ADH substrates, 0.8 g/kg IV or 8 mL/kg po, to maintain serum EtOH level *100–150 mg/dL* (Meth:EtOH ratio = 1:4)
3. **Enhanced elimination:** (1) Urinary *alkalinization* to promote renal excretion of undissociated formic acid; (2) *folic acid*, 150 mg IV q 4 h, to serve as a cofactor promoting the metabolism of formic acid to $CO_2 + H_2O$; (3) *hemodialysis* for methanol levels *≥ 25 mg/dL*

Pesticides

Organochlorines

- **Route:** Ingestion ϖ inhalation > absorption
- **Ex:** DDT, lindane
- **Sx:** Hyperexcitability, seizures
- **Tx:** Decontaminate, supportive, no antidotes
- **Pv:** Elim, bioaccumulates

Organophosphates

- Inhalation > absorption > ingestion
- **Ex:** malathion, TOCP (tri-*ortho*-cresyl phosphate: used in hydraulic fluids)

- Acute—SLUDE; chronic—GBS-like, Alzheimer's
- Decontaminate, atropine, 2-PAM (pralidoxime)
- PPE, RBC cholinesterase

Outline

I. Insecticides
- Organochlorines*
- Organophosphates*
- Carbamates*
- OP nerve gases*
- Pyrethrins*
- DEET*

II. Rodenticides
- High toxicity*
- Moderate toxicity
- Low toxicity

III. Herbicides
- Paraquat
- Diquat
- Chlorphenoxyacetic acids

Organochlorine Classes

I. **DDT:** DDT and its analog, methoxychlor; low-to-moderate toxicity; not biodegradable and bioaccumulating

II. **Lindane (for head lice):** Moderate toxicity and in frequent use; considered in the differential diagnosis of pediatric seizure disorders

III. **Cyclodienes:** Aldrin, dieldrin, endrin, chlordane, chlordecone (Kepone®), and heptachlor (Mirex®); all highly toxic, some carcinogenic, and still in use illicitly (United States) and licitly (developing world)

IV. **Toxaphene:** Moderate toxicity; infrequent use

Organochlorines

Representatives (Reps): DDT, lindane, cyclodienes.

Mechanism: Prolonged opening of Na channels.

Metabolism: Very lipid soluble, GI > inhalation > dermal, cytochrome P450 inducers.

Dx: hx, radiopacities on flat abdominal x-rays.

Antidote: Dextrose and thiamine for seizures.

Acute: Initial N and V, weakness, paresthesias, tremor, clonus, seizures, F 2° sz, resp paralysis.

Chronic: Chlordane—leukemia and TTP; chlordecone—pseudotumor cerebri and male infertility.

---

* Highly neurotoxic pesticides.

Tx: Skin decontamination; careful NG lavage, then AC; sz control—dextrose, thiamine, bzs, ϕbarb; *cholestyramine* to ↓ chlordecone enterohepatic circulation. No oil cathartics- will ↑ absorption of all OCs.

Organophosphates vs. Carbamates

Organophosphates	Carbamates
Reps: parathion, malathion, TOCP (Jamaican/U.S. *ginger-jake* paralysis)	Aldicarb, carbaryl, propoxur
Sx: muscarinic (SLUDGE), nicotinic (NMJ), CNS, miosis	Same, but less CNS penetration
Mech: prolonged, phosphorylated AChE inhibition (aging)	Short-term carbamoylated AChE inhibition
Pharm: all route absorption	Same, all routes
Anti: atropine + 2-PAM	Atropine alone, no oximes
Tx: decon, AC, bzs for sz. Confirm post-**PAM:** plasma (0) and RBC (normal) AChE levels.	Same

Organophosphates: TOCP

- **Uses:** Plasticizer; during prohibition: mixed with alcohols; neuropathies in >50,000 = *ginger jake paralysis.* Jamaica: illicit pharmaceutical solubilizer.
- **Route:** Inhalation > skin. *Syn:* painful motor peripheral neuropathy (resembles lead) after latency of 3–28 days; late UMN disease; CNs not affected.
- **Sx:** Painful cramping hands and feet, then weakness and unsteady gait, then muscle wasting-ataxia-DTRs and + Babinski.
- **Tx:** Supportive.
- **Pv:** remove from the source.

Complications of OP Poisoning

Intermediate Syndrome (IMS)

- Same, OPs
- 24–96 h postcholinergic crisis
- *Inadequate oxime tx*, 2° prolonged nicotinic and ↑ CNS Ach stimulation
- Bulbar, nuchal, and prox limb weakness-paralysis → RF, complete recovery
- Supportive

OP-Induced Delayed Neuropathy (OPIDN)

- **Reps:** OPs only
- **Onset:** 1–3 week postexposure
- **Mech:** *"Dying-back" peripheral neuropathy* 2° to neurotoxic esterase (NTE) inhibition and myelin degeneration
- **Sx:** Weakness, glove and stocking paresthesias, muscle cramps–atrophy, spasticity, ataxia, paralysis
- **Tx:** Supportive

OP Nerve Gases

Mechanism and Classification

- **Mech:** Long-term AChE inhibition with rapid aging
- *German* (G) agents (from 1936–1945):
  GA: Tabun
  GB: Sarin
  GD: Soman
  GF: CMPF
- **British** agent:
  VX

Prophylaxis and Treatment

- **Prophylaxis:** (1) Pyridostigmine, a carbamate anti-AChE oxime that temporarily inhibits and binds AChE protecting enzyme from permanent aging by nerve gas agent; (2) seizure prophylaxis with diazepam
- **Tx:** Neoprene, not latex, gloves for caregivers, immediate skin decontamination, atropine as antimuscarinic, pralidoxime, diazepam for sz, support-IMV

Least Toxic OTC

Pyrethrins

- **Pyrethrins:** Natural extracts from *Chrysanthemum* spp.
- **Pyrethroids:** Synthetics
  Type I: Permethrin
  Type II: Deltamethrin
- **Mech:** Inact and prolonged opening of Na channels
- **Toxicity:** II > I, N, V, dizziness, paresthesias, fasciculations, sz, coma
- **Tx:** Support, atropine, benzodiazepines

n,n-Diethyltoluamide (DEET)

- **Mech:** "Knock-down" agent 2° prolonged opening Na channels, concentration 5–100%, long-acting—4–8 h
- **Toxicity:** Rare 2° ↑ absorbed dose = ataxia, seizures, encephalopathy → RF
- **Predisposition:** Children, women, pregnant, skin diseases-↑absorption
- **Tx:** Supportive

Outline

1. Classification of rodenticides
   a. *High toxicity*—LD_{50} < 50 mg/kg
   b. *Moderate toxicity*—LD_{50} 50–500 mg/kg
   c. *Low toxicity*—LD_{50} 500–5000 mg/kg

2. Epidemiology
3. Toxicology
4. Management of unknown rodenticide exposure

Neurotoxic Rodenticides

Classification

High Toxicity

- Thallium
- SMFA
- Strychnine
- Zinc phosphide
- Yellow phosphorus
- Arsenic
- Barium
- Vacor (pyridyl nitrophenyl urea [PNU])

Moderate Toxicity

- ANTU (alpha napthylthiourea)
- Cholecalciferol (D_3)

Low Toxicity

- Red squill
- Norbormide
- Bromethalin
- Anticoagulants:
- Short-acting warfarins
- Long-acting superwarfarins (hydroxycoumarins)

Low Tox Rodenticides

Epidemiology

1. **Prevalence (1990–1995):** 17,000 cases
2. **Who:** 90% children < 6 yo
3. **CFR:** <6 deaths/year
4. **Risk factors:** Children, elderly, psychotics, exterminators, suicides, homicides, unintentional ingestions of rodenticides stored in food containers

High Toxicity

Strychnine

- **Phys:** Bitter white powder, heroin adulterant

- **Mech:** Blocks glycine motor inhibition in spinal cord
- **Onset:** 10–20 min
- **Sx:** Sensorium remains intact with twitching, hyperextension, opisthotonos → skeletal fxs, trismus → risus sardonicus
- **Anti:** None
- **Tx:** Immediate lavage + AC, bzs, barbs, muscle relaxants; support and quiet room to avoid triggering extensor spasms

Zinc Phosphide

- **Phys:** Dark, gray powder, smells like *rotten fish*
- **Mech:** Releases phosphine and zinc on contact with water and *gastric acid*
- **Onset:** Within hours
- **Sx:** *Rotten fish breath, black vomit,* tetany 2° hypocalcemia, seizures, pulmonary edema 2° inhalation, CV collapse, ATN
- **Anti:** None
- **Tx:** Immediate dilution with water, milk, or $NaHCO_3$; then lavage-AC-cathartic; consider *proton-pump inhibitor to ↓ gastric acid*

High Toxicity: Strychnine

- **Opisthotonos:** Tetanic hyperextension pathognomonic of strychnine poisoning and 2° glycine inhibition

High Toxicity

Barium Carbonate

- **Phys:** Shiny, lumpy water-soluble yellowish powder; unlike insoluble, harmless barium sulfate x-ray contrast media
- **Mech:** ↓↓*K* → NM block
- **Onset:** 1–8 h
- **Sx:** N, V, D, abdominal pain, *hypokalemic paralysis*, dysrhythmias—CV collapse
- **Anti:** None
- **Tx:** Lavage with *Na thiosulfate* to form harmless, insoluble barium sulfate, replace K

Vacor (Pyridyl-Nitro-Phenyl Urea, PNU)

- **Phys:** Smells like **peanuts**, looks like cornmeal, withdrawn in the year 1979
- **Mech:** Stops NAD production and targets and destroys *pancreatic β islet cells*, like *alloxan* and *streptozotocin*
- **Onset:** 4–48 h
- **Sx:** hyperglycemia, *diabetic ketoacidosis* with autonomic (↓ BP) and *peripheral neuropathy*, orthostatic hypotension, GI perforation
- **Anti:** *niacinamide* (nicotinamide), 500 mg IM or IV, then 200 mg q 4 h × 48 h
- **Tx:** Early emesis, then lavage + AC + cathartic; insulin and glucose

High Tox Rodenticides

Barium: Soluble vs. Insoluble?

Insoluble Barium

- **Rep:** Barium sulfate
- **Use:** Oral radiographic contrast agent
- **Tox:** *Insoluble* and harmless when ingested
- **Tx:** None indicated

Soluble Barium

- **Rep:** Acetate, *carbonate*, chloride, hydroxide, nitrate, sulfide
- **Use:** Rodenticides (*carbonate*)
- **Tox:** Profound ↓ K 2° ↑ membrane permeability to K and driving extracellular K into muscles
- **CP and renal**: ↓ K = arrhythmias, CHF; *hypokalemic respiratory paralysis*; acute renal failure
- **Tx:** OG lavage with *Na thiosulfate or* $MgSO_4$ to convert soluble Ba to harmless, insoluble $BaSO_4$

Low Toxicity

Bromethalin

- **Phys:** Green pellets
- **Mech:** Uncouples oxidative phosphorylation in mitochondria, ↓ ATP
- **Onset:** Immediate
- **Sx:** Muscle tremors, myoclonic jerks, severe flexor spasms, *seizures*
- **Anti:** None
- **Tx:** Supportive

Anticoagulants

- **Phys:** Short-acting warfarins and long-acting hydroxycoumarins or superwarfarins
- **Mech:** *Vitamin* K_1 antagonism, clotting factor interference
- **Onset:** 12–48 h to longer
- **Sx:** Bleeding and ↑ PT
- **Anti:** Vitamin K_1
- **Tx:** Vitamin K, FFP, WB

GI decontamination

SH: Bromates vs. Bromides?

Bromates

- **Use:** Hair neutralizers and straighteners, bread preservatives.

- **Tox:** *Like aminoglycosides, bromates target the hair cells of the cochlea and the renal tubules* impairing their unique abilities to regulate electrochemical gradients. Bromate ototoxicity is permanent, but renal failure is reversible.
- **Tx:** Lavage + AC.

Bromides

- **Use:** Old nerve—HA tonics and sedatives (*Bromo-Seltzer®*); gas fumigant for soil, fruits–vegetables; vehicle for some drugs—bromopheniramine and dextromethorphan.
- **Tox:** Severe GI mucosal irritant, *brown-stained tongue*, progressive CNS depression = *Bromism*: HA, apathy, irritability → confusion, ataxia, tremor, dysarthria, psychosis → coma. Later *Bromoderma* = like ioderma with ulcerating facial acne; *tx*: antibiotics + Retin-A®.
- **Tx:** Lavage + AC, hemodialysis.

Psychotropics

SH: Bromates vs. Bromides?

- *Bromoderma acne* resembles *ioderma acne* (photo) with weeping and ulcerating facial pustules and indicates long-term exposure to brominated or iodinated products.

Additives Tox: Bariums, Bromates, Bromides, Boron			
Rodenticides			
Bariums	**Bromates**	**Bromides**	**Boron**
Barium–potassium; insoluble barium carbonate is a rodenticide that drives K into cells, ↓↓↓ K. Tx: Na thiosulfate or $MgSO_4$ converts $BaCO_3$ → $BaCO_4$	*Bromate—Hair straight?*	*Bromide–chloride; Robitussin®*-distributes like Cl = spurious *hyperchloridemia and bromism-ioderma-like* acne, lethargy. Tx: support	*Boron-boil on; boric acid roach pills*, boiled lobster-erythroderma, green blue vomitus, later alopecia.
	Tx: Na thiosulfate to convert to less toxic bromides		Tx: no AC, need HD

Unknown Rodenticide Ingestions

Immediate Supportive Care

1. Assure ABCs.
2. Identify type and quantity of rodenticide ingested.
3. Identify toxidrome by careful PE.
4. **Order precise labs:** CBC, PT, glucose, K, Ca, HCO_3, LFTs, BUN, creatinine.

Toxidrome DDx

1. Careful PE for unusual findings, for example, alopecia.
2. Smell breath; smell and examine vomit and stool.
3. Look for salient lab abnormalities within an almost completely normal lab panel.
4. Assess clotting status—anticoagulants are the most commonly ingested rodenticides.

Insecticides

Toxidrome DDx

1. Painful paresthesias + alopecia = *thallium*
2. Irritability → sz = *SMFA*
3. Opisthotonos + awake → sz = *strychnine*
4. Rotten fish breath, black vomitus → CV collapse = *zinc phosphide*
5. Smoking vomit and stool = *yellow phosphorus*
6. Dysphagia → bloody vomit and diarrhea = *arsenic*
7. Diabetic ketoacidosis, peanut breath, and diabetic neuropathy = *Vacor*
8. Dyspnea → pulmonary edema = *ANTU*
9. Hypercalcemia and its associated findings = *cholecalciferol*
10. Bruising and bleeding = *warfarins*

Herbicides

Chlorphenoxyacetic Acids

- **Reps:** 2,4-D and 2,4,5-T = di- and trichlorophenoxyacetic acids; *Agent Orange* = 2,4-D + 2,4,5-T + dioxin (TCDD) as a contaminant: chloracne, ↑ LFTs, carcinogenic?
- **Mech:** Rapid GI absorption of fat-soluble acids that target muscle and CNS and *uncouple oxidative phosphorylation, like ASA*
- **Onset:** Acute GI (N, V, D) then muscle twitching → seizures → coma
- **Sx:** Muscular weakness, twitching, seizures, ↑ HR and ↓ BP, hyperthermia and metabolic acidosis
- **Tx:** No antidote, OG lavage + AC, *alkaline diuresis* with *$NaHCO_3$* to trap weak acids in blood and urine

Making the Final Diagnosis

- Key point in formulating diagnosis:
    - Most toxic CNS disorders are diffuse without focal pathology.
    - Most toxic CNS disorders are symmetrical.
    - Most toxic CNS disorders will have a temporal association with occupational exposures.
    - Many toxic CNS disorders exhibit unique physical findings (see study questions).

Hierarchy of Prevention

1. Elimination or substitution
2. Engineering controls (encasement, ventilation, exhaust, robotics, etc.)
3. Administrative controls (STELs, shifts)
4. Biologic monitoring (urine better than blood except for lead [blood] and organophosphates [RBC cholinesterase])

Conclusions

1. Lipid-soluble neurotoxins (solvents, VOCs, pesticides) seek lipid targets (*white matter* of cortex and *myelin* of cord and peripheral nerves).
2. The longest *axons* in the LEs (feet) are the most vulnerable to neurotoxins ("dying-back," "*stocking*" before "glove" axonopathies).
3. Toxic neuropathies are always *diffuse and symmetrical.*
4. Neurotoxic syndromes often *mimic common primary neurologic disorders*, such as Alzheimer's disease, Parkinson's disease, MS, ALS, GBS, and even cumulative trauma disorders, such as CTS (an LMN disease).
5. Neurotoxic syndromes are easily prevented; poorly treated. Chelation is controversial, some chelators are contraindicated, and antidotes are few. *Prevention is key.*

Section II

Environmental Toxicology

Chapter 17

Food Poisoning

Outline . . . 360
Clinical Manifestations 1 . . . 360
Clinical Manifestations 2 . . . 360
Potential Etiologic Agents 1 . . . 360
Potential Etiologic Agents 2 . . . 361
Top Etiologic Agents 1 . . . 361
Top Etiologic Agents 2 . . . 361
Bioterrorism—BW Agents . . . 362
Bacillus cereus (d-toxin) . . . 362
Bacillus cereus (enterotoxin) . . . 363
Bacterial: *Brucella* spp. . . . 364
Bacterial: *Campylobacter jejuni* . . . 364
Bacterial: *Clostridium botulinum* . . . 365
Clostridium perfringens . . . 366
Bacterial: *Escherichia coli* . . . 367
Listeria monocytogenes . . . 368
Bacterial: *Salmonella* spp. . . . 369
Outbreaks: Etiologies . . . 370
Bacterial: *Vibrio cholerae* . . . 371
Bacterial: Noncholera *Vibrios* . . . 372
Bacterial: *Y. enterocolitica* . . . 373
Viral: Hepatitis A Virus . . . 374
Viral: Hepatitis E Virus . . . 374

Viral: "Norwalk-Like," Now Noroviruses 375
Viral: Rotaviruses.. 376
Acute Gastrointestinal Illness (AGI) Outbreaks on Cruise Ships 376
Practice Tests 376
Practice Tests: Answers 378

Outline

- Introduction
- Clinical manifestations of acute gastrointestinal illness (AGI)
- Potential etiologic agents
- Top etiologic agents
- Biological warfare (BW) agents
- Differential diagnosis
- Bacterial AGIs
- Viral AGIs
- Practice test questions

Clinical Manifestations 1

- **Acute gastroenteritis:** Vomiting as the primary symptom; diarrhea may also be present.
- **Noninflammatory diarrhea:** Watery diarrhea without high fever or dysentery (bloody diarrhea); low-grade fevers possible.
- **Inflammatory diarrhea (dysentery):** Grossly bloody diarrhea with mucus and pus; often high fever. Fecal leukocytes are present.
- **Persistent diarrhea:** Diarrhea lasting for more than 14 days.

Clinical Manifestations 2

- **Neurologic manifestations:** Gastroenteritis and/or diarrhea with paresthesias, respiratory depression, weakness, or any other peripheral or central neurologic manifestation
- **Systemic illness:** A multisystem disease of the GI tract and other systems, particularly the joints and the circulatory, nervous, and renal systems

Potential Etiologic Agents 1 (See Figure 17.1)

- **Acute gastroenteritis:** Norwalk-like virus (vomitoxin), *Staphylococcus aureus* toxin[bw], *Bacillus cereus* toxin, and all heavy metals (Hg, As)
- **Noninflammatory diarrhea:** ETEC, *Vibrio cholerae*, astroviruses, caliciviruses (genus Norovirus), rotaviruses, and adenoviruses; coccidian protozoans: *Cryptosporidium parvum, Cyclospora cayetanensis, and Isospora belli*

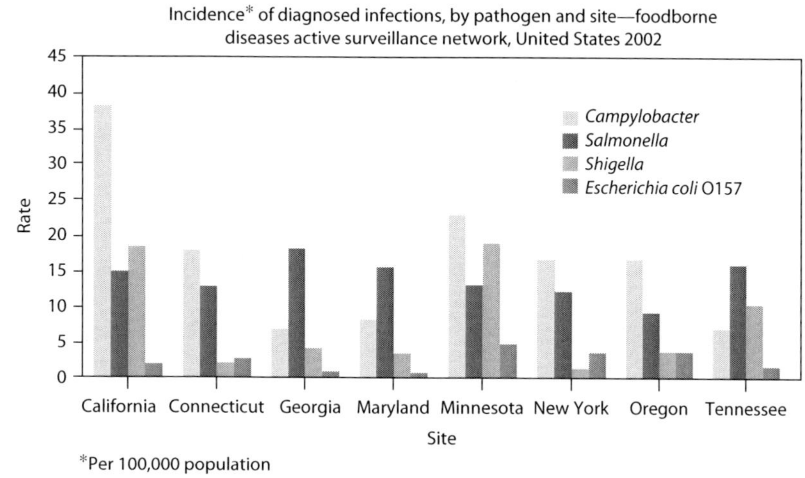

FIGURE 17.1 Active surveillance for food-borne infectious diseases by the pathogen and site, United States, 2002. The incidence of diagnosed food-borne infectious diseases by causative pathogen and state of occurrence in the United States in 2002. (From U.S. Government Document, CDC, FoodNet, U.S. Foodborne Diseases Active Surveillance Network, 2002.)

- **Inflammatory diarrhea (dysentery):** *Shigella* spp.[bw], *Campylobacter* spp., *Salmonella* spp., EIEC, EHEC, *Vibrio parahemolyticus*, *Yersinia enterocolitica*, and *Entamoeba histolytica*

Potential Etiologic Agents 2

- **Persistent diarrhea:** *C. cayetanensis*, *C. parvum*, *E. histolytica*, and *Giardia lamblia*
- **Neurologic manifestations:** Botulinum toxin[bw], OP pesticides[cw], thallium, scombrotoxin, ciguatoxin, tetrodotoxin, brevitoxin, saxitoxin, domoic acid, mushroom toxins, and post-*Campylobacter* Guillain–Barré syndrome
- **Systemic illness:** *Listeria monocytogenes*, *Brucella* spp.[bw], *Trichinella spiralis*, *Toxoplasma gondii*, *Vibrio vulnificus*, and HAV

Top Etiologic Agents 1

- **Acute gastroenteritis**—Norwalk-like virus > *S. aureus* > *B. cereus*
- **Noninflammatory diarrhea**—ETEC (traveler's diarrhea) > *V. cholerae*
- **Inflammatory diarrhea (dysentery)**—*Campylobacter* spp. > *Shigella* spp.
- **Persistent diarrhea**—*C. parvum* > *C. cayetanensis*

Top Etiologic Agents 2

- **Neurologic manifestations:** *Campylobacteriosis* > botulism[bw] > OP poisoning[cw]
- **Systemic illness:** *L. monocytogenes* > *Brucella* spp.[bw]

Table 17.1 Differential Diagnosis

Acute Onset		Unpasteurized	
<6 h = Toxin	Fecal WBCs = Dysentery	Milk/Cheese	Dysentery + High Fever
S. aureus	*Shigella*	*Salmonella (eggs)*	*Salmonella*
B. cereus	*Salmonella*	Campy (chicken)	*Shigella*
Enterotoxigenic *E. coli* (ETEC)	Campy	*Brucella* (goat)	Campy
Ciguatera	Entero-invasive *E. coli* (EIEC)	*Listeria* (processed meats)	EIEC
Scombroid			
Cholera	*Yersinia*	Tuberculosis (TB)	*Yersinia*

Bioterrorism—BW Agents

- *Bacillus anthracis* (bw-A list, October 2001)
- *Botulinum* toxin (bw-A)
- *Brucella* species (bw-B, Greece—WWI)
- *Shigella* species (bw-B, North Africa—WWII)
- *S. aureus* toxin (bw-B)
- *Salmonella typhimurium* (bw-B, Oregon salad bar, 1984)

Food poisoning
Differential diagnosis 1
Food poisoning
Differential diagnosis 2 (Table 17.1)

Bacillus cereus (D-Toxin)

Microbiology

- Large, spore-forming Gram-positive bacilli in long chains
- **Reservoir:** Like *B. anthracis*, stable spores long lived in the environment
- Looks like *B. anthracis* in culture, but hemolytic on blood agar
- *B. cereus*, Gram

Epidemiology

- **Transmission:** Fecal–oral > direct contact
- **Vehicle:** Contaminated meats (*subs*, *po-boys*), gravies, and vanilla sauces
- **Inoculum:** Low (toxin)
- **Incubation:** 10–16 h
- ***Warning*:** *French dip*, roast beef "*po-boys*" (aka "*subs*"), sweet sauces, and gravies

Clinical Manifestations

- **Acute gastroenteritis:** 24–48 h of nausea, usually no vomiting, abdominal cramps, and watery diarrhea without blood or pus
- **Wound infections:** More common with anthrax
- Subacute bacterial endocarditis (SBE)—Possible, but rare

Prevention

- **1°:** No vaccine, avoid high-risk foods
- **2°:** Food and stool culture, diarrheal toxin identification in stool
- **3°:** Self-limiting, no antibiotics, and only supportive care
- *B. anthracis*/*B. cereus*

Bacillus cereus **(Enterotoxin)**

Microbiology

- Large, spore-forming Gram+ bacilli
- **Reservoir:** Like anthrax, environmentally stable spores
- Indistinguishable from *B. cereus*—diarrhea toxin
- Hemolytic on blood agar, such as *B. cereus* (d-toxin)
- *B. cereus*, Gram+

Epidemiology

- **Transmission:** Fecal–oral > direct contact
- **Vehicle:** Improperly refrigerated cooked and fried meats and especially, Chinese fried rice
- **Inoculum:** Low (toxin)
- **Incubation:** 1–6 h
- **Warning:** Chinese food, especially spoiled or unrefrigerated fried rice dishes > meats and veggies

Clinical Manifestations

- **Acute gastroenteritis:** Sudden onset of severe nausea, projectile vomiting, watery diarrhea without blood or pus may be rarely present, self-limiting within 12–48 h, and severe dehydration possible

Prevention

- **1°:** No vaccine, avoid high-risk foods
- **2°:** Food and stool culture, enterotoxin identification in stool
- **3°:** Self-limiting, no antibiotics, and supportive care only—rehydration
- *B. anthracis*/*B. cereus*

Bacterial: *Brucella* spp.

Microbiology

- Small, Gram– coccobacilli
- **Reservoir:** Infected livestock–cattle (*B. abortus*), pigs (*B. suis*), sheep, and goats (*B. melitensis*—most common)
- Rose Bengal test for screening of *B. abortus* Abs in infected cattle
- Dye inhibition tests to differentiate among spp.
- *B. abortus*, Gram–

Epidemiology

- **Transmission:** Fecal–oral > direct contact > aerosol[bw] (suspect bioterrorism).
- Vehicle; unpasteurized milk and cheeses, undercooked meats.
- **Inoculum:** Low.
- **Incubation:** 7–21 days.
- **Warning:** Unpasteurized cheeses and milk, especially goat cheese (*chevre*). Travel to Mexico.

Clinical Manifestations

- **Brucellosis:** A systemic illness with undulating ⟨ fever, chills, sweats, weakness, myalgias, joint pain, lymphadenopathy, acute bloody diarrhea, and then irritable bowel syndrome. Chronic illness mimics chronic fatigue syndrome and *fibromyalgia*.
- **Complications:** SBE osteomyelitis, anemia, and depression.

Prevention

- **1°:** No vaccine, avoid unpasteurized milk and cheeses, especially from goats.
- **2°:** Blood C&S, serology, Rose-Bengal screening of cattle, and *Brucella* blue-ring agglutination tests on raw milk.
- **3°: Rifampin** and **doxycycline** q day × 6 weeks. For complications, add an aminoglycoside.
- *Brucella* blue-ring milk test.

Bacterial: *Campylobacter jejuni*

Microbiology

- Gram-, thin, spiral, "gull wing," and motile-darting bacilli, one flagella
- **Reservoir:** Wild and domestic birds (especially *chickens* and *turkeys*) and mammals
- **United States:** #1 cause of food-borne bacterial diarrheas, alternates with *Salmonella* spp.
- **World:** #2 causes of traveler's diarrhea (#1 ETEC)

Epidemiology

- **Transmission:** Fecal–oral
- **Vehicle:** #1 undercooked poultry (chicken > turkey) > #2 unpasteurized milk > contaminated water
- **Inoculum:** 10^4–10^6 orgs
- **Incubation:** 1–5 days
- **Warning:** Common, mimics Crohn's d. vs. CUC; serious complications = *Guillain–Barré* syndrome and arthritis

Clinical Manifestations

- **Prodrome:** fever (F), headache (HA), nausea (N), vomiting (V), malaise, and myalgias
- **Colitis:** Cramps, 1–10-day diarrhea + mucus, blood (50%), pus (75%), and chronic relapsing colitis (DDx—Crohn's disease and chronic ulcerative colitis [CUC])
- **Complications:** Guillain–Barré syndrome (10–20%), reactive arthritis (1–14%)

Prevention

- **1°:** No vaccine, avoid undercooked poultry and raw, unpasteurized milk
- **2°:** Fecal polymorphonuclear leukocytes (pmns), Gram stain, culture, and antibiotic sensitivity testing—C&S, stool radioimmunoassay—RIA
- **3°:** Macrolides are best (erythromycin, azithromycin) > quinolones > tetracycline—TCN; resistant to penicillin—pcn, vancomycin, and trimethoprim–sulfamethoxazole—TMP/SMX
- **Warning:** Grocery chickens

Raw, Grocery-Bought Chickens

- ***Campylobacter*:** Now the most common cause of U.S. food-borne illnesses found in 42% of grocery chickens; 90% of cultures demonstrated multiple antibiotic resistances.
- ***Salmonella*:** Found in 12% of grocery chickens; 34% antibiotic resistant.
- ***Campylobacter* and *Salmonella*:** Found in 5% of grocery-bought chickens.
- **Antibiotic resistance:** 2° ⟨ use of antibiotics in chickens (quinolones > TCN > pcn).

50% of grocery chickens contain *Campylobacter and Salmonella*
(Cook all chicken thoroughly; sanitize all knives and cutting surfaces.)

Bacterial: *Clostridium botulinum*

Microbiology

- Anaerobic, spore-forming Gram+ bacilli
- **Reservoir:** Ubiquitous environmentally stable spores
- Hemolytic on blood agar
- Botulism, mechanism

Epidemiology

- **Trans:** Environment > fecal–oral > aerosol[bw]
- **Vehicle:** Contaminated home-canned fruits, veggies, herbs (garlic), fish, and raw marine mammals (dolphin, whale-*muktuk*); herb-infused salad oils; unpasteurized honey
- **Lethal dose:** 1 pg/kg
- **Incubation:** Adults, 12–72 h; infants, 3–30 days
- **Warning:** Home canning, dented tuna cans, and *muktuk*

Clinical Manifestations

- **Adult botulism:** N&V, diarrhea, then blurred vision, diplopia, dysphagia, descending paralysis begins with CNs, respiratory failure, CFR 50 + %, and *paralysis + normal mental status*
- **Infant botulism:** <12 months of age, lethargic—weak, poor feeding, poor gag and suck, and hypotonia = floppy baby/floppy head
- **Warning:** Honey in milk bottle

Prevention

- **1°:** Avoid high-risk foods
- **2°:** Food and stool cultures, identification of Botulinum toxin in food and stool
- **3°:** Trivalent Botulinum antitoxin (adults), Botulinum-immune globulin and pentavalent antitoxin (infants), and life support; broad-spectrum antibiotics to ↓ toxin production in gut—controversial
- Management, mild hypoventilation

Clostridium perfringens

Microbiology

- Anaerobic, spore-forming Gram+ bacilli
- **Reservoir:** Domestic livestock and poultry, environmentally stable spores
- Unique double zone of hemolysis on blood agar
- *C. perfringens*, Gram+

Epidemiology

- **Transmission:** Fecal–oral
- **Vehicle:** Contaminated poultry, meats, gravies, dried, and precooked foods
- **Inoculum:** Low (toxin)
- **Incubation:** 8–16 h
- **Warning:** Dried meats, beef "jerky," chitterlings ("*chitlins*"), and unrefrigerated meat gravies

Clinical Manifestations

- **Acute gastroenteritis:** 24–48 h of watery diarrhea without blood or pus, N, no V, and F is rare
- **Wound infections:** Gas gangrene potential
- **Enteritis necroticans:** Pseudomembranous enterocolitis + pneumatosis intestinalis ("*pigbel*"—Papua New Guinea)
- *C. perfringens*: Pigbel enteritis
- **Pigbel:** Pneumotosis intestinalis
- **Pigbel:** *C. perfringens*, Gram+, and ileal bx

Prevention

- **1°:** No vaccine, avoid high-risk foods
- **2°:** Quantitative stool culture to rule out normal flora, Gram stain on stool and pus, and identification of enterotoxin in stool
- **3°:** Self-limiting, supportive care only
- *C. perfringens*, double hemolysis

Bacterial: *Escherichia coli*

Microbiology

- Aerobic, flagellated Gram– bacilli
- **Reservoir:** GI flora of animals > humans
- **Three Ag groups:** O, K, and H
- **Five clinical groups:** Enterotoxigenic *E. coli* (ETEC), Enteropathogenic *E. coli* (EPEC), Entero-invasive *E. coli* (EIEC), Enterohemorrhagic *E. coli* (EHEC) (zoonosis), and Entero-adhesive *E. coli* (EAEC)
- ETEC > EPEC > EAEC as causes of traveler's diarrhea

Epidemiology

- **Trans:** Fecal–oral, person to person
- **Vehicle:** Food (ground beef, apple/orange juice) > water
- **Inoculum:** 10–100 organisms
- **Incubation:** 3–14 days
- **Duration:** 5–7 days (unless HUS or TTP with EHEC)
- **Warning:** Water parks, wading pools, day care, petting zoos, undercooked hamburgers, and unpasteurized fruit juices

Clinical Manifestations

- **ETEC:** Two Shiga-like toxins, 1–7 days watery diarrhea without blood or pus
- **EPEC:** Same as ETEC, 3–6 d, diarrhea— blood/pus, high F
- **EA(I)EC:** Rare, 0124:B17, 3–7 d low F, cramps, diarrhea + blood, and pus

- **EHEC:** O157:H7, 3–10 d low F, cramps, diarrhea+ blood, pus, HUS 5–10% children, and TTP 5% adults

Prevention

- **1°:** No vaccine, "boil it—cook it—peel it—or forget it," bottled drinks, consider prophylactic antibiotics, and Pepto-Bismal®
- **2°:** Fecal pmns, Gram stain, C&S, and ELISAs for ETEC and EHEC
- **3°:** Quinolones, resistant to doxy and TMP/SMX, avoid antimotility agents

Listeria monocytogenes

Microbiology

- Small, aerobic Gram+ bacilli, nonspore forming
- **Reservoir:** Humans, livestock (cattle), and environment
- Pale colonies on blood agar
- *Listeria*, Gram– CSF

Epidemiology

- **Transmission:** Fecal–oral > direct contact
- **Vehicle:** Unpasteurized milk and soft cheeses, ready-to-eat deli/luncheon meats, and hot dogs—all processed meats
- **Inoculum:** Low
- **Incubation:** GI, 8–28 h; systemic, 2–6 weeks
- ***Warning*:** Hot dogs and "cold cuts" (processed meats)

Clinical Manifestations

- **Acute gastroenteritis:** Fever, myalgias, nausea, no vomiting, and diarrhea
- **Perinatal listeriosis:** SAB, preterm delivery, stillbirths, and puerperal fever—sepsis, neonatal sepsis
- **Geriatric listeriosis:** Meningitis, sepsis

Listeria: Processed meats

Processed meat production and packaging facility: Little barrier protection and sterile procedure.

Prevention

- **1°:** No vaccine, avoid high-risk foods
- **2°:** Blood and CSF C&S, serology—listerolysin-o endotoxin antibodies
- **3°:** GI, supportive; systemic-IV pcn or ampicillin > TMP/SMX
- *Listeria* culture, blood agar

Bacterial: *Salmonella* spp.

Microbiology

- Flagellated, Gram− bacilli
- **Reservoir:** Humans (typhoidal), birds/reptiles (commensal nontyphoidal strains)
- **Three Antigens—Ags:** Somatic (O), flagellar (H), and caps (Vi)
- Env stable—FW/sewage
- Nontyphoidal (*S. choleraesuis* spp.) vs. typhoidal—*S. typhi* and paratyphi
- **CFR:** *Typhi* > *paratyphi* > nontyphoidal spp.

Epidemiology

- **Trans:** Typhoidal—fecal–oral, nontyphoidal—direct
- **Vehicle:** Contam food/water, raw eggs, poultry, and reptiles/amphibians (turtles)
- **Inoc:** 10^5–10^7 organisms
- **Incub:** Nontyphoidal 12–48 h, typhoidal—7–21 days
- **Warning:** Typhoidal female carriers > approximately a 40-year-old female with cholelethiasis and a chronically infected gall bladder becomes a chronic shedder of *Salmonella* in stool = "*Typhoid Mary*"

Clinical Manifestations

- **Nontyphoidal:** 3–10 days of diarrhea + blood, pus, F, cramps, and chronic biliary carriage
- **Typhoidal:** 5-day prodrome, F, chills, sore throat, joint pain, and rose spots (30%); cramps, H/S (50%), neuropsychiatric symptoms—sx, lymphadenopathy, constipation, no diarrhea, bradycardia, and CFR≤ 30%
- **Comp:** Perforated Peyer's patch, osteomyelitis
- ***S. typhi*:** Rose spots, colon perforation

Epidemiology

- **Trans:** Typhoidal—fecal–oral, nontyphoidal—direct
- **Vehicle:** Contaminated food/water, raw eggs, poultry, and reptiles/amphibians (turtles)
- **Inoc:** 10^5–10^7 organisms
- **Incub:** Nontyphoidal 12–48 h, typhoidal—7–21 days
- **Warning:** Infants and elderly in homes with pet amphibians and reptiles; turtles > iguanas > snakes

Prevention

- **1° Prevention—Three typhoidal vaccines:** 1 po live, 2 intramuscular—IM, 70% efficacy; "boil-it, bottle-it, peel-it, or forget it"; no amphibian/reptile pets (especially with children and elderly in household)
- **2° Prevention**—Blood (50%)/urine/rose spot (70%)/BM (90%) C&S; Widal H/O Abs

- **3°Prevention**—Non-typh—quinolones, TMP/SMX; typhoidal—quinolones > ampicillin
- The problem with *Salmonella* 1

Increasing Worldwide Resistance

- Food poisoning
- The problem with *Salmonella* 2

Outbreaks: Etiologies

- **<1960s:** *S. typhi, paratyphi*—water and food
- **1960–1980:** *S. choleraesuis*, *S. enteritidis*, and *S. typhimurium*—poultry
- **1980–2000:** *S. anatum*, javiana, and montevideo—reptiles
- **>2000:** *S. newport, S. oranienburg*—Antibiotic therapy + H_2-blockers + PPIs + ↓ HCL + hospital food = ↑ *C. difficile* and hospital-acquired *Salmonella* spp.

Typhoidal GI Perforation: Terminal Ileum

- Food poisoning
- Bacterial: *Shigella sonnei* 1

Microbiology

- Aerobic Gram– bacilli
- **Reservoir:** Humans only
- Environmentally stable and GI acid—resistant
- Four serotypes; A—*Shigella dysenteriae*, B—*S. flexneri*, C—*S. boydii*, and D—*S. sonnei*
- **World:** *S. dysenteriae* most pathogenic
- **United States:** *S. sonnei* > *S. flexneri*

Epidemiology

- **Trans:** Fecal–oral, food > water
- **Vehicle:** Food, water, anal–oral sex, and flies = mechanical vectors
- **Inoc:** 10–100 organisms
- **Incub:** 6–72 h
- **Warning:** Salad bars[bw], day care, mental institutions, wading pools, and male homosexuals—MSM

Clinical Manifestations

- ***S. sonnei, flexneri, and boydii*:** F, cramps, watery—then—bloody, mucoid diarrhea + pus, and seizures (children)
- ***S. flexneri*: Reiter's Syn** in HLA-B27 genotypes
- ***S. dysenteriae*:** *Shiga* toxin, severe dysentery, tenesmus, rectal prolapse, HUS (children), and TTP (adults)
- **Shigella:** Fecal leukocytes always heavily present

Prevention

- **1°:** No vaccine, hand washing, hygienic food preparation, and avoid contaminated DW and RW
- **2°:** Fecal pmns, Gram stain, stool C&S, Shiga toxin ELISA, and flex—sig with biopsy
- **3°:** Quinolones, resistant to ampicillin, TMP/SMX, and TCN

Microbiology

- Aerobic Gram+ cocci in chains
- **Reservoir:** Ubiquitous, man, animals, and environment
- Yellow-gold colonies on blood agar
- Catalase and coagulase positive
- *S. aureus*, Gram, and pus

Epidemiology

- **Transmission:** Direct > food > fecal–oral > aerosol[bw] (suspect bioterrorism)
- **Vehicle:** Contaminated egg/potato/chicken/seafood salads with mayonnaise > cream pastries > meats
- **Inoculation:** Low (toxin)
- **Incubation:** 1–6 h
- **Warning:** Cream-filled pastries: eclairs, cream puffs, and *doberge* cakes > salads

Clinical Manifestations

- **Acute gastroenteritis:** Sudden onset of nausea, projectile vomiting, low-grade fever, diarrhea may be present, and lasts for 24–48 h
- **Skin infections and complications:** Boils, abscesses, impetigo, osteomyelitis, and sepsis

Prevention

- **1°:** No vaccine, avoid high-risk foods, and personal hygiene
- **2°:** Identification of Staph enterotoxins in food, vomitus, and stool
- **3°:** Self-limiting, supportive care only

Bacterial: *Vibrio cholerae*

Microbiology

- Aerobic, Gram–, flagellated, "comma" bacilli
- **Reservoir:** Humans
- Chlorine-resistant, acid-sensitive, thrives in brackish estuaries
- O1 and O139 strains—Cholera toxin blocks Cl pump; O1 = classical cholera, *El Tor* = current epidemic strain
- Non-O strains—Mild diarrhea, wound infections
- Bacterial: Cholera pandemics (Figure 17.2)

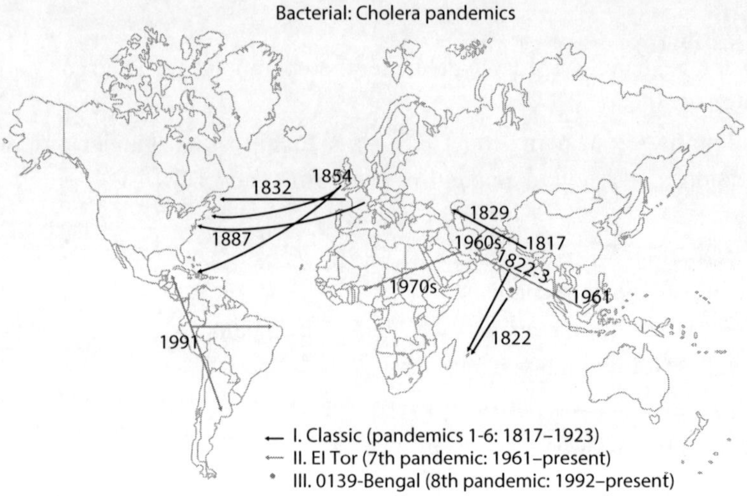

FIGURE 17.2 **The historical global cholera pandemics. A world map indicating the major pandemics and the pandemic-spreading routes of historical global cholera pandemics of the nineteenth and twentieth centuries.**

Epidemiology

- **Transmission:** Fecal–oral, especially during warm periods
- **Vehicle:** Contaminated water > shellfish > nonacidic fish
- **Inoculum:** 10^5–10^8 org
- **Incubation:** 1–5 days
- **Warning:** Raw/underboiled shellfish, low gastric pH (B12 deficiency, pernicious anemia), blood type O, and hemosiderosis

Clinical Manifestations

- **Classical and El Tor (90%):** Early N&V, *no fever*, painless watery diarrhea, no blood–pus, dehydration, and cholera excreters for days
- **Cholera gravis (10%):** Abdominal cramps, fulminant rice–water diarrhea, metabolic acidosis, hypovolemic shock, and excreters for weeks; CFR 40%

Bacterial: Noncholera *Vibrios*

Vibrio parahemolyticus

- Marine, noncholera *Vibrio*
- Salt tolerant, acid sensitive
- **Transmission:** Raw shellfish (especially raw oysters) > water
- **Clinical manifestations:** 1 week F, N&V, and watery diarrhea—no blood or pus
- **Warning:** Avoid raw/undercooked shellfish, especially in warm months, do not count on months with "Rs" and Tabasco

Vibrio vulnificus

Marine, noncholera *Vibrios*, salt and acid resistant

- **Trans:** Raw shellfish—oysters, direct inoculums—seawater
- **Clin:** Ulcerating cellulitis, *ecthyma gangrenosa*, and sepsis has high CFRs
- **Prevention:** No raw shellfish, treat all penetrating injuries in seawater with quinolones
- **Warning:** Alcoholism, liver disease, esp. hemochromatosis

Prevention

1°: Vaccination < 50% effective, adequate sewage tx, breast feeding (maternal IgA antibodies transferred), and avoid raw and undercooked shellfish

2°: Dark-field microscopy, stool C&S → blue–green colonies on TCBS agar, and rapid stool cholera screens

3°: Oral Rehydration Solutions (ORS), antibiotics may decrease diarrhea and *Vibrio* shedding—doxycycline 300 or ciprofloxacin 1 g po × 1

Cholera Gravis: "rice–water stool"

Bacterial: *Y. enterocolitica*

Microbiology

- Gram-negative "*safety pin*" bacilli, resembling other *Yersinia* spp.
- **Reservoir:** Humans and many domestic animals, esp. pigs
- Acid and cold stable (Canada, Northern Europe > United States), heat sensitive
- **Three spp.:** *Y. enterocolitica*, *Y. pseudotuberculosis* (rare in the United States), and *Y. pestis*—plague (four corners)
- Requires special media for C/S (CIN)

Epidemiology

- **Trans:** Fecal–oral, food > DW > RW > blood > nosocomial (households)
- **Vehicle:** Contaminated pork, tofu, milk, and well water
- **Inoculum:** High, 10^9 org
- **Incubation:** 1–3 days
- **Warning:** Raw, undercooked pork and pork prods (chitterlings = pork SI), and tofu; mimics acute appendicitis, especially during winter (Canada and Northern Europe)

Clinical Manifestations

- **Enterocolitis:** Canada, Northern Europe, and Russia > rare in the United States; F, cramps, and diarrhea
- **Acute mesenteric lymphadenitis:** Mimics acute appendicitis in adolescents
- **Comp:** Erythema nodosum (30%): 2:1 female:male ratio; polyarthritis (<30%): HLA-B27; purulent pharyngitis (<10%)

Prevention

- **1°:** No vaccine, cook pork well, esp. frozen; deep freeze pork < 4 °C
- **2°:** Stool and blood C&S c special media, HAI and ELISA rarely available
- **3°:** Susceptible to most antibiotics; quinolones > macrolides

Viral: Hepatitis A Virus

Microbiology

- Small, ssRNA picornavirus, such as polio
- **Reservoir:** Humans only
- **Environmentally stable:** Heat (to 60°C), and acid (to pH 1)—resistant
- Replicates in duodenal epithelial cells and spreads hematogenously to hepatocytes

Epidemiology

- **Trans:** Fecal–oral, direct person–person > food (fecal contamination, shellfish–oysters) > water
- **Vehicle:** Human sewage—contam water and food—berries, tomatoes, and greens (lettuce, spring mix)
- **Inoculum:** 10^4–10^8 virions
- **Incubation:** 2–6 weeks
- **Warning:** Day care/mental facilities, ♂ homosexuals, sewer workers, and primate handlers

Clinical Manifestations

- **Prodrome:** Anorexia, F, N&V, malaise, and lethargy
- **Hepatitis:** RUQ pain, hepatomegaly, dark urine, pale feces, jaundice for up to 6 weeks (adults 66%), and infants/toddlers often asymptomatic (80%); lifelong immunity, CFR 0.5%

Prevention

- **1°:** Two formalin-inactivated vaccines, two doses, 90% efficacy
- **2°:** IgM RIA or ELISA, IEM, and PCR for RNA amplification
- **3°:** Supportive therapy, liver transplant

Viral: Hepatitis E Virus

Microbiology

- Small, round ssRNA calicivirus
- **Reservoir:** Humans only
- **Environmentally stable:** Acid, salt, and cold resistant; probably chlorine sensitive
- Never successfully cultured *in vitro*

Epidemiology

- **Transmission:** Fecal–oral, water > food (especially shellfish)
- **Vehicle:** Human waste-contaminated drinking water
- **Inoculum:** High
- **Incubation:** 2–8 weeks
- **Warning:** Pregnant women traveling in developing countries (high CFR)

Clinical Manifestations

- **Hepatitis:** Occurs predominantly in developing areas in 15–40-year olds, especially pregnant women; high bilirubin levels, deeper jaundice than HAV, otherwise same as HAV; no chronic carriers. CFR 0.5–3%, in pregnancy 10–20% (mechanism unknown)

Prevention

- **1°:** No vaccine; boiled or bottled DW in developing countries
- **2°:** IFEM, viral RNA amplification by PCR; ELISA and Western blot for Abs not widely available
- **3°:** Supportive therapy only

Viral: "Norwalk-Like," Now Noroviruses

Microbiology

- Small, round caliciviruses (six-pointed stars) and astroviruses (snowflakes)
- **Reservoir:** Humans and shellfish
- Linear, ssRNA genome
- Intracellular replication within jejunal villi
- Heat (to 60°C), acid (to pH 3), and chlorine—resistant

Epidemiology

- **Trans:** Fecal–oral, shellfish > salad > person–person > water
- **Vehicle:** Human sewage—contam shellfish
- **Inoculum:** Low $<10^2$ virions
- **Incubation:** Short, 24–48 h
- **Warning:** Raw/inadequately cooked shellfish, seafood salads, food handlers, travel cruises, and naval vessels (*Bon Voyage*!)

Clinical Manifestations

- **Acute gastroenteritis:** 12–60 h of watery diarrhea (80%)—no mucus, blood, and pus: abdominal cramps (80%), N&V (50%), fever (50%), HA (50%), and myalgias (<50%)
- Always self-limited

Prevention

- **1°:** No vaccine, well-cooked shellfish; proper human waste disposal on harvesting (especially oyster-fishing) boats.
- **2°:** EM, IEM; EIA–RIA–PCR are not widely available.
- **3°:** Rehydration, supportive therapy.

Viral: Rotaviruses

Microbiology

- Small round wheels (rotors), two concentric icosahedral shells, and surface protein bumps
- **Reservoir:** Humans, domestic animals, mammals, and birds
- **Environmentally stable:** Acid, salt, cold, and Cl—resistant
- **Six serotypes:** A–F (A most common); infection confers limited immunity

Epidemiology

- **Transmission:** Fecal–oral
- **Vehicle:** Contam water > food > person to person
- **Inoculum:** 10^5–10^{10} virions
- **Incubation:** 1–3 days
- **Warning:** Nurseries, day care, and diaper-change stations (Diaper changers acquire 10^6 virions on their hands per change!)

Clinical Manifestations

- **Acute gastroenteritis:** N&V precede 4–5 days of watery diarrhea without mucus, blood, or pus; low K^+/Cl^- metabolic alkalosis mixed c hypoperfusion metabolic acidosis possible; most common in infants who are 6–24-months old. Mimics pyloric stenosis during prodrome.

Prevention

- **1°:** RotaShield® live vaccine, 80% efficacy, withdrawn 2° infant intussusception; breastfeeding confers IgA protection. New vaccine in trials (Merck).
- **2°:** Stool EM, ELISA, and latex particle agglutination; serum ELISA.
- **3°:** Oral rehydration, supportive treatment, and no antimotility agents (Tables 17.2 through 17.5).

Acute Gastrointestinal Illness (AGI) Outbreaks on Cruise Ships

See Tables 17.2 through 17.5.

Practice Tests

1. A 31-year-old toxicology fellow presented at midnight afebrile with projectile vomiting, watery diarrhea, and postural hypotension. He was unable to eat dinner, but ate

Table 17.2 Diarrhea Outbreaks (31): 1986–1993

Agents	Number of Outbreaks (%)	People Sick
Bacteria	12 (39)	2150
ETEC	5	1155
Shigella	4	450
Salmonella	2	380
S. aureus	1	165
Norwalk/NLV	9 (29)	3028
Unknown	10 (32)	3049
Total	**31 (100)**	**10,377**

Table 17.3 Diarrhea Outbreaks (5): 2002

Lines and Ships	People Sick	People Aboard
Carnival *Fascination*	203	3348
Carnival *Conquest* (#1)	230	4320
Disney *Magic*	160	3488
Holland Am. *Amsterdam*	181	1878
Radisson *7-Seas Mariner*	21	1035
Totals (Source: CDC–VSP)	**795 (Incid. rate = 5.99%)**	**14,069 (Attack rate = 5.65%)**

Table 17.4 Diarrhea Outbreaks (4): 2003

Lines and Ships	People Sick	People Aboard
Sun Princess	296	2906
Sun Cruises Sundream	107	1488
Royal Olympic Olympia Voyager	40	1112
Carnival Spirit	112	3045
Totals (Source: VSP to 3/1/2003)	**555 (Incid rate = 6.94%)**	**8551 (Attack rate = 6.49%)**

Table 17.5 Food Items (31 Outbreaks)[a]: 1986–1993

Food Items Implicated	No of Outbreaks/Agent id	Organisms
Scallops (undercooked)	3	ETEC
Eggs (unpasteurized)	2	*Salmonella*
Potato salad (onshore)	2	*Shigella* spp.
Fresh-sliced fruits	1	Norovirus—NLV
Calamari (marinated)	1	Unknown
Chicken or lobster salad	1	Norovirus—NLV
Smoked fish salad	1	Unknown
Flan (Sp., custard)	1	*S. aureus*
Ice cream	1	Norwalk virus

[a] 31 outbreaks aboard ships were investigated, but the implicated food items were only identified in 13 outbreaks, and the causative organisms in the implicated food items were only identified in 11 of the 13 outbreaks.

lunch at a local Chinese restaurant near the medical center. The most likely etiology of this acute illness was

A. *B. cereus* enterotoxin
B. *C. perfringens* enterotoxin
C. Enterotoxigenic *E. coli*
D. *S. aureus* enterotoxin B

2. Three weeks after a hurricane, a Gulf Coast commercial fisherman in prior good health presented with a 2-day history of fever, myalgias, vomiting, severe watery diarrhea, and postural hypotension. He was successfully treated in the ED with aggressive rehydration and discharged on ciprofloxacin. No stool specimens were taken. The most likely cause of this illness was
   A. *V. cholerae* non-O1, non-O139
   B. *V. cholerae* O1, biotype—El Tor
   C. *V. parahemolyticus*
   D. *V. vulnificus*
3. You are asked to reassess a 55-year-old TV anchorwoman with a 2-month history of malaise, fever, night sweats, nonproductive cough, and generalized arthralgias. Prior medical history was noncontributory, but the patient reported a 1-week stay at a naturopathic spa in northern Mexico 6 months ago. The most likely cause of this chronic illness was
   A. Bovine tuberculosis (*M. bovis*)
   B. Chronic brucellosis (*B. melitensis*)
   C. *Salmonella* spp.—Induced Reiter's syndrome
   D. *Yersinia* spp.—Induced polyarthritis
   E. Seafood Tox
   F. Practice tests
4. A 6-year-old boy had bloody diarrhea of 10 days' duration, abdominal cramps, vomiting, and fever to 104°F. No other family members reported illnesses. The boy shared his room with his pet blue iguana. The most likely cause of his illness was
   A. *C. jejuni*
   B. *Salmonella marina*
   C. *Salmonella paratyphi*
   D. *Shigella boydii*
   E. Seafood Tox

Practice Tests: Answers

1. A
2. B
3. B
4. B

Chapter 18

Seafood Poisoning

Outline 380
Epidemiology. 380
Definitions 381

Outline

1. **Epidemiology:** Disease burden, determinants, and distribution
2. **Definitions:** Plankton, marine toxins, marine habitats, and marine feeding habits
3. **Shellfish poisoning:** Paralytic, neurotoxic, diarrhetic, and amnesic shellfish poisoning
4. *What about Pfiesteria piscicida*?
5. **Crustacean poisoning:** Palytoxic and tetrodotoxic poisoning
6. **Finfish poisoning:** Ciguatera, scombroid, tetrodotoxic, miscellaneous saltwater and freshwater finfish poisoning, marine botulism
7. General management strategies and practice tests

Epidemiology

Burden of Disease

- **Most shellfish and 300+ finfish species:** Can cause poisonings with potentially lethal (CFR *1–62%*) toxins not inactivated by cooking, freezing, smoking, or salting
- **70% of the world's population:** Lives near sea coasts; seafood provides *40%* of world's protein
- **25,000–50,000 cases of ciguatera occur/year:** 2300 cases/year in the United States and Canada, and 5 cases/10,000 in Florida
- **Scombroid fish poisoning:** Causes *5%* of all United States-reported foodborne diseases and *37%* of all reported seafood-borne disease (Figure 18.1)

Determinants of Disease

- ↑ **Harmful algal blooms (HABs):** 2° *global warming*; *runoff* = agricultural (high nitrogen—*N*) + sewage (high sulfur—*S*) + household detergent (high

FIGURE 18.1 Yellowfin tuna, *Thunnus albacares*, a scombroid finfish, Gulf of Mexico. (From NOAA Photo Library.)

FIGURE 18.2 (See color insert.) The crown-of thorns starfish, *Acanthaster planci*, is damaging Australia's Great Barrier Reef. (From NOAA Photo Library.)

phosphorous—*P*) + soil sediment (*pesticides*); *natural disasters* = hurricanes–typhoons, earthquakes; and *trade and industrialization* = port docks/seawalls; ship ballast/sewage.

- ↑ **Coral reef destruction:** 2° deep sea nuclear and ABIM testing; drag-net fishing methods; and the crown-of-thorns starfish, *Acanthaster planci* (Figure 18.2).
- ↑ **Long-line commercial fishing:** Scombrotoxins are produced by the action of gut bacteria such as *Proteus* spp. on decomposing muscle tissues in deep sea pelagic or finfish (tuna, cobia, mahi mahi, and wahoo) hooked on long lines and dying in warm water over 20+ h. As a class, scombrotoxins resemble histamine-like compounds and include toxic proteins such saurine. Scombroid fish poisonings are characterized by allergic manifestations, such as facial flushing and redness, watery eyes, runny nose, scratchy throat, and wheezing. Gastrointestinal symptoms may also occur with nausea, vomiting, and diarrhea. Treatment is with oral antihistamines and rehydration.

Definitions

- **Plankton:** Phytoplankton vs. zooplankton
- **Marine toxins:** Exotoxins vs. endotoxins
- **Marine habitats:** Reef vs. deep sea
- **Feeding habits:** Filtering (*L*) vs. reef-grazing (*R*)

Definition 1: Plankton

Toxic Phytoplankton* (Figure 18.3)

- **Chlorophyta:** Green algae
- **Chrysophyta:** Yellow-brown algae and *diatoms**
- **Cyanophyta:** Freshwater blue-green algae*

* Toxin-producing organisms among the phytoplankton and zooplankton.

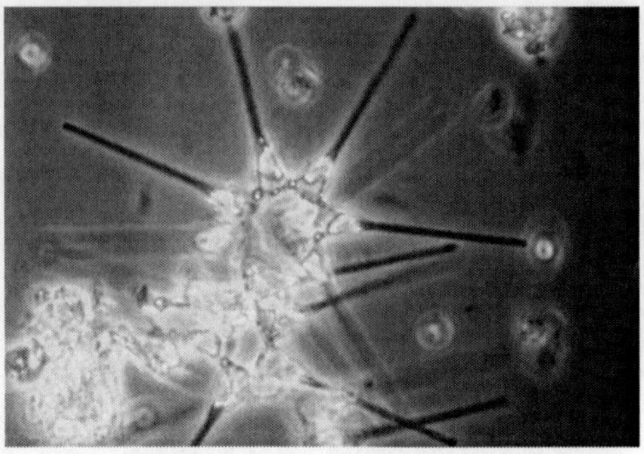

FIGURE 18.3 Phytoplankton species are the foundation of the oceanic food chain. (From NOAA Photo Library.)

- **Euglenophyta:** Freshwater euglenoids—nontoxic pond dwellers
- **Pyrrophyta:** Red tide dinoflagellates*—largest number of toxic plankton species (10%), includes *Pfiesteria piscicida*

Toxic Zooplankton (Figure 18.4)

- **Larval crustaceans:** Xanthid (Xanthidae) crabs—bioaccumulate palytoxin
- **Larval coelenterates:** Zoanthid corals—1° palytoxin producers in reef habitats
- **Larval marine round and flatworms:** Tetrodotoxin (TTX) producers
- **Larval copepods, krill, and shrimp:** Nontoxic; preferred by marine mammals, esp. whales

Harmful Algal Blooms (HABs) (Figures 18.5 and 18.6)

1. **Cyanophyta**
   Freshwater blue-green HAB
2. **Pyrrophyta**
   Saltwater red tide HAB

FIGURE 18.4 Zooplankton species include copepods such as these as well as krill and larval shrimp and are important components of the marine food chain. (From NOAA Photo Library.)

FIGURE 18.5 A cyanobacterial or blue-green harmful algal bloom in a freshwater ecosystem. (From USGS.)

FIGURE 18.6 A red tide or dinoflagellate harmful algal bloom in a saltwater ecosystem. (From NOAA Photo Library.)

Definition 2: Marine Toxins

Bioaccumulated Exotoxins: 1° Sources

- **Saxitoxin:** *Alexandrium* spp.
- **Gonyautoxins:** *Alexandrium* spp.
- **Brevetoxins:** *Gymnodinium breve*
- **Okadaic acid:** *Dinophysis* spp.
- **Domoic acid:** *Pseudonitzschia pungens*
- **Palytoxin:** Zoanthid coral-feeding parrotfish (rarely triggerfish) and all tidal xanthid crabs
- **Ciguatoxins:** *Gambierdiscus toxicus*
- **Shark carchatoxins:** Bull and tiger sharks; 1° source of exotoxin is unknown
- **Buffalo fish myotoxin:** 1° source unknown, could be endogenous?

Endogenous Endotoxins: 1° Sources

- **Scombrotoxins:** Produced by gut bacteria-catalyzed L-histidine decarboxylation to histamine, and saurine in decomposing deep sea finfish (tuna, mackerel, mahi mahi, wahoo, and cobia). See Figure 18.1.

FIGURE 18.7 A tiny spiny pufferfish or porcupine fish, *Diodon holocanthus*, contains tetrodotoxin. (From NOAA Photo Library.)

- **Tetrodotoxin:** Produced by endosymbiotic bacteria in all pufferfish, porcupine fish, marine sunfish, and many other marine animals (stored in fish skin, gonads, liver, roe) and invertebrates (blue-ringed octopus—saliva), and amphibians (newts and toads—skin secretions) (Figure 18.7).

Potency of Biological Toxins

Biotoxins: In Potency Order

- #1 = Botulinum toxin
- #2 = Palytoxin (parrotfish)
- #3 = Frog batrachotoxin
- #4 = Taipan venom
- #5 = Tetrodotoxin (puffers)
- #5 = Saxitoxin (shellfish)
- #6 = Tiger snake venom
- #7 = Cobra venom

LD_{50} (mcg/kg IV in mice)

- 0.0026
- 0.15 (top)
- 2.0
- 2.0
- 9.0 (bottom)
- 9.0
- 25.0
- 75.0

Definition 3: Feeding Habitats and Habits

Reef: Filter-Feeders

1. **Bivalved mollusks:** Clams (*Saxidomus* spp.), cockles, blue mussels (*Mytilus* spp.), oysters, and scallops bioaccumulate and concentrate both dinoflagellate and diatom exotoxins.
2. **Coelenterates:** Some anemones and all zoanthid corals produce palytoxin (parrotfish feed on these and bioaccumulate palytoxin).

Deep Sea/Reef: Baitfish-Feeders (Figures 18.8 through 18.10)

- **Predatory deep sea finfish:** Mackerel and tuna (*Scombridae*), and nonscombrid bonito, cobia, wahoo, and mahi mahi can produce endogenous scombrotoxins on slow, high water temperature decomposition of muscle protein (histidine).
- **Predatory reef fish:** All can bioaccumulate ciguatoxins and some bioaccumulate palytoxin.

FIGURE 18.8 The red grouper, *Epinephelus morio*, can bioaccumulate ciguatoxins. (From NOAA Photo Library.)

FIGURE 18.9 Red snapper (*Lutjanus campechanus*) arranged for fresh purchase in a seafood market may also bioaccumulate ciguatoxins. (From NOAA Photo Library.)

FIGURE 18.10 (See color insert.) The sargassum triggerfish, *Xanthichthys ringens*, can bioaccumulate both ciguatoxins and palytoxin. (From NOAA Photo Library.)

- **Carnivorous:** *Barracuda* > grouper, jacks, and all snappers (especially red snapper).
- **Herbivorous:** *Triggerfish*> surgeonfish and parrotfish (palytoxic).

Stationary Filter-Feeders

- **Blue mussels:** *Mytilus edulis*
- **Zoanthid coral:** *Palythoa* spp.

Predatory Baitfish Feeders

- **Predatory deep sea finfish:** *Cobia*
- **Predatory reef finfish:** *Nassau grouper*

Paralytic Shellfish Poisoning

- **Agents:** *Alexandrium* spp., *Gymnodinium catenatum*, *Pyrodinium bahamense*
- **Toxins:** *Saxitoxin*, neosaxitoxin, gonyautoxins #1–#8, epigonyautoxin
- **LD_{50} (IV in mice):** 9 mcg/kg
- **Mechanism:** Reversible binding to the outer pore of the Na channel, blocking Na influx, preventing depolarization and nerve action potential (NAP) propagation
- **Vectors:** Mussels and clams > oysters, scallops, and Southern pufferfish (most puffers are tetradotoxic; Gulf Stream puffers may also be saxitoxic) (Figure 18.11)
- **Incubation:** 30 min to 2 h
- **Sx:** Perioral burning and tingling, then paresthesias that spread to throat; generalized weakness and numbness; N and V; descending paralysis with dysphagia; respiratory failure; CV instability
- **Dx:** Mouse bioassay, thin layer chromatography (TLC), high-press liquid chromatography (HPLC), radioimmunoassay (RIA), enzyme-linked immunosorbent assay (ELISA)
- **Tx:** Protect AW, gastric lavage then activated charcoal (AC), intravenous (IV) fluids, mechanical ventilation, vasopressors

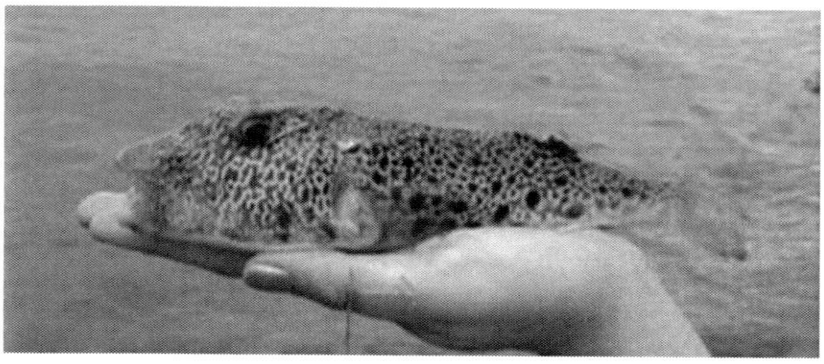

FIGURE 18.11 The Florida pufferfish can bioaccumulate saxitoxins and cause neurologic illness if consumed, even if cooked. (Courtesy of the CDC.)

- **Prognosis:** Sx peak in 12–24 h and resolve in 3–4 days, CFR 8.5–14%; rare complications and/or sequelae
- **Prevention (Prev):** Close beds when toxin levels > 80 mcg/kg, *avoid eating all pufferfish*, and adhere to shellfish advisories

Neurotoxic Shellfish Poisoning

- **Agent:** *Gymnodinium* (Karenia) *breve*, formerly *Phytodiscus brevis*
- **Toxins:** *Brevetoxins* (polycyclic ethers)
- **LD_{50}:** Unknown; no human fatalities
- **Mechanism:** *Forced opening of Na channels* with ↑ Na influx and prolonged depolarization (opposite of saxitoxin and TTX)
- **Vectors:** Clams > oysters
- **Incubation:** 15 min to 3 h
- **Sx:** Mild ciguatera-like sx with perioral paresthesias and temp reversal; rarely N and D; unique conjunctivitis, rhinitis, and/or asthmatic bronchitis 2° aerosolized brevetoxins
- **Dx:** By history (hx), and by high performance liquid chromatography (HPLC) is more sensitive than thin layer chromatography (TLC)
- **Tx:** Supportive only
- **Px:** Full recovery in 48 h
- **Prev:** Monitor shellfish bed dinoflagellate counts, adhere to shellfish consumption advisories

Diarrhetic Shellfish Poisoning

- **Agents:** *Dinophysis acuminata* (Atlantic) and *Dinophysis fortii* (Pacific)
- **Toxins:** *Okadaic acid* > dinophysotoxins, pectenotoxins, and yessotoxin
- **LD_{50}:** Unknown; no human fatalities
- **Mechanism:** *Inhibits protein phosphatases* disrupting cell metabolism; deregulates mitosis promoting neoplasia, specifically benign gastric tumors

- **Vectors:** Blue mussels—*Mytilus edulis* (Atlantic) and *Mytilus californianus* (Pacific) > clams (*Saxidomus* spp.) > cockles, oysters, and scallops
- **Incubation:** 30 min to 15 h (mean 5–6 h)
- **Sx:** Exclusively GI with N, V, cramping abdominal pain, severe diarrhea (>20 stools/day), no CNS sx
- **Dx:** Mouse bioassay, HPLC
- **Tx:** Supportive, IV fluid and electrolyte replacement
- **Px:** Self-limited, sx resolved within 3 days; no fatalities
- **Prev:** Monitor shellfish bed dinoflagellate counts; adhere to local shellfish consumption advisories

What about Pfiesteria?

- **Agents:** *Pfiesteria piscicida* and 10–12 related dinoflagellates, or *Pfiesteria*-complex organisms (PCOs).
- **Toxins:** (1) Water-soluble, ichthyotoxic neurotoxin; (2) lipid-soluble necrotoxin causing "punched out" necrotic fish lesions.
- **LD_{50}:** No human fatalities, but neurotoxin is always lethal in fish.
- **Mechanism:** Like brevetoxins, *aerosolized neurotoxins* force open Na channels, prolonging depolarization, especially in brain.
- **Vectors:** No seafood vectors; does not enter human seafood chain.
- **Incub:** Two weeks after aerosol exposures.
- **Sx:** Confusion and/or memory loss and ≥3 of the following sx: HA, skin rash, conjunctivitis, URT irritation and sensitivity, muscle cramps, and any type of GI sx (abdominal cramps, N, V, *usually no diarrhea*).
- **Dx:** By hx of aerosol exposure only.
- **Tx:** Supportive only.
- **Px:** Sx resolve in 1–2 weeks.
- **Prev:** Avoid swimming, skiing, fishing, and all other exposures in all waters with extensive fish kills; citizens should immediately report large fish kills to state environmental and public health agencies and to the CDC.

Amnesic Shellfish Poisoning

- **Agents:** The *diatom*, *Pseudonitzschia* (*Nitzschia*) *pungens*, and *some red algae* (*Chondria* spp.)
- **Toxin:** *Domoic acid* (from the Japanese "*domoi*" for seaweed); used in Japan as a very effective antihelminthic
- **LD_{50}:** Four deaths reported in elderly > 70
- **Mechanism:** *CNS glutamate receptor stimulation* causing Na channel upregulation and unopposed, prolonged depolarization with ↑ Na and Ca influx and neuronal cell lysis
- **Vectors:** Blue mussels (*Mytilus* spp.) > razor clams (*Seliqua patula*)
- **Incubation:** <24 h

- **Sx:** Initial N, V, D, and cramping abdominal pain; then ataxia, confusion, dizziness, HA, seizures, potentially chronic antegrade and short-term memory loss, especially in the elderly
- **Dx:** Mouse bioassay, HPLC
- **Tx:** Supportive only
- **Px:** Full recovery within 48 h; persistent short-term memory loss possible (*mimics Alzheimer's disease*), especially in the elderly
- **Prev:** Closure of shellfish beds when domoic acid levels >20 mcg/g shellfish; always adhere to local shellfish consumption advisory advisories (particularly in Canada)

Crustacean Poisoning

- **Agents and toxins:** Bioaccumulated red algal gonyautoxins and zoanthid coral palytoxin; endogenous tetrodotoxin.
- **LD_{50}:** Gonyautoxins and tetrodotoxin (TTX)—9 mcg/kg; paly-0.15 mcg/kg.
- **Mech:** Gony and TTX reversibly bind to outer pore of Na channels ↓ Na influx and depolarization; paly inhibits Na–K ATPase, Na and K can enter but not leave axon, Ca cannot enter, causing *hypocalcemic tetanic contractions.*
- **Vectors:** Most Indo-Pacific xanthid crabs, terrestrial coconut crab, and Asian horseshoe crabs; herbivorous reef triggerfish and parrotfish (palytoxin).
- **Incubation:** 10–15 min to 3–4 h.
- **Sx:** Palytoxin—initial nausea (N), vomiting (V), diarrhea (D), facial-to-limb paresthesias; tonoclonic seizures (sz) with rhabdomyolysis, myoglobinuria, acute tubular necrosis (ATN); cardiovascular (CV) collapse. TTX–respiratory paralysis.
- **Dx:** Mouse bioassay, TLC, HPLC, ↑↑ serum CPK 2° *rhabdomyolysis.*
- **Tx:** Protect AW; gastric emptying, OG lavage with $NaHCO_3$, then activated charcoal (AC), 1 g/kg; mechanical ventilation; consider multidose AC.
- **Px:** CFR-TTX: 62%, CFR-palytoxin: >60%; most recover in ICU by 48 h to 5 days.
- **Prev:** Avoid unusual crab species and local crab *miso* soups made from *tidal xanthid crabs*; always adhere to local seafood consumption advisories.

Ciguatera Fish Poisoning

- **Agents:** Dinoflagellates—*Gambierdiscus toxicus* (worldwide), *Ostreopsis lenticularis* (Caribbean only).
- **Toxins:** Three neurotoxins = *ciguatoxin*, gambierol, and scaritoxin; 1 myotoxin = maitotoxin.
- **LD_{50}:** Cig—0.45 mcg/kg; maito—0.05 mcg/kg.
- **Mechanism:** *Cig-forced opening of Na channels with ↑ Na influx*, prolonged depolarization, and myospastic contractures. Maitotoxin-forced opening of calcium (Ca) channels with ↑ Ca influx and prolonged myospasticity.
- **Vectors:** >100 reef fish species; *predatory reef fish*—barracuda, grouper, snapper, all jacks, wrasse, Moray eel; *herbivorous reef fish*—filefish, parrotfish, surgeonfish, triggerfish.

- **Incubation:** Within 24 h.
- **Sx:** Cramps, N, V, D (75%); metallic taste, perioral and distal paresthesias, glove and stocking numbness, palmar pruritus, hot–cold reversal, tremor, ataxia, vertigo, ↓ DTRs then sz, myopathy, arthralgias, weakness, stupor—coma.
- **Dx:** Mouse bioassay, RIA, stick-enzyme IA (Cigua-check®) on suspected seafood, GC/MS.
- **Tx:** Supportive; anticonvulsants (benzodiazepines-BZs preferred); IV mannitol 1 g over 45 m × 2 within 24–48 h and gabapentin 1200–2400 mg/day po for chronic sx (untested); avoid fish, alcohol, nuts × 3–6 mo 2° ↑ pruritus.
- **Px:** Sx resolve 10–58 h; persistent distal numbness, pruritus and temperature reversal possible.
- **Prev:** Avoid ciguatoxic species, esp. *barracuda* and *fish organs* (esp. liver, ovaries, and roe); adhere to all advisories; promote healthy coral reefs- ↓ drag-line fishing and nuclear/ABIM tests, ↑ crown-of-thorns starfish control (*Acanthaster planci*).

Scombroid Fish Poisoning

- **Agents:** Toxic decomposition metabolites called *scombrotoxins*; not bioaccumulated dinoflagellate or diatom exotoxins
- **Toxins:** *Scombrotoxins* = histamine and its 1° *n*-methylhistamine metabolite, and saurine
- **LD_{50}:** No known fatalities
- **Mechanism:** *Scombrotoxins form during gut bacteria-catalyzed, normothermic decarboxylation* (*Proteus*, *Klebsiella*, *Lactobacillus*, *E. coli*, *Enterobacter* spp.) of muscle L-histidine in decomposing finfish
- **Vectors:** *Nonscombroid fish* (amberjack, bonito, bluefish, mahi mahi, anchovies, sardines, herrings) >*scombroid fish* (albacore, cobia, tuna, mackerel, wahoo)
- **Incubation:** Minutes to 3–4 h
- **Scombrotoxins:** "Spoiled" canned anchovies, herrings, and sardines
- **Sx:** Sudden warm, facial flushing and "sunburn"—rash, metallic-peppery taste, perioral burning and blistering sensations; then urticaria, pruritus, bronchospasm, palpitations-↑ HR, ↓ BP; fewer GI sx of abdominal cramps, N, V, and D
- **Dx:** Histidine-to-histamine spot indicator tests, TLC, GC/MS, ↑ serum and urine histamine levels
- **Tx:** Severe poisoning—gastric emptying, then AC gut decontamination; otherwise H_1 and H_2 blockers, β-agonists, and consider steroids for allergic bronchospasm and urticaria/pruritus
- **Px:** Sx resolve in 12–24 h even without tx
- **Prev:** Patients on INH (GI hitaminase inhibitor) @ ↑ risk; avoid nonrefrigerated and spoiling (pale gills) deep sea fish; avoid seafood with [histamine] >50 mg/100 mg fish (FDA); regulate long-line fishing; mandatory cold-chain (0°C) for all seafood from harvest until cooking—consumption

Tetrodotoxic Fish Poisoning

- **Agent:** *Tetrodotoxin*, endogenous toxin
- **Toxin: Endogenous toxin production by endosymbiotic gut bacteria** (*Bacillus, Micrococcus, Acinetobacter, Altermonas, Vibrio*, and other enterobacterial species)
- **LD_{50}:** 9 mcg/kg
- **Mechanism:** Reversible binding to the outer pore of the Na channel, ↓ Na influx, preventing depolarization and NAPs
- **Vectors:** All pufferfish (balloonfish, blowfish, *fugu* fish, globefish, swellfish), porcupine fish, marine sunfish; xanthid crabs, marine worms; blue-ringed octopus bites; skin secretions of some newts
- **Incubation:** 10–20 min
- **Sx:** Initial paresthesias, perioral burning, then salivation, HA, N and V (D rare), sweating, glove and stocking paresthesias then numbness, tremor, ataxia, dysarthria, dysphagia, respiratory depression then paralysis, CV instability, stupor and coma
- **Dx:** Mouse bioassay, TLC, HPLC, GC/MS
- **Tx:** Supportive = protect AW, gastric lavage then AC-MDAC, IV fluids, vasopressors, and mechanical ventilation
- **Px:** CFR = 62%; survivors will recover within 1 week of ICU care (not universally available, esp. in developing world)
- **Prev:** Avoid eating *all pufferfish*; travelers may consume *fugu only in Japan*, prepared by commercially licensed chefs

Misc. Saltwater Fish Poisoning

- **Shark poisoning:** Consumption of cooked shark meat from large bull and tiger sharks has caused an initial ciguatera-like illness with perioral paresthesias, ataxia, and pruritus, then coma and death (↑ CFR = 30%). Structure of two toxins (*carchatoxins A and B*) unknown.
- **Mackerel poisoning:** Mild, self-limited diarrhea after consumption of cooked mackerel (Figure 18.12) species due to a *castor oil-like toxin*. Mackerel liver consumption has also caused a *hypervitaminosis* A-like syndrome with HA, N, V, D, and a macular rash that later desquamates. A similar hypervitaminosis A-like syndrome occurs after *polar bear liver* consumption.
- **Mullet poisoning:** Mild, self-limited intoxication with delusions, hallucinations, ataxia, and nightmares within minutes to hours after consumption of reef-schooling mullet. Toxin unidentified.

Freshwater Fish Poisoning

- **Fish egg (fish roe) poisoning:** HA, N, V, D, cold sweats, metallic taste, tinnitus, and syncope after the consumption of raw or cooked roe during the spawning season of several freshwater fish species, including *barbel, bream, carp, catfish, pike, salmon,*

FIGURE 18.12 The bull shark, *Carcharhinus leucas*, can bioaccumulate carchartoxins, which can cause a neurologic illness like ciguatera fish poisoning when consumed, even if cooked. (From NOAA Photo Library.)

and sturgeon. The uncharacterized toxin is probably a phospholipid egg-white nutrient. *Prevention*: Avoid fish roe.

- **Haff (Haff–Iuksov–Sartlen) disease:** Paroxysmal myalgias and myospastic contractures with *rhabdomyolysis and myoglobinuria* (↑↑ creatine phosphokinase (CPK)) within 6–21 h (mean 8 h) of consuming cooked *buffalo fish* (*Ictiobus cyprinellus*) from the Mississippi–Missouri (*MS–MO) River Basin* and similar basins (Volga–Caspian) worldwide. Toxin unknown; CFR = 1% (Figure 18.13).
- **Prevention:** *No buffalo fish.*

FIGURE 18.13 The large-mouth buffalo fish, *Ictiobus cyprinellus*, is caught commercially in freshwater bodies within the Mississippi and Missouri River drainage basin, and sold often for the preparation of gefilte fish dishes by Eastern European immigrants to the United States. Consumption of buffalo fish, even if cooked, can cause Haff disease with severe muscle and chest pain mimicking myocardial infarction and rhabdomyolysis manifesting as reddish brown urine. (From James H. Diaz, MD, DrPH, private collection.)

Marine Botulism

- **Agent:** *Clostridium botulinum* (marine)
- **Toxin:** Botulinum toxin, exclusively Type E
- **LD_{50}:** 0.0026 mcg/kg IV in mice
- **Mech:** Clostridial contamination of raw or improperly preserved seafood with exclusive production of botulinum toxin Type E on skin, in tissue, and muscle, particularly near gut
- **Vectors:** All home-canned salt or freshwater seafood, raw seafood, raw marine mammals, especially dolphin, seal, whale—*muktuk* (raw skin and underlying pink blubber)
- **Incubation:** ≤36 h
- **Sx:** A febrile, weakness, oriented × 3, descending flaccid paralysis progressing to respiratory fail, CN palsies (blurred vision, diplopia, dysphagia, dysarthria), autonomic dysfunction (↓ HR and BP, N, V, constipation > diarrhea)
- **Dx:** Normal CSF, +EMG, +stool E toxin on mouse bioassay
- **Tx:** Polyvalent equine antitoxin, ICU support, mechanical ventilation
- **Px:** High CFR without ICU
- **Prev:** Boil all raw or fermented Alaskan native dishes and home-canned seafood ≥ 10 min before eating, notify state OPH and CDC (for botulinum antitoxin)

General Management Strategies

- **Seek pathognomonic sx:** Temp reversal = ciguatera and *sunburn-like* rash = scombroid; submit fish samples to toxicology labs for TLC, HPLC, GC/MS.
- **Protect AW and empty the stomach:** Induce vomiting in witnessed ingestions only; orogastric lavage, then activated charcoal (AC). Avoid cathartics.
- **Provide supportive ICU care:** IV fluids and vasopressors, mechanical ventilation.
- **Consider specific pharmacotherapy:** H_1 and H_2 blockers for scombroid; initial IV *mannitol*, then po *gabapentin* for neuropathic pain in ciguatera (untested).
- **Notify PH authorities:** To conduct epidemiologic outbreak analysis.

Conclusions

- All shellfish, >300 finfish species, and marine mammals can cause poisoning with potent biological toxins and ↑ CFRs ranging from 1% to 62%. Example: Botox is #1, palytoxin is #2, TTX and saxitoxin are #5 among the living world's most potent biological toxins.
- Seafood toxins are not inactivated by cooking, smoking, salting, marinating, or freezing, and cannot be detected by human sight (*pale gill color is very nonspecific*), smell, or taste.
- Seafood poisonings affect the autonomic and central nervous systems and/or the GI tract causing symptoms ranging from mild GI distress to fatal respiratory paralysis.

- Although FDA monitors interstate sales, seafood is not federally (USDA) inspected, and there are few available tests to assess seafood quality (e.g., Cigua-Check®), and few specific therapies to manage toxicity. Prevention is key!

Practice Tests

1. A patient complained of headache, sore throat, nausea, diarrhea, and facial burning 1 h after consuming a tuna burger for lunch at a beachfront restaurant. Select the most likely diagnosis.
   A. Ciguatera fish poisoning
   B. Marine botulism
   C. Scombroid poisoning
   D. Tetrodotoxin poisoning
2. A patient vacationing in the Bahamas complained of numb lips, headache, disorientation, dizziness, and diarrhea 8 h after attending an "all-you-can" eat seafood buffet at her hotel. Select the most likely diagnosis.
   A. Amnesic shellfish poisoning
   B. Ciguatera fish poisoning
   C. Diarrhetic shellfish poisoning
   D. Neurotoxic shellfish poisoning
3. A patient complained of weakness, drowsiness, incoordination, and shortness of breath 2 h after a dinner of steamed mussels at a "Belgian"-cuisine restaurant on the California coast. Select the most likely diagnosis.
   A. Amnesic shellfish poisoning
   B. Neurotoxic shellfish poisoning
   C. Paralytic shellfish poisoning
   D. Tetrodotoxin poisoning
4. You are rotating at the local poison control center and answer a call from a concerned ED physician about a 34-year-old man who had numbness and tingling in his hands shortly after consuming a cooked meal of a fish caught locally today. Select the fish species most likely to cause such an illness.
   A. Catfish
   B. Grouper
   C. Flounder
   D. Pufferfish

Test Answers

1. C
2. B
3. C
4. D

Chapter 19

Mushroom Poisonings

Outline 396
Toxicologic Classification 396
Cyclopeptide Toxicity 397
Gyromitrin (MMH) Toxicity 400
Edible or Poisonous? 401
Muscarine Toxicity 401
Ibotenic Acid and Muscimol Toxicity 403
Acute Anuric RF (Allenic Norleucine Toxicity) 406
Rhabdomyolysis: *Tricholoma equestre* 406
Miscellaneous GI Toxicity 1 408
Conclusions 410

Outline

- Epidemiology of mushroom poisoning
- Anatomy of a mushroom
- Toxicologic classification of mushroom poisonings
- Rapid identification of poisonous mushrooms
- Evaluation and management of the mushroom-poisoned patient

Descriptive Epidemiology

- Incidence rate (United States): Five mushroom poisoning per 100,000 persons per year.
- 95% of toxic mushrooms ingested *cannot* be identified.
- 50% of patients are asymptomatic, 25% require treatment, 15% of these have minor toxicity, 5% moderate toxicity, and 0.2% major toxicity.
- 1–2 patients die of mushroom poisoning/year.
- 95% of deaths are due to *Amanita* spp. ingestions; CFRs for *Amanita* ingestions are 25–50%.

Anatomy of a Mushroom (Figure 19.1)

Toxicologic Classification (Table 19.1)

- **Cyclopeptide***-containing mushrooms (potentially lethal *hepatotoxicity*).
- **Monomethylhydrazine***-containing mushrooms (*B_6-inhibitors*, mimic isoniazid [INH] toxicity).
- **Muscarine***-containing mushrooms (muscarinic, cholinergic toxidrome).
- **Coprine-**containing mushrooms ("*disulfiram reaction*" following ethanol intake).
- **Ibotenic and muscimol-containing mushrooms**—Muscimol is a GABA-agonist and its toxidromic manifestations predominate in adult ingestions with dysphoria and hallucinations. Ibotenic acid structurally mimics the excitatory neurotransmitter, glutamic acid, and its toxidromic manifestations predominate in pediatric ingestions with myoclonus and seizures.
- **Psilocybin-**containing mushrooms (*hallucinogenic*, "mellow mushrooms").
- **Orelline/Orellanine***-containing mushrooms (*nephrotoxic*, delayed oliguric renal failure).
- **Allenic norleucine***—*Amanita smithiana*, acute renal failure.
- **Rhabdomyolysis***—*Tricholoma equestre*.
- **Paxillus syndrome**—*Paxillus involutus*, immune-mediated hemolytic anemia.
- **Miscellaneous GI** toxin-containing mushrooms (nonlethal nausea, vomiting, and diarrhea).

* Fatalities after ingestions reported.

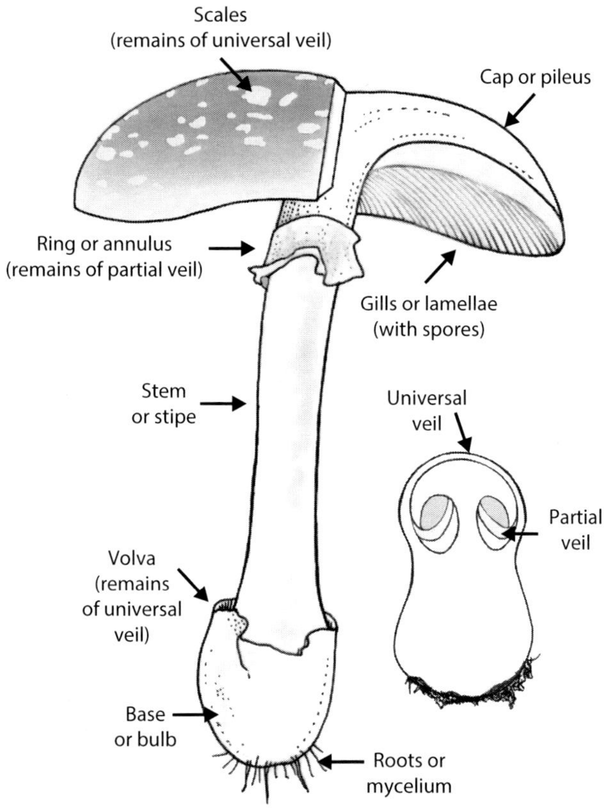

FIGURE 19.1 Anatomy of a poisonous mushroom, *Amanita muscaria* or fly amanita, with the juvenile mushroom button (right) and the mature adult mushroom or toadstool (left).

- **Puff ball poisoning** or **lycoperdonosis** (extrinsic allergic asthma following spore inhalation).

Rapid Diagnosis

- Save mushrooms (dry paper bag) and vomitus (zip-lock bag).
- Photo shop on web.
- *Meixner reaction* for amanitin. HCl + newsprint = *blue*.
- Spore print for interpretation by mycologist.

Cyclopeptide Toxicity

- **Reps:** *Amanita*, *Galerina*, *Lepiota* spp. (Figures 19.2 through 19.5)
- **Toxins:** *Amatoxin* (delayed hepatotoxicity) > phallotoxin (initial GI sx) > virotoxin (nontoxic)

Table 19.1 An Onset Time and Target System Classification of Mushroom Poisoning by Common Mushroom Species

Early Onset Toxicity (<6 h)	Late Onset Toxicity (within 6–24 h)	Delayed Onset Toxicity (1 or More Days)
Neurotoxic	Hepatotoxic	Nephrotoxic
Cholinergic	Amatotoxic	Orellanine
Clitocybe spp. (funnel caps) *Inocybe* spp.	*Amanita* spp. *Galerina* spp. *Lepiota* spp.	*Cortinarius* spp. (corts)
Glutaminergic	Nephrotoxic	Rhabdomyolytic
Amanita muscaria (fly amanita)	*Amanita proxima*	*Tricholoma equestre* (yellow trich)
Amanita pantherina (pantheramanita)	*Amanita smithiana* (toxic lepidella)	*Russula subnigricans* (blackening russula)
Epileptogenic	Erythromelalgia	Neurotoxic
Gyromitra spp. (false morels)	*Clitocybe acromelalga* *Clitocybe amoenolens* (poison dwarf bamboo mushroom)	*Hapalopilus rustilans* (purple-dye polypore)
Hallucinogenic		
Psilocybe spp. (mellow mushrooms)		
Allergic		
Immunohemolytic		
Paxillus involutus (poison pax)		
Pneumonic		
Lycoperdon spp. (puffballs)		
Gastrointestinal (GI)		
Disulfiran reaction		
Coprinus atramentarius (alcohol inky caps)		
Miscellaneous GI		
Boletus spp.		
Chlorophyllum spp.		
Entoloma spp.		

- **Possible Antidotes:** Penicillin, thioctic acid, cimetidine—inhibits CYP450?, silibinin from milk thistle, NAC
- **Dx:** Onset 6–10 h, phase 1—GI toxicity—N, V, D; phase 2—quiescent, liver fx deteriorates; phase 3—jaundice, liver failure, hepatorenal syn; phase 4—death
- **Tx:** Activated charcoal (AC), liver transplant

FIGURE 19.2 (See color insert.) *Amanita phalloides*, the death angel, is an amatoxin-containing highly poisonous mushroom. (From Wikipedia Creative Commons.)

FIGURE 19.3 *Galerina marginata*, a deadly Galerina, is also an amatoxin-containing highly poisonous mushroom. (From Wikipedia Creative Commons.)

FIGURE 19.4 *Lepiota cristata* is an amatoxin-containing highly poisonous mushroom. (From Wikipedia Creative Commons.)

FIGURE 19.5 *Lepiota cristata*, an amatoxin-containing highly poisonous mushroom part of a "fairy ring." Note the free, unattached gills and the rings on the stems, remnants of the partial veils. (Courtesy of David K. Lirette, PhD, LSU School of Public Health, New Orleans, LA.)

Gyromitrin (MMH) Toxicity

- **Reps:** *Gyromitra* spp. (Figure 19.6).
- **Toxin:** *Gyromitrin*, a monomethylhydrazine and B_6/GABA inhibitor. Binds B_6, inhibits pyridoxine phosphokinase, and stops production of GABA from glutamate.
- **Antidote:** B_6 or pyridoxine, 25 mg/kg IV.
- **Dx:** *Delayed onset 5–10 h*, initial GI sx, then seizures mimic INH toxicity 2° GABA inhibition; hepatorenal failure.
- **Tx:** Pyridoxine, anticonvulsants.

FIGURE 19.6 **(See color insert.)** The brain mushroom or false morel, *Gyromitra esculenta*, contains the epileptogenic monomethylhydrazine, gyromitrin, which can cause seizure activity on ingestion. The poisonous brain mushroom may be confused with a look-alike mushroom, the edible conifer or yellow morel, *Morchella esculenta*. (From Wikipedia Creative Commons.)

Edible or Poisonous?

Yellow Morel or False Morel? (Figures 19.7 through 19.9)

Muscarine Toxicity

- **Reps:** All *Inocybe* and some *Clitocybe* spp. (Figures 19.10 and 19.11)
- **Toxin:** Muscarine

FIGURE 19.7 The edible conifer or yellow morel, *Morchella esculenta*, should not be confused with the poisonous brain mushroom or false morel, *Gyromitra esculenta*. (Courtesy of Charles P. Sea, MD, Department of Emergency Medicine, Ochsner Clinic Foundation Hospital, New Orleans, LA. Original source: U.S. Government Document, U.S. Forest Service Document, 1979, "Wild Mushrooms of North America.")

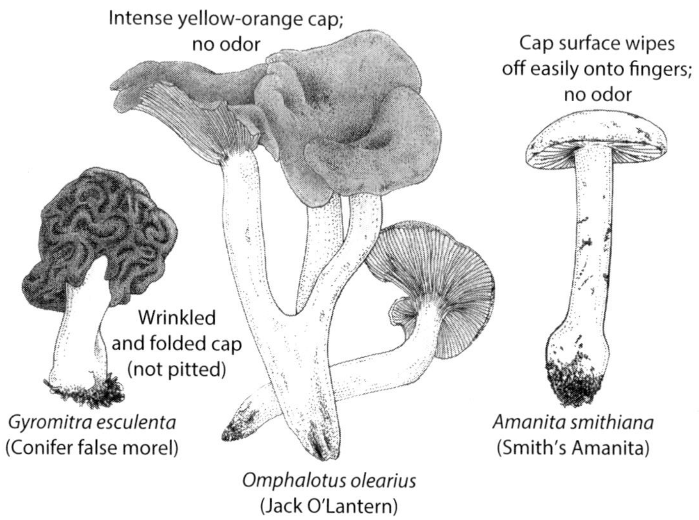

FIGURE 19.8 A study of three poisonous mushrooms and their unique identifying features. Left: *Gyromitra esculenta* (brain mushroom or false morel). Center: *Omphalotus olearius* (Jack O'Lantern). Right: *Amanita smithiana* (Smith's Amanita).

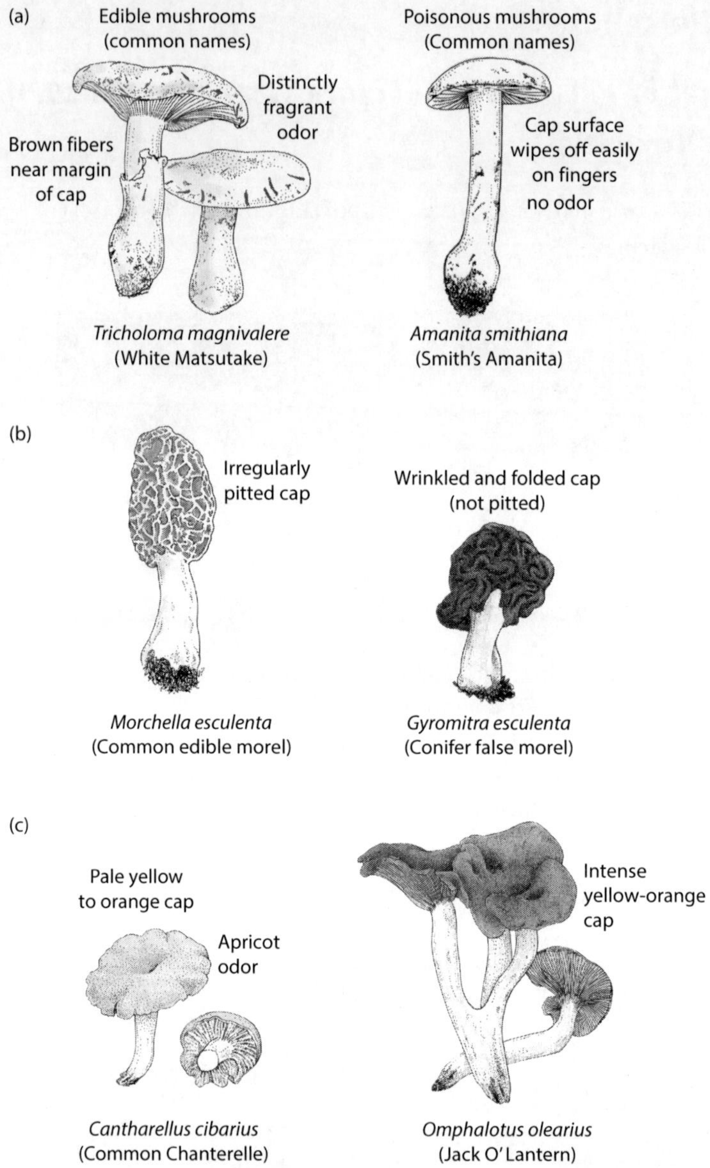

FIGURE 19.9 Many mushrooms look alike. Here is a study of edible and poisonous look-alike mushrooms; some commonly confused look-alike mushrooms.

- **Antidote:** Atropine, 1–2 mg/kg IV
- **Dx:** Onset 0.5–2 h, seizures (sx)—muscarinic cholinergic effects, *SLUDE*,* no CNS effects
- **Tx:** IV Atropine titrated to anticholinergic effects

* Salivation, lacrimation, urination, defecation, emesis. Includes sweating.

FIGURE 19.10 The muscarine-containing sweating mushroom, *Clitocybe dealbata*. (From Wikipedia Creative Commons.)

FIGURE 19.11 Another muscarine-containing mushroom that causes a cholinergic or muscarinic toxidrome when ingested, *Inocybe geophylla*, the white fiber head. (From Wikipedia Creative Commons.)

Ibotenic Acid and Muscimol Toxicity

Ibotenic Acid and Muscimol-Containing Poisonous Mushrooms

Unlike the muscarine-containing mushrooms, these mushrooms are neurotoxic and epileptogenic and do not cause muscarinic toxidromes.

- **Reps:** *Amanita muscaria*, *A. pantherina*, *A. gemmata* (Figures 19.12 and 19.13)
- **Toxins:** *Ibotenic acid*, a *glutamate* agonist = excitation, and its 1° metabolite, *muscimol*, a *GABA* agonist = ataxia, somnolence, hallucinations
- **Antidote:** Benzodiazepines

FIGURE 19.12 A red fly agaric, *Amanita muscaria*, can cause a biphasic toxidrome following ingestion with initial somnolence followed by agitation and seizure activity. (Courtesy of Charles P. Sea, MD, Department of Emergency Medicine, Ochsner Clinic Foundation Hospital, New Orleans, LA. Original source: U.S. Government Document, U.S. Forest Service Document, 1979, "Wild Mushrooms of North America".)

- **Dx:** Onset 0.5–2 h, vertigo, somnolence, delirium, hallucinations; myoclonus and seizures in children
- **Tx:** Anticonvulsants (BZs)

Psilocybin Toxicity

- **Reps:** *Psilocybe* spp. (Figure 19.14).
- **Toxins:** "*Mellow mushrooms*" contain both *psilocin* and *psilocybin*; derived from tryptamine and are serotonergic agonists and analogs of *LSD*.
- **Antidote:** Benzodiazepines.
- **Dx:** Onset rapid 0.5–1 h, hyperkinesis, ataxia, hallucinations.
- **Tx:** Anticonvulsants.

FIGURE 19.13 An orange fly agaric, *Amanita muscaria*, can cause a biphasic toxidrome following ingestion with initial somnolence followed by agitation and seizure activity. Note the caps are dotted with white scales, the remnants of the universal veils of juvenile buttons. (Courtesy of Charles P. Sea, MD, Department of Emergency Medicine, Ochsner Clinic Foundation Hospital, New Orleans, LA. Original source: U.S. Government Document, U.S. Forest Service Document, 1979, "Wild Mushrooms of North America".)

FIGURE 19.14 The hallucinogenic mellow mushroom, *Psilocybe cubensis*, contains LSD-like substances. (From Wikipedia Creative Commons.)

Coprine Toxicity

- **Reps:** *Coprinus* spp. (Figure 19.15)
- **Toxin:** Coprine metabolite = *1-aminocyclopropanol*, acetaldehyde dehydrogenase inhibitor, like disulfiram and diethyldithiocarbamate
- **Antidote:** None
- **Dx:** *Delayed* onset 0.5–2 h, *disulfiram reaction* following ingestion of alcohol within 24–48 h with facial flushing, N and V, tachycardia, hypertension
- **Tx:** Supportive, IV fluids

Orelline Nephrotoxicity

- **Reps:** *Cortinarius* spp. (Figures 19.16 and 19.17).
- **Toxins:** *Orelline and orellanine*, both *nephrotoxic bipyridyls* related to diquat (nephrotoxic) and paraquat (pulmonary toxin)
- **Antidote:** None

FIGURE 19.15 The alcohol inky cap, *Coprinus atramentarius*, can cause a disulfiram-type reaction with nausea and vomiting if any alcohol is ingested after its consumption for 24–48 h. (From Wikipedia Creative Commons.)

FIGURE 19.16 *Cortinarius orellanus* contains the nephrotoxins, orelline and orellanine, which are bipyridyls related to the herbicide diquat. (From Wikipedia Creative Commons.)

FIGURE 19.17 *Cortinarius collinitus* also contains the nephrotoxins, orelline and orellanine, which are bipyridyls related to the herbicide diquat.

- **Dx:** Initial GI sx with HA and chills in 24–36 h, then *delayed oliguric renal failure* may develop days to weeks later
- **Tx:** Hemoperfusion, hemodialysis, renal transplant

Acute Anuric RF (Allenic Norleucine Toxicity)

- **Epid:** Starting in the 1990s-↑ reports *acute anuric RF* 1–6 days postingestion *Amanita smithiana* (United States, Canada), *A. proxima* (France, Spain, Italy), *A. pseudoporphyria* (Japan) 2° confusion with edible *matsutake* mushrooms (Figure 19.18)
- **Toxin:** Nephrotoxin = *allenic norleucine* (2-amino-4,5-hexadienoic acid)
- **Antidote:** None
- **Dx:** Phase 1 = severe N and V in 1–6 h; phase 2 = acute anuric RF-↑ BUN/Cr and AST/ALT in 1–6 days
- **Tx:** Hemodialysis × 1–4 weeks

Rhabdomyolysis: *Tricholoma equestre* (Figure 19.19)

- **Rep:** *Tricholoma equestre* (aka *T. flavovirens*, the "*edible*" yellow knight mushroom) (Figure 19.19)

FIGURE 19.18 *Amanita smithiana* also contains a nephrotoxin, allenic norleucine, which can cause acute anuric renal failure 1–6 days following ingestion, unlike the *Cortinarius* species, which can cause oliguric renal failure several weeks following ingestion. (From Wikipedia Creative Commons.)

- **Epid:** 1992–2001: 12 French patients experienced *delayed rhabdomyolysis* 24–72 h after ingesting cooked *T. equestre* mushrooms; 3 died
- **Myotoxins:** Unidentified, metabolites include triterpenoids, sterols, indoles, acetylenic compounds, and *yellow* pigment = 7, 7′-bi-physicion
- **Antidote:** None
- **Clin:** Initial N, but no V, *facial erythema*, and diaphoresis simulate a disulfiram reaction; then weakness, leg myalgias, dark urine = myoglobinuria in 24–72 h
- **Tx:** Cooling blanket, IV fluid loading, mannitol-forced diuresis, continuous venovenous hemofiltration, exchange tx, vasopressors

FIGURE 19.19 (See color insert.) *Tricholoma equestre*, the yellow knight, can cause rhabdomyolysis with myalgias and myoglobinuria 24–72 h following ingestion. The precise myotoxin has yet to be identified. (From Wikipedia Creative Commons.)

FIGURE 19.20 *Paxillus involutus* can cause an immune-mediated hemolytic anemia with hemoglobinuria and later renal failure following ingestion. (From Wikipedia Creative Commons.)

Paxillus Syndrome

Paxillus involutus

The ingestion of *Paxillus involutus* can cause an *immune-mediated hemolytic anemia followed by hemoglobinuria*, oligurua, and renal failure, known as the paxillus syndrome (Figure 19.20).

Miscellaneous GI Toxicity 1

- **Reps:** Most "*little brown mushrooms*" = *Boletes, Lactarius, Tricholoma, Chlorophyllum* spp. (Figure 19.21)
- **Toxins:** Ill-defined GI toxins
- **Antidote:** None
- **Dx:** Onset 0.5–3 h, severe epigastric pain, nausea, vomiting, diarrhea, hypovolemic shock
- **Tx:** Supportive, fluids and electrolytes

FIGURE 19.21 *Lactarius volemus*, the milky-latex mushroom, is an example of a little brown mushroom that may cause gastrointestinal disturbances that are usually short-lived and do not result in significant morbidity. (Courtesy of David K. Lirette, PhD, LSU School of Public Health, New Orleans, LA.)

Miscellaneous GI Toxicity

Lycoperdonosis

- **Def:** Acute extrinsic allergic alveolitis following the inhalation of *aerosolized puff ball spores*
- **Reps:** *Lycoperdon* spp. puff balls (Figures 19.22 through 19.24)
- **Toxins:** Myco-allergens
- **Dx:** Onset rapid, in hours, acute nasopharyngitis, N, V, inflammatory pneumonitis
- **Tx:** IV steroids, amphotericin B, mechanical ventilation

Summary: Mushroom Poisoning

Select the gourmet edible mushrooms, *Morchella esculenta* (morel) *Tricholoma magnivalere* (matsutake)

The rest are potentially lethal!

FIGURE 19.22 Common white puffballs (*Lycoperdon candidum*), release spores when crushed, which can cause acute bronchospasm or lycoperdonosis when inhaled. (Courtesy of Charles P. Sea, MD, Department of Emergency Medicine, Ochsner Clinic Foundation Hospital, New Orleans, LA. Original source: U.S. Government Document, U.S. Forest Service Document, 1979, "Wild Mushrooms of North America.")

FIGURE 19.23 *Scleroderma geaster*, the earthstar, is a large, dark brown-to-purplish-colored puffball filled with powdery spores. (Courtesy of David K. Lirette, PhD, LSU School of Public Health, New Orleans, LA.)

FIGURE 19.24 *Scleroderma geaster*, the earthstar, peeled open to reveal its powdery spores, which can be aerosolized when the puffball is crushed and cause an acute asthmatic-like attack if inhaled. (Courtesy of David K. Lirette, PhD, LSU School of Public Health, New Orleans, LA.)

Conclusions

"There are *old* mushroom hunters, and *bold* mushroom hunters, but *no old, bold* mushroom hunters."

Avoid pure *white* mushrooms, little (and large) *brown* mushrooms, *red- or pink*-pored boletes (*Boletus* spp.), and all decomposing mushrooms.

Cook all wild mushrooms. *Cooking* does not inactivate all mushroom toxins, and even edible mushrooms, if allowed to age or deteriorate, may become toxic.

Select mushrooms at the *grocery*, not in the woods (except in *Scandinavian* countries—few toxic species).

- Mycotoxins—*Biological warfare agents (BW):* Microorganisms/fungi
- Mycotoxins—*1° Health effects: Mycotoxins*

Mycotoxins (See Table 19.2)

Fusarium Keratitis

- **Def:** Severe fungal infection of cornea; airborne > direct inoculation; permanent damage possible
- **Epid:** Incidence ↑ as temp and humidity ↑; 2005–2006, n = 102; 1% of microbial keratitis in NY, 35% in SE United States
- **Risk factors:** *Use of contact lens solutions* = ReNu® with MoistureLoc® (withdrawn 4/06) > MultiPlus® > extended wear *soft contact lens* users; 4–21 cases/10,000 lens users > trauma/ocular foreign body—*plant material* > chronic ocular surface disease > immunodeficiencies
- **Tx:** Topical and oral antifungals; medical failures—surgical corneal resurfacing; corneal transplant (n = 8)

Table 19.2 Classification of Mycotoxins

Mycotoxins	Main Health Effects	Fungi Producing
Aflatoxins	Hepatotoxic, carcinogenic contaminates peanuts, almonds, pistachios	*Aspergillus flavus* *Aspergillus parasiticus*
Ergot alkaloids	Ergotism	*Claviceps purpura*
Fumonisins	Neurotoxic, carcinogenic; *Fusarium* spp. keratitis = 1% (NY)–35% (U.S. South) microbial keratitis	*Fusarium moniliforme* *Fusarium proliferatum* *Aspergillus ochraceus*
Tricothecenes: Satratoxins Vomitoxin[bw] (deoxynivalenol) T2 toxin[bw]	Inhibit protein synthesis, pulmonary/GI hemorrhage Emesis Emesis, pulm hemorrhage	*Stachybotrys chartarum* *Fusarium cerealis, Fusarium culmorum, Fusarium graminearum* *Fusarium sporotrichoides*

Tricothecene Mycotoxins

- **Microbiology:** Easily aerosolized mycotoxins that are produced by several filamentous molds, including *Stachybotrys* > *Fusarium* > *Myrotecium* and *Trichoderma*, and, *like ricin, all inhibit protein synthesis.*
- **Pathology:** Mycotoxins can cause immediate toxicity on exposure to intact skin and mucosa by inducing inflammatory lesions with early necrosis of skin and mucosa, and throughout tracheobronchial tree. The onset of action is more rapid than with liquid CWs, like mustard and VX. If ingested, mycotoxins can cause alimentary toxic aleukia with fever, chills, gastroenteritis, bone marrow suppression, and sepsis.
- **DDx:** Vesicant CW exposure, especially sulfur mustard, and acute radiation sickness (*dirty bomb*).
- **Tx:** Supportive only.

Stachybotryotoxicosis 1

- **Definition:** A common disease of farm animals caused by the common saprophytic fungus *Stachybotrys chartarum* (aka *S. atra* and *S. alternans*) with initial conjunctivitis, rhinitis, and stomatitis; later followed by leukopenia, thrombocytopenia, and coagulopathy. *S. chartarum* grows well on straw and cellulose-rich, damp material such as wet wallpaper and sheetrock. Two-thirds of colonies produce *satratoxins*.

Stachybotrys atra: Bronchoalveolar lavage (BAL) culture from 7 year-old (y.o.) male with pulmonary hemosiderosis; note its conidiospores.

Stachybotryotoxicosis 2

- **Cleveland, 1993–1996:** 10 ex-preemie infants <1 y.o. living in water-damaged public housing developed *acute idiopathic pulmonary hemorrhage* (AIPH), aka pulmonary hemosiderosis. High spore counts of *S. atra* were detected in 9 of 10 homes. CDC investigations during 1996–2000, demonstrated shortcomings in earlier spore detection methods and found no causative link between AIPH and *S. atra*.

Stachybotryotoxicosis 3

- **Houston, 1999:** A 7 y.o. male living in a previously flooded, 25 y.o. farmhouse being renovated by family developed a chronic cough with fever and recurrent pneumonia and later left lower lobe consolidation. Bronchoalveolar lavage fluid showed hemosiderin-ladened macrophages and grew out *S. atra* in later cultures. Multiple home room cultures also grew *S. atra*, *Aspergillus*, and *Penicillium* spp. Home was mold-remediated and patient recovered completely.
- **Boston, 2002–2003:** Four cases of AIPH in full-term infants reported; three had von Willebrand disease; one home had flooded and the other three were being renovated. Common *Cladosporium* and *Penicillium* molds were cultured from all four homes; one *S. atra* spore found in one home; seven in another.

Stachybotryotoxicosis 4

Stachybotryotoxicosis is more common in cattle and horses than man.

Chronic *S. atra* (aka *S. chartarum*, *S. alternans*) and other mycotoxin-producing mold exposures may rarely induce *pulmonary hemosiderosis with AIPH in infants and children*, especially those with preexisting coagulopathies, such as von Willebrand disease, or chronic respiratory diseases, such as bronchopulmonary dysplasia in ex-preemies.

Aflatoxins

- **Microbiology:** Metabolic by-products of *Aspergillus* spp. molds (*A. flatus*, *A. parasiticus*) that often contaminate foods, grains, and feeds under ↑ temperature and humidity conditions, especially nuts, corn, wheat, and barley, and cause toxic effects when ingested or inhaled.
- **Pathology:** Hepatitis, esp. A-B1, causing interference with fatty acid met., inhibition of RNA synthesis, and mitochondrial failure. Acute exposures more common in tropics with massive GI hemorrhage and liver failure. Chronic exposures cause dose-related *hepatocellular carcinomas.*
- **DDx:** Acute-ricin, iron overdose (OD). Chronic-HBV, HCV, alcoholism.
- **Tx:** Avoid contaminated foodstuffs; FDA monitors levels in grains and peanut butter.

Chapter 20

Herbal Poisonings

Outline .414
Descriptive Epidemiology .414
Pharmacology .414
Toxicology .415
System-Oriented Classification of Herbal Poisons .417
Antidote for Poisonings with Herbal and Plant Cardiac Glycosides 421
Neurotoxic Herbal Poisonings 422
Neurotoxic Herbs and Plants 422
CNS Toxicity: Absinthe 426
Sympathomimetics 430
GI Toxins—Outline 432
Gastrointestinal Toxicity 434
Miscellaneous Herbal Hepatotoxins 435
Hypervitaminosis 438
Tryptophan 441
Conclusions 442

Outline

1. Descriptive *epidemiology* of herbal and vitamin poisonings
2. *Pharmacology* of herbal and vitamin poisonings
3. *Toxicology* of herbal and vitamin poisonings
4. Rapid *identification*, patient evaluation, and management

Descriptive Epidemiology

An herb is a leafy plant without a woody stem, but herbal preparations include any *natural, alternative, or traditional remedy. Today,* 25% of the current traditional pharmaceuticals come from plant–herb sources.

As a result of the *Dietary Supplement and Health Education Act of 1994 (DSHEA),* the FDA has no authority over regulating herbal and vitamin products, *unless they prove to be toxic. The DSHEA resulted from the E-ferol/polysorbate 80 tragedy of the early 1990s—38 neonates died, half of the survivors were impaired.*

80% of the world's population use herbal products and vitamins daily; most of them are benign, and offer no health benefit at all, for example, vitamin C, *Echinacea*, and *Gingko;* or potentially fatal drug–drug interactions, for example, St. John's wort and SSRIs, garlic and ASA, *Gingko,* and ASA.

The most common herb and vitamin delivery forms include *capsules* (50+%), tablets (15+%), teas, and drinks (10+%).

The most common herb supplement types are *single herbs* (50+%) and combinations (30+%).

The most popular herb sales in the United States include *Echinacea* (10%), *garlic* (10%), *goldenseal** (7%), ginseng (6%), *Gingko* (4.5%), and saw palmetto (4.4%).

There are *no toxicologic databases* on herbal and vitamin toxicity in the United States.

In Hong Kong, herbal medicine toxicity accounts for <1% of all acute hospital admissions, and modern *western medicine toxicity and drug–drug interactions account for 4.4%* of all acute hospital admissions.

Regarding vitamins and complementary agents, fatalities have resulted from megadoses of vitamins A, D, and E; and "*therapeutic*" (homeopathic) doses of niacin (B3) and tryptophan.

Pharmacology

- Volatile oils
- Plant resins
- Alkaloids (belladonna alkaloids, pyrrolizidine alkaloids)
- Glycosides (sugar esters)
- Fixed oils (cooking oils)

* For illicit use to adulterate THC+ urine samples.

Table 20.1 Pharmacology: Plant Oils

Classes	Toxicities	Examples
Volatile oils: Evaporate at room temperature	Mucous membrane and CNS irritants	Catnip, garlic, and chamomile
Resins: Mixtures of oily plant resins	Strong gastrointestinal irritants	Dandelion, elder, and black cohosh root
Fixed oils: Long-chain fatty acids	Safe emollients and cooking oils	Olive oil, peanut oil, canola oil, and safflower oil
Alkaloids = belladonnas, pyrrolizidines	Anticholinergic, hepatic veno-occlusion	Jimson weed, comfrey, and goldenseal
Gylcosides: Anthroquinones	Irritating cathartics	Aloe, senna (Sennakot®)
Saponins	Mucous membrane irritants, steroids, and anticoagulants	Licorice, ginseng
Cyanophores	Release cyanide	Prunus pits (apple, apricot, peach, etc.)

Pharmacology 1—Plant Oils

See Table 20.1.

Toxicology

- Abortifacients
- Cardiovascular toxins
- Central nervous system (CNS) toxins
- Gastrointestinal toxins
- Hepatotoxins
- Nephrotoxins and miscellaneous toxins

Abortifacients

Aloe
Aristolochia (birthwort)[*]
Bitter melon
Black and blue cohosh root
Cantharidin[†]
Compound Q
Ergots[*]
Feverfew
aka *Spanish fly*

[*] Highly effective abortifacients
[†] Insect toxin (blister beetle)

Juniper
Mugwort
Nutmeg
*Pennyroyal oil (pulegone)**
*Quinine (↑ oxytocin)**
Rue
Sage

Most Effective Abortifacients

Aristolochia (birthwort)*
Ergots*
Pennyroyal oil (pulegone)* *Rx: NAC*
Quinine (↑ oxytocin)*

Mentha pulegium (Pennyroyal-Mint Family)

See Figure 20.1.

What Is Compound Q?

- Compound Q is an herbal preparation of the Chinese *Trichosanthes* plant (*Chinese cucumber*) that can *inactivate viral ribosomes and inhibit HIV replication.*
- **Pharmacology:** Poor oral availability and *intense diarrhea po*; severe *biphasic neurotoxicity* on parenteral admin.
- **Toxicity:** CNS/PNS (paresthesias) > Derm (hypersensitivity and anaphylaxis) > Metabolic (*hypoglycemia*, also used to treat DM).

FIGURE 20.1 The pennyroyal herb, *Mentha pulegium*, has been used in teas and potions to induce abortion and contains the hepatotoxin, pulegone, which can cause centrilobular hepatic necrosis similar to acetaminophen toxicity. (From Wikipedia Creative Commons.)

* Highly effective abortifacients.

- **CNS toxicity:** (1) *Encephalomyelitis* in 24–72 h with fever, delirium, dementia, myalgias, paresis (2) *coma* within 1 week.
- **Tx:** Immediate ipecac, lavage + AC, supportive.

Compound Q vs. CoQ-10?

Summary *Compound Q* is an herbal supplement derived from *Trichosanthes kirilowii,* the *Chinese cucumber*, which may increase the CD4 lymphocyte count and reduce the viral load in HIV/AIDS. It is also sold as a dietary supplement often mixed with other herbs and alternative natural products, including CoQ-10.

Coenzyme Q10

- *CoQ-10* is a fat-soluble antioxidant (aka ubidecarenone, ubiquinone, or CoQ-10) both endogenously synthesized and absorbed from dietary *yeast–grain sources*; an essential cofactor in *mitochondrial electron transport*, sold as a dietary supplement in the United States.
- **Antidote for drug and environmental toxicities:** (1) *Anthracyclines*: 60–200 mg/d may prevent ↓ *doxorubicin* (Adriamycin®) and other anthracycline-/antibiotic-induced cardiomyopathies with CHF. (2) *Statins*: 60–300 mg/d may cause myopathies that CoQ-10 may prevent. (3) *Dermal photoaging*: Topical application of 0.3% CoQ-10 for 6 months reduced photoaging of human skin.

Summary *CoQ-10* or *ubiquinone* is a fat-soluble antioxidant and essential cofactor in mitochondrial electron transport stored in cardiac and striated muscle, kidney, liver; and endogenously produced from dietary yeast–grain sources and approved for chemotoxicity rescue from anthracycline, especially doxorubicin (Adriamycin®) cardiotoxicity. Sold as a dietary supplement.

System-Oriented Classification of Herbal Poisons

Cardiovascular Toxins

- **Na Channel Openers:** *Monkshood, death camas, and hellebore* (*Veratrum*)
- **Na Channel Openers**: *Aconitine Group*
    - **Representative:** Monkshood (wolfsbane)
    - **Toxin:** Parasympathomimetic aconitine *alkaloids—cause prolonged opening of sodium channels (phase 0)*
    - **Antidote:** None
    - **Dx:** Salivation, nausea (N), vomiting (V), diarrhea (D), bradycardia, muscle weakness, ventricular-tachycardia (VT), ventricular fibrillation (VF), and respiratory failure
    - **Tx:** Atropine, pacemaker, and gastrointestinal (GI) decontam (lavage + activated charcoal [AC]) (Figure 20.2)

FIGURE 20.2 (See color insert.) Monkshood, *Aconitum napellus*, contains the cardiotoxic alkaloid, aconitine, a sodium channel opener, and can cause fatal cardiac arrhythmias and conduction defects on ingestion. (From Wikipedia Creative Commons.)

Aconitum napellus (Monkshood) (Figure 20.2)

- Na Channel Openers: Veratrum Group
    - **Rep:** Green hellebore (hellbane) (*Veratrum viride*)
    - **Toxins:** Primarily veratrine, and others
    - **Antidote:** None
    - **Dx:** Initial N, V, D, then bradycardia, VT–VF, RR, and resp. failure
    - **Tx:** GI decontamination (lavage + AC)

Veratrum viride (Green Hellbane) (Figure 20.3)

- **Na Channel Openers: Zygadenine-containing**

Zigadenus glaberrimus (Death Camas) (Figure 20.4)

FIGURE 20.3 Green hellbane, *Veratrum viride* contains the cardiotoxic alkaloid, veratrine, a sodium channel opener, and can cause fatal cardiac arrhythmias and conduction defects on ingestion. (From Wikipedia Creative Commons.)

FIGURE 20.4 *Zigadenus* spp.: death camas or death lilies are perennial, onion-like bulbs with showy flower stalk with six-petal flowers with green hearts. All parts of the plant are cardiotoxic and potentially fatal on ingestion. (Courtesy of David K. Lirette, PhD, LSU School of Public Health, New Orleans, LA.)

CV Toxins: Na and Ca Channel Blockers

- **Mech:** Plant alkaloids from rare *Pacific yew tree bark* (*Taxus brevifolia*) can act as Na and Ca channel blockers and metaphase inhibitors of tubulin disassembly
- **Indic:** Breast cancer treatment and prevention
- **Tox:** N, V, abdominal pain, ↓ HR–conduction blocks, ventricular dysrhythmias, paresthesias, ataxia, and seizures
- **Tx:** Atropine, amiodarone, BZs, and Na bicarbonate; DigiBind® ineffective
- ***Taxus* spp. (*T. baccata*):** Yew shrub–tree; most parts toxic: leaves and seeds, not the red aril

The Cardiac Glycosides: Foxglove, oleander, lily-of-the valley, and red squill

CV Toxins: Cardiac Glycosides

- **Rep:** Foxglove, oleander, red squill, and lily-of-the-valley
- **Toxin:** Digitalis and digitoxigenin (foxglove, red squill), oleandrin
- Antidote: DigiBind®
- **Dx:** "**dig-toxicity**" = N, V, D, abdominal cramps, and bradydysrhythmias
- **Tx:** Monitor digoxin levels and ECG, GI decontamination (lavage? + AC)

Digitalis purpurea (Common Foxglove)

See Figure 20.5.

Nerium oleander (Oleander)

See Figure 20.6.

FIGURE 20.5 **(See color insert.)** The foxgloves, *Digitalis* species, are a large group of flowering herbaceous perennials that contain digitalis-like cardiac glycosides and are capable of causing digitalis-like poisoning with potentially fatal cardiac arrhythmias and conduction defects on ingestion. Treatment is the same as for digitalis (digoxin) overdose. (From Wikipedia Creative Commons.)

FIGURE 20.6 Oleander, *Nerium oleander*, is an evergreen shrub, all parts of which also contain digitalis-like cardiac glycosides, primarily oleandrin. Reactions to ingestion of this plant can mimic digitalis poisoning with both gastrointestinal and cardiac effects. Contact with its sap can cause irritation and dermatitis reactions. (Courtesy of David K. Lirette, PhD, LSU School of Public Health, New Orleans, LA.)

FIGURE 20.7 The lily-of-the-valley, *Convallaria majalis*, is a flowering herbaceous perennial plant, all parts of which contain cardiac glycosides, such as convallarin, capable of causing digitalis-like poisoning with potentially fatal cardiac arrhythmias and conduction defects on ingestion. Treatment is the same as for digitalis (digoxin) overdose. (From Wikipedia Creative Commons.)

Convallaria majalis (Lily-of-the-Valley)
See Figure 20.7.

Cardiac Glycosides

Urginea (*Drimia*) *maritima*, aka sea onion, sea squill, and red squill, is a bulb native to the coastal Mediterranean that sends out a tall stalk capped with a spike of white flowers (red in some spp., hence red squill). It contains the cardiac glycosides, scillirosides, which can cause digoxin-like toxicity if ingested. Has been used as a rodenticide and insecticide. Treatment of ingestion is the same as for digitalis (digoxin) overdose.

Antidote for Poisonings with Herbal and Plant Cardiac Glycosides

Digoxin-Specific Fab

Properties

Chem: Purified Fb fragments of intact IgG anti-digoxin Abs. *No Fc fragments*, which do not bind Ag and ↑ *hypersensitivity* reaction potential.

Mech: Direct Ag/Ab antagonism of intravascular-free digoxin with enough cross-reactivity to also bind digitoxin and the natural cardiac glycosides from garden plants (oleander) and amphibians (toad bufodienolides).

Contra: Hypercalcemia, concomitant Ca administration—as in CCB overdose.

Applications

Use: Dig toxicity = worsening AV block, VT, VF, and rising K > 5 mEq/L; natural glycoside poisonings—from plants—foxglove, oleander, and red squill; animals—toad bufodienolides.

Dose: Empiric 10–20 vials → *38 mg Fab per vial will bind 0.5 mg of digoxin.*

SE: Acute hypokalemia, worsening of CHF, rash, potential for hypersensitivity, and serum sickness.

Calculations

- Each vial of Dig Fab contains 38 mg of purified Fabs that will bind 0.5 mg of digoxin.
- Digoxin has a bioavailability of 80%.
- Digoxin dose known = digoxin dose ingested in mg × 0.8/0.5 mg = # vials of Dig Fab rounded up.
- Digoxin level known = digoxin level in ng/mL × wt in kg/100 = # vials of Dig Fab rounded up.
- Always round up the number of vials of Dig Fab to administer IV.

Neurotoxic Herbal Poisonings

- Hallucinogens—Absinthe (wormwood)
- Anticholinergics—Belladonna alkaloids
- Sympathomimetics—*Ephedra*
- Nicotinic (tobacco-like) agents
- Methamphetamine-like nutmeg and mace
- Selective serotonin reuptake inhibitor (SSRI)-like St. John's wort
- Sedatives—Kava, valerian root

Neurotoxic Herbs and Plants

Anticholinergics, the Belladonna Alkaloid-Containing Plants: "*Red as a beet, blind as a bat, hot as Hades, mad as a hatter*"

- Ex: Nightshade, Jimson weed, and angel's trumpets = *Brugmasia*, *Solandra*

Nicotinic plants: Nicotine + caffeine-like overdoses

- Ex: Poison hemlock, lobelia, and tobacco

Convulsants: Seizures, paralysis

- Ex: Water hemlock, strychnine, and camphor

Belladonna Alkaloids

Reps: Nightshade, jessamine, Jimson weed (thornapple), *Brugmasia* and *Solandra* spp. (angel's trumpet, common in the southern United States), mandrake, and henbane

Toxins: *Atropine* = hyoscyamine, *scopolamine* = hyoscine
Antidote: Physostigmine for CNS effects
Dx: Atropine tox = F, dry mouth, tachycardia, ileus, urinary retention, hallucinations, and seizures, "*red as a beet, etc.*"
Tx: GI decontamination

Datura stramonium (Jimson Weed [Thornapple])

See Figure 20.8.

Brugmasia suaveolens (Angel's Trumpet)

See Figure 20.9.

Nicotine Group

- **Reps:** Poison hemlock (**Socrates**)—resembles Queen Anne's lace (wild carrot); wild tree tobacco.
- **Toxin: Coniine, nicotine.**
- **Antidote:** None.
- **Dx:** Initial N and V; then diaphoresis, tachycardia, tremors, seizures, ascending paralysis, respiratory failure, and coma.
- **Tx:** GI decontamination (lavage + AC), supportive care.

FIGURE 20.8 Jimson weed (thornapple), *Datura stramonium*. The belladonna alkaloid containing Jimson weed or thornapple plant (*D. stramonium*). The legend holds that early American colonists encouraged occupying British troops to consume salads of local "Jimson" (for Jamestown, Virginia) weed and to suffer the central and peripheral anticholinergic consequences. (From Wikipedia Creative Commons.)

FIGURE 20.9 (See color insert.) The angel's trumpet plants, *Brugmasia* spp. and *Solandra* spp. are very common perennials in the southern United States, and contain a scopolamine-like belladonna alkaloid that can cause a central anticholinergic syndrome on ingestion. The angel's trumpet plant was introduced into the temperate and tropical areas of the United States from southeastern Brazil for landscaping purposes. All parts of the plants are toxic and contain a combination of several anticholinergic tropine alkaloids, including atropine, hyoscyamine, and scopolamine. Since the 1990s, there have been increasing U.S. reports of central anticholinergic syndromes following the ingestion of teas and potions made from angel's trumpet in adolescents seeking legal hallucinogens. (Courtesy of David K. Lirette, PhD, LSU School of Public Health, New Orleans, LA.)

Conium maculatum (Poison Hemlock, *Note*: Fern-Like Leaves)

See Figure 20.10.

Nicotiana glauca (Wild Tree Tobacco)

See Figure 20.11.

Neurotoxicity: Convulsants

- **Rep:** Water hemlock, also resembles the herb—Queen Anne's lace (wild carrot).
- **Toxin:** Cicutoxin.
- **Antidote:** None.
- **Dx:** N, V, abdominal cramps, *status epilepticus*, subsequent rhabdomyolysis, ↑ CPK, CFR = 30%.
- **Tx:** GI decontamination (lavage + AC), anticonvulsants (barbiturates, benzodiazepines [BZs]), and *cicutoxin is dialyzable* = by hemodialysis (HD).

Cicuta maculata (Epileptogenic Water Hemlock) (Leaves Non-Fernlike, Yellow Flowers)

See Figure 20.12.

FIGURE 20.10 *Conium maculatum* (poison hemlock) resembles common herbs, such as wild carrot, parsnip, and Queen Anne's lace, and contains the nicotinic receptor blocker, coniine, which induces seizures and paralysis on ingestions. (Courtesy of Charles P. Sea, MD, Department of Emergency Medicine, Ochsner Clinic Foundations Hospital, New Orleans, LA. From U.S. Government Document, U.S. Department of Health and Human Services, 1981, "Common Poisonous and Injurious Plants.")

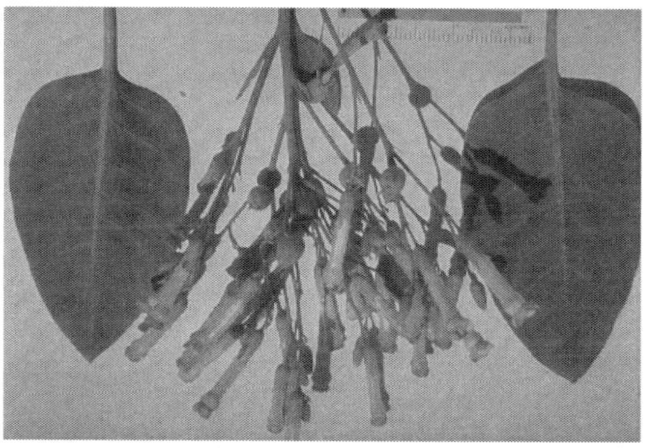

FIGURE 20.11 *Wild tree tobacco, Nicotiana glauca*. Like poison hemlock, *N. glauca* or wild tobacco contains epileptogenic nicotine-like alkaloids. (Courtesy of Charles P. Sea, MD, Department of Emergency Medicine, Ochsner Clinic Foundation Hospital, New Orleans, LA. From U.S. Government Document, U.S. Department of Health and Human Services, 1981, "Common Poisonous and Injurious Plants.")

Miscellaneous Neurotoxic Plants

Hallucinogens—LSD-like effects. Ex: Peyote, morning glory, nutmeg and mace, wormwood, and Hawaiian baby woodrose.

Grass peas and neurolathyrism—The neurotoxic protein, β-oxalylamino-L-alanine (BOAA) causes spastic ataxic paraplegia (mimics MS) following chronic consumption of wild grass peas, *Lathyrus* spp., during famines in Africa and the Middle East.

FIGURE 20.12 Water hemlock, *Cicuta maculata. C. maculata* or water hemlock grows ubiquitously on riverbanks, resembles edible herbs, and contains cicutoxin, which can induce seizures and rhabdomyolysis following ingestion. (Courtesy of David K. Lirette, PhD, LSU School of Public Health, New Orleans, LA.)

Palms and Parkinsonism dementia syndrome—Amyotrophic lateral sclerosis: Cyanobacteria of *Cycas* spp. sago palms produce the neurotoxic protein, β-methylamino-L-alanine (BMAA) that causes PDS-ALS.

Neurotoxicity: Hallucinogens 1

- **Reps:** Wormwood—absinthe, morning glory, nutmeg, and mace (*Myristica fragrans*, resembles MDMA = *ecstasy* toxicity, Hawaiian baby woodrose
- **Toxins:** Morning glory *lysergamide* (LSD-like), peyote *mescaline*, and nutmeg *myristicin* (MMDA)
- Antidote: None
- **Dx:** Initial N and V, diaphoresis, mental status changes, deep sleep (nutmeg), and hallucinations
- **Tx:** GI decontamination, supportive

CNS Toxicity: Absinthe

- **Reps:** Absinthe (wormwood)
- **Indications:** Croup, asthma
- **Latin:** *Artemisia absinthium*
- **Toxin:** *Thujones* (artemisins). (1) Neurotoxicity resembles *camphor*. (2) Antimalarial—Effectively used in SE Asia (Vietnam), even for mefloquine and doxycycline-resistant *Plasmodium falciparum* (Myanmar)

FIGURE 20.13 Wormwood or absinthe, *Artemesia absinthium*, is an herb containing the hallucinogenic neurotoxins, the artemisins, which are also highly effective antimalarials. (From Wikipedia Creative Commons.)

- **Dx:** *Absinthism*—Hallucinations, intellectual deterioration, psychosis, and seizures (most celebrated case of self-mutilation is that of Vincent Van Gogh)
- **Tx:** GI decontamination (lavage + activated charcoal—AC), supportive tx

Wormwood *Artemisia absinthium*

See Figure 20.13.

Morning Glory (Contains Lysergamide) *Ipomoea purpurea*

See Figure 20.14.

FIGURE 20.14 All parts of the morning glory, *Ipomoea purpurea*, especially the seeds, contain an LSD-like lysergamide compound which can produce visual and auditory hallucinations on ingestion. (Courtesy of David K. Lirette, PhD, LSU School of Public Health, New Orleans, LA.)

FIGURE 20.15 Peyote cactus, *Lophophora williamsii*, contains mescaline that can induce a trance-like state with visual and auditory hallucinations on ingestion of the cactus buttons or teas or alcoholic drinks made from the cactus. (From Wikipedia Creative Commons.)

Lophophora williamsii (Peyote Cactus [Contains Mescaline])
See Figure 20.15.

CNS Tox: Hallucinogens

Nutmeg: *Powdered spice grated from the enclosed seed kernel*
Mace: *The soft red cover, or aril, of the kernel*

CNS Tox: Nutmeg and Mace

- **Rep:** East and West (Grenada) Indian nutmeg tree
- **Indic:** Intentional hallucinations, exorcizing demons
- **Latin:** *Myristica fragrans*
- **Toxin:** Myristicin– > meth*amphetamine* metabolites
- **Antidote:** None
- **Dx:** N, V, delirium, euphoria, and deep sleep with hypothermia (such as *Ecstasy,* MDMA, or 4-methyl-2-dimethoxy*amphetamine*)
- **Tx:** GI decontamination (lavage and AC), supportive therapy

CNS Tox: Ephedra

- **Rep:** Ephedra (*ma-huang*)
- **Indic:** Asthma, COPD
- **Toxin:** Ephedrine, pseudoephedrine
- **Antidote:** None
- **Dx:** Sympathomimetic causes HA, nervousness, anxiety, flushing, vomiting (V), increased blood pressure (BP) and heart rate (HR), mania and psychosis, seizures, myocardial infarction (MI), and cerebrovascular accident (CVA) or stroke possible
- **Tx:** GI decontamination (lavage and AC), supportive

FIGURE 20.16 *Ephedra viridis* contains the sympathomimetic amines, ephedrine and pseudoephedrine, both of which are powerful vasoconstrictors and bronchodilators and can cause hypertension and tachycardia on ingestion. Ephedrine-containing preparations are still used in cough and cold preparations to reduce nasal stuffiness. (From Wikipedia Creative Commons.)

Ephedra viridis (Ephedra, *Ma-Huang)*

See Figure 20.16.

Argyreia nervosa (Hawaiian Baby Woodrose)

See Figure 20.17.

FIGURE 20.17 Hawaiian baby woodrose, *Argyreia nervosa*: Like its relative's morning glory seeds, the seeds of the Hawaiian baby woodrose contain ergine, an *LSD-like compound* detected by mass spectrometry. Purchase 100 for $10 seeds online and use 10–12 per hallucinogenic trip. (From Wikipedia Creative Commons.)

Sympathomimetics

Synephrine vs. Ephedrine

- **Rep:** *Citrus aurantium* (Bitter orange)
- **Toxin:** *Synephrine*, an indirect-acting sympathomimetic amine used in dietary supplements (ephedra-free Xanadrine®)
- **Antidote:** None
- **Dx:** Sympathomimetic causes HA, nervousness, anxiety, flushing, syncope, ↑BP and HR, ↑ QT, MI, and CVA reported
- **Tx:** GI decontamination (lavage and AC), supportive

CNS Tox: Nutmeg and Mace

- **Rep:** East and West Indian nutmeg tree
- **Latin:** *Myristica fragrans*
- **Toxin:** *Myristicin*–> an MAOI with a meth*amphetamine* metabolite (methoxy-methylene–dioxyamphetamine), *greater amount in mace*
- **Antidote:** None
- **Dx:** N, V, delirium, euphoria, and deep sleep with hypothermia (such as *ecstasy,* MDMA, or 4-methyl-2-dimethoxy*amphetamine*)
- **Tx:** GI decontamination (lavage and AC), supportive therapy

Plant Hallucinogens

Salvia divinorum (Figure 20.18)

- **Chem:** *Salvia divinorum*: Diviner—Seer's sage long used by Mazatec shamans of Oaxaca to induce visionary trances in spiritual ceremonies contains the diterpiniod, *salvinorum A*, and unique *kappa opioid receptor agonist.*
- **Epid (United States):** 2006: 1.8 M over age 12 had used salvia, 750 k that year; 2007:1 M users that year.
- **Methods:** Ingesting fresh leaves, extracts of dried leaves in seasonings, and tinctures of leaves soaked in H_2O/EtOH.
- Salvia leaves and flowers (such as shade and rarely blooms).
- **Clin:** Spiritual and other visions, fluctuating mood–insight–connectedness–self-confidence concentration–temperature sensations; lightheadedness, flying–floating; calmness—"afterglow."
- **Addiction potential:** Possible, low. Driving impaired.
- **Regulation:** Not scheduled, use is illegal in several states, including LA.
- **Availability:** Increasingly available on the Internet.

Salvia is locally sold in states where legal and on the Internet everywhere.

FIGURE 20.18 A species of *Salvia* or sage, *Salvia divinorum*, long used by Mazatec shamans of Oaxaca to induce visionary trances in spiritual ceremonies, contains the diterpiniod, *salvinorum A*, a unique *kappa opioid receptor agonist*. Salvia is being increasingly abused by adolescents seeking drug-induced highs from drinking mixtures of Salvia leaves in alcohol or smoking dried and rolled Salvia leaves. (From Wikipedia Creative Commons.)

CNS Tox: St. John's Wort

- **Rep:** St. John's wort (*Hypericum perforatum*) is used very *effectively* to self-medicate mild anxiety, nervousness, and depression.
- **Toxins:** Hyperforin > hypericin, and pseudohypericin; inhibit central reuptake of serotonin, dopamine, epinephrine, and norepinephrine.
- **Antidote:** None.
- **Dx:** Serotonin syndrome alone or with SSRIs or MAOIs.
- **Tx:** Supportive, antipyretics, and BZs.

Hypericum perforatum (St. John's Wort)

See Figure 20.19.

CNS Tox: Sedatives—Sleep Aids

Kava kava, *Piper methysticum*. Sedative and sleep aid associated with muscle weakness, potentiates alcohol and sedative—hypnotics, especially the BZs, such as Xanax®. Long-term use causes kava dermopathy (kavaism): yellowish discolored, dry flakey skin.

FIGURE 20.19 St. John's wort, *Hypericum perforatum*, contains several selective reuptake inhibitors and has proven to be effective in some cases of depression, but can induce the serotonin syndrome if taken with other serotonin reuptake inhibitors, serotonin releasers, or monoamine oxidase inhibitors. (From Wikipedia Creative Commons.)

CNS Tox: Sedatives—Sleep Aids

Valerian root Valeriana officinalis Perennial with scented pink–white flowers whose roots are dried for extracts that are *GABA agonists orally* taken as sedatives, anxiolytics, and sleep aids. Potentiates alcohol, sedative—hypnotics (BZs).

GI Toxins—Outline

- Goldenseal
- Pokeweed
- Herbal poisonings

GI Tox: Goldenseal

- **Rep:** Goldenseal is an herb frequently used as an oral astringent for canker sores and to mask the presence of illicit drugs on urine screens. Goldenseal is **ineffective as an undetected adulterant** and is easily detected by GC/MS (=+ drug test)

- **Latin:** *Hydrastis canadensis*
- **Toxin:** Hydrastine
- **Antidote:** None
- **Dx:** N, V, D, convulsions, paralysis, and respiratory failure
- **Tx:** GI decontamination (lavage and AC), supportive

Miscellaneous GI Tract Toxicity

"Poke-Salad Annie"

- **Reps:** Pokeweed, English ivy, yew, and horse chestnut
- **Toxin:** *Phytolaccine* (pokeweed)
- **Antidote:** None
- **Dx:** N, V, D, and abdominal cramps—colic, lymphocytosis (pokeweed)
- **Tx:** GI decontamination (lavage and AC)

Phytolacca americana (Pokeberry or Pokeweed)

See Figure 20.20 and Table 20.2.

FIGURE 20.20 Pokeberries from the pokeweed or pokeberry plant, *Phytolacca americana*, contain phytolaccine that can cause gastrointestinal distress if consumed raw and not detoxified by prior parboiling. Pokeberry can also induce an increase in the number of circulating lymphocytes or lymphocytosis for unknown reasons. (Courtesy of David K. Lirette, PhD, LSU School of Public Health, New Orleans, LA.)

Table 20.2 Hepatotoxins

Class	Toxins	Diagnosis	Antidote/Treatment
Pennyroyal	Pulegone—CYP450 toxin, glutathione depleter	Minty breath, seizures, and external and vaginal bleeding	Gastrointestinal decontamination, NAC
Pyrrolizidines = comfrey and coltsfoot	Pyrrolizidine alkaloids	Hepatic veno-occlusion, cirrhosis, and liver cancer	Gastrointestinal decontamination, supportive therapy, and monitors liver function

Gastrointestinal Toxicity

Hepatotoxicity Group

Hypoglycemic group: Hypoglycin A: Causes severely low blood sugar.

Ex: Ackee fruit (*Blighia sapida*)—Florida and Caribbean (Jamaica).

Pyrrolizidine alkaloids: Block veins in the liver (Budd–Chiari syndrome—OCPs are the only other chemicals that can do this) and the lungs. Ex: Comfrey and coltsfoot.

Hepatotoxicity

Ackee and Vomiting Sickness

- **Rep:** Ackee tree and Ackee tree fruit.
- **Toxins**; *hypoglycin* A inhibits G-6-PD and causes *Jamaican vomiting sickness.*
- **Antidote:** 50% dextrose.
- **Dx:** Severe N and V, hypoglycemia—2° decreased gluconeogenesis, mental status Δs, hypothermia, metabolic acidosis, seizures, and ↓ liver fx—centrilobular hepatic necrosis.
- **Tx:** GI decontamination (lavage + AC).

Hepatotoxicity: Pyrrolizidine Alkaloids (See Table 20.2)

- **Reps**: Comfrey, coltsfoot.
- **Toxins:** Hepatotoxic *pyrrazolidine alkaloids.* Sassafras contains *safrole*, a possible hepatic carcinogen.
- **Antidote:** None.
- **Dx:** Hepatotoxicity, specifically hepatic veno-occlusive disease (comfrey, coltsfoot), hepatocellular carcinoma (sassafras).
- **Tx:** GI decontamination (lavage + AC).

Herbal hepatotoxins: Both comfrey and coltsfoot are capable of causing hepatotoxicity with hepatic vein occlusion (Budd–Chiari syndrome) following chronic ingestion of teas, tablets, tinctures, or powders containing the pyrrolizidine alkaloids in these herbs.

FIGURE 20.21 All parts of the common comfrey, *Symphytum officinale*, have been distilled for internal use by folk medicine practitioners into teas and tinctures to treat gastrointestinal and neuromuscular disorders. All contain hepatotoxic pyrrolizidine alkaloids that have been associated with hepatic vein occlusion (Budd–Chiari syndrome). (From Wikipedia Creative Commons.)

Symphytum officinale (Comfrey)
See Figure 20.21.

Tussilago farfara (Coltsfoot)
See Figure 20.22.

Miscellaneous Herbal Hepatotoxins

***Sassafras albidum* (sassafras, gumbo filé powder, and *mamou* tea):** Contains the potential hepatotoxin and carcinogen = safrole, a potential carcinogen, and a potential inducer of hepatocellular carcinoma

Kidney stones, renal cancer: *Aristolochia* spp. (clematis vines), Balkan endemic nephropathy (Table 20.3)

Nephrogenic diabetes insipidus: Excessive excretion of dilute urine

Tx: DDAVP

***Colchicum autumnale* (autumn crocus):** Colchicine, glory lily

FIGURE 20.22 All parts of the coltsfoot, *Tussilago farfara*, have been distilled for internal use by folk medicine practitioners into teas and syrups for treatment of common colds, especially for cough suppression. All contain hepatotoxic pyrrolizidine alkaloids that have been associated with hepatic vein occlusion (Budd–Chiari syndrome). (From Wikipedia Creative Commons.)

Miscellaneous DI drugs: # 1 = lithium, methoxyflurane, propoxyphene, demeclocycline, and ifosfimide

SIADH: Reduced urine output, hypervolemia, and dilutional hyponatremia

Tx: ↓ Fluids, ↑ Na

Vinca alkaloids: Vinblastine, vincristine

Table 20.3 Miscellaneous Herbal Toxins

Class	Toxins	Diagnosis	Antidote/Treatment
Aristolochia (birthwort—abortifacient)	Aristolochic acid	Renal fibrosis and renal failure, vaginal bleeding	Supportive therapy, gastrointestinal decontamination
Garlic	Sulfoxides—alliin and allicin and ajoene (ASA like)	Nausea, vomiting, diarrhea, dermatitis, external bleeding, and ASA potentiation	Supportive therapy, gastrointestinal decontamination
Ginseng	Panax acid = ginseng abuse syndrome (GAS)	Hypertension, tachycardia, agitation, insomnia, and morning diarrhea	Supportive therapy, gastrointestinal decontamination
Chamomile	Histamine	Cross-reactions with Compositae annuals (ragweed, daisy, and chrysanthemums)	Antihistamines, bronchodialators

Other chemotherapeutics: Cyclophosphamide, cisplatinum

Misc. drugs causing SIADH: # 1 = thiazides, chlorpropamide, TCAs, SSRIs, phenothiazines, and valproic acid

Herbal Nephrotoxicity: Balkan Endemic Nephropathy

Balkan Endemic Nephropathy

- **Dist:** First described in 1950s in Balkans among local ages 50s–60s
- **Clin:** Renal tubular acidosis, glycosuria, hyperuricosuria, hypouricemia, and proteinuria <1 g/d
- **Path:** Interstitial and peri-glomerular fibrosis, no inflammatory cell infiltrates, and normal glomeruli; transitional cell cancers develop in upper tracts in 30–40%
- **Etiol:** Exact etiology unknown, aristolochic acid-contaminated flour by seeds of *Aristolochia clematis* versus recently isolated coronavirus versus transmissible gastroenteritis virus
- **Tx:** HD, screen for papillary transitional cell cancer

CRF: Chinese Herbal Nephropathy

Herbal (Chinese) Endemic Nephropathy

- **Dist:** First described in 1991 in Belgium among women consuming Chinese herbal meds at a weight-loss clinic
- **Clin:** Abnormalities of tubal function predominate as in BEN
- **Path:** Interstitial and periglomerular fibrosis, no infiltrates, glomeruli normal, ↑ and incidence transitional cell cancers
- **Etiol:** *Aristolochia* spp. herbs containing aristolochic acid that can form DNA adducts in patients with HEN
- **Tx:** HD, screen for cancer

Toxic Herb–Drug Interactions

- **Compositae cross-sensitizers:** Allergic rhinitis, "hay fever." Ex: *Echinacea*, chrysanthemum, and daisy
- **Antiplatelet effects/bleeding:** Hemorrhagic stroke. Ex: feverfew, Gingko, garlic, and ginseng
- **Cardiac effects:** Hypertension, MI. Ex: *Ephedra*, licorice, and *Yohimbe*
- **Sedative/CNS effects:** Sedation, serotonin syndrome. Ex: Kava, valerian

Steroid Effects: Licorice

Glycyrrhiza glabra (*licorice*) contains the glycoside, *glyzyrrhizin*, which inhibits conversion of cortisol into cortisone causing aldosterone-like effects with ↑ Na and ↑ water retention, ↓ K, weakness, HTN, and arrhythmias. Will potentiate digitalis toxicity.

Table 20.4 Toxic Herb–Drug Interactions

Herbs	Drugs	Toxicities
Ephedra[a]	BP drugs	Hypertension, MI, and CVA
Feverfew	ASA, anticoagulants	Bleeding
Gingko[a]	ASA, anticoagulants	Bleeding
Ginseng[a]	ASA, anticoagulants	Bleeding
Kava	BZs (Xanax®)	Delirium
Licorice[a]	Digoxin	Hypertension, CHF
St. John's wort[a]	MAOIs, SSRIs	Depression, suicide, and serotonin syndrome
Yohimbe[a]	Antihypertensives	Hypertension, MI, and CVA

Note: ASA = acetyl–salicylic acid; CVA = cerebrovascular accident; CHF = congestive heart failure; MAOIs = monoamine oxidase inhibitors; MI = myocardial infarction; SSRIs = selective serotonin reuptake inhibitors.

[a] Fatal cases reported.

Toxic Herb–Drug Interactions: Cardiovascular (See Table 20.4)

Yohimbe: Yohimbine is a plant alkaloid and α-2 antagonist derived from the bark of the West African evergreen, Pausinystalia yohimbe, which is effective for ED, but causes hypertensive crises and serotonin syndrome when combined with amphetamines SSRIs, SSNRIs, and all other indirect vasopressors, including dextromethorphan, tramadol, and meperidine (Table 20.4).

Hypervitaminosis

Megadose Vitamin Poisoning

Vitamin Therapy

1. Vitamins are used therapeutically to manage several diseases. Ex: Vitamin A for acne.
2. Vitamins are not usually reported as medications.
3. With the exception of folic acid for women of childbearing age and vitamin D for women with osteoporosis, there are *no indications* for empiric vitamin therapy in developed countries.

Potential Toxins (*Fatalities)

- Vitamin A*
- Vitamin E*
- Vitamin K
- Vitamin C
- Vitamin B_6

- Vitamin D*—Also a commonly used rat poison
- Niacin B_3 and nicotinic acid*
- Tryptophan* (amino acid and serotonin precursor)

Hypervitaminosis A

Toxicology

- **Name:** Vitamin A, deficiency = *xerophthalmia*
- **Chem:** Retinol
- **Source:** Liver and vegetable carotenoids
- **RDI (females, 25–50):** 2700 IU, males slightly higher
- **Toxic dose:** 25,000 IU/kg bolus, 25,000 IU/d × 30 d—such doses have been used to treat cystic acne
- **Antidote:** None

Clinical Findings

- **Dx:** Thinning of skin and nails, desquamation, alopecia, bone changes, hepatotoxicity = *cirrhosis, benign intracranial hypertension* (BIH), or *pseudotumor cerebri* = HA, blurred vision, diplopia from CN VI palsy, optic nerve atrophy, and blindness
- **Tx:** Withdrawal, support, and spinal taps + diuretics + prednisone for BIH

Hypervitaminosis E

Toxicology

- **Name:** Vitamin E
- **Chem:** α-Tocopherol
- **Source:** Meats, grains, and nuts
- **RDI (females, 25–50):** 15 mg/d, males 20 mg/d
- **Toxic dose:** 400 mg/d
- **Antidote:** None

Clinical Findings

- **Dx:** Nausea, vomiting, diarrhea, flatulence, increases *epoxidation of vitamin K to its inactive epoxide form, and potentiates warfarin and ASA with bleeding* from decreased platelet adhesiveness
- **Tx:** Withdrawal, support

Vitamin K

The vitamin K group includes fat-soluble vitamins derived from green leafy vegetables, phylloquinones, meats/fish, menaquinones that are activated by VK 2,3 epoxide reductase and VK quinone/hydroquinone reductase to active vitamin K hydroquinone (quinol). Both enzymes are blocked by warfarin (coumadin) and the supercoumarin rodenticides. Menaquinones are produced in the gut by bacterial action (deficient in newborns).

Hypervitaminosis C

Toxicology

- **Name:** Vitamin C, deficiency = *scurvy* = anemia, gingivitis, petechiae, poor wound healing, and bleeding
- **Chem:** Ascorbic acid
- **Source:** Citrus fruits, red fruits, and vegetables
- **RDI:** 60 mg/d
- **Toxic dose:** 2 g/d
- **Antidote:** None
- **Use:** Converts hexavalent Cr to less-toxic trivalent Cr

Clinical Findings

- **Dx:** Diarrhea, *localized esophagitis*, cystine and oxalic acid urinary crystals and stones, unlikely *nephrolithiasis*, and urosepsis; ↑ uric acid excretion → acute *gout*; ↑ Fe absorption → hemosiderosis, *siderophagic* ↑ *Vibrio* and *Yersinia* sepsis risks. *Nephrolithiasis* risks ↑ by concomitant vitamin D, as in vitamin D-fortified milk.
- **Tx:** Withdrawal, fluid loading, and ESWL.
- **Hypervitaminosis C:** *Urinary calcium oxalate crystals* associated with *kidney stones*. Potentiated by concomitant *vitamin D intake*; not vitamin C alone.

Vitamin Deficiencies

Avitaminosis A—*Xerophthalmia*
Avitaminosis C—*Scurvy*

Pyridoxine (B_6) Neuropathy

Toxicology

- **Name:** Vitamin B_6
- **Chem:** Pyridoxine
- **Source:** Meats, cereals, and vegetables
- **RDI (adults):** 2 mg/d
- **Toxic dose:** 150–500 mg bolus, 150–500 mg/d
- **Antidote:** None

Clinical Findings

- **Dx:** Distal, "glove and stocking" *sensory, vibratory, and positional (ataxic) peripheral axonopathy* 2° axonal degeneration; crippling, painful, and sensory peripheral neuropathy may be permanent.
- **Tx:** Withdrawal, support.

Hypervitaminosis D

Toxicology

- **Name:** Vitamin D, deficiency = *rickets* = softening and deformation of long bones
- **Chem:** Cholecalciferol
- **Source:** Produced in skin by cholesterol + UV exposure
- **RDI:** Females, 200 IU/d (5 mcg)—males, 400 IU/d (10)
- **Toxic dose:** > RDA, vitamin D-fortified milk
- **Antidote:** None

Clinical Findings

- **Dx:** Anorexia, N, V, D, HTN, hypercalcemia, cardiac and vascular, and ectopic calcifications
- Hypercalcuria
- Nephrocalcinosis
- **Tx:** Withdrawal, support, fluids, diuretics, prednisone, calcitonin, and biphosphonates

Niacin (B_3) Toxicity

Toxicology

- **Name:** Niacin, vitamin B_3, def = *pellagra* = *3Ds* = *d*iarrhea, *d*ermatitis, *d*ementia, stomatitis, and glossitis
- **Chemical:** Nicotinic acid Vacor® poisoning → niacin, ↓ cholesterol
- **Source:** Meat, fish, poultry, cereals, nuts, and vegetables
- **RDI (adults):** 6–13 mg/d
- **Toxic dose:** 60+ mg po bolus, 60–1000 mg/d
- **Antidote:** Preemptive ASA

Clinical Findings

- **Dx:** Prostaglandin D2-mediated cutaneous *flushing* and vasodilation → potentiates migraine, pruritus, HA, N, V, D, abdominal cramping, *niacin hepatitis → centrilobular cholestasis, and parenchymal necrosis*
- **Tx:** Withdrawal, support, and prostaglandin inhibitors

Vitamin Deficiencies

Niacin Deficiency—*Pellagra*
Avitaminosis D—*Infantile Rickets*

Tryptophan

Eosinophilia-Myalgia Syndrome

Toxicology

- **Name:** Tryptophan, an amino acid (protein) and serotonin (5-HT) precursor

- **Chem:** l-Tryptophan
- **Source:** All animal proteins
- **RDI (adults):** 30–60 mg/d
- **Toxic dose:** 150+ mg/d × 2+ weeks
- **Antidote:** None

Clinical Findings

- **Dx:** *Eosinophilia* + no indication of infection or neoplasm + generalized *myalgias*, pulmonary infiltrates, polyarteritis, and sclerodermiform skin lesions. Resembles *toxic rapeseed oil syndrome* (aniline toxicity, Spain, 1981).
- **Tx:** Market withdrawal of recombinant l-tryptophan, formerly used for PMS and insomnia.

Conclusions

There cannot be two kinds of medicine—conventional and alternative. There is only medicine that has been adequately tested and medicine that has not .... Alternative treatments should be subjected to scientific testing no less rigorous than required for conventional treatments.

Angell M, Kassirer J: NEJM 339, 1998.

Chapter 21

Common Poisonous Household and Garden Plants

Outline 444
Poisonous Plants 444
Na Channel Openers 447
Na and Ach Channel Openers 449
Neutotoxic Herbs and Plants 452
Neurotoxicity 455
Miscellaneous Herbal Hepatotoxins 467
Plant Poisonings. 471
Toxicodendron Group 472

Outline

- Epidemiology (the causes and outcomes) of plant poisonings
- The most common plant poisonings
- The most common lethal plant poisonings
- The toxicology of plant poisonings
- Rapid site identification of poisonous plants
- Syndromic ("toxidromic") evaluation and management of the plant-poisoned patient

Poisonous Plants

Epidemiology (See Tables 21.1 and 21.2)

- 10% of all calls to U.S. Poison Control Centers concern plant ingestion and toxicity.
- 80% of these calls involve children less than 6 years of age.
- **Household plant poisonings are most common:** 80% asymptomatic, <20% symptomatic, <7% hospital admits, case fatality rate = ingesting the poisonous plant and died/all who ingested the poisonous plant = 0.001%.
- Outdoor plant ingestions are now increasing among adolescents and adults seeking hallucinogenic effects, and have greater toxicity than indoor plant ingestions.

Plant Toxicology

- Cardiovascular (CV) toxicity = heart arrhythmias*

Table 21.1 Substances Poisoning Children <6 Years

Ranking	Substance	Frequency	Percent
1	Cosmetics/personal care products	168,021	13.4
2	Cleaning agents	124,021	10.0
3	Analgesics	98,237	7.9
4	Topical preparations	93,482	7.4
5	Foreign bodies	91,101	7.4
6	Cough/cold products	67,494	5.4
7	Plants	55,078	4.4
8	Pesticides	52,174	4.2
9	Vitamins	48,989	3.9
10	Antihistamines	34,401	2.8

Source: AAPCC-TESS.

* Fatalities reported in the United States.

Table 21.2 Frequency of Plant Poisonings by Types (All Ages)

Rank	Botanical Name	Common Name	Frequency
1	*Spathiphyllum* spp.	Peace lily	2972
2	*Ilex* spp.	Holly	2597
3	*Philodendron* spp.[a]	Philodendron	2421
4	*Euphorbia pulcherrima*	Poinsettia	2206
5	*Phytolacca americana*	Pokeweed	1697
6	*Toxicodendron radicans*	Poison ivy	1490
7	*Ficus* spp.	Weeping fig, rubber tree	1136
8	*Solanum* spp.[a]	Nightshade	1046
9	*Malus* spp.[a]	Apple (kernels-seeds)	920
10	*Schlumbergera bridgesii*	Christmas cactus	918
11	*Crassula* spp.	Jade plant	817
12	*Nerium oleander*[a]	Oleander	785

Source: AAPCC-TESS.
[a] Deaths.

- *Neurotoxicity* = Seizures, paralysis, coma*
- *Cytotoxicity* = Acidosis, multi-organ failure*
- *Nephrotoxicity* = Kidney stones, cancer, or failure*
- *Gastrointestinal toxicity* = Nausea (N), vomiting (V), diarrhea (D), dehydration, hypovolemic shock*
- *Dermatotoxicity* = #1 poison ivy > oak > sumac vs. *phytophototoxicity* = #1 limes, then celery and parsnips; no deaths reported, but urushiol from poison ivy + oak + sumac has now been *weaponized* for chemical-tear gas warfare

Cardiovascular Toxicity

- **Cardiac glycoside group*:** All cause digitalis (digoxin)-like poisoning
  Ex: Foxglove, oleander, lily-of-the-valley, summer snowflake (Star-of-Bethlehem), red squill
- **Sodium channel openers*:** All cause both digitalis-like poisoning and neuromuscular paralysis
  Ex: Monkshood, mountain laurel, hellebore (hellbane), azalea, rhododendron, death camas
- **Sodium and calcium channel blockers*:** Digitalis-like poisoning, Vtach-severe ↓BP; mitotic inhibition
  Ex: *Taxus* spp. (yews) only; can both treat and prevent breast cancer

* Fatalities reported in the United States.

CV Tox: Cardiac Glycosides

- **Reps:** Oleander, foxglove, lily-of-the-valley and summer snowflake (Star-of-Bethlehem)
- **Toxins:** *Digitalis*, oleandrin, digitoxigenin
- **Antidote:** DigiBind® (digoxin-specific Fab's)
- **Dx:** N, V, dysrhythmias
- **Tx:** GI decontamination (lavage + AC), monitor ECG and dig levels

Nerium oleander (Oleander—Contains Oleandrin)

See Figure 21.1.

Digitalis purpurea (Foxglove—Contains Digitalis-Like Glycosides)

See Figure 21.2.

Convallaria majalis (Lily-of-the-Valley—Contains Digitalis-Like Plant Glycosides)

See Figure 21.3.

FIGURE 21.1 (See color insert.) All parts of the oleander shrub are highly toxic and contain digitalis glycosides that can cause nausea, vomiting, tachyarrhythmias, and cardiac conduction disturbances, including complete heart block, on ingestion. Oleander grows up to 9 m tall in warm beachfront locations and produces abundant white, yellow, pink, or red flowers. Oleander has poisoned beach-goers who have selected oleander branches to use as skewers to roast their hot dogs over beachside bonfires. (Courtesy of David K. Lirette, PhD, LSU School of Public Health, New Orleans, LA.)

FIGURE 21.2 The cardiotoxic *Digitalis purpurea* (foxglove) plant, a common garden flower, contains high concentrations of digitalis-like glycosides (digitalis, digitoxigenin), especially in its leaves. (From Wikipedia Creative Commons.)

FIGURE 21.3 Lily-of-the-valley, *Convallaria majalis.* Like foxglove and oleander, *Convallaria majalis* (lily-of-the-valley), a common household plant, also contains cardiac glycosides, such as convallotoxin, that will heighten vagal tone and cardiac automaticity following ingestion. (From Wikipedia Creative Commons.)

Na Channel Openers

CV Tox: Aconitine Group

- **Rep:** Monkshood (wolfsbane).
- **Toxin:** Parasympathomimetic *aconitine* alkaloids cause prolonged opening cardiac Na channels with ↑ vagomimesis and ventricular automaticity = ↓ HR + arrhythmias.
- **Antidote:** None.

FIGURE 21.4 *Aconitum napellus* (monkshood), so named for its purple flower that resembles a helmet or monk's hood, contains the cardiotoxin, aconitine, which prolongs the opening of cardiac sodium channels inducing ventricular dysrhythmias. (From Wikipedia Creative Commons.)

- **Dx:** N, V, D, paresthesias, atrioventricular (AV) block, ventricular (V) tachycardia, ventricular (V) fibrillation, respiratory failure.
- **Tx:** GI decontamination (lavage + AC), temporary pacemaker.

Monkshood, *Aconitum napellus*
See Figure 21.4.

CV Tox: Veratrum Group

- **Rep:** Green hellbane or hellebore (*Veratrum viride*)
- **Toxins:** Veratrin and others
- **Antidote:** None
- **Dx:** Initial N, V, D, then bradycardia, VT-VF, respiratory failure
- **Tx:** GI decontamination (lavage + AC), atropine, vasopressors (dopamine)

Veratrum viride (Green Hellebore)
See Figure 21.5.

CV Tox: Zigadenus Group

- **Rep:** *Zigadenus* species, death camas or death lilies
- **Toxins:** Veratrin and others
- **Antidote:** None
- **Dx:** Initial profound gastrointestinal toxicity with N, V, D, then bradycardia and hypotension, potentially fatal tachyarrhythmias, ventricular tachycardia (VT), ventricular fibrillation (VF), cardiorespiratory failure
- **Tx:** GI decontamination (lavage + AC), atropine and dopamine

FIGURE 21.5 Like monkshood, green hellbane or hellebore, *Veratrum viridae*, also contains a cardiotoxin, veratrin, which prolongs the opening of cardiac sodium channels inducing ventricular dysrhythmias. (From Wikipedia Creative Commons.)

Zigadenus glaberrimus (Death Camas or Death Lilies)
See Figure 21.6.

Na and Ach Channel Openers

CV Tox: Grayanotoxins

- **Reps:** Azalea, rhododendron, mountain laurel. Note: Honey made by honeybees from local azalea and rhododendron, and laurel plant nectar may contain grayanotoxins.

FIGURE 21.6 **(See color insert.)** *Zigadenus glaberrimus*. Death camas or death lilies are perennial, onion-like bulbs with showy flower stalk with 6-petal flowers with green hearts. All parts of the plant are cardiotoxic and potentially fatal on ingestion. (Courtesy of David K. Lirette, PhD, LSU School of Public Health, New Orleans, LA.)

- **Toxins:** Parasympathomimetic oily diterpene-*grayanotoxins* force open both cardiac nicotinic and muscarinic Na channels.
- **Antidote:** None.
- **Dx:** GI sx, salivation–lacrimation–urination–defecation–emesis–SLUDE, weakness, bradydysrhythmias, ataxia, paresthesias, seizures, ↓BP.
- **Tx:** GI decontamination (lavage + activated charcoal [AC]), atropine and vasopressors as indicated.

***Azalea, Rhododendron* spp. (Azalea)**
See Figure 21.7.

***Rhododendron ponticum* (True Rhododendron)**
See Figure 21.8.

CV Tox: Na and Ca Channel Blocker (Phases 0 and 2)

- **Mech:** Plant alkaloid from rare *Pacific yew tree bark* (*Taxus brevifolia*); Na and Ca channel blocker and metaphase inhibitor of tubulin disassembly
- **Indic:** Breast cancer treatment and prevention
- **Tox:** N, V, abdominal pain, ↓ HR-conduction blocks, ventricular dysrhythmias, paresthesias, ataxia, seizures
- **Tx:** Atropine, amiodarone, BZs, Na bicarbonate; DigiBind® ineffective
- **Taxus spp. (*T. baccata*):** Yew shrub-tree; most parts toxic: leaves and seeds, not red aril

FIGURE 21.7 Azalea (grayanotoxins), *Rhododendron azalea* spp. Rhododendrons and azaleas are beautiful spring-flowering perennials of the same family, commonly cultivated throughout the temperate United States, which contain the cardiotoxic grayanotoxins, veratrine and andromedotoxin. (Courtesy of Charles P. Sea, MD, Department of Emergency Medicine, Ochsner Clinic Foundation Hospital, New Orleans, LA. Original Source: U.S. Government Document, U.S. Department of Health and Human Services, 1981, "Common Poisonous and Injurious Plants.")

FIGURE 21.8 True rhododendron, *Rhododendron ponticum*. (From Wikipedia Creative Commons.)

Taxine is a plant alkaloid derived from *Pacific yew tree bark* (*Taxus brevifolia*) that is both a Na and Ca channel blocker (phases 0 and 2) and a metaphase inhibitor of tubulin disassembly. Used to treat and prevent breast cancer.

Taxus Species (Yew)

See Figure 21.9.

FIGURE 21.9 Yew, *Taxus* species. One of the many varieties of yew shrub or tree that contains taxine, a cardiac sodium–potassium channel blocker that can cause cardiac arrest on ingestion. The anticancer drug, tamoxifen, is derived from a *Taxus* spp. shrub or tree, the Pacific yew. (Courtesy of Charles P. Sea, MD, Department of Emergency Medicine, Ochsner Clinic Foundation Hospital, New Orleans, LA. Original Source: U.S. Government Document, U.S. Department of Health and Human Services, 1981, "Common Poisonous and Injurious Plants.")

Neurotoxic Herbs and Plants

- **Anticholinergics, the belladonna alkaloid-containing plants:** *"Red as a beet, blind as a bat, hot as Hades, mad as a hatter"*
  Ex: Nightshade, Jimson weed, angel's trumpets = *Brugmasia*, *Solandra*
- **Nicotinic plants:** Nicotine + caffeine-like overdoses
  Ex: Poison hemlock, lobelia, tobacco
- **Convulsants:** Seizures, paralysis
  Ex: Water hemlock, strychnine, camphor

Neurotoxicity Belladonna Alkaloids

- **Reps:** Nightshade, jessamine, Jimson weed (thornapple), *Brugmasia* and *Solandra* spp. (Angel's trumpet, common in the southern United States), mandrake, henbane
- **Toxins:** *Atropine* = hyoscyamine, *scopolamine* = hyoscine
- **Antidote:** Physostigmine for CNS effects
- **Dx:** Atropine tox = F, dry mouth, tachycardia, ileus, urinary retention, hallucinations, seizures, *"red as a beet, etc"*
- **Tx:** GI decontamination

Datura stramonium (Jimson Weed, Thornapple)

See Figure 21.10.

FIGURE 21.10 Jimson weed (thornapple), *Datura stramonium*. The belladonna alkaloid containing Jimson weed or Thornapple plant (*Datura stramonium*). Legend holds that early American colonists encouraged occupying British troops to consume salads of local "Jimson" (for Jamestown, Virginia) weed and to suffer the central and peripheral anticholinergic consequences. (From Wikipedia Creative Commons.)

FIGURE 21.11 The angel's trumpet plants, *Brugmasia* spp. and *Solandra* spp. are very common perennials in the southern United States, and contain a scopolamine-like belladonna alkaloid that can cause a central anticholinergic syndrome on ingestion. The angel's trumpet plant was introduced into the temperate and tropical areas of the United States from southeastern Brazil for landscaping purposes. All parts of the plants are toxic and contain a combination of several anticholinergic tropine alkaloids, including atropine, hyoscyamine, and scopolamine. Since the 1990s, there have been increasing U.S. reports of central anticholinergic syndromes following the ingestion of teas and potions made from angel's trumpet in adolescents seeking legal hallucinogens. (Courtesy of David K. Lirette, Ph.D., LSU School of Public Health, New Orleans, LA.)

Brugmasia suaveolens (Angel's Trumpet)

See Figure 21.11.

Nicotine Group

- **Reps:** Poison hemlock*: Resembles Queen Anne's lace (wild carrot); wild tree tobacco (Socrates was a famous victim)
- **Toxin:** *Coniine, nicotine*
- **Antidote:** None
- **Dx:** Initial N and V; then diaphoresis, tachycardia, tremors, seizures, ascending paralysis, respiratory failure, coma
- **Tx:** GI decontamination (lavage + AC), supportive care

Conium maculatum (Poison Hemlock, Note: Fern-Like Leaves)

See Figure 21.12.

* Fatalities reported in the United States.

FIGURE 21.12 *Conium maculatum* (poison hemlock) resembles common herbs, such as wild carrot, parsnip, and Queen Anne's lace, and contains the nicotinic receptor blocker, coniine, which induces seizures and paralysis on ingestions. (Courtesy of Charles P. Sea, MD, Department of Emergency Medicine, Ochsner Clinic Foundations Hospital, New Orleans, LA. Original Sources: U.S. Government Document, U.S. Department of Health and Human Services, 1981, "Common Poisonous and Injurious Plants.")

Nicotiana glauca (Wild Tree Tobacco)

See Figure 21.13.

Neurotoxicity: Convulsants

- **Rep:** Water hemlock, also resembles the herb—Queen Anne's lace (wild carrot)
- **Toxin:** Cicutoxin
- **Antidote:** None

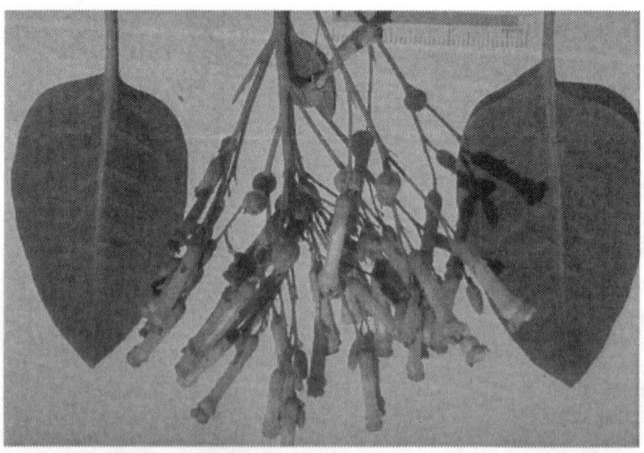

FIGURE 21.13 Wild tree tobacco, *Nicotiana glauca*. Like poison hemlock, *Nicotiana glauca* or wild tobacco contains epileptogenic nicotine-like alkaloids. (Courtesy of Charles P. Sea, MD, Department of Emergency Medicine, Ochsner Clinic Foundation Hospital, New Orleans, LA. Original Source: U.S. Government Document, U.S. Department of Health and Human Services, 1981, "Common Poisonous and Injurious Plants.")

FIGURE 21.14 Water hemlock, *Cicuta maculata. C. maculata* or water hemlock grows ubiquitously on riverbanks, resembles edible herbs, and contains cicutoxin, which can induce seizures and rhabdomyolysis following ingestion. (Courtesy of David K. Lirette, PhD, LSU School of Public Health, New Orleans, LA.)

- **Dx:** N, V, abdominal cramps, *status epilepticus*, subsequent rhabdomyolysis, ↑ CPK, CFR = 30%
- **Tx:** GI decontamination (lavage + AC), anticonvulsants (barbiturates, benzodiazepines), *cicutoxin is dialyzable* = by hemodialysis HD

***Cicuta maculata* (Epileptogenic Water Hemlock) (Leaves Nonfern-Like, Yellow Flowers)**

See Figure 21.14.

Neurotoxicity

Miscellaneous Neurotoxic Plants

Hallucinogens: LSD-like effects. Ex: Peyote, morning glory, nutmeg and mace, wormwood, Hawaiian baby woodrose.

Grass peas and Neurolathyrism: The neurotoxic protein, β-oxalylamino-L-alanine (BOAA) causes spastic ataxic paraplegia (mimics MS) following chronic consumption of wild grass peas, *Lathyrus* spp., during famines in Africa and the Middle East.

Palms and Parkinsonism Dementia Syndrome: Amyotrophic Lateral Sclerosis: Cyanobacteria of *Cycas* spp. sago palms produce the neurotoxic protein, β-methylamino-L-alanine (BMAA) which causes PDS-ALS.

Neurotoxicity: Hallucinogens

- **Reps:** Wormwood–absinthe, morning glory, nutmeg and mace (*Myristica fragrans*, resembles MDMA = *Ecstasy* toxicity), Hawaiian baby woodrose
- **Toxins:** Morning glory *lysergamide* (LSD-like), peyote *mescaline*, and nutmeg *myristicin* (MMDA)

- **Antidote:** None
- **Dx:** Initial N and V, diaphoresis, mental status changes, deep sleep (nutmeg), hallucinations
- **Tx:** GI decontamination, supportive

CNS Toxicity: Absinthe

- **Representative:** Absinthe (wormwood)
- **Indications:** Croup, asthma
- **Latin:** *Artemisia absinthium*
- **Toxin:** *Thujones* (artemisins), (1) Neurotoxicity resembles *camphor*, (2) Antimalarial—effectively used in SE Asia (Vietnam), even for mefloquine and doxycycline-resistant *P. falciparum* (Myanmar)
- **Dx:** *Absinthism*—hallucinations, intellectual deterioration, psychosis, seizures (most celebrated case of self-mutilation = Vincent Van Gogh)
- **Tx:** GI decontamination (lavage + activated charcoal—AC), supportive tx

Wormwood *Artemisia absinthium*

See Figure 21.15.

Morning Glory (Contains Lysergamide) *Ipomoea purpurea*

See Figure 21.16.

FIGURE 21.15 Wormwood or absinthe, *Artemesia absinthium*, is an herb containing the hallucinogenic neurotoxins, the artemisins, which are also highly effective antimalarials. (From Wikipedia Creative Commons.)

FIGURE 21.16 All parts of the morning glory, *Ipomoea purpurea*, especially the seeds, contain an LSD-like lysergamide compound which can produce visual and auditory hallucinations on ingestion. (Courtesy of David K. Lirette, PhD, LSU School of Public Health, New Orleans, LA.)

Lophophora williamsii Peyote Cactus (Contains Mescaline)
See Figure 21.17.

CNS Tox: Hallucinogens

- **Nutmeg:** Powdered spice grated from the enclosed seed kernel
- **Mace:** The soft red cover, or aril, of the kernel

CNS Tox: Nutmeg and Mace

- **Rep:** East and West (Grenada) Indian nutmeg tree
- **Indic:** Intentional hallucinations, exorcising demons

FIGURE 21.17 Peyote cactus, *Lophophora williamsii*, contains mescaline that can induce a trance-like state with visual and auditory hallucinations on ingestion of the cactus buttons or teas or alcoholic drinks made from the cactus. (From Wikipedia Creative Commons.)

- **Latin:** *Myristica fragrans*
- **Toxin:** Myristicin –> meth*amphetamine* metabolites
- **Antidote:** None
- **Dx:** N, V, delirium, euphoria, deep sleep with hypothermia (like *Ecstasy,* MDMA, or 4-methyl-2-dimethoxy*amphetamine*)
- **Tx:** GI decontamination (lavage and AC), supportive therapy

CNS Tox: Ephedra

- **Rep:** Ephedra (*ma-huang*)
- **Indic:** Asthma, COPD
- **Toxin:** Ephedrine, pseudoephedrine
- **Antidote:** None
- **Dx:** Sympathomimetic causes HA, nervousness, anxiety, flushing, vomiting (V), increased blood pressure (BP) and heart rate (HR), mania and psychosis, seizures, myocardial infarction (MI) and cerebrovascular accident (CVA) or stroke possible
- **Tx:** GI decontamination (lavage and AC), supportive

Ephedra viridis **(Ephedra,** ***Ma-Huang*****)**
See Figure 21.18.

Neurotoxicity: Lathyrism Wild Grass or Everlasting Peas (Lathyrus *spp.*)

- **Reps:** *Lathyrus* spp. wild peas; major supplemental food source in Africa and Asia
- **Toxins:** β-*n*-oxalyl-amino-L-alanine

FIGURE 21.18 *Ephedra viridis* contains the sympathomimetic amines, ephedrine and pseudoephedrine, both of which are powerful vasoconstrictors and bronchodilators and can cause hypertension and tachycardia on ingestion. Ephedrine-containing preparations are still used in cough and cold preparations to reduce nasal stuffiness. (From Wikipedia Creative Commons.)

- **Antidote:** None
- **Dx:** No initial GI sx, chronic ingestion results in spastic ataxic paraplegia, mimics *multiple sclerosis*
- **Tx:** Supportive, irreversible paraplegia
- Wild grass peas-everlasting peas (*Lathyrus sativus*)—note climbing pea tendrils

Cytotoxic Plants: All Cause Cell Death

Toxalbumins*: Block protein synthesis in all organs = multi-organ failure. Ex: Castor bean, jequirty (rosary) pea, mistletoe.

Mitotic inhibitors*: Block cell division by mitosis in all rapidly dividing cells (including cancer cells = plant cancer chemotherapy). Ex: Crocus, vinca (periwinkle), mayapple.

Cyanogenic glycosides*: Release cyanide in the GI tract. Ex: Kernels and seeds of all *Prunus* spp. = apple, crab apple, plum, prune, apricot, cherry.

Cytotoxicity: Toxalbumins

- **Reps:** Castor bean, jequirty (rosary) pea, black locust
- **Toxins:** *Ricin* (castor bean), *abrin* (rosary pea)-protein synthesis inhibitors by inactivating *60S* ribosomes, rapid cell death (esp. in GI tract)
- **Antidote:** None
- **Dx:** Severe hemorrhagic gastroenteritis, seizures, CNS depression, cerebral edema, 2° hepatorenal failure
- **Tx:** GI decontamination, whole bowel irrigation

Cytotoxicity Ricin Mechanisms

Ricin is composed of two subunit chains. *Chain B binds* to cell surfaces to allow *chain A to enter and stop protein synthesis by inactivating the 60S ribosomal subunit.*

Castor bean seed has to be *chewed* to release ricin.

Ricin A and B subunit chains

Ricinus communis (Castor Bean Seed Pods)

See Figure 21.19.

Ricinus communis (Castor Bean Seeds)

See Figure 21.20.

Abrus precatorius (Rosary Peas in Pods)

See Figure 21.21.

Abrus precatorius (Rosary Peas Seeds)

See Figure 21.22.

* Fatalities reported in the United States.

FIGURE 21.19 (See color insert.) The castor bean seed pods. *Ricinus communis*, is the source of the ricin-containing castor bean seed. (Courtesy of David K. Lirette, PhD, LSU School of Public Health, New Orleans, LA.)

Christmas Cytotoxicity Toxalbumins

- American mistletoe: *Phoradendron serotinum* (toxalbumin = phoratoxin)
- European mistletoe: *Viscum album* (toxalbumin = phoratoxin)

Antimitotic Plants

- **Antimitotic—Vinca alkaloids:** The cancer chemotherapeutics, vinblastine and vincristine, are derived from the vinca alkaloids in the common vinca or periwinkle groundcover plants.
- **Antimitotic—Colchicine:** Derived from the autumn crocus (or glory lily) and still used to treat gout; causes tubulin damage, mitotic dysfunction, metaphase arrest.
- **Antimitotic—Podophyllotoxin:** A tubulin disruptor derived from the may apple plant and still used to treat venereal warts topically. *Etoposide* is a podophyllotoxin derivative used for cancer chemotherapy.
- **Antimitotic—The Pacific yew (*Taxus*):** Taxol® to prevent breast cancer.

FIGURE 21.20 The castor bean seeds of the castor bean plant, *Ricinus communis*. The castor bean seeds have to be chewed to release the ricin contained within the seed. (Courtesy of David K. Lirette, PhD, LSU School of Public Health, New Orleans, LA.)

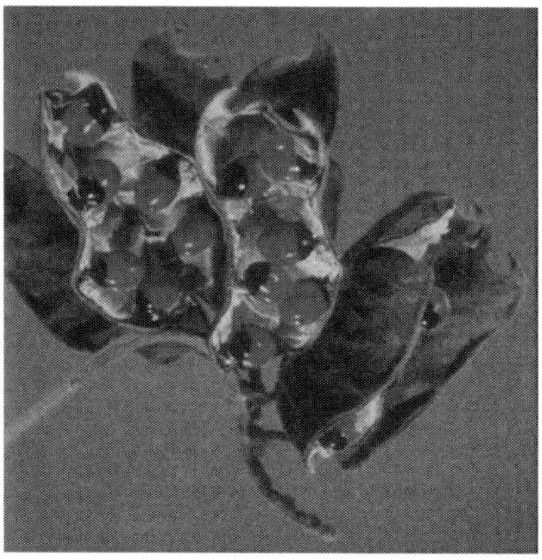

FIGURE 21.21 Rosary pea, *Abrus precatorius* seeds in pods. *Abrus precatorius* (the rosary orjequirty pea) is a tropical shrub, whose seeds contain the toxalbumin, abrin, which can induce hemorrhagic gastroenteritis following chewing and ingestion of seeds. (Courtesy of Charles P. Sea, MD, Department of Emergency Hospital, New Orleans, LA. Original Source: U.S. Government Document, U.S. Department of Health and Human Services, 1981, "Common Poisonous and Injurious Plants.")

FIGURE 21.22 Rosary pea seeds are still used in the Caribbean tropics to make colorful jewelry and rosaries, and may be swallowed whole without serious gastrointestinal toxicity. On the other hand, chewing the seeds can release the protein synthesis inhibitor, abrin, which, like ricin, can cause delayed hemorrhagic gastroenteritis with hypovolemic dehydration, shock, and high case fatality. (Courtesy of Charles P. Sea, MD, Department of Emergency Medicine, Ochsner Clinic Foundation Hospital, New Orleans, LA. Original Source: U.S. Government Document, U.S. Department of Health and Human Services, 1981, "Common Poisonous and Injurious Plants.")

Antimitotic Vinca Alkaloids

- **Mech:** VCR and VB are *periwinkle plant alkaloids* that, like *colchicine (crocus)* and *podophyllin (mayapple)*, bind to *tubulin* to prevent its polymerization into *microtubules*, arresting *mitosis* at metaphase, and inhibiting cell movements and cell division.
- **Indic:** Leukemias, lymphomas, solid tumors.

- **VCR toxicities:** Central nervous system **CNS** > Bone marrow **BM** > Cardiovascular **CV**.
- **CNS:** Ascending peripheral neuropathy (axonopathy), seizures, encephalopathy, autonomic dysfunction = paralytic ileus, atonic bladder; hypothalamic stimulation = fever and *SIADH*.
- **BM:** Myelosuppression, vinblastine (VB) > vincristine (VCR).
- **CV:** Necrotic MI 2° alkaloid-induced coronary vasospasm and platelet aggregation.

Vinca minor **(Note Purple-Periwinkle Color)**
See Figure 21.23.

Anticancer Alkaloids: Autumn Crocus, Contains Colchicine

- **Mech:** Binds to intracellular microtubules and causes mitotic arrest at metaphase
- **Indic:** Acute gout, gout prophylaxis, amyloidosis, biliary cirrhosis
- **Tox:** Initial GI-N, V, D; BM suppression, leukopenia, then rebound leukocytosis, myoneuropathy, later alopecia, sudden cardiac arrest—2–7 days
- **Tx:** Immediate lavage and MDAC, volume of distribution V_d = 2.2 L/kg, HD ineffective

Colchicum autumnale **(Autumn Crocus)**
See Figure 21.24.

Anticancer Alkaloids: Mayapple, Contains Podophyllin (Podophyllotoxin [Etoposide®])

- **Mech:** Tubulin disruptor.
- **Indic:** Topical treatment of venereal warts and as a chemotherapeutic (Etoposide®) for many cancers.
- **Tox:** Delayed (up to 10 h) severe diarrhea, myelosuppression, acute severe sensorimotor peripheral neuropathy, lethargy, confusion, ataxia, autonomic instability, encephalopathy.
- **Tx:** Glutamic acid for peripheral neuropathy. HD ineffective.

FIGURE 21.23 The vinca or periwinkle plant contains antimitotic alkaloids. (From Wikipedia Creative Commons.)

FIGURE 21.24 The autumn crocus, *Colchium autumnale*, contains the mitotic inhibitor, colchicine, used historically to treat gout and other inflammatory-cell-mediated conditions. (From Wikipedia Creative Commons.)

FIGURE 21.25 The mayapple, *Podophyllum peltatum*, contains podophyllin, a mitotic inhibitor used to treat venereal warts (*Condyloma acuminata*) topically and cancer intravenously. (From Wikipedia Creative Commons.)

Podophyllum peltatum (Mayapple—Contains Podophyllin)
See Figure 21.25.

Anticancer Alkaloids: Pacific Yew, Contains Taxine (Paclitaxel [Taxol®])

- **Mech:** Plant alkaloids from rare Pacific yew (*Taxus brevifolia*); Na and Ca channel blocker and metaphase inhibitor of tubulin disassembly
- **Indic:** Breast cancer, breast cancer prevention
- **Tox:** N, V, abdominal pain, ↓ HR-conduction blocks, ventricular dysrhythmias, paresthesias, ataxia, seizures
- **Tx:** Atropine, amiodarone, BZs, ? glutamic acid for neuropathies

***Taxus* spp. (*T. baccata*)**: Yew shrub-tree; all parts toxic: Leaves > berries

Plant Chemotherapy

Paclitaxel (Taxol®)

- **Mech:** Plant alkaloid from rare Pacific yew tree bark (*Taxus brevifolia*); *Na* and *Ca channel blocker* and metaphase inhibitor of tubulin disassembly
- **Indic:** Breast cancer, breast cancer prevention
- **Tox:** N, V, abdominal pain, ↓ HR-conduction blocks, ventricular dysrhythmias—refractory Vtach, ataxia, szs
- **Tx:** Atropine, amiodarone, BZs, ? Na bicarbonate

***Taxus* spp. (*T. baccata*)**: Yew shrub-tree; most parts toxic: Leaves and seeds, not red aril

Cyanide Poisonings

Cytotoxic: Cyanogenic Group

- **Reps:** *Prunus* spp., esp. seeds of almond, apricot, plum, peach, cherry; elderberry, hydrangea, cassava (tapioca)
- **Toxin:** *Amygdalin* → cyanide (hydrocyanic acid, HCN = *Laetrile®* from apricot pits)
- **Antidote:** Cyanide Kit® amyl nitrite + Na nitrite + Na thiosulfate, OH-cobalamin
- **Dx:** HA, vertigo, sz, ↑ T, stupor, tissue hypoxia-acidosis, coma
- **Tx:** GI decontamination

Steve McQueen

Steve McQueen (1930–1980) starred in *Bullitt* and *The Towering Inferno.* What hobby did he share with Paul Newman? He was an amateur race car driver during the days when the drivers wore fireproof suits containing asbestos. McQueen died in Mexico following treatment for asbestos-induced mesothelioma with Laetrile®, an unapproved chemotherapeutic drug made from cyanogenic apricot seeds.

Hydrangea macrophylla (Contains Cyanogenic Amygdalin)

See Figure 21.26.

FIGURE 21.26 Hydrangeas contain cyanogenic amygdalin alkaloids in all parts of the plant. (From Wikipedia Creative Commons.)

FIGURE 21.27 With the exception of the berries, other parts of the elderberry tree or shrub also contain cyanogenic amygdalin alkaloids. (Courtesy of David K. Lirette, PhD, LSU School of Public Health, New Orleans, LA.)

Sambucus nigra mexicana (Elderberry)
See Figure 21.27.

Nephrotoxic Plants

- **Kidney stones, renal cancer:** *Aristolochia* spp. (clematis vines), Balkan endemic nephropathy.
- **Nephrogenic diabetes insipidus:** Excessive excretion of dilute urine.
- **Tx:** Desamino-D-arginine-vasopressin (DDAVP or vasopressin).
- ***Colchicum autumnale* (autumn crocus):** Colchicine, glory lily.
- **Syndrome of inappropriate antidiuretic hormone secretion or SIADH:** Vinca alkaloids can cause SIADH characterized by reduced urine output, hypervolemia, dilutional hyponatremia.
- **Tx:** ↓ Fluids, ↑ Na.

Gastrointestinal (GI) Toxicity Hepatotoxicity Group

Hypoglycemic group* = hypoglycin A: Causes severely low blood sugar

Ex: Ackee fruit (*Blighia sapida*)—Florida and Caribbean (Jamaica) and available at *Whole Foods*

Pyrrolizidine alkaloids*: Block veins in the liver (Budd–Chiari syndrome—OCPs are the only other chemicals that can do this) and the lungs

Ex: *Comfrey, Crotalaria, Heliotropium*

* Fatalities reported in the United States.

Plant Hepatotoxicity: Hypoglycemia Ackee and Jamaican Vomiting Sickness

- **Rep:** Ackee tree.
- **Toxins:** *Hypoglycin* A inhibits G-6-PD and causes *Jamaican vomiting sickness.*
- **Antidote:** 50% dextrose.
- **Dx:** Severe N and V, hypoglycemia—2° decreased gluconeogenesis, mental status Δs, hypothermia, metabolic acidosis, seizures, ↓ liver fx-centrilobular hepatic necrosis.
- **Tx:** GI decontamination (lavage + AC).

Plant and Herbal Hepatotoxicity: Veno-Occlusive Disease

- **Reps:** Comfrey, coltsfoot
- **Toxins:** Hepatotoxic *pyrrazolidine alkaloids*
- **Antidote:** None
- **Dx:** Hepatotoxicity, specifically hepatic veno-occlusive disease (comfrey)
- **Tx:** GI decontamination (lavage + AC)

Herbal hepatotoxins: Both comfrey and coltsfoot are capable of causing hepatotoxicity with hepatic vein occlusion (Budd–Chiari syndrome) following chronic ingestion of teas, tablets, tinctures, or powders containing the pyrrolizidine alkaloids in these herbs.

Symphytum officinale **(Comfrey)**
See Figure 21.28.

FIGURE 21.28 All parts of the common comfrey, *Symphytum officinale*, have been distilled for internal use by folk medicine practitioners into teas and tinctures to treat gastrointestinal and neuromuscular disorders. All contain hepatotoxic pyrrolizidine alkaloids that have been associated with hepatic vein occlusion (Budd–Chiari syndrome). (From Wikipedia Creative Commons.)

FIGURE 18.2 The crown-of thorns starfish, *Acanthaster planci*, is damaging Australia's Great Barrier Reef. (From NOAA Photo Library.)

FIGURE 18.10 The sargassum triggerfish, *Xanthichthys ringens*, can bioaccumulate both ciguatoxins and palytoxin. (From NOAA Photo Library.)

FIGURE 19.2 *Amanita phalloides*, the death angel, is an amatoxin-containing highly poisonous mushroom. (From Wikipedia Creative Commons.)

FIGURE 19.6 The brain mushroom or false morel, *Gyromitra esculenta*, contains the epileptogenic monomethylhydrazine, gyromitrin, which can cause seizure activity on ingestion. The poisonous brain mushroom may be confused with a look-alike mushroom, the edible conifer or yellow morel, *Morchella esculenta*. (From Wikipedia Creative Commons.)

FIGURE 19.19 *Tricholoma equestre*, the yellow knight, can cause rhabdomyolysis with myalgias and myoglobinuria 24–72 h following ingestion. The precise myotoxin has yet to be identified. (From Wikipedia Creative Commons.)

FIGURE 20.2 Monkshood, *Aconitum napellus*, contains the cardiotoxic alkaloid, aconitine, a sodium channel opener, and can cause fatal cardiac arrhythmias and conduction defects on ingestion. (From Wikipedia Creative Commons.)

FIGURE 20.5 The foxgloves, *Digitalis* species, are a large group of flowering herbaceous perennials that contain digitalis-like cardiac glycosides and are capable of causing digitalis-like poisoning with potentially fatal cardiac arrhythmias and conduction defects on ingestion. Treatment is the same as for digitalis (digoxin) overdose. (From Wikipedia Creative Commons.)

FIGURE 20.9 The angel's trumpet plants, *Brugmasia* spp. and *Solandra* spp. are very common perennials in the southern United States, and contain a scopolamine-like belladonna alkaloid that can cause a central anticholinergic syndrome on ingestion. The angel's trumpet plant was introduced into the temperate and tropical areas of the United States from southeastern Brazil for landscaping purposes. All parts of the plants are toxic and contain a combination of several anticholinergic tropine alkaloids, including atropine, hyoscyamine, and scopolamine. Since the 1990s, there have been increasing U.S. reports of central anticholinergic syndromes following the ingestion of teas and potions made from angel's trumpet in adolescents seeking legal hallucinogens. (Courtesy of David K. Lirette, PhD, LSU School of Public Health, New Orleans, LA.)

FIGURE 21.1 All parts of the oleander shrub are highly toxic and contain digitalis glycosides that can cause nausea, vomiting, tachyarrhythmias, and cardiac conduction disturbances, including complete heart block, on ingestion. Oleander grows up to 9 m tall in warm beachfront locations and produces abundant white, yellow, pink, or red flowers. Oleander has poisoned beach-goers who have selected oleander branches to use as skewers to roast their hot dogs over beachside bonfires. (Courtesy of David K. Lirette, PhD, LSU School of Public Health, New Orleans, LA.)

FIGURE 21.6 *Zigadenus glaberrimus*. Death camas or death lilies are perennial, onion-like bulbs with showy flower stalk with 6-petal flowers with green hearts. All parts of the plant are cardiotoxic and potentially fatal on ingestion. (Courtesy of David K. Lirette, PhD, LSU School of Public Health, New Orleans, LA.)

FIGURE 21.19 The castor bean seed pods. *Ricinus communis*, is the source of the ricin-containing castor bean seed. (Courtesy of David K. Lirette, PhD, LSU School of Public Health, New Orleans, LA.)

FIGURE 22.1 Southern or Southeastern copperhead (*Agkistrodon contortrix contortrix*). Copperheads are commonly encountered venomous crotalid pit vipers in the southeastern United States. (Courtesy of the CDC.)

FIGURE 22.2 A southeastern cottonmouth or water moccasin, *Agkistrodon piscivoris piscivoris,* an aquatic relative of the copperhead, is aggressive if disturbed. In this photograph, the snake is coiled atop floating water hyacinths and waiting for a frog or fish to strike. Note the cotton-white color of the snake's mouth. (Courtesy of David K. Lirette, PhD, LSU School of Public Health, New Orleans, LA.)

FIGURE 22.5 The timber or canebrake rattlesnake, *Crotalus horridus horridus*, is a south-central U.S. relative of the eastern diamondback rattlesnake with more complex venom that includes neuromuscular toxins. Rather than a diamond pattern, the dorsal pattern is best characterized as a series of black chevrons, and the caudal body and tail are very dark to black in color. (Courtesy of the CDC.)

FIGURE 22.11 The Texas or western coral snake (*Micrurus tener tener*). The Texas or western coral snake closely resembles its relative, the eastern coral snake, *Micrurus fulvius fulvius,* which differs only in its distribution of black mottling within its red segments. In contrast to the crotalids or pit vipers, the fangs of coral snakes are sort and are permanently fixed in position on the anterior maxillary bones. Therefore, coral snakes do not strike with forward protruding fangs like the pit vipers and most envenoming bites occur on the hands when brightly colored coral snakes are misidentified as king snakes and handled. (Courtesy of the CDC.)

FIGURE 22.20 The Oregon or western rough-skinned newt, *Taricha granulosa granulosa*, is related to the salamander that ranges from coastal Alaska to California and has rough dull-colored skin which secretes a tetrodotoxin to discourage predation. Ingestions of these newts usually on a dare have been fatal.

FIGURE 22.23 The black widow (female), *Latrodectus mactans*, is identified by its black color and a distinctive red hourglass marking on the ventral surface of its abdomen, which may take on different shapes and an orange-red color in some specimens and other *Latrodectus* species. Deaths in healthy adults from *Latrodectus* bites are relatively rare in terms of the number of bites per thousand people. Sixty-three deaths were reported in the United States between 1950 and 1959. Since the species range worldwide, the highest number of deaths worldwide is caused by members of the genus *Latrodectus*. Widow spiders have more potent venom than most spiders, and prior to the development of antivenom, 5% of reported bites resulted in fatalities. Improvements in plumbing have greatly reduced the incidence of bites and fatalities in areas where outdoor privies have been replaced by flush toilets. (Courtesy of David K. Lirette, PhD, LSU School of Public Health, New Orleans, LA.)

FIGURE 22.24 The brown recluse or violin spider, *Loxosceles reclusa*, is medium to very dark brown in color and most species have distinctive violin or fiddle-shaped patterns on the dorsal aspect of the cephalothorax. Since not all brown recluses have the violin markings, the arrangement of the eyes will allow positive identification with 8 eyes instead of the typical 6 arranged in pairs with 1 median pair and 2 lateral pairs. An envenoming bite may result in blistering progressing to skin necrosis or loxoscelism, also referred to as necrotic arachnidism. (Courtesy of the CDC.)

FIGURE 22.40 The io moth, *Automeris io*, caterpillar is bright green with two lateral stripes, the top one is red and the lower white. It is covered with urticating hairy spines which can break off and inject venom into victims. (Courtesy of David K. Lirette, PhD, LSU School of Public Health, New Orleans, LA.)

FIGURE 22.42 The gypsy moth, *Lymantria dispar*, caterpillar, a voracious feeder, is black with long, hair-like setae and five pairs of raised blue spots and six pairs of raised red spots along the back. The caterpillars will climb up any object in their way in search of food including telephone poles and people.

FIGURE 22.43 The white-marked tussock moth, *Orgyia leucostigma*, caterpillar is related to the destructive gypsy moth caterpillar and can also damage trees and sting humans when present in large numbers. (Courtesy of David K. Lirette, PhD, LSU School of Public Health, New Orleans, LA.)

FIGURE 25.1 Blue-ringed octopus (*Hapalochlaena maculosus*). The blue-ringed octopus can inflict a painful bite and inject a tetradotoxin containing paralyzing venom. (With permission from Dietrich Mebs, *Venomous and Poisonous Animals*, 2002, CRC Press, Boca Raton, FL, p. 72, Figure 2.34.)

FIGURE 25.2 Masked pufferfish, *Arothron diadematus*, Red Sea. The meat of the pufferfish is often consumed raw as "fugu" fish in Japan. The pufferfish and marine sunfish contain high concentrations of paralyzing tetradotoxin in the skin, liver, bile, ovaries, and roe, and must be filleted precisely in order to be eaten raw or cooked without risk of tetradotoxin poisoning. (With permission from Dietrich Mebs, *Venomous and Poisonous Animals*, 2002, CRC Press, Boca Raton, FL, p. 139, Figure 2.91.)

FIGURE 25.6 Lionfish (*Pterosis volitans*). The lionfish has dorsal fins tipped with sharp spines attached to separate venom glands, which can inflict painful envenoming injuries in divers and saltwater aquaria enthusiasts. A polyvalent Scorpaenid antivenom is available for the management of moderate-to-severe envenomings caused by lionfish, scorpionfish, and stonefish. (Courtesy of Charles P. Sea, Department of Emergency Medicine, Ochsner Clinic Foundation Hospital, New Orleans, LA. Original Source: U.S. Government Document, Information Bulletin #12, 1980, "Toxic Fish and Mollusks.")

FIGURE 21.29 All parts of the coltsfoot, *Tussilago farfara*, have been distilled for internal use by folk medicine practitioners into teas and syrups for treatment of common colds, especially for cough suppression. All contain hepatotoxic pyrrolizidine alkaloids that have been associated with hepatic vein occlusion (Budd–Chiari syndrome). (From Wikipedia Creative Commons.)

Tussilago farfara (Coltsfoot)
See Figure 21.29.

Miscellaneous Herbal Hepatotoxins

Sassafras albidum (sassafras, gumbo filé powder, *mamou* tea): Contains the potential hepatotoxin and carcinogen = safrole, a potential carcinogen, a potential inducer of hepatocellular carcinoma.

Plants Causing Gastrointestinal (GI) Toxicity on Ingestion GI Toxicity Group

- **Calcium oxalate group:** Stab the GI tract with calcium oxalate crystals stored in raphides. Ex: *Caladium, Diffenbachia.*
- **Solanine group:** Do not eat potato and tomato eyes and leaves.
- **"Christmas" group:** Probably nonpoisonous, except for mistletoe. Ex: *Poinsettia.*
- **Miscellaneous (Poke-Salad Annie group) GI toxicity group:** Always parboil and decant × 3 young pokeweed leaves before making salads and cookies or pokeweed berries before making jams or jellies; or to become *Poke-Salad Annie.*

GI Toxicity: Calcium Oxalate

- **Reps:** Species of *Diffenbachia, Philodendron, Brassaia, Schefflera, Pothos, Caladium, Spathiphyllum.*

FIGURE 21.30 *Diffenbachia* or dumbcane is a popular household decorative plant whose leaves contain idioblasts that discharge sharply pointed and irritant calcium oxalate crystals when damaged. (Courtesy of Charles P. Sea, MD, Department of Emergency Medicine, Ochsner Clinic Foundation Hospital, New Orleans, LA. Original Source: U.S. Government Document, U.S. Department of Health and Human Services, 1981, "Common Poisonous and Injurious Plants.")

- **Toxin:** *Calcium oxalate* crystals are bundled in raphides →; and loaded into idioblasts to be fired into the oral and gastrointestinal mucosa of any person ingesting the plant. Ex: *Diffenbachia.*
- **Antidote:** None.
- **Dx:** Salivation, dysphagia, dysarthria, mucosal edema and oral bullae, contact dermatitis, and conjunctivitis.
- **Tx:** Cold milk/ice cream, nonsteroidal anti-inflammatory drugs vs. steroids.

Diffenbachia spp. (Dumbcane—Contains Sharp Calcium Oxalate Crystals)

See Figure 21.30.

Caladium hortulanum (Caladium)

See Figure 21.31.

Philodendron pertusum (Philodendron)

See Figure 21.32.

GI Tract Toxicity Not! Calcium Oxalate!

The jade plant (*Crassula argentea*) is a very popular houseplant from which no toxin has been isolated, yet there is a case report of a 1-year-old who ingested several leaves and had persistent diarrhea and perianal dermatitis (Schilling et al.: *Vet Hum Tox*, 1980).

FIGURE 21.31 Like *Diffenbachia* or dumbcane, philodendrons, caladiums, and pothos plants or parlor ivy are all also very popular indoor decorative plants whose leaves contain idioblasts that discharge irritant calcium oxalate crystals when damaged, causing salivation and oropharyngeal edema. (Courtesy of David K. Lirette, PhD, LSU School of Public Health, New Orleans, LA.)

FIGURE 21.32 Like *Diffenbachia* or dumbcane and caladiums, philodendrons are all also very popular indoor decorative plants whose leaves contain idioblasts that discharge irritant calcium oxalate crystals when damaged, causing salivation and oropharyngeal edema. (Courtesy of Charles P. Sea, MD, Department of Emergency Medicine, Ochsner Clinic Foundation Hospital, New Orleans, LA. Original Source: U.S. Government Document, U.S. Department of Health and Human Services, 1981, "Common Poisonous and Injurious Plants.")

- In 2005, Czechs reported successful thoracic surgical repair of a hemorrhaging aorto-esophageal fistula in a 12 1/2-year-old girl who had attempted suicide by ingesting one leaf of *Diffenbachia picta*. (Snajdauf J et al.: *J Ped Surg*, 2005).

GI Tract Toxicity Solanine Group

- **Reps:** Leaves of green potatoes (especially potato "eyes" and vines) and tomatoes (leaves and stems)
- **Toxins:** Solanine, solanidine
- **Antidote:** None
- **Dx:** 2–24 h—N, V, D, abdominal cramps, later delirium, hallucinations, coma, death, no deaths since 1960s
- **Tx:** GI decontamination (lavage and AC)

GI Tract Toxicity Christmas Group

- **Reps:** The Euphorbiaceae include poinsettia, crown-of-thorns, and spurges.
- **Toxins:** Miscellaneous; *Diterpene and phorbol esters in milky saps can cause contact dermatitis.*
- **Antidote:** None.
- **Dx:** N, V, D, abdominal cramps, oral mucosal burns, last death 2° poinsettia ingestion—Hawaii, 1919.
- **Tx:** GI decontamination (lavage and AC).

Euphorbia milii **(Crown-of-Thorns)**
See Figure 21.33.

FIGURE 21.33 The crown-of-thorns, *Euphorbia milii*, contains diterpene and phorbol esters in a sap that can cause gastrointestinal distress if ingested or chemical contact dermatitis from prolonged topical application. (Courtesy of David K. Lirette, PhD, LSU School of Public Health, New Orleans, LA.)

Misc. GI Tract Toxicity "Poke-Salad Annie"

- **Reps:** Pokeweed, English ivy, yew, horse chestnut
- **Toxin:** *Phytolaccine* (pokeweed)
- **Antidote:** None
- **Dx:** N, V, D, abdominal cramps—colic, lymphocytosis (pokeweed)
- **Tx:** GI decontamination (lavage and AC)

Pokeweed leaves (salads, teas, baked goods following multiple par-boilings)
Pokeweed berries (jellies, juices following multiple par-boilings)

Phytolacca americana (Pokeberry or Pokeweed)

See Figure 21.34.

Plant Poisonings

Dermatotoxicity Group

Toxicodendron-Containing Plants

- The Toxicodendron group of vines and shrubs can induce severe chemical contact dermatitis on exposure to their oily resin, toxicodendrol, which contains the suspended active toxin, urushiol.

FIGURE 21.34 Pokeberries from the pokeweed or pokeberry plant, *Phytolacca americana*, contain phytolaccine, which can cause gastrointestinal distress if consumed raw and not detoxified by prior par-boiling. Pokeberry can also induce an increase in the number of circulating lymphocytes or lymphocytosis for unknown reasons. (Courtesy of David K. Lirette, PhD, LSU School of Public Health, New Orleans, LA.)

- The Toxicodendron group of plants includes poison ivy (*Toxicodendron radicans*), poison oak (*Toxicodendronpubescens* [*toxicarium*]), and poison sumac (*Toxicodendron vernix*).

Toxicodendron Group (See Figures 21.35 through 21.37)

- **Reps:** Poison ivy and poison oak ("*leaves of 3, let them be*"); poison sumac.

FIGURE 21.35 Poison ivy, *Toxicodendron radicans*, is a member of the Toxicodendron group and contains the oily resin, urushiol, which can induce a highly pruritic chemical contact dermatitis. Note the three leaves on a red stem. (Courtesy of Charles P. Sea, MD, Department of Emergency Medicine, Ochsner Clinic Foundation Hospital, New Orleans, LA. Original Source: U.S. Government Document, U.S. Department of Health and Human Services, 1981, "Common Poisonous and Injurious Plants.")

FIGURE 21.36 Poison oak, *Toxicodendron pubescens (toxicarium)*, is a member of the Toxicodendron group and contains the oily resin, urushiol, which can induce a highly pruritic chemical contact dermatitis. Unlike poison ivy which is a climbing vine, poison oak is a ground-cover shrub that prefers the shaded areas near tree bases. Note the three leaves on a green stem. (From Wikipedia Creative Commons.)

FIGURE 21.37 Poison sumac, *Toxicodendron vernix*, is a member of the Toxicodendron group and contains the oily resin, urushiol, which can induce a highly pruritic chemical contact dermatitis. Poison sumac is a tall shrub with a palmate leaf pattern. (From Wikipedia Creative Commons.)

- **Toxin:** The active toxin, *urushiol*, is suspended in the oily and sticky resin, *toxicodendrol*, of all *Rhus* family plants.
- **Antidote:** None.
- **Dx:** Pruritic linear vesiculobullous dermatitis.
- **Tx:** Antihistamines, topical-systemic steroids.

Toxicodendron radicans **(Poison Ivy)**
See Figure 21.35.

Toxicodendron pubescens (toxicarium) **(Poison Oak)**
See Figure 21.36.

Toxicodendron vernix **(Poison Sumac)**
See Figure 21.37.

Dermatotoxicity: Lantana

- **Rep:** Lantana (*Lantana camara*), ham and eggs
- **Toxins:** Lantandene A and B, phylloerythrin
- **Antidote:** None
- **Dx:** Allergic contact dermatitis with photosensitivity, few fatalities reported
- **Tx:** Oral antihistamines, topical-systemic corticosteroids

Lantana camara **(Lantana = Ham and Eggs)**
See Figure 21.38.

FIGURE 21.38 *Lantana* is a shrub often called *ham-and-eggs* because of the mixed colors of its flowers; it contains toxins which can induce allergic contact dermatitis. (Courtesy of David K. Lirette, PhD, LSU School of Public Health, New Orleans, LA.)

Dermatotoxicity: Trumpet Vine

- **Rep:** Trumpet vine (*Campsis radicans*)
- **Toxin:** *Oleoresin*, like urushiol
- **Antidote:** None
- **Dx:** Allergic and chemical contact dermatitis, no fatalities reported
- **Tx:** Antihistamines, allergic-systemic corticosteroids

Campsis radicans **(Trumpet Vine)**
See Figure 21.39.

Phytophototoxicity

Phytophototoxicity = Contact with lemons, limes, mangos, celery. Psoralens are activated by ultraviolet waves in sunlight to cause erythematous, pruritic rashes in regions of contact (lips) or even distant regions exposed to sunlight (back and extremities).

Plant Poisonings: Summary of Toxidrome Evaluation and Management

See Tables 21.3 and 21.4.

Plant Poisonings: Summary and Conclusions

Plant poisonings are most common in children <6 years and up in adolescents seeking hallucinogens.

FIGURE 21.39 The trumpet vine, *Campsis radicans*, is a vine with bright reddish-orange flowers that contains an oily resin, oleoresin, similar to the urushiol resin of the Toxicodendron group that can cause an allergic and/or chemical contact dermatitis. (Courtesy of David K. Lirette, PhD, LSU School of Public Health, New Orleans, LA.)

Table 21.3 Plant Poisonings: Toxidrome Evaluation and Mx 1

Toxidrome Groups	Specific Antidotes	Supportive Therapy
Cardiac glycosides	Digoxin FAB	Decon. = GI lavage + AC ± pacemaker
Na channel openers	None	Same ± pacemaker
Grayanotoxins	Atropine	Same ± pacemaker
Anticholinergics	Physostigmine	Decontamination
Nicotinics	None	Decon; benzo-diazepines (BZs)
Convulsants	None	Same
Hallucinogens	None	Same

Table 21.4 Plant Poisonings: Toxidrome Evaluation and Mx 2

Toxidrome Groups	Specific Antidotes	Supportive Therapy
Cytotoxics	None	Decontamination
Mitotic inhibitors	None; Colchicine FAB IND?	Decon
Cyanogens	Lilly CN kit® and/or hydroxocobalamin	Decon
Hepatotoxins	None; cimetidine?; *n*-acetylcystine?	Decon ± liver transplant?
GI toxins	None	Decon
Ca oxalate injectors	None	Demulcents
Dermatotoxins	None	Decon; + antihistamines ± steroids

- Household plant poisonings are *rarely serious*, but *can be fatal*.
- Outdoor plant poisonings are *more serious* and more often fatal than household plant poisonings.
- Grandmothers' *purses contain drugs* (heart and BP pills) that fatally poison more children than plant poisonings.
- Today, 70% of newly discovered drugs come from *plants*. Ex: *Tamiflu®*.
- 25–50% of all existing drugs come from *plants*.
- <1% ($n = 350$) of existing drugs come from *animals* (*Armor* thyroid, beef lung heparin); <0.5% ($n = 121$) from fish (protamine).
- Many new drugs to *treat cancer* and other chronic diseases remain undiscovered in the world's *tropical rain forests* which are now being harvested and burned.
- *New drugs from plants: Tamiflu®* for influenza.
  Ex: Star anise (China)
- *Existing drugs from plants: Taxol®* for breast cancer.
  Ex: Pacific yew bark (China)

Chapter 22

Bites and Stings

Terrestrial Envenomings

Outline 478
Taxonomy 479
Taxonomy II: Simplified Reptile Taxonomy 480
Southern or Southeastern Copperhead 481
Eastern or Southeastern Cottonmouth (Water Moccasin) 482
Western Cottonmouth 483
Eastern Diamondback Rattlesnake 484
Canebrake Rattlesnake 484
Mojave or Sidewinder Rattlesnake 486
Northern Pacific Rattlesnake 486
Western Massasauga 487
Pygmy Rattlesnake 488
Desert Massasauga 488
Texas or Western Coral Snake 490
Milk Snake 490
Central American Coral Snake 491
Eastern Coral Snake 491
Some Central and South American Exotic Snakes 498
Gila Monster 500
Mexican Beaded Lizard 500
Oregon or Western Rough-Skinned Newt 501
Colorado River Toad 502
Cane Toad 503

Black Widow Female.......... 505
Brown Recluse or Violin Spider.......... 506
Hobo Spider.......... 508
U.S. Desert Tarantula.......... 509
Australian or Sydney Funnel Web Spider 510
Bark Scorpion 511
Honeybee Workers.......... 512
Bumblebee.......... 512
Carpenter Bee.......... 514
Yellow Jackets 514
Mud Dauber Wasp 514
Oriental Hornet 514
Red Fire Ant.......... 517
Hymenoptera Venoms and Hypersensitivity Reactions.......... 518
Io Moth.......... 518
Buck Moth 519
Gypsy Moth 519
White-Marked Tussock Moth Caterpillar 520
Hag Moth.......... 520
Puss or Flannel Moth.......... 521
Saddleback Moth 521
Miscellaneous: Centipedes and Millipedes 523
Centipede.......... 523
Reference.......... 524

Outline

Terrestrial Animals

- Reptiles
  - Snakes
  - Lizards
- Amphibians
  - Newts
  - Salamanders
  - Toads

Arthropods (Insects)

- Arachnids (spiders)
- *Hymenoptera* spp.
  - Bees
  - Wasps
  - Fire ants

Lepidoptera spp.
Caterpillars

Pre-Test Question 1

1. Necrotic arachnidism is most likely to follow envenoming bites by which of the following spiders?
   a. *Dugesiella henzia*
   b. *Latrodectus mactans*
   c. *Loxosceles reclusa*
   d. *Tegenaria agrestis*

Pre-Test Question 2

2. On an early spring wildflower walking tour of the Grand Canyon, a tourist was bitten on her thumb by a small rattlesnake as she steadied her camera on a boulder. Although the bite was virtually painless, had only one fang puncture mark, and was not surrounded by expanding ecchymoses or edema, the tour guide recommended immediate evacuation to a local ED for evaluation and antivenom therapy. Select the species of rattlesnake most likely to have inflicted such a bite.
   a. *Crotalus adamanteus*
   b. *Crotalus horridus*
   c. *Crotalus scultulatus*
   d. *Crotalus viridis*

Taxonomy

Phylum Chordata

Class Reptilia: Reptiles

Order Squamata: Snakes and lizards
Suborder Serpentes: Snakes
Suborder Sauria: Lizards

Class Amphibia: Amphibians

Order Anura: Frogs, toads
Order Caudata: Salamanders

Phylum Arthropoda

Class Arachinida

Order Araneae: Spiders
Order Scorpiones: Scorpions
Order Acari: Ticks, mites

Class Insecta

Order Hymenoptera

Family Apidae: Bees

Family Vespidae: Wasps, hornets, yellow jackets

Family Formicidae: Ants

Order Lepidoptera: Caterpillars—moths and butterflies

Miscellaneous orders: Hemiptera (true bugs), Siphonoptera (fleas), Diptera (flies) (see Chapter 23)

Definitions: Bites vs. Stings

What Is a Bite?

An intentionally inflicted injury from an animal's oral pole for the purposes of defending self or territory, obtaining and devouring prey, or blood feeding.

Can bites be envenoming? Yes: Gila monster (venom delivery via specialized grooved teeth).

What Is a Sting?

An intentional injection of venom stored in an animal's venom glands or sacs by highly modified nonreproductive structures, including teeth, spines, and stingers, or highly modified ovipositors no longer used for egg laying (arthropods only).

Can Some Animals Bite and Sting?

Yes: Fire ants (bite—oral pole; sting—aboral stinger), sting rays (mouth—ventral; stinger—dorsal).

Taxonomy II: Simplified Reptile Taxonomy

Snakes

Reptiles: Snakes

Order Squamata

Suborder Serpentes

Family Viperidae: Pit vipers

Subfamily Crotalidae: American pit vipers

Family Elapidae: Only 1 U.S. genus = coral snakes

Family Colubridae: Largest family, nonvenomous in the United States (except for the rear-fanged species) still regarded as nonvenomous, that is, "harmless" in the United States

Crotalids (pit vipers)

Agkistrodon spp.

Copperheads

Moccasins

Rattlesnakes

Crotalus spp.

Sistrurus spp.

Elapids (coral snakes)

Micrurus spp.

Micuroides

Lizards/Amphibians

Lizards

Gila monster

Beaded lizard

Amphibians

Newts

Salamanders

Toads

Class Reptilia

Nonpoisonous Snakes as Pets

Garter snake (*Thamnophis sirtalis*)

- Most widely distributed snake in North America
    - Found in Alaska
- Mild neurotoxin
    - 3FTx (three-finger toxin)

Hognose snake (*Heterodon nasicus*)

- Distribution: United States and Northern Mexico

Major Problems with Nonpoisonous Snakes as Pets

- Family *Colubridae* (United States)
- Reptilian *Salmonella* spp.—deaths in infants and elderly
- Grooved teeth break off and deliver "venom" in bites
- Toxic venoms = Duvernoy's glands in species once thought "harmless": hognose,* garter,* ringneck,* parrot
- **Tx:** Tetanus toxoid—Ttox + antibiotics

Southern or Southeastern Copperhead

Agkistrodon contortrix contortrix

Crotalids: Pit Vipers

- **Name:** Southern/southeastern copperhead (Figure 22.1)
- **Latin:** *Agkistrodon contortrix contortrix*

---

* Species once felt to be nonpoisonous and sold as pets, and now known to have poison glands and capable of inflicting envenoming bites by backward facing fangs.

FIGURE 22.1 (See color insert.) Southern or Southeastern copperhead (*Agkistrodon contortrix contortrix*). Copperheads are commonly encountered venomous crotalid pit vipers in the southeastern United States. (Courtesy of the CDC.)

- **Venom:** Nucleic acid—NA/acetylcholine—Ach-ases, serotonin-5HT, kinins, phospholipases, collaginase, hyaluronidase
- **Dx:** Hemorrhagic blisters, proximal edema, minimal systemic toxicity
- **Antidote:** Polyvalent antivenin—CroFab®
- **Tx:** Tetanus toxoid—Ttox, antibiotics—Abs for infection (cephalosporins 1° > penicillins), wound mx, and polyvalent antivenin—CroFab®

Many copperhead bites are either nonenvenoming or demonstrate minimal envenoming. CroFab is not indicated for dry or nonenvenoming bites. Tetanus prophylaxis is indicated. Antibiotic coverage with a third- or fourth-generation cephalosporin is indicated only for evidence of infection (Figure 22.1).

Eastern or Southeastern Cottonmouth (Water Moccasin)

Agkistrodon piscivoris piscivoris

Crotalids: Pit Vipers

- **Name:** Eastern or southeastern cottonmouth (water moccasin) (Figure 22.2)
- **Latin:** *Agkistrodon piscivorus piscivorus*
- **Venom:** "Mosaic of antigens"
- **Dx:** Slightly more severe envenomations than copperhead bites

FIGURE 22.2 (See color insert.) A southeastern cottonmouth or water moccasin, *Agkistrodon piscivoris piscivoris,* an aquatic relative of the copperhead, is aggressive if disturbed. In this photograph, the snake is coiled atop floating water hyacinths and waiting for a frog or fish to strike. Note the cotton-white color of the snake's mouth. (Courtesy of David K. Lirette, PhD, LSU School of Public Health, New Orleans, LA.)

- **Antidote:** CroFab rarely indicated
- **Tx:** Same as copperhead (Figure 22.2)

Crotalids: Cottonmouth Envenoming Bite

- **History:** A 56-year-old male with a history of cutaneous porphyria was bitten on his right index finger by a cottonmouth while trimming bushes in late March.
- **Physical examination:** Intense pain, edema, ecchymoses, and later cyanotic color changes at the bite site, hypotension.
- **Management:** Five vials of CroFab were administered at a local Emergency Department, and the patient was transferred to a regional referral hospital ICU.
- **Course:** Platelet count on admission = *56,000.* Five more vials of CroFab were administered; later, a finger fasciotomy was performed for a digital compartment syndrome. Prophylactic antibiotics were administered along with tetanus toxoid. The platelet count rose to 104,000, and the patient was discharged home in 48 h (Figure 22.3).

Western Cottonmouth (Figure 22.3)

Agkistrodon piscivoris leucostoma

FIGURE 22.3 A western cottonmouth, *Agkistrodon piscivoris leucostoma,* another aquatic relative of the copperhead and close relative of the eastern cottonmouth, is smaller than other subspecies, but is also aggressive if disturbed. The cottonmouths inhabit the hurricane-prone regions of the United States, and have posed significant threats to both residents and first responders following hurricanes and other major flooding disasters. (Courtesy of the CDC.)

Eastern Diamondback Rattlesnake

Crotalus adamanteus

Crotalids: Vipers/Rattlesnakes

- **Name:** Eastern diamondback rattlesnake (Figure 22.4)
- **Latin:** *Crotalus adamanteus*
- **Venom:** "Mosaic of antigens"
- **Dx:** Hemorrhagic bullae, tissue necrosis, massive edema, nausea, and vomiting, cardiovascular instability, potential for disseminated intravascular coagulation (DIC), hemolysis and rhabdomyolysis possible with secondary acute renal failure
- **Antidote:** Mod envenom—5–10 vials CroFab, severe—10–40 vials CroFab
- **Tx:** Immobilize limb, no ice, tetanus toxoid, vasopressors for hypotension, blood products as indicated, wound debridement as indicated, rarely fasciotomy following adequate treatment with antivenom, antibiotic coverage for infection (Figure 22.4)

Canebrake Rattlesnake

Crotalus horridus horridus

Crotalids: Vipers/Rattlesnakes

- **Name:** Timber or canebrake rattlesnake (Figure 22.5).
- **Latin:** *Crotalus horridus horridus.*

FIGURE 22.4 An eastern diamondback rattlesnake, *Crotalus adamanteus*, photographed in Bienville Parish, Louisiana. This nonretreating eastern diamondback is poised to strike. (Courtesy of Dino Ferri, herpetologist and assistant curator of reptiles and amphibians, Audubon Nature institute, New Orleans, LA. With permission.)

FIGURE 22.5 (See color insert.) The timber or canebrake rattlesnake, *Crotalus horridus horridus*, is a south-central U.S. relative of the eastern diamondback rattlesnake with more complex venom that includes neuromuscular toxins. Rather than a diamond pattern, the dorsal pattern is best characterized as a series of black chevrons, and the caudal body and tail are very dark to black in color. (Courtesy of the CDC.)

- **Venom:** Same as diamondback, + hematoxic.
- **Dx:** Same as diamondback, + *persistent muscular quivering (myokymia)*, hemolysis, *thrombocytopenia.*
- **Tx:** Same treatment recommended for all envenoming rattlesnake bites. All Mojave rattlesnake bites require treatment with CroFab (Figure 22.5).

Mojave or Sidewinder Rattlesnake

Crotalus scutulatus scutulatus

Crotalids: Vipers/Rattlesnakes

- **Name:** Mojave rattler or sidewinder (Figure 22.6)
- **Latin:** *Crotalus scutulatus scutulatus*
- **Venom:** Some species have potent *neurotoxins* and fewer tissue-destructive antigens—Ags = minor local symptoms—sx and delayed neurotoxicity—lethargy, obtundation, cranial nerve—CN palsies, weakness, respiratory paralysis, tissue damage, and coagulopathy possible
- **Antidote:** *CroFab as indicated and not prophylactically*
- **Tx:** Tetanus toxoid—Ttox, antibiotics—Abx indicated for infection only (Figures 22.6 through 22.10)

Northern Pacific Rattlesnake (Figure 22.7)

Crotalus viridis oreganus

FIGURE 22.6 The Mojave or sidewinder rattlesnake, *Crotalus scutulatus scutulatus*, is indigenous to the U.S. desert southwest, smaller than diamondback rattlesnakes, with venom that includes neuromuscular toxins. Like a coral snake bite, a Mojave rattlesnake bite may initially be relatively painless. The Mojave rattlesnake is also known as a sidewinder because of its unique and very swift sideways movement across desert sand.

FIGURE 22.7 Northern Pacific rattlesnake (*Crotalus viridis oreganus*), American Pacific Northwest. The Northern Pacific rattlesnake (*Crotalus viridis oreganus*) is one of the many regional species of crotalid rattlesnakes in North America. (Courtesy of Dino Ferri, herpetologist and assistant curator of reptiles and amphibians, Audubon Nature Institute, New Orleans, LA. With permission.)

Western Massasauga (Figure 22.8)

Sistrurus milieris streckeri

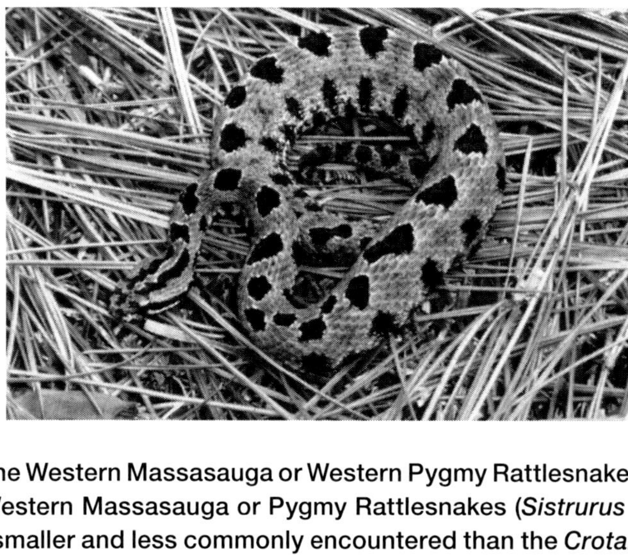

FIGURE 22.8 The Western Massasauga or Western Pygmy Rattlesnake (*Sistrurus milieris streckeri*). The Western Massasauga or Pygmy Rattlesnakes (*Sistrurus milieris streckeri*) are significantly smaller and less commonly encountered than the *Crotalus* species rattlesnakes, but can still inflict envenoming snakebites. (Courtesy of the CDC.)

FIGURE 22.9 The Eastern or Carolina Pygmy Rattlesnake (*Sistrurus miliaris miliaris*). The Eastern or Carolina Pygmy Rattlesnakes (*Sistrurus miliaris miliaris*) are significantly smaller than the *Crotalus* species rattlesnakes, but can still inflict envenoming snakebites. They range from eastern North Carolina south to Georgia and west through Alabama to central Mississippi. They prefer the pine-oak forests of the Atlantic Coastal Plain. (Courtesy of the CDC.)

Pygmy Rattlesnake (Figure 22.9)

Sistrurus catenatus catenatus

Desert Massasauga (Figure 22.10)

Sistrurus catenatus edwardsi

Coral Snakes (See Figures 22.11 through 22.14)

Family Elapidae: Only 1 U.S. genus = coral snakes

The shared characteristics of the U.S. coral snakes include red, yellow/rarely white, and black bands.

Red on yellow, kill a fellow; red on black, friend of Jack.
Red on yellow, kill a fellow; red on black, venom lack.

Note: This old adage only applies in North America; not with albinos-cross breeds or other species of coral snakes in Central and South America.

Proterolgyphous—Small, short, hollow fangs that are permanently fixed on the anterior maxillary bones.

FIGURE 22.10 The desert Massasauga (*Sistrurus catenatus edwardsi*). The desert Massasauga is lighter colored than the western Massasauga and is distributed along the Texas Gulf Coast. Despite its name, it may be encountered in marshy areas. The Massasaugas are small gray to tan rattlesnakes with a pattern of round or irregular blotches that run from neck to tail. They are related to the pygmy rattlesnakes, copperheads, and cottonmouths. (Courtesy of the CDC.)

FIGURE 22.11 (**See color insert.**) The Texas or western coral snake (*Micrurus tener tener*). The Texas or western coral snake closely resembles its relative, the eastern coral snake, *Micrurus fulvius fulvius,* which differs only in its distribution of black mottling within its red segments. In contrast to the crotalids or pit vipers, the fangs of coral snakes are sort and are permanently fixed in position on the anterior maxillary bones. Therefore, coral snakes do not strike with forward protruding fangs like the pit vipers and most envenoming bites occur on the hands when brightly colored coral snakes are misidentified as king snakes and handled. (Courtesy of the CDC.)

<1% of U.S. bites.

The second most potent venom in North America (NA).

Venom: Neurotoxic.

Distribution: Florida, Louisiana, Alabama, Arizona, Texas = western and eastern coral snakes. Southeastern Florida has the highest distribution.

Texas or Western Coral Snake

Micrurus tener tener

Coral Snakes: "Red-on-yellow"

Elapids: Coral Snakes

- **Name:** Texas (western) coral snake (Figure 22.11)
- **Latin:** *Micrurus fulvius tenere*
- **Venom:** Delayed neurotoxin
- **Dx:** Same as the eastern
- **Antidote:** Equine Elapid bivalent antivenin
- **Tx:** Mandatory admit as for eastern coral snake bites (Figures 22.11 through 22.13)

Milk Snake (Figure 22.12, Often Mistaken for a Coral Snake)

Lampropeltis triangulum annulata

Coral Snakes: Misidentification

FIGURE 22.12 The nonvenomous milk snake (*Lampropeltis triangulum annulata*) is similar in its coloration and habitat to both the eastern and western coral snakes. Most envenoming bites from coral snakes occur on the hands when brightly colored coral snakes are misidentified as either harmless milk snakes or king snakes with similar color banding patterns and intentionally handled. (Courtesy of the CDC.)

Central American Coral Snake (Figure 22.13)

Micrurus alleni

Sonoran Coral Snake, *Micuroides euryxanthus*

- **Name:** Sonoran coral snake
- **Latin:** *Micuroides euryxanthus*
- **Distribution:** Arizona, Mexico, Central and South Americas
- **Venom:** *Much less potent delayed neurotoxin*
- **Diagnosis:** Less severe neurotoxicity than the other U.S. coral snake bites
- **Antivenom:** Not available in the United States but available in Mexico and Costa Rica; only bivalent elapid antivenom—United States
- **Tx:** Consider importing antivenom; supportive, observe for apnea and respiratory dysfunction for 24 h

Eastern Coral Snake

Micrurus fulvius fulvius

- **Name:** Eastern coral snake (Figure 22.14).
- **Latin:** *Micrurus fulvius fulvius.*
- **Venom:** Neurotoxin.
- **Dx:** Shy, docile, nocturnal, bites and chews when disturbed, few local symptoms, 12–24 h later—paresis, paresthesias, fasciculation, dysarthria, dysphagia, ptosis, stridor, diplopia, and respiratory arrest.

FIGURE 22.13 Central American coral snake (*Micrurus alleni*), Osa Peninsula, Costa Rica. North and Central American *Micrurus* species coral snakes are all brightly colored, docile and nocturnal, and may rarely inflict neurotoxic snakebites, especially if handled. (Courtesy of Dino Ferri, herpetologist and assistant curator of reptiles and amphibians, Audubon Nature Institute, New Orleans, LA. With permission.)

FIGURE 22.14 The eastern coral snake, *Micrurus fulvius fulvius*, resembles the western coral snake in size and banding arrangement, but the black bands have more mottled appearances. Note the iridescent blue mottling in the black bands of this specimen. Eastern coral snakes are very prevalent in Florida and prefer to forage and feed at night in pine and palmetto forests. They inflict the majority of coral snake bites in Florida excluding those inflicted by imported coral snakes.

- **Antidote:** Equine bivalent (eastern + Texas)—5–10 vials.
- **Tx:** Mechanical ventilation will be required in approximately 15% of significant coral snake envenomations, especially those not immediately treated with coral snake antivenom (Figure 22.14).

Coral Snake Bites: Florida, 2004–2009

Presenting manifestations, N = 234:

- Fang marks 85%
- Local edema 40%
- Paresthesia 35%
- Nausea 30%
- Vomiting 25%
- Euphoria 15%
- Vertigo and/or
- Tinnitus 15%
- Diplopia 10%

- Dyspnea 10%
- Diaphoresis 10%
- Muscle pain 10%
- Fasciculation 5%
- Confusion 5%
- **Management:** Antivenom
- **Manufacturer:** Wyeth, equine, bivalent, since 1967
- **Dose:** 3–5 vials; repeat × 1
- **Administer:** *Prior to sx onset; will not reverse presenting signs or sx*
- **AEs:** Urticaria 35%, serum sickness 10%
- **Problem:** *Wyeth stopped production in* 2005; *all vials now expired*
- **Availability:** Coralmyn®, equine, polyvalent—Mexico; Suero Autiofidico Anti-coral®, equine, monovalent—Costa Rica

A Recent Coral Snake Bite Case: Florida, 2009

- **Source, Personal communication:** J.N. Bernstein, MD, FACEP, medical director Miami—Dade County, FL, Poison Control Center—PCC.
- **Bite:** Intoxicated 39-year-old woman picks up a small brightly colored snake on a picnic and is bitten on the right hand.
- **1st hour:** Presents to local ED, + fang marks; observed × 3 h and discharged as intoxicated.
- **6th hour:** Returns to the same ED—c/o widespread allodynia, tinnitus, metallic taste; DC'ed as intoxicated.
- **16 hours post-bite:** Drives to a distant ED with a Poison Control Center (PCC) c/o unbearable tinnitus, allodynia; PE: opisthotonic posture, no gag, dysarthric.
- **Mx:** Intubated, mechanical ventilation × 5 weeks.
- **Outcomes:** Discharged at 6 weeks, left foot drop 5th–7th weeks; neurologically intact by week 8.
- **Moral:** Antivenom for all documented cases; even if expired or imported.

Exotic Snakebites: The United States vs. The World

Incidence of attack

7000–8000 reptile bites per year in the United States

- Rattlers majority
- 10–15% are dry bites

300,000–400,000 venomous snake bites per year internationally

Mortality

- Fewer than 12 deaths/year in the United States

- 30,000–110,000 deaths/year worldwide
    - Up to 5× that amount face permanent morbidity

U.S. Mortality Rate

- With antivenom treatment–0.28%
- Without antivenom treatment–2.6%

Data derived from estimates
Worldwide:

- 5.4 million bites w/2.5 million envenomations and 125,000 deaths

Highest Rates of Prevalence

Number of bites:

■ S Asia	121,000
■ SE Asia	111,000
■ East Sub-Saharan Africa	43,000

Envenomations/year:

■ India	81,000
■ Sri Lanka	33,000
■ Vietnam	30,000
■ Brazil	30,000
■ Mexico	28,000
■ Nepal	20,000

Exotic Snakebites: Elapidae

Tropical and subtropical regions, except Europe

- Indian Ocean and Pacific Ocean
    - *Pelamis plature*—found across the Pacific Ocean in CA and SA

Proteroglyphous fangs—point downward, longer bites for envenomation

- Hollow fixed fangs

Round pupils

Primarily neurotoxic

- Paralysis, asphyxiation

Examples:

- Black mamba—most dangerous
- Green mamba
- Island Taipan—most venomous land snake
- Belcher's sea snake—most toxic venom
- Cobras
- Corals (see Figure 22.13)

- Kraits
- Sea snakes

Black Mamba (*Dendroaspis polylepis*)

- Africa
- 2.4–3 m long
- Given name from inky black mouth
- Diurnal, living in termite mounds and hollow trees
- Mainly neurotoxin venom
    - Block neuromuscular junctions between the brain and nervous system causing paralysis
        - Victim usually dies from suffocation
- Pressure immobilization and respiratory support very important
- Polyvalent antivenom
    - 99% of victims survive without complication

Island Taipan (*Oxyuranus microlepidotus*)

- Eastern Australia to NW New South Wales
    - Isolated species in South Australia
    - Disappeared for almost 100 years
- Most venomous land snake
    - Maximum venom yield recorded for one bite is 110 mg
    - Pre- and post-synaptic neurotoxins, myotoxins, and procoagulants
        - Enough to kill 100 people
    - Neurotoxic venom
- Highly reclusive
    - No confirmed deaths
- **Sx:** Vomiting, flaccid paralysis, respiratory paralysis

King Cobra (*Ophiophagus hannah*)

- S China, SE Asia, India
    - Mainly rainforests and plains of India
- Neurotoxic venom
    - Can deliver 7 mL per bite, enough to kill 20 people
    - Venom used as pain relievers and arthritis medication
    - 75% mortality rate
- **Sx:** Severe pain, blurred vision, vertigo, paralysis
    - Cardiovascular collapse within 2 min → coma → respiratory failure
- Proteroglyphous fangs
- Territorial (build nests)
- Largest venomous snake
- Feed on other snakes

- Fiercely aggressive when cornered
- Can reach 18 ft
  - Ability to "stand up" and spit venom—aims at eyes of attackers

Sea Snakes

- **Species:** *Aipysurus laevis*, *Astrotia stokesii*, *Enhydrina schistosa*, *Hydrophis ornatus*, *J. cyanocinctus*, *Lapemis hardwickii*
- **Adaptations:**
  - Paddle-like tail, excrete salts, respire through skin (up to 20%)
- **Venom:** Neurotoxin alters Na/Cl permeability but no effect on Na–K ATPase pump
  - Hemolytic and myotoxic (olive sea snake)
- **Antidote:** Equine-derived bivalent antivenom
- **Dx:** No local rxn, peripheral and cranial nerve neuropathies w/in 3–6 h, paralysis, respiratory failure, myonecrosis, myoglobinuria (especially olive sea snake), RF
- **Tx:** Supportive, antivenom, analgesics, tetanus prophylaxis

Belcher's Sea Snake (*Hydrophis belcheri*)

- Indian Ocean, Gulf of Thailand Australia, Solomon Islands, especially near Ashmore Reef in the Timor Sea
- Most toxic venom
  - Only 25% of bites lead to envenomations

Multi-Banded Krait (*Bungarus multicinctus*)

- Taiwan, S China, Burma, Laos, N Vietnam
- Neurotoxin
    - Alpha-bungarotoxin
  - Generalized paralysis and respiratory failure with hypertension
  - **Tx:** Ventilatory support, treatment with anticholinesterase and antivenom
- 50% chance of survival if treated with antivenom

Exotic Viperidae

- Found all over except Australia and Madagascar
- Solenoglyphous fangs
  - Long, hollow front fangs with the ability to fold and enclose in a membranous sheath
  - Control venom output (capable of giving dry bites)
- Venom gland at base of the neck gives characteristic triangle head
- Elliptical eyes
- Nocturnal
- Venom contains proteases
  - Pain, local swelling necrosis, coagulopathy
  - Death from collapse due to blood pressure

- Examples:
  - Fea's viper
  - Night adders
  - Pit vipers
  - True or pitless vipers

Rhombic Night Adder (*Causus rhombeatus*)

- Sub-Saharan Africa
- **Venom:** Cytotoxic
- **Dx:** Pain, minor swelling with minimal necrosis
  - Symptoms disappear within 2–3 days
  - No well-documented case of fatality

Gaboon Viper (*Bitis rhinoceros*)

- True viper—lacks heat sensing pit
- Sub-Saharan Africa
  - Rainforests and savannas
- Largest fangs
- **Venom:** Highest venom yield
  - 200–1000 mg of dried venom
- **Sx:** Rapid swelling, intense pain, severe shock, local blistering, hypotension, coagulation dysfunction

Colubridae

- 2/3 of all snakes
- Found everywhere except Antarctica
- Opisthoglyphous fangs
  - Elongated grooved teeth at the rear of the jaw
- Examples:
  - Boiga species
  - Boomslang
  - Twig snake

Brown Tree Snake (*Boiga irregularis*)

- E and N coastal Australia, Papua New Guinea, NW Melanesia
- Invasive species in Guam
  - Devitalizing to local bird species
- Nocturnal
- Aggressive
- Opisthoglyphous
- **Venom:** Weakly neurotoxic and cytotoxic

Boomslang snake (*Dispholidus typus*)

- Sub-Saharan Africa
- Diurnal
- Arboreal
- **Venom:** Hemotoxic
  - Slow acting (up to several hours)
- **Dx:** Internal and external bleeding, headache, nausea, mental disorders, organ degeneration, and generalized tissue damage
  - Death from massive bleeding from every orifice
- **Antivenom:** Monovalent

Some Central and South American Exotic Snakes (See Figures 22.13, 22.15 through 22.17)

Porthidium ophyromegas *(Figure 22.16)*

Formerly *Bothrops orphyromegas*

Porthidium nasutum, *Northwestern Costa Rica (Figure 22.17)*

Formerly *Bothrops nasutum*

Lizards

Order Squamata

- **Name:** Gila monster
- **Latin:** *Heloderma suspectum*

FIGURE 22.15 Latin American Fer-de-Lance (*Bothrops asper*), Northern Costa Rica. *Bothrops* species, such as the Fer-de-Lance (*Bothrops asper*), account for many of the seriously envenoming snakebites in tropical Latin America. Note the distinct triangular or lance-like head. (Courtesy of Dino Ferri, herpetologist and assistant curator of reptiles and amphibians, Audubon Nature Institute, New Orleans, LA. With permission.)

FIGURE 22.16 *Porthidium ophyromegas*, formerly *Bothrops orphyromegas*, Northwestern Costa Rica. *Porthidium* species venomous snakebites are relatively common in tropical Central America and northern South America, but fatalities are exceedingly rare. (Courtesy of Dino Ferri, herpetologist and assistant curator of reptiles and amphibians, Audubon Nature Institute, New Orleans, LA. With permission.)

- **Venom:** Similar to Crotalid, but more complex with kallekrein, serotonin, helothermine; inefficient grooved teeth and no fangs
- **Dx:** Shy, slow, nocturnal, macerating bite, cyanosis, edema, respiratory distress, MI, anaphylaxis, coagulopathy
- **Antidote:** 0
- **Tx:** Supportive (Figure 22.18)

FIGURE 22.17 *Porthidium nasutum*, Northwestern Costa Rica. *Porthidium*, formerly *Bothrops*, species snakes are not as aggressive when disturbed as the *Bothrops* species, such as the Fer-de-Lance, but still capable of inflicting mildly to moderately envenoming snakebites. (Courtesy of Dino Ferri, herpetologist and assistant curator of reptiles and amphibians, Audubon Nature Institute, New Orleans, LA. With permission.)

FIGURE 22.18 Gila monster (*Heloderma suspectum*), desert Southwest United States. The shy, slow-moving, and nocturnally active Gila monster (*Heloderma suspectum*), once a very common inhabitant of the American desert southwest, may rarely inflict painful, macerating, envenoming bite, especially if handled. Venom injection is inefficiently delivered by grooved teeth that communicated with poison glands and not by fangs as in pit vipers. *Heloderma* species (*H. suspectum*, *H. horridum*) lizard venoms are complex in chemical composition and may induce anaphylaxis, respiratory depression, and coagulopathy. There is no antivenom available in the United States, and treatment of envenoming bites is supportive. (Courtesy of Dino Ferri, herpetologist and assistant curator of reptiles and amphibians, Audubon Nature Institute, New Orleans, LA. With permission.)

Gila Monster

Heloderma suspectum

Lizards

Order Squamata

- **Name:** Beaded lizard or Mexican beaded lizard, no coloration on head, duller in color and larger than the Gila monster
- **Latin:** *Heloderma horridum*
- **Venom:** Same as Gila
- **Dx:** Same as Gila, but less severe systemic effects
- **Antidote:** No antivenin
- **Tx:** Same as for Gila monster bite, supportive, aggressive wound management, Ttox, antibiotics (Figure 22.19)

Mexican Beaded Lizard

Heloderma horridum

Venomous Lizards: Gila Monster vs. Beaded Lizard. What Is the Difference?

FIGURE 22.19 The Mexican beaded lizard, *Heloderma horridum*, is native to the border areas of Mexico and the desert southwest U.S. states, especially Arizona. It is differentiated from the Gila monster by its color patterns and its heavily beaded skin.

- *Gila monster, Heloderma suspectum*: Smaller bright pink to red colored bands on the tail
- *Mexican beaded lizard, Heloderma horridum*: Larger, duller, and more gray in color, no coloration on the head, less banding and more beading

Newts and Salamanders

Newts and Salamanders: What Is the Difference?

The differences between newts and salamanders are really minor as newts are types of salamanders. Newts usually have rougher and less slimy skins than other salamanders, and most newts return to semi-aquatic habitats for their adult lives.

The Pacific newts (genus *Taricha*) are terrestrial as adults, but return to water to breed. During the breeding season, they develop a flat tail, unlike salamanders which have round tails.

Salamanders are predators, most eat insects, earthworms, and spiders, but some will also eat small mammals and other amphibians.

Oregon or Western Rough-Skinned Newt

Taricha granulosa granulosa

- **Name:** Oregon or western rough-skinned newt
- **Latin:** *Taricha granulosa granulosa*
- **Venom:** Secretes neurotoxic *tetrodotoxins* (same as *pufferfish*—Fugu and *blue-ringed octopus*) through the skin
- **Dx:** Neurotoxicity, ingestion > contact

FIGURE 22.20 (See color insert.) The Oregon or western rough-skinned newt, *Taricha granulosa granulosa*, is related to the salamander that ranges from coastal Alaska to California and has rough dull-colored skin which secretes a tetrodotoxin to discourage predation. Ingestions of these newts usually on a dare have been fatal.

- **Antidote:** None
- **Tx:** Supportive (Figure 22.20)

Newts and Salamanders

- **Name:** *Salamandra* spp. salamanders
- **Latin:** *Salamandra* spp.
- **Venom:** Potent CNS neurotoxin—*salamandrin*
- **Dx:** Neurotoxicity
- **Antidote:** None
- **Tx:** Supportive

Colorado River Toad

Bufo alvarius

Toads

- **Name:** Colorado River toad
- **Latin:** *Bufo alvarius*

FIGURE 22.21 The Colorado River toad, *Bufo alvarius*, is a native of the lower Colorado River Valley and its large salivary glands secrete a toxic substance containing hallucinogenic bufotenins. Note: Just behind the large golden eye with a horizontal pupil is a bulging kidney-shaped parotid gland that secretes bufotenins. Below this is the large circular pale green ear drum. (Courtesy of U.S. National Park Service.)

- **Venom:** *Bufotenins*, skin-secreted biogenic amines that are serotonin agonists → can cause LSD-like hallucinations
- **Dx:** Hallucinations after toad licking and toad soup; characterized by salivation, euphoria, seizures, dysrhythmias
- **Antidote:** None
- **Tx:** Supportive (Figure 22.21)

Cane Toad

Bufo marinus, *Now* Rhinella marina

Toads

- **Name:** Cane toad
- **Latin:** *Bufo marinus*, now *Rhinella marina*
- **Venom:** Parotid and sebaceous gland secretions of toads contain *bufotoxins*, including (1) the cardiac glycoside-like *bufadienolides* and (2) the serotonergic *bufotenines;* used as a traditional Chinese topical aphrodisiac, *Ch'an su*
- **Dx:** "Dig-toxic"—N, V, bradycardia, dysrhythmias, hyperkalemia; LSD-like hallucinations
- **Antidote:** DigiBind® (Dig Fab antibodies)
- **Tx:** Mx dig-tox, reduce K^+ (Figure 22.22)

FIGURE 22.22 The cane or marine toad, formerly *Bufo marinus* and now *Rhinella marina*, was introduced into the southern United States from South America for biological control use against the cane beetle and is now considered a pest and an invasive species. When threatened, its salivary glands secrete a milky-white fluid containing bufotoxins which are digitalis-like cardiotoxins. (Courtesy of David K. Lirette, PhD, LSU School of Public Health, New Orleans, LA.)

Arthropods: Outline

Arachnids

- Spiders
  - Black widow
  - Brown recluse
  - Hobo spider
  - Tarantulas
  - Funnel web
- Scorpions
- Ticks

Order Hymenoptera

- Apids (bees)
- Vespids (wasps)
- Formicids (fire ants)

Order Lepidoptera

- Caterpillars of butterflies and moths

Miscellaneous

- Blister beetles
- Centipedes

Black Widow Female

Latrodectus mactans

Arachnids: *Latrodectus*

- **Name:** Black widow or red hourglass spider (Figure 22.23)
- **Latin:** *Latrodectus mactans*
- **Venom:** Alpha-latrotoxin causes Ach release and presynaptic stimulation of all muscarinic and nicotinic cholinergic receptors
- **Dx:** *Two painful red spots*—in hours—latrodectism = *facies latrodectismica*, N, V, salivation, urine retention, priapism, bronchorrhea, abdominal muscle cramps—rigidity, ↑ HR, and BP, restlessness, seizures
- **Name:** Black widow
- **Antidote:** *Latrodectus mactans* antivenin—a crude monovalent hyperimmune horse serum (IgG) antivenin

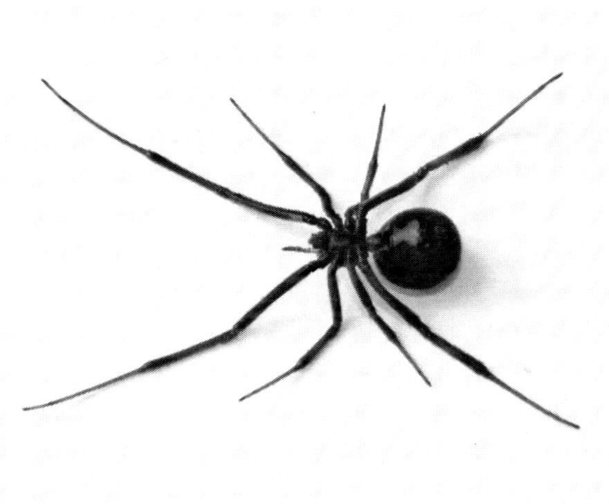

FIGURE 22.23 (See color insert.) The black widow (female), *Latrodectus mactans*, is identified by its black color and a distinctive red hourglass marking on the ventral surface of its abdomen, which may take on different shapes and an orange-red color in some specimens and other *Latrodectus* species. Deaths in healthy adults from *Latrodectus* bites are relatively rare in terms of the number of bites per thousand people. Sixty-three deaths were reported in the United States between 1950 and 1959. Since the species range worldwide, the highest number of deaths worldwide is caused by members of the genus *Latrodectus*. Widow spiders have more potent venom than most spiders, and prior to the development of antivenom, 5% of reported bites resulted in fatalities. Improvements in plumbing have greatly reduced the incidence of bites and fatalities in areas where outdoor privies have been replaced by flush toilets. (Courtesy of David K. Lirette, PhD, LSU School of Public Health, New Orleans, LA.)

- **Tx:** Tetanus toxoid—Ttox, cold packs, benzodiazepines preferred over >10% calcium gluconate for cramping abdominal muscular pain (Figure 22.23)

Brown Recluse or Violin Spider (See Figure 22.24)

Loxosceles reclusa

Arachnids: ***Loxosceles***

- **Name:** Brown recluse.
- **Latin:** *Loxosceles reclusa.*
- **Venom:** *Sphingomyelinase D.*
- **Dx:** *Painless* bite, bleeding blister—2 hours, necrotic ulcer and regional edema (*necrotic arachnidism*)—8 hours, eschar—1 week (Figure 22.25). Systemic loxoscelism = F, N, chills, rash, arthralgias, seizures, DIC, low platelets methemoglobinemia and hemolysis, ARF, coma.

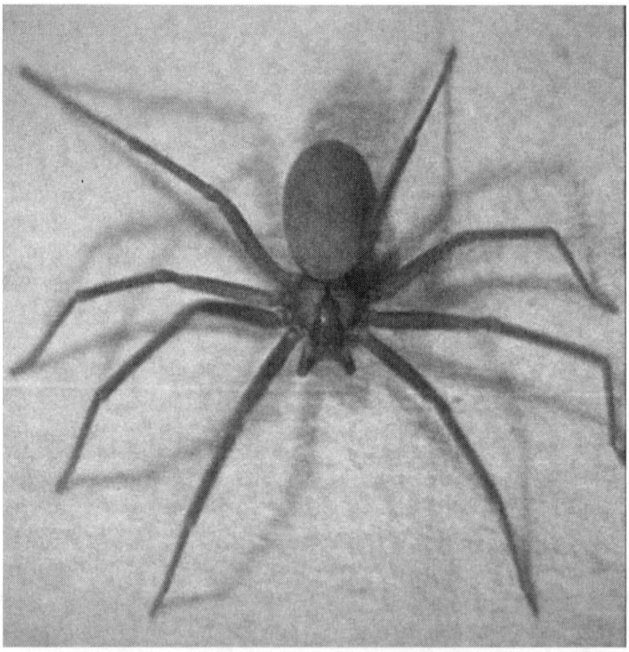

FIGURE 22.24 (See color insert.) The brown recluse or violin spider, *Loxosceles reclusa*, is medium to very dark brown in color and most species have distinctive violin or fiddle-shaped patterns on the dorsal aspect of the cephalothorax. Since not all brown recluses have the violin markings, the arrangement of the eyes will allow positive identification with 8 eyes instead of the typical 6 arranged in pairs with 1 median pair and 2 lateral pairs. An envenoming bite may result in blistering progressing to skin necrosis or loxoscelism, also referred to as necrotic arachnidism. (Courtesy of the CDC.)

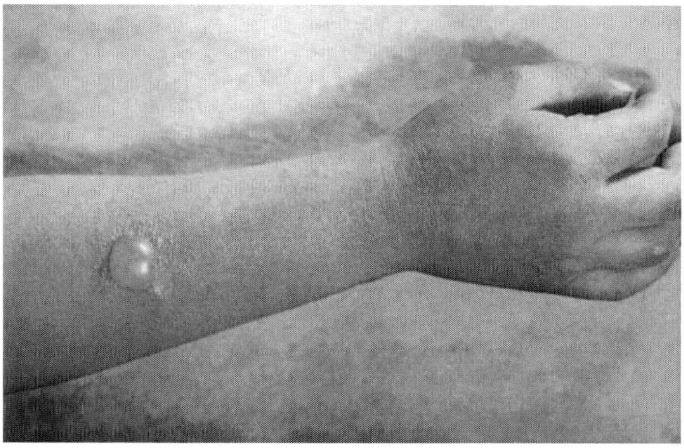

FIGURE 22.25 A blistering or bullous skin lesion on the dorsal forearm of a patient 24 h after being bitten by a *Loxosceles* species spider, the Chilean recluse, *Loxosceles laeta*. (Courtesy of the CDC.)

- **Antidote:** Experimental rabbit hyperimmune antivenin, not commercially available.
- **Tx:** Ttox, antibiotics for infection, wound care, surgical debridement, hyperbaric O_2? Consider polymorphonuclear leukocyte (pmn) microtubule inhibitors = dapsone (hemolysis in G-6-PD deficiency) and colchicine.

Loxosceles Species Spider Bite at 4 Months (See Figure 22.26)

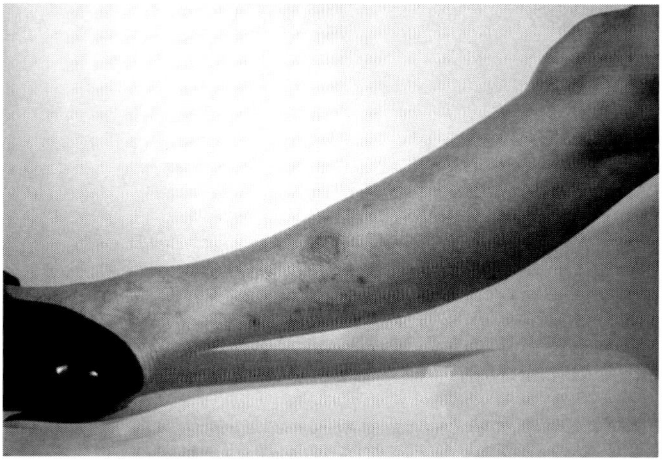

FIGURE 22.26 This patient displayed permanent tissue necrosis with annular scarring 4 months following the confirmed bite on the back of the lower leg by a brown recluse female spider, *Loxosceles reclusa.* (Courtesy of the CDC.)

Hobo Spider

Tegenaria agrestis

Arachnids: Hobo Spider

- **Name:** Hobo spider, aggressive house spider (recent European immigrant to NW United States—Washington and Oregon).
- **Latin:** *Tegenaria agrestis.*
- **Venom:** Locally cytotoxic venom, similar to brown recluse venom in causing necrotic arachnidism (often overdiagnosed).
- **Exception:** *Male hobo spiders are larger, more aggressive, more venomous than females and inflict more bites.*
- **Dx:** Initial painless bite, expanding erythema in hours, blister in 15–35 hours, necrotic ulcer—eschar, sloughs with scar over months to years. Comp: N, V, D, aplastic anemia, death.
- **Antidote:** None.
- **Tx:** Ttox, wound care, skin graft, consider systemic steroids (Figure 22.27).

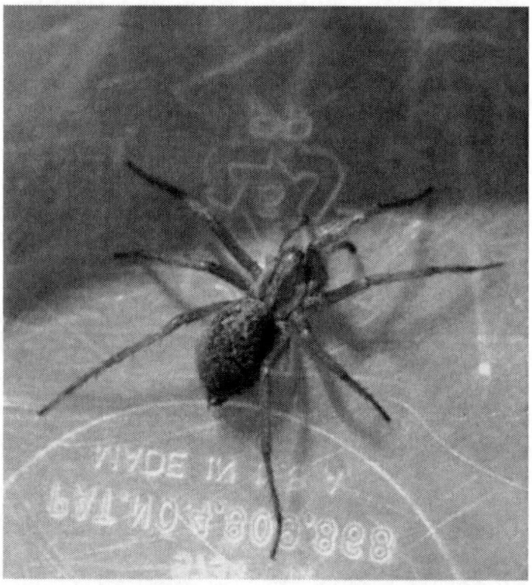

FIGURE 22.27 The hobo spider, *Tegenaria agrestis*, was introduced into the Pacific Northwest from Western Europe prior to World War II, was first identified in Seattle, and now occurs in southern Oregon. Hobo spiders are dark brown in color and often have darker brown to black midline chevrons and lateral longitudinal stripes on the dorsal surface of the cephalothorax. Misidentification often with beneficial spider species occurs commonly. The aggressiveness and venom toxicity of U.S. hobo spiders are disputed because bites by European species have not resulted in necrotic skin lesions. (Photograph taken by Dr. Lee Ostrom.)

U.S. Desert Tarantula

Aphonopelma chalcodes

Arachnids: Therapsids (Tarantulas) (See Figure 22.28)

- **Name:** Tarantulas of the desert SW United States
- **Latin:** *Dugesiella henzi*
- **Venom:** ATPase, spermine, hyaluronidase
- **Dx:** Rarely bites, local histamine triple resp, barbed urticating hairs fired from abdomen—can lodge in the cornea
- **Antidote:** None
- **Tx:** H_1 and H_2 blockers, adhesive removal hairs, slit-lamp examination of the cornea for embedded urticating hairs

Arachnids: The Problem with Pet Tarantulas

Slit-lamp examination: Tarantula urticating hairs may be released into a pet owner's face and *embedded in the cornea.* On electron microscopic examination, tarantula urticating hairs are barbed, and if embedded in the cornea can be difficult to remove surgically and can incite a severe inflammatory reaction known as *opthalmia nodosa* (Figure 22.28).

FIGURE 22.28 Tarantulas comprise a group of often hairy and very large arachnids belonging to the Theraphosidae family of spiders, of which approximately 900 species have now been identified. Most species of North American tarantulas are brown and not dangerous to humans. The desert tarantula (*Aphonopelma chalcodes*) or western desert tarantula is one of about 50 species of terrestrial tarantulas native to the southwestern and central United States. Some species have become popular in the exotic pet trade. Tarantulas have developed a unique defensive strategy by launching urticating hairs from their legs and cephalothorax at the faces of pursuing predators. In some cases, pet tarantula owners have suffered from skin reactions to embedded tarantula hairs or have experienced significant corneal foreign body reactions to hairs lodged in the cornea. (Courtesy of the CDC.)

Australian or Sydney Funnel Web Spider

Atrax robustus

Arachnids: Funnel-Web Spiders

Name: Australian funnel web spiders, large (3–5 cm) ground-burrowing or tree-dwelling black spiders with the world's most potent neurotoxin, *atraxotoxin*

Exception: Males more venomous than females—same as the hobo spiders

- **Latin:** *Atrax* (ground) and *Hadronyche* (trees)
- **Venom:** Massive release of acetylcholine—Ach, norepinephrine—NE, and epinephrine
- **Dx:** *Stage I:* piloerection, fasciculation, adrenergic (↑ HR and BP) and cholinergic (SLUDE = salivation, lacrimation, urination, defecation, emesis) crises in 5 min; *Stage II:* ↓ BP, respiratory depression, pulmonary edema, metabolic acidosis, death, especially kids who are less than 4 years of age
- **AD:** Rabbit IgG AV, 2 amps q 5 m
- **Tx:** Atropine, vasodilators, MRs, mechanical ventilation (Figure 22.29)

FIGURE 22.29 The Australian or Sydney funnel-web spider, *Atrax robustus*, is a species of Australian funnel-web spider usually found within a 100 km radius of Sydney, New South Wales, Australia. It is a venomous mygalomorph spider with a bite capable of causing serious injury or death in humans if left untreated. Sydney funnel-web spiders are mostly terrestrial spiders and typically build silk-lined tubular burrow retreats with collapsed "tunnels" or open "funnel" entrances from which irregular trip-lines radiate over the ground. Funnel-web spider venom contains a compound known as atraxotoxin (or atracotoxin), an ion channel inhibitor. Funnel webs usually deliver a full envenomation when they bite, often striking repeatedly due to their defensiveness and large chitinous cheliceral fangs. The bite of a Sydney funnel web is initially very painful, with clear fang marks separated by several millimeters. Since the funnel web antivenom became available in 1981, there have been no recorded fatalities from Sydney funnel-web spider bites.

Are All Spiders Venomous? Can Only Female Spiders Inflict Envenoming Bites?
With few exceptions, most spiders have venom glands to store venom for use in paralyzing prey for consumption, but only large spiders especially the female spiders have chelicerae long and strong enough to penetrate the human skin and significantly deliver envenoming bites. Necrotic skin ulcers are frequently misdiagnosed as spider bites and are usually caused by methicillin-resistant *Staphylococcus aureus* (MRSA) skin and soft-tissue infections following minor trauma, including other insect bites.

Arachnids: Scorpion

- **Name:** Bark scorpion
- **Latin:** *Centruroides sculpturatus*
- **Venom:** Complex with acetylcholinesterase—Achase, 5HT, hyaluronidase, phospholipases, Na-channel opening neurotoxins that cause massive autonomic discharge, both adrenergic (↑ HR and BP) and cholinergic (SLUDE)
- **Dx:** Grade I—pain + tap test; II—spreading paresthesias and numb; III—restless shakes, chorea, CN palsies, dysarthria; IV—CN and neuromuscular dysfunction
- **Antidote:** New equine Fab antivenom
- **Tx:** Sym + cholinergic blockers, Ca gluconate, consider ASA and quinine

Centruroides antivenom

Properties

- **Chem:** Fab antivenom produced in horses, very expensive
- **Mech:** Direct Ag/Ab antagonism
- **Contra:** Most adults, reserve for severe envenomations in children

Applications

- **Use:** Severe (grades III–IV) U.S. scorpion envenomations in children <age 6
- **Dose:** 1–2 vials over 30 min each
- **SE:** Serum sickness less likely (Figure 22.30)

Bark Scorpion

Centruroides sculpturatus

Hymenoptera: Apids (Bees) 1

- **Names:** Honeybee, bumblebee, carpenter bee
- **Latin:** *Apis mellifera, Bombus* spp., *Xylocopa* spp.
- **Venom:** Phospholipase A_2, hyaluronidase, *mellitin*, *apamin*, acid phosphatase, *allergen C*, mast cell degranulating peptide
- **Dx:** Local pain—edema, systemic-GI sx, F, HA, syncope, seizures, resp failure. Anaphylaxis (Type I HS rxn)—urticaria, bronchospasm, throat and chest tightness, stridor, CV collapse and arrest

FIGURE 22.30 The Arizona bark scorpion, *Centruroides sculpturatus*, is a small light brown scorpion common to the Sonoran Desert in south west United States and northern Mexico. An adult male can reach 8 cm in length (3.14 inches), while a female is slightly smaller. The bark scorpion is the most venomous scorpion in North America, and its venom can cause severe pain lasting between 24 and 72 h. Temporary numbness and weakness in the area stung is common, and many victims describe sensations of electrical jolts (positive tap signs) after envenoming's. Fatalities from scorpion envenomation in the United States are rare and confined to small children and adults with compromised immune systems. Extreme reaction to the venom is indicated by numbness, frothing at the mouth, paralysis, and epileptogenic activity. An antivenin was developed for this species at Arizona State University, and produced in quantities sufficient to treat individuals within the state of Arizona. However, this antivenom was not FDA approved, but use within the state of Arizona was permitted, and was very successful in shortening the duration of symptoms and hospitalization. Production of this local antivenom ceased by 2000, and the product became unavailable by 2004. However, a Mexican-produced antivenom, Anascorp (Antivenin Centruroides [scorpion] F[ab′]^2, Laboratorios Silanes, Instituto Bioclon SA de CV), received U.S. FDA approval on August 3, 2011, and is now in use in the Americas.

- **Antidote:** None, prophylactic desensitization with venoms from apids and vespids
- **Tx:** Scrape out stingers, subcutaneous—subq epi, support AW and circ (Figures 22.31 through 22.33)

Honeybee Workers

Apis mellifera *(Figure 22.31)*

Bumblebee

Bombus terrestris *(Figure 22.32)*

FIGURE 22.31 Honeybee workers, *Apis mellifera*, have been domesticated worldwide to produce honey and beeswax. They are related to bumble bees, *Bombus* species, and to carpenter bees, *Xylocopa* species. Africanized honeybees, also called "killer bees," are hybrids of the European honeybees, such as the Italian honeybee, *Apis mellifera linguistica*, and the Spanish honeybee, *Apis mellifera iberiensis*, cross-bred with the African honeybee, *Apis mellifera scultellata*. Africanized honeybees are the most defensive of all domesticated bees and will invade other honeybee hives, kill the reigning queen, and install their own queen bee. (Courtesy of David K. Lirette, PhD, LSU School of Public Health, New Orleans, LA.)

FIGURE 22.32 The bumblebee, *Bombus terrestris*, has black and yellow hairs arranged in bands, and, like the honeybee, feeds on nectar and gathers pollen to feed its young. Bumblebees form less extensive colonies than honeybees either underground or on the ground and under tall grasses, unlike carpenter bees that burrow into wood. Unlike the barbed honeybee stinger, a bumblebee stinger lacks barbs allowing a bumble bee to sting repeatedly unlike the honeybee which is disemboweled by a sting and dies shortly thereafter leaving its stinger and pulsating venom gland in its victim. (Courtesy of David K. Lirette, PhD, LSU School of Public Health, New Orleans, LA.)

FIGURE 22.33 The carpenter bee, *Xylocopa virginica*, which burrows into wood to form its nests, also has a barbless stinger, and can sting repeatedly. Although carpenter bees do not eat wood, they can damage trees and wood construction materials with their extensive tunneling. They resemble bumblebees in size, but are usually darker, have less banding; and are more docile and less likely to sting, unless handled. (Courtesy of the CDC.)

Carpenter Bee

Xylocopa virginica *(Figure 22.33)*

Hymenoptera: Vespids (Wasps and Hornets)

- **Name:** Paper wasp, gold wasp, "mud-dauber" wasp, yellow jacket, white-faced hornet.
- **Latin:** Vespids.
- **Venom:** *Kinins*, *antigen 5*, phospholipases, hyaluronidase, mast cell degranulating peptide.
- **Dx:** Same as Apids, consider desensitization.
- **Tx:** Scrape out stingers if present, prepare for anaphylaxis (Figures 22.34 through 22.37).

Yellow Jackets (Figure 22.34)

Vespula squamosa

Mud Dauber Wasp (Figure 22.36)

Sceliphron caementarium

Oriental Hornet

Vespa orientalis *(Figure 22.37)*

Wasps and Hornets: What Is the Difference?

Hornets are also wasps and belong to the same family as wasps, Vespidae. Hornets are the largest of the wasps and have much larger heads than other wasps. Hornets build aerial

FIGURE 22.34 Two yellow jacket wasps, *Vespula squamosa*, with a larger queen (left) compared to a worker (right). Yellow jackets are easily identified by the pair of longitudinal and parallel yellow stripes on the dorsal surface of the thorax. Yellow jackets build concealed nests underground, unlike hornets which build aerial nests, and will sting aggressively and repeatedly, if disturbed. Approximately 2 million Americans have allergies to stinging insect venoms, especially honeybee, yellow jacket, and hornet venoms. (Courtesy of the CDC.)

nests of chewed tree bark and wood pulp either in tree holes or suspended on tree limbs or buildings. Hornets are aggressive like yellow jacket wasps and will sting repeatedly with their barbless stingers. Unlike the venom of other wasps, hornet venom contains up to 5% acetylcholine.

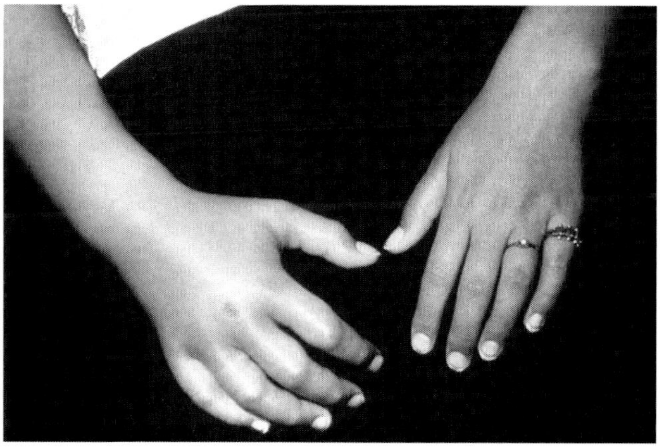

FIGURE 22.35 This figure demonstrates the significant edema that can follow yellow jacket stings and depicts the dorsal surfaces of a woman's hands and forearms 24 h after having been stung on the dorsum of the right hand by a yellow jacket, *Vespula squamosa*. Note the circular erythema surrounding the bite site and the marked swelling of the right hand and wrist compared to the left side. (Courtesy of the CDC.)

FIGURE 22.36 The mud dauber wasp, *Sceliphron caementarium*, is long and slender black with a thread-like waist and black and yellow in color. Female mud daubers build nests of mouth-molded mud in high places in which stockpile paralyzed spiders for their young to feed on with only one developing wasp per nest cell. Mud daubers are rarely aggressive and stings are uncommon compared to honeybee and yellow jacket stings. (Courtesy of the CDC.)

Hymenoptera: Formicids

- **Name:** Southern fire ants
- **Latin:** *Solenopsis* spp. (*S. invicta* most common)
- **Venom:** Phospholipase, hyaluronidase, *glucosaminidase*, *piperidines*
- **Dx:** Initial red wheals, clear vesicles in hours, then pustules by 12 h, umbilicate at 24 h, anaphylaxis possible

FIGURE 22.37 The oriental hornet, *Vespa orientalis*, is a relative of the widely distributed European hornet, *Vespa crabo*. Hornets are the largest wasps and can be differentiated from other wasps, such as yellow jackets and mud daubers, by their larger heads and aerial nests of chewed tree bark. As the hornet colony size grows, these nests in tree hollows or suspended from trees or even buildings can become very large. Hornets are aggressive and will sting multiple times. Their venom contains up to 5% acetylcholine, and allergic reactions in humans may require treatment with parenteral epinephrine.

- **Antidote:** None
- **Tx:** Salt/vinegar wash, cold, topical lidocaine, H_1-blockers

Red Fire Ant

Solenopsis invicta *(Figure 22.38)*

Can Some Animals Bite and Sting?

Yes: Fire ants (bite—oral pole; sting—aboral stinger), sting rays (mouth—ventral; stinger—dorsal) (Figure 22.39).

Fire ant Bite

Lepidoptera: Caterpillars

- **Names:** Nettling caterpillars = browntail moth caterpillar (*Euproctis* spp.), io moth caterpillar, buck moth caterpillar (*Hemileuca maia*), saddleback moth caterpillar, and puss moth caterpillar.

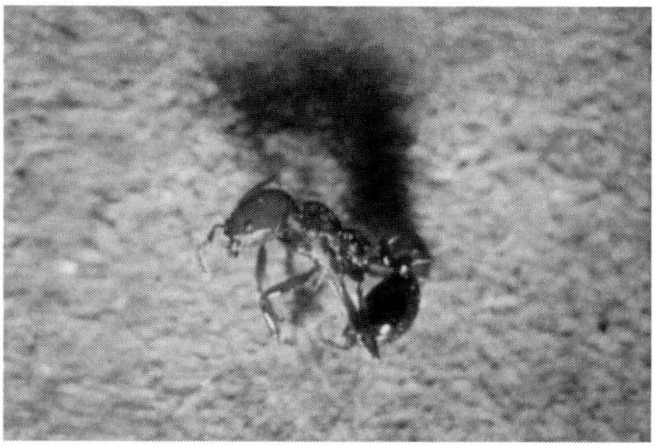

FIGURE 22.38 The red fire ant, *Solenopsis invicta*, is a native of South America that has become an unwelcomed imported pest in the United States as a result of its large persistent colonies and painful stings. Fire ants actually both bite initially to anchor themselves to their victims and then pivot in a circular fashion stinging repeatedly.

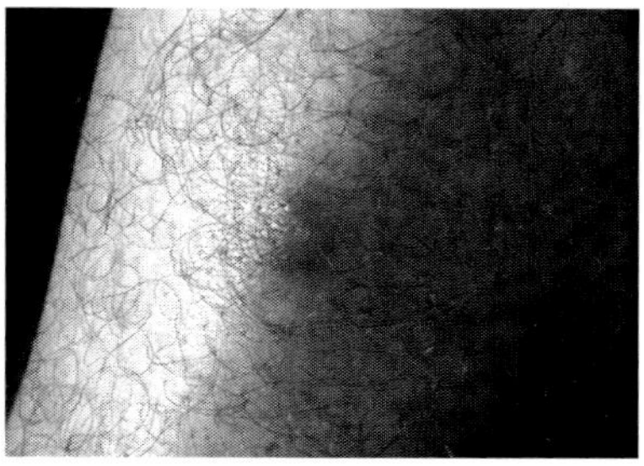

FIGURE 22.39 This figure demonstrates the clinical characteristics of a red fire ant bite on the leg. Note the ring of erythema surrounding the papular and pustular center. (Courtesy of the CDC.)

- **Puss moth caterpillar stings:** Shooting pain, nausea—N, vomiting—V, syncope possible.
- **Venoms:** Urticarial toxins.
- **Dx:** Painful sting, white-red papules → adenopathy, muscle cramps, seizures—sz possible, shock.
- **Antidote:** None.
- **Tx:** Adhesive removal spines? IV calcium gluconate probably ineffective, topical corticosteroids (Figures 22.40 through 22.46).

Hymenoptera Venoms and Hypersensitivity Reactions

See Tables 22.1 and 22.2.

Io Moth

Automeris io *(Figure 22.40)*

Table 22.1 Hymenoptera: Unique Venoms

Apid (Bees)	Vespids (Wasps)	Formicids (Fire Ants)
Unique components: Allergen C, apamin, mellitin, minimine	Unique components: Antigen 5, kinins, acetylcholine	Unique components: Glucosaminidase, piperidines (2,6-disubstituted piperidine) Misc. amines: *Sol i* I–IV
Common components: Hyaluronidase	Common components: Hyaluronidase	Common components: Hyaluronidase
Phospholipases	Phospholipases	Phospholipases
Acid phosphatase	Acid phosphatase	
Mast cell degranulating peptide	Mast cell degranulating peptide	

Table 22.2 Hypersensitivity (HS) Reactions to Foreign Antigens

Type	Definitions	Mediators	Onset Times	Examples
I	Immediate HS Anaphylaxis	IgE	Immediate to minutes	Bee stings Baker's asthma
II	Complement fixation	IgM, IgG, and complement	Hours	Transfusion reactions Trimetallic anhydrides
III	Antigen–antibody complex formation-deposition	IgM and IgG	12 h to 1–2 weeks	Serum sickness HS pneumonitis
IV	Delayed HS cellular immunity	T-lymphocytes	24–72 h	Beryllium dis. poison ivy PPD +

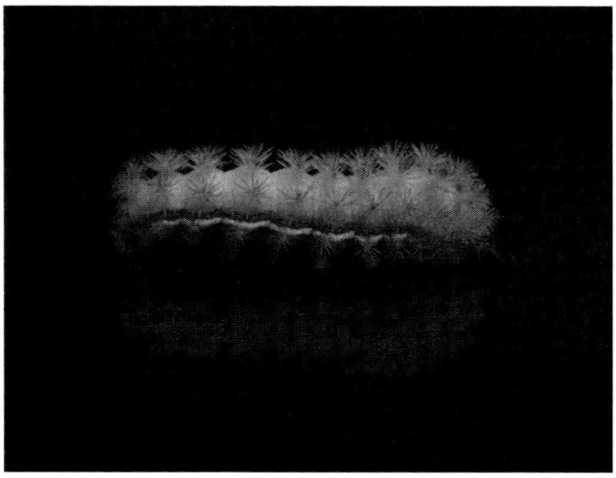

FIGURE 22.40 (**See color insert.**) The io moth, *Automeris io*, caterpillar is bright green with two lateral stripes, the top one is red and the lower white. It is covered with urticating hairy spines which can break off and inject venom into victims. (Courtesy of David K. Lirette, PhD, LSU School of Public Health, New Orleans, LA.)

Buck Moth (Figure 22.41)

Hemileuca maia

Gypsy Moth

Lymantria dispar *(Figure 22.42)*

FIGURE 22.41 The buck moth, *Hemileuca maia*, caterpillar is often found on oak and willow trees and is brownish black with white spots and covered with spines attached to venom glands which can break off on contact to inject venom into victims. (Courtesy of David K. Lirette, PhD, LSU School of Public Health, New Orleans, LA.)

FIGURE 22.42 (See color insert.) The gypsy moth, *Lymantria dispar*, caterpillar, a voracious feeder, is black with long, hair-like setae and five pairs of raised blue spots and six pairs of raised red spots along the back. The caterpillars will climb up any object in their way in search of food including telephone poles and people.

White-Marked Tussock Moth Caterpillar

Orgyia leucostigma *(Figure 22.43)*

Hag Moth

Phobetron pithecium *(Figure 22.44)*

FIGURE 22.43 (See color insert.) The white-marked tussock moth, *Orgyia leucostigma*, caterpillar is related to the destructive gypsy moth caterpillar and can also damage trees and sting humans when present in large numbers. (Courtesy of David K. Lirette, PhD, LSU School of Public Health, New Orleans, LA.)

FIGURE 22.44 The hag moth, *Phobetron pithecium*, caterpillar, so named because its six pairs of brown curly projections resemble a bad hair day, is not a notorious stinger; but its spines can break off in victims and deliver a venom-induced chemical allergic reaction in susceptible victims. (Courtesy of USDA Forest Service and the University of Georgia.)

Puss or Flannel Moth

Megalopyge opercularis *(Figure 22.45)*

Saddleback Moth

Sibene stimulea *(Figure 22.46)*

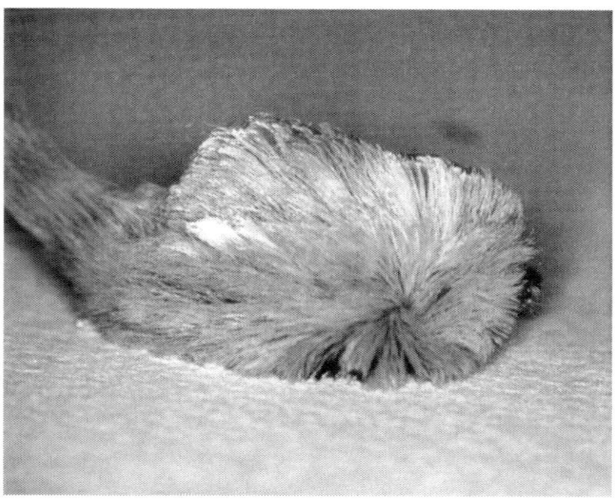

FIGURE 22.45 The puss moth or southern flannel moth, *Megalopyge opercularis*, caterpillar is covered with hair-like yellowish-brown setae and resembles a tiny cat, hence its name. Hollow spines are hidden within its flannel-like "fur" and will break off and release venom on contact causing extremely painful reactions in victims leaving a "tire tread" mark from spine punctures on sting wounds. (Courtesy of the CDC.)

FIGURE 22.46 Saddleback moth, *Sibene stimulea*, caterpillars are devouring a leaf. (Courtesy of David K. Lirette, PhD, LSU School of Public Health, New Orleans, LA.)

Lytta vesicatoria

("Spanish Fly")

Miscellaneous Venomous True Bugs (Hemiptera):

Blister Beetles

- **Name:** Blister beetle (eastern United States), Spanish fly (Europe)
- **Latin:** *Cantharis vesicatoria* (Eur), *Tegrodera aloga* (United States), *Lytta vesicatoria* (United States) (Figure 22.47).
- **Venom:** Cantharidin, an irritating skin and mucosal vesicant

FIGURE 22.47 Potions or powders of dried blister beetles, especially *Lytta vesicatoria*, the "Spanish fly" were used either as aphrodisiacs or abortifacients because of the irritating properties of cantharidin on the mucosal surfaces of the genitourinary tract.

- **Dx:** Blistering, vesicular dermatitis, stomatitis, cystitis, hematuria, priapism, vaginal bleeding, spontaneous abortion
- **Antidote:** None
- **Tx:** Supportive (Figure 22.47)

Miscellaneous: Centipedes and Millipedes

Centipedes vs. Millipedes: What Is the Difference?

Centipedes belong to the order Chilopoda and are flattened, worm-like arthropods with a pair of well-developed antennae on their heads. Centipedes have one pair of legs per body segment with the first pair modified into fangs or chelicerae connected to venom glands. Centipedes can grow up to 6 inches long, and some species can run fast. Centipedes are venomous and can inflict painful bites with their fangs. Millipedes are rounded, worm-like arthropods with 2 pairs of legs per body segment. Their legs are shorter than centipede legs and their movement is slow and wave-like. Millipedes are typically 1.5 inches long, but some species can grow up to 4 inches in length. Millipedes do not bite, but, if provoked, can release or even squirt an irritating and malodorous fluid from glands opening at the bases of their legs. This fluid may blister the skin and cause allergic reactions in sensitive individuals.

Centipede

Scolopendra *Species*

- **Name:** Centipedes.
- **Latin:** *Scolopendra* species centipedes (Figure 22.48).
- **Venom:** Toxin(s) undefined, poison glands are connected to a pair of chelicerae that will bite if provoked. The larger species of centipedes will have larger jaws or chelicerae and can inflict more painful bites. Some individuals may be allergic to centipede venom.
- **Dx:** Painful sting.
- **Antidote:** None.
- **Tx:** Supportive (Figure 22.48).

Post-Test Question 3

3. You receive a frantic phone call from a local grammar school principal seeking advice on a plague of fuzzy, tan caterpillars dropping from oak trees on kids at recess and causing painful stings that leave a red, tire-grid welt mark. Select the species of venomous caterpillar capable of inflicting such injuries.
   a. *Autumeris io*
   b. *Lymantria dispar*
   c. *Megalopyge opercularis*
   d. *Sibene stimulea*

FIGURE 22.48 *Scolopendra* species centipede. Note the curved antennae on the head and the single pair of legs per body segment which serve to differentiate centipedes from millipedes. Centipedes are venomous and can inflict painful bites with their fangs which are connected to venom glands.

Post-Test Question 4

4. Antigen 5 is a unique, highly immunoreactive protein constituent of the venom of which of the following arthropods?
   a. Bumblebees
   b. Fire ants
   c. Honeybees
   d. Wasps

Answers to Practice Test Questions 1–4

1. b
2. c
3. c
4. d

Reference

The Epidemiology of Coral Snake Bites in Florida

J.N. Bernstein, MD, FACEP, medical director, Miami-Dade County, FL, Poison Control Center-PCC, personal communication.

Chapter 23

Common Arthropod Vectors of Infectious Diseases

Outline 526
Mosquitoes and Flies: Outline 526
Mosquitoes (Culicidae) 526
Flies (Diptera): Outline 531
Fleas, Lice, Ticks, Mites: Outline 540
Conclusions 555

Outline

- Mosquitoes, flies, and myiasis (human infestation with maggots)
- Bugs, fleas, lice, ticks, and mites

Mosquitoes and Flies: Outline

Mosquitoes (Culicidae)

1. Anophelines (Anophelinae)
2. Culicines (Culicinae)

Flies (Diptera)

1. Blackflies (Simuliidae)
2. Sandflies (Phlebotominae)
3. Biting midges (Ceratopogonidae)
4. Horseflies (Tabinidae)
5. Tsetse flies (Glossinidae)
6. Domestic flies and myiasis:
   a. House and stable flies (Muscidae)
   b. Latrine flies (Fanniidae)

Mosquitoes (Culicidae)

Anophelines (Anophelinae)

- **Adult:** Only females feed after mating to obtain nutrient blood meals for eggs; rest at angle to feed; digest over 3 days–2 weeks; lifespan 1–4 weeks; infective for life
- **Disease:** Malaria × 5 species of *Plasmodium*, filariasis (*Wuchereria bancrofti, Brugia malayi, Brugia timori*), zoonotic arborvirus (*O'Nyong-nyong*—"joint-breaker" fever)
- **Mechanism:** PM-biting, anthropophagic vs. zoophagic, endophagic vs. exophagic, endophilic vs. exophilic; the mosquito must ingest gametocytes to start sexual cycle—infective sporozoites stored in salivary glands; microfilaria—no sexual cycle, nonsalivary release on biting (Figure 23.1)

Culicines (Culicinae)

- **Adult:** The same feeding behaviors and lifespan; rest parallel to host to feed (Figure 23.2)
- **Disease:** *Culex-Wuchereria bancrofti, Brugia malayi*; *Aedes* cause yellow fever and dengue; both—zoonotic arborviruses (Ross River—Australia, Chikungunya—Africa, Asia; Sindbis—Af, As; West Nile—Af, As, Am); encephalitis viruses (JE, Japan, Asia; SLE, EEE-WEE-VEE-Am)

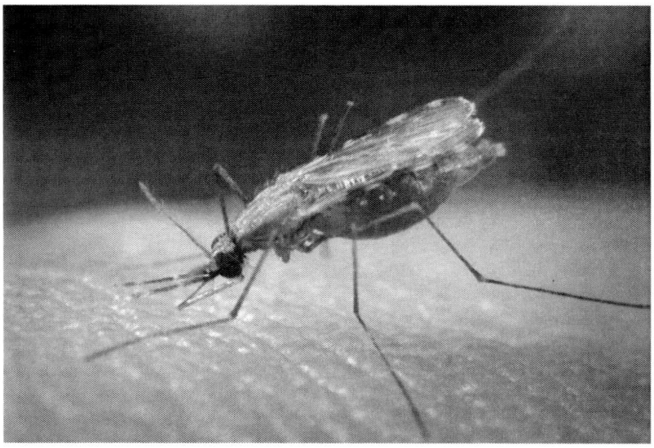

FIGURE 23.1 Blood-feeding behavior of a female *Anopheles* species mosquito. (Courtesy of the CDC.)

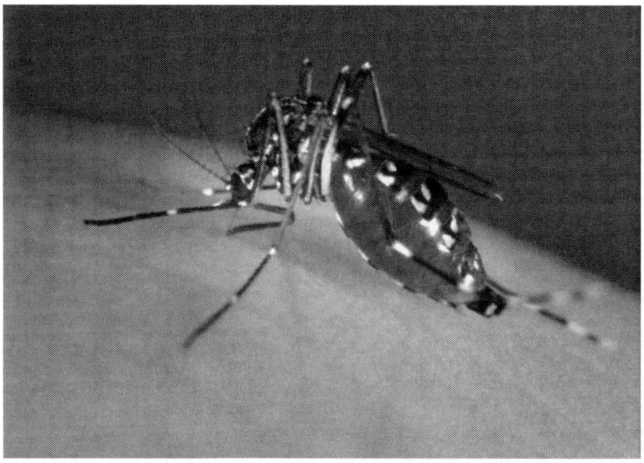

FIGURE 23.2 Blood-feeding behavior of an *Aedes* species mosquito—female *Aedes albopictus*, competent vector for yellow fever virus, Chikungunya virus, West Nile virus, and many viral encephalitides. (Courtesy of the CDC.)

- **Mech:** Day biting, anthropophagic and zoophagic, exophagic, and endophilic; no malaria transmission, same microfilaria and viral transmission

Mosquitoes: Stages

Anophelines

- **Adults:** Females have nonplumose antennae, palps as long as proboscis, black and white block-like wing scales; always feed at angle to host
- **Eggs:** Always laid singly with floats ("little canoes")

- **Larvae:** No siphon, rest parallel to water surface
- **Pupae:** Breathing trumpets short and broad apically (little "*Shreks*"), hairy spines on segments 2–7

Culicines

- **Adults:** Females have nonplumose antennae too, palps much shorter than proboscis, wing veins not block-like scales; feed parallel (horizontal) to host
- **Eggs:** Laid in rafts or singly with no floats ("life rafts")
- **Larvae:** Always have siphons, rest at 45° angle to water surface
- **Pupae:** Trumpets short or long, but not broad apically, non-"*Shrek*," no spines on segments 2–7 (Figure 23.3)

Mosquitoes: *Malaria*

See Figures 23.4 and 23.5.

Note: P. falciparum trophozoites within human RBCs.

Note: P. falciparum sexual gametocytes within human RBCs—infect female Anopheles.

Mosquitoes: Filiariasis

See Figure 23.6.

Note: Wuchereria bancrofti larvae develop within mosquito (Aedes, Culex, Mansonia) thorax muscle.

Mosquito Vector for Dengue: Aedes aegypti

Range: *Aedes aegypti*

See Figure 23.7.

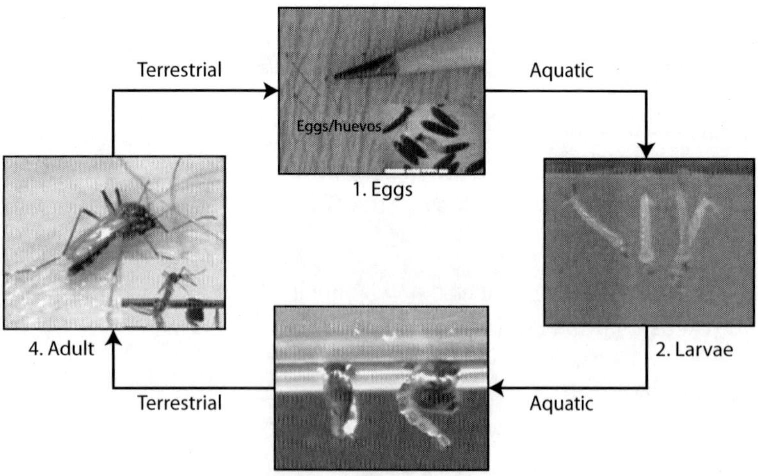

FIGURE 23.3 Life cycle of the mosquito. (Courtesy of the CDC.)

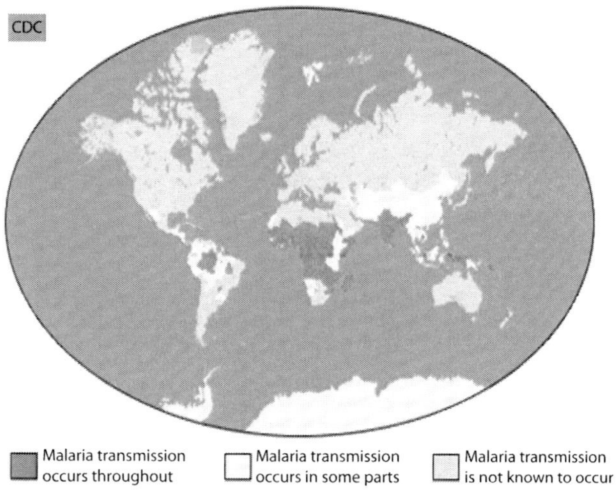

FIGURE 23.4 Global distribution and regional transmission of malaria. (Courtesy of the CDC.)

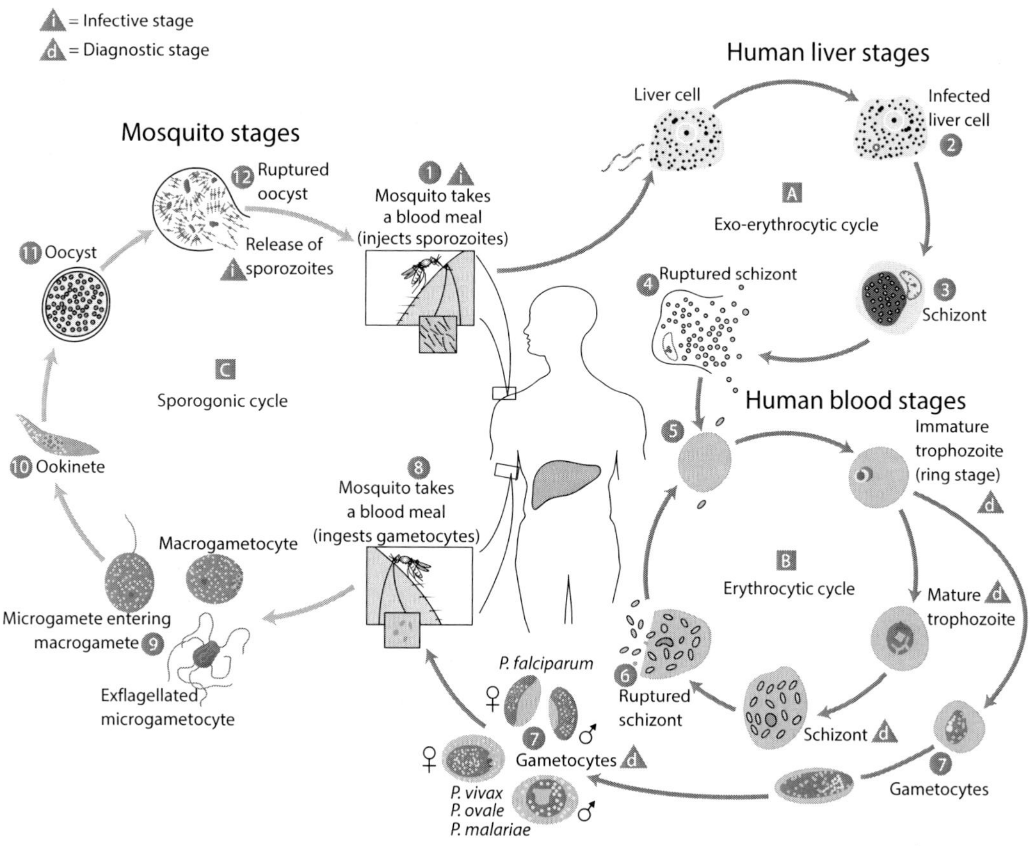

FIGURE 23.5 Various stages of the malaria infection. (Courtesy of the CDC.)

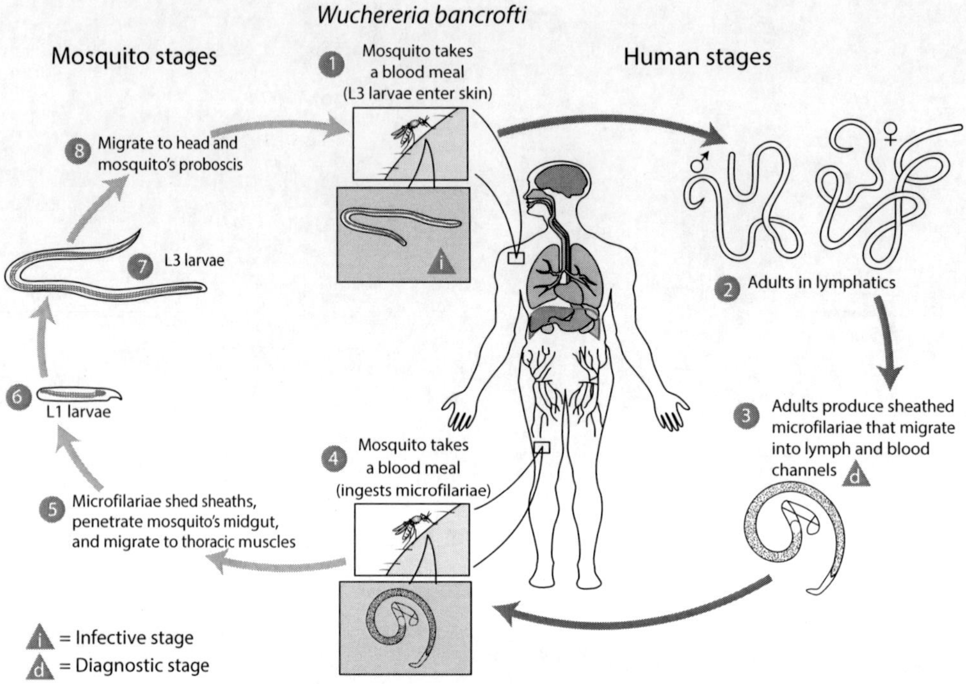

FIGURE 23.6 Filarial worm life cycle for *Wuchereria bancrofti*. (Courtesy of the CDC.)

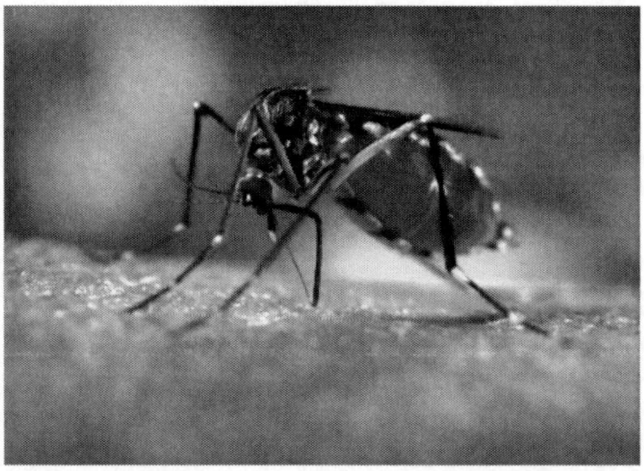

FIGURE 23.7 Blood-feeding posture for the female *Aedes aegypti* mosquito, the preferred vector for the yellow fever virus. (Courtesy of the CDC.)

Mosquitoes: Yellow Fever Mosquito Vector Transmission Cycles

See Figure 23.8.

Mosquitoes: Control and Prevention

- **Hierarchy of vector control:** Genetic control > physical > biological > chemical > personal protection

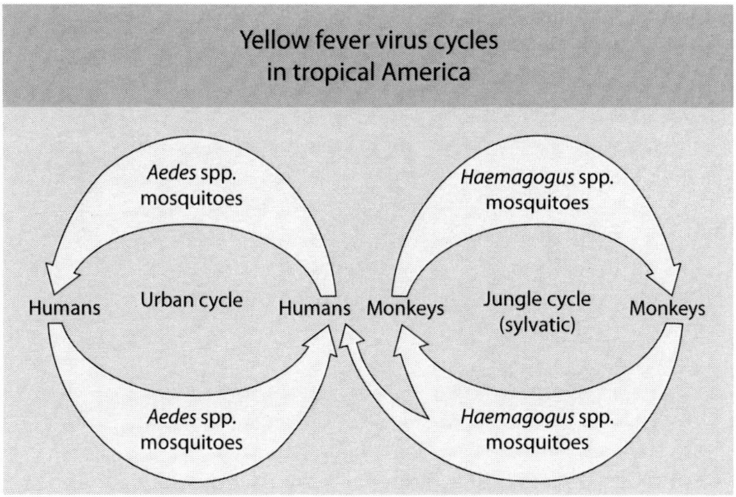

FIGURE 23.8 The urban and sylvatic vector transmission cycles for the yellow fever virus in the tropical Americas. (Courtesy of the CDC.)

- **Genetic:** Complex and expensive, #1 release of infertile and impotent males (hybrids, irradiated, or chemo-sterilized males) > #2 lethal genomic reengineering (USNR > USAMRID)
- **Physical:** Drainage > landfills > habitat changes = ↓ water flow, marsh impoundment to create deep ponds and lakes
- **Chemical:** Oil spraying > insecticides: *Pyrethroids* (deltamethrin, permethrin) > bio-degrading *organophosphates* (malathion, fenitrothion, chlorpyrifos, pirimiphos, temephos) and *carbamates* (aldicarb, bendiocarb, propoxur) > bioaccumulating; Organochlorines: DDT, lindane
- **Personal protection:** Pyrethroid-impregnated blinds, coils, mats, nets, screens > pyrethroid-impregnated clothing > body repellants (diethyltoluamide [DEET])> dimethylphthlate [DIMP])

Flies (Diptera): Outline

- Blackflies (Simuliidae)
- Sandflies (Phlebotaminae)
- Biting midges (Ceratopogonidae)
- Horseflies (Tabinidae)
- Tsetse flies (Glossinidae)
- Domestic (house, stable, and latrine flies) flies (Muscidae)
- Myiasis (human maggot infestation)—producing flies

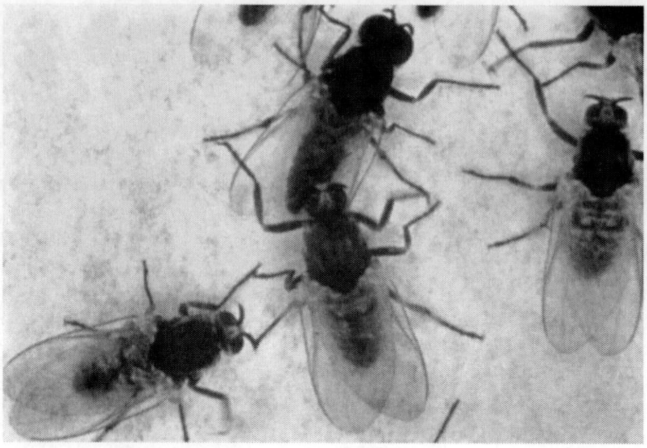

FIGURE 23.9 Simuliid species black flies, arthropod vectors of *Onchocerca volvulus*, a filarial worm. (Courtesy of the CDC.)

Blackflies (Simuliidae) 1

- **Family:** Simuliidae
- **Genus:** *Simulium* blackflies or buffalo flies (Figure 23.9)
- **Adult:** Tiny black flies with buffalo-humped thorax, hairless wings, and 3–4 week lifespan
- **Disease:** African and Latin American River Blindness (*Onchocerca volvulus*), SA filariasis (*Mansonella ozzardi*) (Figures 23.10 and 23.11)
- **Mechanism:** Daytime-biting females, stretch skin with toothed labrum, then use their raspy maxilla and mandible to chew into fine capillaries creating a blood pool filled with host's circulating microfilaria to drink from

Blackflies (Simuliidae) 2

- **Eggs:** 200–800 laid in sticky masses at water level in fast-flowing rivers and streams
- **Larvae:** Sedentary passive filter feeders anchored by posterior circlet; characteristic gill spot and apical mouth brush
- **Pupae:** Slipper-shaped brown cocoon anchored to submerged rocks; simultaneous adult emergence (hatch)
- **Control:** OPs (temephos) > DDT into flowing streams; consider biological control (*Bacillus thuringiensis*)
- **Prevention:** Personal protection with DEET > DIMP

Sandflies (Phlebotaminae) 1

- **Genus:** *Phlebotomus* (Old World) and *Lutzomyia* (New World)
- **Adult:** Tiny black flies covered with hair, large black eyes, stilt-like legs, hairy wings held erect over body at rest (Figure 23.12)

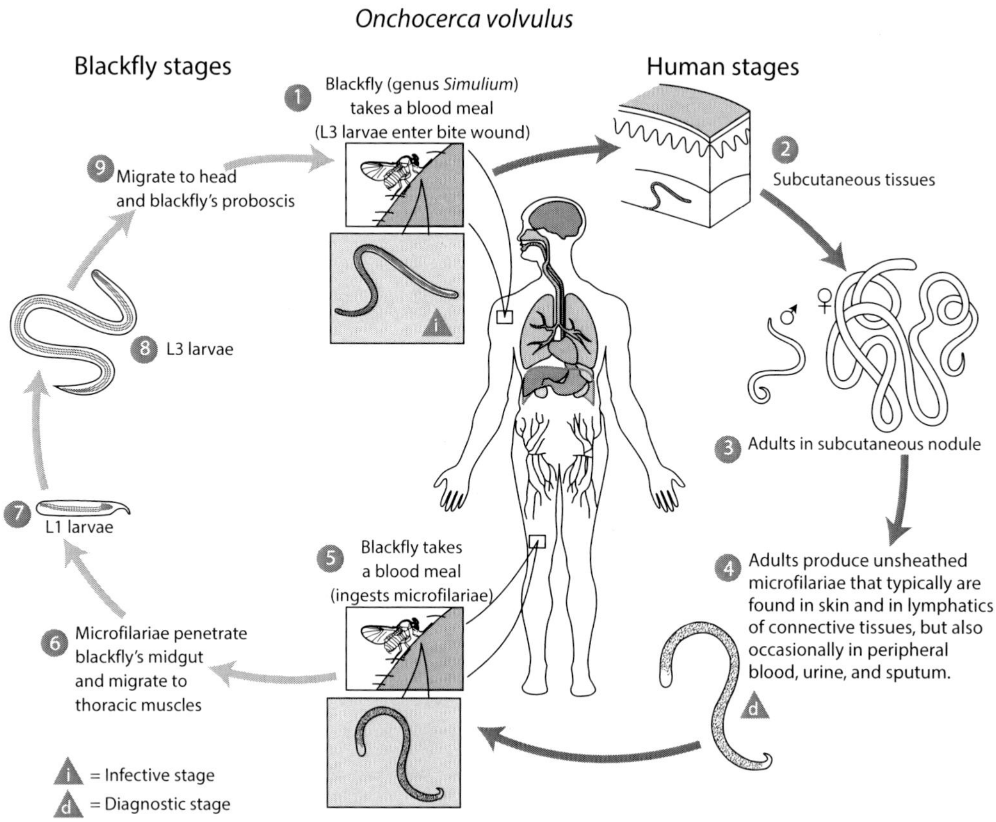

FIGURE 23.10 Transmission cycle of *Onchocerca volvulus*, a filarial worm. (Courtesy of the CDC.)

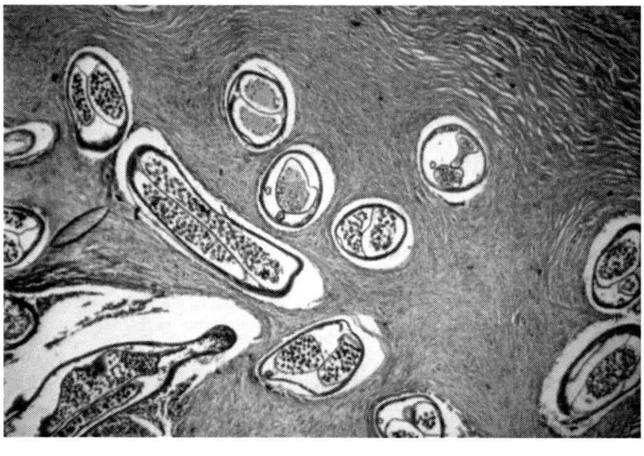

FIGURE 23.11 Encysted adult *Onchocerca volvulus*, a filarial worm, in a subcutaneous skin nodule. (Courtesy of the CDC.)

FIGURE 23.12 *Phlebotomus* species sandfly, arthropod vector for the Old World leishmanias, blood feeding on a human host. (Courtesy of the CDC.)

- **Diseases:** Leishmaniasis—cutaneous (*L. tropica* and *L. major*), mucocutaneous espundia (*L. braziliensis* and *L. panamensis*), diffuse cutaneous (*L. aethiopica* and *L. amazonensis*), visceral-kala-azar (*L. donovani* and *L. chagasi*); Bartonellosis (Carrion's disease); viral sandfly fever (transovarian passage) (Figure 23.13)
- **Mechanism:** Nocturnal blood-sucking exophagic females ingest amastigotes to midgut, metacyclic promastigotes regurgitated into host at blood meal

Sandflies (Phlebotaminae) 2

- **Eggs:** 30–70 min ovoid eggs with brick patterns oviposited on moist ground, masonry, or leaf litter
- **Larvae:** Four stages of segmented instars, all have dark heads, are bristled with matchstick hairs, and tipped with caudal bristles
- **Pupae:** Comma-shaped pupa with larval skin remaining attached caudally with its characteristic matchstick hair and caudal bristles
- **Control:** Pyrethroid-impregnated blinds, screens, nets, and clothing
- **Prevention:** Personal protection—DEET > DIMP > trimethyl pentanediol

Biting Midges 1

- **Family:** Ceratopogonidae.
- **Genus:** *Culicoides*, "no-see-ums" (Figure 23.14).
- **Adult:** Only minute females bite, small head, prominent eyes, long nonplumose antennae, two dark depressions or humeral pits on the head end of the thorax, patterned black and white wings.

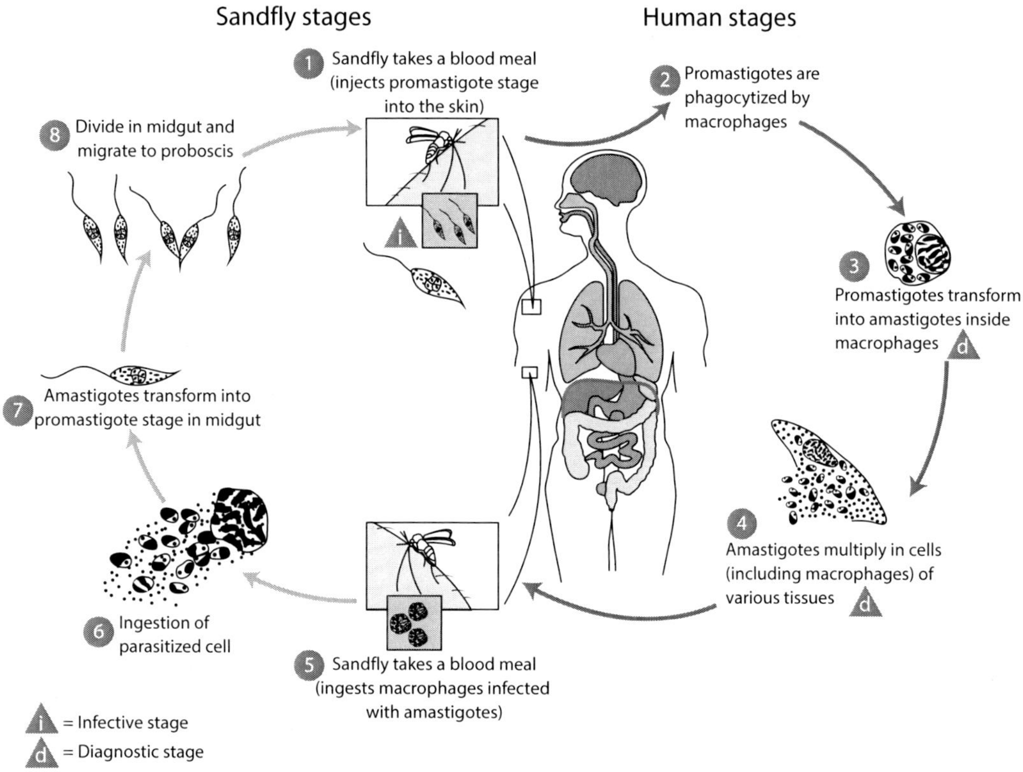

FIGURE 23.13 Transmission cycle for leishmaniasis. (Courtesy of the CDC.)

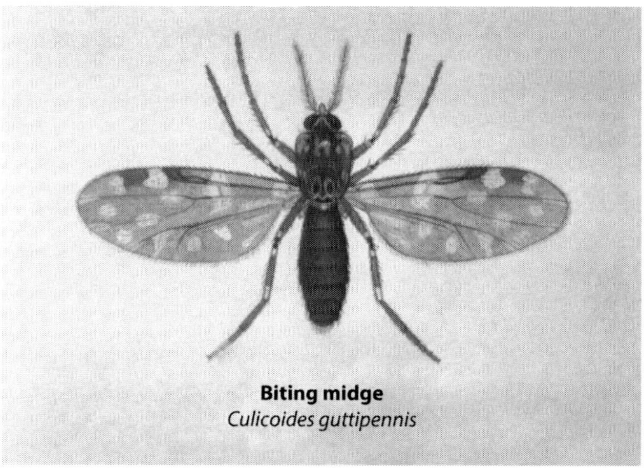

FIGURE 23.14 *Culicoides guttipennis*, a competent arthropod vector for filarial diseases. (Courtesy of the CDC.)

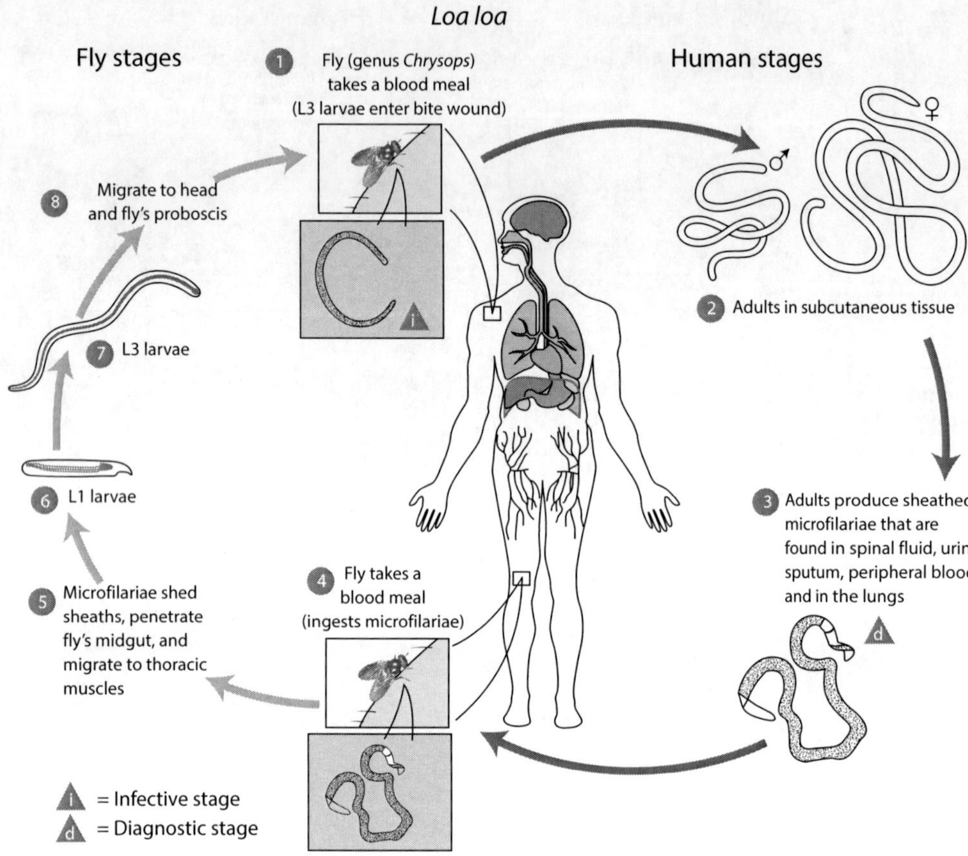

FIGURE 23.15 Transmission life cycle of *Loa loa,* another filarial worm. (Courtesy of the CDC.)

- **Disease:** Filiariasis: Africa—*Mansonella perstans* and *Streptocerca*; Americas—*Mansonella ozzardi* (Figure 23.15).
- **Mechanism:** Females ingest dermal microfilaria with blood meals, invade thoracic wing muscles to develop, and then migrate to head and proboscis in 10 days, and ultimately rupture via nonsalivary transmission blood feeds.

Biting Midges 2

Eggs: 30–250 banana-shaped eggs per oviposition on wet mud or manure

Larvae: 4 nematode-like instars with dark conical heads, 12 segments, 4-lobed retractable papillae

Pupae: Paired 2-segment breathing trumpets on head and paired spiny thorns on tail

Control: Marsh impoundment; aquatic vegetation and bottomland spraying, OPs > OCs

Prevention: Small-mesh pyrethroid-impregnated screens, DEET > DIMP > trimethyl pentanediol (TP)

Horseflies (Tabanidae) 1

- **Family:** Tabanidae
- **Genus:** *Chrysops* (deerflies) and *Tabanus* (horseflies)
- **Adult:** Large dark flies with semilunar heads and iridescent compound eyes separated in females by a dichoptic space, short stout antennae, wings rest at roof-like angle over abdomen
- **Disease:** Loiasis (*Loa loa*), mechanical transmission of bacterial (anthrax, tularemia) and trypanosomal zoonoses (Figure 23.15)
- **Mechanism:** Females inflict deep, painful bites (often interrupted and repeated) sucking up dermal microfilaria, which develop in thoracoabdominal fat and then migrate to the proboscis for nonsalivary transmission on the next blood meal

Horseflies and Deerflies (Tabanidae) 2

- **Eggs:** 100–1000 creamy to dark-colored eggs oviposited on the undersides of vegetation close to the aquatic larval sites
- **Larvae:** Creamy to dark, large and cylindrical, pointed at both ends, 11 segments separated by tire-like rings—the mid 4–10 of which have pseudopods; characteristic caudal Graber's sensory organ
- **Pupae:** Comma-shaped and brown, buries itself into mud and resembles a butterfly chrysalis
- **Control:** Marsh drainage
- **Prevention:** Personal protection

Tsetse flies (Glossinidae) 1

- **Family:** Glossinidae
- **Genus:** *Glossina*
- **Adult:** Both sexes are daytime biters, especially through dark clothing, large yellow-brown to black with rigid, forward projecting proboscis and characteristic upside-down hatchet wing venation, wings rest over abdomen like scissors
- **Diseases:** Human (*T. brucei gambiense*—chronic sleeping sickness, *T. brucei rhodesiense*—virulent sleeping sickness) and animal (*T. brucei brucei*) African trypanosomiasis (Figure 23.16)
- **Mechanism:** Amastigotes sucked up on blood feed migrate to paired salivary glands and mature into infective metacyclic trypomastigotes, ready for human/animal transmission on the next blood meal

Tsetse flies (Glossinidae) 2

- **Eggs:** No eggs, direct single-larva larvipositors
- **Larvae:** Nourished by paired milk glands, has 12 segments with paired black polyneustic lobes to burrow into 2–5 cm of moist, shady soil on oviposition after 9-day gestation

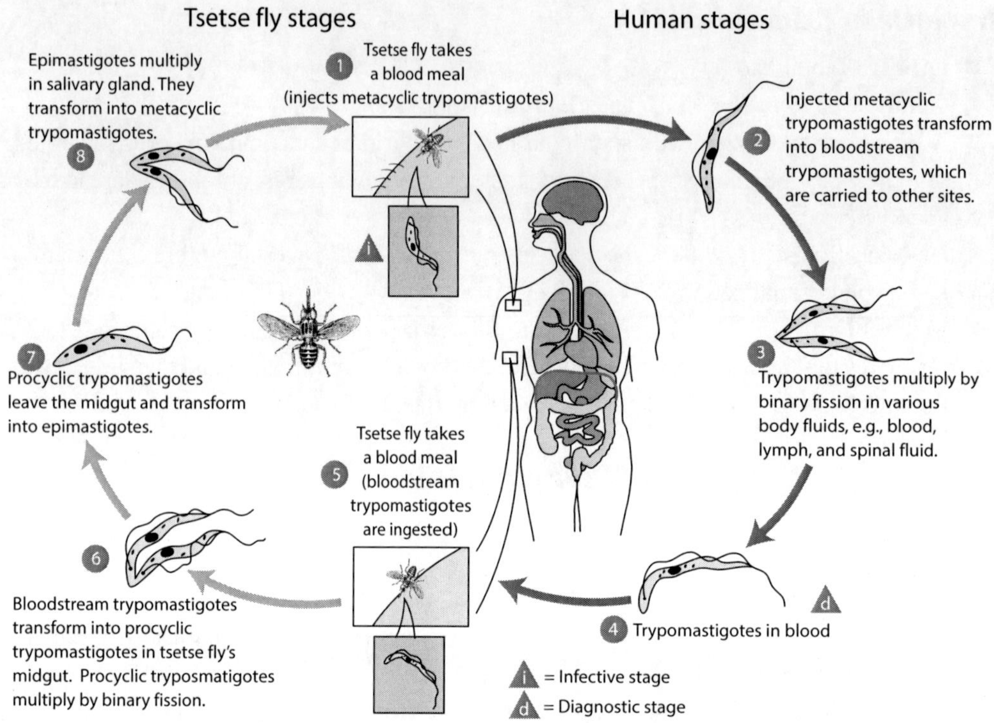

FIGURE 23.16 **Transmission life cycle of *African trypanosomiasis* (African sleeping sickness), transmitted by the bite of an infected tsetse fly. (Courtesy of the CDC.)**

- **Pupae:** Resembles a contracted, barrel-shaped larva with prominent polyneustic lobes; adult fly emerges from buried pupa
- **Control:** OCs (dieldrin, DDT) directed at adults since larvae develop within females and pupae are buried; clearing waterfront vegetation; OP-impregnated blue cloth target screens and conical flytraps
- **Prevention:** Avoid dark clothes, personal protection

Domestic flies (Muscidae)

Outline

- Domestic house fly (*Musca domestica*)
- Stable fly (*Stomoxys calcitrans*)
- Latrine fly (*Fannia* spp.)

Domestic House Flies (Muscidae) 1

- **Family:** Muscidae
- **Genus:** *Musca domestica*

- **Adult:** Medium-sized, nonmetallic color, four dark thoracic stripes, telescoping proboscis designed for siphoning semisolid fluids, three pairs of legs equipped with glandular hairs secreting sticky substances
- **Diseases:** Mechanical vectors of bacterial (*Shigella*, *Salmonella*, cholera, ETEC, *Campylobacter*); protozoan (amebic), and viral IDs
- **Mechanism:** Feed on feces then human food, mechanically transmitting, vomiting, or defecating infectious microbes

Domestic House Fly (Muscidae) 2

- **Eggs:** 75–120 banana-shaped eggs oviposited on decaying matter, feces
- **Larvae:** Creamy white 11-segment cylindrical maggot with a pointed head, 2 mouth hooks, and a posterior pair of breathing spiracles
- **Pupae:** Dry, brown, barrel-shaped pupa develops in dry soil beneath larval habitats
- **Control:** Physical screens, ultraviolet-light traps, toxic baits; environmental-refuse disposal; larvicides-OP spraying garbage cans; adulticides-OPs > pyrethroids
- **Prevention:** Sanitary food preparation, food and restaurant service monitoring and inspection

Stable Fly (Muscidae) 1

- **Family:** Muscidae
- **Genus:** *Stomoxys calcitrans*
- **Adult:** Resembles house fly, but frequents stables and barns; and has distinctly unique forward-projecting proboscis
- **Diseases:** Same as house flies
- **Mechanism:** Same as house flies

Stable Fly (Muscidae) 2

- **Eggs:** 50–200 creamy white eggs oviposited in horse manure
- **Larvae:** Cream-colored maggots resembling house-fly maggots, but with widely separated posterior spiracular slits
- **Pupae:** Brown and barrel-shaped resembling house-fly pupa, but with characteristic posterior spiracular slits
- **Control:** Remove manure; fly traps; OC > OP spraying of breeding sites in stables, barns, and animal shelters
- **Prevention:** Sanitary food preparation and consumption away from barns and stables
- **Family:** Fanniidae
- **Genus:** *Fannia*
- **Adult:** Smaller than house flies with three longitudinal stripes on the thorax
- **Disease:** Same as house flies
- **Mechanism:** Same as house flies
- **Eggs:** 50–100 oviposited on feces

- **Larva:** Uniquely distinctive, not maggot-shaped, flattened dorsoventrally and segmented with spines
- **Pupa:** Brown and resembles larva
- **Control:** OC > OP spraying of latrine breeding sites
- **Prevention:** Proper latrine design and sanitation; sanitary food preparation and consumption

Myiasis-Causing Flies: Outline

- Definitions: Obligatory vs. facultative myiasis
- Fly classification: Calliphoridae; Sarcophagidae, Oestridae
- Tumbu and Congo floor-mat flies
- Screw-worms: Old World vs. New World
- Blowflies: Greenbottles and bluebottles
- Sarcophagidae
- Ostridae: Human bot flies

Fleas, Lice, Ticks, Mites: Outline

Myiasis: Definitions

Obligatory myiasis

- **Def:** Fly larvae (maggots) must live and feed on a live human or other animal host for a part of their life cycle (Figure 23.17).

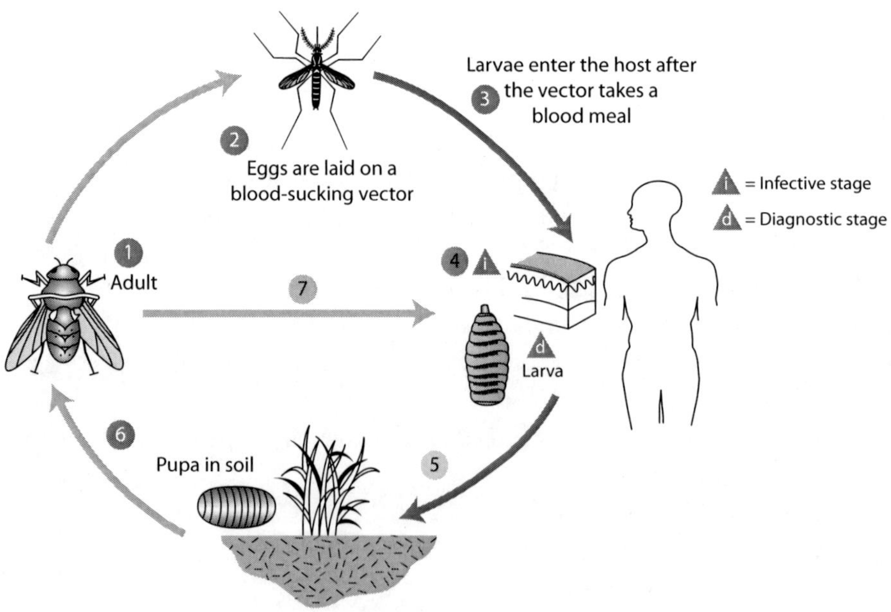

FIGURE 23.17 Transmission cycle of myiasis. (Courtesy of the CDC.)

FIGURE 23.18 *Dermatobia hominis*, the human bot fly. (Courtesy of the CDC.)

FIGURE 23.19 *Cochliomyia hominivorax,* the New World Screw-worm fly. (Courtesy of the CDC.)

- **Ex:** *Cordylobia anthropophagia* (tumbu fly), *Cochliomyia hominivorax* (New World screw-worm), *Chrysomya bezziana* (Old World screw-worm), *Dermatobia hominis* (bot fly), *Wohlfahrtia magnifica* (Figures 23.18 and 23.19).

Facultative Myiasis

- **Def:** Normally free-living fly larvae that preferentially feed on carrion and other decaying matter, and only incidentally attack and feed on sores and wounds of live human and animal hosts
- **Ex:** *Calliphora* (bluebottles), *Lucilia* (greenbottles), *Phormia*, *Sarcophaga*

Bugs: Fleas, Lice, Ticks, Mites

Fleas, Lice, and True Bugs

Fleas (Siphonaptera)

Lice (Anophura)

True Bugs

1. Bedbugs (Cimicidae)
2. Triatomids (Triatominae)
3. Cockroaches (Blattaria)

Ticks and Mites

Ticks

1. Soft ticks (Argasidae)
2. Hard ticks (Ixodidae)

Mites

1. Scabies mites (Sarcoptidae)
2. Scrub typhus mites (Trombiculidae)

Fleas (Siphonaptera) 1

- **Family:** Siphonaptera
- **Genus:** *Xenopsylla cheopsis* (rat flea), *Pulex irritans* (human flea), *Ctenocephalides* (dog and cat fleas)
- **Adult:** Small oval, compressed laterally; hairy, conspicuous black eyes, three pairs of powerful legs with hind legs specialized for jumping (specialized protein = elastin)
- **Disease:** *Yersinia pestis*—sylvatic rodent zoonosis → urban rodent zoonosis → rats die off → human bubonic plague → epidemic pneumonic plague; murine typhus-rodent zoonosis → overcrowding (*Rickettsia typhi*) (Figure 23.20)
- **Mechanism:** Both sexes infected; plague—*Yersinia* block proventricularis, regurgitated undigested + infected feces; *R. typhi* digested, defecated, and rubbed into wounds and delicate mucosal membranes (Figures 23.20 and 23.21)

Fleas (Siphonaptera) 2

- **Eggs:** Females lay 3–25 sticky, yellow-white eggs/day in dusty crevices near host dwellings; egg lifespan 1 year
- **Larvae:** Hatch in 2–14 days, 2–3 instars, pale brown, 13 segments, conspicuous black head and caudal pair of anal struts; dwell in dusty cracks near host, dining on regurgitated blood meals of adult fleas and on host feces
- **Pupae:** Develop in sticky, white cocoons, camouflaged with dust and mammal dander; adults emerge in 7–14 d 2° vibrations or CO_2 emitted by nearby potential hosts

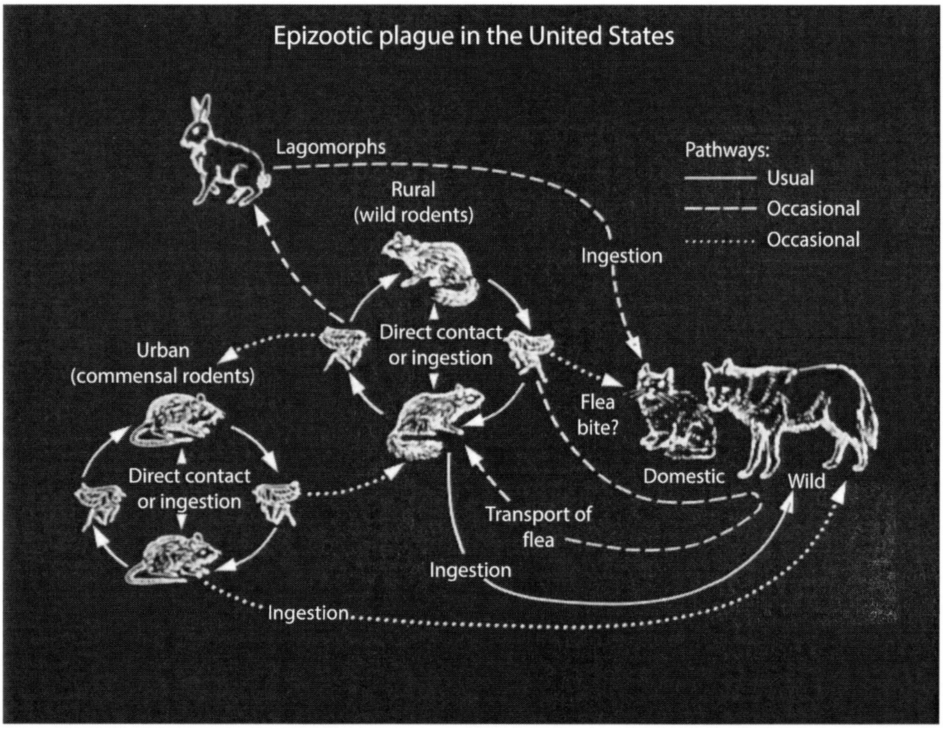

FIGURE 23.20 The epizoonotic maintenance of the plague organism, *Pastuerella pestis*, in its sylvatic cycle in the United States. (Courtesy of the CDC.)

- **Control and Prev:** OP-impregnated pet spot-on solns > flea collars; treat kennels-OPs > pyrethroids > OCs; epidemics-insecticides 1st, then rodenticides; tuck pants in socks, DEET > DIMP > benzoyl benzonate

Fleas 3: Tunga penetrans

- **Family:** Siphonaptera
- **Genus:** *Tunga penetrans* (chigoe or jigger flea)
- **Adults:** Smaller than most fleas, hairless, no head combs on compressed thorax
- **Diseases:** None; burrow deeply into skin
- **Mechanism:** Gravid female burrows deeply into peripheral skin-soles, between toes, under fingernails and toenails, buttocks; swells 1000× (Figure 23.22)
- **Eggs:** 150–200 oviposited on mud hut floors from genital opening, which remains exteriorized with anus
- **Larva:** Hatch 3–4 days; pupate in 2 weeks
- **Control:** Same chemical control; extract gravid females aseptically
- **Prevention:** Wear shoes; do not sit on ground naked

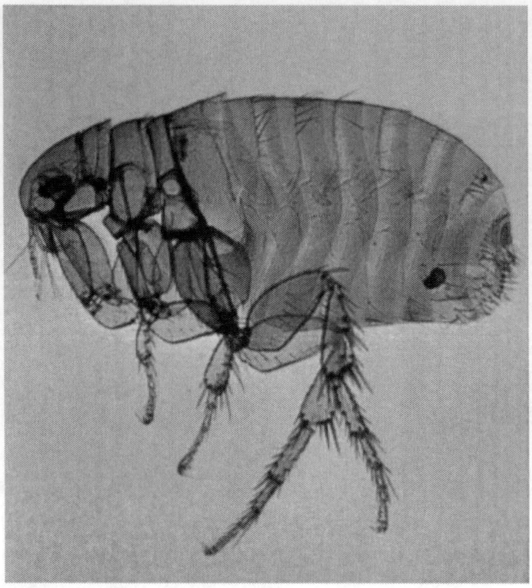

FIGURE 23.21 The rat flea, *Xenopsylla cheopsis*, the arthropod vector of the plague organism, *Pastuerella pestis*. (Courtesy of the CDC.)

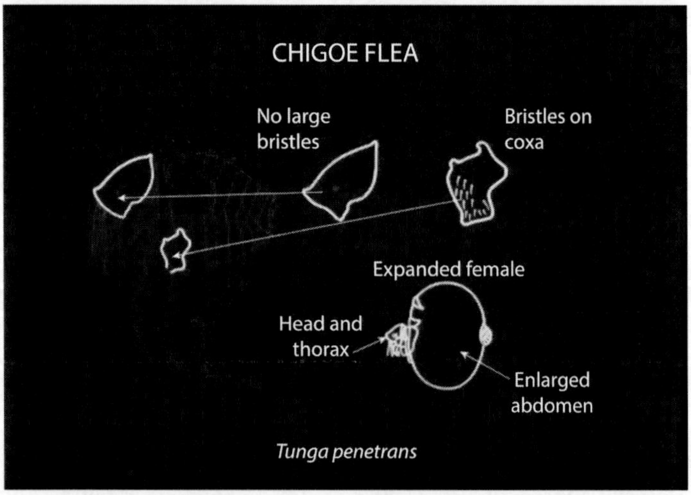

FIGURE 23.22 The egg-engorged female chigoe or jigger flea, *Tunga penetrans*, causing painful tungiasis. (Courtesy of the CDC.)

Lice (Anoplura) 1

Lice: Epidemic Typhus

Rickettsia prowazekii: Body lice, *Pediculus humanus,* feeding and defecating

Rickettsia prowazekii: Louse-borne epidemic typhus, maculopapular rash

Body Louse (Pediculus corporis)

See Figure 23.23.

Crab Louse (Pthirus pubis)

See Figure 23.24.

Bedbugs (Cimicidae) 1

- **Family:** Cimicidae
- **Genus:** Cimex lectularius (common bedbug, worldwide) and Cimex hemipterus (tropical)
- **Adult:** Brown, oval, flattened dorsoventrally, wingless-vestigial hemelytra, short-broad head with retractable proboscis, 8-segment abdomen; male has curved penis

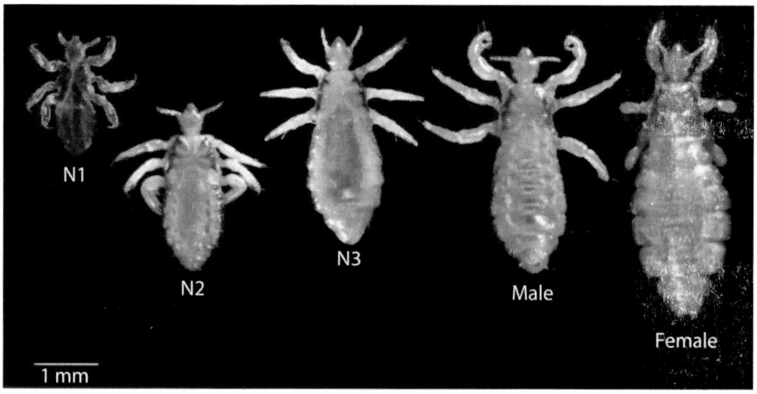

FIGURE 23.23 The larval (L) developmental stages and adult forms of the body louse, *Pediculus corporis*. (Courtesy of the CDC.)

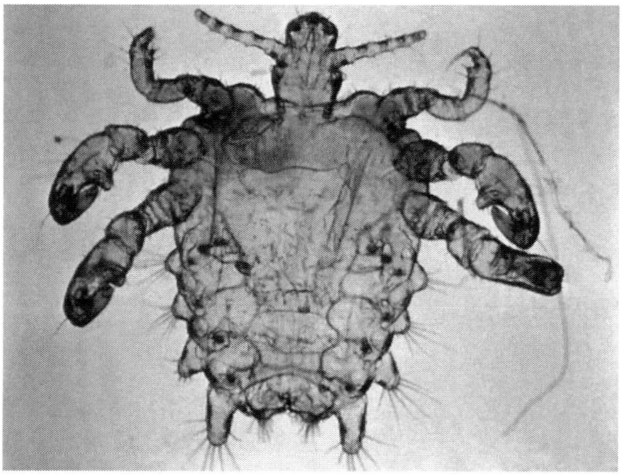

FIGURE 23.24 The crab or pubic louse, *Pthirus pubis*. (Courtesy of the CDC.)

FIGURE 23.25 The common bedbug (adult), *Cimex lectularius*. (Courtesy of the CDC.)

and female has a spermatheca or sperm receptacle ("vagina"), known as the organ of Berlese. Adult lifespan: 2–5 years (Figures 23.25 and 23.26)

- **Diseases:** Potential transmission of HBV; infant iron deficiency in tropics
- **Mechanism:** Both sexes reside comfortably in dark bedroom crevices, and between mattresses and box-springs; enjoy pre-dawn nighttime blood meals; and then return to gregarious communal living at dawn

FIGURE 23.26 The common bedbug (adult), *Cimex lectularius*, feeding on a human. (Courtesy of the CDC.)

Bedbugs (Cimicidae) 2

- **Eggs:** 6–10 eggs/week, pearly white with fine and delicate mosaic patterns on shell and slight anterior upturn at operculum; cemented between comfortable bedding layers, wallpaper layers, and drywall cracks; hatch within 8–11 days with empty shells remaining as thoughtful calling cards from guests
- **Nymphs:** Five nymphal instars enjoy blood meals on any mammal and mature into adults within 5–8 weeks
- **Control:** Recognize infestation; spray or "bomb" floors, walls, and beds (then air) with organophosphates OPs > pyrethroids > OCs
- **Prevention:** Select appropriate nighttime dwellings

Triatomid Bugs (Triatominae) 1

- **Family:** Triatominae
- **Subfamily:** Reduviidae ("assassin, cone-nose, kissing, and stink" bugs)
- **Genera:** *Triatoma*, *Rhodnius*, and *Panstrongylus* spp.
- **Adult:** Big 1–2 in. bugs with long snout and dark eyes; 4-seg antennae; thin, straight, retractable proboscis; triangular thorax, folding wings with contrasting dark (brown-orange) and light (yellow-pink) colors; powerful flyers
- **Diseases:** Chagas disease (*Trypanosoma cruzi*)—a wild animal—zoonosis, especially armadillos, opossums, squirrels (Figures 23.27 and 23.28)
- **Mechanism:** Nymph/adults of both sexes feed vociferously and nocturnally × 10–30 min on sleeping human hosts snug in bed up to their eyes/noses; adult females soon defecate infective feces, later rubbed into bite wounds and delicate EEN mucosa

Triatomid Bugs (Triatominae) 2

- **Eggs:** 200–300 white-to-pinkish oval eggs with constricted neck just before operculum deposited in cracks and crevices in walls, floors, and thatched roofs
- **Nymphs:** Emerge after 15–30 days, small and pale, resemble adults, but cannot fly, five instars—all voracious nocturnal blood feeders and can transmit *Trypanosoma cruzi*—triatomid infection rates in Latin America are 25–40%
- **Control:** Interior spraying of residual insecticides—OPs > pyrethroids > OCs; OP—impregnated interior paints
- **Prevention:** Plaster or sheetrock interior walls, replace mud-sealed walls with bricks/concrete blocks to eliminate cracks; replace thatched roofs with corrugated metal roofs

Cockroaches (Blattaria) 1

- **Family:** Blattaria
- **Genus:** *Periplaneta americana*, *Blatta orientalis*
- **Adult:** Large 1–5 cm long, chestnut brown, flattened dorsoventrally, shiny-smooth and tough integument; prominent paired antennae; chewing mouthparts—no

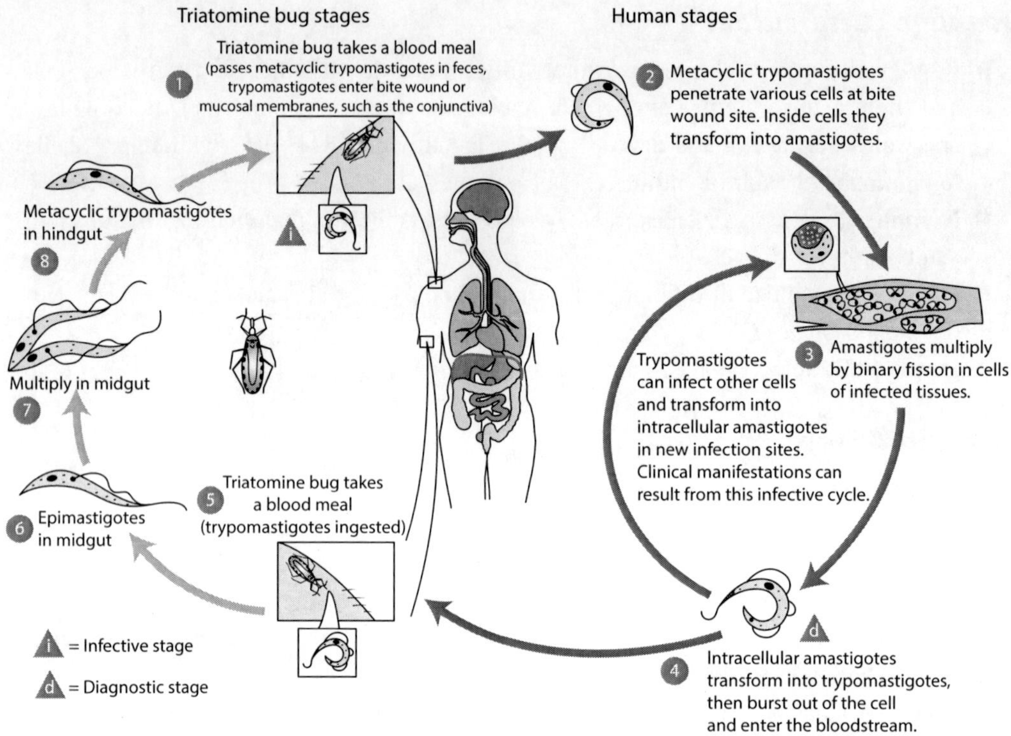

FIGURE 23.27 The transmission life cycle of American trypanosomiasis or Chagas disease. (Courtesy of the CDC.)

FIGURE 23.28 The kissing or triatomid (reduviid) bug, *Triatoma infestans*, a common cause of Chagas disease in the Americas. (Courtesy of the CDC.)

stylets—cannot suck blood; three pairs hairy legs; wings scissor-folded over abdomen, rarely fly; lifespan 2+ years

- **Diseases:** Viruses (polio), protozoa (amoebae, Toxo), helminths (pinworms), bacteria (*Salmonella/Shigella, Staph, Klebsiella*)
- **Mechanism:** Mechanical transmission and regurgitate and excrete partially digested omnivorous meals (blood, hair, feces, dead insects, etc.) over foods

Cockroaches (Blattaria) 2

- **Eggs:** Oothecae containing 12–15 eggs deposited in cracks and crevices in warm, dark, and secluded places within homes, empty buildings, and hospitals
- **Nymphs:** Hatch within 1–3 months, six instars, cannot fly, wings develop gradually to operational adult wings
- **Control:** Domestic spraying (OPs + pyrethroids > OPs [malathion, primiphos, fenthion, diazinon, chlorpyrifos] and carbamates [carbaryl, propoxur, bendiocarb] > pyrethroids [permethrin, deltamethrin, cypermethrin, lambdacyhalothrin] > OCs); boric acid tablets/powder; pheromone-impregnated roach traps
- **Prevention:** Kitchens and households cleaned of dirty utensils and food spills; pyrethroid and OP-impregnated varnishes and lacquers

Ticks and Mites: Outline

- **Class:** Arachnida
- **Subclass:** Acari
- **Ticks:** Worldwide dist.; much larger than mites; toothed hypostome; no claws on palps.
    - Soft-bodied ticks (Argasidae)
        - **Genus:** *Ornithodoros*
    - Hard-bodied ticks (Ixodidae)
        - **Genera:** *Ixodes, Dermacentor, Amblyomma, Hyalomma*
- **Mites:** Worldwide dist.; miniscule: 0.45 mm-scabies mites to 1–2 mm for scrub typhus mites
    - Scabies mites (Sarcoptidae)
        - **Genus:** *Sarcoptes scabiei*
    - Scrub typhus mites (Trombiculidae): *Leptotrombidium*

Soft Ticks (Argasidae) 1

- **Genus:** *Ornithodoros moubata* complex
- **Adult:** Oval, flat, wrinkled-leathery integument, ventral mouthparts not visible dorsally except in larvae, four pairs of legs with terminal claws; unique paired coxal glands open between base of 1st two paired legs and filter excess Na and H_2O from blood meals (Figures 23.29 and 23.30)
- **Diseases:** Tick paralysis, tick-borne relapsing fever (*Borrelia duttoni*), Q-fever (*Coxiella burneti*)

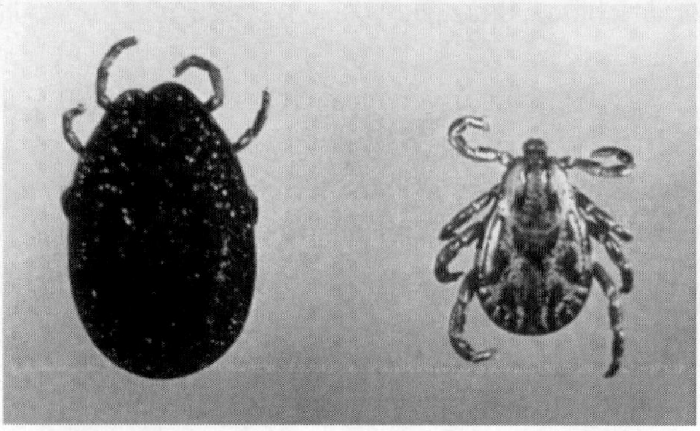

FIGURE 23.29 A soft-bodied Argasidae species tick on the left compared to a hard-bodied Ixodidae species tick on the right. (Courtesy of the CDC.)

FIGURE 23.30 A soft-bodied Argasidae species tick, *Ornithodorus* spp. (Courtesy of the CDC.)

- **Mechanism:** Both salivary and coxal glands can transmit ID agents into bite wounds during prolonged blood meals; transovarial and transstadial transmission common

Soft Ticks (Argasidae) 2

- **Eggs:** Following a blood meal up to 12× BW, females lay 4–6 batches of 15–100 spherical eggs in cracks, crevices, mud, and debris near host dwellings
- **Larvae:** Hatch within 1–3 weeks and resemble adults with three pairs of legs and forward projecting capitellum; blood-feed-transstadial transmission
- **Nymphs:** Four to seven instars; all blood feed
- **Control:** Home spray—OPs, carbamates
- **Prevention:** Coat tick with volatile antiseptics and then forcep removed *in toto*; personal protection: pant legs tucked into socks, pyrethroid-impregnated clothing, DEET > DIMP > dibutyl phthalate > dimethyl carbamate

Hard Ticks (Ixodidae) 1

- **Genera:** *Ixodes, Dermacentor, Amblyomma*
- **Adult:** Oval, flat, capitulum projects forward, festooned, male scutum > female, four pairs of legs with terminal claws; no coxal glands. (See Figures 23.31 through 23.33)
- **Diseases:** Bacterial (Lyme d, tularemia); Rickettsial (Rocky Mountain spotted fever [RMSF], Boutonneuse and Q-fevers, Siberian tick typhus); protozoal (babesiosis, ehrlichiosis); toxic (tick paralysis); arboviral (Russian spring-summer encephalitis [RSSE], tick-borne encephalitis [TBE], Omsk hemorrhagic fever [OHF], Kyasanur Forest hemorrhagic fever [KFD], Crimean-Congo hemorrhagic fever [CCHF])

FIGURE 23.31 A hard-bodied Argasidae species tick, *Dermacentor andersoni*, the preferred tick vector of the rickettsial disease, Rocky Mountain spotted fever. (Courtesy of the CDC.)

FIGURE 23.32 A hard-bodied Argasidae species tick, *Ixodes scapularis*, or black-legged tick, a rick vector for Lyme disease caused by the spirochete, *Borrelia burgdorferi*. (Courtesy of the CDC.)

FIGURE 23.33 A hard-bodied Argasidae species tick, *Amblyomma americanum*, the lone star tick, the preferred tick vector for the transmission of Southern Tick Associated Illness (STARI) in the southern United States. (Courtesy of the CDC.)

- **Mechanism:** All stages exhibit questing behavior and blood feed on up to three hosts; salivary–transovarial–transstadial transmission

Hard Ticks (Ixodidae) 2

- **Eggs:** 1000–8000 small, spherical eggs laid in sticky, gelatinous mass in front and atop female scutum over 10 days, then the female dies
- **Larvae:** Minute, seed-tick larvae hatch in 10–20 days, and resemble small adults with three pairs of legs; quest for hosts (by warmth, CO_2, vibrations); feed × 1 week, drop off and mature into nymphs
- **Nymphs:** One instar, 8-legged
- **Control:** Peridomestic spraying; acaricide dips (sheep, cattle) and pet solutions: OPs, carbamates
- **Prevention:** Skin inspection, tick removal, pants stuck into socks, DEET > DIMP

Scabies Mites (Sarcoptidae) 1

- **Genus:** *Sarcoptes scabiei*
- **Adult:** Tiny, white, disk-shaped, numerous dorsal pegs; four pairs short-fat legs, mouthparts project anteriorly; smaller males are suckers on the 4th pair of legs (Figure 23.34)
- **Diseases:** Scabies (female tunnels—fecal pepper spots, larval moulting pockets, pruritic allergic rash); Norwegian crusted scabies—immunocompromised

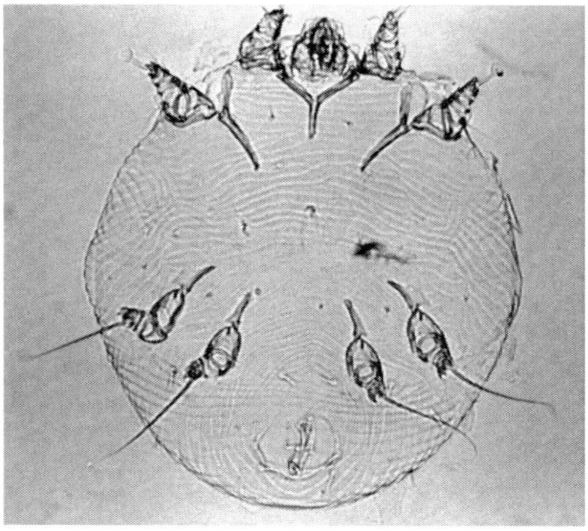

FIGURE 23.34 The human scabies mite, *Sarcoptes scabiei*. (Courtesy of the CDC.)

- **Mechanism:** Highly contagious on close contact-holding hands, sharing beds and clothing, overcrowding-refugees; females burrow into thin skin → hands, scrotum, buttocks → thin twisting mating tunnels → larvae form moulting pockets in hair follicles (Figure 23.35)

Scabies Mites (Sarcoptidae) 2

- **Eggs:** Females mature mate in moulting pocket, then tunnel into epidermis, feed on lymph and stratum corneum; lay 1–3 eggs; hatch in 3–5 days
- **Larva:** Six-legged and resemble adults; create a moulting pocket within a hair follicle and mature into nymphs
- **Nymphs:** Eight legs; males surface then burrow into moulting pockets to fertilize young females, which then remain in their tunnels to lay eggs
- **Control:** Topical 20–25% benzoyl benzonate, liquid sulfur (Mitigal, Tetmosol), 0.5% malathion
- **Prevention:** ↑ personal hygiene, washing and not sharing clothes and bedding

Scrub Typhus Mites 1

- **Family:** Trombiculidae.
- **Genera:** Eutrombicula-red bugs or chiggers (scrub itch); *Leptotrombiculidium* (scrub typhus).
- **Adult:** Small, red, figure-8 shape, velvety hairs, four pairs of legs-terminal claws, forward projecting palps and mouthparts (Figure 23.36).
- **Diseases:** Scrub-chigger itch, scrub typhus (*Rickettsia tsutsugamushi*).
- **Mechanism:** Only larvae transmit disease via transovarial transmission, especially in fringe habitats or "mite islands" separating two vegetation zones; larval mites leave eggshells in 5–7 days, feed via hypostomes × 2–10 days on host lymph and skin in warm moist crural, perianal, waist and ankle areas; anywhere clothing is tight against skin.

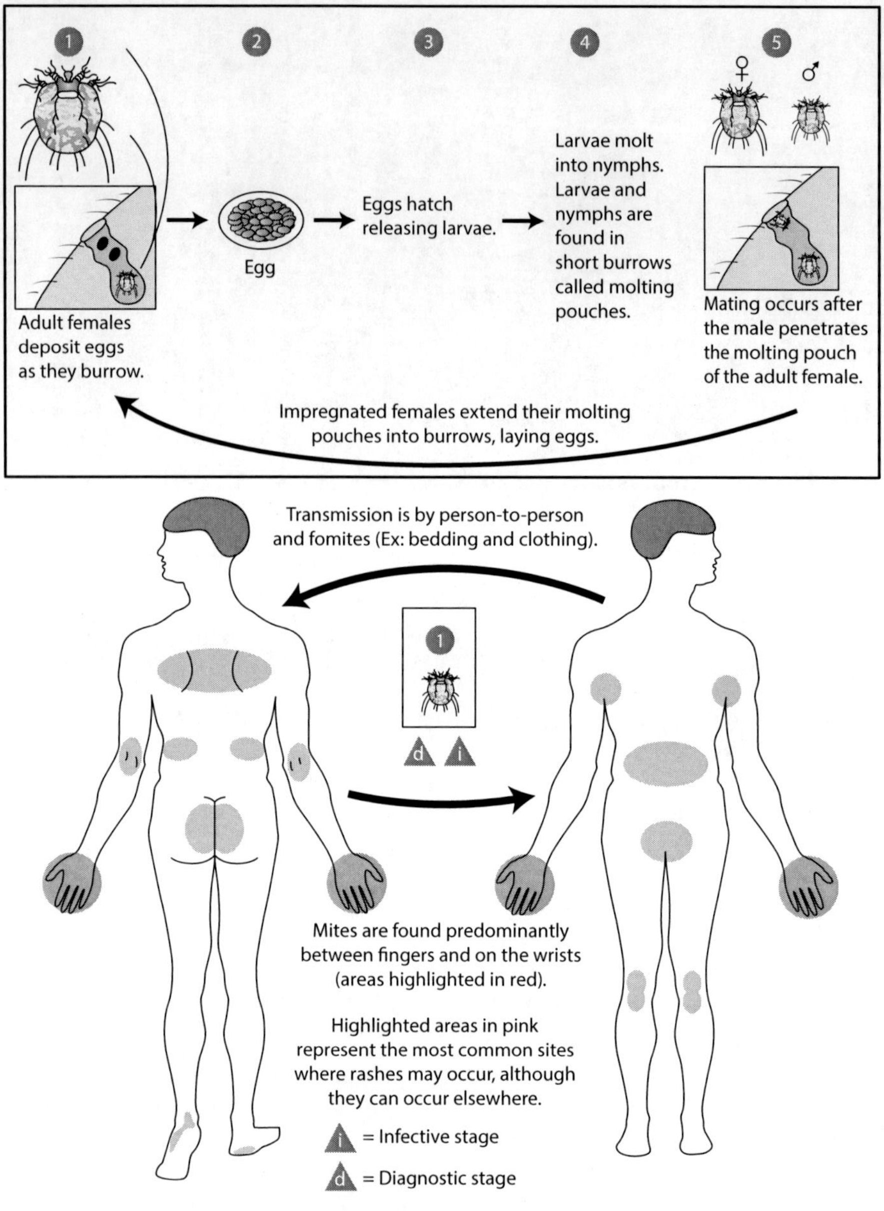

FIGURE 23.35 The life cycle of the human scabies mite, *Sarcoptes scabiei*. (Courtesy of the CDC.)

Scrub Typhus Mites 2

- **Eggs:** Gravid female lays 1–5 spherical eggshells/day in leaf litter in mite islands in damp, well-drained soil; eggshell splits by 1 week, larvae remain × 1 week, then emerge to quest and attach to mammalian hosts

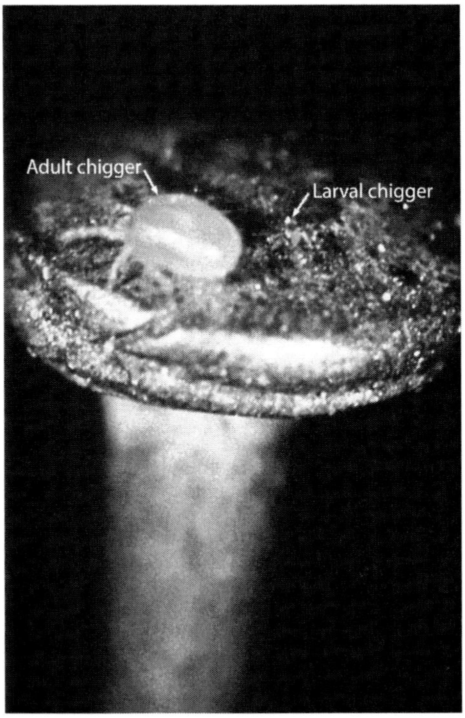

FIGURE 23.36 Diminutive adult and larval trombiculid "chigger" mites poised on the head of a pin. (Courtesy of the CDC.)

- **Larvae:** Very small, red-orange, with three pairs of legs terminating in large claws; resemble adults, but less hairy; highly infectious 2° transovarial transmission and prolonged blood feeding × 2–10 days
- **Nymphs:** Engorged larvae drop off host after 2–10 days, bury in leaf litter, mature in complex life cycle: eggshell → infective pre-larval deutovum → infective larva → infective protonymph → nymph → infective preadult → noninfectious adult
- **Control:** Herbicide →insecticide spraying: OPs > pyrethroids > OCs
- **Prevention:** Impregnated clothing, DEET

Conclusions

- **Mosquitoes** remain the most important vectors of the most unique and virulent IDs: protozoal (malaria), parasitic (filariasis), and arboviral (dengue, YF, EEs).
- **Flies** are often overlooked as mechanical vectors of foodborne bacterial ID outbreaks (*Shigella* and *Salmonella*) and as livestock devastators (screw-worms).
- **Fleas** and **lice** are important vectors of highly contagious (fleas plague) and easily transmissible (murine and louse-borne typhus) IDs, especially in crowded human shelters and refugee camps.

- **Ticks** are the most versatile insect vectors able to transmit all microbes (viral, bacterial, protozoal) due to unique combinations of transovarial and transstadial transmission, and prolonged blood feeding on multiple mammalian hosts.
- **The HIV–AIDS epidemic**, especially in Africa and SE Asia, has created an enlarging population of immunocompromised human hosts at greater risk of developing complicated vector-borne IDs, even relatively innocuous insect-borne diseases, for example, scabies (Norwegian-crusted scabies) and arboviral meningoencephalitis (West Nile virus, Rift Valley fever).

Chapter 24

Tick Paralysis

Introduction 558
Tick Biology, Behavior, and the Mechanisms of Tick Paralysis 559
Evolving Global Epidemiology of Tick Paralysis 560
Clinical Manifestations of Tick Paralysis 563
DDx of Tick Paralysis 564
Management of Tick Paralysis 564
Control and Prevention of Tick Paralysis 567
Conclusions 568
References 568

Introduction

1. The emergence of Lyme disease (LD) in the United States in the early 1970s, whose causative agent, the spirochete *Borrelia burgdorferi*, was not identified until 1982, sparked renewed interest in tick-borne diseases worldwide.
2. By the early 1990s, LD had become the most common arthropod-borne infectious disease in the United States and Europe.
3. Climate changes, especially global warming with milder winters, and human lifestyles and leisure activities now place humans and ticks together outdoors for longer periods for tick breeding, blood feeding, and disease transmission.
4. Since ticks are not afflicted by most of the microorganisms they may transmit or they may inject the paralytic salivary toxins during prolonged blood feeding, ticks will remain among the most competent and versatile of all arthropod vectors of human diseases.
5. Tick paralysis (TP), a uniquely tick-borne poisoning, is an ascending flaccid neuromuscular paralysis with sensory sparing caused by salivary neurotoxins secreted by gravid hard ticks (Acari: Ixodidae) while blood feeding.
6. Although reported worldwide since 1912 and transmitted by 43 tick species, TP usually occurs in the same regions of North America and Australia during predictable spring–summer tick-breeding seasons.
7. North American TP is most commonly transmitted by *Dermacentor andersoni*, the Rocky Mountain wood tick, in the U.S. Pacific Northwest, U.S. West, and Southwestern Canada (British Columbia, Alberta) (Figure 24.1).

FIGURE 24.1 A "questing" female Rocky mountain wood tick, *Dermacentor andersoni*, a primary vector of tick paralysis in the U.S. Pacific Northwest and a vector of Rocky Mountain spotted fever (RMSF) throughout the U.S. Mid-West. (From U.S. Centers for Disease Control and Prevention [CDC], Atlanta, GA, USA. CDC Public Health Image Library [PHIL]. PHIL ID # 10865.)

FIGURE 24.2 **A "questing" female American dog tick, *Dermacentor variabilis*, a vector of tick paralysis in the Southeastern United States, and a secondary vector of Rocky Mountain spotted fever (RMSF) in addition to the Rocky Mountain wood tick, *Dermacentor andersoni*, in the U.S. Mid-West. (From U.S. Centers for Disease Control and Prevention [CDC], Atlanta, GA, USA. CDC Public Health Image Library [PHIL]. PHIL ID # 170.)**

8. In the Southeast United States, TP is usually transmitted by *Dermacentor variabilis*, the American dog tick (Figure 24.2).
9. In Eastern Australia, TP is usually transmitted by *Ixodes holocyclus*, the marsupial or paralysis tick.

Tick Biology, Behavior, and the Mechanisms of Tick Paralysis

1. There are four stages in the tick's life cycle: egg, six-legged larva, nymph, and adult. TP is only transmitted by blood-feeding gravid adult female ticks by an incompletely characterized neurotoxin produced by the tick's salivary glands.
2. Ticks are classified into three families: (1) the Ixodidae, or hard ticks; (2) the Argasidae, or soft ticks; and (3) the Nuttalliellidae, a much lesser known family, with characteristics of both hard and soft ticks.
3. Ixodid ticks have a hard dorsal plate or scutum, which is absent in the soft-bodied, argasid ticks. Although TP is most commonly transmitted by ixodid species ticks, all tick species may transmit TP.
4. Ixodid ticks have mouthparts that are attached anteriorly and visible dorsally. They live in open, exposed environments, such as woodlands, grasslands, meadows, and scrub brush areas.
5. Argasid ticks prefer to live in more sheltered environments, such as animal nests, caves, and crevices.
6. All ticks feed by cutting a small hole in the host's epidermis with their chelicerae and then inserting their toothed hypostomes into the cut with blood flow maintained by salivary anticoagulants.

7. Ticks are attracted to warm-blooded hosts by vibration and exhaled CO_2. Ixodid ticks will actually "quest" for hosts by climbing onto vegetation with their forelegs outstretched; waiting to embrace passing hosts (Figures 24.1 and 24.2).
8. Some ticks spend relatively short periods of their lives mating and blood-feeding on hosts with soft ticks feeding rapidly for hours and dropping off; compared to hard ticks, which often blood-feed for many days (6–12) before dropping off for egg-laying.
9. The exact mechanism of neurotoxic paralysis in *Dermacentor* tick paralysis is unknown, but neuroelectrophysiological studies suggest that sodium flux across axonal membranes is blocked at the nodes of Ranvier, leaving neuromuscular transmission unimpeded.
10. In Australia, the marsupial ixodid tick, *Ixodes holocyclus*, can cause a more severe, delayed form of ascending neuromuscular paralysis by producing a botulinum-like neurotoxin that blocks neuromuscular transmission by inhibiting the presynaptic release of acetylcholine.

Evolving Global Epidemiology of Tick Paralysis

1. First reported simultaneously in North America and Australia in 1912, TP is a recurring neurotoxic poisoning that occurs in regional pockets worldwide with demographic, regional, and seasonal predictabilities. Although the demographics and spring–summer seasonalities of North American and Australian ixodid TP do not differ substantially, their neurotoxidromes do differ considerably and are compared in Table 24.1.
2. In addition to *Dermacentor* species ixodid ticks, other much less common vectors of TP in the United States have included *Amblyomma americanum* (the Lone Star tick), *Amblyomma maculatum* (the Gulf Coast tick), *Ixodes scapularis* (the Eastern black-legged or wood tick), and *Ixodes pacificus* (the Western black-legged or wood tick).
3. In Australia, there are 70 tick species, with 22 species of ixodid ticks, only 3 of which can cause TP: (1) *Ixodes holocyclus*, (2) *I. cornuatus*, and (3) *I. hirsti*.
4. In the American Pacific Northwest, most cases of TP occur during April through June when *Dermacentor* ticks emerge from hibernation to mate and to seek blood meals.
5. Most cases of TP in North America have occurred sporadically in young girls with long hair and felt to be predisposed to unnoticed tick blood-feeding on the scalp or neck. However, a four-patient-cluster of *Dermacentor* TP including a 6-year-old girl with a tick on her hairline, and three adults with ticks on the neck ($n = 1$) and back ($n = 2$), was reported by the U.S. Centers for Disease Control and Prevention (CDC) from Colorado in 2006 [1]. Although children, especially girls younger than age 8 years, are most commonly afflicted with TP, boys and adults may also be affected and may present with ticks attached at sites other than the scalp and head.
6. Today, more cases of TP in children in the United States are being misdiagnosed and treated as the Guillain–Barré syndrome (GBS), especially in children, before

Table 24.1 Epidemiological, Clinical, and Neurophysiological Comparison of North American and Australian Tick Paralysis

Regional Tick Paralysis	North American Tick Paralysis	Australian Tick Paralysis
Geographic distribution	Southwest Canada (British Columbia, Alberta) U.S. Pacific Northwest and Rocky Mountain West U.S. Southeast Atlantic and Gulf of Mexico Coasts	Eastern Australia: Southeast Queensland and New South Wales
Incidence (NB: The true annual U.S. incidence is unknown)	Rare, Colorado reports one case per year. May occur in clusters	Rare in humans, more common in animals, especially dogs
Seasonality	Spring–summer	Spring–summer
Preferred tick vectors	Canada and U.S. Northwest and West: *Dermacentor andersoni* (Rocky Mountain wood tick) U.S. Southeast: *Dermacentor variabilis* (American dog tick) Other gravid female ixodid ticks may also rarely transmit TP in the United States	*Ixodes holocyclus* (marsupial or paralysis tick) Two other gravid female *Ixodes* spp. may rarely transmit TP in Australia
Other potential tick vectors	*Amblyomma americanum* (Lone Star tick), *Amblyomma maculatum* (Gulf Coast tick), *Ixodes pacificus* (Western black-legged or Western wood tick)	*Ixodes cornuatus* (one human case reported), *Ixodes hirsti* (only animal cases reported to date)
Preferred tick attachment sites	Scalp, often behind the ears	Scalp, often behind the ears
Neurotoxins	Neurotoxin produced by gravid female ixodid ticks and concentrated in salivary glands; not fully characterized at present; *not* botulinum-like	Neurotoxin produced by gravid female ixodid ticks and concentrated in salivary glands; not fully characterized at present; botulinum-like
Age predilections	Children, aged 1–8 years. May occur in adults much less commonly	Children, aged 1–5 years. May occur in adults much less commonly
Sex predilections	Females <8 years old	Children <5 years old
Prodromes	Present, short duration (24 h): No to low-grade fever, irritability, fatigue, weakness, muscle pain and paresthesias	Present, longer duration (48–72 h): afebrile, fatigue, sleepiness–drowsiness, weakness, leg pain, unsteady gait
Fever	Rare, but may be low grade during prodrome	Rare, but may be low grade during prodrome. Fever occurs commonly following canine antitoxin administration

(*continued*)

Table 24.1 (continued) Epidemiological, Clinical, and Neurophysiological Comparison of North American and Australian Tick Paralysis

Regional Tick Paralysis	North American Tick Paralysis	Australian Tick Paralysis
Exanthem	Rare, prodromal pruritic popular rash possible	Absent. Urticarial rashes are common following antitoxin administration
Incubation periods (days)	Short, 1–1.5 days	Longer, 3–5 days
Paralysis onset (hours)	Within 24 h of tick attachment	Later, within 48–72 h of tick attachment
Maximum intensity of paralysis (hours)	Within 24–48 h if tick is not removed	Worsens to maximum intensity 48 h after tick removal
Tick bite site eschars	Absent	Absent
Regional lymphadenopathy	Absent	Absent
Cranial nerve involvement	Present later: Drooling, dysphagia, dysphonia, facial weakness. Facial nerve palsies more common than internal and external ophthalmoplegia	Present early: Internal and external ophthalmoplegia common
Cerebrospinal fluid (CSF) analysis	Normal	Normal
Treatment	Tick removal	Tick removal Temporary mechanical ventilation may be indicated, especially in children Canine antitoxin recommended (serum sickness common). Antipyretics and antihistamines are recommended for fever and urticarial rashes following antitoxin administration
Neurological recovery time (days)	Rapid, 1–1.5 days	Prolonged, 1–3 + weeks
Nerve conduction studies	Reduced amplitude of compound muscle action potentials (CMAPs) Normal sensory nerve action potentials (SNAPs) Normal response to repetitive nerve stimulation Decreased nerve conduction velocities Prolonged distal motor nerve latencies	Reduced amplitude of CMAPs. Normal SNAPs Normal response to repetitive nerve stimulation
Case fatality rates (without tick removal)	Canada: 10–12% (before 1954). United States: 6–10% (1940s–present, deaths occurred in the 1940s)	Unknown. 20 deaths were reported from TP in New South Wales, Australia, over the period, 1900–1945

conducting careful body searches for ticks at preferred attachment sites. In their series of six pediatric cases of TP in Mississippi, Venkataraman and coinvestigators reported that half of their patients ($n = 3$) were misdiagnosed as GBS and treated with intravenous gamma globulin G (IVIG) before attached ticks were discovered, often by nurses or parents grooming the patient [2].

7. In 2010, Diaz reported the results of a meta-analysis of the scientific literature on TP in the United States using Internet search engines to assess the evolving epidemiology of TP [3]. Fifty well-documented cases of TP were analyzed over the study period, 1946–2006. Cases were stratified by demographics, clinical manifestations, and outcomes. TP occurred seasonally and sporadically in individuals and in clusters of children and adults of both sexes in urban and rural locations. The case fatality rate (CFR) for TP was 6.0% over 60 years. The proportion of misdiagnoses of TP as GBS was significantly greater ($p = 0.005$) in more recently collected series of TP cases, 1992–2006, than the proportion of misdiagnoses in earlier series, 1946–1996.

Clinical Manifestations of Tick Paralysis

1. North American TP is characterized by a distinct prodrome that begins some time after a gravid ixodid tick bite and secretion of an unidentified salivary neurotoxin, and comprises two distinct phases, including: (1) a nonspecific prodromal phase of lethargy and weakness; and (2) a subsequent neurotoxic phase of acute ataxia (often described as an inability to sit up and to walk without assistance) progressing to ascending flaccid paralysis with preserved sensorium.
2. Unlike Australian TP, the recovery time to normal neurological function in North American TP is rapid and occurs within 1.5 days of tick removal (Table 24.1).
3. Australian TP is also characterized by an initial nonspecific, 2–3 day prodrome of drowsiness, lethargy, weakness, muscle pain, and an unsteady gait. This prodrome is then followed by the neurotoxic phase with an acute onset of ascending neuromuscular paralysis, often accompanied by both internal and external ophthalmoplegia [4].
4. Although fever and pruritic, papular rashes may occur rarely during the prodrome of North American TP, febrile exanthems are very rare in Australian TP and, if present, usually follow the administration of antitoxin [4].
5. Fever and rash in combination with ascending flaccid paralysis and an embedded tick suggest the possibility of a tick-borne coinfection.
6. The incubation period from tick attachment to ascending paralysis is significantly longer in Australian TP (3–5 days) than in North American TP (1–1.5 days). The maximum intensity of neuromuscular paralysis in North American TP will occur within 24–48 h if the tick is not removed.
7. The maximum intensity of neuromuscular paralysis in Australian TP usually occurs 48 h after the tick is removed and, therefore, observation for hypoventilation after tick removal is recommended [4].

8. Cranial nerve involvement occurs in both North American and Australian TP; with ophthalmoplegia more common in Australian TP, and facial nerve palsy more common in North American TP.
9. All laboratory and cerebrospinal fluid (CSF) parameters remain normal in both North American and Australian TP.
10. The nerve conduction abnormalities are also similar for both poisonings with reduced amplitude of compound muscle action potentials (CMAPs), normal sensory nerve action potentials (SNAPs), and normal responses to repetitive nerve stimulation (Table 24.1).

DDx of Tick Paralysis

1. A bedside clinical differential diagnosis of acute ascending flaccid paralysis with a preserved sensorium is relatively narrow and should include TP, GBS, spinal cord tumor, botulism, and poliomyelitis (Table 24.2).
2. Botulism causes a descending neuromuscular paralysis with a preserved sensorium and ophthalmoplegia, and poliomyelitis has been nearly eradicated by vaccination worldwide. However, poliomyelitis may occur in unvaccinated patients with positive travel histories to polio-endemic regions of the world or following vaccination with live oral polio-virus vaccines (OPV).
3. Since TP and GBS both have identical electrophysiological signatures on nerve conduction testing, the only way to differentiate the diseases is to find and remove an attached, blood-feeding tick and observe the rapidity of neurological recovery.
4. Postmortem examinations of persons who have died suddenly of unexplained paralytic illnesses have demonstrated attached ticks on the head and neck of decedents.

Management of Tick Paralysis

1. Most patients with TP do not recall painless tick bites, and attachment sites may be unseen, or hidden by long hair. Nevertheless, tick localization and removal as soon as possible, preferably within 24 h, remain recommended strategies to reverse TP.
2. Ticks should always be removed with forceps (or tweezers), not fingers (as squishing ticks can transmit several tick-borne microbial diseases across dermal barriers or create infectious aerosols), and in contiguity with their feeding mouthparts, rather than burning ticks with spent matches, or painting embedded ticks with adhesives or nail polishes (Figure 24.3). Ticks should be removed with forceps or fine-tipped tweezers applied close to the point of skin attachment with gentle, steady traction applied to avoid decapitating ticks and leaving imbedded mouthparts with toxin-filled salivary glands (Figure 24.3).
3. Although *I. holocyclus* TP is also treated by tick removal, transient neuromuscular deterioration may occur for 24–72 h following tick removal, with a peak paralysis often at 48 h after tick removal. Therefore, prolonged observation for hypoventilation has been recommended following *I. holocyclus* removal in cases of Australian TP.

Table 24.2 Clinical Differential Diagnosis of Tick Paralysis versus Neuromuscular Paralysis with Preserved Sensorium

Presenting Clinical Features	Tick Paralysis	Guillain–Barré Syndrome	Cervical Spinal Cord Lesion	Botulism	Poliomyelitis
Onset of neuromuscular paralysis	Acute, rapid, within 24–48 h of tick attachment in North American TP; longer onset, 48–72 h, in Australian TP	Slower onset, days to weeks	Abrupt to gradual onset	Gradual and often following acute gastrointestinal prodrome of nausea, vomiting, diarrhea Recent history of ingestion of unpasteurized honey, home-canned or pickled foods and salad dressings may be present	Gradual onset, following a prodrome of fever, meningeal signs, and asymmetrical weakness
Direction of neuromuscular paralysis	Ascending	Ascending	Ascending	Descending	Ascending
Ataxia	Present	Absent	Absent	Absent	Absent
Deep tendon reflexes	Hyporeflexia progressing to areflexia	Hyporeflexia progressing to areflexia	Variable	Variable	Hyporeflexia progressing to areflexia
Babinski sign	Absent	Absent	Present	Absent	Absent
Sensory loss	None	Mild	Present	Absent	Absent
Meningeal signs	Absent	Rarely present	Absent	Absent	Present
Ophthalmoplegia (external and internal)	May be present in North American TP. Often present and pathognomonic of Australian TP	Absent	Absent	Often present and also pathognomonic	Absent
Other cranial nerve palsies	Present	May be present	Absent	Present	Absent

(*continued*)

Table 24.2 (continued) Clinical Differential Diagnosis of Tick Paralysis versus Neuromuscular Paralysis with Preserved Sensorium

Presenting Clinical Features	Tick Paralysis	Guillain–Barré Syndrome	Cervical Spinal Cord Lesion	Botulism	Poliomyelitis
Fever	Low grade, if present. Often follows antitoxin administration in Australian TP	Rarely present	Absent	Often present	Present
Exanthem	May be present. Urticarial rashes often present following antitoxin administration in Australian TP	Absent	Absent	Absent	Absent
CSF findings: Protein levels (mg/dL) White cells per mm^3 Differential counts	Normal <10 Normal	High (≥40) <10 <10 mononuclear cells/mm^3	Normal to high Variable Normal	Normal <10 Polymorphonuclear leukocytosis possible	High (≥40) >10 Lymphocytosis possible
Nerve conduction studies	↓ Amplitude of compound muscle action potentials (CMAPs) Normal sensory nerve action potentials (SNAPs) Normal response to repetitive nerve stimulation ↓ Nerve conduction velocities. Prolonged distal motor nerve latencies	Similar	Similar	Similar with a reduction in compound motor nerve action potentials (CMAPs). However, with exercise or following rapid, repetitive stimulation, the amplitude of CMAPs may be further reduced	Similar
Time to neurologic recovery (hours)	Rapid, ≤24 h after tick removal in north American TP; more prolonged, 48–72 h, in Australian TP	Weeks to months	Variable	Prolonged	Prolonged
Permanent neurologic deficits	None after tick removal in North American TP; prolonged weakness possible in Australian TP	Permanent paresis possible	Permanent paresis possible	Permanent paresis possible and frequent	Permanent paresis common

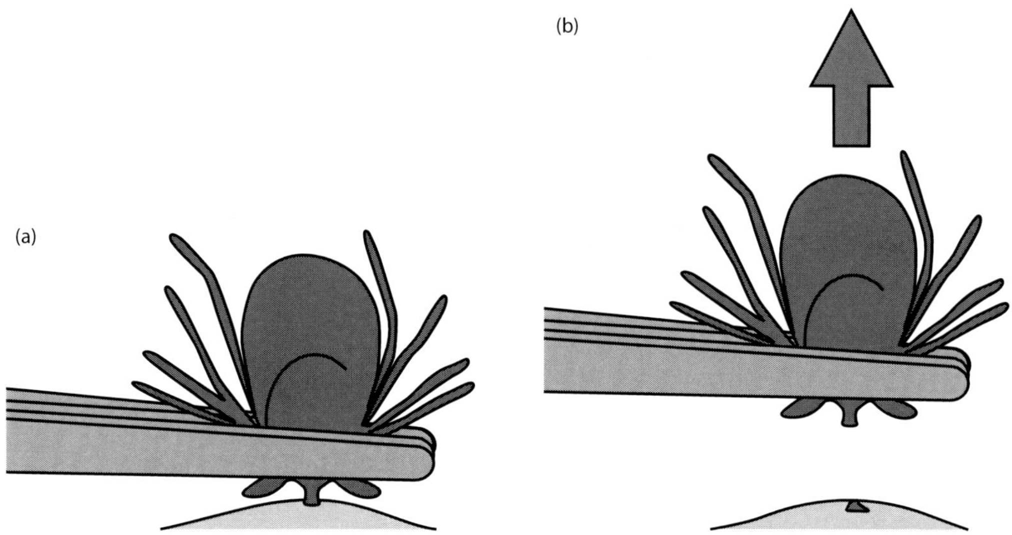

FIGURE 24.3 The steps of proper tick removal: (1) Use fine-tipped tweezers and always protect your fingers with a tissue, paper towel, or latex gloves. Do not remove ticks with your bare hands. (2) Grasp the tick as close to the skin surface as possible and pull upward with steady, even traction. Do not twist or jerk the tick as this could cause the mouth parts to break off and remain embedded in the skin. If this happens, remove the mouth parts separately with tweezers. (3) After removing the tick, thoroughly disinfect the bite site and your hands with rubbing alcohol, iodine scrub solution, or soap and water. (4) Avoid all folklore remedies aimed at coaxing the tick to detach including painting the tick with nail polish or petroleum jelly or using a spent match or other source of heat to make the tick detach from the skin. (5) Your goal is to remove the tick as soon as possible, preferably within 24 h or less. (From U.S. Centers for Disease Control and Prevention [CDC], Atlanta, GA, USA. Available at http://www.cdc.gov/ticks/removing_a_tick.html.)

Although a hyperimmune, canine antitoxin for ixodid TP in Australia has had widespread use in dogs, its use in humans, primarily children, has been limited due to acute reactions including fever, rash, and serum sickness.

Control and Prevention of Tick Paralysis

1. Effective strategies for the prevention and control of TP include personal protective measures, landscape management, and wildlife management.
2. Personal protective measures to prevent TP include wearing appropriate clothing, applying insect repellants to clothing and exposed skin, and performing regular tick checks. Wearing long pants tucked into socks, long-sleeved shirts, and light-colored clothing can aide in keeping ticks off of the skin and in making them easier to spot on clothing.

3. Spraying and/or impregnating clothing with pyrethrin/pyrethroid-containing insecticides (permethrin, deltamethrin, etc.) are highly effective repellant strategies against ticks and other insects.
4. The topical application of insect repellants containing 10–50% formulations of *N*, *N*-diethyl-*meta*-toluamide (DEET) or 20% picardin (only available in the United States as a 7% formulation) directly on exposed skin is another effective and recommended measure while outdoors in tick-infested areas, with less concentrated formulations of DEET (≤20–30%) recommended for children.
5. Landscape management strategies to prevent tick-borne diseases include widespread application of acaricides over tick-preferred ecosystems, removal of vegetation and leaf litter near homes and recreation sites, and creation of dry barriers of gravel, stone, rocks, or wood chips between forested areas and yards or playgrounds.
6. Domestic and wild animal management strategies to prevent tick-borne diseases include encouraging the development of better veterinary vaccines and topical pesticides for tick-borne diseases with large domestic and wild animal reservoirs; applying the safest acaricides actively and routinely to domestic animals and passively to wild animals. Deer and cattle can be humanely treated at baited feeding or watering stations, tick dips, and salt licks.
7. Effective rodent control measures may include setting out rodenticide-baited rodent houses for rodents to occupy or acaricide-baited cotton, lint, or fabric balls for rodents to adopt as nesting materials, especially in crawl spaces under homes and near playgrounds, to control several rodent infectious disease-transmitting ectoparasites, including ticks, mites, and fleas.

Conclusions

TP should be added to and excluded from the differential diagnoses of acute ataxia and ascending flaccid paralysis in adults and children visiting and returning home from the TP-endemic regions of the United States, Canada, and Australia in order to curtail a highly significant trend toward the misdiagnosis of TP as GBS and to delay the immediate management of TP by prompt tick removal.

References

1. Cluster of tick paralysis—Colorado, 2006. *MMWR* 2006;55:933–935.
2. Vedanarayanan VV, Evans OB, Subramony SH. Tick paralysis in children: Electrophysiology and possibility of misdiagnosis. *Neurology* 2002;59:1088–1090.
3. Diaz JH. A 60-year meta-analysis of tick paralysis in the United States: A predictable, preventable, and often misdiagnosed poisoning. *J Med Toxicol* 2010;6:15–21.
4. Grattan-Smith PJ, Morris JG, Johnston HM, et al. Clinical and neurophysiological features of tick paralysis. *Brain* 1997;120:1975–1987.

Chapter 25

Bites and Stings

Marine Envenomings

Marine Envenomings 570
Toxic Coelenterates 572
Toxic Vertebrates 575

Marine Envenomings

Pre-Test Question

1. Soft-tissue infections caused by *Vibrio vulnificus* are most likely to complicate envenoming injuries by which of the following marine animals?
   A. *Dasyatis americana**
   B. Fire coral
   C. *Hapalochlaena maculosa*
   D. *Physalia physalis*
2. Life-threatening respiratory insufficiency is most likely to follow envenoming injuries by which of the following marine animals?
   A. *Dasyatis americana*
   B. *Hapalochlaena maculosa**
   C. *Linuche unguiculata*
   D. *Physalia physalis*

Outline

- *Taxonomy* of marine envenomations (Tables 25.1 and 25.2)
- *Epidemiology* of marine envenomations

TABLE 25.1 Marine Invertebrates

Phyla	Species
Porifera	Sponges
Cnidaria	Corals, hydroids, anemones, jellyfish
Annelida	Worms
Mollusca	Snails, octopuses
Echinodermata	Starfish, sea urchins, sea cucumbers

TABLE 25.2 Chordates (Vertebrates)

Classes of the Vertebrate Chordates (Phylum Chordata)	Species
Chondrichthyes	Stingrays and sharks
Osteichthyes	Bony fishes
Scorpaenidae	Lionfish, stonefish, scorpionfish, zebrafish
Trachinidae	Weeverfish
Reptilia	Sea snakes and sea kraits
Hydrophiliidae	Sea snakes

* Correct.

- *Toxicology* of marine envenomations
- Rapid identification, patient evaluation, and management

Taxonomy—Invertebrates

Coelenterate Phyla

Porifera
Cnidaria
Annelida
Mollusca
Echiodermata

Coelenterate Species

Sponges
Corals, hydroids, anemones, jellyfish
Worms
Snails, octopuses
Starfish, sea urchins, sea cucumbers

Taxonomy—Vertebrates

Chordate Classes

- Chondrichthyes
- Osteichthyes
  - Scorpaenidae
  - Trachinidae
- Reptilia
  - Hydrophiliidae

Chordate Species

- Stingrays and sharks
- Bony fishes
  - Lionfish, stonefish, scorpionfish, zebrafish
  - Weeverfish
- Sea snakes and sea kraits
  - Sea snakes

Descriptive Epidemiology 1

- *Coelenterates*, especially corals and jellyfish, cause most marine envenomations.
- The Australian *box jellyfish* (*Chironex fleckeri*) is the most venomous and deadly (CFR 20+%) of all toxic marine life.
- The *fire coral* is the most toxic Cnidarian; the *blue-ringed octopus* is the most toxic mollusk; and the *crown-of-thorns* starfish is the most toxic Echinoderm.

Descriptive Epidemiology 2

- *Stingrays* cause 1800 painful envenomations per year in the United States.
- The *stonefish* (*Synanceja horrida*) is the most venomous Scorpaenid bony fish.
- The *lionfish* (*Pterosis volitans*) is the most common Scorpaenid in home aquaria.
- Marine venoms are very *complex* mixtures of low and high MW proteins, including histamine, prostaglandins, serotonin, kinins, indoles, and many other *vasoactive* compounds.

Toxic Coelenterates

- Echinoderms—starfish and sea urchins
- Cnidarians—corals and jellyfish
- Mollusks—cone shells (sea snails) and octopuses

Echinoderms—Starfish

- **Name:** Crown-of-thorns
- **Latin:** *Acanthaster planci*
- **Venom:** Toxic saponins—hemolytic, anticoagulant, and histaminergic
- **Antidote:** None
- **Dx:** Puncture wounds, pain, erythema, N, V, muscular paralysis, syncope, ataxia
- **Tx:** Hot water immersion (110–115°F), analgesics, ttox

Echinoderms—Sea Urchins

- **Name:** Long-spined sea urchin
- **Latin:** *Diadema antillarum*
- **Venom:** Hemolysins, proteases, serotonin, and steroid glycosides
- **Antidote:** None
- **Dx:** Edema, erythema, N, V, syncope ↑ respiratory paralysis, paresthesias ↑ ataxia, later FB granuloma
- **Tx:** Hot soak, ttox, spines out

Cnidarians—Corals (Hydroids)

- **Name:** Fire coral
- **Latin:** *Millepora* spp.
- **Venom:** Histaminergic kinins
- **Antidote:** None
- **Dx:** Burning/stinging, pruritus, regional urticaria, prolonged wound healing, eventual scarring
- **Tx:** Sea water irrigation, vinegar soak, papain meat tenderizer, skin shave, antihistamines, steroids, ttox

Cnidarians—Jellyfish 1

- **Name:** Box jellyfish, sea wasp
- **Latin:** *Chironex fleckeri*
- **Venom:** Myospastic, neurotoxic
- **Antidote:** Sheep-derived antivenin (Australia)
- **Dx:** Myospasm, respiratory paralysis, hypotension, cardiac arrest
- **Tx:** CPR, ttox, ovine antivenom is whole IgG and not an Fab fragment like stonefish and sea snake antivenom
- Box jellyfish sting (linear ribbon welts)

Cnidarians—Jellyfish 2

- **Name:** Portuguese man-of-war, tentacles trail up to 30 m
- **Latin:** *Physalia physalis*
- **Venom:** Neurotoxic
- **Antidote:** None
- **Dx:** Painful linear papules—welts, N, V, HA, myalgias, chills, respiratory distress, CV collapse
- **Tx:** Vinegar soak, papain meat tenderizer, skin shave, ttox, antihistamines

Cnidarians—Jellyfish 3

- **Name:** Sea lice—larval jellyfish
- **Latin:** *Linuche unguiculata*
- **Venom:** Histamine, kinins
- **Antidote:** None
- **Dx:** Sea bather's eruption-blisters-hives in swimsuit distribution, N, V, HA
- **Tx:** Seawater wash, vinegar soak, topical–systemic antihistamines and steroids

Cnidarians—Misc. Jellyfish

Pelagia noctiluca: Mauve Stinger

- **Name:** Mauve stinger, a bioluminescent pink jellyfish
- **Latin:** *Pelagia noctiluca*
- **Venom:** High MW uncharacterized proteins
- **Antidote:** None
- **Dx:** Slow healing, often hyperpigmented blisters, possible systemic toxicity
- **Tx:** Topical anesthetics > antihistamines, corticosteroids

Chrysaora quinquecirrha: Sea Nettle

- **Name:** Sea nettle
- **Latin:** *Chrysaora quinquecirrha*

- **Venom:** Complex mixture of esterases, proteases, and hyaluronidase
- **Antidote:** None
- **Dx:** Severe pain then blistering tentacle tracks, then skip areas of skin necrosis
- **Tx:** Topical baking soda plaster to inactivate venom

Misc. Cnidarians—Hydroids

Aglaophenia spp.: Stinging Hydroids

- **Name:** Stinging hydroids
- **Latin:** *Aglaophenia* spp.
- **Venom:** Contained in nematocysts distributed over branches and stems of fernlike hydroid colonies growing on rocks and dead coral
- **Dx:** Stinging, then erythema, edema, blistering within minutes, hemorrhagic blebs within hours
- **Tx:** Topical antihistamines, corticosteroids

Mollusks—Cone Shells

Conus spp. (Cone Shells)

Cone shell envenomation apparatus

- **Name:** Cone shells
- **Latin:** *Conus* spp.
- **Venom:** Conotoxins injected by radular tooth, block Na channels like TTX, saxitoxins
- **Antidote:** None
- **Dx:** Burning, numbness, ischemia, local–distal paresthesias, dysphagia, diplopia, CV collapse
- **Tx:** Seawater wash, vinegar soak, topical–systemic steroids and antihistamines, no antivenom

Mollusks—Octopuses

- **Name:** Blue-ringed octopus (Figure 25.1)
- **Latin:** *Hapalochlaena maculosa*
- **Venom:** Parrot-like beak, two venom glands, neurotoxic *tetrodotoxin* (as in all puffer fish and Oregon rough-skinned newt)
- **Antidote:** None
- **Dx:** Burning–numbness, ischemia, paresthesia, aphonia, dysphagia, diplopia, CV collapse, respiratory failure, coma, death
- **Tx:** Inotropic support, hot water soak, ttox

Other Marine Tetrodotoxins

Masked puffer fish (Figure 25.2)

FIGURE 25.1 (See color insert.) Blue-ringed octopus (*Hapalochlaena maculosus*). The blue-ringed octopus can inflict a painful bite and inject a tetradotoxin containing paralyzing venom. (With permission from Dietrich Mebs, *Venomous and Poisonous Animals*, 2002, CRC Press, Boca Raton, FL, p. 72, Figure 2.34.)

"Fugu," raw puffer fish, can cause tetrodotoxin poisoning with respiratory paralysis following the consumption of improperly cleaned and prepared "fugu" fish, even if cooked.

Toxic Vertebrates

- Chondrichthyes—Stingrays
- Scorpaenidae—Scorpaenid bony fish
- Trachinidae—Weeverfish
- Reptilia—Sea snakes

Chondrichthyes—Stingrays 1

Dasyatis americana (Southern Stingray)

- **Name:** Southern stingray (see Figures 25.3 through 25.5).
- **Latin:** *Dasyatis americana.*
- **Venom:** Serotonin, 5′-nucleotidase, and phospho-diesterase-injected by tail barb-dorsal serrated spines into deep, jagged lacerations, usually on foot-leg; death not rare 2° chest (cardiac) punctures or *Vibrio* sepsis. Steve "*Crocodile Hunter*" Irwin, ς 09/04/06.
- **Antidote:** None.

Chondrichthyes—Stingrays 2

- **Latin:** *Dasyatis americana*

FIGURE 25.2 (See color insert.) Masked pufferfish, *Arothron diadematus*, Red Sea. The meat of the pufferfish is often consumed raw as "fugu" fish in Japan. The pufferfish and marine sunfish contain high concentrations of paralyzing tetradotoxin in the skin, liver, bile, ovaries, and roe, and must be filleted precisely in order to be eaten raw or cooked without risk of tetradotoxin poisoning. (With permission from Dietrich Mebs, *Venomous and Poisonous Animals*, 2002, CRC Press, Boca Raton, FL, p. 139, Figure 2.91.)

- **Dx:** Intensifying burning pain often in cyanotic deep wound, muscle cramping, weakness, tremor, syncope, hypotension, CV collapse, seizures, *potential paralysis*, 2° *Vibrio* infections—*ecthyma gangrenosa* (*V. vulnificus*) and osteomyelitis common
- **Tx:** Hot water immersion, third-generation cephalosporins, ttox, debridement, analgesics

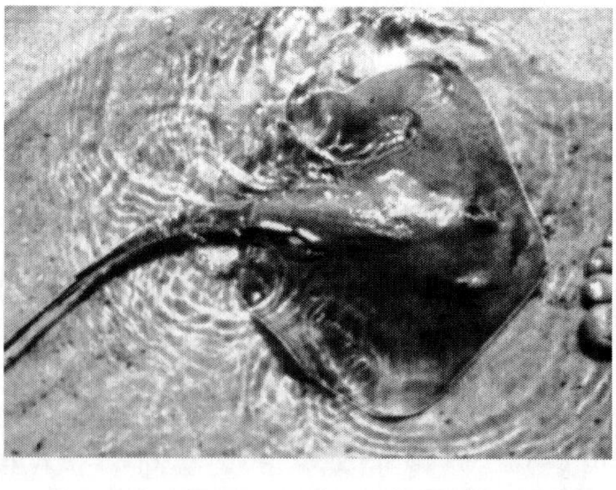

FIGURE 25.3 Southern stingray (*Dasyatis americana*) injuries: diagnosis and treatment. Southern stingrays are commonly found in shallow waters off the U.S. Atlantic and Gulf of Mexico coasts and can inflict serious penetrating injuries with sharp spines on their long, whip-like tails.

FIGURE 25.4 Southern stingray (*Dasyatis americana*). Southern stingray-inflicted human injuries usually occur on the feet and shins when the stingrays are stepped upon in shallow water and whip their barbed tails over their bodies. (Courtesy of Charles P. Sea, Department of Emergency Medicine, Ochsner Clinic Foundation Hospital, New Orleans, LA. Original Source: U.S. Government Document, Information Bulletin #12, 1980, "Toxic Fish and Mollusks.")

Scorpaenids—Lionfish

- **Name:** Lionfish (Figure 25.6).
- **Latin:** *Pterosis volitans.*
- **Venom:** $PGF_2\alpha$, PGE_2, TXB_2 injected by long, curved dorsal spines with separate venom glands.

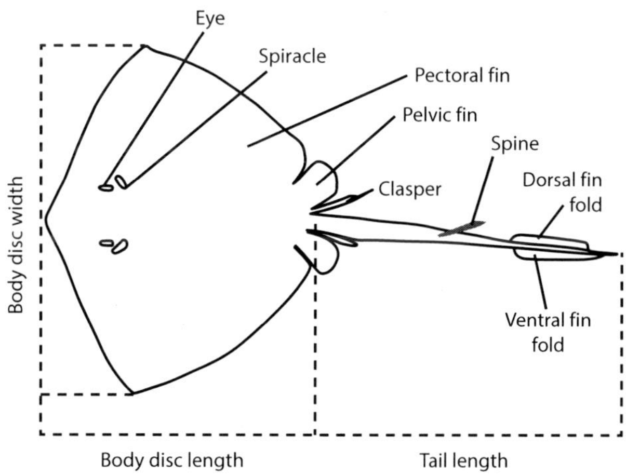

FIGURE 25.5 Barbed tail spine, southern stingray (*Dasyatis americana*). The hollow barbed spine on the dorsal aspect of the stingray's tail can cause jagged lacerations and inject a heal-labile toxin. (Courtesy of Charles P. Sea, Department of Emergency Medicine, Ochsner Clinic Foundation Hospital, New Orleans, LA. Original Source: U.S. Government Document, Information Bulletin #12, 1980, "Toxic Fish and Mollusks.")

FIGURE 25.6 (See color insert.) Lionfish (*Pterosis volitans*). The lionfish has dorsal fins tipped with sharp spines attached to separate venom glands, which can inflict painful envenoming injuries in divers and saltwater aquaria enthusiasts. A polyvalent Scorpaenid antivenom is available for the management of moderate-to-severe envenomings caused by lionfish, scorpionfish, and stonefish. (Courtesy of Charles P. Sea, Department of Emergency Medicine, Ochsner Clinic Foundation Hospital, New Orleans, LA. Original Source: U.S. Government Document, Information Bulletin #12, 1980, "Toxic Fish and Mollusks.")

- **Antidote:** No specific antivenom for lionfish. Scorpaenid polyvalent Fab antivenin (CDC and local aquaria) is reserved for stonefish/scorpionfish injuries.
- **Dx:** Local severe pain/edema.
- **Tx:** Hot water soak, digital block, analgesics, ttox.

Scorpaenids—Stonefish

- **Name:** Stonefish (Figure 25.7)
- **Latin:** *Synanceja horrida*
- **Venom:** Cytolytic, hemolytic, myotoxic heat-labile high MW proteins (stonustoxins)
- **MoA:** Hydrophilic pores in cell membranes permit Ca entry
- **Antidote:** Contact aquaria for Fab stonefish antivenom
- **Dx:** Intensifying local pain erythema, ecchymoses, induration, hyperesthesia–dysesthesia, N, V, dyspnea, diaphoresis, later lymphadenopathy, syncope, hypotension, dysrhythmias
- **Tx:** Hot water immersion (110–115°F), digital block 0.25% bupivacaine plain, antivenin not universally available—contact CDC and local aquaria, analgesics—po ASA + NSAIDs + opioids, parenteral opioids often required, drain and unroof blisters filled with venom

Trachinidae—Weeverfish

- **Name:** Weeverfish—small, bottom-feeders that burrow into muddy/sandy-bottomed bays of eastern Atlantic, sharp dorsal and single opercular spines surrounded by venom-containing glandular tissue will penetrate thick boots.

FIGURE 25.7 Stonefish (*Synanceja* spp.). Stonefish are flattened dorsoventrally, lie camouflaged by sand on the ocean floor, and can inflict painful envenoming injuries with dorsal spines when stepped on by swimmers or divers. (Courtesy of Charles P. Sea, Department of Emergency Medicine, Ochsner Clinic Foundation Hospital, New Orleans, LA. Original Source: U.S. Government Document, Information Bulletin #12, 1980, "Toxic Fish and Mollusks.")

- **Latin:** *Trachinus* spp. (weeverfish venomous spines) (Figure 25.7).
- **Venom:** High MW proteins, serotonin, epinephrine, norepinephrine, histamine.
- **Antidote:** None.
- **Dx:** Pain, edema, HA, fever, chills, N, V, diaphoresis, hypotension, seizures, dysrhythmias. Initial, local edema ↑ induration can involve entire extremity and may persist for months.
- **Tx:** Analgesics, digital block, ttox, supportive care.

Marine Wound Infections

Bacterial contamination of marine wounds, often puncture wounds inflicted by stingrays (Figure 25.4) or catfish (Figures 25.8 and 25.9), are usually caused by a mixed microbial flora of marine pathogens including:

- Non-cholera *Vibrios*
- *Mycobacterium marinum*
- MRSA
- *Clostridium tetani* (rare)

Recommended Management

- Debridement and cultures
- Place PPD for mycobacterial reactions (rxns) (10–20 mm of induration)
- Antibiotic prophylaxis
- Tetanus toxoid prophylaxis
- ***M. marinum*:** Rifampin + ethambutol × 4–6 months
- **MRSA:** Trimethoprim—sulfamethoxazole
- ***Vibrios*:** Quinolones (except tenosynovitis) vs. azithromycin

FIGURE 25.8 Saltwater gafftopsail or gafftop catfish (*Bagre marinus*) washed up on the beach and is still capable of inflicting a serious and frequently infected wound from the venomous barbed spine in its dorsal and pectoral fins. The gafftopsail catfish is found in the central western Atlantic Ocean, the Gulf of Mexico, and the Caribbean Sea. Although not prized as table fare, Many prefer to skin the fish and then fry the filets. (Courtesy of Dr. David K. Lirette, LS School of Public Health, New Orleans, LA.)

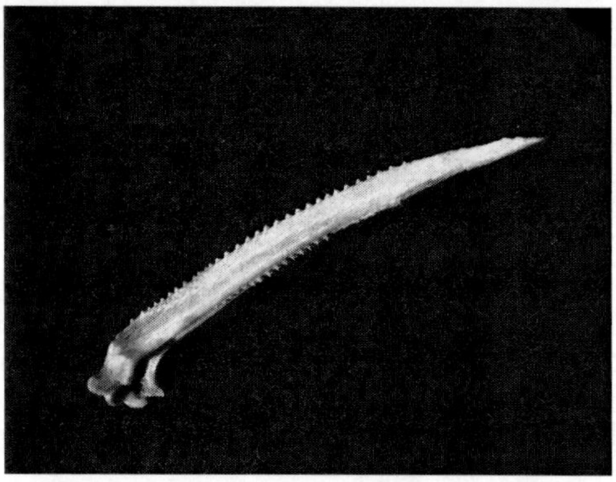

FIGURE 25.9 The bony, barbed spine of a saltwater gafftopsail or gafftop catfish, *Bagre marinus*. (Courtesy of Dr. David K. Lirette, LSU School of Public Health, New Orleans, LA.)

Bact: Non-Cholera Vibrios

Vibrio parahemolyticus

- Marine, non-cholera *Vibrio*
- Salt-tolerant, acid-sensitive (use Tabasco®?)
- Transmission (Trans): raw shellfish (especially raw oysters) > water
- Clinical manifestations (Clin): 1 wk F, N and V, watery diarrhea—no blood or pus
- **Warning:** Avoid raw/under-cooked shellfish, esp. in warm months, do not count on months with "Rs" and Tabasco

Vibrio vulnificus

Marine, non-cholera *Vibrios*, salt and acid-resistant

- **Trans:** Raw shellfish—oysters, direct inoculums—seawater
- **Clin:** Ulcerating cellulitis, *ecthyma gangrenosa*, sepsis has high CFRs
- **Pv:** No raw shellfish, treat all penetrating injuries in seawater with quinolones
- **Warning:** Alcoholism, liver disease, esp. hemochromatosis

M. marinum Hand Infection

A marine lab researcher abraded the back of her left hand. 4 days later a very tender erythematous nodule appeared and drained yellow fluid. Gram and AFB stains were negative. Cultures grew *M. marinum*—white colonies in dark turn yellow in light. Tx: *Rifampin* ± *ethambutol* po × 4 months

M. marinum granuloma

A man lacerated the dorsum of his left index finger while cleaning his saltwater fish tank. 3 months later, he noted crusted, verrucous plaque at the site and 2 subcutaneous nodules along the lymphatic drainage track. Bx of the granuloma was + for *M. marinum* by AFB and culture. Tx: *rifampin* and *ethambutol* × 4 months.

M. marinum tenosynovitis

A beachcomber pulled a splinter out of the left thumb during beach vacation 3 months ago. PE: afebrile, L hand swollen, fingers semi-flexed, palm warm and puffy, 7 × 5-cm inflamed area volar forearm proximal to L wrist. MRI: edema around flexor tendon sheaths and metacarpals, 2 fluid collections (insert = normal hand). PPD +, aspirate + for *M. marinum*. Tx: debridement, *ethambutol, rifampin, trimethoprim-sulfamethoxazole (TMP-SMX)* × 4 months.

M. marinum—Not CTS!

A beach explorer collected seashells 8 months before presenting with a 4 mo. hx of 4 nodular lesions dorsum R hand + palmar numbness and tingling. Underwent CT release by orthopod—no C&S. Sx persisted. MRI: inflamed flexor tendons, wrist and forearm. PPD + at 10 mm – neg Quantiferon-TBGold. Skin bx and culture + for AFB (*M. marinum*). Tx: ethambutol + clarithromycin × 9 months.

Reptilia—Sea Snakes

- **Name:** Sea snakes and kraits.
- **Latin:** *Aipysurus laevis*, *Astrotia stokesii*, *Enhydrina schistosa* (most toxic), *Hydrophis ornatus*, *H. cyanocinctus*, *Lapemis hardwickii*, and so on.
- **Venom:** Neurotoxin alters Na/Cl permeability and *postsynaptically blocks NMJ receptors like nondepolarizing muscle relaxants*. No effect on Na–K ATPase pump—some venoms also hemolytic and myotoxic (olive sea snake).

Beaked Sea Snake (*Enhydrina schistosa*)

- **Name:** Sea snakes
- **Antidote:** Equine-derived bivalent antivenin used for all envenomations
- **Dx:** No local reaction, peripheral and CN neuropathies within 3–6 h, paralysis, respiratory failure, myonecrosis and myoglobinuria (esp. olive sea snake), renal failure
- **Tx:** Supportive, antivenin, analgesics, tetanus toxoid (ttox)

Reptilia—Sea Snakes vs. Kraits

Sea snakes
  Olive sea snake (myotoxic)
Banded sea krait (neurotoxic venom)

Post-Test Question

1. An effective antivenom is available for severely envenoming injuries inflicted by which of the following marine animals?
   A. *Acanthaster planci*
   B. *Dasyatis americana*
   C. *Physalia physalis*
   D. *Synanceja horrida**
2. The most sought-after venomous marine animal for home aquariums today is
   A. *Acanthaster planci*
   B. *Diadema antillarum*
   C. *Pterosis volitans**
   D. *Synanceja horrida*

* Correct

Chapter 26

Voodoo, Hoodoo, and Cajun Traditions and Poisonings

Outline 584
Introduction 584
Cajun Healing Practitioners 585
Herbal and Plant Poisonings 595
Voodoo–Hoodoo 603
Arthropods 607
Conclusions 610

Outline

Introduction
Definitions and History
- Voodoo vs. Hoodoo
- Cajuns vs. Acadians
- Gris-Gris
- Zombification
- Traiteurs vs. Traiteusses
- Los Curanderos
- Stimulating, Healing, Punishing Services

Pharmacology and Formulary
Plant-Derived Remedies and Toxins
- Classification
- Herbs
- Plants and Cacti

Other Remedies and Toxins—Mushrooms and Heavy Metals
Animal-Derived Remedies and Toxins
- Classification
- Marine
- Terrestrial

Conclusions

Introduction

Voodoo, hoodoo, and Louisiana Cajun have magical–religious healing practices that originated from the sixteenth to the eighteenth centuries mergers of the ethno-cultural practices of indigenous (*Native Americans*) and imported or exiled populations of *West Africans*, *Caribbeans*, and *French Canadian Catholics* and *Huguenots* with Western European beliefs and religions, predominantly Roman Catholicism and Protestantism.

All New World traditional practitioners relied on both *native plant and animal potions* and on *inanimate transfer objects* (amulets, cordons, dolls, talismans, "poisoned" notes and letters, etc.) to *stimulate, heal, or punish* their clients or patients.

Many of these practices have recently been determined to have significant physiochemical effects, to induce potentially toxic drug–drug and drug–food interactions, and to open possibilities for investigational new drug therapies, including cancer chemotherapy.

However, many of these traditional practices are *more psychic and religious than scientific and physiologic*; and have absolutely no therapeutic values, other than placebo effects, which are often very powerful treatment adjuncts.*

* This chapter presents only those plant and animal toxins that are commonly employed in voodoo–hoodoo, Cajun, and Curanderos treatment practices, and does not include all agents used in the past and present formularies.

Placebo effects have been observed to provide *20–30% improvements* in conditions treated.

Voodoo vs. Hoodoo

Voodoo

A folk religion emanating in *French Haiti* (sixteenth to nineteenth centuries) that emerged from the interaction of *West African* ethno-theologies with European Christian rituals, mostly *Roman Catholic.* Voodoo *priests and priestesses* practice the arts of stimulating, healing, and punishing using native plant and animal toxins and inanimate objects.

Hoodoo

A folk religion emanating in *isolated barrier islands* off the coasts of *Georgia* and *South Carolina* (seventeenth to nineteenth centuries) from the interaction of *West African Gullah* (coastal) and *Geechee* (inland) ethno-theologies with Native American and Western European rituals. Hoodoo practitioners use native plants, animals, and inanimate objects to heal their clients.

Cajun Healing Practitioners

Cajuns vs. Creoles

- **Cajuns (from Acadians):** White descendants of Catholic French exiled to Louisiana from Protestant British Canada (Nova Scotia) and British Caribbean, mid-eighteenth century
- **Creoles (nonnatives):** *West African-French speakers*, imported as slaves from Caribbean to Louisiana by European slave traders, or exiled as prisoners to Louisiana by Caribbean colonials, or moved to Louisiana as free-persons-of-color (*noires libres*); often intermarried Cajuns

Traiteurs, Traiteusses, and Los Curanderos

- **Traiteurs:** Male Cajun/Creole health practitioners (treaters)
- **Traiteusses:** Female Cajun and Creole healing practitioners
- **Curanderos:** Mexican-American male and female healing practitioners in Texas and Louisiana
- **"Medical" Instruments:** Chants, touch > objects—amulets > plants—herbs, mushrooms, animals—fish, frogs, insects

The Practitioners

	Voodoo	Hoodoo	Cajun
Designation	Priests (male)	Healers (both sex)	*Traiteurs* (M)
	Priestesses (female)		*Traiteusses* (F)
			Los Curanderos (Mex. M and F)

(*continued*)

	Voodoo	Hoodoo	Cajun
Professional Calling	Caul (amnion) birth; twins	None	Caul birth
			Twins
Professional Code	None	None	Strict code
Dispense	Heal, stimulate, and punish	Heal, stimulate	Heal, stimulate, and punish
Instruments	Chants—prayers, plant–animal toxins, objects	Plant > animal toxins, objects, seashells	Prayers, hands, objects, plant > animal toxins

Unique Practices

Stimulating–Healing–Punishing

- **Stimulating practices:** Most commonly abortion, erection, labor, libido, mood, and spirits
- **Healing practices:** Mental—depression, melancholia > medical—musculoskeletal and skin, psoriasis, skin infections, headache (HA), ear, and toothaches > surgical—boils, ganglion cysts (*Bible bumps*)
- **Punishing practices:** Zombification > *Gris-Gris* (bad luck hexes)

Zombification vs. Gris-Gris

- **Zombification:** Voodoo punishment practices of inducing *cataleptic trances* on victims (zombies) using animal > plant and mushroom toxins
- **Gris-Gris:** Cajun/Creole treaters' punishment practices of inducing *bad luck outcomes* on victims using chants—prayers, inanimate objects, letters—notes, transfer dolls, plant and animal parts

Cajun Treater's Practice Code

- The patient must *contact* the treater.
- The treater works in *secret* and may *not advertise*.
- The treater *cannot accept payment* for services, but gifts are OK for the treater and his/her family.
- Treaters may treat at a *distance*, but not across bodies of water.
- Treaters *touch* patients near chief complaint sites.
- Treaters *whisper* chants-prayers to themselves.
- Treaters may pass on their skills, but always *older to younger*, one sex *to opposite sex*.

Formulary 1

	Plants	Animals	1° Objects
Voodoo	Abortifacients, oxytocics, aphrodisiacs, hallucinogens	Fish, shellfish, amphibian—frogs and newts	Amulets, necklaces, dolls, notes, black magic
Hoodoo	Same + Spanish moss, poultices, topicals, teas	Spider webs for wounds	Seashell amulets, necklaces
Cajuns and Curandos	Same	Spider webs for wounds	Crucifixes, buried nails, cordons, notes

Formulary 2

	Stimulating	Healing	Punishing
Plant	Abortifacients Oxytocics	Teas topicals	Hallucinogens
Animal	Abortifacients Aphrodisiacs	Spider webs	Tetrodotoxins Saxitoxins Ciguatoxins
Heavy metals	Inorganic mercury for teething	Lead for diarrhea	Inorganic mercury for trances and STDs

Stimulating Agents

Libido and erection:*

Bufotoxins—"rock hard," *chan-su*, amphibian (toads) toxic secretions
Cantharidin—"Spanish fly," arthropod (blister beetles) toxic secretion—mucosal irritant
Yohimbe bark—"yo-yo," α_2-antagonist and cholinergic agonist

Healing Agents

Balsam apple (*giddy-giddy*)
Cayenne
Elemental lead
Gentian (violet)
Mayapple (podophyllin)
Pine needles
Sassafras
Spanish moss (*Tilandsia* spp.)
Spider webs (all species)
Witch hazel
Yew

Punishing Agents

Hallucination

Brugmasia and *Datura* spp.
Bufotoxins—amphibian
Ephedra
Lizard's tail (*Saururus* spp.)
Ibotenic acid and psilocybin MRs
Morning glory (*Ipomoea pandurata*)

---

* Ginseng is recommended by Chinese herbalists for erectile dysfunction (ED); not traditionally used by voodoo–hoodoo–Cajuns (Figure 26.1).

FIGURE 26.1 The southern toad frog, *Anaxyrus terrestris*, resembles the Asian toad, which secretes bufotoxins through its skin to defer predators. Toad secretions and dried skin continue to be used as traditional, especially oriental, medications for erectile dysfunction. Some bufotoxins are, however, cardiotoxic and can cause digitalis-like toxicity with potentially fatal cardiac arrhythmias. (Courtesy of David K. Lirette, PhD, LSU School of Public Health, New Orleans, LA.)

Peyote cactus
Wormwood (*Artemesia* spp.)
Nutmeg and mace

Zombification

Cassava
Palytoxins and saxitoxins—marine toxins
Tetrodotoxins—marine and terrestrial toxins

Other Punishments

Cassava—cyanide poisoning
Cantharidin—arthropod blistering secretion
Camphor (*Cinnamonum* spp.)
Capsaicin—cayenne peppers (*Capsicum* spp.)
Ciguatoxin—marine
Inorganic mercury (mercury bichloride)
Scombrotoxins—marine

Miscellaneous Traditional Medications

Trees and Plants

Teas: Sassafras—flu, willow—for headache. Note: aspirin was originally derived from the bark of willow trees.

Wormwood, *Artemesia*—malaria.

Prickly ash bark—toothache.
White balsam—boils and superficial skin infections.
Yohimbe bark and Boar hog, *Ligusticum canadense*—impotence.
Casearia ilicifolia and *Rhoeo spathacea*—oxytocics to stimulate labor.
Cassava (yucca), lizard's tail (*Saururus cernuus*), nutmeg—hallucinogens.

Herbs and Cacti

Cayenne peppers, *Capsicum* spp. (Subs P-depleter)—OA, RA, fibromyalgia, LBP, psoriasis
Cow cabbage, *Nymphaea odorata*—earache
Gentian—athlete's foot, candidiasis
Spanish moss—DM, HTN
Peyote cactus, *Lophophora williamsi*—hallucinogen
Psilocybe and ibotenic *Amanita* spp. MRs—hallucinogens
Mayapple-podophyllin—warts, skin cancer, venereal warts. Note: Topical podophyllin preparations are still used to treat venereal warts and intravenous preparations are administered as cancer chemotherapeutics.

Animal Secretions

Hallucinogens—frog bufotoxins
Zombification—marine and newt tetrodotoxins, marine saxitoxins
Punishments—marine saxitoxins and palytoxins, ant formic acid, beetle cantharidin.
Spider webs—wounds dressings, topical anticoagulants

Heavy Metals

Lead (Los Curanderos)—for diarrhea, parasites, AGIs = empacho; *Alarcon, Azarcon, Rueda, Maria Luisa*
Inorganic Hg—mercuric chloride ($HgCl_2$) for *empacho*—parasites, STDs—syphilis, hallucinations
Iron oxide (rebar rods in water)—anemia, hookworm, Pb poisoning = hemolysis = anemia
Note: *Hippocrates* placed used iron swords contributed by ancient Greek soldiers into buckets of water to prepare solutions of iron oxide to administer orally to women with postpartum anemias.

Inanimate Transfer Treatments

Toothaches*—Buried Nail Tx** The treater uses a small nail to make the ***Sign of the Cross near the afflicted tooth, and then buries the nail in the patient's backyard during chanted prayers. The nail is exhumed and inspected daily by the treater or patient. When the nail rusts, the decayed tooth will fall out.

***Extremity Sprains/Strains*—Cordon** The treater puts a series of knots in a *long cord or string called a cordon that is then looped like a rosary during chanting prayers.* The healer wraps the cordon like a bracelet around the afflicted limb of the patient. The patient wears the cordon until healed.

Herbal and Plant Poisonings

- Abortifacients (mostly oxytocics used to stimulate the premature onset of contractions)
- Central nervous system (CNS) toxins
- Gastrointestinal toxins
- Miscellaneous toxins

Abortifacients

- Aloe
- *Aristolochia* (birthwort)*
- Bitter melon
- Black cohosh root
- Blue cohosh root

Note: Black and blue cohosh root extracts—teas were used as herbal abortifacients by causing vaginal, cervical irritation leading to bleeding, like cantharidin, a blistering acid secreted by beetles.

- Ergot fungi
- Cantharidin
- Juniper
- Mugwort
- Nutmeg
- Pennyroyal oil (pulegone)†
- Quinine (directs posterior pituitary gland to secrete oxytocin)†
- Rue
- Sage
- Tricosanthin root (compound Q)

What Is Compound Q? Indications for Its Use

- **Compound Q** is an herbal preparation of the Chinese *Trichosanthin* plant and roots (*Tian Hua Fen*) which can *inactivate viral ribosomes and inhibit HIV replication.*
- **Pharmacology:** Poor oral availability and *intense diarrhea po*; severe *biphasic neurotoxicity* on parenteral admin.
- **Toxicity:** CNS/PNS (paresthesias) > derm (hypersensitivity and anaphylaxis) > metabolic (hypoglycemia).
- **CNS neurotoxicity:** (1) *Encephalomyelitis* in 24–72 h with fever, delirium, dementia, myalgias, paresis; (2) *coma* within 1 week.
- **Tx:** Immediate NG lavage + AC, supportive.

---

* Insect (blister beetle) toxin.

† Highly effective abortifacients.

CNS Neurotoxins: Outline

- Absinthe hallucinogen (wormwood)
- Belladonna alkaloids (anticholinergics)
- *Ephedra* (sympathomimetics)
- Nicotinic (tobacco-like) agents
- Nutmeg and mace (meth-like)
- St. John's wort (SSRI-like)

CNS Toxicity: Absinthe

- **Representative:** Absinthe (wormwood) (Figure 26.2)
- **Indications:** Croup, asthma
- **Latin:** *Artemisia absinthium*
- **Toxin:** *Thujones* (artemisins). (1) Neurotoxicity resembles *camphor*. (2) Antimalarial—effectively used in SE Asia (Vietnam), even for mefloquine and doxycycline-resistant *P. falciparum* (Myanmar)
- **Dx: Absinthism**—hallucinations, intellectual deterioration, psychosis, seizures (most celebrated case of self-mutilation = Vincent Van Gogh)

FIGURE 26.2 Wormwood or absinthe, *Artemesia absinthium*, is an herb containing the hallucinogenic neurotoxins, the artemisins, which are also highly effective antimalarials. (From Wikipedia Creative Commons.)

- **Tx:** GI decontamination (lavage + activated charcoal [AC]), supportive tx

Wormwood

Artemisia absinthium

- **CNS toxins:** Belladonna alkaloids
- **Reps:** Jimson weed (thornapple), nightshade, jessamine, *Solandra* spp. (angel's trumpet, very common in NO)
- **Toxins:** *Scopolamine* = hyoscine >
- ***atropine*** = Hyoscyamine
- **Antidote:** Physostigmine for CNS effects
- **Dx:** Atropine tox = F, dry mouth, tachycardia, ileus, urinary retention, hallucinations, seizures, *"red as a beet, blind as a bat, hot as Hades, mad as a hatter."*
- **Tx:** GI decontamination

CNS: Miscellaneous Belladonna Alkaloids

- *Datura stramonium* (Jimson weed)
- *Atropa belladonna* (deadly nightshade)
- Angel's trumpet (*Brugmansia suaveolens*); see Figure 26.3

FIGURE 26.3 All parts of the angel's trumpet, *Brugmansia suaveolens*, contain anticholinergic neurotoxins, including scopolamine, hyoscine, and hyoscyamine. On ingestion of the plant or teas made from its seeds, flowers, or leaves, these toxins can induce visual and auditory hallucinations and produce an anticholinergic toxidrome characterized by confusion, tachycardia, dry mouth, diarrhea, mydriasis, rapid onset cycloplegia, and smooth muscle paralysis. (Courtesy of David K. Lirette, PhD, LSU School of Public Health, New Orleans, LA.)

Hallucinogen Group

- **Hallucinogens:** Morning glory,* nutmeg and mace,† peyote cactus,‡ and wormwood

CNS Toxicity: Hallucinogens

- **Reps:** Morning glory ("LSD"), peyote cactus, nutmeg and mace (*Myristica fragrans*, resembles MDMA = *ecstasy* toxicity)
- **Toxins:** *Lysergamide* (LSD-like), *mescaline*, and *myristicin* (MMDA—nutmeg), respectively
- **Antidote:** None
- **Dx:** Initial N and V, diaphoresis, mental status changes, deep sleep (nutmeg), hallucinations
- **Tx:** GI decontamination, supportive (Figures 26.4 and 26.5)
- Morning glory (contains lysergamide)
  Ipomoea purpurea; see Figure 26.4
- Peyote cactus (contains mescaline)
  Lophophora williamsii; see Figure 26.5

CNS Tox: Hallucinogens

- **Nutmeg:** Powdered spice grated from the enclosed seed kernel
- **Mace:** Soft red cover, or aril, of the kernel

FIGURE 26.4 All parts of the morning glory, *Ipomoea purpurea*, especially the seeds, contain an LSD-like lysergamide compound which can produce visual and auditory hallucinations on ingestion. (Courtesy of David K. Lirette, PhD, LSU School of Public Health, New Orleans, LA.)

* Used by voodoo practitioners for inducing trance, not zombification.

† Used by the *Curanderos* for exorcism.

‡ Used by Cajun treaters for fevers of unknown origin. Effective for *P. falciparum* malaria. Not effective against hypnozoites (add primaquine).

FIGURE 26.5 Peyote cactus, *Lophophora williamsii*, contains mescaline which can induce a trance-like state with visual and auditory hallucinations on ingestion of the cactus buttons or teas or alcoholic drinks made from the cactus. (From Wikipedia Creative Commons.)

CNS Tox: Nutmeg and Mace

- **Rep:** East and West (Grenada) Indian nutmeg tree
- **Indic:** Intentional hallucinations, exorcising demons
- **Latin:** *Myristica fragrans*
- **Toxin:** Myristicin –> meth*amphetamine* metabolites
- **Antidote:** None
- **Dx:** N, V, delirium, euphoria, deep sleep with hypothermia (like *Ecstasy,* MDMA, or 4-methyl-2-dimethoxy*amphetamine*)
- **Tx:** GI decontamination (lavage and AC), supportive therapy

CNS Tox: Ephedra

- **Rep:** Ephedra (*ma-huang*) *Ephedra viridis*; see Figure 26.6
- **Indic:** Asthma, COPD
- **Toxin:** Ephedrine, pseudoephedrine
- **Antidote:** None
- **Dx:** Sympathomimetic causes HA, nervousness, anxiety, flushing, vomiting, increased blood pressure (BP) and heart rate (HR), mania and psychosis, seizures, myocardial infarction MI, and cerebrovascular accident (CVA) or stroke possible
- **Tx:** GI decontamination (lavage and AC), supportive (Figure 26.6)

CNS Tox: Nicotine Group

- **Rep:** Betel nut, tobacco, blue cohosh, broom, chestnut, *Lobelia* (wild tobacco)
- **Indic:** Depression, insect bites, and stings

FIGURE 26.6 *Ephedra viridis* contains the sympathomimetic amines, ephedrine and pseudoephedrine, both of which are powerful vasoconstrictors and bronchodilators and can cause hypertension and tachycardia on ingestion. Ephedrine-containing preparations are still used in cough and cold preparations to reduce nasal stuffiness. (From Wikipedia Creative Commons.)

- **Toxin:** Arecholine (betel nut), lobeline (*Lobelia*), nicotine (tobacco)
- **Antidote:** None
- **Dx:** Bronchospasm, COPD, CAD, oral and lung cancers
- **Tx:** GI decontamination (lavage and AC), supportive

CNS Tox: St. John's Wort

- **Rep:** St. John's wort (*Hypericum perforatum*) used very *effectively* to self-medicate mild anxiety, nervousness, and depression (Figure 26.7)
- **Toxins:** Hyperforin > hypericin and pseudohypericin; inhibit central reuptake of serotonin, dopamine, epinephrine, norepinephrine
- **Antidote:** None
- **Dx:** Serotonin syndrome alone or with SSRIs or MAOIs
- **Tx:** Supportive, antipyretics, BZs

Herbal and Plant Poisonings

GI Toxins: Outline

- Goldenseal
- Pokeweed

FIGURE 26.7 St. John's wort, *Hypericum perforatum*, contains serotonin agonist and other sympathomimetic amines and is an effective antidepressant, but can cause serotonin syndrome with muscular rigidity and rhabdomyolysis if ingested along with other serotonin agonists, especially the selective serotonin reuptake inhibitors (SSRIs) and the monoamine oxidase inhibitors (MAOIs). (From Wikipedia Creative Commons.)

- Gentian
- Balsam apple
- Witch hazel
- Hepatotoxins

GI Tox: **Goldenseal**

- **Rep:** Goldenseal is a herb frequently used as an astringent and to reputedly mask the presence of illicit drugs on urine screens. Goldenseal is ineffective as an undetected adulterant and is easily detected by GC/MS (=+ drug test).
- **Other indications:** Allergies.
- **Latin:** *Hydrastis canadensis.*
- **Toxin:** Hydrastine.
- **Antidote:** None.
- **Dx:** Nausea N, Vomiting V, Diarrhea D, convulsions, paralysis, respiratory failure.
- **Tx:** GI decontamination (lavage and activated charcoal AC), supportive.

GI Tox: Pokeweed

- **Rep:** Pokeweed, English ivy, yew, horse chestnut
- **Indic:** Fever, infection
- **Toxin:** Phytolaccine (pokeweed), enterotoxins = terpene—resins
- **Antidote:** None
- **Dx:** N, V, D, cramps, hemorrhagic gastritis, weakness; later diplopia, seizures sz, dysrhythmias, respiratory failure, *lymphocytosis*
- **Tx:** GI decontamination (lavage + AC), supportive (Figure 26.8)

Phytolacca americana (pokeweed or pokeberry); see Figure 26.8

GI Tox: Gentian

- **Rep:** Bottle gentian, gentian violet
- **Indications:** Anorexia, indigestion, athlete's foot, candidiasis, ringworm, color for liquors—gin

FIGURE 26.8 Pokeweed or pokeberry (*Phytolacca americana*) is a common shrub which can grow very tall in the summer producing dark purple berries containing the enterotoxin and neurotoxin, phytolaccine. The shrub will die back in the winter and produce leafy new growth in the early spring. Both the leaves and the berries can be initially parboiled several times for detoxification, if desired, and consumption in salads (*Poke-Salad Annie*) or jams and baked goods, respectively. (Courtesy of David K. Lirette, PhD, LSU School of Public Health, New Orleans, LA.)

- **Toxin:** Gentian dye
- **Antidote:** None
- **Dx:** N, V, D, cramps, hemorrhagic gastritis, weakness; tattooing of the skin; allergic reactions—possible toxic epidermal necrolysis = Steven Johnson syndrome
- **Tx:** GI decontamination (lavage + AC), supportive

GI : Balsam apple (*giddy-giddy*) (See Figure 26.9)

- **Rep:** An inedible orange thorny "apple" ("*giddy-giddy*"); invasive Caribbean vine related to cucumber. Boiled leaf tea is mixed with isopropyl alcohol to make an effective antiseptic astringent.
- **Indic:** Herpes labialis, warts, sores/boils, burns, bites/stings.
- **Toxin:** Unidentified, resembles pokeberry or phytolaccine enterotoxic and anticholinergic components = GI + anticholinergic.
- **Antidote:** None.
- **Dx:** HA, N, V, D, cramps, salivation, weakness, facial erythema, mydriasis.
- **Tx:** GI decontamination (lavage + AC), supportive.

FIGURE 26.9 Balsam apple (*Mormordica balsamina*) or in Cajun French, *giddy-giddy*, is a vine that produces an apple-shaped orange-red inedible fruit whose juice has been used as an effective topical astringent for inflammatory skin conditions, such as allergic and chemical contact dermatitis. (From Wikipedia Creative Commons.)

GI Tox: Witch hazel

- **Rep:** Witch hazel "elm" shrub, *Hamamelis virginiana*, unrelated to hazel/elm trees, seed capsules (arils) explode to release edible seeds. Leaves boiled then mixed in isopropyl alcohol to make antiseptic astringent.
- **Indic:** Bites and stings, sores, cuts—lacerations, burns, boils, rashes, warts, herpes labialis.
- **Toxin:** Hamellitannin—anticoagulant and antiviral effects, effective antiseptic astringent.
- **Antidote:** None.
- **Dx:** N, V, D, cramps, nonspecific acute GI sx.
- **Tx:** GI decontamination (lavage + AC), supportive.

Hepatotoxins

- **Herbal hepatotoxins:** Both are capable of causing hepatotoxicity with hepatic vein occlusion (Budd–Chiari syndrome) following chronic ingestion of teas, tablets, tinctures, or powders containing the pyrrolizidine alkaloids in these herbs (Figures 26.10 and 26.11).

FIGURE 26.10 All parts of the common comfrey, *Symphytum officinale*, have been distilled for internal use by folk medicine practitioners into teas and tinctures to treat gastrointestinal and neuromuscular disorders. All contain hepatotoxic pyrrolizidine alkaloids that have been associated with hepatic vein occlusion (Budd–Chiari syndrome). (From Wikipedia Creative Commons.)

FIGURE 26.11 All parts of the coltsfoot, *Tussilago farfara*, have been distilled for internal use by folk medicine practitioners into teas and syrups for treatment of common colds, especially for cough suppression. All contain hepatotoxic pyrrolizidine alkaloids that have been associated with hepatic vein occlusion (Budd–Chiari syndrome). (From Wikipedia Creative Commons.)

Symphytum officinale (comfrey); see Figure 26.10
Tussilago farfara (coltsfoot); see Figure 26.11

Miscellaneous Herbal Hepatotoxins

***Sassafras albidum* (sassafras, gumbo filé powder, mamou tea):** Contains the potential hepatotoxin and carcinogen = safrole, a potential carcinogen, a potential inducer of hepatocellular carcinoma?

Common Household Herbs/Plants

Miscellaneous Common Household Herbs

Anticoagulants:

- Garlic—*Allium sativum*, anticoagulant effects
- Ginseng—*Panax quinquefolium*, anticoagulant effects
- Ginkgo—*Ginkgo biloba*, the maidenhair tree

Anticancer alkaloids:

- Crocus—*Colchium autumnale* (autumn crocus), contains colchicine, a mitotic inhibitor
- Mayapple—*Podophyllum peltatum*, contains podophyllin, another mitotic inhibitor
- Chili pepper—contains capsaicin, a substance P depleter, may have potential as a cancer chemotherapeutic

Purported herbal antiallergens:

- Chamomile—*Matricaria chamomilla*
- Echinacea—*Echinacea purpurea*

The purported herbal antiallergens, chamomile and *Echinacea*, are members of the daisy-sunflower or Compositae (or Asteraceae) family of angiosperms, all of which produce oily terpenes capable of causing contact allergies and asthmatic manifestations in atopic individuals. Their oily leaves have been used in teas as desensitizers for individuals with outdoor plant and pollen allergies, but the therapeutic effects of Compositae herbs have not been confirmed by randomized, placebo-controlled trials.

Anticancer Alkaloids

- **Colchicine:** Derived from the autumn *crocus* and still used to treat gout; causes metaphase arrest (see Figure 26.12).
- **Podophyllotoxin:** A tubulin disruptor derived from the *mayapple* (mandrake) plant and still used to treat venereal warts topically.
- **Etoposide** is a podophyllotoxin derivative used for cancer chemotherapy.
- **Capsaicin:** The chemical that makes *chilli peppers* hot; a known substance P inhibitor and a human prostate cancer cell growth inhibitor in vitro and in mice.

Anticancer Alkaloids: Autumn Crocus, Contains Colchicine

- **Mech:** Binds to intracellular microtubules and causes mitotic arrest at metaphase
- **Indic:** Acute gout, gout prophylaxis, amyloidosis, biliary cirrhosis
- **Tox:** Initial GI—N, V, D; BM suppression, leukopenia, then rebound leukocytosis, myoneuropathy, later alopecia, sudden cardiac arrest—2–7 days
- **Tx:** Immediate lavage and MDAC, volume of distribution $V_d = 2.2$ L/kg, HD ineffective

FIGURE 26.12 The autumn crocus, *Colchium autumnale*, contains the mitotic inhibitor, colchicine, used historically to treat gout and other inflammatory-cell-mediated conditions. (From Wikipedia Creative Commons.)

Colchicum autumnale **(Autumn Crocus)**

- **Anticancer alkaloids:** Mayapple, contains podophyllin (podophyllotoxin [Etoposide®]) (See Figure 26.13).
- **Mech:** Tubulin disruptor.
- **Indic:** Topical treatment of venereal warts and as a chemotherapeutic (Etoposide®) for many cancers.
- **Tox:** Delayed (up to 10 h) severe diarrhea, myelosuppression, acute severe sensorimotor peripheral neuropathy, lethargy, confusion, ataxia, autonomic instability, encephalopathy.
- **Tx:** Glutamic acid for peripheral neuropathy; HD ineffective.
- **Anticancer alkaloids:** Pacific yew, contains taxine (paclitaxel [Taxol®]).
- **Mech:** Plant alkaloids from rare Pacific yew (*Taxus brevifolia*); Na and Ca channel blocker and metaphase inhibitor of tubulin disassembly.
- **Indic:** Breast cancer, breast cancer prevention.
- **Tox:** N, V, abdominal pain, ↓ HR—conduction blocks, ventricular dysrhythmias, paresthesias, ataxia, seizures.
- **Tx:** Atropine, amiodarone, BZs, glutamic acid for neuropathies.
- **Taxus spp. (*T. baccata*):** Yew shrub tree; all parts toxic: leaves > berries.
- **Chilli pepper:** Contains capsaicin (Zostrix®) (Figure 26.14).
- **Mech:** Capsaicin inhibits the growth of human prostate cancer cells in Petri dishes and mice by inhibiting NF-kappa beta, a tumor growth factor.
- **Indications:** Prostate cancer, leukemia.
- **Toxicities:** Unknown, gastritis, diarrhea. Still under investigation. Dose per kg is high and yet to be determined.

FIGURE 26.13 The mayapple, *Podophyllum peltatum*, contains podophyllin, a mitotic inhibitor used to treat venereal warts (*Condyloma acuminata*) topically and cancer intravenously. (From Wikipedia Creative Commons.)

FIGURE 26.14 The chilli pepper, *Capsicum annuum*, contains the substance P deplete capsaicin, used in ointments as a topical analgesic for musculoskeletal and neuropathic pain (herpetic neuralgia). (Courtesy of David K. Lirette, PhD, LSU School of Public Health, New Orleans, LA.)

Toxic Herb–Drug Interactions

Herbs	Drugs	Toxicities
Ephedra*	Amphetamines	CNS stimulation, seizures
Nutmeg	Amphetamines	CNS stimulation, seizures
St. John's wort*	MAOIs, SSRIs	Serotonin syndrome
Valerian	Alcohol, sedatives, BZs (Xanax®)	Delirium, sedation
Kava	Alcohol, sedatives, BZs (Xanax®)	Delirium, sedation
Feverfew	ASA, warfarin, antiplatelet, vit. E	Bleeding
Ginkgo	ASA, warfarin, antiplatelet, vit. E	Bleeding
Ginseng	ASA, warfarin, antiplatelet, vit. E	Bleeding
Garlic	ASA, warfarin, antiplatelet, vit. E	Bleeding

*Fatalities.

Voodoo–Hoodoo

Hallucinogenic Mushrooms (See Chapter 19): Outline

1. Muscimol-containing mushrooms:
   - *Amanita muscaria*
   - *Amanita pantherina*
   - *Amanita gemmata*
2. Psilocybin-containing mushrooms:
   - *Psilocybe cubensis*
   - *Psilocybe* spp.

Ibotenic Acid—Muscimol

- **Reps:** *Amanita muscaria, A. pantherina, A. gemmata*
- **Toxins:** *Ibotenic acid* and its 1° metabolite, *muscimol*, a GABA-nergic glutamic acid analog
- **Antidote:** Benzodiazepines
- **Dx:** Onset 0.5–2 h, vertigo, somnolence, delirium, hallucinations; myoclonus and seizures in children
- **Tx:** Anticonvulsants (BZs)

Psilocybin Toxicity

- **Reps:** *Psilocybe* spp.
- **Toxins:** *Psilocybin* (serotonin agonist and antagonist) and *psilocin* indoles, both analogs of *LSD*
- **Antidote:** Benzodiazepines
- **Dx:** Onset rapid 0.5–1 h, hyperkinesis, ataxia, hallucinations
- **Tx:** Anticonvulsants

Animal-Derived Toxins (See Chapters 18 and 25)

Ciguatera Fish Poisoning 1

- **Agents:** Dinoflagellates—*Gambierdiscus toxicus* (worldwide), *Ostreopsis lenticularis* (Caribbean only).
- **Toxins:** Three neurotoxins = ciguatoxin, gambierol, and scaritoxin; One myotoxin = maitotoxin.
- **LD_{50}:** Cig—0.45 mcg/kg; maito—0.05 mcg/kg.
- **Mechanism:** Cig—forced opening of Na channels with ↑ Na influx, prolonged depolarization, and myospastic contractures. Maito—forced opening of Ca channels with ↑ Ca influx and prolonged myospasticity.
- **Vectors:** > 100 reef fish species; *predatory reef fish*—barracuda, grouper, snapper, all jacks, wrasse, Moray eel; *herbivorous reef fish*—filefish, parrotfish, surgeonfish, triggerfish.
- **Incubation:** Within 24 h.

Ciguatera Fish Poisoning 2

- **Sx:** Cramps, N, V, D (75%); metallic taste, perioral and distal paresthesias, glove and stocking numbness, palmar pruritus, hot–cold reversal, tremor, ataxia, vertigo, ↓ DTRs then sz, myopathy, arthralgias, weakness, stupor-coma.
- **Dx:** Mouse bioassay, RIA, stick-enzyme IA (Cigua-check®) on suspected seafood, GC/MS.
- **Tx:** Supportive; anticonvulsants (BZs); IV mannitol 1 g over 45 m × 2 within 24–48 h and gabapentin 1200–2400 mg/day po for chronic sx (untested); avoid fish, alcohol, nuts × 3–6 mo 2° ↑ pruritus.

- **Px:** Sx resolve 10–58 h; persistent distal numbness, pruritus, and temperature reversal possible.
- **Prev:** Avoid ciguatoxic species, esp. *barracuda* and *fish organs* (esp. liver, ovaries, and roe); adhere to all advisories; promote healthy coral reefs— ↑ drag-line fishing and nuclear/ABIM tests, ↑ crown-of-thorns starfish control (*Acanthaster planci*).

Scombroid Fish Poisoning 1

- **Agents:** Toxic decomposition metabolites called *scombrotoxins*; not bioaccumulated dinoflagellate or diatom exotoxins
- **Toxins:** Scombrotoxins = histamine and its 1° *n*-methylhistamine metabolite, and saurine
- **LD_{50}:** No known fatalities
- **Mechanism:** Scombrotoxins form during gut bacteria-catalyzed, normothermic decarboxylation (*Proteus, Klebsiella, Lactobacillus, E. coli, Enterobacter* spp.) of muscle L-histidine in decomposing finfish
- **Vectors:** *Non-scombroid fish* (amberjack, bonito, bluefish, mahi mahi, anchovies, sardines, herrings) > *Scombroid fish* (albacore, cobia, tuna, mackerel, wahoo)
- **Incubation:** Minutes to 3–4 h
- **Scombrotoxins:** *"Spoiled" canned anchovies, herrings, sardines, and tuna (especially frozen tuna burgers)*

Scombroid Fish Poisoning 2

- **Sx:** Sudden warm, facial flushing and *"sunburn"—rash*, metallic-peppery taste, perioral burning and blistering sensations; then urticaria, pruritus, bronchospasm, palpitations—↑ HR, ↓ BP; fewer GI sx of abdominal cramps, N, V, and D
- **Dx:** Histidine-to-histamine spot indicator tests, TLC, GC/MS, ↑ serum and urine histamine levels
- **Tx:** Severe poisoning—gastric emptying, then AC gut decontamination; otherwise H_1 and H_2-blockers, β-agonists, and steroids for allergic bronchospasm and urticaria/pruritus
- **Px:** Sx resolve in 12–24 h even without tx
- **Prev:** Pts on INH (GI histaminase inhibitor) at ↑ risk; avoid nonrefrigerated and spoiling (*pale gills*) deep sea fish; avoid seafood with [histamine] > 50 mg/100 mg fish (FDA); regulate long-line fishing; *mandatory cold-chain* (0°C) for all seafood from harvest until cooking consumption

Tetrodotoxic Fish Poisoning 1

- **Agent:** Endogenous toxin
- **Toxin:** Endogenous toxin production by endosymbiotic gut bacteria (*Bacillus, Micrococcus, Acinetobacter, Altermonas, Vibrio,* and other enterobacterial species)
- **LD_{50}:** 9 mcg/kg
- **Mechanism:** Reversible binding to the outer pore of the Na channel, ↓ Na influx, preventing depolarization and NAPs

- **Vectors:** All pufferfish (balloonfish, blowfish, *fugu* fish, globefish, swellfish), porcupine fish, marine sunfish; xanthid crabs, marine worms; blue-ringed octopus bites; skin secretions of some newts, frogs, and toads
- **Incubation:** 10–20 min

Tetrodotoxic Fish Poisoning 2

- **Sx:** Initial paresthesias, perioral burning, then salivation, HA, N, and V (D rare), sweating, glove and stocking paresthesias then numbness, tremor, ataxia, dysarthria, dysphagia, respiratory depression then paralysis, CV instability, stupor, and coma
- **Dx:** Mouse bioassay, TLC, HPLC, GC/MS
- **Tx:** Supportive = protect AW, gastric lavage then AC-MDAC, IV fluids, vasopressors, and mechanical ventilation
- **Px:** CFR = 62%; survivors will recover within 1 wk of ICU care (not universally available, esp. in developing world)
- **Prev:** Avoid eating *all pufferfish*; travelers may consume *fugu only in Japan*, prepared by commercially licensed chefs

Amphibian Secretions (See Chapter 22): Outline

1. Newts and salamanders
   Newts—Tetrodotoxin: nondepolarizing MR
   Salamanders—Salmanderin: CNS neurotoxin
2. *Frogs* (specifically *toads*, family *Anura*)
   Bufotenines: "Toad licking"—serotonin agonists
   Bufotoxins: Digoxin-like cholinergics (N, V, heart blocks, brady/tachyarrhythmias) and α_2-antagonists (impotence/ED = *chan-su*) contains bufadienolides and bufotalins

Newts and Salamanders

- **Name:** Oregon (western) rough-skinned newt > CA newt
- **Latin:** *Taricha granulosa* > *T. californicus*
- **Venom:** Secretes neurotoxic *tetrodotoxins* (same as *pufferfish*—Fugu and Australian *blue-ringed octopus*) through skin
- **Dx:** Neurotoxicity, ingestion > contact
- **Antidote:** None
- **Tx:** Supportive

Toads (Anura) 1

- **Name:** Colorado River toad
- **Latin:** *Bufo alvarius*
- **Venom:** Bufotenines, skin-secreted biogenic amines that are serotonin agonists → LSD-like hallucinations

- **Dx:** Hallucinations after toad licking and toad soup, salivation, euphoria, seizures, dysrhythmias
- **Antidote:** None
- **Tx:** Supportive

Toads (Anura) 2

- **Name:** Cane-bamboo toad
- **Latin:** *Bufo marinus*
- **Venom:** *Bufotoxins*—Chinese aphrodisiac—*chan-su* (*bufadienolides* and *bufotalins*), all resemble digoxin in toxicity
- **Dx:** "Dig-toxic"—N, V, bradycardia, dysrhythmias, hyperkalemia
- **Antidote:** DigiBind® (Dig Fab antibodies)
- **Tx:** Manage as digitalis toxicity, reduce potassium K^+

Arthropods

Arachnids

Spiders*
Scorpions

Argiope aurantia
(Black and gold garden spider); see Figure 26.15

Order Hymenoptera

Apids (bees)
Vespids (wasps)
Formicids (fire ants)

Order Lepidoptera

Venomous caterpillars of moths

Miscellaneous
Blister beetles
Centipedes

Arachnids: Latrodectus 1

- **Name:** Black widow
- **Latin:** *Latrodectus mactans*

* Have frequently been used as voodoo remedies and punishments. Spider webs used as wound dressings and anticoagulants. Often combined with crushed roaches (palm beetles) (Figure 26.15).

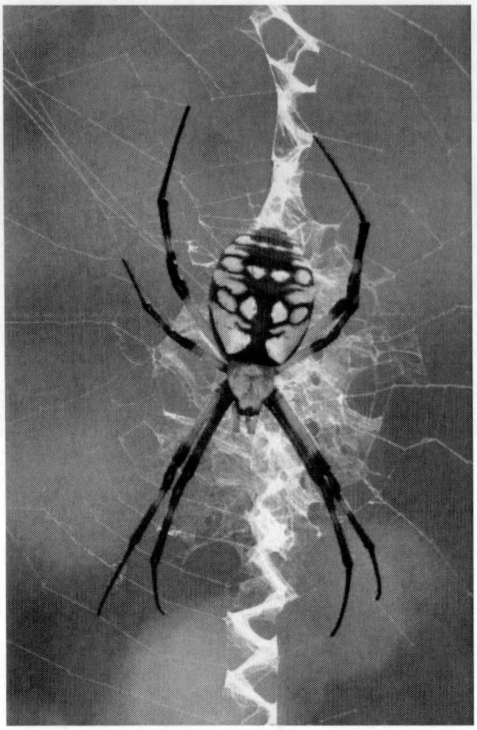

FIGURE 26.15 Spider webs have been used by healers as wound dressings to stop bleeding probably by serving as a hemostatic matrix for platelets to adhere to. The black and yellow garden spider, *Argiope aurantia*, is a compulsive silk weaver that usually remains in the center of its web during the day. These webs would have been collected as wound dressings. Note the characteristic "X" or zigzag pattern of the web with the spider straddling the center of the pattern. (Courtesy of David K. Lirette, PhD, LSU School of Public Health, New Orleans, LA.)

- **Venom:** Alpha-latrotoxin causes Ach release and presynaptic stimulation of all muscarinic and nicotinic cholinergic receptors
- **Dx:** *Two painful red spots*—in hrs—latrodectism = *facies latrodectismica*, N, V, salivation, urine retention, priapism, bronchorrhea, abdominal muscle cramps—rigidity, ↑ HR, and BP, restlessness, seizures

Arachnids: Latrodectus 2

- **Name:** Black widow, red hourglass spider (Figure 26.16)
- **Latin:** *Latrodectus mactans*
- **Antidote:** *Latrodectus mactans* antivenin—a crude monovalent hyperimmune horse serum (IgG) antivenin
- **Tx:** Ttox, cold packs, benzodiazepines > 10% calcium gluconate for cramps, antivenom available (Figure 26.16)

FIGURE 26.16 The female black widow spider, *Latrodectus mactans*, produces a neurotoxic venom containing alpha-latrotoxin, a cholinergic and nicotinic agonist, capable of causing a cholinergic crisis with painful abdominal muscle contractions. Note the characteristic red-to-orange hourglass pattern on the ventral surface of the abdomen. (Courtesy of David K. Lirette, PhD, LSU School of Public Health, New Orleans, LA.)

Misc. Arthropods: Blister Beetles

- **Name:** Blister beetle (eastern United States), Spanish fly (Europe). All produce a defensive secretion of a blistering agent, cantharidin. There are many multicolored species from the family Meloidae distributed worldwide.
- **Latin:** *Cantharis vesicatoria* (Europe), *Tegrodera aloga* (United States), *Lytta vesicatoria* is best known as the "Spanish fly" (Figure 26.17).

FIGURE 26.17 Potions or powders of dried blister beetles, especially *Lytta vesicatoria*, the "Spanish fly" were used either as aphrodisiacs or abortifacients because of the irritating properties of cantharidin on the mucosal surfaces of the genitourinary tract. (From Wikipedia Creative Commons.)

- **Venom:** Cantharidin, an irritating skin and mucosal vesicant.
- **Dx:** Blistering, vesicular dermatitis, stomatitis, cystitis, hematuria, priapism, vaginal bleeding, spontaneous abortion.
- **Antidote:** None.
- **Tx:** Supportive.

Conclusions

- Geographically *isolated* and frequently *underserved* (exiles, refugees, slaves) ethnic cultures have relied on *self-treatments with medicinal and toxic plants, herbs, metals—minerals, and animal secretions for generations.*
- Many traditional therapies now have modern therapeutic efficacies, such as *artemisins* for *P. falciparum* malaria, and *capsaicin*, a substance P depleter, for herpes zoster.
- The *few remaining traditional practitioners are aging and not being replaced.* Few are left to identify and to catalogue useful plant and animal species, and to train their successors.
- As in oriental medicine, *more side effects and interactions will occur with modern Western therapies and procedures than with traditional treatments.*

Section III

Industrial and Occupational Toxicology

Chapter 27

Volatile Organic Chemicals

Outline .614
VOC Uses .614
VOC Stratification .614
VOC Stratification: "Splitting" .615
Hydrocarbons .615
Toxic Alcohols 620

Outline

- Halogenated hydrocarbons (HCs)
  - Petroleum distillates
  - Wood distillates
- Toxic alcohols
  - Ethanol
  - Isopropanol
  - Ethylene glycol
  - Methanol

VOC Uses

- Adhesives and cements
- Fuels and propellants
- Paints and coatings
- Lacquers and varnishes
- Lubricants and oils
- Polishes and waxes
- Paint removers and strippers
- Paint thinners
- Solvents and degreasers
- Spot removers and dry cleaners
- Typewriter correction fluids (Liquid Paper®)

VOC Stratification

Most are petroleum distillates

- Acetone and toluene
- Gasoline and benzene
- Kerosene and mineral spirits
- Stoddard solvent
- Butane and propane
- Carbon tetrachloride
- Methylene chloride
- Trichloroethane
- Trichloroethylene
- Tetrachloroethylene (perchloroethylene [perc])
- *n*-Hexane and *n*-heptane
- Methyl-*n*-butyl-ketone
- Methyl-isobutyl ketone

Few are wood (camphor, pine) distillates

- Pine oil
- Turpentine
- Camphor—may be synthesized from turpentine, or derived from *Cinnamomum camphora* (camphor tree)

VOC Stratification: "Splitting"

- **Aliphatics**: *Choking cyanosis, honeymoon-pneumonitis, extrapulmonary air, pneumomediastinum on chest x-ray*
  - **Petroleum derivatives:** gasoline, diesel, kerosene, mineral spirits
- **Aromatics:** *Central nervous system (CNS) toxicity and cancer*
  - **Benzene:** Acute myeloid (myelogenous or nonlymphocytic) leukemia (AML)
  - **Toluene:** Renal tubular acidosis (RTA), embryopathy
  - **Xylene, styrene (peripheral neuropathy):** Biphasic CNS toxicity
  - **Polycyclic aromatic hydrocarbons (PAHs):** Combustion by-products, carcinogens, benzo-*a*-pyrene (B[*a*]P)
- **Terpenes**: *From plants, pneumonitis and hemorrhagic cystitis*
  - **Pine oil:** Pneumonitis
  - **Turpentine:** Hemorrhagic cystitis
  - **Camphor:** Seizures

Halogenated Hydrocarbons

Historically used as the first anesthetics, solvents, and degreasers. All are myocardial sensitizers and can cause "sudden sniffing deaths" from fatal tachyarrhythmias in abusers from "sniffing," "bagging," or "huffing."

- **Chloroform:** Centrilobular hepatoxicity and liver cancer
- **Carbon tetrachloride:** Hepatic necrosis, liver cancer?
- **Methylene chloride:** Delayed hepatic carbon monoxide (CO) production
- **Trichloroethylene:** Degreaser's flush, trigeminal neuralgia, chloral hydrate metabolite—trichloroethanol
- **Trichloroethane:** Sudden sniffing deaths
- **Tetrachloroethylene (perchloroethylene):** Elevated liver function tests (LFTs), liver cancer?
- **Vinyl chloride:** Raynaud's phenomenon, acroosteolysis, scleroderma, hepatic angiosarcoma

Hydrocarbons

Outline

- Epidemiology of HC poisoning

- Toxicology of HC poisoning
- Treatment of HC poisoning
- Volatile HC substance abuse: "*sniffing*" → "*huffing*" → "*bagging*"

HC Epidemiology

- There are 60,000 HC exposures per year; 95% are unintentional; 60% involve children; 50% demonstrate minimal toxic effects; and 20% require treatment.
- There are 20 deaths per year from HC poisoning; 90% of these deaths occur in children under age 5; 30% of these deaths involve gasoline/motor oils; and 10% involve Freon® and propellants (usually in adolescent HC inhalation abusers engaging in sniffing, huffing, or bagging of volatile hydrocarbons).

HC Toxicity

- **Pulmonary toxicity predominates:** Pulmonary (50%) > GI (5%) > CNS (3%) > CV > dermal > hematologic
- **Pulmonary toxicity** 2° aspiration → ↓ surfactant → acute respiratory distress syndrome (ARDS)
  - **HC pulmonary toxicity:** Determined by HC physical properties: ↓ *surface tension,* ↓ *viscosity,* ↑ *volatility*
  - **Sx:** Gagging, coughing, choking → bronchospasm, rales, rhonchi, tachypnea, hypoxia → **hemorrhagic pulmonary edema**, methemoglobinemia (nitro-, nitrites, chlorates), cyanosis → chronic URIs → bronchiectasis and pulmonary fibrosis
  - **X-ray:** Pneumonitis, infiltrates, consolidating pneumonias, pleural effusions, barotrauma, upright gastric "double-bubble" sign = (1) air–HC + (2) HC–gastric fluid interfaces
- **Extrapulmonary air trapping:** Pneumothorax, pneumomediastinum, obstructive emphysema
- **Gastrointestinal toxicity (GI) (5%):** Nausea, vomiting, hematemesis, GI mucosal ulcerations
- Neurotoxicity
  - **CNS toxicity (3%):** All are "*anesthetics*" with progression from Stage II (excitement) to Stage IV (coma). In overdoses (ODs), seizures occur first then coma 2° hypoxia.
  - **PNS:** Peripheral neuropathies (styrene, trigeminal neuralgia [TCE]).
- **Cardiovascular (CV) toxicity:** *Myocardial sensitization* → dysrhythmias
- **Dermal toxicity:** Defatting dry dermatitis, *oil boils, degreaser's flush* (trichloroethylene)
- **Hematologic toxicity:** Methemoglobinemia, hemolysis, anemia, DIC

What are the drugs and chemicals most likely to cause methemoglobinemia? (Tables 27.1 through 27.3)

Table 27.1 Drugs and Chemicals Most Likely to Cause Methemoglobinemia

Antibiotics	Local Anesthetics	Nitrates and Nitrites	Miscellaneous Drugs	Toxicants
Dapsone Chloroquine Primaquine Nitrofurantoin Sulfonamides Sulfamethoxazole	Benzocaine EMLA cream (prilocaine) Prilocaine (toluidine and nitroso-toluidine metabolite) Aminobenzoate	Amyl nitrite Sodium nitrite Nitric oxide Nitro-glycerin Silver nitrate Sodium nitroprusside	Acetaminophen Phenacetin Phenytoin Phenylhydrazine Phenazopyridine (Pyridium®)	Acetanilide Aniline dyes Benzene derivatives Chlorates Dinitrophenol Napthalene Potassium permanganate

Table 27.2 Clinical Manifestations of Methemoglobinemia

Methemoglobin Levels (%)	Symptoms and Signs
≤2–3	None (physiologic)
2–15	None
15–20	Cyanosis
20–30	Mental changes: HA, fatigue, dizziness, exercise intolerance, syncope, tachycardia
30–50	Fatigue, confusion, tachypnea, tachycardia
50–70	Dysrhythmias, seizures, coma, acidosis
>70	Death

Table 27.3 Difficulties in Measuring Blood Methemoglobin Levels

Hemoglobin Species	Spectrophotometric Absorption by Peak Wavelengths (nm)	Impact on SpO2
Oxygenated hemoglobin (OxyHb)	Two peaks: 660 and 940 nm	None: SpO2 ↑
Deoxygenated hemoglobin (DeoxyHb)	Two peaks: 660 and 940 nm	None: SpO2 ↓
Methemoglobin (MetHb)	Peak: 630, equal absorption @ 660 and 940 nm (ratio pulse ox uses to calculate SpO2)	Significance: As metHb ↑ SpO2 85–90%, as metHb ↓ SpO2 fixes at 85%
Methylene blue	Peak: 668 nm	Significance: SpO2 ↓ after IV dosing

HC Ingestion

Summary

- HCs most likely to cause aspiration pneumonia have *high volatility, low viscosity, and low surface tension.*
- Ranked by likelihood of aspiration pneumonia: furniture polish > gasoline > kerosene > heavy fuel oil > motor oil > mineral oil > paraffin.

HC Poisoning: Treatment

- **Careful GI decontamination:** No emesis! No activated charcoal! Possibly gastric lavage with small NG for large volumes, intentional ingestions, and highly toxic HCs: (*CHAMP*) = *C*amphor, *H*alogenated HCs, *A*romatic HCs, HCs associated with *M*etals, HCs associated with *P*esticides.
- No cathartics, especially *no olive or mineral oil cathartics* (will increase absorption of lipophilic HCs), no prophylactic antibiotics or corticosteroids.
- **Mechanical ventilation for ARDS:** Barotrauma risk = start with PEEP > HFJV > ECMO.
- **CV:** Consider avoiding inotropic support during PEEP due to *myocardial sensitization* and arrhythmogenesis.

Volatile Organic Chemical: Substance Abuse

VOCs Commonly Abused by Adolescents

1. Butane lighter refills
2. Typewriter correction, dry cleaning, and degreasing fluids
   Trichloroethane
   Perchloroethylene
   Trichloroethylene
3. Aerosol propellants
   Nitrous oxide gas
   CFCs
4. Propane gas canisters

VOCs Commonly Abused by Workers

Occupational/industrial workers

1. Glues and paints
   Benzene
   Toluene
   Napthalene
   n-Hexane
   Xylene
2. Gasoline, kerosene
   Health care industry workers

3. Liquid anesthetics
   Ether, enflurane, desflurane

- **Techniques:** Sniffing → huffing → bagging
- **Agents:** Toluene (glues, paints) → fuels (butane, gasoline) → TCE and PCE (typewriter correction fluids, Liquid Paper®) → dry cleaning fluids (acetone, CCl_4, TCE, PCE) → propellants (CFCs, nitrous oxide)
- **Acute toxicity:** CNS—excitation, inebriation, *euphoria*, hallucinations, ataxia, seizures, HA, respiratory depression > CV—tachyarrhythmias → "*sudden sniffing death*" > hematological toxicity—methemoglobinemia > *hepatotoxicity* (CCL_4) and *CO poisoning* (*methylene chloride*)
- **Chronic toxicity:** *"Glue-sniffers"* or toluene *encephalopathy*/chronic "painter's syndrome": leukoencephalopathies characterized by memory and cognitive losses, dementia, insomnia, anxiety and depression, personality disorder, ataxia and chorea, peripheral neuropathy (*n*-hexane, methyl-*n*-butyl ketone, 2,3-hexanedione)
- **Epidemiology:** 5–10% HS students; > 60 deaths year/United States and much greater among street children in SE Asia and Africa; male:female = 5:1; *butane lighter refills* are the most commonly abused VOCs

Carcinogenic vs. Neurotoxic VOCs

Carcinogenic HCs

- Benzene—AML
- Vinyl chloride—hepatic angiosarcoma
- PAHs—colon cancer
- Formaldehyde—nasal and sinus cancers
- Chloroform and methylene chloride—liver cancers?
- CCl_4, TCE, perc—animal cancers only

CNS Leukoencephalopathies

- Toluene—paints and glues
- Trichloroethylene (TCE)—trigeminal neuralgia
- Glycol ethers

Peripheral Neuropathies

- *n*-Hexane—axonopathy
- Acrylamide, styrene, and xylene
- Methyl-*n*-butyl ketone—axonopathy (*methyl-ethyl ketone [MEK] and methyl-isobutyl ketone [MIBK] nontoxic*)
- 2,5-*Hexanedione* (MNBK is a metabolite)
- Carbon disulfide (CS_2) gas
- Ethylene oxide gas

Wood Distillates

Pine Oil

- PineSol®
- Pine terpenes
- *Pulm > CNS toxicity*
- **Pulmonary toxicity:** Aspiration pneumonitis
- *CNS toxicity* excitation → depression
- **Tx:** Same as for the petroleum distillates

Turpentine

- Pine terpenes
- *Pulmonary > renal > hematological > CNS toxicity*
- **Pulmonary:** Aspiration pneumonitis, ARDS
- **Renal:** Pathognomonic *hemorrhagic cystitis* 2° acrolein metabolite → ATN; urine smells like violets
- **Turpentine hematological toxicity:** Pathognomonic of turpentine = *TP thrombocytopenic purpura*
- **CNS:** Excitation → depression
- **Tx:** Same as for petroleum distillates

Camphor

- **Chemistry:** Derived from turpentine or synthesized from camphor tree.
- **Uses:** OTC poultices—*Camphophenique*®, *Chloroseptic*®, *Mentholatum*®, *Ben-gay*®, *Vick's Vapo-Rub*®.
- **Pharmacology:** Rapid absorption and hepatic metabolism.
- **Toxicity:** Approximately 8 deaths/year. *Note*: recent accidental *Ben-gay* death in female high school marathon runner.
- **Clinical manifestations:** Rapid sx—15–30 min = abdominal pain, vomiting; then confusion, tremor, ataxia, *seizures*; then apnea, aspiration followed by coma and death. ↑ LFTs if recover.
- **American Academy of Pediatrics (AAP) Position:** 1978, 1993: "Camphor! Who needs it? No one!"
- **Tx:** CPR, benzodiazepines (BZs), no ipecac, rapid gastric lavage, then activated charcoal (AC).

Toxic Alcohols

Outline

- High anion gap vs. high osmol gap metabolic acidosis
- Ethanol (ethyl alcohol [EtOH])
- Isopropanol (isopropyl alcohol = rubbing alcohol)

- Ethylene glycol (antifreeze)
- Methanol (methyl alcohol, wood alcohol)

High Anion Gap Metabolic Acidosis

- **Definition:** [measured cations − measured anions] = $[Na^+] - [Cl^- + HCO_3^-]$ = 140 − [110 + 24] = 6.
- **Normal range:** 3–11.
- **High:** MUDPPIILEESS = *M*ethanol, *U*remia, *D*iabetic ketoacidosis, *P*araldehyde, *P*henformin, *I*NH, *I*ron, *L*actic acidosis, *E*thanol, *E*thylene glycol, *S*alicylates, and *S*olvents.
- **Low:** *Bromides* (lab interpreted as *falsely elevated chloride levels, not a true low anion gap metabolic acidosis*). Most metabolic acidosis has a high anion gap.

High Osmol Gap Metabolic Acidosis

- **Definition:** [Measured osmolality − calculated osmolarity] = [mOsm/kg] − $[2Na^+]$ + [BUN/2.8] + [Glu/18]
- **Normal range:** −14 to +10, nonspecific, very wide range
- **High:** Ethanol, all toxic alcohols, lactic acidosis, renal failure, hyperlipidemias, hypertriglyceridemias, and hyperproteinemias (multiple myeloma)

Ethanol

Ethanol: Pharmacology and Toxoxicology

- **Chemistry:** Colorless, odorless hydrocarbon; highly water soluble and highly lipid soluble; dependence and addiction possible
- **Pharmacology:** Low MW, low volume of distribution—*Vd = 0.6 L/kg*, rapidly diffusible; rapid gastric emptying and drinking without food increase absorption; hepatically oxidized by three pathways: (1) *ADH* (EtOH—[alcohol dehydrogenase—Alc DH] → acetaldehyde—[acetaldehyde dehydrogenase—Acet DH] → acetyl CoA—[thiamine cofactor] → Kreb's tricarboxylic acid [TCA] cycle → $CO_2 + H_2O$) > (2) *CYP450* (inducible metabolism)> and (3) *hepatic peroxidase–catalase*
- **Toxicity:** CNS > GI > metabolic toxicity
- **CNS:** Drunkenness—inebriation, disinhibition, incoordination, blurred vision, diplopia, confusion, CNS and respiratory depression
- **GI:** Nausea, vomiting, cramping abdominal pain, gastric bleeding
- **Metabolic toxicity:** High anion gap metabolic acidosis, *hypoglycemia*, hypokalemia, hypomagnesemia, hypophosphatemia, hyperamylasemia → acute pancreatitis

Ethanol Metabolism (See Figure 27.1)

Acute EtOH Intoxication

- Blood ethanol levels
    - 0.05% (50 mg/dL)

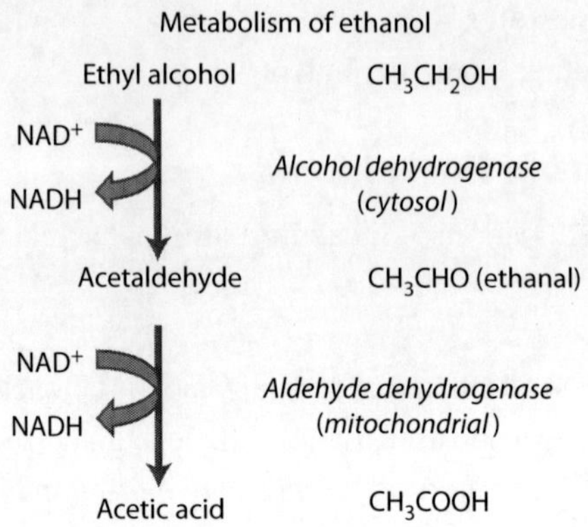

FIGURE 27.1 Metabolism of ethanol.

- 0.08% (80 mg/dL)*
- 0.20% (200 mg/dL)
- 0.30% (300 mg/dL)
- 0.40% (400 mg/dL)
- 0.70% (700 mg/dL)

Clinical Manifestations

- Disinhibition and incoordination
- ↓ Reaction time, auto driving impaired
- N, V, confusion, staggering gait
- Slurred speech, ↓ vision and ↓ sensation
- ↓ Temp, ↓ glucose, amnesia, seizures
- ↓ DTRs, respiratory depression, loss of AW protective reflexes, aspiration pneumonia, coma, death

Ethanol Overdose (OD): Diagnosis and Management

Diagnosis EtOH OD

1. **Blood ethanol levels:** Determine stage of intoxication
2. **Blood glucose:** r/o *hypoglycemia*
3. **CBC and electrolytes:** ↓ Na, ↓ K, ↓ Mg, ↓ Ca, ↓ P
4. **ABGs:** High anion gap metabolic acidosis
5. **Serum amylase:** r/o *pancreatitis*
6. **Serum ammonia:** r/o hepatic encephalopathy 2° alcoholic nutritional *cirrhosis*

Management of Ethanol Overdose

- Ipecac contraindicated

* Legally intoxicated (United States).

- **OG lavage and AC:** *Especially for coingestions*
- **Coma cocktail**: $D_{50}W$ 0.5–1.0 g/kg + *thiamine 100 mg IV*
- *Multivitamins and folate* 1–5 mg IV
- *Slow rewarming*
- **Correct electrolytes:** ↓ K–Mg–P
- **Enhanced elimination:** Hemodialysis is very effective 2° ↓ MW and Vd, but rarely indicated

Ethanol: Causes of Disulfiram (Antabuse®) Reactions

- **Disulfiram reaction = Acetaldehyde poisoning:** *Flushing*, diaphoresis, N, V, disorientation, vertigo, headache, palpitations, chest pain
- **Antibiotics:** Chloramphenicol, *n*-methylthiotetrazole (nMTT) side chain cephalosporins, sulfonamides
- **Antifungals**: Griseofulvin, metronidazole
- **Mickey Finn:** Chloral hydrate from trichloroethylene (and its trichloroethanol metabolite)
- **Miscellaneous:** *Coprinus* spp. mushrooms, industrial chemicals: carbamate pesticides and oximes, diethyldithiocarbamate (precursor of disulfiram—Antabuse®)

Isopropanol

Isopropanol: Pharmacology and Toxicity

- **Chemistry:** 70% isopropyl alcohol or rubbing alcohol; a clear, colorless volatile liquid with an acetone smell; used in toiletries, disinfectants, window cleaners, and solvents. **Exception**: *Adsorbed by AC.*
- **Pharmacology:** Rapid all-route absorption, esp. dermal and inhalation; ↓Vd = 0.6 L/kg; 80% rapidly *metabolized by ADH to acetone*, remaining 20% not metabolized and excreted by kidneys > or lungs, exhalation. *Acetone is detected by ± nitroprusside test on serum or urine.*
- **Toxicity:** CNS > GI > pulmonary > metabolic toxicity.
- **CNS:** *3× more CNS depression than EtOH*, lethargy, weakness, HA, ataxia, apnea, respiratory depression, hypotension.
- **Pulmonary and GI toxicity:** Acetone breath, hemorrhagic gastritis and hemorrhagic tracheobronchitis.
- **Metabolic:** Another *exception*: only toxic alcohol *not causing metabolic acidosis or hypoglycemia*, euglycemia, ketonemia → ketonuria.

Isopropanol Metabolism (See Figure 27.2)

Isopropanol OD: Diagnosis and Management

- Determine *serum* acetone level
- Anticipate *falsely* elevated creatinine
- **ABGs**: *pH will be normal, no acidosis*

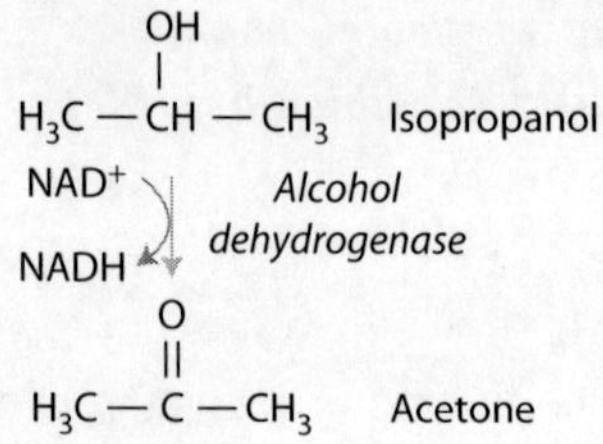

FIGURE 27.2 Metabolism of isopropanol.

- **Glucose:** *No hypoglycemia*
- Anticipate *ketonemia and ketonuria* 2° acetone
- **Breath:** *Acetone odor*

Management

- Immediate skin decontamination
- **OG lavage, then AC:** *Exception*: only toxic alcohol to be well adsorbed by AC
- **Enhanced elimination:** *Hemodialysis* very effective in serious ODs, especially in children

Ethylene Glycol

Ethylene Glycol: Pharmacology and Toxicity

- **Chemistry:** A toxic alcohol similar to methanol in toxicity and lethality with a characteristic delayed onset of toxicity; used in antifreeze (95%), refrigerating fluids, fire extinguishers, solar energy fluids.
- **Pharmacology:** Rapidly absorbed orally (po), peaks 1–4 h; rapidly metabolized by ADH to glycoaldehyde, then by Ald DH to *glycolic, glyoxalic,* and *oxalic acids. Pyridoxine* and *thiamine* serve as cofactors to promote nontoxic alternative routes of metabolism.
- **Toxicity:** (1) CNS > (2) metabolic > (3) renal > initial GI N and V.
- **Toxic phases 1–3:** *Phase 1—CNS*: N, V, *intoxication*, inebriation, nystagmus, myoclonus, seizures, progressing to lethargy and coma in 4–8 h. *Phase 2—Metabolic*: profound *high anion gap metabolic acidosis* causing CV collapse. Phase 3—Renal: urinary excretion of toxic metabolites (calcium oxalate and hippuric acid); *calcium oxalate crystalluria* → nephrolithiasis → proteinuria and hematuria → ATN.

Ethylene Glycol Metabolism (See Figure 27.3)

Ethylene Glycol OD: Dx and Mx

- **Dx:** Calcium oxalate *crystalluria*, urine *fluorescein* staining under ultraviolet Wood's lamp, serum EG levels by gas chromatography
- **Initial mx:** AC ineffective 2° rapid absorption and delayed sx onset of 4–8 h; ipecac contraindicated 2° vomiting; $NaHCO_3$ to correct acidosis and ↑ excretion weak acids;

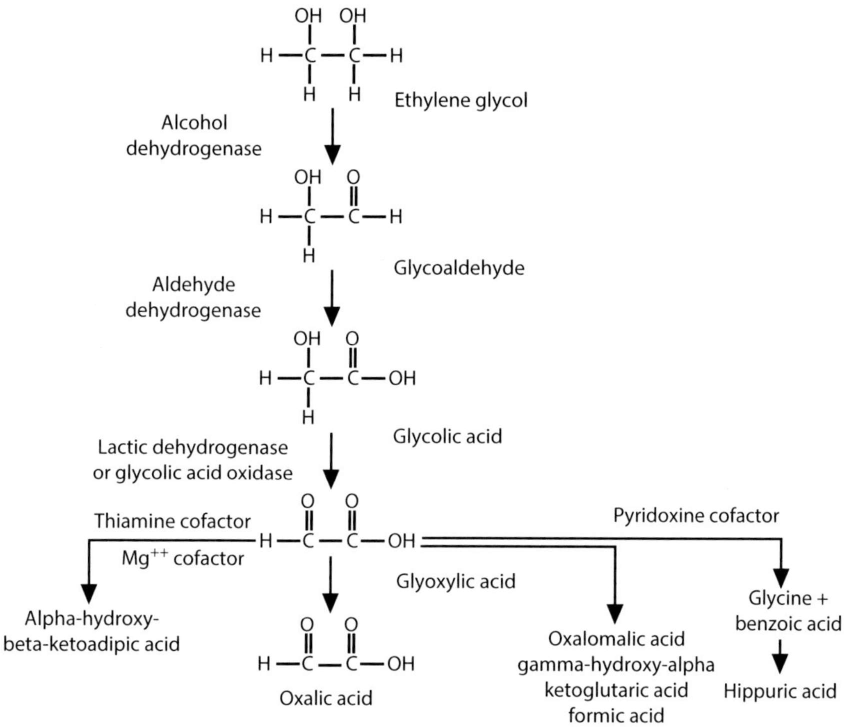

FIGURE 27.3 Metabolism of ethylene glycol.

antidotes = *fomepizole* (15 mg/kg load, then 10 mg/kg q 12 h × 48 h, then 15 mg/kg q 12 h until EG levels < 20 mg/dL) as the preferred ADH inhibitor, or *ethanol* 0.8 g/kg IV or 8 mL/kg po, to maintain serum EtOH level of *100–150 mg/dL = blood alcohol 0.15% = really drunk* (EG:EtOH ratio = 1:4)

- **Enhanced elimination:** (1) Urinary *alkalinization* to promote urinary excretion of *weak acid metabolites*; (2) *thiamine*, 100 mg IV, and *pyridoxine*, 50 mg IV, q 6 h, to promote alternative nontoxic routes of metabolism; (3) *hemodialysis* for EG levels ≥ *25 mg/dL*
- **Correct hypocalcemia:** Treat hypocalcemia 2° massive calcium losses from calcium oxalate crystalluria

Ethylene Glycol Ingestion

- *Urinary calcium oxalate crystals* (ethylene glycol ingestion → *ethanol* and/or *4-MP* therapy indicated with *HD* for serum EG level > *25 mg/dL* to prevent ATN)

Methanol

Methanol: Pharmacology and Toxicity

- **Chemistry:** Methyl alcohol or wood alcohol; used in windshield washing fluids, de-icing solutions, carburetor cleaners, model airplane and canned heat (Sterno®) fuels, paint removers/thinners

- **Pharmacology:** Rapid all-route absorption, peaks 1/2–1 h; 85% rapidly metabolized by hepatic ADH to *formaldehyde* and then oxidized to *formic acid*, which is responsible for *retinal toxicity*
- **Toxicity:** Eye/CNS > metabolic > initial GI—N, V, and cramping
- **Eye:** Dimmed and blurred vision, scotomata, dilated and sluggishly reactive pupils, *hyperemic optic disks*, retinal edema, blindness
- **Metabolic:** *24 h delayed onset* of high anion gap metabolic acidosis, followed by oculotoxicity
- **CNS:** Inebriation, HA, vertigo, meningismus, seizures, coma, later Parkinsonism

Methanol Metabolism (See Figures 27.4 and 27.5)

Methanol Poisoning: Dx and Mx (See Table 27.4, Figures 27.5 and 27.6)

- **Dx:** Lactic acidosis, unique eye findings, increased serum levels by gas chromatography.
- **Initial mx:** AC ineffective 2° rapid absorption and delayed symptom onset; ipecac contraindicated 2° vomiting; *$NaHCO_3$* to correct acidosis; antidotes = *fomepizole* (15 mg/kg load, then 10 mg/kg q 12 h × 48 h, then 15 mg/kg every 12 h until ME levels, <20 mg/dL) as the preferred ADH inhibitor, or *ethanol*, 0.8 g/kg IV or 8 mL/kg po, to maintain serum EtOH level *100–150 mg/dL* (Meth:EtOH ratio = 1:4).
- **Enhanced elimination:** (1) Urinary *alkalinization* to promote renal excretion of undissociated formic acid; (2) *folinic acid (reduced folic acid) is preferred over folic*

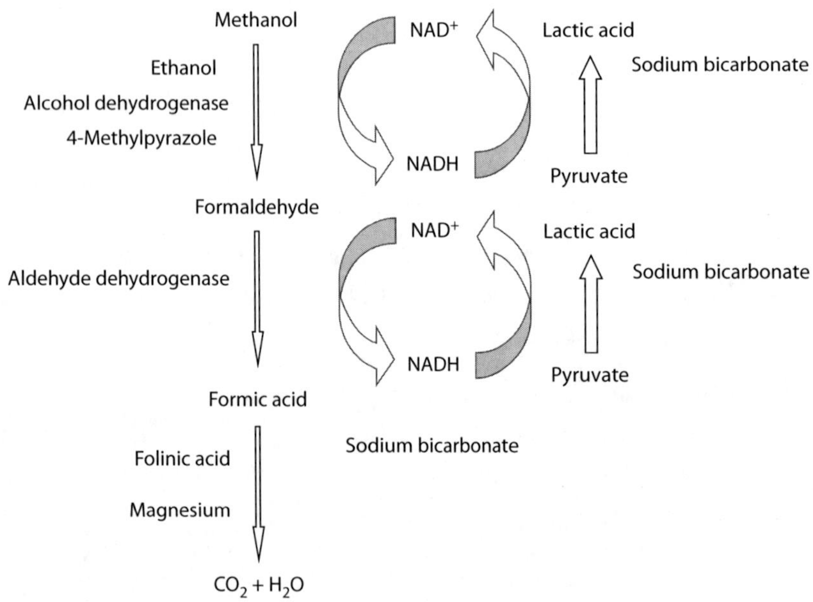

FIGURE 27.4 Metabolism of methanol.

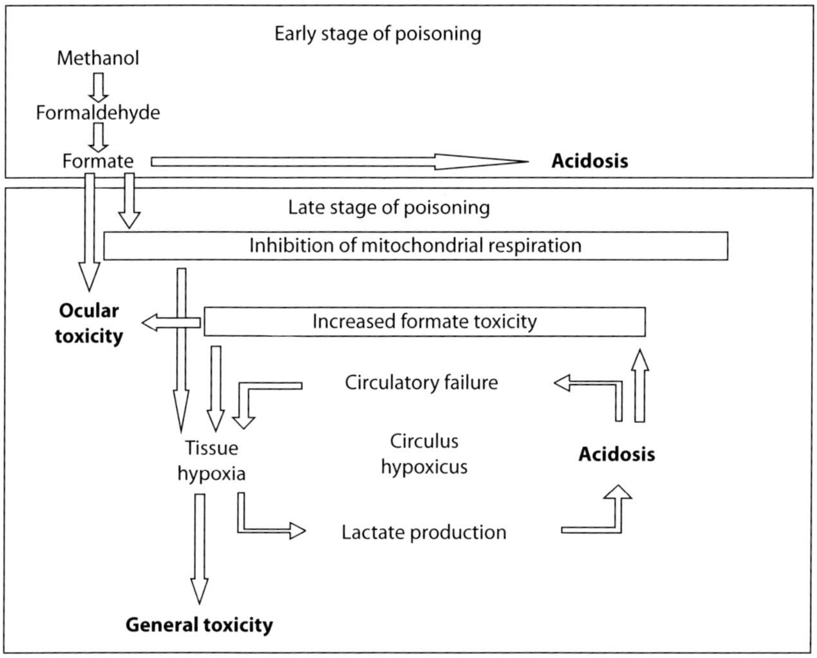

FIGURE 27.5 Mechanisms of methanol toxicity.

acid, 150 mg IV q 4 h, to serve as a cofactor promoting the metabolism of formic acid to $CO_2 + H_2O$; (3) *hemodialysis* for methanol levels ≥*25 mg/dL*.

- **Treatment:** *Fomepizole therapy for ethylene glycol and methanol poisoning* (Figure 27.6).

Table 27.4 Diagnostic Indications and Dosing Schedules for Fomepizole Therapy for Ethylene Glycol or Methanol Poisoning

Indications and Doses	Ethylene Glycol	Methanol
Indications:		
Plasma level, or	≥20 mg/dL	≥20 mg/dL
Osmolal gap, or	>10 mOs m/L <7.3	>10 mOs m/L < 7.3
Arterial pH, or oxalate crystalluria	Present	Not applicable
Doses:		
Loading IV in 30 min	15 mg/kg	15 mg/kg
Maintenance × 48 h	10 mg/kg q 12 h	10 mg/kg q 12 h
Maintenance until plasma level < 20 mg/dL	15 mg/kg q 12 h	15 mg/kg q 12 h

Note: Osmolal gap = measured serum osmolality – calculated serum osmolality.
Serum osmolality = [2 × Na] + [BUN/2.8] + [glucose/18].

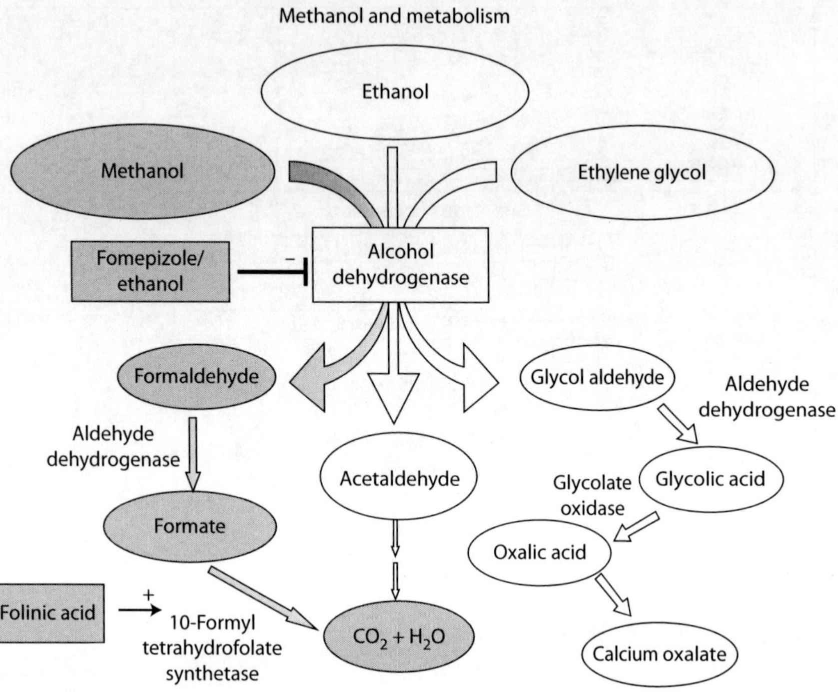

FIGURE 27.6 Summary: Metabolism of toxic alcohols.

Chapter 28

Petrochemical Toxicity

Introduction 630
Case Report 630
Objectives. 631
Human Toxicities of Crude Oil 631
Human Toxicities of Dispersants 636
Prior Acute Health Effects Following Oil Tanker Spills 638
Conclusions 643
References 643

Introduction

In April 2010, the *Deepwater Horizon* oil platform exploded, burned, and sank in the Gulf of Mexico off the Louisiana coast triggering a massive oil spill. From April until July 2010, Louisiana light crude oil was released into the deepwater column at an unprecedented rate, making this oil spill the largest oil spill in the history of petroleum exploration. The *Deepwater Horizon* oil spill dwarfed all prior oil tanker spills in magnitude and impacted environments and caused extensive ecosystem damage to the Gulf Coast and its commercial fisheries. A massive cleanup effort was launched and manned by over 50,000 oil field workers, untrained volunteers, commercial and recreational fishermen; and coordinated by BP, the responsible party, and the U.S. government. This chapter will describe the chemical constituents of light crude oil and dispersants and their known acute and chronic toxic effects in man by documenting and comparing the acute and chronic health effects of similar chemicals on oil spill cleanup workers following prior oil tanker spills worldwide.

Case Report

At 9:45 p.m. CDT on April 20, 2010, the *Deepwater Horizon*, a 9-year-old floating deep-sea oil-drilling platform, exploded and burned for 36 h before sinking and triggering a massive oil spill in the northern Gulf of Mexico, 41 miles off of the Mississippi River Delta in Louisiana (Figure 28.1). The explosion killed 11 platform workers; two platform workers died from fatal injuries; and 15 workers survived serious injuries. From April 22, 2010, until the seafloor wellhead was capped

FIGURE 28.1 The *Deepwater Horizon* Gulf of Mexico oil spill slick as viewed from space on May 24, 2010, by the moderate-resolution imaging spectroradiometer (MODIS) on the U.S. National Aeronautics and Space Administration (NASA) Terra satellite. The oil spill stemmed from a methane gas explosion on the Deepwater Horizon oil rig 48 miles off of the Mississippi River Delta in Louisiana on the evening of April 20, 2010, which killed 13 platform workers (11 perished in the explosion and two died of fatal injuries) and injured 15 others. As much as 4.9 million barrels (200 million U.S. gallons) were released into the northern Gulf of Mexico between April 22 and July 15, 2010, when the leak was capped. (From U.S. National Oceanographic and Space Administration (NASA), NASA/GSFC MODIS rapid response.)

on July 15, 2010, Louisiana light crude oil was released into the deepwater column at a rate ranging from 53,000 barrels/day (8400 m^3/day) to 62,000 barrels/day (9900 m^3/day) for a total crude oil spill of 185 million gallons or 4.9 million barrels over an area up to 6800 square miles (180,000 km^2). The volume of oil-dispersant chemicals used in the cleanup effort has been estimated to be between 2 and 4 million gallons, but may have been as high as 7 million gallons. The predominant dispersant used in the first month of the oil spill was the Nalco Company's *Corexit* 9527 A®, later replaced by *Corexit* 9500 A®. A massive cleanup effort was launched as dispersed and weathered crude oil approached the U.S. coastline (Figure 28.1). The oil spill cleanup was manned by over 55,000 oil field workers, untrained volunteers, mostly commercial and recreational fishermen; and coordinated by BP, the responsible party, and the U.S. government.

This oil spill was the largest oil spill in the history of the petroleum industry, dwarfed all prior oil tanker and oil rig spills in magnitude and impacted ecosystems, and caused extensive damage to marine and wildlife habitats. It impacted over 1600 miles of shoreline and significantly spoiled over 800 miles of beach and marsh shoreline from Texas to Florida, and threatened the viability of the northern Gulf's commercial fishing and tourism industries. Table 28.1 compares the magnitudes of the *Deepwater Horizon* oil spill with the *Ixtoc I* oil spill, the only other massive offshore oil spill from a rig explosion and sinking in the Gulf of Mexico in June 1979.

Objectives

1. This chapter will describe the chemical constituents of light crude oil and dispersants and their known toxic effects in man, document the acute health effects of similar chemicals on oil spill cleanup workers following prior oil tanker spills worldwide, and assess the potential chronic health outcomes of prolonged exposures to crude oil and dispersants in coastal southeastern Louisiana populations with high seroprevalence rates of specific genetic polymorphisms.
2. These polymorphisms regulate the hepatic biotransformation and systemic toxicity of polycyclic aromatic hydrocarbons (PAHs) in crude oil and glycol ethers in dispersants used in the *Deepwater Horizon* oil spill cleanup and may increase risks of adverse health outcomes including carcinogenesis, anemia, and chronic liver and kidney disease.

Human Toxicities of Crude Oil

Light Crude Oil

The American Petroleum Institute characterizes crude oil both by geographic source (e.g., Louisiana sweet crude) and by physicochemical attributes (e.g., class A light crude oil). The Louisiana *sweet* crude oil spilled in the *Deepwater Horizon* disaster is a class A, volatile crude oil, and is the highest-quality crude oil, which requires the least amount of refining into fuels and other petrochemicals. Light crude oils are clear colored with a strong odor and high volatility and flammability. Light crude oils can be washed off surfaces, but will deeply penetrate porous surfaces, such as dirt and sand, and become persistent in the environment. They are

Table 28.1 Comparison of the Magnitudes and Outcomes of the *Ixtoc I* and the *Deepwater Horizon* Gulf of Mexico Oil Spills

	***Ixtoc I* Oil Spill**	***Deepwater Horizon* Oil Spill**
Location—Gulf of Mexico	Bay of Campeche (62 miles northwest of Cuidad del Carmen, Yucatan, Mexico)	Macondo Canyon (41 miles off of the mouth of the Mississippi River)
Water depth (feet) Gulf water depth record = 10,011 ft	160	5067
Drill depth (feet) Gulf drill depth record = >30,000 ft	11,800	18,360 (13,293 ft below seafloor)
Date of spill	June 3, 1979	April 20, 2010
Ultimate causes of spill	(1) Flawed well-designed plan; and (2) failed blowout preventer (BOP)	(1) Drilling mud circulatory failure; and (2) failed (BOP)
Operator	*Pemex/Sedco* (*Sedco* later became *Transocean*)	*BP/Transocean*
Crew	63	146
Deaths	0	13 (11 deaths on rig and two later deaths from injuries)
Injuries	0	17 (two fatalities)
Maximum spill flow rate 1 barrel of crude oil = 42 U.S. gallons	30,000 barrels = 1.26 million gallons	62,000 barrels = 2.6 million gallons
Total volume of spill 1 barrel of crude oil = 42 U.S. gallons	3 million barrels = 126 million gallons	4.28 million barrels = 180 million gallons
Dispersants used	*Corexit* 9527 (only in Mexican waters)	*Corexit* 9527, later *Corexit* 9500
Area of Gulf impacted (square miles)	1100	6800
Shorelines impacted (miles)	162 (Texas, Mexico)	1600 (Texas to Florida)
Plugging strategies	"Sombrero" containment cap, drilling mud plug, and "junk shot" plug	Containment dome, "top hat" containment cap, drilling mud plug, and "junk shot" plug
Spill stopped	March 28, 1980 by relief wells permitting cementing	September 19, 2010 by relief wells permitting cementing
Cleanup costs	$100 million	$40.9 billion to date

lighter than water (lower specific gravity) and float on the surface, where they evaporate rapidly in sunlight. As the VOCs in light crude oils evaporate, the surface oil will lose 20–40% of its volume and become denser and more viscous forming floating mats. Some of this weathered crude will dissolve in the water column to form a thick *mousse* and other dense particles will congeal and sink forming tar balls that may be washed ashore by wave action. Although consumed by several species of marine bacteria, light crude oils may be highly toxic to humans, fish, and higher benthic organisms.

Chemical Constituents of Crude Oil

The chemical constituents of crude oil are often referred to as the total petrochemical hydrocarbons and are divided into (1) the VOCs that will burn or evaporate quickly in surface spills and minimally bioaccumulate in seafood; and (2) the PAHs that are more stable, can be activated by sunlight, and bioaccumulate to a greater extent in the seafood chain. The major monitored VOCs and PAHs and their levels of concern (LOC) in air and in seafood during the *Deepwater Horizon* oil spill are depicted in Tables 28.2 through 28.4. On April 30, 2010, and again on June 15, 2010, trace levels of PAHs were detected in four seafood samples, but remained below LOCs.[1] VOCs remained below LOCs in air and seafood throughout the *Deepwater Horizon* oil spill.[1]

Acute Health Effects of Volatilized Crude Oil

The acute health effects of liquid volatile crude may be divided into the shared effects of exposures to the total petrochemical hydrocarbons and the specific effects of exposures to VOCs and PAHs, which may be compounded by sunlight (phototoxicity) and by heat. The shared acute health effects of crude exposures include dermal erythema, conjunctival irritation, lacrimation, mucosal irritation, sneezing, coughing, bronchospasm, nausea, and vomiting if ingested, and chemical pneumonitis if aspirated. Both PAHs and VOCs can cause myocardial depression with sensitization to endogenous catecholamines and precipitate angina or

Table 28.2 Air and Seafood Surveillance for PAHs during the Deepwater Horizon Gulf Oil Spill, 2010

PAHs	Air Surveillance	Seafood Surveillance
Sampling and analyzing agencies	EPA, LADEQ	LADHH, LADWF, and NOAA
Established LOCs	24-h screening LOCs	Screening LOCs in specific seafood by weight
Units for LOCs	ng/m^3	mg/kg
Benzo(*a*)anthracene	8.7	490–2000
Benzo(*a*)pyrene	0.87	0.35–1.43
Benzo(*b*)fluoranthene	8.7	0.035–0.143
Benzo(*k*)fluoranthene	8.7	3.5–14.3
Chrysene	87	35–143
Dibenzo(*a,h*)anthracene	0.8	0.035–0.143
Indeno(1,2,3-*cd*)pyrene	8.7	0.35–1.43
Fluoranthene	Not reported (NR)	65–267
Fluorene	NR	65–267
Phenanthrene	NR	490–2000
Pyrene	NR	490–2000

Note: EPA: U.S. Environmental Protection Agency; LADEQ: Louisiana Department of Environmental Quality; LADHH: Louisiana Department of Health and Hospitals; LADWF: Louisiana Department of Wildlife and Fisheries; NOAA: U.S. National Oceanographic and Atmospheric Administration.

Table 28.3 Air and Seafood Surveillance for VOCs during the Deepwater Horizon Gulf Oil Spill, 2010

VOCs	Air Surveillance	Seafood Surveillance
Sampling and analyzing agencies	EPA, LADEQ	LADHH, LADWF, and NOAA
Established LOCs	24-h screening LOCs	Screening LOCs in specific seafood by weight
Units for LOCs	μg/m³	mg/kg
Total C12–C13 aliphatics	Not reported (NR)	233
Ethylbenzene	43,000	NR
Isopropylbenzene	4000	NR
Naphthalene	30	33–133
Toluene	3800	NR
m-, *p*-, or *o*-xylene	8700	NR

Note: EPA: U.S. Environmental Protection Agency; LADEQ: Louisiana Department of Environmental Quality; LADHH: Louisiana Department of Health and Hospitals; LADWF: Louisiana Department of Wildlife and Fisheries; NOAA: U.S. National Oceanographic and Atmospheric Administration.

myocardial infarction during inhalation exposures, especially in enclosed and underventilated spaces. PAHs are phototoxic and can cause skin bronzing and hyperpigmentation with solar keratosis formation and later skin cancers. In addition, viscous hydrocarbons can plug hair follicles if not washed off, causing oil acne ("oil boils") or oil folliculitis (Figure 28.2). The solvents in dispersants and VOCs can cause defatting dermatitis with lichenification and secondary infection, chemical contact dermatitis, and allergic, eczematous contact dermatitis in sensitive individuals (Figure 28.3).

Table 28.4 Pollutants, Particulates, and Dispersants Monitored in Air during the Deepwater Horizon Gulf Oil Spill, 2010

Air Pollutants, Particulates, and Dispersants	Air Surveillance
Sampling and analyzing agencies	EPA, LADEQ
Established LOCs	LOCs in air: 24-h screening levels (or longer), 1-time screening reference toxic concentration
Units for LOCs	μg/m³, ppb
Pollutant: H_2S	0.07 μg/m³ over ≤14 days
Pollutant: SO_2	10.0 μg/m³ over ≤14 days
Particulate: PM10	150 μg/m³ over 24 h
Particulate: PM2.5	35 μg/m³ over 24 h
Dispersant: 2-butoxyethanol	330 ppb (1-time screening reference toxic concentration)
Dispersant metabolite: 1-(2-butoxy-1-methylethoxy-2-propanol)	7 ppb (1-time screening reference toxic concentration)

Note: EPA: U.S. Environmental Protection Agency; LADEQ: Louisiana Department of Environmental Quality.

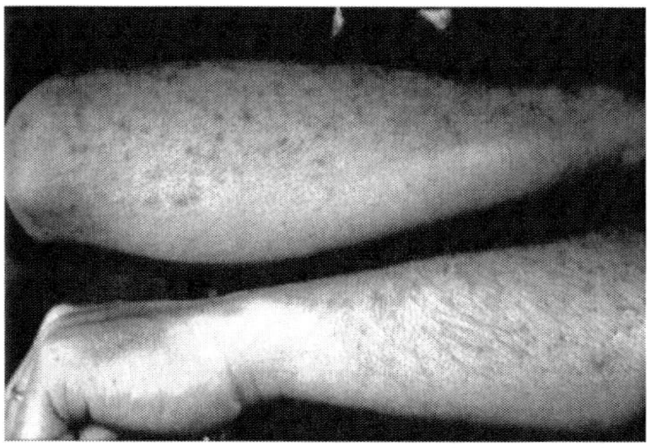

FIGURE 28.2 Oil folliculitis, also called oil boils, on the forearms of a worker with a history of prolonged, unprotected skin contact with oil is characterized by multiple sterile comedones and pustules. (From U.S. National Institute of Occupational Safety and Health, *Occupational Dermatoses: A Program for Physicians*. Available at http://www.dpd.cdc.gov/niosh/topics/skin/occderm-slides/occderm5.)

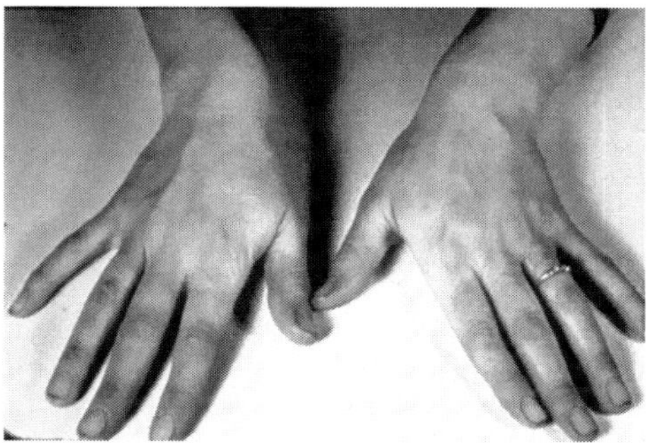

FIGURE 28.3 Solvent-induced nummular eczema on the hands of a worker chronically exposed to organic solvents derived from petroleum by-products and frequently used as cleansers, dispersants, and degreasers. (From U.S. National Institute of Occupational Safety and Health, *Occupational Dermatoses: A Program for Physicians*. Available at http://www.dpd.cdc.gov/niosh/topics/skin/occderm-slides/occderm8.)

The VOCs are highly lipophilic and neurotoxic compounds that can cause biphasic central nervous system effects with initial headache, dizziness, intoxication, vertigo, and ataxia; followed by obtundation, stupor, and coma with respiratory depression. Temporary glove-and-stocking peripheral neuropathies with allodynia, anesthesia, and paresthesias may occur after short-term VOC exposures to unprotected skin with permanent painful, permanent peripheral sensory neuropathies not uncommon after long-term exposures, especially to hexanes and xylenes.

Acute Health Effects of Exposures to Burning Crude Oil

When crude oil is burned on the sea surface, the VOCs are mostly consumed or vaporized, PAHs are pyrolized into anthracenes and pyrenes, and particulates of the burned hydrocarbons are released into the atmosphere. The major contaminants of burned crude oil that were monitored in the atmosphere and their LOCs are depicted in Table 28.3.

In addition to PAHs and VOCs, burning weathered and dispersed crude oil will release toxic gases (carbon monoxide, hydrogen sulfide, ozone, sulfur dioxide, and nitrogen oxides), traces of heavy metals ranging from arsenic to zinc, and particulate matter ranging from visible ash to PM 2.5 particulates, associated with immediate cardiorespiratory symptoms and premature death. Although the 24-h averages for PM 2.5 levels on June 12 and June 14, 2010, at Grande Isle, Jefferson Parish, Louisiana, exceeded the Environmental Protection Agency's (EPA) LOCs, atmospheric particulates remained generally present at normal levels for the Louisiana Gulf coastline, from April through July 2010.[1] Finally, burning crude oil on the sea surface, rather than burning crude oil on shore or on barges, will provide all the ingredients for the formation of bioaccumulating polychlorinated dibenzodioxins, including seawater chloride sources, petrochemical hydrocarbons, and heavy metal catalysts both in crude oil and seawater.[2]

Human Toxicities of Dispersants

Crude oil dispersants were developed for water surface application to break up oil slicks, to increase the rate of oil biodegradation by marine microorganisms, and to protect fragile coastlines supporting commercial fisheries and wildlife-breeding habitats. Once the process of chemical oil dispersion begins, the physical turbulence created by winds, waves, and tides further disperses micelles of crude oil in the water column. To be effective, dispersants are composed of two types of chemicals, surfactants and solvents. The surfactants are the least-toxic ingredients of dispersants and are designed to make the dispersants bind to spilled crude oil. The common surfactants in dispersants include petroleum distillates and dioctyl sodium sulfosuccinate (DOSS), the derivatives of which continue to be used in enemas and laxatives, respectively. The solvents in surfactants are more toxic and are used to disperse and to dissolve spilled crude oil.

The commonly used solvents in dispersants include propylene glycol, a solvent used in many intravenous drug preparations, and 2-butoxyethanol, an industrial solvent used in paint thinners and strippers and in industrial and household- cleaning compounds. Both propylene glycol and 2-butoxyethanol are glycol ethers that are hepatically metabolized to lactic and pyruvic acids by the alcohol dehydrogenase (ADH) enzyme system that also metabolizes ethanol (ethyl alcohol). Butoxyethanol can also be metabolized to ethylene glycol (antifreeze), a highly nephrotoxic glycol ether, by an alternate route in rodent models; and it is unclear if this toxic, alternate route of metabolism occurs in humans when the ADH detoxification system becomes saturated by overdoses. The chemical constituents and the acute health effects of the two *Corexit*® dispersants used in the *Deepwater Horizon* oil spill cleanup 2010 are summarized in Table 28.5, and their chronic health effects are summarized in Table 28.6.

Although there are many proprietary dispersants that are approved for use in oil spill cleanup efforts, only two dispersants were used in the *Deepwater Horizon* oil spill; *Corexit*® 9527, which contains 2-butoxyethanol and was used initially in April to May 2010, and *Corexit*® 9500, which does not contain 2-butoxyethanol and was used later in June through September

Table 28.5 Comparison of the Acute Health Effects of the Two Corexit Dispersants Used during the Deepwater Horizon Oil Spill Cleanup, 2010

Dispersants Used	Corexit 9527	Corexit 9500
MSDS-listed hazardous ingredients	2-Butoxyethanol (ethylene glycol monobutyl ether)	Hydro-treated light petroleum distillates
	Propylene glycol	Propylene glycol
	(1,2-propanediol)	(1,2-propanediol)
	DOSS	DOSS
MSDS-listed other ingredients	Butanedioic acid	Butanedioic acid
	Sorbitan	Sorbitan
	2-Propanol	2-Propanol
Mucosal EENT	Lacrimation, acute irritation of eyes, nose, throat, and metallic taste	Same
Dermal	Acute irritation and erythema	Same
Pulmonary	Cough, bronchospasm, and aspiration pneumonitis if ingested	Same
Cardiovascular	Blood pressure instability, hypo/hypertension, and bradycardia	Same
Gastrointestinal	Acute nausea, then vomiting	Same
Neurological	Acute headache, inebriation, intoxication, depressed mental status, and tremor	Same
Hematological	Oxidizing stress on red blood cells with hemolysis and hemolytic anemia, especially in patients with G-6-PD deficiency	Same
Renal	Hemoglobinuria following acute hemolysis	Same

2010. These dispersants were used in unprecedented amounts in the oil spill, were directly injected into the deepwater column for the first time, and were supplemented with repeated applications to surface waters by ship and aircraft.

On June 30, 2010, the U.S. EPA reported its results of toxicity testing on eight oil dispersants, only one of which, *Corexit* 9500, was used in the *Deepwater Horizon* oil spill cleanup.[3] The toxicity tests included a variety of cytotoxicity tests and tests of both androgenic and estrogenic receptor disruption.[3] The EPA concluded that all the dispersants tested manifested some degree of cytotoxicity at concentrations between 10 and 100 ppm, but none of the eight dispersants tested demonstrated any significant endocrine-disrupting activity via the androgen- or estrogen-signaling pathways.[3]

The unprecedented use of such a large volume of dispersants for a prolonged period in the *Deepwater Horizon* oil spill has created uncertainties regarding the potential human health impacts. The most significant potential, long-term human health effects of *Corexit* dispersant use in the *Deepwater Horizon* oil spill include (1) the potential for hemolytic anemia and renal damage in exposed cleanup workers with glucose-6-phosphate dehydrogenase (G-6-PD)

Table 28.6 Comparison of the Chronic Health Effects of the Two Corexit Dispersants Used during the Deepwater Horizon Oil Spill Cleanup, 2010

Dispersants Used	Corexit 9527	Corexit 9500
MSDS-listed hazardous ingredients	2-Butoxyethanol (ethylene glycol monobutyl ether)	Hydro-treated light petroleum distillates
	Propylene glycol	Propylene glycol
	(1,2-propanediol)	(1,2-propanediol)
	DOSS	DOSS
MSDS-listed other ingredients	Butanedioic acid	Butanedioic acid
	Sorbitan	Sorbitan
	2-Propanol	2-Propanol
Mucosal—EENT	"Gas eye"—chronic blepharitis and conjunctivitis	Same
Dermal	Dry skin, lichenification, fissuring, and secondary infection	Same
Pulmonary	Exacerbation of preexisting obstructive airways disease, occupational asthma	Same
Cardiovascular	Not reported	Same
Gastrointestinal	Elevated hepatic transaminases	Not reported
Neurological	Chronic tremor	Not reported
Hematological	Anemia, initially hemolytic, then renal	Same
Renal	Acute tubular necrosis followed by chronic renal failure possible in patients predisposed by genetic polymorphisms	Same

deficiency, mostly males with this common X-linked recessive genetic polymorphism, and (2) the risks of fetal alcohol syndrome (FAS) from the metabolism of solvents in the *Corexits* by the ADH enzyme system in pregnant cleanup workers. In addition, genetic polymorphisms in the enzyme systems that regulate the metabolism of alcohols and glycols could increase an individual's susceptibility to a wide range of fetal alcohol spectrum disorders (FASDs), which include the complete or partial FAS with or without maternal alcohol exposures, alcohol-related birth defects, and the alcohol-related neurodevelopmental disorder.[4–6]

Prior Acute Health Effects Following Oil Tanker Spills

The acute health effects of prior oil tanker spills are compared in Table 28.7.[7–17]

Chronic Health Predictions Based on Prior Experiences

Only two prior oil tanker spills have provided comparative peer-reviewed and evidence-based results on the longer-term health effects of human exposures to coastal oil spills; the tanker

Table 28.7 Acute Health Effects of Prior Oil Tanker Spills

Tanker Spills (Location, Year)	Study Designs	Acute Health Effects
Exxon Valdez (Alaska, 1989)	Closed-claims study	1811 claims: 506 sprains/strains, 264 respiratory symptoms, 150 cuts, and 144 contusions
MV Braer (Scotland, 1993)	Case–control study	Significant increase in headache, throat, and eye symptoms by day 1 of exposures; health quality remained significantly reduced in exposed cases at 6 months postexposures
Sea Empress (Wales, 1996)	Case–control study	Significant increase in medical and mental health complaints in exposed cases
Nakhodka (Sea of Japan, 1997)	Home interviews of 282 cleanup workers; 97 submitted urine samples.	Low back and leg pain, headache, eye, and throat irritation related to duration of exposures; no increase in urine benzene indicator; three workers had slight increases in urine toluene indicator
Erika (Bay of Biscay, France, 1999)	Cross-sectional study in 1465 professional and volunteer cleanup workers.	Skin exposures from decontaminating oiled birds associated with increased risks of dermatitis and eye irritation
Prestige (NW Spain, 2002)	Before and after cross-sectional study	Significantly increased DNA damage and immunosuppression as measured by comet assays, CD_4 counts, interleukins (ILs)-2, 4, 10, and interferon gamma in pre- versus postexposed case—patient blood samples
Tasman Spirit (Pakistan, 2003)	Case–control study	Significant abnormalities in pulmonary function in exposed cases
Heibei Spirit (South Korea, 2007)	Exposed cleanup workers versus exposed coastal residents study	Significant increases in urine volatile organic chemicals and in mental health complaints in exposed cases; both cases and controls reported cough, sore eyes and throats, and skin rashes

Source: Gorman RW, Beradinelli SP, Bender TR. *Exxon/Valdez* Alaska oil spill. HATA 89-200 and 89-273-2111. Cincinnati: Hazard Evaluation and Technical Assistance Branch, NIOSH, U.S. Department of Health and Human Services; 1991. Available at http://www.cdc.gov/niosh/hhe/reports/pdfs/1989-0200-2111.pdf; Campbell D et al. *Brit Med J* 1993; 307: 1251–5; Campbell D et al. *Brit Med J* 1994; 309: 773–4; Lyons LA et al. *J Epidemiol Commun Health* 1999; 53: 306–10; Morita A et al. *Environ Res* 1999; 81:185–94; Schvoerer C et al. Etude épidémiologique des troubles de santé survenus à court term chez les personnes ayant participle au nettoyage des sites pollutés par le fioul de l'Erika. Paris: Institut de Veille Sanitaire, 2000; Meo SA et al. *Mar Poll Bull* 2008; 56: 88–94; Meo SA et al. *Int J Occup Med Environ Health* 2009; 22: 35–41; Lee J et al. *Biomed Chromatogr* 2010; 24: 562–8; Lee CH et al. *Prev Med Public Health* 2010; 43: 166–73; O'Neill AK. Self-reported exposures and health status among workers from the Exxon Valdez oil spill: Cleanup (master's thesis). New Haven, CT: Yale University; 2003.

Exxon Valdez oil spill in Alaska in 1989, and the tanker *Prestige* oil spill in Spain in 2002. In a master's thesis, O'Neil studied the health status of oil spill workers 14 years after the *Exxon Valdez* oil spill and found a significantly greater prevalence of the symptoms of chronic airway disease among workers with higher exposures to weathered crude oil and dispersants, as well as a greater prevalence of self-reported neurological disorders and multiple chemical sensitivities.[17] In 1993, Palinkas et al.[18] reported their results of a validated mental health instrument survey study 1 year after the *Exxon Valdez* oil spill and again 6 years postspill in 599 exposed subjects. There was a statistically increased odds ratio of anxiety, posttraumatic stress disorder, and depression following the oil spill that significantly remained 6 years postspill.[18]

In 2007, Zock et al.[19] obtained self-reported questionnaire data from 6780 fishermen exposed to crude oil and dispersants following the *Prestige* oil spill of the northeast Spanish coast in 2002 and found a significantly higher prevalence of the lower respiratory tract symptoms 2 years after oil spill activities with a significant dose-response effect exhibited by the 4271 higher-exposed oil spill cleanup workers. In 2010, Rodriguez-Trigo et al.[20] reported their results of a cross-sectional study among exposed case fishermen (n = 501) and unexposed control fishermen (n = 177) 2 years following the *Prestige* oil spill in 2002. The authors reported the following results: (1) significantly increased prevalence of persistent lower respiratory tract symptoms in exposed subjects; (2) significantly higher levels of biomarkers of chronic airway injury and repair (8-isoprostane, a basic fibroblast growth factor) in non-smoking-exposed cleanup workers; (3) a dose-response effect with greater levels of injury biomarkers reflecting the increasing intensity of oil spill cleanup exposures; and (4) a higher proportion of structural chromosomal damage, predominantly unbalanced chromosome alterations, in exposed study subjects.[20]

From a perspective of years of follow-up on first responders and cleanup workers in the *Exxon Valdez* oil spill in 1989, the WTC Twin Towers attacks in 2001, and the *Prestige* oil spill in 2002, several similar chronic health effects in early responders to vaporizing and burning crude oil and jet fuels were observed including persistent lower respiratory tract symptoms; dose-response effects with greater reported symptoms following more intense exposures; elevated biomarkers of lung tissue injury, inflammation, and repair; pulmonary function abnormalities; and evidence of structural damage to chromosomes suggesting DNS damage and potential for carcinogenesis.[21–23] In addition, varying degrees of neurological impairments and mental health disorders, primarily posttraumatic stress disorder and depression, have been reported following these disasters.[21]

Since the exposures to the particulates and the chemicals in evaporating or burning oils sustained by WTC, *Exxon Valdez*, *Prestige*, and *Deepwater Horizon* oil spill first responders were similar in chemical composition, the chronic effects of such inhalational exposures may be predicted to be similar.[21–23] Such similarities may be anticipated in terms of both subacute effects in the first 5 years postexposure including PFT abnormalities and, possibly, sarcoid-like granulomatous pulmonary disease (SLGPD), and any latent carcinogenic effects from a combination of high-dose petrochemical and pyrogenic PAH exposures.[21–23] The compounding effects of smoking, environmental tobacco smoke exposures, and genetic polymorphisms regulating the detoxification of the chemical constituents of crude oil and dispersants cannot be anticipated and must be controlled in longitudinal cohort investigations with biomarker monitoring. The chronic health effects following prior oil tanker spills are summarized in Table 28.8.[17,24–26]

Table 28.8 Chronic Health Effects of Prior Oil Tanker Spills

Tanker Spills (Location, Year)	Study Designs	Chronic Health Effects
Exxon Valdez (Alaska, 1989)	Follow-up study of closed-claim participants 14 years later	Increased prevalence of reactive airway diseases, neurological impairments, and multiple chemical sensitivities
Exxon Valdez (Alaska, 1989)	Mental health survey study 1 year postspill and again at 6 years postspill	N = 599; increased odds ratios for anxiety = 3.6; posttraumatic stress disorder = 2.9; and depression = 2.1. These adverse mental health effects were observed at similar levels up to 6 years postspill
Erika (Bay of Biscay, France, 1999)	Cancer-risk analysis based on water column and beach PAH measurements 4 months after spill and on modeling of atmospheric PAH levels	PAH residues were greatest on rocky soil; the highest estimated cancer risk approximated 10^{-5} per lifetime
Prestige (NW Spain, 2002)	Survey study sent to 38 commercial fishermen's cooperatives, N = 6780 (76% response rate) 1–2 years postspill	Significantly increased prevalence of lower respiratory tract symptoms in fishermen participating in cleanup with a significant dose–response effect for exposures by hours, days, and activities
Prestige (NW Spain, 2002)	Cross-sectional case–control study among exposed case fishermen (n = 501) and unexposed control fishermen (n = 177) 2 years postspill	Significantly increased prevalence of persistent lower respiratory tract symptoms, elevated markers of airway injury (8-isoprostane, vascular endothelial growth factor, and basic fibroblast growth factor) in breath condensates, and chromosomal lesions and structural alterations in circulating lymphocytes 2 years postspill

Source: O'Neill AK. Self-reported exposures and health status among workers from the Exxon Valdez oil spill: Cleanup (master's thesis). New Haven, CT: Yale University; 2003; Zock JP et al. *Prestige. Am J Resp Crit Care Med* 2011; June 30 (Epub ahead of print); Rodriguez-Trigo G, Zock JP, Isidro Montes I. *Arch Broncopneumol* 2007; 43: 628–35; Dor F et al. *Risk Anal* 2003; 23:1199–208.

Chronic Health Predictions Based on Common Genetic Polymorphisms among Oil Spill-Related Workers and the General Population

The enzyme systems with frequently inherited genetic polymorphisms that may impact an individual's ability to metabolize and to detoxify the chemical constituents of crude oil and dispersants include aryl hydrocarbon hydroxylase (AHH), uridine diphosphoglucuronyl transferase (UDPT), glutathione-*S*-transferase (GST), G-6-PD, and the alcohol–acetaldehyde dehydrogenases (AADHs).[27–31] The most common genetic polymorphisms in both exposed oil spill-cleanup workers and the general population in Louisiana that could pose a potential chronic health impact are summarized by mechanisms of toxicity and adverse health effects in Table 28.9.[27–31] Many

Table 28.9 Common Genetic Polymorphisms among Oil Spill Workers and the General Population of South Louisiana

Genetic Polymorphisms	Hepatic Enzyme Phase	Mechanisms of Adverse Effects	Populations at Risk	Potential Adverse Health Outcomes
Glucose-6-phosphate dehydrogenase deficiency (G6PDD)	Phase 1 G6PDD is an X-linked recessive trait and the most common genetic polymorphism	Failure to protect RBCs from oxidative stresses imposed by solvents in dispersants and VOCs in crude oil	Up to 50% of Americans of Southern European ancestry. Up to 40% of Americans of Middle Eastern ancestry. 12% African-American males 4% Asian-American males 4% African-American females	Hemolytic anemia, chronic anemia, gall stones, jaundice, and renal insufficiency—failure, cirrhosis, and liver failure
ADHs 1B *2 and *3	Phase 1—ADH–acetaldehyde dehydrogenase system	Hyper- versus hypo-metabolism of ethyl alcohol and related compounds such as the glycols in dispersants: 2-butoxyethanol, propylene glycol	Native Americans Asian Americans	Lactic and metabolic acidosis. Increased risk of FASDs, including FAS
Cytochrome P1A1 aryl hydrocarbon hydroxylase	Phase 1	Activates carcinogenic benzo-*a*-pyrenes in PAHs in crude oil, volatilized crude, burning crude, ingested PAHs, and cigarette smoke.	Asian-Americans All populations with high smoking prevalence: African-American and Asian-American males	Increased susceptibility to the following cancers: oral, throat, lung, prostate, colorectal, breast, and skin
UDTP 1A7	Phase 2	Failure to supply adequate amount of glutathione to detoxify PAHs, especially the carcinogenic benzo-*a*-pyrenes	Asian-Americans All populations with high smoking prevalence: African-American and Asian-American males	Increased susceptibility to the following cancers: oral, throat, lung, prostate, colorectal, breast, and skin
GST	Phase 2	Failure to detoxify activated PAH–epoxide free radicals, which are cancer promoters	Up to Asian-Americans All populations with high smoking prevalence: African-American and Asian-American males	Increased susceptibility to the following cancers: oral, throat, lung, prostate, colorectal, breast, and skin

Source: Kiyohara C et al. *Pharmacogenetics* 1998; 8: 315–23; Kiyohara C, Ohno Y. *Nippon Koshu Eisei Zasshi* 1999; 46: 241–9; Wang Y et al. *J Occ Environ Med* 2009; 51: 682–9; Strassburg CP et al. *Gut* 2002; 50: 851–6; Chinevere TD et al. *Mil Med* 2006; 171: 905–7.

Note: PAHs: Polycyclic aromatic hydrocarbons; RBCs: red blood cells; VOCs: volatile organic compounds.

of the genetic polymorphisms compared in Table 28.9 are overrepresented in three minority populations in Louisiana: African-Americans (AHH, G-6-PD), Vietnamese–Americans (AHH, UDP, and GST), and Native Americans (AADH) that may promote chronic health disparities.[27–31]

Conclusions

The *Deepwater Horizon* oil spill of 2010 was an environmental and economic disaster for the northern Gulf Coast with the potential for longer-term adverse ecosystem and human health impacts. Reliable biomarkers must be selected now and monitored longitudinally over many years to measure the impact of adverse chemical exposures on the ecosystem, on the marine food chain, and on humans. Cohorts of highly exposed offshore and onshore cleanup workers and their spouses and children are now being assembled for prospective longitudinal studies. These studies must account for many confounders to establish causal outcomes including smoking, smokeless tobacco use, second-hand tobacco smoke exposures, ethnicity, and, especially, genetic polymorphisms regulating the detoxification of crude oil and dispersants.

Respiratory, neurological, and dermal disorders may be anticipated now based on the outcomes of prior exposures to crude oil spills, burning petrochemical fuels, particulates, and VOCs. Screening for adverse mental health outcomes has also begun and may be predicted to extend to the general population of lesser exposed and nonexposed individuals as a result of economic uncertainty, loss of culture and identity, stress, anxiety, and depression. Several populations will require special monitoring and long-term studies, including children of exposed cleanup workers and ethnic groups with high prevalence of genetic polymorphisms regulating the metabolism of PAHs and solvents. Finally, the chronic effects of chemical exposures with prolonged latencies of decades, such as cancer and demyelinating neurological diseases, will need to be assessed frequently in prospective cohorts of exposed and nonexposed subjects with reliable biomarkers of DNA damage and repair, inflammation and cytokine stimulation, autoimmune effects, immunosuppression and infection, and chromosomal alterations.

References

1. Canyon MS. 252. Oil Spill Surveillance Reports. Louisiana Department of Health and Hospitals Office of Public Health Section of Environmental Epidemiology and Toxicology, 2010.
2. Shibamoto T, Yasuhara A, Katimi T. Dioxin formation from waste incineration. *Rev Environ Contam Toxicol* 2007; 190: 1–41.
3. Hemmer MJ, Barron MG, Greene RM. Comparative toxicity of eight oil dispersant products on two Gulf of Mexico aquatic test species. U.S. Environmental Protection Agency Office of Research and Development, June 30, 2010. Available at http://www.epa.gov/bpspill/dispersants.
4. Haycock PC. Fetal alcohol spectrum disorders: The epigenetic perspective. *Biol Repro* 2009; 81: 607–17.
5. Green RF, Stoler JM. Alcohol dehydrogenase 1B genotype and fetal alcohol syndrome: A HuGe minireview. *Am J Obstet Gynecol* 2007; 197: 12–25.
6. May PA, Gossage JP, Kalberg WO et al. Prevalence and epidemiologic characteristics of FASD from various research methods with an emphasis on recent in-school studies. *Dev Disab Res Rev* 2009; 15: 176–92.

7. Gorman RW, Beradinelli SP, Bender TR. *Exxon/Valdez* Alaska oil spill. HATA 89-200 and 89-273-2111. Cincinnati: Hazard Evaluation and Technical Assistance Branch, NIOSH, U.S. Department of Health and Human Services; 1991. Available at http://www.cdc.gov/niosh/hhe/reports/pdfs/1989-0200-2111.pdf.
8. Campbell D, Cox D, Crum J et al. Initial effects of the grounding of the tanker *Braer* on health in Shetland. The Shetland Health Study Group. *Brit Med J* 1993; 307: 1251–5.
9. Campbell D, Cox D, Crum J et al. Later effects of grounding of tanker *Braer* on health in Shetland. *Brit Med J* 1994; 309: 773–4.
10. Lyons LA, Temple JM, Evans D et al. Acute health effects of the *Sea Empress* oil spill. *J Epidemiol Commun Health* 1999; 53: 306–10.
11. Morita A, Kusaka Y, Deguchi Y et al. Acute health problems among people engaged in the cleanup of the Nakhodka oil spill. *Environ Res* 1999; 81:185–94.
12. Schvoerer C, Gourier-Fréry C, Ledrans M et al. Etude épidémiologique des troubles de santé survenus à court term chez les personnes ayant participle au nettoyage des sites pollutés par le fioul de l'Erika. Paris: Institut de Veille Sanitaire, 2000.
13. Meo SA, Al-Drees AM, Meo IM et al. Lung function in subjects exposed to crude oil spill into sea water. *Mar Poll Bull* 2008; 56: 88–94.
14. Meo SA, Al-Drees AM, Rasheed S et al. Effect of duration of exposure to polluted air environment on lung function in subjects exposed to crude oil spill in sea water. *Int J Occup Med Environ Health* 2009; 22: 35–41.
15. Lee J, Kim M, Ha M, Chung BC. Urinary metabolic profile of volatile organic compounds in acute exposed volunteers after an oil spill in Republic of Korea. *Biomed Chromatogr* 2010; 24: 562–8.
16. Lee CH, Kang YA, Chang KJ et al. Acute health effects of the *Heibei* oil spill on the residents of Taean, Korea. *Prev Med Public Health* 2010; 43: 166–73.
17. O'Neill AK. Self-reported exposures and health status among workers from the Exxon Valdez oil spill: Cleanup (master's thesis). New Haven, CT: Yale University; 2003.
18. Palinkas LA, Petterson JS, Russell J, Downs MA. Community patterns of psychiatric disorders after the *Exxon Valdez* oil spill. *Am J Psychiatry* 1993; 150: 1517–23.
19. Zock JP, Rodriguez-Trigo G, Pozo-Rodriguez F et al. SEPAR-*Prestige* Study Group. Prolonged respiratory symptoms in clean-up workers of the *Prestige* oil spill. *Am J Resp Crit Care Med* 2007; 176: 610–6.
20. Rodriguez-Trigo G, Zock JP, Pozo-Rodriguez F et al. SEPAR-*Prestige* Study Group. Health changes in fishermen 2 years after clean-up of the *Prestige* oil spill. *Ann Intern Med* 2010; 153: 540–1.
21. Samet JM, Geyh AS, Utell MJ. The legacy of World Trade Center dust. *N Engl J Med* 2007; 356: 2233–6.
22. Edelman P, Osterloh J, Pirkle J et al. Biomonitoring of chemical exposure among New York City firefighters responding to the World Trade Center fire and collapse. *Environ Health Perspect* 2003; 111: 1906–11.
23. Banauch GI, Hall C, Weiden M et al. Pulmonary function after exposure to the World Trade Center collapse in the New York City Fire Department. *Am J Resp Crit Care Med* 2006; 174: 312–9.
24. Zock JP, Rodrigez-Trigo G, Pozo-Rodriguez F, Barbera JA. Health effects of oil spills: Lessons from the *Prestige*. *Am J Resp Crit Care Med* 2011; June 30 (Epub ahead of print).
25. Rodriguez-Trigo G, Zock JP, Isidro Montes I. Health effects of exposures to oil spills. *Arch Broncopneumol* 2007; 43: 628–35.
26. Dor F, Bonnard R, Gourier-Fréry C et al. Health risk assessment after decontamination of the beaches polluted by the wrecked ERIKA tanker. *Risk Anal* 2003; 23:1199–208.
27. Kiyohara C, Nakanishi Y, Inutsuka S et al. The relationship between CYP1A1 aryl hydrocarbon hydroxylase activity and lung cancer in a Japanese population. *Pharmacogenetics* 1998; 8: 315–23.
28. Kiyohara C, Ohno Y. Role of metabolic polymorphisms in lung carcinogenesis. *Nippon Koshu Eisei Zasshi* 1999; 46: 241–9.
29. Wang Y, Duan H, Dai Y et al. Uridine diphosphoglucuronyltransferase 1A7 gene polymorphism and susceptibility to chromosomal damage among polycyclic aromatic hydrocarbon exposed workers. *J Occ Environ Med* 2009; 51: 682–9.
30. Strassburg CP, Vogel A, Kneip S et al. Polymorphisms of the human UDP-glucuronyltransferase (UGT) 1A7 gene in colorectal cancer. *Gut* 2002; 50: 851–6.
31. Chinevere TD, Murray CK, Grant E Jr. et al. Prevalence of glucose-6-phosphate dehydrogenase deficiency in U.S. Army personnel. *Mil Med* 2006; 171: 905–7.

Chapter 29

Industrial Gas Exposures and Occupational Lung Diseases

Outline . . . 646
Pathophysiology . . . 646
Asphyxiants: Noble Gases . . . 647
Asphyxiants: Crude Oil-Derived Hydrocarbons . . . 647
Irritant Gases . . . 647
Metal and Polymer Fume Fevers . . . 648
ALI vs. RADS . . . 648
Irritant Toxic Mechanisms . . . 649
Smoke Inhalation (SI) . . . 650
Carbon Monoxide Poisoning . . . 651
CO Poisoning: Effects on the Oxyhemoglobin Dissociation Curve . . . 653
Cyanide Poisoning . . . 656
Hydrogen Sulfide . . . 657
"Tear" Gases . . . 660
Poison Gas: Personal Protective Equipment Levels A–D . . . 662
Pneumoconioses . . . 662
Occupationally-Related Lung Cancer . . . 666
Occupational "Asthma" . . . 669
Inhalation Fevers . . . 671
Conclusions . . . 671

Outline

- Simple asphyxiants
- Pulmonary irritants
    - High water solubility
    - Intermediate water solubility
    - Low water solubility
- Smoke inhalation
- Carbon monoxide poisoning
- Cyanide poisoning
- Hydrogen sulfide poisoning
- Occupational lung diseases
- Occupational airway diseases

Pathophysiology

Simple Asphyxiants

- Definition of simple asphyxiants
- **Noble gases:** Helium, neon, argon, xenon, radon
- **Hydrocarbon gases:** Methane, ethane, propane, butane
- **Physiologic simple asphyxiants:** Carbon dioxide, nitrogen

Asphyxiants: Definitions

- Asphyxiants include physiologic gases, noble gases, and HCs. Nonirritating, colorless, and odorless gases with no pharmacologic or physiologic activities except physiologic gases: (1) CO_2: hyper/hypocarbia and pH changes, (2) N_2: N_2 narcosis and caisson disease.
- All are easily compressible and expand logarithmically on depressurization.
- Produce hypoxic tissue damage, mainly to the brain and myocardium, by *displacing* O_2.
- Treatment includes evacuation, supplemental O_2, ventilatory assistance, and support.
- Hyperbaric oxygenation (HBO) is not indicated unless there is coexposure to CO or H_2S.

Asphyxiants: Pathophysiology

Carbon Dioxide

- **Uses:** Carbonating beverages, fire-fighting, solid "dry ice," formerly laparoscopic insufflation (metabolic acidosis—premature ventricular contractions [PVCs], ventricular tachycardia [VT], ventricular fibrillation [VF])
- **Toxicity:** Respiratory acidosis 2° carbonic acid accumulation, compensatory respiratory alkalosis → hypokalemia, arrhythmias

Nitrogen

- **Uses:** Fertilizer, cryosurgery (liquid N_2), compressed gas for power tools
- **Toxicity:** Nitrogen narcosis ("rapture of the deep"); use helium in deep sea diving operations > air with 80% N_2 as the preferred diluent gas for O_2 in deep sea diving operations and ascend slowly to prevent N_2 bubble decompression and CNS–lung–GI air emboli, belly pain ("bends"), and osteonecrosis (caisson workers' disease)

Asphyxiants: Noble Gases

- **Helium:** Used in deep sea diving, asthmatics, and IABP because of its compressibility, inflammability, low viscosity, and low lipid (tissue) solubility
- **Argon and neon:** Lighting manufacture, thermal windows (argon)
- **Xenon:** General anesthetic at 1 atm
- **Radon:** Alpha particle emitter and carcinogen (↑ lung cancer in uranium miners)

Asphyxiants: Crude Oil-Derived Hydrocarbons

- **Methane:** "Swamp gas" used as fuel for cooking, drying, driving autos, and generating electrical power
- **Ethane:** A natural gas component used as a refrigerant
- **Propane:** A compressed gas fuel and liquid solvent
- **Butane:** A cigarette lighter and fire-starter fuel and liquid volatile solvent; often abused by adolescents—"huffing"

Irritant Gases

- Impact of increasing water solubility on irritant gas toxicity (See Table 29.1)

Table 29.1 Irritant Gases Stratified by Their Water Solubilities

Highly Soluble	Intermediate	Poorly Soluble
Prompt escape	Less escape prompting	No escape prompting
Rapidly irritating to mucosa	Less irritating to mucosa	No mucosal irritation
Target upper airway and EENT mucosa	Target tracheobrochial tree	Target pulmonary parenchyma
Acute lung injury (ALI) possible	ALI common	Delayed, severe pneumonitis
Reactive airways dysfunction syndrome (RADS) possible	RADS common	Pulmonary edema

Note: The more water soluble the gas, the more irritant effect it will have on the upper respiratory tract mucosa.

- Outcomes of irritant gas poisoning: (1) acute lung injury (*ALI = pulmonary edema*), (2) subacute injury = bronchiolitis obliterans, and (3) chronic reactive airways dysfunction syndrome (*RADS*)
- Pathophysiology of irritant gas toxicity
- Caustic (acid–base) effects of irritant gases
- "Tear gases" = irritant gases with high toxicity and decreased morbidity and mortality *Kinder and gentler* tear gases = capsaicin–pepper spray

Highly Soluble Irritants

- Ammonia (NH_3)
- Chloramines
- Hydrogen chloride (HCl)
- Hydrogen fluoride (HF)
- Sulfur dioxide (SO_2)
- Acrolein
- "Tear gases"

Poorly Soluble Irritants

- Phosgene
- Nitric oxide
- Ozone

Intermediate Solubility Irritants

- Chloride/chlorine (CL_2)
- Methylisocyanate (MIC) (Bhopal)
- Immune sensitizers → occ asthma
    - Toluene *diisocyanate* (TDI)
    - Diphenylmethane *diisocyanate*
    - Trimetallic *anhydrides* (TMI)

Metal and Polymer Fume Fevers

- **Zn and Cu:** Most often, polymer—Teflon®.
- *Cadmium* causes acute pneumonitis, not metal fume fever.

ALI vs. RADS

Acute Lung Injury

- **Pathology:** Acute pulmonary inflammation and alveolar filling = pulmonary edema

- **Signs and sx:** Dyspnea, chest tightness, chest pain, cough, frothy sputum, rales, pulmonary edema
- **X-ray:** Pulmonary infiltration, normal cardiac silhouette

Reactive Airways Dysfunction Syndrome (RADS)

- **Path:** Chronic hyperreactive lower airways and asthmatic bronchospasm—bronchiolitis
- **Sx:** Wheezing, tachypnea, air hunger, "irritant-induced asthma"
- **X-ray:** Air trapping = hyperinflation, flat diaphragms, elongated cardiac silhouette, barotrauma = pneumothorax, pneumomediastinum

Irritant Toxic Mechanisms

1. *Local caustic generation on tissue hydration → mucosal neutralization burns*
   - **Ammonia** → ammonium hydroxide
   - **Chloramines** → hypochlorous acid
   - **Hydrogen chloride** → hydrochloric acid
   - **Hydrogen cyanide** → hydrocyanic acid → cytochrome oxidase inhibition
   - **Hydrogen fluoride** → hydrofluoric acid
   - **Hydrogen sulfide** → cytochrome oxidase inhibition → lactic acid
   - **Sulfur dioxide** → sulfuric acid
   - **Chlorine** → hypochlorous and hydrochloric acids
   - **Zinc phosphide** → phosphine gas (Tables 29.2 and 29.3)
2. *Free radical generation on lung tissue absorption → pulmonary parenchymal damage*
   - **Oxygen** → superoxide and singlet O^- radicals

Table 29.2 Highly Water-Soluble Irritant Gases Will Combine with Mucosal Water to Generate Caustic Chemicals

Irritant Gases	Mucosal Caustics Produced
Ammonia	Ammonium hydroxide
Chloramines	Hypochlorous acid
Hydrogen chloride	Hydrochloric acid
Hydrogen fluoride	Hydrofluoric acid
Hydrogen sulfide	Cytochrome oxidase inhibition, lactic acid (metabolic acidosis)
Sulfur dioxide	Sulfuric acid
Chlorine	Hypochlorous and hypochloric acids

Table 29.3 Occupational Exposures to Irritant Gases Occur in Many Industries Ranging from Agriculture to Petrochemical Refining

Gas	Exposure	Toxicity
NH_3	Fertilizer/explosives, cleansers	Reactive airways dysfunction syndrome (RADS)
Chloramines	Water treatment	ALI, RADS
Hydrogen chloride (HCl)	PVC	RADS
Hydrogen fluoride (HF)	Rust removal	Reduced Ca/Mg (treatment: Ca glue)
Hydrogen sulfide (H_2S)	Oil refinery, sewage	Cytochrome poison (treatment: consider HBO)
Sulfur dioxide (SO_2)	Autos, smog, acid rain	RADS
Chloride (Cl)	Water treatment	ALI (consider nebulized $NaHCO_3$)
Acrolein	Polypropylene	Pulmonary edema

Table 29.4 Least Water-Soluble Irritant Gases May Be Deeply Inhaled to the Lower Respiratory Tract Causing Free Radical Injury at the Alveolar Level

Irritant Gases	Free Radicals Generated
Oxygen	Superoxide and single O radicals
Oxides of nitrogen (NO_x)	NO, NO_2, N_2O, and N_2O_3, all generate perosynitrite free radicals; NO_x also dissolve in lung water generating nitric and nitrous acids, causing further caustic burn injury to pulmonary parenchyma
Ozone generated by air	Superoxide and singlet O free radicals pollution, lightning, electrical fires, and welding

- **Oxides of nitrogen** (NO_x) → NO, NO_2, N_2O, and N_2O_3 → (1) generate *peroxynitrite free radicals*, (2) NO_x also dissolve in lung water → releasing *nitric and nitrous acids*, causing caustic injury
- **Ozone** → superoxide and singlet O^- free radicals (Table 29.4)

Smoke Inhalation

- Epidemiology
- Pathophysiology
- Clinical manifestations
- Management

SI: Epidemiology

- There are 3600 fire-related deaths and nearly 30,000 fire-related injuries/year in the United States.
- 50–80% of the fire deaths are due to smoke inhalation.
- The United States has the highest fire death rates in the world.
- Pyrolysis of wood produces nearly 200 toxic combustion products; pyrolysis of PVC and nitrogen-containing plastics and fabrics produces at least 75 toxic combustion products.
- Cyanide is produced from combustion of nitrogen-containing *plastics, polyurethanes, polyacrylonitriles, nitrocellulose, wool, silk, nylon, synthetic rubber,* and *paper.*
- Combustion products of PVC include *carbon monoxide, hydrogen chloride, chlorine,* and *phosgene.*

SI: Pathophysiology

Pathology and Outcome

- **CNS toxicity:** Hypoventilation, unconsciousness–coma, cardiorespiratory arrest
- **Upper airway (AW) edema:** Stridor, dyspnea
- **AW obstruction:** Cough/wheeze bronchospasm, hypoxemia
- **Atelectasis:** Rales, pneumonia, respiratory failure, pulmonary edema, first x-ray changes appear
  - **Impaired O_2 transport 2° CO, CN, metHb:** Neurologic depression, arrhythmias, angina, metabolic acidosis
  - **Impaired tissue oxygenation (2° CO, CN, H_2S):** Same

Management

- O_2, AW support
- O_2, endotracheal intubation for mechanical ventilation
- O_2, bronchoscopy to remove obstructive soot and debris, β_2-agonists
- O_2, ventilator modalities: Continuous positive airway pressures (CPAP), intermittent mandatory ventilation (IMV), positive end expiratory pressure (PEEP), and others
- O_2, HBO, methylene blue (for methemoglobin [metHb] levels >20–30%)
- O_2, pressors, HBO (COHb levels >25%), Cyanide Kit®—amyl, then sodium nitrite; IV sodium thiosulfate or Cyanokit®—hydroxocobalamin to form less toxic cyanocobalamin or vitamin B12

Carbon Monoxide Poisoning

- Epidemiology
- Pathophysiology
- Clinical manifestations
- Delayed effects

- Diagnosis
- Management

CO: Epidemiology 1

- CO is the leading cause of poisoning morbidity and mortality in the United States, causing >5000 deaths/year.
- 50+% of the CO deaths/year are caused by auto exhausts; 500 CO deaths/year are caused by stoves, fireplaces, gas heaters, generators, propane-powered indoor equipment (forklifts, Zamboni® ice resurfacers—also ↑ NO_x).
- 3–24% of symptomatic patients with flu-like sx of HA, N, and dizziness, reporting to EDs/year have CO poisoning.
- CO is the most common cause of fire deaths; smokers can have COHb levels of 6–10% increasing their susceptibility to CO poisoning.

CO: Epidemiology 2

- 14–40% of discharged patients treated for CO poisoning will have delayed, permanent neurologic dysfunction, such as Parkinsonism.
- Besides combustion of fossils fuels (oil, gas, coal, wood) and cigarette smoking, methylene chloride-containing paint strippers are the next highest contributors to human COHb levels. Methylene chloride is rapidly absorbed through the skin and lungs and metabolically converted to CO by the liver within 24 h.

Basal Ganglia Toxins

The basal ganglia toxins target specific nuclei in the basal ganglia and can cause postexposure toxic Parkinsonism.

- Carbon monoxide (globus pallidus)
- Carbon disulfide
- Hydrogen cyanide (globus pallidus)
- Hydrogen sulfide
- Manganese (substantia nigra)
- Methanol (putamen)
- 1-Methyl-4-phenyl-1,2,3,6-tetrahydropyridine = MPTP (substantia nigra)

CO Poisoning: Clinical Manifestations

Severity =% COHb

- **Mild:** 5–15%
- **Moderate:** 15–25%
- **Severe:** >25%

Symptoms → Signs

- Headache, nausea, dizziness → vomiting, no sequelae

- Obtundation, weakness, chest tightness, dyspnea → tachycardia, angina, tachypnea, ataxia, myonecrosis from disrupted myoglobin
- Chest pain, palpitations, disorientation → PVCs, MI → BP, seizures (sz), coma, skin bullae, *cherry-red skin color—postmortem*, CNS damage, death

CO Poisoning: Pathophysiology

- CO *binds to hemoglobin (Hb)* with an affinity *250* × greater than for O_2.
- CO *shifts the oxyhemoglobin (oxyHb) dissociation curve leftward, decreasing oxygen unloading to tissues*, causing tissue hypoxia and lactic acidosis (see Figures 29.1 and 29.2).
- CO also *binds to myoglobin*, impairing myocardial performance and causing *myonecrosis and myoglobinuria.*
- CO can *displace NO from platelets*, causing peripheral vasodilation and hypotension.
- CO interferes with cellular respiration by *binding to mitochondrial cytochrome oxidase (aa3)*, like CN and H_2S, *inhibiting oxidative phosphorylation*, promoting anaerobic metabolism, tissue hypoxia, and lactic acidosis.

CO Poisoning: Effects on the Oxyhemoglobin Dissociation Curve

CO Poisoning: Delayed Effects

- Fetuses and patients rendered unconscious or >30-years-old (yo) during CO exposure are more susceptible to delayed, often permanent, neurologic effects of CO poisoning.

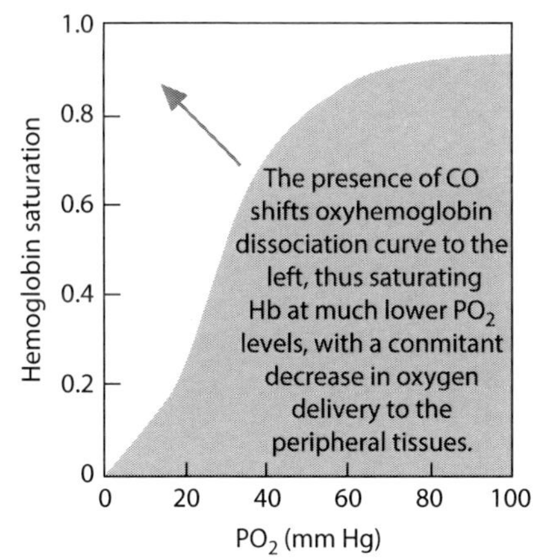

FIGURE 29.1 The normal oxyhemoglobin dissociation curve and the mechanism of action of carbon monoxide inhalation on the normal oxyhemoglobin dissociation curve. The presence of carbon monoxide (CO) in the blood following its inhalation will shift the orientation of the oxyhemoglobin dissociation curve leftwards, causing hemoglobin to become saturated at lower oxygen tension levels (PO_2), and delivering less oxygen to the organs and tissues.

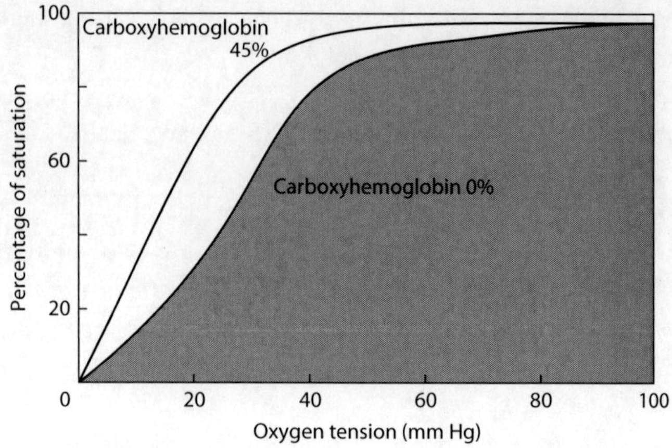

FIGURE 29.2 A comparison of a normal oxyhemoglobin dissociation curve and an abnormal oxyhemoglobin dissociation curve shifted leftward by 45% carboxyhemoglobin in the blood. The presence of carbon monoxide (CO) in the blood following its inhalation will shift the orientation of the oxyhemoglobin dissociation curve leftwards, causing hemoglobin to become saturated at lower oxygen tension levels (PO_2), and delivering less oxygen to the organs and tissues. This diagram depicts a comparison of a normal oxyhemoglobin dissociation curve and an abnormal oxyhemoglobin dissociation curve shifted leftward by 45% carboxyhemoglobin in the blood.

- Delayed neurologic effects = amnesia, agnosia, apraxia, dementia, incontinence, psychosis, chorea, cortical blindness, peripheral neuropathy, Parkinsonism.
- Delayed neurologic sequelae can be predicted from acute changes on CT and MRI scans, especially *basal ganglia lesions* (globus pallidus) and ischemia of subcortical white matter.

CO Poisoning: CT Scan Findings

- **Delayed CNS damage in CO poisoning:** Bilateral lucent lesions of *globus pallidus*, 2° ischemia–reperfusion

CO: Dx and Tx

Lab Diagnosis

- COHb level monitoring by *cooximetry* only
- ABGs (usually normal PaO_2) and pulse oximetry (often normal too) very unreliable
- ABGs to confirm metabolic = lactic acidosis
- Mildly elevated CPK 2° myonecrosis

Indications for Hyperbaric Oxygenation (HBO)

Immediate HBO

- COHb > 25%

- COHb > *15% in pregnancy*
- **Any local CNS findings:** syncope, seizures, coma, lateralizing neurologic signs
- **ECG:** myocardial ischemia, PVCs/any tachydysrhythmias
- **HBO after initial tx (100% $O_2 \times$ 2–4 h):** Persistent neurologic findings = HA, dizziness, confusion, and ataxia

Cyanide: Outline

- Exposures and settings
- Mechanisms of toxicity
- Clinical manifestations
- Diagnosis and management

CN: Exposures and Settings

CN Exposures

- Suicides/homicides involving chemists and lab workers
- Consumer product tampering
- Residential fires involving all fabrics and synthetics: synthetic rubber, wool, silk, polyurethane, nitrocellulose
- Ingesting *acetonitrile-based* fake nail glue removing solutions
- **Plants:** (1) *Prunus* spp. pitted fruits = apricots, cherries, peaches, almonds; (2) *hydrangeas* → gut-transformed—*amygdalin* → HCN; (3) cassava
- Iatrogenic SCN infusions

Clinical Settings for CN Toxicity

- Sudden collapse of an academic or industrial lab or chemical worker
- Fire victims with coma and metabolic acidosis
- Suicide or unexplained coma and acidosis
- Ingestion of or access to *artificial nail removers*
- Cancer pts on "*Laetrile®*" (amygdalin or CN-containing "anticancer" hoax) tx
- ICU pts on prolonged SCN^- infusions

CN: Mechanisms

- *Rapid absorption* via all routes with rapid membrane transit due to nonionization and low MW.
- Initial *inhibition of cytochrome oxidase and oxidative phosphorylation*, shutting down electron transport chain, *blocking aerobic ATP-generating energy production during the Krebs cycle in mitochondria*, causing cellular hypoxia.
- Stimulation of alternative *anaerobic routes of ATP-energy production* from pyruvate with lactate production, metabolic = lactic acidosis.

- Direct *CNS neurotoxicity* through lipid peroxidation and ischemia with greatest damage to the most O_2-sensitive areas of the brain in the *basal ganglia.*

Cytotoxic: Cyanide Poisonings

Cyanogenic Plant Group (See Chapter 21)

- **Reps:** *Prunus* spp. seeds = apple, crab apple, apricot (*Laetrile*®), plum, peach, cherry; elderberry leaves–stems (berries OK); hydrangea; cassava roots (tapioca)—all contain the cyanogenic glycoside, amygdalin
- **Toxin:** *Amygdalin* → amygdalase → *hydrocyanic acid*
- **Antidote:** CN kit® amyl nitrite + Na nitrite + Na thiosulfate; or hydroxocobalamin → B12
- **Dx:** HA, vertigo, sz, ↑T, stupor, tissue hypoxia–acidosis, coma
- **Tx:** GI decontamination

Mass Plant Cyanide Poisonings

- Do not drink kool aid/juice @ picnics 8/26/83-mass HCN poisoning in Ca.
- **Monterey, California, Church Picnic:** 8 people of a 25-person religious-philanthropic group urgently EMS-evacuated to SF with cramps, N, V, weakness, dizziness, numbness 15 min after enjoying a 12-h-old homemade elderberry juice-crushed berries, leaves, stems in apple juice–sugar water juice mix. HCN poisoning suspected; but antidotes not indicated 2° stability of all poisoned pts. 1 hospitalized pt consumed 5 glasses juice = dose-response effects +.
- **American Elderberry, *Sambucus nigra/mexicana*:** Berries OK for wines–liqueurs (*Sambuca*), and jams; but leaves, buds, flowers, and roots contain cyanogenic glycosides.

Cyanide Poisoning

By Foods: Cassava

Cassava, *Manihot escuelenta*: Tropical plant that provides the third most important carbohydrate source in the tropics and has edible tuberous roots that *must be soaked* before cooking (*tapioca*) to remove cyanogenic glycoside, *linamarin*. Chronic ingestion of unsoaked cassava roots during drought causes a tropical ataxic neuropathy (tropical spastic paraparesis), similar to neurolathyrism.

CN: Acute vs. Delayed Effects

Acute Manifestations

- **Unique:** Bitter almond breath and body odor detectable by only 40% of the population
- **CNS:** Predominant progressive sx of anxiety, agitation, confusion, lethargy, seizures, coma, central tachypnea → agonal bradypnea

- **CV:** Initial ↓ HR and ↑ BP, then ↑ HR and ↓ BP, then myocardial failure
- **Skin:** Cherry-red skin color postmortem → cyanosis

Delayed Manifestations

- **CNS neurotoxicity predominates:** Confined to basal ganglia = globus pallidus, putamen, hippocampus (CT confirmation) → *Parkinsonism*, bradykinesia, dystonia, dysarthria, rigidity, L-dopa resistant.
- **Chronic low-level CN toxicity occurs in** (1) *tobacco amblyopia* (male smokers); (2) *tropical (cassava root) ataxic neuropathy*; and (3) *Leber's hereditary optic atrophy* (males). Mechanism: low endogenous stores of CN-detoxifying *hydroxocobalamin* and *thiosulfate*.

CN: Management

Lab Diagnosis

- Assess for metabolic acidosis with ABGs, central venous gas, serum lactate, glucose, electrolytes, renal function tests—BUN, creatinine
- Request serum and gastric aspirate CN levels
- Obtain baseline ECG
- Monitor with cooximetry for metHb and cyanmethemoglobin (cyanmetHb) after nitrites

Treatment

- **Decontamination (Decon):** Lavage + 1 g/kg activated charcoal (AC), remove all contaminated clothes and wash skin.
- **Antidote:** Cyanide kit® = (1) *amyl nitrite* insufflation and/or (2) IV 3% *sodium nitrite*, 10 mL over 30 min, (3) IV 25% *sodium thiosulfate*, 50 mL, to form less toxic excretable thiocyanate by the rhodanase–thiosulfate pathway.
- **Latest tx:** The B_{12} precursor, *hydroxocobalamin*, uses its cobalt to displace CN from cytochrome oxidase to form cyanocobalamin (vitamin B_{12}) subsequently metabolized to nontoxic metabolites by the same rhodanase–thiosulfate pathway.

Hydrogen Sulfide

- H_2S exposures and settings for poisoning
- Mechanisms of toxicity
- Clinical manifestations
- Management: Diagnosis and treatment

H_2S: Sources and Mechanisms

H_2S Sources of Exposures

- **Natural gas:** Bacterial decomposition of proteins, including vegetation, human sewage, animal remains and wastes, decaying fish → marsh–swamp gas

- **Natural events:** Volcanoes, sulfur springs, natural gas fields, marine vents, and tube worms
- **Industrial:** Paper mills, oil/gas refineries, leather tanning and manufacture

H_2S Toxic Pathophysiology

- *Rapid absorption* via lungs and easy membrane transit 2° high lipid solubility
- H_2S *inhibits cytochrome oxidase*, like CN, inhibiting oxidative phosphorylation and limiting aerobic ATP-generating energy production with resulting lactic acidosis
- H_2S *binds to endogenous metHb to form sulfmethemoglobin (sulfmetHb)* with even greater affinity than it binds to mitochondrial cytochrome oxidase
- *H_2S causes K-channel-mediated neuronal hyperpolarization* and potentiates neuronal inhibition

H_2S: Clinical Manifestations

Suspect H_2S Poisoning

- Anticipate a rapid "knock down" effect
- Rapid loss of consciousness
- Blackening and/or darkening of pocket change and any jewelry items—watch, necklace, and so on
- **Breath and body odor:** Rotten eggs
- **Low odor threshold:** 0.02–0.13 ppm
- **Mucosal irritation:** 50–150 ppm
- **Rapid olfactory fatigue and paralysis:** 100–150 ppm
- **Knock down, death:** 1000 + ppm

Confirm Clinical Suspicions

- **HEENT:** Severe mucosal irritation and edema, *keratoconjunctivitis* → corneal epithelial ulcers (*gas eye*), rhinitis
- **CV:** Bradycardia, angina
- **Pulm:** Dyspnea, cyanosis, bronchitis, cough, hemoptysis, pulmonary edema
- **GI:** Nonspecific N and V
- **CNS:** HA, weakness, dysequilibrium, seizures, coma, *purple brain* at autopsy
- Poison gas

H_2S: Management

Lab Diagnosis

- Assess for metabolic acidosis (ABGs) and elevated serum lactate levels
- Monitor metHb levels with cooximetry
- **MRI:** To assess delayed and often permanent neuropsychiatric sequelae 2° subcortical white matter demyelination and *globus pallidus* degeneration

Treatment

- **Prehospital:** Evacuate with SCBA, provide high-flow oxygen, provide best AW and support ventilation
- **Hospital:** Manage acidosis and provide inotropic support
- **Antidote:** (1) 3% *sodium nitrite*, 10 mL IV over 15 min, to induce *metHb* → *sulfmetHb*; (2) *HBO* if immediately available (Figures 29.3 and 29.4)

Causes of Methemoglobinemia from Hemolysis

Toxic RBC Oxidative Stressors

- **Nitrites:** Nitrate fertilizers → nitrites in well water; artificial nail removers: acetonitrile, nitroethane
- **Phenols:** Pentachlorophenol, dinitrophenol, creosol, creosote
- **Aniline dyes:** MBOCA—methylene-bis-chloroaniline (bladder cancer)
- **Poison gases:** Arsine, stilbene
- **Mothballs:** Naphthalene
- **Aromatics:** Benzidine (bladder cancer), xylidine, styrene
- **Hydrazines:** Hydrazine fuels, INH, gyromitrin

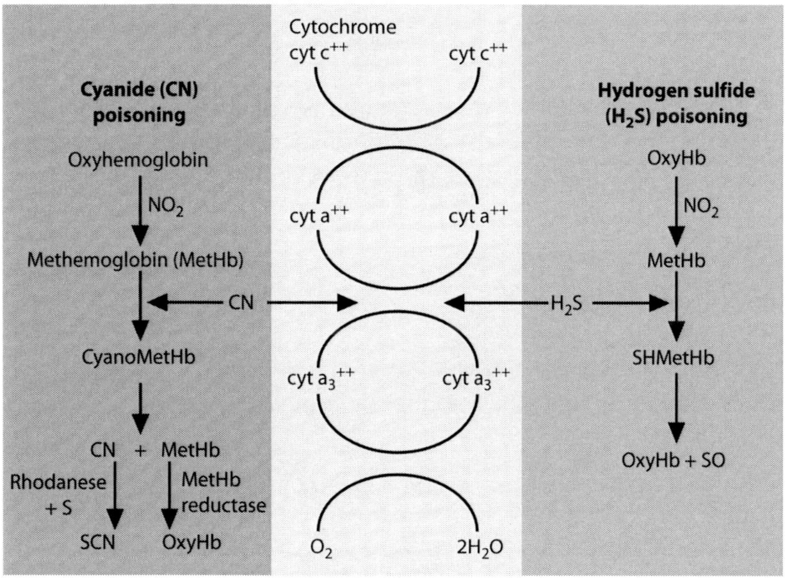

FIGURE 29.3 The shared toxicities and similarities in treatment strategies for cyanide or hydrogen cyanide gas poisonings. The shared impact of cyanide (CN) or hydrogen sulfide (H_2S) gas poisoning on the cytochrome oxidase electron transport system and the oxygenation of hemoglobin. The diagram also depicts the rationale for inducing methemoglobinemia with nitrites in the detoxification of both CN- and H_2S-poisoned patients.

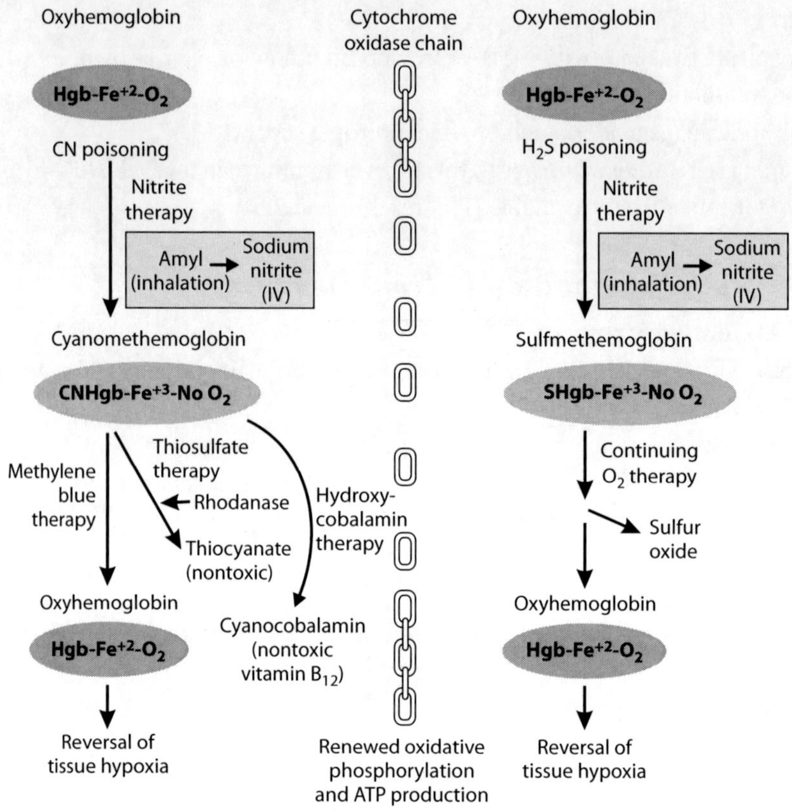

FIGURE 29.4 The pathophysiology and management of cyanide or hydrogen sulfide gas poisoning. Restoring the disrupted cytochrome oxidase chain in cyanide and hydrogen sulfide gas poisoning with specific and shared treatment strategies.

Pharmaceutical Oxidative Stressors

- **Antibiotics:** Sulfonamides, dapsone
- **Antimalarials:** Chloroquine, primaquine
- **Antiseptics:** Chlorates (in toothpastes and antiseptics), potassium permanganate, benzalkonium chloride
- **Antidotes:** High dose methylene blue for CN or H_2S poisoning
- **Vasodilators:** NTG, SCN
- **Misc:** *Metaclopramide* can cause both methemoglobinemai and sulfhemoglobinemia

"Tear" Gases

Riot Control Agents (Tear "Gas")

Agents and Properties (See Table 29.5)

Table 29.5 Most Commonly Used Tear Gases

Aerosol ("Gas")	Mechanism	Toxicity
Chloroacetophenone (CN), mace	Highly water-soluble irritant	Tearing, eye pain, dermal burns, cough, RADS
Chlorobenzylidene malononitrile (CS)	Same	Same
Capsaicin pepper spray = kinder gentler tear gas	Peripheral pain c-fibers release substance P causing neurogenic inflammation	Less oculotoxic, pulmonary edema, bronchospasm, possible RADS

- **Agents:** All are intense dermal and mucous membrane irritants and lacrimators and include (1) **CN:** chloracetophenone = Mace®; (2) **CS:** chlorobenzilidene malononitrile; and (3) **OC:** oleoresin capsicum = *capsaicin* = pepper spray.
- **Prop:** Volatile oily liquids disseminated as aerosols, sprays, and incendiary bombs for crowd control with rapid onset, short duration of action, and high safety profile. Severe reactions and deaths (CN, CS) from status asthmaticus possible after closed space exposures.

Clinical Manifestations and Tx

- **Clin:** Rapid onset of eye and skin burning, lacrimation, conjunctival injection, photophobia, blepharospasm, sneezing, rhinorrhea, cough, chest tightness, bronchorrhea, bronchospasm, possibly status asthmaticus.
- **Tx:** Initial disrobing then immediate copious cold water irrigation. *0.5% bleach solutions are contraindicated* and could exacerbate injuries. Lidocaine gel patches for topical tx of capsaicin exposure.

Incapacitating Agents

Vomiting Agent

- **DM:** Diphenylamine*arsine gas (Adamsite).*
- **Mech:** Arsine hydrolyzes sulfhydryl groups in mucosa, inhibits glycolysis, depletes glutathione, like Lewisite.
- **Clin:** Arsine gas induces initial eye and upper airway irritation, followed by headache, malaise, nausea, and severe vomiting with dehydration.
- **Tx:** Supportive with IV fluids.

Sedating Agent

- **BZ:** 3-Quinuclidinyl benzylate.
- **Mech:** A CNS-acting *anticholinergic*, 25× more potent than atropine (*Note:* Israel, 1991: >200 casualties occurred from self-inflicted atropine injection during the first Gulf War).

- **Clin:** Anticholinergic syndrome = "*Mad as a hatter, blind as a bat, hot as Hades, dry as a bone.*" Initial dry mouth and mydriasis, then delayed onset of incapacitating drowsiness, incoordination, reduced cognition, delirium, ↑ awakening over 2–3 days.
- **Tx:** Supportive only.

Poison Gas: Personal Protective Equipment Levels A–D (See Table 29.6)

Occupational Lung Diseases

Outline and Definitions

- **Pneumoconioses and occupational lung cancers:** Progressive pulmonary fibrosis and parenchymal lung diseases due to the inhalation (asbestos = 1 fiber) and deposition of mineral dusts in the lungs. Bronchogenic carcinoma > adenocarcinoma > mesothelioma.
- **Occupational asthma:** 5–15% of asthma; >250 workplace substances can cause asthma by (1) exacerbating preexisting asthma (work-aggravated asthma), (2) by exposing upper airways to potent water-soluble irritants (irritant asthma or reactive airways dysfunction syndrome [RADS]), or (3) by sensitizing the airways to allergic antigens (allergic asthma). Preexisting atopy predisposes to irritant, not allergic, asthma.
- **Inhalation fevers:** Self-limited fever with peripheral leukocytosis and little to no lung inflammation 6–12 h after inhalation exposure to causative workplace agents. Caused by soldering (colophony) and welding fluxes: Cu and Zn.

Pneumoconioses

Fibrogenic Dust Exposures

- Coal dust (CWP)
- Silica dust (silicosis)
- Asbestos fibers (asbestosis)
- Beryllium fumes (berylliosis)
- Talc powder (talcosis)
- Graphite particles (graphitosis)
- Mica or kaolin dusts
- Fuller's earth (DE)
- Mixed dust fibrosis

Nonfibrogenic Dust Exposures

- Iron (siderosis)
- Tin (stannosis)

Table 29.6 Personal Protective Equipment (PPE) OSHA/EPA Classification System

OSHA/EPA Classification Levels	Level A	Level B	Level C	Level D
Protection provided	Highest level of skin, eye, and respiratory protection	Highest level of respiratory protection, but lower level of skin protection	Lower levels of respiratory and skin protection, but adequate for radiation event response without other hazards present	Lowest level of respiratory and skin protection
Indications	Provides maximum protection for working in confined areas with unknown hazards	Provides maximum respiratory protection for working in hypoxic atmospheres (<19.5% oxygen)	Hazards have been identified, will not affect exposed skin, and all criteria for using an air purifying respirator have been met: (1) concentrations of all airborne known contaminants; (2) appropriate filters available; (3) oxygen levels >19.5%	The atmosphere contains no known hazards, and there is low to no risk for unexpected respiratory of skin contact with environmental hazards
Who should wear?	First responders to biological or chemical hazards	First responders in radiation zones or hypoxic atmospheres	First responders and first receivers when caring for radiation-contaminated victims	First receivers when working in post-decontamination areas for infection control purposes
Example		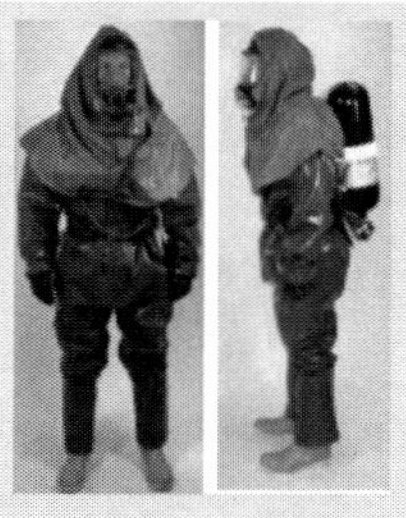		

Source: U.S. Department of Health and Human Services.

- Barium (baritosis)
- Tungsten (diamond polisher's lung)
- Cobalt (hard metal disease)

Granulomatous Pneumoconioses

- Berylliosis
- Silicotuberculosis
- Talcosis

Nongranulomatous Pneumoconioses

- Coal worker's pneumoconiosis (CWP)
- Silicosis
- Asbestosis
- Graphitosis

Pneumoconioses: Epidemiology 1

1. During 1968–2000, there were *124,846 deaths* from pneumoconiosis as recorded by the CDC National Center for Health Statistics (NCHS).
2. Comparing 1968–1981 male deaths to 1982–2000 deaths, death rates from *CWP declined by 36%*, death rates from *silicosis declined by 70%*, but death rates from *asbestosis increased by 400%* due to its latency period of 30–40 years.
3. CWP was the most frequently reported pneumoconiosis from 1968 until 1998, when it was *surpassed by asbestosis.*
4. Asbestosis deaths are increasing substantially in the United States, especially in *coastal states*, including Louisiana, where asbestosis was frequently used in *shipbuilding* until the 1970s.

Pneumoconioses: Epidemiology 2

1. In Western Europe, the incidence of asbestos-induced mesothelioma will peak between 2010 and 2020, and will cause over 250,000 deaths over the next 35 years, especially in family members of asbestos-exposed workers. The incidence of *erionite-induced mesothelioma* in Eastern Europe, Turkey, and Iraq remains incalculable. In these areas, *erionite* continues to be used in home, sidewalk, and road construction.
2. For 27 years, *asbestos-contaminated vermiculite ore* was shipped to 250 sites in the United States, including 4 sites in the New Orleans, Louisiana Metropolitan area.

Coal Worker's Pneumoconiosis (CWP) 1

- **Pathology:** Coal dust-filled pulmonary macrophages coalesce into *macules* and then migrate toward mediastinal nodes releasing proteolytic enzymes and attracting fibroblasts.

- **Risks:** Simultaneous coal and silica dust inhalation; smoking is not an independent risk factor for CWP.
- **CWP, lung bx:** Note the coal macules.

Coal Worker's Pneumoconioses 2

- **CXR:** Note *upper lobe* and mediastinal nodular opacities that appear to consolidate in a winged pattern of progressive massive pulmonary fibrosis (PMF) across the upper lobes and mediastinum (*"angel wings"* sign).
- **Tx:** Supportive only.

Coal Worker's Pneumoconioses 3

- **CWP gross section:** Note macules, nodules, necrosis, and peripheral obstructive emphysema.
- **CWP CXR:** Note the fluffy, nodular pattern of "angel wings."

Asbestosis 1

- **Pathology:** Sharp, pointed amphibolic (usually crocidolite) asbestos fibers penetrate parenchyma, resist degradation by macrophages, form *ferruginous asbestos bodies* in airspaces and interstitium, and migrate peripherally to cause reactive fibrosis in the lower lobes and pleurae (plaques).
- **Risks:** Smoking synergistically increases bronchogenic lung cancer risks (but not mesothelioma risks) 10× (RR smoking = 5, RR smoking + asbestos = 50). Mesothelioma, or pleural cancer, risks are independent of smoking and are shared by worker and family contacts (*"foul nest"*).
- **Asbestosis, lung bx:** Note ferruginous asbestos bodies in airspaces and interstitium.
- **Sputum specimen:** Note asbestos bodies.

Asbestosis 2

- **CXR:** Calcified pleural plaques in lower lobes and spread out over visceral and parietal pleurae, especially on diaphragmatic surfaces. Pleural effusions possible. All pathognomonic of asbestos exposure.
- **Tx:** Monitor for lung cancer and mesothelioma.
- **Asbestosis, LAO CXR:** Note calcified pleural plaques and densities confined to lower lobes.

Asbestosis 3

- **Asbestosis, gross lung specimen:** Note lower lobe fibrosis and pleural thickening.
- **Asbestosis, gross lung specimen:** Parietal pleural plaques.

Occupationally Related Lung Cancer

Smoking potentiates the risks of lung cancer from occupational exposures = (occupational exposures ± smoking = lung cancer)*

Squamous Cell (Bronchogenic) Carcinoma Etiologies

- Arsenic
- Asbestos
- Cadmium
- Chromium
- Mustard gas
- Nickel
- Uranium → Radon
- Silica
- Soot, tar (PAHs)

Small-Cell (Oat Cell) Adenocarcinoma Etiologies

Asbestos

- Bis-chloromethyl and other methylethyl ethers
- Second-hand tobacco smoke (ETS)

Mesothelioma

Asbestos

- Asbestos workers or their clothes or lunchboxes
- **Erionite**—an asbestos-like mineral fiber mined in Turkey and used in domestic whitewashes and cements

Asbestos and Cancer 1

- **Source:** Autopsy evaluation of known asbestos exposure
- **Authors:** King JAC, Wong SW, USA, Mobile. SMJ 1996; 89: 380–5
- **Design:** Retrospective study of 135 autopsies, mostly male shipyard workers
- **Mean age at death:** 72 years
- **Smoking hx:** 73%

Results

- **Pleural plaques:** 61%
- **Asbestos bodies:** 30% H&E, 80% Clorox® digestion
- **Lung/pleural cancer:** 62.4%
- **Mesothelioma:** 21

* U.S. lung cancers: 95% from smoking or ETS ± 5% occupational exposures.

- **Adenocarcinoma:** 19
- **Squamous cell:** 17
- **Small (oat) cell:** 8
- **Large cell:** 6
- **Total:** n = 71

Asbestosis and Cancer 2

- **Nodular adenocarcinoma:** Forms in peripheral pleural plaque—scar.
- **CXR, nodular adenocarcinoma:** Note nodular shape of scar cancer originating in pleural plaque.

Asbestosis and Cancer 3

- **Squamous cell carcinoma:** Hilar tumor invading bronchus
- **Pleural mesothelioma:** Inoperable cancer encasing lung; invading fissure, chest wall, pericardium

Asbestosis and Cancer 4

- **Mesothelioma, R lung:** Note hemorrhagic pleural effusion.
- **Mesothelioma, R lung, CXR:** Note shadow over entire R lung + pleural effusion.

Familial Mesothelioma—Foul Nest Syndrome

- **Denmark, 1989:** Three members of a family of six home-producing an asbestos (amosite)-contaminated gypsum board filler, *Rollfix*
- **United Kingdom, 1991:** 17 familial cases 15 known exposures +2 unexposed sisters of asbestos workers
- **Italy, 1993:** 8 cases, 2 pairs exposed father and son; 2 pairs exposed husband worker + unexposed wife
- **Rollfix:** A locally made asbestos (amosite)-contaminated home repair product

Silicosis 1—Pathology

- **Pathology:** Quartz-like silica (sand) crystals are ingested by macrophages which then release proteolytic enzymes and attract fibroblasts to form fibrous nodules (*silicotic nodules*) of concentric collagen fibers in pathognomonic "onionskin" arrangements that later migrate to the mediastinum and upper lobes and often calcify.
- **Risks:** Silicosis significantly increases risks of contracting TB (not that communicable) and TB + silicosis = silicotuberculosis = accelerated progressive massive fibrosis (PMF).
- **Typical silicotic nodule, lung biopsy:** Note "*onionskin*" arrangement of collagen.

Silicosis 2—Early Stage

- **CXR:** *Simple silicosis* demonstrates a bilateral upper lobe pattern of numerous interstitial nodules ("*silicotic nodules*"). In this case, there has been increasing pulmonary hypertension with smoking-associated COPD and cardiomegaly (note enlarged heart > 50% CT width).

- **Tx:** Supportive only, prevention is best.

Silicosis 3—Progression

- **CXR:** In *later silicosis*, hilar lymph nodes will calcify and silicotic nodules in the upper lobes will coalesce in a pattern of bilateral massive fibrosis. In this case, progressive fibrosis is present in the right upper lobe only (black arrows). A similar pattern will develop in the left upper lobe to create the "angel's wings" pattern of progressive massive fibrosis (PMF).
- **Tx:** Supportive only, prevention is best.

Silicosis 4—Late (PMF) Stage

- **CXR:** In late stage silicosis, the fibrosis in the upper lobes will coalesce in a pattern of bilateral massive fibrosis filling the upper lobes and mediastinum in a unique "angel wings" pattern with hyperlucency in the spared bases from secondary obstructive emphysema. Note flattened hemidiaphragms and "hanging heart."
- **Tx:** Supportive only, prevention is best.

Silicosis 5—PMF Pathology

- **Complicated silicosis:** Note massive nodular fibrosis (PMF) and thick adhesive pleura.
- **CXR, PMF:** Note "angel wing" fibrotic opacification and basilar obstructive emphysma.
- **Complications:** Silicotuberculosis.
- **Silicotb, gross:** Note cavitary TB superimposed on silicotic nodules.
- **Silicotb, CXR:** Note upper lobe cavitary TB + nodular fibrosis.

Silicosis ± Rheumatoid Arthritis ± CWP

- **Caplan's syn:** Note rheumatoid (Caplan's) nodules + silicotic nodules + coal macules.
- **Caplan's syndrome:** Note bilateral Caplan's nodules and diffuse fibrosis.

Berylliosis 1

- **Pathology:** An immunologic allergic response to the beryllium antigen may result in a sarcoid or TB-like lung disease characterized by the development of reactive granulomas with central multinucleated giant cells and an inner surrounding cuff of lymphocytes and outer fibrous collagen. Similar lesions may also develop in the skin and upper airway mucosa.
- **Dx:** + lymphocyte proliferation test.
- **Risks:** Only short exposures to the strategic metal may result in berylliosis in uniquely immunologically predisposed individuals.
- **Tx:** Supportive.
- **Beryllium granuloma:** Sarcoid-like granuloma with central giant cells and ringing cuffs of lymphocytes and collagen.

Berylliosis 2—Dx

- **Beryllium lymphocyte proliferation test:** A peripheral blood response to beryllium antigen that causes an organized granulomatous proliferation of lymphocytes in beryllium-sensitized workers at risk of chronic beryllium disease.

Berylliosis 3

- **Chronic beryllium disease:** Granuloma
- **Chronic beryllium disease:** Multinucleated giant cells with Schaumann bodies

Miscellaneous Fibropneumoconioses

- **Kaolin pneumoconiosis:** Note whorled fibrous nodules and smaller nodules.
- **Fuller's earth pneumoconiosis:** Note masses of earth-colored (brown) pigment within macrophages in perivascular orientation.

Miscellaneous Fibropneumoconioses

- **Graphitosis, lung bx:** Note black graphite deposits within macrophages and extensive fibrosis.
- **Mixed dust fibrosis, lung bx—welder:** Note fibrosis surrounding deposits of iron oxide (rust), silica, and carbon.

Miscellaneous Nonfibrogenic Pneumoconioses

- **Siderosis:** Brick-colored discoloration + mild nodular fibrosis. Normal CXR.
- **Tungsten (diamond polisher's lung):** Note WBCs and giant cells in alveoli + interstitial inflammation and ↑ collagen.

Occupational "Asthma"

Runny Noses and Nasal Ulcers: Not Asthma

Rhinorrhea

- Cold air.
- Most pesticides, esp. OPs, carbamates, pyrethrins and pyrethroids. OCs = shakes and seizures.

Nasal Ulcers, Septal Perforation

- Arsenic
- Chromium
- Copper
- Nickel

Allergen-Induced Occ Asthma Extrinsic Allergic Alveolitis

- **Baking dusts:** Wheat, rye, soy, buckwheat, gluten, amylase—all of which can contain allergenic mites and fungi
- Animal feed, grain and wood dusts
- **Latex:** On exam and surgical gloves and cornstarch coatings
- Pollen and mold spores
- **Experimental animal antigens:** Rats, hamsters, guinea pigs
- **Acid anhydrides:** TMAs
- **Psyllium seeds:** Metamucil®, Konsyl®

Asthma-Inducing Irritants

- Acid–alkaline solvents
- Ammonia
- Environmental tobacco smoke
- Hypochlorous bleaches (Chlorox®)
- **Cutting oils:** For metalworking
- **Ozone:** Welding fumes
- Sulfur dioxide
- **VOCs:** Paints, thinners, solvents, dry cleaners—CCL_4, perchloroethylene

Asthma-Inducing Organic Toxins and Inorganic Toxicants

- Acid anhydrides (TMIs), aldehydes, and aryl acrylates
- All animal proteins
- **Cadmium:** Not just metal fume fever, but small AWs disease = asthma
- Cobalt fumes and dust
- Ethylene diamines and most amines
- **Formaldehydes and most glutaraldehydes:** Tissue preserving and medical instrument cleaning solutions
- **Most isocyanates:** Especially toluene diisocyanates

Occupational "Asthma"—Farmer's Lung

- **Farmer's lung (and mushroom picker's lung):** From inhalation of moldy hay dust with the thermophilic actinomycete, *Micropolyspora faeni*.
- **Farmer's lung:** Note massive subpleural and interstitial inflammatory cell infiltration with extensive fibrosis.

Occupational "Asthma"—Bagassosis

- **Bagassosis:** From inhalation of dried bagasse dust containing spores of the thermophilic actinomycete, *Thermoactinomyces saccharii*.
- **Bagassosis, chronic:** Note massive fibrosis and bullous emphysema. Note vacuolated macrophages filling alveoli on the lung biopsy.

Inhalation Fevers

Organic Fevers

- **Definition:** Transient fever, cough, dyspnea, and leukocytosis with normal CXR resulting from indoor inhalation of microbially contaminated humidified air or dusts from decomposing vegetation or cotton dust. Include:
  - Byssinosis (cotton dust)
  - Flax, hemp, jute dusts
  - Humidifier fever
  - Moldy hay
  - Grass clippings
  - Compost—mulch
  - Wood chips—western red cedar

Fume Fevers and Pneumonias

Metal Fume Fevers

- Zinc (zinc oxide): Zinc and copper welding fumes are the most common causes of metal fume fevers.
- Copper.
- **Mn and Cd:** Acute pneumonitis, manganic pneumonia.

Metal Fume Pneumonias and Interstitial Pneumonitis

- Cadmium
- Manganese (manganic pneumonia [pn])
- **Cobalt:** Diamond polishers' lung

Polymer Fume Fever

- Polytetrafluoroethylene
- (Teflon®)

Conclusions

- All industrial exposures and occupational lung diseases are *not specifically treatable, but preventable.*
- People who *smoke are at logistically increased risks of contracting occupational asthma and lower airway diseases.*
- Up to *15% of all asthma is due to workplace allergens. Most (>90%) asthma is caused by exposure to workplace and domestic (home) allergens.*
- All workers can be protected by *substitution, engineering controls, and PPEs.*

Chapter 30

Metal and Metalloid Poisonings

Outline 674
Metal Poisoning 674
Arsenic 674
Cadmium 677
Chromium 679
Iron 680
Lead 682
Heme Inhibition and Anemia 687
Clinical Findings in Children and Adults 689
Lead Poisoning: Public Health Case Correlations 693
Where Are the Soil Lead Hot Spots in Cities? 694
Mercury 694
Thallium 697
Heavy Metal Poisoning: Minor Metal Toxicities 699

Outline

- Major metal toxicity
  - Arsenic
  - Cadmium
  - Chromium
  - Iron
  - Lead
  - Mercury
  - Thallium
- Minor metal toxicity
  - Aluminum
  - Bismuth
  - Cobalt
  - Copper
  - Manganese
  - Nickel
  - Selenium
  - Tin
  - Zinc

Metal Poisoning

Definitions

- **Metalloids:** Elements with the characteristics of both metals and nonmetals that often combine with metals to form alloys; metalloids make good semiconductors (Intel® processors). Ex: As and Sb.
- **Transition metals:** Elements that can only donate and not accept electrons and are characterized by multiple valences and many colors. Ex: Cu and Mn.
- Metals, metalloids, and nonmetals metalloids = transition metals.

Arsenic

Forms and Uses

Forms of Arsenic

- **Elemental:** Nontoxic
- **Gaseous:** Arsine gas—highly toxic, ARDS, acute hemolysis with resulting acute tubular necrosis (ATN), high case fatality rate (CFR)
- **Inorganic:** As (arsenic trioxide—As^{3+} and arsenic pentoxide—As^{5+})
- **Organic:** As = arsenobetaine (nontoxic, concentrated by shellfish, especially oysters)

Uses (Inorganic Arsenics)

- **Pesticides:** As^{3+} arsenic trioxide:
  - Wood and deck preservatives.
  - *Chromated copper arsenate*-treated pine decks—*Pets with prolonged contact with arsenic-treated decks have developed skin cancers.*
  - Outdoor furniture and play sets (most replaced by plastic play stations).
  - Antiparasitics.
- **Cancer chemotherapy:** Arsenic trioxide
- **Electronics manufacture:** Semiconductors
  - **Semiconductors:** Gallium arsenide coatings in microprocessors
- **Folk remedies:** Depilatories, elixirs

Arsenic: Toxicology

Absorption/Distribution

- Tasteless and odorless
- Well absorbed rapidly
- Pulmonary inhalation (especially arsine gas) > GI (inorganics) > dermal
- Systemic distribution once absorbed, especially to liver and kidneys, and also to skin, hair, and nails with toxic effects
- Arsenicals can remain as *radiopaque* metal sludge in small intestine (SI)← enterohepatic circulation

Metabolism/Excretion

- Rapid hepatic *methylation* to *methyl*arsonic acid (MAA) and di*methyl*arsinic acid (DMA)—methylation requires *glutathione*
- *Glutathione depletion* is common in alcoholics and malnourished, will ↓ *methylation* and ↑ toxicity of arsenicals
- Renal excretion (90%) > GI—fecal > dermal—hair and nails

Arsenic: Pathophysiology

1. Reduced glucose production from impaired gluconeogenesis from pyruvate
2. Reduced glucose uptake and utilization
3. Reduced production of high-energy ATP by oxidative phosphorylation
4. *Rapid glucose depletion* with severe *hypoglycemia*, especially in the CNS and PNS

Arsenic: Clinical Effects

Acute Toxicity

- **GI:** Initial sx—metallic taste, garlic breath, nausea (N), vomiting (V), cramps, rice-water (cholera-like) diarrhea
- **CV:** Instability, orthostasis

- **CNS:** Encephalopathy, seizures, coma
- **Pulm:** ARDS and respiratory failure
- **Hepatorenal:** Rhabdomyolysis + acute hemolytic anemia → acute tubular necrosis (ATN), especially in glutathione-depleted persons (alcoholics)

Chronic Toxicity

- **PNS:** Stocking (feet) > *glove peripheral sensory neuropathy*, ↓ pain–touch–position–temp–vibration sensation, ↓ DTRs → *ascending flaccid paralysis*; partial sensorimotor recovery only, even after chelation
- **CNS:** Encephalopathy, cranial nerve (CN) palsies, dementia
- **Peripheral vascular system (PVS):** Blackfoot disease (PVD)
- **Dermal:** Hyperpigmentation–hyperkeratosis → *skin cancer* (squamous, basal cell, Bowen's disease), Mees' lines on nails
- **Pulm:** *Lung cancer*
- **Arsenic:** Dermal effects—skin cancers and grooved fingernails (Mees' lines)
- Arsenical hyperkeratosis (premalignant)
- Arsenical epidermoid (squamous) cancer
- Arsenical hyperkeratoses
- Arsenical Bowen's disease
- Arsenical Mees' lines (keratin destruction of nails)

Arsenic: "Blackfoot" Disease

"Blackfoot" Disease 1

Definition: Accelerated *peripheral vascular disease* of the lower extremities causing *dry gangrene and auto-amputation* caused by high arsenic levels in drinking well water (endemic in Taiwan, India, Bangladesh) and also associated with As-induced skin, liver (hepatic angiosarcoma), and lung cancers.

"Blackfoot" Disease 2

- Blackfoot discoloration of toes and feet
- Blackfoot auto-amputation toes and feet

Arsenic: Diagnosis and Treatment

Diagnosis

- **Labs:** *Urine* spot As + 24-h urine As R/O organic As from shellfish ingestion: By liquid separation chromatography CBC, LFTs, RFTs, hair and nail As
- **X-rays:** Flat abdomen for *radiopaque sludge* in stomach and SI

Treatment

1. Orogastric (OG) lavage if radiopaque sludge present, then whole bowel irrigation (WBI) with polyethylene glycol electrolyte (PEG) solution

2. Glucose and nutritional support
3. Monitor for respiratory failure using negative inspiratory forces (NIFs)
4. **Chelation:** *BAL intramuscularly (IM)* > succimer po > penicillamine po
5. Hemodialysis for ATN

Cadmium

Uses and Exposures

Uses of Cadmium

- **Electroplating:** Silverware
- **Glazing:** Pots, pans, utensils
- **Soldering:** Hot and cold vending machines
- **Warning—cadmium:** Coffee and hot chocolate from vending machines
- **Batteries:** Nickel–cadmium
- Paint pigments
- Film manufacture

Exposures to Cadmium

- **Vapor and fume inhalation:** Occupational
- **Ingestion:** Acidic foods and acidic liquids and wines contaminated by cadmium leached from cadmium-glazed containers and pitchers

Cadmium: Toxicology

Absorption/Distribution

- Inhalation > GI absorption
- Rapid transport to liver for binding with its specific metal transport protein, *metallothionein*
- Circulatory transport of *bound Cd to kidneys* for glomerular filtration and proximal tubular reabsorption
- Bound Cd concentrated in *kidneys > bone > liver*

Metabolism/Excretion

- Cadmium is not biotransformed.
- As *hepatic* and *then renal metallothionein production is overwhelmed*, unbound Cd is distributed to *kidneys* and *bone*, where it establishes a reservoir pool (like lead in bone).
- Slow renal elimination with T1/2 = 7–30 years.

Cadmium: Pathophysiology

1. Once the stores of *metallothionein*-binding protein are depleted and the *hepatorenal protein synthesizing capabilities are overwhelmed*, free toxic Cd is distributed to *kidneys ≥ bone ≥ liver.*

2. Chronic Cd nephrotoxicity causes a *Fanconi's syndrome* of *aminoaciduria, glucosuria, calciuria-hyperphosphaturia, and metabolic acidosis* (RTA) ↓ concentrating ability, and nephrolithiasis 2° ↑ excretion of Ca and P.
3. Urinary *calcium loss* results in *osteomalacia* with pathologic fractures (*itai-itai* or "ouch-ouch" disease).
4. Chronic inhalation exposure causes emphysema that *initially mimics metal fume fever* and later causes *pulmonary fibrosis.*
5. Chronic Cd exposures cause ↑ *lung (not prostate) cancers.*

Cadmium: Clinical Effects

Acute Toxicity

- **GI:** Nausea (N), vomiting (V), diarrhea (D)
- **Pulm:** Acute chemical pneumonitis > mimics "metal fume fever" but worse → pulmonary edema, ARDS, later pulmonary fibrosis
- **Renal:** Proximal tubular dysfunction and proteinuria = *Fanconi's syndrome*

Chronic Toxicity

- **Pulm:** Emphysema, pulmonary fibrosis, lung cancer
- **GU/renal:** Reduced GFR, ↑ spilling of Ca and PO_4 in urine, CRF often associated with *nephrolithiasis* (Ca phosphate kidney stones)
- **Bone:** *Demineralization, osteomalacia*, accelerated osteoporosis, pathologic fractures (*itai-itai* or "ouch-ouch" disease)

Cadmium: Diagnosis and Treatment

Diagnosis

- Urine > serum Cd
- **Serum Cd:** Unhelpful and not reflective of body burden as Cd is protein bound to its transporter protein metallothionein in kidneys > liver
- Urine metallothionein levels
- Increasing proteinuria and glucosuria reflecting early Fanconi's syndrome

Treatment

- Gastric evacuation and catharsis.
- Pulmonary support.
- Remove from exposure sources.
- *Chelation is absolutely contraindicated* as it will increase renal cadmium load and further deplete metallothionein, *increasing nephrotoxicity.*

Chromium

Uses and Exposures

Uses of Chromium

- Cement mix
- Electroplating
- Alloys
- Chrome
- Yellow paint pigment
- Wood preservatives
- Leather tanning

Exposures to Chromium

- Mining
- Stainless-steel machining
- Chrome-plating
- Refrigeration plumbing

Chromium: Toxicology

Absorption/Distribution

- Toxicity increases with *valency* of Cr from trivalent +3 to hexavalent +6
- **Hexavalent** Cr^{6+} is more toxic than the relatively nontoxic and insoluble *trivalent* Cr^{3+}
- Inhalation—pulmonary > GI > dermal absorption
- Concentrated in lungs > kidneys > liver

Metabolism/Excretion

- Not metabolized.
- Soluble hexavalent Cr^{6+} is oxidized and reduced on entering the body to trivalent Cr^{3+}, which is trapped in RBCs for 120 days.
- Excretion is primarily renal > bile and feces > sweat, hair, nails, breast milk.

Chromium: Pathophysiology

1. Caustic, *soluble hexavalent chromium* is rapidly absorbed, particularly by the *lungs.*
2. As soon as hexavalent chromium enters the body, it is *reduced to insoluble trivalent chromium*, which is *trapped within RBCs* until they expire in 120 days.
3. Hexavalent chromium is more readily absorbed and concentrated in the *airways and lungs*, where it acts as a pulmonary *irritant, sensitizer, and carcinogen (lung and sinus).*

Chromium: Clinical Effects

Acute Toxicity

- **Pulm:** Caustic irritation—burning, acute bronchitis, rhinitis, sinusitis, mucosal ulceration, *nasal septal perforation*
- **Skin:** Caustic thermal burns and ulcerations = "*chrome holes*"
- **Renal:** Hemolytic anemia, proximal tubular damage (*Fanconi's syndrome*), ATN
- **Hepatic:** Hepatotoxicity

Chronic Toxicity

- **Pulm:** Chronic bronchitis, rhinitis, sinusitis, nasal septal perforation, occupational asthma, pneumoconiosis, ↑ *nasal* and *lung cancers*
- **Skin:** Nonhealing chrome holes, irritant dermatitis = type IV dermal hypersensitivity reactions (rxns)
- **Renal:** Chronic interstitial nephritis → CRF

Chromium: Dermal Effects

1. Cr^{6+} cement irritant dermatitis from cement contact (usually feet and ankles)
2. Cr^{6+} cement caustic burns
3. Chrome holes, fingers
4. Chrome hole, nasal septum

Chromium: Diagnosis and Treatment

Diagnosis

- Urine > blood chromium levels
- Avoid provocative skin patch testing as it frequently causes skin sensitization to future chromium exposures

Treatment

- **Immediate decontamination:** Remove clothing and shower
- Induced *vomiting contraindicated* as Cr^{6+} is a strong caustic alkali
- 10% topical *ascorbic acid* (vitamin C) to (1) *reduce* $Cr^{6\pm}$ *to nontoxic* $Cr^{3\pm}$ then (2) *chelate reduced* $Cr^{3\pm}$ *with topical 10%* $CaNa_2EDTA$
- Consider careful *NG lavage with oral ascorbic acid and NAC*, followed by *IV ascorbic acid and po NAC* for severe poisoning

Iron

Epidemiology of Iron Poisoning

- **Epid:** 30% of pediatric ingestion deaths, 1999–2001
- **Fe content:** Ferrous gluconate 11–12%, ferrous sulfate 20%, ferrous fumarate 33%

- **Dose:** Toxic dose = 20–60 mg/kg, fatal dose > 60 mg/kg; > 500 mcg/dL
- **MoA:** (1) Caustic corrosion GI mucosa, (2) severe metabolic acidosis, (3) inhibition of oxidative phosphorylation, (4) periportal hepatic necrosis, (5) GI strictures in survivors
- **Abdominal x-ray:** Radio-opaque iron containing tabs in the stomach of a child

Stages of Iron Toxicity

- **Stages:** I: Bloody vomit and diarrhea within 6 h, II: latency between 6 and 18 h, III: acidosis and hypovolemic shock by 24 h, IV: liver failure by day 2–3, V: GI strictures within weeks, repeated operations.
- **Dx:** Radio-opaque pills in stomach (CHIPS), serum Fe > 500 mcg/dL, TIBC useless.
- **Tx:** No ipecac or AC, IVFs, $NaHCO_3$, monitor LFTs, consider WBI, deferoxamine chelation = 100 mg chelates 8.5 mg Fe.
- Deferoxamine chelation and urine color is useless; use serum Fe levels to follow efficacy of therapy.

Iron-Containing Preparations	Tab (mg)	% Fe	Mg Fe/tab
Ferrous gluconate	325	12%	40
Ferrous sulfate	325	20%	65
Ferrous fumarate (OB)	325	33%	107
Pedi multivitamin	NA	NA	10–18
Adult multivitamin	NA	NA	3–100
Prenatal multivitamin	NA	NA	10–100
Toxic dose	20–60 mg/kg ingested, >500 mcg/dL blood level		
Fatal dose	>60 mg/kg ingested, >500 mcg/dL blood level		

Is there a potential for iron toxicity in cases of overingestion of pediatric vitamin tablets that contain iron?

How many tabs did he take?

Treatment of Iron Poisoning

Fe Chelating Agent

- **Deferoxamine (desferrioxamine):** A specific chelator for *iron* is extracted from the bacterium, *Streptomyces pilosus*; may be given IV (*15 mg/kg/h*) > IM; *binds only free Fe and not Fe in transferrin or Hgb*; binds Fe on a molar basis 1-to-1, *100 mg binds 9 mg Fe*; can acutely cause histamine-mediated vasodilation with ↓ BP, and *free radical-induced lung injury*; chronically associated with hemosiderosis/iron overload and *Yersinia enterocolitica* and *Vibrio vulnificus* (oysters) septicemia by serving as a siderophore to chelate Fe for bacteria that cannot absorb iron naturally.

Lead

Lead Poisoning

Outline

- Uses and sources of exposure
- Toxicology
- Pathophysiology
- Clinical findings
- Diagnosis
- Treatment
- Public health case correlations

Uses of Lead

Inorganic Leads

- Pb arsenate—insecticides
- Pb azide—explosive bullet primers
- Pb carbonate—white paints
- Pb chromate—*yellow (pastel) paints*
- Pb oxide—*red (dark) and all rust-proof and marine (bridge) paints*
- Pb silicate—ceramic glazes
- Pb sulfide—natural ore galena causes *Burton's lines*

Organic Leads (Antiknock Gasoline Additives)

- Tetraethyl Pb—U.S. gasoline additive until 1978
- Tetramethyl Pb—U.S. gasoline additive until 1978
- Antiknock additives—Replaced by MTBE (LUST* epidemic), but still in use for agricultural and military vehicles and all vehicles in the developing world

Sources of Pb Exposure 1

Primary Sources

- **Paints:** 3 M tons in 57 M pre-1980 buildings
- **Soil:** Paint residues ("yuppie plumbism") + leaded gas emissions + lead recycling/smelting emissions
- **Water:** Lead pipes and solder in pre-1980 buildings; lead glazed crystal, cooking utensils and pots, water coolers

Secondary Sources

- **Air:** 500 tons from battery and radiator recycling, agricultural/military leaded gasoline use

* Leaking underground storage tanks. NB. Organic Pb converted to inorganic in man.

- **Food:** 1% of cans Pb soldering, animal bone—natural Ca supplements, alcohol/wine in lead crystal decanters, acidic fruit juices in ceramic glassware, "moonshine" whisky made in radiator and lead pipe stills

Battery Manufacture (2/3 of All U.S. Lead Use)

Sources of Pb Exposure

Exotic and Underreported Lead Exposures

1. Folk remedies, cosmetics, spices, and homemade "candies"—in every ethnicity (especially Hispanic = Mexican and Cuban, Indian, SE Asian). Ex: "*greta*" *and* "*azarcon*" as prominent indigestion or traveler's diarrhea remedies and after dinner "mints"
2. Lead-beaded jewelry, amulets—"protection strings." India and SE Asia: Cambodia, Vietnam—Hmong, Laos
3. Retained bullets/shrapnel (joint, pleural spaces)
4. Ingested foreign bodies—toys, jewelry
5. Gasoline (leaded) huffing
6. Many hobbies—ceramics, painting, stained glass, target shooting, bullet/cartridge reloading, auto and boat repairs, model boat building, building and restoring cannons

Pathophysiological Effects of Lead Poisoning (Table 30.1, Figures 30.1 through 30.3)

Primary Effects

1. Neurologic
2. Hematologic
3. Renal
4. Reproductive

Secondary Effects

1. Endocrine
2. Skeletal

Table 30.1 Lead Toxicity

Absorption	Distribution	Excretion
Adults: inhalation > ingestion—GI (occupational)	First blood pool—99% RBC bound	Urine > bile > sweat > hair
Particles <1 m	Labile ST pool	Urine 65%
Inhalation 30–40% Ingestion—GI 10–15%	Stable ST pool brain > kid > liver	Bile 35%
Children: GI > inh, GI 40–50%	Lab. trabecular bone pool	T1/2 blood: weeks–months
Rapid placental transfer	Stable cortical bone pool	T1/2 bone: 10–20 years

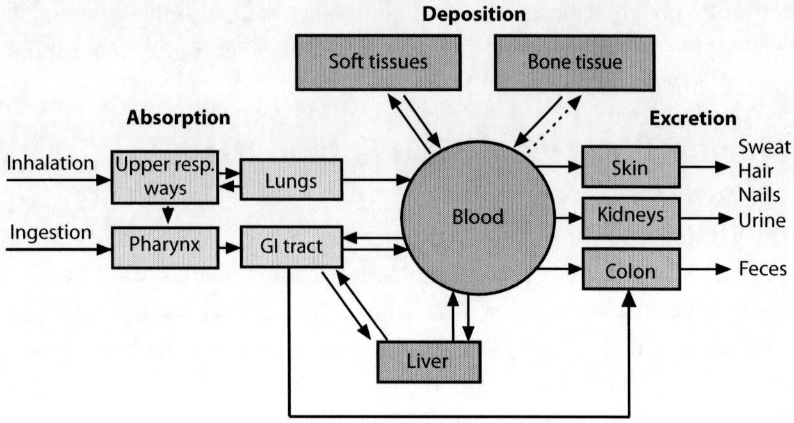

FIGURE 30.1 Biotransformation model of lead poisoning.

3. Gastrointestinal
4. Cardiac

Primary Effects of Lead Poisoning Neurotoxicity

Central Nervous System (Targeted in Children)

- Inhibits Ach, dopa, NE, GABA, NMDA, glutamate trans, blocks vascular Ca channels and Na–K ATPase in mitochondria

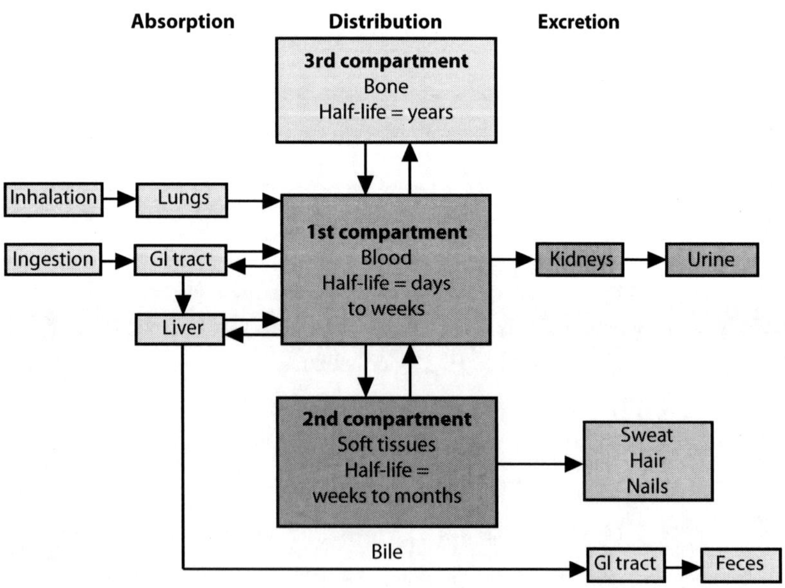

FIGURE 30.2 Ingested lead distribution in a three-compartment model.

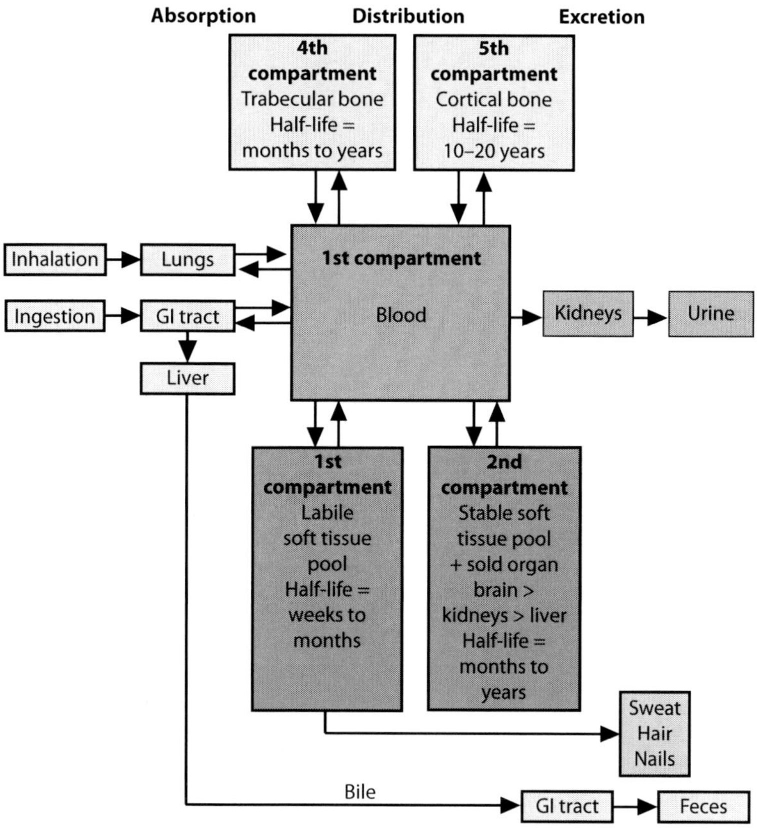

FIGURE 30.3 Ingested lead distribution in a five-compartment model.

- Targets cortex, cerebellum, and occipital lobes
- Acute encephalopathy— ↑ ICP, seizures, and coma
- **Children:** Hearing, cognition, IQ, developmental, motor, and coordination disorders (Figure 30.4)

Peripheral Nervous System (Targeted in Adults)

- Schwann cell necrosis and demyelination (adults)
- Reduced peripheral nerve conduction amplitude and velocity, UE > LE
- *Motor* > sensory neuropathy
- *Wrist drop* ("*dangles*") > foot drop: described by Ben Franklin in colonial printers (Table 30.2)

↓ Hemoglobin Synthesis (Table 30.2)

- **Stimulates:** ALA synthetase
- **Inhibits:** δ-ALA dehydratase (initially), coproporphrinogen decarboxylase, ferrochelatase

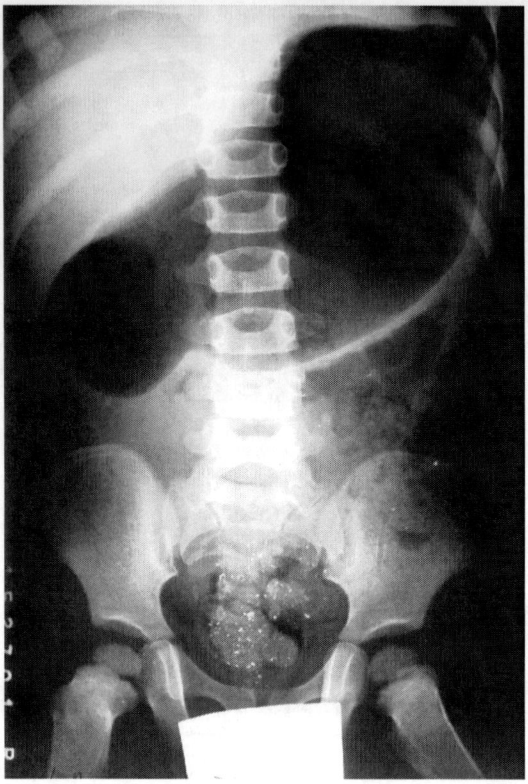

FIGURE 30.4 Lead paint chips in the GI tract of a 3-year-old.

- **Anemia:** Normochromic (early)-to-hypochromic (late) microcytic anemia
- **Organic leads:** (Tetraethyl Pb): trimethyl Pb metabolite—N, V, ↑DTRs, tremor, and encephalopathy; but *do not inhibit heme synthesis or cause anemia*

Reduced RBC Integrity

- ↓ Red blood cell (RBC) survival + ↓ erythropoietin = *anemia*
- ↑ RBC membrane fragility → *hemolysis* → *anemia*
- *Basophilic stippling* of RBCs—2° Pb's inhibition of *pyrimidine-5′-nucleotidase and inability to remove degraded RNA*, which then combines with fragments of damaged mitochondria and other microsomal remnants

Table 30.2 Lead Hemotoxicity

Heme Enzymes Inhibited	Heme Substrates Accumulating	Location of Substrates
Delta ALA dehydratase	Delta aminolevulinic acid	Urine and plasma
Coproporphyrinogen decarboxylase	Coproporphyrinogen III	Urine
Ferrochelatase	Protoporphyrin IX	RBCs

Heme Inhibition and Anemia

See Figure 30.5.

Nephrotoxicity (Table 30.3)

Lead Nephropathy

- Adults > children
- Nuclear inclusions from lead–protein complexes in *proximal tubular cells* and their casts
- **Fanconi's syndrome:** Aminoaciduria, glycosuria, phosphaturia, renal tubular acidosis (RTA)
- *CRF* 2° tubular atrophy initially and later fibrosis
- *Renovascular HTN* 2° ↑ renin (adults only) (Table 30.3)

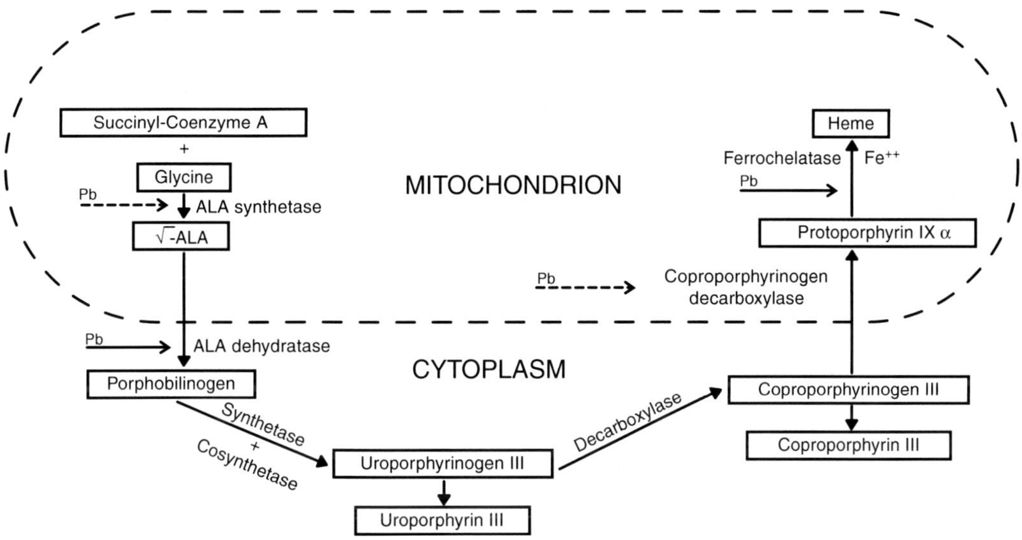

FIGURE 30.5 Mechanism of anemia in lead poisoning.

Table 30.3 Comparative Nephrotoxicities of Heavy Metals

Metal	Proximal Convoluted Tubule (PCT) Necrosis	Fanconi's Syndrome	CRF	Nephrotic Syndrome
Cadmium	+	+	+	0
Copper	+	+	+	0
Gold	+	0	+	+
Mercury	+	0	+	+
Lead	+	+	+	0
Thallium	+	0	0	+

"Saturnine" Gout

- **Saturn:** Roman god of agriculture and vineyards; red wines leach Pb out of lead-glazed and leaded glass decanters, Pb plumbing
- Adults—common > children—rare
- ↓ Renal uric acid excretion
- ↑ Serum uric acid = "saturnine" gout
- **Gout:** Uric acid crystal deposition in joints (gouty arthropathy), kidneys (urolithiasis), and skin (tophi)

Secondary Effects of Lead Poisoning

Reproductive Toxicity

- **Females:** Infertility, stillbirths, SABs, prematurity, possible VACTERL*-associated birth defects?
- **Males:** Infertility from ↓ sperm motility and counts, abnormal sperm morphology

Endocrinopathy

- **Adults:** Hypothyroidism, SIADH
- **Children:** Reduced growth hormone secretion and short stature, reduced adrenopituitary axis function

Skeletal Effects (Children)

- Skeletal effects
- Osteoblast inhibition
- Osteoclast inhibition
- Reduced osteoblast and osteoclast remodeling
- Pb lines: Hypermineralization at pediatric metaphyses of long bones
- Reduced bone growth and short extremities and stature in children (Figure 30.6)

Cardiac Effects (Adults)

- Systolic hypertension (↑ renin)
- AV/IV blocks (↑ QT, ↓ T)

Gastrointestinal Effects

- Metallic taste in mouth
- **Lead colic:** Anorexia, abdominal pain, vomiting, constipation (GI autonomic neuropathy?)

---

* The VACTERL association is defined by a constellation of congenital defects, including vertebral defects, anal (imperforate anus), cardiac anomalies, tracehoesophageal fistula (TEF), and renal and limb anomalies. It remains uncertain as to whether chronic lead toxicity is associated with the VACTERL syndrome.

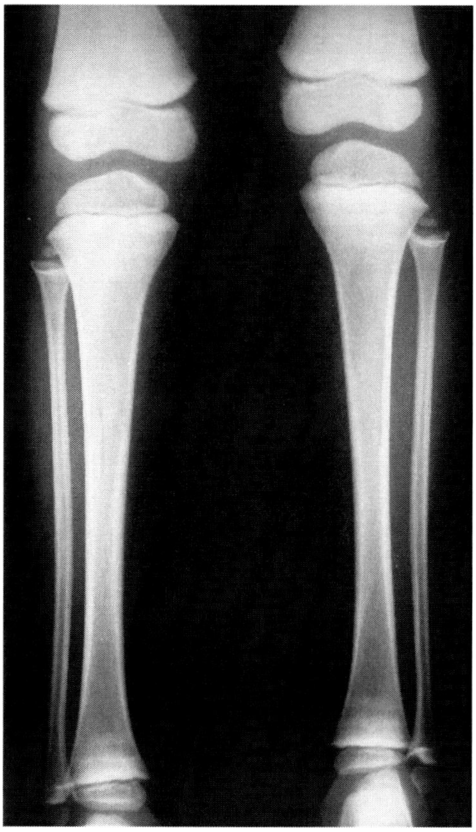

FIGURE 30.6 Metaphyseal lead lines in a child's legs.

- **Burton's blue lines:** Lead sulfide deposits at gingival-dental lines
- **Acute exposure:** ↑ LFT hepatitis and pancreatitis, especially in adults

Clinical Findings in Children and Adults

See Tables 30.4 and 30.5.

Table 30.4 Clinical Findings in Children

Severity	Asymptomatic	Moderate	Severe
BLL	>10–40 mcg/dL	>50–70 mcg/dL	>70–100 mcg/dL
CNS	↓ Cognition, bizarre behavior, ↓ hearing and coordination, mimics ADHD	Irritable-to-lethargic with "difficult" behavior—"terrible twos"	↑ ICP, CN palsies, seizures, encephalopathy
GI	None → constipation	Anorexia, lead colic	Persistent vomiting
Heme	RBC stippling	RBC stippling	Anemia

Table 30.5 Clinical Findings in Adults

Severity	Mild	Moderate	Severe
BLL level	>40 mcg/dL	>80	>100–150 mcg/dL
CNS and PNS	Somnolence, disinterested affect, ↓ libido	HA, loss of memory, infertility	Encephalopathy, neuropathy = wrist > foot drop
GI	Metallic taste	Constipation	Lead colic
Heme/CV	HTN	Anemia, HTN	Anemia, pallor, systolic HTN
Renal	None	Nephropathy	CRF, gout, kidney stones

Lead Poisoning: Diagnosis 1

Figures 30.7 and 30.8.

Laboratory Studies

- Normochromic–hypochromic microcytic anemia
- Basophilic stippling of RBCs
- **U/A:** ↑ Protein and glucose
- **Biomarkers:** Serum > urine

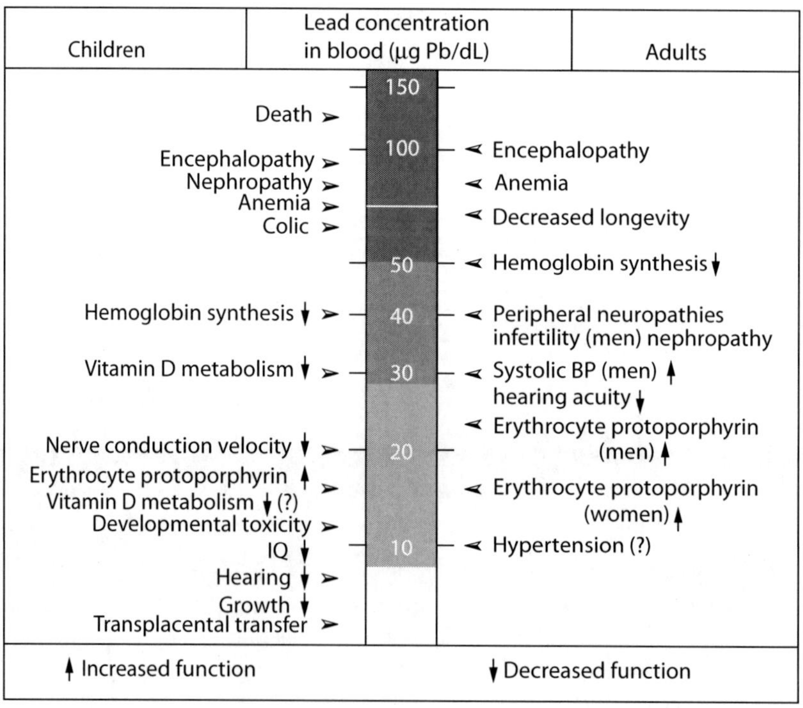

FIGURE 30.7 Correlation of increasing blood lead levels with decreasing IQ in children.

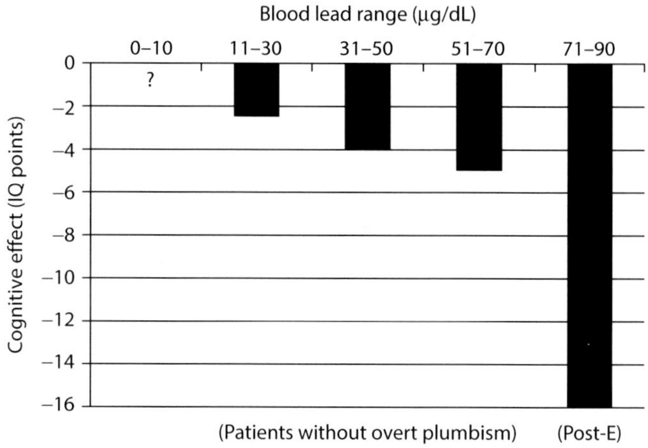

FIGURE 30.8 Correlation of clinical findings with increasing blood lead levels in children and adults.

- Elevated urine δ-ALA, venous blood Pb > total EP > ZPP + FEP (EPs and ZPP insensitive @ BLLs 10–25 mcg/dL)
- Urine, hair assays insensitive
- Tooth assays for research

Radiographic Images

- **Long bones (children):** Metaphyseal lead lines of ↑ calcification @ wrists and knees
- **Shell fragments:** Pleura, joints
- **Flat abdomen:** Radiopaque ingestions of metal foreign bodies (FBs), paint chips, folk medicines
- **CT:** Cerebral edema, ↓ gray–white matter demarcation
- **MRI:** Cortical atrophy, cerebral infarcts

Lead Poisoning: Diagnosis 2

Laboratory Studies

- **Basophilic stippling of *red blood cells*:** Form circumferential *Cabot's rings*
- **Radiographic images:** Ingested foreign bodies (FBs)

Lead Poisoning: Neuroradiographic Diagnosis

CT Scan

- Cerebral edema and loss of gray–white differentiation

MRI

- Cortical atrophy and multiple infarcts

Lead Poisoning: Treatment

Reduce Lead Exposures

- **Reduce preexposures risks:** Children and pregnant > adults; ↑ dietary calories and minerals, especially Fe and Ca; ↑ personal hygiene and PPE; change work clothes ("*foul nest*" syndrome); ↑ plant ventilation and dust reduction
- **Remediation:** Home Pb-paint abatement, relocation, dust control, landscaping, soil removal and replacement

Chelation Therapy

1. **Succimer:** Po, safest
2. **$CaNa_2EDTA$:** IV, can combine with po succimer
3. **BAL:** *IM first*; then add EDTA to avoid ↑ brain Pb from EDTA alone
4. **Penicillamine:** Po, *not recommended* except for tx failures due to BM depression, penicillin (pcn)-like anaphylactic skin reactions, and nephrotoxicity

Lead Poisoning: Chelating Agents

- *BAL* (British anti-Lewisite, dimercaprol): IM only, peanut oil vehicle, developed prior to WWII as antidote for Lewisite (arsine gas) and mustard gases; sulfur donor and nonspecific chelator of Pb, As, Cu; SEs—hemolysis in G-6-PD, nephrotoxic in acid urine, peanut allergy; give prior to EDTA for Pb encephalopathy
- *$CaNa_2EDTA$* (disodium ethylenediamine tetraacetic acid): IV > IM, water-soluble nonspecific chelator of Pb, Hg, Ca, Cu, Zn; SEs–nephrotoxic with oliguria, IM–subcutaneous calcinosis, transient ↑ ALT/AST, redistributes Pb from ST to brain in encephalopathy and should be given after BAL
- *Penicillamine*: IV > po, nonspecific chelator of Pb, As, Hg, Cu, Zn; SEs–BM depression, immunosuppression, nephrotoxic, teratogenic, penicillin-like allergy. Recommended only in *Wilson's disease (hepatolenticular degeneration)*
- *Succimer* (dimercaptosuccinic acid, DMSA): an oral derivative of BAL (note two SH groups), po only, water-soluble specific and least toxic chelator for Pb, As, Hg; will not chelate the essential minerals Fe, Cu, Zn, Ca, and can be given with Fe supplementation; minor, mostly GI SEs, transient ↑AST

Lead Poisoning: Chelation Therapy

Adult Chelation Therapy

- **Encephalopathic:** BAL IM first followed by EDTA IV
- BLL > 100 mcg/dL: Same
- BLL > 70–100 mcg/dL: Succimer po only
- BLL < 70 mcg/dL: Reduce exposure, *no chelation* indicated—chelation contraindicated 2° ↑ BLL levels from mobilized bone stores

Pediatric Chelation

- **Encephalopathic:** BAL IM first followed by EDTA IV

- BLL > 70 mcg/dL: Same
- BLL > 45–69 mcg/dL: Succimer > EDTA
- BLL 35–44 mcg/dL: Succimer if <2 years old
- BLL 20–44, if > 2 years old (yo): reduce exposures, *no chelation*
- BLL <20 mcg/dL : reduce exposures, *no chelation*

Lead Poisoning: Public Health Case Correlations

Case 1: Presentation

- **4 yo M:** 4 day history of abdominal cramps, vomiting; primary care MD diagnosis: viral GE syndrome?
- **2 weeks later:** Recurrence + anemia
- **2 days later:** ED—cramps, severe abdominal pain, anemia, gastric foreign body (FB) (a vending machine bracelet with a lead medallion), later retrieved by EGD along with a quarter; Dx: FB
- **3 days later:** Seizes, bites cheek, BLL = 123 mcg/dL
- **Admit:** IM BAL (25 mg/kg/day × 5) → IV EDTA (50 mg/kg/day × 5 → po succimer (30 mg/kg/day × 5, then 20 mg/kg/day × 2 weeks)

Home Investigation

- **Home:** Built 1996, no lead.
- **Sister:** 6 yo, BLL <5.
- **State EPA lab:** Medallion contained 40% lead, 4% antimony, and 3% tin.
- **U.S. CPSC:** 1.5 M medallions made in India distributed to U.S. vending machine operators. Nationwide recall.
- **CDC:** MMWR alert to LMDs 10 months (mos) later.
- **1.5 medallions distributed:** Few returned despite recall.

Case 2: Presentation

- **1 yo M:** Since a relative in NYC had Pb poisoning, screening @ 6 mos-BLL = 1 μg/dL; @1 year BLL = 10 μg/dL; family denied Pb exposures: paint, candy, spices, food, and jewelry
- **3 mos later:** BLL = 20 μg/dL and family admitted child had worn "protection" amulet (R) since age 3 mos and often mouthed it
- **Pb content amulet:** 450,000 mg/kg = 45% Pb
- **5 mos later, age 18 mos:** BLL = 5 μg/dL

Home Investigation

- **Home inspection:** X-ray fluorescence readings of 29 paint surfaces all < HUD LOCs
- **Spice and rice testing:** Pb levels < LOCs
- **Food item testing:** Pb levels < LOCs
- **Pb source confirmed:** Amulet with Pb content + observed mouthing

Case 3: Lead in Public Playground Soils: New Orleans, Louisiana (NOLA)

Epidemiology

- Elimination of Pb in gas and paints has resulted *in a 98% ↓ in mean BLLs in children from 14.9 μg/dL in 1976 to 1.9 μg/dL in 2004.*
- The main source of Pb exposures *remains leaded paint, but nonpaint sources in imported candy, cosmetics, spices, foods, jewelry, pottery,* and *ceramics are increasing in high-risk children*.
- Children @ ↑ risks of Pb exposures
  - *Latin American and SE Asian children ages 1–5 years*, especially ages 1–2 years 2° mouthing behavior and nonfood sources.
  - African-American children, same ages, living in older, deteriorating housing.
  - Asian-American children in NYC.
  - Children with "*yuppie plumbism*."

Where Are the Soil Lead Hot Spots in Cities?

- Areas near public transit routes
- Playgrounds near public transit routes

How Much Lead Is There?

Epidemiology

- In 2004 (pre-Katrina), *13.8% of all children tested in NOLA had BLL > 10 μg/dL.*
- By 2009, only *5.3% of all children tested in NOLA had BLL > 10 μg/dL*; possibly as a result of reduced Pb levels in central city areas flooded by Katrina.
- NOLA's *park and playground soils* are now being tested for Pb levels and will undergo soil remediation if not in compliance with *EPA action levels of <400 ppm.*
- Soil remediation programs in NOLA require removing 1/2 foot of soil, laying geotextile fabric liner, and covering the soil liner with 1/2 foot of sterile soil. *Is this sufficient Pb abatement? Levels > 400 ppm have been detected @ 2-foot depths.*

Remediating Lead Hot Spots

- Remove Pb-contaminated soil
- Replace Pb-contaminated soil with tested, toxin-free soil

Mercury

Accidental Exposures (Table 30.6)

1. Cantor tube, Hg-filled balloon to decompress small bowel obstruction (SBO).

Table 30.6 Mercury: Forms and Exposures

Elemental Hg	Inorganic Hg	Organic Hg
Ex: "Quicksilver"	Mercuric chloride	Methyl Hg
Dentists: amalgams	Antiseptics, disinfectants	Seafood: long-lived, predatory
Calibrated medical instruments (BP)	Taxidermy, Mad Hatter syndrome	Grain and seed fumigants
NG tubes	Batteries	Insecticides
Jewelers	Explosives	Fungicides
Electroplaters	Plastics (PVC)	Wood preserve

2. Nasogastric (NG) tube removed after balloon rupture-free elemental Hg in the gastrointestinal tract will be expelled and has to be collected as hazardous waste. No danger to the patient unless the elemental mercury is aspirated into lungs or injected.

Mercury: Pathophysiology (Table 30.7)

1. Avid covalent binding to all sulfur-containing groups, especially the *sulfhydryl groups*, throughout the body
2. Widespread destruction of membranes and structural proteins (CNS) and disruption of enzyme and transport systems
3. *Elemental Hg* targets *lungs* (chemical pneumonitis, ARDS) and CNS (*Mad Hatter*); *inorganic Hg* targets *GI* tract, *kidneys* (hemorrhagic gastroenteritis, ATN) and CNS (mercuric chloride, *Mad Hatter*); *organic Hg* targets *CNS*, especially fetal CNS > maternal CNS (*Minamata disease*)

Mercury Poisoning: Clinical Syndromes (Table 30.7)

1. Acute inhalation of elemental Hg vapor
2. Acute ingestion of inorganic Hg salts
3. Chronic elemental Hg poisoning
4. Chronic inorganic Hg poisoning
   - **Mad Hatter syndrome:** 2° to the chronic inhalation exposures to elemental Hg vapor or post inhalation or ingestion of inorganic Hg salts, for example, mercuric chloride and nitrate

Table 30.7 Toxicities of the Different Forms of Mercury

Elemental Hg	Inorganic Hg	Organic Hg
Route: inhalation	Ingestion (GI) > dermal (skin)	Predominantly GI
Distribution: lung, CNS, kidney	CNS > kidney > GI	CNS > fetal > maternal > kidney > liver
Excretion: renal > GI	Renal > GI	Methyl: GI—fecal; Aryl: renal

5. Methyl (organic) Hg poisoning (Minamata disease)
6. Mercurial acrodynia (*pink disease*)

Mercury: Acute Clinical Effects (Table 30.8)

Acute Elemental Inhalation

- Pulmonary > GI > CNS
- **Pulm:** Cough, chills, fever, dyspnea, *chemical pneumonitis*, pulmonary edema, ARDS, interstitial fibrosis
- **GI:** Metallic taste, nausea, vomiting, diarrhea, dysphagia
- **CNS:** Headaches, weakness, visual disturbances, *Mad Hatte*r syndrome possible

Acute Inorganic Ingestion

- GI > renal
- **GI:** Metallic taste, oral pain and burning, nausea, vomiting, diarrhea, abdominal pain, *hemorrhagic gastroenteritis*, dehydration → orthostatic hypotension
- **Renal:** Proximal tubular necrosis → ATN

Mercury: Chronic Clinical Effects

Chronic Elemental Mercury

- Pulm > CNS > renal > GI
- **Pulm:** Pulmonary fibrosis, restrictive lung disease
- **CNS:** Similar to *Mad Hatter* with triad of tremor, gingivitis, erethrism
- **Renal:** *Fanconi's syndrome* = proteinuria → nephrotic syndrome 2° autoimmune glomerulonephritis, CRF
- **GI:** Relatively nontoxic due to *negligible absorption* (e.g., after long-NG tube balloon rupture)

Chronic Inorganic Mercury ("Mad Hatter" Syndrome)

- CNS > renal > GI
- **CNS:** Intention tremor, ballismus and *choreoathetosis* ("mad hatter" syndrome 2° mercuric chloride exposures), *erethism* (anxiety, *easy blushing*, emotional paradox, labile affect, memory loss), *neurasthenia* (HA, depression, fatigue anorexia, weight loss)

Table 30.8 Mercury Poisoning: Diagnosis and Management

Diagnosis	Emergency Management	Specific Treatment
Elemental: urine Hg > blood Hg	Elem: absorb, decontaminate, no vacuuming, notify hazmat 911-PPE	Inorganic: IM BAL + po succimer > penicillamine
Inorganic: urine Hg	Inorganic: EGD, WBI (PEG) for residual	Elemental: same as inorganic tx
Methyl Hg: blood Hg	Methyl Hg: NA	Methyl Hg: tx resist, succimer

- **GI:** Metallic taste and a characteristic triad of (1) *gingivostomatitis*, (2) *loose teeth*, and (3) *salivary gland hyperplasia*

Inorganic Hg-Pink Disease

Mercurial Acrodynia ("Pink Disease")

- **Toxic form:** *Inorganic* HgCl salts—*Calomel*, inorganic mercurial teething powders can cause idiosyncratic hypersensitivity reactions in children = *pink acrodynia*
- **Common name:** "*Pink disease*"
- **Sx:** *Pink papular rash* → hyperkeratoses on palms and soles → later *acral desquamation* → ulceration

Methyl Hg and Minamata Disease

Methyl Hg Poisoning

- **Toxic form**: Inorganic Hg transformed by marine bacteria to *organic* methyl Hg *bio-concentrated in the seafood chain*
- **Common name**: *Minamata disease*
- **Sx:** *Fetal neurotoxicity, methyl Hg crosses fetal blood–brain barrier complexed with* L-cysteine; ↓ birth weight, severe MR, developmental delay, ataxia, seizures hypotonia-spasticity, deafness–blindness

Thallium

Properties and Uses

Properties

- Soft, pliable toxic metal
- Common component of granite and shale
- Behaves like K^+ ion in the body, interfering with nerve conduction, especially in the longest peripheral nerves → *painful, stocking (feet) ≥ glove (hands) peripheral neuropathy*

Uses/Exposures

- Alloys and anticorrosives
- Optical lenses
- Coatings for lamp and lantern filaments (*Coleman lanterns®*)
- Jewelry
- Depilatories
- Rodenticide—outside the United States
- **Radioactive contrast agent**—thallium cardiac scan for ejection fraction (EF) measurements (potential "dirty bomb" radioactive materials)

Thallium: Toxicology (Tables 30.9 and 30.10)

Absorption/Distribution

- Rapidly absorbed by all routes
- Inhalation and ingestion > dermal
- Distributed rapidly throughout the body
- Partitions into a three-compartment model: first—blood, second—well-perfused organs, last—CNS, *no prolonged storage* in reservoirs, like Pb and Cd

Metabolism/Excretion

- Not metabolized
- *Does not persist in tissue storage sites*, like Pb and Cd in bone
- GI—fecal excretion (50 + %), unlike most other heavy metals > renal—urine excretion (25 + %) > sweat, hair, nails (<10%)

Thallium: Pathophysiology

1. Thallium ions preferentially accumulate in all areas of *high K concentration*, particularly peripheral NS first > then CNS *nerves*, liver, and muscle, including cardiac muscle.
2. Thallium *replaces K* in all K-dependent enzyme systems.
3. Thallium *impairs nerve conduction* and *muscle membrane depolarization*: sensory > motor, long nerves (LE, ascends from feet) > short nerves (UE).

Table 30.9 Thallium Poisoning: Clinical Effects

Immediate	Intermediate	Late	Chronic
3–4 h	Hours–days	2–24 weeks	Months
#1 = Gastrointestinal GI	#1 = Peripheral nervous system (PNS)	#1 = Dermatological	#1 = Central nervous system (CNS)
N, V, cramps, constipation (vagal neuropathy)	Painful ascend peripheral neuropathy, CN palsies	Alopecia, Mees' lines	Optic neuritis Ophthalmoplegia
Autonomic (X) neuropathy	Alopecia	Motor neuropathy	Memory and cognitive loss

Table 30.10 Thallium Poisoning: Diagnosis and Treatment

Diagnosis	Early Mx	Late Tx
24-h urine for atomic absorption spectroscopy	Lavage > emesis if no vomiting, WBI if x-ray +	MDAC + mannitol (osmotic cathartics only)
Urine > blood > hair and nails	Oral Prussian blue exchanges K for thallium-Tl	Prussian blue = K ferric ferrocyanide
Abdominal x-ray for radiopaque GI sludge if present, eliminate using whole bowel irrigation (WBI) with polyethylene glycol (PEG) solution	MDAC + cathartic, mannitol > sorbitol due to reduced GI motility	Prussian blue exchanges its K for thallium and cesium ions during chelation

4. Thallium decreases mitotic activity (causing total alopecia) and combines with sulfhydryl groups, like arsenic, weakening keratin in nails → causing Mees' lines.
5. Exception: Unlike other heavy metal salts, thallium salts are substantially adsorbed to activated charcoal (Table 30.9).

Dermal Effects

- Thallium alopecia
- Thallium—Mees' lines

DDx of Alopecia and Mees' Lines

DDx of Total Alopecia

- Thallium
- Arsenic
- Selenium
- Colchicine
- Boron
- Vinca alkaloids and other mitosis-inhibiting cancer chemotherapeutics

DDx of Mees' Lines

- Thallium
- Arsenic
- **Mitotic inhibitors:** Colchicine, dapsone
- Antimetabolites

Heavy Metal Poisoning: Minor Metal Toxicities (See Tables 30.11 through 30.16)

Aluminum

Minor Toxicity: Aluminum

- **Source:** Common metal often combined with *bauxite ore*, many uses—in antacids, antiperspirants, cookware, and transportation

Table 30.11 Cobalt Poisoning

Exposures	Acute Toxicity	Subacute Chronic Toxicity	Treatment
Grinders polishers	Irritant dermatitis	Polycythemia	Remove from source
Machinists tool sharpeners	Allergic dermatitis	Cobalt cardiomopathy Goiter	Decontaminate
Beer foam stabilizers (Canada)	Occupational exposures—occupational asthma, "hard metal" asthma	Pulm. fibrosis Diamond polisher's lung	Chelation with $CaNa_2EDTA$

Table 30.12 Copper Poisoning

Exposures	Acute Toxicity	Chronic Toxicity	Treatment
Alloys Electrical wiring	GI: metallic taste, N, V, D, GI bleed, jaundice	Proximal tubular damage Wilson's disease (congenital)	Lavage Catharsis Chelation for Wilson's
Algicides Fungicides	Metal fume fever Hemolysis	↓ Ceruloplasmin Blindness, cirrhosis	Chelation—D-penicillamine only
Preservative Pigments	Irritant > allergic dermatitis	Encephalopathy	Liver transplant (for Wilson's disease primarily)

Table 30.13 Manganese Poisoning

Exposures	Acute Toxicity	Chronic Toxicity	Treatment
Alloys Welding solders	MnO_2-acute pneumonitis (manganic pneumonia)	Parkinsonism—often l-dopa resistant	Early chelation only
Animal food additives	Conjunctivitis, dermatitis	Globus pallidus manganic madness	$CaNa_2EDTA$
Fertilizers	GI caustic-mucosal and orogastric burns	Intention tremor dystonia Pulm fibrosis	L-Dopa for Parkinson's disease

Table 30.14 Selenium Poisoning

Exposures	Acute Toxicity	Chronic Toxicity	Treatment
Gun bluing solvents	GI: garlic breath, N, V, watery D	GI distress, garlic breath, metal taste	Chelation contraindicated 2° nephrotoxicity
Alloys	Abdominal cramps	Anosomia, reactive AW	Activated charcoal
Antifungal shampoos (Selsun Blue®)	Caustic gastric burns, dry hair, paresthesias ↑ CFR	Antioxidant and anticancer effects?	Add a cathartic

Table 30.15 Tin Poisoning

Exposures	Acute Toxicity	Chronic Toxicity	Treatment
Alloys—bronzes Solders Electroplating	Benign pneumoconiosis	Peripheral demyelinating neuropathy (organotins)	Chelation with BAL
Cook utensils	Stannosis	Encephalopathy	#1 = BAL
Toothpastes Algicides Fungicides	CXR +	Cerebral edema	BAL > DMSA

Table 30.16 Zinc Poisoning

Exposures	Acute Toxicity	Chronic Toxicity	Tx
Alloys Brasses Bronzes Welding solders: Zn is the most common cause metal fume fever	Metal fume fever Contact dermatitis Deficiency: acrodermatitis enteropathica = alopecia, acral and perioral dermatitis, diarrhea	↓ Cu-sideroblastic anemia BM depression ATN, interstitial nephritis	Remove from source; do not chelate; give copper only
Galvanized pipes	Abdominal cramps	Leukopenia	Replace copper
Electroplating	Diarrhea	White cell aplasia	

- **Toxicity:** Greatest risks in those with ↓ renal dysfunction as exposures from dialysates, household products, and acidic liquids can ↑ deposition in *bone and CNS—very* weak association with *Alzheimer's disease*
- **Tx:** Remove from *exposure sources*, deferoxamine chelation
- **Rodenticides:** Al and Zn phosphides release *phosphine gas* when exposed to water or HCl
- **Bauxite ore:** A source for aluminum

Bismuth

- **Minor toxicity:** Bismuth
- **Forms:** Bismuth subsalicylate, *Pepto Bismol®*
- **Uses:** Dyspepsia, diarrhea
- **Dx:** Radio-opaque, bismuth blue lines from bismuth sulfide deposits, black stool—heme negative, black tongue
- **Acute toxicity:** Acute renal failure from PCT damage
- **Chronic toxicity:** *Progressive myoclonic encephalopathy* = weakness, twitching, ataxia, myoclonus, tremors, rarely seizures
- **Tx:** Supportive, *succimer chelation*
- **Interaction:** PPIs ↑ absorption 2° gastric ↑ pH

Cobalt

Minor Metal Poisoning: Cobalt

Copper

Minor Metal Poisoning: Copper

Manganese

Minor Metal Poisoning: Manganese

Toxic Causes of Parkinsonism

1. Manganese
2. Methanol
3. Methyl-phenyl tetrahydropyridine (MPTP)
4. Carbon monoxide
5. Carbon disulfide
6. Hydrogen cyanide
7. Hydrogen sulfide

Nickel

Minor Metal Poisoning: Nickel

Nickel Uses/Exposures

- Steel and other alloys
- Nickel–cadmium batteries
- Electroplating
- **Cooking utensils:** Pots and pans
- Coins
- Ceramic glazes
- Green glass
- Jewelry

Acute Nickel Toxicity

- GI > pulmonary toxicity
- **GI:** N, V, D, abdominal cramps, hemorrhagic gastritis
- **Pulm:** Dyspnea, chest pain, rhinitis, sinusitis, tracheobronchitis—croup; targets upper AW like Cr
- **Derm:** Allergic > irritant contact dermatitis
- **Eye:** Conjunctivitis

Nickel Dermal Effects

- Nickel allergic contact dermatitis

Chronic Nickel Toxicity

#1 = bronchopulmonary

- **Upper airway**: Anosomia, nasal polyposis, *nasal septal perforation*, chronic bronchitis, *nasal cancer; similar to chromium*—"chrome holes" and nasal septal perforation
- **Lower airway**: Chronic bronchitis, pulmonary fibrosis, *lung cancer*

Treatment: Nickel Poisoning

- Remove from the source.

- Specific chelation therapy only with diethyldithiocarbamate (DDC), a disulfiram metabolite that binds nickel and also platinum (platinoid chemotherapeutics).
- *Topical DDC* can be used to manage nickel and platinum allergic contact dermatitis.

Selenium

Minor Metal Poisoning: Selenium

Differential Diagnosis of Garlic Breath

1. Garlic consumption.
2. **Selenium, selenious acid:** Topical or ingested.
3. **Dimethyl sulfoxide (DMSO):** Topical or ingested.
4. **Phosphorus, zinc phosphide (rotten fish):** A common component of rodent and small animal pest (gopher) poisoning. Has also been used to intentionally contaminate heroin.
5. **Arsenic:** Chronic ingestion.
6. **Tellurium:** Chronic ingestion.

Tin

Minor Metal Poisoning: Tin

Zinc

Minor Metal Poisoning: Zinc

Zinc Deficiency

- Acrodermatitis enteropathica.
- Chronic zinc deficiency or *acrodermatitis enteropathica* may either be acquired or inherited as an automosomal recessive genetic disorder characterized by alopecia, diarrhea, and acral (hands and feet) and perioral dermatitis.

Heavy Metal Poisoning Antidotes

Metal Chelators

1. **Calcium disodium edetate ($CaNa_2EDTA$):** Lead
2. **Deferoxamine:** Iron and aluminum
3. **Dimercaprol (British anti-Lewisite, BAL):** Pb, As, Hg
4. **Succimer (dimethylsuccinic acid, DMSA):** Lead
5. **D-Penicillamine:** Cu
6. **Diethylene triamine pentaacetic acid (DTPA):** Chelates radioactive americium, curium, and plutonium
7. **Prussian blue (ferric ferrocyanide):** Chelates radioactive cesium and thallium
8. **Gallic acid:** Uranium

Chelators: EDTA

Properties

- **Chem:** Water-soluble, calcium-containing ring-structured acid
- **Mech:** *Exchanges its ring-bound Ca for a heavy metal*, usually Pb, to form a stable, nonionized, water-soluble chelate that can be renally excreted
- **Contra:** Dehydration, renal dysfunction, CAD chelation, cadmium chelation, *sole therapy (without BAL initially) in Pb encephalopathy*—give BAL first, then EDTA 4 h later to ↓ brain Pb delivery by EDTA

Applications

- **Use:** To chelate Pb in lead poisoning; in conjunction with BAL initially to rapidly chelate Pb in Pb encephalopathy
- **Dose:** IM in procaine or IV (preferred) diluted in NS over 8–24 h
- **SE:** Chelation and subsequent depletion of all essential metals (*minerals*) (Cu, Co, Fe, Mn, Zn); elevated LFTs; calcinosis at injection sites; thrombophlebitis; nephrotoxicity 2° Pb release in kidneys during excretion

Chelators: Deferoxamine

Properties

- **Chem:** A water-soluble, specific iron chelator created by removing ferric iron (Fe^{3+}) from ferrioximine.
- **Mech:** Chelates extra free Fe and Fe in transit between transferrin and ferritin; but *will not chelate Fe complexed to Hb, ferritin, or hemosiderin*. Also *chelates aluminum* best.
- **Contra:** None.

Applications

- **Use:** To chelate Fe in Fe overdoses, massive transfusions, hemosiderosis, and thalassemia. To chelate aluminum in CRF.
- **Dose:** 1 g IM, then 0.5 g q 4–12 h; IV preferred = *15 mg/kg/min slowly.*
- **SE:** ↓ BP; pulmonary toxicity (ARDS); *oculotoxicity* (↓ vision, ↓ color vision, night blindness); and *ototoxicity* (deafness). Acts as *siderophage* for some bacteria that cannot absorb Fe—*Yersinia* and *Vibrio*— ↑ *V. vulnificus* sepsis risk. *Rose (vin rosé)—orange colored urine.*

Chelators: BAL

Properties

- **Chem:** Nonspecific metal chelator formulated in peanut oil and developed during WWII as an antidote for both Lewisite (arsine gas) and mustard vesicant gases
- **Mech:** A sulfur-donating chelator that forms stable bonds with *soft metals*—especially *As* and *Hg*; can also bind borderline soft metals, particularly *Pb*

- **Contra:** Peanut allergy, liver dysfunction, G-6-PD deficiency 2° hemolysis, organic or methyl Hg poisoning

Applications

- **Use:** To chelate As, elemental and inorganic Hg; to treat arsenical dermatitis; to use in conjunction with EDTA as initial chelation in Pb encephalopathy
- **Dose:** Deep IM 2.5 mg/kg q 4–6 h × 4 doses; topical quantity sufficient (qsad)
- **SE:** Local injection site pain, peanut anaphylaxis, fever, ↑ BP *and* HR, N, V, HA; can also chelate essential metals (especially Cu and Zn) and will chelate Fe during concomitant Fe therapy

Chelators: Succimer

Properties

- **Chem:** DMSA, a more water-soluble analog of BAL that is less toxic and more specific for Pb, a borderline soft metal, than BAL
- **Mech:** Same as BAL, but less toxic, *effective orally, will not chelate essential metals* (Cu, Co, Fe, Mn, Zn), and can be used with concomitant Fe therapy; unlike BAL, succimer does not cause hemolysis in G-6-PD deficiency
- **Contra:** None

Applications

- **Use:** Primarily lead poisoning (blood lead—BPb > 45 mcg/dL), unapproved for organic and inorganic Hg poisoning and As poisoning
- **Dose:** 30 mg/kg/day po × 5 days
- **SE:** Transient ↑ AST and multiple abdominal complaints—crampy abdominal pain, flatus, and diarrhea

Chelators: Penicillamine

Properties

- **Chem:** A highly toxic, penicillin-derived, nonspecific metal chelator (Cu > As, Hg, Pb) that is orally titrated over weeks
- **Mech:** Same as succimer, but less effective and ↑ SEs; *works best for Cu*
- **Contra:** Penicillin allergy, preexisting skin diseases, or renal dysfunction

Applications

- **Uses:** Cu chelation in Wilson's disease (hepatolenticular degeneration)
- **Dose:** 10 mg/kg/day po ↑ 10 mg/kg/week to 30 mg/kg/day × 10 weeks
- **SE:** Severe N&V, pcn anaphylaxis, leukopenia, thrombocytopenia, eosinophilia, aplastic anemia, myopathy, *dermatitis—Stevens–Johnson syndrome*, nephrotic syndrome
- **B poisons:** Bariums, bromates, bromides, boron

Bariums	Bromates	Bromides < toxic than bromates, in many drugs: Robitussin®—distributes like chloride—Cl = spurious hyperchloridemia and bromism-ioderma-like acne, lethargy. Tx: support	Boron
Soluble barium, sulfate, is a nontoxic x-ray contrast agent; insoluble barium carbonate is a rodenticide that drives K into cells, ↓↓↓ K. Tx: Na thiosulfate or $MgSO_4$ converts $BaCO_3 \rightarrow BaCO_4$	K+ bromate in hair perms cause inner ear hair cell deafness, just like amino-glycosides. Tx: Na thiosulfate to convert to less toxic bromides		Borax® brighteners, cleansers, and boric acid roach pills, boiled lobster—erythroderma, green blue vomitus, and later alopecia. Tx: no AC, need HD

Chapter 31

Pesticide Poisonings

Insecticides, Rodenticides, and Herbicides

Outline 708
Insecticides. 708
Pesticides: Topical Insect Repellents 713
Rodenticides. 714
Fumigants. 723
Herbicides 724

Outline

I. Insecticides
- Organochlorines
- Organophosphates
- Carbamates
- OP nerve gases
- Pyrethrins and pyrethroids
- DEET

II. Rodenticides
- High toxicity
- Moderate–low toxicity

III. Herbicides
- Paraquat
- Diquat
- Chlorphenoxyacetic acids

IV. Fumigants: methyl bromide

V. Conclusions

Insecticides

Commonly Used Insecticides (Table 31.1)

From Most to Least Toxic (Not Including OP Nerve Gases)

Organochlorines

- **DDT (dichlorodiphenyltrichloroethane):** DDT* and its analog, methoxychlor are *GABA antagonists* (ODs often present with *seizures only*) of low-to-moderate toxicity; not biodegradable and bioaccumulating (Table 31.1).
- **Lindane (used for head lice):** Moderate toxicity; consider in the DDx of any pediatric seizure disorder.
- **Cyclodienes:** Aldrin,* dieldrin,* endrin,* chlordane,† endosulfan, chlordecone (Kepone® shakes), and heptachlor (Mirex®); all highly toxic, some are *carcinogenic* in man† or animals,† and still in use illicitly (U.S. ban*) and licitly (developing world).
- **Toxaphene:** Moderate toxicity; restricted use termites.

Pesticides: Organochlorines

- **Reps:** DDT, lindane, all are fat soluble, bioaccumulate in the environment, and bioconcentrate in fat and breast milk.
- **Mech:** ↑↑ Opening Na channels, *inhibits GABA*.
- **Metabolism:** Very lipid soluble, GI > inhalation > dermal, cytochrome P450 inducers.

* Banned for use in the United States.

† Carcinogenic in animals and/or man.

Table 31.1 Commonly Used Pesticides from Most to Least Toxic

1. Organochlorines (OCs)	2. Organophosphates (Ops)	3. Carbamates	4. Pyrethroids Class II—CN	5. Pyrethroids Class I—No CN
DDT/Mirex	Malathion	Aldicarb	Cyfluthrin	Allathrin
Lindane	Parathion	Carbaryl	Cyhalothrin	Cyclothrin
Chlordane	Diazinon	DDTC[a] antifungal	Cypermethrin	Permethrin
Chlordecone (Kepone shakes)	Chlorpyrifos	Propoxur	Deltamethrin	Phenothrin
Aldrin–dieldrin	Leptophos	Sevin	Flucythrinate	Pyrethrosin
Toxaphene	Tri-ortho-cresyl phosphate (TOCP) (ginger jake)	Oximes	Tralomethrin	Tetramethrin

[a] Diethyl-dithio-carbamate.

- **Dx:** By exposure history, radiopacities (contain chloride [Cl] ions) on flat abdominal x-rays.
- **Antidote:** Dextrose + thiamine, and benzodiazepines (BZs) for seizures.
- **Acute manifestations:** Initial nausea (N) and vomiting (V), weakness, paresthesias, tremor, clonus, seizures, F 2° sz, and respiratory paralysis.
- **Chronic manifestations:** Chlordane = leukemia, thrombotic thrombocytopenic purpura (TTP); chlordecone = "*Kepone shakes,*" animal carcinogen pseudotumor cerebri, and male infertility.
- **Tx:** Skin decontamination; careful NG lavage, then AC; sz control dextrose, thiamine, BZs, phenobarbital; and *cholestyramine* to ↓ chlordecone enterohepatic circulation. *No oil cathartics because they will ↑ absorption of all fat-soluble OCs.*

Organophosphates and Carbamates

Organophosphates

- **Reps:** *Parathion, malathion, TOCP added to ethyl alcohol (EtOH) in the 1920s–1930s Prohibition Era, and Jamaican "ginger-jake" paralysis = organophosphate-induced delayed peripheral neuropathy (OPIDPN) (inhibits neuropathy target esterase [NTE] or neuropathic esterase).*
- **Sx:** Muscarinic (DUMBBELS) > nicotinic (opposite), neuromuscular junction (NMJ)-weakness and paralysis, CNS, miosis, ataxia, and seizures.
- **Dx:** Whole-blood RBC AchE > plasma (butyryl) AchE.
- **Mech:** Prolonged, phosphorylated AchE inhibition (*aging*).
- **Pharmacology:** All route absorptions.
- **Antidote:** Atropine + 2-PAM.
- **Tx:** O_2, decontamination, and BZs. Post-PAM.

Carbamates

- **Reps:** Aldicarb, carbaryl, propoxur, diethyldithiocarbamate, DDTC (binds nickel and platinum)
- **Sx:** Same, mostly muscarinic, less CNS penetration—less risk of ataxia, sz, and coma. *No OPIDPN, no intermediate syndrome (IMS), and no aging*
- **Dx:** Muscarinic SLUDE
- **Mech:** Reversible carbamoylated AchE inhibition—*no aging*
- **Pharm:** Same, all routes
- **Anti:** Atropine alone, *no oximes*
- **Tx:** Same

Pupillary Findings in Pesticide Poisonings

Organophosphates and Carbamates

- *Miosis*, characteristics of OP, and carbamate poisonings
- *Mydriasis*, also possible and may follow miosis

Miosis (Pinpoint Pupils)

CCOOPPS

- **C**holinergics
- **C**lonidine, **c**hloral hydrate
- **O**piates
- **O**rganophosphates
- **P**henothiazines (neuroleptics)
- **P**ilocarpine
- **P**CP (phencyclidine, ketamine)
- **S**edative hypnotics
- **Misc:** Caffeine, ergotamines (including bromocriptine, LSD, and trazodone)

Mydriasis (Dilated Pupils)

AAAAS

- **A**nticholinergics
- **A**tropine
- **A**mphetamines
- **A**ntihistamines
- **A**ntidepressants
- **S**ympathomimetics

Complications of OP Poisoning

Intermediate Syndrome

OPs Only, Not Carbamates

- **Onset:** NM paralysis occurs at 24–96 h as cholinergic crisis resolves.

- **Mech:** Inadequate oxime treatment possible, 2° prolonged nicotinic, and ↑ CNS Ach stimulation.
- **Sx:** Bulbar, nuchal, and proximal limb weakness—paralysis → restrictive renal failure (RF), usually complete recovery.
- **Tx:** Supportive only.

OP-Induced Delayed Neuropathy

Again OPs Only, Not Carbamates

- **Onset:** 1–3 weeks postexposure
- **Mech:** "Dying-back" peripheral neuropathy 2° to inhibition NTE and myelin degeneration (ginger *jake leg* OPIDN)
- **Sx:** Weakness, ascending glove and stocking paresthesias, muscle cramps–atrophy–spasticity, ataxia, and permanent "*jake leg*" paralysis
- **Tx:** Supportive

An Early Example of OPIDPN: TOCP Jake Leg

Prohibition Era (1930s): Patent Drug Remedy

- **Ethanol substitute:** Jamaica ginger "cordial"

OP Nerve Gases

Mechanism and Classification

- **Mech:** *Long-term AchE inhibition* with rapid aging
  German (G) agents (1936–1945)
- **GA: Tabun**
- **GB: Sarin** (*Aum Shrinrikyo* Matsumoto, 1994; Tokyo, 1995)
- **GC:** Stands for *Gonococcus*
- **GD: Soman**
  Br. and Fr.: First to deploy gas
  Br. vesicant mustard agent: *VX*
  Am. not Br. Anti-lewisite: *BAL*

Prophylaxis and Treatment

- **Prophylaxis:** (1) Pyridostigmine, a carbamate and reversible anti-AchE oxime that temporarily inhibits and binds AchE protecting AchE from permanent aging by nerve gas agent; (2) seizure prophylaxis with diazepam
- **Tx:** Neoprene, not latex, gloves for caregivers, immediate skin decontamination, atropine as antimuscarinic, pralidoxime, diazepam for sz, and support-MV

Least Toxic and OTC

Pyrethrins

- **Pyrethrins:** Natural extracts from *Chrysanthemum* spp.

- **Pyrethroids:** Synthetics
  - **Type I—Non-cyano (CN) group:** Permethrin, T (tremors) group
  - **Type II—CN group:** Deltamethrin, CSS (choreoathetosis, salivation, and seizures) group
- **Mech:** Penetrates chitin, Na channel blockers
- **Tox:** Type I ↓ toxic = T-tremors; type II ↑ toxic = C + S + S choreoathetosis + salivation + sz
- **Tx:** Decontamination, support, and BZs for seizures

N,N-Diethyltoluamide

- **Mech:** "Knock-down" agent with unknown mechanism; concentration 5–100%, long acting—4–8 h
- **Tox:** Very rare 2° ↑ absorbed dose or ingestions in children = ataxia, seizures, encephalopathy → and RF from rhabdomyolysis possible
- **Predisposition:** Children, women, pregnant, skin diseases—↑ inhaled and dermal absorption
- **Tx:** Supportive

Synthetic

Pyrethroids

Type I Pyrethroids

- **Chem:** No α-CN group at the central ester linkage. Chemically resembles the naturally occurring insecticides, the pyrethrins, expressed by Compositae family plants, especially chrysanthemums.
- **Env:** Not persistent.
- **Ex:** Permethrin.
- **Tox:** Inhaled > skin absorb, less CNS toxic; ↑ allergic rxns.* Toxidrome: T toxic = *tremors* and *hyperthermia*.
- **Tx:** Decon, support, and BZs.

Type II Pyrethroids

- **Chem: α-CN group present** at the central ester linkage.
- **Env:** More persistent.
- **Ex:** Deltamethrin.
- **Tox:** Inhaled > skin absorb, more CNS toxic; ↑ allergic rxns.* Toxidrome: C + S + S toxic = *choreoathetosis* ± *salivation* ± *seizures*.
- **Tx:** Decon, support, and BZs (Table 31.2).

* *Compositae* family (chrysanthemum, daisy, *Echinacea*, etc.) plant antigen (Ag) look alikes, cross-sensitivities to ragweed, daisy, and *Echinacea*.

Table 31.2 Topical Insect Repellents					
Repellant	**Brands**	**Strength (%)**	**Duration (h)**	**Efficacy Against**	**Comments**
DEET	*Off®* *Cutter®* *Sawyer®*	5–100%	6–12	Mosquitoes, fleas, chiggers, gnats, and flies	≤30% for children; can damage clothing and plastic
Picaridin	*Cutter Advanced®* *Natrapel®*	7% 20%	6–12	Mosquitoes, fleas, chiggers, and flies	No damage for clothing and plastic
Oil of lemon eucalyptus methane—3,8-diol	*Cutter Lemon®* *Repel Lemon®*		6	Mosquitoes	Avoid in children <3 years old
Permethrin	*Sawyer Permethrin Clothing®*	NA	2–4 weeks on clothes	Mosquitoes and ticks	Chemical contact dermatitis
IR3535	*Avon Skin So Soft®* *Bull Frog®*	7.5% 20%	6 h	Mosquitoes and gnats	>10% effective
Citronella	*Generic*	NA	<1	Mosquitoes	Ineffective

Pesticides: Topical Insect Repellents

Repellents

See Table 31.2.

Pesticide Endocrine Activity

See Table 31.3.

Table 31.3 Pesticide Endocrine Activity and Endocrine Disrupters			
Estrogen Agonists	**Estrogen Antagonists**	**Phytoestrogens**	**Xenoestrogens**
Organochlorines: dieldrin	Chlorphenoxyacetic acid herbicides	Estradiol	Some oral contraceptives (OCPs)
Chlorpyrifos	2,4-D	Structures	Ethinyl estradiol
Carbamates	2,4,5-T	Isoflavones	
		Soy, red clover	Endocrine disrupters
		Flavonoids	Bisphenol A
		Cereals	
		Coumarins	

Rodenticides

Outline

- Epidemiology
- Classification of rodenticides (Table 31.4)
    - **High toxicity**—LD_{50} < 50 mg/kg
    - **Moderate toxicity**—LD_{50} 50–500 mg/kg
    - **Low toxicity**—LD_{50} 500–5000 mg/kg
- Toxicology
- The management of unknown rodenticide exposure

Rodenticides: Epidemiology

- **Prevalence (1990–1995):** 17,000 cases
- **Who:** 90% children < 6 years
- **CFR:** < 6 deaths/year
- **Risk factors:** Children, elderly, psychotics, exterminators, suicides, homicides, and unintentional ingestions of rodenticides stored in food containers

Rodenticides: Classification

Classification System (Table 31.4)

High Toxicity

- **Thallium:** Painful sensory neuropathy

Table 31.4 Rodenticides Classification System

High Toxicity	Moderate Toxicity	Low Toxicity
Thallium: Sensory PN, alopecia, Mees, and Prussian	ANTU = α-Naphthyl thiourea: rat pulmonary edema	Anticoagulants = The superwarfarins: inhibit K1 epoxide, II, VII, IX, X, proteins S and C
SMFA: Uncoupler	Cholecalciferol (D3): Very high Ca, Tx: calcitonin	Bromethalin: Uncoupler
Strychnine: Inhibits glycine, opisthotonus	Red squill: Digitalis glycoside, Tx: DigiBind® or DigiFab®	Norbormide: Rat smooth muscle vasoconstrictor
Zn phosphide: ↓Ca, black vomit, and phosphine gas		
Arsenic: Bloody D and V, Mees' lines		
Barium: Very low K		
Valor (PNU): Alloxan, DKA, and niacinamide		
Yellow phosphorus: Smoking vomit and stool, phossy jaw		

- **SMFA:** Metabolic inhibitor
- **Strychnine:** Opisthotonic paralysis
- **Zinc phosphide:** ↓ Ca-tetany
- **Yellow phosphorus:** Phossy jaw
- **Arsenic:** Hemorrhagic GE, carcinogen
- **Barium:** Hypokalemic paralysis
- **Valor (pyridyl nitrophenyl urea [PNU]):** Islet cell destruction

Moderate Toxicity

- **ANTU (alpha naphthylthiourea):** Rat vasoconstrictor
- **Cholecalciferol (D_3):** ↑ Ca
- **Red squill:** Digitalis toxicity

Low Toxicity

- **Norbormide:** Rat pulmonary edema
- **Bromethalin:** Metabolic uncoupler
- **Anticoagulants:** Vitamin K inhibitors
  - Short-acting warfarins
  - Long-acting superwarfarins (hydroxycoumarins)

High-Toxicity Rodenticides

High Toxicity: *Thallium*

- **Phys:** White, crystalline, odorless, and tasteless powder
- **Mech:** Combines with mitochondrial sulfhydryl groups to interfere with oxidative phosphorylation
- **Onset:** Acute GI, later PNS-2-5 d
- **Sx:** N, bloody vomit and diarrhea, ileus; later HA, painful peripheral sensory neuropathy, myalgias, coma, seizures, later alopecia, and Mees' lines
- **Anti:** Prussian blue (potassium ferric ferrocyanide)
- **Tx:** Lavage + AC

High Toxicity: *Sodium Monofluoroacetate* (1080/1081)

- **Phys:** Same, remains in use—very toxic
- **Mech:** Disrupts the Krebs TCA cycle by inhibiting aconitase; ASA-like *metabolic inhibition, and* uncouples oxidative phosphorylation
- **Onset:** Delayed for 1–2 h
- **Sx:** Hyperthermia, initial hypotension, nausea (N), vomiting (V), seizures, coma, tachydysrhythmias, and high case fatality rates (CFRs)
- **Anti:** None
- **Tx:** Lavage + AC, sorbitol cathartic; glycerol monoacetate = possible antidote

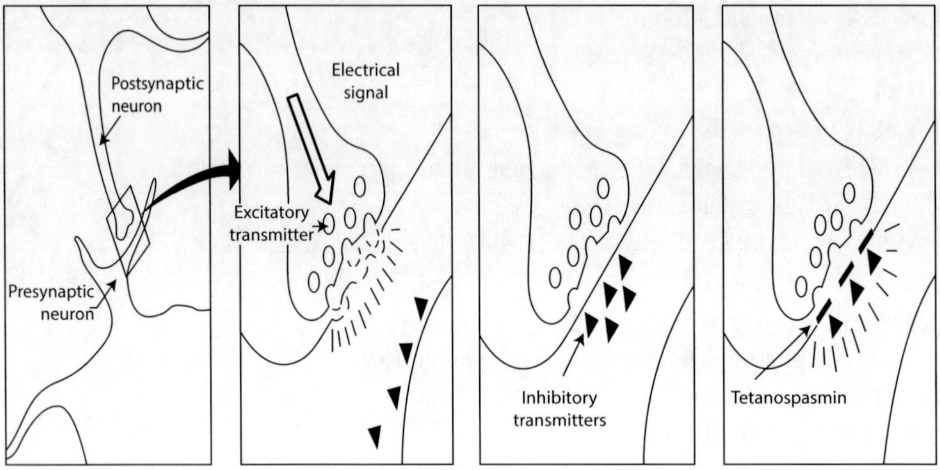

FIGURE 31.1 The mechanism of tetanospasm in strychnine poisoning.

High Toxicity: *Strychnine*

- **Phys:** Bitter white powder, heroin adulterant, and Chinese and Cambodian folk medicine = *Maqianzi.*
- **Mech:** Presynaptic glycine motor inhibition in the spinal cord.
- **Onset:** 10–20 min, T1/2 = 10–16 h.
- **Sx:** Sensorium remains intact with twitching, hyperextension, opisthotonos → skeletal fxs, compartment syn. and rhabdomyolysis, and trismus → risus sardonicus (lockjaw). Pancreatitis possible.
- **Tx:** No antidote; immediate lavage + AC, BZs, barbs, and muscle relaxants; support and quiet room to avoid triggering extensor spasms.

High Toxicity: *Strychnine*

Tetanospasm *Glycine inhibition:* Tetanus causes presynaptic inhibition of the inhibitory transmitter glycine (Figure 31.1).

Mechanism *Opisthotonos:* Tetanic hyperextension causing restrictive respiratory failure pathognomonic of strychnine poisoning and 2° glycine inhibition (Figure 31.2).

Risus Sardonicus (Sardonic Smile)

Strychnine causes postsynaptic inhibition of the inhibitory transmitter *glycine* (Figure 31.3).

High Toxicity: *Zinc Phosphide*

- **Phys:** Dark, gray powder, smells like rotten fish.
- **Mech:** Releases *phosphine gas* and zinc on contact with water and *gastric acid*; also an *AchE inhibitor. Onset:* Within hours.

FIGURE 31.2 Opisthotonic posture characteristic of strychnine poisoning and tetanus. (From Wikipedia Creative Commons.)

- **Sx:** Rotten fish breath, black vomit, rapid ↓ Ca, tetany 2° hypocalcemia–carpopedal spasms, seizures, pulmonary edema 2° inhalation, CV collapse, and acute tubular necrosis—ATN.
- **Anti:** None.
- **Tx:** Immediate dilution with water, milk, or $NaHCO_3$; then lavage–AC–cathartic; and consider proton-pump inhibitor to ↓ gastric acid.

High Toxicity: ***Yellow (White) Phosphorus***

- **Phys:** Whitish-yellow paste
- **Mech:** Burns, phossy jaw
- **Onset:** 1–2 h
- **Sx:** *Garlic breath*, *luminescent* and *smoking vomitus* and *stool*, severe skin and GI mucosal *burns*, CV collapse 2° ↓↓ K and ↓↓ Ca, and coma ↑ hepatic absorption = jaundice

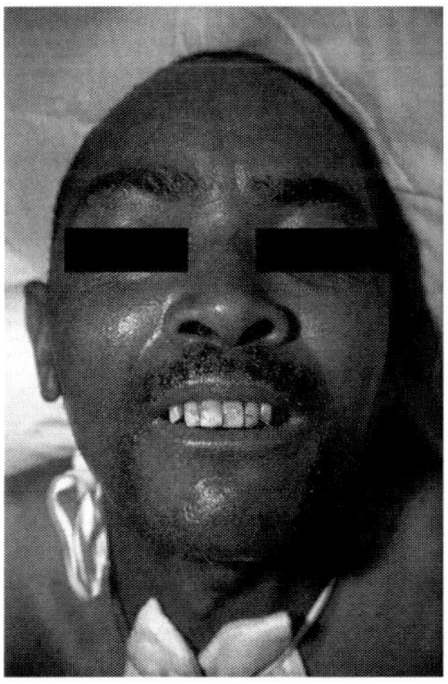

FIGURE 31.3 Risus sardonicus characteristic of strychnine poisoning and tetanus. (Courtesy of the CDC.)

- **Anti:** Orogastric lavage with $KMnO_4$ or H_2O_2 to *oxidize* phosphorus to harmless phosphates
- **Tx:** AC, cathartic, and dextrose; skin burns should be irrigated and debrided under water (MASH episode)

High Toxicity: *Phosphorus: Red vs. Yellow?*

High Toxicity: *Red Phosphorus*

- **Use:** Modern *red "safety"* matches; replaced *yellow* or white phosphorus on exploding matches
- **Tox:** Nonvolatile and insoluble; harmless when ingested
- **Tx:** None indicated

High Toxicity: *Yellow (White) Phosphorus*

- **Use:** Rodenticides and incendiaries
- **Tox:** Volatile and more soluble
- **Skin:** Burns; "phossy jaw" = *mandibular osteonecrosis*
- **GI:** "Smoking" and luminescent vomitus and stools
- **CV:** Direct myocardial depress
- **Tx:** Emesis → OG lavage with 0.1% $KMnO_4$ or 2% H_2O_2 to oxidize P to harmless PO_4s → then AC + sorbitol (not Mg or oil cathartics)
- **Phossy jaw and bisphosphonates:** German white phosphorous match maker nineteenth century; note draining sinus
- Biphosphonates (Fosamax®, Boniva®) twenty-first-century phosphorous-containing compounds capable of causing "phossy jaw" or mandibular osteonecrosis in postmenopausal females taking high-dose or intravenous bisphosphonates for osteoporosis and hip fracture prophylaxis; note swollen R mandible ♀ > 50 (Figure 31.4)

High Toxicity: *Arsenic*

- **Phys:** White crystalline powder
- **Mech:** Combines with sulfhydryl groups
- **Onset:** 1 h, death 24 h
- **Sx:** *Garlic breath*, acute *dysphagia*, muscle cramps, seizures, *vomiting* and *bloody diarrhea*, and then CV collapse; late periph sensory + ascend motor neuropath, Mees' lines
- **Anti:** BAL IM > succimer po > d-penicillamine oral (po) chelation
- **Tx:** Immediate lavage, AC, and cathartic

High Toxicity: *Barium Carbonate*

- **Phys:** Shiny, lumpy water-soluble yellowish powder; unlike insoluble, harmless barium sulfate used in x-ray contrast media. Barium/potassium.
- **Mech:** ↓↓ K as Ba blocks K efflux (phase 3)→ NM block and paralysis.

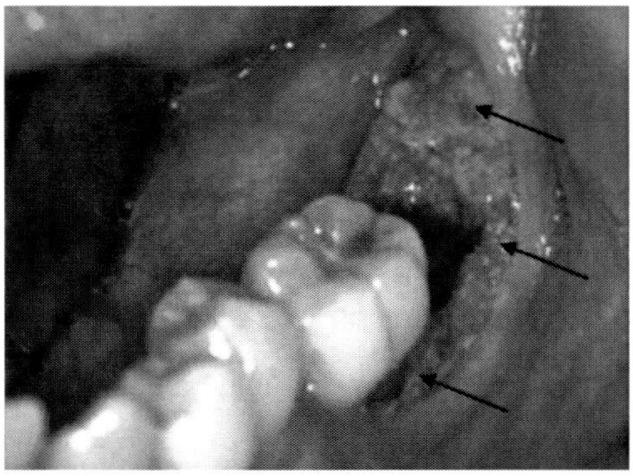

FIGURE 31.4 Phossy jaw. Osteonecrosis of the jaw (arrows) occurred in yellow (or white) phosphorus matchmakers in the mid-eighteenth century that licked the tip of their phosphorus brushes when painting the match tips. Osteonecrosis of the jaw has now reappeared as a result of a complication of bisphosphonate prophylaxis and therapy for osteoporosis. (From American Academy of Family Physicians (AAFP). Available at AAFP.org.)

- **Onset:** 1–8 h
- **Sx:** N, V, D, abdominal pain, *hypokalemic paralysis*, and dysrhythmias—CV collapse
- **Anti:** None
- **Tx:** Lavage with *Na thiosulfate* or *Mg sulfate* to form harmless, *insoluble barium sulfate*, replace K

High Toxicity: *Vacor (Pyridyl-Nitrophenyl Urea)*

- **Phys:** Smells like *peanuts*, looks like cornmeal, and withdrawn in 1979; on ships
- **Mech:** Stops NAD production and targets and destroys *pancreatic β-islet cells*, such as alloxan and streptozotocin
- **Onset:** 4–48 h
- **Sx:** Hyperglycemia, *diabetic ketoacidosis* with autonomic (↓ BP) and peripheral *neuropathy*, orthostatic hypotension, and GI perforation
- **Anti:** *Niacinamide* (nicotinamide), 500 mg IM or IV, then 200 mg q 4 × 48 h
- **Tx:** Early emesis, then lavage + AC + cathartic; insulin and glucose

High Toxicity: Barium: Soluble vs. Insoluble?

Nontoxic: *Insoluble Barium*

- **Rep:** Barium sulfate
- **Use:** Oral radiographic contrast agent: barium swallow, barium enema
- **Tox:** *Insoluble* and harmless when ingested; radio-opaque contrast stays in GI tract
- **Tx:** None indicated

High Toxicity: *Soluble Barium*

- **Rep:** Barium acetate, *carbonate*, Cl, hydroxide, nitrate, and sulfide

- **Use:** Rodenticides (*carbonate*)
- **Tox:** Profound ↓ ↓ > K 2° ↑ muscle membrane permeability, driving extracellular K into muscles
- **CP and renal:** ↓ K = arrhythmias, CHF; *hypokalemic respiratory paralysis;* and acute respiratory failure
- **Tx:** OG lavage with *Na thiosulfate or $MgSO_4$* → soluble $BaCO_3$ → harmless, *insoluble $BaSO_4$*

Moderate-Toxicity Rodenticides

Moderate Toxicity: ***Alpha-Naphthyl Thiourea***

- **Phys:** Odorless, blue–gray powder
- **Mech:** Targets and destroys *rodent pulmonary capillaries* and ↑ capillary permeability with *pulmonary edema* + pleural effusions
- **Onset:** Unknown
- **Sx:** Dyspnea, cyanosis, pulmonary edema, and pleural effusions
- **Anti:** None
- **Tx:** Immediate emesis, lavage, AC, and cathartic

Moderate Toxicity: ***Cholecalciferol (Vitamin D_3)***

- **Phys:** Vitamin D_3 pellets–pills
- **Mech:** Rapidly mobilizes Ca from bones to cause *hypercalcemia*
- **Onset:** Hours to days
- **Sx:** ↑↑ Ca, weakness, metastatic calcifications throughout CV system and kidneys, and osteomalacia
- **Anti:** None
- **Tx:** Emesis or lavage, AC, sorbitol, and fluids—replace K and Mg; diuresis = furosemide, prednisone, and *calcitonin* to reduce high Ca

Moderate-to-Low Toxicity: ***Red Squill = Moderate Toxicity***

- **Phys:** Cardiac glycosides, *scillaren A* and *B*, from the seaside sea onion plant
- **Mech:** "Digitalis toxicity"
- **Onset:** 30 min–6 h
- **Sx:** Digitalis toxicity = N, V, cramps, ventricular dysrhythmias, and AV block
- **Anti:** Digoxin-specific Fabs
- **Tx:** Lavage + AC, lidocaine, and atropine, pacemaker

Low-Toxicity Rodenticides

Low Toxicity: ***Norbormide***

- **Phys:** Yellow cornmeal
- **Mech:** *Specific* rodent-irreversible smooth-muscle vasoconstrictor
- **Onset:** ?

- **Sx:** Hypothermia and hypotension
- **Anti:** None
- **Tx:** Emesis or lavage + AC with cathartic

Red Squill Is Not Red

- **Red squill:** *Urginea maritima* grows near sandy seacoasts
- **Red squill:** *U. maritima* has onion-like bulb and little grayish purple, rarely red flowers

Low Toxicity: *Bromethalin*

- **Phys:** Green pellets
- **Mech:** Uncouples oxidative phosphorylation in mitochondrial electron transport chain, ↓ ATP
- **Onset:** Immediate
- **Sx:** Hyperthermia, muscle tremors, myoclonic jerks, severe flexor spasms, and seizures
- **Anti:** None
- **Tx:** Supportive

Low Toxicity: *Anticoagulants*

- **Phys:** Short-acting warfarins and long-acting hydroxycoumarins or superwarfarins
- **Mech:** Vitamin K_1 antagonism, clotting factor interference-*II (prothrombin), VII, IX, X*
- **Onset:** 12–48 h to longer
- **Sx:** Bleeding and ↑ PT
- **Anti:** Vitamin K_1
- **Tx:** Vitamin K_1 (not K_3), FFP, WB, and GI decontamination

Oxidative Phosphorylation and Rodenticides–Herbicides

- **Oxidative phosphorylation:** An oxidative pathway within the mitochondria that uses the energy released by the oxidation of nutrients to produce ATP to run all cellular processes (Figure 31.5)
- **Inhibitors:** Azide, carbon monoxide, carbon tetrachloride, hydrogen cyanide, hydrogen sulfide, oligomycin, ricin, *rotenone*, salicylates, and *sodium monofluoroacetate*
- **Uncouplers:** Bromethalin, dinitrophenol, dicoumarol, and chlorphenoxyacetic acid herbicides
- **Steps of oxidative phosphorylation:** (1) Glycolysis, (2) fatty acids (FAs) cross outer mitochondrial membrane, and (3) FAs cross inner mitochondrial membrane (Figure 31.5)

Low-Toxicity Rodenticides: Superwarfarins

Low Toxicity: *Anticoagulants*

- **Phys:** Include the short-acting warfarins and long-acting superwarfarins inhibit both *vitamin K 2,3-epoxide reductase* and *vitamin K quinone reductase* reducing active *vitamin K hydroquinone (quinol)*

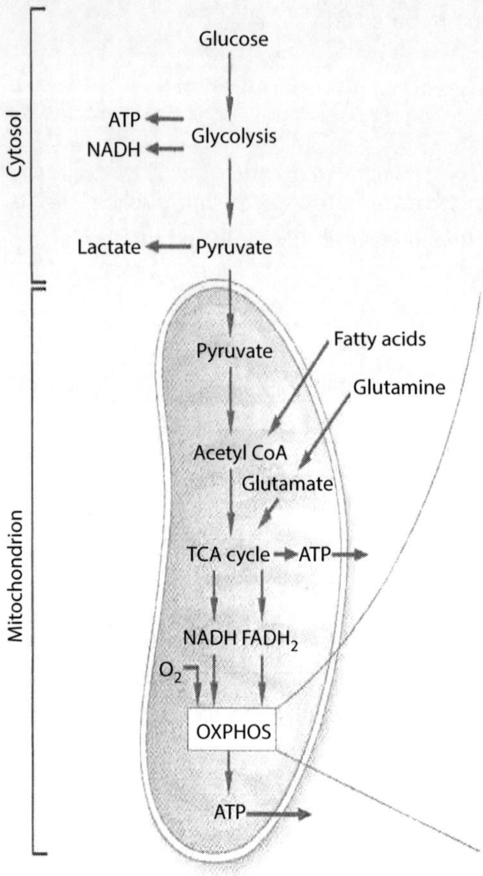

FIGURE 31.5 The steps of oxidative phosphorylation.

- **Mech:** Vitamin K_1 antagonism, clotting factor interference—*II (prothrombin), VII, IX, X* (Figure 31.6)
- **Onset:** 12–48 h to longer
- **Sx:** Bleeding and ↑ PT
- **Anti:** Vitamin K_1
- **Tx:** Vitamin K_1 (not K_3), FFP, WB, and GI decontamination (Figure 31.6)

Superwarfarins: Vitamin K Cycle

Rodenticides: Management of Unknown Ingestions

Immediate Supportive Care

- Assure ABCs
- Identify type and quantity of rodenticide ingested
- Identify *toxidrome* by careful PE
- **Order precise labs:** CBC, PT, glucose, K, Ca, Cl, Mg, HCO_3, LFTs, BUN, and creatinine

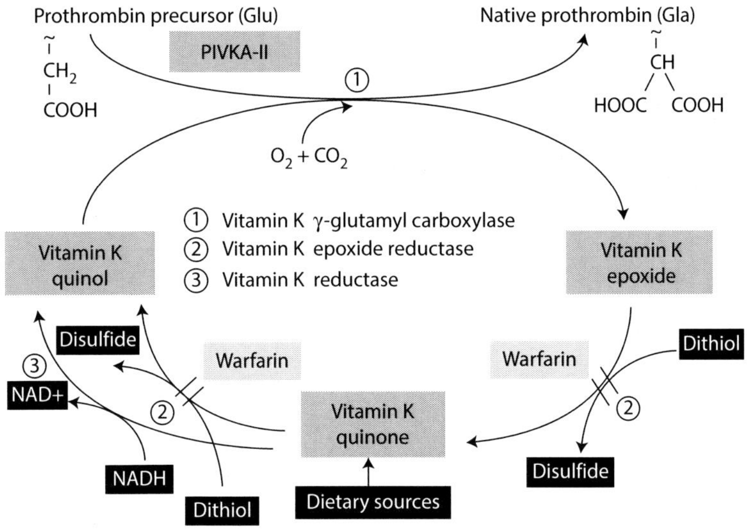

FIGURE 31.6 The vitamin K cycle and its inhibition by warfarin.

Toxidrome DDx

- Careful PE for unusual findings, for example, *alopecia*.
- Smell breath; smell and examine *vomit* and *stool colors*.
- Look for salient *lab (K)* abnormalities within an almost completely normal lab panel.
- Assess *clotting* status—anticoagulants are the most commonly ingested rodenticides.

Rodenticides: Toxidrome DDx

- Painful paresthesias + total alopecia = *thallium*
- Irritability → sz = *SMFA*
- Opisthotonos + awake → sz = *strychnine*
- Rotten fish breath, *black* vomitus → CV collapse = *zinc phosphide*
- Smoking vomit and smoking stool = *yellow phosphorus*
- Dysphagia → bloody vomit and diarrhea = *arsenic*
- Diabetic ketoacidosis, peanut–butter breath, and diabetic neuropathy = *valor*
- Dyspnea → pulmonary edema = *ANTU*
- Hypercalcemia and its associated findings, "stones, bones, moans, groans" = *cholecalciferol*
- Bruising and bleeding = *warfarins*

Fumigants

Fumigants: Methyl Bromide

- **Use:** Soil and seed fumigant, fire extinguishers.
- **Phys:** Colorless, odorless gas; ozone depleter.
- **Mech:** Inhalation/dermal absorption; + chloropicrin added as a lacrimator.

- **Clin:** Initial URI like, CNS dizzy, drowsy, dysarthria, then ataxia, myoclonus, and seizures. Skin: erythema, vesicles. Late peripheral motor neuropathy, epilepsy.
- **Dx:** Bromide levels falsely ↑ Cl.
- **Tx:** BZs and barbs for sz; HD.

Herbicides

Outline

- Paraquat
- Diquat
- Chlorphenoxyacetic acids
- Glyphosate (Round Up®)
- Glufosinate

Herbicides: Paraquat and Diquat

- **Paraquat phys:** Water-soluble, dark-brown liquid, looks like coke; rapid GI absorption, little skin and lung absorption; and a common suicide agent in India and South East Asia.
- **Mech:** Very corrosive to GI tract, O superoxide radical damage to alveolar lining cells > kidneys; ↑↑ pulmonary O_2 toxicity (Figure 31.7).
- **Onset:** Immediate GI effects = N–V–D; subacute ATN in 1–5 days.
- **Sx:** GI ulceration → esophageal perforation → hemorrhagic pulmonary edema → "*diphtheritic membrane*" → late *pulmonary interstitial fibrosis* from O^- superoxide radical toxicity.
- **Tx:** No antidote; immediate adsorbent = AC > Fuller's earth (DE) > bentonite clay; no emesis and lavage 2° ↑ GI perforation risk; sorbitol cathartic; consider bilateral lung tx; and ↓↓ FIO_2.
- **Diquat:** Not taken up by alveolar-lining cells, no oxygen toxicity, no residual interstitial fibrosis, little lung injury, and only renal damage.

Paraquat Tox: Mechanism

- Paraquat cations are reduced by NADPH to cation radicals that chain react with lung O_2 to form superoxide anion radicals (Figure 31.7).

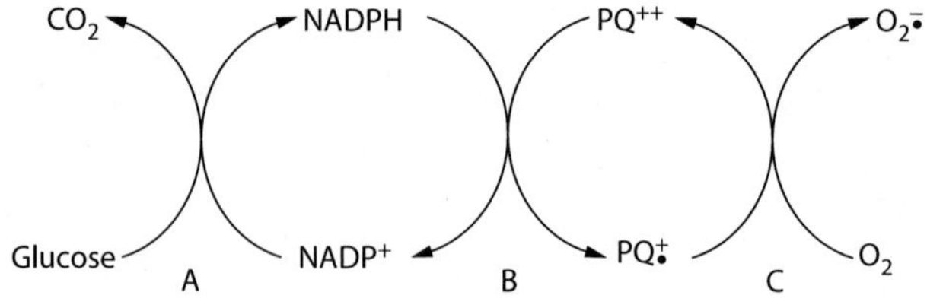

FIGURE 31.7 Paraquat mechanism of toxicity.

Herbicides: Phenols and Chlorphenoxyacetic Acids

- **Reps:** 2,4-D and 2,4,5-T = *dichlorophenoxyacetic* and *trichlorophenoxyacetic* acids; agent orange = 2,4-D + 2,4,5-T + dioxin (TCDD) as a contaminant: chloracne, ↑ LFTs, carcinogenic? Also include *pentachlorophenol creosotes*, the most commonly used pesticides–preservatives on telephone poles.
- **Mech:** Rapid GI absorption of fat-soluble acids that target muscle and CNS and uncouple oxidative phosphorylation, such as *ASA*.
- **Onset:** Acute GI (N, V, and D), then fever and muscle twitching → seizures → coma.
- **Sx:** Muscular weakness, twitching, seizures, ↑ HR and ↓ BP, hyperthermia, and metabolic acidosis.
- **Tx:** No antidote, OG lavage + AC, alkaline diuresis with $NaHCO_3$ to *trap weak acids in blood* and *urine*, and BZs.

Herbicides: Glyphosate (Round Up®)

- **Chem:** An analog of glutamic acid and a member of a new class of herbicides, the phosphonates, which *inhibit AA synthesis required for photosynthesis* and *chlorophyll production* in plants, but do not inhibit AchE in man or animals. Phosphonates do not bioaccumulate in the environment and do not bioconcentrate in man and animals. Among the safest herbicides.
- **LD_{50}:** >5000 mg/kg. Surfactants determine toxicity.

Herbicides: Glufosinate

- **Toxicity:** A commonly used herbicide that on ingestion can inhibit enzymes directing synthesis of both the inhibitory neurotransmitter *GABA* (resulting in seizures) and the excitatory neurotransmitter *glutamate* (resulting in CNS depression) to cause initial CNS depression (drowsiness, disorientation, tremors, ataxia, and then stupor) within 4–8 h; respiratory depression within 24–48 h; and later seizures and respiratory arrest.

Regulatory Federal Legislation

- *Federal Insecticide, Fungicide, and Rodenticide Act—FIFRA* (1972): All pesticides in the United States must be registered with EPA; *general-use* pesticides may be used by *anyone*; and *restricted-use* pesticides that could damage the environment may only be used by *certified applicators.*
- *Toxic Substances Control Act—TSCA* (1976): Maintains the inventory of and regulates all the current *hazardous chemicals*; prevents new potentially hazardous chemicals from entering the market. Most pesticides are exempt from TSCA and are regulated under FIFRA. Under TSCA: PCBs, PCDDs (dioxins), PCDFs, dioxins, CFCs, and asbestos were all banned from manufacture.
- *Asbestos Hazard Emergency Response Act—AHERA* (1986): Amendment to TSCA regarding asbestos abatement in schools.

Conclusions—Posttest

Match the toxidrome below to the pesticide below

1. Easy bruising and bleeding
2. Paresthesias and then seizures
3. Fever and then tremors
4. Salivation and then choreoathetosis
5. Smoking vomit and stool
6. Weakness and then dyspnea
7. Diabetic ketoacidosis and orthostatic hypotension
8. Bloody vomit and diphtheritic pneumonia
9. Peripheral neuropathy and alopecia
10. Hypokalemia and respiratory arrest

a. Paraquat
b. Phosphorous
c. DDT
d. Valor
e. Deltamethrin
f. Permethrin
g. Barium carbonate
h. Hydroxycoumarin
i. Thallium
j. Barium carbonate

Conclusions: Posttest Answers

1.—h.
2.—c.
3.—f.
4.—e.
5.—b.
6.—g.
7.—d.
8.—a.
9.—i.
10.—j.

Chapter 32

Radiation Toxicology

Outline: Radiation Toxicology 728
Introduction 728
Historical Events 728
Definitions 730
Basic Science of Radioactivity 730
Types of Radiation 731
Units of Measurement 732
Sources of Radiation Exposure 734
Radioactive Isotopes 735
Types of Radiation Exposure 736
Outline: Radiation Exposures during Pregnancy 741
Resources 745

Outline: Radiation Toxicology

- Historical information
- Definitions
- Brief basic science of radioactivity
- Types of radiation
- Units of measurement
- Sources of exposure to radiation
- Radioisotopes
- Types of radiation exposure
- Diagnosis
- Management
- Special considerations: Radiation exposures during pregnancy and childhood
- Resources for radiation emergencies

Introduction

- Radiation injuries and the nature of radiation itself have been studied vigorously over the past century as a result of expanding use and prevalence in our society.
- Radiation—(defined): Energy sent out in the form of waves or particles.
- There are two primary forms of radiation, known as ionizing and nonionizing radiation, and these shall be covered in more detail later.
- Major radiation accidents worldwide. Human experiences 1944 to March 1999.

Historical Events

- *1895*—Wilhelm Roentgen discovered x-rays.
- *1896*—Henri Becquerel discovered natural radioactivity.
- Thomas Edison conducted thousands of experiments using an x-ray generator. In 1896, corneal injuries were reported in several of his workers. The death of his assistant, Clarence Dally, became the first radiation-related death in the United States.
- *1899*—Ernest Rutherford discovered that uranium compounds produce three different kinds of radiation. He separated the radiations according to their penetrating abilities and named them α-, β-, and γ-radiation, after the first three letters of the Greek alphabet.
- The British Army used portable x-ray machines to find bullets and shrapnel in wounded soldiers in Sudan.
- Emergence of radioactive substances as health products.
- *1915*—British Roentgen Society recognized the potential hazards for radiation and proposed standards for radiation protection of workers: shields, medical exams, and restricted work hours.

- *1917*—U.S. Radium Luminous Materials Corporation, painted radium-luminescent paint on watches/jewelry. Mostly, female workers would use lips to point the paintbrushes. By 1927, about 100 of the women would die from osteosarcoma, brain tumors, and would develop noncancerous lesions of mouth, related to radium exposure.
- *1945*—The only atomic bomb used in war: Little Boy (Hiroshima) had a uranium core, and the blast was equivalent to 12,500 tons of TNT. Fat Man (Nagasaki) had a plutonium core, and the blast was equivalent to 20,000 tons of TNT.
- Estimates of dead: +200,000 souls.
- Most of them died from bomb blasts, but many thousands died of acute radiation syndrome and radiation-induced cancers.
- *1950s*—Physicians used a thorium-containing contrast agent, thoratrast (α-emitting). It is found to have a very slow elimination rate, accumulated in the hepatic tissue, and cases of angiosarcomas and hepatic carcinomas lead to its abandonment.
- *1979*—Three Mile Island, PN. No deaths or injuries, but a malfunction causes a core meltdown that was contained, which led to drastic changes in nuclear power in the United States.
- *1986*—Chernobyl, Ukraine. 31 acute fatalities; 116,500 exposures. A series of errors led to a fire in the number 4 reactor core, several explosions, and meltdown of the reactor. Over the first 10 days following the incident, a cloud spread to the Baltic States, Scandinavia, and Europe carrying radioactive material (^{131}I and ^{137}Cs). The reactor entombed in a giant concrete sarcophagus. Among the 600 workers present on the site at the time of the accident, 134 received high radiation doses and suffered from acute radiation sickness. The area around Chernobyl closed in a 30-km exclusion zone.
- *1987*—Goiania, Brazil. Locals scavenged the remains of an abandoned medical clinic and found a source of ^{137}Cs. Resulted in over 200 exposures and four deaths. Were weeks before the source of the sickness could be discovered and the proper diagnosis and treatment was given.
- *2011*—Fukushima Prefecture, Japan. A nuclear power plant that opened in 1971 suffered major damage from a tsunami spawned by an undersea magnitude 9.0 earthquake in the Pacific Ocean. The disaster disabled reactor-cooling systems, leading to multiple reactor unit meltdowns with significant immediate radiation releases into the atmosphere that triggered a 30-km evacuation zone surrounding the plant. As piped water to cool reactors initially escaped containment, a significant amount of radioactive water was later released into the Pacific Ocean over several months. Two workers who sought shelter from the tsunami in the basement of reactor unit 4 drowned.
- Since December *1990*—Over 50 accidents have occurred worldwide, involving more than 650 individuals. Of these, more than 250 have had significant exposure and more than 30 have died.
- Approximately 10 million "sealed" sources of radiation exist in more than 50 countries. Sources are encased in metal and used for medicinal, agricultural, industrial, and research purposes.

- 612 sources reported lost or stolen since 1995; 254 have not been recovered. May be more sealed sources not accounted for.

Who Is at Risk? Professions That May Incur Radiation Exposure

- Pharmacists
- Physicians/researchers
- Radiologists/oncologists
- Support staff (nurses/techs)
- Miners: Asbestos, coal, diatomaceous earth, iron, and miscellaneous rare earths
- Nuclear facility workers
- Military
- NASA, aerospace workers
- Patients

Definitions

- *Radiation*—Energy sent out in the form of waves or particles.
- *Ionization*—The ability of high-energy radiation to displace electrons from atoms and cause matter through which it Passes to become electrically charged.
- *Nonionizing radiation*—Long-wavelength, low-frequency, and low-energy form. Ex: ultraviolet rays, visible rays, infrared rays, radio waves, and microwaves. Lasers, ultrasound, and NMR systems.
- *Ionizing radiation*—Short-wavelength, high-frequency, and high-energy forms. Emitted from unstable forms of elements called radioisotopes. Ex: x-rays and γ-rays.
- *Half-life*—The period of time it takes for a radioisotope to lose half of its radioactivity.
- *Isotope*—A variation of an element with a different number of neutrons in the nucleus. All isotopes of an element have the same number of protons; differing neutrons give isotopes of the same element but with different atomic weights.
- *Decay* (disintegration)—Unstable isotopes spontaneously transform to reach a more stable configuration, and may involve the release of ionizing radiation.
- *Radioisotope*—Isotope that releases ionizing radiation during its decay.
- *Criticality*—The chain reaction of fissionable atoms that results in the release of energy. The basic operating principle behind fusion bombs and nuclear reactors is an efficient means of generating energy.

Basic Science of Radioactivity

- Radiation may be due to loss of α-particles, electrons (–charged β-particles or +positrons), γ-rays, and x-rays.

- An atom can decay to a product element through the loss of a negatively or positively charged electron (β-particle or positron).
- γ-Radiation results when the nucleus releases excess energy, usually after an α-, β-, or positron transition.

Types of Radiation

Four Main Types of Radiation

1. Alpha (α): Particulate
2. Beta (β): Particulate
3. Neutron (N): Particulate
4. Gamma (γ): Nonparticulate

Alpha (α) Particles

- Heavy (high mass), highly charged particle composed of two protons and two neutrons.
- Travel at a low velocity and readily interact with matter.
- Deposit a large amount of energy in a small volume of tissue.
    - Easily shielded and cannot penetrate paper. However, they can penetrate the epithelial tissue to a depth of 50 μm, deep enough to damage the epithelium.
    - Significant biologic hazard only when internalized (via inhalation, open wounds, and ingestion).
- Heavy radioisotopes with an atomic number above 82 (uranium, radium, and plutonium) are sources of α-particle emission.
- *Cannot* be detected with standard Geiger counters.

Beta (β) Particles

- Smaller mass and charge, greater velocity than α-particles. High-energy electrons, emitted from the nuclei of unstable atoms (cesium-137 and iodine-131).
- Interact with matter to a lesser extent and create less ionization along its path. Travel further and penetrate deeper than α.
    - 8 mm into the exposed skin and can cause serious burns, especially if allowed to remain on the skin. External coverings offer some protection.
    - Note: Children are more susceptible to adults due to less-keratinized epithelium.
    - Hazard if internally deposited.
- Most radioisotopes decay by β-radiation followed by γ-radiation.
- Can be detected with routine instruments such as Geiger counters.

Neutrons (N)

- Electrically neutral particles (lack of charge prevents deep penetration), wide range of energy, velocity, and penetration power.

- Unique form of exposure. High-level neutron exposure can induce radioactivity (previous stable atoms can become radioactive via neutron collision releasing α- and β-particles).
  - In the human tissue, the induced isotope is usually Na-24, which can be detected in urine and blood.
- Sources limited to nuclear power plants, linear accelerators, and weapon assembly sites.

Gamma (γ) Radiation (and X-Rays)

- Electromagnetic waves (nonparticulate) with no mass or charge that travel at the speed of light.
- γ-Rays are the most penetrating type of ionizing radiation, traveling for many centimeters in the tissue.
- Exposure to an external source of γ- or high-power x-rays represents a significant whole-body radiation hazard and may result in acute radiation syndrome (ARS).
- Frequently accompanied α- and β-particles, can be detected with Geiger counters and dosimeters.

Units of Measurement

Various units describe radiation dose, exposure, and quantity (Table 32.1).

- Roentgen (R) is the unit used to describe radiation *exposure*. Measures radioactivity per unit of air.
- Rad (radiation-absorbed dose) and gray (Gy) both measure *absorbed doses* of radiation.
  - 100 rads = 1 Gy
  - Gy = Absorption of 1 J/ kg
- Dose-equivalent quantification.
- Rem—(Roentgen equivalent man), or seivert (Sv).
  - 100 rem = 1 Sv

Table 32.1 Units of Measurement

Description	Convention	SI	Conversion
Activity	Curie (Ci)	Becquerel (Bq)	1 Bq ~ 2.7×10^{-11} Ci 1 Ci ~ 3.7×10^{10} Bq
Exposure	Roentgen (R)	Coul/kg	1 R = 2.58×10^{-4} Coul/kg
Absorbed dose	Rad (r)	Gray (Gy)	1 rad =0.01 Gy 1 Gy = 100 rad
Dose equivalent	Rem	Sievert (SV)	1 rem = 0.01 Gy 1 Sv = 100 rem
Internalized radiation	Body burden	N/A	

- Dose-equivalent quantification is obtained by multiplying the dose in radiations by a quality factor that describes biologic damage.
- The quality factor for x-rays, β- particles, and γ-radiation is 1. The quality factor for α-particles and neutrons is 20.

Quantity of Radiation

- Measured by the activity or number of atomic disintegrations per unit time.
- Unit is the curie (Ci) and becquerel (bQ).
  - 1 Ci = 1.37×10^{10} transformations/s
  - 1 bQ = 1 transformation/s
  - 1 mCi equals 37 MbQ
- Body burden is the reference to the internally deposited radioactive material. Different radio nucleotides will deliver different amounts of radiation when internalized.

Radiation Units of Measure

- Radiation monitoring.
- *Dosimeters* are small devices that are worn on the upper torso and record cumulative radiation that an individual receives.
  - Film badge measures β-, x-, and γ-radiation.
  - Dose is recorded in rem or sievert.
  - Requires processing.
  - Pocket dosimeters can be read by holding to the light source.
- *Survey meters* are rate meters that record the amount of radiation detected in an area per unit of time.
  - Ion chambers are the common survey meters for recording x- and γ-radiation.
  - Calibrated in mR/h.
  - Geiger–Müeller (GM) instruments are used for surveys for external contamination. Detect lower exposures of x-, γ-, and β-radiation.
  - Recorded in counts/minute: 2500 cpm = ~1 mR/h.

Laws of Radiosensitivity

Three laws developed by observation of radiation damage on the human tissue:

1. Radiosensitivity directly varies with the rate of cell division; rapidly dividing cells are more profoundly affected. (GI tract, skin, and appendages.)
2. Radiosensitivity directly varies with the number of future divisions. (Increased future divisions in gonads–ovaries–oogenesis, embryogenesis; testes–spermatogenesis; bone marrow–hematopoiesis; epithelial linings–GI, skin, and appendages [hair follicles].)
3. Radiosensitivity indirectly varies with the degree of morphological and functional differentiation. (Bone growth plate.)

Sources of Radiation Exposure

The average *annual dose* to persons in the United States is approximately 3.6 mSv (360 mrem).

- Standard *CXR* delivers 6–11 mrem (0.06 –0.11 mSv, 0.06–0.11 mGy).
- Barium enema, 0.7 rem (700 mrem, 7 mSv, or 7 mGy).
- Lowest dose with notable bone marrow suppression with a decrease in blood counts is 10–50 rem (100–500 mSv, 0.1–0.5 Gy).
- Lowest total body dose from ionizing radiation from which death may be seen is in the range of 1.0–2.0 Gy.

Exposure can occur by a variety of means:

1. Background radiation
2. Medical exposure
3. Accidental industrial exposure
4. Nuclear reactor accidents
5. Detonation of nuclear weapons

- Background exposure
  - Numerous sources of background radiation.
    - Cosmic and terrestrial radiation: 60 mrem/year.
    - Natural radioactivity in the body: 40 mrem/year.
    - Radon: (Variable—~200 mrem/year).
      - Radioactive noble gas enters homes/buildings from the materials themselves or cracks in the structure.
      - Risk to humans via inhalation and increases the risk for lung cancer. Smokers have even more increased risk.
      - Areas of NY, NJ, and PA have particularly high levels.
  - Air travel, smoke detection devices, food products, and fluorescent materials: (~10–20 mrem/year).
- Medical exposure
  - Radiation extensively used for diagnosis and treatment.
  - CXR, cardiac catheterization (16 rems), and administration of radioactive elements (technetium, brachytherapy, and radiation therapy).
- Industrial exposure
  - Radiation is used to examine high-pressure pipe welds, valves, and vessels.
    - Industrial accidents account for the largest amount of radiation injuries.
    - Include:
      - Inadvertent discharge of radioactive waste into the environment.
      - Leaks in the irradiation facility containment units.
      - Explosion of underground waste storage tanks.
- Nuclear reactors
  - 438 commercial nuclear-generating units worldwide.

  - 104 of these units operate at 65 locations in the United States.
  - Accidents can occur when barriers that isolate the heated radioactive wastewater are breached and allow water and/or materials, such as radioactive rods, to be released into the environment.
  - Large amounts of γ- and neutron energy are released without a nuclear explosion (criticality accident).
  - Causes large doses of whole-body radiation exposure.
- Nuclear weapons
  - Detonation results in the tremendous release of thermal energy, γ-radiation, α-, and β-particles. Detected in the vicinity of detonation and in fallout.
  - "Dirty bomb," is a combination of radioactive materials and traditional explosives.

Radioactive Isotopes

- Numerous radioisotopes are in use in many different industries.
- *Radioisotope*—Isotope that releases ionizing radiation during its decay.

Pathophysiology of Radiation Exposure

- Ionizing radiation causes direct and indirect damage to the tissue.
- Directly, it impacts the target molecule and causes damage. In DNA, mutations may arise, resulting in the neoplasm or cell death.
- Indirectly, radiation impacts a molecule and creates a reactive species (free radicals) that may chemically react with organic molecules in cells, altering their structure or function.
- Usually, time and oxygen allow the organism to repair radiation damage, molecular scavengers such as glutathione help to protect against free radicals. When these systems are overwhelmed by large doses of radiation, permanent damage may occur.

Preparing for Arrival of Victims

Emergency Department Preparation

- Separate entrance established.
- Area for decontamination/treatment is established.
- Pregnant women, nonessential equipment, and personnel removed.
- Equipment and radiation supply kits are brought from storage (dosimeters, collection containers, and survey meters).
- Boundaries to delineate clean from contaminated areas. Radiation signs, floors covered with nonskid plastic.
- Ventilation system turned off to prevent contamination from the rest of the hospital if airborne contamination is a possibility.

Obtain Detailed Account of the Incident

1. What radioactive substances are involved?
2. What type of exposure occurred?
3. How many victims?

Arrival of Patients

- Emergency team dons protective clothing and dosimeters.
- Contaminated clothing/items placed in bags, containers.
- No one should leave radioactivity triage area/treatment area unless cleared by a radiation safety officer.
- Emergency intervention/treatment should not be delayed because of contamination.
- Mass casualty scenarios may involve only giving palliative care for those who received a known lethal dose of radiation.

Types of Radiation Exposure

May occur alone or simultaneously:

- *Perceived radiation injury* (Fear out of proportion to actual danger, anxiety symptoms)
- External contamination
- Internal contamination
- Partial-body irradiation
- Whole-body irradiation

Clinical Assessment

- **History:** Location of the incident, duration of exposure, interval between exposure and evaluation, activity, and location at the time of exposure, occupation.
- **Physical:** ABCs of CPR, vital signs, neurological assessment, GI exam, and hematologic exam (skin as well).
- **Initial laboratory:** Complete blood count (CBC) with differential, platelet count, and initial chemistries. The time of CBC must be carefully noted. Serial CBCs for 6–12 h for at least three samples.

External Contamination

Radioactive materials are deposited on the patient's skin or clothing.

- Dose from external contamination to the patient or medical staff is rarely significant.
- The main hazard is the spreading of contamination in the environment or potential for internalization.

- The radionuclide itself is not important immediately, and not important to know whether or not it emits β-, γ-, and/or α-radiation.
- An externally contaminated *child* should have all clothing removed, preferably at the scene.
- Once medically stable, analysis with Geiger or α-counters determines the sequence for radionuclide decontamination of intact skin.
- To assess internal contamination, saline-water swabs should be taken of all orifices and wounds and assessed for radioactivity.
- Decontamination:
  - Debridement of open wounds, remove as much debris as possible. Metallic fragments should be removed with thongs or forceps.
  - Copious irrigation of wounds with saline until free of radioactivity, then covered with a waterproof dressing.
  - Contaminated burns should be treated as thermal burns.
    - *Mouth*: Frequent tooth brushing and gargling if the oral cavity is contaminated. Gastric lavage indicated if the radioactive substance is swallowed.
    - *Eyes*: Rinse from *inner* canthus to *outer* canthus, avoid contamination of nasolacrimal duct.
    - *Ears*: Rinse auditory canal with saline if TM is intact.
- Decontamination.
  - Sponge with lukewarm soap and water.
  - Avoid cold water as it closes pores and traps radioactive materials.
  - Avoid hot water because it causes vasodilatation and increases risk of absorption.
  - Avoid further damage to the skin as this may increase risk of absorption.
  - Sponged areas should be reevaluated every 5 min until activity is consistent with background levels.
  - Hair should be clipped if washing is insufficient for decontamination, do not shave.

Internal Contamination

Radioactive material enters the body through (Table 32.2):

1. Inhalation
2. Ingestion
3. Absorption through MM or skin

- Internally deposited radioactive material will continue to irradiate tissues until it decays to a stable isotope or is biologically eliminated.
- Biochemical nature of the radionuclide determines if it is disseminated throughout the body or concentrated in a specific organ.
- *Critical organ*—Organ that receives the highest dose of radiation or is the most damaged by radiation.

Table 32.2 Internal Contamination

Radionuclide	Route	1′ Hazard	Treatment Mechanisms	Agent	Administration
I-131	Inhalation Ingestion Percutaneous	Thyroid	Block thyroid uptake	KI	390 mg QD for 7–14 days
Pu-239	Inhalation Ingestion Wounds	Bone Liver Lung	Chelation, increases excretion	DTPA	1 g/day for 5 days
H-3	Inhalation Ingestion Percutaneous	Whole-body dose	Isotopic dilution, Increase excretion	Water	PO: 3–4 L QD for 2 weeks
Cs-137	Inhalation Ingestion	Whole-body dose	Mobilization, decreases GI uptake	Ferric ferrocyanide (Prussian blue)	1 g PO in 100–200 mL water TID for days

- Identification of radionuclides is important for determining the method and sequence of treatment.
- Internally deposited radionuclides were identified by radioanalysis of substances excreted from the body (saliva, blood, feces, and urine). Known as *bioassay measurement.*
- Collect urine and feces for 4 days to monitor excretion rate.
- If ingested, begin gut decontamination (emetics, gastric lavage) (Table 32.2).

External Irradiation

General Concepts

1. Acute dose gives more biologic damage than the same radiation dose over a more protracted period of time.
2. Biologic injury at the time of exposure, clinical signs, and symptoms manifest over time.
3. Time of exposure to the onset of symptoms is inversely related to the radiation dose received.
4. Penetrating types of radiation result in a whole-body dose.
5. Nonpenetrating types (alpha, beta) do not deliver a whole-body dose.

Whole-Body Radiation/Acute Radiation Syndrome

- Characteristic signs and symptoms develop when an organism is exposed to significant doses of radiation over a short period of time.
- Known as ARS.
- Whole-body dose of γ-radiation in excess of 2 Gy (200 rad) is the main cause of ARS.

Four Distinct Phases

1. Prodromal phase
2. Latent phase
3. Manifested illness phase
4. Recovery phase or death

Prodromal Phase

- First 48 h following exposure, but may develop up to 6 days after exposure.
- Early symptoms include anorexia, apathy, nausea, vomiting, diarrhea, fever, tachycardia, and/or headache.
- Generally mild or absent at total body doses of 1 Gy or less.
- Patients whose symptoms begin more than 2 h after exposure were probably exposed to doses <2 Gy. Recover in about 1 month.
- Onset of symptoms within the first 2 h usually indicates significant and potentially lethal exposures exceeding 2 Gy.
- At high doses (e.g., 10 to >20 Gy), prodromal symptoms occur in virtually all patients within minutes of exposure. Death in days to weeks.

Latent Phase

- Symptom-free interval that follows resolution of the prodromal phase
- May last for 1–3 weeks with a dose <4 Gy (400 rads)
- May last for only a few hours with a dose above 15 Gy received

Manifested Illness Phase

- Often divided into three dose-dependent subsyndromes:
  - Hematopoietic syndrome
  - GI syndrome
  - Cardiovascular and CNS syndrome
- Overlap between the three subsyndromes

Hematopoietic Syndrome

- First system to express injury from whole-body irradiation. Symptoms are seen from doses above 1.5 Gy.
- Radiation damages lymphocytes and damages stem cells in the bone marrow and lymphatic system.
- Rapid decline in lymphocytes is a hallmark of hematopoietic syndrome.
- Granulocytes and platelets display an initial rise and then a decrease to a nadir at about 30 days.
- Mild anemia.
- Effects are pancytopenia and immunosuppression with *hemorrhage and infection* principle that are the causes of morbidity and mortality. Worse at 2–3 weeks.

GI Syndrome

- Doses higher than HS syndrome, 6–7 Gy.
- Onset of N/V, diarrhea within hours of exposure.
- Latent phase of 1 week and then reoccurrence of symptoms and pain.
- Damage to GI mucosa leads to massive fluid loss and electrolyte disturbances.
- Enteric flora often invades blood stream leading to sepsis; immunocompromised state of HS does not help.
- The few documented cases were all fatal.

CNS/CV Syndrome

- Doses above 20–30 Gy
- Immediate prostration, N/V, explosive, bloody diarrhea, and hypotension
- Alterations in consciousness, lethargy, and seizures, within hours of exposure
- Hypotension refractory to treatment
- Universally fatal with death in 24–72 h, mainly from circulatory collapse

Pulmonary

- Radiation doses above 8–9 Gy can damage the pulmonary system leading to pnuemonitis, interstitial edema, and fibrosis.
- Lethal dose:
  - LD 50/60:
    - 4.5 Gy assumes intensive medical care provided.
    - 3.4 Gy, only first aid.
    - High survival rate in Chernobyl victims of doses ~6 Gy.
    - Cytokine administration and stem cell transplant may raise LD 50/60 to 11 Gy.

Treatment of ARS

- Obtain labs, collect specimens, and decontaminate.
- Alleviation of symptoms, pain management.
- The ultimate treatment goal is to provide support during periods of deficient defenses against infection and hemorrhage, until the bone marrow recovers.
- Support includes IV fluids, transfusions (note: blood products should be irradiated), ABX, TPN, and antifungal medications (*Candida* most common in neutropenic patients).
- Monitor for HSV, CMV, and pneumocystis.
- Family and patient should undergo HLA typing if marrow transplant is possible. Doses above 8–9 Gy. (11 of 13 Chernobyl patients who received transplants died—causes are multifactorial.)
- Research into hematopoietic growth factors and cytokines (stimulate stem cells and reconstitute bone marrow).

Local Radiation Exposure

- Partial body exposures.
- Clinical picture consists of cutaneous changes.
- Doses above 2–3 Gy may present with erythema, itching. Occurs within hours.
- Faster occurrence signifies higher doses.
- Other changes include epilation, desquamation, and necrosis.
- Appear similar to thermal burns, but unlike thermal burns, erythema may reappear, delayed onset of pain, and more chronic, severe pain. Exception: High-dose radiation may give third-degree transdermal burn, pain immediate and excruciating, and surgical resection and grafting may be required.
- **Treatment:** Analgesics, routine burn care, and surgical referral. PT and splinting may prevent contractures and preserve ROM.

Special Populations

Prenatal

- Fetal cells are largely undifferentiated and highly proliferative. Damage depends on the phase of gestation.
  - *0–2 weeks*: Irradiation results in death with reabsorption or no obvious damage.
  - *≥2 weeks*: Risk of congenital malformations due to organogenesis. After 7 weeks, organogenesis is complete with the exception of CNS.
  - The most common injuries to CNS are MR and microcephaly.
  - Minimum exposure of 0.1–0.2 Gy needed for injury.
  - Fetal thyroid takes up iodine at 12 weeks.
- *Elderly*—More susceptible due to decreased bone marrow reserve and increased likelihood of comorbidities.

Outline: Radiation Exposures during Pregnancy

- Uses and sources of exposure
- Risks and health effects
- Risk reduction

Exposure of Pregnant Patients

- Prenatal doses from most properly performed diagnostic procedures present no increased risk of prenatal death, malformation, or mental impairment.
- Higher doses such as those from therapeutic procedures can result in significant fetal harm (Tables 32.3 and 32.4).
- Radionuclides such as iodine-131 cross the placenta and can pose fetal risks.
- After 10 weeks of gestational age, the fetal thyroid accumulates iodine.

Table 32.3 Fetal Dose Exposure from Conventional X-Rays

Examination	Dose Mean (mGy)	Maximum Dose (mGy)
Abdomen	1.4	4.2
Chest	<0.01	<0.01
Intravenous urogram— lumbar spine	1.7	10
Pelvis	1.1	4
Skull–thoracic spine	<0.01	<0.01
Thoracic spine		

Table 32.4 Fetal Dose Exposure from CT and Fluoroscopic Studies Exposures from Nuclear Medicine Studies

Examination	Dose Mean (mGy)	Maximum Dose (mGy)
Barium swallow (UGI)	1.1	5.8
Barium enema	6.8	24
Head CT	<0.005	<0.005
Chest CT	0.06	1
Abdomen CT	8	49
Pelvis CT	25	80

- High fetal thyroid doses from radioiodine can result in permanent hypothyroidism.
- If pregnancy is discovered within 12 h of radio-iodine administration, prompt oral administration of stable potassium iodine (60–130 mg) to the mother can reduce the fetal exposure (Tables 32.5 and 32.6).

Table 32.5 Fetal Dose Exposure from Common Nuclear Medicine Studies

Procedure	Early Pregnancy (mGy)	Fetus at Term (mGy)
Tc—99 m		
Bone scan	4.7	1.8
Lung scan	0.9	0.9
Liver colloid scan	0.6	1.1
Thyroid scan	4.4	3.7
Renal DTPA	9	3.5
Red blood cell	6	2.5
I-123 thyroid uptake	0.6	0.3
I-131 thyroid uptake	0.04	0.15

Table 32.6 Risks in Pregnant Patients without Radiation Exposure

Risk	
Spontaneous abortion	>15%
Incidence of genetic abnormalities	4–10%
Intrauterine growth retardation	4%
Incidence of major malformation	2–4%

Fetal Radiation Risks and Health Effects

- Radiation-related risks during pregnancy are related to the stage of pregnancy and absorbed dose.
- Risks are most significant during organogenesis and in the early fetal period, somewhat less in the second trimester, and least in the third trimester.

Gestational Age and Radiation Dose

- <2 weeks gestation (the time after conception): Exposure of >0.1 Gy (10 rads) is the death of the embryo.
- <13 weeks gestation: Permanent retardation of physical growth with increasing dose, particularly above 1 Gy (100 rads). (Atomic bomb survivor data suggest about a 3–4% reduction of height at the age of 18 when the dose is >1 Gy.)
- 26 weeks: The fetus is less sensitive to the noncancer health effects of radiation exposure.
- Anytime: Doses above 1 Gy (100 rads) increase the risk for miscarriage, neonatal death, and stillbirth.
- In all stages of gestation, radiation-induced noncancer health effects are not detectable for fetal doses below about 0.05 Gy (5 rads).

Malformations and CNS Effects from Fetal Exposure

- Malformations have a threshold of >~100–200 mGy and are typically associated with CNS problems.
- Fetal doses >1000 mGy can result in reduction in IQ, severe mental retardation, and microcephaly, particularly during 8–15 weeks and to a lesser extent at 16–25 weeks.
- Preconception irradiation of either parent's gonads has not been shown to result in increased risk of cancer or malformations in children.

Steps to Prevent Exposures

- Be aware of placement of radiological equipment in the workplace.
- Use personal protective shields and equipment.
- Review material safety data sheets to become familiar with reproductive hazards.

- Participate in all safety and health education, training, and monitoring programs offered by the employer.

Pregnancy Confirmation and Evaluation

- In female patients of child-bearing age, an attempt should be made to determine parity prior to radiologic imaging.
- Notices should be posted in patient and work areas warning of radiation exposure hazards (i.e., If it is possible that you might be pregnant, notify the physician or other staff before your x-ray examination, treatment, or before being injected with a radioactive material).

Radiation Exposure of Pregnant Workers

- Informed consent—The pregnant patient or worker has a right to know the magnitude and type of potential radiation effects that might result from *in utero* exposure.
- Communication should be related to the level of risk. Communicating that risk is negligible is adequate for very-low-dose procedures (<1 mGy to the fetus).
- Pregnant employees may work in a radiation environment if assurance exists that the fetal dose can be kept below 1 mGy during the pregnancy.
- Research involving radiation exposure of pregnant patients should be discouraged.

Review of NIOSH Publications

- **National occupational research agenda. DHHS (NIOSH) publication no. 96.115—**Discusses fertility and pregnancy abnormalities as one of 21 priority research areas.
- **The effects of workplace hazards on male reproductive health. DHHS (NIOSH) publication no. 96.132—**Provides general information about reproductive hazards for men in the workplace and suggests methods for preventing exposures.

Termination of Pregnancy

- High fetal doses (100–1000 mGy) during late pregnancy are not likely to result in malformations or birth defects since all the organs have been formed.
- Termination at fetal doses < 100 mGy is not justified based on current risk assessments.
- Fetal doses > 500 mGy can cause significant damage at which point termination may be considered.

Special Populations

Children

- Goals of management:
  - Limit exposure
  - Reduce further damage to the child's cellular systems

- The key is to distance the fetus, infant, or child as far away from the site of exposure and to decontaminate external and internal (ingested) radionuclides. Fallout affects children more due to smaller size and higher absorption.
- KI should be available in schools, nurseries, and so on if it is within 10 miles from a nuclear reactor.

Radiation Safety

Protection is accomplished through:

1. Minimizing the time of exposure
2. Maximizing the distance from the source
3. Using a shield as appropriate

Resources

Department of Energy Radiological Assistance Program:

Oak Ridge Operations Office
P.O. Box E, Oak Ridge, TN 37380
(423) 576-1005, 24 h: (423) 481-1000
www.orau.gov/reacts
http://www.nrc.gov/reading-rm/contact-pdr.html

Chapter 33

Chemical, Biological, and Radiological Weapons and Warfare

Outline 748
Chemical and Biological Weapons and Warfare 748
Biological Weapons 755

Outline

- CBW definitions
- CBW similarities
- CBW differences
- History of CBW
- Chemical weapons
- Biological weapons
- Emergency responsiveness
- Hierarchies of prevention

Chemical and Biological Weapons and Warfare

Definitions: Chemical

- **Chemical warfare:** The intentional use of noxious or toxic chemicals as weapons was designed to terrorize, incapacitate, injure, or kill mass groups of people.
- **Ex:** Chlorine and phosgene: Both gases are frequently transported by rail for use in drinking water purification, and chemical and plastic manufacturing, and are ubiquitously available as potential, simple chemical weapons. *Phosgene gas caused 85% of all gas deaths in WWI.*

Definitions: Biological

- **Biological warfare:** The intentional use of either microorganisms or toxins produced by a variety of living organisms include viruses (smallpox), bacteria (*C. botulinum*), fungi (mycotoxins), and plants (ricin) to cause dysfunction or death in people, livestock, and/or agricultural crops.
- **Ex:** *Bacillus anthracis:* The sporulating anthrax bacillus is the most environmentally stable and easily disseminated of all the class A biological warfare (BW) agents.

CW and BW Similarities

- Both CW and BW are employed as *weapons of terror or mass destruction.*
- CW and BW often use the *same delivery systems*, including artillery shells, missiles, and bombs.
- Both CW and BW are dispersed most effectively as *aerosols or vapors.*
- The atmospheric movement of CW and BW is primarily determined by *wind* and *other weather conditions, especially temperature.*
- Wearing appropriate *personal protective equipment* will prevent injury from both CW and BW.

CW and BW Differences

Differences	Chemical Weapons	Biological Weapons
Confirmation	Easier: 2° rapid onset effects, odors, and simple detectors	Harder: 2° delayed onset effects; no color, no odors, and taste; limited detectors
Incubation	*Immediate: Minutes to hours*	*Delayed: Days to weeks*
Distribution	Close, downwind, and nonrandom	Widely dispersed and random
Persistence	Liquids persist (VX and mustard); gases dissipate	Nonpersistent, biodegradable, except anthrax and communicable plague pn
First response	HAZEMAT/EMTs, fire, and police	EDs, GPs, and public health officials
Decontamination	Necessary and critical	Unnecessary, except acute exposures
Treatment	Antidotes, support	Antibiotics, vaccines, and support
Isolation	Unnecessary	Necessary only for smallpox and plague

CW and BW: Ancient History

Ancient History (hx) of CW

- **429 BC:** Spartans vs. Athenians—Spartans burned tar pitch and brimstone to intentionally release sulfur gas, which mixed with atmospheric water vapor, and human mucosal and lung water to create highly irritant, water-soluble sulfuric acid on mucosal and upper respiratory tract exposure.

Ancient hx of BW

- **600 BC:** Athenians poisoned enemy water sources with *green hellebore* (*cardiotoxic veratrum alkaloids*). Assyrians used ergot to contaminate grain crops and bread.
- **67 BC:** Mithradates V of Pontus forced Pompey's pursuing Roman legions into a Turkish valley where the local honey was poisoned with *grayanotoxins* from *Rhododendron* nectar.
- **1344–1346:** The Tartars besieged the Genoans in the Black Sea port of Kaffa and catapulted plague corpses into the walled city, creating an intentional plague epidemic that fleeing Genoans spread to western Europe as the *Black Death* (fourteenth to seventeenth century).

CW and BW: Modern History

Modern hx of CW

- **1915:** Germans—Ypres, Belgium, and Cl *gas*
- **1917:** Germans vs. Allies, Ypres, and *mustard*
- **1918:** Captain L. W. Lewis, USA—*Lewisite*
- **1936:** Germany (G), *tabun* "gas" (GA)
- **1938:** Germany, *sarin* "gas" (GB)
- **1944:** Germany, *soman* "gas" (GD)
- **1952:** U.K., *VX* vesicant liquid arsenic
- **1963–1967:** Egypt vs. Yemen—mustard and nerve agents

- **1980s:** Iraq vs. Iran—tabun, soman; Kurds—sarin, cyanide?
- **1994:** Matsumoto, sarin (*Aum Shinrikyo*)
- **1995:** Tokyo, sarin (*Aum Shinrikyo*)

Modern hx of BW

- **1763:** French and Indian War (United States)—British General Sir Jeffrey Amherst distributed smallpox-contaminated blankets to Native Americans allied with the French.
- **WWI:** Germans intentionally infected allied livestock with *B. anthracis* and glanders (*Burkholderia pseudomallei*, formerly *Pseudomonas mallei*).
- **1936–1944:** Manchuria, General Shiro Ishii, MD, Unit # 731, infected Chinese POWs and civilians with anthrax and plague.
- **1940:** Porton Down, U.K. (British BW research). Sheep were infected with anthrax on Gruinard Island, off Scotland.
- **1941:** Ft. Detrick, MD (U.S. BW research).

Biological Weapons Modern History

- **1978:** Georgi Markov, a Bulgarian double agent was assassinated in London by KGB with a *ricin* pellet injected by an umbrella gun.
- **1979:** In Sverdlovsk, Russia, 66 *anthrax* deaths followed accidental release from the Russian BW facility.
- **1979–1983:** USSR vs. Afghanistan—"yellow rain," tricothecene *mycotoxins*? No delivery devices discovered.
- **1984:** The Dallas, Oregon, and Rajneeshee cult intentionally contaminated restaurant salad bars with *Salmonella* spp.
- **September–October 2001:** Anthrax-spore-filled *letters* were mailed along the east coast, causing 22 anthrax cases—10 inhalational (four deaths, 40% CFR) and 12 cutaneous. CFR 40% for intentional anthrax < CFR.
- 80% for occupational inhalation anthrax (*Woolsorter's disease*).

CW Outline

- Principles of decontamination
- Nerve agents ("nerve gas")
- Blister agents (vesicants)
- Blood agents (cyanides)
- Pulmonary agents ("poison gas")
- Riot control agents ("tear gas")
- Incapacitating agents (vomiting or sedating agents)

Principles of Decontamination

Objectives of decontamination: (1) To prevent further absorption and spread of toxic substances on victims; (2) to prevent contamination of others; (3) to focus on CW and BW liquids, which can spread to others, and are more amenable to decontamination than gases; and (4) to focus on mass CBW exposure solutions; for example, *all CW* and *BW victims must disrobe* and *then shower immediately prior to further decontamination procedures.* This critical initial decontamination step could be simply and efficiently conducted at home.

CW and BW Decontamination

- **CW decon:** (1) *All nerve agents are hydrolyzed* and *inactivated* by 1:10 dilutions or *0.5%* solutions of *household bleach*; (2) *sulfur mustard must be inactivated within 1–2 min*; (3) copious water or soap and water showering also work well; (4) caustic bleach exacerbates skin lesions from tear gas; and *water* irrigation alone works better.
- **BW decon:** (1) Initial disrobing, then soap and water showering; (2) *0.5% bleach*, then water rinse that is also effective for BW.

Nerve Agents 1

Mechanisms, Properties, and Toxicities

- **Mech:** *Organophosphates (OP) are acetylcholinesterase (AchE) inhibitors*, related to OP and reversible carbamate insecticides, which can complex with AchE rapidly and irreversibly (*aging*).
- **German (G) agents:** Tabun (GA), sarin (GB), and soman (GD—ages fastest)—All OPs are clear, volatile *liquids*, and easily aerosolized. (No GC agent, because GC = gonorrhea.)
- **Vesicant (V) agent:** VX (U.K.), oily liquid, least volatility, and highest environmental persistence such as mustard, but more so.
- **Toxicities:** Soman > VX > sarin > tabun.
- **Aging rapidity:** Soman > tabun > sarin > VX (48 h). 2-PAM is effective only for soman and VX.

Cholinergic Toxidrome

Muscarinic > nicotinic > CNS

- **Muscarinic (DUMBBELS):** Diarrhea, urination, miosis, bronchospasm, bronchorrhea, emesis, lacrimation, and salivation. Miosis > HA > dyspnea > N and V > eye pain > diplopia. Miscellaneous: Localized sweating. *Tx*: *Atropine.*
- **Nicotinic:** Weakness > fasciculations seizures > sphincter incontinence > flaccid paralysis > RF. *Tx: Diazepam*, O_2, and ventilation.
- **Central nervous system:** Apnea, respiratory depression—failure, loss of consciousness, and coma. *Tx: 2-PAM* (pralidoxime).

Nerve Agents 2: Tx

Pretreatment AchE Protection

- **Pyridostigmine:** A reversible carbamate AchE inhibitor that can block nerve agent access to the AchE enzyme by *occupying binding sites* and protecting a portion of

AchE from potential complexing with the nerve agent and later aging irreversibly (soman). Pyridostigmine binding can be later reversed with the oxime, 2-PAM. To offer protection, primarily from soman > tabun (not sarin and VX), 20–40% of AchE must be inhibited by pyridostigmine pretreatment for efficacy. Pretreatment also enhances the efficacy of both atropine and 2-PAM reversal therapy.

Postexposure Management

- **Anti-muscarinic tx:** *Atropine* in 2 mg doses titrated to endpoints of reversing bradycardia and wheezing, and drying up secretions. Mark I kits contain one 2 mg *AtroPen* injector. Only atropine drops can reverse miosis and eye pain.
- **Anti-nicotinic tx:** *Pralidoxime* (2-PAM) reactivates the OP-AchE complex prior to aging. Mark I kit also contains a 600 mg 2-PAM *ComboPen*, which must be *coadministered* with atropine.
- **Anti-epileptogenic tx:** Anticonvulsants, principally *diazepam* 10 mg—the other part of the *ComboPen* in Mark I kits.

Blister (Vesicant) Agents: Sulfur Mustard

Properties, Mechanisms, and PE

- **Prop:** *Yellow–brown oily liquid*, mustard–horseradish odor, ↓ volatility, ↑ environmental persistence, ↑ temps ↑ vaporization, and permeates clothes and skin.
- **Mech:** Arsenic-based alkylating agent that (nitrogen mustard) *alkylates sulfhydryl bonds blistering skin* and *lungs*; breaks DNA cross-links; inhibits glycolysis; and depletes ATP and glutathione.
- **Clin:** *Skin > lungs > eyes*; necrotic bullae, especially in *warm moist skin areas* (axilla, perineum, groin, and neck); and 1st → 3rd° burns in 4–48 h. *Lungs:* Cough, bronchospasm, tracheobronchitis, and pseudomembranes. *Eyes:* Miosis, lacrimation, photophobia, blepharospasm, corneal burns, and rarely blindness.
- **Misc:** Early N&V, later BM depression.

Postexposure Management

- Decontaminate skin with water and 0.5% bleach solution within *1–2 min* to prevent burns.
- Unroof all large blisters and bullae (do not contain mustard).
- Apply atropine eye drops (gtts) to eyes and petroleum jelly to lids to prevent adhesions.
- Inhaled O_2, bronchodilators, and mucolytics.
- Bronchoscopic removal of obstructive tracheobronchial (diphtheritic-like) pseudomembranes.
- Early, elective tracheal intubation for mechanical ventilation.

Blister Agents

Lewisite

Properties, Mechanisms, and PE

- **Prop:** 2-Chlordivinyldichloro*arsine*, oily, colorless *liquid*; more volatile, but less environmentally persistent than mustard, also more amenable than mustard to water and bleach inactivation.
- **Mech:** Same as arsenic and mustard, *alkylates sulfhydryl groups cause skin and lung blistering*, inhibits glycolysis, and depletes glucose and glutathione.
- **Clin:** Similar to mustard but immediately painful, blistering is not as severe as mustard.

Postexposure Management

- Water or *0.5% bleach* decontamination.
- **Administer specific antidote:** British anti-Lewisite (*BAL*) IM, *still used to chelate arsenic* and other heavy metals, such as lead and mercury.
- Other heavy metal chelators may also be used: DMSA, DMPS.

"Blood" Agents (Cyanides)

Agents, Properties, and Mechanisms

- **Agents:** Used ineffectively in WWI by France initially (hydrogen cyanide, cyanogen chloride) and then Austria (cyanogen bromide). 1980s: Used by Iraq against Iran and Kurds.
- **Prop:** Active ingredient, hydrocyanic acid is lighter than air, dissipates rapidly, and either kills victims or permits quick recovery, except for cyanogen chloride that can cause delayed pulmonary edema.
- **Mech:** Initially felt to exert systemic toxicity via the bloodstream; actually *inhibits cellular respiration in the mitochondria.*

Decontamination and Tx

- **Decon:** Initial disrobing, then soap and water showering.
- **Tx:** O_2, cyanide kit = (1) amyl, then Na nitrite, (2) Na thiosulfate, (3) methylene blue; correct metabolic acidosis; and supports urine output.
- **New tx:** (4) Hydroxocobalamin (B_{12}).
- **Tx mech:** (1) Oxidize ferrous oxyHb^{+2} to ferric metHb^{+3} with nitrites to bind free CN and form cyanmethemoglobin (cyanmetHb), (2) competitively pull CN out of the ferrous oxyHb moiety with thiosulfate to form urine-excretable thiocyanate, (3) reverse methemoglobinemia with methylene blue, and (4) form vitamin B12.

Pulmonary Agents ("Poison Gas")

Agents, Properties, and Mechanisms

- **Agents:** Phosgene (>chlorine) caused 85% of gas deaths in WWI; both gases are extensively used in the industry, along with NO_x.

- **Prop:** More water-soluble chlorine forms a *yellow–green cloud* with pungent odor; more insoluble phosgene hydrolyzes in mist forming a white cloud with pleasant odor of *freshly mown grass or hay, or green corn.*
- **Mech:** All pulmonary agents hydrolyze in lung water forming *HCl* that burns tracheobronchial mucosa inducing pulmonary edema.

Clinical Manifestations and Tx

- **Clin:** Rapid onset of cough, dyspnea, chest pain, rhinorrhea, lacrimation, *frothy* and *bloody pulmonary edema within 2–6 h*, and delayed respiratory failure which is common; phosgene is said to cause smoked tobacco to taste bad.
- **Tx:** Mostly supportive with O_2 and *aerosolized inhalation of sodium bicarbonate to neutralize HCl.* Early, elective tracheal intubation is highly recommended during honeymoon period before PE.

Riot Control Agents ("Tear Gas")

Agents and Properties

- **Agents:** All are intense dermal and mucous membrane irritants and lacrimators and include (1) *CN*: *chloracetophenone* = Mace®; (2) *CS:* chlorobenzilidene malononitrile; and (3) *OC:* oleoresin capsicum = *capsaicin* = pepper spray.
- **Prop:** Volatile oily liquids disseminated as aerosols, sprays, and incendiary bombs for crowd control with *rapid* onset, short duration of action, and high safety profile. Severe reactions and deaths (CN, CS) from status asthmaticus possible after closed space exposures.

Clinical Manifestations and Tx

- **Clin:** Rapid onset *of* eye and skin burning, lacrimation, conjunctival injection, photophobia, blepharospasm, sneezing, rhinorrhea, cough, chest tightness, bronchorrhea, bronchospasm, and possibly status asthmaticus.
- **Tx:** Initial disrobing and then immediate copious cold-water irrigation. *0.5% bleach solutions are contraindicated* and could exacerbate injuries. Lidocaine gel patches for topical tx of capsaicin exposure.

Incapacitating Agents

Vomiting Agent

- **DM:** Diphenylamine*arsine gas* (*Adamsite*).
- **Mech:** Arsine hydrolyzes sulfhydryl groups in mucosa, inhibits glycolysis, and depletes glutathione, such as Lewisite.
- **Clin:** Arsine gas induces initial eye and upper airway irritation, followed by headache, malaise, nausea, and severe vomiting with dehydration.
- **Tx:** Supportive *with* IV fluids.

Sedating Agent

- **BZ:** 3-Quinuclidinyl benzylate.
- **Mech:** A CNS-acting *anticholinergic*, 25× more potent than atropine. (Note: Israel, 1991: >2000 casualties occurred from self-inflicted atropine injection during the first Gulf War.)
- **Clin:** Anticholinergic syndrome = "*Mad as a hatter, blind as a bat, hot as Hades, dry as a bone.*" Initial dry mouth and mydriasis, then delayed onset of incapacitating drowsiness, incoordination, reduced cognition, delirium, ↑ awakening over 2–3 days.
- **Tx:** Supportive only.

Biological Weapons

BW: Outline

- BW microorganisms
- Categories of BW
- Likely BW scenarios
- Suspicious syndromes suggesting BW
- BW agents

BW: Microorganisms

Likely CBW Scenarios

- **Most probable:** The intentional aerosolized release of (1) anthrax spores (*Bacillus anthracis*) > (2) crystalline botulinum toxin (*Clostridium botulinum*) > (3) plague (*Yersinia pestis*) > smallpox (*Variola minor*) > (4) tularemia (*Pasteurella tularensis*).
- **Less likely:** Intentional contamination of drinking water, because microorganisms and toxins will be inactivated by dilution, aeration, and chlorination.
- **Least likely:** Intentional contamination of food supplies, crops, cattle; 2° limited impact and slow progression; and will only occur as isolated events.

Suspicious Syndromes

- Acute respiratory distress + fever + no hx trauma or chronic disease = anthrax, plague, tularemia, ricin, and staphylococcal enterotoxin B
- Eruptive fever + rash = smallpox
- Flu-like illness + sepsis = tularemia, arenavirus hemorrhagic fevers, brucellosis, and Q fever
- Acute bilateral descending flaccid paralysis = botulism
- Blistering syndromes = nitrogen mustard, VX (Lewisite), and tricothecene mycotoxins (T2)

Anthrax 1

- **Micro:** *B. anthracis is* a large, spore-forming Gram+ bacillus (rod) that grows in lengthening chains and produces three Ags: protective Ag that is attenuated for the anthrax vaccine and facilitates endocytosis of the other two Ags: edema factor (causes massive swelling) and lethal factor (releases TNF and IL-1).
- **Path:** Inhaled spores enter thoracic lymphatics and germinate within mediastinal lymph nodes causing hemorrhagic mediastinitis with pleural effusions, but no pneumonia. Cutaneous form is 2° direct skin inoculation and is characterized by black eschar and massive edema (unlikely in BW release) (see Figure 33.1).

Anthrax 2

- **Cutaneous anthrax:** Note necrotic eschar.
- **Cutaneous anthrax:** Note massive edema on MRI (see Figures 33.2 and 33.3).

Anthrax 3

- **DDx:** Pulmonary embolism, dissecting thoracic or thoracoabdominal aneurysm
- **Dx:** +CXR with *widened mediastinum* and *pleural effusions*, + Gram stain and +C&S on sputum and blood, ELISA, and PCR
- **Tx:** Ciprofloxacin 400 mg IV q 8 h, doxycycline 200 IV q 8 h, penicillin 2 MU q 2 h + streptomycin IM, or gentamicin IV
- **Pv:** Ciprofloxacin 500 mg or doxycycline mg 100 po bid × 4–6 weeks + six-shot vaccine, or ×8 weeks without the anthrax vaccine

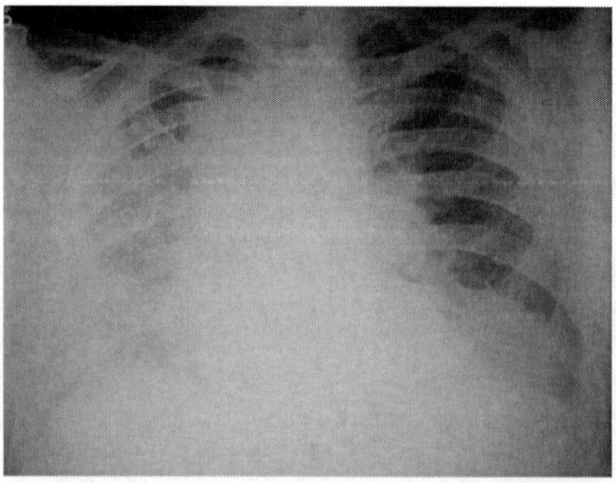

FIGURE 33.1 Pulmonary anthrax. Frontal chest radiograph of a patient with pulmonary or inhalation anthrax that demonstrates the characteristic widening of the mediastinum, bilateral pleural effusions, bilateral perihilar infiltrates, and clear peripheral lung fields. (Courtesy of Carlos R. Gimenez, MD, professor of radiology, LSU School of Medicine, New Orleans, LA. With Permission.)

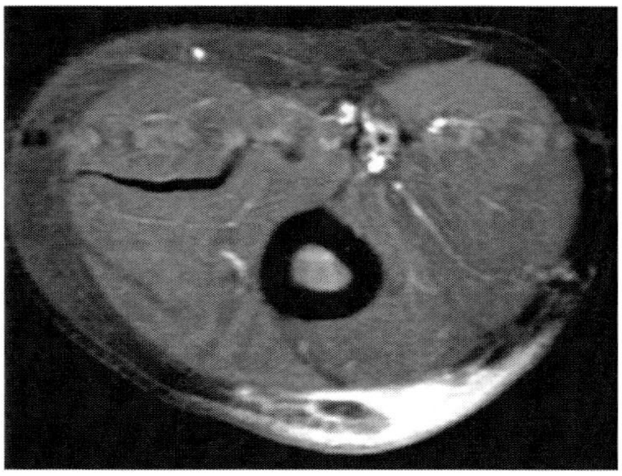

FIGURE 33.2 Cutaneous anthrax. Axial MRI with intravenous gadolinium contrast enhancement of the arm of a patient with cutaneous anthrax that demonstrates massive lymphedema and enhancement of the subcutaneous fat in the lateral compartment. (Courtesy of Carlos R. Gimenez, MD, professor of radiology, LSU School of Medicine, New Orleans, LA. With Permission.)

- **Pulmonary anthrax:** Note mediastinal widening (arrows) and right-sided pleural effusion (Figure 33.1).

Botulism 1

- **Micro:** *C. botulinum* is an aerobic, spore-forming Gram+ bacillus that produces eight toxins (A–H), all of which can be aerosolized.

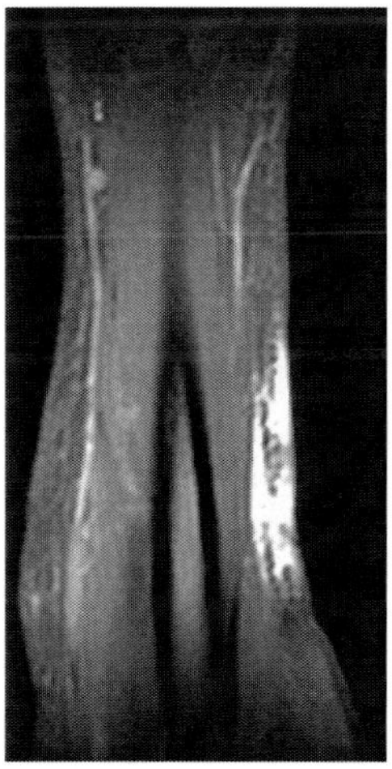

FIGURE 33.3 Cutaneous anthrax. Coronal MRI with intravenous gadolinium contrast enhancement of the arm of a patient with cutaneous anthrax that demonstrates massive lymphedema and enhancement of the subcutaneous fat in the lateral compartment. (Courtesy of Carlos R. Gimenez, MD, professor of radiology, LSU School of Medicine, New Orleans, LA. With Permission.)

- **Path:** After a short 1–5-day incubation period, botulism is characterized by afebrile, *acute descending flaccid paralysis* causing ptosis, diplopia, mydriasis, dysarthria, dysphonia, dysphagia, weakness, hypotonia, paralysis, and terminal respiratory failure. CFR 50%.
- Characteristic facies of mild botulism. Note ptosis, absence of nasolabial folds, and asymmetrical smile.

Botulism 2

- **DDx:** Guillain–Barré syndrome—a subacute postinfectious ascending weakness, paralysis, and sensory loss.
- **Dx:** Ag detection by ELISA in gastric aspirate, vomitus, stool, or blood. Spares cranial nerves, and the toxin acts only peripherally.
- **Tx:** Supportive + pentavalent equine antitoxin for toxins A–E, or IND heptavalent equine Fab antitoxin for serotypes A–G? Guanadine hydrochloride?
- **Pv:** IND heptavelent toxoid vaccine for serotypes A–G under development by U.S. Army at USAMRID (Figures 33.2 and 33.3).

Mild Botulism

- Note asymmetric smile.

Plague 1

- **Micro:** *Y. pestis* is a Gram−, safety-pin-shaped *Coccobacillus.*
- **Path:** Bubonic plague occurs in endemic areas from plague-infected rat flea bites and is characterized by fever, malaise, regional buboes, and possibly pneumonic sepsis. Pneumonic plague occurs with a 2–3-day incubation period after direct respiratory contact or BW release and is characterized by HA, fever, chills, cough, hemoptysis, severe pneumonia, then respiratory failure with CV collapse, and terminal coagulopathy. Only pneumonic plague is transmissible from person to person.
- **Bubonic plague:** Note draining buboes in regional lymphatics.

Plague 2

- **DDx:** Community-acquired pn, hantavirus pulmonary syndrome, and meningococcemia
- **Dx:** CXR with severe pneumonia, sputum, blood, or bubo aspirate for Gram− coccobacilli with bipolar, safety-pin-shape Gram-staining characteristics; blood C&S with growth in 24 h, often misdiagnosed as *Y. enterocolitica*; Abs detected by IgM ELISA, Ag detected by PCR
- **Tx:** *Streptomycin* IM 30 mg/kg/d × 10 d, + doxycycline 200 mg IV push, then 100 mg IV q 12 h × 10 d; or gentamicin IV 5 mg/kg × 10 d
- **Pv:** Tetracycline 500 mg po qid × 7 d, or doxycycline 100 po bid × 7 d

Plague 3: Epizootic–Epidemic

- Rodents die off and fleas move on to new human hosts!
- Domestic animal fleas bite man causing bubonic plague.

Smallpox 1

- **Micro:** *V. minor* is a highly contagious DNA pox virus, related to vaccinia, chicken pox, and monkey pox.
- **Path:** After a typical *14-day incubation*, smallpox causes high fever, malaise, prostration, headache, backache, myalgias, cramping abdominal pain, delirium, and a characteristic *centrifugal rash on the face, trunk,* and *hands with the synchronous appearance* and resolution of initial red macules, then vesicles, pustules, ulcers, crusts, and pitted scars, most prominent on the face and extremities. CFR 30%.
- **Smallpox (*Variola*):** Note pustular lesions on the face in the same stage of development—pustules.

Smallpox 2: r/o Chickenpox

- **DDx:** Chickenpox—has a characteristic centripetal rash sparing the face with asynchronously developing and resolving red macules, vesicles, pustules, ulcers, crusts, scabs, and shallow scars, most marked on the neck and trunk.
- **Dx:** Viral culture, Ag detection by ELISA, and PCR.
- **Tx:** None, possibly ribavirin, or cidofovir.
- **Pv:** Calf-lymph vaccinia vaccine intradermally q 10 years.
- Chicken pox (*Varicella zoster*).
- Note lesions favoring the trunk in varying stages of development.
- Smallpox (*Variola*).

Tularemia 1

- **Micro:** *Franciscella tularensis* is an aerobic and environmentally stable, nonspore-forming, Gram– coccobacillus with an epizootic reservoir in rabbits and ixodid tick transmitting vectors.
- **Path:** A very low inoculum (<50 organisms) may be transmitted via direct contact with infected rabbits, tick bites, or aerosolized organisms (2° BW or just mowing grass). Contact results in *ulceroglandular > oculoglandular > oropharyngeal* (ingestion) tularemia with ulcers at entry sites and regional lymphadenopathy. *Inhalation results in pneumonic tularemia with abrupt onset of high fever, productive cough, pleuro-pneumonitis, hemoptysis, bilateral hilar adenopathy, sepsis (typhoidal tularemia),* and *terminal respiratory failure.*

Tularemia 2

- **DDx:** Influenza, mycoplasma pneumonia, adenoviral, or atypical community-acquired pneumonias

- **Dx:** +CXR with *bilateral pneumonia* and *hilar adenopathy; mediastinum not widened*; +Gram stains or fluorescent Ab stains and +C&S on ulcers, sputum, and blood; serological Ag detection by ELISA and PCR
- **Tx:** *Streptomycin* 30 mg/kg/d bid × 14 d, or gentamicin 3–5 mg/kg/d IV × 14 d
- **Pv:** No vaccine, doxycycline 100 mg po q 12 h × 14 d, or tetracycline 2 g/d po × 14 d

Staph Enterotoxin B 1

- **Micro:** SEB-1 is a superantigenic bacterial toxin that produces profound activation of the immune system when either inhaled or ingested.
- **Path:** If inhaled, SEB-1 causes a pulmonary syndrome with a 3–12 h incubation period that is characterized by prolonged fever, chills, headaches, myalgias, persistent coughing (for weeks), chest pain, hypoxia, and an incapacitating pneumonia that is rarely fatal. If ingested in spoiled dairy products, SEB-1 causes food poisoning characterized by severe vomiting and dehydration without diarrhea.

Staph Enterotoxin B 2

- **DDx:** Ricin, tularemia
- **Dx:** +CXR with pneumonia, Ag, and Ab detection by ELISA
- **Tx:** Supportive
- **Pv:** No toxoid vaccine, respirator mask

Brucellosis 1

- **Micro:** *Brucella* is a small Gram– coccobacillus with a zoonotic reservoir in domestic livestock: cattle (*B. abortus*), pigs (*B. suis*), and goats (*B. melitensis*).
- **Path:** A very low inoculum of *Brucella* may be inhaled (<1-wk incubation) or ingested (7–60-d incubation) and causes a nonspecific illness characterized by *prolonged undulant fevers*, chills, malaise, weakness, joint pain, early acute bloody diarrhea, later chronic fatigue and *depression, and complications include osteomyelitis* and *SBE*. Misdiagnosed as fibromyalgia/chronic fatigue syn.

Brucellosis 2

- **DDx:** Streptococcal SBE, chronic fatigue syndrome, and fibromyalgia
- **Dx:** Blood C&S, Ag and Ab detection by ELISA
- **Tx:** *Doxycycline* 200 mg/d po + *rifampin* 600–900 mg/d po × 6 weeks
- **Pv:** Avoid undercooked meats and unpasteurized milks and cheeses

Miscellaneous BW: Q-Fever

- **Micro:** Q-fever 2° *Coxiella burnetti*, Gram– Rickettsia; is an epizootic reservoir in wild mammals and domestic livestock (cattle, sheep, and goats); transmitted via fecal/gestational aerosols and not usually by tick bites; spore like and extremely stable environmentally; and has a very low infective inoculum (LD50 = 18), U.S. weaponized > 5 K gallons—Pine Bluff.

- **Path:** Nonspecific illness after 10–28 days of incubation with malaise, ↑ fever, rigors, myalgias, no rash, painful hepatosplenomegaly, and persistent pneumonitis; complicated by myocarditis, endocarditis, and encephalitis. Prolonged convalescence, ® CFR (<1%) without endocarditis.
- **DDx:** Influenza, infectious mononucleosis, brucellosis, leptospirosis, and toxoplasmosis.
- **Dx:** +CXR with patchy pneumonic infiltrates, serologic Ag detection by CF, and not Weil–Felix (*Proteus* agglutination) reaction.
- **Tx:** *Tetracycline* 500 mg po q 6 h × 1 week, or doxycycline 100 mg po q 12 h, 1 week.
- **Pv:** Postexposure tetracycline or doxycycline × 1 week within 8–12 days; IND vaccine under development; and avoid domestic livestock aerosols, especially of fecal and gestational products.
  - Q fever = Category B
  - Most common presentation = Q fever pneumonia (CXR)
  - Q fever = Category B
  - Least common presentation = Q fever endocarditis (echo)
  - Q fever endocarditis = Aortic valve vegetations
  - *Burkholderia pseudomallei* = Category B
- **Micro:** Gram– rod—formerly (pre-1992) *Pseudomonas pseudomallei,* the bacterial agent of meliodosis; hyperendemic in soil, freshwater in SE Asia—Thailand, Vietnam, and Northern Australia; rel. to *B. mallei*—glanders in horses; transmitted via aerosols, water-near drowning, and skin punctures; incubation 1–2 weeks.
- **Path:** Chronic TB-like granulomatous nodules and ulcers in skin, lungs, parotid gland, bone joints, liver, spleen, and prostate.
- **DDx:** TB, sporotrichosis.
- **Dx:** Culture from blood, bone marrow, ulcer, and biopsy (bx); indirect hemagglutination, and IFA.
- **Tx:** Acute = IV ceftazidime or imipenem. Chronic = doxycycline or cotrimoxazole × 12–20 weeks.
- **Pv:** Avoid soil–mud and freshwater exposures in endemic areas, especially if immunosuppressed with diabetes, thalassemia, or ESRD.
  - *Burkholderia mallei* = Category B
  - Equine glanders 1
  - Equine glanders 2
  - *Burkholderia pseudomallei* = Category B
  - Meliodosis common presentation 1: Skin puncture, later abscess
  - Meliodosis common presentation 2: Splenic abscesses

Misc. BW: Nipah Virus

- **Micro:** Nipah virus is a previously unrecognized paramyxoviral zoonosis of Malaysian fruit bats, closely related to the Hendra virus of Australia. Caused an outbreak of febrile encephalitis in Malaysian pig farmers in 1998–1999 with 260 cases and 110 deaths.

- **Path:** Natural reservoir in flying fruit bats that transmits mild infections to pigs characterized by mild encephalitis and pneumonitis. Close contact and aerosol transmission to man are characterized by *febrile encephalitis, areflexia, segmental myoclonus, ↑ BP and HR, and CFR 50%.*
- **DDx:** Equine encephalidides, LaCrosse encephalitis.
- **Dx:** +MRI demonstrates high-signal-intensity lesions throughout the brain, viral identification in CSF by EM, and viral isolation from CSF.
- **Tx:** Ribavirin?
- **Pv:** Cull-infected swine.

Henipaviruses

Family Paramyxoviridae, RNA Viruses

- Nipah virus—causes Nipah virus encephalitis.
- Hendra virus—causes Hendra virus disease.
- The known reservoirs are *Pteropus* spp. fruit bats (flying foxes).
- Nipah—Southeast Asia and Africa (human deaths as far as Malaysia, Singapore, India, and Bangladesh).
- Hendra—Australia.
- Bats appear to be unaffected.
- Both cause severe respiratory and neurologic diseases in humans.

Nipah Virus

- Initially isolated in 1999 during an outbreak of encephalitis and respiratory illness among men in Malaysia and Singapore.
- During the Nipah virus disease outbreak in 1998–1999, 257 patients were infected with the virus.
- About 40% of those patients who entered hospitals with serious nervous disease died from the illness (105 deaths, 1 million pigs culled).
- Causes a relatively mild disease in pigs in Malaysia and Singapore.
- Transmitted to humans, cats, and dogs through close contact with infected pigs.
- Eight more outbreaks of Nipah virus have occurred since 1998, all within Bangladesh and neighboring parts of India.
- Antibodies found in flying foxes in Cambodia.

Hendra Virus

- Symptoms of humans may be respiratory, including hemorrhage and edema of the lungs, or encephalitic resulting in meningitis.
- In horses, infection usually causes pulmonary edema and congestion.
- First discovered in 1994 in Brisbane, two outbreaks in Australia (coastal Queensland and northern New South Wales).

- 22 horses, three humans.
- Before 2008, an additional seven equine infections and one human infection.
- In July 2008, five equine infections and two human infections (one fatal).
- Unlike the previous infections, neurologic equine symptoms were present (rather than respiratory).

Coronaviruses

Enveloped RNA Viruses

- Detected in multiple species of bat.
- Can sometimes cause mild respiratory illness in humans.
- Severe acute respiratory syndrome coronavirus (SARS CoV).
- Bats were identified as potential carriers of CoV in China following the 2003 epidemic.
  - Horseshoed-nosed bats of several species.
  - Palm Civet may be the intermediate host.
- Phylogenetic analysis of bat CoVs and other known CoVs suggest that the progenitor of SARS-CoV and all other CoVs in other animal hosts originated in bats.
- Bat CoVs have been detected in China, Hong Kong, North and South America, Africa, Europe, and the Philippines.

Filoviruses

Marburg Virus

- Causative agent of Marburg hemorrhagic fever.
- Found almost exclusively in Africa.
- Can kill almost 90% of those infected.
- Fruit bats have been recently shown to be a natural source of virus.
- Repetitively isolated from fruit bats in Uganda.

Marburg Virus History

- The first filovirus was recognized in 1967 when a number of laboratory workers in Germany and Yugoslavia, who were handling tissues from green monkeys, developed hemorrhagic fever.
- 31 cases, seven deaths.
- Monkeys were from Uganda and kept in holding facility in Lake Victoria with high numbers of fruit bats.
- Second outbreak in 1975, Marburg hemorrhagic fever developed in two tourists who had slept in rooms with insectivorous bats in two locations in Zimbabwe.
- In two separate incidences in 1980 and 1987, infection with Marburg virus was linked with entry into Kitum Cave in Kenya, where fruit and insectivorous bats were present.

Filoviruses

Ebola Virus

- Causative agent in Ebola hemorrhagic fever.
- Highly fatal and mostly found in Africa.
- The virus has not be isolated in bats, but suspects bats as a natural source.

Ebola Virus History

- First identified in 1976 when two outbreaks of Ebola hemorrhagic fever (Ebola HF) occurred in northern Zaire (now the Democratic Republic of Congo) and southern Sudan. The first six patients worked in a cotton factory in Sudan in which insectivorous bats were present.
- In 1994, a clan of chimpanzees in a forest reserve in the Ivory Coast had been observed feeding in a wild fig tree with fruit bats for 2 weeks before an outbreak of the fatal disease, caused by a new strain of Ebola virus, occurred.

Ricin 1

- **Micro:** Ricin is a lethal toxin produced by the *castor bean plant (Ricinus communis)* that *inhibits protein synthesis* at the ribosomal messenger RNA level.
- **Path:** On parenteral exposure, ricin causes a septicemic, hemorrhagic GI syndrome with fever, leukocytosis, shock, and death within 24–72 h. The double agent Georgi Markov, was assassinated by KGB by ricin pellet injection (London, 1978). On inhalation exposure, ricin causes a pulmonary syndrome with fever, weakness, cough, hypoxia, pulmonary edema, and terminal respiratory failure.

Ricin 2

- **DDx:** Staphyloccal enterotoxin B is a community-acquired atypical pneumonia.
- **Dx:** CXR is initially normal, then rapidly develops pneumonia and pulmonary edema; serological Ag detection by ELISA on nasal swabs, sputum, or blood.
- **Tx:** Respiratory support in the ICU.
- **Pv:** An IND toxoid vaccine is under development by U.S. Army.

Mycotoxins

- 1° Health Effects: Mycotoxins

Tricothecene Mycotoxins

- **Micro:** Easily aerosolized mycotoxins that are produced by several filamentous molds including *Stachybotrys* > *Fusarium* > *Myrotecium* and *Trichoderma*, and, like ricin, *inhibit protein synthesis.*

- **Path:** Mycotoxins can cause immediate toxicity on exposure to intact *skin* and *mucosa* by inducing inflammatory lesions with early necrosis of skin and mucosa, and throughout tracheobronchial tree. The onset of action is more rapid than with liquid CWs, such as mustard and VX. If ingested, mycotoxins can cause *alimentary toxic aleukia* with fever, chills, gastroenteritis, bone marrow suppression, and sepsis that *mimic acute radiation sickness.*
- **DDx:** Vesicant CW exposure, especially sulfur mustard or VX, and acute radiation sickness (*dirty bomb*).
- **Tx:** Supportive only.

Emergency Responsiveness

Biological Attack

- Report possible attack to local OPH, CDC, PD, and FBI.
- Diagnose and characterize etiologic agent(s).
- Treat all victims specifically and supportively.
- Provide prompt, specific prophylaxis to all "worried well" possibly exposed.

Chemical Attack

- Report possible attack to local OPH, CDC, PD, and FBI.
- Decontaminate all exposed immediately by disrobing and showering in the appropriate response site outside of the hot zone in a surrounding decon or warm zone, supplied by an outer supporting or cold zone—all aligned upwind.
- Diagnose and characterize etiologic agent(s).
- Triage and treat all victims specifically and supportively, following decontamination.

Hierarchies of Prevention

Biological Attack

- 1° prevention by vaccination (smallpox, anthrax, and plague)
- Antibiotic tx and prophylaxis
- Surveillance and warning systems
- Irradiation of mail/food
- Use electronic > snail mail
- Lab precautions and infection control
- PH education and communication
- PPE-HEPA masks, level A—total SCBA

Chemical Attack

- Plant/property security at safety-sensitive sites
- Surveillance and warning systems
- Chemical release characterization network

- Track-controlled chemicals
- PH education and communication
- Engineering controls—HVAC intakes, decontamination systems
- PPE-gas masks, SCBA: Level A—total SCBA, level B—SCBA or SAR, and level C—air purifier

Radiological Weapons: Outline

- Types of radiation
- Measuring radiation
- Radiation effects
- Monitoring radiation effects
- Treating radiation injuries
- Avoiding radionuclides
- Nuclear/radiological WMD
- Acute radiation illness
- Sickness:
  - Major cause is the depletion of immature parenchymal stem cells in quickly dividing tissues
- Caused by:
  - Penetrating (ionizing) radiation: Causes cell damage and cell death
  - Nonpenetrating (nonionizing) radiation: Dermal burns similar to sunburn
- Types of radiation:
  - α-Particles: Cannot penetrate skin (ingestion or wound contamination)
  - β-Particles: Burn skin or damage eyes
  - γ-Rays: Penetrating radiation
- Sickness is dependent on:
  - Amount of exposure
  - Route of exposure
  - Tissues exposed
  - Duration of exposure
  - Radiological weapons

Types of Radiation

Nonionizing Radiation

Insufficient energy to disrupt atoms/molecules

- Radiowaves
- Microwaves
- Infrared radiation
- Ultraviolet radiation
- Laser: Capable of cell damage to unprotected retina

Ionizing Radiation

Sufficient energy to disrupt atoms/molecules

- α-Particles (helium nuclei)
- β-Particles (fast electrons)
- γ-Rays (EM fields)
- X-Rays (EM fields)
- Cosmic rays

Monitoring Radiation

Atomic Particle Counting

1. Geiger counter
    - Scintillation counter
    - Nuclear emulsion monitoring

Biologic Effect (REM) Monitoring: (Dosimetry)

1. Film badge
2. Pocket ionization dosimeter
3. Thermoluminescent dosimeter

Human Surveillance

1. Onset of vomiting
2. Lymphocyte depletion
3. Chromosomal aberration survey

Radiation Sickness Effects

Radiation-Absorbed Doses: Gy and RADs

- <0.7 Gy or < 70 rads
- 1–2 Gy or 100–200 rads
- 2–3 Gy or 200–300 rads
- 3–4 Gy or 300–400 rads
- 4–5 Gy or 400–500 rads
- 5–8 + Gy or 500–800 rads

Radiation Biological Effects

- No clinical effects, chromosomal damage possible
- Vomiting in 50% in 6 h, ↓ WBC
- Same + ↓ RBC, ↓ platelets
- Same + aplastic anemia, *death*
- Same + slough GI tract, *death*
- Same + CV and CNS damage, *death*

Treating Radiation Injuries

Nonspecific Treatments

- Treat life-threatening injuries first.
- **External decon:** Remove clothes, shower.
- **Internal decon:** Antacids, cathartics-to-empty GI tract.
- **Protect vulnerable organs:** KI for thyroid protection from ^{131}I.
- **Chelate isotopes:** KI for ^{131}I, Prussian blue (Radiogardase) for ^{137}Cs, and thallium. Diethylene triamine pentaacetic acid (DTPA) ±Zn for americium, curium, and plutonium.
- **Draw baseline labs:** CBC/diff q 6 h, *absolute lymphocyte count* ASAP.

Specific Treatments

- First, stimulate the hematopoietic system
  a. Anabolics for RBCs: 5-androstendiol
  b. Colony-stimulating factors for WBCs
- Next, restore/replace the hematopoietic system
  a. Stem cell transplants
  b. Cord/placenta blood progenitor cell transplants
  c. Peripheral blood progenitor cell transplants
  d. Bone marrow transplants

Nuclear Regulatory Commission Sources and PELs

NRC 1° Sources of Human Irradiation

- *Radon* (basements and mines): 55%
- Medical x-rays: 11%
- Internal (milk, etc.): 11%
- Cosmic: 8%
- Terrestrial (^{238}U): 8%
- Nuclear meds: 4%

NRC Lifetime Dose Limits of Irradiation

- Annual: 5 REMs/year
- Cumulative lifetime: 5 REMs/year
- During pregnancy: 0.5 REM/pregnancy, not to exceed 5 REMs/year

Chapter 34

Workplace Substance Abuse Monitoring

Outline 770
Introduction 771
Federal Regulations 771
Epidemiology 772
Chemical Dependency 775
Abused Substances 778
Substance Abuse Professionals 787
Medical Review Officers 788
Employee Assistance 790
Rehabilitation 792
Alcohol Testing 794
Drug Testing 795
Chain of Custody 798
MRO Responses 807

Outline

- **Introduction**
  - Americans with Disabilities Act (ADA)
- Federal regulations
  - Components of a comprehensive drug-free workplace program
  - Definition of a disabled individual
  - ADA and employment drug testing
- Epidemiology
  - Some measures of the impact of drugs in the workplace
  - Marijuana is the most commonly used illicit drug in the United States
  - Types of drug testing
- Chemical dependency
  - Substance dependency (APA, DSM-IV)
  - Tolerance develops
  - Withdrawal develops
  - Recurrent substance abuse
  - Experimental substance abuse
  - Recreational substance abuse
  - Circumstantial substance abuse
- Abused substances
  - Five basic categories of psychoactive substances
  - Opioids/opiates
  - Sedatives
  - Psychedelics/hallucinogens
  - Four basic categories of psychoactive of stimulant substances
- Substance abuse professionals
  - Substance abuse professionals medical review officer (MRO)
- Medical review officers
  - The practical MRO
  - MRO qualifications
- Employee assistance programs
- Rehabilitation
  - Rehabilitation and individual treatment
  - Rehabilitation and therapeutic medications
  - Rehabilitation and psychiatric medications
  - 1991 Omnibus Transportation Employee Testing Act (PL102-143)
  - Omnibus Transportation Employee Testing Act 1991
- Alcohol testing
  - Random alcohol testing
- Drug testing

  - DOT drug testing procedures
- Chain of custody
  - Unique screening characteristics of commonly abused drugs
  - Opiate metabolism
- MRO responses
  - Medical Miranda

Introduction

Americans with Disabilities Act

- "The Federal Government, as the largest employer in the nation, can and should show the way toward achieving drug-free workplaces through a program designed to offer drug users a helping hand..." Executive order 12564, 1986.
- The ADA prohibits discrimination against individuals with disabilities in employment, public services and transportation, public accommodations, and telecommunications services. The ADA also impacts drug-free workplace efforts. Legislated 1992–1994; enacted 1994.

Federal Regulations

Components of a Comprehensive Drug-Free Workplace

- **1986:** Executive order 12564 initiated drug testing of over 1.8 million safety- or security-sensitive federal employees in executive branch agencies.
- **1988:** U.S. Department of Health and Human Services (DHHS) Mandatory Guidelines for Federal Workplace Drug Testing Programs set scientific and technical standards for drug testing of federal employees and for certification of drug testing laboratories.
- **1988:** U.S. Department of Transportation (DOT) Regulations impact 4 million private-sector employees in DOT-regulated industries, requiring sanctions, training/education, and testing.
- **1988:** Drug-Free Workplace Act required federal contractors and grantees to provide a drug-free workplace written drug policy, employee drug abuse awareness, and sanctions for convictions of drug crimes in the workplace. (No drug testing required.)
- **1989:** U.S. Nuclear Regulatory Commission (NRC) Rules required nuclear power facilities to implement fitness-for-duty testing programs.
- **1991:** Omnibus Transportation Employee Testing Act (PL 102–135) enacted by Congress and mandated drug and alcohol testing for over 6 million transportation industry employees.
- **1994:** DOT Alcohol Misuse Rules mandated breath alcohol testing of transportation employees.

- **1994:** Americans with Disabilities Act
- Formal written policy
- Employee assistance program
- Supervisor training
- Employee education
- Methods for deterring and detecting illicit drug users (i.e., drug testing)

Definition of a Disabled Individual

- An individual with a disability "has a physical or mental impairment that substantially limits one or more major activities of daily living (e.g., caring for oneself, walking, seeing, hearing, speaking, and working), a record of such impairment, or who is regarded as having such an impairment."

ADA and Employment Drug Testing

- The ADA does not interfere with an employer taking appropriate action for alcohol or drug abuse on the job (Figure 34.1).
- The ADA does not impact an employer's ability to perform drug testing for job applicants or employees.
- Drug tests are not medical examinations under ADA and are not subject to the same restrictions as other employment physicals (Figure 34.2).

Epidemiology

Some Measures of the Impact of Drugs in the Workplace

- Absenteeism

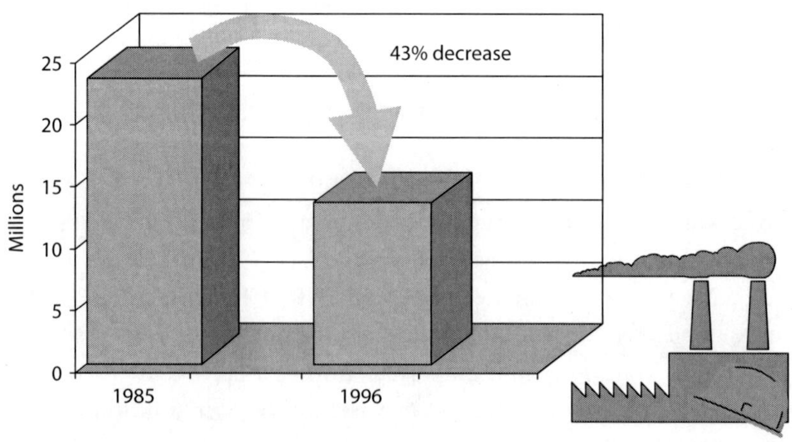

FIGURE 34.1 Substance abuse: Past month use of any illicit drug (ages 12 and over). (From National Household Survey on Drug Abuse, 1996.)

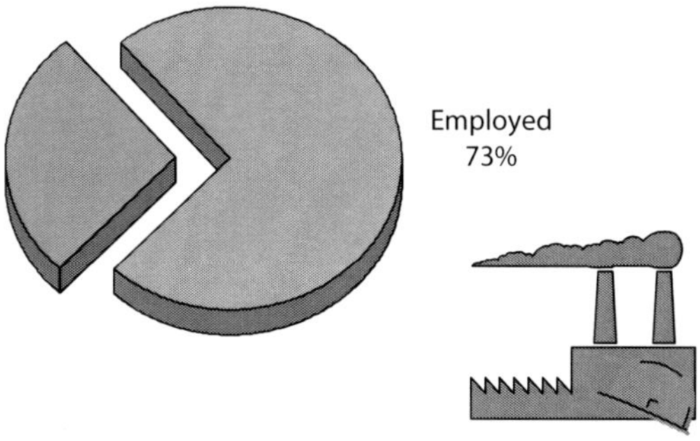

FIGURE 34.2 Substance abuse: The majority of current drug users are employed (current users of illicit drugs, ages 18 and over). (From National Household Survey on Drug Abuse, 1996.)

- Accidents and injuries
- Increased health care utilization
- Lost productivity
- Theft, property damage, reduced security
- Increased training requirements

Marijuana Is the Most Commonly Used Illicit Drug in the United States

- The 1996 National Household Survey estimated the number of marijuana users as
  - Occasionally—8.6 million
  - Monthly—9.8 million
  - Weekly—6.1 million

Types of Drug Testing

- Applicant testing (preemployment) (Table 34.1)
- Accident/unsafe practice testing
- Reasonable suspicion testing (for cause)
- Follow-up to treatment testing (for compliance)
- Random testing
- Voluntary testing

Table 34.1 Clinical Laboratory Improvement Act + Amendments

	Forensic Testing	Workplace Drug Testing	Testing as Part of a Treatment Program
Drugs	Not covered	Not covered	Covered
Alcohol	Not covered	Not covered	Covered except by breathalyzer

Goals of Changing Opiate Testing Cutoffs (Tables 34.2 and 34.3)

- To substantially reduce the total number of specimens reported as positive for opiates by laboratories, but verified as negative by the MRO
- To shift the emphasis of testing for opiates to the deterrence and detection of heroin use
- To reduce unnecessary and excessive costs of retesting without compromising the original drug deterrent objectives (Figures 34.3 through 34.6)

Urine Drug Tests after Ingesting Food Products Containing Hemp Seeds

- Specimens that showed immunoreactivity (not necessarily = or > cutoff) were tested by gas chromatography/mass spectrometry; some screened positive, most did not.
- Gas chromatography/mass spectrometry results were 0 or very close to 0 ng/mL; none were close to cutoff (50 ng/mL).
- Immunoreactivity was likely due to cannabinoids other than delta-9-THC acid; may be a problem for on-site testing.

Urine Drug Tests after Ingesting Hemp Oil

- 14 employees screened positive at 20 ng/mL; 7 screened positive at 50 ng/mL; 2 screened positive at 100 ng/mL.
- All specimens were tested by gas chromatography/mass spectrometry; 14 of the 18 contained 5 ng/mL or more delta-9-THC acid; several exceeded 15 ng/mL.

Table 34.2 HHS Cutoffs

Drug/Metabolite	Initial (ng/mL)	Confirmation (ng/mL)
Marijuana metabolite	50	15 (delta-9-THC acid)
Cocaine metabolite	300	150 (benzoylecgonine)
Opiates	2000	2000 (morphine), 2000 (codeine)
Phencyclidine	25	500 (phencyclidine)
Amphetamines	1000	500 (amphetamine), 500 (methamphetamine[a])

[a] To be reported there must be 200 ng/mL amphetamine.

Table 34.3 Revisions to Opiate Cutoffs, Effective in 1998

Drug/Metabolite	Initial (ng/mL)	Confirmation (ng/mL)
Opiates	2000	
Morphine		2000[a]
Codeine		2000
6-Acetylmorphine		10

[a] If morphine equals or exceeds 2000 ng/mL, then the laboratory must analyze for 6-acetylmorphine by gas chromatography/mass spectrometry (6-MAM).

- Hemp oil is more of a problem than hemp seed ingestion.

Drug Tests

- The Americans with Disabilities Act does not impact an employer's ability to perform drug testing for applicants or employers.
- Drug tests are not medical examinations under ADA and are not subject to the same restrictions as other employment physicals.

Omnibus Transportation Employee Testing Act of 1991 (See Figures 34.3 through 34.6)

- Requires drug and alcohol testing of safety-sensitive employees in the aviation, rail, truck, bus, and mass transit sectors.
- Types of testing include
  - Preemployment
  - Reasonable suspicion
  - Random
  - Postaccident
- All drug testing is to be conducted according to the HHS Mandatory Guidelines.

Chemical Dependency

- A positive toxicology screen alone does not equate with chemical dependency, substance dependence, or substance abuse.

Substance Dependency (APA, DSM-IV)

- "A maladaptive pattern of substance use, leading to clinically significant impairment or distress, as manifested by three (or more) of the following, occurring at any time in the same 12-month period."

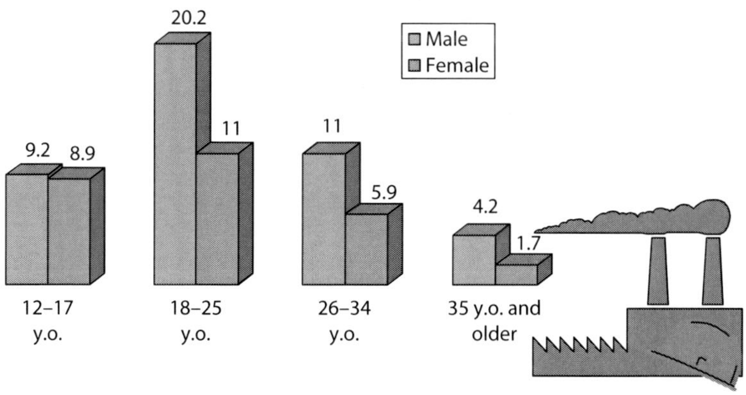

FIGURE 34.3 Substance abuse: Percent past month use of any illicit drug by age and sex. (From National Household Survey on Drug Abuse, 1996.)

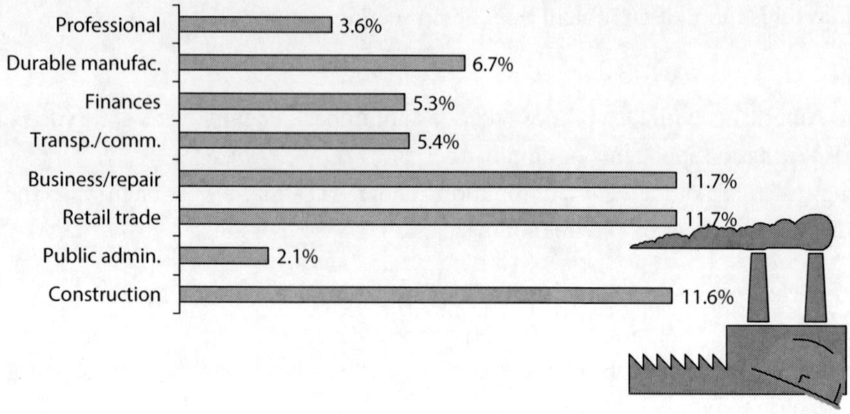

FIGURE 34.4 Substance abuse: Current illicit drug use among 18–49-year olds (full-time employed by industry). (From Drug Use among U.S. Workers, 1993.)

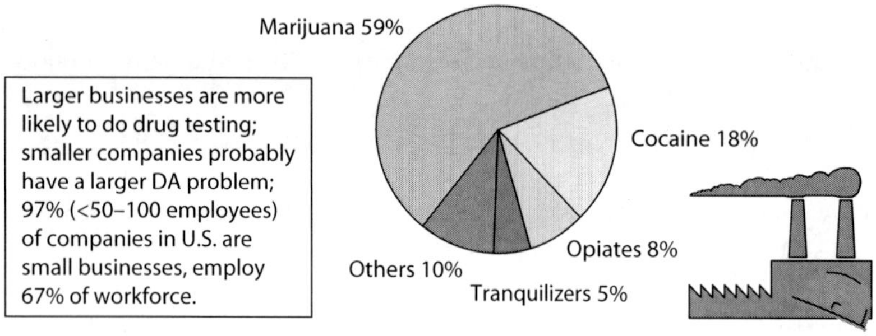

FIGURE 34.5 Substance abuse: Drug distribution of positive urine tests among U.S. workforce tested by SKB Clinical Labs 1/97–6/97.

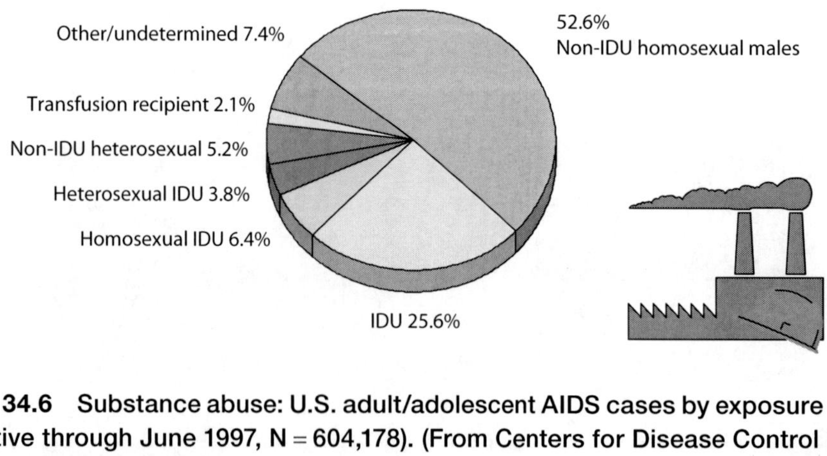

FIGURE 34.6 Substance abuse: U.S. adult/adolescent AIDS cases by exposure category (cumulative through June 1997, N = 604,178). (From Centers for Disease Control HIV/AIDS Surveillance Report, 1997.)

- Tolerance.
- Withdrawal.
- The substance is often taken in larger amounts or over a longer period than was intended.
- There is a persistent desire or unsuccessful effort to cut down or control substance use.
- A great deal of time is spent in activities necessary to obtain the substance or recover from its effects.
- Important social, occupational, or recreational activities are given up or reduced because of substance use.
- The substance use is continued despite knowledge of having a persistent or recurrent physical or psychological problem that is likely to have been caused or exacerbated by the substance.

Tolerance Developments

- A need for markedly increased amounts of the substance to achieve intoxication or desired effect, or
- Markedly diminished effect with continued use of the same amount of the substance.

Withdrawal Developments

- The characteristic withdrawal syndrome for the substance, or
- The same (or closely related) substance is taken to relieve or avoid withdrawal symptoms.

Recurrent Substance Abuse

- Recurrent substance use results in a failure to fulfill major role obligations at work, school, or home
- Recurrent substance use in situations in which it is physically hazardous
- Recurrent substance-related legal problems
- Continued substance use despite having persistent or recurrent social or interpersonal problems caused or exacerbated by the effects of the substance

Experimental Substance Abuse

- Short-term, random trials of one or more drugs, motivated by curiosity or a desire to experience an altered mood state

Recreational Substance Abuse

- Substance abuse that occurs in a social setting among friends or acquaintances who desire to share an experience that they define as both acceptable and pleasurable. Use is both voluntary and patterned.

Circumstantial Substance Abuse

- Substance abuse for the purpose of achieving an anticipated effect in order to cope with a specific problem, situation or condition of a personal or vocational nature.

The U.S. Substance Abuse and Mental Health Services Administration (SAMHSA) five drugs of abuse

- Amphetamines/methamphetamines
- Cocaine
- Marijuana
- Opioids
- Phencyclidine

Abused Substances

Five Basic Categories of Psychoactive Substances

1. Opioids/opiates
2. Sedatives
3. Psychedelics/hallucinogens
4. Stimulants
5. Inhalants

Opioids/Opiates

- Heroin
- Morphine
- Codeine
- Propoxyphene
- Hydromorphone
- Diphenoxylate
- Hydrocodone
- Dihydrocodone
- Oxycodone
- Pentazocine
- Methadone
- Meperidine
- Fentanyl
- Sufentanil
- Butorphanol

Opioid Use and Induced Disorders

- Dependency
- Abuse
- Intoxication
- Withdrawal
- Intoxication delirium

- Induced psychotic disorder, with delusions
- Induced psychotic disorder, with hallucinations
- Induced mood disorder
- Induced sexual dysfunction
- Induced sleep disorder

Opioids/Opiates—Routes of Administration

- Heroin, morphine, Dilaudid®, fentanyl, sufentanil, and meperidine are usually injected.
- Codeine, oxycodone, hydrocodone, MS Contin®, pentazocine, and methadone are usually taken orally.
- Opium is usually smoked. Heroin and morphine may be smoked or insufflated nasally.
- Fentanyl may also be administered by patch.

Signs and Symptoms of Opioid Intoxication

Physical

- Nodding out
- Drowsiness
- Respiratory depression
- Constricted pupils
- Nausea
- Vasodilation ("flush and rush")
- Slurred speech

Psychological

- Impaired judgment
- Impaired social functioning
- Euphoria
- Impaired attention
- Impaired memory

Signs of Opioid Overdose

- Slow and shallow breathing
- Clammy skin
- Convulsions
- Coma
- Death

Signs and Symptoms of Opioid Withdrawal (A "Flu-Like" Syndrome)

- Dysphoric mood
- Nausea or vomiting

- Muscle aches
- Lacrimation
- Rhinorrhea
- Dilated pupils
- Diarrhea
- Yawning
- Fever
- Insomnia

Sedatives

Sedative Examples

- Alcohol—Beer, wine, spirits
- Benzodiazepines—Valium®, Librium®, Ativan®, Xanax®, Halcion®, Restoril®, Klonopin®, benzodiazepine-like Ambien®
- Barbiturates—Phenobarbital, secobarbital, pentobarbital, butabarbital, amobarbital
- Barbiturate like—Chloral hydrate, meprod-bamae, glutethimide, carisoprodol (Soma®)

Sedative-, Hypnotic-, or Anxiolytic-Induced Disorders

- Dependence
- Abuse
- Intoxication
- Withdrawal
- Intoxication delirium
- Withdrawal delirium
- Induced persistent amnesic disorder
- Induced psychotic disorders
  - With delusions
  - With hallucinations
- Induced mood disorder
- Induced anxiety disorder
- Induced sexual disorder
- Induced sleep disorder

Alcohol

- Approximately 66% of all adult Americans take at least one alcoholic drink in the course of a year.
- Men drink more than women.
- Women metabolize alcohol slower than men.
- Among males of 18–29 years of age, 77% report drinking alcohol.
- Approximately 47% of alcoholics meet the criteria for another psychiatric disorder.
- Alcohol withdrawal should be treated.

Common Alcohol Withdrawal Signs and Symptoms

- Nausea and vomiting
- Tremor
- Paroxysmal sweats
- Anxiety
- Agitation
- Tactile disturbances
- Auditory disturbances
- Seizures
- Visual disturbances
- Headache, head fullness
- Disorientation and clouding of sensorium
- Increased blood pressure and pulse rate
- Hypertension

Benzodiazepines

- Widely prescribed for
  - Anxiety disorders
  - Muscle relaxation
  - Seizure disorders
  - Sleep disturbances
  - Alcohol withdrawal
- Anxiolytic properties are reinforcing
- May affect motor performance
- No U.S. National Institute of Drug Abuse (NIDA) laboratory standards

Barbiturates

- About 4% of the population have taken barbiturates for nonmedical purposes.
- Males, ages 26–34, living in large metropolitan areas, are more likely to have used barbiturates.
- Barbiturates abuse is less popular now, preempted by abuse of the safer benzodiazepines.
- Some increase in prescribing barbiturates is now noted in states that monitor benzodiazepine use.

Common Sedative Withdrawal Symptoms

- Anxiety
- Irritability
- Insomnia
- Fatigue
- Headache

- Muscle twitching or aching
- Tremor, shakiness
- Nausea, loss of appetite
- Observable depression
- Depersonalization
- Increased sensory perception
- Abnormal perception or sensation of movement
- Seizures
- Death

Psychedelics/Hallucinogens

- Hallucinogens consist of a variety of compounds that alter perceptions and feelings.
- Hallucinogens rarely produce hallucinations.
- PCP is often grouped as a hallucinogen, but is really a dissociative anesthetic, related to ketamine.
  - Ketamine dissociates awareness from the body.
- Ketamine permits abusers to self-induce altered perceptions and feelings.

Hallucinogen Use and Induced Disorders (DSM-IV)

- Dependence
- Abuse
- Intoxication
- Persisting perceptual disorder (Flashbacks—LSD, PCP)
- Intoxication
- Delirium
- Induced psychotic disorders
  - With delusions
  - With hallucinations
- Induced mood disorder
- Induced anxiety disorder

Psychedelics/Hallucinogens Examples

- Marijuana (THC)
- PCP
- LSD
- Psilocybin (mushrooms)
- Mescaline (peyote)
- Methylenedioxymethamphetamine (MDMA, Ecstasy)
- Methylenedioxyethamphetamine (MDE)

Marijuana

Marijuana Route of Administration

- Most often smoked.
    - Onset of effects within several minutes. Effects may last approximately 2 h.
- May be taken orally.
    - Onset of effects in 30+ min.
    - Effects may last 3–5 h.
- Variable absorption of THC in digestive system.

Inhalants

- Glue
- Gasoline
- Solvents
- Correction fluids
- Anesthetics
- Paint/lacquer thinners
- Polishes
- Amyl nitrates

Inhalant Uses and Induced Disorders

- Dependence
- Abuse
- Intoxication
- Intoxication delirium
- Persisting dementia
- Induced psychotic disorder
    - With delusions
    - With hallucinations
- Induced mood disorder
- Induced anxiety disorder
- Dementia/organic brain syndromes

Lysergic Acid Diethylamide

- No legal therapeutic use.
- Schedule I drug.
- A little drug goes a long way (doses average only 50–100 μg).
- Detected in urine using radioimmunoassay (RIA) at levels of 0.5 ng/mL or above.
- Not a National Institute of Drug Abuse (NIDA) five substance of abuse.
- Doses often sold on the street on blotter paper.
- May also be used in pill or liquid form.
- Efficient oral and digestive system absorption.
- The blotter paper or sticker on to which the LSD is deposited is often a pop-art form; "Beavis and Butt-Head," for example.

- There can be a "brand name" quality to the blotter paper.
- Blotter → LSD "stickers."

Mescaline—Peyote

- Mescaline is found in peyote and San Pedro cacti of the desert in Southwest United States and Latin America.
- **Typical dose:** 300–500 mg or 6–12 peyote "buttons."
- About 1/2000th the potency of LSD.
- About 1/20th the potency of psilocybin.
- **Duration:** 6+ h.
- Efficient oral and digestive system absorption.

Psilocybin/Psilocin

- Found in numerous species of mushrooms.
- About 1/100th the potency of LSD.
- **Typical dose:** 10–20 mg.
- **Duration:** 4–6 h.
- Efficient oral and digestive system absorption.
- Dry weight in mushrooms is about 1%.
- Psilocin is a dephosphorylated moiety of psilocybin.

Phencyclidine

- Routes of administration
- Smoked
- Oral ingestion
- Intranasal snorting
- Intravenous injection

Stimulants

Four Basic Categories of Psychoactive or Stimulant Substances

- Cocaine
- Amphetamine/methamphetamine
- Nicotine
- Caffeine

Signs and Symptoms of Stimulant Overdose

- Agitation
- Increased body temperature (hyperthermia)
- Hallucinations
- Convulsions
- Arrhythmias
- Death

Signs and Symptoms of Stimulant Withdrawal

- Dysphoric mood
- Fatigue
- Vivid, unpleasant dreams
- Increased appetite
- Psychomotor retardation or agitation
- Insomnia or hypersomnia

Treatment Issues for Stimulant Users

- An overdose of stimulants constitutes a medical emergency that requires immediate attention. Seizures and cardiac arrhythmias may require medications. Anxiety reaction can be managed by reassurance. Sedative–hypnotic medications may be required.

Stimulant Use and Induced Disorders

- Dependence
- Abuse
- Intoxication
- Withdrawal
- Intoxication delirium
- Induced psychotic disorders
    - With delusions
    - With hallucinations
- Induced mood disorder
- Induced anxiety disorder
- Induced sexual disorder
- Induced sleep disorder

Routes of Administration

- May be injected, snorted, smoked, or consumed orally

Cocaine

Illicit Dispensing Characteristics

- Small vials
- Basic substance
- Not water soluble
- Inexpensive
- Usually smoked

Cocaine Routes of Administration Profile

- Intranasal

    - Onset in 30 s to 2 min
    - Peak levels of 150 ng/mL
    - Postdrug dysphoric state
- Intravenous
    - Onset in 15 s or less
    - Peak levels in 3–5 min
    - Duration 15–20 min
- Smoking
    - Onset in 10 s or less
    - Peak levels in 3–5 min
    - Duration of high 15 min

Amphetamines

Amphetamine/Methamphetamine Routes of Administration

- May be injected, snorted, smoked, or consumed orally

Signs and Symptoms of Amphetamine Intoxication

- Tachycardia or bradycardia
- Pupillary dilation
- Hypertension or hypotension
- Perspiration or chills
- Nausea or vomiting
- Psychomotor agitation or retardation
- Evidence of weight loss
- Muscular weakness, respiratory depression, chest pain, or cardiac arrhythmias
- Confusion, seizures, dyskinesias, dystonia, or coma
- Impairment in attention or memory

Physical Signs of Injection Drug Use

- Track marks along veins
- Needle puncture sites

Track Marks along Veins

- Arms
- Forearms
- Dorsa of hands
- Dorsa of feet
- Thighs (inguinal crease)
- Neck
- Dorsal veins (penis or clitoris)

Dermatologic Masquerades, Hiding Track Marks

- Tattoos
- Arm hair
- Body hair
- Abscesses
- Old scars

Substance Abuse Professionals

- A trained health professional engaged in the counseling and monitoring of substance abuses.
- The SAP may determine the number and the frequency of the unannounced follow-up testing.

Substance Abuse Professional versus MRO

- With the advent of 1994 regulations, the SAP has broader functions than the MRO, a licensed physician. The SAP is involved in alcohol testing. The MRO is not. The SAP is involved in assistance determination. The MRO is not. The SAP is involved in follow-up testing. The MRO is not (See Table 34.4).

SAPs: Who Can Be One?

- A licensed physician (MD or DO)
- A licensed or certified
  - Psychologist
  - Social worker
  - Employer Assisted Program (EAP) officer or providers
- Additional counselor whose certification is recognized by DOT (e.g., National Association of Alcoholism and Drug Abuse Certification Commission Certification)

Table 34.4 SAP versus MRO

Activity	SAP	MR
Interpret drug test results		X
Evaluate employee for help for drug use	X	
Evaluate employee for help for alcohol use	X	
Determine employee compliance	X	
Determine need for cross-training	X	
Determine follow-up testing	X	

SAPs: What Do They Do?

- The generic function of the SAP is to evaluate an employee who has tested positive for alcohol or drugs to determine what assistance, if any, the employee needs in resolving problems associated with alcohol misuse or controlled substance abuse.

SAPs: What Else Do They Do?

- Through a second evaluation, the SAP determines whether an employee who has tested positive for alcohol or drugs has properly followed the prescribed rehabilitation program, where offered or required.

Medical Review Officers

- Must be a licensed physician with knowledge of substance abuse disorders (See Figure 34.7).
- Must afford an opportunity for the tested individual to discuss the test results prior to making a final decision to verify a test as positive.
- Must review all medical records made available by a tested individual when a confirmed positive could have resulted from a legally prescribed drug.
- To confirm heroin, urine must contain 6-monoacetylmorphine (6-MAM) or MRO must find clinical evidence, such as venous track marks (in addition to the positive urine test) of drug abuse.
- Only the MRO can authorize reanalysis of the original sample.
- If the MRO finds a legitimate medical explanation, the specimen is reported as negative.

California Proposition 215 and Arizona Proposition 200

- The MROs shall not accept a prescription, or the verbal or written recommendation of a physician, for a Schedule I substance as a legitimate medical explanation for the presence of a Schedule I drug or metabolite in a Federal employee/applicant specimen.

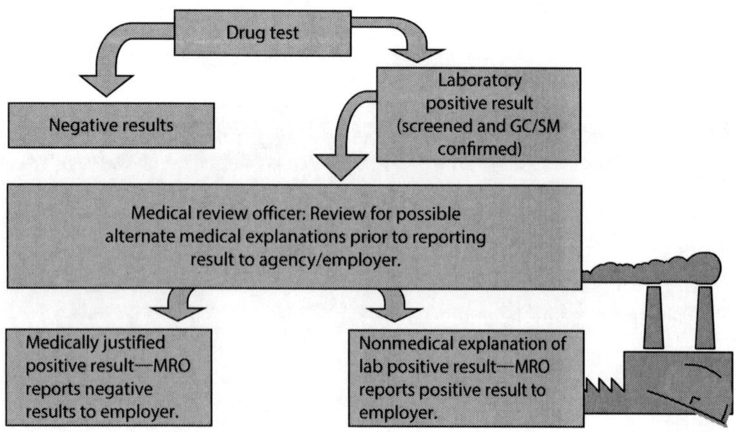

FIGURE 34.7 Substance abuse: The MRO chain.

- This policy applies to all Federal agencies. This affects approximately 1.8 million employees in all 50 states and territories, as well as those stationed abroad (Figure 34.7).

The Practical MRO

- The MRO–employee interview
  - Documentation
  - "Medical Miranda"
  - Interview tips
  - The denying donor
  - Common excuses
- 5- and 14-day rule
- Specimen not suitable
- Opiates
- Amphetamines
- Split samples
- Reporting issues
- Return to work determination
- Commercial driver's license (CDL) exams and controlled substances testing
- Shy bladder evaluation
- Reporting requirements
- DOT guidance to Third-Party Administrators (TPAs) and MROs
- Announcement to change opiate cutoffs
- MRO/LAB conflict of interest prohibitions

Medical Review Officer Qualifications

- "The Medical Review Officer shall be a licensed physician (MD or DO) responsible for receiving laboratory results generated by an employer's drug testing program who has knowledge of substance abuse disorders and has appropriate medical training to interpret and evaluate an individual's confirmed positive test result together with his or her biomedical history and any other relevant biomedical information."—49 U.S. CFR Part 40.3

The Medical Review Interview Is Not...

- A normal encounter with a patient
- A popularity contest
- A way to build your practice
- A criminal investigation
- A personal crusade
- A tool for use by the employer
- A chemical dependency evaluation
- A normal doctor–patient relationship

The Medical Review Interview

- Use standard form
- One size fits all?
- Review of Chain of Custody (CoC)
  - Fatal flaws
  - Correctable flaws
  - Noncritical flaws
- Identify self and affiliation
- Confirm identity of the donor (have donor confirm last four digits of SS#)
- Inquire about collection procedures
- Present medical Miranda
- Inquire about illicit drug use
- Offer split sample or retest (required by RSPA, USCG)

Employee Assistance

Employee Assistance Programs

- Programs concerned with drug, alcohol, and other problems that have an adverse impact on work performance in businesses and industries (See Tables 34.5 and 34.6, and Figures 34.8 through 34.10).

Employee Assistance Program Functions

- Educating employees about alcohol and drugs
- Exploring personal problems affecting work performance
- Training supervisors as referral agents
- Consulting on specific cases
- Referring employees to treatment
- Evaluating employees for return to work

EAP Prevalence

- Only one-third of all private worksites in the United States with 50 or more full-time employees have an EAP.
- However, 55% of all U.S. employees in private worksites with 50 or more employees are covered by EAP services.

Table 34.5 Size of Worksites with EAPs

Worksite Size	% with EAPS
50–99 employees	20.8
100–259 employees	33.2
250–999 employees	48.4
1000+ employees	76.1

Table 34.6 Types of Industries with EAPs

Industry	% with EAPs
Manufacturing	33.3
Wholesale/retail	33.7
Communication/utilities/transportation	53.4
Finance/realty/insurance	41.5
Mining/construction	20.4
Services	25.4

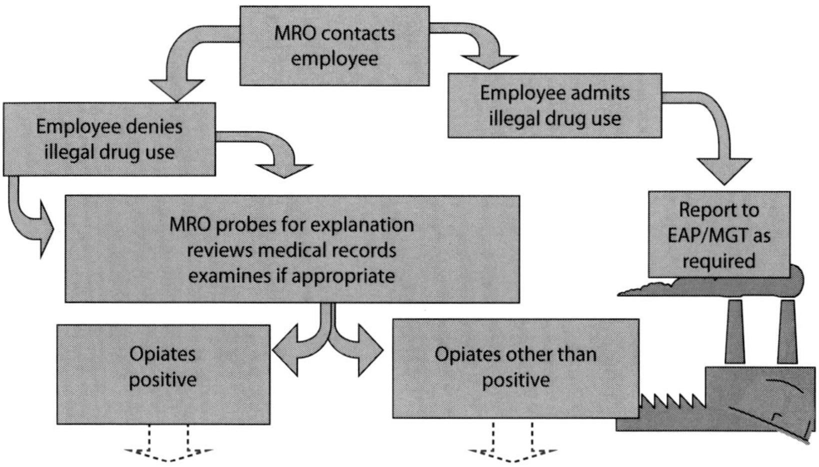

FIGURE 34.8 Substance abuse: How MRO reporting works—I.

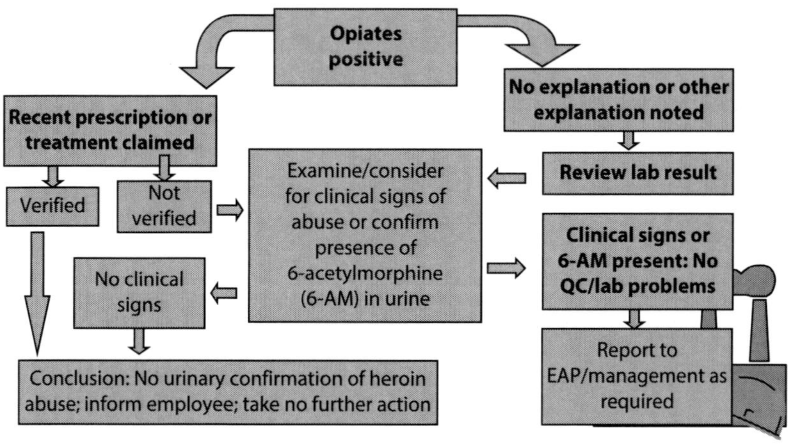

FIGURE 34.9 Substance abuse: How MRO reporting works—II.

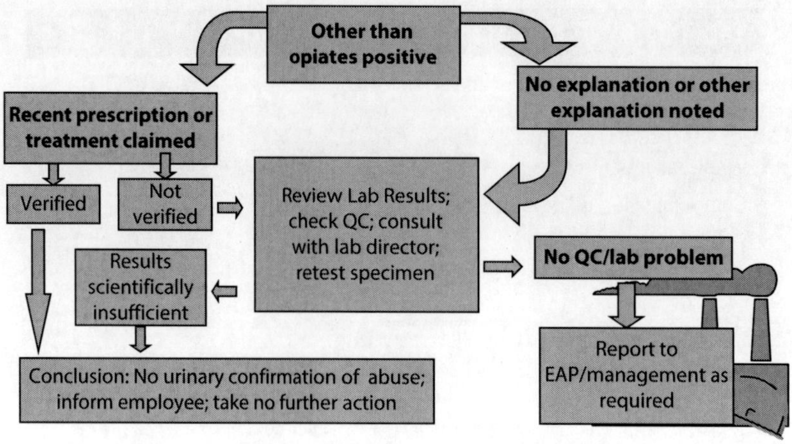

FIGURE 34.10 Substance abuse: How MRO reporting works—III.

Employee Assistance Program Organizations

- Internal (operated by the company)
- External (operated by an outside contractor)
- Operated by management or union
- May do simple evaluations or more complex ones
- May offer short-term or long-term treatments

Rehabilitation

- Rehabilitation begins with the detection of the proscribed substance and the admission by the positive employee that there is a problem.
- Rehabilitation is often linked with some form of treatment providers.
- U.S. Department of Transportation (DOT) regulations *do not* mandate that an employer provide treatment for an affected employee.

Rehabilitation and Individual Treatment

- Medical detoxification
- Outpatient psychoeducation
- Outpatient relapse prevention
- Residential therapeutic treatment
- Family therapy
- Self-help support systems
  - 12-step programs (e.g., Alcoholics Anonymous, Narcotics Anonymous, Cocaine Anonymous, Methamphetamine Anonymous)
  - Rational Recovery or Secular Organizations for Sobriety (SOS)
- Toxicology screens

Breath Alcohol Analysis

See Table 34.7.

Rehabilitation and Therapeutic Medications

- Naltrexone (ReVia®) can be used as an anticraving agent for alcoholics.
- Naltrexone can be used as an opioid blocker for those at risk for using opioids.
- Antabuse® may be used as an aversive for those at risk for using alcohol.
- Methadone can be used for opioid maintenance for those unable to remain opioid-free. (Cannot be used under DOT regulations. Methadone is proscribed by DOT.)

Rehabilitation and Psychiatric Medications

- Antidepressants may be beneficial for early withdrawal states or for concomitant primary depression.
- Antipsychotics may be necessary for those suffering from psychotic symptoms either secondary to or concomitant with substance abuse.

1991 Omnibus Transportation Employee Testing Act (PL 102–143)

- Enacted after NYC transit (subway) accident
- Mandated drug and alcohol testing programs in transportation industries
- Affected over 7 million safety sensitive employees
- Required DOT to issue implementing regulations
- Applies to aviation, railroad, transit, and commercial motor vehicle operations
- Requires preemployment, postaccident, reasonable suspicion, and random urine drug testing

Table 34.7 Principles and Devices for Breath Alcohol Analysis[a]

Principle	Typical Commercial Device	Features[a]
Chemical oxidation and photometry	Breathalyzer models 900, 900A	4
Electrochemical oxidation/fuel cell	Alco-Sensor II, III	2, 5, 7
Gas chromatography	BAC DataMaster	1, 2, 3, 5
	Intoxilyzer Models 1400, 5000	1, 2, 3, 5
Infrared spectrometry	A.L.E.R.T Model 14	2, 5, 7

[a] Features:
1 = Automatic purge and zero
2 = Digital result readout
3 = Integral printer
4 = Liquid reagents
5 = Reagentless
6 = Compressed gas required
7 = Battery operated

- Mandates use of DHHS procedures for urine drug testing
- Requires "split specimens" for drug testing

Omnibus Transportation Employee Testing Act 1991

- Includes all common driver's license (CDL) required vehicle operators
- Includes air traffic controllers
- Requires opportunity for treatment for individuals who engage in prohibited conduct

Prohibited Alcohol Conduct

- Performance of safety-sensitive functions is prohibited under the following conditions:
    - While having an indicated alcohol concentration of greater of 0.04 or greater
    - While using alcohol
    - Within 4 h (flight crew: 8 h) after using alcohol
    - Use of alcohol for 8 h following an accident or until tested, when an employee knows of the accident and an alcohol test is required
    - Refusal to submit to a required alcohol test

Alcohol Testing

- Postaccident
- Random
- Reasonable suspicion
- Return-to-duty and follow-up

Random Alcohol Testing

- Initial annual rate of 25%.
- Adjustable (10–50%) based on "violation" rate.
- Random alcohol testing must be conducted just before, during, or just after performance of safety-sensitive duties.
- Random testing must be announced and must be conducted immediately after notification of employee.

Alcohol Testing Procedures

- Alcohol testing must be conducted using testing devices listed on a National Highway and Traffic Safety Administration (NHTSA) conforming products list.
- Alcohol testing procedures include accuracy, reliability, and confidentiality protections.
- Screening test may be conducted using an alcohol screening device (ASD) or an evidential breath-testing device (EBT).
- Confirmation evidential breath test must be completed within 30 min of presumptive positive screening test (≥0.02) and must use EBT.
- Blood alcohol test not authorized under DOT rules.

Drug Testing

DOT Drug Testing Procedures

- Require testing in federally certified laboratories
  - Five classes of drugs
  - Two separate analytical processes
  - Stringent internal and external quality control procedures
  - Employee confidentiality protected
- Include physician review and interpretation of test results
  - Established MRO concept and functions
  - Provide for donor interview
  - Protect employee confidentiality

Receipt of Drug Test Results

- Lab reports all test results to MRO
- Lab reporting of test results cannot be by telephone
- Lab must send chain-of-custody (CoC) copy on all results
- Collection site must send MRO copy of CoC directly to MRO
- No routine reporting of quantitative levels (except opiates)
- Receipt of test results must be secure and confidential

Review of Negative Test Results

- Administrative review only
- CoC fatal flaws/corrective statements
- Conducted by MRO staff
- MRO signature stamp/staff initials OK

Review of Positive Test Results

- MRO copy of CoC
- Lab copy of CoC—signed by certifying scientist
- Special requests (quantitative levels, additional analysis); DOT → opiate specification

Review of Atypical Test Results

- Dilute specimens
- Unsuitable for testing specimens
- Adulterated specimens

Atypical Specimen Analysis: Dilute Specimen

- Report as negative—must report
- Inform employer of dilute result, including possible explanations for dilution

- Employer decision on direct observation for subsequent collections
- Do not require retesting of donor

Atypical Specimen Analysis: Specimen Unsuitable for Testing

- Explore tampering possibility
  - Inform donor of adulteration suspicion
  - Inform employer that specimen was unsuitable
  - Report is canceled
  - Retesting of donor under direct observation

Interpretation of Positive Results

- Donor contact
  - If unable to contact donor, contact company representative
  - Once notified by company representative, donor has five days to contact MRO for an explanation
  - If donor fails to contact MRO, or expressly refuses to discuss test results with MRO, result is verified as positive
  - If MRO or company cannot contact donor, verify as positive after 14 days
- Medical interview
  - Must be conducted by physician, MRO
  - Limits of confidentiality explained
  - Review of medications and medical procedures
  - Offers an opportunity for split specimen analysis
  - Offers opportunity for reanalysis of primary specimen (U.S. Resource Services and Pipelines Administration [RSPA] and U.S. Coast Guard [USCG] only)
  - Document donor contact, medical interview, and findings

Split Specimen (MRO Processing)

- Inform donor of opportunity to have split urine specimen analyzed on verified positive test
- Process request for split analysis (72 h window for donor decision)
- Provide written request to laboratory
  - Include specimen ID#, drug(s) to second lab
- Review split analysis result from second lab
- Report reconfirmation result to employer and donor
- Report failure to reconfirm to employer, donor, and DOT
- Failure to reconfirm, inability to locate split, or lack of split collection requires canceled test result

Interpretation of Opiate Results

- Obtain codeine and morphine quantitation

- Order 6-mono-acetylmorphine (6-MAM) analysis, if appropriate >2000 μg/mL cut-off exceeds
- Obtain medical history regarding opiate use
- Demonstrate clinical evidence of unauthorized use of opiates needed
- Establish policy on prescription drug sharing, foreign medication use, and use of "old" prescriptions

Reporting Results

- Telephone reporting to employer authorized
- Ensure confidentiality of reporting
- Provide written documentation of verified result
- Verified positives must be signed by MRO
- Federal Aviation Administration (FAA) requires MRO reporting to FAA on pilots

Urine Specimen Collection Procedures

- Collection site personnel—need some training in collection techniques
- Preparation of collection site
- Supplies and equipment
- Chronological steps of collection process
- Process ensures specimen identity, security and integrity
- Based on principles of search and seizure of evidence—a legal procedure
- Custody and control form documentation required
- A search and seizure collecting evidence (urine) must assure integrity of evidence

Specimen Collection Supplies

- Specimen collection "kit"
  - Specimen bottle(s)*
  - Shipping container
  - Specimen bag/pouch
  - Collection container
  - Temperature device
- Custody and control form
  - 6 or 7 copies of form
  - Bottle seal(s)/label(s) attached
  - Shipping container seal attached
  - Requires donor's and collector's signatures
  - "Chain of custody" block
- Pen, rubber gloves, bluing agent, tape

* Must be a freshly voided specimen.

Chain of Custody

"Fatal Flaws" Resulting in Canceled (or Rejected) Urine Specimen

- No preprinted specimen ID number
- No donor SSN or ID# unless noted in remarks
- No collector signature on collector statement*
- Incomplete CoC block*—indicated by absence of any of the following:
    - Collector name
    - Shipping entity
    - Date
    - Purpose of CoC entry
    - Recoverable by signed statement
- On positive results
    - No donor signature on specimen*
- No certifying scientist signature

Specimen Rejection Criteria

- Fatal CoC error
- Quantity-not-sufficient (QNS) specimen (30 mL minimum)
- Bottle seal broken or absent
- Specimen ID# on bottle and CoC form do not match
- Specimen obviously contains "foreign matter"

Specimen Collection Privacy Issues

- No undressing and gowning
- No pocket searches without cause
- No medication inquiries
- Private enclosure for urination
- "Monitored" collection

Collection Security Issues

- Wrapped collection container
- Wrapped specimen bottle(s)
- Specimen always in donor's sight
- Donor signature and initials obtained after specimen bottle is sealed
- Specimen bottle(s) CoC form secured until sealed in shipping container
- Restricted access to shipping container
- Always keep collection bottle in sight of donor

---

* Recoverable by signed statement.

Direct Observation

- Collector must notify site supervisor or employer representative
- Observation by same-gender individual
- Direct observation noted in remarks section
- Limited to special circumstances

Direct Observation Criteria Required

- Specimen temperature out of range (90–100°F)
  - Offer body temperature measurement
- Tampering attempt observed
  - Donor conduct or specimen qualities
- Send suspect specimen to laboratory
- Use new CoC and kit for witnessed collection

Direct Observation Criteria Optional

- Previous specimen dilute (SG < 1.003, low urine creatinine, <20 mg/dL)*
- Compared to next collection opportunity
- Previous specimen canceled as unsuitable
- Recollection of specimen required
- Return-to-duty or follow-up tests

Shy Bladder

- Provide up to 40 oz of fluids at collection site to provide urination
- Provide up to 3 h to urinate
- Discontinue collection attempt after 3 h
- Report to employer as shy bladder
- Refer donor for medical evaluation by employer-designated physician

Split Specimens Collection

- Mandatory for Federal Highway Administration (FHWA), Federal Aviation Administration (FAA), Federal Transit Administration (FTA), and Federal Railway Administration (FRA) supervised industries and companies
- Collect 30 mL for primary specimen, 15 mL for split specimen
- No combination of voided specimens
- Subdivide specimens at collection site
- Use 7-part CoC on each specimen bottle
- Ship bottles + 3 copies of the CoC to lab for testing of primary

* Decision about direct observation made by employer.

Goals for a Forensic Urine Drug Testing Laboratory

- To discriminate reliably between those specimens that contain drug or its metabolite at or above the cut-off and those that do not
- To do this in a legally defensible manner

Initial Test (Screening Test)

- An immunoassay screen used to eliminate "negative" urine specimens from further consideration should have high sensitivity.
- The initial test shall use an immunoassay that meets the requirements of the U.S. Food and Drug Administration (FDA) for commercial distribution.

Negative Specimen

- Any specimen whose apparent concentration of drug or metabolite is less than the preestablished cut-off concentration for that drug or metabolite
- *Not* necessarily a specimen containing no drug or metabolite

Positive Specimen

- Any specimen whose apparent concentration of drug or metabolite is greater than or equal to the preestablished cut-off concentration for that drug or metabolite

What Is the Cutoff?

- An arbitrary point on a continuum of possible drug or metabolite concentrations
- Used to divide specimens into negatives and positives
- Methods of estimating will vary according to immunoassay used

Mandated Cutoffs (ng/mL)

- Marijuana metabolites—50
- Cocaine metabolites—300
- Opiate metabolites—2000*
- PCP—25
- Amphetamines—1000

Confirmatory Test

- A second analytical procedure used to confirm the identity of a specific drug or metabolite which is independent of the initial test and which uses a different technique or chemical principle from that used in the initial test. The most commonly used technique is gas chromatography/mass spectrometry. Confirmatory tests must have high sensitivity.

---

* 25 ng/mL if immunoassay is specific for free morphine.

Confirmation Cutoffs (ng/mL)

- Marijuana metabolites—15
- Cocaine metabolites—150
- Opiate metabolites—2000
- Phencyclidine—25
- Amphetamines
  - Amphetamine—500
  - Methamphetamine—500

Unexpected Methamphetamine Issues

- Conversions of large amounts of ephedrine and ephedrine-containing over-the-counter (OTC) pharmaceuticals to methamphetamine during gas chromatography/mass spectrometry confirmation.
- No conversion to methamphetamine's metabolite, amphetamine.
- **Reporting rule:** Specimens must contain at least 500 ng/mL of methamphetamine and at least 200 ng/mL of amphetamine to be reported positive for methamphetamine.

Other Gas Chromatography/Mass Spectrometry Procedures

- **Identify 6-mono-acetylmorphine (6-MAM):** The initial metabolite of heroin.
- Differentiate the D- and L-stereoisomers of methamphetamines: Vicks Inhaler® contains the L-stereoisomer of amphetamine (L-stereoisomer = legal stereoisomer).

Adulteration/Dilution Testing

- Specific testing not presently required under guidelines
- Creatinine reported as <20 mg/dL
- Specific gravity reported as <1.003
- Presence of adulterant must be "forensically validated"
- *In vivo* adulteration/dilution
- *In vitro* adulteration/dilution

In Vivo *Adulterants*

- Ingested water (most common adulterant)
- Ingested herbals—used most commonly to mask THC
  - Golden seal—to mask THC (yellow root)
  - Herbal teas
  - "Test Pure"
  - "THC Free"
- Oral diuretics
- Chemicals
  - Vinegar
- Vitamin C

In Vitro *Adulteration*

- **Definition:** The addition of a substance to a urine specimen for the purpose of altering drug resting results
- **Most commonly used adulterants:**
  - "Freeze Dried Urine" urinaid (bleach)
  - "Urine Acid" (glutaraldehyde)
  - "Mary Jane's Super Clean 13" (crystal clear soy)
  - "Urine Luck Plus" (concentrated HCl)
  - "Klear" (oxidizing agent—potassium nitrite)
  - "Stealth"
  - Many other unknown urine adulterants

Contents of a Typical Litigation Package

- Chain of custodies (external and internal)
- Immunoassay data (specimens, calibrators, controls)
- Gas chromatography/mass spectrometry data (specimens, calibrators, controls)
- Reports (electronic, certified chain of custody)

Interception of Negative Urine Drug Test Results

- No drug use?
- No drug use recently?
- Urine dilution and/or adulteration?
- Creatinine as a marker (<20 mg/dL)?
- Specific gravity as a marker (<1.003)?
- Urinaid, bleach, Mary Jane Super Clean, Golden Seal tea, diuretics, used as *in vitro* adulterants?
- Drug present, but below preestablished cut-off level?

Interpretation of Positive Urine Drug Test Results

- Indicates use only?
- Does not correlate with impairment?
- Does not indicate route of administration?
- Cannot tell time of use or amount of use?

Unique Screening Characteristics of Commonly Abused Drugs

Cannabinoids

- 61 Cannabinoids in marijuana.
- Delta-9-tetrahydrocannabinol (THC) is the psychoactive constituent.
- 11-NOR-THC-9-carboxylic acid is the major metabolite in urine.

- Have at least 20 other oxygenated metabolites, including hydroxylated compounds, other monocarboxylic acids, and dicarboxylic acids.
- Pattern of metabolites may depend on type of user.

Cannabinoids Issues

- Passive inhalation
- Unknown digestion—"Seedy Sweeties" hemp seeds
- Tim e since last use
- Release from lipid depots
- Degradation postcollection

Cocaine

- **Metabolites in humans:** Benzoylecgonine and ecgonine methyl ester are major metabolites. Norcocaine is a minor metabolite.
- Cocaine's plasma half-life is very short; that of benzoylecgonine is much longer.
- Benzoylecgonine can be detected for days after use.
- Urine concentrations of benzoylecgonine can be extremely high (100,000s of ng/mL).
- **Preferred routes of administration:** Smoking, snorting, and injection.
- Oral route reported to be ineffective but!
- **Therapeutic uses:** Ear–nose–throat (ENT) surgical procedures and tetracaine–cocaine–adrenalin (TAC) solution for open wound instillation and topical anesthesia for suture repair of lacerations.

Cocaine Issues

- Passive inhalation
- Unknown ingestion
- Degradation postcollection
- Herbal teas (e.g., Health Inca Tea, "HIT," decocainized teas from Columbia)

Opiate Metabolism

Morphine

- Major metabolite of heroin
- Also a metabolite of codeine
- Constituent of opium
- **Routes of administration of heroin:** Injection, snorting, and smoking
- **Therapeutic uses of morphine:** Many, including narcotic analgesics

Codeine

- **Metabolites:** Morphine and norcodeine

- Codeine concentrations during use can be in the 10,000s of ng/mL; morphine concentrations are significantly lower.
- **Therapeutic uses:** Many, including narcotic analgesics and antitussives.

Opiate Issues

- **Codeine versus morphine:** After use, concentrations of morphine and codeine similar late in the excretion curve. Morphine may be higher than codeine. Latter can be lower than cut-off and therefore reported as negative.
- Synthetic opiates (e.g., hydrocodone, hydromorphone) cannot be detected and reported.
- 6-MAM as a marker of heroin use
  - Concentrations very low, particularly after single use, and half-life very short.
  - Infrequently detected in workplace programs.
  - If 6-MAM absent, need "clinical signs of opiate abuse" for a positive-use test.
- Poppy seeds
  - Morphine present in poppy seeds, amount dependent on geographical origin.
  - Urine morphine concentration can be found in the thousands of ng/mL, usually in the hundreds.
  - Codeine is usually very low, often cannot be detected.
- **Poppy seeds:** General guidelines
  - Concentration of morphine greater than 5000 ng/mL suggests use of heroin (or opium), particularly when codeine concentrations are much lower.
  - High codeine concentrations (>300 ng/mL) with morphine to codeine ratios less than two generally rule out poppy seed ingestion.
- Remember presence of 6-MAM indicates heroin use!

Amphetamines

- **Only ones that can be reported:** Methamphetamine and amphetamine.
- Amphetamine is a metabolite of methamphetamine.
- Excretion is pH dependent, an acidic urine enhances excretion.
- In the United States, methamphetamine generally represents the abused form of the drug. In Europe, amphetamine is more commonly abused.
- **Methamphetamine routes of administration:** Injection, snorting, smoking ("ice"), and oral.
- Both are still used therapeutically.

Amphetamine Issues

- Metabolites of other preparations, for example, benzphetamine, *p*-chlorobenzphetamine (Ascetin® from Mexico), and selegeline (as the L-isomers).
- **Isomers of methamphetamine:** L-Isomer in Vicks Inhaler®. Can be differentiated from psychoactive D-isomer by gas chromatography/mass spectrometry.

- Immunoassays detect other sympathomimetics, for example, ephedrine, pseudoephedrine, and phenylpropanolamine, often at only very high concentrations. Can be differentiated by gas chromatography/mass spectrometry.
- Temporary reporting rule for methamphetamine (at least 500 ng/mL of methamphetamine, plus at least 200 ng/mL of amphetamine as methamphetamine metabolite).
- Methamphetamine still very much a Western U.S. issue.
- **Designer amphetamines (Ecstasy, Eve):** MDMA, MDA, and MDE: generally regionalized. Cannot be detected and reported.

Phencyclidine

- No legitimate use.
- Excretion pH dependent. An acidic urine enhances excretion.
- Normally smoked.
- Regional use patterns.

Other Drugs

- **Barbiturates:** Urine positives almost always butalbital and phenobarbital.
- **Benzodiazepines:** Oxazepam common metabolite of several; most labs focus on this one metabolite. Gas chromatography/mass spectrometry methods not in common use for several "newer" benzodiazepines, including alprazolam. Xanax® (Alprazolam) is the most commonly prescribed one today.
- **Methadone and methaqualone:** Very few (if any) positives.
- Other drugs not a real issue in the workplace.
- Specific "workplaces" have their own problems (e.g., athletics—anabolic steroids, anesthesiologists—fentanyls).

Other Specimens

- **Blood:** Not routinely used, may be collected postaccident or for alcohol.
- **Saliva:** Little information on drug detection. Proposed as a specimen for alcohol.
- **Hair:** Still not widely accepted. Difficult to confirm marijuana use because of technology limitations.
- **Breath:** Accepted only for alcohol testing.

Forensic Laboratory Drug Testing Laboratory Selection Questions

- Is the laboratory licensed and/or accredited to perform drug analyses?
- What drugs are included in the screening test(s) and the confirmation test(s)?
- What is the cost of testing?
- What is the turnaround time?
- Is a chain of custody procedure available?

- What supplies (urine containers, etc.) are provided?
- What is the laboratory's report mechanism and how is confidentiality ensured?
- How long can positive specimens be stored at the laboratory?
- Can the laboratory offer support (technical testimony) at hearing or in court-related cases? (Figures 34.11 through 34.15)

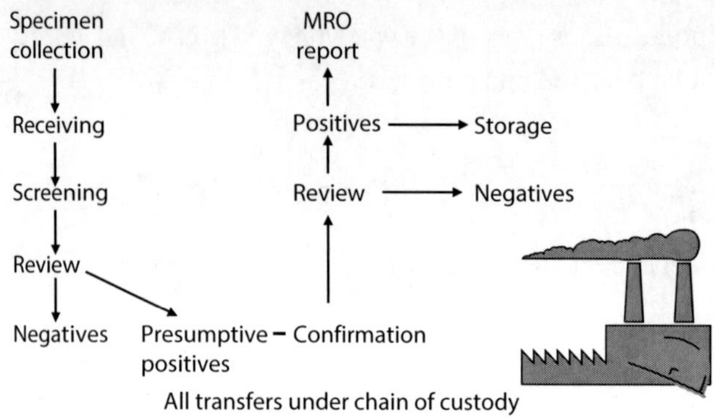

FIGURE 34.11 Substance abuse: The laboratory flowchart 1.

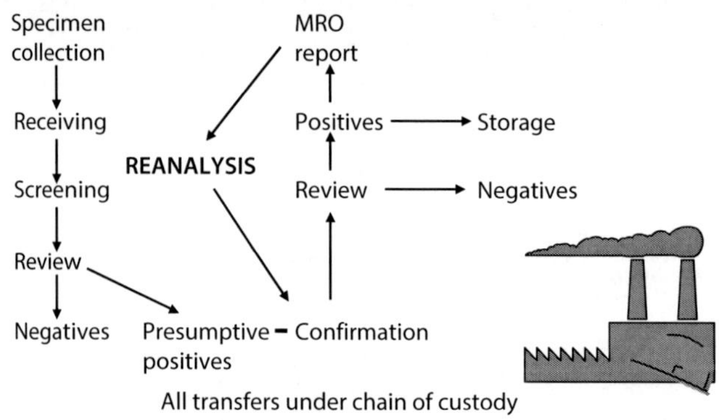

FIGURE 34.12 Substance abuse: The laboratory flowchart 2.

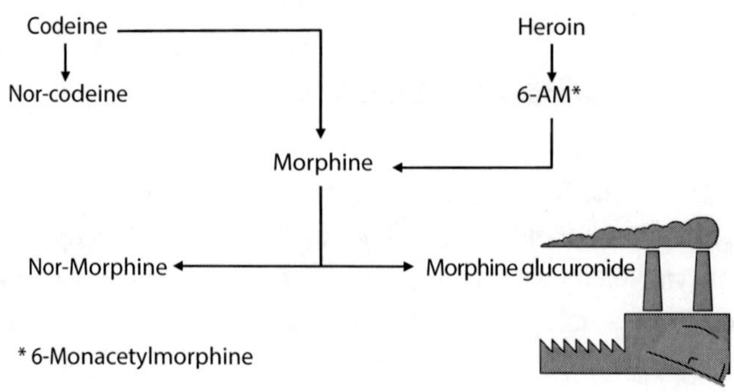

FIGURE 34.13 Substance abuse: Opiate metabolism.

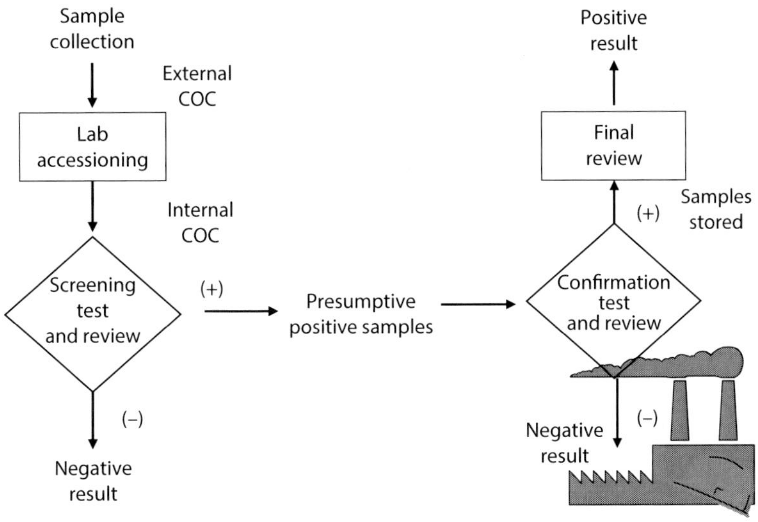

FIGURE 34.14 Substance abuse: The laboratory flowchart 3.

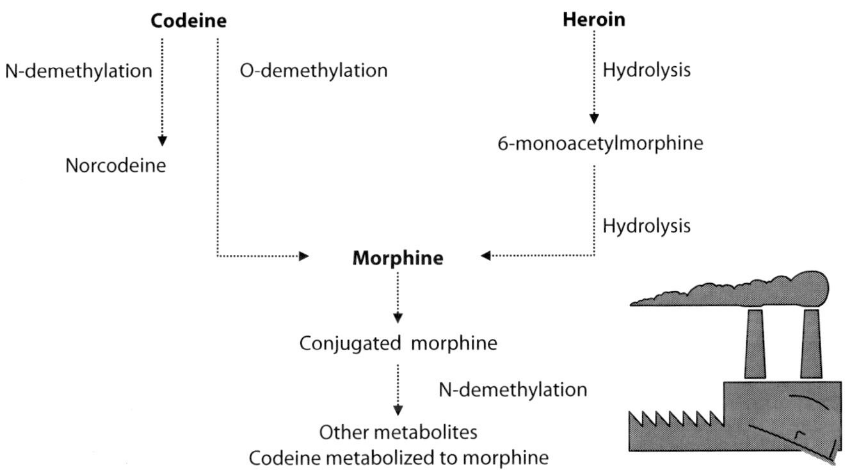

FIGURE 34.15 Substance abuse: The drugs of abuse.

MRO Responses

Medical Miranda

- "The reason I am speaking to you personally is because the results of your urine drug test have been received and it is a positive test. The purpose of this interview is to provide you with an opportunity to voluntarily share information with me that might explain a positive result, such as anything from your medical history, prescriptions, recent treatment, or something in your diet. Before I ask you any further questions, I want to tell you that any information that you may disclose will be *treated confidentially* and not be released unless a U.S. Department of Transportation regulation requires or permits such a disclosure. You have the option of not discussing the matter with me, if you choose. Do you have any questions at this point?" Noncontact positive test donor declines interview—refuses medical interview—report as positive drug test.

5-Day Noncontact Positive

- Verified positive results without donor interview (Table 34.8).
- Document that donor knew to call MRO.
- 14-day noncontact positive.
- Document efforts to contact donor.
- Report as "subject to further review?"

Specimen Not Suitable

- Medical review interview procedure similar to positive test interview (Table 34.9).

Table 34.8 Medical Review Officer's Conclusions in Complex Opioid Cases

Urinalysis	Employee Presents Prescription	Claims Poppy Seed Eating	Signs of Abuse	MRO's Conclusion of Probable Explanation
1. 6-Monoacetylmorphine with or without other findings	NR	NR	NR	Urinary confirmation of heroin abuse
2. Morphine	Morphine	NR	NR	No urinary confirmation of opioid abuse
3. Morphine	None	Yes	Yes	Urinary confirmation of heroin abuse
4. Morphine predominates, some codeine	Morphine	NR	None	No urinary confirmation of opioid abuse
5. Morphine predominates, some codeine	Codeine	No	Yes	Urinary confirmation of morphine or heroin abuse
6. Morphine predominates, some codeine	Codeine	Yes	NR	No urinary confirmation of opioid abuse
7. Codeine predominates, some morphine	Codeine	NR	NR	No urinary confirmation of opioid abuse
8. Codeine predominates, some morphine	None	Yes	Yes	Urinary confirmation of codeine abuse
9. Codeine predominates, some morphine	None	Yes	None	No urinary confirmation of opioid abuse

Note: NR = not relevant.

Table 34.9 Atypical Specimens

Laboratory Research	MRO and Employer Action
1. Specific gravity <1.003 and creatine <0.2 g/L	The MRO can, but is not required to, inform the employer that the specimen's specific gravity is less than 1.003 and its creatinine is less than 0.2 g/L (20 ng/mL). Given this information, the employer can, but is not required to, direct that the donor's next urine drug test specimen be collected under direct observation.
2. Specimen not suitable	The MRO attempts to determine the reason for the specimen's unsuitability. If the specimen remains "not suitable" and the reason remains unclear, the MRO reports the test as "test not performed" and advises the employer that another specimen should be collected immediately and under direct observation.
3. Specimen adulterated: Presence of <adulterant> detected	The MRO reports the outcome as "test not performed" and notifies the employer that the specimen was adulterated. An adulterated specimen is considered a refusal to submit to testing.

- MRO's duty is to ascertain if an acceptable explanation exists for the specimen's unsuitability.
- Declare final, verified, results accordingly.
- Recollection under direct observation.

Amphetamine Interpretation

- Not as difficult as it may seem.
- Remember D and L isomers of methamphetamines are the key (d "drug" and l "legal" amphetamines not at issue—exception is selegiline).
- 200 ng/mL or more of amphetamine must be present to report a methamphetamine-positive result.
- <500 ng/mL amphetamine will not be reported.
- Know your laboratory—isomers by request?

Opiate Interpretation

- Clinical evidence of unauthorized use of an opiate (burden of proof on the MRO).
- Verify prescriptions—codeine and morphine only.
- Old prescription?
- Spouse's prescription?
- Foreign preparations?
- Unexplained result with no admission of use and urinary findings of
  - Low morphine only
  - Morphine and codeine
  - Codeine only
  - High morphine levels
- Perform physical examination.

- Poppy seed ingestion (alone) rarely will produce morphine in excess of 2000 ng/mL; morphine/codeine 2:1 or more.
- 6 mg heroin (IM) produces peak morphine level of 8721 ng/mL.
- 20 mg morphine (IM) produces peak urinary concentration of 18,000 ng/mL.
- 60 mg IM codeine produces peak urinary excretion of 15,682 ng/mL codeine.
- Morphine peaked at 3096 ng/mL following cocaine ingestion (both codeine and morphine peaked at 2.8 h).
- At 36 h, morphine remained reportable (491 ng/mL) while codeine was not (207 ng/mL).
- Codeine in body converted to morphine → morphine sulfate + morphine glucuronide.

Opiate Interpretations: Rules of Thumb

- Poppy seeds are usually not responsible for urinary opiates 24–36 h after ingestion.
- Morphine/codeine ratios of less than 2–3:1 usually rule out poppy seed ingestion as the sole source for urinary opiates (suggest codeine use).
- Morphine levels over 1000–2000 ng/mL without reportable codeine or over 4000–5000 ng/mL with codeine reported usually rule out poppy seed ingestion as the sole source for urinary opiates.
- Low morphine levels only (<2000 ng/mL) can be found with poppy seed ingestion, the "tail end" of codeine ingestion, or several days after morphine or heroin use.
- Very high levels of morphine (>10,000 ng/mL) with little or no codeine almost always mean heroin or morphine use.
- A finding of 6-MAM in the urine is specific evidence of heroin abuse.

Split Sample Issues

- Splits optional for two operating administration, RSPA and USCG.
- MRO's responsibility to offer split test.
- Regulations moot on financial responsibility for split sample testing.
- Request for split should not delay reporting of result to employer.
- Donor must request split within 72 h.
- Lab will not routinely report lack of split sample availability.
- Failure of split to confirm initial test result requires cancelation of report to DOT.
- Also cancel if specimen is unavailable, inadequate for testing, or untestable.
- Report cases where donor request for split test results in cancelation on standard form.
- Do not cancel test if collector failed to mark split not collected.
- MRO must request split test in writing.
- **MRO can order primary reanalysis:** Donor can request split specimen analysis (for drug only).

Return to Work Determination

- Clearance by MRO necessary for USCG and RSPA.
- USCG requires statement related to "cure."

- FAA asks for statement of drug "dependence or nondependence."
- MRO should evaluate all clinical information; interview donor.

Shy Bladder Evaluation

- Required after failure to produce an adequate urine sample (45 mL/30 mL).
- MRO may perform evaluation.
- MRO may receive information from outside physician evaluator and transmit to employer.
- Examination must develop pertinent data that might explain the donor's inability to produce a sample.
- Evaluation may consist of
  - Medical history (renal diagnosis, output problems)
  - Medication history (anticholinergics, antihypertensives, antihistamines)
  - General physical (turgor, orthostatic changes)
  - Simple lab tests (U/A, BUN, creatinine)
  - Cystoscopy, IVP usually not needed
- Written report required.
- DOT July 25, 1995 notice defines "medical condition" (for shy bladder purposes) as an "ascertainable physiologic condition (e.g., urinary system dysfunction) as distinct from assertions of 'situational anxiety' or unsupported claims of dehydration."

Chapter 35

Miscellaneous Toxicants

Acrolein .814
Acrylamides 815
Acrylates .816
Amines .816
Aniline Compounds .817
Azides .817
Azides—Sodium Azide .818
Bromide Compounds .818
Bromide Compounds: Bromides vs. Bromates .819
Butadienes .819
Carbon Disulfide (CS_2) 820
Chlorates 821
Coal Tar Products 822
Coal Tar Products: Naphthalene 822
Diamines 823
Dibromochloropropane 823
Dimethylacetamide 824
Dimethylformamide 825
Dinitrobenzene 825
Dinitrotoluene 826
Epichlorohydrin 826
Ethylene Dibromide 827

Ethylenediamine 828
Fluoride Compounds 828
Fuels.... 829
Hexachloro-1,3-Butadiene.... 831
Isocyanates.... 831
Isocyanates—Toluene Diisocyanate 831
Maleic Anhydride.... 832
Mercaptans.... 833
Methylene Diamine 834
Nitriles 835
o-Phenylenediamine.... 835
Phosphorus/Phosphides 836
Phthalates.... 837
Polymers 838
Resins.... 838
Styrene 838
Trimellitic Anhydride.... 839
Triorthocresylphosphate.... 839
Xylidine 840

Acrolein

2-Propenal

- **Chemical:** Flammable, volatile, poison
- **Properties:** Water white or yellow liquid, disagreeable odor
- **Sources/Usage:** 1° acrylic acid production, burning tobacco (smoking) and gasoline/fuels; small amounts in some fried foods, cooking oils, modified starch production, and roasted coffee; herbicide/algicide; chemical weapon WWI
- **Absorption:** Inhalation, dermal, ocular, ingestion

Acute Toxicity

- **Respiratory**: Concentrations at 10 ppm can lead to pulmonary edema and death; asthmatic reaction
- **Dermal:** Skin irritant, burns, erythema, and edema
- **Ocular/ophthalmic:** Eye irritation, damage to cornea
- **Gastrointestinal:** Burns of lips, mouth, throat, esophagus, and stomach; nausea, vomiting, and diarrhea
- **Cardiovascular:** Hypertension and tachycardia
- **CNS:** CNS depression
- **Immunologic:** Potential immunotoxin

Chronic Toxicity

- **Inhalation:** General respir congestion; eye, nose, throat irritation
- **Dermal:** Strong irritant, skin burns
- **Carcinogen**: Potential
- **Dosage:** Odor threshold 0.16 ppm; OSHA permissible exposure limit 0.1 ppm
- **Diagnosis**: Biological or environmental samples; no specific medical tests available
- **Treatment:** Removal, decontamination (decon), flush exposed or irritated eyes and skin with tepid water for 15 min, do not induce emesis, activated charcoal at a dose of 1 g/kg (infant, child, and adult dose), 4–8 ounces of milk or water; if bronchospasm—aerosolized bronchodilator (albuterol), corticosteroids if patient wheezing or hypersensitivity pneumonitis; children with stridor—racemic epinephrine aerosol (dose 0.25–0.75 mL of 2.25% racemic epinephrine solution as needed every 20 min); adults with systolic pressure less than 80 mm Hg, bolus perfusion of 1,000 mL/h intravenous saline or lactated Ringer's solution, children—20 mL/kg bolus of normal saline over 10–20 min, then infuse at 2–3 mL/kg/h

Acrylamides

2-Propenamide

- **Chemical:** Toxic, mutagen
- **Properties:** A white odorless crystalline solid; soluble in water, ethanol, ether, chloroform
- **Use:** Synthesize polyacrylamides (thickeners) including water treatment, gel electrophoresis (SDS-PAGE), papermaking, ore; baking or frying foods produce acrylamide (overcooking = ↑levels)—Rxn btw aspargine and reducing sugars
- **Absorption**: Inhalation, ingestion, dermal

Acute Toxicity

- **Dermal, ocular, respiratory:** Sweating, urinary incontinence, nausea, myalgia, speech disorders, numbness, and weakened legs and hands
- **Ingestion:** Drowsiness, off-balance, confusion, memory loss, hallucinations

Chronic Toxicity

- **Neurotoxicant:** Polyneuropathy with motor and sensory impairment marked by numbness, paresthesias, ataxia, tremor, dysarthria, and mid-brain lesions
- **Reproduction:** Large doses suspected to affect male reproductive glands
- **Carcinogen:** Studies inconsistent but suspected
- **Mutagen:** Chromosomal aberrations, dominant lethality, sister chromatid exchanges and unscheduled DNA synthesis *in vivo* and *in vitro* animals
- **Diagnosis:** Test air, water, foods
- **Misc:** One case well-water poisoning

Acrylates

Propenoates

- **Definition:** Salts and esters of *acrylic acid*
- **Chemical:** Corrosive
- **Properties:** Colorless liquid; miscible with water; acrid odor
- **Use:** Plastics, latex applications, floor polish, polymer solutions for coatings applications, emulsion polymers, paint formulations, leather finishing, and paper coatings; produced by some algae
- **Absorption:** Inhalation, ingestion, ocular, dermal

Toxicity

- **Dermal:** Corrosive, inflammation, skin rashes systemic poisoning
- **Inhalation:** Potentially fatal as a result of spasms, inflammation/swelling of larynx and bronchi, chemical pneumonitis, pulmonary; may trigger allergic reaction; coughing, wheezing, laryngitis, shortness of breath, headache, nausea, and vomiting
- **Ocular:** Irritant, eye damage, or blindness
- **Ingestion:** Pain/burning in mouth, pharynx, stomach; diarrhea, ↓blood pressure, asphyxia via throat swelling, GI tract mucous membranes destruction
- **Diagnosis:** Primarily environmental testing

Treatment

- **Dermal:** Flush with soap and water, remove contaminated clothing and shoes
- **Inhalation:** Removal, oxygen, artificial respiration (if not breathing)
- **Ocular:** Flush eyes with water lifting occasionally
- **Ingestion:** Dilution

Amines

- **Definition:** Group of organic compounds considered as derived from ammonia by replacement of one or more hydrogen by organic radicals
- **Types:** Aliphatic amines, aromatic amines
- **Examples:** Methylamine, ethanolamine, 2-aminoethanol, trisamine (tris), dimethylamine, methylethanolamine, aziridine, azetidine, pyrrolidine, piperidine, trimethylamine, dimethylethanolamine
- **Use:** *Dyes* (methyl orange, direct brown 138, sunset yellow), *pharmaceuticals* (chlorpheniramine—antihistamine; chlorpromazine—tranquilizer; ephedrine and phenylephrine—decongestants; amphetamine, methamphetamine, and methcathinone = controlled substances), *gas treatment* (used to remove carbon dioxide (CO_2) and hydrogen sulfide (H_2S) from natural gas)
- **Absorption:** Inhalation, ingestion, or dermal

Toxicity

- **Diagnosis:** By exposure history

Treatment

- **Dermal:** Flush with soap and water, remove contaminated clothing and shoes
- **Inhalation:** Removal, oxygen, artificial respiration (if not breathing)
- **Ocular:** Flush eyes with water lifting occasionally
- **Ingestion:** Dilution

Aniline Compounds

- **Chemical:** Toxic, carcinogen, mutagen
- **Properties:** Colorless oily liquid; aromatic taste; rotten fish smell (amines)
- **Sources/use:** Pharmaceuticals, explosives, petroleum refining, photographic chemicals intermediate for dyes, agricultural, polymer, and rubber; pollutants in outdoor air, burning plastics, burning tobacco; made from benzene; drugs (starting product for paracetamol—acetaminophen, Tylenol); staining dye
- **Absorption:** Inhalation, dermal, ocular, ingestion
- **Acute toxicity:** Inhalation of high levels causes upper respiratory tract irritation and congestion; very toxic—lethal dose 50–500 milligrams per kilogram body weight (mg/kg); tiredness, loss of appetite, headache, and dizziness
- **Chronic toxicity:** *Inhalation*—methemoglobin formation (inability to transport O_2 and CO_2) resulting cyanosis (bluish coloration of the skin, nail beds, lips, mucous membranes due to $\downarrow O_2$ of the blood); irritating to mucous membranes eyes, skin, upper respiratory; carcinogen; nervous system
- **Pathophysiology:** Binds hemoglobin—iron normal ferrous state Fe^{2+} oxidizes to Fe^{3+} alters absorption and discolorization
- **Diagnosis:** Arterial blood sample (chocolate brown—methemoglobinemia detection)
- **Treatment:** (1) In methemoglobin levels >30%, methylene blue IV at 1–2 mg/kg (oxidant)—*contraindicated if glucose-6-phosphate dehydrogenase deficiency hemolysis*; (2) ascorbic acid (antioxidant)
- **Misc:** Aniline dye used in diaper production—methemoglobinemia; Spain 1981 epidemic—rapeseed oil denatured with aniline linked to toxic oil syndrome

Azides

- **Definition:** Anion with the formula N_3^-
- **Chemical:** Toxic, explosive
- **Inorganic azides:** Sodium azide—airbags, trimethylsilylazide
- **Organic azides:** Phenyl azide, zidovudine—AZT, drug, tosyl azide

- **Uses:** NaN_3 propellant in airbags; anhydrous source of N_3^-; pharmaceuticals; azide salts mutagenesis studies; rotary evaporators, freeze-drying equipment, cooling traps, water baths, waste pipes
- **Toxicity:** Inhibits cytochrome c oxidase by binding irreversibly to heme cofactor (similar carbon monoxide); explosive in [↑] and vapors

Azides—Sodium Azide

- **Chemical:** ↑Toxic
- **Properties:** Odorless white solid
- **Use:** Airbags, chemical preservative, biocide
- **Absorption:** Inhalation, dermal, ingestion
- **Symptoms:** Rapid breathing, restlessness, dizziness, weakness, headache, nausea and vomiting, rapid heart rate, red eyes (gas or dust exposure), clear drainage from the nose (gas or dust exposure), cough (gas or dust exposure), skin burns and blisters (explosion or direct skin contact); convulsions, ↓ blood pressure, slow heart rate, loss of consciousness, lung injury, respiratory failure leading to death
- **Toxicity:** Uncouples oxidative phosphorylation cytochrome oxidase (cytotoxic hypoxia and metabolic acidosis), potential CN production
- **Clinical poisoning:** Cardiovascular, and eye > initial gastrointestinal (nausea, vomiting, diarrhea)
- **Cardiovascular:** Vasodilation = hypotension
- **CNS:** Biphasic—initial headache and seizures, then hyporeflexia and coma
- **Eye:** Deeply penetrating liquefaction necrosis
- **EMS risks:** Ingestion: Combines w/gastric HCl liberating hydrazoic acid posing toxicity to all attending personnel
- **Treatment:** Supportive, ICU monitoring, copious eye irrigation (pH 7.4 saline > Ringer's lactate > tap water); adequate ventilation and PPE

Bromide Compounds

- **Definition:** Chemical compounds containing bromine.
- **Examples:** Aluminum bromide ($AlBr_3$), ammonium bromide (NH_4Br), bromine monofluoride (BrF), bromine pentafluoride (BrF_5), bromine trifluoride (BrF_3), ethidium bromide ($C_{21}H_{20}BrN_3$), tetrabromomethane (CBr_4), hydrobromic acid (HBr), iron(III) bromide ($FeBr_3$), lithium bromide (LiBr), phosphorus pentabromide (PBr_5), phosphorus tribromide (PBr_3), potassium bromide (KBr), potassium bromate ($KBrO_3$), silver bromide (AgBr), sodium bromide (NaBr), sodium bromate ($NaBrO_3$).
- **Chemical:** Volatile.
- **Properties:** Only liquid nonmetallic element at room temperature.

- **Use:** 1,2-Dibromoethane was used as gasoline antiknock agent for leaded gasoline; fumigants, brominated flame retardants, water purification compounds, dyes, medicines, sanitizers, inorganic bromides for photography; intermediates in organic synthesis; brominated vegetable oil (emulsifier—citrus soft drinks; tests for alkenes and phenols; hair neutralizer and straightener, bread preservative.
- **Overdose:** Old nerve tonics (Bromo-Seltzer) and nematocidal fumigants; irritates GI = vomiting; ↑sedation = stupor and coma; bromism = strange neurologic and psychological effects.
- **Bromism:** Bizarre behavior, delusions, hallucinations, headache, apathy, irritation, headache, apathy, irritability, confusion, dysarthria, tremors, ataxia, anorexia—weight loss, bromoderma.
- **Miscellaneous:** Spurious hyperchloridemia.

Bromide Compounds: Bromides vs. Bromates

Bromates

- **Use:** Hair neutralizers and straighteners, bread preservatives

Toxicity

- Like aminoglycosides, bromates target hair cells of cochlea and renal tubules—impairing the ability to regulate electrochemical gradients.
- Bromate ototoxicity is permanent, but renal failure is reversible.
- **Treatment:** Lavage and AC.

Bromides

- **Use:** Old nerve-headache tonics and sedatives (Bromo-Seltzer); gas fumigant for soil, fruits, and vegetables; vehicle for some drugs (bromopheniramine and dextromethorphan)
- **Toxicity:** Severe gastrointestinal mucosal irritant, brown stained tongue, progressive CNS depression = bromism, later bromoderma—like ioderma w/ulcerating facial acne; treatment = antibiotics and Retin-A®
- **Bromoderma:** Acne resembles ioderma w/weeping and ulcerating facial pustules—indicative to brominated or iodinated long-term exposure
- **Treatment:** Lavage and AC, hemodialysis

Butadienes

1,3-Butadiene

- **Definition:** A colorless, highly flammable hydrocarbon, C_4H_6, obtained from petroleum and used in the manufacture of synthetic rubber

- **Chemical:** Flammable, irritant
- **Sources/use:** Vehicle exhaust; rubber and plastics; petroleum processing; acrylics; forest fires; cigarette smoke
- **Absorption:** Inhalation, dermal

Acute Toxicity

- **Inhalation:** Irritation of eyes, nasal passages, throat, and lungs; neurological effects—blurred vision, fatigue, headache, and vertigo @ ↑levels
- **Dermal**: Sensation of cold, followed by burning sensation; potential frostbite

Chronic Toxicity

- **Inhalation:** ↑Cardiovascular diseases—rheumatic and arteriosclerotic heart diseases
- **Carcinogen:** Increased incidence of respiratory, bladder, stomach, and lymphatohematopoietic cancers

Diagnosis

- **Clinical based**—Respiratory distress or symptoms of CNS depression; lab tests for CBC, glucose, electrolytes, liver enzymes, and kidney function tests; chest radiography and pulse oximetry (or ABG measurements) for severe inhalation exposure.
- Metabolites rapidly eliminated from the body via lungs and kidney; breath levels of epoxides and urine levels of mercapturic acids are not clinically useful, but can be used to document an exposure.
- **Treatment:** Supportive.

Carbon Disulfide (CS_2)

- **Chemical:** Highly flammable, CNS toxin
- **Properties:** *Pure*–colorless liquid with pleasant odor resembling chloroform; *impure*–yellowish liquid with unpleasant odor (rotting radishes)
- **Use**: Manufacture of rayon, cellophane, carbon tetrachloride, rubber chemicals, and pesticides; volcanic eruptions or marshes; flotation agents in mineral processing; soil fumigant
- **Absorption**: Inhalation, ingestion, dermal

Acute Toxicity

- **Inhalation:** Changes in breathing, chest pains, nausea, vomiting, dizziness, fatigue, headache, mood changes, lethargy, blurred vision, delirium, and convulsions
- **CNS:** Excitation resembling alcoholic followed by depression, stupor, restlessness, unconsciousness, and possible death; if recovery, possible narcosis, nausea, vomiting, and headache

Chronic Toxicity

- **CNS:** Behavioral and neurophysiological changes, reduced nerve conduction velocity, peripheral neuropathy, and polyneuropathy
- **Circulatory:** ↑ Risk coronary heart disease, angina
- **Misc:** Effects vision, possible blisters and eczematous lesions on hands
- **Reproductive/developmental:** *Men*—decreased sperm count, decreased libido in men; *women*—menstrual disturbances; *pharmacokinetic* studies—may cross placenta and localize in target organs of fetus (brain, blood, liver, and eyes)
- **Cancer risk:** ↑ Risk lymphatic leukemia in some studies
- **Diagnosis:** Blood, urine and breath test—determine breakdown substances from carbon disulfide are higher than normal (test not specific for carbon disulfide exposure); *chronic exposure*—presence of sensory and motor neuropathy, neuropsychiatric changes, *parkinsonism*, renal and hepatic damage, sleep disturbance, fatigue, anorexia and weight loss
- **Treatment:** No antidote; removal from contaminated area, support of respiratory and cardiovascular functions, and irrigation of contaminated eyes or skin

Chlorates

- **Definition:** Compound that contains chlorine in an oxidation state; salts of chloric acid. *Examples*—potassium chlorate ($KClO_3$), sodium chlorate ($NaClO_3$), magnesium chlorate ($Mg(ClO_3)_2$)
- **Chemical:** Oxidant
- **Use:** Antiseptics (obsolete), matches, explosives, herbicides
- **Absorption:** Ingestions, inhalation

Toxicity

- GI irritant (elimination by kidneys mostly)—may cause mild CNS depression
- Oxidizes hemoglobin and ↑RBC membrane rigidity = methemoglobinemia (hypoxic stress) and hemolytic anemia (which may result in 2° disseminated intravascular coagulation and potentiate renal toxicity)

Clinical

- **Symptoms:** Usually 1–4 h after ingestion. GI irritation including nausea, vomiting, diarrhea, and abdominal cramps; cyanosis from methemoglobinemia—"black-brown urine"; obtundation and anuria may ensue.
- **Case study—Potassium chlorate:** 120 matches ingested w/MRI revealing symmetric abnormal signal intensity within deep gray matter and medial temporal lobes (basal ganglia ↑ vulnerability to O_2 deprivation). Follow-up MRI 2 months later was normal.

- **Treatment:** Orogastric lavage, activated charcoal, exchange transfusions, hemodialysis, and peritoneal dialysis.
- **Misc:** Sodium chlorate used to control morning glory, Canada thistle, Johnson grass, bamboo, ragwort and St John's wort; once treated ulcerative lesions with mouthwash and toothpaste.

Coal Tar Products

- **Definition:** Brown-black liquid of high viscosity, naphthalene smell and aromatic hydrocarbons; liquid by-product coal distillation to make coke (carbonaceous material from destructive distillation of low-ash, low-sulfur bituminous coal)
- **Examples:** Acetanilid, antikamnia, antipyrin, creosote (disinfectant, laxative, and a cough treatment), phenacetin, naphthalene (mothballs; most abundant component of coal tar)
- **Use:** Kerosene production, heating or to fire boilers, coal tar soap, medicated shampoo (head lice, psoriasis, and dandruff), OTC drugs (Balnetar), insecticides, fungicides

Accidental Poisoning

- Patent fever remedies, and headache powders

Toxicology

- **General:** Fatigue, lack of appetite, restlessness, pale skin; exposure to large amounts causes nausea, vomiting, diarrhea, blood in the urine, and jaundice.
- **Creosotes exposure:** Burning in the mouth, throat, stomach pains, rash or severe irritation of the skin, chemical burns on surfaces of eyes, convulsions, and mental confusion, kidney or liver problems, unconsciousness, and death; light sensitivity, damage to the cornea.
- **Carcinogen:** Long-term exposure can cause skin cancer and cancer of the scrotum (Sir Percival Potts, London, 1775: first described scrotal skin cancer in chimney sweeps from prolonged skin exposures to coal tars).
- **Naphthalene exposure:** Damage or destroy RBCs; can occur by ingesting mothballs or deodorant blocks; *glucose-6-phosphate dehydrogenase deficiency*—exposure may cause hemolytic anemia (erythrocytes break down).

Coal Tar Products: Naphthalene

- **Other names:** Tar camphor, white tar, moth flakes
- **Properties:** Crystalline, aromatic, white, solid hydrocarbon; primary ingredient mothballs
- **Use:** Household fumigant, manufacture of dyes, synthetic resins, celluloid, solvents, and fuels
- **Absorption:** Most common in children that ingest mothballs; also dermal, and inhalation

Toxicology

- **Ingestion and inhalation:** Headache, nausea, vomiting, diarrhea, abdominal pain, fever, altered mental status
- **Dermal:** Dermatitis
- **Liver:** Hepatic metabolites cause oxidant stress—hemolysis and methemoglobinemia

Pathophysiology

- **Methemoglobinemia**—Hemoglobin oxidized ($Fe^{2+} \rightarrow Fe^{3+}$) and hemoglobin denatured and precipitate Heinz bodies

Diagnostic Testing

- Blood and urine test to detect 1-naphthol and 2-naphthol; reticulocytosis; Coombs test negative; ↑lactate dehydrogenase because hemolyzed RBCs; peripheral blood smear
- **Treatment:** Activated charcoal with polyethylene glycol electrolyte lavage solution with large ingestions; transfusion if high risk and methylene blue

Diamines

- **Definition:** Type of polyamine with exactly two amino groups
- **Examples:** Ethylene diamine, putrescine, cadaverine, hexamethylene diamine, ethambutol, phenylenediamine
- **Properties:** Colorless to yellowish liquid, ammonia-like odor
- **Use:** Color photography developing, lubricants for the molding and processing of plastics, fuel additives, carbamate fungicides, binders, adhesives, fabric softeners, surfactants, curing agents for epoxys, and dyes; solvent for proteins like albumins or casein, as a part of electroplating baths, lubricant for textiles, stabilizer in latex emulsions, and in polyamide adhesives
- **Absorption:** Ingestion, inhalation, dermal

Toxicity

- Skin irritation
- **Ingestion and inhalation:** Human carcinogen
- **Diagnosis:** By history of exposures
- **Treatment:** Remove from exposure sources

Dibromochloropropane

- **Definition:** An active ingredient in soil fumigants
- **Properties:** Colorless liquid when pure; commercial grades as dark-amber to dark-brown liquid

- **Use:** Soil fumigant, nematocide, synthesis of organic chemicals
- **Absorption:** Ingestion, inhalation, dermal

Acute Toxicity

- **Inhalation:** CNS and pulmonary congestion; nausea, lightheadedness, and weakness
- **Ingestion:** Gastrointestinal distress and pulmonary edema
- **Dermal:** Irritant to skin and eyes
- **Reproductive/developmental effects:** Chronic exposure decreased sperm counts (some men with irreversible damage to testicular tissue); *men:* azoospermia, oligospermia; *women:* affects thyroid hormone, ↓ovulation (FSH and LF decrease while normal testosterone)
- **Diagnosis:** Measured in exhaled air, blood, and samples of tissues; sperm counts and the blood levels of certain hormones (follicular stimulating hormone, luteinizing hormone)
- **Treatment:** Prevention (PPE), irrigate skin, activated charcoal, water or milk ingestion, facilitate eye irrigation, oxygen and ventilation
- **Misc:** Costa Rica banana workers found sterile due to DBCP; 1985—banned in the United States

Dimethylacetamide

- **Definition:** Commonly used as a solvent in organic synthesis
- **Properties:** Colorless, water miscible, high boiling, polar and hygroscopic liquid
- **Use:** Solvent for fibers or in adhesive industry, pharmaceuticals and plasticizers as a reaction medium
- **Absorption:** Inhalation, ingestion, dermal, ocular

Toxicity

- **Inhalation:** Irritation to respiratory tract; symptoms—coughing, shortness of breath.
- **Ingestion:** Irritation to GI tract; may cause abdominal spasm, vomiting, sweating, weakness, and headache; large oral doses may cause depression, lethargy, disorientation, visual and auditory hallucinations, perceptual distortions, delusions, emotional detachment, and kidney damage.
- **Dermal:** Irritation to skin; symptoms include redness, itching, and pain; absorption through skin is rapid.
- **Eye contact:** Causes irritation, redness, and pain.
- **Chronic exposure:** Prolonged or repeated exposure may cause liver damage with yellow jaundice.
- **Treatment:** Removal, artificial respiration, oxygen, dilution w/water, flush skin or eyes with water.

Dimethylformamide

- **Definition:** Industrial solvent and in the production of fibers, films, and surface coatings.
- **Properties:** Clear liquid, miscible with water, pure—odorless, technical-grade—fishy/unpleasant smell.
- **Use:** Used to process polymer fibers, films, and surface coatings; to permit easy spinning of acrylic fibers; to produce wire enamels, and as a crystallization medium in pharmaceutical industry. LSUHSC—peptide production.

Acute Toxicity

- **Inhalation:** Irritation to respiratory tract; symptoms include coughing, shortness of breath; causes liver, kidney, cardiovascular system, and central nervous system disorders; abdominal pain, loss of appetite, nausea, weakness, dizziness, headache, constipation, vomiting, diarrhea, increased blood pressure anxiety, and palpitations; flushing of the face and skin may occur, especially with ingestion of alcoholic beverages.
- **Ingestion:** Irritation to GI tract; symptoms parallel inhalation; fatal dose—10 g.
- **Dermal:** Irritation to skin; symptoms include redness, itching, and pain; absorption through the skin can readily occur, resulting in symptoms paralleling inhalation.
- **Ocular:** Causes irritation, conjunctivitis, and pain; blurred vision.

Chronic Toxicity

- Liver and digestive damage
- **Reproductive/developmental effects:** Increased rate of spontaneous abortion (females normally not chosen to work in proximity)
- **Diagnosis:** Measurement of a metabolite of dimethylformamide, methyl formamide, in urine as guide to monitor exposure; liver needle biopsy
- **Treatment:** Symptomatic, removal, supportive, liver function monitoring; support of respiratory and cardiovascular functions

Dinitrobenzene

- **Definition:** Substances that are used in explosives
- **Properties:** Crystal-like solids at room temperature; may exist in air as dust or a vapor; if under very high heat—explosive; no odor or taste
- **Sources/use:** Army ammunitions plant or chemical manufacturer
- **Absorption:** Inhalation, dermal, ingestion, ocular

Toxicity

- Reduces ability of blood to carry oxygen causing skin to become bluish (methemoglobin); headache, nausea, and dizziness; potentially fatal if swallowed, inhaled or absorbed through the skin

- **Chronic:** Anemia, liver damage, visual impairment
- **Symptoms:** Anoxia, cyanosis; visual disturbance, central scotomatas; bad taste, burning mouth, dry throat, thirst; yellowing hair, eyes, skin; anemia; liver damage
- **Target organs:** Eyes, skin, blood, liver, cardiovascular system, central nervous system
- **Diagnosis:** Liver function tests, blood test
- **Treatment:** Removal, induce vomiting, charcoal slurry—aqueous or mixed with saline cathartic or sorbitol

Dinitrotoluene

- **Definition:** Intermediate for polyurethanes
- **Chemical:** Explosive (precursor to trinitrotoluene, TNT)
- **Properties:** Pale yellow to orange crystalline solid
- **Use:** Explosives industry, dyes, polyurethanes, smokeless gunpowder
- **Absorption:** Inhalation or dermal

Toxicity

- **Chronic inhalation:** Affects the CNS, resulting in unpleasant metallic taste in mouth, muscular weakness, headache, appetite loss, giddiness, dizziness, nausea, insomnia, and tingling pains in the extremities in humans
- **Blood:** Causing pallor, cyanosis, and anemia; ↑mortality from heart disease
- **Reproductive/developmental effects:** Potential cause for low sperm counts, spontaneous abortions
- **Diagnosis:** 24 h testing detected in blood and urine (measured by quantification of excreted DNT metabolites in the urine); methemoglobinemia testing, which are reversible 2–3 days after removal from exposure; liver function (nephrotoxic effects directed to the tubular system)
- **Treatment:** Hemodialysis, forced diuresis, hyperbaric oxygen, or hemoperfusion for methemoglobinemia; methylene blue (tetramethylthionine chloride); exchange/RBC transfusion if not responding to methylene blue

Epichlorohydrin

- **Chemical:** Volatile and flammable
- **Properties:** Clear liquid at room temperature; pungent, garlicky, sweet odor
- **Use:** Production of epoxy resins used in coatings, adhesives, and plastics; manufacture of synthetic glycerine, textiles, paper, inks and dyes, solvents, surfactants, and pharmaceuticals; inert ingredient in pesticides

Acute Toxicity

- **Inhalation:** Irritation to the eyes, respiratory tract, and skin of workers; ↑ level exposure, nausea, vomiting, cough, labored breathing, chemical pneumonitis (inflammation of the lung), pulmonary edema, and renal lesions
- **Dermal:** Irritation and burns of the skin
- **Lethal dosage:** Expected between 1360 and 3000 mg/m^3

Chronic Toxicity

- **Inhalation:** Respiratory tract illness and hematological effects (decreased hemoglobin concentration and decreased erythrocyte and leukocyte counts)
- **Carcinogen:** Potential lung cancer
- **Diagnosis:** Chest x-ray, expired air, liver function tests, pulmonary function tests, urinalysis
- **Treatment:** Removal, administer oxygen or pulmonary resuscitation, flush contaminated areas with water

Ethylene Dibromide

- **Chemical:** Extremely toxic to humans
- **Properties:** Colorless liquid; sweet odor, like chloroform
- **Use:** Additive to leaded gasoline (obsolete); treatment of felled logs for bark beetles and termites, and control of wax moths in beehives; intermediate for dyes, resins, waxes, and gums; fumigant for pests and turf

Acute Toxicity

- **Respiratory:** Irritation of nose and throat; moderate to severe exposure produces respiratory manifestations ranging from cough, chest pain, and dyspnea to bronchitis, pneumonitis, pulmonary edema, and hemorrhage; pulmonary edema 3 days after oral poisoning in 1 fatal human case; children ↑risk—hydrocarbon pneumonitis possible.
- **CNS:** Mild depressant; drowsiness from ingestion and inhalation; inhalation in a confined oxygen-deficient space causes loss of consciousness, coma, and death; if survive, potential CNS and PNS effects likely to persist indefinitely.
- **Dermal:** Skin irritant; brief contact can cause erythema and discomfort; splashing causes cooling; prolonged contact may cause blistering and skin ulcers; can lead to reactive airway dysfunction syndrome (RADS), a chemically or irritant-induced type of asthma.
- **Ocular/ophthalmic:** Conjunctivitis, temporary loss of vision (destruction of eye tissue).
- **Hepatic:** Significant liver damage, necrosis, elevated serum aspartate aminotransferase and lactic dehydrogenase found in autopsies.
- **Renal:** Severe renal lesions—necrosis of the tubular epithelium, cytoplasmic vacuolization of proximal convoluted tubules, and tubular protein casts.

- **Gastrointestinal:** Abdominal pain, nausea, vomiting, and diarrhea after ingestion.
- **Reproductive:** Potential infertility in men.
- **Incompatibilities:** With strong oxidizers, magnesium, alkali metals, and liquid ammonia.
- **Diagnosis:** Serum bromide levels; routine lab—CBC, glucose, and electrolyte determinations; liver function and renal function tests; chest radiography and arterial blood gas readings.
- **Treatment:** *Inhalation*—oxygen, bronchodilator (albuterol), racemic epinephrine aerosol for children who develop stridor; *ingestion*—no emesis, charcoal slurry.

Ethylenediamine

- **Chemical:** Flammable, corrosive
- **Properties:** Colorless to yellowish liquid, with an ammonia-like odor
- **Use:** Solvent for proteins, electroplating baths, textiles lubricant, latex emulsions stabilizer, polyamide adhesives, corrosion inhibitor in paints and coolants, chelating agent, building block in pharmaceuticals (e.g., aminophylline and some antihistamines), cattle feed additive (ethylenediamine dihydroiodide [EDDI]).

Toxicity

- **Target organs:** Skin, respiratory system, liver, kidneys
- Red-brown generalized erythema, anuria, tachycardia, hemolysis: increased blood potassium, ↓RBC count, ↑body temp and pulse, coughing with expectoration, abdominal cramps, diarrhea, blackish vomiting, anuria resulting in ↑ blood urea, cardiac collapse—death
- **Chronic respiratory:** Rhinitis, congestion, coughing, wheezing, dyspnea; asthma
- **Diagnosis:** Chest x-ray, eosinophil counts
- **Treatment:** Removal, supportive

Fluoride Compounds

- **Definition:** Fluorides are naturally occurring compounds.
- **Examples:** Hydrofluoric acid (HF), sodium fluoride (NaF), calcium fluoride (CaF_2), and uranium hexafluoride (UF_6).
- **Properties:** Naturally occurring, pale yellow-green gas with a sharp odor.
- **Use:** Sodium fluoride, calcium fluoride, and sodium monofluorophosphate—added to toothpaste, drinking water, prescribed treatments (oral hygiene).
- Hydrofluoric acid—etching of glass and industrial applications.
- Fluoride in concentrated form is used as prescription drug.
- Fluorine—used in drug molecules to resist detoxification in the liver by the cytochrome P450 oxidase (strong C–F bonds are not easily broken) ensuring orally administered medication not inactivated before reaching the blood stream.

- Fluoride ion—synthetic organic chemistry.
- Sulfur hexafluoride—mostly inert, nontoxic propellant.
- Uranium hexafluoride—separates isotopes of uranium between the fissile isotope U-235 and the nonfissile isotope U-238 in preparation of nuclear reactor fuel and atomic bombs.
- **Absorption**: Ingestion, inhalation, ocular.

Acute Toxicity

- **Ingestion:** High concentrations extremely toxic, potential death (child fatality reported 5 mg/kg)
- **GI:** Fluoride compounds readily absorbed by intestines, excreted in hours, trace amounts found in bone; irritant in doses as low as 0.1–0.3 mg/kg
- **Ocular/dermal**: Irritant in high concentrations

Chronic Toxicity

- Chronic exposure at *low levels* have *beneficial* effect—dental cavity prevention and treatment of osteoporosis (*high levels* can cause tooth and bone damage)
- **Oral:** *Fluorosis*—"excessive" (generally above 0.7–1.2 ppm—amounts recommended for fluoridated water) intake of fluorine compounds—yellowing of teeth, white spots, and pitting, damage in tooth development (6 months to 5 years) or mottling of enamel
- **Diagnosis:** Urine sample, bone sample (measures long-term exposure)
- **Treatment:** Accidental swallowing milk, calcium carbonate, or milk of magnesia slows absorption

Fuels

- **Definition:** Variety of yellowish to light brown liquid mixtures that come from crude petroleum; produce hydrocarbons
- **Properties:** Toxic, flammable, carcinogen
- **Use:** Kerosene, diesel fuel, jet fuel, range oil, home heating oil

Pathophysiology

- **Pulmonary:** Aspiration (most frequently reported)—despite aliphatic hydrocarbons having ↓GI absorption, aspiration occurs, either initially or delayed as patient coughs or vomits; postaspiration, severe pneumonitis from toxic effects on lung parenchyma type II pneumocytes (have altered surfactant production and function); end result aspiration = interstitial inflammation, intra-alveolar hemorrhage and edema, hyperemia, bronchial necrosis, vascular necrosis
- **Nervous system:** CNS toxicity—by direct injury to brain or indirectly via severe hypoxia or simple asphyxiation; direct = hydrocarbons diffuse blood–brain b/c

highly lipophilic; huffing or bagging (the act of rebreathing) can result in hypercarbia (decreased level of arousal); prolonged abuse = leukoencephalopathy and peripheral neuropathy

- **Cardiovascular:** May cause cardiotoxicity—myocardium sensitized to effects of catecholamines → which predisposes patient to tachydysrhythmias→ which can result in syncope or sudden death; *sudden sniffing death syndrome*—teenager huffing or bagging alone and then startled by parent/person causing cardiac arrest (results in ventricular fibrillation or ventricular tachycardia, following large catecholamine exposure to a myocardium that is sensitized by effects of catecholamines)
- **Gastrointestinal:** Irritate GI mucosa = burning sensation; vomiting in one-third of all exposures
- **Hepatic:** Chlorinated hydrocarbons (e.g., carbon tetrachloride) very hepatotoxic; hepatotoxicity results after the hydrocarbon phase I metabolism, introducing free radical formation → free radicals bond hepatic macromolecules causing lipid peroxidation; common histopathologic pattern = centrilobular (zone III) necrosis
- **Renal:** Chronic exposure to toluene (hydrocarbon in octane booster in gasoline fuel); can result in distal renal tubular acidosis and anion gap acidosis (occupational or recreational risk)
- **Hematologic:** Prolonged exposure ↑ risk aplastic anemia, multiple myeloma, and acute myelogenous leukemia; hemolysis from acute ingestion

Frequency

- **United States:** 2004—54,766 cases of hydrocarbon poisoning were reported to U.S. poison control centers (27,000 aged 19 years or younger); account for 2% calls to U.S. Poison Control centers.
- **Internationally:** Developing nations—kerosene implicated in one-third of pediatric poisonings.
- **Age:** Fatalities ↑ in children <5 years (accidental ingestions); inhalant abuse increasingly common among adolescents (study 8th graders: 17.1%).

Toxicity

- **Respiratory:** Pulmonary toxicity after ingestion and subsequent aspiration; symptoms—coughing, gagging, choking.
- **Nervous system:** Headache, lethargy, and decreased mental status, weakness, fatigue, transient euphoria, possible axonopathy—peripheral neuropathy usually begins in extremities and the progresses more proximally.
- **Cardiovascular:** Dyspnea or syncope; sensitization of myocardium to catecholamines; *sudden sniffing death syndrome.*
- **Gastrointestinal:** Mild nausea, vomiting, and sore throat; diarrhea, melena, and hematemesis are rare.

- **Diagnosis:** Liver function test (abnormal within 24 h after ingestion), clinically apparent jaundice can occur within 48–96 h, pulse oximetry (evaluate O_2), complete blood count (benzene exposure may produce myelogenous leukemia or aplastic anemia, ingestion may show leukocytosis, or anemia due to intravascular hemolysis), chest radiography (detect aspiration), electrocardiogram (to assess arrhythmia or ischemia).
- **Treatment:** GI decon controversial (activated charcoal does not absorb hydrocarbons well; secured airway via endotracheal intubation prior to instituting gastric lavage), circulation (oxygen), cardiac monitoring; if arrhythmias, electrolytes replacement, including magnesium and potassium; antibiotics if pneumonitis.

Hexachloro-1,3-Butadiene

- **Properties:** Colorless liquid with a turpentine-like odor
- **Use:** Intermediate in manufacturing of rubber compounds, lubricants, as fluid for gyroscopes, heat transfer liquid, hydraulic fluids
- **Toxicity:** No human studies
- **Animal studies:** Effects on kidney and respiratory system from acute inhalation and ingestion exposure; carcinogen—kidney tumors reported
- **Diagnosis**: Testing HCBD breakdown levels in urine or fat

Isocyanates

- **Definition:** The functional group of atoms –N=C=O
- **Examples:** Toluene diisocyanate, methyl isocyanate
- **Chemical:** Very toxic, carcinogen
- **Use:** Manufactured for reaction with polyols in polyurethanes production
- **Absorption:** Ocular, inhalation, ingestion, dermal

Toxicity

- Irritants to mucous membranes of the eyes and gastrointestinal and respiratory tracts; severe asthma in repeat exposures—death from severe asthma reported
- **Dermal:** Inflammation

Isocyanates—Toluene Diisocyanate

- **Production:** Made by reacting toluene diamine with carbonyl chloride (phosgene)
- **Chemical:** Very toxic, carcinogen
- **Properties:** Clear, pale yellow liquid with a sharp, pungent odor
- **Use:** Chemical intermediate in the production of polyurethane foams, elastomers, coatings, paints, varnishes, wire enamels, sealants, adhesives, and binders

Routes of Exposure

- **Inhalation:** Main route of exposure; lung absorption—irritates respiratory tract and lungs even at low concentrations (odor threshold of 2.1 ppm is 100 times greater than the OSHA permissible exposure limit 0.02 ppm—odor not adequate warning indicator); asphyxiation in enclosed, poorly ventilated, or low-lying areas; children ↑ risk—greater lung surface area: body weight ratios and increased minute volumes: weight ratios, short stature—higher levels nearer to the ground.
- **Dermal/ocular:** Direct contact = severe eye and skin irritation; inflammation mucous membranes; dermal absorption slow.
- **Ingestion:** Potential chemical burns of lips, mouth, throat, esophagus, and stomach.

Toxicity

- **Respiratory:** Irritation of the respiratory tract, chest tightness, cough, breathlessness, and inflammation of the bronchi with sputum production and wheezing; fluid and inflammation in lungs possible; flu-like symptoms such as fever, malaise, shortness of breath, and cough result; asthmatic attacks possible @ 0.0001 ppm; reactive airway dysfunction syndrome (RADS); also euphoria, ataxia, mental aberrations, vomiting, abdominal pain, bronchospasm, chemical bronchitis, hypersensitivity pneumonitis, and noncardiogenic pulmonary edema.
- **CNS:** Lightheadedness, headache, insomnia, mental aberrations, impaired gait, loss of consciousness, and coma.
- **Dermal:** Irritant; liquid form—second- and third-degree skin burns possible; respiratory sensitization rare.
- **Ocular:** Irritation, inflammation of the eye membrane, cornea inflammation, clouding, secondary glaucoma.
- **Potential sequelae:** Potential development nonspecific bronchial hyperresponsiveness and toluene diisocyanate hypersensitization; narrowing of the bronchi could last years; neurologic effects—difficulty concentrating, poor memory, and dull headache from high-level exposure (possible neurotoxic effects or lack of oxygen in the blood).
- **Chronic exposure**: Sudden asthma.
- **Diagnosis:** Chest x-ray.
- **Treatment:** Bronchodilators, respiratory and cardiovascular support, NO emesis—slurry of activated charcoal at 1 g/kg (usual adult dose 60–90 g, child dose 25–50 g), 4–8 ounces of milk or water (not to exceed 15 mL/kg in a child).

Maleic Anhydride

- **Definition:** Organic compound manufactured by the oxidation of benzene or other aromatic compounds

- **Properties:** Colorless or white solid with a penetrating odor
- **Use:** Formation of unsaturated polyester resins for boats, autos, trucks, buildings, piping, and electrical goods; used to make copolymers, pesticides, and other organic compounds, and in Diels–Alder syntheses; prolong engine oil life
- **Symptom(s):** Conjunctivitis, photophobia, double vision; nasal, upper respiratory irritation; bronchial asthma; dermatitis
- **Target organs:** Eyes, respiratory system, skin

Acute Toxicity

- **Inhalation:** Cause irritation of the respiratory tract, burning in the larynx, reflex cough, lacrimation, headaches, eye irritation, and corneal burns (healed within 48 h)

Chronic Toxicity

- Chronic bronchitis, asthma-like attacks, pulmonary edema, upper respiratory tract irritation, eye irritation, and dermatitis; people with allergies may not be able to tolerate low levels.
- **Pathophysiology:** Radioallergosorbent testing (RAST)—showed IgE antibodies against human serum albumin conjugates.
- **Diagnosis:** Neurotoxicity.
- **Treatment:** Decon, removal, supportive.

Mercaptans

- **Definition:** Sulfur-containing organic compound; *thiol*
- **Use:** Released from decaying organic matter (marshes); detect natural gas leaks (methyl mercaptan); pharmaceuticals, pesticides, plastics livestock feed additives; in vegetables (such as garlic and onions), in "sour" gas oil fields, in coal tar and petroleum; skunk spray

Pathophysiology

- Depresses CNS and affects respiratory center (similar to hydrogen sulfide)—death by respiratory paralysis; paralysis of the locomotor muscles and pulmonary edema; primary mechanism = interference with cytochrome oxidase

Acute Lethality

- Hemolytic anemia, methemoglobinemia (↑ risk if G-6-PD deficiency), internal bleeding, coma, myoclonic tremors, emboli in pulmonary arteries

Clinical Diagnosis

- **Symptoms:** Eye and mucous membrane irritation, headache, dizziness, staggering gait, nausea, and vomiting.

- **Autopsy:** Detected in liver, kidneys, lungs, blood, urine, and washout solution of trachea; transfusions = hematological.
- **Clinical:** ↑ blood pressure; *testing*—CBC, glucose, and electrolyte determinations, pulse oximetry (or ABG measurements), chest radiography.
- **Treatment:** Removal, decon, transfusions; if bronchospasm—aerosolized bronchodilator (albuterol); seizures with benzodiazepine (diazepam); nitroprusside—good choice for hypertension; children with stridor—racemic epinephrine aerosol (dose 0.25–0.75 mL of 2.25% racemic epinephrine solution, repeat every 20 min as needed); if frostbite—rewarm in water bath (104–108°F); if pulmonary edema develops—maintain ventilation and oxygenation (monitor frequent arterial blood gas or pulse oximetry); prophylactic antibiotic may reduce respiratory infection.
- **Misc:** Natural gas in native state = colorless and odorless; mercaptan added to natural gas to make it detectable for leaks; mercaptan has distinct smell of rotten eggs (sulfur containing); detected by smell @ 1.6 PPB.

Methylene Diamine

- **Properties:** Pale yellow crystals that darken when exposed to air and are slightly soluble in cold water; faint amine-like odor
- **Use:** Primarily for 4,4-′methylenedianiline diisocyanate production and other polymeric isocyanates—used to manufacture polyurethane foams; curing agent for epoxy resins and urethane elastomers, corrosion preventative iron, lubricating oils antioxidant, rubber processing chemical, intermediate in the manufacture of elastomeric fibers (Spandex), preparation of azo dyes

Acute Toxicity

- **Ingestion/dermal:** Liver damage; "Epping jaundice"—symptoms include jaundice, tender liver, weakness, abdominal pain, nausea, vomiting, headache, fever, chills, and muscle pain
- **Ocular/dermal:** Irritating
- **Carcinogen:** Animal testing shows ↑ liver and thyroid tumors
- **Pathophysiology:** After inhalation, dermal, or ingestion—enters stomach, lungs, skin → then absorbed by the blood stream
- **Toxicokinetics:** Metabolized by cytochrome P450 to polar metabolites → undergo conjugation with glutathione; can also be acetylated and metabolites detected in urine
- **Diagnosis:** Urine can be tested; serum bilirubin, alkaline phosphatase activity, and glutamic oxaloacetic transaminase affected; liver biopsy—cellular infiltration and cholestasis and evidence of damage to liver parenchyma and biliary tree
- **Treatment:** Supportive; blood exchange/transfusion therapy
- **Misc:** "Epping jaundice"—1965 Epping, England—sack of flour contaminated with MDA during transport to a bakery producing hepatitis

Nitriles

- **Definition:** *Also called cyano compounds*, class of organic compounds having a cyano group—C ≡ N attached to a carbon atom; capable of releasing highly toxic CN^- cyanide ion
- **Properties:** Colorless or pale-blue solids or liquids with distinctive odors
- **Amyl nitrite and alkyl nitrites:** Aphrodisiac usage
- **Absorbed** via skin, lungs, mucous membranes and GI tract
- **Metabolized** in liver and excreted partially in urine
- **Inhalation:** Relaxation of vascular smooth muscle—vasodilation, reflex tachycardia, and hypotension; rapid blood pressure ↓within 30 s (five drops butyl nitrile)
- **Cardiovascular:** Cardiovascular collapse in intravenous injection; vasodilation cerebral blood vessels = ↑intracranial pressure and cerebral aneurysm rupture possible (amyl nitrite)

Toxicity

- **Inhalation:** Headache, nausea, syncope; dangerous if glaucoma—transient increase in intraocular pressure; causes methemoglobinemia—*antidote methylene blue* hemolytic anemia reported (due to oxidizing effect on hemoglobin); "*popper dermatitis*"—characteristic rash around nose, lips, face, penis, scrotum and presents erythematous, edematous, and lesions (appearance of impetigo and seborrheic dermatitis)

Applications

- **Nitric oxide:** Inhalant used to treat persistent pulmonary hypertension of new born and other cardiopulmonary diseases associated; potent vasodilator; @ doses <40 ppm—methemoglobin production possible
- **Cyanide poisoning:** Cyanide antidote kit contains—amyl nitrite pearls, 3% sodium nitrite intravenous solution, 25% sodium thiosulfate
- **Mechanism:** Induces methemoglobinemia in order to preferentially bind CN, forming cyanomethemoglobin and limit cytochrome oxidase poisoning

o-Phenylenediamine

- **Definition:** Aromatic diamine
- **Properties:** Brown to yellow crystals; turns dark when exposed to light
- **Sources/use:** Synthesis of fungicides, corrosion inhibitors, pigments, and pharmaceuticals; removal of elemental sulfur in mining ores, and aldehyde color formers in polymeric products

Absorption

- **Inhalation/ingestion:** Blue lips or finger nails, blue skin, confusion, convulsions, dizziness, headache, nausea, unconsciousness

- **Dermal:** Redness
- **Ocular:** Redness, pain

Acute Toxicity

- **Inhalation/ingestion:** Irritates eyes and mildly irritating to skin and respiratory tract. The effects may be delayed. Medical observation is indicated.
- **Circulatory**: Effects blood, resulting in the formation of methemoglobin.

Chronic Toxicity

- Dermal sensitization, anemia, carcinogenic
- **Treatment:** Supportive; activated charcoal

Phosphorus/Phosphides

- **Properties:** Waxy white/yellow (ignites in air forming white fumes and greenish light), red, black, colorless; garlic smell
- **Use:** Fertilizers, fireworks, nerve agents, friction matches, pesticides, toothpaste, and detergents; *white/yellow phosphorus:* extremely toxic—rodenticides and explosives

Pathophysiology

- **Hepatic:** ↑O_2 hepatocyte consumption, ↓intrahepatocyte ATP levels—mitochondrial injury and visible swelling electron microscopy; massive hepatic steatosis (hallmark white phosphorus toxicity)—rise in hepatic triglycerides w/I 2 h and peaking in 36 h; hepatic necrosis, ↓hepatic glycogen and blood glucose; massive rough endoplasmic reticulum observed
- **Skin, mucous membranes, GI:** Thermal and chemical injury—subcutaneous tissue damage; GI spared likely ↓ [O_2]
- **Cardiovascular:** Interstitial edema and vascuolated cytoplasm with pale linear areas
- **Nervous system:** Radiolabeled phosphorus minimal effects
- **Electrolyte homeostasis:** Calcium complexes with phosphate cause hypocalcemia—precipitates within tissues (forms such as hydroxyapatite); possible hyperkalemia from hypocalcemia (as in hydrofluoric acid poisoning) or renal failure
- **Renal:** Glomerulus injury following systemic absorption; fatty degeneration, fatty deposition, and necrosis in renal tissues

Acute Toxicity

- **Ingestion:** Three stages—first stage: gastrointestinal effects; second stage: symptom-free and lasts about 2 days; third stage: rapid decline in condition with severe gastrointestinal (vomiting, abdominal cramps and pain), kidney, liver, cardiovascular, and CNS effects
- **Inhalation:** Respiratory tract irritation and coughing

- **Dermal:** Severe burns, which are necrotic, yellowish, fluorescent under ultraviolet light, and have a garlic-like odor

Chronic Toxicity

- White phosphorus causes necrosis of the jaw, "phossy jaw"—local inflammation or irritation followed by swelling, ulceration, and destruction of jawbone with perforation to sinus or nasal cavities and externally to cheek; anemia and leukopenia possible.

Miscellaneous Phosphorous Uses and Toxicities

- Matches once used white phosphorus until switching to red phosphorus—vapors gave match workers a necrosis of bones and jaw = "phossy jaw"
- WWII Molotov cocktails—benzene and phosphorus
- Red, white (yellow) phosphorus
- **Use:** Matches; replaced white/yellow phosphorus
- **Toxicity:** Nonvolatile and insoluble; no harm when ingested
- **Treatment:** None
- White/yellow phosphorus
- **Use:** Rodenticides, explosives
- **Toxicity:** Volatile and soluble
- **Skin:** Second- and third-degree burns
- **Gastrointestinal:** "Smoking" and luminescent emesis and excretion
- **Cardiovascular:** Myocardial depression
- **Treatment:** Emesis, orogastric lavage w/0.1% $KMnO_4$ or 2% H_2O_2 (oxidizes phosphorus to harmless phosphates), then AC and sorbitol

Phthalates

- **Use:** Used in flexible polyvinyl chloride (PVC) plastics, such as plastic bags, garden hoses, inflatable recreational toys, blood-storage bags, intravenous medical tubing, and children's toys; *also* vinyl flooring, adhesives, detergents, lubricating oils, solvents, automotive plastics, plastic clothing such as raincoats, personal-care products, such as soap, shampoo, deodorants, fragrances, hair spray, nail polish; and some medical pharmaceuticals.

Potential Exposure

- **Food:** Can migrate into food from plastics during processing and storage
- **Medical procedures:** Blood transfusions and kidney dialysis and use of respirators
- **Household:** Drinking water, newly painted room, room with newly installed flooring
- **Occupational:** Workers in factories that manufacture or use the chemical

Acute Toxicity

- Mild gastrointestinal disturbances, nausea, vertigo

Chronic Toxicity

- Damage to liver and testes; reproductive effects; cancer; abdominal obesity and insulin resistance
- **Treatment:** Dialysis, transfusions

Polymers

- **Use:** Plastic production; comprise a large class of natural and synthetic materials with a variety of properties and purposes
- **Examples:** Natural polymers—shellac and amber; naturally occurring—cellulose (polysaccharide); biopolymers—starches, proteins, and nucleic acids (biological processes)

Toxicity

- **Inhalation:** Fluoropolymer pyrolysis (e.g., Teflon) products cause "polymer fume fever"; symptoms include fever, chills, pneumonitis, myalgias, and nonproductive cough (often mistaken for acute viral illness)
- **Diagnosis:** Chest x-rays
- **Treatment:** Supportive; supplemental oxygen (has completely resolved "polymer fume fever" within 24 h in some cases)

Resins

- **Definition:** Complex chemical mixtures of acrid resins, resin alcohols, resinol, tannols, esters, and resenes
- **Use:** Herbal preparations (dandelion—*Taraxacum officinale*, elder—*Sambucus* spp., black cohosh root—*Cimicifuga racemosa*), tooth repair, incense, perfume, varnishes, cement, string instrument upkeep (rosin)
- **Absorption:** Dermal
- **Toxicity:** Chemical contact dermatitis
- **Gastrointestinal:** Strong irritant
- **Diagnosis:** Skin rash
- **Treatment:** Remove from the source, topical corticosteroids

Styrene

- **Properties:** Colorless liquid, evaporates easily, sweet smell (often mixed with other chemicals giving unpleasant smell)

- **Use:** Make products such as rubber, plastic, resins, insulation, fiberglass, pipes, automobile parts, food containers, and carpet backing; occur naturally in foods such as fruits, vegetables, nuts, beverages, and meats; vapors from building materials, consumer products, and tobacco smoke
- **Pathophysiology:** Metabolized via the styrene 7,8-oxide pathway to be excreted in urine as mandelic and phenylglyoxylic acids

Acute Toxicity

- **Respiratory:** Mucous membrane irritation, eye irritation, and gastrointestinal effects

Chronic Toxicity

- **CNS:** Headache, fatigue, weakness, depression, CNS dysfunction (reaction time, memory, visual-motor speed and accuracy, intellectual function), loss, peripheral neuropathy
- **Renal:** Minor effects on some kidney enzyme functions and blood
- **Diagnosis:** Measured in your blood, urine, and body tissues
- **Treatment:** No emesis; activated charcoal followed by saline purge; gastric lavage (if no lung aspiration present: if aspiration = dilution with water and absorption by activated charcoal is necessary, followed by a saline purge)

Trimellitic Anhydride

- **Chemical:** Flammable
- **Properties:** Colorless or white crystalline powder with musty odor
- **Use:** Preparation of resins, dyes, adhesives, polymers, printing inks, plasticizer and chemical intermediate, agricultural chemicals, pharmaceuticals
- **Absorption:** Ingestion, inhalation or dermal

Acute Toxicity

- Irritation of mucous membranes, cough, rhinorrhea, and potential allergic reactions

Chronic Toxicity

- Rhinitis, wheezing, dyspnea, malaise, chills, fever, and aching muscles and joints; in addition, hemoptysis, compromised respiratory function, hypoxemia, anemia, allergic reactions with flu-like symptoms and "pulmonary disease–anemia syndrome"
- **Treatment:** Symptomatic and supportive therapy

Triorthocresylphosphate

- **Properties:** Colorless, odorless liquid
- **Sources/use:** Flame retardant, plasticizer, lubricant, additive to gasoline and hydraulic fluids, intermediate for pharmaceuticals

- **Absorption:** Inhalation, dermal, ingestion, ocular
- **Symptoms:** GI disturbances; peripheral neuropathy; cramps in calves; paresthesia in feet or hands; weakness in feet, wrist drop, paralysis
- **"Ginger Jake Paralysis":** Popular ethanol substitute of Jamaican ginger (sold as "the Jake") in south and Midwestern United States during prohibition; sold legally to treat headaches and aid digestion; sold with adulterated castor oil, but 1930 price rose and TOCP used; 1930–1931—50,000 drank the Jake, developed TOCP poisoning (potent neurotoxin)
- Organophosphate-induced delayed neuropathy—reduced plasma cholinesterase activity and peripheral neuropathy, manifested by upper and lower extremity weakness ("ginger Jake paralysis") and gait impairment ("Jake walk" or "Jake leg")
- **Oral dosage:** Serious paralysis 6.6 mg/kg; lethal >28 mg/kg
- **Diagnosis:** Clinical; electromyograms and nerve conduction velocity studies
- **Treatment:** Removal, decon; treatment symptomatic and supportive; no emesis, gastric lavage, airway protection (endotracheal intubation)

Xylidine

- **Definition:** Derived from xylene, used chiefly as dye intermediates
- **Chemical:** Combustible
- **Properties:** Pale-yellow to brown liquid with a weak, aromatic, amine-like odor
- **Use:** Production of pigments, dyes, various antioxidants, agrochemicals, pharmaceuticals, organic chemicals, and component of the Tonka rocket fuel
- **Symptoms:** Central cyanosis, headache, lethargy, dizziness, fatigue, syncope, dyspnea, CNS depression, seizures, dysrhythmia, and shock

Acute Toxicity

- Irritating to the eyes, the skin and the respiratory tract; high levels may result in methemoglobin formation.

Chronic Toxicity

- Effects blood—anemia; effects on kidneys, liver; possible carcinogenic
- **Diagnosis:** Hemoglobin level, electrolytes, arterial blood gases, chest x-ray, ECG, methemoglobin level
- **Treatment:** Emesis: ipecac-induced emesis is not recommended because of the potential for CNS depression and seizures, activated charcoal slurry (240 mL water/30 g charcoal), oxygen, methemoglobinemia—administer 1–2 mg/kg of 1% methylene blue slowly IV in symptomatic patients, exchange transfusions and hyperbaric oxygen useful in severe cases

Section IV

Epidemiology and Statistics for Toxicology

Chapter 36

Epidemiology and Statistics for Toxicology

Outline 844
Probability 844
Descriptive Statistics 845
Differential Statistics 847
Analytical Epidemiological Investigations 851

Outline

- Probability
  - Likelihood ratios
  - Probability rules
  - Binomial distribution
- Descriptive statistics
  - Types of data
  - Summary analysis
  - Variation
  - Distribution
- Differential statistics
  - Testing for trends
  - Hypothesis testing
  - Rates, proportions, and associations
  - Cohort studies
  - Case–control studies
  - Error and power

Probability

Likelihood Ratios

Probability = number of ways events can occur; number of equally likely events that can occur.

Probability Rules

- Multiplication rule = P (A and B) = P (A) P (B) (Figure 36.1)
  - (Both A + B)
- Conditional probability = P (A/B) = P (B) • P (A/B)
  - (A given B)

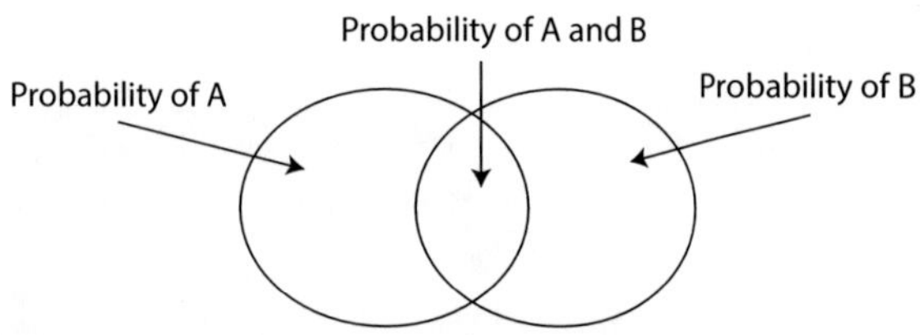

Probability of (A or B) = P(A) + P(B) – P(A and B)
Probability of (A and B) = P(A) × P(B) (if independent)
Probability of (A and B) = 0 (if mutually exclusive)
Probability of (A or B) = P(A) + P(B) (if mutually exclusive)

FIGURE 36.1 Probability rules.

- Addition rule = P (A or B)
  - (*Mutually exclusive*) = P (A) + P (B)
- Additional rule = P (A or B or both)
  - (*Not mutually exclusive*) = P (A) + P (B)–P (A) P (B)

Mutual Exclusivity

- A and B are independent events.
- A and B cannot occur simultaneously.
- A and B are not related.
- Opposite for nonmutual exclusivity.
  - (A and/or B).

Binomial Distribution

- Outcomes are limited to two choices.
- **Decision tree analysis:** Dead or alive, sick or well, treat medically or surgically, radiotherapy, or chemotherapy.
- Decision tree cost-effectiveness analysis.
- Marginal cost-effectiveness analysis.
- Threshold (break-even) analysis.

Descriptive Statistics

Types of Data

- **Continuous (interval) data:** Measured on an arithmetic scale. Examples: height, weight, blood pressure, heart rate, and FEV1.
- **Nominal (categorical) data:** Divided into two (binomial) or more unordered, discrete categories.
- **Examples:** Sex, race, and religion.
- **Ordinal data:** A predetermined ordering (ranking) of nominal (categorical) data. Examples: SES, Likert scale, qualitative, and functional scales.

Summary Analysis

Central Tendency (Table 36.1)

- Mean = average
- Median = middle
- Mode = repeating

Variation

- Range = highest–lowest (Table 36.1)
- Variance = sum of squared deviations from the mean
- Standard deviation = square root of variance

Table 36.1 Summary Analysis		
Quantity	**Sample**	**Population**
Mean	X	μ (mu)
Variation	s^2	α^2 (sigma squared)
Standard deviation	S[a]	α (sigma)
Standard error	SE (X)	SE (μ)

[a] Preferred measure of variation.

Distribution

Normal Distribution

- Bell shaped (Figure 36.2)
- Unimodal
- Symmetric about mean, X
- Compared to test the null hypothesis (H_o)
- **Examples:** t and z distributions
- Central limit theorem applies
- Central tendency = mean
- **SE (X):** Not applicable
- Variation = s = σ

Skewed Distribution

- Not bell shaped (Figure 36.3)
- Often multimodal
- Asymmetric about mean, X
- Transformed to test H_o
- **Example:** F distribution (ANOVA)

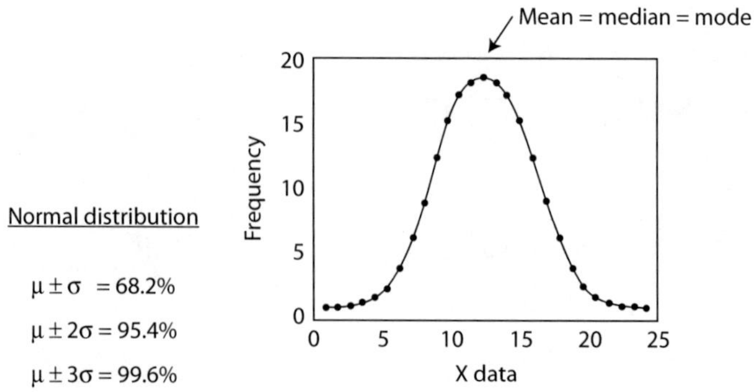

FIGURE 36.2 Normal distribution.

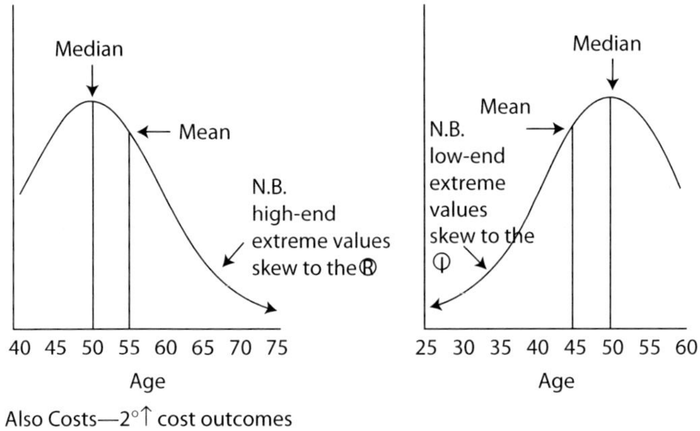

FIGURE 36.3 Skewed distribution.

- No central limit
- Central tendency = median
- SE (X) = SE (ξ)
- Variation = s ≠ σ

Differential Statistics

Testing for Trends

- **Linear regression:** How much one dependent (Y) variable increases or decreases on the average as another independent (X) variable changes.
- **Multiple regression:** How much one dependent variable (Y) increases or decreases on the average as multiple other independent variables (Xs) change. Xs = predictor variables. Us = outcomes.
- **Correlation:** A measure (*r*) of the strength of an association.

Trend Variables

- **Independent (input):** Variable (X) is independent of a dependent (outcome) variable, placed on x-axis.
- **Dependent (outcome):** Variable (Y) is entirely dependent on the input variable, placed on y-axis.

Correlation Coefficient (*r*) for Least Squares Regression

- *r* = a measure of the strength of linear association between the independent (x) and dependent (y) variables (Figures 36.4 through 36.7, Table 36.2).
- *r* has no units and takes on values between –1 (strongest inverse relationship) and +1 (strongest positive relationship).

$$r = \sqrt{\frac{1 - \text{sum of squared deviations from regression}}{\text{Sum of squared deviations from mean}}}$$

FIGURE 36.4 Least-squares regression.

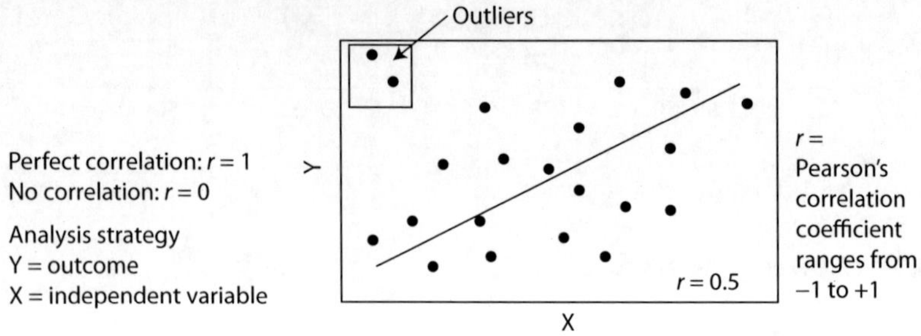

FIGURE 36.5 The scatterplot.

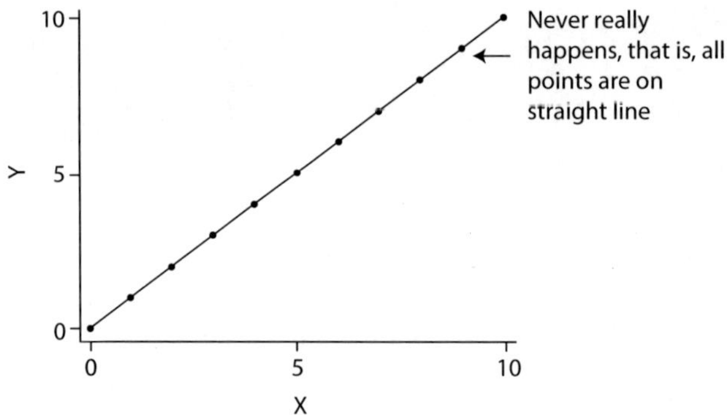

FIGURE 36.6 Perfect correlation: $r = 1$.

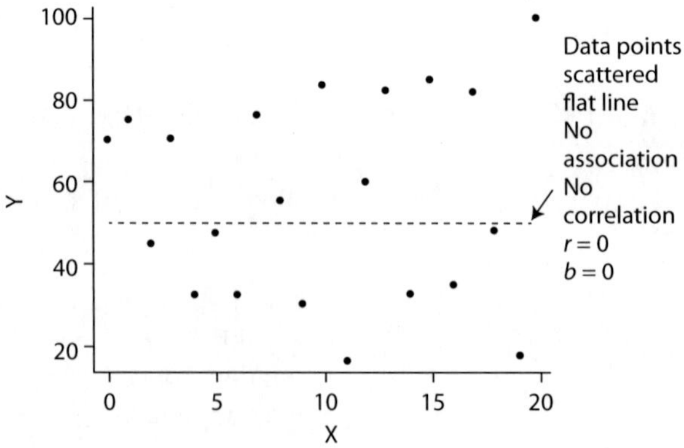

FIGURE 36.7 No correlation: $r = 0$.

Table 36.2 Correlation and Type of Variable		
Correlation Coefficient	**Variable**	**Distribution**
Pearson product moment (r)	Continuous	Normal
Spearman rank (r_S)	Ordinal	Skewed

- When $r = 0$, there is no relationship between the two variables, x + y.
- The stronger a correlation r, the more nearly the regression linc y approximates a straight line.
- Regression lines can be compared to test H_o using the t-test.
- y = a + bx = straight line.

Hypothesis Testing

What Experimental Design to Use?

See Figures 36.8 through 36.10.

What Statistical Test to Use

- **z → continuous:** Compare sample mean versus population mean (Tables 36.3 and 36.4).
- **t → continuous:** Compare two sample means.
- **X^2 → categorical:** Compare two probabilities or percentages from two samples.

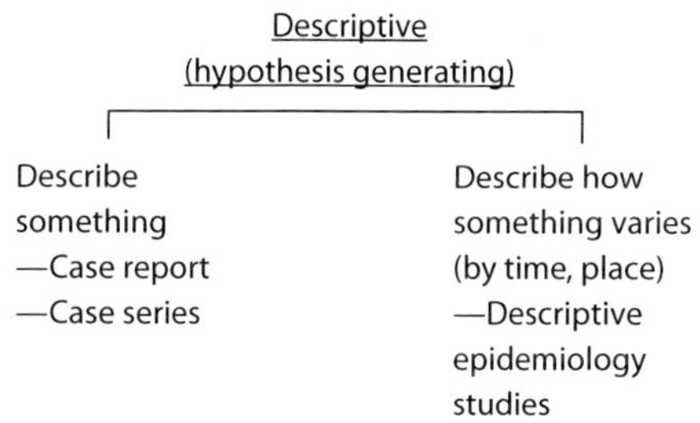

FIGURE 36.8 Overview diagram of research designs 1.

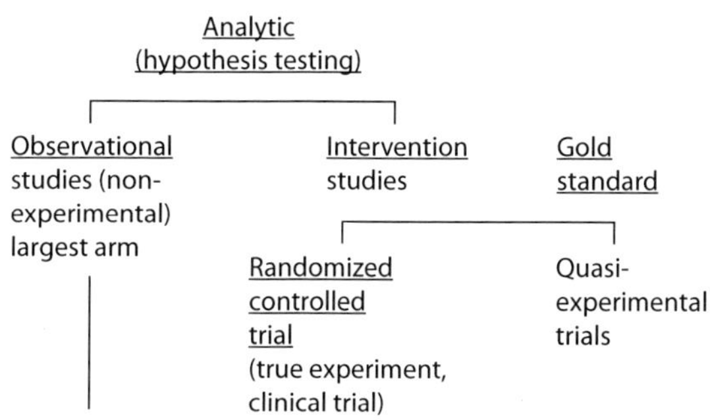

FIGURE 36.9 Overview diagram of research designs 2.

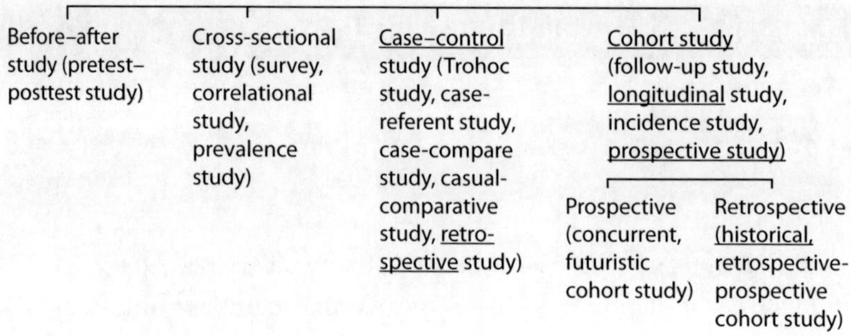

FIGURE 36.10 Overview diagram of research designs 3.

Table 36.3 Rough Guide to the Use of Statistical Methods

	Independent Variables	
Dependent Variable	**Continuous**	**Categorical**
Continuous	Scatterplot	t-Tests
	Linear regression	ANOVA ANCOVA[a]
Categorical	Discriminate analysis	Contingency tables Stratified analysis Logistic regression[a]
Outcome = dependent variable. Predictor = independent variable		

[a] Special case.

Table 36.4 Differential Statistics Comparative Groups

Date	Two Groups	Three or More Groups
Continuous	t-Test (paired vs. unpaired)	ANOVA
Nominal	χ-Square test, McNemar's test	χ-Square test
Ordinal	Mann–Whitley test	Kruskal–Wallis test

Assume the Null Hypothesis (H_0) of No Difference

- Note degrees of freedom based on rows and columns (df = {r–1} × {c–1}) for X^2.
- Small test statistics (t, F) indicate H_o true.
- Large test statistics lead to rejection of H_o.

Rates, Proportions, and Associations

χ-Square

- Positively skewed distribution.
- High test statistic values lead to rejection of H_o.

- Square of the difference of observed minus expected numbers per cell divided by expected numbers per cell.
- Expected = computed by proportion of observed on *n*.
- Less rigidity than continuous comparisons.
- Use the z-test statistic, often with Yates (continuity) correction, $x^2 = z^2$.
- Replace with Fisher's exact test when any expected value is <5.

Confidence Intervals

- Tells us how close an estimate is to the population parameter.
- An interval of numbers in which we have a specific (95–99%) degree of assurance or confidence that the value of the test parameter was captured.

Analytical Epidemiological Investigations

Cohort Studies

Relative Risk

- The risk of disease in people (study cohort) exposed to a factor relative to the risks in people not exposed (control cohort) (Figure 36.11 and Tables 36.5 through 36.9).

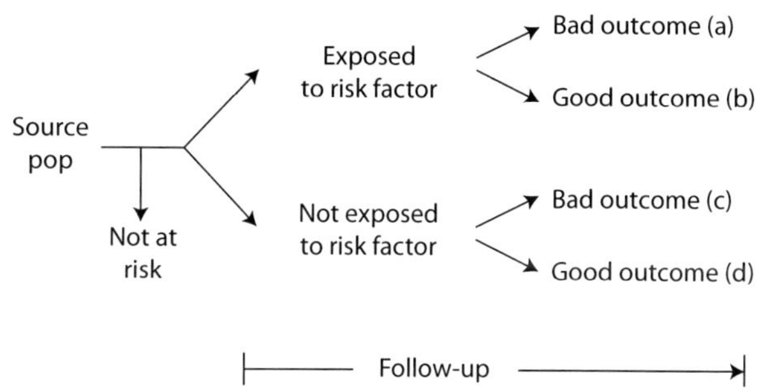

FIGURE 36.11 Cohort study.

Table 36.5 Analytical Investigations in Epidemiology

	Cohort	Case–Control	Experimental
Time	Pro/retro	Retro	Pro
Cost	Moderate	Low	High
Disease	Rare	Rare	Common
Compare	Incidence	Prevalence	Outcomes
Measure	RR	OR, X2	Test statistics (T, F)
Control	No	Yes	Yes
Randomize	No	No	Yes
Rigidity	Intermediate	Lowest	Highest
Gold standard	No	No	Yes

Table 36.6 Epidemiologic Measures of Association

Measure	Study
RR	Cohort study
OR	Case–control study

Table 36.7 RR: 2 × 2 Table from Cohort Study

	Disease		
	Yes	No	Total
Exposure	a	b	a + b
Nonexposure	c	d	c + d
Total	a + c	b + d	

Table 36.8 OR: 2 × 2 Table from Case–Control Study

	Controls	
	Disease	No Disease
Exposed	a	b
Unexposed	c	d

Table 36.9 2 × 2 Table: Exposure and Disease

	Disease Status		
Test Result	Disease	No Disease	
Exposed	a	b	a + b
Unexposed	c	d	c + d
	a + c	b + d	Total

Odds ratio = (a × d)/(b × c).
Relative risk = [a/(a + b)]/[c/(c + d)].

RR Formula

RR = disease rate in exposed = [a/(a + b)]. Disease rate in unexposed = [c/(c + d)].

- RR > 1 = positive association
- RR < 1 = negative (protective) association
- RR = 0 = no association
- RR > 2–3 = significant association

Attributable Risk

- **Definition:** Incidence in exposed population – incidence in unexposed population
- **Formula:** AR = [a/(a + b)] – [c/(c + d)] = disease attributable to exposure

Population-Attributable Risk

- **Definition:** Proportion (%) of disease in a population attributable to an exposure
  - Total incidence – incidence exposed
- Allows investigators to say that 95% (99%) of all sample means from *n* fall within ±1.96 (±2.58) SEs of the population mean
- Can also be used to test Hs using the *t* distribution
- A measure of the strength of association between an exposure and a disease
- Requires presentation of data in a 2 × 2 table
- **Formula:** [(a + c)/(a + b + c + d)] – [c/(a + b)] – [c/(c + d)] = disease in population attributable to exposure

Case–Control Studies

Odds Ratio

- Since disease incidence cannot be calculated in case–control studies, RR cannot be calculated.
- OR is an estimate of the RR. Best for rare diseases and widespread exposures.
- OR is a measure of increasing risk of disease from exposure. OR = risk ratio.
- Requires presentation of data in a 2 × 2 table.

OR Formula

- OR = proportion of diseased people in general population = (a/b) = (ad)
- Proportion of nondiseased in general population = (c/d) = (bc)

Error and Power

Error

- Types of error (I, II) (Tables 36.10 through 36.12)
- Significance levels (α, β)
- P-value

Power

- Relationship to error

Table 36.10 Types of Error

	Type I (False Positive)	Type II (False Negative)
Definition	Falsely rejecting H_0	Falsely accepting H_0
True difference	Does not exist	Exists
Probability	α (1–5%)	β (10–20%)
Significance level	0.01–0.05	0.10–0.20
Power	NA	1–β (80–90%)

Table 36.11 Hypothesis Testing: Type I and II Errors

	Truth in Population	
Results in the Study Sample	**The Means Are Different**	**The Means Are Not Different**
Reject the null hypothesis	Correct	Type 1 α-error
Fail to reject the null hypothesis	Type II β-error	Correct

Table 36.12 Power Relationships

Determinants of Power	Effect on Power
N ↑	↑
N ↓	↓
n ↑[a]	↑
n ↓	↓
α ↑	↑
α ↓	↓
δ ↑	↑
δ ↓	↓

[a] Power is the greatest when there are equal subject numbers in treatment groups.

- Sample size (*n*)
- Effect size (δ)

Error Definitions

- **Error types:** False positive (I) and false negative (II)
- **Significance level (α):** P of rejecting H_o when H_o is true, or the P of making a Type I error (false positive)
- **Significance level (β):** P of accepting H_o when H_o is false, or the P of making a Type II error (false negative)
- **P-value:** P of observing a study result by chance alone; should be low ($P < 0.05$) to reject H_o

Power Definitions

- **Power:** The P of correctly recognizing a true difference or the P of rejecting H_o when H_o is false (false negative).
- Power is the complement of β (P of making a Type II error) = 1–β.
- Power is related to population sample size (*N*), subject sample size (*n*), significance level (α), and effect or treatment size (δ).

Index

A

AADHs, *see* Alcohol–acetaldehyde dehydrogenases (AADHs)
AAP, *see* American Academy of Pediatrics (AAP)
AAPCCs, *see* American Association of Poison Control Centers (AAPCCs)
Abdominal x-rays, 45; *see also* Diagnosis in poisoned patient
  body stuffer, 45
  intestinal ischemia, 46
  opioid bowel, 45
Abortifacients, 219, 590; *see also* Plant-derived remedies and toxins; Reproductive toxicology
Absinthe (*Artemesia absinthium*), 591, 592; *see also* Cajun healing practice
Absorption, 4; *see also* Poisoning and envenoming pharmacology
  delayed GI, 4–5
  rates vs. bioavailabilities, 5–6
  routes of, 4, 5
  toxin transport mechanisms, 6–7
Absorption prevention, 22
  activated charcoal, 25–26
  alternative GI emptying, 28–29
  categorizing, 36
  compartment models, 33–34
  diagnostic odors of xenobiotics, 33
  elimination kinetics, 34–35
  emesis vs. lavage, 24
Abused drug screening characteristics, 802; *see also* Drug testing—laboratory selection questions; Workplace substance abuse monitoring
  amphetamines, 804–805
  barbiturates, 805
  benzodiazepines, 805
  cannabinoids, 802–803
  cocaine, 803
  codeine, 803–804
  laboratory selection questions, 805–807
  methadone, 805
  methaqualone, 805
  morphine, 803
  opiate issues, 804
  PCP, 805
  poppy seeds, 804
AC, *see* Activated charcoal (AC)
ACE, *see* Angiotensin-converting enzyme (ACE)
Acetaminophen, see *N*-Acetyl-para-aminophenol (APAP)
Acetic acid, 106; *see also* Acids
Acetylcholinesterase (AchE), 751; *see also* Specific antagonists
  AchE antag, 69
  inhibitor, 751–752
Acetyl salicylic acid (ASA), 22, 90; *see also* *N*-Acetyl-para-aminophenol (APAP); Nonsteroidal anti-inflammatory drugs (NSAIDs); Opioid
  APAP vs. ASA poisoning, 92
  chronic poisoning, 92
  clinical manifestations, 91
  epidemiology, 90
  poisoning, 92, 93
  toxicology, 90
  treatment, 93
AchE, *see* Acetylcholinesterase (AchE)
Acids, 106–107; *see also* Cleansers and caustics
  esophageal stenosis, 108
  sources and uses of, 106
Ackee and Jamaican vomiting sickness, 235; *see also* Hypoglycemia
Acquired methemoglobinemia, 77; *see also* Nonspecific antidotes
Acrodynia, 327; *see also* Mercury poisoning
Acroelin, 121–122, 156, 814; *see also* Aldehydes; Toxicants
  toxicity, 815
Acrylamides, 156, 815; *see also* Toxicants
Acrylates, 157, 816; *see also* Toxicants
ACT, *see* Activated clotting time (ACT)
Activated charcoal (AC), 16, 19, 57, 387, 657; *see also* Gastrointestinal decontaminants
Activated clotting time (ACT), 70

Active transport, 7; *see also* Absorption
Acute anuric RF, 287; *see also* Acute renal failure (ARF)
Acute gastrointestinal illness (AGI), 360; *see also* Food poisoning
  diarrhea outbreaks, 377
  food items, 377
  outbreaks on cruise ships, 376
Acute idiopathic pulmonary hemorrhage (AIPH), 411
Acute lung injury (ALI), 647, 648–649
Acute myeloid leukemia (AML), 615
Acute Radiation Syndrome (ARS), 738; *see also* Radiation toxicology
  CNS/CV syndrome, 740
  GI syndrome, 740
  hematopoietic syndrome, 739
  latent phase, 739
  manifested illness phase, 739
  prodromal phase, 739
  pulmonary disorders, 740
  treatment of, 740
Acute renal dysfunction, 284; *see also* Acute renal failure (ARF)
Acute renal failure (ARF), 284; *see also* Cadmium; Chronic renal failure (CRF); Lead poisoning; Mercury poisoning; Nephrotoxicology; Renal dysfunction
  causes of, 285, 286–287, 288–293, 294, 299
  crustacean poisoning, 291
  glomerular nephropathy, 298, 301–302
  Haff disease, 289
  hemlock poisoning, 288–290
  herbicides causing, 302–303
  hymenoptera causing, 303
  hypersensitivity reactions causing, 300
  mushroom poisonings, 287
  nephrotoxins causing, 284
  rodenticide ingestions, 292
  from toxic alcohols, 299–300
Acute respiratory distress syndrome (ARDS), 616
Acute tubular necrosis (ATN), 389, 674
ADA, *see* Americans with Disabilities Act (ADA)
Addition rule, 845
Additives, *see* Excipients
ADH, *see* Alcohol dehydrogenase (ADH)
ADHD, *see* Attention deficit hyperactivity disorder (ADHD)
Aedes aegypti, 528; *see also* Mosquitoes
  blood-feeding posture, 530
African trypanosomiasis life cycle, 537; *see also* Flies
AGI, *see* Acute gastrointestinal illness (AGI)
Agkistrodon contortrix contortrix, 481–482; *see also* Terrestrial envenomings
Agkistrodon piscivoris, 482–483, 484; *see also* Terrestrial envenomings
AHERA, *see* Hazard Emergency Response Act (AHERA)
AHH, *see* Aryl hydrocarbon hydroxylase (AHH)
AIPH, *see* Acute idiopathic pulmonary hemorrhage (AIPH)
Albumin, 8
Alcohol, 213, 780; *see also* Sedative-hypnotics (SHs)
  prohibited conduct, 794
  testing, 794
  withdrawal signs, 781
Alcohol dehydrogenase (ADH), 73, 636
Alcohol inky cap (*Coprinus atramentarius*), 405; *see also* Mushroom poisoning
Alcohol screening device (ASD), 794
Alcohol–acetaldehyde dehydrogenases (AADHs), 641
Alcohols and glycols, 122; *see also* Hydrocarbons (HCs)
  diethylene glycol, 122–123
  ethylene glycol, 123–124
  glycol ethers, 124–125
  isopropanol, 125
  methanol, 125, 127
  poison management and pathophysiology, 126
Aldehyde dehydrogenase (ALDH), 127
Aldehydes, 119; *see also* Hydrocarbons (HCs)
  acroelin, 121–122
  formaldehyde, 119–121
ALDH, *see* Aldehyde dehydrogenase (ALDH)
ALI, *see* Acute lung injury (ALI)
Aliphatic hydrocarbon, 127; *see also* Hydrocarbons (HCs)
  fuel oils/kerosene, 130–131
  gasoline, 128–129
  hexane, 127–128
Alkali, 107; *see also* Cleansers and caustics
  sources and uses of, 108
Alkaline dieresis, 16; *see also* Enhanced elimination
Alpha agonists, 180; *see also* Cocaine
α-Blockers and vasodilators, 218, 219; *see also* Reproductive toxicology
Alpha napthylthiourea (ANTU), 351
α-1-Acid glycoprotein, 8
Alpha radiation, 731
ALS, *see* Amyotropic lateral sclerosis (ALS)
Aluminum, 154–155; *see also* Aromatic hydrocarbons
  poisoning, 699, 701
Amanita; *see also* Mushroom poisoning
  phalloides, 399
  smithiana, 407
American Academy of Pediatrics (AAP), 620
American Association of Poison Control Centers (AAPCCs), 245

American dog tick (*Dermacentor variabilis*), 559; *see also* Ticks
American trypanosomiasis life cycle, 548; *see also* Bedbugs
Americans with Disabilities Act (ADA), 771
  and employment drug testing, 772
Amines, 157, 816; *see also* Toxicants
  toxicity, 817
Aminoglycosides, 259; *see also* Antibiotic toxicity
  toxicity, 259–260
Amitriptyline, 143–144; *see also* Aromatic hydrocarbons
AML, *see* Acute myeloid leukemia (AML)
Ammonia, 107; *see also* Alkali
Amphetamines, 182; *see also* Drug abuse
  acute vs. chronic toxicity, 183
  interpretation, 809
  intoxication symptoms, 786
  issues, 804–805
  OD management, 184
  pharmacology and abuse, 182
  phentermine–fenfluramine cardiomyopathy, 183, 184
  Rx vs. designer, 182
  signs of injection, 786
  street names, 168
  track marks, 786, 787
Amphibian secretions, 606; *see also* Animal toxins
Amphibians, 481; *see also* Terrestrial envenomings
Amphotericin B, 261–262; *see also* Antifungals
Amyotrophic lateral sclerosis(ALS), 317, 318; *see also* Neurotoxicology
Anabolic steroids (AS), 238
Analytical epidemiological investigations, 851; *see also* Epidemiology and statistics for toxicology; Hypothesis testing
  attributable risk, 853
  cohort studies, 851
  error, 853, 854
  odds ratio, 853
  OR formula, 853
  population-attributable risk, 853
  power, 853, 854
  relative risk, 851
  RR formula, 852
Aneurysm, 174; *see also* Cocaine
Angel's trumpet (*Brugmasia suaveolens*), 424, 453, 592; *see also* Neurotoxic plants
Angiotensin blockers, 253; *see also* Antihypertensives
  adenosine, 253
  classification, 253
  mechanisms, 254
  quinidine, 254
  side effects, 253
Angiotensin receptor blockers (ARBs), 254
Angiotensin-converting enzyme (ACE), 253
Aniline compounds, 157, 817; *see also* Toxicants
Animal therapeutics, 143; *see also* Aromatic hydrocarbons
Animal toxins; *see also* Cajun healing practice
  amphibian secretions, 606
  ciguatera fish poisoning, 604–605
  newts and salamanders, 606
  scombroid fish poisoning, 605
  tetrodotoxic fish poisoning, 605–606
  toads, 606–607
Anophelines, 526; *see also* Mosquitoes
  blood-feeding, 527
  stages, 527–528
Anosmia, 331; *see also* Gustatory toxicity
Anthrax, 756–757
Antiarrhythmics, 11; *see also* Cardiovascular drug toxicity
  classification of, 250
  Vaughan–Williams classifications of, 251
Antibiotic toxicity, 258; *see also* Aminoglycosides; Antifungals; Antimalarial toxicity; Antimalarials; Anti-TB agents; Cephalosporins; Isonicotinyl hydrazide (INH)
  antituberculous agent toxicity, 262
  chloramphenicol, 260
  coprine toxicity, 259
  disulfiram reactions, 259
  fluoroquinolones, 260–261
  macrolides, 261
  mushroom poisonings 259
  penicillins, 258
  streptomycin, 266
  sulfonamides, 261
  TB and INH epidemiology, 262
  tetracyclines, 261
  vancomycin, 260
Antibiotics, 11
Anticancer alkaloids, 462, 601; *see also* Plant-derived remedies and toxins; Poisonous household plants
  autumn crocus, 463
  mayapple, 463
  Taxus baccata, 464
Anticancer drug toxicity; *see also* Methotrexate (MTX); Vincristine (VCR)
  anthracyclines, 275
  carcinogens, 270, 276–280
  chemotoxicity, 270
  classification, 270, 271
  epidemiology, 271
  nitrogen mustards, 275
  platinoid toxicity, 275–276

Anticholinergic toxidrome, 54, 69; *see also* Toxidromes
Anticoagulants, 721
Anticonvulsants, 11, 17, 208; *see also* Sedative-hypnotics (SHs)
Antidiarrheals, 101, 179.; *see also* Cocaine; Opioid
Antidote, 709
Anti-epileptogenic treatment, 752
Antifungals, 11, 261; *see also* Antibiotic toxicity
  amphotericin B, 261–262
  azoles, 262
Antihypertensives, 250; *see also* Angiotensin blockers; Cardiovascular drug toxicity; Diuretics; Sympatholytics; Vasodilators
Antimalarials, 266; *see also* Antibiotic toxicity
  chloroquine toxicity, 268
  cinchonism, 267
  current, 267
  mefloquine, 268
  primaquine, 268
  quinine/quinidine OD, 267–268
Antimalarial toxicity, 266; *see also* Antimalarials
Antimicrobial-induced disulfiram reactions, 259; *see also* Antibiotic toxicity
Antimitotic plants, 460; *see also* Poisonous household plants
  colchicine, 460
  podophyllotoxin, 460, 462
  vinca alkaloids, 460, 461
  Vinca minor, 462
Anti-muscarinic treatment, 752
Anti-nicotinic treatment, 752
Antiretrovirals, 11
Antiseptic toxicity, 83
  additives toxicity, 82
  benzalkonium chloride, 85
  benzyl alcohol, 84
  bromines/bromides, 84
  chlorobutanol, 84–85
  diethylene glycol, 85
  parabens, 86
  pharm additive tragedies, 86–87
  phenol, 86
  polyethylene glycol, 83
  propylene glycol, 82–83
  thimerosal, 85
Anti-TB agents, 265; *see also* Antibiotic toxicity
  ethambutol, 266
  pyrazinamide, 266
  rifampin, 265–266
  toxicity, 262
Antitoxin, 62; *see also* Antivenom; Poison antidotes
  botulinum antitoxin, 66–67
  digoxin-specific fab, 67
Antivenom, 62; *see also* Antitoxin; Poison antidotes
  centruroides antivenom, 66
  crotalid antivenom, 63
  elapid antivenom, 64–66
  elapids, 63–64
  indications, 67
  latrodectus antivenom, 668
ANTU, *see* Alpha napthylthiourea (ANTU)
Anxiolytics, 208, 214; *see also* Sedative-hypnotics (SHs)
APAP ODs, 224–225; *see also* Poisoning in pregnancy
Aphrodisiacs, 220; *see also* Reproductive toxicology
Aquarium products, 145; *see also* Aromatic hydrocarbons
Arachnids, 607, 608; *see also* Arthropods
ARBs, *see* Angiotensin receptor blockers (ARBs)
ARDS, *see* Acute respiratory distress syndrome (ARDS)
ARF, *see* Acute renal failure (ARF)
Argon as asphyxiants, 647
Arizona bark scorpion (*Centruroides sculpturatus*), 512; *see also* Terrestrial envenomings
Aromatic hydrocarbons, 131; *see also* Hydrocarbons (HCs)
  benzene, 131–132
  PCA hydrocarbons, 132–134
  toluene, 134–136
  veterinary products, 136
ARS, *see* Acute Radiation Syndrome (ARS)
Arsenic, 322, 674, 718; *see also* Heavy metal poisoning; Metal poisoning; Neurotoxicology
  absorption, 322
  Blackfoot disease, 676
  clinical effects, 323, 675–676
  diagnosis, 323–324, 676
  metabolism, 322–323
  pathophysiology, 323, 675
  toxicology, 322, 323, 675
  treatment, 324, 676–677
Arthropoda, 479; *see also* Terrestrial envenomings
  lepidoptera, 607
Arthropod vectors, 478, 526, 555–556; *see also* Bedbugs; Cajun healing practice; Fleas; Flies; Mites; Mosquitoes; Myiasis; Ticks; Terrestrial envenomings
  arachnids, 607, 608
  black widow spider, 609
  blister beetles, 609–610
  hymenoptera, 607
  lepidoptera, 607
  spider webs as wound dressings, 607, 608
Art products, 144; *see also* Aromatic hydrocarbons
Aryl hydrocarbon hydroxylase (AHH), 641
AS, *see* Anabolic steroids (AS)

ASA, *see* Acetyl salicylic acid (ASA)
Asbestos Hazard Emergency Response Act (AHERA), 725
Asbestosis, 665, 667; see also *Pneumoconioses*
ASD, *see* Alcohol screening device (ASD)
Asphyxiants, 646; *see also* Industrial exposures
  carbon dioxide, 646
  hydrocarbons, 647
  nitrogen, 647
  noble gases, 647
Aspirin, *see* Acetyl salicylic acid (ASA)
ATN, *see* Acute tubular necrosis (ATN)
Atomic particle counting, 767
Attention deficit hyperactivity disorder (ADHD), 204
Attributable risk, 853
Atypical specimens, 809
Australian or Sydney funnel-web spider (*Atrax robustus*), 510; *see also* Terrestrial envenomings
Autumn crocus (*Colchicum autumnale*), 463, 601–602; *see also* Anticancer alkaloids; Cajun healing practice
Axonopathy, 314; *see also* Neurotoxicology
  examples, 315
Azalea (*Rhododendron* spp.), 450; *see also* Channel openers
Azides, 158, 817–818; *see also* Toxicants
Azoles, 262; *see also* Antifungals

B

B1, *see* Thiamine (B1)
B6, *see* Pyridoxine (B6)
B[*a*]P, *see* Benzo-*a*-pyrene (B[*a*]P)
Bacillus cereus, 362, 363; *see also* Food poisoning
Baitfish-feeders, 385; *see also* Feeding habits
BAL, *see* Bronchoalveolar lavage (BAL)
Balkan endemic nephropathy (BEN), 305, 437; *see also* Herbal hepatotoxins
Balsam apple (*Mormordica balsamina*), 598; *see also* Cajun healing practice
Barbiturates, 210, 780, 781, 805; *see also* Sedative-hypnotics (SHs)
  classification, 210
  drug interactions, 211
  pharmacology, 210
  toxicity, 211
Barium, 718, 719; *see also* Neurotoxic rodenticides
  carbonate, 352–353
Basal ganglia toxins, 332; *see also* Poison gas
Bath salts, 191–192; *see also* Drug abuse
Batteries, 150; *see also* Aromatic hydrocarbons
BBB, *see* Blood–brain barrier (BBB)
BD, *see* 1,4-Butanediol (BD)
Bedbugs, 545–547; *see also* Fleas; Flies; Mites; Mosquitoes; Myiasis; Ticks
  American trypanosomiasis, 548
  bedbug, 547
  cockroaches, 547, 549
  kissing bug, 548
  triatomid bugs 2, 547
Belcher's sea snake (*Hydrophis belcheri*), 496; *see also* Eastern coral snake
Belladonna alkaloids, 54, 188–189, 422–423, 592; *see also* Neurotoxic plants; Plant hallucinogens; Toxidromes
BEN, *see* Balkan endemic nephropathy (BEN)
Benign intracranial hypertension (BIH), 439
Benzalkonium chloride, 107; *see also* Alkali
Benzene, 131–132; *see also* Aromatic hydrocarbons
Benzo-*a*-pyrene (B[*a*]P), 615
Benzodiazepine (BZ), 168, 709, 780, 781, 805; *see also* Sedative-hypnotics (SHs); Specific antagonists; Toxidromes
  antagonism, 68
  classification, 211
  drug interactions, 212
  toxicity, 211
  toxidrome, 56
Benzyl alcohol, 346; *see also* Neurotoxicology
  pharmacokinetics, 346–347
Berylliosis, 305, 668–669; *see also* Chronic renal failure (CRF)
β-Adrenergic physiology, 245; *see also* β-Blockers
β-Blockers, 245; *see also* Cardiovascular drug toxicity
  β-adrenergic physiology, 245
  β1-selective blockers, 246
  classification, 245
  diagnosis, 246–247
  indications, 246
  nonselective β-blockers, 245
  overdose epidemiology, 245
  overdose management, 248
  side effects, 246
  toxicity, 246
β-Methylamino-L-alanine (BMAA), 426, 455
β-Oxalylamino-L-alanine (BOAA), 425
β1-Selective blockers, 246; *see also* β-Blockers
Beta radiation, 731
BIG, *see* Botulinum hyperimmune globulin (BIG)
BIH, *see* Benign intracranial hypertension (BIH)
Binding agents, 28
Binomial distribution, 845
Bioaccumulated exotoxins, 383; *see also* Marine toxins
Biological warfare (BW), 360, 362, 748; *see also* Biological weapons (BW); Food poisoning
  Black Death, 749
  and CW, 748–749

Biological warfare (*Continued*)
  decontamination, 750–751
  history, 749–750
  Salmonella spp., 750
Biological weapons (BW), 755; *see also* Radiological weapons
  anthrax, 756–757
  botulism, 757–758
  brucellosis, 760
  coronaviruses, 763
  Ebola HF, 764
  emergency response, 775
  filoviruses, 763
  Guillain–Barré syndrome, 758
  hendra virus, 762–763
  henipaviruses, 762
  microorganisms, 755
  mycotoxins, 763
  nipah virus, 761–762
  plague, 758–759
  prevention, 765–766
  Q-fever, 760
  ricin, 763, 764
  smallpox, 759
  staph enterotoxin B 1, 760
  suspicious syndromes, 755
  tricothecene mycotoxins, 764–765
  tularemia, 759–760
Bioterrorism, 362; *see also* Biological warfare (BW); Food poisoning
Bismuth poisoning, 701
Bismuth subsalicylate abuse, 41
Bite, 480; *see also* Flies; Terrestrial envenomings
  midges, 534, 536
Black Death, 749
Blackflies, 532; *see also* Flies
Black mamba (*Dendroaspis polylepis*), 495; *see also* Eastern coral snake
Black widow (*Latrodectus mactans*), 505, 609; *see also* Cajun healing practice; Terrestrial envenomings
Black-legged tick (*Ixodes scapularis*), 551; *see also* Ticks
Bleach, 108–109; *see also* Cleansers and caustics
Blister agents, 752, 753
Blister beetles (*Lytta vesicatoria*), 609; *see also* Cajun healing practice
Blood agents, 753
Blood–brain barrier (BBB), 312
Blue-ringed octopus (*Hapalochlaena maculosus*), 575; *see also* Coelenterates, toxic
BMAA, *see* β-Methylamino-L-alanine (BMAA)
BOAA, *see* β-Oxalylamino-L-alanine (BOAA)
Body louse (*Pediculus corporis*), 545
Body packers, cocaine vs. heroin, 103; *see also* Opioid
Body stuffer, 45, 104; *see also* Opioid
Boomslang snake (*Dispholidus typus*), 498; *see also* Eastern coral snake
Boric acid, 106; *see also* Acids
Botulinum antitoxin, 66–67; *see also* Antitoxin; Antivenom
Botulinum hyperimmune globulin (BIG), 67
Botulism, 757–758
Bound drugs, 8; *see also* Distribution
Brain mushroom (*Gyromitra esculenta*), 400; *see also* Mushroom poisoning
Breath alcohol analysis devices, 793
British anti-Lewisite (BAL), 60, 61, 692; *see also* Metal chelators
Bromates, 354, 819
Bromethalin, 353–354, 721; *see also* Neurotoxic rodenticides
Bromides, 214, 354, 819; *see also* Sedative-hypnotics (SHs); Toxicants
  compounds, 158, 818–819
Bronchoalveolar lavage (BAL), 411
Brown recluse (*Loxosceles reclusa*), 506; *see also* Terrestrial envenomings
  blistering, 507
Brown tree snake (*Boiga irregularis*), 497; *see also* Eastern coral snake
Brucella spp., 364; *see also* Food poisoning
Brucellosis, 760
Buck moth (*Hemileuca maia*), 519; *see also* Terrestrial envenomings
Bufo marinus, *see* Cane toad (*Rhinella marina*)
Bufotoxins, 220; *see also* Reproductive toxicology
Bull shark (*Carcharhinus leucas*), 392; *see also* Seafood poisoning
Bumblebee (*Bombus terrestris*), 513; *see also* Terrestrial envenomings
Buprenorphine, 205
Buspirone, 214; *see also* Sedative-hypnotics (SHs)
Butadienes, 158, 819–820; *see also* Toxicants
  as asphyxiants, 647
1,4-Butanediol (BD), 192, 193; *see also* Date-rape drugs
Butorphanol, 778
BW, *see* Biological warfare (BW); Biological weapons (BW)
BZ, *see* Benzodiazepine (BZ)

C

Cacosmia, 331–332; *see also* Gustatory toxicity
Cadmium, 149, 295, 677; *see also* Acute renal failure (ARF); Aromatic hydrocarbons; Heavy metal poisoning; Metal poisoning; Nephrotoxicology
  clinical effects, 296, 678

diagnosis, 296, 678
exposures, 295, 677
pathophysiology, 295–296, 677–678
toxicology, 295, 677
Cajun healing practice, 585; *see also* Animal toxins; Arthropods; Hoodoo; Mushroom poisoning; Plant-derived remedies and toxins; Voodoo
Cajun treater's practice code, 586
Creoles, 585
gris-gris, 586
healing, 586, 587
peyote cactus, 594
punishing, 586, 587, 588
stimulating, 586, 587
Traiteurs, 585
Traiteusses, 585
unique practices, 586
zombification, 586, 588
Cajuns, 585; *see also* Cajun healing practice
Caladium (*Caladium hortulanum*), 469; *see also* GI toxicity
Calcium channel blockers (CCB) , 22, 248; *see also* Cardiovascular drug toxicity
classification, 249
clinical effects, 249–250
indications, 249
overdose, 248, 250
pharmacology, 249
physiology, 248
poisoning, 249
Campylobacter jejuni, 364–365; *see also* Food poisoning
Canebrake rattlesnake, 484, 485; *see also* Terrestrial envenomings
Cane toad (*Rhinella marina*), 504; *see also* Terrestrial envenomings
Cannabinoids, 802
issues, 803
Cantharidin, 220; *see also* Reproductive toxicology
Capsaicin, 601; *see also* Cajun healing practice
Carbamates, 710
Carbonates, 107; *see also* Alkali
Carbon disulfide, 159, 338, 820–821; *see also* Neurotoxicology; Toxicants
Carbon monoxide poisoning, 74, 226–227, 332–333, 615, 651; *see also* Asphyxiants; Poison gas; Poisoning in pregnancy; Specific antidotes
basal ganglia toxins, 652
clinical effects, 333, 652–653
CT scan findings, 654
delayed effects, 334
diagnosis and treatment, 334, 654
on OxyHb, 653–654
pathophysiology, 333–334, 653
Carcinogenic metals, 322; *see also* Neurotoxicology
Cardiac glycosides, 242; *see also* Cardiovascular drug toxicity
diagnosis, 243
digoxin-specific fabs, 244
etiology, 242
immunoreactive substances, 243
management, 244
mechanisms, 242
pathophysiology, 242–243
pharmacology, 242
plant glycosides, 242
serum digoxin levels, 243
toxicity effects, 243
Cardiovascular (CV), 389
adrenergic physiology, 247; *see also* Cardiovascular drug toxicity
Cardiovascular drug toxicity, 241; *see also* Antiarrhythmics; Antihypertensives; β-Blockers; Calcium channel blockers (CCB); Cardiac glycosides
adrenergic pharmacology, 247
QT prolongation drugs, 254, 255
Cardiovascular toxins, 417; *see also* Herbal poisoning
channel blockers, 419
death camas, 419
foxglove, 420
glycosides, 419, 421
green hellbane, 418
lily-of-the-valley, 421
monkshood, 418
oleander, 420
Carfentanil, 139–140; *see also* Aromatic hydrocarbons
Carolina pygmy rattlesnake, *see* Eastern pygmy rattlesnake (*Sistrurus miliaris miliaris*)
Carpenter bee (*Xylocopa virginica*), 514; *see also* Terrestrial envenomings
Carrier protein, 7; *see also* Absorption
Case fatality rate (CFR), 563, 674
Castor bean seed pods (*Ricinus communis*), 460; *see also* Cytotoxic plants
CBC, *see* Complete blood count (CBC)
CCB antag, 68; *see also* Specific antagonists
CCHF, *see* Crimean-Congo hemorrhagic fever (CCHF)
CDC, *see* Centers for Disease Control and Prevention (CDC)
CDL, *see* Commercial driver's license (CDL)
Centers for Disease Control and Prevention (CDC), 202, 308, 560
Centipedes, 523; *see also* Scolopendra species; Terrestrial envenomings
Central American coral snake (*Micrurus alleni*), 491; *see also* Terrestrial envenomings

Central and South American exotic snakes, 498; *see also* Terrestrial envenomings
  Latin American Fer-de-Lance (*Bothrops asper*), 498
  Porthidium, 499
Central nervous system (CNS), 56, 415, 590, 635, 751; *see also* Toxidromes
Central nervous system toxicity, 426; *see also* Herbal poisoning
  ephedra, 428, 429
  hallucinogens, 428
  Hawaiian baby woodrose, 429
  morning glory, 427
  nutmeg and mace, 428
  peyote cactus, 428
  wormwood, 427
Central tendency, 845
Centruroides antivenom, 66; *see also* Antitoxin; Antivenom
Cephalosporins, 258; *see also* Antibiotic toxicity
  mechanism, 258–259
  toxicities, 259
Cerebral perfusion pressure (CPP), 312
Cerebrospinal fluid (CSF), 564
Cerebrovascular accident (CVA), 59
CFDs, *see* Craniofacial defects (CFDs)
CFR, *see* Case fatality rate (CFR)
Chagas disease 547, 548
Chain of custody (CoC), 771, 798, 790 *See also* Abused drug screening characteristics; Drug testing—laboratory selection questions
  adulteration, 801–802
  collection issues, 798
  confirmatory test, 800
  cut-off, 800
  direct observation, 799
  litigation package, 802
  methamphetamine issues, 801
  MRO responses, 807
  shy bladder, 799
  specimen rejection, 798
  split specimens, 799
Channel openers, 449; *see also* Poisonous household plants
  azalea, 450
  grayanotoxins, 449
  Na and Ca channel blocker, 450
  true rhododendron, 451
  yew, 451
Charcoal hemoperfusion, 30
Chelators, 5, 225, 226; *see also* Poisoning in pregnancy
Chemical dependency, 775, 777
Chemical spot tests, 38
Chemical warfare (CW), 748, 749; *see also* Biological warfare (BW); Chemical weapons (CW)
  and BW, 748–749
  chlorine, 748
  decontamination, 750–751
  history, 749–750
  phosgene, 748
Chemical weapons (CW), 748, 749; *see also* Chemical warfare (CW)
  acrolein as, 814
Chemoreceptor trigger zone (CTZ), 58
Chest x-rays; *see also* Diagnosis in poisoned patient
  airspace filling, 42
  aortic dissection, 44
  interstitial patterns, 42
  lungs, 42
  osteonecrosis, 43
  pleura, 44
  pneumomediastinum, 44
  pulmonary edema, 43
CHF, *see* Congestive heart failure (CHF)
Chilli pepper (*Capsicum annuum*), 603; *see also* Cajun healing practice
Chinese endemic nephropathy, *see* Herbal endemic nephropathy (HEN)
χ-Square, 850
Chloral hydrate, 213; *see also* Sedative-hypnotics (SHs)
  toxicity, 51
Chloramphenicol, 260; *see also* Antibiotic toxicity
Chlorates, 159, 821–822; *see also* Toxicants
Chlorine, 748
Chloroquine toxicity, 268; *see also* Antimalarials
Chlorphenoxyacetic acids, 356, 725; *see also* Herbicides
Chlorpromazine (CPZ), 8
Cholecalciferol, 720
Cholinergic toxidrome, 54, 69, 751; *see also* Toxidromes
Chordata, 479, 570; *see also* Marine envenomings; Terrestrial envenomings
Chromatographic assays, 38–39
Chromium, 679; *see also* Heavy metal poisoning; Metal poisoning
  clinical effects, 680
  diagnosis, 680
  exposures, 679
  pathophysiology, 679
  toxicology, 679
  treatment, 680
  uses of, 679
Chromosomal damage, 767
Chronic obstructive pulmonary disease (COPD), 246
Chronic renal dysfunction, 284; *see also* Chronic renal failure (CRF)

Chronic renal failure (CRF), 258, 284, 305; *see also* Acute renal failure (ARF); Nephrotoxicology; Renal dysfunction
- berylliosis and urolithiasis, 305
- malignancies, 306
- nephrotoxicology, 303–304
- nephrotoxic plants, 304–305
- turpentine, 306

Chronic ulcerative colitis (CUC), 365
Ciguatera fish poisoning, 604–605; *see also* Animal toxins
Cinchonism, 267; *see also* Antimalarials
Cl, *see* Clearance (Cl)
Clay, 149; *see also* Aromatic hydrocarbons
Cleansers and caustics, 104; *see also* Household poisoning
- acids, 106–107
- alkali, 107
- antimicrobials, 111
- bleach, 108–109
- detergents, 109–110
- disinfectants and topical anti-infectives, 110, 112
- iodines, 111
- mercurochrome, 113
- mothballs, 111
- OTC mercury bichloride, 112
- swimming pool products, 113–114

Clearance (Cl), 14
Clenbuterol, 140–144; *see also* Aromatic hydrocarbons
CLIA, *see* Clinical Laboratory Improvement Act + Amendments (CLIA)
Clinical Laboratory Improvement Act + Amendments (CLIA), 773
Clitocybe dealbata, 403; *see also* Mushroom poisoning
Clonidine, 102, 180; *see also* Cocaine; Opioid
Clostridium; *see also* Food poisoning
- *botulinum*, 365–366, 757
- *perfringens*, 366–367

CMAPs, *see* Compound muscle action potentials (CMAPs)
CNS, *see* Central nervous system (CNS)
Coal tar products, 822
Coal worker's pneumoconiosis (CWP), 664
Cobalt poisoning, 699
CoC, *see* Chain of custody (CoC)
Cocaine, 803; *see also* Drug abuse
- abuse methods, 169
- agonists/antagonists, 178
- alpha agonists, 180
- aneurysm, 171, 174
- antidiarrheals, 179
- body stuffers, 176–177
- CT, 170
- CXR and ECG, 170
- epidemiology, 169
- hemorrhage, 172
- vs. heroin body packers, 177
- history, 168
- intestinal ischemia, 46
- long-acting opioids, 178
- meperidine, 178–179
- mesenteric infarction, 175
- miosis, 178
- MPTP, 179
- OD, 175–176
- opioid agonists, 180
- opioid OD, 181
- parkinsonism, 180
- pentazocine, 179–180
- pharmacology, 169
- pneumomediastinum, 173
- propoxyphene, 179
- pulmonary edema, 170
- septic cerebral emboli, 172
- specific OD, 176
- street names, 168
- toxicology, 169
- toxidrome diagnosis, 174–175

Cockroaches, 547, 549
Codeine, 778, 803–804
Coelenterates, toxic, 572; *see also* Marine envenomings
- blue-ringed octopus, 575
- cone shells, 574
- corals, 572–573
- hydroids, 574
- jellyfish, 573–574
- masked pufferfish, 576
- octopuses, 574–575
- sea urchins, 572
- starfish, 572

Cohort studies, 851
Colchicine, 460, 601; *see also* Antimitotic plants; Cajun healing practice
Colorado river toad (*Bufo alvarius*), 503; *see also* Terrestrial envenomings
Coltsfoot (*Tussilago farfara*), 436, 467, 600; *see also* Cajun healing practice; Gastrointestinal toxicity; Plant chemotherapy
Comfrey (*Symphytum officinale*), 435, 466, 599; *see also* Cajun healing practice; Gastrointestinal toxicity; Plant chemotherapy
Commercial driver's license (CDL), 789
Common bedbug (*Cimex lectularius*), 546, 547; *see also* Bedbugs
Common foxglove (*Digitalis purpurea*), 420; *see also* Cardiovascular toxins

Common white puffballs (*Lycoperdon candidum*), 409; *see also* Mushroom poisoning
Compartment models, 9, 33–34; *see also* Distribution
Complete blood count (CBC), 736
Compound muscle action potentials (CMAPs), 564
Compound Q, 590; *see also* Plant-derived remedies and toxins
Computed tomography (CT), 315
Conditional probability, 844
Confidence intervals, 851
Congestive heart failure (CHF), 243
Consumer Product Safety Commission (CPSC), 36
Contact time, 5; *see also* Absorption
Continuous data, 845
Continuous hemofiltration, 30
Continuous positive airway pressures (CPAP), 651
Convallaria majalis, 447; *see also* Poisonous plants
COPD, *see* Chronic obstructive pulmonary disease (COPD)
Copper poisoning, 700
Copper sulfate, 144; *see also* Aromatic hydrocarbons
Coprine toxicity, 259, 405; *see also* Antibiotic toxicity; Mushroom poisoning
Corexit dispersant, 637, 638; *see also* Petrochemical toxicity
Coronaviruses, 763
Correlation, 847
  χ-Square, 850
  coefficient, 847–848
  confidence intervals, 851
  no, 848
  perfect, 848
  and variable type, 849
Cortinarius, 406; *see also* Mushroom poisoning
Cosmetics, 151; *see also* Aromatic hydrocarbons
CPAP, *see* Continuous positive airway pressures (CPAP)
CPK, *see* Creatine phosphokinase (CPK)
CPP, *see* Cerebral perfusion pressure (CPP)
CPSC, *see* Consumer Product Safety Commission (CPSC)
CPZ, *see* Chlorpromazine (CPZ)
Crab louse (*Pthirus pubis*), 545
Crack cocaine; *see also* Cocaine
  dispensing characteristics, 785
  routes of administration, 785–786
Craniofacial defects (CFDs), 222; *see also* Reproductive toxicology
Creatine phosphokinase (CPK), 392
Creoles, 585; *see also* Cajun healing practice
CRF, *see* Chronic renal failure (CRF)
Crimean-Congo hemorrhagic fever (CCHF), 551
Criticality, 730
Crotalid antivenom, 63; *see also* Antitoxin; Antivenom
Crotalus Adamanteus, 484, 485; *see also* Terrestrial envenomings
Crown-of-thorns (*Euphorbia milii*), 381, 470; *see also* GI toxicity; Seafood poisoning
Crude oil; see also *Deepwater Horizon* oil spill; Petrochemical toxicity
  constituents of, 633
  effects of exposures to burning, 635–636
  effects of volatilized, 633–635
  light, 631
  toxicities of, 631
CSF, *see* Cerebrospinal fluid (CSF)
CT, *see* Computed tomography (CT)
CTZ, *see* Chemoreceptor trigger zone (CTZ)
CUC, *see* Chronic ulcerative colitis (CUC)
Culicines, 526; *see also* Mosquitoes
  blood-feeding behavior, 527
  stages, 528
Culicoides guttipennis, 535; *see also* Flies
CV, *see* Cardiovascular (CV)
CVA, *see* Cerebrovascular accident (CVA)
CW, *see* Chemical warfare (CW); Chemical weapons (CW)
CWP, *see* Coal worker's pneumoconiosis (CWP)
CY, *see* Cytochrome (CY)
Cyanide poisoning, 334, 464, 655; *see also* Neurotoxicology; Nonspecific antidotes; Poisonous household plants
  acute vs. delayed effects, 335–336, 656–657
  cyanogenic group, 464
  cyanogenic plants, 656
  and cytochrome oxidase electron transport system, 659
  elderberry, 465
  exposures, 335, 655
  Hydrangea macrophylla, 464
  kit, 77, 78
  lab diagnosis, 657
  management, 336
  mechanisms, 335, 655–656
  pathophysiology, 660
  toxicity, 655
Cyclodienes, 708
Cyclopeptide toxicity, 397; *see also* Mushroom poisoning
CYP450 hepatic enzymes, 10
Cytochrome (CY), 10
Cytotoxic chemotherapeutics, 42
Cytotoxic plants, 459; *see also* Poisonous household plants
  castor bean seed pods, 460
  cytotoxicity, 459
  rosary peas in pods, 461
  toxalbumins, 459, 460

D

Date-rape drugs, 192, 212; *see also* Drug abuse; Sedative-hypnotics (SHs)
BD, 193
clinical effects, 212
flunitrazepam, 193
GBL, 192
GHB, 192
overdose management, 212
toxicology, 212
DBCP, *see* Dibromochloropropane (DBCP)
DCTs, *see* Distal convoluted tubules (DCTs)
DDAVP, *see* Desamino-d-arginine-vasopressin (DDAVP)
DDT, *see* Dichlorodiphenyltrichloroethane (DDT)
DDTC, *see* Diethyldithiocarbamate (DDTC)
DDx, *see* Differential diagnosis (DDx)
Death camas (*Zigadenus glaberrimus*), 419; *see also* Cardiovascular toxins; Sodium channel openers
Death lilies, *see* Death camas (*Zigadenus glaberrimus*)
Decay, 730
Decontamination, 750–751
Deepwater Horizon oil spill, 630–631, 643; *see also* Crude oil; Petrochemical toxicity
health effects, 637, 638
surveillance, 633, 634
Deerflies, 537; *see also* Flies
DEET, see *N,N*-Diethyl-*meta*-toluamide (DEET)
Deferoxamine, 59–61; *see also* Metal chelators
DEG, *see* Diethylene glycol (DEG)
Delayed GI absorption, 4; *see also* Absorption
delayed gastric emptying, 4
drug coatings, 5
pylorospasm, 5
Delta-9-tetrahydrocannabinol (THC), 214, 802; *see also* Marijuana
Dental products, 151; *see also* Aromatic hydrocarbons
Dependent variable, 847
Dermacentor andersoni, 551; *see also* Ticks
Desamino-D-arginine-vasopressin (DDAVP), 465
Desert Massasauga (*Sistrurus catenatus edwardsi*), 489; *see also* Terrestrial envenomings
Desert tarantula (*Aphonopelma chalcodes*), 509; *see also* Terrestrial envenomings
Detergents and soaps, 109–110; *see also* Cleansers and caustics
Dextromethorphan, 102, 180, 194; *see also* Cocaine; Drug abuse; Opioid
Dextrose, 76; *see also* Nonspecific antidotes
DHFR, *see* Dihydrofolate reductase (DHFR)
DHHS, *see* U.S. Department of Health and Human Services (DHHS)
DI, *see* Diabetes insipidus (DI)
Diabetes insipidus (DI), 75
Diagnosis (Dx), 709
Diagnosis in poisoned patient, 37; *see also* Abdominal x-rays; Chest x-rays; Electrocardiogram (ECG)
bismuth subsalicylate abuse, 41
blood/serum levels, 39
chemical spot tests, 38
chromatographic assays, 38–39
decreased bone density, 41
head CT, 46
immunoassays, 38
increased bone density, 40–41
lab assessment, 38
lab tests, 38
metaphyseal lead lines, 42
radiographic assessment, 40
routine serum toxicity, 39
spectrophotometric tests, 38
testing methods, 38
toxic skeletal changes, 40
toxins detection, 39, 40
visualizing toxins, 40
Diamantes, 159–160; *see also* Toxicants
Diamines, 823
Dibromochloropropane (DBCP), 160, 823–824; *see also* Toxicants
Dichlorodiphenyltrichloroethane (DDT), 708
Dietary Supplement and Health Education Act of 1994 (DSHEA), 414
Diethyldithiocarbamate (DDTC), 276
Diethylene glycol (DEG), 83, 86, 126–127, 301; *see also* Alcohols and glycols; Antiseptic toxicity; Nephrotoxicology
Diethylene triamine pentaacetic acid (DTPA), 60, 768
Differential diagnosis (DDx), 708
Differential statistics, 847; *see also* Correlation
dependent variable, 847
independent variable, 847
least-squares regression, 848
linear regression, 847
multiple regression, 847
scatterplot, 848
Digibind, 67; *see also* Antitoxin; Antivenom
Digitalis purpurea, 447; *see also* Poisonous plants
Digoxin toxicity, 49, 50; *see also* Antitoxin; Antivenom
digoxin-specific fab, 67
Digoxin-like immunoreactive substances (DLIS), 243
Dihydrocodone, 778
Dihydrofolate reductase (DHFR), 70
Dimethyl sulfoxide (DMSO), 142, 331; *see also* Aromatic hydrocarbons

Dimethylacetamide (DMAC), 160, 824; *see also* Toxicants
Dimethylarsinic acid (DMA), 322, 675
Dimethylformamide (DMF), 160–161, 825; *see also* Toxicants
Dimethylphthlate (DIMP), 531
Dimethylsuccinic acid (DMSA), 60
DIMP, *see* Dimethylphthlate (DIMP)
Dinitrobenzene, 161, 825–826; *see also* Toxicants
Dinitrotoluene (DNT), 161, 826; *see also* Toxicants
Dioctyl sodium sulfosuccinate (DOSS), 636
Diphenoxylate, 101, 179, 778; *see also* Cocaine; Opioid
Diquat, 724
Disinfectants, 110, 112; *see also* Cleansers and caustics
Disodium edetate (Na_2EDTA), 59
Distal convoluted tubules (DCTs), 16
Distribution, 8; *see also* Poisoning and envenoming pharmacology
- bound drugs, 8
- compartment models, 9
- distribution volume, 8–9
- physiochemical determinants, 8
- unbound drugs, 8

Disulfiram reactions, 259; *see also* Antibiotic toxicity
Diuretics, 252; *see also* Antihypertensives
DLIS, *see* Digoxin-like immunoreactive substances (DLIS)
DMA, *see* Dimethylarsinic acid (DMA)
DMAC, *see* Dimethylacetamide (DMAC)
DMF, *see* Dimethylformamide (DMF)
DMSA, *see* Dimethylsuccinic acid (DMSA)
DMSO, *see* Dimethyl sulfoxide (DMSO)
DNT, *see* Dinitrotoluene (DNT)
Domestic flies (Muscidae), 538–539; *see also* Flies
Dose–response relationships, 13; *see also* Liver zones
- efficacy, 13
- potency, 14
- receptor, 13

Dosimetry, 767
DOSS, *see* Dioctyl sodium sulfosuccinate (DOSS)
DOT, *see* U.S. Department of Transportation (DOT)
Drug abuse, 168, 200; *see also* Amphetamines; Cocaine; Date-rape drugs; Hallucinogens; LSD; Marijuana; Plant hallucinogens; Propofol; Substance abuse
- anesthetic, 196
- bath salts, 191–192
- dextromethorphan, 194
- drug-induced deaths, 204
- nonprescription drug abuse, 194
- opioid analgesic overdose deaths, 203
- opioids adulterants, 181
- overdose emergency, 202
- prescription drug abuse, 193–194
- response roles for physicians, 200–205
- synthetic cannabis, 191
- unintentional overdose deaths, 203

Drug elimination kinetics, 14–15; *see also* First-order kinetics; Poison elimination; Poisoning and envenoming pharmacology; Zero-order kinetics
Drug testing, 775
- HHS cut-offs, 774
- laboratory selection questions, 805–807
- Omnibus Transportation Employee testing Act, 775
- opiate cut-offs, 774
- types of, 773

Drug–drug interactions, 11
Drugs and teratogens, 222; *see also* Pregnancy pharmacokinetics
DSHEA, *see* Dietary Supplement and Health Education Act of 1994 (DSHEA)
DTPA, *see* Diethylene triamine pentaacetic acid (DTPA)
Dumbcane (*Diffenbachia* spp.), 468; *see also* GI toxicity
Dx, *see* Diagnosis (Dx)

E

EAEC, *see* Entero-adhesive *E. coli* (EAEC)
EAP, *see* Employer Assisted Program (EAP); Employee assistance programs (EAPs)
Ear–nose–throat (ENT), 803
Eastern coral snake, 491; *see also* Terrestrial envenomings
- Belcher's sea snake, 496
- bites epidemiology, 492–493
- black mamba, 495
- boomslang snake, 498
- brown tree snake, 497
- colubridae, 497
- exotic viperidae, 496–497
- gaboon viper, 497
- Island Taipan, 495
- King Cobra, 495–496
- *Micrurus fulvius fulvius*, 492
- multi-banded krait, 496
- prevalence, 494
- rhombic night adder, 497
- sea snakes, 496
- snakebites, 493–494, 494–495

Eastern pygmy rattlesnake (*Sistrurus miliaris miliaris*), 488; *see also* Terrestrial envenomings
Ebola hemorrhagic fever (Ebola HF), 764
Ebola HF, *see* Ebola hemorrhagic fever (Ebola HF)
EBT, *see* Evidential breath-testing device (EBT)
ECC, *see* Excitation–contraction coupling (ECC)

ECG, *see* Electrocardiogram (ECG)
Ecgonine methyl ester (EME), 169
ED, *see* Erectile dysfunction (ED)
ED_{50}, *see* Effective dose 50 (ED_{50})
EDA, *see* Ethylenediamine (EDA)
EDB, *see* Ethylene dibromide (EDB)
Edible conifer (*Morchella esculenta*), 401; *see also* Mushroom poisoning
EDs, *see* Emergency Departments (EDs)
EDTA, 60; *see also* Metal chelators
E-Ferol tragedy, 87; *see also* Antiseptic toxicity
Effective dose 50 (ED_{50}), 14
Efficacy, 13; *see also* Dose–response relationships
EHEC, *see* Enterohemorrhagic *E. coli* (EHEC)
EIEC, *see* Entero-invasive *E. coli* (EIEC)
Elapids, 63–64; *see also* Antitoxin; Antivenom
  antivenom, 64–66
Elderberry (Sambucus nigra mexicana), 465; *see also* Cyanide poisoning
Electrocardiogram (ECG), 47, 135; *see also* Diagnosis in poisoned patient
  bradyarrhythmias, 52
  chloral hydrate toxicity, 51
  digoxin, 48
  electrolyte disturbances, 47
  hypercalcemia, 48
  hyperkalemia, 47
  hypothermia, 48, 49
  ischemia and ectopy, 52
  lytes and temp, 47
  tachyarrhythmias, 50
  tricyclic antidepressant overdose, 50
  ventricular tachycardia, 51
Electrolyte lavage solution (ELS), 59, 209
ELISA, *see* Enzyme-linked immunosorbent assay (ELISA)
ELS, *see* Electrolyte lavage solution (ELS)
EME, *see* Ecgonine methyl ester (EME)
Emergency Departments (EDs), 18
Emergency responsiveness, 775
Employee assistance programs (EAPs), 772, 790
  functions, 790
  of industries with, 791
  organizations, 790
  prevalence, 790
Employer Assisted Program (EAP), 787
Encephalopathy, 319; *see also* Neurotoxicology
Endocrine; *see also* Hormones; Hypoglycemia
  antithyroid agents, 237
  bone-active agents, 238
  electrolyte abnormalities, 239
Endogenous endotoxins, 383; *see also* Marine toxins
Endotracheal tube (ETT), 209
Enhanced elimination, 16; *see also* First-order kinetics; Zero-order kinetics
  corporeal enhanced elimination, 16
  drug factors favoring use of, 17
  extracorporeal, 16
  indications for, 16–17
  techniques, 17
ENT, *see* Ear–nose–throat (ENT)
Enteral administration, 4; *see also* Absorption
Entero-adhesive *E. coli* (EAEC), 367
Enterohemorrhagic *E. coli* (EHEC), 367
Entero-invasive *E. coli* (EIEC), 367
Enteropathogenic *E. coli* (EPEC), 367
Enterotoxigenic *E. coli* (ETEC), 367
Environmental Protection Agency (EPA), 136, 636
Enzyme-linked immunosorbent assay (ELISA), 386
Eosinophilia–Myalgia Syndrome, 87, 441–442; *see also* Antiseptic toxicity; Herbal poisoning
EPA, *see* Environmental Protection Agency (EPA)
EPEC, *see* Enteropathogenic *E. coli* (EPEC)
Ephedra (*Ephedra viridis*), 428, 429, 458, 595; *see also* Cajun healing practice; Central nervous system toxicity; Poisonous household plants
Epichlorohydrin, 161–162, 826–827; *see also* Toxicants
Epidemiology and statistics for toxicology, 844; *see also* Analytical epidemiological investigations; Differential statistics; Hypothesis testing; Probability rules
  binomial distribution, 845
  central tendency, 845
  continuous data, 845
  nominal data, 845
  normal distribution, 846
  probability for events, 844
  skewed distribution, 846, 847
  variation, 845, 846
Erectile dysfunction (ED), 587
Error, 853, 854
Escherichia coli, 367–368; *see also* Food poisoning
Esophageal stenosis, 105
ETEC, *see* Enterotoxigenic *E. coli* (ETEC)
Ethambutol, 266; *see also* Anti-TB agents
Ethane as asphyxiants, 647
Ethanol, *see* Ethyl alcohol (EtOH)
Ethchlorvynol, 213; *see also* Sedative-hypnotics (SHs)
Ethyl alcohol (EtOH), 73, 621, 709; *see also* Neurotoxicology; Specific antidotes; Toxic alcohols
  acute intoxication, 344
  clinical effects, 622
  diagnosis and management, 344–345
  disulfiram reactions, 623
  intoxication, 621–622
  metabolism, 622
  overdose, 622–623
  toxicity, 344, 621

Ethylene dibromide (EDB), 162, 827–828; *see also* Toxicants
Ethylene glycol, 123–124, 624; *see also* Alcohols and glycols; Nephrotoxicology; Neurotoxicology; Toxic alcohols
  diagnosis, 346
  fomepizole therapy, 627
  ingestion, 346, 625
  metabolism, 300–301, 624–625
  toxicity, 345–346, 624
Ethylene oxide, 338; *see also* Neurotoxicology
Ethylenediamine (EDA), 162, 828; *see also* Toxicants
EtOH, *see* Ethyl alcohol (EtOH)
Etomidate, 215; *see also* Sedative-hypnotics (SHs)
Etoposide, 460, 601; *see also* Cajun healing practice
ETT, *see* Endotracheal tube (ETT)
Euglycemia, 234
Euthanasia drugs, 137; *see also* Aromatic hydrocarbons
Evidential breath-testing device (EBT), 794
Exchange transfusion, 31
Excipients, 12, 82; *see also* Antiseptic toxicity; Benzyl alcohol;Liver zones; Methanol; Neurotoxicology
  toxicity, 346
Excitation–contraction coupling (ECC), 248
Excretion, *see* Drug elimination kinetics
Exotoxins, 383; *see also* Marine toxins
Extrapyramidal toxidrome, 56; *see also* Toxidromes

F

FAA, *see* Federal Aviation Administration (FAA)
False morel, *see* Brain mushroom (*Gyromitra esculenta*)
FAS, *see* Fetal alcohol syndrome (FAS)
FASDs, *see* Fetal alcohol spectrum disorders (FASDs)
Fatal mesenteric infarction, 175; *see also* Cocaine
FCS, *see* Fetal cocaine syndrome (FCS)
FDA, *see* U.S. Food and Drug Administration (FDA)
Fe chelating agent, 226; *see also* Poisoning in pregnancy
Fe ODs, 225; *see also* Poisoning in pregnancy
Federal Aviation Administration (FAA), 799
Federal Highway Administration (FHWA), 799
Federal Insecticide, Fungicide, and Rodenticide Act (FIFRA), 725
Federal Railway Administration (FRA), 799
Federal Transit Administration (FTA), 799
Feeding habits, 385; *see also* Seafood poisoning
  baitfish-feeders, 385
  filter-feeders, 385
  predatory feeders, 386
  red grouper, 385
  red snapper, 385
  sargassum triggerfish, 386
  stationary filter-feeders, 386
Fentanyl, 778
  analogs, 104; *see also* Opioid
Fetal alcohol spectrum disorders (FASDs), 638
Fetal alcohol syndrome (FAS), 229, 638; *see also* Reproductive toxicology
Fetal cocaine syndrome (FCS), 229; *see also* Reproductive toxicology
FHWA, *see* Federal Highway Administration (FHWA)
Fibropneumoconioses, 669
Fick's law of diffusion, 6; *see also* Absorption
FIFRA, *see* Federal Insecticide, Fungicide, and Rodenticide Act (FIFRA)
Filoviruses, 763
Filter-feeders, 385; *see also* Feeding habits
First-order kinetics, 14, 15; *see also* Enhanced elimination; Poisoning and envenoming pharmacology; Renal elimination
  elimination kinetics, 14, 15
  plasma clearance, 14–15, 17
  vs. zero-order kinetics, 14
Fleas, 542; *see also* Bedbugs; Flies; Mites; Myiasis; Ticks
  jigger flea, 543, 544
  plague maintenance, 543
  rat flea, 544
Flies, 526, 531; *see also* Bedbugs; Fleas; Leishmanias; Mites; Mosquitoes; Myiasis; Onchocerca volvulus; Ticks
  African trypanosomiasis, 537
  biting midges, 534, 536
  blackflies, 532
  Culicoides guttipennis, 535
  deerflies, 537
  flies, 537, 538–539
  Loa loa transmission, 536
  myiasis-causing flies, 540
  sandflies, 532, 534
  stable fly, 539–540
  tsetse flies, 537
Florida pufferfish, 387; *see also* Seafood poisoning
Flunitrazepam, 193, 212; *see also* Date-rape drugs
  clinical effects, 213
  toxicokinetics, 212–213
Fluoride, 152–153; *see also* Aromatic hydrocarbons; Toxicants
  compounds, 162–163, 828–829
Fluoroquinolones, 260–261; *see also* Antibiotic toxicity
Fluoxetine, 144; *see also* Aromatic hydrocarbons
Fly amanita (*Amanita muscaria*), 397; *see also* Mushroom poisoning

Folic acids, 70; *see also* Vitamins
Fomepizole, 73; *see also* Specific antidotes
Food additives, 115; *see also* Household poisoning
  monosodium glutamate, 115
  sulfites, 115–116
Food poisoning, 360; *see also* Acute gastrointestinal illness (AGI)
  Bacillus cereus, 362, 363
  bioterrorism, 362
  Brucella spp., 364
  Campylobacter jejuni, 364–365
  clinical manifestations, 360
  Clostridium, 365–367
  Escherichia coli, 367–368
  etiologic agents, 360, 361
  food-borne diseasesurveillance, 361
  Hepatitis virus, 374–375
  Listeria monocytogenes, 368
  Noroviruses, 375–376
  outbreaks, 370–371
  practice tests, 376, 378
  Rotaviruses, 376
  Salmonella spp., 369–370
  typhoidal GI perforation, 370
  vibrios, 371–372, 373
  Y. enterocolitica, 373–374
Forced dieresis, 30
Forensic Urine Drug Testing Laboratory, 800
Formaldehyde, 106, 119–121; *see also* Acids; Aldehydes
Formic acid, 106; *see also* Acids
Foul nest syndrome, 667
FRA, *see* Federal Railway Administration (FRA)
Fragrance, 155–156; *see also* Aromatic hydrocarbons
FTA, *see* Federal Transit Administration (FTA)
Fuels, 829; *see also* Aliphatic hydrocarbon
  frequency, 830
  kerosene, 130–131
  pathophysiology, 829–830
  toxicity, 830–831
Fumigants, methyl bromide, 723–724; *see also* Heavy metal poisoning; Insecticides; Pesticide poisoning; Metal poisoning; Rodenticides

G

GABA, *see* Gamma-aminobutyric acid (GABA)
Gaboon viper (*Bitis rhinoceros*), 497; *see also* Eastern coral snake
Gafftop catfish, *see* Saltwater gafftopsail (*Bagre marinus*)
Galerina marginata, 399; *see also* Mushroom poisoning
Gamma radiation, 731, 732
Gamma-aminobutyric acid (GABA), 258
Gamma-butyrolactone (GBL), 192; *see also* Date-rape drugs
Gamma-hydroxybutyrate (GHB), 168, 192; *see also* Date-rape drugs
Gamma-hydroxybutyric acid, *see* Gamma-hydroxybutyrate (GHB)
Gas Chromatography (GC), 39
Gas Chromatography/Mass Spectrometry (GC/MS), 39
Gasoline, 128–129; *see also* Aliphatic hydrocarbon
Gasping baby syndrome, 12, 87; *see also* Antiseptic toxicity; Liver zones
Gastric emptying, 22
Gastrointestinal decontaminants, 57; *see also* Poison antidotes
  activated charcoal, 57
  cathartics, 57
  diluents, 58
  ipecac, 58
  multiple-dose AC, 57–58
  WBI, 59
Gastrointestinal toxicity, 434, 467, 616; *see also* Herbal poisoning; Poisonous household plants
  caladium, 469
  calcium oxalate, 467
  Christmas group, 470
  coltsfoot, 436
  comfrey, 435
  crown-of-thorns, 470
  dumbcane, 468
  GI toxins, 432
  goldenseal, 432–433
  hepatotoxicity, 434
  philodendron, 469
  plants causing, 467
  pokeberry, 433, 471
  pyrrolizidine alkaloids, 434
  solanine group, 470
Gastrointestinal toxins, 595–599; *see also* Plant-derived remedies and toxins
Gastrointestinal tract (GI tract), 106
GBL, *see* Gamma-butyrolactone (GBL)
GBS, *see* Guillain–Barré syndrome (GBS)
GC, *see* Gas Chromatography (GC)
GC/MS, *see* Gas Chromatography/Mass Spectrometry (GC/MS)
Geiger counter, 767
Genetic polymorphisms, 11; *see also* Liver zones
Genitourinary malignancies, 306; *see also* Chronic renal failure (CRF)
Gentian, 597–598; *see also* Cajun healing practice
German agents, 751

GF, *see* Glomerular filtration (GF)
GF rate (GFR), 15
GFR, *see* GF rate (GFR)
GHB, *see* Gamma-hydroxybutyrate (GHB)
GI tract, *see* Gastrointestinal tract (GI tract)
Gila monster (*Heloderma suspectum*), 500; *see also* Terrestrial envenomings
Ginseng, 587; *see also* Cajun healing practice
Glomerular filtration (GF), 15; *see also* Renal elimination
Glucagon, 76; *see also* Nonspecific antidotes
Glucose-6-phosphate dehydrogenase, 637
  deficiency, 11
Glufosinate, 725
Glutathione-S-transferase (GST), 641
Glutethimide, 213; *see also* Sedative-hypnotics (SHs)
Glycol ethers, 122–123; *see also* Alcohols and glycols
Glyphosate, 725
Goldenseal, 432–433, 596; *see also* Cajun healing practice; Gastrointestinal toxicity
Grayanotoxins, 449; *see also* Channel openers
Green hellbane (*Veratrum viride*), 418, 449; *see also* Cardiovascular toxins; Sodium channel openers
Gris-gris, 586; *see also* Cajun healing practice
GST, *see* Glutathione-S-transferase (GST)
Guillain–Barré syndrome (GBS), 317, 318, 560, 758; *see also* Neurotoxicology
  diagnosis of, 319
Gustatory toxicity, 331; *see also* Metal poisoning
  anosmia, 331
  cacosmia, 331–332
Gut dialysis, 16; *see also* Enhanced elimination
Gypsy moth (*Lymantria dispar*), 520; *see also* Terrestrial envenomings
Gyromitrin toxicity, 400; *see also* Mushroom poisoning

H

H_2-blockers and proton-pump inhibitors, 11
HABs, *see* Harmful algal blooms (HABs)
Haff disease, 289; *see also* Acute renal failure (ARF)
Hag moth (*Phobetron pithecium*), 521; *see also* Terrestrial envenomings
Hair products, 153; *see also* Aromatic hydrocarbons
Half-life, 730
Hallucinogens, 782; *see also* Drug abuse; Phencyclidine (PCP); Plant-derived remedies and toxins
  common, 186
  group, 593
  LSD intoxication, 187
  mushroom, 603
  plant hallucinogens, 188
  toxicity, 187
  use and induced disorders, 782
Harmful algal blooms (HABs), 380, 382, 383; *see also* Seafood poisoning
Hawaiian baby woodrose (*Argyreia nervosa*), 429; *see also* Central nervous system toxicity
HBO, *see* Hyperbaric oxygen (HBO)
HCBD, *see* Hexachloro-1,3-Butadiene (HCBD)
HCs, *see* Hydrocarbons (HCs)
HD, *see* Hemodialysis (HD)
Heavy metal poisoning, 699; *see also* Metal chelators
  aluminum poisoning, 699, 701
  antidotes, 703–706
  bismuth poisoning, 701
  cobalt poisoning, 699
  copper poisoning, 700
  manganese poisoning, 700
  nickel poisoning, 702–703
  and parkinsonism, 702
  selenium poisoning, 700, 703
  tin poisoning, 700
  zinc poisoning, 700
Helium as asphyxiants, 647
Hemlock (*Cicuta maculata*), 426; *see also* Neurotoxic plants
Hemodialysis (HD), 16, 17, 30, 83; *see also* Antiseptic toxicity; Poison elimination
Hemofiltration (HF), 16, 17; *see also* Hemodialysis (HD); Hemoperfusion (HP)
Hemoperfusion (HP), 16, 17; *see also* Hemodialysis (HD)
HEN, *see* Herbal endemic nephropathy (HEN)
Hendra virus, 762–763
Henipaviruses, 762
Heparin antag, 69–70; *see also* Specific antagonists
Hepatic enzyme inducers, 11
Hepatic enzyme inhibitors, 11
Hepatic reactions, 10
Hepatitis; *see also* Food poisoning
  A virus, 374
  E virus, 374–375
Hepatotoxins, 434, 599–600; *see also* Gastrointestinal toxicity; Herbal poisoning; Plant-derived remedies and toxins
  herbal, 467
Herbal endemic nephropathy (HEN), 305, 437; *see also* Hepatotoxins
Herbal hepatotoxins, 435, 436; *see also* Herbal poisoning
  Balkan endemic nephropathy, 437

herbal endemic nephropathy, 437
toxic herb–drug interactions, 437–438
Herbal poisoning, 54, 414, 442, 590, 595–600; *see also* Cardiovascular toxins; Central nervous system toxicity; Gastrointestinal toxicity; Herbal hepatotoxins; Hypervitaminosis; Neurotoxic plants; Sympathomimetics; Toxidromes
abortifacients, 415–416
antidote, 421
cardiac glycosides, 421–422
eosinophia–myalgia syndrome, 441–442
epidemiology, 414
herbal hepatotoxins, 467
neurotoxic, 422
pennyroyal-mint family, 416–417
pharmacology, 414–415
system-oriented classification, 417
toxicology, 415
tryptophan, 441
Herbicides, 356; *see also* Heavy metal poisoning; Insecticides; Metal poisoning; Neurotoxicology; Pesticide poisoning; Rodenticides
chlorphenoxyacetic acids, 356, 725
diquat, 724
glufosinate, 725
glyphosate, 725
paraquat, 724
Heroin, 778; *see also* Opioid
body packers, 105
Hexachloro-1,3-Butadiene (HCBD), 162, 831; *see also* Toxicants
Hexane, 127–128; *see also* Aliphatic hydrocarbon
HF, *see* Hemofiltration (HF); Hydrofluoric acid (HF)
High pressure liquid chromatography (HPLC), 38, 386
Hobo spider (*Tegenaria agrestis*), 508; *see also* Terrestrial envenomings
Honey bee workers (*Apis mellifera*), 513; *see also* Terrestrial envenomings
Hoodia Gordonii, 189–190; *see also* Plant hallucinogens
Hoodoo, 584, 585; *see also* Cajun healing practice; Voodoo
Hormones, 238; *see also* Endocrine; Hypoglycemia
Hornets, 514; *see also* Terrestrial envenomings
Horseflies, 537; *see also* Flies
Household antimicrobials, 111; *see also* Cleansers and caustics
Household herbs, 600–601; *see also* Plant-derived remedies and toxins
Household poisoning, 105; *see also* Cleansers and caustics; Food additives; Household products; Hydrocarbons; Toxicants
Household products, 116, 145; *see also* Aromatic hydrocarbons; Household poisoning
aquarium products, 116
art products, 117
batteries, 117–118
cosmetics, 118–119
HP, *see* Hemoperfusion (HP)
HPLC, *see* High pressure liquid chromatography (HPLC)
Human bot fly (*Dermatobia hominis*), 541; *see also* Myiasis
Human scabies mite (*Sarcoptes scabiei*), 552, 554; *see also* Mites
Hydrocarbons (HCs), 58, 119, 340, 614, 647; *see also* Alcohols and glycols; Aldehydes; Aliphatic hydrocarbon; Aromatic hydrocarbons; Household poisoning; Methemoglobinemia; Neurotoxicology; Volatile organic compounds (VOCs)
and alcohols, 338
carcinogenic vs. neurotoxic, 341
classification, 339
epidemiology, 339, 616
halogenated, 615
hexacarbons, 342
ingestion, 618
poisoning, 618
TCE, 341–342
toxicity, 616
toxicology, 340
treatment, 340
uses, 339
volatile substance abuse, 341
wood distillates, 342–343
Hydrochloric acid, 106; *see also* Acids
Hydrocodone, 778
Hydrofluoric acid (HF), 68
Hydrogen sulfide poisoning, 336, 657; *see also* Neurotoxicology
clinical effects, 337, 658
diagnosis, 658
management, 337
methemoglobinemia, 659
sources, 336–337, 657
treatment, 659
Hydromorphone, 778
Hydroxocobalamin, 70–71; *see also* Vitamins
Hymenoptera, 607; *see also* Arthropods; Terrestrial envenomings
venoms, 518
Hyperbaric oxygen (HBO), 75, 79, 654, 646; *see also* Nonspecific antidotes
Hypercalcemia, 48
Hyperkalemia, 47
Hypermetabolic toxidrome, 55, *see also* Toxidromes

Hypervitaminosis, 438; *see also* Herbal poisoning
A, 439
B_3 toxicity, 441
B_6 neuropathy, 440
C, 440
D, 441
E, 439
K, 439–440
poisoning, 438–439
Hypnotics, 208
Hypoglycemia, 234; *see also* Endocrine; Hormones; Oral hypoglycemics; Plant chemotherapy
Ackee and Jamaican vomiting sickness, 235, 466
clinical effects, 235
electrolyte abnormalities, 239
epidemiology, 234
etiologies, 235
hepatotoxicity and, 235
insulin pharmacokinetics, 234
OD management, 236–237
sulfonylureas, 236
surreptitious, 237
toxicity, 234
Hypothermia, 49
Hypothesis testing, 849
differential statistics comparative groups, 850
research designs, 849–850

I

Ibotenic acid, 604; *see also* Mushroom poisoning
and muscimol toxicity, 403
ICH, *see* Intracranial hemorrhage (ICH)
ICP, *see* Intracranial pressure (ICP)
ICU, *see* Intensive care unit (ICU)
IDDM, *see* Insulin-dependent diabetes mellitus (IDDM)
IFE, *see* Intravenous fat emulsion (IFE)
Ileus, 99; *see also* Opioid
Imidazolines, 102, 180–181; *see also* Cocaine; Opioid
Immunoassays, 38
IMS, *see* Intermediate syndrome (IMS)
IMV, *see* Intermittent mandatory ventilation (IMV)
Incapacitating agents, 754
Independent variable, 847
Industrial exposures, 671; *see also* Asphyxiants; Carbon monoxide poisoning; Irritant gases; Occupational lung diseases; Pneumoconioses
hydrogen sulfide 657
inhalation fevers, 671
poison gas, 662
smoke inhalation, 650–651
INH, *see* Isonicotinyl hydrazide (INH)
Inhalants, 783; *see also* Drug abuse
abuse, 196–197
Insecticides; *see also* Fumigants; Heavy metal poisoning; Insecticides; Pesticide poisoning; Metal poisoning; Rodenticides
carbamates, 710
organochlorines, 708–709
Insulin pharmacokinetics, 234
Insulin-dependent diabetes mellitus (IDDM), 243
Intensive care unit (ICU), 198
Intermediate syndrome (IMS), 349, 710
Intermittent mandatory ventilation (IMV), 651
Intracranial and interventricular hemorrhage, 172; *see also* Cocaine
Intracranial aneurysm, 171; *see also* Cocaine
Intracranial hemorrhage (ICH), 247
Intracranial pressure (ICP), 312
Intravenous (IV), 4
Intravenous drug users (IVDUs), 32, 101; *see also* Opioid
Intravenous fat emulsion (IFE), 79; *see also* Nonspecific antidotes
Intravenous gamma globulin G (IVIG), 563
Intravenous pyelogram (IVP), 308
Intrinsic sympathetic activity (ISA), 245
In vitro adulteration, 802
Io moth, 519; *see also* Terrestrial envenomings
Iodines, 111; *see also* Cleansers and caustics
Ionization, 730
Ionizing radiation, 730
Ipecac, 58, *see also* Gastrointestinal decontaminants
emesis, 22–23, 24
Iron poisoning, 680; *see also* Heavy metal poisoning; Metal poisoning
-containing preparations, 681
epidemiology, 680–681
toxicity, 681
treatment, 681
Irradiation dose limits, 768
Irritant gases, 647; *see also* Asphyxiants
ALI vs. RADS, 648
fume fevers 648
irritants, 648
occupational exposures to, 650
tear gases, 648
toxic mechanisms, 649
ISA, *see* Intrinsic sympathetic activity (ISA)
Island Taipan (*Oxyuranus microlepidotus*), 495; *see also* Eastern coral snake
Isocyanates, 163, 831; *see also* Toxicants
Isocyanates—toluene diisocyanate, 831
routes of exposure, 832
toxicity, 832
Isoniazid, 71, 88

Isonicotinyl hydrazide (INH), 262; *see also* Antibiotic toxicity
INH epidemiology, 262
metabolism, 263, 264
overdose management, 264
pharmacology, 262–263
TB and INH epidemiology, 262
toxicity, 264, 265
Isopropanol, 125, 623; *see also* Alcohols and glycols; Toxic alcohols; Neurotoxicology
diagnosis, 345
metabolism, 623–624
toxicity, 345, 623
Isotope, 730
IV, *see* Intravenous (IV)
IVDUs, *see* Intravenous drug users (IVDUs)
Ivermectin, 142–143; *see also* Aromatic hydrocarbons
IVIG, *see* Intravenous gamma globulin G (IVIG)
IVP, *see* Intravenous pyelogram (IVP)
Ixtoc I oil spill, 631; *see also* Petrochemical toxicity

J

Jamaican vomiting sickness, 466; *see also* Plant chemotherapy
Jigger flea (*Tunga penetrans*), 543, 544; *see also* Fleas
Jimson weed (*Datura stramonium*), 423, 452; *see also* Neurotoxic plants

K

Ketamine, 138–139; *see also* Aromatic hydrocarbons
KFD, *see* Kyasanur Forest hemorrhagic fever (KFD)
King Cobra (*Ophiophagus hannah*), 495–496; *see also* Eastern coral snake
Kissing bug (*Triatoma infestans*), 548; *see also* Bedbugs
Kyasanur Forest hemorrhagic fever (KFD), 551

L

LA, *see* Long-acting (LA)
LAAM, *see* Levo-alpha-acetyl methadol (LAAM)
Large-mouth buffalo fish (*Ictiobus cyprinellus*), 392; *see also* Seafood poisoning
Latin American Fer-de-Lance (*Bothrops asper*), 498; *see also* Central and South American exotic snakes
Latrodectus antivenom, 66; *see also* Antitoxin; Antivenom
LD, *see* Lyme disease (LD)
Lead poisoning, 146–149, 296, 324, 682; *see also* Acute renal failure (ARF); Aromatic hydrocarbons; Heavy metal poisoning; Metal poisoning; Nephrotoxicology; Neurotoxicology; Reproductive toxicology
additives, 220
cardiac effects, 688
clinical findings, 689–691
CNS, 324
endocrinopathy, 688
exposure sources, 682–683
GI effects, 688
hemoglobin reduction, 685–687
nephrotoxicity, 297, 687–688
neurotoxicity, 324, 684–685
pathophysiology, 296–297, 683
peripheral nervous system, 324
public health case, 693–694
reproductive toxicity, 688
skeletal effects, 688, 689
soil lead hot spots, 694
treatment, 692–693
uses of, 682
Least-squares regression, 848
Leishmanias; *see also* Flies
Phlebotomus species sandfly, 534
transmission cycle for, 535
Levels of concern (LOC), 633
Levo-alpha-acetyl methadol (LAAM), 100; *see also* Opioid
LFTs, *see* Liver function tests (LFTs)
Lice, 544; *see also* Bedbugs; Fleas; Flies; Mites; Mosquitoes; Myiasis; Ticks
Lily-of-the-valley (*Convallaria majalis*), 421; *see also* Cardiovascular toxins
Lindane, 708
Linear regression, 847
Lionfish (*Pterosis volitans*), 578; *see also* Toxic vertebrates
Liver function tests (LFTs), 31, 615
Liver zones, 11; *see also* Poisoning and envenoming pharmacology
dose–response relationships, 13–14
excipients, 12
pharmacogenetics, 11–12
therapeutic index, 12
Lizards, 481; *see also* Terrestrial envenomings
Loa loa transmission life cycle, 536; *see also* Flies
LOC, *see* Levels of concern (LOC)
Long-acting (LA), 234
Loperamide, 101, 179; *see also* Cocaine; Opioid
Louisiana Cajun, 584; *see also* Cajun healing practice; Hoodoo; Voodoo
LSD, *see* Lysergic acid diethylamide (LSD)
Lycoperdonosis, 409; *see also* Mushroom poisoning

Lye relaxers, 153–154; *see also* Aromatic hydrocarbons
Lyme disease (LD), 558
Lysergic acid diethylamide (LSD), 168, 782, 783; *see also* Drug abuse; Hallucinogens
  intoxication, 187
  pharmacology, 187
  street names, 168

M

MAA, *see* Methylarsinic acid (MAA)
Macrolides, 261; *see also* Antibiotic toxicity
Mad Hatter syndrome, 695, 696
Magnetic resonance imaging (MRI), 316
Malaria, 528; *see also* Mosquitoes
Maleic anhydride, 163, 832–833; *see also* Toxicants
6-MAM, *see* 6-Mono-acetylmorphine (6-MAM)
Manganese, 329; *see also* Aromatic hydrocarbons; Neurotoxicology
  dioxide, 150–151
  heavy metal poisoning, 330
  -induced parkinsonism, 329
  neurotoxicity, 330
  poisoning, 700
MAOIs, *see* Monoamine oxidase inhibitors (MAOIs)
MAP, *see* Mean arterial pressure (MAP)
Marijuana, 190, 215, 782; *see also* Drug abuse; Sedative-hypnotics (SHs)
  epidemiology, 190, 215
  intoxication, 191, 216
  pharmacology, 190, 215
  route of administration, 782–783
  street names, 168
  toxicity, 190–191, 215–216
Marine envenomings, 570; *see also* Coelenterates, toxic; Toxic vertebrates
  chordates, 570, 571
  coelenterates, 571
  epidemiology, 571–572
  invertebrates, 570, 571
  marine invertebrates, 570
  marine wound infections, 579
  M. marinum, 581
  non-cholera vibrios, 580
  post-test question, 582
  pre-test question, 570
  recommended management, 579–580
  sea snakes, 581–582
  taxonomy, 571
  vertebrates, 571
  vibrios, 580–581
Marine toad, *see* Cane toad (*Rhinella marina*)
Marine toxins, 383; *see also* Seafood poisoning
  bioaccumulated exotoxins, 383
  endogenous endotoxins, 383
  potency of biological toxins, 384
  pufferfish or porcupine fish, 384
  tetrodotoxin, 384
Masked pufferfish (*Arothron diadematus*), 576; *see also* Coelenterates, toxic
Mayapple (*Podophyllum peltatum*), 463, 602; *see also* Anticancer alkaloids; Cajun healing practice
MCADD, *see* Medium-chain acyl-coenzyme A dehydrogenase deficiency (MCADD)
MDA, *see* Methylene diamine (MDA)
MDAC, *see* Multi-dose-activated charcoal (MDAC)
MDE, *see* Methylenedioxyethamphetamine (MDE)
MDMA, *see* Methylenedioxymethamphetamine (MDMA)
MDPV, *see* Methylenedioxypyrovalerone (MDPV)
Mean arterial pressure (MAP), 312
Mechanisms of action (MoAs), 79, 681
Medical review of officer (MRO), 770, 774, 788; *see also* Chain of custody (CoC); Opioid case conclusions
  medical review interview, 790
  practical, 789
  qualifications, 789
  reporting, 791, 792
Medium-chain acyl-coenzyme A dehydrogenase deficiency (MCADD), 200
Mees' Lines, 328; *see also* Thallium
  diagnosis and treatment, 329
Mefloquine, 268; *see also* Antimalarials
MEK, *see* Methyl-ethyl ketone (MEK)
Meperidine, 100, 178, 778; *see also* Cocaine; Opioid
Meprobamate, 214; *see also* Sedative-hypnotics (SHs)
Mercaptans, 163–164, 833–834; *see also* Toxicants
Mercurial acrodynia, 697
Mercurochrome, 113; *see also* Cleansers and caustics
Mercury bichloride tablets, 112; *see also* Cleansers and caustics
Mercury poisoning, 297, 325, 326, 694; *see also* Acute renal failure (ARF); Heavy metal poisoning; Metal poisoning; Nephrotoxicology
  accidental exposures, 325
  and acrodynia, 326
  acrodynia, 327
  acute clinical effects, 326
  acute elemental inhalation, 326
  clinical effects, 297, 298, 325, 326, 695–697
  diagnosis and management, 696
  elemental mercury, 326
  exposures, 325, 694–695
  inorganic mercury, 326
  mad hatter syndrome, 695, 696

mercurial acrodynia, 697
minamata disease, 697
pathophysiology, 297–298, 695
toxicology, 325
Mescaline, 782, 784
Mesothelioma, 666
Metabolic reactions, 10; *see also* Poisoning and envenoming pharmacology
Metal chelators, 59; *see also* Heavy metal poisoning; Poison antidotes
BAL, 61, 704–705
clinical findings, 62
deferoxamine, 59–61, 704
EDTA, 60, 704
penicillamine, 61, 705
succimer, 60, 705
Metal poisoning, 330, 674; *see also* Arsenic; Cadmium; Chromium; Iron; Lead; Mercury; Neurotoxicology; Thallium
copper, 330
gustatory toxicity, 331
ototoxicity, 331
selenium, 330, 331
tin, 332
Metalloids, 674
Metaphyseal Lead Lines, 42
Methadone, 778, 805
Methane as asphyxiants, 647
Methanol, 125, 625; *see also* Alcohols and glycols; Neurotoxicology; Toxic alcohols
diagnosis, 347
dosing for fomepizole therapy, 627
metabolism, 127, 626
toxicity, 347, 625, 627
Methaqualone, 214, 805; *see also* Sedative-hypnotics (SHs)
Methemoglobinemia, 616; *see also* Hydrocarbons (HCs)
clinical manifestations of, 617
factors causing, 617
methemoglobin level measurement, 617
Methicillin-resistant Staphylococcus aureus (MRSA), 511
Methotrexate (MTX), 70, 271; *see also* Anticancer drug toxicity
action mechanisms, 272
overdose management, 272–273
toxicity, 272
Methyl alcohol, 144–146; *see also* Aromatic hydrocarbons
Methyl bromide, 723–724
Methyl n-butyl ketone (MNBK), 315
Methylarsinic acid (MAA), 322, 675
Methylene blue, 76–77; *see also* Nonspecific antidotes
Methylene diamine (MDA), 834
Methylenedioxyethamphetamine (MDE), 782
Methylenedioxymethamphetamine (MDMA), 782
Methylenedioxypyrovalerone (MDPV), 191
Methylisocyanate (MIC), 648
Methyl-ethyl ketone (MEK), 619
Methyl-isobutyl ketone (MIBK), 619
Methyl-phenyl-tetra-hydropyridine (MPTP), 101, 168, 179, 314; *see also* Opioid
Methyprylon, 213; *see also* Sedative-hypnotics (SHs)
Mexican beaded lizard (*Heloderma horridum*), 501; *see also* Terrestrial envenomings
MIBK, *see* Methyl-isobutyl ketone (MIBK)
MIC, *see* Methylisocyanate (MIC)
Michaelis–Menten kinetics, 14, 15
Milk snake (*Lampropeltis triangulum annulata*), 490; *see also* Terrestrial envenomings
Millipedes, 523; *see also* Terrestrial envenomings
Minamata disease, 697
Miosis, 54, 55, 98.; *see also* Opioid; Toxidromes
Mississippi–Missouri (*MS–MO*), 392
Mites, 549; *see also* Bedbugs; Fleas; Flies; Mosquitoes; Myiasis; Ticks
scabies mite, 552, 553, 554
scrub typhus mites, 553, 554–555
trombiculid mites, 555
MMH, *see* Monomethylhydrazine (MMH)
MNBK, *see* Methyl n-butyl ketone (MNBK)
MoAs, *see* Mechanisms of action (MoAs)
Molecular weight (MW), 5
Monitoring radiation, 767
Monkshood (*Aconitum napellus*), 418; *see also* Cardiovascular toxins; Sodium channel openers
6-Mono-acetylmorphine (6-MAM), 797, 801
Monoamine oxidase inhibitors (MAOIs), 596
Monomethylhydrazine (MMH), 71
Monosodium Glutamate (MSG), 115; *see also* Food additives
Morning glory (*Ipomoea purpurea*), 188, 427, 457, 593; *see also* Cajun healing practice; Central nervous system toxicity; Plant hallucinogens; Poisonous household plants
Morphine, 778, 803
poppy seeds, 804
Mosquitoes, 526; *see also* Anophelines; Bedbugs; Culicines; Fleas; Flies; Mites; Myiasis; Ticks
control and prevention, 530
filarial life cycle, 530
filiariasis, 528
malaria, 528, 529
stages, 527, 528
vector for dengue, 528
yellow fever vector transmission, 530, 531
Mothballs, 111; *see also* Cleansers and caustics

Motor neuron, 312; *see also* Neuroanatomy
MPTP, *see* Methyl-phenyl-tetra-hydropyridine (MPTP)
MPTP-induced parkinsonism, 180; *see also* Cocaine
MRI, *see* Magnetic resonance imaging (MRI)
MRO, *see* Medical review of officer (MRO)
MRSA, *see* Methicillin-resistant Staphylococcus aureus (MRSA)
MS, *see* Multiple sclerosis (MS)
MS–MO, *see* Mississippi–Missouri (*MS–MO*)
MSG, *see* Monosodium Glutamate (MSG)
MTX, *see* Methotrexate (MTX)
Mud dauber wasp (*Sceliphron caementarium*), 516; *see also* Terrestrial envenomings
Multi-banded krait (*Bungarus multicinctus*), 496; *see also* Eastern coral snake
Multi-dose-activated charcoal (MDAC), 19, 26–27, 57–58; *see also* Gastrointestinal decontaminants
Multiple regression, 847
Multiple sclerosis (MS), 317, 318; *see also* Neurotoxicology
Multiplication rule, 844
Muscarine toxicity, 401, 403; *see also* Mushroom poisoning
Mushroom poisoning, 259, 396; *see also* Antibiotic toxicity; Cajun healing practice
- acute anuric RF, 406
- alcohol inky cap, 405
- *Amanita*, 399, 407
- brain mushroom, 400
- classification, 398
- *Clitocybe dealbata*, 403
- coprine toxicity, 405
- *Cortinarius*, 406
- cyclopeptide toxicity, 397
- diagnosis, 397
- edible conifer, 401
- epidemiology, 396
- *Galerina marginata*, 399
- GI toxicity, 408
- gyromitrin toxicity, 400
- hallucinogenic mushroom, 603
- ibotenic acid, 604
- *Inocybe geophylla*, 403
- *Lactarius volemus*, 408
- *Lepiota cristata*, 399, 400
- lycoperdonosis, 409
- muscarine toxicity, 401, 403
- orange fly, 404
- orelline nephrotoxicity, 405
- *Paxillus*, 408
- poisonous mushroom, 397, 401, 402
- *Psilocybe cubensis*, 405
- psilocybin toxicity, 404, 604
- red fly agaric, 404
- Rhabdomyolysis, 406
- *Scleroderma geaster*, 409, 410
- toxicologic classification, 396–397
- *Tricholoma equestre*, 407
- white puffballs, 409
- Yellow knight, 407

Mutual exclusivity, 845
MW, *see* Molecular weight (MW)
Mycotoxins, 410, 763; *see also* Mushroom poisoning
- aflatoxins, 412
- classification of, 411
- *Fusarium keratitis*, 410
- stachybotryotoxicosis, 411–412
- tricothecene mycotoxins, 411

Mydriasis, 54, 55; *see also* Toxidromes
Myeloneuropathy, 320; *see also* Neurotoxicology
Myiasis, 540; *see also* Bedbugs; Fleas; Flies; Mites; Mosquitoes; Ticks
- causing flies, 540
- facultative, 541
- human bot fly, 541
- obligatory, 540
- screw-worm fly, 541
- transmission cycle of, 540

N

NAC, *see* N-Acetyl-cysteine (NAC)
N-Acetyl-cysteine (NAC), 72, 73–74, 416; *see also* Specific antidotes
N-Acetyl-para-aminophenol (APAP), 8, 90; *see also* Acetyl salicylic acid (ASA); Nonsteroidal anti-inflammatory drugs (NSAIDs); Opioid
- vs. ASA poisoning, 92
- clinical effects, 90
- diagnosis, 92
- epidemiology, 90
- poisoning, 92, 93
- toxicity, 90, 91, 92
- treatment, 93

N-Acetyl-p-benzoquinoneimine (NAPQI), 90
Na_2EDTA, *see* Disodium edetate (Na_2EDTA)
NAP, *see* Nerve action potential (NAP)
Naphthalene, 822–823
NAPQI, *see* *N*-Acetyl-p-benzoquinoneimine (NAPQI)
Narcotic adulterants, 102, 104, 181; *see also* Cocaine; Opioid
Nasogastric (NG), 695
National Center for Health Statistics (NCHS), 664
National Highway and Traffic Safety Administration (NHTSA), 794

National Institute of Drug Abuse (NIDA), 783
NIDA "5", 168
Natural cathinone, 191; *see also* Synthetic cannabis
Natural glycosides, 242; *see also* Cardiac glycosides
NCHS, *see* National Center for Health Statistics (NCHS)
NCPE, *see* Noncardiogenic pulmonary edema (NCPE)
NE, *see* Norepinephrine (NE)
Negative inspiratory forces (NIFs), 324, 677
Neon as asphyxiants, 647
Neonatal withdrawal syndrome (NWS), 229; *see also* Reproductive toxicology
Nephrotoxicology, 283; *see also* Acute renal failure (ARF); Cadmium; Chronic renal failure (CRF); Lead poisoning; Mercury poisoning; Renal dysfunction
causing ARF and CRF, 284
environmental, 307
epidemiology, 283
mushroom poisonings, 287
orelline nephrotoxicity, 288
pathophysiology, 283
phosphorous ingestions, 293
post-test questions, 307
pretest questions, 282
rodenticides, 293–294
schistosomiasis, 308
Nerve action potential (NAP), 386
Nervous system (NS), 312
vulnerability, 311–312
Neural tube defects (NTDs), 222; *see also* Reproductive toxicology
Neuraxis, 312; *see also* Neuroanatomy
Neuroanatomy, 312; *see also* Neurotoxicology
LMN lesion, 313
motor neuron, 312
neuraxis, 312
UMN lesion, 313
Neurodiagnostic investigations, 315; *see also* Neurotoxicology
CNS, 316
functional integrity, 316
neurotoxicity, 316
structural integrity, 315–316
Neuromuscular junction (NMJ), 709
Neuronopathy, 314
Neuropathology, 319; *see also* Neurotoxicology
Neurotoxic esterase (NTE), 350, 709
Neurotoxic gases, 332
Neurotoxic heavy metals, 321; *see also* Neurotoxicology
essential minerals, 321–322
Neurotoxic metals, 322; *see also* Neurotoxicology
Neurotoxicity, 314
Neurotoxicology, 310; *see also* Additives toxicity; Arsenic; Carbon monoxide poisoning; Cyanide; Herbicides; Hydrocarbons (HCs); Hydrogen sulfide; Lead; Manganese; Mercury; Mercury poisoning; Metal poisoning; Neuroanatomy; Neurodiagnostic investigations; Neurotoxic rodenticides; Neurotoxic syndromes; Occupational neurotoxicity; Parkinsonism; Pesticide poisoning; Psychotropics; Thallium; Toxic alcohols; Volatile organic compounds (VOCs)
additives toxicity, 346–347
axonopathy, 314
carbon disulfide, 338
carcinogenic vs. neurotoxic, 322
diagnosis, 319–321
ethylene oxide, 338
mechanisms, 314
metals vs. minerals, 321
neuronopathy, 314
neuropathology, 319
neurotoxic gases, 332
neurotoxic opioids, 314
objectives, 311
poison gas, 332
pyramidal vs. extrapyramidal, 313
toxic CNS disorders, 315
toxic vs. nontoxic disorders, 317
transmissionopathy, 315
Neurotoxic opioids, 314; *see also* Neurotoxicology
Neurotoxic plants, 422, 425, 452, 455; *see also* Herbal poisoning; Plant hallucinogens
angel's trumpet, 424, 453
belladonna alkaloids, 422–423, 452
convulsants, 424, 454
epileptogenic water hemlock, 426
hallucinogens, 426
jimson weed, 423, 452
nicotine group, 423, 453
poison hemlock, 425, 454
poisonings, 189
water hemlock, 455
wild tree tobacco, 425, 454
Neurotoxic rodenticides, 351, 353; *see also* Neurotoxicology
anticoagulants, 354
barium carbonate, 352–353
bromethalin, 353–354
classification, 351
epidemiology, 352
strychnine, 352
toxicity, 352, 353
toxidrome diagnosis, 355
vacor, 353

Neurotoxic syndromes, 320; *see also* Neurotoxicology
gases, 320–321
heavy metals, 320
hydrocarbons, 321
pesticides, 321
Neutron, 731–732
New world screw-worm fly (*Cochliomyia hominivorax*), 541; *see also* Myiasis
Newts, 501, 606; *see also* Animal toxins; Terrestrial envenomings
NG, *see* Nasogastric (NG)
NHTSA, *see* National Highway and Traffic Safety Administration (NHTSA)
Niacin, 72; *see also* Vitamins
Nickel poisoning, 702–703
NIDA, *see* National Institute of Drug Abuse (NIDA)
NIFs, *see* Negative inspiratory forces (NIFs)
Nipah virus, 761–762
Nitriles, 164, 835; *see also* Toxicants
Nitrites, 220; *see also* Reproductive toxicology
Nitrous oxide, 196–197; *see also* Drug abuse
n-Methylthiotetrazole (nMTT), 259, 623
NMJ, *see* Neuromuscular junction (NMJ)
nMTT, *see* n-Methylthiotetrazole (nMTT)
N,N-Diethyl-*meta*-toluamide (DEET), 350, 568
Nominal data, 845
Nonamphetamine appetite suppressants, 189; *see also* Plant hallucinogens
Noncardiogenic pulmonary edema (NCPE), 43, 91, 100, 103, 250, 254; *see also* Opioid
Noncholera *Vibrios*, 372; *see also* Food poisoning
Noncontact positive, 808
Nondissolving radiopacities, 23
Nonfibrogenic pneumoconioses, 669
Nonionizing radiation, 730
Nonrenal genitourinary tract abnormalities, 306; *see also* Chronic renal failure (CRF)
Nonselective β-blockers, 245; *see also* β-Blockers
Nonspecific antidotes, 75; *see also* Poison antidotes; Specific antidotes
acquired methemoglobinemia, 77
cyanide kit, 77, 78
dextrose, 76
glucagon, 76
HBO, 79
hyperbaric oxygen, 78
intravenous fat emulsion, 79
methylene blue, 76–77
sodium bicarbonate, 78, 79
Nonsteroidal anti-inflammatory drugs (NSAIDs), 90; *see also* Acetyl salicylic acid (ASA); *N*-Acetyl-para-aminophenol (APAP); Opioid
adverse effects, 96
classification of, 95
drug–drug interactions, 96
epidemiology, 94
poison management, 96–97
toxicities, 95–96, 97
Nontoxic exposures, 35
home products, 23, 36
orogastric lavage, 24–25
Nontoxic home products, 23
Norbormide, 720
Norepinephrine (NE), 245
Normal distribution, 846
Noroviruses, 375–376; *see also* Food poisoning
Northern Pacific rattlesnake (*Crotalus viridis oreganus*), 487; *see also* Terrestrial envenomings
NRC, *see* Nuclear Regulatory Commission (NRC)
NS, *see* Nervous system (NS)
NSAIDs, *see* Nonsteroidal anti-inflammatory drugs (NSAIDs)
NTDs, *see* Neural tube defects (NTDs)
NTE, *see* Neurotoxic esterase (NTE)
Nuclear Regulatory Commission (NRC), 768, 771
Nutmeg, 188; *see also* Plant hallucinogens
NWS, *see* Neonatal withdrawal syndrome (NWS)

O

Occupational lung cancer, 666; *see also* Occupational lung diseases
asbestosis, 667
berylliosis, 668–669
fibropneumoconioses, 669
foul nest syndrome, 667
mesothelioma, 666
nonfibrogenic pneumoconioses, 669
silicosis, 667–668
small-cell adenocarcinoma, 666
squamous cell carcinoma, 666
Occupational lung diseases, 662; *see also* Asbestosis; Occupational lung cancer; Pneumoconioses
asthma, 669–670
fume fevers, 671
inhalation fevers, 671
Occupational neurotoxicity, 316, 354; *see also* Neurotoxicology
bromates, 354
bromides, 354
diagnosis, 356
neurotoxicity, 316–317
prevention hierarchy, 356
OCPs, *see* Oral contraceptive pills (OCPs)
OD, *see* Order for diagnosis (OD); Overdose (OD)
Odds ratio, 853
OG, *see* Orogastric (OG)

OHF, *see* Omsk hemorrhagic fever (OHF)
Oleander (*Nerium oleander*), 420; *see also* Cardiovascular toxins
Omnibus Transportation Employee testing Act, 775, 793, 794
Omsk hemorrhagic fever (OHF), 551
Onchocerca volvulus, 533; *see also* Flies
One compartment, 33
  model, 9; *see also* Distribution
OP, *see* Organophosphate (OP)
OPD, *see* o-Phenylenediamine (OPD)
o-Phenylenediamine (OPD), 835
  absorption, 835–836
  toxicity, 836
OPIDN, *see* OP-Induced Delayed Neuropathy (OPIDN)
OPIDPN, *see* Organophosphate-induced delayed peripheral neuropathy (OPIDPN)
OP-Induced Delayed Neuropathy (OPIDN), 350, 711
Opioid, 56, 98; *see also* Acetyl salicylic acid (ASA); Amphetamines; Cocaine; Codeine; Morphine; *N*-Acetyl-para-aminophenol (APAP); Nonsteroidal anti-inflammatory drugs (NSAIDs); Specific antagonists; Toxidromes
  adulterants, 104, 178, 181
  agonists, 100, 180
  antagonists, 68–69, 100
  antidiarrheals, 101
  body packers, 102, 104, 176, 177
  bowel, 45
  clinical effects of, 98
  clonidine, 102
  dextromethorphan, 102
  diagnosis, 98–99
  diphenoxylate, 101
  ileus, 99
  imidazolines, 102
  induced disorders, 778
  intoxication symptoms, 779
  long-acting, 100
  loperamide, 101
  meperidine, 100
  miosis, 99
  MPTP, 101
  noncardiogenic pulmonary edema, 103, 104
  overdose management, 104, 779
  pentazocine, 101
  propoxyphene, 100
  receptors, 98
  routes of administration, 779
  special consideration, 100
  toxidrome, 56, 101
  tramadol, 101
  withdrawal symptoms, 779
Opioid case conclusions, 807; *see also* Chain of custody (CoC); Workplace substance abuse monitoring
  amphetamine interpretation, 809
  atypical specimens, 809
  laboratory selection questions, 805–807
  noncontact positive, 808
  opiate interpretation, 809, 810
  returning to work, 810–811
  shy bladder evaluation, 811
  split sample issues, 810
  unsuitable specimen, 808
OPV, *see* Oral polio-virus vaccines (OPV)
Oral contraceptive pills (OCPs), 10
Oral hypoglycemics, 235; *see also* Hypoglycemia
  α-glucosidase inhibitors, 236
  biguanides, 235
  drugs causing, 236
  sulfonylureas, 235
  thiazolidinedione, 236
Oral polio-virus vaccines (OPV), 564
Oral Rehydration Solutions (ORS), 373
Order for diagnosis (OD), 39
Orelline nephrotoxicity, 288, 405; *see also* Mushroom poisoning; Nephrotoxicology
OR formula, 853
Organochlorines, 347–348, 349, 708–709; *see also* Neurotoxicology; Pesticide poisoning
Organophosphate (OP), 348, 709, 751; *see also* Insecticides; Neurotoxicology; Pesticide poisoning
  vs. carbamates, 349
  IMS, 349
  nerve gases, 711
  OPIDN, 350, 711
  OP nerve gases, 350
  pesticides, 315
  poisoning complications, 349
  prophylaxis and treatment, 711
  TOCP, 349
Organophosphate-induced delayed peripheral neuropathy (OPIDPN), 709
Oriental hornet (*Vespa orientalis*), 516; *see also* Terrestrial envenomings
Orogastric (OG), 676
  lavage, 24
ORS, *see* Oral Rehydration Solutions (ORS)
OTC, *see* Over-the-Counter (OTC)
Overdose (OD), 88, 412
Over-the-Counter (OTC), 54, 801
  mercury bichloride tablets, 112
Oxycodone, 778
oxyHb, *see* Oxyhemoglobin (oxyHb)
Oxyhemoglobin (oxyHb), 653

P

Paclitaxel, 464
PAHs, *see* Polycyclic aromatic hydrocarbons (PAHs)
Paints, 144; *see also* Aromatic hydrocarbons
2-PAM, *see* Pralidoxime (2-PAM)
p-ANCA, *see* Perinuclear-ANCA (p-ANCA)
Paraldehyde, 214; *see also* Sedative-hypnotics (SHs)
Paraquat, 724
Parenteral administration, 4; *see also* Absorption
Parkinsonism, 318; *see also* Neurotoxicology
  extrapyramidal, 320
  Mn-induced, 329
Passive diffusion, 6, 7; *see also*Absorption
Pastuerella pestis, 543; *see also* Fleas
Paxillus involutus, 408; *see also* Mushroom poisoning
Paxillus syndrome, 408; *see also* Mushroom poisoning
PCC, *see* Poison Control Center (PCC)
Pcns, *see* Penicillins (Pcns)
PCOs, *see Pfiesteria*-complex organisms (PCOs)
PCP, *see* Phencyclidine (PCP)
PDMP, *see* Prescription drug monitoring programs (PDMP)
PEEP, *see* Positive end expiratory pressure (PEEP)
PEG, *see* Polyethylene glycol (PEG)
Penicillamine, 61; *see also* Metal chelators
Penicillins (Pcns), 258; *see also* Antibiotic toxicity
Pennyroyal herb (*Mentha pulegium*), 416
Pennyroyal-mint family (*Mentha pulegium*), 416–417; *see also* Cardiovascular toxins
Pentazocine, 101, 179–180, 778; *see also* Cocaine; Opioid
Perinuclear-ANCA (p-ANCA), 307
Peripheral vascular resistance (PVR), 249
Peritoneal dialysis, 16, 30; *see also* Enhanced elimination
Personal hygiene products, 154; *see also* Aromatic hydrocarbons
Personal Protective Equipment (PPE), 662
  classification, 663
Pesticide poisoning, 347, 708; *see also* Fumigants; Heavy metal poisoning; Insecticides; Metal poisoning; Neurotoxicology; Organophosphate (OP); Rodenticides
  common, 709
  dilated pupils, 710
  endocrine activity, 713
  insect repellents, 713
  intermediate syndrome, 710–711
  least toxic OTC, 350–351
  legislation, 725
  N,N-diethyltoluamide, 712
  OPIDN, 711
  organochlorines, 347–348, 349
  pesticide and toxidrome, 726
  pinpoint pupils, 710
  pyrethrins, 711
  pyrethroids, 712
PET, *see* Positron emission tomography (PET)
Petrochemical toxicity, 630, 643; *see also* Crude oil; *Deepwater Horizon* oil spill
  corexit dispersant, 637, 638
  Deepwater Horizon oil spill, 630–631
  dispersant toxicities, 636–638
  genetic polymorphisms, 642
  health predictions, 641–643
  Ixtoc I oil spill, 631, 632
  oil folliculitis, 635
  oil spill and health effects, 638–641
  solvent-induced nummular eczema, 635
Petroleum-based products, 151; *see also* Aromatic hydrocarbons
Pfiesteria, 388; *see also* Seafood poisoning
Pfiesteria-complex organisms (PCOs), 388; *see also* Seafood poisoning
Pharmaceutical excipients, 12; *see also* Liver zones
Pharmacodynamics, 4
Pharmacogenetics, 11; *see also* Liver zones
Pharmacokinetics, 4
Phencyclidine (PCP), 168, 185, 782, 784, 805; *see also* Drug abuse; Hallucinogens
  clinical and lab findings, 185–186
  OD management, 186
  pharmacology, 185
  street names, 168
Phentermine–fenfluramine cardiomyopathy, 183, 184
Phenylpropanolamine (PPA), 54, 247
PHIL, *see* Public Health Image Library (PHIL)
Philodendron (*Philodendron pertusum*), 469; *see also* GI toxicity
Phosgene, 748
Phosphates, 107; *see also* Alkali
Phosphides, 164; *see also* Toxicants
  pathophysiology, 836
  toxicity, 836–837
Phosphorus, 717, 718
Phthalates, 164, 837; *see also* Toxicants
  potential exposure, 837
  toxicity, 838
Physical assessment, 31
  bowel irrigation, 27–28
  overdose, 32
  primary survey, 31
  secondary survey, 32
  unusual exposures, 32–33
Phytoplankton, 382; *see also* Plankton
Pink disease, *see* Mercurial acrodynia
Piperidinediones, 213; *see also* Sedative-hypnotics (SHs)

Plague, 758–759
Plankton, 381; *see also* Seafood poisoning
  HABs, 382, 383
  phytoplankton, 382
  toxic zooplankton, 382
  zooplankton species, 382
Plant chemotherapy, 464; *see also*Poisonous household plants
  coltsfoot, 467
  comfrey, 466
  hepatotoxicity, 465
  hypoglycemia Ackee, 466
  Jamaican vomiting sickness, 466
  veno-occlusive disease, 466
Plant-derived remedies and toxins; *see also* Cajun healing practice
  abortifacients, 590
  anticancer alkaloids, 601
  belladonna alkaloids, 592
  CNS toxicity, 591–592, 593–595
  compound Q, 590
  GI toxins, 595–599
  hallucinogen group, 593
  hepatotoxins, 599–600
  household herbs, 600–601
  plant poisonings, 590, 595–600
  toxic herb, 603
  traditional medications, 588–589
Plant glycosides, 242; *see also* Cardiac glycosides
Plant hallucinogens, 188; *see also* Drug abuse; Hallucinogens
  appetite suppressants, 189
  belladonna alkaloids, 188–189
  Hoodia Gordonii, 189–190
  morning glory, 188
  neurotoxicity, 188
  neurotoxic poison, 189
  nutmeg, 188
  Salvia divinorum, 189
  serotonergic hallucinogens, 190
Plasmapheresis, 31
Platinoid toxicity, 275; *see also* Anticancer drug toxicity
  mechanism and toxicity, 275–276
  OD, 276
PMS, *see* Pre-menstrual syndrome (PMS)
Pneumoconioses, 662; *see also* Asbestosis
  CWP, 664
  epidemiology, 664–665
  fibrogenic dust exposures, 662
  granulomatous, 664
  nonfibrogenic dust exposures, 662
  nongranulomatous, 664
  PPE, 663
Pneumomediastinum, 44, 173; *see also* Cocaine
PNU, *see* Pyridyl nitrophenyl urea (PNU)
Podophyllotoxin, 460, 462, 601; *see also* Antimitotic plants; Cajun healing practice
Poison antidotes, 54; *see also* Antitoxin; Antivenom; Gastrointestinal decontaminants; Metal chelators; Nonspecific antidotes; Specific antagonists; Specific antidotes; Toxidromes; Vitamins
Poison Control Center (PCC), 493
Poison elimination, 29–31
  epid, 35–36
  gastric emptying, 22
  ipecac emesis, 22–23, 24
  MDAC, 26–27
  nondissolving radiopacities, 23
Poison gas, 332; *see also* Carbon monoxide poisoning; Neurotoxicology
Poison hemlock (*Conium maculatum*), 425, 454; *see also* Neurotoxic plants
Poisoning and envenoming pharmacology, 3; *see also* Absorption; Distribution; Excretion; First-order kinetics; Liver zones; Metabolic reactions; Poison pharmacology; Zero-order kinetics
Poisoning in pregnancy, 223–224; *see also* Reproductive toxicology
  APAP ODs, 224–225
  chelators, 225, 226
  CO poisoning, 226–227
  Fe chelating agent, 226
  Fe ODs, 225
  iron, 225–226
  pediatric iron OD, 225, 226
Poison ivy (*Toxicodendron radicans*), 472; *see also* Toxicodendron group
Poison management, 21; *see also* Absorption prevention; Nontoxic exposures; Physical assessment; Poison elimination, 33
Poison oak (*Toxicodendron pubescens*), 472; *see also* Toxicodendron group
Poisonous household plants, 444, 474, 476; *see also* Anticancer alkaloids; Antimitotic plants; Channel openers; Cyanide poisoning; Cytotoxic plants; GI toxicity; Neurotoxic plants; Plant chemotherapy; Poisonous plants; Sodium channel openers; Toxicodendron group
  absinthe, 456
  dermatotoxicity group, 471
  ephedra, 458
  hallucinogens, 455–456, 457
  Lathyrus spp., 458–459
  morning glory, 457
  neurotoxicity, 455
  nutmeg and mace, 457–458

Poisonous household plants (*Continued*)
- peyote cactus, 457
- plant poisonings, 471
- wormwood, 456

Poisonous plants, 444; *see also* Poisonous household plants
- cardiac glycosides, 446
- cardiovascular toxicity, 445
- *Convallaria majalis*, 447
- *Digitalis purpurea*, 447
- epidemiology, 444
- *Nerium oleander*, 446
- plant toxicology, 444–445
- poisoning children, 444
- poisoning frequency, 445

Poison pharmacology, 18; *see also* Poisoning and envenoming pharmacology
- in children, 18
- ED management, 18–19
- in elderly, 19
- hydrocarbons, 18
- ingested agents, 18
- PICU management, 19

Poison sumac (*Toxicodendron vernix*), 473; *see also* Toxicodendron group

Pokeberry (*Phytolacca americana*), 433, 471, 597; *see also* Cajun healing practice; Gastrointestinal toxicity

Pokeweed, *see* Pokeberry (*Phytolacca americana*)

Polycyclic aromatic hydrocarbons (PAHs), 11, 132–134, 615, 631; *see also* Aromatic hydrocarbons; Crude oil; Petrochemical toxicity
- surveillance for, 633

Polyethylene glycol (PEG), 59, 209
- electrolyte, 324, 676

Polymers, 165, 838; *see also* Toxicants

Polyneuropathy, 320; *see also* Neurotoxicology

Polyvinyl chloride (PVC), 164

Poppy seeds, 804

Population-attributable risk, 853

Porcupine fish, *see* Pufferfish

Porthidium nasutum, 499; *see also* Central and South American exotic snakes

Porthidium ophyromegas, 499; *see also* Central and South American exotic snakes

Positive end expiratory pressure (PEEP), 651

Positron emission tomography (PET), 316

Potency, 14; *see also* Dose–response relationships

Power, 853
- relationships, 854

PPA, *see* Phenylpropanolamine (PPA)

PPE, *see* Personal Protective Equipment (PPE)

Pralidoxime (2-PAM), 72, 74–75; *see also* Specific antidotes

Predatory baitfish feeders, 386; *see also* Feeding habits

Pregnancy pharmacokinetics, 221; *see also* Reproductive toxicology
- D drugs and X teratogens, 222
- free drug concentration, 221
- placental transfer, 222–223
- teratogenic syndromes, 223
- VACTREL association, 223, 224

Premature ventricular contractions (PVCs), 243, 646

Pre-menstrual syndrome (PMS), 87; *see also* Antiseptic toxicity

Prescription drug monitoring programs (PDMP), 205

Priapism-inducing agents, 218; *see also* Reproductive toxicology

Primaquine, 268; *see also* Antimalarials

Primary neurologic diseases, 317; *see also* Neurotoxicology

PRIS, *see* Propofol Infusion Syndrome (PRIS)

Probability rules, 844
- addition rule, 845
- conditional probability, 844
- multiplication rule, 844
- mutual exclusivity, 845

Propane as asphyxiants, 647

Propofol, 197, 215; *see also* Drug abuse; Sedative-hypnotics (SHs)
- abuse, 197-, 198
- case study, 198
- mechanism of action, 197

Propofol Infusion Syndrome (PRIS), 198
- clinical manifestations, 199
- diagnosis, 199, 200
- epidemiology, 199
- history, 198
- recommendations, 199–200
- risk factors, 198

Propoxyphene, 100, 179, 778; *see also* Cocaine; Opioid

Propylthiouracil (PTU), 237

Psilocybin, 782, 784; *see also* Mushroom poisoning
- toxicity, 404, 604

Psychedelics, *see* Hallucinogens

Psychoactive stimulant substances, 784

Psychotropics, 354; *see also* Neurotoxicology
- bromates vs. bromides, 354
- rodenticide ingestions, 355

PTU, *see* Propylthiouracil (PTU)

Public Health Image Library (PHIL), 308

Pufferfish, 384; *see also* Marine toxins

Pulmonary agents, 753–754

Pulmonary hemosiderosis, *see* Acute idiopathic pulmonary hemorrhage (AIPH)

Puss moth (*Megalopyge opercularis*), 521; *see also* Terrestrial envenomings

PVC, *see* Polyvinyl chloride (PVC)

PVCs, *see* Premature ventricular contractions (PVCs)

PVR, *see* Peripheral vascular resistance (PVR)
Pyrazinamide, 266; *see also* Anti-TB agents
Pyridostigmine, 751–752
Pyridoxine (B6), 71; *see also* Vitamins
Pyridyl nitrophenyl urea (PNU), 351
  rodenticide, 236
Pyrrolizidine alkaloids, 434; *see also* Gastrointestinal toxicity

Q

Q-fever, 760
QNS, *see* Quantity-not-sufficient (QNS)
QT prolongation, 254, 255; *see also* Cardiovascular drug toxicity
Quantity-not-sufficient (QNS), 798
Quinine, 100, 104; *see also* Antimalarials; Opioid
  and quinidine, 267

R

RAA, *see* Renin–angiotensin–aldosterone (RAA)
Radiation, 728, 730; *see also* Radiation toxicology
  alpha, 731
  beta, 731
  exposure, 734–735
  gamma, 731, 732
  historical events, 728–730
  isotopes, 735
  laws of radiosensitivity, 733
  measurement units, 732–733
  neutron, 731–732
  radioactivity, 730–731
Radiation toxicology, 728; *see also* Acute Radiation Syndrome (ARS); Radiation; Radiological weapons
  on elderly, 741
  exposure types, 736
  external contamination, 736–737
  external irradiation, 738
  on fetal cells, 741, 742, 743
  injury treatment, 768
  internal contamination, 737–738
  local radiation exposure, 741
  pathophysiology, 735
  during pregnancy 741–743
  preparing for victims, 735–736
  to prevent exposures, 743–744
  at risk population, 730, 744–745
  safety, 745
Radioimmunoassay (RIA), 243, 386, 783
Radioisotope, 730
Radiological weapons, 766; *see also* Biological weapons (BW); Radiation toxicology
  absorbed doses, 767
  biological effects, 767
  chromosomal damage, 767
  dose limits, 768
  ionizing radiation, 767
  NRC, 768
  radiation types, 766
  treating injuries, 768
Radon as asphyxiants, 647
RADS, *see* Reactive airways dysfunction syndrome (RADS)
Rat flea (*Xenopsylla cheopsis*), 544; *see also* Fleas
Reactive airways dysfunction syndrome (RADS), 162, 647, 649
Red squill, 720, 721
Relative risk, 851
  formula, 852
Renal dysfunction; *see also* Acute renal failure (ARF); Chronic renal failure (CRF); Nephrotoxicology
  acute, 284
  anuric RF, 287
  biomarkers of, 285
  chronic, 284–285
  tests, 285, 286
Renal elimination, 15; *see also* First-order kinetics; Zero-order kinetics
  distal tubular reabsorption, 16
  glomerular filtration, 15
  proximal tubular secretion, 16
Renal failure (RF), 711
Renal tubular acidosis (RTA), 297, 615; *see also* Nephrotoxicology
Renin–angiotensin–aldosterone (RAA), 254
Representative enzyme substrates, 10
Reproductive toxicology, 218; *see also* Pregnancy pharmacokinetics; Poisoning in pregnancy; Theophylline OD in pregnancy
  abortifacients, 221
  α-blockers and vasodilators, 218, 221
  aphrodisiacs, 220
  breastfeeding, 231
  epidemiology, 218
  female infertility, 220
  male infertility, 219
  opioid abuse and NWS, 230–231
  priapism-inducing agents, 218
  sexual dysfunction, 219, 220
  substance abuse, 229, 230
  withdrawal syndromes, 230
Reptilia, 481; *see also* Terrestrial envenomings
Resins, 165, 838; *see also* Toxicants
Return to work determination, 810–811
RF, *see* Renal failure (RF)
Rhombic night adder (*Causus rhombeatus*), 497; *see also* Eastern coral snake

RIA, *see* Radioimmunoassay (RIA)
Ricin, 763, 764
Rifampin, 265–266; *see also* Anti-TB agents
Riot Control Agents, 754
RMSF, *see* Rocky mountain spotted fever (RMSF)
Rocky mountain spotted fever (RMSF), 551
Rocky mountain wood tick (*Dermacentor andersoni*), 558; *see also* Ticks
Rodenticides; *see also* Heavy metal poisoning; Insecticides; Pesticide poisoning; Metal poisoning
  anticoagulants, 721
  arsenic, 718
  barium, 718, 719
  bromethalin, 721
  cholecalciferol, 720
  epidemiology, 714
  ingestions management, 722–723
  norbormide, 720
  phosphorus, 717, 718
  red squill, 720, 721
  sodium monofluoroacetate, 715
  strychnine, 716
  thallium, 715
  toxicity, 714–715, 715–720, 720–722
  vacor, 719
  zinc phosphide, 716
Rosary peas in pods (*Abrus precatorius*), 461; *see also* Cytotoxic plants
Rotaviruses, 376; *see also* Food poisoning
Rough-skinned newt (*Taricha granulosa granulosa*), 502; *see also* Terrestrial envenomings
RSSE, *see* Russian spring-summer encephalitis (RSSE)
RTA, *see* Renal tubular acidosis (RTA)
Russian spring-summer encephalitis (RSSE), 551

S

SA, *see* Sinoatrial (SA)
Saddleback moth (*Sibene stimulea*), 522; *see also* Terrestrial envenomings
SAH, *see* Subarachnoid hemorrhage (SAH)
Salamanders, 501, 606; *see also* Animal toxins; Terrestrial envenomings
Salmonella spp., 369–370, 750; *see also* Food poisoning
Saltwater gafftopsail (*Bagre marinus*), 580; *see also* Toxic vertebrates
Salvia divinorum, 189, 430, 431; *see also* Plant hallucinogens; Sympathomimetics
SAMHSA, *see* Substance Abuse and Mental Health Services Administration (SAMHSA)
Sandflies, 532, 534; *see also* Flies
SAP, *see* Substance Abuse Professional (SAP)
Sarcoidlike granulomatous pulmonary disease (SLGPD), 640
Sargassum triggerfish (*Xanthichthys ringens*), 386; *see also* Feeding habits
SARS CoV, *see* Severe acute respiratory syndrome coronavirus (SARS CoV)
Saturnine gout, 688
SBE, *see* Subacute bacterial endocarditis (SBE)
SBO, *see* Small bowel obstruction (SBO)
Scatterplot, 848
Schistosomiasis, 308; *see also* Nephrotoxicology
SCN, *see* Sodium nitroprusside (SCN)
Scolopendra species, 523, 524; *see also* Terrestrial envenomings
Scombroid fish poisoning, 605; *see also* Animal toxins
Scopolamine, 104; *see also* Opioid
Scrub typhus mites, 553, 554–555; *see also* Mites
SE, *see* Side effects (SE)
Seafood poisoning, 380; *see also* Feeding habits; Marine toxins; Plankton
  buffalo fish, 392
  bull shark, 392
  ciguatera fish poisoning, 389–390
  crown-of thorns starfish, 381
  crustacean poisoning, 389
  disease determinants, 380–381
  epidemiology, 380
  Florida pufferfish, 387
  freshwater fish poisoning, 391
  management strategies, 393
  marine botulism, 393
  Pfiesteria, 388
  practice tests, 394
  saltwater fish poisoning, 391
  scombroid fish poisoning, 390
  shellfish poisoning, 386–387, 387–388, 388–389
  tetrodotoxic fish poisoning, 391
  yellowfin tuna, 380
Secondary neurotoxic syndromes, 317; *see also* Neurotoxicology
Sedating agent, 755
Sedative-hypnotics (SHs), 208; *see also* Barbiturates; Benzodiazepine (BZ); Date-rape drugs; Flunitrazepam; Marijuana
  anxiolytics, 214
  bromates, 209–210
  carbamates and bromides, 214
  classification, 208
  diagnosis, 208–209
  ethchlorvynol, 213
  mechanism, 208
  overdose management, 209
  pharmacology, 208
  piperidinediones, 213

short-term anesthetics, 215
withdrawn, 214
Sedatives, 11, 208, 780; *see also* Sedative-hypnotics (SHs)
withdrawal symptoms, 781–782
Selective Serotonin Re-uptake Inhibitors (SSRIs), 144, 596; *see also* Aromatic hydrocarbons
Selenium poisoning, 700, 703
Sensory nerve action potentials (SNAPs), 564
Septic cerebral emboli, 172; *see also* Cocaine
Serotonergic hallucinogens, 190; *see also* Plant hallucinogens
Severe acute respiratory syndrome coronavirus (SARS CoV), 763
Short-term anesthetics, 215; *see also* Sedative-hypnotics (SHs)
SHs, *see* Sedative-hypnotics (SHs)
Shy bladder evaluation, 811
SI, *see* Smoke Inhalation (SI)
SIADH, *see* Syndrome of inappropriate antidiuretic hormone (SIADH)
Side effects (SE), 76
Sidewinder rattlesnake (*Crotalus scutulatus scutulatus*), 486; *see also* Terrestrial envenomings
Silica dust, 149–150; *see also* Aromatic hydrocarbons
Silicates, 107; *see also* Alkali
Silicosis, 667–668
Simplified reptile taxonomy, 480; *see also* Terrestrial envenomings
Sinoatrial (SA), 243
Skewed distribution, 846, 847
SLGPD, *see* Sarcoidlike granulomatous pulmonary disease (SLGPD)
SLS, *see* Sodium lauryl sulfate (SLS)
Small bowel obstruction (SBO), 57, 325
Small-cell adenocarcinoma, 666
Smallpox, 759
Smoke Inhalation (SI), 650–651
SN, *see* Substantia nigra (SN)
Snakes, 480; *see also* Terrestrial envenomings
SNAPs, *see* Sensory nerve action potentials (SNAPs)
Sodium
azide, 818
bicarbonate, 78, 79; *see also* Nonspecific antidotes
borates, 107; *see also* Alkali
hydroxide, 107; *see also* Alkali
monofluoroacetate, 715
Sodium channel openers, 447; *see also* Poisonous household plants
aconitine group, 447
channel blocker, 450
death camas, 449
green hellebore, 449
monkshood, 448
veratrum group, 448
Zigadenus group, 448
Sodium lauryl sulfate (SLS), 154; *see also* Aromatic hydrocarbons
Sodium nitroprusside (SCN), 252
Southern flannel moth, *see* Puss moth (*Megalopyge opercularis*)
Southern stingray (*Dasyatis americana*), 576, 577; *see also* Toxic vertebrates
Southern toad frog (*Anaxyrus terrestris*), 588; *see also* Cajun healing practice
Spanish fly (*Lytta vesicatoria*), 522; *see also* Terrestrial envenomings
Specialized carrier proteins, 8
Specific antagonists, 67; *see also* Poison antidotes
AchE antag, 69
BZ antagonism, 68
CCB antag, 68
heparin antag, 69–70
opioid antagonists, 68–69
Specific antidotes, 72; *see also* Poison antidotes
cerebral effects of carbon monoxide poisoning, 74
ethanol, 73
fomepizole, 73
miscellaneous, 75
n-acetylcysteine, 73–74
pralidoxime, 74–75
Spectrophotometric tests, 38
Split sample issues, 810
Squamous cell carcinoma, 666
SSRIs, *see* Selective Serotonin Re-uptake Inhibitors (SSRIs)
Stable fly, 539–540; *see also* Flies
Staph enterotoxin, 760
Stationary filter-feeders, 386; *see also* Feeding habits
Steroid-induced osteonecrosis, 43
Stimulants
and induced disorders, 785
overdose symptoms, 784
routes of administration, 785
treatment issues, 785
withdrawal symptoms, 785
Sting, 480; *see also* Terrestrial envenomings
St. John's wort (*Hypericum perforatum*), 431, 432, 596; *see also* Cajun healing practice; Sympathomimetics
Stonefish (*Synanceja* spp.), 578; *see also* Toxic vertebrates
Streptomycin, 266; *see also* Antibiotic toxicity
Strychnine, 352, 716; *see also* Neurotoxic rodenticides

Styrene, 165, 838; *see also* Toxicants
  pathophysiology, 839
Subacute bacterial endocarditis (SBE), 32, 363
Subarachnoid hemorrhage (SAH), 47, 243
Substance abuse, 194, 201, 777; *see also* Drug abuse
  carcinogenic HCs, 195–196
  CNS leukoencephalopathies, 196
  dependency, 775–777
  high-risk groups for, 204, 205
  methods, 195
  peripheral neuropathies, 196
  poppers, 195
Substance Abuse and Mental Health Services Administration (SAMHSA), 215, 778
Substance Abuse Professional (SAP), 770, 787
  function of, 788
  vs. MRO, 787
Substantia nigra (SN), 313
Succimer, 60; *see also* Metal chelators
Sufentanil, 778
Sulfites, 115–116; *see also* Food additives
Sulfonamides, 261; *see also* Antibiotic toxicity
Sulfur Mustard, 752
Sulfuric acid, 106; *see also* Acids
Supraventricular tachycardia (SVT), 244
SVT, *see* Supraventricular tachycardia (SVT)
Swimming pool products, 113–114; *see also* Cleansers and caustics
Sx, *see* Symptoms (Sx)
Sympathetic, 54, *see also* Toxidromes
Sympatholytics, 250; *see also* Antihypertensives
  classification, 250–251
  management, 252
  mechanisms, 251
  toxicity, 252
Sympathomimetics, 430; *see also* Herbal poisoning; Toxidromes
  nutmeg and mace, 430
  plant hallucinogens, 430
  Salvia divinorum, 430, 431
  sedatives, 431, 432
  St. John's wort, 431, 432
  synephrine vs. ephedrine, 430
  toxidrome, 54–56
Symptoms (Sx), 709
Syndrome of inappropriate antidiuretic hormone (SIADH), 465
Synthetic cannabis, 191; *see also*Drug abuse

T

T-61, 138; *see also* Aromatic hydrocarbons
TAB, *see* Therapeutic abortions (TAB)
TAC, *see* Tetracaine–cocaine–adrenalin (TAC)
Taxine, 451
Taxus baccata, 464; *see also* Anticancer alkaloids
TB, *see* Tuberculosis (TB)
TBE, *see* Tick-borne encephalitis (TBE)
TCAs, *see* Tricyclic antidepressants (TCAs)
TCE, *see* Trichloroethylene (TCE)
TDI, *see* Toluene *diisocyanate* (TDI)
Tear gase, 648, 660; *see also* Asphyxiants
  commonly used, 661
  incapacitating agents, 661
  sedating agent, 661–662
  treatment, 661
TEF, *see* Tracehoesophageal fistula (TEF)
Terrestrial animals, 478; *see also* Terrestrial envenomings
Terrestrial envenomings, 478; *see also* Central and South American exotic snakes; Eastern coral snake
  Agkistrodon, 481–484
  arthropoda, 479
  arthropods, 478
  bark scorpion, 511, 512
  black widow female, 505
  brown recluse, 506, 507
  buck moth, 519
  bumblebee, 512, 513
  cane toad, 503, 504
  canebrake rattlesnake, 484–485
  carpenter bee, 514
  centipede, 523–524
  Central American coral snake, 491
  chordata, 479
  colorado river toad, 502–503
  coral snake, 489, 490
  Crotalus adamanteus, 484, 485
  desert massasauga, 488, 489
  diamondback rattlesnake, 484
  eastern cottonmouth, 482
  funnel web spider, 509–511
  Gila monster, 500
  gypsy moth, 519, 520
  hag moth, 520, 521
  hobo spider, 507–508
  honey bee workers, 512, 513
  hymenoptera venom, 518
  io moth, 518, 519
  lizards/amphibians 481
  Mexican beaded lizard, 500, 501
  milk snake, 490
  millipedes, 523
  mud dauber wasp, 514, 516
  newts, 501
  Northern Pacific rattlesnake, 486, 487
  oriental hornet, 514, 516
  pre-test question, 479

puss or flannel moth, 521
pygmy rattlesnake, 488
red fire ant, 517
reptilia, 481
rough-skinned newt, 501, 502
saddleback moth, 521, 522
salamanders, 501
sidewinder rattlesnake, 486
simplified reptile taxonomy, 480
snakes, 480
Southern copperhead, 481
taxonomy, 479
terrestrial animals, 478
U.S. desert Tarantula, 508, 509
Western cottonmouth, 483
Western Massasauga, 487
white-marked tussock moth caterpillar, 520
yellow jackets, 514, 515
Testosterone and estradiol, 141–142; *see also* Aromatic hydrocarbons
Tetracaine–cocaine–adrenalin (TAC), 803
Tetracyclines, 261; *see also* Antibiotic toxicity
Tetrodotoxic fish poisoning, 605–606; *see also* Animal toxins
Tetrodotoxin, 384; *see also* Marine toxins
Texas coral snake (*Micrurus tener tener*), 489, 490; *see also* Terrestrial envenomings
Thallium, 327, 697, 715; *see also* Heavy metal poisoning; Neurotoxicology
alopecia, 699
clinical effects, 328, 698
dermal effects, 328, 699
diagnosis, 328, 698, 699
Mees' lines, 328, 329
pathophysiology, 328, 697
toxicology, 327–328, 697–697
treatment, 698, 699
uses, 327, 697
THC, *see* Delta-9-tetrahydrocannabinol (THC)
Theophylline OD in pregnancy, 227, 228; *see also* Reproductive toxicology
enhanced elimination, 229
metabolism, 227
pharmacology, 227
toxicity, 227
Therapeutic abortions (TAB), 221; *see also* Reproductive toxicology
Therapeutic euglycemia maintenance, 234
Therapeutic index (TI), 12; *see also* Liver zones
Thiamine (B1), 72; *see also* Vitamins
Thin layer chromatography (TLC), 38, 386
Third-Party Administrators (TPAs), 789
Thornapple, *see* Jimson weed (*Datura stramonium*)
Three to five compartment, 34
ingested lead distributes in, 34, 35
Thrombocytopenic purpura (TTP), 709
TI, *see* Therapeutic index (TI)
Tick paralysis (TP), 558; *see also* Ticks
Australian, 561–562
clinical manifestations of, 563–564
control and prevention of, 567–568
differential diagnosis of, 564
global epidemiology of, 560, 563
management of, 564, 567
mechanisms of, 559–560
vs. neuromuscular paralysis, 565–566
North American, 561–562
regional, 561–562
tick removal, 567
Tick-borne encephalitis (TBE), 551
Ticks, 549; *see also* Bedbugs; Fleas; Flies; Mites; Mosquitoes; Myiasis; Tick paralysis (TP)
American dog tick, 559
biology and behavior, 559–560
black-legged tick, 551
Dermacentor andersoni, 551
hardbodied Ixodidae species, 550, 551, 552
life cycle, 559
Ornithodorus species, 550
rocky mountain wood tick, 558
soft-bodied Argasidae species tick, 549, 550
tick removal, 567
Tilmicosin, 136–137; *see also* Aromatic hydrocarbons
Tin poisoning, 700
TLC, *see* Thin layer chromatography (TLC)
TMI, *see* Trimetallic *anhydrides* (TMI)
TNT, *see* Trinitrotoluene (TNT)
Toads, 606–607; *see also* Animal toxins
cane or marine toad, 504
Colorado river toad, 503
Southern toad frog, 588
TOCP, *see* Triorthocresylphosphate (TOCP)
Toluene, 134–136; *see also* Aromatic hydrocarbons
Toluene *diisocyanate* (TDI), 648
Toxaphene, 708
Toxic alcohols, 343, 620; *see also* Ethanol; Ethylene glycol; Hydrocarbons (HCs); Isopropanol; Methanol; Neurotoxicology; Volatile organic compounds (VOCs)
anion gap metabolic acidosis, 343, 621
metabolism of, 628
osmol gap metabolic acidosis, 343, 621
Toxicants, 156; *see also* Household poisoning
acrolein, 156
acrylamides, 156
acrylates, 157
amines, 157
aniline compounds, 157
azides, 158

Toxicants (*Continued*)
- bromide compounds, 158
- butadienes, 158
- carbon disulfide, 159
- chlorates, 159
- diamantes, 159–160
- dibromochloropropane, 160
- dimethylacetamide, 160
- dimethylformamide, 160–161
- dinitrobenzene, 161
- dinitrotoluene, 161
- epichlorohydrin, 161–162
- ethylene dibromide, 162
- ethylenediamine, 162
- fluoride compounds, 162
- hexachloro-1,3-butadiene, 162
- isocyanates, 163
- maleic anhydride, 163
- mercaptans, 163–164
- nitriles, 164
- phosphorus/phosphides, 164
- phthalates, 164
- polymers, 165
- resins, 165
- styrene, 165
- trimellitic anhydride, 165–166
- triorthoscresyl phosphate, 166
- xylidine, 166

Toxic CNS disorders, 315
Toxic herb–drug interactions, 603; *see also* Plant-derived remedies and toxins
Toxicodendron group, 472; *see also* Poisonous household plants
- *Lantana camara*, 473, 474
- phytophototoxicity, 474
- poison ivy, 472
- poison oak, 472
- poison sumac, 473
- toxicodendron-containing plants, 471
- toxidrome evaluation, 474, 475
- trumpet vine, 474, 475

Toxic Substances Control Act (TSCA), 725
Toxic vertebrates, 575; *see also* Marine envenomings
- lionfish, 577, 578
- saltwater gafftopsail, 580
- stingrays, 575, 576, 577
- stonefish, 578–579
- weeverfish, 579

Toxic zooplankton, 382; *see also* Plankton
Toxicodynamics, 4
Toxicokinetics, 4
Toxidromes, 54
- anticholinergic, 54
- belladonnas, 54
- benzodiazepine, 56
- cholinergic, 54
- CNS, 56
- extrapyramidal, 56
- herbal poisonings, 54
- hypermetabolic, 55
- miosis, 54, 55
- mydriasis, 54, 55
- opioid, 56
- parasympathetic, 54
- sympathetic, 54
- sympathomimetic, 54–56
- withdrawal, 56

Toxin transport mechanisms, 6–7; *see also* Absorption
TP, *see* Tick paralysis (TP); Trimethyl pentanediol (TP)
TPAs, *see* Third-Party Administrators (TPAs)
Tracehoesophageal fistula (TEF), 688
Traditional medications, 588–589; *see also* Plant-derived remedies and toxins
Traiteurs, 585; *see also* Cajun healing practice
Tramadol, 102, 180; *see also* Cocaine; Opioid
Transition metals, 674
Transmissionopathy, 315; *see also* Neurotoxicology
Treatment, 709
Trichlorfon, 145–146; *see also* Aromatic hydrocarbons
Trichloroethylene (TCE), 315, 619
Tricholoma magnivalere, 288; *see also* Nephrotoxicology
Tricothecene mycotoxins, 764–765
Tricyclic antidepressants (TCAs), 8, 32
- overdose, 50

Trimellitic anhydride, 165–166, 839; *see also* Toxicants
Trimetallic *anhydrides* (TMI), 648
Trimethyl pentanediol (TP), 536
Trinitrotoluene (TNT), 161
Triorthocresylphosphate (TOCP), 839–840
Triorthoscresyl phosphate, 166; *see also* Toxicants
True rhododendron (*Rhododendron ponticum*), 451; *see also* Channel openers
Trumpet vine (*Campsis radicans*), 474, 475; *see also* Toxicodendron group
TSCA, *see* Toxic Substances Control Act (TSCA)
Tsetse flies, 537; *see also* Flies
TTP, *see* Thrombocytopenic purpura (TTP)
Tuberculosis (TB), 362; *see also* Antibiotic toxicity
- epidemiology, 262

Tularemia, 759–760
Turpentine, 306; *see also* Chronic renal failure (CRF)
Two compartment, 33; *see also* Distribution
- model, 9

U

UDPT, *see* Uridine diphosphoglucuronyl transferase (UDPT)
Ultraviolet (UV), 119
Unbound drugs, 8; *see also* Distribution
United States Department of Agriculture (USDA), 136
Unsuitable specimen, 808
Uridine diphosphoglucuronyl transferase (UDPT), 641
Urinary alkalinization, 29–30
Urolithiasis, 305; *see also* Chronic renal failure (CRF)
USDA, *see* United States Department of Agriculture (USDA)
U.S. Department of Health and Human Services (DHHS), 771
U.S. Department of Transportation (DOT), 771, 791
- drug testing, 795
- result interpretation, 796–797
- results review, 795
- specimen analysis, 795–796
- specimen collection, 797
- split specimen, 796

U.S. Food and Drug Administration (FDA), 115, 800
UV, *see* Ultraviolet (UV)

V

V agent, *see* Vesicant agent (V agent)
Vacor, 353, 719; *see also* Neurotoxic rodenticides
VACTERL association, 688
Vancomycin, 260; *see also* Antibiotic toxicity
Variation, 845, 846
Vasodilators, 253; *see also* Antihypertensives
Vasopressin, *see* Desamino-d-arginine-vasopressin (DDAVP)
VCR, *see* Vincristine (VCR)
Vd, *see* Volume of distribution (Vd)
Veno-occlusive disease, 466; *see also* Plant chemotherapy
Ventricular fibrillation (VF), 243, 646
Ventricular tachycardia (VT), 243, 646
Vesicant agent (V agent), 751
Vetanarcol, 137; *see also* Aromatic hydrocarbons
Veterinary products, 140; *see also* Aromatic hydrocarbons
VF, *see* Ventricular fibrillation (VF)
Vibrio; *see also* Food poisoning
- *cholerae*, 371–372
- *parahemolyticus*, 372
- *vulnificus*, 373

Vinca alkaloids, 460, 461; *see also* Antimitotic plants
Vinca minor, 462; *see also* Antimitotic plants
Vincristine (VCR), 273; *see also* Anticancer drug toxicity
- toxicity, 274

Violin spider, *see* Brown recluse (*Loxosceles reclusa*)
Vitamins, 70; *see also* Poison antidotes
- folic and folinic acids, 70
- hydroxocobalamin, 70–71
- niacin, 72
- pyridoxine, 71
- thiamine, 72
- vitamin K, 71

VOCs, *see* Volatile organic compounds (VOCs)
Volatile organic compounds (VOCs), 338, 346, 614; *see also* Hydrocarbons (HCs); Neurotoxicology; Toxic alcohols
- air and seafood surveillance for, 634
- carcinogenic vs. neurotoxic, 619
- ethylene glycol ingestion, 346
- splitting, 615
- stratification, 614–615
- styrene vs. xylene, 342
- substance abuse, 618–619
- uses, 614
- volatile substance abuse, 341
- wood distillates, 620

Volatile substance abuse, 341; *see also* Neurotoxicology
Volume of distribution (Vd), 8–9; *see also* Distribution
Voodoo, 584, 585; *see also* Cajun healing practice; Hoodoo
VT, *see* Ventricular tachycardia (VT)

W

Wasps, 514; *see also* Terrestrial envenomings
Water hemlock (*Cicuta maculata*), 455; *see also* Neurotoxic plants
WBI, *see* Whole bowel irrigation (WBI)
Weapons, *see* Biological weapons (BW); Chemical weapons (CW); Radiological weapons
Western coral snake, *see* Texas coral snake (*Micrurus tener tener*)
Western Massasauga (*Sistrurus milieris streckeri*), 487; *see also* Terrestrial envenomings
Western pygmy rattlesnake, *see* Western Massasauga (*Sistrurus milieris streckeri*)
White-marked tussock moth (*Orgyia leucostigma*), 520; *see also* Terrestrial envenomings
Whole bowel irrigation (WBI) , 27–28, 57, 59, 252, 676, 324; *see also* Gastrointestinal decontaminants
Wild tree tobacco (*Nicotiana glauca*), 425; *see also* Neurotoxic plants

Witch hazel, 599; *see also* Cajun healing practice
Withdrawal toxidrome, 56; *see also* Toxidromes
Wood distillates, 620; *see also* Volatile organic compounds (VOCs)
Workplace substance abuse monitoring, *see* Abused drug screening characteristics; Americans with Disabilities Act (ADA); Opioid; Sedatives
  abused substances, 778
  alcohol testing, 794
  breath alcohol analysis, 793
  California and Arizona Proposition 200, 788
  CLIA, 773
  drug impact in workplace, 772
  drug testing, 773, 795
  disabled individual, 772
  drug-free workplace, 771
  employee assistance programs, 790
  epidemiology, 772
  Federal regulations 771
  marijuana, 773
  MRO, 788
  opiate testing cut-offs, 774
  opioids, 778
  psychoactive substances, 778
  rehabilitation, 791, 792, 793
  substance abuse professionals, 787
  urine drug tests, 774
Wormwood (*Artemisia absinthium*), 427, 456; *see also* Central nervous system toxicity; Poisonous household plants
Wuchereria bancrofti, 530; *see also* Mosquitoes

X

Xenobiotics, 4, 9
Xenon as asphyxiants, 647
Xylidine, 166, 840; *see also* Toxicants

Y

Yellow fever transmission cycles, 530, 531
Yellow jacket wasps (*Vespula squamosa*), 515; *see also* Terrestrial envenomings
Yellow knight (*Tricholoma equestre*), 407; *see also* Mushroom poisoning
Yellow morel, *see* Edible conifer (*Morchella esculenta*)
Yellowfin tuna, 380; *see also* Seafood poisoning
Yersinia enterocolitica, 226, 373–374; *see also* Food poisoning
Yew (*Taxus* species), 451; *see also* Channel openers
Yohimbine, 220; *see also* Reproductive toxicology

Z

Zero-order kinetics, 14, 15
Zigadenus group, 448; *see also*Sodium channel openers
Zinc, 151–152; *see also* Aromatic hydrocarbons
  phosphide, 716
  poisoning, 700
Zolpidem, 214; *see also* Sedative-hypnotics (SHs)
Zombification, 586, 588; *see also* Cajun healing practice
Zooplankton species, 382; *see also* Plankton